HOLT
ELEMENTS OF
LITERATURE

World Literature

HOLT, RINEHART AND WINSTON

A Harcourt Education Company

Orlando • **Austin** • New York • San Diego • Toronto • London

Language Arts Standards

The following chart lists the **North Carolina Course of Study for English Language Arts.** The Course of Study for English II is comprised of six goals. Under each goal, there is a list of objectives. An explanation and an example accompany each objective.

COMPETENCY GOAL I

The learner will react to and reflect upon print and non-print text and personal experiences by examining situations from both subjective and objective perspectives.

1.01 Produce reminiscences (about a person, event, object, place, animal) that engage the audience by:

- using specific and sensory details with purpose.
- explaining the significance of the reminiscence from an objective perspective.
- moving effectively between past and present.
- recreating the mood felt by the author during the reminiscence.

You are required to write about personal experiences.

EXAMPLE: Writing a Reflective Essay

The Writing Workshop "Writing a Reflective Essay" on pages 88–93 shows you how to write about a personal experience and its significance.

1.02 Respond reflectively (through small group discussion, class discussion, journal entry, essay, letter, dialogue) to written and visual texts by:

- relating personal knowledge to textual information or class discussion.
- showing an awareness of one's own culture as well as the cultures of others.
- exhibiting an awareness of culture in which text is set or in which text was written.
- explaining how culture affects personal responses.
- demonstrating an understanding of media's impact on personal responses and cultural analyses.

Show a connection to a variety of texts.

EXAMPLE: Making Connections

The Cultural Points of View feature "Beginnings and Endings" on pages 305–320 provides an opportunity for you to read three selections from different cultures that share a similar theme. Before reading the selections, though, you will share stories from your own culture of origin or family to connect to the stories you are about to read.

1.03 Demonstrate the ability to read, listen to and view a variety of increasingly complex print and non-print expressive texts appropriate to grade level and course literary focus, by:

- selecting, monitoring, and modifying as necessary reading strategies appropriate to readers' purpose.
- identifying and analyzing text components (such as organizational structures, story elements, organizational features) and evaluating their impact on the text.
- providing textual evidence to support understanding of and reader's response to text.
- demonstrating comprehension of main idea and supporting details.
- summarizing key events and/or points from text.
- making inferences, predicting, and drawing conclusions based on text.
- identifying and analyzing personal, social, historical or cultural influences, contexts, or biases.
- making connections between works, self and related topics.
- analyzing and evaluating the effects of author's craft and style.
- analyzing and evaluating the connections or relationships between and among ideas, concepts, characters and/or experiences.
- identifying and analyzing elements of expressive environment found in text in light of purpose, audience, and context.

This standard requires you to use a variety of strategies to understand, analyze, and evaluate expressive texts.

EXAMPLE: Reading Expressive Texts

The Thinking Critically and Extending and Evaluating questions on the Response and Analysis pages give you practice on analyzing and evaluating expressive texts. For example, see the questions about "The Hunger Artist" on page 880.

COMPETENCY GOAL 2

The learner will evaluate problems, examine cause/effect relationships, and answer research questions to inform an audience.

2.01 Demonstrate the ability to read, listen to and view a variety of increasingly complex print and non-print informational texts appropriate to grade level and course literary focus, by:

- selecting, monitoring, and modifying as necessary reading strategies appropriate to readers' purpose.
- identifying and analyzing text components (such as organizational structures, story elements, organizational features) and evaluating their impact on the text.
- providing textual evidence to support understanding of and reader's response to text.
- demonstrating comprehension of main idea and supporting details.
- summarizing key events and/or points from text.
- making inferences, predicting, and drawing conclusions based on text.
- identifying and analyzing personal, social, historical or cultural influences, contexts, or biases.
- making connections between works, self and related topics.
- analyzing and evaluating the effects of author's craft and style.
- analyzing and evaluating the connections or relationships between and among ideas, concepts, characters and/or experiences.
- identifying and analyzing elements of informational environment found in text in light of purpose, audience, and context.

You must use many strategies, such as comparing main ideas across texts and drawing conclusions, to respond to informational texts.

EXAMPLE: Comparing Main Ideas Across Texts

The Reading Skills activity on page 971 asks you to analyze several selections and present their common ideas.

2.02 Create responses that examine a cause/effect relationship among events by:

- effectively summarizing situations.
- showing a clear, logical connection among events.
- logically organizing connections by transitioning between points.
- developing appropriate strategies such as graphics, essays, and multimedia presentations to illustrate points.

As you read different types of texts, you must ask questions and conduct research.

EXAMPLE: Persuading with Cause and Effect

The Writing feature on page 381 helps you respond to a poem by prompting you to use cause and effect to write a persuasive essay to the main character.

2.03 Pose questions prompted by texts (such as the impact of imperialism on *Things Fall Apart*) and research answers by:

- accessing cultural information or explanations from print and non-print media sources.
- prioritizing and organizing information to construct a complete and reasonable explanation.

As you read different types of texts, you must ask questions and conduct research.

EXAMPLE: Asking Questions and Conducting Research

The Writing Workshop "Reporting Literary Research" on pages 1098–1111 guides you through the process of developing research questions about an author and his or her works, conducting research, organizing your ideas, and producing a research paper.

COMPETENCY GOAL 3

The learner will defend argumentative positions on literary or nonliterary issues.

3.01 Examine controversial issues by:

- sharing and evaluating initial personal response.
- researching and summarizing printed data.
- developing a framework in which to discuss the issue (creating a context).
- compiling personal responses and researched data to organize the argument.
- presenting data in such forms as a graphic, an essay, a speech, or a video.

You must examine a controversial issue by identifying your own opinions and those of others that you discovered through research. In addition, you are required to record your findings and present them.

EXAMPLE: Analyzing an Issue

The Writing Workshop "Examining a Controversial Issue in an Editorial" on pages 726–731 allows you to research a controversial issue by reviewing both sides. Then, you will determine your position on the issue and gather evidence to support it. You will share your opinion and your findings by writing an editorial.

3.02 Produce editorials or responses to editorials for a neutral audience by providing:

• a clearly stated position or proposed solution.
• relevant, reliable support.

You must present a clear opinion and make sure the support for your argument pertains to your stated topic and is credible.

EXAMPLE: Writing an Editorial

The Writing Workshop "Examining a Controversial Issue in an Editorial" on pages 726–731 will lead you through the steps of writing an editorial on an issue that includes relevant support.

3.03 Respond to issues in literature in such a way that:

• requires gathering of information to prove a particular point.
• effectively uses reason and evidence to prove a given point.
• emphasizes culturally significant events.

This standard requires many steps, from identifying an issue in literature to defending your ideas about the issue with evidence you gathered from research.

EXAMPLE: Conducting and Reporting Research

The "Reporting Literary Research" Writing Workshop on pages 1098–1111 directs you in finding reliable sources to support your ideas and guides you to report your findings in the correct format.

3.04 Demonstrate the ability to read, listen to and view a variety of increasingly complex print and non-print argumentative texts appropriate to grade level and course literary focus, by:

• selecting, monitoring, and modifying as necessary reading strategies appropriate to readers' purpose.

• identifying and analyzing text components (such as organizational structures, story elements, organizational features) and e valuating their impact on the text.

• providing textual evidence to support understanding of and reader's response to text.

• demonstrating comprehension of main idea and supporting details.

• summarizing key events and/or points from text.

• making inferences, predicting, and drawing conclusions based on text.

• identifying and analyzing personal, social, historical or cultural influences, contexts, or biases.

• making connections between works, self and related topics.

• analyzing and evaluating the effects of author's craft and style.

• analyzing and evaluating the connections or relationships between and among ideas, concepts, characters and/or experiences.

• identifying and analyzing elements of argumentative environment found in text in light of purpose, audience, and context.

You are required to use many strategies to respond to argumentative texts.

EXAMPLE: Using Reading Strategies

The Response and Analysis questions on page 189 ask you to analyze and evaluate a persuasive speech.

COMPETENCY GOAL 4

The learner will critically interpret and evaluate experiences, literature, language, and ideas.

4.01 Interpret a real-world event in a way that:
- makes generalizations about the event supported by specific references.
- reflects on observation and shows how the event affected the current viewpoint.
- distinguishes fact from fiction and recognizes personal bias.

You must use your knowledge of facts and opinions to evaluate an event and understand its significance.

EXAMPLE: Interpreting an Event

The Reading Skills feature "Interpreting Real-World Events" on page 913 prepares you to distinguish between the facts and personal feelings Elie Wiesel shares in his memoir of the Holocaust.

4.02 Analyze thematic connections among literary works by:
- showing an understanding of cultural context.
- using specific references from texts to show how a theme is universal.
- examining how elements such as irony and symbolism impact theme.

This standard requires you to identify and understand shared ideas of literary works.

EXAMPLE: Comparing Themes

The Reading Skills feature "Comparing Universal Themes Across Texts" on page 305 asks you to compare the similar ideas about life you find in three selections.

4.03 Analyze the ideas of others by identifying the ways in which writers:

- introduce and develop a main idea.
- choose and incorporate significant, supporting, relevant details.
- relate the structure/organization to the ideas.
- use effective word choice as a basis for coherence.
- achieve a sense of completeness and closure.

You must analyze writers' ideas by examining how the parts of a piece of writing work together to produce an effect on the reader.

EXAMPLE: Analyzing Style

The Literary Focus feature "Style" on page 456 provides you with a chart with definitions of different elements of style. On the same page, the Reading Skills feature "Analyzing Style" directs you to use those definitions to describe Lady Shōgan's style in an excerpt from *The Pillow Book*.

4.04 Evaluate the information, explanations, or ideas of others by:

- identifying clear, reasonable criteria for evaluation.
- applying those criteria using reasoning and substantiation.

Before you evaluate a writer's or speaker's ideas, you must first develop criteria for assessment. Then, you can discuss your findings using evidence from the text or speech.

EXAMPLE: Evaluating Peers

Every Writing Workshop gives you the opportunity to evaluate the writing of a fellow student. See, for example, "Peer Evaluation" on pages 729–730 in the Writing Workshop "Examining a Controversial Issue in an Editorial."

4.05 Demonstrate the ability to read, listen to and view a variety of increasingly complex print and non-print critical texts appropriate to grade level and course literary focus, by:

- selecting, monitoring, and modifying as necessary reading strategies appropriate to readers' purpose.
- identifying and analyzing text components (such as organizational structures, story elements, organizational features) and evaluating their impact on the text.
- providing textual evidence to support understanding of and reader's response to text.
- demonstrating comprehension of main idea and supporting details.
- summarizing key events and/or points from text.
- making inferences, predicting, and drawing conclusions based on text.
- identifying and analyzing personal, social, historical or cultural influences, contexts, or biases.
- making connections between works, self and related topics.
- analyzing and evaluating the effects of author's craft and style.
- analyzing and evaluating the connections or relationships between and among ideas, concepts, characters and/or experiences.
- identifying and analyzing elements of critical environment found in text in light of purpose, audience, and context.

Use strategies, including making connections between selections and evaluating those relationships, to respond to argumentative texts.

EXAMPLE: Examining Critical Texts

"From Middle Ages to Middle-Earth" on page 593 offers a critique that explains the influence of medieval literature on J.R.R. Tolkien's writing.

COMPETENCY GOAL 5

The learner will demonstrate understanding of selected world literature through interpretation and analysis.

5.01 Read and analyze selected works of world literature by:

- using effective strategies for preparation, engagement, and reflection.
- building on prior knowledge of the characteristics of literary genres, including fiction, non-fiction, drama, and poetry, and exploring how those characteristics apply to literature of world cultures.
- analyzing literary devices such as allusion, symbolism, figurative language, flashback, dramatic irony, situational irony, and imagery and explaining their effect on the work of world literature.
- analyzing the importance of tone and mood.
- analyzing archetypal characters, themes, and settings in world literature.
- making comparisons and connections between historical and contemporary issues.
- understanding the importance of cultural and historical impact on literary texts.

You are required to analyze world literature texts by looking for, in part, common themes, historical and cultural contexts, and the impact of literary devices and elements.

EXAMPLE: Analyzing and Comparing Literature

The Skills Review section for Collection 6 on pages 832–835 asks you to draw on your knowledge of literary elements, such as tone, symbolism, imagery, and mood, to analyze and compare two poems from separate cultural traditions that share a common theme.

5.02 Demonstrate increasing comprehension and ability to respond personally to texts by:

- selecting and exploring a wide range of works which relate to an issue, author, or theme of world literature.
- documenting the reading of student-chosen works.

You must read and respond to different types of world literature pieces.

EXAMPLE: Responding to Literature

The Writing Workshop "Analyzing Literature" and the Speaking and Listening Workshop "Presenting Literary Analysis" on pages 824–831 give you a chance to respond to a literary work by writing an essay or by giving a speech.

5.03 Demonstrate the ability to read, listen to and view a variety of increasingly complex print and non-print literacy texts appropriate to grade level and course literary focus, by:

- selecting, monitoring, and modifying as necessary reading strategies appropriate to readers' purpose.
- identifying and analyzing text components (such as organizational structures, story elements, organizational features) and evaluating their impact on the text.
- providing textual evidence to support understanding of and reader's response to text.
- demonstrating comprehension of main idea and supporting details.
- summarizing key events and/or points from text.
- making inferences, predicting, and drawing conclusions based on text.
- identifying and analyzing personal, social, historical or cultural influences, contexts, or biases.
- making connections between works, self and related topics.
- analyzing and evaluating the effects of author's craft and style.

- analyzing and evaluating the connections or relationships between and among ideas, concepts, characters and/or experiences.
- identifying and analyzing elements of literary environment found in text in light of purpose, audience, and context.

As you read different literary texts, you are required to use varying strategies, such as analyzing style and text structures, in order to show an understanding of the text.

EXAMPLE: Analyzing Style

The Reading Skill "Appreciating a Writer's Style" on page 709 gives you an opportunity to analyze Voltaire's humorous style in an excerpt from *Candide.*

COMPETENCY GOAL 6

The learner will apply conventions of grammar and language usage.

6.01 Demonstrate an understanding of conventional written and spoken expression by:

- employing varying sentence structures (e.g., inversion, introductory phrases) and sentence types (e.g., simple, compound, complex, compound-complex).
- analyzing authors' choice of words, sentence structure, and use of language.
- using word recognition strategies to understand vocabulary and exact word choice (Greek, Latin roots and affixes, analogies, idioms, denotation, connotation).
- using vocabulary strategies such as context clues, resources, and structural analysis (roots, prefixes, etc.) to determine meaning of words and phrases.
- examining textual and classroom language for elements such as idioms, denotation, and connotation to apply effectively in own writing/speaking.
- using correct form/format for essays, business letters, research papers, bibliographies.
- using language effectively to create mood and tone.

Be deliberate in your choice of words and your construction of sentences in order to achieve the effects you want your writing and speaking to have.

EXAMPLE: Developing Style

Page 1217 of the Language Handbook provides instruction on combining sentences.

Pages 1155–1156 of the Writer's Handbook have many examples of aspects of style, in particular, using language to achieve a specific tone.

6.02 Edit for:

- subject-verb agreement, tense choice, pronoun usage, clear antecedents, correct case, and complete sentences.
- appropriate and correct mechanics (commas, italics, underlining, semicolon, colon, apostrophe, quotation marks).
- parallel structure.
- clichés, trite expressions.
- spelling.

Eliminate errors in your writing by editing carefully. By adhering to grammatical conventions, you will ensure that your writing is understood by your audience.

EXAMPLE: Editing for Clarity and Correctness

The Language Handbook on pages 1200–1236 gives you a ready resource for answering any grammar, usage, and mechanics questions that may arise during revision. (See, for example, page 1224 for rules and examples in using colons.) Be sure to consult this handbook for help in writing, revising, and proofreading your essays.

The North Carolina Writing Assessment, Grade 10

This year, you will take the **Writing Assessment.** This test will measure your ability to express yourself clearly and effectively and determine whether you are ready for eleventh-grade writing assignments.

On the pages that follow, you will find information that will help you prepare for the Writing Assessment.

Taking the Writing Assessment

When you take the Writing Assessment, you will be asked to write an informational response to a prompt. This response requires you to explain your stance and support it with the ideas and information from the prompt, your own experiences, other readings, and/or observations. It will be scored based on its **content** and on your use of **writing conventions.** You will receive a score for content, a score for conventions, and a total writing score. The rubrics below and on page NC19 tell you which content and conventions elements scorers will look for in your paper.

CONTENT RUBRIC

A 4-point response

- has a clear topic or subject. This topic may not be stated in a topic sentence, but the whole response focuses on the topic.

- is organized to reflect the way the ideas or events in the response go together.

- logically relates ideas or events to one another and has no gaps in logic or information.

- contains only information that clearly supports the topic.

- uses plenty of specific details to support the topic.

- uses appropriate, precise vocabulary and a variety of correct sentence structures.

A 3-point response

- has a fairly clear topic or subject. This may not be stated in a topic sentence, but almost all of the response focuses on the topic.

- is mostly organized to reflect the way the ideas or events in the response go together.

- logically relates ideas or events to one another and has few gaps in logic or information.

- contains information that supports the topic.

- uses some specific details to support the topic.

- generally uses appropriate, precise vocabulary and a variety of correct sentence structures.

A 2-point response

- has a vague topic or subject. Some of the response focuses on the topic.

- is generally not organized to reflect the way the ideas or events in the response go together.

- may not logically relate ideas or events to one another and has major gaps in logic or information.

- may contain a large amount of information that does not support the topic.

- uses general, undeveloped details to support the topic.

- generally does not use appropriate, precise vocabulary or a variety of correct sentence structures.

A 1-point response

- has an unclear or confusing topic or subject. The response may not focus on the topic.

- is not organized to reflect the way the ideas or events in the response go together.

- does not logically relate ideas or events to one another and has major gaps in logic or information.

- may contain a large amount of information that does not support the topic.

- uses few details. These details do not support the topic or are confusing.

- does not use appropriate, precise vocabulary and may not use a variety of correct sentence structures.

A NS (non-scorable) response

- cannot be read.

- is blank.

- is written in a foreign language.

- restates the prompt.

- is off-topic or incoherent.

CONVENTIONS RUBRIC

A 2-point response

- uses correctly formed sentences.

- shows correct agreement, tense, and case.

- uses correct capitalization, punctuation, and spelling.

A 1-point response

- uses some correctly formed sentences.

- sometimes shows correct agreement, tense, and case.

- uses some correct capitalization, punctuation, and spelling.

A 0-point response

- does not use correctly formed sentences.

- does not show correct agreement, tense, and case.

- does not use correct capitalization, punctuation, and spelling.

HOW THE WRITING ASSESSMENT IS SCORED

As stated previously, your response will receive a content score, a conventions score, and an overall writing score. Unlike multiple-choice tests, which are scored by a machine, this test has readers. Two readers will independently evaluate your response using the rubrics you've just read. Each reader will assign a content score of 1 to 4 and a conventions score of 0 to 2. The content scores will be added together and multiplied by 2; the conventions scores will be added together and multiplied by 1. These figures will then be added together to determine your overall writing assessment score. The minimum score your response can receive is 4, and the maximum is 20. Here's an example of how a response might be scored.

	Content Score	Conventions Score
Reader 1:	4	2
Reader 2:	+ 3	+ 2
Total:	7	4
	× 2	× 1
Overall Writing Score:	14 +	4 = 18

STEPS FOR TAKING THE WRITING ASSESSMENT

Here are some steps and a suggested timetable you can use when responding to the writing prompt on the Writing Assessment, Grade 10. You'll probably find these steps in the writing process comfortable and familiar.

Watch Your Time

Prewriting	15 min.
Drafting	40 min.
Editing and Revising	20 min.
Proofreading	10 min.
Writing the Final Draft	15 min.

STEP 1   **Analyze the writing prompt.** Read the prompt, and think about what it means. Look for key words (such as *define, cause, effect*) that define your writing task. Identify your audience and purpose.

STEP 2   **Plan what you'll say.** You have about one hundred minutes to write your response, so take about fifteen minutes for prewriting. Brainstorm ideas, make an outline or chart, and think about organization. You may use a cluster diagram or other graphic organizer to list main ideas and supporting details.

STEP 3   **Draft your response.** Allow about forty minutes to draft your response. Pay special attention to a strong opening paragraph and a definite closing. Strive to express your ideas as clearly as you can, and add relevant details to support and elaborate each main point. Make sure you write your ideas in an order that is easy to follow.

One way to visualize an appropriate structure for your response is shown below.

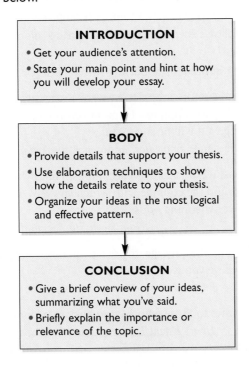

INTRODUCTION
- Get your audience's attention.
- State your main point and hint at how you will develop your essay.

BODY
- Provide details that support your thesis.
- Use elaboration techniques to show how the details relate to your thesis.
- Organize your ideas in the most logical and effective pattern.

CONCLUSION
- Give a brief overview of your ideas, summarizing what you've said.
- Briefly explain the importance or relevance of the topic.

Don't forget to vary the kinds of sentences (simple, compound, complex, compound/complex) you use.

STEP 4   **Edit and revise your draft.** Allow about twenty minutes to re-read and revise your first draft. Look for places where you can add transitions or combine sentences to make your sentences flow smoothly together. Strengthen your response by inserting additional supporting details and by moving sentences or paragraphs so that they are in a more logical order.

STEP 5   **Proofread your response.** Take at least ten minutes to search for and correct errors in grammar, usage, and mechanics. Be mindful of correct spelling and capitalization.

STEP 6   **Write the final draft.** Allow about fifteen minutes to copy your final draft into the response booklet. Make sure your handwriting is readable! If you need to make corrections, neatly cross out words and rewrite them correctly.

FIRST SAMPLE WRITING PROMPT

As you already know, the Writing Assessment in grade ten will ask you to respond to an informational prompt. Here is a sample prompt for the Writing Assessment. A set of guidelines follows the prompt. Each guideline refers to a content or conventions element.

Read the following quotations about the meaning of success.

Success is not the key to happiness. Happiness is the key to success. If you love what you are doing, you will be successful.

Albert Schweitzer, Alsatian medical missionary, theologian, and musician in Africa

Success is not measured by what you accomplish, but by the opposition you have encountered, and the courage with which you have maintained the struggle against overwhelming odds.

Orison Swett Marden, author of motivational books

Success means having the courage, the determination, and the will to become the person you believe you were meant to be.

George Sheehan, American physician, author, and running enthusiast

Success usually comes to those who are too busy to be looking for it.

Henry David Thoreau, American essayist, poet, and philosopher

---

Write a speech to be given to teachers and students at a school assembly on the meaning of success. You may use ideas presented above, your own experiences, observations, and/or readings.

As you write your speech, remember to:

- Identify clearly the meaning of success.

- Consider the audience, purpose, and context of your speech.

- Use specific details to support the topic.

- Present your ideas in a logical order that reflects the way the ideas should go together.

- Use correctly structured sentences and a variety of words.

- Correct any errors in grammar, usage, and mechanics.

PREWRITING: ORGANIZING YOUR IDEAS

Decide on a controlling point or main idea. The prompt presents a topic you can respond to without doing research. Your main idea must be directly related to the prompt. For this prompt, the main idea of your speech will relate to your definition of success.

Gather your ideas. You might create a chart, an outline, or a graphic organizer in which you can write your thoughts. Below is a cluster diagram by a writer who chose to define success as achieving a personal goal. Before drafting his speech, this writer thought about the topic presented in prompt, and then he brainstormed ideas to use when writing his response.

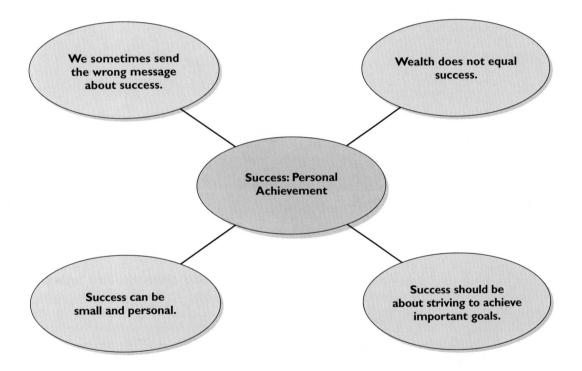

DRAFTING: GETTING IT DOWN ON PAPER

Time to write. You have a big head start because you know what you are going to say and roughly how you're going to organize your ideas. Keep in mind your **purpose** and **audience** so that you'll use appropriate language.

Don't keep the reader or listener guessing. Early in your introductory paragraph, include a clear statement of your main idea in a **thesis statement.**

The structure of introductory paragraphs frequently moves from general information to a more specific statement, which is typically the thesis statement. You might think of the structure as an inverted triangle, with the flat top as the **general opening** and the pointed bottom as the **precisely stated thesis**—the main idea that your response will support or prove. The graphic below is a visual representation of this structure.

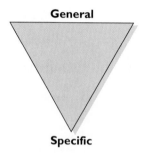

Add the details. As you draft, concentrate on **elaborating** (supporting) each paragraph's **main idea.** Each reason should be different and should be supported with details and examples. Be specific; test graders will be looking for precise words.

Find your own voice. Write with your own style and create your own "sound." However, since you are writing a formal speech, avoid using slang and contractions.

REVISING AND PROOFREADING: POLISHING YOUR DRAFT

The final step. Allow enough time to re-read your response. Read it once for sense and clarity. Read it a second time for style and sentence variety. Then, proofread it to catch mistakes in grammar, usage, mechanics, and spelling.

An especially important area to check is your use of transitions. Transitions are the words or phrases, like "for example" or "moreover," that tie your ideas together. They help your response not to sound like a listing of ideas.

WRITING THE FINAL DRAFT

Here is one writer's final draft in response to the writing prompt.

What Is Real Success?

What is success? Is it expensive sports cars? a three-story house in the hills? the latest fashions? Sadly, our culture—as seen in movies, songs, and TV ads—sometimes seems to say yes. However, I believe that success comes from personal achievement. Because wealth can be a sign of achievement, we sometimes confuse the two.

The messages society sends might be subtle, but we hear them and see them constantly: Own these products, dress this way, or live like these people, and you will be successful. However, there is a problem with that message; wealth and the "things" you can buy with it do not actually make you a success. In my opinion, some of the wealthiest people are not very successful. Although they might meet our culture's superficial definition of success, I think it is important to ask what they have achieved—at what have they succeeded? You have to look beyond the cars, the clothes, and the lifestyles and to the person within.

To me, real success is not necessarily about having wealth, accumulating the most stuff, or even being the very best. Success can be smaller and more personal. Author Orison Swett Marden said that "success is not measured by what you accomplish, but by the opposition you have encountered, and the courage with which you have maintained the struggle against overwhelming odds." That is, it is about people overcoming obstacles and striving to achieve something meaningful. It is the athlete who works out every day or the student who studies at night to earn a degree or the mother who works hard to take care of her family.

Success has the power to make a person feel proud and fulfilled in a way that wealth on its own cannot. Take, for example, my uncle Ken. I think he used to make a lot of money as an accountant. However, last year, he took a big risk: He quit his high-paying job so that he could pursue his dream of opening a restaurant. With a lot of hard work, he eventually did it. Today, Uncle Ken makes less money, but you can see that he seems proud of his accomplishment. Now _that_ is success. The problem is, powerful personal successes and triumphs get less attention than messages about wealth.

Wealth is definitely not a bad thing. Who does not want to be prosperous? However, I believe we, as a culture, need to look beyond the simple message that wealth equals success. I believe we need to send a new and truly invaluable message: Real success comes with achieving a meaningful goal or dream.

CHARACTERISTICS OF AN EXCELLENT RESPONSE

Now that you have finished your response, how can you tell whether it will earn a high score? Evaluate your writing by comparing it with the characteristics of an excellent response below.

- The writing is exceptionally engaging, clear, and focused.

- Ideas and content are thoroughly developed with relevant details and examples where appropriate.

- The writer's control over organization and the connections between ideas moves the reader smoothly and naturally through the text.

- The writer shows a mature command of language including precise word choice that results in a compelling piece of writing.

- Tight control over language use and mastery of writing conventions contribute to the effect of the response.

SECOND SAMPLE WRITING PROMPT

Here is another sample prompt. Remember that the bulleted guidelines below the prompt refer to a content or conventions element that scorers will look in your response.

Read the following quotations about the meaning of courage.

Courage—the state or quality of mind that enables one to face danger with self-possession, confidence, and resolution.

American Heritage Dictionary

We can never be certain of our courage until we have faced danger.

Francois de la Rochefoucauld, French classical author

Whatever you do, you need courage. Whatever course you decide upon, there is always someone to tell you that you are wrong.

Ralph Waldo Emerson, American poet, lecturer, and essayist

Courage is doing what you're afraid to do. There can be no courage unless you're scared.

Edward Vernon Rickenbacker, American pilot, businessman, and aviator

---

Write a speech to be given to your city council on the meaning of courage.

As you write your speech, remember to:

- Identify clearly the meaning of courage.

- Consider the audience, purpose, and context of your speech.

- Present your ideas in a logical order that reflects the way the ideas should go together.

- Use correctly structured sentences and a variety of words.

- Correct any errors in grammar, usage, and mechanics.

PREWRITING: ORGANIZING YOUR IDEAS

Decide on a controlling point or main idea. Again, your main idea must be directly related to the prompt. For this prompt, the main idea of your speech will relate to your definition of courage.

Gather your ideas. You might create a chart, an outline, or a graphic organizer in which you write your thoughts.

To help you gather ideas, you can also ask yourself the following questions as needed.

- *To what larger class does this term belong? What is it?*
  Answering this question puts your term in a category with similar terms.

- *What is it not?*
  Showing how a term is different from ideas your audience knows can help them to better understand the term.

- *What are its characteristics? What is it like?*
  By answering this question, you will find the qualities or features of your term—the things that make it unique among the other members of its class.

- *How can the definition be extended? What are some examples?*
  There is no single right way to extend a definition. There are many methods for defining, and each one adds a different kind of information to a definition. The best definitions combine several methods to define a term. Some of these are opinions, examples, quotations, comparisons, descriptions, and personal anecdotes and feelings.

Below is a cluster diagram by a writer who chose to define courage. Before drafting his speech, this writer thought about the topic presented in the prompt, the quotations given, and then he brainstormed ideas to use when writing his response. Pay particular attention to the questions that triggered his ideas: "What is it not?" "What are the characteristics?" "What are some examples?"

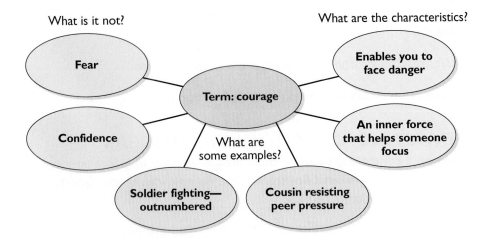

DRAFTING: GETTING IT DOWN ON PAPER

Time to write. Now it's time to draft your response. As you write, keep in mind your **purpose** and **audience** so that you'll use appropriate language.

State your point. Remember that you need to include a **thesis statement,** or main point, early in your introductory paragraph. A thesis gives the reader or listener a clear picture of how your response will proceed. One way of developing a thesis is by showing that a term can mean one thing, despite the fact that many people think it means something else. Another way to develop a thesis is to show how a term's extended definition differs from its short definition.

Add the details. Support your ideas by elaborating each paragraph's main idea. Provide examples and be specific with your explanations and illustrations of the term.

Find your own voice. Even though your tone should be formal, write with our own style and create your own "sound." The unique way you express yourself should be natural, not stilted.

Sum it up. Give a brief overview of your definition, and, if applicable, concentrate on the ways it differs from the dictionary or common definition. You might also explain why your definition is more accurate or useful than the brief definition given in a dictionary.

REVISING AND PROOFREADING: POLISHING YOUR DRAFT

The final step. Before you turn in your test booklet, read your response a couple of times. Make sure that your points are clear and expressed with style. Also, proofread it to catch mistakes in grammar, usage, and mechanics.

WRITING THE FINAL DRAFT

Here is one writer's final draft in response to the writing prompt.

The Meaning of Courage

We all know courage when we see it. It is the "special something" that enables firefighters to run into burning buildings to save people. It prompts a soldier to rush headlong into a losing battle or a mother to dash into a busy street to whisk her child out of traffic. In all these examples, people take action despite physical dangers, and they seem self-possessed and resolved when they do. Believe it or not, however, their behavior does not fit the common definition of courage. The American Heritage Dictionary defines courage as "the state or quality of mind" that differs from others because it "enables one to face danger with self-possession, confidence, and resolution." I think these examples actually show that confidence is not always a necessary part of courage. Moreover, I think that in order to understand courage, you need to think about what danger means.

It may help first to examine the confidence of the soldier and the firefighter. Both have been thoroughly trained to meet the physical dangers and psychological challenges of their assignments. They recognize the risks that go along with their jobs, and they assume that their training will help them face those risks. To that extent, they are confident. Nevertheless, both of these people have moments on the job when they do not feel confident about what they have to do. In fact, both can be confronted by situations that defy confidence. Still, an inner strength—courage—sustains them, and they act despite their lack of confidence.

Confidence is trust, not just in yourself but also in the situation. The soldier who lands on a beach where his army is outnumbered four to one may have confidence in his training, but he may not have much confidence that his situation will turn out for the best. He fights to protect his fellow soldiers (and perhaps even to defend an idea like liberty), even as he may have doubts that he and his comrades will live. No one I know would dare say he acts without courage just because he acts without confidence. Similarly, when a firefighter dashes into a burning building, he hopes rather than trusts that he and the people trapped in the fire will emerge safely. He chooses to disregard his lack of confidence and tries to save people anyway.

French author François de la Rochefoucauld said, " We can never be certain of our courage until we face danger." However, I think this it is a false assumption to think that it must be physical danger. Many times it does, but more often courage is what lets people risk being hurt emotionally. Take, for instance, the case of my cousin Lucia, who resisted peer pressure to cheat on a test. When she told her friends she would not do it, she was pretty sure that they would not openly call her a wimp. However, she suspected that they would not talk to her in school the next day, and that they might convince other students to avoid her, which would make her feel miserable. In fact, Lucia's friends did not reject her, but it still took courage for her to speak her mind when she knew how she would feel if they had rejected her.

In conclusion, I think we need to stop thinking of courage as a state of mind that requires confidence. Not every person who acts heroically can honestly say, "I am confident that everything is going to be all right." Sometimes, people who act heroically are acting on instinct and not thinking anything at all. Other times, they lack confidence but push aside their doubts and fears to do what they need to do. Also, we should consider that acting with courage does not always involve putting your life on the line. More often, it means taking an emotional risk because you believe you must do so. By understanding more thoroughly the characteristics of courage, we can appreciate that most of us have the capacity to be courageous—at least a little bit—every day of our lives.

Preparing to Take Tests

You have studied and taken practice tests, and now you are ready to take the Writing Assessment. However, you feel you may get nervous moments before the test. What do you do? The section below offers strategies you can use to combat your nerves and to prepare yourself mentally and physically for the test.

THE NIGHT BEFORE

- Review any test-taking notes you might have. Be familiar with the types of questions you will encounter.

- Prepare your materials. Get together everything you will need for your test, such as sharp pencils, scratch paper, or anything else you will need.

- Get plenty of sleep. Go to bed at your usual time. If you are nervous, try reading a magazine or listening to soothing music.

THE MORNING OF THE TEST

- Eat breakfast. Even if you feel nervous, your brain will need energy. Avoid sugary foods that could make you sleepy later.

- Double check to make sure you have everything you need for the test.

- Leave in plenty of time to get to school. You don't want to feel rushed when you arrive at the testing site.

DURING THE TEST

- Stay calm. Remind yourself that you have prepared carefully and can expect to do well.

- Keep breathing. Breathing deeply helps keep you calm and supplies the brain with oxygen.

- Check the time periodically. You want to make sure that you have enough time to finish the test.

HOLT
ELEMENTS OF
LITERATURE

World Literature

HOLT
ELEMENTS OF
LITERATURE®

World Literature

HOLT, RINEHART AND WINSTON

A Harcourt Education Company

Orlando • **Austin** • New York • San Diego • Toronto • London

EDITORIAL
Editorial Vice President: Ralph Tachuk
Executive Book Editor: Patricia McCambridge
Senior Book Editor: Leslie Griffin
Senior Product Manager: Don Wulbrecht
Managing Editor: Marie Price
Editorial Staff: Julie Hill, Kerry Johnson, Michael Zakhar
Copyediting Manager: Michael Neibergall
Senior Copyediting Supervisor: Mary Malone
Copyediting Supervisor: Kristen Azzara
Copyeditors: Christine Altgelt, Elizabeth Dickson, Emily Force, Leora Harris, Anne Heausler, Stephanie Jones, Kathleen Scheiner, Nancy Shore, Lisa Vecchione
Associate Managing Editor: Elizabeth LaManna
Editorial Support: Christine Degollado, Betty Gabriel, Janet Jenkins, Alissa LeViness, Erik Netcher, Gloria Shahan, Emily Stern
Editorial Permissions: Ann Farrar
Index: M. L. Pilkinton

DESIGN
Book Design
Director, Book Design: Kay Selke
Senior Design Director: Betty Mintz
Page Designers: Paul Caullett, Peter Sawchuk

Media Design
Design Director: Richard Metzger
Developmental Designer: Chris Smith

Image Acquisitions
Director: Curtis Riker
Senior Picture Researcher: Mary Monaco

PRODUCTION
Production Manager: Carol Trammel
Senior Production Coordinators: Carol Marunas, Dolores Keller
Manufacturing Supervisor: Shirley Cantrell
Inventory Analyst: Mark McDonald
Inventory Supervisor: Ivania Quant Lee
Media Manufacturing Coordinator: Amy Borseth

Cover
Photo Credits: (inset) Japanese six-fold screen depicting reeds and cranes, by Suzuki Kiitsu. Edo period (19th century). Color on gilded silk. © The Detroit Institute of Art, USA/Founders Society Purchase/Bridgeman Art Library. (background) Photograph of Sakura (cherry blossom) season, park in Kyoto, Japan. © Chad Ehlers/Index Stock Imagery

Printed in the United States of America

ISBN 0-03-037722-6   3 4 5 048 08 07 06

Program Author

Kylene Beers established the reading pedagogy for *Elements of Literature*. A former middle-school teacher, Dr. Beers has turned her commitment to helping readers having difficulty into the major focus of her research, writing, speaking, and teaching. Dr. Beers is currently Senior Reading Researcher at the Child Study Center of the School Development Program at Yale University and was formerly a Research Associate Professor at the University of Houston. Dr. Beers is also currently the editor of the National Council of Teachers of English journal *Voices from the Middle.* She is the author of *When Kids Can't Read: What Teachers Can Do* and the co-editor of *Into Focus: Understanding and Creating Middle School Readers.* Dr. Beers is the 2001 recipient of the Richard Halle Award from the NCTE for outstanding contributions to middle-level literacy education. She has served on the review boards of the *English Journal* and *The Alan Review.* Dr. Beers currently serves on the board of directors of the International Reading Association's Special Interest Group on Adolescent Literature.

Writers

Claire Miller Colombo holds a doctorate in English from the University of Texas at Austin. She has taught literature and composition at both the college and the secondary levels and has published articles on Romantic poetry, drama, and culture. She has been a freelance writer of educational materials for fifteen years.

Kathleen Daniel has edited and directed middle-school and secondary literature and language arts programs for over forty years, specializing in the development of literature anthologies. She currently works as a writer, editor, and educational consultant.

Mescal K. Evler has been writing and editing educational materials for more than twenty years. A former middle-school and high school teacher and English department chair, she has a masters degree in English and a Ph.D. in English education.

Phyllis Goldenberg graduated from the University of Chicago and did graduate work in literature at Columbia University. She has over thirty years' experience as an educational writer and editor specializing in literature, grammar, and composition materials for secondary-school students. She is the author of a student guide to writing a research paper and the author and series editor of a grammar and composition program for middle-school and high school students.

Christopher LeCluyse holds a doctorate in English Language and Linguistics from the University of Texas at Austin. He has taught college-level courses in writing, literature, linguistics, and information technology and administrated UT's Undergraduate Writing Center. Dr. LeCluyse has edited and written instructional materials in grammar, usage, and mechanics since 1997.

Carroll Moulton holds a Ph.D. in classics from Yale University. He has taught literature at the university and secondary levels for over thirty years. Author of numerous books and articles, he served on the editorial board of *Classical World* and as editor-in-chief of *Ancient Greece and Rome: An Encyclopedia for Students.* Besides his interests in classical, English, and comparative literature, he has written and lectured extensively in the field of conservation and the environment. His most recent publication is *Kanha Tiger Reserve: Portrait of an Indian National Park.*

Fannie Safier, a former teacher, has written and edited language arts materials for thirty-five years.

Mairead Stack has a master's degree in English from New York University. A former teacher, she has edited and written educational materials for literature and language arts for more than twenty years.

Reviewers

Charles (Rick) Craddock
Garfield High School
Akron, Ohio

Melinda Darrow
Westlake High School
Austin, Texas

Margaret Garrison
Peninsula High School
Gig Harbor, Washington

Bonnie McMurray
Union County Public
   Schools
Monroe, North Carolina

Traci Saxton
Content Specialist, English
   Language Arts 6–12
East Orange Board of
   Education
East Orange, New Jersey

John R. Williamson
Highlands High School
Fort Thomas, Kentucky

Research Participants

Todd Bertsch
Newport High School
Newport, Kentucky

Ruth Feinman
Trinidad High School
Trinidad, Colorado

Andrea Ferraro
Nandua High School
Onley, Virginia

Gary Hale
Woodlawn High School
Woodlawn, Maryland

Kaley Keenan
North Monterey County
   High School
Castroville, California

Scott Legan
West Geauga
   High School
Chesterland, Ohio

Mike Messmore
Brighton High School
Brighton, Michigan

Madonna Mezzanotte
Sprayberry High School
Marietta, Georgia

Laura Schneider
Simon Kenton
   High School
Independence, Kentucky

Carol Hollar-Watson
Kinston High School
Kinston, North Carolina

CONTENTS IN BRIEF

Collection 1

THE ANCIENT MIDDLE EAST

c. 3000 B.C. – A.D. 100
ANCIENT VOICES, ANCIENT WISDOM

COLLECTION 1: SKILLS REVIEW

Comparing Literature

Collection 2

ANCIENT GREEK AND ROMAN LITERATURE

800 B.C. – A.D. 200
THE LIFE WORTH LIVING

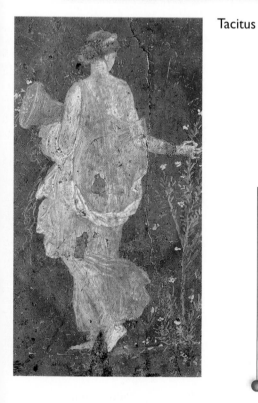

Collection 3

Literature of India, China, and Japan

2500 B.C. – A.D. 1800s
THE SEARCH FOR TRUTH AND ENLIGHTENMENT

JAPANESE LITERATURE

Collection 4

LITERATURE OF AFRICA AND THE MIDDLE EAST

700 B.C. – A.D. 1800s
THE POWER OF THE WORD

ARABIC AND PERSIAN LITERATURE

Collection 5

European Literature from the Middle Ages to the Enlightenment

500–1800
A TIME OF TRANSITION

RENAISSANCE AND ENLIGHTENMENT LITERATURE

Collection 6

European Literature in the Nineteenth Century

1800–1900
IMAGINATION AND REALITY

Collection 7

Modern and Contemporary World Literature

1900 – Present
A WORLD WITHOUT BORDERS

Resource Center

SELECTIONS BY THEME

SELECTIONS BY GENRE

LYRIC POETRY

SELECTIONS BY REGION

SKILLS, WORKSHOPS, AND FEATURES

SKILLS

LITERARY SKILLS

READING SKILLS

READING MATTERS

VOCABULARY SKILLS

WORKSHOPS

WRITING WORKSHOPS

LISTENING AND SPEAKING WORKSHOPS

MEDIA WORKSHOP

Creating a Multimedia Presentation 1114

FEATURES

A CLOSER LOOK

That Mysterious Wedge-Shaped Writing 10
The Discovery of the Dead Sea Scrolls 17
Classical Allusions in Modern English 110
Mughal Masterpieces 356
Teaching to the Test .359
Where Nasrudin Goes, Laughter Follows 499
From the Middle Ages to Middle-Earth 593
Drama During the Enlightenment 603
Preserving a National Heritage:
The Brothers Grimm .750
The Gold Standard:
The Nobel Prize in Literature 852

CRITICAL COMMENTS

Tragedy and the Tragic Hero 263
Dante's Allegory 664
The Utopia as a Literary Genre 720

GRAMMAR LINK

Connecting Ideas: Using Adjective
and Adverb Clauses 75
Getting Along: Subject-Verb Agreement 266
Pointing to the Right Place: Agreement
of Pronoun and Antecedent 400
From Time to Time: Keeping Verb
Tenses Consistent 536
Avoiding Misplaced and Dangling Modifiers 634
Make Your Meaning Clear: Avoiding
Sentence Fragments and Run-on Sentences 822
Building Coherence: Using Direct References,
Transitions, and Conjunctions 1001

LANGUAGE HANDBOOK

The Parts of Speech .1200
Agreement 1201

Using Verbs 1203
Using Pronouns 1205
Using Modifiers 1207
Phrases 1208
Clauses 1210
Sentence Structure 1211
Sentence Style 1214
Sentence Combining .1217
Capitalization 1218
Punctuation 1221, 1224
Spelling 1229
Glossary of Usage 1231

SKILLS REVIEW

Comparing Literature 94, 338, 480, 576,
732, 832, 1122
Vocabulary 98, 342, 484, 580,
736, 836, 1124
Writing .99, 343, 485, 581,
737, 837, 1125

THE WORLD OF WORK

Reading for Work and Life 1143
Informative Documents 1143
Persuasive Documents 1145
Writing for Work and Life 1146
Job Applications and Résumés 1146
Business Letters 1147
Word-Processing Features 1147

WRITER'S HANDBOOK

The Writing Process .1149
Paragraphs 1151
The Writer's Language 1155
Designing Your Writing 1157

TEST SMARTS

Strategies for Taking Multiple-Choice Tests 1161
Strategies for Taking Writing Tests 1170

Elements of Literature on the Internet

TO THE STUDENT

At the *Elements of Literature* Internet site, you can analyze the work of skilled writers and learn inside stories about your favorite authors. You can also build your word power and analyze messages in the media. As you move through *Elements of Literature*, you will find the best online resources at **go.hrw.com**.

Here's how to log on:

1. Start your Web browser, and enter **go.hrw.com** in the Address or Location field.

2. Note the keyword in your textbook.

INTERNET

Vocabulary Practice

Keyword:
LE5 WL-1

3. Enter the keyword, and click "go."

FEATURES OF THE SITE

More About the Writer
Author biographies provide the inside stories behind the lives and works of great writers.

More Writer's Models
Interactive Writer's Models present annotations and reading tips to help you with your own writing.

Interactive Reading Workshops
Interactive Reading Workshops guide you through high-interest informational articles and allow you to share your opinions through pop-up questions and polls.

Vocabulary Practice
Interactive vocabulary-building activities help you build your word power.

Cross-Curricular Connections
Short informational readings relate the literature you read in your textbook to your other studies and to real life.

Projects and Activities
Projects and activities help you extend your study of literature through writing, research, art, and public speaking.

Speeches
Video clips from historical speeches provide you with the tools you need to analyze elements of great speechmaking.

Media Tutorials
Media tutorials help you dissect messages in the media and learn to create your own multimedia presentations.

THE ANCIENT MIDDLE EAST

c. 3000 B.C.–A.D. 100

Ancient Voices, Ancient Wisdom

Writing is the mother of eloquence and the father of artists.

—Mesopotamian proverb

(Opposite) Sumerian votive statues from the Square Temple of Abu, Ashnunak, Iraq (c. 2900–2600 B.C.E.).

The Oriental Institute of the University of Chicago.

go.hrw.com

INTERNET

Collection Resources

Keyword: LE5 WL-1

The Ancient Middle East

5000 B.C.	3000 B.C.	2500 B.C.	2000 B.C.

c. 4500 B.C. Sumerians settle in Mesopotamia

c. 3500 B.C. City-states emerge in Sumer

c. 3500–3000 B.C. Sumerians develop cuneiform writing; Sumerians build temples at Eridu, Ur, and Uruk; Egyptians invent hieroglyphic writing

c. 3000–2500 B.C. Cuneiform tablets are inscribed with Sumerian writings

c. 2750 B.C. Gilgamesh is king in Uruk

c. 2575–2130 B.C. Old Kingdom in Egypt

c. 2500 B.C. The Pyramids and the Great Sphinx are built in Egypt; legends about Gilgamesh begin to appear on cuneiform tablets

c. 2334 B.C. Sargon I seizes control of Sumer; Akkadian Empire begins

c. 2000 B.C. Egyptian *Coffin Texts* are compiled

c. 1938–c. 1630 B.C. Middle Kingdom in Egypt

c. 1792 B.C. Babylon reaches its cultural and artistic peak under Hammurabi

c. 1750 B.C. Hammurabi's Code is set down in Babylon

c. 1600 B.C. Hittites invade Babylon

c. 1580–1350 B.C. Egyptian Book of the Dead is assembled

Pyramid and Sphinx, Giza.

5000 B.C.	3000 B.C.	2500 B.C.	2000 B.C.

c. 5000–c. 3000 B.C. Yangshao culture grows in China

c. 3500 B.C. Civilization begins to develop in southwest Asia

c. 3000–c. 1100 B.C. The rise and fall of Minoan civilization

c. 3000 B.C. The beginning of the Bronze Age in Crete and the Cyclades

c. 2500 B.C. Indus Valley civilization in northwest India reaches its height

c. 2300 B.C. Indus Valley people use pictographs and trade with people of the Tigris and Euphrates river valleys

c. 2000–c. 1500 B.C. Minoans on the island of Crete use the decimal numbering system

c. 1750 B.C. Indo-Aryan speakers begin migrating to India

c. 1600–c. 1200 B.C. Mycenaean culture prospers on the Greek mainland

Gold vessel in the shape of a ship (c. 2300 B.C.E.). From the Schliemann treasure, discovered in Troy.

Museum für Vor- und Frühgeschichte, Staatliche Museen zu Berlin.

(Opposite) Mound of Hissarlik, site of the ancient city of Troy (3000–1100 B.C.E.).

c. 3000 B.C.–A.D. 100

THE ANCIENT MIDDLE EAST

1500 B.C.	1000 B.C.	500 B.C.	A.D. 1
c. 1550–1085 B.C. New Kingdom in Egypt	c. 1000 B.C. The Torah is assembled from earlier Hebrew texts	c. 380–343 B.C. Last Egyptian dynasty	c. A.D. 30 Jesus of Nazareth dies
c. 1375–1362 B.C. Akhenaten institutes religious reforms in Egypt	c. 1000–c. 587 B.C. The writings of the Hebrew Bible prophets are composed	c. 330 B.C. Alexander the Great conquers Mesopotamia and Egypt	c. A.D. 50–c. 150 The books of the New Testament are written
c. 1354 B.C. Assyrians rise to power in Mesopotamia	c. 950–c. 750 B.C. The biblical Book of Ruth is written	c. 6–c. 4 B.C. Jesus of Nazareth is born	c. A.D. 70 Romans destroy Jerusalem
c. 1300 B.C. The *Epic of Gilgamesh* is written down by Babylonians in Mesopotamia	c. 750–c. 655 B.C. Kushite kingdom in Africa gains control of Egypt		
	c. 587 B.C. Many Hebrews are taken into exile by Babylonian King Nebuchadnezzar II		

Gold coin of Alexander the Great (336–323 B.C.E.).
The Granger Collection, New York.

1500 B.C.	1000 B.C.	500 B.C.	A.D. 1
c. 1500 B.C. Hinduism starts to develop in India	c. 1000 B.C. Earliest hymns from the Rig-Veda are written down in India; the first ancestors of today's Japanese population arrive in Japan	c. 551–479 B.C. Chinese sage Confucius teaches ethical principles known as Confucianism, which are recorded in his *Analects*	c. A.D. 1–c. A.D. 200 The *Bhagavad-Gita* is written down in India
c. 1500–1122 B.C. Art of writing is developed in China during the Shang dynasty	c. 900–500 B.C. Later Vedas, Upanishads, and Brahmanas are compiled in India	c. 387 B.C. Plato founds the Academy in Athens, Greece	A.D. 64 Rome is destroyed by fire under the emperor Nero
c. 1250 B.C. Mycenaeans destroy rival city of Troy	c. 753 B.C. Rome is founded	c. 100 B.C.–c. A.D. 500 *Panchatantra* is written in India	c. A.D. 200 Christianity is introduced to northern Africa by way of the Roman Empire
	c. 700 B.C. In Greece, Homer writes the *Iliad*	c. 27 B.C. Roman Empire is established	

The Ancient Middle East **3**

Cultural and Historical

The Invention of Writing

4000–3000 B.C.

Between 4000 and 3000 B.C., the Sumerians invented cuneiform, among the world's oldest known writing systems. Cuneiform, which means "wedge-shaped," consists of roughly triangular markings inscribed on clay tablets with a pointed stick. Cuneiform was used by numerous cultures that came after the Sumerians and became the standard writing system of the region.

Around the end of the fourth millennium B.C., the Egyptians developed hieroglyphs, a script in which pictures represent ideas. The ornamental and beautiful hieroglyphic writing was often painted on or carved into wood or stone. Over time, hieroglyphic symbols evolved to represent syllables and sounds, rather than ideas.

Mery, scribe and head of the royal archives. Dynasty 4 (c. 2575–2450 B.C.E.). Relief from Saqqara.

Musée du Louvre, Paris.

The Origin of Legal Systems

c. 1792–c. 1200 B.C.

In about 1792 B.C., a great Babylonian ruler named Hammurabi began developing the Code of Hammurabi. This list of 282 laws covered almost every aspect of daily life, from marriage and divorce to theft and slavery. The laws set fines and punishments for crimes: People who were found guilty of major offenses could have a hand or arm broken or severed or an eye gouged out; execution of the criminal or his family members was the punishment for the worst crimes. Despite its harshness, the Code of Hammurabi created a consistent and predictable legal system in the region.

The Hebrews codified and followed another ancient set of laws, which were attributed to Moses and believed to have come directly from God. Known as Mosaic law, these principles, which include the Ten Commandments, instructed the Hebrews on ethics, or moral conduct, and covered every aspect of daily life. Mosaic law remains central to the Jewish faith.

The Walls and Hanging Gardens of Babylon. Wood engraving and original coloring after a drawing from 1886 by Ferdinand Knab.

Monuments to Greatness

c. 2575–c. 562 B.C.

The great rulers of the ancient world displayed their power in structures so large, so beautiful, and so original that they continue to capture our imagination. The Hanging Gardens of Babylon, supposedly built by the Babylonian king Nebuchadnezzar II (c. 605–c. 561 B.C.), was a magnificent "mountain" of stone terraces draped with lush plants and leafy trees.

Desiring to assert their power even after death, the pharaohs of ancient Egypt built immense pyramid tombs to house their mummified bodies and royal possessions. Two of the greatest of these pyramids were built over four thousand years ago in Giza.

The Hebrew king Solomon, the son of King David, also undertook many building projects. The most famous of his buildings was the Temple of Jerusalem, which stood for four centuries until the Babylonians destroyed it in the sixth century B.C. But the truly great monument left by the Hebrews was neither an empire nor a structure: It was the Hebrew Bible, the lasting record of the Hebrews' historical experience and uniting faith.

Code of Hammurabi (c. 1792–1750 B.C.E.). Babylonian stele from Susa, Iran.

Musée du Louvre, Paris.

The Ancient Middle East
c. 3000 B.C.–A.D. 100

PREVIEW

Think About . . .

In the ancient Middle East, highly developed civilizations flourished thousands of years ago. The cultures of Mesopotamia preserved the record of their existence by making inscriptions on clay tablets. The Egyptians left records of their culture in hieroglyphic script. The Hebrew people left behind a powerful legacy in the Hebrew Bible. The literature of these ancient civilizations has contributed to our institutions and helped to shape our traditions and beliefs.

As you read about the history and literature of the ancient Middle East, look for answers to the following questions:

- What is probably the most important legacy of the ancient Mesopotamians?
- What cultural contributions did the ancient Egyptians make to civilization?
- How were the Hebrews different from their neighboring cultures in both their history and their beliefs?

North Carolina Competency Goal
1.02; 1.03;
4.02; 4.05;
5.01; 5.03

Collection introduction (pages 6–18) covers

Literary Skills Evaluate the philosophical, historical, and cultural influences of the historical period.

The first three thousand years of Western history were played out in two great river-valley civilizations: Mesopotamia in southwest Asia and Egypt in upper Africa. Agriculture was born in these regions, as were the first cities. Scientific and mathematical knowledge, architectural advancements, legal systems, forms of government, religious systems, and countless other innovations that still influence our lives came out of these ancient cultures. These cultures were also responsible for the world's first writing systems—and the literature and historical records that have enabled us to understand these ancient peoples.

Mesopotamian Literature

Mesopotamia (mes′ə·pə·tā′mē·ə), a word that means "land between rivers," is the name given by the Greeks to an ancient area of the Middle East. Today the region corresponds roughly to much of Iraq and parts of Iran, Turkey, and Syria. This area, an agriculturally rich land watered by the Tigris and Euphrates (yoo·frāt′ēz) rivers, is also known as the **Fertile Crescent.**

The Standard of Ur (detail) (c. 2500 B.C.E.). Sumerian, from Ur, southern Iraq.

The British Museum, London.

A Civilization Built on Mud

Mesopotamia attracted a series of peoples who successively dominated the region, starting with the **Sumerians.** Drawn to the fertile delta land formed by the Tigris and Euphrates rivers, these nomadic people settled in Sumer between 5000 and 4000 B.C.

The Sumerians dug canals to drain the delta marshlands and to provide irrigation for their crops. There was no stone in the region, and virtually no timber, so the Sumerians used mud to build their houses and to make an excellent grade of pottery. Mud also provided the raw material for the clay tablets on which the Sumerians recorded their laws, financial transactions, and literature. The entire Sumerian civilization, one might say, was fashioned out of river mud.

The Sumerians lived in city-states, each consisting of a large town or city and its surrounding lands. These city-states were laid out around great pyramid-like temples called **ziggurats** (zig′ oo·rats′), buildings as high as six or seven stories. Unlike the pyramids of the Egyptians, the ziggurats were layered, like wedding cakes, and they were probably brightly decorated, with each story painted a different color. Each ziggurat was presided over by a priest-king, believed to be the earthly representative of the local god. The largest city-states, such as Ur and Uruk, had a population in the tens of thousands. Oddly, though many of the city-states were in sight of one another, the Sumerians seem never to have developed a central, unifying government.

Cultural Legacy of the Sumerians

With farming and trade as their economic base, the Sumerians were able to turn their energies to artistic and scientific achievements. Renowned for their beautiful stonework, metalwork, and sculpture,

> *No matter where the Sumerians came from, and whatever type of culture they brought with them, this much is certain: their arrival led to an extraordinary ethnic and cultural fusion with the native population that brought about a major creative spurt for the history of civilization.*
>
> —Samuel Noah Kramer

Ziggurat of Inshushinak and Napirisha in Choqa Zanbil, Iran.

they were also highly skilled architects, as their ziggurats and other buildings show. Among other accomplishments, the Sumerians were able to develop a mathematical system with a number base of sixty, and they devised a remarkably precise twelve-month calendar based on the cycles of the moon.

Perhaps the Sumerians' chief cultural achievement, however, was their invention of one of humanity's oldest systems of writing: **cuneiform** (kyo͞o·nē′ə·fôrm′). The distinctive wedge-shaped cuneiform markings (the word is from the Latin *cuneus,* meaning "wedge") were made by pressing a stylus, or pointed stick, on wet clay tablets.

The Pyramids first, which in Egypt were laid; / Next Babylon's Garden for Amytis made. . . .

—from "Seven Wonders of the Ancient World," Anonymous

The Rise of Babylon

Sometime before 2000 B.C., the Sumerians were conquered by a Semitic people who established a magnificent capital city on the banks of the Euphrates River. The city was called **Babylon,** meaning "gate of the gods"; it was located close to what we know today as Baghdad, in Iraq. Under the Babylonians, as the newcomers came to be called, the Sumerians lost all political power and identity. Recognizing the value of the Sumerian culture, however, the Babylonians adapted the Sumerian cuneiform script to their own Semitic language, Akkadian. The Babylonians translated many Sumerian writings, including the *Epic of Gilgamesh,* and they continued to use Sumerian as a literary language, much as Europeans used Latin throughout the Middle Ages.

About 1792 B.C., under the reign of **Hammurabi** (hä′mo͞o·rä′bē), Babylon became the religious and cultural center of western Asia. The **Code of Hammurabi,** a collection of 282 laws, regulated every aspect of Babylonian life, from building codes to marriage and divorce. Highly detailed and harshly punitive, the code was based on the rigid concept of "an eye for an eye, a tooth for a tooth."

The Great Library of Nineveh

For years, Babylon suffered invasion after invasion by mountain peoples looking for a better life in the rich valley region of the Tigris and Euphrates rivers. Then, in about 900 B.C., the **Assyrians** (ə·sir′ē·ənz), a fiercely warlike people, came into Mesopotamia.

The Assyrians built their capital, **Nineveh** (nin′ə·və), on the banks of the Tigris, about 230 miles north of present-day Baghdad. There they created a magnificent library in which the clay tablets containing Sumerian and Babylonian literature were carefully stored and preserved. In the mid–nineteenth century, archaeologists excavated tablets containing the priceless remains of Sumerian-Babylonian writings from the ruins of Nineveh.

Bronze portal of King Nebuchadnezzar of Babylon (12th century C.E.).

The Rebirth and Fall of Babylon

In 612 B.C., the Assyrians were overthrown, and Babylon rose once again to enjoy a period of glory. The ruler **Nebuchadnezzar** (neb′yə·kəd·nez′ər) rebuilt Babylon, creating spectacular palaces and temples. The city became famous for its Hanging Gardens, one of the Seven Wonders of the World recognized by the ancient Greeks. Babylon was also known for a great ziggurat that some historians have identified as the biblical Tower of Babel. ("Babel" was the Hebrew name for Babylon.)

Babylon fell to Cyrus the Great of Persia in 539 B.C. It remained a center of trade and culture for several centuries, until a new port was established at a more favorable site on the Euphrates. After that, Babylon, the last of the great ancient Mesopotamian empires, fell into ruins.

A CLOSER LOOK: CULTURAL INFLUENCES

That Mysterious Wedge-Shaped Writing

INFORMATIONAL TEXT

Cuneiform tablet with part of the *Babylonian Chronicle* (605–594 B.C.E.). Babylonian, from Babylon, southern Iraq.

The British Museum, London.

Our knowledge of the culture of the Sumerians comes from clay tablets inscribed in cuneiform, which date from between 3500 and 2000 B.C. Archaeologists' excavation of cuneiform tablets began in the mid–nineteenth century.

Linguists found Sumerian texts, with their wedge-shaped markings, virtually impossible to translate. Fortunately, Babylonian scribes recorded many of their own texts twice: once in Sumerian (the literary language), and once in Akkadian (the Babylonians' everyday language). The meaning of the Sumerian cuneiform could be deciphered when it was compared with the corresponding Akkadian texts.

Archaeologists found few complete tablets to work from, but because diligent Sumerian and Babylonian scribes tended to make several copies of texts, scholars were able to reconstruct the contents of many broken tablets by piecing together various copies. An important feature of the Sumerian literary style—the repetition of key passages—also helped

scholars. A missing fragment from a passage of text could often be filled in when the same passage was encountered later on.

Several hundred thousand clay tablets, some as small as one or two inches, have been excavated. Examples of practical record keeping, such as tax records and financial receipts, make up the greater number of Sumerian tablets. Thousands more tablets contain imaginative literature, including myths, epics, hymns, laments, proverbs, and fables. The Babylonians' own literature included creation myths, hymns, and stories of the Great Flood. These tablets now reside in universities and museums all over the world. Many others have been lost to the ravages of time—either disintegrated or buried under four thousand years' accumulation of soil.

Egyptian Literature

Ancient Egypt, one of the most powerful civilizations the world has ever known, existed for almost three thousand years. Images of this exotic, almost otherworldly ancient land—the Sphinx, shrouded mummies, the Great Pyramids, animal-headed gods—haunt our imaginations even today.

The "Gift of the Nile"

The Greek historian Herodotus (hə·räd′ə·təs) (485–425 B.C.) called Egypt the "gift of the Nile." Just as the ancient Mesopotamians were able to thrive in the fertile valleys of the Tigris and Euphrates rivers, the earliest Saharan settlers were sustained by the Nile. The Nile provided water and, during the flood season, the fertilizing silt necessary for growing crops. The great river also made ancient

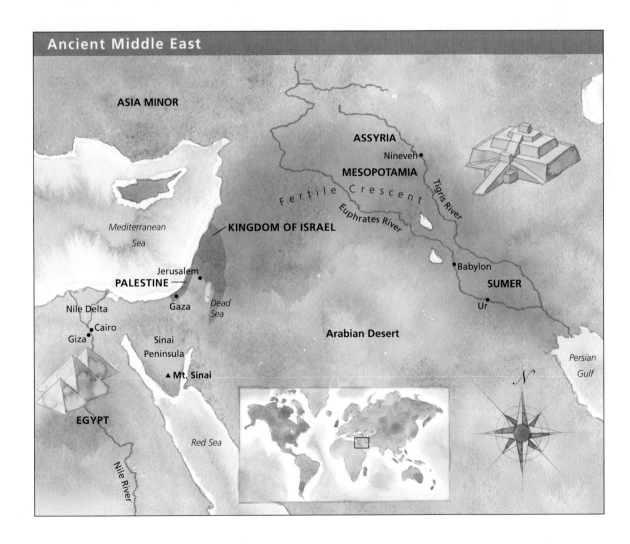

Ancient Middle East

Fishermen with nets and baskets. Dynasty 19 (c. 1279–1212 B.C.E.). Wall painting from tomb of Ipy, Deir el-Medina, Thebes.

Musée du Louvre, Paris.

Egypt's thriving trade with neighboring peoples possible. Boats laden with gold, hardwood, and metals—all the resources that Egypt itself lacked—were transported along the Nile. Without the Nile, Egypt would simply have been part of the vast and arid Sahara.

Papyrus and Paper

The Nile provided another gift that enabled Egypt to grow into a remarkable and enduring civilization: the **papyrus** (pə·pī′rəs) reeds that grew along its banks. From these reeds the Egyptians developed an early form of paper, a more convenient writing material than the clay tablets used by the Mesopotamians. (Our word *paper*, in fact, comes from *papyrus*.) Using papyrus, Egyptians could keep written records and carry out the practical tasks of a complex society. In addition, ideas and literature could be shared far and wide and be recorded for future generations.

Twenty-seven Centuries of Civilization

Egyptian civilization flourished for more than twenty-seven centuries under thirty-one dynasties, or successive ruling families. Its greatest years are divided into three eras. During the **Old Kingdom**—c. 2700 to c. 2200 B.C.—the famous pyramids were constructed. Prayer and autobiography, two literary genres, reached their highest levels of sophistication during this time. The **Middle Kingdom**—c. 2000 to c. 1800 B.C.—was characterized by Egypt's expanding economy and political power. Hymns and songs first appeared during the Middle Kingdom. Egypt was at the peak of its political power during the **New Kingdom**—c. 1600 to c. 1100 B.C. This period is known for its lyric love poems.

Pyramid Power

The organization of Egyptian society resembled the triangular shape of its pyramids. A single, powerful ruler, the **pharaoh,** was at the top of the social pyramid. Priests and scribes formed the next level. Then came the upper class, consisting of merchants and professionals. At the bottom of the pyramid was its largest class—the workers, the peasants, and the slaves.

Religion infused every aspect of daily life in ancient Egypt. The pharaoh was not only a political leader but also a spiritual leader. Indeed, he was seen as a god. It was the pharaoh's destiny to live with the gods after death. To ease the pharaoh's journey to the afterlife, the Egyptians built magnificent pyramids, which contained the pharaoh's mummified body and earthly possessions.

Literature and the Cult of the Dead

Along with the Sumerians, the Egyptians were among the earliest peoples to create a system of writing: **hieroglyphs** (hī′ər·ō·glifs′), a script in which pictures represented ideas. The Egyptians believed that their system of writing was invented by Thoth, the ibis-headed god of wisdom and the patron of scribes. Hence, they called hieroglyphs "the words of the god."

Virtually everything the Egyptians wrote was in some way tied to their religious beliefs. A fascination with death pervaded Egyptian culture. This "cult of the dead" largely dictated Egyptian morality and ethics. The New Kingdom saw the ultimate expression of

Colossal statue of Ramses II at the Temple of Amun, Karnak. Dynasty 19 (c. 1279–1212 B.C.E.).

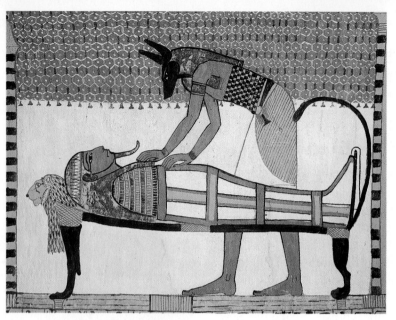

Anubis attends Sennedjem's mummy. Dynasty 19 (c. 1279–1212 B.C.E.). Painted mural from the tomb of Sennedjem, Deir el-Medina, Thebes.

Egyptian funerary literature: The Book of the Dead, a kind of "traveler's guide" to the afterlife, contained everything the deceased needed to have and know after death.

Religious literature did not stop with the Book of the Dead. Other strictly religious texts included praise songs and hymns as well as sacred, or ritual, dramas—plays enacted in religious ceremonies.

During the period of the New Kingdom, when the social structure and morality of Egyptian culture had become less rigid, a flowering of secular poetry occurred. Much of it was **pastoral poetry**—lyric poems that portray everyday life in idyllic terms. Even by today's standards, the New Kingdom pastoral poetry delivers a fresh and honest view of romantic love.

Hebrew Literature

For much of their history, the Hebrews were wanderers. Instead of building great monuments or far-reaching empires, the Hebrews forged a rich cultural life based on their religious beliefs. Unlike most of their neighbors in the Middle East, the Hebrews were monotheists—that is, they worshiped one God, whom they called Yahweh.

The beliefs of the Hebrews are given form in the **Hebrew Bible,** known to Christians as the **Old Testament.** In a way, the Hebrew Bible is the great "monument" left by the ancient Hebrews, for it is the enduring record of their spiritual, literary, and historical experience. It contains diverse literary forms—from psalms, or sacred hymns, to historical narrative and proverbs.

The Early Hebrew Patriarchs

The first Hebrew patriarch, or founding father, was Abraham. According to the Book of Genesis, the first book in the Hebrew Bible, Abraham and Sarah, his wife, left the Babylonian city of Ur and crossed the Jordan River to the land of Canaan. The descendants of

Scenes of Exodus from the *Golden Haggadah* (14th century C.E.).

The British Library, London.

Abraham and Sarah came to be called Hebrews, which means "people from across the river."

The Hebrews lived in Canaan for four generations under the great patriarchs: Abraham, his son Isaac, and his grandson Jacob. Jacob, who was later named Israel, lent his name to the Hebrews, who came to be called the **Israelites.**

Captivity and the Flight from Egypt

The Book of Genesis tells the story of Joseph, Jacob's favorite son, who was betrayed and sold into slavery in Egypt by his eleven jealous brothers. Joseph, who won the favor of the pharaoh, saved the Israelites from starvation by bringing them into Egypt.

In Egypt the Israelites organized themselves into twelve tribes. But years later a new Egyptian pharaoh enslaved them. Around 1200 B.C., a leader named **Moses** led the Hebrews on an exodus, or going out, to freedom across an arm of the Red Sea and into the Sinai Desert. The Book of Exodus in the Hebrew Bible describes this daring escape from slavery in Egypt.

According to the Hebrew Bible, while traveling through the desert toward Canaan, called the Promised Land, Moses received from Yahweh the **Ten Commandments,** a code of ethics, or moral conduct. The Ten Commandments laid the foundation for **Mosaic law.** Moses died during the difficult years in the Sinai Desert, but one of his followers, Joshua, eventually led the Israelites into Canaan.

The Promised Land

Canaan was already inhabited by other peoples, among them the Canaanites and the Philistines. (The Romans called Canaan Palestine, after the Philistines.) The Israelites struggled to make a place for themselves over the next two hundred years. Their task was difficult because of disagreements among the twelve tribes. Eventually, around 1020 B.C., a Hebrew leader named Saul unified the twelve tribes and became the first king of Israel. Under his rule the Israelites became the most powerful group in Canaan.

An Interlude of Peace and Stability

For almost one hundred years, the Hebrews enjoyed prosperity and stability. Saul's successor, King David, who reigned from 1010 to 970 B.C., captured the city of the Jebusites (jeb′yə·sīts′) and transformed it into the Hebrew capital city, **Jerusalem.** David's son Solomon, who reigned until about 925 B.C., launched many ambitious projects to beautify Jerusalem. His greatest contribution was the construction of the magnificent **Temple of Jerusalem,** which became an important symbol of the Hebrews' spiritual unity.

He that is slow to anger is better than the mighty; and he that ruleth his spirit than he that taketh a city.

—Proverbs 16:32
King James Bible

Conflict and Division

After Solomon's death, internal conflicts drove the twelve tribes apart. To the south, the tribes of Benjamin and Judah founded **Judah,** or Judea, from which the words *Judaism* and *Jew* come. To the north, the remaining ten tribes founded **Israel,** later called Samaria. Although the twelve tribes had split into two kingdoms, they continued to think of themselves as one people spiritually.

In 722 B.C., the Assyrian rulers of Mesopotamia conquered Israel. The ten tribes of Israel scattered and were gradually absorbed into the surrounding cultures. Hebrew tradition refers to these groups as the Ten Lost Tribes.

In Exile

In 586 B.C., the king Nebuchadnezzar conquered Judah. He destroyed the Temple of Jerusalem and took many Hebrews into slavery in Babylon. Thus began one of the most bitter periods in Hebrew history, the **Babylonian Exile.**

In exile, the Hebrews remembered their culture and kept it alive. When the Persian leader Cyrus the Great conquered Babylon and freed the Hebrew slaves in 539 B.C., many Hebrews returned to Jerusalem to rebuild the Temple and reestablish their society. Some Hebrews stayed in Babylon, however, sowing the first seeds of the Diaspora (dī·as′pə·rə)—literally, "a scattering"—that would come to characterize the state of the Hebrew people.

The Hebrews who returned to Jerusalem were not granted independence. For the next three and a half centuries, the Hebrews lived under the domination of a series of foreign rulers. None of these rulers, however, succeeded in suppressing their beliefs.

A CLOSER LOOK: CULTURAL INFLUENCES

The Discovery of the Dead Sea Scrolls

INFORMATIONAL TEXT

In 1947, a Bedouin shepherd, out looking for his herd, stumbled upon some ancient scrolls in a cave near the Dead Sea. Many more scrolls—some intact, but many in fragments—were eventually found in caves in the same area. Some of the scrolls dated back to 200 B.C. Many scrolls were found in pottery jars near the ruins of Qumran, an area associated with a Jewish sect called the Essenes. The Dead Sea Scrolls, as they have been named, were written mainly in Hebrew on papyrus and animal skin. They contain most of the contents of the Hebrew Bible and in fact represent the oldest written fragments of the Bible ever discovered. The scrolls also contain many writings not included in the Hebrew Bible. They show that a unified Hebrew Bible existed by A.D. 70 and prove that later versions of the Hebrew Bible (in circulation from antiquity until now) were fairly faithful transcriptions of the earliest sources.

In 1991, the Huntington Library in California at long last released photographs of the Dead Sea Scrolls to the public. There are still many unanswered questions about the scrolls, and articles on the subject continue to be published.

Musée du Louvre, Paris.

(Left) jar that contained some of the Dead Sea Scrolls (1st century C.E.); (right) fragments of the Scroll of the Rule.

The Ark of the Covenant
by Luigi Ademollo
(1764–1849).

Palazzo Pitti, Florence, Italy.

The Hebrew Identity: A Covenant with God

Since ancient times, Jews have focused on their God, Yahweh, as their source of unity. They believe that Yahweh established with his people a special agreement, or **covenant.** The terms of this covenant mean that God would always guide Hebrew history, protecting his people if they fulfilled divine law. Thus, even when the Hebrew people lost their homeland, they found a sense of identity and belonging in their ongoing relationship with Yahweh.

R E V I E W

Talk About . . .

Turn back to the Think About questions at the beginning of this introduction (page 6). Write down your responses, and get together with classmates to compare answers and discuss your views.

Reading Check

1. What system of writing was developed by the Sumerians? by the Egyptians?
2. What are the Code of Hammurabi and Mosaic law?
3. What ancient documents were uncovered by archaeologists and others in the nineteenth and twentieth centuries?

4. Name two major literary works from the ancient Middle East that have survived to our time.
5. What are the terms of the covenant between the Hebrews and Yahweh?

The Ancient Middle East: Ancient Voices, Ancient Wisdom

Mesopotamian Literature

In the marshland may the fish and birds chatter,
In the canebreak may the young and old reeds
  grow high,
In the steppe may the *mashgur*-trees grow high,
In the forests may the deer and wild goats
  multiply,
In the orchards may there be honey and wine,
In the gardens may the lettuce and cress grow
  high,
In the palace may there be long life.
May there be floodwater in the Tigris and
  Euphrates,
May the plants grow high on their banks and fill
  the meadows,
May the Lady of Vegetation pile the grain in heaps
  and mounds.

—*from* "The Cycle of Inanna:
    The Courtship of Inanna and Dumazi"
    translated by Diane Wolkstein *and*
    Samuel Noah Kramer

Ur-Ningirsu, prince of Lagash and son of Gudea
(c. 2100 B.C.E.). Sumerian, from Lagash, Iraq.
Musée du Louvre, Paris.

Epic of Gilgamesh

The *Epic of Gilgamesh,* the Sumerian story of a superhuman hero's quest for eternal life, was composed before 2000 B.C. It is probably the oldest surviving epic. Like many epics, it contains an element of truth: Gilgamesh was an actual historical figure, the king of the city-state of Uruk sometime between 2700 and 2500 B.C. His legendary exploits were the basis of an oral tradition that gradually took on epic features and trappings and was eventually recorded in cuneiform on clay tablets. It was then revised, adapted, expanded, and edited through the centuries by a succession of scribes in various regions of Mesopotamia. Around 1300 B.C., a scribe named Sinleqqiunninni is said to have compiled the version of the epic that was placed in King Assurbanipal's library at Nineveh. After the library was destroyed by the Chaldeans in 612 B.C., the eleven tablets, containing nearly three thousand lines of the epic, lay damaged and buried in ruins until they were uncovered during nineteenth-century British archaeological digs. Since the British discovery, numerous clay fragments of older versions of the epic have been found as far north as the Black Sea and as far south as Jerusalem and from the Mediterranean coast eastward to the Persian Gulf. These shards of the epic have helped scholars restore or clarify missing details and obliterated lines. Some scholars now believe that the epic could be the **archetype,** or model, for later heroic myths in Greece, India, and Persia.

The epic begins with the statement "When the gods created Gilgamesh they gave a perfect body...." It is the combination of superhuman abilities with human weaknesses that helps us empathize with Gilgamesh and understand his

Gilgamesh, or the Lion Spirit (detail) (8th century B.C.E.). Stone relief from Khorsabad, Assyria.

Musée du Louvre, Paris.

appeal to listeners and readers through the ages. Although he is a powerful leader who has built a great city, he allows excessive pride to cloud his judgment as he searches for fame. He rejects Ishtar, the goddess of love and war, and insults the gods. They respond by sending a fatal illness to his beloved friend, Enkidu. The death of Enkidu shakes Gilgamesh to his core and spurs him on a quest for eternal life. Although he overcomes a number of obstacles on his journey, he must finally accept that mortality is his human destiny.

The *Epic of Gilgamesh* dramatizes aspects of culture that concerned the Mesopotamians: love, friendship, the pursuit of fame, fear of oblivion, and the relationship of humans to the spiritual world. Those ancient concerns touch us still.

Before You Read

from the Epic of Gilgamesh

Make the Connection

The search for everlasting life is a persistent theme in world mythology and literature. Think of stories you have read or films you have seen that explore this theme. Why do you think so many of them end with failure or disaster or with an ironic twist that surprises you?

Literary Focus

Epic Hero

Gilgamesh is the earliest known **epic hero,** and he shares many traits with later epic heroes, such as the Anglo-Saxon hero Beowulf. The epic hero is a leader of his people who embodies the values of his society and is endowed with superior strength, knowledge, cunning, and courage. The epic hero often undertakes a long, dangerous journey or quest to supernatural realms to achieve a particular goal. However, epic heroes also possess human weaknesses. And unlike gods, they can die.

> An **epic hero** is an epic's larger-than-life main character whose mighty deeds reflect the values admired by the society that created the epic.
>
> *For more on Epic Hero, see the Handbook of Literary and Historical Terms.*

Reading Skills

Visualizing the Epic

Epics are full of action. You can improve your comprehension of the epic if you try to form mental images of what is happening. Try these strategies:

- Describe the events on the page in your own words either to yourself or to a partner.

- Draw a picture of the scene you are reading about.

- Read aloud and try to picture the events in your mind.

Background

Mesopotamian societies faced constant threats such as floods, droughts, and attacks from hostile neighbors. It is no wonder that their religious beliefs were somewhat pessimistic: Their gods were vengeful and offered no hope of a joyful afterlife. When Gilgamesh realizes that even he will die, he sets off on a quest to gain immortality.

> ### Vocabulary Development
>
> **somber** (säm′bər) *adj.:* dark; dismal.
>
> **ominous** (äm′ə·nəs) *adj.:* seeming to threaten evil or misfortune; sinister.
>
> **deluge** (del′yōōj′) *n.:* great flood.
>
> **transgression** (trans·gresh′ən) *n.:* act that goes beyond limits set by laws.
>
> **pestilence** (pes′tə·ləns) *n.:* deadly disease.

North Carolina Competency Goal
1.03; 5.01; 5.03

INTERNET

Vocabulary Practice

•

More About the Epic of Gilgamesh

Keyword: LE5 WL-1

Literary Skills
Understand characteristics of an epic hero.

Reading Skills
Visualize the epic.

from the

Epic of Gilgamesh

translated by N. K. Sandars

CHARACTERS IN THE EPIC

Anu (ä′nōō): god of the heavens; the father-god.

Ea (ā′ə): god of wisdom; usually a friend to humans.

Enkidu (en′kē·dōō): Gilgamesh's friend; a wild man whom the gods created out of clay.

Enlil (en·lil′): god of the air, the wind, and the earth.

Gilgamesh (gil′gə·mesh′): king of Uruk and the epic's hero.

Ishtar (ish′tär): goddess of love and war; the queen of heaven.

Ninurta (nə·nʉr′tə): god of war and of irrigation.

Shamash (shä′mäsh): god associated with the sun and human laws.

Siduri (sə·dōō′rē): goddess of wine and brewing.

Urshanabi (ʉr′shə·nä′·bē): ferryman who travels daily across the sea of death to the home of Utnapishtim.

Utnapishtim (ōōt′nə·pēsh′təm): survivor of a flood sent by the gods to destroy humanity; the gods granted him eternal life.

The epic opens with an introduction to Gilgamesh, the king of the city-state of Uruk. Gilgamesh, who is two-thirds god and one-third man, is handsome, courageous, and powerful. But he is also arrogant, and he continually oversteps his bounds as a ruler. His people, upset over the liberties Gilgamesh takes with them, pray to the gods for relief. In response, the gods send a match for Gilgamesh: the wild man Enkidu, reared by wild animals and unfamiliar with civilization. When the two men meet, they engage in a fierce wrestling match, which Gilgamesh wins. But the two men become close friends, and Enkidu, now civilized, joins Gilgamesh on a series of adventures. First they destroy Humbaba, the demon who guards the great cedar forest, and then they level the forest. When they dare to criticize the goddess Ishtar, who makes romantic overtures to Gilgamesh, she sends the Bull of Heaven to ravage the land as punishment. Gilgamesh and Enkidu destroy the bull. The gods cannot tolerate such disrespect, and they decree that one of the heroes must die. In this section of the epic, Enkidu has fallen mortally ill.

(Opposite) Gilgamesh, or the Lion Spirit (8th century B.C.E.).
Stone relief from Khorsabad, Assyria.

Musée du Louvre, Paris.

The demon Humbaba (c. 1800–1600 B.C.E.). Babylonian clay mask from Sippar, southern Iraq.
The British Museum, London.

The Death of Enkidu

As Enkidu slept alone in his sickness, in bitterness of spirit he poured out his heart to his friend. "It was I who cut down the cedar, I who leveled the forest, I who slew Humbaba and now see what has become of me. Listen, my friend, this is the dream I dreamed last night. The heavens roared, and earth rumbled back an answer; between them stood I before an awful being, the somber-faced man-bird; he had directed on me his purpose. His was a vampire face, his foot was a lion's foot, his hand was an eagle's talon. He fell on me and his claws were in my hair, he held me fast and I smothered; then he transformed me so that my arms became wings covered with feathers. He turned his stare towards me, and he led me away to the palace of Irkalla,[1] the Queen of Darkness, to the house from which none who enters ever returns, down the road from which there is no coming back.

"There is the house whose people sit in darkness; dust is their food and clay their meat. They are clothed like birds with wings for covering, they see no light, they sit in darkness. I entered the house of dust and I saw the kings of the earth, their crowns put away forever; rulers and princes, all those who once wore kingly crowns and ruled the world in the days of old. They who had stood in the place of the gods like Anu and Enlil, stood now like servants to fetch baked meats in the house of dust, to carry cooked meat and cold water from the water skin. In the house of dust which I entered were high priests and acolytes,[2] priests of the

---

1. **Irkalla** (ir·kä′lə): also called Ereshkigal; goddess of the underworld.

2. **acolytes** (ak′ə·līts′) *n. pl.*: priests' assistants.

Vocabulary
somber (säm′bər) *adj.*: dark; dismal.

incantation and of ecstasy; there were servers of the temple, and there was Etana, that king of Kish whom the eagle carried to heaven in the days of old. I saw also Samuqan, god of cattle, and there was Ereshkigal, the Queen of the Underworld; and Belit-Sheri squatted in front of her, she who is recorder of the gods and keeps the book of death. She held a tablet from which she read. She raised her head, she saw me and spoke: 'Who has brought this one here?' Then I awoke like a man drained of blood who wanders alone in a waste of rushes; like one whom the bailiff[3] has seized and his heart pounds with terror."

Gilgamesh had peeled off his clothes, he listened to his words and wept quick tears, Gilgamesh listened and his tears flowed. He opened his mouth and spoke to Enkidu: "Who is there in strong-walled Uruk who has wisdom like this? Strange things have been spoken, why does your heart speak strangely? The dream was marvelous but the terror was great; we must treasure the dream whatever the terror; for the dream has shown that misery comes at last to the healthy man, the end of life is sorrow." And Gilgamesh lamented, "Now I will pray to the great gods, for my friend had an ominous dream."

This day on which Enkidu dreamed came to an end and he lay stricken with sickness. One whole day he lay on his bed and his suffering increased. He said to Gilgamesh, the friend on whose account he had left the wilderness, "Once I ran for you, for the water of life, and I now have nothing." A second day he lay on his bed and Gilgamesh watched over him but the sickness increased. A third day he lay on his bed, he called out to Gilgamesh, rousing him up. Now he was weak and his eyes were blind with weeping. Ten days he lay and his suffering increased, eleven and twelve days he lay on his bed of pain. Then he called to Gilgamesh, "My friend, the great goddess cursed me and I must die in shame. I shall not die like a man fallen in battle; I feared to fall, but happy is the man who falls in the battle, for I must die in shame." And Gilgamesh wept over Enkidu. . . .

Gilgamesh laments Enkidu's death for seven days and nights. Finally he has the people of Uruk fashion a magnificent statue of Enkidu as a memorial. Then the grieving Gilgamesh leaves Uruk.

The Search for Everlasting Life

Bitterly Gilgamesh wept for his friend Enkidu; he wandered over the wilderness as a hunter, he roamed over the plains; in his bitterness he cried, "How can I rest, how can I be at peace? Despair is in my heart. What my brother is now, that shall I be when I am dead. Because I am afraid of death I will go as best I can to find Utnapishtim whom they call the Faraway, for he has entered the assembly of the gods." So Gilgamesh traveled over the wilderness, he wandered over the grasslands, a long journey, in search of Utnapishtim, whom the gods took after the deluge; and they set him to live in the land of Dilmun,[4] in the garden of the sun; and to him alone of men they gave everlasting life.

At night when he came to the mountain passes Gilgamesh prayed: "In these mountain passes long ago I saw lions, I was afraid and I lifted my eyes to the moon; I prayed and my prayers went up to the gods, so now, O moon god Sin,[5] protect me." When he had prayed he lay down to sleep, until he was woken from out of a dream. He saw the lions round him glorying

---

3. **bailiff** *n.:* sheriff's assistant whose duties include making arrests and serving people with court summonses and other legal documents.

4. **Dilmun:** land beyond the seas (the Persian Gulf); paradise of the Sumerians.
5. **Sin:** father of Shamash, the sun god, and Ishtar, the goddess of love; son of Enlil, the chief god.

Vocabulary

ominous (ăm′ə·nəs) *adj.:* seeming to threaten evil or misfortune; sinister.
deluge (del′yo͞oj′) *n.:* great flood.

in life; then he took his axe in his hand, he drew his sword from his belt, and he fell upon them like an arrow from the string, and struck and destroyed and scattered them.

So at length Gilgamesh came to Mashu,[6] the great mountains about which he had heard many things, which guard the rising and the setting sun. Its twin peaks are as high as the wall of heaven and its paps reach down to the underworld. At its gate the Scorpions stand guard, half man and half dragon; their glory is terrifying, their stare strikes death into men, their shimmering halo sweeps the mountains that guard the rising sun. When Gilgamesh saw them he shielded his eyes for the length of a moment only; then he took courage and approached. When they saw him so undismayed the Man-Scorpion called to his mate, "This one who comes to us now is flesh of the gods." The mate of the Man-Scorpion answered, "Two thirds is god but one third is man."

Then he called to the man Gilgamesh, he called to the child of the gods: "Why have you come so great a journey; for what have you traveled so far, crossing the dangerous waters; tell me the reason for your coming?" Gilgamesh answered, "For Enkidu; I loved him dearly, together we endured all kinds of hardships; on his account I have come, for the common lot of man has taken him. I have wept for him day and night, I would not give up his body for burial, I thought my friend would come back because of my weeping. Since he went, my life is nothing; that is why I have traveled here in search of Utnapishtim my father; for men say he has entered the assembly of the gods, and has found everlasting life. I have a desire to question him concerning the living and the dead." The Man-Scorpion opened his mouth and said, speaking to Gilgamesh, "No man born of woman has done what you have asked, no mortal man has gone into the mountain; the length of it is twelve leagues[7] of darkness; in it

there is no light, but the heart is oppressed with darkness. From the rising of the sun to the setting of the sun there is no light." Gilgamesh said, "Although I should go in sorrow and in pain, with sighing and with weeping, still I must go. Open the gate of the mountain." And the Man-Scorpion said, "Go, Gilgamesh, I permit you to pass through the mountain of Mashu and through the high ranges; may your feet carry you safely home. The gate of the mountain is open."

Gilgamesh successfully makes his way through the twelve leagues of darkness. When he comes out on the other side of Mashu, he is greeted with an astounding sight.

There was the garden of the gods; all round him stood bushes bearing gems. Seeing it he went down at once, for there was fruit of carnelian with the vine hanging from it, beautiful to look at; lapis lazuli[8] leaves hung thick with fruit, sweet to see. For thorns and thistles there were hematite and rare stones, agate, and pearls from out of the edge of the sea. While Gilgamesh walked in the garden by the edge of the sea Shamash saw him, and he saw that he was dressed in the skins of animals and ate their flesh. He was distressed, and he spoke and said, "No mortal man has gone this way before, nor will, as long as the winds drive over the sea." And to Gilgamesh he said, "You will never find the life for which you are searching." Gilgamesh said to glorious Shamash, "Now that I have toiled and strayed so far over the wilderness, am I to sleep, and let the earth cover my head forever? Let my eyes see the sun until they are dazzled with looking. Although I am no better than a dead man, still let me see the light of the sun."

Beside the sea she lives, the woman of the vine, the maker of wine; Siduri sits in the garden at the edge of the sea, with the golden bowl and the golden vats that the gods gave her. She is covered with a veil; and where she sits she sees

---

6. **Mashu:** in the Lebanon ranges.
7. **leagues** *n.:* units used for measuring length; one league equals three miles or 4.8 kilometers.

---

8. **lapis lazuli** *n.:* semiprecious sky-blue colored stone.

Gilgamesh coming towards her, wearing skins, the flesh of the gods in his body, but despair in his heart, and his face like the face of one who has made a long journey. She looked, and as she scanned the distance she said in her own heart, "Surely this is some felon; where is he going now?" And she barred her gate against him with the cross-bar and shot home the bolt. But Gilgamesh, hearing the sound of the bolt, threw up his head and lodged his foot in the gate; he called to her, "Young woman, maker of wine, why do you bolt your door; what did you see that made you bar your gate? I will break in your door and burst in your gate, for I am Gilgamesh who seized and killed the Bull of Heaven, I killed the watchman of the cedar forest, I overthrew Humbaba who lived in the forest, and I killed the lions in the passes of the mountain."

Then Siduri said to him, "If you are that Gilgamesh who seized and killed the Bull of Heaven, who killed the watchman of the cedar forest, who overthrew Humbaba that lived in the forest, and killed the lions in the passes of the mountain, why are your cheeks so starved and why is your face so drawn? Why is despair in your heart and your face like the face of one who has made a long journey? Yes, why is your face burned from heat and cold, and why do you come here wandering over the pastures in search of the wind?"

Gilgamesh answered her, "And why should not my cheeks be starved and my face drawn? Despair is in my heart and my face is the face of one who has made a long journey, it was burned with heat and with cold. Why should I not wander over the pastures in search of the wind? My friend, my younger brother, he who hunted the wild ass of the wilderness and the panther of the plains, my friend, my younger brother who seized and killed the Bull of Heaven and over-threw Humbaba in the cedar forest, my friend who was very dear to me and who endured dangers beside me, Enkidu my brother, whom

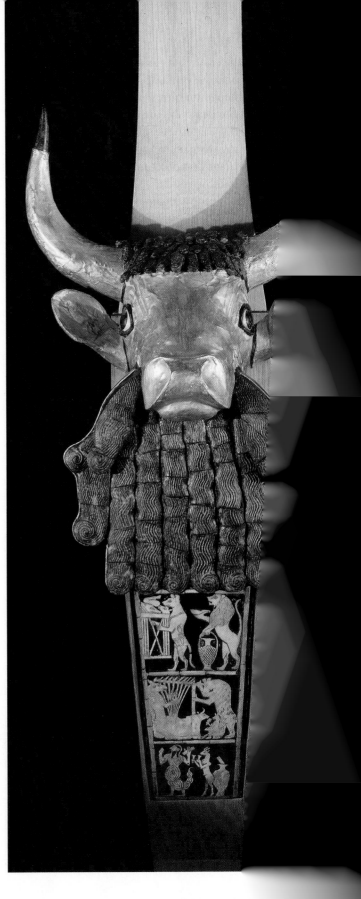

Great lyre with bull's head and inlaid front panel (c. 2680 B.C.E.). Sumerian, from Ur.
University of Pennsylvania Museum, Philadelphia (B17694).

Epic of Gilgamesh

I loved, the end of mortality has overtaken him. I wept for him seven days and nights till the worm fastened on him. Because of my brother I am afraid of death, because of my brother I stray through the wilderness and cannot rest. But now, young woman, maker of wine, since I have seen your face do not let me see the face of death which I dread so much."

She answered, "Gilgamesh, where are you hurrying to? You will never find that life for which you are looking. When the gods created man they allotted to him death, but life they retained in their own keeping. As for you Gilgamesh, fill your belly with good things; day and night, night and day, dance and be merry, feast and rejoice. Let your clothes be fresh, bathe yourself in water, cherish the little child that holds your hand, and make your wife happy in your embrace; for this too is the lot of man."

But Gilgamesh said to Siduri, the young woman, "How can I be silent, how can I rest, when Enkidu whom I love is dust, and I too shall die and be laid in the earth. You live by the seashore and look into the heart of it; young woman, tell me now, which is the way to Utnapishtim, the son of Ubara-Tutu? What directions are there for the passage; give me, oh, give me directions. I will cross the Ocean if it is possible; if it is not I will wander still farther in the wilderness."

Siduri sends Gilgamesh into the woods to find Urshanabi, the ferryman, who is building a boat. In anger and ignorance, Gilgamesh smashes some sacred stones that Urshanabi is fashioning into a prow to protect his boat. Gilgamesh then builds another boat, and Urshanabi guides him across the ocean and over the waters of death.

So Urshanabi the ferryman brought Gilgamesh to Utnapishtim, whom they call the Faraway, who lives in Dilmun at the place of the sun's transit, eastward of the mountain. To him alone of men the gods had given everlasting life.

Now Utnapishtim, where he lay at ease, looked into the distance and he said in his heart, musing to himself, "Why does the boat sail here without tackle and mast; why are the sacred stones destroyed, and why does the master not sail the boat? That man who comes is none of mine; where I look I see a man whose body is covered with skins of beasts. Who is this who walks up the shore behind Urshanabi, for surely he is no man of mine?" So Utnapishtim looked at him and said, "What is your name, you who come here wearing the skins of beasts, with your cheeks starved and your face drawn? Where are you hurrying to now? For what reason have you made this great journey, crossing the seas whose passage is difficult? Tell me the reason for your coming."

He replied, "Gilgamesh is my name. I am from Uruk, from the house of Anu." Then Utnapishtim said to him, "If you are Gilgamesh, why are your cheeks so starved and your face drawn? Why is despair in your heart and your face like the face burned with heat and cold; and why do you come here, wandering over the wilderness in search of the wind?"

Gilgamesh explains his quest and asks Utnapishtim for the secret of eternal life. The old man's reply is not what Gilgamesh expects.

Utnapishtim said, "There is no permanence. Do we build a house to stand forever, do we seal a contract to hold for all time? Do brothers divide an inheritance to keep forever, does the flood time of rivers endure? It is only the nymph of the dragonfly who sheds her larva and sees the sun in his glory. From the days of old there is no permanence. The sleeping and the dead, how alike they are, they are like a painted death. What is there between the master and the servant when both have fulfilled their doom? When the Anunnaki,[9] the judges, come together, and Mammetun the mother of destinies, together they decree the fates of men. Life and death they allot but the day of death they do not disclose."

Then Gilgamesh said to Utnapishtim the Faraway, "I look at you now, Utnapishtim, and your appearance is no different from mine; there

---

9. **Anunnaki** (ă·noo·nä′kē): underworld gods who serve Ereshkigal by judging the dead.

is nothing strange in your features. I thought I should find you like a hero prepared for battle, but you lie here taking your ease on your back. Tell me truly, how was it that you came to enter the company of the gods and to possess everlasting life?" Utnapishtim said to Gilgamesh, "I will reveal to you a mystery, I will tell you a secret of the gods."

The Story of the Flood

"You know the city Shurrupak,[10] it stands on the banks of Euphrates? That city grew old and the gods that were in it were old. There was Anu, lord of the firmament, their father, and warrior Enlil their counselor, Ninurta the helper, and Ennugi watcher over canals; and with them also was Ea. In those days the world teemed, the people multiplied, the world bellowed like a wild bull, and the great god was aroused by the clamor. Enlil heard the clamor and he said to the gods in council, 'The uproar of mankind is intolerable and sleep is no longer possible by reason of the babel.' So the gods agreed to exterminate mankind. Enlil did this, but Ea because of his oath warned me in a dream. He whispered their words to my house of reeds, 'Reed-house, reed-house! Wall, O wall, hearken reed-house, wall reflect; O man of Shurrupak, son of Ubara-Tutu; tear down your house and build a boat, abandon possessions and look for life, despise worldly goods and save your soul alive. Tear down your house, I say, and build a boat. These are the measurements of the bark as you shall build her: let her beam equal her length, let her deck be roofed like the vault that covers the abyss; then take up into the boat the seed of all living creatures.'"

"When I had understood I said to my lord, 'Behold, what you have commanded I will honor and perform, but how shall I answer the people, the city, the elders?' Then Ea opened his mouth and said to me, his servant, 'Tell them this: I have learned that Enlil is wrathful against me, I dare no longer walk in his land nor live in his city; I will go down to the Gulf to dwell with Ea my lord. But on you he will rain down abundance, rare fish and shy wildfowl, a rich harvesttide. In the evening the rider of the storm will bring you wheat in torrents.'

"In the first light of dawn all my household gathered round me, the children brought pitch and the men whatever was necessary. On the fifth day I laid the keel and the ribs, then I made fast the planking. The ground-space was one acre, each side of the deck measured one hundred and twenty cubits, making a square. I built six decks below, seven in all, I divided them into nine sections with bulkheads between. I drove in wedges where needed, I saw to the punt-poles, and laid in supplies. The carriers brought oil in baskets, I poured pitch into the

Gilgamesh between two demigods supporting the sun (9th century B.C.E.). Syrio-Hittite stele from Tell Halaf, Syria.
Archaeological Museum, Aleppo, Syria.

---

10. **Shurrupak** (shə·rŏŏp´ak): ancient city of Sumer.

furnace and asphalt and oil; more oil was consumed in caulking, and more again the master of the boat took into his stores. I slaughtered bullocks for the people and every day I killed sheep. I gave the shipwrights wine to drink as though it were river water, raw wine and red wine and oil and white wine. There was feasting then as there is at the time of the New Year's festival; I myself anointed my head. On the seventh day the boat was complete.

"Then was the launching full of difficulty; there was shifting of ballast above and below till two thirds was submerged. I loaded into her all that I had of gold and of living things, my family, my kin, the beast of the field both wild and tame, and all the craftsmen. I sent them on board, for the time that Shamash had ordained was already fulfilled when he said, 'In the evening, when the rider of the storm sends down the destroying rain, enter the boat and batten her down.' The time was fulfilled, the evening came, the rider of the storm sent down the rain. I looked out at the weather and it was terrible, so I too boarded the boat and battened her down. All was now complete, the battening and the caulking; so I handed the tiller to Puzur-Amurri the steersman, with the navigation and the care of the whole boat.

"With the first light of dawn a black cloud came from the horizon; it thundered within where Adad, lord of the storm was riding. In front over hill and plain Shullat and Hanish, heralds of the storm, led on. Then the gods of the abyss rose up; Nergal[11] pulled out the dams of the nether waters, Ninurta the warlord threw down the dikes, and the seven judges of hell, the Annunaki, raised their torches, lighting the land with their livid flame. A stupor of despair went up to heaven when the god of the storm turned daylight to darkness, when he smashed the land like a cup. One whole day the tempest raged, gathering fury as it went, it poured over the people like the tides of battle; a man could not see his brother nor the people be seen from heaven. Even the gods were terrified at the flood, they fled to the highest heaven, the firmament of Anu; they crouched against the walls, cowering like curs. Then Ishtar the sweet-voiced Queen of Heaven cried out like a woman in travail: 'Alas the days of old are turned to dust because I commanded evil; why did I command this evil in the council of all the gods? I commanded wars to destroy the people, but are they not my people, for I brought them forth? Now like the spawn of fish they float in the ocean.' The great gods of heaven and of hell wept, they covered their mouths.

---

11. **Nergal:** god of plagues of the underworld.

Ishtar (8th century B.C.E.). Assyrian ivory plaque from Nimrud, Iraq.

Iraq Museum, Baghdad.

"For six days and six nights the winds blew, torrent and tempest and flood overwhelmed the world, tempest and flood raged together like warring hosts. When the seventh day dawned the storm from the south subsided, the sea grew calm, the flood was stilled; I looked at the face of the world and there was silence, all mankind was turned to clay. The surface of the sea stretched as flat as a rooftop; I opened a hatch and the light fell on my face. Then I bowed low, I sat down and I wept, the tears streamed down my face, for on every side was the waste of water. I looked for land in vain, but fourteen leagues distant there appeared a mountain, and there the boat grounded; on the mountain of Nisir[12] the boat held fast, she held fast and did not budge. One day she held, and a second day on the mountain of Nisir she held fast and did not budge. A third day, and a fourth day she held fast on the mountain and did not budge; a fifth day and a sixth day she held fast on the mountain. When the seventh day dawned I loosed a dove and let her go. She flew away, but finding no resting-place she returned. Then I loosed a swallow, and she flew away but finding no resting-place she returned. I loosed a raven, she saw that the waters had retreated, she ate, she flew around, she cawed, and she did not come back. Then I threw everything open to the four winds, I made a sacrifice and poured out a libation[13] on the mountain top. Seven and again seven cauldrons I set up on their stands, I heaped up wood and cane and cedar and myrtle. When the gods smelled the sweet savor, they gathered like flies over the sacrifice. Then, at last, Ishtar also came, she lifted her necklace with the jewels of heaven that once Anu had made to please her. 'O you gods here present, by the lapis lazuli round my neck I shall remember these days as I remember the jewels of my throat; these last days I shall not forget. Let all the gods gather round the sacrifice, except Enlil. He shall not approach this offering,

for without reflection he brought the flood; he consigned my people to destruction.'

"When Enlil had come, when he saw the boat, he was wroth[14] and swelled with anger at the gods, the host of heaven, 'Has any of these mortals escaped? Not one was to have survived the destruction.' Then the god of the wells and canals Ninurta opened his mouth and said to the warrior Enlil, 'Who is there of the gods that can devise without Ea? It is Ea alone who knows all things.' Then Ea opened his mouth and spoke to warrior Enlil, 'Wisest of gods, hero Enlil, how could you so senselessly bring down the flood?

Lay upon the sinner his sin,
Lay upon the transgressor his transgression,
Punish him a little when he breaks loose,
Do not drive him too hard or he perishes;
Would that a lion had ravaged mankind
Rather than the flood,
Would that a wolf had ravaged mankind
Rather than the flood,
Would that famine had wasted the world
Rather than the flood,
Would that pestilence had wasted mankind
Rather than the flood.

It was not I that revealed the secret of the gods; the wise man learned it in a dream. Now take your counsel what shall be done with him.'

"Then Enlil went up into the boat, he took me by the hand and my wife and made us enter the boat and kneel down on either side, he standing between us. He touched our foreheads to bless us saying, 'In time past Utnapishtim was a mortal man; henceforth he and his wife shall live in the distance at the mouth of the rivers.' Thus it was that the gods took me and placed me here to live in the distance, at the mouth of the rivers."

---

14. **wroth** (rôth) *adj.*: (British) angry.

Vocabulary

transgression (trans·gresh'ən) *n.*: act that goes beyond limits set by laws.
pestilence (pes'tə·ləns) *n.*: deadly disease.

---

12. **Nisir:** sometimes identified with Ararat.
13. **libation** *n.*: ritual offering in which wine or oil is poured out on the ground as a sacrifice to a god.

The Return

Utnapishtim said, "As for you, Gilgamesh, who will assemble the gods for your sake, so that you may find that life for which you are searching? But if you wish, come and put it to the test: only prevail against sleep for six days and seven nights." But while Gilgamesh sat there resting on his haunches, a mist of sleep like soft wool teased from the fleece drifted over him, and Utnapishtim said to his wife, "Look at him now, the strong man who would have everlasting life, even now the mists of sleep are drifting over him." His wife replied, "Touch the man to wake him, so that he may return to his own land in peace, going back through the gate by which he came." Utnapishtim said to his wife, "All men are deceivers, even you he will attempt to deceive; therefore bake loaves of bread, each day one loaf, and put it beside his head; and make a mark on the wall to number the days he has slept."

So she baked loaves of bread, each day one loaf, and put it beside his head, and she marked on the wall the days that he slept; and there came a day when the first loaf was hard, the second loaf was like leather, the third was soggy, the crust of the fourth had mold, the fifth was mildewed, the sixth was fresh, and the seventh was still on the embers. Then Utnapishtim touched him and he woke. Gilgamesh said to Utnapishtim the Faraway, "I hardly slept when you touched and roused me." But Utnapishtim said, "Count these loaves and learn how many days you slept, for your first is hard, your second like leather, your third is soggy, the crust of your fourth has mold, your fifth is mildewed, your sixth is fresh and your seventh was still over the glowing embers when I touched and woke you." Gilgamesh said, "What shall I do, O Utnapishtim, where shall I go? Already the thief in the night has hold of my limbs, death inhabits my room; wherever my foot rests, there I find death."

Stone vessel fragment with depiction of a goddess (c. 2400 B.C.E.). Sumerian.

Antikensammlung, Staatliche Museen zu Berlin.

Then Utnapishtim spoke to Urshanabi the ferryman: "Woe to you Urshanabi, now and forevermore you have become hateful to this harborage; it is not for you, nor for you are the crossings of this sea. Go now, banished from the shore. But this man before whom you walked, bringing him here, whose body is covered with foulness and the grace of whose limbs has been spoiled by wild skins, take him to the washing-place. There he shall wash his long hair clean as snow in the water, he shall throw off his skins and let the sea carry them away, and the beauty of his body shall be shown, the fillet[15] on his forehead shall be renewed, and he shall be given clothes to cover his nakedness. Till he reaches his own city and his journey is accomplished, these clothes will show no sign of age, they will wear like a new garment." So Urshanabi took Gilgamesh and led him to the washing-place, he washed his long hair as clean as snow in the water, he threw off his skins, which the sea carried away, and showed the beauty of his body. He renewed the fillet on his forehead, and to cover his nakedness gave him clothes which would show no sign of age, but would wear like a new garment till he reached his own city, and his journey was accomplished.

Then Gilgamesh and Urshanabi launched the boat onto the water and boarded it, and they made ready to sail away; but the wife of Utnapish-

---

15. **fillet** (fil'it) *n.:* narrow headband.

tim the Faraway said to him, "Gilgamesh came here wearied out, he is worn out; what will you give him to carry him back to his own country?" So Utnapishtim spoke, and Gilgamesh took a pole and brought the boat in to the bank. "Gilgamesh, you came here a man wearied out, you have worn yourself out; what shall I give you to carry you back to your own country? Gilgamesh, I shall reveal a secret thing, it is a mystery of the gods that I am telling you. There is a plant that grows under the water, it has a prickle like a thorn, like a rose; it will wound your hands, but if you succeed in taking it, then your hands will hold that which restores his lost youth to a man."

When Gilgamesh heard this he opened the sluices so that a sweet-water current might carry him out to the deepest channel; he tied heavy stones to his feet and they dragged him down to the water-bed. There he saw the plant growing; although it pricked him he took it in his hands; then he cut the heavy stones from his feet, and the sea carried him and threw him onto the shore. Gilgamesh said to Urshanabi the ferryman, "Come here, and see this marvelous plant. By its virtue a man may win back all his former strength. I will take it to Uruk of the strong walls; there I will give it to the old men to eat. Its name shall be 'The Old Men Are Young Again'; and at last I shall eat it myself and have back all my lost youth." So Gilgamesh returned by the gate through which he had come, Gilgamesh and Urshanabi went together. They traveled their twenty leagues and then they broke their fast; after thirty leagues they stopped for the night.

Gilgamesh saw a well of cool water and he went down and bathed; but deep in the pool there was lying a serpent, and the serpent sensed the sweetness of the flower. It rose out of the water and snatched it away, and immediately it sloughed its skin and returned to the well. Then Gilgamesh sat down and wept, the tears ran down his face, and he took the hand of Urshanabi; "O Urshanabi, was it for this that I toiled with my hands, is it for this I have wrung out my heart's blood? For myself I have gained nothing; not I, but the beast of the earth has joy of it now. Already the stream has carried it twenty leagues back to the channels where I found it. I found a sign and now I have lost it. Let us leave the boat on the bank and go."

After twenty leagues they broke their fast, after thirty leagues they stopped for the night; in three days they had walked as much as a journey of a month and fifteen days. When the journey was accomplished they arrived at Uruk, the strong-walled city. Gilgamesh spoke to him, to Urshanabi the ferryman, "Urshanabi, climb up onto the wall of Uruk, inspect its foundation terrace, and examine well the brick work; see if it is not of burnt bricks; and did not the seven wise men lay these foundations? One third of the whole is city, one third is garden, and one third is field, with the precinct of the goddess Ishtar. These parts and the precinct are all Uruk."

This too was the work of Gilgamesh, the king, who knew the countries of the world. He was wise, he saw mysteries and knew secret things, he brought us a tale of the days before the flood. He went a long journey, was weary, worn out with labor, and returning engraved on a stone the whole story.

Frieze with inlays of cows from a Ninhursanga temple (c. 2400–2250 B.C.E.). Sumerian, from Tell al Ubaid, Iraq.

University of Pennsylvania Museum, Philadelphia (B15880).

The following interview from National Public Radio's All Things Considered *is with Martha Roth, professor of Assyriology at the University of Chicago. She is working with a group of researchers to decipher Sumerian cuneiform tablets and to put together a dictionary of all the words in the Sumerian texts. As they translate letters, lists, and business documents, the team is learning the details of daily life in Mesopotamia in 3000 B.C. Daniel Zwerdling is the host of the radio program. He is talking about the old clay tablets.*

INFORMATIONAL TEXT

Sumerian Tablets

from All Things Considered, May 2, 1998

ZWERDLING: I would love to know what they [the tablets] look like, feel like, what it's like to hold one of them in your hands. . . .

ROTH: The first time I held one, it was an incredible rush. They range in size from the size of a matchbook to massive pieces that might be tablets, or cylinders, or prisms that could be fourteen or eighteen inches on a side. They are inscribed with a very fine stylus, impressed into the damp clay, making wedges.

The wedges are what we call a cuneiform script from the wedge-shaped impressions made by the stylus. Some of them are very lightweight. Some are very heavy. They're fragile now. They've been preserved in the sands of the deserts for thousands of years. . . .

But it's thrilling to hold this lump of dirt that is two, three, four thousand years old and that records such fascinating details about individuals who lived and died lives very much like our own.

The Flood Tablet, relating part of the *Epic of Gilgamesh* (7th century B.C.E.). Assyrian, from Nineveh, Iraq.

The British Museum, London.

ZWERDLING: And how did people use them? Did each family keep its own, you know, tablets like a personal notebook? Was it kept only by the government officials about the community? What?

ROTH: Both. The largest archives, of course, of tablets that we have will come from the great bureaucracies—from the palaces, from the temples, from the big business enterprises. And these places will keep for many, many years records of the income and outgo and so forth. . . .

But individuals also kept their own documents. They kept records of marriages; they kept records of land sales; they kept records of adoptions. And they kept their own family records, sometimes for generations. There are some times and places in which we can track several generations of individual families and through their soap operas, if you will—the marriages, and divorces, and trials and tribulations.

ZWERDLING: Boy, what a feeling to be able to peep at those ancient soap operas. Give us an example of one of the dramas you've come across, a family soap opera.

ROTH: OK. One example [is] a letter that is sent by a young man, who's probably off in school, misses his mother, and is quite dependent upon her, I suppose, for his clothing and maintenance and so forth. He sends a letter to his mother and it reads as follows: "May the gods, Shamashmarduk and Ilebra, keep you forever in good health for my sake. From year to year the clothes of the other young men here become better, but you let my clothes get worse from year to year. Indeed, you persist in making my clothes poorer and more scanty.

"At a time when in our house, wool is used up like bread, you have made me but poor clothes. The son of another man, whose father is only an assistant to my father, has two new sets of clothes, while you fuss even about a single set of clothes for me.

"In spite of the fact that you bore me and his mother only adopted him, his mother loves him, while you—you do not love me at all.". . .

ZWERDLING: . . . Do you find yourself almost being back in that time, you know, internally in your mind?

ROTH: Well, I do feel like I know some of the people. Depending on what the work is, I'm doing my own research and in recent years focused on family history. And I became very well acquainted with a couple of hundred young women who were marrying and divorcing and became widowed in the first millennium B.C.

And I felt I knew these women. I knew something about them. I knew their trials and tribulations, their loves, their financial details, details of their housekeeping and so forth.

It's exciting to be able to look inside their lives and to find that the . . . most interesting and amazing thing is the human continuity, that these people were doing the same things we are. They had the same problems and the same questions. And they sought the same sorts of solutions.

According to Dr. Roth, what facts about ancient Sumerian life do the cuneiform tablets reveal? In addition to facts, what opinions and personal feelings does Dr. Roth express about the material she is studying? Give specific examples from the interview.

Response and Analysis

Reading Check

1. Why does Gilgamesh want to find Utnapishtim?

2. According to Utnapishtim, why did the gods decide to destroy humanity?

3. What happens to the magic plant? How does Gilgamesh react?

Thinking Critically

4. How well did Enkidu's description of his dream help you visualize the Sumerian afterlife? Identify **images** that particularly struck you, and describe their effect.

5. Why is Enkidu's dream important for an understanding of the **motivation,** or reason, for Gilgamesh's quest?

6. Could Gilgamesh be satisfied with the simple joys of life that Siduri describes? Explain.

7. Summarize Utnapishtim's response to Gilgamesh when Gilgamesh asks him for the secret of eternal life. Do you think Utnapishtim's argument is convincing? In what ways is Utnapishtim not what Gilgamesh expected?

8. **Irony** is the contrast between what we expect to happen and what actually happens. Explain the irony in what happens to the plant of eternal youth.

9. An **epic hero** embodies the highest values of his society and acts with his people in mind. What does Gilgamesh ultimately bring back to share with his people in Uruk?

10. The *Connection* on page 34 gives us a more human view of the ancient Sumerians. What details in *Gilgamesh* give you a picture of what the Sumerians might have been like?

Extending and Evaluating

11. Some people feel that consciousness of the inevitability of death makes people more aware that life is precious and that they should make the most of time. Other people feel that knowing life must eventually come to an end makes it impossible to enjoy life's pleasures fully. What do you think about this issue? How do you think the ancient Sumerians felt about it, judging from the excerpt from the epic you have just read?

WRITING

Gilgamesh the Sequel

What if Gilgamesh decided to go back to retrieve the magic plant—and succeeded? Would he share it with others—perhaps try to restore life to Enkidu? Write a mini-sequel that describes the outcome of Gilgamesh's "second chance."

Vocabulary Development
Question and Answer

Answer the following questions to test your understanding of the underlined Vocabulary words.

1. What is the opposite of a somber mood?

2. What type of situation might be ominous?

3. What is the difference between a deluge and a drought?

4. How does transgression differ from compliance?

5. Is a pestilence more serious than an illness?

SKILLS FOCUS

Literary Skills
Analyze characteristics of an epic hero.

Reading Skills
Visualize the epic.

Writing Skills
Write a sequel.

Vocabulary Skills
Answer questions about vocabulary words.

The Ancient Middle East: Ancient Voices, Ancient Wisdom

Egyptian Literature

The sky is a dark bowl, the stars die and fall.
The celestial bows quiver,
the bones of the earthgods shake and
    planets come to a halt
when they sight the king in all his power,
the god who feeds on his father and eats his
    mother.
The king is such a tower of wisdom
even his mother can't discern his name.
His glory is in the sky, his strength lies in
    the horizon
like that of his father the sungod Atum who
    conceived him.

—*from* "The Cannibal Hymn"
translated by Tony Barnstone
and Willis Barnstone

Inner coffin of Tutankhamun's sarcophagus, from the
tomb of Tutankhamun. Dynasty 18 (1336–1327 B.C.E.).
Valley of the Kings, near Deir el-Bahri.

Egyptian Museum, Cairo.

Before You Read

The Great Hymn to the Aten

Make the Connection

Quickwrite ✏

Think of an aspect of nature that is meaningful to you, such as the stars, the ocean, or mountains. Jot down words and phrases that best capture the attributes, or qualities, of this aspect of the natural world, as well as your feelings about it.

Literary Focus

Epithet

An **epithet** is a descriptive name, adjective, phrase, or title that is repeatedly used to describe or characterize a quality or characteristic of a person, place, or thing. We use epithets when we refer to "America the Beautiful," "Richard the Lionhearted," or "Paris, the City of Lights." In "The Great Hymn to the Aten," epithets are used to honor and show respect for the attributes of the Egyptian sun god, Aten.

> An **epithet** is an adjective or other descriptive phrase that is regularly used to characterize a person, place, or thing.
>
> *For more on Epithet, see the Handbook of Literary and Historical Terms.*

North Carolina Competency Goal
1.02; 1.03; 4.05; 5.01; 5.03; 6.01

Background

"The Great Hymn to the Aten" is the longest of several New Kingdom praise poems to the sun god Aten. This poem, composed as a **hymn,** or sacred song, was found on the wall of a tomb built for a royal scribe named Ay and his wife. It was intended to assure their safety in the afterlife.

The Egyptians had worshiped the sun—along with a host of other gods—since the Old Kingdom. But during the Amarna period of the New Kingdom, the pharaoh Amenhotep IV, who later took the name Akhenaten ("he who serves the Aten"), declared that the sun god, Aten, was the one true god. Thus, Egypt was introduced to one man's concept of **monotheism,** or belief in one god.

Akhenaten (ä′ke·nät′'n), who came to power as a child and ruled from 1379 B.C. to 1362 B.C., was an unusual ruler. Under his reign, conservative, tradition-bound Egypt experienced a revolution that affected every aspect of life. Akhenaten was a talented poet, and this poem, as well as several others, has been attributed to him. But Akhenaten's break with tradition must have seemed too shockingly revolutionary for the Egyptians, who for centuries had recognized and worshiped approximately eighty gods, each of whom took a different form and represented a different power. As soon as their radical pharaoh died, the Egyptians returned to the worship of their traditional deities.

SKILLS FOCUS

Literary Skills
Understand epithets.

Head of colossal painted
statue of Akhenaten from the
temple of Aten at Karnak.
Dynasty 18 (1353–1336 B.C.E.).

Egyptian Museum, Cairo.

The Great Hymn to the Aten

translated by Miriam Lichtheim

Splendid you rise in heaven's lightland,°
O living Aten, creator of life!
When you have dawned in eastern lightland,
You fill every land with your beauty.
5   You are beauteous, great, radiant,

1. **lightland** *n.:* sky.

High over every land;
Your rays embrace the lands,
To the limit of all that you made.
Being Re,° you reach their limits,

10   You bend them <for> the son whom you love;
Though you are far, your rays are on earth,
Though one sees you, your strides are unseen.

When you set in western lightland,
Earth is in darkness as if in death;

15   One sleeps in chambers, heads covered,
One eye does not see another.
Were they robbed of their goods,
That are under their heads,
People would not remark it.

20   Every lion comes from its den,
All the serpents bite;
Darkness hovers, earth is silent,
As their maker rests in lightland.

Earth brightens when you dawn in lightland,

25   When you shine as Aten of daytime;
As you dispel the dark,
As you cast your rays,
The Two Lands° are in festivity.
Awake they stand on their feet,

30   You have roused them;
Bodies cleansed, clothed,
Their arms adore your appearance.
The entire land sets out to work,
All beasts browse on their herbs;

35   Trees, herbs are sprouting,
Birds fly from their nests,
Their wings greeting your *ka*.°
All flocks frisk on their feet,
All that fly up and alight,

40   They live when you dawn for them.
Ships fare north, fare south as well,
Roads lie open when you rise;
The fish in the river dart before you,
Your rays are in the midst of the sea. . . .

45   How many are your deeds,
Though hidden from sight,
O Sole God beside whom there is none!
You made the earth as you wished, you alone,
All peoples, herds, and flocks;

50   All upon earth that walk on legs,

9. Re (rā): another name for the sun god.

28. The Two Lands: Upper and Lower Egypt.

37. *ka* *n.:* life force.

All on high that fly on wings,
The lands of Khor and Kush,°
The land of Egypt.
You set every man in his place,
55 You supply their needs;
Everyone has his food,
His lifetime is counted.
Their tongues differ in speech,
Their characters likewise;
60 Their skins are distinct,
For you distinguished the peoples.

52. Khor and Kush: Syria and Nubia.

Pyramid, Egypt.

You made Hapy in *dat*,°
You bring him when you will,
To nourish the people,
65 For you made them for yourself.
Lord of all who toils for them,
Lord of all lands who shines for them,
Aten of daytime, great in glory!
All distant lands, you make them live,
70 You made a heavenly Hapy descend for them;
He makes waves on the mountains like the sea,
To drench their fields and their towns.
How excellent are your ways, O Lord of eternity!
A Hapy from heaven for foreign peoples,
75 And all lands' creatures that walk on legs,
For Egypt the Hapy who comes from *dat*.

Your rays nurse all fields,
When you shine they live, they grow for you;
You made the seasons to foster all that you made,
80 Winter to cool them, heat that they taste you.
You made the far sky to shine therein,
To behold all that you made;
You alone, shining in your form of living Aten,
Risen, radiant, distant, near.
85 You made millions of forms from yourself alone,
Towns, villages, fields, the river's course;
All eyes observe you upon them,
For you are the Aten of daytime on high. . . .

<Those on> earth come from your hand as you made them,
90 When you have dawned they live,
When you set they die;
You yourself are lifetime, one lives by you.
All eyes are on <your> beauty until you set,
All labor ceases when you rest in the west;
95 When you rise you stir [everyone] for the King,
Every leg is on the move since you founded the earth.
You rouse them for your son who came from your body,
The King who lives by Maat,° the Lord of the Two Lands,
Neferkheprure, Sole-one-of-Re,
100 The Son of Re who lives by Maat, the Lord of crowns,
Akhenaten, great in his lifetime;
(And) the great Queen whom he loves, the Lady of the
    Two Lands,
Nefer-nefru-Aten Nefertiti,° living forever.

62. Hapy in *dat*: Hapy is the river Nile; *dat* is the underworld. Ancient Egyptians thought that the Nile came from a river in the underworld.

98. Maat: personification of truth, order, and moral law. The ancient Egyptians believed that only those who had followed Maat in life would achieve immortality.

103. Nefertiti (nef′ər·tē′tē): Akhenaten's wife, renowned for her beauty.

Pharaohs of the Sun

Rick Gore

from National Geographic, April 2001

Akhenaten, Nefertiti, and the boy pharaoh Tutankhamun—perhaps Akhenaten's son born to a secondary wife—have been called the Pharaohs of the Sun. Their reign was brief. Akhenaten ruled just 17 years, and within a few years after his death in 1336 B.C., the old orthodoxy[1] was restored. Akhenaten's enemies soon smashed his statues, dismantled his temples, and set out to expunge[2] all memory of him and Nefertiti from Egypt's historical record.

But the controversy the couple created lives on. Egyptologists still struggle to piece together the story of this renegade pair. Swept up in

---

1. **orthodoxy** (ôr′thə·däk′sē) *n.:* conventional beliefs.

2. **expunge** (ek·spunj′) *v.:* remove completely.

Akhenaten and his family under the rays of Aten. Dynasty 18 (c. 1345 B.C.E.). Relief from Akhetaten.

Egyptian Museum, Cairo.

religious passion, they brought the vast and powerful Egyptian empire to the brink of collapse.

"You're never going to find two Egyptologists who agree on this period," said Nicholas Reeves, a British Egyptologist.

Barry Kemp, an archaeologist at Cambridge University, is even more pessimistic: "The minute you begin to write about those people you begin to write fiction."

The same may be true of the likenesses left of them. . . .

In the Egyptian Museum in Cairo are colossal statues—troubling and mesmerizing—of Akhenaten. His face is elongated and angular with a long chin. His eyes are mystical and brooding. His lips are huge and fleshy. Although he wears a pharaoh's headdress and holds the traditional symbols of kingship, the crook and flail,[3] across his chest, the chest is spindly, and the torso flows into a voluptuous belly and enormous feminine hips.

Because of the strangeness of these and so many other images of Akhenaten, scholars speculated for decades that the pharaoh had a deforming disease. But now many believe that the odd appearance of the colossi[4] might be rooted in Akhenaten's new religion, for Aten had both male and female aspects. They also point out that in the early years of his reign, when Akhenaten was a young radical fighting an established religion, he had reasons for the exaggeration. He wanted to break down more than a thousand years of artistic tradition, so he instructed his artists to portray the world as it really was.

Instead of the standard static depictions of physically perfect pharaohs smiting[5] enemies or making offerings to the gods, artists gave the new king a much more realistic appearance. "Akhenaten probably didn't have the greatest physique by American standards," says James Allen, a specialist on the period at the Metropolitan Museum of Art in New York. "He had the easy life in the palace."

For the first time, artists routinely portrayed the pharaoh in informal situations—being affectionate with Nefertiti or playing with his children. They also painted scenes of life and nature—wheat rippling in the wind, farmers plowing, birds taking flight. In truth, Akhenaten unleashed a creative furor that gave rise to perhaps the finest era of Egyptian art. . . .

We walk to a 40-foot-high relief Akhenaten had carved on a wall of Amun-Re's[6] temple soon after taking power. It's a traditional "smiting scene" for pharaohs. Akhenaten holds his enemies by their hair and is about to kill them. . . .

"His was a strange new vision," says Robert Vergnieux of the University of Bordeaux in France. "Since the Egyptians' god was now the sunlight, they didn't need statues in dark inner sanctums. So they built temples without roofs and performed their rituals directly under the sun."

"For a short time the Egyptians believed the sun god had come back to Earth in the form of the royal family," says Ray Johnson.[7] "There was a collective excitement that becomes tangible in the art and architecture. The whole country was in jubilee. It's one of the most astonishing periods in world history."

---

6. **Amun-Re:** king of the Egyptian gods.
7. **Ray Johnson:** expert on Akhenaten at the University of Chicago.

According to the article, what effect did Akhenaten's "strange new vision" have on Egyptian art and culture during his brief reign?

---

3. **crook and flail:** curved staff and a tool used to thresh grain.
4. **colossi** (kə·läs′ī′) *n. pl.:* gigantic statues.
5. **smiting** (smīt′iŋ) *v.* used as *adj.:* defeating; striking down.

Response and Analysis

Reading Check

1. The speaker describes the sun's rising as a joyous occasion. How does he (or she) describe the setting of the sun?

2. Re-read lines 45–88. Make a list of the things that Aten creates or makes possible.

3. What attributes, or characteristics, of Aten does the speaker praise?

Thinking Critically

4. **Apostrophe** is a figure of speech in which a writer directly addresses a thing, concept, or absent person. An apostrophe is written in the second person, using the pronouns *you* and *yours*. Find three examples of apostrophe in "The Great Hymn to the Aten." How does the use of apostrophe convey a deep reverence for Aten?

5. An **epithet** is a brief descriptive name, title, or adjective that characterizes a person, place, or thing. An epithet appears in the second line of the poem: "living Aten, creator of life!" Find two or three other epithets in the poem. To what major characteristics of Aten do they refer? What do the epithets tell you about the relationship between Aten and his people?

6. This praise poem is a **hymn**, a sacred song composed for performance in a religious context. What aspects of the poem make it particularly suitable for oral presentation? (Consider such features of the poem as repetition, parallelism, and the use of apostrophe.) Read the poem aloud to hear other characteristics that make it suitable for oral performance.

Extending and Evaluating

7. "The Great Hymn to the Aten" is a declaration of reverence to a deity, but to us today it is also a celebration of an aspect of nature. Name some of the ways that people today show a reverence for nature. How is our attitude toward nature similar to or different from that of the ancient Egyptians?

WRITING

Writing a Praise Poem

Write your own praise poem that addresses another element or force in the natural world, such as the oceans, moon, trees, animals, or the earth itself. Your praise poem, like Akhenaten's, should be written in the form of an **apostrophe,** or direct address to your subject. You should also use at least two **epithets** in your poem. Refer to the Quickwrite notes you made earlier for ideas. You may wish to set your poem to music or illustrate it.

North Carolina Competency Goal
1.03; 2.01; 4.01; 4.05; 5.03; 6.01

go.hrw.com

INTERNET
Projects and Activities
Keyword: LE5 WL-1

SKILLS FOCUS

Literary Skills
Analyze epithets.

Writing Skills
Write a praise poem.

Akhenaten and his family worshiping Aten. Dynasty 18 (c. 1348–1335 B.C.E.).

Egyptian Museum, Cairo.

New Kingdom Love Lyrics

Make the Connection

Quickwrite ✏️

Love poems and songs often create a vivid, expressive testament to a speaker's thoughts or emotional state. Think of some love songs you have heard. Brainstorm a list of common characteristics of popular love songs: the feelings they address, the figures of speech they use, the situations they describe. What qualities do these songs emphasize? What emotions do they celebrate?

Literary Focus

Speaker

The **speaker** of a poem is the voice that addresses us. The speaker expresses emotions or ideas that may or may not be those of the poet. It is helpful to think of the speaker as a character who may be very different from the poet: a different age, race, or gender, for example. Readers should not assume that the speaker and the poet are one and the same.

In both of the following poems, the speaker is someone quite different from the poet. Although the language in the poems is fresh and simple, conveying the heartfelt language of young lovers, the lyrics' complex figures of speech and careful meter suggest that the poets were highly skilled and well educated, probably wealthy men who were members of the pharaoh's court.

North Carolina Competency Goal
1.02; 1.03; 4.05; 5.01; 5.03; 6.01

SKILLS FOCUS

Literary Skills
Understand speaker.

> The **speaker** is the imaginary voice, or persona, assumed by the author of a poem.
>
> *For more on Speaker, see the Handbook of Literary and Historical Terms.*

Background

Lyric poetry was already being composed in Egypt during the Middle Kingdom period. However, love lyrics—a specific type of lyric poetry—come to us only from the New Kingdom. The two lyrics you are about to read come from a battered New Kingdom papyrus containing three sets of love lyrics, now in the British Museum. This papyrus is one of only four known manuscripts containing Egyptian love lyrics.

Lyrics like these were probably sung to musical accompaniment at dinner parties and other festive occasions. Such poems may also have been acted out or accompanied by dance. While we may know the setting for the performance of the songs, we know little about the background of the poems themselves. The speakers of the poems are usually adolescent girls and boys, but the authors were undoubtedly adult men who were talented artists.

Most of the love songs are written in the form of interior monologues in which the speaker is addressing himself or herself. In the lyrics that do address other people, the speaker is almost always a young woman who is speaking to a boy or man she loves. The lyrics cover a range of motifs, or themes, but some of the most common ones are descriptions of longing, hopes for the future, and the pain of love. As you read the following lyrics, watch for one or more of these motifs.

(Opposite, background) Maya, overseer of King Tutankhamun's treasury. Dynasty 18 (c.1336–1327 B.C.E.). Relief from Tutankhamun's tomb at Saqqara.

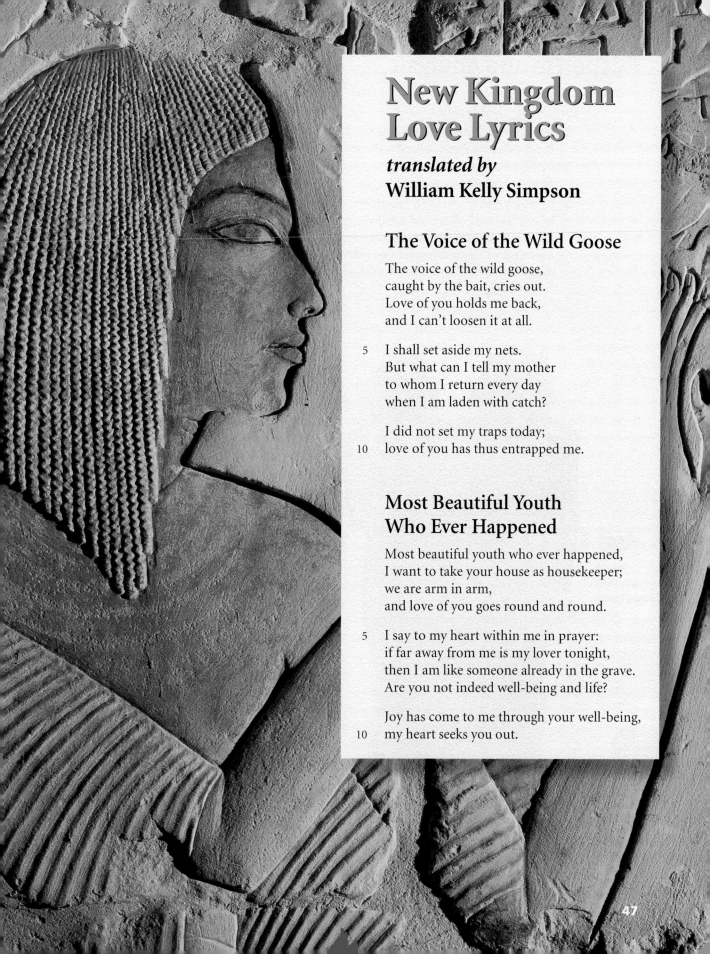

New Kingdom Love Lyrics

translated by
William Kelly Simpson

The Voice of the Wild Goose

The voice of the wild goose,
caught by the bait, cries out.
Love of you holds me back,
and I can't loosen it at all.

5   I shall set aside my nets.
But what can I tell my mother
to whom I return every day
when I am laden with catch?

I did not set my traps today;
10   love of you has thus entrapped me.

Most Beautiful Youth Who Ever Happened

Most beautiful youth who ever happened,
I want to take your house as housekeeper;
we are arm in arm,
and love of you goes round and round.

5   I say to my heart within me in prayer:
if far away from me is my lover tonight,
then I am like someone already in the grave.
Are you not indeed well-being and life?

Joy has come to me through your well-being,
10   my heart seeks you out.

Response and Analysis

Thinking Critically

1. What can you **infer,** or guess, about the speakers in these poems?

2. What is the speaker's **tone,** or attitude, toward love in each poem?

3. In "The Voice of the Wild Goose," love is seen as a kind of trap. How is this **metaphor,** or comparison, appropriate? What comment does the metaphor make about the notion of "true love"?

4. What is "modern" about these poems, and what marks them as products of an earlier time? In what ways are the poems specific to their time and culture, and in what ways are they timeless and universal?

5. How do the characteristics of popular love songs that you listed in your Quickwrite compare with the way love is described in the two poems you just read?

WRITING

Comparing Love Poems

The American poet Emily Dickinson (1830–1886) wrote poems that expressed tremendous feelings of love and desire, often using strikingly original images and metaphors. Compare the following poem by Dickinson with the two Egyptian love poems you have read. In two or three paragraphs, explain the similarities and differences you see in these poems. Consider the speaker in each, the emotions that are expressed, and the imagery.

> **It's All I Have to Bring Today—**
> Emily Dickinson
>
> It's all I have to bring today—
> This, and my heart beside—
> This, and my heart, and all the fields—
> And all the meadows wide—
> Be sure you count—should I forget
> Some one the sum could tell—
> This, and my heart, and all the Bees
> Which in the Clover dwell.

North Carolina Competency Goal
1.02; 1.03; 4.05; 5.01; 5.03; 6.01

SKILLS FOCUS

Literary Skills
Analyze speaker.

Writing Skills
Compare love poems.

King Menkaure (Mycerinus) and Queen. Dynasty 4 (c. 2490–2472 B.C.E.). Giza.

Museum of Fine Arts, Boston. Harvard University—Museum of Fine Arts Expedition, (II.1738).

The Ancient Middle East: Ancient Voices, Ancient Wisdom

Hebrew Literature

The heavens declare the glory of God;
and the firmament sheweth his handiwork.
Day unto day uttereth speech,
and night unto night sheweth knowledge.
There is no speech nor language,
where their voice is not heard.
Their line is gone out through all the earth,
and their words to the end of the world.

—*from* Psalm 19
King James Bible

Moses Destroying the Tablets of the Law
(1659) by Rembrandt van Rijn.
Gemäldegalerie, Staatliche Museen zu Berlin.

49

The Hebrew Bible

J ews have often been called the "people of the book." The "book" is the Hebrew Bible, which tells the history of the Hebrews and presents the basic laws and teachings of the Jewish faith. The contents existed first as oral tradition. Then, from approximately 1000 to 100 B.C., the various parts were recorded in Hebrew and Aramaic and assembled. (Aramaic is a Semitic language that replaced Hebrew around 400 B.C. It was spoken by the Hebrews and other peoples throughout Mesopotamia.)

The Hebrew Bible contains twenty-four books, beginning with Genesis and ending with Chronicles. Christians refer to the Hebrew Bible as the Old Testament and accept it as sacred, but they also include a second collection of sacred writings, the Christian Scriptures, also called the New Testament (see page 82), in their Bible.

Jewish people call their Bible **Tanakh,** an acronym formed from the first letters of the Hebrew words for the three categories of books contained in it: **Torah** (Law), **Nevi'im** (Prophets), and **Ketuvim** (Writings).

The Torah, or Law, is the first and oldest part of the Hebrew Bible. Sometimes called the Five Books of Moses—according to tradition, they were written by Moses—the Torah consists of five books that contain the earliest historical narratives of the Jews: Genesis, Exodus, Leviticus, Numbers, and Deuteronomy. It also contains the laws of Judaism, with detailed instructions for religious rituals and the conduct of daily life. The Torah is so greatly revered that no copy of it, no matter how old or worn, is ever destroyed. (If a Torah is seriously damaged, it must be given a full funeral and be buried.)

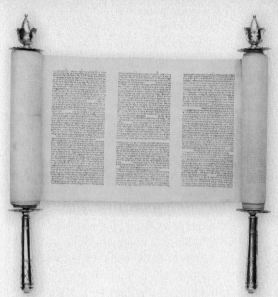

Torah scroll from Germany (c. 1840–1850).
The Jewish Museum, New York.

Nevi'im, or Prophets, contains the powerful words of social and spiritual reformers such as Isaiah, Jeremiah, and Ezekiel, who called on the people of Israel to repent and lead purer lives. These books also contain narratives about Hebrew rulers such as Saul, David, and Solomon.

The final volume, Ketuvim, or Writings, contains a rich variety of **genres,** or types, of literature. The Book of Psalms contains lyrical hymns of praise that overflow with emotions and vivid imagery. The Book of Ruth, sometimes called the first short story, is a tender work about compassion, loyalty, and tolerance. The Book of Job features a dramatic dialogue between God and a man named Job in which the question of human suffering is movingly probed.

In the Hebrew Bible, God, or Yahweh, tests human beings, who must suffer the consequences of their actions when they fail to obey him. But they may also experience the mercy of God and the eternal promise of spiritual renewal.

In the Beginning
from Genesis

Make the Connection
Quickwrite

Jot down anything you recall about the biblical account of creation in Genesis. As you read, see whether you remembered the details correctly. Does anything in the account of creation surprise you?

Literary Focus
Repetition

Repetition is the recurrence of words, phrases, or even entire sentences or passages. It is an important feature of biblical style. Repetition can create rhythm and build suspense and dramatic intensity in a work of literature. It can also help emphasize important words and ideas.

> **Repetition** is the recurrence of words, phrases, or other parts of a text to create a particular literary effect.
>
> *For more on Repetition, see the Handbook of Literary and Historical Terms.*

Reading Skills
Comparing and Contrasting

When you **compare** and **contrast,** you point out likenesses and differences between two things. There are two accounts of creation in Genesis. As you read, look for similarities and differences between the two versions.

Background

The Greek word *genesis* means "coming into being." The name is appropriate, since the Book of Genesis begins with the birth of the universe and goes on to explain such things as the emergence of evil, the cause of the Great Flood, and the establishment of God's covenant with the Hebrews. The Book of Genesis is the first book of the Torah; it reflects the Hebrews' beliefs about the origins of the world and contains the core teachings of the Jewish faith.

Most scholars today believe that Genesis is a combination of narratives by different writers collected over several hundred years. This may explain why Genesis contains two accounts of creation. Taken together, the two creation accounts give us a fuller picture of the Hebrews' concept of God.

Vocabulary Development

dominion (də·min′yən) *n.*: rule; absolute authority.

replenish (ri·plen′ish) *v.*: refill or make complete again; resupply.

subdue (səb·dōō′) *v.*: conquer; cultivate.

beguiled (bē·gīld′) *v.*: deceived.

enmity (en′mə·tē) *n.*: hostility.

North Carolina Competency Goal
1.02; 1.03; 4.05; 5.01; 5.03; 6.01

INTERNET

Vocabulary Practice
•
More About Genesis
Keyword: LE5 WL-1

Literary Skills
Understand repetition.

Reading Skills
Compare and contrast.

The last days of creation, from the *Sarajevo Haggadah* (14th century).

In the Beginning

from **Genesis**

King James Bible

The Creation

In the beginning God created the heaven and the earth. And the earth was without form, and void; and darkness was upon the face of the deep. And the Spirit of God moved upon the face of the waters.[1]

And God said "Let there be light": and there was light. And God saw the light, that it was good: and God divided the light from the darkness. And God called the light Day, and the darkness he called Night. And the evening and the morning were the first day.

And God said, "Let there be a firmament[2] in the midst of the waters, and let it divide the waters from the waters." And God made the firmament, and divided the waters which were under the firmament from the waters which were above the firmament: and it was so. And God called the firmament Heaven. And the evening and the morning were the second day.

And God said, "Let the waters under the heaven be gathered together unto one place, and let the dry land appear": and it was so. And God called the dry land Earth; and the gathering together of the waters he called Seas: and God saw that it was good. And God said, "Let the earth bring forth grass, the herb[3] yielding seed,

and the fruit tree yielding fruit after his[4] kind, whose seed is in itself, upon the earth": and it was so. And the earth brought forth grass, and herb yielding seed after his kind, and the tree yielding fruit, whose seed was in itself, after his kind: And God saw that it was good. And the evening and the morning were the third day.

And God said, "Let there be lights in the firmament of the heaven to divide the day from the night; and let them be for signs, and for seasons, and for days, and years. And let them be for lights in the firmament of the heaven to give light upon the earth": and it was so. And God made two great lights; the greater light to rule the day, and the lesser light to rule the night: he made the stars also. And God set them in the firmament of the heaven to give light upon the earth, and to rule over the day and over the night, and to divide the light from the darkness: and God saw that it was good. And the evening and the morning were the fourth day.

And God said, "Let the waters bring forth abundantly the moving creature[5] that hath life, and fowl that may fly above the earth in the open firmament of heaven." And God created great whales, and every living creature that moveth, which the waters brought forth

---

1. **waters** *n.:* According to Hebrew belief, only water existed before the creation began.
2. **firmament** *n.:* sky, imagined as an arch or a vault.
3. **herb** *n.:* vegetation.

4. **his** *pron.:* its. (*Its,* the neuter form of the pronoun, did not come into common use until late in the seventeenth century, after the King James Bible was published.)
5. **creature** *n. pl.:* old plural form, without the *s.*

abundantly, after their kind,[6] and every winged fowl after his kind: and God saw that it was good. And God blessed them, saying, "Be fruitful, and multiply, and fill the waters in the seas, and let fowl multiply in the earth." And the evening and the morning were the fifth day.

And God said, "Let the earth bring forth the living creature after his kind, cattle, and creeping thing, and beast of the earth after his kind": and it was so. And God made the beast of the earth after his kind, and cattle after their kind, and every thing that creepeth upon the earth after his kind: and God saw that it was good.

And God said, "Let us make man in our image, after our likeness: and let them have dominion over the fish of the sea, and over the fowl of the air, and over the cattle, and over all the earth, and over every creeping thing that creepeth upon the earth." So God created man in his own image, in the image of God created he him; male and female created he them. And God blessed them, and God said unto them, "Be fruitful, and multiply, and replenish the earth, and subdue it: and have dominion over the fish of the sea, and over the fowl of the air, and over every living thing that moveth upon the earth."

And God said, "Behold, I have given you every herb bearing seed, which is upon the face of all the earth, and every tree, in the which is the fruit of a tree yielding seed; to you it shall be for meat.[7] And to every beast of the earth, and to every fowl of the air, and to every thing that creepeth upon the earth, wherein there is life, I have given every green herb for meat": and it was so. And God saw every thing he had made, and, behold, it was very good. And the evening and the morning were the sixth day.

Thus the heavens and the earth were finished, and all the host[8] of them. And on the seventh day God ended his work which he had made; and he rested on the seventh day from all his work which he had made. And God blessed the

seventh day, and sanctified it: because that in it he had rested from all his work which God created and made.

The Garden of Eden

These are the generations of the heavens and of the earth when they were created, in the day that the Lord God made the earth and the heavens, and every plant of the field before it was in the earth, and every herb of the field before it grew: for the Lord God had not caused it to rain upon the earth, and there was not a man to till the ground. But there went up a mist from the earth, and watered the whole face of the ground. And the Lord God formed man of the dust of the ground, and breathed into his nostrils the breath of life; and man became a living soul.

And the Lord God planted a garden eastward in Eden; and there he put the man whom he had formed. And out of the ground made the Lord God to grow every tree that is pleasant to the sight, and good for food; the tree of life also in the midst of the garden, and the tree of knowledge of good and evil. And a river went out of Eden to water the garden; and from thence it was parted, and became into four heads. The name of the first is Pison: that is it which compasseth the whole land of Havilah,[9] where there is gold; and the gold of that land is good: there is bdellium[10] and the onyx stone. And the name of the second river is Gihon: the same is it that compasseth the whole land of Ethiopia. And the name of the third river is Hiddekel:[11] that is it which goeth toward

---

6. **their kind:** their nature.
7. **meat** *n.:* In the King James Bible, *meat* simply means food in general. Animal meat is called flesh.
8. **host** *n.:* multitude.

9. **Pison** (pē′sən) ... **Havilah** (hav′ə·lə): land rich in gold, perhaps located in Arabia.
10. **bdellium** (del′ē·əm) *n.:* kind of jewel—either a crystal, a pearl, or a deep red gem such as a garnet.
11. **Gihon** (gē′hän) ... **Hiddekel** (hid′ə·kəl): Hiddekel is the biblical name for the Tigris River.

Vocabulary

dominion (də·min′yən) *n.:* rule; absolute authority.

replenish (ri·plen′ish) *v.:* refill or make complete again; resupply.

subdue (səb·doo′) *v.:* conquer; cultivate.

Paradise (detail) (c. 1650) by Jan Brueghel the Elder.
Gemäldegalerie, Staatliche Museen zu Berlin.

the east of Assyria. And the fourth river is Euphrates.[12] And the Lord God took the man, and put him into the garden of Eden to dress it and to keep it. And the Lord God commanded the man, saying, "Of every tree of the garden thou mayest freely eat. But of the tree of the knowledge of good and evil, thou shalt not eat of it: for in the day that thou eatest thereof thou shalt surely die."

And the Lord God said, "It is not good that the man should be alone; I will make him an help meet[13] for him." And out of the ground the Lord God formed every beast of the field, and every fowl of the air; and brought them unto Adam to see what he would call them: and whatsoever Adam called every living creature, that was the name thereof. And Adam gave names to all cattle, and to the fowl of the air, and to every beast of the field; but for Adam there was not found an help meet for him. And the Lord God caused a deep sleep to fall upon Adam, and he slept: and he took one of his ribs, and closed up the flesh instead thereof; and the rib, which the Lord God had taken from man, made he a woman, and brought her unto the man. And Adam said, "This is now bone of my bones, and flesh of my flesh: she shall be called Woman, because she was taken out of Man." Therefore shall a man leave his father and his mother, and shall cleave unto his wife: and they shall be one flesh.

---

12. **Euphrates** (yōō·frāt′ēz): longest river in western Asia.
13. **help meet** *n.*: helpful companion; often a spouse.

The Fall

And they were both naked, the man and his wife, and were not ashamed.

Now the serpent[14] was more subtil[15] than any beast of the field which the Lord God had made. And he said unto the woman, "Yea, hath God said, 'Ye shall not eat of every tree of the garden'?" And the woman said unto the serpent, "We may eat of the fruit of the trees of the garden. But of the fruit of the tree which is in the midst of the garden, God hath said, 'Ye shall not eat of it, neither shall ye touch it, lest ye die.'" And the serpent said unto the woman, "Ye shall not surely die. For God doth know that in the day ye eat thereof, then your eyes shall be opened, and ye shall be as gods, knowing good and evil." And when the woman saw that the tree was good for food, and that it was pleasant to the eyes, and a tree to be desired to make one wise, she took of the fruit thereof, and did eat, and gave also unto her husband with her; and he did eat. And the eyes of them both were opened, and they knew that they were naked; and they sewed fig leaves together, and made themselves aprons. And they heard the voice of the Lord God walking in the garden in the cool of the day: and Adam and his wife hid themselves from the presence of the Lord God amongst the trees of the garden. And the Lord God called unto Adam, and said unto him, "Where art thou?" And he said, "I heard thy voice in the garden, and I was afraid, because I was naked; and I hid myself." And he said, "Who told thee that thou wast naked? Hast thou eaten of the tree, whereof I commanded thee that thou shouldest not eat?" And the man said, "The woman whom thou gavest to be with me, she gave me of the tree, and I did eat." And the Lord God said unto the woman, "What is this that thou hast done?" And the woman said, "The serpent beguiled me, and I did eat." And the Lord God said unto the serpent, "Because thou hast done this, thou are cursed above all cattle,[16] and above every beast of the field; upon thy belly shalt thou go, and dust shalt thou eat all the days of thy life. And I will put enmity between thee and the woman, and thy seed and her seed; it shall bruise thy head, and thou shalt bruise his heel." Unto the woman he said, "I will greatly multiply thy sorrow and thy conception;[17] in sorrow thou shalt bring forth children; and thy desire shall be to thy husband, and he shall rule over thee." And unto Adam he said, "Because thou hast hearkened unto[18] the voice of thy wife, and hast eaten of the tree, of which I commanded thee, saying, Thou shalt not eat of it: cursed is the ground for thy sake; in sorrow shalt thou eat of it all the days of thy life; thorns also and thistles shall it bring forth to thee; and thou shalt eat the herb of the field; in the sweat of thy face shalt thou eat bread, till thou return unto the ground: for out of it wast thou taken, for dust thou art, and unto dust shalt thou return." And Adam called his wife's name Eve; because she was the mother of all living. Unto Adam also and to his wife did the Lord God make coats of skins, and clothed them.

And the Lord God said, "Behold, the man[19] is become as one of us, to know good and evil: and now, lest he put forth his hand, and take also of the tree of life,[20] and eat, and live for ever": therefore the Lord God sent him forth from the garden of Eden, to till the ground from whence he was taken. So he drove out the man; and he placed at the east of the garden of Eden, Cherubims[21] and a flaming sword which turned every way, to keep the way of[22] the tree of life.

---

14. **the serpent:** traditionally understood to be, or to be possessed by, Satan. Formerly the angel Lucifer, Satan was cast out of heaven because he set himself up as God's enemy.
15. **subtil** *adj.:* subtle, here meaning "crafty" or "sly."
16. **cattle** *n. pl.:* general term for all animals.
17. **conception** *n.:* childbearing pains.
18. **hearkened unto:** listened to and obeyed.
19. **man** *n.:* man and woman.
20. **tree of life:** second tree in Eden, apparently a source of immortality.
21. **Cherubims** (cher′yoo·bimz′): warrior angels who act as guardian spirits and support the throne of God.
22. **keep the way of:** deny access to.

Vocabulary

beguiled (bē·gīld′) *v.:* deceived.
enmity (en′mə·tē) *n.:* hostility.

Response and Analysis

Reading Check

1. In "The Creation," what responsibilities and privileges does God give to humans?
2. In "The Garden of Eden," how are Adam and Eve created?
3. In "The Fall," how do Adam and Eve change after they eat the forbidden fruit?

Thinking Critically

4. **Repetition** occurs in "The Creation" with the phrases "And God said . . . : and it was so" and "God saw that it was good." Why do you think these phrases are repeated so often? How do they help to characterize God?
5. Make a list that compares and contrasts the two accounts of the creation of man and woman. Why do you think people tend to forget the first account and remember only the story of Adam and Eve? How did your memories of the accounts compare with the actual texts? Refer to your Quickwrite notes.
6. Does God seem to consider Adam and Eve equally guilty, or does he punish one more harshly than the other? Explain.

Extending and Evaluating

7. What aspects of the human condition are explained in "The Fall"? What do you think the outcome might have been if Adam and Eve had rejected the fruit the serpent offered?

WRITING

Exploring a Theme

One **theme,** or central insight, of the Hebrew Bible is that the relationship between God and humans is often shaped by humanity's struggles with temptation. Find examples from "In the Beginning"—episodes, conflicts, characterization—that anticipate or support this theme. Organize your evidence under these headings: *The Creation, The Garden of Eden,* and *The Fall.* Then, write a three-paragraph essay explaining how your examples illustrate the theme.

North Carolina Competency Goal
1.02; 1.03; 4.05; 5.03; 6.01

INTERNET
Projects and Activities
Keyword: LE5 WL-1

SKILLS FOCUS

Literary Skills
Analyze repetition.

Reading Skills
Compare and contrast.

Writing Skills
Explore a theme.

Vocabulary Skills
Answer questions about vocabulary words.

Vocabulary Development
What's the Difference?

Answer the following questions on a separate sheet of paper using each underlined Vocabulary word in the same sense in which it is used in the selection.

1. What's the difference between <u>dominion</u> and *influence*?
2. What's the difference between <u>replenish</u> and *assist*?
3. What's the difference between <u>subdue</u> and *plant*?
4. What's the difference between <u>beguiled</u> and *flattered*?
5. What's the difference between <u>enmity</u> and *distaste*?

Boy reading from the Torah at his bar mitzvah.

Vocabulary Development

Analyzing Word Analogies

An **analogy** is a similarity between two things that are unlike in other ways. A **word analogy** is a formula for comparing the relationships between pairs of words.

Reading word analogies. In a valid word analogy the first pair of words have the same relationship as the second pair. Study the following analogy:

SLIM : THIN :: sad : gloomy

The colon (:) stands for the phrase "is related to." The double colon (::) between the pairs of words stands for the phrase "in the same way that." Here are two ways to read the analogy:

> *Slim* is related to *thin* in the same way that *sad* is related to *gloomy.*
> *Slim* is to *thin* as *sad* is to *gloomy.*

Identifying relationships. Two types of relationships are often expressed in analogies. The example above expresses a **synonymous** relationship, one based on similarity. The following analogy expresses an **antonymous** relationship, one based on opposition:

LAUGH : CRY :: wake : sleep

Laugh is the opposite of *cry*, just as *wake* is the opposite of *sleep.*

Solving word analogies. Follow these steps to solve an analogy question:

1. Identify the relationship between the first pair of words. Also note the part of speech of the pair.
2. Eliminate all pairs of words among the answer choices that do not have the same relationship and part of speech as the first pair.

3. Choose as your answer the remaining pair of words, whose relationship and part of speech should match the first pair.

PRACTICE

For each of the following items, choose the pair of words whose relationship most closely matches the relationship between the first pair of words. Write the letter of your answer, and identify the type of relationship being expressed.

1. ENMITY : FRIENDSHIP ::
   a. courage : bravery
   b. courtesy : tenderness
   c. loyalty : treachery
   d. king : monarch

2. BEGUILED : DECEIVED ::
   a. abandoned : accompanied
   b. reduced : diminished
   c. whispered : screamed
   d. succeeded : failed

3. DOMINION : RULE ::
   a. riches : wealth
   b. dominant : submissive
   c. palace : hut
   d. tuition : refund

4. SUBDUE : CONQUER ::
   a. terrify : soothe
   b. reveal : conceal
   c. massive : huge
   d. modify : change

5. REPLENISH : DEPLETE ::
   a. repeat : resemble
   b. ascend : descend
   c. excite : stimulate
   d. remote : distant

North Carolina Competency Goal
1.03; 4.05; 5.03; 6.01

SKILLS FOCUS

Vocabulary Skills
Analyze analogies.

Before You Read

Noah and the Flood
from Genesis

Make the Connection

"Noah and the Flood" tells of a terrifying deluge that apparently occurred in Mesopotamia in the distant past. Floods still cause extreme destruction throughout the world. In what ways might a flood be seen as something that not only destroys but creates? Is the same true of other types of natural disasters?

Literary Focus

Theme

Theme is the central insight about life revealed in a work of literature. Whereas the subject or topic of a work can be stated in a word, such as *heroism* or *destruction,* a theme is stated in a sentence, one that makes a generalization about human behavior. For example, *A natural disaster can motivate ordinary people to perform heroic acts* is a statement of a theme. In most literature a theme is the view of a particular writer, but the themes of the Hebrew Bible express the beliefs and concerns of the Hebrew people.

> **Theme** is the central insight about life in a work of literature.
>
> *For more on Theme, see the Handbook of Literary and Historical Terms.*

Reading Skills

Identifying Theme

Sometimes the theme of a work is stated directly. In many fables, for example, the moral is given at the end in the form of a proverb or statement. Most themes, however, are **implied**—the reader must determine the theme from details in the text. The actions of the characters often help reveal the theme.

Background

By the time Genesis was assembled, Hebrew storytellers knew many different versions of the ancient story of the Flood and had combined these accounts into one long narrative. Like the creation stories of Genesis, the story of Noah explains beginnings—the most important of which is the origin of the covenant, the abiding pact between the Hebrews and God.

Vocabulary Development

terminate (tʉr′mə·nāt′) *v.:* end.

covenant (kuv′ə·nənt) *n.:* solemn agreement or contract.

subsided (səb·sīd′id) *v.:* sank; moved to a lower level.

reckoning (rek′ən·iŋ) *n.:* assignment of rewards or punishments for actions.

North Carolina Competency Goal
1.03; 4.05; 5.01; 5.03

INTERNET

Vocabulary Practice
•
More About Genesis

Keyword: LE5 WL-1

Noah's ark, from an allegorical manuscript addressed to King Charles VIII of France (16th century).

Bodleian Library, University of Oxford, England (Rawl. A. 417, fol. 11V).

SKILLS FOCUS

Literary Skills
Understand theme.

Reading Skills
Identify theme.

Noah's Ark (1846) by Edward Hicks.

Noah and the Flood

from **Genesis**

Jewish Publication Society of America

The Lord saw how great was man's wickedness on earth, and how every plan devised by his mind was nothing but evil all the time. And the Lord regretted that He had made man on earth, and His heart was saddened. The Lord said, "I will blot out from the earth the men whom I created—men together with beasts, creeping things, and birds of the sky; for I regret that I made them." But Noah found favor with the Lord.

This is the line of Noah. Noah was a righteous man; he was blameless in his age; Noah walked with God. Noah begot three sons: Shem, Ham, and Japheth.

The earth became corrupt before God; the earth was filled with lawlessness. When God saw how corrupt the earth was, for all flesh had corrupted its ways on earth, God said to Noah, "I have decided to put an end to all flesh, for the earth is filled with lawlessness because of them: I am about to destroy them with the earth. Make yourself an ark of gopher wood;[1] make it an ark with compartments, and cover it inside and out with pitch.[2] This is how you shall make it: the length of the ark shall be three hundred cubits,[3] its width fifty cubits, and its height thirty cubits. Make an opening for daylight in the ark, and terminate it within a cubit of the top. Put the entrance to the ark in its side; make it with bottom, second, and third decks.

"For My part, I am about to bring the Flood waters upon the earth to destroy all flesh under the sky in which there is breath of life; everything on earth shall perish. But I will establish My covenant with you, and you shall enter the ark, with your sons, your wife, and your sons' wives. And of all that lives, of all flesh, you shall take two of each into the ark to keep alive with you; they shall be male and female. From birds of every kind, cattle of every kind, every kind of creeping thing on earth, two of each shall come to you to stay alive. For your part, take of everything that is eaten and store it away, to serve as food for you and for them." Noah did so; just as God commanded him, so he did.

Then the Lord said to Noah, "Go into the ark, with all your household, for you alone have I found righteous before Me in this generation. Of every clean[4] animal you shall take seven pairs, males and their mates, and of every animal which is not clean, two, a male and its mate; of the birds of the sky also, seven pairs, male and female, to keep seed alive upon all the earth. For in seven days' time I will make it rain upon the earth, forty days and forty nights, and I will blot out from the earth all existence that I created." And Noah did just as the Lord commanded him.

Noah was six hundred years old when the Flood came, waters upon the earth. Noah, with his sons, his wife, and his sons' wives, went into the ark because of the waters of the Flood. Of the clean animals, of the animals that are not clean, of the birds, and of everything that creeps on the ground, two of each, male and female, came to Noah into the ark, as God had commanded Noah. And on the seventh day the waters of the Flood came upon the earth.

In the six hundredth year of Noah's life, in the second month, on the seventeenth day of the month, on that day

All the fountains of the great deep burst apart,
And the floodgates of the sky broke open.

The rain fell on the earth forty days and forty nights. That same day Noah and Noah's sons, Shem, Ham, and Japheth, went into the ark, with Noah's wife and the three wives of his sons— they and all beasts of every kind, all cattle of every kind, all creatures of every kind that creep on the earth, and all birds of every kind, every bird, every winged thing. They came to Noah into the ark, two each of all flesh in which there was breath of life. Thus they that entered comprised male and female of all flesh, as God had commanded him. And the Lord shut him in.

The Flood continued forty days on the earth, and the waters increased and raised the ark so that it rose above the earth. The waters swelled and increased greatly upon the earth, and the ark drifted upon the waters. When the waters had swelled much more upon the earth, all the highest mountains everywhere under the sky were covered. Fifteen cubits higher did the waters swell, as the mountains were covered. And all flesh that stirred on earth perished—birds, cattle, beasts, and all the things that swarmed upon the earth, and all mankind. All in whose nostrils was the

---

1. **gopher wood** *n.:* unidentified type of wood.
2. **pitch** *n.:* gummy, tarlike substance used for waterproofing.
3. **cubits** (kyo͞o′bits) *n. pl.:* A cubit is a measure of 17 to 22 inches.
4. **clean** *adj.:* The Hebrews considered some animals clean, or fit for eating and for ritual sacrifice, and others unclean.

Vocabulary

terminate (tʉr′mə·nāt′) *v.:* end.
covenant (kuv′ə·nənt) *n.:* solemn agreement or contract.

merest breath of life, all that was on dry land, died. All existence on earth was blotted out—man, cattle, creeping things, and birds of the sky; they were blotted out from the earth. Only Noah was left, and those with him in the ark.

And when the waters had swelled on the earth one hundred and fifty days, God remembered Noah and all the beasts and all the cattle that were with him in the ark, and God caused a wind to blow across the earth, and the waters subsided. The fountains of the deep and the floodgates of the sky were stopped up, and the rain from the sky was held back; the waters then receded steadily from the earth. At the end of one hundred and fifty days the waters diminished, so that in the seventh month, on the seventeenth day of the month, the ark came to rest on the mountains of Ararat.[5] The waters went on diminishing until the tenth month; in the tenth month, on the first of the month, the tops of the mountains became visible.

At the end of forty days, Noah opened the window of the ark that he had made and sent out the raven; it went to and fro until the waters had dried up from the earth. Then he sent out the dove to see whether the waters had decreased from the surface of the ground. But the dove could not find a resting place for its foot, and returned to him to the ark, for there was water over all the earth. So putting out his hand, he took it into the ark with him. He waited another seven days, and again sent out the dove from the ark. The dove came back to him toward evening, and there in its bill was a plucked-off olive leaf! Then Noah knew that the waters had decreased on the earth. He waited still another seven days and sent the dove forth; and it did not return to him any more.

In the six hundred and first year, in the first month, on the first of the month, the waters began to dry from the earth; and when Noah removed the covering of the ark, he saw that the surface of the ground was drying. And in the second month, on the twenty-seventh day of the month, the earth was dry.

God spoke to Noah, saying, "Come out of the ark, together with your wife, your sons, and your sons' wives. Bring out with you every living thing of all flesh that is with you: birds, animals, and everything that creeps on earth; and let them swarm on the earth and be fertile and increase on earth." So Noah came out, together with his sons, his wife, and his sons' wives. Every animal, every creeping thing, and every bird, everything that stirs on earth came out of the ark by families.

Then Noah built an altar to the Lord and, taking of every clean animal and of every clean bird, he offered burnt offerings on the altar. The Lord smelled the pleasing odor, and the Lord said to Himself: "Never again will I doom the earth because of man, since the devisings of man's mind are evil from his youth; nor will I ever again destroy every living being, as I have done.

> So long as the earth endures,
> Seedtime and harvest,
> Cold and heat,
> Summer and winter,
> Day and night
> Shall not cease."

God blessed Noah and his sons, and said to them, "Be fertile and increase, and fill the earth. The fear and the dread of you shall be upon all the beasts of the earth and upon all the birds of the sky—everything with which the earth is astir—and upon all the fish of the sea; they are given into your hand. Every creature that lives shall be yours to eat; as with the green grasses, I give you all these. You must not, however, eat flesh with its life-blood in it. But for your own life-blood I will require a reckoning: I will require it of every beast; of man, too, will I require a reckoning for human life, of every man for that of his fellow man!

---

5. **Ararat** (ar′ə·rat′): highest mountain in Turkey.

Vocabulary

subsided (səb·sīd′id) v.: sank; moved to a lower level.
reckoning (rek′ən·in) n.: assignment of rewards or punishments for actions.

Whoever sheds the blood of man,
By man shall his blood be shed;
For in His image
Did God make man.

Be fertile, then, and increase; abound on the earth and increase on it."

And God said to Noah and to his sons with him, "I now establish My covenant with you and your offspring to come, and with every living thing that is with you—birds, cattle, and every wild beast as well—all that have come out of the ark, every living thing on earth. I will maintain My covenant with you: never again shall all flesh be cut off by the waters of a flood, and never again shall there be a flood to destroy the earth."

God further said, "This is the sign that I set for the covenant between Me and you, and every living creature with you, for all ages to come. I have set My bow[6] in the clouds, and it shall serve as a sign of the covenant between Me and the earth. When I bring clouds over the earth, and the bow appears in the clouds, I will remember My covenant between Me and you and every living creature among all flesh, so that the waters shall never again become a flood to destroy all flesh. When the bow is in the clouds, I will see it and remember the everlasting covenant between God and all living creatures, all flesh that is on earth. That," God said to Noah, "shall be the sign of the covenant that I have established between Me and all flesh that is on earth."

The sons of Noah who came out of the ark were Shem, Ham, and Japheth—Ham being the father of Canaan. These three were the sons of Noah, and from these the whole world branched out.

Noah, the tiller of the soil, was the first to plant a vineyard. He drank of the wine and became drunk, and he uncovered himself within his tent. Ham, the father of Canaan, saw his father's nakedness and told his two brothers outside. But Shem and Japheth took a cloth, placed it against both their backs and, walking backwards, they covered their father's nakedness; their faces were turned the other way, so that they did not see their father's nakedness. When Noah woke up from his wine and learned what his youngest son had done to him, he said,

"Cursed be Canaan;
The lowest of slaves
Shall he be to his brothers."

And he said,

"Blessed be the Lord,
The God of Shem;
Let Canaan be a slave to them.
May God enlarge Japheth,
And let him dwell in the tents of Shem;
And let Canaan be a slave to them."

Noah lived after the Flood 350 years. And all the days of Noah came to 950 years; then he died.

The Dove Returns to Noah by James J. Tissot. (1836–1902). Jewish Museum, New York.

---

6. bow *n.*: rainbow.

If you've already read the excerpts from the Epic of Gilgamesh *in this book, you probably noticed that its story of Utnapishtim and the flood shares many similarities with the story of Noah and the Flood. In fact, dozens of cultures throughout the world, not just ancient Mesopotamia, have accounts of a great flood. The following short myths—the first from ancient Greece and the second from the Aztecs of Mesoamerica—are also about great floods. Look for details in each that you have seen before in the stories of Utnapishtim and Noah.*

Deucalion

A Greek Myth
retold by J. F. Bierlein

At a very early point in history, perhaps even before the end of the golden age, humankind grew very wicked and arrogant. They grew more tiresome by the day until Zeus finally decided to destroy them all. Prometheus, Titan creator of mankind, was warned of this coming flood and he in turn warned his human son, Deucalion, and Deucalion's wife, Pyrrha. Prometheus placed the two of them in a large wooden chest. And it rained for nine days and nine nights until the entire world was flooded except for two mountain peaks in Greece, Mount Parnassus and Mount Olympus, the latter being the home of the gods.

Finally the wooden chest landed on Mount Parnassus, and Deucalion and Pyrrha got out of it only to see that the entire world around them had been destroyed. From the trunk, they took out

Deucalion and Pyrrha (c. early 17th century) by Peter Paul Rubens.
Museo Nacional del Prado, Madrid.

enough provisions to feed themselves until the waters subsided. Then when they came down from the mountain, they were horrified. Everywhere around them were dead bodies of humans and animals; everything was covered with silt, slime, and algae. The couple was grateful to be saved and they gave thanks to the gods for their deliverance.

Zeus spoke to them out of the sky, saying, "Veil your heads and cast behind you the bones of your mother." Pyrrha responded, "We have no mother with us, only my husband and I were in the chest." But Deucalion knew what Zeus meant and threw some rocks behind him. For rocks are the bones of Mother Earth, the mother of all. These rocks were transformed into people who repopulated the earth.

Tata and Nena

An Aztec Myth
retold by J. F. Bierlein

During the era of the Fourth Sun, the Sun of Water, the people grew very wicked and ignored the worship of the gods. The gods became angry and Tlaloc, the god of rains, announced that he was going to destroy the world with a flood. However, Tlaloc was fond of a devout couple, Tata and Nena, and he warned them of the flood. He instructed them to hollow out a great log and take two ears of corn—one for each of them—and eat nothing more.

So Tata and Nena entered the tree trunk with the two ears of corn, and it began to rain. When the rains subsided and Tata and Nena's log landed on dry land, they were so happy that they caught a fish and ate it, contrary to the orders of Tlaloc. It was only after their stomachs were full that they remembered Tlaloc's command.

Tlaloc then appeared to them and said, "This is how I am repaid for saving your lives?" They were then changed into dogs. It was at this point, where even the most righteous people were disobedient, that the gods destroyed the world, ushering in the present era of the Fifth Sun.

? What parallels, or similarities, do you see between these two accounts of a great flood? Discuss which details in these myths seem to be universal, or common to many cultures, and which seem to be culturally specific— that is, unique to the culture (Greek or Aztec) that produced the myth. What theories might explain the existence of cultural parallels in unrelated cultures from different time periods and different parts of the world?

Response and Analysis

Reading Check

1. Why does God spare Noah?

2. What does the return of the dove with an olive leaf tell Noah?

3. What is the first thing Noah does after the ark is unloaded?

Thinking Critically

4. Water can symbolize rebirth as well as destruction. How are both destruction and rebirth involved in the account of the Flood?

5. What details can you find that show the virtuous side of Noah's **character**? What main idea can you infer about his character from the final paragraph dealing with his three sons?

6. What is the covenant that God establishes with Noah? What does this covenant reveal about God's attitude toward his creation?

7. In a sentence, state the **theme,** or central insight about life, in "Noah and the Flood." Your general statement should take into account what the text reveals about the relationship between a supreme being and humanity.

8. Compare the story of Noah with the creation account. Is God characterized the same way in the two selections? Is he more forgiving or more vengeful in one than the other? Explain.

WRITING

Comparing and Contrasting Accounts of the Flood

The story of the flood in the *Epic of Gilgamesh* (page 29) is strikingly similar to "Noah and the Flood." The myths "Deucalion" and "Tata and Nena" in the **Connection** on pages 64–65 are similar as well. Compare and contrast "Noah and the Flood" with any one of the three flood accounts mentioned above. Consider the following ideas in your essay:

- What is the relationship between humanity and a supreme being in each account?

- How is each account about both destruction and rebirth?

North Carolina Competency Goal
1.03; 4.02; 4.05; 5.03; 6.01

INTERNET

Projects and Activities

Keyword:
LE5 WL-1

SKILLS FOCUS

Literary Skills
Analyze theme.

Reading Skills
Identify theme.

Writing Skills
Compare and contrast two flood accounts.

Vocabulary Skills
Write sentences about the story.

Vocabulary Development
Sentence Sense

terminate	subsided
covenant	reckoning

On a separate sheet of paper, use each Vocabulary word listed above in an original sentence based on the characters and events in "Noah and the Flood."

Noah's Ark. Clay sculpture from Mexico.

Caplan Collection of The Children's Museum of Indianapolis.

Before You Read

The Book of Ruth

Make the Connection

Have you ever felt like an outsider, as if you didn't belong? What caused you to feel this way? Who or what helped you overcome this feeling?

Literary Focus

Narrative

A **narrative** is a type of written or oral literature that tells about a series of events, usually in chronological order—the order in which the events occurred. Many kinds of literature are written in narrative form—fiction, nonfiction, even poetry. Most of the accounts in the Hebrew Bible, like the selections from Genesis you have just read, are narratives. Unlike a short story, a narrative doesn't necessarily have a definite plot or developed characters. The Book of Ruth is a complex narrative; its characters, setting, and sequence of events come as close to a short story as any book in the Hebrew Bible.

> A **narrative** is any work of literature, written or oral, that tells a story.
>
> *For more on Narrative, see the Handbook of Literary and Historical Terms.*

Reading Skills

Making Inferences About Motivation

Why do characters act the way they do? For a story to be convincing, we need to be able to infer the characters' **motivations**—the causes of their behavior. Literary characters, like real people, are motivated by their wants and needs. As you read this story, see if you can **infer,** or make intelligent guesses about, the characters' motivations from the way they interact with one another.

Background

Ruth is from Moab (mō′ab′), where people worship idols, a practice the Hebrews condemn. She marries a Hebrew man but is soon left widowed and childless, a precarious position for a woman. However, the Hebrews practice a custom called levirate (lev′ə·rit) marriage. According to this custom, a brother or another close male relative of the dead husband is obliged to marry the widow if the husband has left no son to be his heir. The firstborn son of this second marriage is raised in the dead husband's name and is considered his legal heir. Despite being an outsider, Ruth goes to Israel and ultimately marries Boaz (bō′az′), a relative of her husband. The story emphasizes compassion toward outsiders who accept the Jewish faith.

North Carolina Competency Goal
1.03; 2.01; 3.04; 4.05; 5.01; 5.03

Vocabulary Development

entreat (en·trēt′) v.: beg; plead with.

afflicted (ə·flikt′id) v.: brought suffering upon.

kindred (kin′drid) n.: family; relatives.

recompense (rek′əm·pens′) v.: repay; reward.

sufficed (sə·fist′) v.: satisfied; had a need met.

reproach (ri·prōch′) v.: scold; express disapproval.

INTERNET

Vocabulary Practice
•
More About the Book of Ruth
Keyword: LE5 WL-1

SKILLS FOCUS

Literary Skills
Understand narrative.

Reading Skills
Make inferences about motivation.

Naomi entreating Ruth and Orpah to return to the Land of Moab (c. 1795) by William Blake.
Victoria & Albert Museum, London.

The Book of Ruth

King James Bible

Chapter 1

Now it came to pass in the days when the judges ruled that there was a famine in the land. And a certain man of Bethlehem-Judah[1] went to sojourn in the country of Moab,[2] he, and his wife, and his two sons.

And the name of the man was Elimelech, and

---

1. **Bethlehem-Judah:** that is, Bethlehem in Judah. Judah was a region in southern Palestine that eventually became a kingdom rivaling Israel to the north.

2. **Moab:** kingdom of the Dead Sea, in what is today called Jordan.

the name of his wife Naomi, and the names of his two sons Mahlon and Chilion, Ephrathites[3] of Bethlehem-Judah. And they came into the country of Moab and continued there.

And Elimelech, Naomi's husband, died; and she was left, and her two sons.

And they took them wives of the women of Moab; the name of the one was Orpah, and the name of the other Ruth: and they dwelled there about ten years.

And Mahlon and Chilion died also, both of them; and the woman was left of her two sons and her husband.

Then she arose with her daughters-in-law, that she might return from the country of Moab: for she had heard in the country of Moab how that the Lord had visited his people in giving the bread.

Wherefore she went forth out of the place where she was, and her two daughters-in-law with her; and they went on the way to return unto the land of Judah.

And Naomi said unto her two daughters-in-law, "Go, return each to her mother's house: the Lord deal kindly with you, as ye have dealt with the dead and with me. The Lord grant you that ye may find rest, each of you in the house of her husband." Then she kissed them; and they lifted up their voice and wept.

And they said unto her, "Surely we will return with thee unto thy people."

And Naomi said, "Turn again, my daughters: why will ye go with me? Are there yet any more sons in my womb, that they may be your husbands?

"Turn again, my daughters, go your way; for I am too old to have a husband. If I should say I have hope, if I should have a husband also tonight and should also bear sons, would ye tarry for them till they were grown? Would ye stay for them from having husbands? Nay, my daughters; for it grieveth me much for your sakes that the hand of the Lord is gone out against me."

And they lifted up their voice and wept again: and Orpah kissed her mother-in-law, but Ruth clave unto[4] her.

And she said, "Behold, thy sister-in-law is gone back unto her people and unto her gods: Return thou after thy sister-in-law."

And Ruth said, "Entreat me not to leave thee or to return from following after thee: for whither thou goest, I will go; and where thou lodgest, I will lodge: thy people shall be my people, and thy God my God: where thou diest, will I die, and there will I be buried: the Lord do so to me, and more also, if ought[5] but death part thee and me."

When she saw that she was steadfastly minded to go with her, then she left speaking unto her.

So they two went until they came to Bethlehem. And it came to pass, when they were come to Bethlehem, that all the city was moved about them, and they said, "Is this Naomi?" And she said unto them, "Call me not Naomi, call me Mara:[6] for the Almighty hath dealt very bitterly with me. I went out full, and the Lord hath brought me home again empty: Why then call ye me Naomi, seeing the Lord hath testified against me, and the Almighty hath afflicted me?"

So Naomi returned, and Ruth the Moabitess, her daughter-in-law, with her, which returned out of the country of Moab: and they came to Bethlehem in the beginning of barley harvest.

Chapter 2

And Naomi had a kinsman of her husband's, a mighty man of wealth, of the family of Elimelech; and his name was Boaz.

---

4. **clave** (archaic form of *cleaved*) **unto:** clung to; was faithful to.
5. **ought** *n.:* alternative spelling of *aught* (ôt), meaning "anything."
6. **Naomi...Mara:** *Naomi* means "pleasantness" or "my pleasant one" in Hebrew; *Mara* means "bitterness" or "the bitter one."

Vocabulary

entreat (en·trēt′) *v.:* beg; plead with.
afflicted (ə·flikt′id) *v.:* brought suffering upon.

---

3. **Ephrathites** (efˈrə·thīts): natives of Bethlehem, once known as Ephrath; members of the clan of Ephrah.

And Ruth the Moabitess said unto Naomi, "Let me now go to the field and glean ears of corn after him in whose sight I shall find grace."[7] And she said unto her, "Go, my daughter."

And she went, and came, and gleaned in the field after the reapers: and her hap[8] was to light on a part of the field belonging unto Boaz, who was of the kindred of Elimelech.

And, behold, Boaz came from Bethlehem and said unto the reapers, "The Lord be with you." And they answered him, "The Lord bless thee."

Then said Boaz unto his servant that was set over the reapers, "Whose damsel is this?"

And the servant that was set over the reapers answered and said, "It is the Moabitish damsel that came back with Naomi out of the country of Moab. And she said, 'I pray you, let me glean and gather after the reapers among the sheaves': so she came, and hath continued even from the morning until now, that she tarried a little in the house."

Then said Boaz unto Ruth, "Hearest thou not, my daughter? Go not to glean in another field, neither go from hence, but abide here fast by my maidens. Let thine eyes be on the field that they do reap, and go thou after them. Have I not charged the young men that they shall not touch thee? And when thou art athirst, go unto the vessels, and drink of that which the young men have drawn."

Then she fell on her face and bowed herself to the ground and said unto him, "Why have I found grace in thine eyes, that thou shouldest take knowledge of me, seeing I am a stranger?"

And Boaz answered and said unto her, "It hath fully been showed me all that thou hast done unto thy mother-in-law since the death of thine husband: and how thou hast left thy father and thy mother, and the land of thy nativity and art come unto a people which thou knewest not heretofore. The Lord recompense thy work, and a full reward be given thee of the Lord God of Israel, under whose wings thou art come to trust."

Then she said, "Let me find favor in thy sight, my lord; for that thou hast comforted me, and for that thou hast spoken friendly unto thine handmaid, though I be not like unto one of thine handmaidens."

And Boaz said unto her, "At mealtime come thou hither, and eat of the bread, and dip thy morsel in the vinegar." And she sat beside the reapers: and he reached her parched corn, and she did eat, and was sufficed, and left.

And when she was risen up to glean, Boaz commanded his young men, saying, "Let her glean even among the sheaves, and reproach her not. And let fall also some of the handfuls on purpose for her, and leave them, that she may glean them, and rebuke her not."

So she gleaned in the field until even, and beat out that she had gleaned: and it was about an ephah[9] of barley.

And she took it up and went into the city: and her mother-in-law saw what she had gleaned: and she brought forth and gave to her what she had reserved after she was sufficed.

And her mother-in-law said unto her, "Where hast thou gleaned today? and where wroughtest thou? Blessed be he that did take knowledge of thee." And she showed her mother-in-law with whom she had wrought, and said, "The man's name with whom I wrought today is Boaz."

And Naomi said unto her daughter-in-law, "Blessed be he of the Lord, who hath not left off his kindness to the living and to the dead." And Naomi said unto her, "The man is near of kin unto us, one of our next kinsmen."

---

9. **ephah** (ē'fə) *n.*: amount slightly greater than a bushel.

---

7. **glean . . . grace:** According to biblical law, the poor were entitled to glean in the fields—to gather any grain left or dropped by the reapers. The corners of the fields were also left for the poor to reap.
8. **hap** *n.*: luck.

Vocabulary

kindred (kin′drid) *n.*: family; relatives.
recompense (rek′əm·pens′) *v.*: repay; reward.
sufficed (sə·fist′) *v.*: satisfied; had a need met.
reproach (ri·prōch′) *v.*: scold; express disapproval.

Epreuve d'artiste

Marc Chagall

Meeting of Ruth and Boaz (1960) by Marc Chagall.

And Ruth the Moabitess said, "He said unto me also, 'Thou shalt keep fast by my young men, until they have ended all my harvest.'"

And Naomi said unto Ruth her daughter-in-law, "It is good, my daughter, that thou go out with his maidens, that they meet thee not in any other field."

So she kept fast by the maidens of Boaz to glean unto the end of barley harvest and of wheat harvest; and dwelt with her mother-in-law.

Chapter 3

Then Naomi her mother-in-law said unto her, "My daughter, shall I not seek rest for thee,[10] that it may be well with thee? And now is not Boaz of our kindred, with whose maidens thou wast? Behold, he winnoweth barley tonight in the threshing floor. Wash thyself therefore, and anoint thee, and put thy raiment upon thee, and get thee down to the floor: but make not thyself known unto the man, until he shall have done eating and drinking. And it shall be, when he lieth down, that thou shalt mark the place where he shall lie, and thou shalt go in and uncover his feet and lay thee down; and he will tell thee what thou shalt do."

And she said unto her, "All that thou sayest unto me I will do."

And she went down unto the floor and did according to all that her mother-in-law bade her.

And when Boaz had eaten and drunk and his heart was merry, he went to lie down at the end of the heap of corn: and she came softly and uncovered his feet and laid her down.

And it came to pass at midnight, that the man was afraid and turned himself: and, behold, a woman lay at his feet.

And he said, "Who art thou?" And she answered, "I am Ruth thine handmaid: Spread therefore thy skirt[11] over thine handmaid; for thou art a near kinsman."

And he said, "Blessed be thou of the Lord, my daughter: for thou hast showed more kindness in the latter end than at the beginning, inasmuch as thou followedst not young men,[12] whether poor or rich. And now, my daughter, fear not; I will do to thee all that thou requirest: for all the city of my people doth know that thou art a virtuous woman. And now it is true that I am thy near kinsman: howbeit, there is a kinsman nearer than I. Tarry this night, and it shall be in the morning that if he will perform unto thee the part of a kinsman, well; let him do the kinsman's part: but if he will not do the part of a kinsman to thee, then will I do the part of a kinsman to thee, as the Lord liveth: lie down until the morning."

And she lay at his feet until the morning: and she rose up before one could know another. And he said, "Let it not be known that a woman came into the floor."

Also he said, "Bring the veil that thou hast upon thee, and hold it." And when she held it, he measured six measures of barley and laid it on her: and she went into the city.

And when she came to her mother-in-law, she said, "Who art thou, my daughter?" And she told her all that the man had done to her.

And she said, "These six measures of barley gave he me; for he said to me, 'Go not empty unto thy mother-in-law.'"

Then said she, "Sit still, my daughter, until thou know how the matter will fall: for the man will not be in rest until he have finished the thing this day."

Chapter 4

Then went Boaz up to the gate and sat him down there and, behold, the kinsman of whom Boaz spake came by; unto whom he said, "Ho, such a one! turn aside, sit down here." And he turned aside and sat down.

---

10. **seek rest for thee:** seek a husband. Naomi wants to fulfill the duty of a parent to arrange a marriage for a child.
11. **Spread therefore thy skirt:** formal act of betrothal.

12. **thou followedst not young men:** Boaz, who is much older than Ruth, is praising Ruth for her willingness to fulfill the levirate marriage obligation by marrying him even though he is old.

And he took ten men of the elders of the city and said, "Sit ye down here." And they sat down.

And he said unto the kinsman, "Naomi, that is come again out of the country of Moab, selleth a parcel of land, which was our brother Elimelech's. And I thought to advertise thee, saying, Buy it before the inhabitants and before the elders of my people. If thou wilt redeem it, redeem it: but if thou wilt not redeem it, then tell me, that I may know: for there is none to redeem it beside thee; and I am after thee." And he said, "I will redeem it."

Then said Boaz, "What day thou buyest the field of the hand of Naomi, thou must buy it also of Ruth the Moabitess, the wife of the dead, to raise up the name of the dead upon his inheritance."

And the kinsman said, "I cannot redeem it for myself, lest I mar mine own inheritance:[13] Redeem thou my right to thyself; for I cannot redeem it."

Now this was the manner in former time in Israel concerning redeeming and concerning changing, for to confirm all things; a man plucked off his shoe, and gave it to his neighbor: and this was a testimony in Israel.

Therefore the kinsman said unto Boaz, "Buy it for thee." So he drew off his shoe.

And Boaz said unto the elders and unto all the people, "Ye are witnesses this day, that I have bought all that was Elimelech's, and all that was Chilion's and Mahlon's, of the hand of Naomi. Moreover, Ruth the Moabitess, the wife of Mahlon, have I purchased to be my wife, to raise up the name of the dead upon his inheritance, that the name of the dead be not cut off from among his brethren and from the gate of his place: Ye are witnesses this day."

And all the people that were in the gate and the elders said, "We are witnesses. The Lord make the woman that is come into thine house like Rachel and like Leah,[14] which two did build the house of Israel: and do thou worthily in Ephrath, and be famous in Bethlehem. And let thy house be like the house of Pharez, whom Tamar bare unto Judah,[15] of the seed which the Lord shall give thee of this young woman."

So Boaz took Ruth, and she was his wife: and when he went in unto her, the Lord gave her conception, and she bare a son.

And the women said unto Naomi, "Blessed be the Lord, which hath not left thee this day without a kinsman, that his name may be famous in Israel. And he shall be unto thee a restorer of thy life and a nourisher of thine old age: for thy daughter-in-law, which loveth thee, which is better to thee than seven sons, hath born him."

And Naomi took the child and laid it in her bosom and became nurse unto it.

And the women her neighbors gave it a name, saying, "There is a son born to Naomi";[16] and they called his name Obed: He is the father of Jesse, the father of David.

Now these are the generations of Pharez: Pharez begat Hezron, and Hezron begat Ram, and Ram begat Amminadab, and Amminadab begat Nahshon, and Nahshon begat Salmon, and Salmon begat Boaz, and Boaz begat Obed, and Obed begat Jesse, and Jesse begat David.

---

13. **lest I mar mine own inheritance:** that is, by spending money on property that will go to the son legally regarded as Mahlon's rather than to his own son.

14. **like Rachel and like Leah:** two sisters who were Jacob's wives. Their sons were among the twelve sons of Jacob, founders of the twelve tribes of Israel.

15. **Pharez . . . Judah:** Judah was the fourth son of Jacob and Leah. After his daughter-in-law Tamar had twice been left a childless widow after two of his sons died, she tricked Judah into becoming the father of her twin sons, Pharez and Zarah.

16. **son born to Naomi:** not literally, but rather a son in the sense of a legal heir to both her husband and her son. Some biblical scholars suggest that the child may have been legally regarded as Naomi's.

Response and Analysis

Reading Check

1. How does Naomi try to persuade Ruth and Orpah to return home?
2. How does Boaz meet Ruth?
3. What must Boaz do to redeem the land and marry Ruth?

North Carolina Competency Goal
1.03; 4.02; 4.05; 5.01; 5.03; 6.01

Thinking Critically

4. What did you **infer** about Ruth's **motivation** for leaving her people and devoting herself to Naomi? List the details that led to your inferences.

5. If the relationship between Ruth and Boaz is truly a love story, what attitudes toward love and marriage does it express?

6. From this narrative we learn that David, the greatest king of Israel, is descended from Ruth. What is **ironic,** or unexpected, about this detail?

7. Is the Book of Ruth a more fully developed **narrative** than the stories from Genesis? Can it be considered a short story? Analyze such elements as plot, character, setting, and theme.

INTERNET
Projects and Activities
Keyword:
LE5 WL-1

Literary Criticism

8. To some feminist critics, Ruth and Naomi are courageous women who defy social conventions and make their own decisions, taking control of their own lives in a male-dominated society. Male characters are seen as playing relatively minor roles in the narrative. Do you agree or disagree with this view of the Book of Ruth? Explain.

Literary Skills
Analyze narrative.

Reading Skills
Make inferences about motivation.

Writing Skills
Write a reflective essay.

Vocabulary Skills
Write a summary of the story.

WRITING

Reflecting on an Experience

Have you ever willingly or unwillingly found yourself in the position of being an outsider— someone who is not yet part of a new place, a new situation, or a new group of people? Write a short **reflective essay** about a personal experience when you felt like the new kid on the block. Describe your situation and the choices you made. What did you learn from the experience? What was its significance in your life?

▷ Use "Writing a Reflective Essay," pages 88–93, for help with this assignment.

Vocabulary Development
Summarizing the Book of Ruth

entreat   recompense

afflicted   sufficed

kindred   reproach

Use the Vocabulary words above to write a summary of the story. You do not have to use a Vocabulary word in every sentence, and you may use any word more than once.

Boaz and Ruth by Gustave Doré. Engraving.

Grammar Link

Connecting Ideas: Using Adjective and Adverb Clauses

How can you combine choppy sentences, relate ideas more clearly, and add variety to your sentences? Try using adjective and adverb clauses. An **adjective clause** is a subordinate clause that modifies a noun or pronoun and usually begins with *who, whom, whose, which, that, where,* or *when.* Consider these two choppy sentences:

> Ruth promises to follow Naomi. Naomi is Ruth's mother-in-law.

You can combine these short sentences by turning one of them into an adjective clause.

> Ruth promises to follow Naomi, <u>who is Ruth's mother-in-law</u>.

If an adjective clause can be removed without changing the basic meaning of the sentence, as in the sentence above, it is a **nonrestrictive clause.** Set off non-restrictive clauses with commas.

If an adjective clause cannot be removed without changing the basic meaning of the sentence, it is a **restrictive clause** (*Ruth is the woman* **who promises to follow Naomi**). No commas should be used.

An **adverb clause** is a subordinate clause that modifies a verb, an adjective, or an adverb. An adverb clause begins with a subordinating conjunction, such as *after, although, because, before, if, since, when,* or *while.* Here are two more choppy sentences:

> Naomi's husband dies. He leaves her with two sons.

By turning one of these sentences into an adverb clause, you can combine them and add variety.

> <u>When Naomi's husband dies</u>, he leaves her with two sons.

When an adverb clause comes first, as in the sentence above, separate it from the rest of the sentence with a comma.

PRACTICE

Combine each of the following sets of sentences by turning one or more sentences into an adjective or adverb clause. Identify the kind of clauses that you use.

1. Naomi's sons, Mahlon and Chilion, die ten years later. She suffers another tragedy.

2. Naomi plans to return to her home. Naomi is from the land of Bethlehem.

3. Naomi does not expect Ruth and Orpah to stay with her. They can seek help from their own families.

4. Orpah returns to her family. Ruth makes a promise. She will keep this promise for the rest of her life.

Apply to Your Writing

Look through a writing assignment you are working on now or have already completed. Can you find any short, choppy sentences? Use adjective and adverb clauses to combine those sentences and add variety to your writing.

▶ **For more help, see The Adjective Clause, 7d, and The Adverb Clause, 7f, in the Language Handbook.**

SKILLS FOCUS

Grammar Skills
Understand adjective and adverb clauses.

Psalms 8, 23, 121, 137

Make the Connection

Quickwrite ✏️

Think of some popular songs whose lyrics have a special meaning for you. Jot down some lines or phrases from these lyrics, and briefly describe the thoughts and feelings they bring to mind.

Literary Focus

Parallelism

Parallelism, or **parallel structure,** is the repetition of words, phrases, or sentences that have the same grammatical structure or restate or contrast an idea, such as *"It was the best of times, it was the worst of times."* Parallelism is often used in speeches, poetry, and other works that are meant to be read aloud. The technique is a common feature of Hebrew writings, but it is especially apparent in the psalms. Instead of depending on the usual poetic devices of rhyme and meter, the psalms use parallelism to create a sense of balance and order. While parallel structure shows the relationship between similar ideas, it also creates rhythm, emphasizes images, and adds emotional intensity. Try reading each of these psalms aloud. Listen for the repetition of words or sentence structures, the restatement of ideas, and the use of contrasting ideas.

North Carolina Competency Goal
1.02; 1.03; 4.05; 5.01; 6.01

INTERNET

More About the Psalms

Keyword: LE5 WL-1

SKILLS FOCUS

Literary Skills
Understand parallelism.

> **Parallelism** is the repetition of words, phrases, or sentences that are grammatically similar or that compare or contrast ideas.
>
> *For more on Parallelism, see the Handbook of Literary and Historical Terms.*

Background

The Book of Psalms, which appears in the section of the Hebrew Bible called Writings, contains 150 poems that were combined into a single collection around the fourth century B.C. Although nearly half the psalms carry the title "Song of David," not all the poems were composed by King David, who lived around 1000 B.C. Some psalms were recited in sacred rituals long before David ruled; others, such as Psalm 137, were composed after his reign.

The origin of the word *psalm,* from the Greek word *psalmos* (meaning "a plucking of strings"), implies that the psalms were sung to musical accompaniment. Many psalms, like Psalm 8, offer praise to God; not surprisingly, their Hebrew title, *Tehillim,* means "songs of praise." But adoration is not the only emotion the psalms express. Like other lyric poems, they range in emotion from joyous exultation to bitter anger. The Book of Psalms includes laments, personal meditations, and even battle songs. What makes the psalms unique among the books of the Hebrew Bible is their emphasis on personal, heartfelt responses to God.

Biblioteca del Studio Teologico Accademico, Bressanone, Italy.

Illuminated letter B with King David singing the psalms, from a breviary of Ludovic de Teck, patriarch of Aquileia, Italy (c. 1350).

In this psalm, look for imagery that recalls images from "The Creation" in the Book of Genesis. How would you describe the tone of this psalm? Why do you think the psalmist asks, "What is man, that thou art mindful of him?"

Psalm 8
King James Bible

O Lord our Lord,
How excellent is thy name in all the earth!
Who hast set thy glory above the heavens.
Out of the mouth of babes and sucklings° hast thou
    ordained strength
5   Because of thine enemies,
That thou mightest still° the enemy and the avenger.
When I consider thy heavens, the work of thy fingers,
The moon and the stars, which thou hast ordained;°
What is man, that thou art mindful of him?
10 And the son of man, that thou visitest him?
For thou hast made him a little lower than the angels,
And hast crowned him with glory and honor.
Thou madest him to have dominion over the works
    of thy hands;
Thou hast put all things under his feet:
15 All sheep and oxen,
Yea, and the beasts of the field;
The fowl of the air, and the fish of the sea,
And whatsoever passeth through the paths of the seas.
O Lord our Lord,
20 How excellent is thy name in all the earth!

---

4. sucklings *n.:* infants who are still being nursed.
6. still *v.:* put down; silence.
8. ordained *v.:* decreed; called into being.

Genesis, page from a Hebrew Bible from Avignon, France (c. 1422).

The Pierpont Morgan Library, New York (MS. G.48, f.17v).

The Twenty-third Psalm is probably the most frequently recited of all the psalms. Many people find comfort in this psalm; it is often recited at funerals. What comparison is explored at length in the psalm?

Psalm 23

King James Bible

The Lord is my shepherd;
I shall not want.°

He maketh me to lie down in green pastures:
He leadeth me beside the still waters.

5   He restoreth my soul:
He leadeth me in the paths of righteousness for his name's sake.

Yea, though I walk through the valley of the
      shadow of death, I will fear no evil: for thou art with me;
Thy rod and thy staff they comfort me.

Thou preparest a table before me in the presence
      of mine enemies:
Thou anointest my head with oil;° my cup
10   runneth over.

Surely goodness and mercy shall follow me all the
      days of my life:
And I will dwell in the house of the Lord for ever.

---

2. **want** *v.:* lack the necessities of life.
10. **anointest . . . oil:** It was a Hebrew custom to show respect or hospitality toward a man by pouring oil on his head, since his hair and beard might be dusty from the roads or fields.

The Good Shepherd (c. 4th century).
Museo Pio Cristiano, Musei Vaticani, Rome.

This psalm, like several others, has often been adapted as a church hymn. What features does it share with the Twenty-third Psalm?

Psalm 121
King James Bible

I will lift up mine eyes unto the hills,
From whence cometh my help.
My help cometh from the Lord,
Which made heaven and earth.
5   He will not suffer thy foot to be moved:
He that keepeth thee will not slumber.
Behold, he that keepeth Israel
Shall neither slumber nor sleep.
The Lord is thy keeper:
10   The Lord is thy shade upon thy right hand.
The sun shall not smite thee by day, nor the moon by night.
The Lord shall preserve thee from all evil:
He shall preserve thy soul.
The Lord shall preserve thy going out
15   And thy coming in from this time forth, and even for evermore.

Israeli landscape.

This psalm expresses the sorrow of the Hebrews during their exile in Babylon, after King Nebuchadnezzar destroyed Jerusalem. At what point in the psalm is there a shocking change in tone?

Psalm 137
King James Bible

By the rivers of Babylon, there we sat down,
Yea, we wept, when we remembered Zion.°

We hanged our harps upon the willows in the midst thereof.

For there they that carried us away captive required of us a
      song;
And they that wasted us required of us mirth, saying,
5   Sing us one of the songs of Zion.

How shall we sing the Lord's song in a strange land?

If I forget thee, O Jerusalem, let my right hand forget her
      cunning.

If I do not remember thee, let my tongue cleave to the roof
      of my mouth;
If I prefer not Jerusalem above my chief joy.

Remember, O Lord, the children of Edom° in the day of
10   Jerusalem;

Who said, Raze it, raze it, even to the foundation thereof.

O daughter of Babylon, who art to be destroyed;
Happy shall he be, that rewardeth thee as thou hast served us.

Happy shall he be, that taketh and dasheth thy little ones
      against the stones.

Jerusalem (2002) by Vivian Linder.

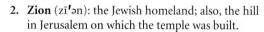

2. **Zion** (zī'ən): the Jewish homeland; also, the hill
   in Jerusalem on which the temple was built.
10. **Edom** (ē'dəm): country south of the Dead Sea.

Response and Analysis

Thinking Critically

1. In Psalm 8, how does the poet answer the question "What is man, that thou art mindful of him?"

2. How would you describe the poet's **tone,** or attitude toward his subject, in Psalm 23? What **image** do you think is most effective in conveying this tone?

3. In Psalm 121, what do "keep" and "keeper" suggest about human relationships with God?

4. Identify the line of Psalm 137 where the **mood,** or emotional atmosphere, changes sharply. Describe this shift. How did the final line of the psalm affect you?

5. Each of the psalms you've just read contains many examples of **paral-lelism,** places where words, phrases, and sentence structures are repeated or an idea is restated. Find at least one example of parallelism in each psalm. Then, describe the effect this kind of repetition produces, especially in an oral reading.

Extending and Evaluating

6. Think of contemporary poems or song lyrics in which parallelism or other forms of repetition are used. What is the purpose and effect of repetition in each case? Refer to your Quickwrite notes for ideas.

WRITING

Comparing Translations of Psalm 23

The following translation of Psalm 23 is from the Anchor Bible, published in 1965. The translations in this Bible were designed to convey the meaning of the original Hebrew to contemporary readers. Compare this version with the King James translation you have just read, from the early seventeenth century. Which version seems more poetic? Which seems more literal? Which do you prefer? Present your responses in a brief essay. Support your evaluation with specific examples from the two versions.

North Carolina Competency Goal
1.02; 1.03; 4.05; 5.03; 6.01

> Psalm 23
> The Anchor Bible Translation
>
> Yahweh is my shepherd,
>   I shall not lack.
> In green meadows he will make me lie
>   down;
> Near tranquil waters will he guide me,
> 5   to refresh my being.
> He will lead me into luxuriant pastures,
>   as befits his name.
> Even though I should walk
>   in the midst of total darkness,
> 10 I shall fear no danger
>   since you are with me.
> Your rod and your staff—
>   behold, they will lead me.
> You prepare my table before me,
> 15   in front of my adversaries.
> You generously anoint my head with oil,
>   my cup overflows.
> Surely goodness and kindness will attend
>   me
>   all the days of my life;
> 20 And I shall dwell in the house of Yahweh
>   for days without end.

INTERNET

Projects and Activities
Keyword: LE5 WL-1

SKILLS FOCUS

Literary Skills
Analyze parallelism.

Writing Skills
Compare two translations of a psalm.

The New Testament

The Four Evangelists (c. 18th century).
Ashmolean Museum, Oxford.

The Christian Bible consists of the Hebrew Bible and the New Testament, a collection of twenty-seven books written within the first two centuries A.D. Although recorded in Greek, the New Testament is a product of Hebrew culture and tradition, since its writers were Hebrews.

The New Testament opens with the four Gospels, which explain the origins and key beliefs of Christianity—just as the Hebrew Bible opens with the Five Books of Moses, explaining the origins of the Hebrew people and their beliefs. *Gospel* comes from the Old English word *godspel,* or "good news," a direct translation of *evangelium,* the Greek name for these books. The "good news" of the Gospels is that of the life and message of Jesus Christ, a Jewish teacher who lived during the period when the Romans ruled Judea. *Christ,* meaning "the anointed one," implies divinity; Christians believe that Jesus is the divine son of God. According to Christian belief, God established a new covenant, or testament, with humanity by sending Christ, his only son, to die for people's sins. Christians see the New Testament as a continuation of the Hebrew covenant with God.

The four Gospels are attributed to Matthew, Mark, Luke, and John, but scholars do not know the exact identity of these writers. Each writer wrote for a different audience and emphasized different aspects of Jesus' life and works. The accounts by Matthew, Mark, and Luke parallel one another closely, however, and are sometimes called the synoptic (si·näp'tik) gospels, from the Greek words *syn* ("same") and *optic* ("vision").

The New Testament also includes the Acts of the Apostles, the Epistles, and Revelation. The Acts of the Apostles continues Luke's Gospel and describes the deeds of the missionary Paul, a convert to Christianity. Paul contributed to the next section of the New Testament, the Epistles—letters written to various people and communities to spread the teachings of Jesus. The final book of the New Testament, Revelation (the name is a direct translation of the Greek word *apokalypsis*), is filled with symbols and images representing the age-old struggle between good and evil during the "end times." Sometimes considered a work of prophecy, Revelation brings the Christian Bible full circle: It unites the Hebrew Bible and the New Testament through the use of images associated with the accounts of creation in Genesis: "a new heaven and a new earth" and a new "tree of life" (Revelation 21:1 and 22:2).

The Prodigal Son
The Talents

Make the Connection

Which of the following approaches do you think would be a more effective way to convince others of the value of forgiveness: saying "Forgive your enemies" or telling a brief story to illustrate what happens when someone forgives an enemy? Explain.

Literary Focus

Parable

A **parable** is a brief narrative that teaches a moral, a lesson about life. Parables rely on the use of **allegory**—a story in which the characters, settings, and events stand for, or symbolize, abstract or moral concepts. Allegories can be read on one level for their literal meaning and on another for their symbolic meaning. Since symbols can suggest numerous meanings, even a brief, seemingly simple parable can be interpreted in several ways. *Parable* comes from a Greek word meaning "comparison," indicating that the surface details in these brief stories can be compared to underlying abstract concepts.

> A **parable** is a brief allegorical story that teaches a moral lesson about life.
>
> *For more on Parable, see the Handbook of Literary and Historical Terms.*

Reading Skills

Making Inferences About Theme

The **theme** is the central insight about life in a story. The theme of a parable does not need to be directly stated; it can usually be **inferred**, or guessed, from the text itself. You should be able to state the theme in the form of a sentence that makes a generalization about the human experience: *Forgiving your enemies is necessary for your own peace of mind.*

Background

About forty parables—all of which are attributed to Jesus—appear throughout the four Gospels of the New Testament. The biblical scholar Joachim Jeremias says of Jesus' down-to-earth figurative language that "the parables' imagery is drawn from the daily life of Palestine. . . . The hearers find themselves in a familiar scene where everything is so clear and simple that a child can understand it, and so obvious that again and again those who hear cannot help saying 'Yes, that's how it is.'"

The parables involve everyday subjects: a shepherd who searches for a sheep that has gone astray; a traveler who helps a man who has been robbed and beaten; a poor woman who loses a coin. But beneath the easily grasped action and everyday imagery of the parables are important messages about moral conduct.

**North
Carolina
Competency
Goal**
1.03; 2.01;
3.04; 4.05;
5.01; 5.03

Literary Skills
Understand
parables.

Reading Skills
Make inferences
about theme.

The word prodigal *usually means "recklessly extravagant" or "wasteful," but it can also imply great generosity. To which son does the word* prodigal *apply? Could it apply to the father as well?*

The Prodigal Son
New English Bible

Again he[1] said: "There was once a man who had two sons; and the younger said to his father, 'Father, give me my share of the property.' So he divided his estate between them.[2] A few days later the younger son turned the whole of his share into cash and left home for a distant country, where he squandered it in reckless living. He had spent it all, when a severe famine fell upon that country and he began to feel the pinch. So he went and attached himself to one of the local landowners, who sent him on to his farm to mind the pigs.[3] He would have been glad to fill his belly with the pods that the pigs were eating; and no one gave him anything. Then he came to his senses and said, 'How many of my father's paid servants have more food than they can eat, and here am I, starving to death! I will set off and go to my father, and say to him, "Father, I have sinned, against God and against you; I am no longer fit to be called your son; treat me as one of your paid servants."' So he set out for his father's house. But while he was still a long way off his father saw him, and his heart went out to him. He ran to meet him, flung his arms round him, and kissed him. The son said, 'Father, I have sinned, against God and against you; I am no longer fit to be called your son.' But the father said to his servants, 'Quick! fetch a robe, my best one, and put it on him; put

Return of the Prodigal Son (1668–1669) by Rembrandt van Rijn.
Hermitage, St. Petersburg, Russia.

a ring on his finger and shoes on his feet. Bring the fatted calf and kill it, and let us have a feast to celebrate the day. For this son of mine was dead and has come back to life; he was lost and is found.' And the festivities began.

"Now the elder son was out on the farm; and on his way back, as he approached the house, he heard music and dancing. He called one of the servants and asked what it meant. The servant told him, 'Your brother has come home, and your father has killed the fatted calf because he has him back safe and sound.' But he was angry and refused to go in. His father came out and

1. **he:** Jesus.
2. **So he divided his estate between them:** The younger son's share would be one third.
3. **mind the pigs:** Because the Hebrews considered pigs unclean animals, tending pigs was seen as degrading work.

pleaded with him; but he retorted, 'You know how I have slaved for you all these years; I never once disobeyed your orders; and you never gave me so much as a kid, for a feast with my friends. But now that this son of yours turns up, after running through your money with his women, you kill the fatted calf for him.' 'My boy,' said the father, 'you are always with me, and everything I have is yours. How could we help celebrating this happy day? Your brother here was dead and has come back to life, was lost and is found.'"

Luke 15:12–30

This parable is called "The Talents" because in earlier translations the name of a valuable gold coin, the talent, was used instead of the phrase "bags of gold." What does the word talent *usually mean today? How might this parable apply to both meanings of* talent?

The Talents
New English Bible

"It is like a man going abroad, who called his servants and put his capital in their hands; to one he gave five bags of gold, to another two, to another one, each according to his capacity. Then he left the country. The man who had the five bags went at once and employed them in business, and made a profit of five bags, and the man who had the two bags made two. But the man who had been given one bag of gold went off and dug a hole in the ground, and hid his master's money. A long time afterwards their master returned, and proceeded to settle accounts with them. The man who had been given the five bags of gold came and produced the five he had made: 'Master,' he said, 'you left five bags with me; look, I have made five more.' 'Well done, my good and trusty servant!' said the master. 'You have proved trustworthy in a small way; I will now put you in charge of something big. Come and share your master's delight.'° The man with the two bags then came and said, 'Master, you left two bags with me; look, I have made two more.' 'Well done, my good and trusty servant!' said the master. 'You have proved trustworthy in a small way; I will now put you in charge of something big. Come and share your master's delight.' Then the man who had been given one bag came and said, 'Master, I knew you to be a hard man: you reap where you have not sown, you gather where you have not scattered; so I was afraid, and I went and hid your gold in the ground. Here it is— you have what belongs to you.' 'You lazy rascal!' said the master. 'You knew that I reap where I have not sown, and gather where I have not scattered? Then you ought to have put my money on deposit, and on my return I should have got it back with interest. Take the bag of gold from him, and give it to the one with the ten bags. For the man who has will always be given more, till he has enough and to spare; and the man who has not will forfeit even what he has. Fling the useless servant out into the dark, the place of wailing and grinding of teeth!'"

Matthew 25:14–31

° **share your master's delight:** enjoy the same prosperity as the master.

Response and Analysis

Reading Check

1. In "The Prodigal Son," why does the younger son return home?
2. How do the father and older brother react to the return of the younger son in "The Prodigal Son"?
3. In "The Talents," why is the master angry with the third servant?

Thinking Critically

4. Look up definitions of the word *prodigal* in a dictionary. Could the parable have been titled "The Prodigal *Father*"? Explain.
5. An **allegory** is a story in which the characters, settings, and events stand for abstract or moral concepts. On an allegorical level, what might "The Prodigal Son" be saying about any parent's love for his or her children? What might it be saying about God's feelings for those who make mistakes but repent for their actions?
6. On an allegorical level, what has the servant who hides his gold in "The Talents" really done? If the master symbolizes God, what does this parable say about God's expectations of people?
7. Choose one of the two parables, and state its **theme,** or central insight about life, in a sentence.

Extending and Evaluating

8. How might a person identify with each of the three characters in "The Prodigal Son" at different times in his or her life? In what ways is the theme of this parable universal—that is, meaningful to anyone, regardless of culture or religion?

North Carolina Competency Goal
1.03; 4.02; 4.05; 5.03

INTERNET

Projects and Activities
Keyword:
LE5 WL-1

SKILLS FOCUS

Literary Skills
Analyze parables.

Writing Skills
Update a parable.

WRITING

Updating a Parable

Choose either "The Prodigal Son" or "The Talents," and rewrite it using a contemporary setting, current usage, and familiar characters that a modern reader could relate to. To plan your updated parable, make a chart like the one below. Identify the details of the original parable and the allegorical meaning of those details. Then, decide how you will change the details in your parable while keeping the allegorical meaning the same.

Original Details (characters, places, things)	Allegorical Meaning	Updated Details (characters, places, things)
the father	forgiveness; God	school principal
the younger son	recklessness; sinner	high school student who skips classes
the older son	obedience; faithful follower who is jealous	honor student who never misses a class

Roman coins (69–96 C.E.).
The Granger Collection, NY.

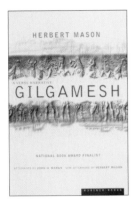

EPIC
It's the Same Old Story—or Is It?

Like most epics, the *Epic of Gilgamesh* was composed in verse rather than prose. Several fine verse translations of the epic are available, but one of the most personal and accessible versions is Herbert Mason's translation. Mason was a student at Harvard when he experienced his eye-opening introduction to the epic. Having lost his father as a child, Mason was deeply moved by and empathized with Gilgamesh's grief over the loss of Enkidu and his quest to overcome death. Mason's retelling of the epic is a poignant and affecting translation that speaks to modern sensibilities.

SACRED TEXT
Ancient Wisdom

In *The Illustrated Hebrew Bible: 75 Stories,* Ellen Frankel presents a new translation of stories from the Hebrew Scriptures. The collection consists of forty stories from the Torah, or Law, and thirty-five selections from the Prophets and Writings sections of the Hebrew Bible. Frankel's translation is accompanied by vibrant illustrations, including reproductions of mosaics, paintings, and illuminated manuscripts.

NONFICTION
An Exploration of Egypt's Past

The Oxford History of Ancient Egypt, edited by Ian Shaw, is a comprehensive archaeological history of Egyptian civilization from its beginnings to A.D. 311. This account, which focuses on the information archaeology has revealed about Egypt's past, consists of twelve essays written by Egyptologists, scholars who specialize in the study of ancient Egypt. Some of the topics covered include the rule of the pharaohs, advances in art and literature, and the Roman conquest of Egypt.

ADDITIONAL READING

• Have you ever wondered who created the first legal system, the first library catalog, or even the first aquarium? You'll find the answers to these questions and more in Samuel Noah Kramer's *History Begins at Sumer.* This text describes the significant contributions that the Sumerians made to civilization, which helped shape the course of world history.

• *Love Songs of the New Kingdom,* translated by John L. Foster, gives us a glimpse of life in ancient Egypt through the Egyptians' passionate, funny, and elegant poetry. Many of the poems are accompanied by hieroglyphs and illustrations depicting daily life in ancient Egypt.

• In *The Complete World of the Dead Sea Scrolls,* the scholars Philip R. Davies, George J. Brooke, and Phillip R. Callaway present a comprehensive account of the history, discovery, and interpretation of these mysterious scrolls, which have captured the popular imagination.

Writing a Reflective Essay

Writing Assignment
Write an essay in which you reflect on the meaning of a personal experience and share it with others.

Turning points are events that change the direction of our lives by teaching us something about ourselves, our cultures, or other people. By reflecting on these experiences, we make discoveries about ourselves and the world; by writing about them, we let other people share in our discoveries. In this workshop you'll have a chance to reflect on an experience and share its meaning with others in a personal essay.

Prewriting

Think About Your Purpose and Experiences

Why and What A reflective essay has two purposes: to explore the meaning of a personal experience and to share its significance with others. Keep these purposes in mind as you search for an experience to write about. The experience you choose shouldn't be just funny, frightening, or weird—it should be one that taught you something or changed you in a significant way. It should also be one you feel comfortable sharing.

Here are some strategies to help you recall that special experience:

• Skim through your diaries, journals, and photo albums.

• Ask friends or family members to help you recall important moments in your life.

• Read memoirs or reflective poems to see how professional writers used experiences in their lives as springboards for self-reflection.

Reflect on the Experience

A Defining Moment Take some time to think about how and why the experience you chose is important to you, and how and why it may be important to others. Does your experience illustrate a universal truth about life? Does it offer a lesson about love, friendship, betrayal, dishonesty, or courage? Reflect on your experience by asking yourself the following questions:

SKILLS FOCUS

Writing Skills
Write a reflective essay about a personal experience.

North Carolina Competency Goal
1.01; 6.01

- How did I feel during this event? How did I feel afterward? What do I feel now as I look back on the experience?

- How did the experience change my attitudes or behavior?

- What universal truth did the experience teach me? How might others benefit from learning about the experience?

Remember, Record, and Organize

Details Count Your experience may have included a defining moment, but it consisted of a series of smaller events and related details that are woven together to make that moment happen. Consult your journals and photo albums, or ask friends and family members to help you remember all of the little events that made up your experience. Jot down these events in chronological order, the order in which they occurred. Then, add concrete images and details to bring the events to life for a reader. The chart below gives examples of the kinds of narrative and descriptive details you should include.

NARRATIVE AND DESCRIPTIVE DETAILS

Types of Details	Examples
Narrative details	
• details that reveal the actions and thoughts of the people involved	"He watched me with intent, unwavering interest . . ."
• dialogue—the actual words that people said	" 'Your grandpa has had a heart attack.' "
• interior monologue—what you were thinking while the events were occurring or afterward	"I kept thinking, 'I love Grandpa and want to be there for him, but I can't give up my goals, can I?' "
Descriptive details	
• details that paint a picture for the reader—descriptions of settings, people's appearance, and sounds, tastes, and smells	"Whenever I glanced in his direction, I could see the pride in his expression."

TIP You may want to use more than one form of organization in your reflective essay.

- In general, you should use **chronological order**—the exact order in which events occurred—when you're describing what happened. You may want to relate certain parts of your story out of sequence, using **flash-backs** or **flash-forwards,** for effect.

- **Spatial order** may work best for an extended description of a scene. Start your description at a certain point in space, and then move in a logical way around your subject: left to right, up to down, fore-ground to background, and so on.

- In discussing the meaning or significance of the experi-ence, you might use **order of importance:** Arrange your ideas according to their significance, starting with the least important idea and leading up to the most important idea.

North Carolina Competency Goal
1.01; 6.01

PRACTICE & APPLY 1 First, choose a subject for your reflective essay. Then, reflect upon your subject and gather narrative and descriptive details.

SKILLS FOCUS

Writing Skills
Think about the significance of the experience. Use details to create concrete images.

Writing

Writing a Reflective Essay

A Writer's Model

Courage Counts

BEGINNING
Quotation as a hook to engage readers

"When you see what is right, have the courage to do it." That's an old Chinese proverb that my grandfather always used. When I was only five years old, I decided I would be courageous in all things and make my grandfather proud. It wasn't until much later that I understood what real courage is.

Hint at significance of experience

When I entered high school, I became interested in swimming competitively. I was intimidated by the students who had been swimming since they were children, but as usual, Grandpa was a big supporter. "Courage, Molly. Don't let a little competition scare you away." So I tried out for the swim team.

MIDDLE
First event

Dialogue

Semiretired, Grandpa found time to attend all of my swim meets. He watched me with intent, unwavering interest, like a spectator at a horse race. Whenever I glanced in his direction, I could see the pride in his expression.

Descriptive details

Before long I was coming in third, then second, then an occasional first. By my senior year, college scouts were coming to watch me swim. Grandpa and my parents were telling me I could probably get a scholarship. I even began to dream of the Olympics. As far as I was concerned, I had the true spirit of courage.

Later events

Thoughts and feelings

Event building to the defining moment

Finally, the state finals—the culminating event of my high school swimming career—approached, and I knew I had a chance to earn

(continued)

first place in the fifty-yard freestyle. At my last practice before the big meet, Grandpa said he didn't feel well and left early. When I arrived home two hours later, Dad rushed out the door and said, "Your grandpa has had a heart attack. We've got to hurry to the hospital." Shortly after we arrived at the hospital, Grandpa's doctor came to see us. He had scheduled Grandpa for a quadruple bypass.

Dialogue

Narrative details

I began to sob hysterically, and my parents tried to console me. "Your grandpa loves you so much; he'll pull through just so he can see you again." But they didn't understand. I was crying because the surgery was scheduled for the day of my big meet. I couldn't miss it— I told myself Grandpa would want me to go through with it. Then I stopped crying and told my parents that I was going to my swim meet. My parents were very upset, but they said I would have to search my own heart for the right thing to do.

Dialogue

Thoughts and feelings
Later events
Narrative details

That night I couldn't sleep. I kept thinking, "I love Grandpa and want to be there for him, but I can't give up my goals, can I?" I remembered the Chinese proverb about courage: You needed to have the courage to do what you knew was right. Suddenly I knew what I had to do.

Interior monologue

Defining moment

At 6:00 A.M., I called my coach and told her I wouldn't be attending the meet. She said she understood and that it didn't have to mean the end of my swimming career. "I'm glad to hear that," I told her, "but you know, I'd still do this, even if it did affect my swimming career. I love my grandfather. If I didn't go to the hospital today and something happened to him, I'd never forgive myself. No swimming match is worth that." I finally understood that courage and doing the right thing are one and the same.

Thoughts and feelings

END
Effect of the experience on the writer

Significance of the experience

 Using the framework and Writer's Model on these pages as your guide, write the first draft of your essay.

INTERNET
More Writer's Models
Keyword:
LE5 WL-1

Revising

Self-Evaluation

Focus on Form It's important to evaluate your first draft so that you can improve it. Read your essay, focusing on content, organization, and style. Use the rubric on page 92 as a guide.

Rubric: Writing a Reflective Essay

Evaluation Questions	▶ Tips	▶ Revision Techniques
❶ Does the beginning engage the reader's interest, provide background, and hint at the significance of the experience?	▶ **Circle** the opening attention grabber. **Bracket** background information. **Underline** the part that hints at the significance of the experience.	▶ **Add** an interesting anecdote, fact, or quotation. **Add** helpful background information. **Add** a sentence that hints at the significance of the event.
❷ Is the essay clearly organized? Does it progress logically from event to event?	▶ **Bracket** words that show relationships between ideas. **Number** each event.	▶ **Rearrange** events and details to make the sequence clear. **Add** words to show relationships between events. **Cut** any irrelevant details.
❸ Does the essay include narrative and descriptive details that bring the events and people to life?	▶ **Circle** sentences that include narrative and descriptive details that bring the events and people to life.	▶ **Add** details that show what people say and do. **Add** descriptions of thoughts and feelings that hint at the significance of the event.
❹ Does the essay effectively convey the defining moment of the experience and reveal its significance to you?	▶ **Draw** a wavy line under the description of the defining moment. **Star** the sentence that expresses the significance of the experience.	▶ **Add** details to make the defining moment of the experience striking and vivid. **Add** a sentence that reveals your insight about life.

ANALYZING THE REVISION PROCESS
Study the revisions below, and answer the questions that follow.

> —*the culminating event of my high school swimming career*—
> Finally, the state finals⌃approached, and I knew I had a
> *in the fifty-yard freestyle*
> chance to earn first place. ~~I was really swimming well.~~ At my
> *before the big meet* *early*
> last practice, Grandpa said he didn't feel well and left⌃.

TIP A reflective essay usually has an informal **tone.** As you review your essay, determine whether you need to make the tone more conversational by adding contractions and using everyday, informal language.

Responding to the Revision Process
1. What does the writer achieve by adding details to these sentences?
2. Why do you think the writer decided to delete the second sentence?

 **PRACTICE & APPLY 3** Using the guidelines on these pages, revise your essay to bring your experience to life and reveal its significance.

Publishing

Proofread and Publish Your Essay

Last Pass You have taken time to make this essay interesting and polished; don't mar the final product with errors in usage or mechanics. Review your essay, and correct any mistakes you find.

Time to Share Once you've polished your reflective essay, share it with others so that they can learn from your experience. Here are some ways to publish or share your essay:

- Take advantage of the Internet. Submit your essay to a bulletin board where similar postings are welcome. If you have your own Web site, post it there.

- Create an essay collection with some of your classmates who also wrote reflective essays. Use publishing software to give the collection a professional appearance, and give copies to the school library.

Reflect on Your Essay

Lessons Learned We learn more from any experience—work, study, or play—by reflecting on it. Take the time now to think about what you learned while writing your reflective essay.

- What process did you use to choose the experience you wrote about? What other methods might you have used to choose your subject?

- What part of your experience was the most difficult to put into words: dialogue? your thoughts and feelings? Why do you think this part was so hard to write?

 PRACTICE & APPLY 4 Proofread your essay, and correct any errors you find in mechanics or usage. Then, publish your essay using one of the options outlined above. Finally, answer the reflection questions.

TIP The spellchecker on a computer will catch most misspellings. However, you'll need to do a separate check for words easily confused, such as *its/it's* and *their/there.*

North Carolina Competency Goal
1.01; 6.01; 6.02

SKILLS FOCUS

Writing Skills
Revise for content and style.
Proofread your essay.

Test Practice The story of Abraham, the father of the Hebrew people, appears in Genesis, the first book of the Hebrew Bible. In Genesis 21, God blesses Abraham and his wife, Sarah, in their old age with a son, Isaac. In Genesis 22, as you will see, God again intervenes in Abraham's life.

Wilfred Owen, the author of "The Parable of the Old Man and the Young," wrote poetry while serving in the deadly trenches of World War I. He died in battle at the age of twenty-five. In his poem, Owen uses the biblical story of Abraham and Isaac to comment on the old men of his time who sent the young to war.

DIRECTIONS: Read the following selections. Then, read each multiple-choice question that follows and write the letter of the best response.

Abraham and Isaac

King James Bible

And it came to pass after these things, that God did tempt Abraham, and said unto him, Abraham: and he said, Behold, here I am.

And he said, Take now thy son, thine only son Isaac, whom thou lovest, and get thee into the land of Moriah; and offer him there for a burnt offering upon one of the mountains which I will tell thee of.

And Abraham rose up early in the morning, and saddled his ass, and took two of his young men with him, and Isaac his son, and clave the wood for the burnt offering, and rose up, and went unto the place of which God had told him.

Then on the third day Abraham lifted up his eyes, and saw the place afar off.

And Abraham said unto his young men, Abide ye here with the ass; and I and the lad will go yonder and worship, and come again to you.

And Abraham took the wood of the burnt offering, and laid it upon Isaac his son; and he took the fire in his hand, and a knife; and they went both of them together.

And Isaac spake unto Abraham his father, and said, My father: and he said, Here am I, my son. And he said,

North Carolina Competency Goal
1.03; 4.05; 5.02; 5.03

Pages 94–97 cover
Literary Skills
Compare and contrast literary works.

Behold the fire and the wood: but where is the lamb for a burnt offering?

And Abraham said, My son, God will provide himself a lamb for a burnt offering: so they went both of them together.

And they came to the place which God had told him of; and Abraham built an altar there, and laid the wood in order, and bound Isaac his son, and laid him on the altar upon the wood.

And Abraham stretched forth his hand, and took the knife to slay his son.

And the angel of the Lord called unto him out of heaven, and said, Abraham, Abraham: and he said, Here am I.

And he said, Lay not thine hand upon the lad, neither do thou any thing unto him: for now I know that thou fearest God, seeing thou hast not withheld thy son, thine only son from me.

And Abraham lifted up his eyes, and looked, and behold behind him a ram caught in a thicket by his horns: and Abraham went and took the ram, and offered him up for a burnt offering in the stead of his son.

And Abraham called the name of that place Jehovah-jireh: as it is said to this day, In the mount of the Lord it shall be seen.

And the angel of the Lord called unto Abraham out of heaven the second time,

And said, By myself have I sworn, saith the Lord, for because thou hast done this thing, and hast not withheld thy son, thine only son,

That in blessing I will bless thee, and in multiplying I will multiply thy seed as the stars of the heaven, and as the sand which is upon the sea shore; and thy seed shall possess the gate of his enemies;

And in thy seed shall all the nations of the earth be blessed; because thou hast obeyed my voice.

—Genesis 22:1–18

The Parable of the Old Man and the Young

Wilfred Owen

So Abram rose, and clave the wood, and went,
And took the fire with him, and a knife.
And as they sojourned both of them together,
Isaac the first-born spake and said, My Father,
5   Behold the preparations, fire and iron,
But where the lamb for this burnt-offering?
Then Abram bound the youth with belts and straps,
And builded parapets and trenches there,
And stretchèd forth the knife to slay his son.
10 When lo! an angel called him out of heaven,
Saying, Lay not thy hand upon the lad,
Neither do anything to him. Behold,
A ram, caught in a thicket by its horns;
Offer the Ram of Pride instead of him.
15 But the old man would not so, but slew his son,
And half the seed of Europe, one by one.

---

1. In the Genesis story, God commands Abraham to—

A abandon Isaac in the wilderness

B leave his son with two servants

C kill his son as an offering to God

D protect Isaac from God's anger

2. Which word best describes Isaac's relationship with his father, Abraham, in Genesis?

F distant

G fearful

H disrespectful

J trusting

3. In the first verse of the Genesis story, God is said to "tempt" Abraham. What is Abraham tempted to do?

A make a forbidden offering

B disobey God and save his son

C lie to Isaac

D run away

4. In Genesis, Abraham is rewarded for—

F his leadership of a great dynasty

G his love for his son

H his faithful obedience to God

J his belief in angels

Collection 1: Skills Review

5. Which words reveal the **setting** of Owen's poem?
   A "Isaac the first-born spake"
   B "fire and iron"
   C "parapets and trenches"
   D "an angel called him"

6. In Owen's poem, who does Abram, or "the old man," represent?
   F those who send the young to war
   G fathers who love their sons
   H mature men who think for themselves
   J those who obey orders

7. A **parable** teaches a moral lesson. What moral point is Owen making?
   A In wartime the older generation willingly sacrifices the young.
   B Those who decide to go to war face difficult choices.
   C The young agree to be sacrificed to uphold the pride of the fathers.
   D Personal feelings must be sacrificed for the public good.

8. How would you describe the **tone,** or attitude, of Owen's poem?
   F angry
   G objective
   H proud
   J disillusioned

9. What question does Isaac ask his father in both the biblical story and the poem?
   A What is the purpose of their journey?
   B Where is the lamb for the burnt offering?
   C Why can't he stay behind?
   D Why must he carry the wood?

10. How is Abram's response to the angel in the poem different from Abraham's response to the angel in Genesis?
    F Abram debates with the angel.
    G Abram disobeys the angel.
    H Abram hides from the angel.
    J Abram refuses to kill his son.

Essay Question

Both in the biblical story of Abraham and Isaac and in Owen's poem, the older generation is presented with a challenge in regard to the young. In each there is an order that comes from a divine source. Write a brief essay in which you compare and contrast the order given, Abraham's (or Abram's) response, and the way Abraham's (or Abram's) choice affects the young. Keep in mind that in the biblical account, God can be viewed as a father to Abraham, so Abraham has obligations to him as well as to his son Isaac. End your essay with a generalization about how "fathers" are viewed in each selection.

Collection 1: Skills Review

Vocabulary Skills

Test Practice

Analogies: Synonyms and Antonyms

DIRECTIONS: For each item, choose the pair of words whose relationship is most *like* the relationship between the pair of capitalized words.

1. RECOMPENSE : REPAY ::
   A   victory : defeat
   B   lose : regain
   C   stretch : lengthen
   D   hint : declare

2. TRANSGRESSION : SIN ::
   F   mountain : plain
   G   infant : baby
   H   noise : silence
   J   walk : foot

3. REPROACH : APPROVE ::
   A   advance : retreat
   B   mimic : imitate
   C   forgive : forget
   D   reply : respond

4. ENTREAT : IMPLORE ::
   F   flatter : insult
   G   advertise : disguise
   H   recede : appear
   J   lift : raise

5. SOMBER : CHEERFUL ::
   A   calm : placid
   B   similar : synonymous
   C   ignorant : stupid
   D   confident : timid

6. TERMINATE : INITIATE ::
   F   torture : torment
   G   restore : rebuild
   H   liberate : imprison
   J   award : grant

7. OMINOUS : THREATENING ::
   A   criminal : lawful
   B   indolent : lazy
   C   miserable : content
   D   poverty : destitution

8. KINDRED : STRANGERS ::
   F   kindness : parents
   G   computer : machines
   H   correspondence : letters
   J   children : adults

SKILLS FOCUS

Vocabulary Skills
Identify analogies.

Collection 1: Skills Review
Writing Skills

DIRECTIONS: Read the following paragraph from a draft of a student's reflective essay. Then, answer the questions below it.

(1) No matter how hard I try, I can't seem to keep my room from being messy and cluttered. (2) In the past I've misplaced many things in my room because of the mess, but I never lost anything important. (3) Last week my disorganization almost made me lose an essay competition. (4) On the morning the essay was due, I couldn't find it anywhere among the mounds of clothing and piles of magazines and books littering my room. (5) My friends had all turned in their essays a week before the deadline. (6) I began to panic when I couldn't find the essay and begged my mom to help me look for it. (7) She couldn't hide her annoyance; she had been warning me for years that something like this would happen because of my messy habits.

1. Which word or phrase could the writer add to the beginning of sentence 3 to improve the transition between sentences 2 and 3?
   A However,
   B In fact,
   C As a result,
   D In conclusion,

2. Which sentence should be deleted to improve the paragraph's organization?
   F 2
   G 3
   H 5
   J 6

3. What information could the writer add after sentence 2 to provide more background about his or her situation?
   A Examples of other items the writer has lost in the room
   B A description of the writer's other bad habits
   C A list of all the essays the writer has ever composed
   D Information about the essay competition and its significance

4. The writer could add narrative details by
   F including dialogue between the writer and his or her mother
   G describing his or her room and its contents
   H urging others to learn from his or her mistakes
   J describing his or her appearance

5. If the writer wanted to include a sentence later in the essay expressing an insight about life gained from this experience, which would be the *best* choice?
   A I'll always remember this incident.
   B Parents don't like it when their children's rooms are messy.
   C I've learned that a lack of organization can have serious consequences.
   D My friends have much cleaner rooms than I do.

North Carolina Competency Goal
1.03; 4.03; 6.01

SKILLS FOCUS

Writing Skills
Answer questions about a reflective essay.

Collection 2

ANCIENT GREEK AND ROMAN LITERATURE

800 B.C.–A.D. 200

The Life Worth Living

The life which is unexamined

is not worth living.

—Socrates, quoted in
the *Apology* by Plato

(Foreground) bust of Alexander the Great from Pergamon,
Turkey (c. 3rd century B.C.E.); (background) colonnade of the
Parthenon, Acropolis, Athens (5th century B.C.E.).

Archaeological Museum, Istanbul.

**go.
hrw
.com**

INTERNET

**Collection
Resources**
Keyword:
LE5 WL-2

Ancient Greece and Rome

Before 700 B.C.	600 B.C.	500 B.C.	400 B.C.
c. 3000–c. 1100 B.C. Minoan civilization	**600s–400s B.C.** Lyric poetry flourishes in Greece	**500–479 B.C.** Greek city-states fight in the Persian Wars	**399 B.C.** Socrates is put on trial in Athens for his teachings
c. 1100–c. 1000 B.C. Dorians invade Greece; period known as the Greek Dark Ages begins	**c. 500s B.C.** Aesop composes fables; Sappho composes lyrics	**400s B.C.** Classical era of Greek drama: Aeschylus, Sophocles, and Euripides write tragedies	**c. 387 B.C.** Plato founds the Academy in Athens
776 B.C. Olympic Games in honor of Zeus begin	**594–593 B.C.** Athenians elect Solon to run the government	**431–404 B.C.** Athens loses to Sparta in the Peloponnesian War	**c. 384–c. 322 B.C.** Lifetime of Aristotle, writer of *Poetics*
c. 753 B.C. Rome is founded	**c. 518–c. 438 B.C.** Lifetime of Pindar, composer of odes		**359–336 B.C.** Philip II becomes king of Macedonia and conquers Greece
c. 700 B.C. Homer composes the *Iliad*	**509 B.C.** Roman Republic is established		**336–323 B.C.** Alexander the Great conquers Mesopotamia, Persia, and part of India
700–500 B.C. Emergence of Greek city-states			

Relief of two wrestlers from the base of a Greek *kouros* (c. 500 B.C.E.). National Archaeological Museum, Athens.

Before 700 B.C.	600 B.C.	500 B.C.	400 B.C.
c. 1000 B.C. Earliest hymns from the Rig-Veda are written down; first ancestors of today's Japanese population arrive in Japan	**c. 600 B.C.** Zoroastrianism becomes the dominant religion in Persia	**c. 400s B.C.** The Maya use the earliest known solar calendars; written form of Sanskrit is developed	**c. 400 B.C.–c. A.D. 1000** Classical period of Indian epic and wisdom literature
c. 950–c. 750 B.C. The biblical Book of Ruth is written	**c. 500s B.C.** *The Book of Songs* is compiled in China	**475 B.C.** Era of Warring States begins in China	**380–343 B.C.** Last Egyptian dynasty
	587 B.C. Many Hebrews are taken into exile by the Babylonian king Nebuchadnezzar II		
	c. 551–479 B.C. Chinese sage Confucius teaches ethical principles known as Confucianism, recorded in his *Analects*		
	c. 539 B.C. Persians capture Babylon; some Hebrews return to Israel		

Figure of a Chac-Mool at Kukulcan Pyramid at Chichen Itza, Mexico.

800 B.C.–A.D. 200

Augustus of Prima Porta (c. 1st century C.E.).
Braccio Nuovo, Musei Vaticani, Vatican City.

ANCIENT GREECE AND ROME

300 B.C.	200 B.C.	100 B.C.	A.D. 1
c. 289 B.C. First Roman mint is established	**c. 190–c. 159 B.C.** Terence, a former slave from North Africa, writes comedies	**70–19 B.C.** Lifetime of Virgil, author of the *Aeneid*	
264–241 B.C. First Punic War between Rome and Carthage is fought	**149–146 B.C.** Carthage is destroyed in the Third Punic War	**44 B.C.** Julius Caesar becomes dictator for life, but is assassinated	**c. 6 B.C.–A.D. 30** Lifetime of Jesus of Nazareth
234–149 B.C. Lifetime of Cato, writer of prose in Latin	**133 B.C.** Roman Republic controls the entire Mediterranean region	**27 B.C.** Augustus Caesar becomes emperor of Rome	**A.D. 8** Ovid's *Metamorphoses* is complete
218–202 B.C. Second Punic War			**A.D. 64** Rome is destroyed by fire under the emperor Nero
			c. A.D. 70 Romans destroy Jerusalem

Relief depicting spoils from the Temple of Jerusalem, from the passageway of the Arch of Titus, Rome (c. 81 C.E.).
Museo Nazionale, Naples.

THE WORLD

300 B.C.	200 B.C.	100 B.C.	A.D. 1
c. 300 B.C. The *Ramayana* is compiled	**c. 200 B.C.–c. A.D. 500** Rise and fall of the African kingdom of Aksum	**c. 100 B.C.** The Silk Road stretches four thousand miles, linking China, central Asia, and the Mediterranean	**c. A.D. 1–c. 200** The Bhagavad-Gita is written down in India
221–206 B.C. Ch'in dynasty unites China into an empire; Great Wall of China is built	**c. 200 B.C.–c. A.D. 600** Nazca culture emerges in South America	**c. first century B.C.** Bantu speakers from the Cameroon Highlands move south and east through Africa	**c. A.D. 124–c. 170** Algerian-born Apuleius writes *The Golden Ass,* the oldest surviving Latin novel
c. 200 B.C. The earliest Buddhist sculptures appear	**c. 168–c. 142 B.C.** Jews gain independence from the Seleucids during the Maccabee rebellion	**c. 73 B.C.** Han emperor Hsüan Ti conquers part of the Hsiung-nu territory	
	c. 150 B.C. The Chinese invent paper	**28 B.C.** Chinese astronomers observe sunspots	

Illustration of a Chinese astronomer (1675).
The Granger Collection, New York.

Cultural and Historical

A Conversation between Philosophers (also known as *The School of Plato*) (1st century C.E.). Mosaic from Pompeii, Italy.

The Peloponnesian War

431–404 B.C.

The Peloponnesian War was a prolonged conflict at the end of the fifth century B.C. between the city-states of Athens and Sparta and their respective allies. It was begun by Sparta in 431 B.C. as a preemptive war. Although Sparta had the best army in

Plato's Academy

c. 387 B.C.–A.D. 529

Plato founded his Academy in approximately 387 B.C. as a school to train future statesmen. The Academy was named for Academus, a mythological hero whose tomb was supposedly located in the sacred wood near Athens where Plato set up the Academy. The school became a center for philosophical training and research that brought together many exceptional minds. Legal experts at the Academy gave rulers advice about state issues and laws. The Academy has been called the forerunner of today's think tanks. In A.D. 529, the emperor Justinian I closed the Academy because it was not a Christian school.

Greece, it was worried about Athenian naval supremacy and power over other Greek city-states. The war ended in 404 B.C., after the Spartans received help from Persia to blockade Athens and force the Athenians to surrender. The Peloponnesian War brought to an end the Golden Age of Greece.

Copper engraving depicting a naval battle near Corinth during the Peloponnesian War (17th century).

Augustus and Lictors (detail) (13–9 B.C.E.). Relief from the *Ara Pacis*. Museum of the Ara Pacis, Rome.

The Roman Empire

27 B.C.—A.D. 1453

The Roman Empire emerged after a period of civil unrest and struggle for power. In 27 B.C., Octavian, Julius Caesar's heir, became the first Roman emperor. The Senate gave him the title Augustus. (The word means "holy" or "revered" in Latin.) The emperor extended Rome's control over new territories. After Augustus's death, in A.D. 14, the empire had a succession of rulers, some of whom were infamous for their cruelty. By the second century A.D., the empire was weakened by crises in the provinces. As Rome declined, the empire broke into two parts: The Western Roman Empire fell in A.D. 476, when barbarian peoples forced the emperor out, and the Byzantine Empire, or Eastern Roman Empire, continued until A.D. 1453, when Constantinople was captured by the Turks.

Ancient Greece and Rome
800 B.C.–A.D. 200

PREVIEW

Think About ...

In Western culture the ancient civilizations of Greece and Rome are often called "the classical world," for these two cultures have profoundly influenced the development of Western thought and achievement. Ancient Greek and Roman writers produced epics, poems, dramas, histories, oratory, and other works that endure to the present day. These two cultures also left a lasting legacy in such fields as art, architecture, politics, and philosophy. Both the Greeks and the Romans also contributed a legacy of language, for many English words and word parts that we commonly use today came to us from Greek and Latin.

As you read about the Greeks and the Romans, look for answers to the following questions:

- What elements of ancient Greek culture have influenced modern Western civilization?
- What are some characteristics of Greek literature, including drama and lyric poetry?
- How did Roman culture exert its influence over much of Europe?
- What are the main characteristics of Roman literature, religion, and philosophy?

North Carolina Competency Goal
1.02; 1.03; 4.02; 4.05; 5.01; 5.03

SKILLS FOCUS

Collection introduction (pages 106–118) covers

Literary Skills
Evaluate the philosophical, historical, and cultural influences of the historical period.

Greek Literature

The achievements of the ancient Greeks flowed mainly from their ability to wonder, to ask the question *why?* The Greeks' efforts to understand themselves and the world they lived in produced an intense love of intellectualism and rational thought. This Greek mind-set gave rise to poems, dramas, histories, and political and philosophical theories that have endured for centuries.

Relief of Apollo holding a cithara with Victory (4th century B.C.E.).

Musée du Louvre, Paris.

The Heroic Age

Greek civilization began in Crete. By 3000 B.C., a remarkable culture had developed on this rugged, mountainous island located sixty miles south of mainland Greece. This civilization is called **Minoan** (mi·nō′ən), after the legendary King Minos (mī′näs′) of Crete, who supposedly sacrificed twelve young men and women each year to feed a half-man, half-bull monster called the Minotaur.

Minoan civilization directly influenced the rise of the **Mycenaean** (mī′sə·nē′ən) culture, which flourished between 1500 and 1200 B.C. on the Greek mainland. But while the Minoans were peaceful, the Mycenaeans were both aggressive and enterprising. Scholars believe that around 1250 B.C., under the leadership of King Agamemnon (ag′ə·mem′nän′), the Mycenaeans organized an expedition against the city of Troy in Asia Minor. Four centuries later the poet Homer immortalized the heroes of this "Trojan War" in the *Iliad,* one of the earliest epics in Western literature. To the Greeks of Homer's time, the Mycenaean era was known as the **Heroic Age.** The great figures in the epic were looked on as the ancestors of the Greeks and were held up as models of heroic behavior.

The Epic Age

The earliest surviving works of Greek poetry are two epics now known as the *Iliad* and the *Odyssey,* both attributed to a blind storyteller called Homer (see page 120). Shortly after Homer composed his epics, the

Victory of Samothrace
(c. 3rd–2nd century B.C.E.).
Musée du Louvre, Paris.

Greeks developed a script for their language, based on a system borrowed from the Phoenicians. This system became what we know as the alphabet, named for its two initial letters, *alpha* and *beta*. Whether its purpose was to aid commercial dealings or, as one theory holds, to record Homer's epics for posterity, the Greek invention of the alphabet opened the door to a remarkable era of literary achievement.

The Rise of the City-States

Between 700 and 500 B.C., small, fragmented settlements in mainland Greece banded together to form communities. Soon a number of **city-states** emerged. The typical city-state, called a *polis* (from which the word *politics* is derived), was ruled by a king.

In this period of city-states, the Greeks did not think of themselves as a single nation. However, they did feel some common cultural bonds. They called themselves **Hellenes** (hel′ēnz′), believing themselves direct descendants of Hellen, the son of Deucalion (doo·kāl′ē·ən), who, according to a Greek myth, was the sole survivor of a great flood and thus the ancestor of all Greeks. This cultural identity made the Greeks feel superior to their "barbarian" neighbors, and the resulting sense of unity found expression in various social and religious institutions. A regular series of athletic contests brought the main Greek city-states in contact with one another and fostered a sense of Greek identity. The most important games were those held at Olympia every four years in honor of the god Zeus. The Olympic games that we hold today are a continuation of this tradition.

Bust of Homer.
Museo Capitolino, Rome.

Ritual and myth are the two forms in which Greek religion presents itself to the historian. . . . There are no founding figures and no documents of revelation, no organizations of priests and no monastic orders.

—Walter Burkert

School scenes depicting the teaching of a double flute (left) and the correction of a writing tablet (center), from a red-figure kylix (480 B.C.E.).

Antikensammlung, Staatliche Museen zu Berlin.

109

The Lyric Age

From about the seventh to the fifth centuries B.C., **lyric poetry** began to flourish among the Greeks. Unlike the epic, this new poetry did not tell of the heroic deeds of warriors and gods. Instead, lyric poetry was brief, intensely personal, emotional, and down-to-earth. For the first time in human history, poets told us their names and sang of their loves, their hates, their triumphs and failures.

Sparta and Athens

Bitter rivalries often occurred between the Greek city-states. By the start of the fifth century B.C., two rival states—**Sparta** and **Athens**—had emerged from these conflicts as the most powerful in Greece. Sparta owed its prominence to an extremely militaristic and conservative culture, where boys were taken from their homes at the age of twelve to undergo years of rigorous physical training. Frail infants were left on mountaintops to die.

Athens emerged as a power to be reckoned with when the city played a leading role in defeating the Persians in the **Persian Wars,** which began in 500 B.C. and ended in 479 B.C. The Persian emperor Darius launched these wars when the cities established by the Greeks in Asia Minor revolted against Persian rule.

As a result of the Persian Wars, Athens took its place as the wartime leader of all the city-states and the chief naval power of Greece. At home (though not in conquered territories), the Athenians established

Bust of Leonidas, King of Sparta (490–480 B.C.E.).
Archaeological Museum, Sparta.

A CLOSER LOOK: CULTURAL INFLUENCES

Classical Allusions in Modern English

INFORMATIONAL TEXT

An **eponym** (ep′ə·nim′) is a person—either mythical or real—from whose name the name of a nation, idea, or term has been derived. Classical Greek and Roman myths and literature have lent English dozens of eponymous expressions. You may be familiar with some of the following terms.

Achilles' heel. According to Homer's *Iliad,* the hero Achilles is fated to win great glory but to die an early death. Achilles' mother, the sea nymph Thetis, tries to forestall her son's destiny when he is still an infant by dipping every part of his body in the waters of the Styx, a river in the Underworld. The magic waters are supposed to protect Achilles against all wounds in battle. However, Thetis forgets to immerse one part of her son's body: the heel by which she holds him. Years later the Trojan prince Paris slays Achilles with an arrow that pierces him—you guessed it—in the heel. Nowadays, *Achilles' heel* is used to refer to any vulnerable point in a plan or a person's character.

Midas touch. The Greeks told several legends about Midas, who ruled in the kingdom of Phrygia (frij′ē·ə) in Asia Minor (now Turkey).

In the most famous story the god Dionysus grants Midas one wish. Midas wishes that everything he touches will turn to gold. Dionysus takes him literally, and Midas becomes the original "Goldfinger" and an instant billionaire. Unfortunately, the king's food, wine—even his

a **democratic government,** or rule by the people (or free adult males, at least—women and slaves could not vote). Athenian democracy was one of the earliest democratic governments in the world, and it had a tremendous influence on the formation later of both the Roman Republic and American democracy.

Pericles and the Golden Age of Athens

Starting in the late 460s B.C., at the height of the Athenian Golden Age, the great general and statesman **Pericles** (per′ə·klēz′) (c. 494–429 B.C.) guided the fortunes of Athens for more than three decades. Pericles was a skillful politician who steered a middle course between extremist views in the democratic assembly. He was also a patron of literature, philosophy, and the arts. It was Pericles who organized the campaign to build Athens's most famous temple, the Parthenon, dedicated to the city's patron goddess, Athena.

The Rise of Greek Drama

Three of the greatest authors of tragedy in the history of Western literature—**Aeschylus** (es′ki·ləs), **Sophocles** (säf′ə·klēz′), and **Euripides** (yōō·rip′ə·dēz′)—all lived during the period of intellectual ferment of Athens in the fifth century B.C. Their plays pose

> *Our way is to consider each separate thing alone by itself; the Greeks always saw things as parts of a whole, and this habit of mind is stamped upon everything they did.*
>
> — Edith Hamilton

daughter—are transformed to gold as soon as he touches them. Today the expression *Midas touch* applies to anyone who easily acquires riches.

Pandora's box. Hesiod (hē′sē·əd), a poet who was roughly contemporary with Homer, tells the story of Zeus's creation of the first woman, Pandora. Before he sends Pandora to live on earth, Zeus gives her a mysterious box, instructing her never to open it. Once on earth, however, Pandora's curiosity gets the better of her. She opens the box, and war, plague, and famine escape and take up permanent residence in the world. Only hope remains inside the box, as a consolation prize to mortals. The expression *opening a Pandora's box* now refers to an action likely to lead to unforeseen—and unpleasant—consequences.

Pandora Opening the Box by Walter Crane. (c. 19th century)

profound questions about human suffering, individual free will, moral responsibility, and the limits of knowledge.

Sophocles (c. 496–406 B.C.) was the most highly regarded playwright of his day and the winner of more than twenty prizes for his dramas. As a general and a friend of the statesman Pericles, he was involved in many of the great events of his time. Sophocles explores the issues of pride, loyalty, and personal responsibility in works such as *Oedipus Rex* (see page 199) and *Antigone.*

The Historians: Herodotus and Thucydides

During the fifth and fourth centuries B.C., the Greeks' search for knowledge resulted in the development of historical writing. Now, for the first time, historians did not merely report events; they also asked rigorous questions. **Herodotus** (hə·räd′ə·təs) (c. 485–c. 425 B.C.), for example, investigated the causes of the Persian Wars, and **Thucydides** (tho͞o·sid′i·dēz′) (c. 460–401 B.C.) analyzed Athens's rise to power and its conflict with Sparta in the Peloponnesian War.

The Great Greek Philosophers: Socrates, Plato, and Aristotle

The Golden Age of Greece also saw the emergence of great philosophical thinkers and writers. According to tradition, the Greek philosopher **Socrates** (säk′rə·tēz′) (469–399 B.C.) once asked a young Athenian boy whether he thought a great deal. The boy modestly replied no but said that at least he had wondered a great deal. The response Socrates gave the boy sums up his own philosophy: "Wisdom," he replied, "begins in wonder." Socrates called himself a philosopher, a Greek word meaning "lover of wisdom."

Socrates' pupil **Plato** (plāt′ō) (c. 429–c. 347 B.C.) preserved his teacher's method of questioning in a series of dialogues, or conversations, in which the "character" Socrates poses and answers philosophical questions. Plato's writings examine such concepts as freedom of conscience, the nature of reality, the existence of the soul, ideal government, and the way to lead a virtuous and happy life.

Plato's greatest pupil, **Aristotle** (ar′is·tät″1) (c. 384–c. 322 B.C.), wrote about subjects such as logic, ethics, political theory, rhetoric, and biology. The *Poetics,* his analysis of the principles of tragedy, is still referred to by drama critics today.

The Decline of Athens

Increasing resentment toward Athenian expansion led to clashes and then to full-scale war between Athens and its chief rival, Sparta. The **Peloponnesian War,** which involved other city-states on the

(Top) Greek gold coin depicting Zeus sitting on a *diphros* (chair) with eagle in his right hand and scepter in his left.
Muenzkabinett, Staatliche Museen zu Berlin.

(Bottom) Greek silver coin with the head of Dionysus (461–430 B.C.E.).

BRITAIN

GAUL

IBERIA

Peloponnesian peninsula, lasted from 431 to 404 B.C. Sparta was victorious, and Athens spiraled into a decline from which it never recovered.

In the middle of the fourth century B.C., the kingdom of Macedon (in what is now the Balkan peninsula), ruled first by Philip and then by his son **Alexander the Great,** emerged as the most powerful state in the Greek-speaking world.

By the time Alexander died, in 323 B.C., his conquests had spread Greek language and culture throughout the Mediterranean, North Africa, and western Asia. The Romans, who conquered the Macedonians in 197 B.C., were awed by the Greeks and would be responsible for the preservation and spread of Greek knowledge in the West.

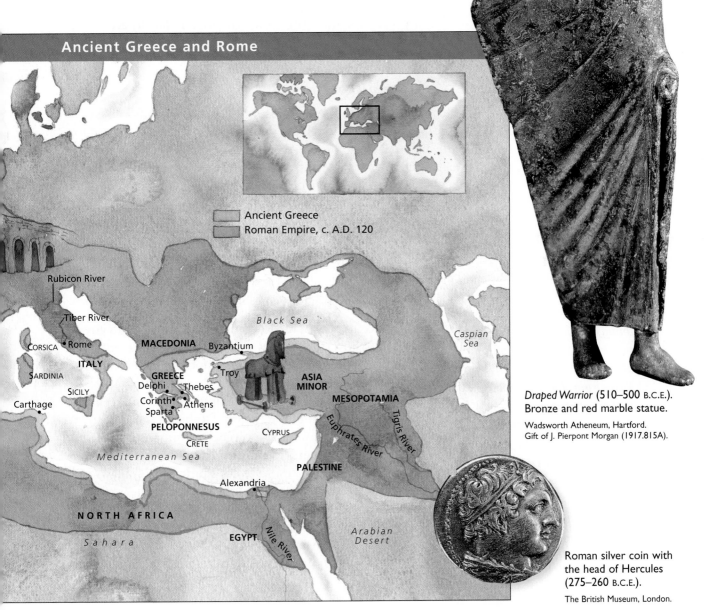

Ancient Greece and Rome

Ancient Greece
Roman Empire, c. A.D. 120

Rubicon River
Tiber River
Black Sea
Caspian Sea
CORSICA • Rome
MACEDONIA • Byzantium
ITALY
SARDINIA
GREECE • Troy
SICILY
Delphi • Thebes
ASIA MINOR
Carthage
Corinth • Athens
Sparta •
MESOPOTAMIA
PELOPONNESUS
CYPRUS
Euphrates River
Tigris River
CRETE
Mediterranean Sea
PALESTINE
Alexandria
NORTH AFRICA
Sahara
EGYPT
Nile River
Arabian Desert

Draped Warrior (510–500 B.C.E.). Bronze and red marble statue.

Wadsworth Atheneum, Hartford. Gift of J. Pierpont Morgan (1917.815A).

Roman silver coin with the head of Hercules (275–260 B.C.E.).

The British Museum, London.

Ancient Greek and Roman Literature 113

Roman Literature

After the death of Alexander the Great, in 323 B.C., the center of power in the Mediterranean world gradually shifted westward to Rome. During their supremacy the Romans proved themselves to be able soldiers, administrators, and engineers. They also produced literary and artistic works that imitated and often rivaled those of their Greek teachers.

The Romans were a practical people. They valued order, thrift, ambition, and loyalty. Three Latin words sum up traditional Roman values: *pietas* (pē′ā·täs), duty to family; *gravitas* (grav′i·täs′), seriousness of conduct and purpose; and *fides* (fē′dās), patriotism and loyalty. (The English words *piety, gravity,* and *fidelity* are derived from them.)

The Founding of Rome

To give themselves the noblest possible past, the Romans looked to the Greek epics as models. In Virgil's *Aeneid* (ē·nē′id), written to be the national epic of Rome, the Trojan prince Aeneas flees from the flaming ruins of Troy. After a long journey, guided by the gods, Aeneas reaches Italy, where he establishes a colony of Trojan survivors (see page 269).

In reality, the founding of Rome was less dramatic. The city of Rome began in the year 753 B.C. as an agricultural settlement on the east bank of the river Tiber in the fertile region known as Latium.

The Republic and Roman Expansion

In the late sixth century B.C., the Romans set up a republican government, that is, a government in which voters elect representatives to make political decisions. This republican form of government lasted nearly five centuries and was looked to as a model by the framers of the United States Constitution in the eighteenth century.

By 270 B.C., all of Italy south of the river Rubicon was in Roman hands. During the centuries that followed, the Romans conquered Spain and established colonies in Britain. They also waged three costly and lengthy conflicts, known as the **Punic** (pyōō′nik) **Wars,** with their rival city, Carthage, situated across the Mediterranean in North Africa. During these wars a daring attack by the Carthaginian general Hannibal, who led a troop of African elephants across Spain and over the Alps, nearly brought the terrified Romans to their knees. In 146 B.C., however, the Romans finally reduced Carthage to ruins.

> One of the great strengths of their empire was their willingness . . . to borrow and to adapt freely from others whatever they found useful. This made possible the transmission of religions, ideas, and ideals from older cultures, and it helped them construct . . . a respectable literature, an efficient military machine, a formidable bureaucracy, and the world's greatest legal system.
>
> —Frank C. Bourne

Painting depicting the reconstruction of the Roman Forum in Imperial Times (1893).

Soprintendenza alle Antichita, Rome.

The Breakdown of the Republic

As Roman armies pushed farther from home, full-time professional troops replaced citizen soldiers. Far from home, an army commander could—and did—make major decisions entirely on his own and could acquire enormous personal wealth. By far the most successful of these army commanders was **Julius Caesar** (102–44 B.C.).

In 48 B.C., in a power struggle for the control of Rome, Caesar was the victor. He later became dictator for life—but he did not grow old

Assassination of Julius Caesar (c. 1793) by Vincenzo Camuccini.
Galleria Nazionale d'Arte Moderna, Rome.

in office. On March 15 in 44 B.C., a conspiracy of senators who disliked Caesar's reforms and feared his power stabbed him to death in the senate house. But the assassins had underestimated Caesar's great popularity with the people, and angry crowds forced the leaders of the conspiracy to flee from Rome.

Years of civil war ensued. The Roman Republic formally became an empire in 27 B.C., when Caesar's great-nephew, who had won firm control of the Roman world, was given the name Augustus, meaning "of good omen," and the title imperator, meaning "emperor."

The Age of Augustus and the Early Empire

Augustus spent much of his vast wealth rebuilding the city of Rome. It has been said that Augustus "found Rome brick, and left it marble." During his long reign (27 B.C.–A.D. 14), peace returned at last to the Roman world.

The cruelty and incompetence of Augustus's successors—Tiberius, Caligula, Claudius, and Nero—were amply detailed by Roman historians. It was said of these emperors that an arch deceiver was succeeded by a madman and a fool by a monster.

In contrast to Augustus's corrupt immediate successors, a line of capable rulers upheld order and prosperity throughout the empire in the second century A.D. At the start of this period, the Roman Empire reached its greatest geographical extent, stretching from Spain and Britain in the west to the borders of Persia in the east.

Roman Religion and Philosophy

The Romans gradually adopted the Greek gods, but by the end of the republic, few Romans seemed to have real belief in these divinities.

After about 150 B.C., various philosophical schools competed with religion in the search for ways to live in the world. The **Epicureans** (ep′i·kyo͞o·rē′ənz), for example, held that people are merely collections of atoms, which disappear at death. The object of life, they held, is to seek pleasure, avoid pain, and value true friendship. The **Stoics** (stō′iks) disagreed, arguing that human beings are the repository of reason, and thus the goal of the individual is to achieve wisdom and virtue through the practice of asceticism—to regard with indifference public opinion, private misfortune, even death itself.

Latin Literature of the Empire

Augustus gathered at his court the most gifted writers to celebrate the achievements of their age. Chief among them was the poet **Virgil** (70–19 B.C.). His epic, the *Aeneid*, links Rome with the glory of Greece's Heroic Age by imagining that a prince fleeing the Trojan War founded the city of Rome. Virgil even wove the emperor Augustus into the epic by linking him through family lines to Aeneas (see page 269). In this way, Virgil gave Rome a national epic that connected history to contemporary life. Other writers who enjoyed the patronage of Augustus were the poets **Horace** (65–8 B.C.) and **Ovid** (43 B.C.–A.D. 17) (see pages 302 and 306).

The Later Empire: Rome's Decline and Fall

During the late second and third centuries A.D., the Roman Empire began its slow decay. Poor supervision of the far-flung empire resulted in corruption and inefficiency.

In the late third century A.D., the emperor Diocletian (ruled 284–305) tried to solve the problem of governing

Fragments from the colossal statue of Emperor Constantine from the Roman Forum (4th century C.E.).

Museo Capitolino, Rome.

Cultural Influences

- Around 750 B.C., Greeks invent an alphabet based on a system used by the Phoenicians.
- Greek city-states participate in Olympic games held every four years.
- Romans adapt Greek rhetorical styles for use in debates.

the enormous Roman Empire by dividing it into two administrative units. Rome remained the capital of the western region, while the eastern part was ruled from Byzantium (now Istanbul, in Turkey). In the fourth century, Byzantium was renamed Constantinople in honor of the emperor Constantine (ruled 306–337). Constantine's conversion to Christianity and his efforts to Christianize his entire empire had far-reaching effects on the history of medieval Europe.

During the later fourth and fifth centuries, a weakened Rome became increasingly vulnerable to the invasions of Germanic tribes. The date usually given for the fall of Rome is A.D. 476, when the city was overrun by the forces of the German barbarian chief Odoacer. The eastern empire continued to exist until 1453, when the Ottoman Turks besieged and conquered Constantinople.

REVIEW

Talk About ...

Turn back to the Think About questions at the beginning of this introduction (page 106). Write down your responses, and get together with a classmate to compare and discuss your views.

Reading Check

1. What are the earliest surviving works of Greek poetry?
2. Name one way in which people of the Greek city-states fostered a common identity.

3. Why did Greek culture thrive even after the decline of Athens?
4. What form of government did Rome have before becoming an empire?
5. What was the primary philosophical belief of the Epicureans? of the Stoics?

Collection 2

**Ancient Greek and Roman Literature:
The Life Worth Living**

Greek Literature

Numberless are the world's wonders, but none
More wonderful than man; the stormgray sea
Yields to his prows, the huge crests bear him high;
Earth, holy and inexhaustible, is graven
With shining furrows where his plows have gone
Year after year, the timeless labor of stallions....

Words also, and thought as rapid as air,
He fashions to his good use; statecraft is his,
And his the skill that deflects the arrows of snow,
The spears of winter rain: from every wind
He has made himself secure—from all but one:
In the late wind of death he cannot stand.

—*from* Antigone, Scene 1, Ode 1
by Sophocles, *translated by*
Dudley Fitts *and* Robert Fitzgerald

Oedipus and Antigone (also known as
The Plague of Thebes) (detail) (1843)
by Charles-François Jalabert.
Musée des Beaux-Arts, Marseille.

119

Introduction

The Iliad

We know very little about Homer, the legendary Greek bard who is said to have composed the Greek epics the *Iliad* and the *Odyssey* around 700 B.C. He was probably from Ionia in western Asia Minor and belonged to a class of traditional oral bards, or professional storytellers, called rhapsodes, who performed their works before live audiences. These oral poets played a vitally important role in Greek society, serving as both historians and entertainers. The traditional belief that Homer was blind is a detail probably based more on convention than on fact, since in Greek culture physical blindness was often a metaphor for profound insight.

A few centuries after they were first composed, the written versions of Homer's epics became a staple of Greek education. These epics not only told rousing tales of gods and heroes grounded in history and legend but also gave literary form to Greek values and ideals. In the epics, Homer brought coherence to an otherwise chaotic pantheon, or family of gods. He also depicted beloved Greek heroes who embodied the ideal of *arete* (arʹə·tāʹ), or excellence, for which the ancient Greeks strived.

The Origin of the Trojan War

The events of the *Iliad* take place during the Trojan War. Although the siege of Troy was a real event, probably caused by competition for trade and control of shipping passages, Homer based his epic on a popular legend that blamed the war on the abduction of a beautiful woman, Helen of Troy. According to this legend, the cause of the Trojan War began with a beauty contest. Paris, a young and handsome prince of Troy, was chosen by the goddesses Aphrodite, Athena, and Hera to decide which one of them was the fairest. Paris chose Aphrodite, the goddess of love, who had bribed him to make the choice by offering him marriage to the world's most beautiful woman, Helen. After the beauty contest, Paris abducted Helen from her husband, King Menelaus of Sparta. As a result, the various Greek chieftains, bound by oaths of loyalty, banded together to attack Troy. Under the leadership of Menelaus's brother Agamemnon, the Greeks laid siege to Troy for ten years. Finally, thanks to the cunning strategies of the clever hero Odysseus, they succeeded in sacking Troy and recapturing Helen.

Conventions of the Homeric Epics

Certain features of Homer's work were so widely imitated in later written epics, such as Virgil's *Aeneid* (see page 269), that they became recognizable characteristics, or **conventions,** of the epic genre. Some of those conventions are listed here.

1. **Invocation.** The *Iliad* begins with an **invocation,** or formal plea for aid, to Calliope, one of the nine Muses, the Greek goddesses who preside over the arts and sciences.

2. ***In medias res.*** The epic plunges us into the middle of the action, or *in medias res* (in mā′dē·äs′ res′), a Latin expression meaning "into the midst of things." **Flashbacks** are then used to inform the audience of prior events.

3. **Epic similes.** Homer uses elaborate, extended comparisons called **epic,** or **Homeric, similes.** These lengthy similes compare heroic events to familiar, everyday events that the audience could easily understand.

4. **Metrical structure.** The *Iliad* was composed in dactylic hexameter, a meter consisting of six stressed syllables per line. The use of formulas, or fixed phrases of a particular metrical shape, aided the speaker's memorization of lines and passages.

5. **Stock epithets.** A **stock epithet** is a descriptive adjective or phrase that is repeatedly used with—or in place of—a noun or proper name. Thus, the audience repeatedly hears of "gray-eyed Athena" and "swift-footed Achilles." The repetition of these epithets, which are also called Homeric epithets, helped the listeners to follow the narrative, since they could associate recurring characters and places with familiar identifying tags. Epithets also aided the rhapsode, who could rely on his stockpile of conventional descriptions as he improvised the poem in performance.

Mask of Agamemnon, from the royal tombs at Mycenae (c. 1600–c. 1550 B.C.E.).

National Archaeological Museum, Athens.

Before You Read

from the Iliad

Make the Connection

Greek warriors strove to achieve *arete,* or personal honor and excellence. What does personal excellence mean to you? Discuss your ideas with a small group.

Literary Focus

Foreshadowing and Flashback

Foreshadowing is the use of clues to hint at what is going to happen later in a plot. This technique increases suspense. A **flashback** is a scene that interrupts present action to narrate the events of an earlier time. Watch for foreshadowing and flashbacks as you read the *Iliad.*

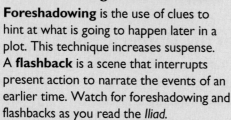

> **Foreshadowing** hints at future events; a **flashback** interrupts the plot to narrate past events.
>
> *For more on Foreshadowing and Flashback, see the Handbook of Literary and Historical Terms.*

Reading Skills

Evaluating Historical Context

As you read, keep in mind the three key beliefs listed below held by Homer's Greek warriors. Jot down notes on how the historical context affects the plot of the epic.

- The spoils of war won in combat were a measure of a Greek warrior's honor and prestige. Losing material possessions was the equivalent of being publicly shamed, the worst insult a hero could suffer.

- The Greeks believed that their gods actively intervened in the affairs of humans and even took sides in conflicts. At the same time, humans had free will and were responsible for their own actions.

- An unburied corpse was considered an offense to the gods. The soul of a person whose body was not buried was doomed to wander the earth forever.

Background

As the *Iliad* begins, the war between the Greeks and the Trojans has been at a stalemate for almost ten years. On the tenth day of a plague that has swept through the Greek forces, the hero Achilles calls an assembly of the entire army to discuss the crisis. This meeting leads to the quarrel between Achilles and Agamemnon that opens the epic.

Vocabulary Development

revere (ri·vir′) *v.:* respect deeply.

formidable (fôr′mə·də·bəl) *adj.:* causing fear.

loath (lōth) *adj.:* reluctant.

implacable (im·plak′ə·bəl) *adj.:* incapable of being pacified.

destitute (des′tə·tōōt′) *adj.:* abandoned.

allay (ə·lā′) *v.:* to relieve; calm.

(Opposite) relief of Trojan horse and Greek soldiers from an earthenware amphora. Mykonos Archeological Museum, Greece.

from the ILIAD

Homer

translated by Robert Fitzgerald

THE CHARACTERS OF THE *ILIAD*

THE GREEKS

Achilles (ə·kil′ēz′): son of a mortal king, Peleus, and the sea goddess Thetis. King of the Myrmidons, Achilles is the mightiest of the Greek warriors.

Agamemnon (ag′ə·mem′nän′): king of Mycenae and commander of the Greek forces. He is Menelaus's older brother.

Ajax (ā′jaks′): one of the strongest Greek warriors.

Calchas (kal′kəs): seer, or prophet, who counsels the Greeks.

Clytemnestra (klī′təm·nes′trə): Agamemnon's wife; Helen's sister.

Helen (hel′ən): wife of Menelaus, whose abduction by Paris causes the war.

Menelaus (men′ə·lā′əs): king of Sparta; husband of Helen.

Nestor (nes′tər): king of Pylos. The oldest of the Greek leaders at Troy, he serves as a counselor.

Odysseus (ō·dis′ē·əs): wily middle-aged Greek warrior. He is the protagonist of Homer's *Odyssey*.

Patroclus (pə·trō′kləs): Greek warrior and closest friend of Achilles.

THE TROJANS

Andromache (an·dräm′ə·kē): faithful wife of Hector.

Astyanax (as·tī′ə·naks′): youngest son of Hector and Andromache.

Briseis (brī′si·əs): girl captured from the Trojans by Achilles as a prize of war.

Cameo bust of Menelaus (1842).
Hermitage, St. Petersburg.

Helen and Priam, from a red-figure kylix (detail) (c. 5th century B.C.E.).
Museo Archeologico, Tarquinia, Italy.

Cassandra (kə·san′drə): daughter of King Priam and Queen Hecuba; she has the gift of prophecy.

Chryseis (kri′si·əs): girl captured by Agamemnon during the plunder of Chryse. Her father, Chryses, is a priest of the god Apollo.

Hector (hek′tər): son of King Priam and Queen Hecuba; commander of the Trojan forces.

Hecuba (hek′yōō·bə): queen of Troy; King Priam's wife.

Paris (par′is): son of King Priam and Queen Hecuba. He is also known as Alexandros.

Priam (prī′əm): king of Troy; father of Hector and Paris.

GODS AND GODDESSES

Aphrodite (af′rə·dīt′ē): goddess of love. She sides with the Trojans during the war.

Apollo (ə·päl′ō): god of poetry, music, and prophecy; he also sides with the Trojans. He is often referred to only as the son of Zeus and Leto, the daughter of Titans.

Athena (ə·thē′nə): goddess of wisdom; she takes the Greeks' side in the conflict.

Hera (hir′ə): wife of Zeus; enemy of the Trojans.

Hermes (hur′mēz′): messenger of the gods, also called the Wayfinder.

Thetis (thēt′is): sea goddess; mother of Achilles.

Zeus (zōōs): father god, the most powerful of all the gods; he remains more or less neutral throughout the conflict.

Achilles, from a red-figure amphora (detail) (c. 5th century B.C.E.).
Museo Gregoriano Etrusco, Musei Vaticani, Vatican City, Italy.

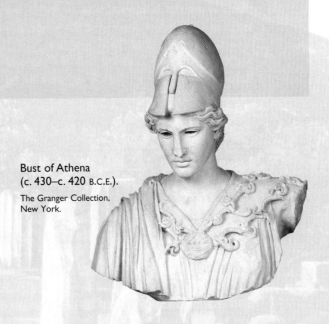

Bust of Athena
(c. 430–c. 420 B.C.E.).
The Granger Collection, New York.

(Background) Tholos, ruins at Delphi (early 4th century B.C.E.).

Detail of Trojan heroes competing for the arms and armor of the slain Achilles (c. 490 B.C.E.). Red figure kylix.

Kunsthistorisches Museum, Vienna, Austria.

from BOOK 1: Quarrel, Oath, and Promise

Anger be now your song, immortal one,
Achilles' anger, doomed and ruinous,
that caused the Achaeans° loss on bitter loss
and crowded brave souls into the undergloom,
5   leaving so many dead men—carrion
for dogs and birds; and the will of Zeus was done.
Begin it when the two men first contending
broke with one another—

                    the Lord Marshal
Agamemnon, Atreus' son, and Prince Achilles.

10   Among the gods, who brought this quarrel on?
The son of Zeus by Leto.° Agamemnon
angered him, so he made a burning wind
of plague rise in the army: rank and file
sickened and died for the ill their chief had done
15   in despising a man of prayer.
This priest, Chryses, had come down to the ships
with gifts, no end of ransom for his daughter;
on a golden staff he carried the god's white bands
and sued for grace from the men of all Achaea

3. Achaeans (ə·kē′ənz): one of the names used in the *Iliad* for the Greeks.

11. The son . . . Leto (lē′tō): Apollo.

? 10–15. *How does Apollo respond after he is angered by Agamemnon's actions?*

the two Atridae° most of all:

20   "O captains
Menelaus and Agamemnon, and you other
Achaeans under arms!
The gods who hold Olympus, may they grant you
plunder of Priam's town and a fair wind home,
25   but let me have my daughter back for ransom
as you <u>revere</u> Apollo, son of Zeus!"

Then all the soldiers murmured their assent:

"Behave well to the priest. And take the ransom!"

But Agamemnon would not. It went against his desire,
30   and brutally he ordered the man away:

"Let me not find you here by the long ships
loitering this time or returning later,
old man; if I do,
the staff and ribbons of the god will fail you.
35   Give up the girl? I swear she will grow old
at home in Argos, far from her own country,
working my loom and visiting my bed.
Leave me in peace and go, while you can, in safety."

So harsh he was, the old man feared and obeyed him,
40   in silence trailing away
by the shore of the tumbling clamorous whispering sea,
and he prayed and prayed again, as he withdrew,
to the god whom silken-braided Leto bore:

"O hear me, master of the silver bow,
45   protector of Tenedos and the holy towns,
Apollo, Sminthian,° if to your liking
ever in any grove I roofed a shrine
or burnt thighbones in fat upon your altar—
bullock or goat flesh—let my wish come true:
50   your arrows on the Danaans° for my tears!"

Now when he heard this prayer, Phoebus Apollo
walked with storm in his heart from Olympus's crest,
quiver and bow at his back, and the bundled arrows
clanged on the sky behind as he rocked in his anger,
55   descending like night itself. Apart from the ships

---

20. Atridae (ə·trī′dē):
Agamemnon and Menelaus
are the sons of Atreus
(ā′trē·əs), the king of Mycenae.
At the time of the Trojan War
and in Homer's own day,
Greece was not a unified
country but a mixture of
diverse kingdoms. The Atridae
were one of many families
of kings.

27–38. How do the soldiers think Agamemnon
should respond to the priest?
How does Agamemnon
actually respond?

46. Sminthian (smin′thē·ən):
epithet for Apollo, probably
in reference to his role as
destroyer of mice; the Greek
for *mouse* is *sminthos*.

50. Danaans (dān′ənz): one
of the names for the Greeks.

Vocabulary
revere (ri·vir′) v.: respect deeply.

he halted and let fly, and the bowstring slammed
as the silver bow sprang, rolling in thunder away.
Pack animals were his target first, and dogs,
but soldiers, too, soon felt transfixing pain
60 from his hard shots, and pyres burned night and day.
Nine days the arrows of the god came down
broadside upon the army. On the tenth,
Achilles called all ranks to assembly. Hera,
whose arms are white as ivory, moved him to it,
65 as she took pity on Danaans dying.
All being mustered, all in place and quiet,
Achilles, fast in battle as a lion,
rose and said:

                    "Agamemnon, now, I take it,
the siege is broken, we are going to sail,
70 and even so may not leave death behind:
if war spares anyone, disease will take him. . . .
We might, though, ask some priest or some diviner,
even some fellow good at dreams—for dreams
come down from Zeus as well—
75 why all this anger of the god Apollo?

Has he some quarrel with us for a failure
in vows or hecatombs?° Would mutton burned
or smoking goat flesh make him lift the plague?"

Putting the question, down he sat. And Calchas,
80 Calchas Thestorides, came forward, wisest
by far of all who scanned the flight of birds.
He knew what was, what had been, what would be,
Calchas, who brought Achaea's ships to Ilion°
by the diviner's gift Apollo gave him.
85 Now for their benefit he said:

                                      "Achilles,
dear to Zeus, it is on me you call
to tell you why the Archer God° is angry.
Well, I can tell you. Are you listening? Swear
by heaven that you will back me and defend me,
90 because I fear my answer will enrage
a man with power in Argos, one whose word
Achaean troops obey.
                    A great man in his rage is formidable

Vocabulary
formidable (fôr′mə·də·bəl) *adj.:* causing fear.

68–78. *What does Achilles want to know?*

77. hecatombs (hek′ə·tōmz′) *n. pl.:* sacrifices to the gods; originally a hecatomb consisted of a hundred oxen.

83. Ilion (il′ē·ən): another name for Troy; the founder of Troy was Ilus, who named the city for his father, Tros.

87. the Archer God: Apollo.

for underlings: though he may keep it down,
he cherishes the burning in his belly
95   until a reckoning day. Think well
if you will save me."

Said Achilles:

                    "Courage.
Tell what you know, what you have light to know.
I swear by Apollo, the lord god to whom
100   you pray when you uncover truth,
never while I draw breath, while I have eyes to see,
shall any man upon this beachhead dare
lay hands on you—not one of all the army,
not Agamemnon, if it is he you mean,
105   though he is first in rank of all Achaeans."

The diviner then took heart and said:

                    "No failure
in hecatombs or vows is held against us.
It is the man of prayer whom Agamemnon
treated with contempt: he kept his daughter,
110   spurned his gifts: for that man's sake the Archer
visited grief upon us and will again.

> **106–117.** *What does Calchas say must occur in order for the Greeks to be released from the plague?*

The embassy of Chryses to Agamemnon. Mosaic from the House of Nymphs, Nabeul, Tunisia.
Museum, Nabeul.

Relieve the Danaans of this plague he will not
until the girl who turns the eyes of men°
shall be restored to her own father—freely,
115 with no demand for ransom—and until
we offer up a hecatomb at Chryse.
Then only can we calm him and persuade him."

He finished and sat down. The son of Atreus,
ruler of the great plain, Agamemnon,
120 rose, furious. Round his heart resentment
welled, and his eyes shone out like licking fire.
Then, with a long and boding look at Calchas,
he growled at him:

                              "You visionary of hell,
never have I had fair play in your forecasts.
125 Calamity is all you care about, or see,
no happy portents; and you bring to pass
nothing agreeable. Here you stand again
before the army, giving it out as oracle
the Archer made them suffer because of me,
130 because I would not take the gifts
and let the girl Chryseis go; I'd have her
mine, at home. Yes, if you like, I rate her
higher than Clytemnestra, my own wife!
She loses nothing by comparison
135 in beauty or womanhood, in mind or skill.

For all of that, I am willing now to yield her
if it is best; I want the army saved
and not destroyed. You must prepare, however,
a prize of honor for me, and at once,
140 that I may not be left without my portion—
I, of all Argives.° It is not fitting so.
While every man of you looks on, my girl
goes elsewhere."

Prince Achilles answered him:

145 "Lord Marshal, most insatiate of men,
how can the army make you a new gift?
Where is our store of booty? Can you see it?
Everything plundered from the towns has been
distributed; should troops turn all that in?
150 Just let the girl go, in the god's name, now;
we'll make it up to you, twice over, three
times over, on that day Zeus gives us leave
to plunder Troy behind her rings of stone."

113. the girl . . . of men: He is referring to Chryseis.

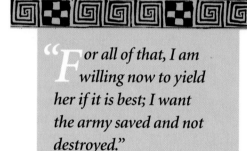

"*For all of that, I am willing now to yield her if it is best; I want the army saved and not destroyed.*"

141. Argives (är′gīvz′): Greeks from Argos, in the northeastern part of the Peloponnesus.

Agamemnon answered:

"Not that way

155 will I be gulled, brave as you are, Achilles.
Take me in, would you? Try to get around me?
What do you really ask? That you may keep
your own winnings, I am to give up mine
and sit here wanting her? Oh, no:

160 the army will award a prize to me
and make sure that it measures up, or if
they do not, I will take a girl myself,
your own, or Ajax's, or Odysseus' prize!
Take her, yes, to keep. The man I visit

165 may choke with rage; well, let him.
But this, I say, we can decide on later.

Look to it now, we launch on the great sea
a well-found ship, and get her manned with oarsmen,
load her with sacrificial beasts and put aboard

170 Chryseis in her loveliness. My deputy,
Ajax, Idomeneus,° or Prince Odysseus,
or you, Achilles, fearsome as you are,
will make the hecatomb and quiet the Archer."

Achilles frowned and looked at him, then said:

175 "You thick-skinned, shameless, greedy fool!
Can any Achaean care for you, or obey you,
after this on marches or in battle?
As for myself, when I came here to fight,
I had no quarrel with Troy or Trojan spearmen:

180 they never stole my cattle or my horses,
never in the black farmland of Phthia°
ravaged my crops. How many miles there are
of shadowy hills between, and foaming seas!
No, no, we joined for you, you insolent boor,

185 to please you, fighting for your brother's sake
and yours, to get revenge upon the Trojans.
You overlook this, dogface, or don't care,
and now in the end you threaten to take my girl,
a prize I sweated for, and soldiers gave me!

190 Never have I had plunder like your own
from any Trojan stronghold battered down
by the Achaeans. I have seen more action
hand to hand in those assaults than you have,
but when the time for sharing comes, the greater

195 share is always yours. Worn out with battle
I carry off some trifle to my ships.

154–166. What does Agamemnon demand in return for his agreement to send Chryseis back to her father?

171. Idomeneus
(ī·däm′i·no͞os′): king of Crete and leader of the Cretan forces against Troy.

175–199. What does Agamemnon say that enrages Achilles? What injustice does Achilles see in the proposal?

181. Phthia (thī′ə): Achilles' home in northern Greece.

Apollo of Belvedere (detail) (c. 350–c. 320 B.C.E.).

Museo Pio Clementino, Musei Vaticani, Vatican City.

Well, this time I make sail for home.
Better to take now to my ships. Why linger,
cheated of winnings, to make wealth for you?"

200   To this the high commander made reply:

"Desert, if that's the way the wind blows. Will I
beg you to stay on my account? I will not.
Others will honor me, and Zeus who views
the wide world most of all.

                                                    No officer
205   is hateful to my sight as you are, none
given like you to faction, as to battle—
rugged you are, I grant, by some god's favor.
Sail, then, in your ships, and lord it over
your own battalion of Myrmidons.° I do not
210   give a curse for you, or for your anger.
But here is warning for you:

                                                    Chryseis

being required of me by Phoebus Apollo,
she will be sent back in a ship of mine,
manned by my people. That done, I myself
215   will call for Briseis at your hut, and take her,
flower of young girls that she is, your prize,
to show you here and now who is the stronger
and make the next man sick at heart—if any
think of claiming equal place with me."

220   A pain like grief weighed on the son of Peleus,°
and in his shaggy chest this way and that
the passion of his heart ran: should he draw
longsword from hip, stand off the rest, and kill
in single combat the great son of Atreus,
225   or hold his rage in check and give it time?
And as this tumult swayed him, as he slid
the big blade slowly from the sheath, Athena
came to him from the sky. The white-armed goddess,
Hera, sent her, being fond of both,
230   concerned for both men. And Athena, stepping
up behind him, visible to no one
except Achilles, gripped his red-gold hair.

Startled, he made a half turn, and he knew her
upon the instant for Athena: terribly
235   her gray eyes blazed at him. And speaking softly
but rapidly aside to her he said:

209. Myrmidons
(mʉr′mə·dänz′): warriors
from Thessaly, in northern
Greece; followers of Achilles.

212–219. In these lines,
Agamemnon threatens
Achilles.
*What is the threat? How
do you think Achilles will
respond?*

220. son of Peleus: Achilles.

"What now, O daughter of the god of heaven
who bears the stormcloud,° why are you here? To see
the wolfishness of Agamemnon?
240 Well, I give you my word: this time, and soon,
he pays for his behavior with his blood."

The gray-eyed goddess Athena said to him:

"It was to check this killing rage I came
from heaven, if you will listen. Hera sent me,
245 being fond of both of you, concerned for both.
Enough: break off this combat, stay your hand
upon the sword hilt. Let him have a lashing
with words, instead: tell him how things will be.
Here is my promise, and it will be kept:
250 winnings three times as rich, in due season,
you shall have in requital for his arrogance.
But hold your hand. Obey."
                                    The great runner,

Achilles, answered:

                    "Nothing for it, goddess,
but when you two immortals speak, a man

237–238. god . . . who bears
the stormcloud: Zeus.

243–252. *Why has
Athena arrived to speak
with Achilles? What does she
advise him to do?*

*Minerva Preventing Achilles from
Killing Agamemnon* (1757) by
Giovanni Battista Tiepolo.

Villa Valmarana, Vicenza, Italy.

255 complies, though his heart burst. Just as well.
Honor the gods' will, they may honor ours."
On this he stayed his massive hand
upon the silver pommel,° and the blade
of his great weapon slid back in the scabbard.
260 The man had done her bidding. Off to Olympus,
gaining the air, she went to join the rest,
the powers of heaven in the home of Zeus.

But now the son of Peleus turned on Agamemnon
and lashed out at him, letting his anger ride
in execration:°
265   "Sack of wine,
you with your cur's eyes and your antelope heart!
You've never had the kidney to buckle on
armor among the troops, or make a sortie
with picked men—oh, no; that way death might lie.
270 Safer, by god, in the middle of the army—
is it not?—to commandeer the prize
of any man who stands up to you! Leech!
Commander of trash! If not, I swear,
you never could abuse one soldier more!

275 But here is what I say: my oath upon it
by this great staff: look: leaf or shoot
it cannot sprout again, once lopped away
from the log it left behind in the timbered hills;
it cannot flower, peeled of bark and leaves;
280 instead, Achaean officers in council
take it in hand by turns, when they observe
by the will of Zeus due order in debate:
let this be what I swear by then: I swear
a day will come when every Achaean soldier
285 will groan to have Achilles back. That day
you shall no more prevail on me than this
dry wood shall flourish—driven though you are,
and though a thousand men perish before
the killer, Hector. You will eat your heart out,
290 raging with remorse for this dishonor
done by you to the bravest of Achaeans."

He hurled the staff, studded with golden nails,
before him on the ground. Then down he sat,
and fury filled Agamemnon, looking across at him.
295 But for the sake of both men Nestor arose,
the Pylians'° orator, eloquent and clear;
argument sweeter than honey rolled from his tongue.

258. pommel *n.:* knob on the end of the hilt of a sword or dagger.

264. execration *n.:* the act of speaking abusively of someone or something.

Mycenaean bronze dagger (1300–1100 B.C.E.).
The British Museum, London.

296. Pylians (pīl′ē·ənz): people from Pylos (pī′läs), a town in the Peloponnesus.

By now he had outlived two generations
of mortal men, his own and the one after,
300   in Pylos land, and still ruled in the third.
In kind reproof he said:

                               "A black day, this.

Bitter distress comes this way to Achaea.
How happy Priam and Priam's sons would be,
and all the Trojans—wild with joy—if they
305   got wind of all these fighting words between you,
foremost in council as you are, foremost
in battle. Give me your attention. Both
are younger men than I, and in my time
men who were even greater have I known
310   and none of them disdained me. Men like those
I have not seen again, nor shall: Peirithous,
the Lord Marshal Dryas, Caereus, Exadius,
Polyphemus, Theseus°—Aegeus's son,
a man like the immortal gods. I speak
315   of champions among men of earth, who fought
with champions, with wild things of the mountains,
great centaurs° whom they broke and overpowered.
Among these men I say I had my place
when I sailed out of Pylos, my far country,
320   because they called for me. I fought
for my own hand among them. Not one man
alive now upon earth could stand against them.
And I repeat: they listened to my reasoning,
took my advice. Well, then, you take it too.
It is far better so.

325   Lord Agamemnon,
do not deprive him of the girl, renounce her.
The army had allotted her to him.
Achilles, for your part, do not defy
your King and Captain. No ones vies in honor
330   with him who holds authority from Zeus.
You have more prowess, for a goddess bore you;
his power over men surpasses yours.

But, Agamemnon, let your anger cool.
I beg you to relent, knowing Achilles
335   a sea wall for Achaeans in the black waves of war."

Lord Agamemnon answered:

                               "All you say

is fairly said, sir, but this man's ambition,
remember, is to lead, to lord it over
everyone, hold power over everyone,

**311–313. Peirithous…
Theseus:** heroes of Nestor's
generation.

317. centaurs *n. pl.:* legendary
creatures, half man and
half horse.

325–335. *What does
Nestor advise each of
the men to do to settle their
dispute?*

340 give orders to the rest of us! Well, one
will never take his orders! If the gods
who live forever made a spearman of him,
have they put insults on his lips as well?"

Achilles interrupted:
                              "What a poltroon,°
345 how lily-livered I should be called, if I
knuckled under to all you do or say!
Give your commands to someone else, not me!
And one more thing I have to tell you: think it
over: this time, for the girl, I will not
350 wrangle in arms with you or anyone,
though I am robbed of what was given me;
but as for any other thing I have
alongside my black ship, you shall not take it
against my will. Try it. Hear this, everyone:
355 that instant your hot blood blackens my spear!"

They quarreled in this way, face to face, and then
broke off the assembly by the ships. Achilles
made his way to his squadron and his quarters,
Patroclus by his side, with his companions.

360 Agamemnon proceeded to launch a ship,
assigned her twenty oarsmen, loaded beasts
for sacrifice to the god, then set aboard
Chryseis in her loveliness. The versatile
Odysseus took the deck, and, all oars manned,
365 they pulled out on the drenching ways of sea.
The troops meanwhile were ordered to police camp
and did so, throwing refuse in the water;
then to Apollo by the barren surf
they carried out full-tally hecatombs,
370 and the savor curled in crooked smoke toward heaven.

That was the day's work in the army.
                              Agamemnon
had kept his threat in mind, and now he acted,
calling Eurybates and Talthybios,
his aides and criers:
                              "Go along," he said,
375 "both of you, to the quarters of Achilles
and take his charming Briseis by the hand
to bring to me. And if he balks at giving her
I shall be there myself with men-at-arms
in force to take her—all the more gall for him."

344. poltroon (päl·trōōn′) *n.*: coward.

"*You shall not take it against my will. Try it. Hear this, everyone: that instant your hot blood blackens my spear!*"

380 So, ominously, he sent them on their way,
and they who had no stomach for it went
along the waste sea shingle° toward the ships
and shelters of the Myrmidons. Not far
from his black ship and hut they found the prince
385 in the open, seated. And seeing these two come
was cheerless to Achilles. Shamefast, pale
with fear of him, they stood without a word;
but he knew what they felt and called out:

                                  "Peace to you,
criers and couriers of Zeus and men!
390 Come forward. Not one thing have I against you:
Agamemnon is the man who sent you
for Briseis. Here then, my lord Patroclus,
bring out the girl and give her to these men.
And let them both bear witness before the gods
395 who live in bliss, as before men who die,
including this harsh king, if ever hereafter
a need for me arises to keep the rest
from black defeat and ruin.

                                  Lost in folly,
the man cannot think back or think ahead
400 how to come through a battle by the ships."

Patroclus did the bidding of his friend,
led from the hut Briseis in her beauty
and gave her to them. Back along the ships
they took their way, and the girl went, <u>loath</u> to go.

405 Leaving his friends in haste, Achilles wept,
and sat apart by the gray wave, scanning the endless sea.
Often he spread his hands in prayer to his mother:°

"As my life came from you, though it is brief,
honor at least from Zeus who storms in heaven
410 I call my due. He gives me precious little.
See how the lord of the great plains, Agamemnon,
humiliated me! He has my prize,
by his own whim, for himself."

                                Eyes wet with tears,
he spoke, and her ladyship his mother heard him
415 in green deeps where she lolled near her old father.

Vocabulary

loath (lōth) *adj.:* reluctant.

382. **shingle** *n.:* beach covered with coarse gravel.

388–398. Agamemnon's aides have arrived to take Briseis from Achilles.

[?] *Why does Achilles bear no ill will toward the men Agamemnon has sent? What does Achilles' behavior tell you about his character?*

Briseis being taken away, from a red-figure *skyphos* (detail) (5th century B.C.E.).
Musée du Louvre, Paris.

407. **mother** *n.:* the goddess Thetis (thēt'is), a daughter of Nereus, the old man of the sea.

Gliding she rose and broke like mist from the inshore
gray sea face, to sit down softly before him,
her son in tears; and fondling him she said:

"Child, why do you weep? What grief is this?
420 Out with it, tell me, both of us should know."
Achilles, fast in battle as a lion,
groaned and said:
                                    "Why tell you what you know?
We sailed out raiding, and we took by storm
that ancient town of Eetion° called Thebe,
425 plundered the place, brought slaves and spoils away.
At the division, later,
they chose a young girl, Chryseis, for the king.
Then Chryses, priest of the Archer God, Apollo,
came to the beachhead we Achaeans hold,
430 bringing no end of ransom for his daughter;
he had the god's white bands on a golden staff
and sued for grace from the army of Achaea
mostly the two Atridae, corps commanders.
All of our soldiers murmured in assent:
435 'Behave well to the priest. And take the ransom!'
But Agamemnon would not. It went against his desire,
and brutally he ordered the man away.
So the old man withdrew in grief and anger.
Apollo cared for him: he heard his prayer
440 and let black bolts of plague fly on the Argives.

One by one our men came down with it
and died hard as the god's shots raked the army
broadside. But our priest divined the cause
and told us what the god meant by the plague.

445 I said, 'Appease the god!' but Agamemnon
could not contain his rage; he threatened me,
and what he threatened is now done—
one girl the Achaeans are embarking now
for Chryse beach with gifts for Lord Apollo;
450 the other, just now, from my hut—the criers
came and took her, Briseus' girl, my prize,
given by the army.
                                    If you can, stand by me:
go to Olympus, pray to Zeus, if ever
by word or deed you served him—
455 and so you did, I often heard you tell it
in Father's house: that time when you alone
of all the gods shielded the son of Cronus°

424. Eetion (ē·ē′tē·än): king of Thebe (thē′bē), a city near Troy.

457. son of Cronus: Zeus; Cronus ruled over the Titans until his son Zeus dethroned him and became ruler over the Olympians.

from peril and disgrace—when other gods,
Pallas Athena, Hera, and Poseidon,
460 wished him in irons, wished to keep him bound,
you had the will to free him of that bondage,
and called up to Olympus in all haste
Aegaeon, whom the gods call Briareus,°
the giant with a hundred arms, more powerful
465 than the sea-god, his father. Down he sat
by the son of Cronus, glorying in that place.
For fear of him the blissful gods forbore
to manacle Zeus.

463. **Briareus** (brī·är′ē·əs):
giant who helped Zeus and
the Olympians overcome the
Titans.

                    Remind him of these things,
cling to his knees and tell him your good pleasure
470 if he will take the Trojan side
and roll the Achaeans back to the water's edge,
back on the ships with slaughter! All the troops
may savor what their king has won for them,
and he may know his madness, what he lost
475 when he dishonored me, peerless among Achaeans."

452–472. Achilles asks
his mother to intervene
with Zeus on his behalf.
The ancient Greeks
believed that the gods
would help those who
were loyal to them.
? *How has Thetis served
Zeus in the past?*

Her eyes filled, and a tear fell as she answered:

"Alas, my child, why did I rear you, doomed
the day I bore you? Ah, could you only be
serene upon this beachhead through the siege,
480 your life runs out so soon.
Oh early death! Oh broken heart! No destiny
so cruel! And I bore you to this evil!

? **477–482.** *According to
Thetis, what fate does
the future hold for Achilles?*

But what you wish I will propose
To Zeus, lord of the lightning, going up
485 myself into the snow-glare of Olympus
with hope for his consent.
                            Be quiet now
beside the long ships, keep your anger bright
against the army, quit the war.
                            Last night
Zeus made a journey to the shore of Ocean
490 to feast among the Sunburned,° and the gods
accompanied him. In twelve days he will come
back to Olympus. Then I shall be there
to cross his bronze doorsill and take his knees.
I trust I'll move him."
                            Thetis left her son

490. the Sunburned:
Ethiopians.

495 still burning for the softly belted girl
whom they had wrested from him. . . .

Response and Analysis

from Book 1

Reading Check

1. What crisis in the Greek camp confronts the leaders at the opening of the epic? How does this crisis lead to a conflict between Achilles and Agamemnon?

2. What action does Agamemnon take to appease Apollo? Whom does he take from Achilles?

3. What oath does Achilles swear? Why does he withdraw from the battle?

4. What does Thetis promise to do for her son Achilles?

Thinking Critically

5. What impression do you form of Agamemnon's character from his own words and actions and the reactions of Calchas and Achilles?

6. What ominous, or threatening, images can you identify in the first fifteen lines of Book 1 of the *Iliad*? What future events do these images **foreshadow**?

7. In the scene between Achilles and his mother, Thetis, there is a **flashback** to an earlier time when Thetis helped defend Zeus. What purpose does this flashback serve?

8. What role do the gods play in Book 1? Are they aloof observers, fair intermediaries, or meddling nuisances? Describe the roles played by Apollo, Athena, and Thetis in this book of the *Iliad*.

Extending and Evaluating

9. Do you think that Achilles is justified in his wrath against Agamemnon and his subsequent withdrawal from battle? Imagine that Achilles is a modern-day military officer. Would a modern general be justified in withdrawing from combat if his personal honor were at stake? If so, under what circumstances?

WRITING

Writing a Screenplay

One of the most enjoyable aspects of the *Iliad* is its vivid portrayal of character and action. Select one of the scenes you have read from Book 1 of the epic, and write a screenplay for a film version of the scene. Your script should include not only dialogue but also notes on costumes, casting choices, and special effects that you think would contribute to an effective film version of the scene. Experiment with different settings in place and time. For example, you might set your film during World War II, the Vietnam War, or even an imaginary intergalactic conflict.

The embassy of Chryses to Agamemnon (detail). Mosaic from the House of Nymphs, Nabeul, Tunisia.
Museum, Nabeul.

Battle between the Greeks and
Persians (late 4th century B.C.E.).
Relief from the *Alexander Sarcophagus*.

Archaeological Museum, Istanbul.

from the Iliad
from Books 22 and 24
Homer
translated by **Robert Fitzgerald**

*Without Achilles' help, the Greeks are at a serious disadvantage
against the Trojans, who are led by their great warrior Hector, the
son of the Trojan king, Priam. In Book 6, we glimpse Hector's
humanity as he shares a loving moment with his wife, Andromache,
and his son Astyanax. Book 6 also reveals to us Hector's pride, for
we learn that although he believes Troy is doomed, honor will not
allow him to surrender.*

    *Hector returns to battle, fighting fiercely for the Trojans. As
fear grows in the Greek camp, Agamemnon admits that he has*

wronged Achilles. He sends a delegation of ambassadors to offer
amends and to ask Achilles and his comrades to return to battle.
Achilles' immense pride is revealed as he stubbornly refuses to
accept Agamemnon's gifts. He tells the delegates that he has
decided to return to his kingdom and live out his life in comfort,
forgoing the honor of dying a hero's death in battle.

When the Trojans break through the Greek defenses, Achilles'
best friend, Patroclus, pleads with the hero to permit him to
rejoin the fighting. Achilles reluctantly agrees (Books 11–15). As
the battle rages, the god Apollo strikes Patroclus from his horse,
giving Hector the opportunity to slay the warrior and strip the
corpse of its armor.

On hearing of Patroclus's death, Achilles is overcome with grief
and rage. Vowing to avenge his friend, he finally returns to the
battle, mercilessly slaying the Trojan forces (Books 19–21). As Book
22 opens, the exhausted Trojans take refuge behind the high walls
of the city. One Trojan remains outside the walls: Hector.

BOOK 22: Desolation Before Troy

Once in the town, those who had fled like deer
wiped off their sweat and drank their thirst away,
leaning against the cool stone of the ramparts.°
Meanwhile Achaeans with bright shields aslant
5   came up the plain and nearer. As for Hector,
fatal destiny pinned him where he stood
before the Scaean Gates, outside the city.

Now Achilles heard Apollo calling
back to him:
                              "Why run so hard, Achilles
10   mortal as you are, after a god?
Can you not comprehend it? I am immortal.
You are so hot to catch me, you no longer
think of finishing off the men you routed.
They are all in the town by now, packed in
15   while you were being diverted here. And yet
you cannot kill me; I am no man's quarry."

Achilles bit his lip and said:

"Archer of heaven, deadliest
of immortal gods, you put me off the track,
20   turning me from the wall this way. A hundred
might have sunk their teeth into the dust

3. **ramparts** *n. pl.*: defensive embankments surrounding a town.

9–16. Why does Apollo question the wisdom of Achilles' pursuit?

before one man took cover in Ilion!
You saved my enemies with ease and stole
my glory, having no punishment to fear.
25   I'd take it out of you, if I had the power."

Then toward the town with might and main he ran,
magnificent, like a racing chariot horse
that holds its form at full stretch on the plain.
So light-footed Achilles held the pace.
30   And aging Priam was the first to see him
sparkling on the plain, bright as that star
in autumn rising, whose unclouded rays
shine out amid a throng of stars at dusk—
the one they call Orion's° dog, most brilliant,
35   yes, but baleful as a sign: it brings
great fever to frail men. So pure and bright
the bronze gear blazed upon him as he ran.
The old man gave a cry. With both his hands
thrown up on high he struck his head, then shouted,
40   groaning, appealing to his dear son. Unmoved,
Lord Hector stood in the gateway, resolute
to fight Achilles.
                              Stretching out his hands,
old Priam said, imploring him:
                                              "No, Hector!

Cut off as you are, alone, dear son,
45   don't try to hold your ground against this man,
or soon you'll meet the shock of doom, borne down
by the son of Peleus. He is more powerful
by far than you, and pitiless. Ah, were he
but dear to the gods as he is dear to me!
50   Wild dogs and kites would eat him where he lay
within the hour, and ease me of my torment.
Many tall sons he killed, bereaving me,
or sold them to far islands. Even now
I cannot see two sons of mine, Lycaon°
55   and Polydorus,° among the Trojans massed
inside the town. A queen, Laothoe,
conceived and bore them. If they are alive
amid the Achaean host, I'll ransom them
with bronze and gold: both I have, piled at home,
60   rich treasures that old Altes, the renowned,
gave for his daughter's dowry. If they died,
if they went under to the homes of Death,
sorrow has come to me and to their mother.
But to our townsmen all this pain is brief,
65   unless you too go down before Achilles.

34. Orion: constellation named after a hunter who was loved and accidentally killed by the goddess Artemis.

42–70. *What reasons does Priam give in his attempt to convince Hector not to confront Achilles?*

54. Lycaon (lī·kā′än).
55. Polydorus (päl·i·dō′rəs).

Come inside the wall, child; here you may
fight on to save our Trojan men and women.
Do not resign the glory to Achilles,
losing your own dear life! Take pity, too,
70   on me and my hard fate, while I live still.
Upon the threshold of my age, in misery,
the son of Cronus° will destroy my life
after the evil days I shall have seen—
my sons brought down, my daughters dragged away,
75   bedchambers ravaged, and small children hurled
to earth in the atrocity of war,
as my sons' wives are taken by Achaeans'
ruinous hands. And at the end, I too—
when someone with a sword-cut or a spear
80   has had my life—I shall be torn apart
on my own doorstep by the hounds
I trained as watchdogs, fed from my own table.
These will lap my blood with ravenous hearts
and lie in the entranceway.

Everything done
85   to a young man killed in war becomes his glory,
once he is riven° by the whetted bronze:
dead though he be, it is all fair, whatever
happens then. But when an old man falls,
and dogs disfigure his gray head and cheek
90   and genitals, that is most harrowing
of all that men in their hard lives endure."

The old man wrenched at his gray hair and pulled out
hanks of it in both hands, but moved
Lord Hector not at all. The young man's mother
95   wailed from the tower across, above the portal,
streaming tears, and loosening her robe
with one hand, held her breast out in the other,
saying:

"Hector, my child, be moved by this,
and pity me, if ever I unbound
100   a quieting breast for you. Think of these things,
dear child; defend yourself against the killer
this side of the wall, not hand to hand.
He has no pity. If he brings you down,
I shall no longer be allowed to mourn you
105   laid out on your bed, dear branch in flower,
born of me! And neither will your lady,
so endowed with gifts. Far from us both,
dogs will devour you by the Argive ships."

72. son of Cronus: Zeus.

86. riven *v.:* split or torn apart.

98–108. *What does Hector's mother predict will happen if Hector fights Achilles?*

With tears and cries the two implored their son,
110 and made their prayers again, but could not shake him.
Hector stood firm, as huge Achilles neared.
The way a serpent, fed on poisonous herbs,
coiled at his lair upon a mountainside,
with all his length of hate awaits a man
115 and eyes him evilly: so Hector, grim
and narrow-eyed, refused to yield. He leaned
his brilliant shield against a spur of wall
and in his brave heart bitterly reflected:
"Here I am badly caught. If I take cover,
120 slipping inside the gate and wall, the first
to accuse me for it will be Polydamas,°
he who told me I should lead the Trojans
back to the city on that cursed night
Achilles joined the battle. No, I would not,
125 would not, wiser though it would have been.
Now troops have perished for my foolish pride,
I am ashamed to face townsmen and women.
Someone inferior to me may say:
'He kept his pride and lost his men, this Hector!'
130 So it will go. Better, when that time comes,
that I appear as he who killed Achilles
man to man, or else that I went down
fighting him to the end before the city.
Suppose, though, that I lay my shield and helm
135 aside, and prop my spear against the wall,
and go to meet the noble Prince Achilles,
promising Helen, promising with her
all treasures that Alexandros° brought home
by ship to Troy—the first cause of our quarrel—
140 that he may give these things to the Atridae?
Then I might add, apart from these, a portion
of all the secret wealth the city owns.
Yes, later I might take our counselors' oath
to hide no stores, but share and share alike
145 to halve all wealth our lovely city holds,
all that is here within the walls. Ah, no,
why even put the question to myself?
I must not go before him and receive
no quarter, no respect! Aye, then and there
150 he'll kill me, unprotected as I am,
my gear laid by, defenseless as a woman.
No chance, now, for charms from oak or stone
in parley with him—charms a girl and boy
might use when they enchant each other talking!

121. Polydamas
(pō·lid′ə·məs): Trojan leader.

119–146. *What three options must Hector choose between as he ponders his difficult decision? What do you learn about Hector through his self-questioning?*

138. Alexandros: another name for Paris. *Alexandros* means "champion."

155 Better we duel, now at once, and see
  to whom the Olympian awards the glory."

  These were his shifts of mood. Now close at hand
  Achilles like the <u>implacable</u> god of war
  came on with blowing crest, hefting the dreaded
160 beam of Pelian ash° on his right shoulder.
  Bronze light played around him, like the glare
  of a great fire or the great sun rising,
  and Hector, as he watched, began to tremble.
  Then he could hold his ground no more. He ran,
165 leaving the gate behind him, with Achilles
  hard on his heels, sure of his own speed.
  When that most lightning-like of birds, a hawk
  bred on a mountain, swoops upon a dove,
  the quarry dips in terror, but the hunter,
170 screaming, dips behind and gains upon it,
  passionate for prey. Just so, Achilles
  murderously cleft the air, as Hector
  ran with flashing knees along the wall.
  They passed the lookout point, the wild fig tree
175 with wind in all its leaves, then veered away
  along the curving wagon road, and came
  to where the double fountains well, the source
  of eddying Scamander.° One hot spring
  flows out, and from the water fumes arise
180 as though from fire burning; but the other
  even in summer gushes chill as hail
  or snow or crystal ice frozen on water.
  Near these fountains are wide washing pools
  of smooth-laid stone, where Trojan wives and daughters
185 laundered their smooth linen in the days
  of peace before the Achaeans came. Past these
  the two men ran, pursuer and pursued,
  and he who fled was noble, he behind
  a greater man by far. They ran full speed,
190 and not for bull's hide or a ritual beast
  or any prize that men compete for: no,
  but for the life of Hector, tamer of horses.
  Just as when chariot-teams around a course
  go wheeling swiftly, for the prize is great,
195 a tripod° or a woman, in the games

160. Pelian (pēl′ē·ən) **ash:** wood cut from trees on Mount Pelion, one of the highest mountains in Greece.

157–166. How does Hector respond as Achilles gets close to him?

178. Scamander (skə·man′dər): river of Troy.

193–198. Homer often uses **similes,** or comparisons, to convey events. What does Homer compare Achilles and Hector to in these lines? What effect does this comparison create?

195. tripod *n.:* bronze altar used in sacrifices.

Vocabulary

implacable (im·plak′ə·bəl) *adj.:* incapable of being pacified.

held for a dead man, so three times these two
at full speed made their course round Priam's town,
as all the gods looked on. And now the father
of gods and men° turned to the rest and said:

200   "How sad that this beloved man is hunted
around the wall before my eyes! My heart
is touched for Hector; he has burned thigh flesh
of oxen for me often, high on Ida,°
at other times on the high point of Troy.

205   Now Prince Achilles with devouring stride
is pressing him around the town of Priam.
Come, gods, put your minds on it, consider
whether we may deliver him from death
or see him, noble as he is, brought down
by Peleus' son, Achilles."

210   Gray-eyed Athena
said to him:
                 "Father of the blinding bolt,
the dark stormcloud, what words are these? The man
is mortal, and his doom fixed, long ago.
Would you release him from his painful death?
215   Then do so, but not all of us will praise you."

The Lion Gate at Mycenae
(detail) (c. 1250 B.C.E.).

147

Zeus who gathers cloud replied:

"Take heart,
my dear and honored child. I am not bent
on my suggestion, and I would indulge you.
Act as your thought inclines, refrain no longer."

220 So he encouraged her in her desire,
and down she swept from ridges of Olympus.
Great Achilles, hard on Hector's heels,
kept after him, the way a hound will harry
a deer's fawn he has startled from its bed
225 to chase through gorge and open glade, and when
the quarry goes to earth under a bush
he holds the scent and quarters till he finds it;
so with Hector: he could not shake off
the great runner, Achilles. Every time
230 he tried to spring hard for the Dardan gates°
under the towers, hoping men could help him,
sending missiles down, Achilles loomed
to cut him off and turn him toward the plain,
as he himself ran always near the city.
235 As in a dream a man chasing another
cannot catch him, nor can he in flight
escape from his pursuer, so Achilles
could not by his swiftness overtake him,
nor could Hector pull away. How could he
240 run so long from death, had not Apollo
for the last time, the very last, come near
to give him stamina and speed?

Achilles
shook his head at the rest of the Achaeans,
allowing none to shoot or cast at Hector—
245 none to forestall him, and to win the honor.
But when, for the fourth time, they reached the springs,
the Father poised his golden scales.

He placed
two shapes of death, death prone and cold, upon them,
one of Achilles, one of the horseman, Hector,
250 and held the midpoint, pulling upward. Down
sank Hector's fatal day, the pan went down
toward undergloom, and Phoebus Apollo left him.
Then came Athena, gray-eyed, to the son
of Peleus, falling in with him, and near him,
saying swiftly:

"Now at last I think
255 the two of us, Achilles loved by Zeus,
shall bring Achaeans triumph at the ships

Great Achilles, hard on Hector's heels, kept after him, the way a hound will harry a deer's fawn...

230. Dardan gates: gates of Troy. Dardania, a city built near the foot of Mount Ida, became part of Troy.

? **246–252.** How does Zeus's weighing of Hector's and Achilles' fates **foreshadow** the ending of the conflict between Achilles and Hector?

by killing Hector—unappeased
though he was ever in his thirst for war.
260 There is no way he may escape us now,
not though Apollo, lord of distances,
should suffer all indignity for him
before his father Zeus who bears the stormcloud,
rolling back and forth and begging for him.
265 Now you can halt and take your breath, while I
persuade him into combat face to face."

These were Athena's orders. He complied,
relieved, and leaning hard upon the spearshaft
armed with its head of bronze. She left him there
270 and overtook Lord Hector—but she seemed
Deiphobus° in form and resonant voice,
appearing at his shoulder, saying swiftly:

"Ai! Dear brother, how he runs, Achilles,
harrying you around the town of Priam!
Come, we'll stand and take him on."

275   To this,
great Hector in his shimmering helm replied:

"Deiphobus, you were the closest to me
in the old days, of all my brothers, sons
of Hecuba and Priam. Now I can say
280 I honor you still more
because you dared this foray for my sake,
seeing me run. The rest stay under cover."

Again the gray-eyed goddess spoke:

"Dear brother, how your father and gentle mother
285 begged and begged me to remain! So did
the soldiers round me, all undone by fear.
But in my heart I ached for you.
Now let us fight him, and fight hard.
No holding back. We'll see if this Achilles
290 conquers both, to take our armor seaward,
or if he can be brought down by your spear."

This way, by guile, Athena led him on.
And when at last the two men faced each other,
Hector was the first to speak. He said:

295 "I will no longer fear you as before,
son of Peleus, though I ran from you

271. Deiphobus (dē′ə·fō′bəs):
one of Hector's brothers.

269–292. *How does Athena trick Hector into agreeing to fight Achilles?*

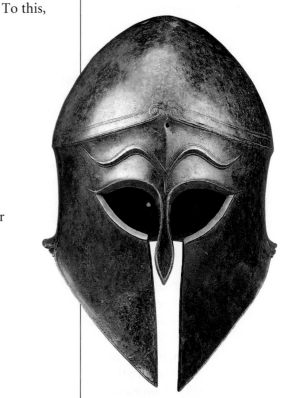

Corinthian bronze helmet
(c. 540 B.C.E.).

The Minneapolis Institute of Arts.
Gift of funds from Ruth and Bruce
Dayton (2001.80.1).

round Priam's town three times and could not face you.
Now my soul would have me stand and fight,
whether I kill you or am killed. So come,
300   we'll summon gods here as our witnesses,
none higher, arbiters° of a pact: I swear
that, terrible as you are,
I'll not insult your corpse should Zeus allow me
victory in the end, your life as prize.
305   Once I have your gear, I'll give your body
back to Achaeans. Grant me, too, this grace."

But swift Achilles frowned at him and said:

"Hector, I'll have no talk of pacts with you,
forever unforgiven as you are.
310   As between men and lions there are none,
no concord between wolves and sheep, but all
hold one another hateful through and through,
so there can be no courtesy between us,
no sworn truce, till one of us is down
315   and glutting with his blood the wargod Ares.
Summon up what skills you have. By god,
you'd better be a spearman and a fighter!
Now there is no way out. Pallas Athena
will have the upper hand of you. The weapon
320   belongs to me. You'll pay the reckoning
in full for all the pain my men have borne,
who met death by your spear."
                           He twirled and cast
his shaft with its long shadow. Splendid Hector,
keeping his eye upon the point, eluded it
325   by ducking at the instant of the cast,
so shaft and bronze shank passed him overhead
and punched into the earth. But unperceived
by Hector, Pallas Athena plucked it out
and gave it back to Achilles. Hector said:

330   "A clean miss. Godlike as you are,
you have not yet known doom for me from Zeus.
You thought you had, by heaven. Then you turned
into a word-thrower, hoping to make me lose
my fighting heart and head in fear of you.
335   You cannot plant your spear between my shoulders
while I am running. If you have the gift,
just put it through my chest as I come forward.
Now it's for you to dodge my own. Would god
you'd give the whole shaft lodging in your body!

301. arbiters *n. pl.:* judges.

303–322. Hector vows to treat Achilles' corpse with respect if Hector wins the fight. However, Achilles refuses to extend the same courtesy to Hector.

? *What reason does Achilles give for refusing Hector's request?*

Athena constructing the Trojan Horse, from a red-figure kylix (detail) (6th century B.C.E.).
Museo Archaeologico, Florence.

340   War for the Trojans would be eased
       if you were blotted out, bane° that you are."

       With this he twirled his long spearshaft and cast it,
       hitting his enemy mid-shield, but off
       and away the spear rebounded. Furious
345   that he had lost it, made his throw for nothing,
       Hector stood bemused. He had no other.
       Then he gave a great shout to Deiphobus
       to ask for a long spear. But there was no one
       near him, not a soul. Now in his heart
350   the Trojan realized the truth and said:

       "This is the end. The gods are calling deathward.
       I had thought
       a good soldier, Deiphobus, was with me.
       He is inside the walls. Athena tricked me.
355   Death is near, and black, not at a distance,
       not to be evaded. Long ago
       this hour must have been to Zeus's liking
       and to the liking of his archer son.°
       They have been well disposed before, but now
360   the appointed time's upon me. Still, I would not
       die without delivering a stroke,
       or die ingloriously, but in some action
       memorable to men in days to come."

       With this he drew the whetted blade that hung
365   upon his left flank, ponderous and long,
       collecting all his might the way an eagle
       narrows himself to dive through shady cloud
       and strike a lamb or cowering hare: so Hector
       lanced ahead and swung his whetted blade.
370   Achilles with wild fury in his heart
       pulled in upon his chest his beautiful shield—
       his helmet with four burnished metal ridges
       nodding above it, and the golden crest
       Hephaestus° locked there tossing in the wind.
375   Conspicuous as the evening star that comes,
       amid the first in heaven, at fall of night,
       and stands most lovely in the west, so shone
       in sunlight the fine-pointed spear
       Achilles poised in his right hand, with deadly
380   aim at Hector, at the skin where most
       it lay exposed. But nearly all was covered
       by the bronze gear he took from slain Patroclus,
       showing only, where his collarbones

341. bane *n.:* cause of distress, death, or ruin.

349–360. *What does Hector realize once he finds that Deiphobus is not really by his side?*

358. archer son: Apollo.

374. Hephaestus (hē·fes′təs): blacksmith of the gods, who forged new arms for Achilles after Patroclus, wearing Achilles' armor, was slain by Hector.

divided neck and shoulders, the bare throat
385 where the destruction of a life is quickest.
Here, then, as the Trojan charged, Achilles
drove his point straight through the tender neck,
but did not cut the windpipe, leaving Hector
able to speak and to respond. He fell
390 aside into the dust. And Prince Achilles
now exulted:

                    "Hector, had you thought
that you could kill Patroclus and be safe?
Nothing to dread from me; I was not there.
All childishness. Though distant then, Patroclus's
395 comrade in arms was greater far than he—
and it is I who had been left behind
that day beside the deep-sea ships who now
have made your knees give way. The dogs and kites
will rip your body. His will lie in honor
400 when the Achaeans give him funeral."

Hector, barely whispering, replied:

"I beg you by your soul and by your parents,
do not let the dogs feed on me
in your encampment by the ships. Accept
405 the bronze and gold my father will provide
as gifts, my father and her ladyship
my mother. Let them have my body back,
so that our men and women may accord me
decency of fire when I am dead."

410 Achilles the great runner scowled and said:

"Beg me no beggary by soul or parents,
whining dog! Would god my passion drove me
to slaughter you and eat you raw, you've caused
such agony to me! No man exists
415 who could defend you from the carrion pack—
not if they spread for me ten times your ransom,
twenty times, and promise more as well;
aye, not if Priam, son of Dardanus,
tells them to buy you for your weight in gold!
420 You'll have no bed of death, nor will you be
laid out and mourned by her who gave you birth.
Dogs and birds will have you, every scrap."

Then at the point of death Lord Hector said:

375–390. Hector is wearing Achilles' old armor. Achilles had given the armor to his friend Patroclus, whom Hector killed.

? *How does Achilles wound Hector?*

402–422. Hector begs Achilles to return his body to his parents so that they can cremate and bury it. His plea emphasizes the idea that his soul will never be allowed to rest if his body is not properly buried.

? *How does Achilles respond to Hector's request? How does his response reinforce the rage and bitterness Achilles feels toward Hector?*

"I see you now for what you are. No chance
425   to win you over. Iron in your breast
your heart is. Think a bit, though: this may be
a thing the gods in anger hold against you
on that day when Paris and Apollo
destroy you at the Gates,° great as you are."

430   Even as he spoke, the end came, and death hid him;
spirit from body fluttered to undergloom,
bewailing fate that made him leave his youth
and manhood in the world. And as he died
Achilles spoke again. He said:

435   "Die, make an end. I shall accept my own
whenever Zeus and the other gods desire."

At this he pulled his spearhead from the body,
laying it aside, and stripped
the bloodstained shield and cuirass° from his shoulders.
440   Other Achaeans hastened round to see
Hector's fine body and his comely face,
and no one came who did not stab the body.
Glancing at one another they would say:

"Now Hector has turned vulnerable, softer
445   than when he put the torches to the ships!"

And he who said this would inflict a wound.
When the great master of pursuit, Achilles,
had the body stripped, he stood among them,
saying swiftly:
                              "Friends, my lords and captains
450   of Argives, now that the gods at last have let me
bring to earth this man who wrought
havoc among us—more than all the rest—
come, we'll offer battle around the city,
to learn the intentions of the Trojans now.
455   Will they give up their strongpoint° at this loss?
Can they fight on, though Hector's dead?

                                             But wait:

why do I ponder, why take up these questions?
Down by the ships Patroclus's body lies
unwept, unburied. I shall not forget him
460   while I can keep my feet among the living.
If in the dead world they forget the dead,
I say there, too, I shall remember him,
my friend. Men of Achaea, lift a song!
Down to the ships we go, and take this body,

428–429. Paris . . . Gates:
Achilles is later slain by Paris,
who shoots an arrow into
Achilles' heel, the only part of
his body that is vulnerable.

439. cuirass (kwi·ras′) *n.:*
armor protecting the breast
and back.

440–446. *What do
other Achaeans do to
Hector's body after he is
killed by Achilles?*

455. strongpoint *n.:* Troy.

465 our glory. We have beaten Hector down,
     to whom as to a god the Trojans prayed."

     Indeed, he had in mind for Hector's body
     outrage and shame. Behind both feet he pierced
     the tendons, heel to ankle. Rawhide cords
470 he drew through both and lashed them to his chariot,
     letting the man's head trail. Stepping aboard,
     bearing the great trophy of the arms,°
     he shook the reins, and whipped the team ahead
     into a willing run. A dustcloud rose
475 above the furrowing body; the dark tresses
     flowed behind, and the head so princely once
     lay back in dust. Zeus gave him to his enemies
     to be defiled in his own fatherland.
     So his whole head was blackened. Looking down,
480 his mother tore her braids, threw off her veil,
     and wailed, heartbroken to behold her son.
     Piteously his father groaned, and round him
     lamentation spread throughout the town,
     most like the clamor to be heard if Ilion's
485 towers, top to bottom, seethed in flames.
     They barely stayed the old man, mad with grief,
     from passing through the gates. Then in the mire
     he rolled, and begged them all, each man by name:

     "Relent, friends. It is hard; but let me go
490 out of the city to the Achaean ships.
     I'll make my plea to that demonic heart.
     He may feel shame before his peers, or pity
     my old age. His father, too, is old.
     Peleus, who brought him up to be a scourge
495 to Trojans, cruel to all, but most to me,
     so many of my sons in flower of youth
     he cut away. And, though I grieve, I cannot
     mourn them all as much as I do one,
     for whom my grief will take me to the grave—
500 and that is Hector. Why could he not have died
     where I might hold him? In our weeping, then,
     his mother, now so destitute, and I
     might have had surfeit° and relief of tears."

     These were the words of Priam as he wept,
505 and all his people groaned. Then in her turn

Vocabulary

destitute (des′tə·tōōt′) *adj.*: abandoned.

467–478. *What does this description make you realize about Achilles?*

472. great trophy of the arms: Hector's armor.

Zeus gave him to his enemies to be defiled in his own fatherland.

503. surfeit *n.*: excess.

Achilles dragging the body
of Hector around the walls
of Troy (detail). Attic black
figure. Hydria.

Attributed to the Antiope Group.
William Francis Warden Fund, Museum
of Fine Arts, Boston (63.473).

Hecuba led the women in lamentation:

"Child, I am lost now. Can I bear my life
after the death of suffering your death?
You were my pride in all my nights and days,
510   pride of the city, pillar to the Trojans
and Trojan women. Everyone looked to you
as though you were a god, and rightly so.
You were their greatest glory while you lived.
Now your doom and death have come upon you."

515   These were her mournful words. But Hector's lady
still knew nothing; no one came to tell her
of Hector's stand outside the gates. She wove
upon her loom, deep in the lofty house,
a double purple web with rose design.
520   Calling her maids in waiting,
she ordered a big caldron on a tripod
set on the hearthfire, to provide a bath
for Hector when he came home from the fight.
Poor wife, how far removed from baths he was

> **509–513.** *In these
> lines, what do you learn
> about the way Hector was
> viewed by his fellow Trojans?*

525   she could not know, as at Achilles' hands
Athena brought him down.

                               Then from the tower
she heard a wailing and a distant moan.
Her knees shook, and she let her shuttle° fall,
and called out to her maids again:

                                 "Come here.
530   Two must follow me, to see this action.
I heard my husband's queenly mother cry.
I feel my heart rise, throbbing in my throat.
My knees are like stone under me. Some blow
is coming home to Priam's sons and daughters.
535   Ah, could it never reach my ears! I die
of dread that Achilles may have cut off Hector,
blocked my bold husband from the city wall,
to drive him down the plain alone! By now
he may have ended Hector's deathly pride.
540   He never kept his place amid the chariots
but drove ahead. He would not be outdone
by anyone in courage."

                             Saying this, she ran
like a madwoman through the megaron,°
her heart convulsed. Her maids kept at her side.
545   On reaching the great tower and the soldiers,
Andromache stood gazing from the wall
and saw him being dragged before the city.
Chariot horses at a brutal gallop
pulled the torn body toward the decked ships.
550   Blackness of night covered her eyes; she fell
backward swooning, sighing out her life,
and let her shining headdress fall, her hood
and diadem,° her plaited band and veil
that Aphrodite once had given her,
555   on that day when, from Eetion's house,
for a thousand bridal gifts, Lord Hector led her.
Now, at her side, kinswomen of her lord
supported her among them, dazed and faint
to the point of death. But when she breathed again
560   and her stunned heart recovered, in a burst
of sobbing she called out among the women:

"Hector! Here is my desolation. Both
had this in store from birth—from yours in Troy
in Priam's palace, mine by wooded Placus
565   at Thebe in the home of Eetion,
my father, who took care of me in childhood,
a man cursed by fate, a fated daughter.

528. shuttle *n.:* as used here, an instrument that carries thread back and forth, used in weaving.

? 527–549. *How does Andromache learn that her husband has been killed?*

543. megaron (meg′ə·rän) *n.:* central hall of the house.

553. diadem *n.:* ornamental headband.

How I could wish I never had been born!
Now under earth's roof to the house of Death
570 you go your way and leave me here, bereft,
lonely, in anguish without end. The child
we wretches had is still in infancy;
you cannot be a pillar to him, Hector,
now you are dead, nor he to you. And should
575 this boy escape the misery of the war,
there will be toil and sorrow for him later,
as when strangers move his boundary stones.°
The day that orphans him will leave him lonely,
downcast in everything, cheeks wet with tears,
580 in hunger going to his father's friends
to tug at one man's cloak, another's chiton.°
Some will be kindly: one may lift a cup
to wet his lips at least, though not his throat;
but from the board some child with living parents
585 gives him a push, a slap, with biting words:
'Outside, you there! Your father is not with us
here at our feast!' And the boy Astyanax
will run to his forlorn mother. Once he fed
on marrow only and the fat of lamb,
590 high on his father's knees. And when sleep came
to end his play, he slept in a nurse's arms,
brimful of happiness, in a soft bed.
But now he'll know sad days and many of them,
missing his father. 'Lord of the lower town'
595 the Trojans call him. They know, you alone,
Lord Hector, kept their gates and their long walls.
Beside the beaked ships now, far from your kin,
the blowflies' maggots in a swarm will eat you
naked, after the dogs have had their fill.
600 Ah, there are folded garments in your chambers,
delicate and fine, of women's weaving.
These, by heaven, I'll burn to the last thread
in blazing fire! They are no good to you,
they cannot cover you in death. So let them
605 go, let them be burnt as an offering
from Trojans and their women in your honor."

Thus she mourned, and the women wailed in answer.

571–594. *What does Andromache predict will happen to her son now that Hector is dead?*

577. move his boundary stones: steal his land and estates.

581. chiton (kī′tən) *n.*: tunic.

597–606. These lines convey the importance of proper burial of the dead. *Do you predict that Hector will be buried properly? Why or why not?*

Funeral of Patroclus,
from a red-figure krater
(c. 5th century B.C.E.).

Museo Archeologico Nazionale, Naples.

from BOOK 24: A Grace Given in Sorrow

*After he slays Hector in Book 22, Achilles prepares for Patroclus's
ceremonial funeral. When the Greeks burn Patroclus's body, they
also hold elaborate athletic contests, a custom in funeral services for
distinguished men (Book 23).*

*As Book 24 opens, Achilles is still so enraged at Hector's killing of
Patroclus that he refuses to give up Hector's body for burial. This is
a particularly offensive form of revenge, for both the Greeks and the
Trojans believed that certain funeral rites were necessary before the
soul of a dead person could find rest. Achilles' shameful treatment
of Hector's body offends Zeus, who finally orders Achilles to give up
the body to Priam. The aged king, bowed with grief and bearing a
rich ransom to exchange for his son's corpse, is escorted to the Greek
camp by the god Hermes, who is disguised as a young man.*

Now night had fallen,
bringing the sentries to their supper fire,
but the glimmering god Hermes, the Wayfinder,
showered a mist of slumber on them all.
5   As quick as thought, he had the gates unbarred
and open to let the wagon enter, bearing
the old king and the ransom.

                                Going seaward

they came to the lofty quarters of Achilles,
a lodge the Myrmidons built for their lord
10 of pine trees cut and trimmed, and shaggy thatch
from mowings in deep meadows. Posts were driven
round the wide courtyard in a palisade,°
whose gate one crossbar held, one beam of pine.
It took three men to slam this home, and three
15 to draw the bolt again—but great Achilles
worked his entryway alone with ease.
And now Hermes, who lights the way for mortals,
opened for Priam, took him safely in
with all his rich gifts for the son of Peleus.
20 Then the god dropped the reins, and stepping down
he said:

                      "I am no mortal wagoner,
but Hermes, sir. My father° sent me here
to be your guide amid the Achaean men.
Now that is done, I'm off to heaven again
25 and will not visit Achilles. That would be
to compromise an immortal's dignity—
to be received with guests of mortal station.
Go take his knees, and make your supplication:
invoke his father, his mother, and his child;
30 pray that his heart be touched, that he be reconciled."

Now Hermes turned, departing for Olympus,
and Priam vaulted down. He left Idaeus°
to hold the teams in check, while he went forward
into the lodge. He found Achilles, dear
35 to Zeus, there in his chair, with officers
at ease across the room. Only Automedon°
and Alcimus° were busy near Achilles,
for he had just now made an end of dinner,
eating and drinking, and the laden boards
lay near him still upon the trestles.

                                    Priam,
40 the great king of Troy, passed by the others,
knelt down, took in his arms Achilles' knees,
and kissed the hands of wrath that killed his sons.

1–7. Hermes is the messenger of the gods. He also brings the spirits of the deceased to the Underworld.
? *How does Hermes get Priam into Achilles' camp?*

12. palisade *n.:* barrier.

22. father *n.:* Zeus.

? **28–30.** *What does Hermes suggest Priam do to win over Achilles?*

32. Idaeus (ī′dē′əs): herald of the Trojans.

36. Automedon (ô·täm′ə·dän): Achilles' charioteer.

37. Alcimus (al·sī′məs): one of Achilles' officers.

When, taken with mad Folly in his own land,
45   a man does murder and in exile finds
refuge in some rich house, then all who see him
stand in awe.
So these men stood.

                                                    Achilles
gazed in wonder at the splendid king,
50   and his companions marveled too, all silent,
with glances to and fro. Now Priam prayed
to the man before him:

                          "Remember your own father,
Achilles, in your godlike youth: his years
like mine are many, and he stands upon
55   the fearful doorstep of old age. He, too,
is hard pressed, it may be, by those around him,
there being no one able to defend him
from bane of war and ruin. Ah, but he
may nonetheless hear news of you alive,
60   and so with glad heart hope through all his days
for sight of his dear son, come back from Troy,
while I have deathly fortune.

                                              Noble sons
I fathered here, but scarce one man is left me.
Fifty I had when the Achaeans came,
65   nineteen out of a single belly, others
born of attendant women. Most are gone.
Raging Ares cut their knees from under them.
And he who stood alone among them all,
their champion, and Troy's, ten days ago
70   you killed him, fighting for his land, my prince,
Hector.

                          It is for him that I have come
among these ships, to beg him back from you,
and I bring ransom without stint.°

                                              Achilles,
be reverent toward the great gods! And take
75   pity on me, remember your own father.
Think me more pitiful by far, since I
have brought myself to do what no man else
has done before—to lift to my lips the hand
of one who killed my son."

                                    Now in Achilles
80   the evocation of his father stirred
new longing, and an ache of grief. He lifted
the old man's hand and gently put him by.
Then both were overborne as they remembered:
the old king huddled at Achilles' feet

52–62. In what ways are Achilles' father and Priam similar? In what ways are they different?

73. **stint:** limit; restriction.

79–93. What images in these lines emphasize Priam's age and frailty?

85 wept, and wept for Hector, killer of men,
while great Achilles wept for his own father
as for Patroclus once again; and sobbing
filled the room.

But when Achilles' heart

had known the luxury of tears, and pain
90 within his breast and bones had passed away,
he stood then, raised the old king up, in pity
for his gray head and graybeard cheek, and spoke
in a warm rush of words:

"Ah, sad and old!

Trouble and pain you've borne, and bear, aplenty.
95 Only a great will could have brought you here
among the Achaean ships, and here alone
before the eyes of one who stripped your sons,
your many sons, in battle. Iron must be
the heart within you. Come, then, and sit down.
100 We'll probe our wounds no more but let them rest,
though grief lies heavy on us. Tears heal nothing,
drying so stiff and cold. This is the way
the gods ordained the destiny of men,
to bear such burdens in our lives, while they
105 feel no affliction. At the door of Zeus
are those two urns° of good and evil gifts
that he may choose for us; and one for whom
the lightning's joyous king dips in both urns
will have by turns bad luck and good. But one
110 to whom he sends all evil—that man goes
contemptible by the will of Zeus; ravenous
hunger drives him over the wondrous earth,
unresting, without honor from gods or men.
Mixed fortune came to Peleus. Shining gifts
115 at the gods' hands he had from birth: felicity,
wealth overflowing, rule of the Myrmidons,
a bride immortal at his mortal side.
But then Zeus gave afflictions too—no family
of powerful sons grew up for him at home,
120 but one child, of all seasons and of none.
Can I stand by him in his age? Far from my country
I sit at Troy to grieve you and your children.
You, too, sir, in time past were fortunate,
we hear men say. From Macar's isle of Lesbos
125 northward, and south of Phrygia and the Straits,°
no one had wealth like yours, or sons like yours.
Then gods out of the sky sent you this bitterness:
the years of siege, the battles and the losses.
Endure it, then. And do not mourn forever

Bust of Zeus (c.150–c. 200 C.E.)
Ammon. Marble.

The British Museum, London.

106. urns *n. pl.:* vases with pedestals.

105–128. *How does Achilles explain good and bad fortune? How have the fortunes of his father (Peleus) and King Priam been similar?*

125. the Straits: the Dardanelles, a narrow waterway between the Aegean Sea and the Sea of Marmara.

130   for your dead son. There is no remedy.
You will not make him stand again. Rather
await some new misfortune to be suffered."

The old king in his majesty replied:

"Never give me a chair, my lord, while Hector
135   lies in your camp uncared for. Yield him to me
now. Allow me sight of him. Accept
the many gifts I bring. May they reward you,
and may you see your home again.
You spared my life at once and let me live."

140   Achilles, the great runner, frowned and eyed him
under his brows:
                    "Do not vex me, sir," he said.
"I have intended, in my own good time,
to yield up Hector to you. She who bore me,°
the daughter of the Ancient of the sea,
145   has come with word to me from Zeus. I know
in your case, too—though you say nothing, Priam—
that some god guided you to the shipways here.
No strong man in his best days could make entry
into this camp. How could he pass the guard,
or force our gateway?
150
                         Therefore, *let me be*.
Sting my sore heart again, and even here,
under my own roof, suppliant though you are,
I may not spare you, sir, but trample on
the express command of Zeus!"

                         When he heard this,
155   the old man feared him and obeyed with silence.
Now like a lion at one bound Achilles
left the room. Close at his back the officers
Automedon and Alcimus went out—
comrades in arms whom he esteemed the most
160   after the dead Patroclus. They unharnessed
mules and horses, led the old king's crier
to a low bench and sat him down.
Then from the polished wagon
they took the piled-up price of Hector's body.
165   One chiton and two capes they left aside
as dress and shrouding for the homeward journey.
Then, calling to the women slaves, Achilles
ordered the body bathed and rubbed with oil—

143. She who bore me:
Thetis.

> **141–154.** *What does Achilles realize about the way Priam was able to enter the camp? How does he threaten Priam?*

but lifted, too, and placed apart, where Priam
170 could not see his son—for seeing Hector
he might in his great pain give way to rage,
and fury then might rise up in Achilles
to slay the old king, flouting Zeus's word.
So after bathing and anointing Hector
175 they drew the shirt and beautiful shrouding over him.
Then with his own hands lifting him, Achilles
laid him upon a couch, and with his two
companions aiding, placed him in the wagon.
Now a bitter groan burst from Achilles,
who stood and prayed to his own dead friend:
180   "Patroclus,
do not be angry with me, if somehow
even in the world of Death you learn of this—
that I released Prince Hector to his father.
The gifts he gave were not unworthy. Aye,
185 and you shall have your share, this time as well."

The Prince Achilles turned back to his quarters.
He took again the splendid chair that stood
against the farther wall, then looked at Priam
and made his declaration:
          "As you wished, sir,
190 the body of your son is now set free.
He lies in state. At the first sight of Dawn
you shall take charge of him yourself and see him.
Now let us think of supper. We are told
that even Niobe in her extremity
195 took thought for bread—though all her brood had perished,
her six young girls and six tall sons. Apollo,
making his silver longbow whip and sing,
shot the lads down, and Artemis with raining
arrows killed the daughters—all this after
200 Niobe had compared herself with Leto,
the smooth-cheeked goddess.
        She has borne two children,
Niobe said, How many have I borne!
But soon those two destroyed the twelve.
             Besides,
nine days the dead lay stark, no one could bury them,
205 for Zeus had turned all folk of theirs to stone.
The gods made graves for them on the tenth day,
and then at last, being weak and spent with weeping,
Niobe thought of food. Among the rocks
of Sipylus' lonely mountainside, where nymphs

163–173. Achilles is careful not to allow Priam to see Hector's body.
? Why does Achilles insist that Hector's body be hidden from Priam?

"As you wished, sir, the body of your son is now set free. He lies in state. At the first sight of Dawn you shall take charge of him yourself and see him."

210 who race Achelous's° river go to rest,
     she, too, long turned to stone, somewhere broods on
     the gall immortal gods gave her to drink.°

     Like her we'll think of supper, noble sir.
     Weep for your son again when you have borne him
215 back to Troy; there he'll be mourned indeed."

     In one swift movement now Achilles caught
     and slaughtered a white lamb. His officers
     flayed it, skillful in their butchering
     to dress the flesh; they cut bits for the skewers,
220 roasted, and drew them off, done to a turn.
     Automedon dealt loaves into the baskets
     on the great board; Achilles served the meat.
     Then all their hands went out upon the supper.
     When thirst and appetite were turned away,
225 Priam, the heir of Dardanos, gazed long
     in wonder at Achilles' form and scale—
     so like the gods in aspect. And Achilles
     in his turn gazed in wonder upon Priam,
     royal in visage° as in speech. Both men
230 in contemplation found rest for their eyes,
     till the old hero, Priam, broke the silence:

     "Make a bed ready for me, son of Thetis,
     and let us know the luxury of sleep.
     From that hour when my son died at your hands
235 till now, my eyelids have not closed in slumber
     over my eyes, but groaning where I sat
     I tasted pain and grief a thousandfold,
     or lay down rolling in my courtyard mire.
     Here for the first time I have swallowed bread
     and made myself drink wine.
240   Before, I could not."

     Achilles ordered men and serving women
     to make a bed outside, in the covered forecourt,
     with purple rugs piled up and sheets outspread
     and coverings of fleeces laid on top.
245 The girls went out with torches in their hands
     and soon deftly made up a double bed.
     Then Achilles, defiant of Agamemnon,
     told his guest:
                        "Dear venerable sir,
     you'll sleep outside tonight, in case an Achaean
250 officer turns up, one of those men

210. Achelous (ə·kel′ō·əs): river god.

194–212. Niobe (nī′ō·bē′) . . . **drink:** woman whose children were killed by the goddess Artemis and the god Apollo because she boasted of her superiority to their mother, Leto; Niobe was then turned into a rock, from which her tears are still said to flow. This rock is believed to be on a mountain called Sipylus (si′pil·əs) in Turkey.

229. visage *n.:* face; expression.

232–244. Priam has not been able to sleep since his son's death.
? What is the significance of Achilles' offering of hospitality to Priam?

King Priam begging Achilles to let him have the body of Hector, from a red-figure *skyphos* (detail) (c. 490 B.C.E.).

Kunsthistorisches Museum, Vienna.

who are forever taking counsel with me—
as well they may. If one should see you here
as the dark night runs on, he would report it
to the Lord Marshal Agamemnon. Then
255   return of the body would only be delayed.
Now tell me this, and give me a straight answer:
How many days do you require
for the funeral of Prince Hector?—I should know
how long to wait, and hold the Achaean army."

260   Old Priam in his majesty replied:

"If you would have me carry out the burial,
Achilles, here is the way to do me grace.
As we are penned in the town, but must bring wood
from the distant hills, the Trojans are afraid.
265   We should have mourning for nine days in hall,
then on the tenth conduct his funeral
and feast the troops and commons;

261–269. *What conditions does Priam set for Hector's burial?*

on the eleventh we should make his tomb,
and on the twelfth give battle, if we must."

Achilles said:

270   "As you command, old Priam,
the thing is done. I shall suspend the war
for those eleven days that you require."

He took the old man's right hand by the wrist
and held it, to <u>allay</u> his fear.

                                    Now crier
275   and king with hearts brimful retired to rest
in the sheltered forecourt, while Achilles slept
deep in his palisaded lodge. Beside him,
lovely in her youth, Briseis° lay.
And other gods and soldiers all night long,
280   by slumber quieted, slept on. But slumber
would not come to Hermes the Good Companion,
as he considered how to ease the way
for Priam from the camp, to send him through
unseen by the formidable gatekeepers.
285   Then Hermes came to Priam's pillow, saying:

"Sir, no thought of danger shakes your rest,
as you sleep on, being great Achilles' guest,
amid men fierce as hunters in a ring.
You triumphed in a costly ransoming,
290   but three times costlier your own would be
to your surviving sons—a monarch's fee—
if this should come to Agamemnon's ear
and all the Achaean host should learn that you are here."

The old king started up in fright, and woke
295   his herald. Hermes yoked the mules and horses,
took the reins, then inland like the wind
he drove through all the encampment, seen by no one.
When they reached Xanthus,° eddying and running
god-begotten river, at the ford,
300   Hermes departed for Olympus. Dawn
spread out her yellow robe on all the earth,
as they drove on toward Troy, with groans and sighs,
and the mule-team pulled the wagon and the body.
And no one saw them, not a man or woman,
305   before Cassandra.° Tall as the pale-gold

278. Briseis: In order to appease Achilles, Agamemnon had Briseis returned to him.

298. Xanthus (zan′thəs): also called Scamander.

305. Cassandra (kə·san′drə): daughter of Priam and Hecuba; in Greek mythology, Apollo gives her the gift of prophecy, but when she rejects his advances, he decrees that no one will believe her predictions. She figures more prominently in other versions of the Trojan War legend, such as Euripides' drama *The Trojan Women*.

Vocabulary

allay (a·lā′) v.: to relieve; calm.

goddess Aphrodite, she had climbed
the citadel of Pergamus° at dawn.
Now looking down she saw her father come
in his war-car, and saw the crier there,
310 and saw Lord Hector on his bed of death
upon the mulecart. The girl wailed and cried
to all the city:

307. Pergamus (pʉr′gə·məs):
citadel, or fortress, of Troy.

? 311–320. *How do the
Trojans react to the sight
of Hector's body?*

"Oh, look down, look down,
go to your windows, men of Troy, and women,
see Lord Hector now! Remember joy
315 at seeing him return alive from battle,
exalting all our city and our land!"

Now, at the sight of Hector, all gave way
to loss and longing, and all crowded down
to meet the escort and body near the gates,
320 till no one in the town was left at home.
There Hector's lady and his gentle mother
tore their hair for him, flinging themselves
upon the wagon to embrace his person
while the crowd groaned. All that long day
325 until the sun went down they might have mourned
in tears before the gateway. But old Priam
spoke to them from his chariot:
"Make way,
let the mules pass. You'll have your fill of weeping
later, when I've brought the body home."

*N ow, at the sight of
Hector, all gave way
to loss and longing, and
all crowded down to meet
the escort and body near
the gates . . .*

330 They parted then, and made way for the wagon,
allowing Priam to reach the famous hall.
They laid the body of Hector in his bed,
and brought in minstrels, men to lead the dirge.°
While these wailed out, the women answered, moaning.
335 Andromache of the ivory-white arms
held in her lap between her hands
the head of Hector who had killed so many.
Now she lamented:
"You've been torn from life,
my husband, in young manhood, and you leave me
340 empty in our hall. The boy's a child
whom you and I, poor souls, conceived; I doubt
he'll come to manhood. Long before, great Troy
will go down plundered, citadel and all,
now that you are lost, who guarded it
345 and kept it, and preserved its wives and children.
They will be shipped off in the murmuring hulls

333. dirge *n.:* funeral hymn.

? 340–355. *What does
Andromache predict will
happen to herself and her
son? What reasons does she
give for her prediction?*

one day, and I along with all the rest.
You, my little one, either you come with me
to do some grinding labor, some base toil
350 for a harsh master, or an Achaean soldier
will grip you by the arm and hurl you down
from a tower° here to a miserable death—
out of his anger for a brother, a father,
or even a son that Hector killed. Achaeans
355 in hundreds mouthed black dust under his blows.
He was no moderate man in war, your father,
and that is why they mourn him through the city.
Hector, you gave your parents grief and pain
but left me loneliest, and heartbroken.
360 You could not open your strong arms to me
from your deathbed, or say a thoughtful word,
for me to cherish all my life long
as I weep for you night and day."

Her voice broke,

and a wail came from the women. Hecuba
365 lifted her lamenting voice among them:

"Hector, dearest of sons to me, in life
you had the favor of the immortal gods,
and they have cared for you in death as well.
Achilles captured other sons of mine
370 in other years, and sold them overseas
to Samos, Imbros, and the smoky island,
Lemnos.° That was not his way with you.
After he took your life, cutting you down
with his sharp-bladed spear, he trussed and dragged you
375 many times round the barrow° of his friend,
Patroclus, whom you killed—though not by this
could that friend live again. But now I find you
fresh as pale dew, seeming newly dead,
like one to whom Apollo of the silver bow
380 had given easy death with his mild arrows."

Hecuba sobbed again, and the wails redoubled.
Then it was Helen's turn to make lament:

"Dear Hector, dearest brother to me by far!
My husband is Alexandros,
385 who brought me here to Troy—God, that I might
have died sooner! This is the twentieth year
since I left home, and left my fatherland.
But never did I have an evil word
or gesture from you. No—and when some other
390 brother-in-law or sister would revile me,

351–352. hurl you down from a tower: Indeed, after the fall of Troy, Astyanax was thrown by the Greek conquerors from the walls of the city.

371–372. Samos (sā′mäs′), **Imbros** (ēm′brôs) **...Lemnos** (lem′näs′): islands in the Aegean Sea.

375. barrow *n.:* mound of earth and stones built over a grave.

383–398. *How does Helen say most Trojans treated her? How did Hector treat Helen?*

or if my mother-in-law spoke to me bitterly—
but Priam never did, being as mild
as my own father—you would bring her round
with your kind heart and gentle speech. Therefore
395 I weep for you and for myself as well,
given this fate, this grief. In all wide Troy
no one is left who will befriend me, none;
they all shudder at me."

                                              Helen wept,
and a moan came from the people, hearing her.
400 Then Priam, the old king, commanded them:

"Trojans, bring firewood to the edge of town.
No need to fear an ambush of the Argives.
When he dismissed me from the camp, Achilles
told me clearly they will not harass us,
405 not until dawn comes for the twelfth day."

Then yoking mules and oxen to their wagons
the people thronged before the city gates.
Nine days they labored, bringing countless loads
of firewood to the town. When Dawn that lights
410 the world of mortals came for the tenth day,
they carried greathearted Hector out at last,
and all in tears placed his dead body high
upon its pyre, then cast a torch below.
When the young Dawn with finger tips of rose
415 made heaven bright, the Trojan people massed
about Prince Hector's ritual fire.
All being gathered and assembled, first
they quenched the smoking pyre with tawny wine
wherever flames had licked their way, then friends
420 and brothers picked his white bones from the char
in sorrow, while the tears rolled down their cheeks.
In a golden urn they put the bones,
shrouding the urn with veiling of soft purple.
Then in a grave dug deep they placed it
425 and heaped it with great stones. The men were quick
to raise the death-mound, while in every quarter
lookouts were posted to ensure against
an Achaean surprise attack. When they had finished
raising the barrow, they returned to Ilion,
430 where all sat down to banquet in his honor
in the hall of Priam king. So they performed
the funeral rites of Hector, tamer of horses.

King Priam before the Tomb of Hector in the Temple of Apollo, from *History of the Destruction of Troy* (c. 1500). From the workshop of Jean Colombe.

Bibliothèque nationale de France, Paris.

414–432. *What are the key details of Hector's funeral rites? Why do you think these details about a Trojan enemy's funeral have been included in this Greek epic?*

CRITICAL COMMENT

Two Translations of Homer's *Iliad*

INFORMATIONAL TEXT

A work of literature in translation is the creation of at least two individuals: the original writer and the translator(s). Translators do much more than transcribe words; they practice a complex and challenging art that involves constant aesthetic choices and a good deal of subjective interpretation. They must understand the meaning, structure, and style of a work in its original language, then decide how best to preserve and convey those elements artfully in a second language. The original language may have qualities—in terms of grammatical structure, meter, sound (alliteration, rhyme, consonance, onomatopoeia), idiomatic expressions, and other attributes—that the second language does not possess.

Translators must strike a balance between the two extremes of upholding form over content or content over form. The best translators preserve the integrity of the original text while crafting a new text that has literary merit in its own right.

There are many English translations of Homer's *Iliad*, both in prose and in verse. Below is an excerpt from Book 22 of Robert Fagles's recent translation of the *Iliad*. Read these lines of verse; then, on page 146, re-read lines 157–173 of the Fitzgerald translation.

Achilles Defeating Hector (detail) (17th century) by Peter Paul Rubens.
Musée des Beaux-Arts, Paris.

                           So he wavered,
waiting there, but Achilles was closing on him now
like the god of war, the fighter's helmet flashing,
over his right shoulder shaking the Pelian ash spear,
that terror, and the bronze around his body flared
like a raging fire of the rising, blazing sun.
Hector looked up, saw him, started to tremble,
nerve gone, he could hold his ground no longer,
he left the gates behind and away he fled in fear—
and Achilles went for him, fast, sure of his speed
as the wild mountain hawk, the quickest thing on wings,
launching smoothly, swooping down on a cringing dove
and the dove flits out from under, the hawk screaming
over the quarry, plunging over and over, his fury
driving him down to break and tear his kill—
so Achilles flew at him, breakneck on in fury
with Hector fleeing along the walls of Troy,
fast as his legs would go.

? What different images does each translator emphasize in showing Hector's fear, Achilles' wrath and determination, and the speed with which Hector flees? What are the differences in the way each translator handles the epic simile that compares Achilles' pursuit of Hector to a hawk hunting its prey? Which version do you prefer? Why?

Response and Analysis

from Books 22 and 24

Reading Check

1. What advice do Priam and Hecuba give to Hector as he stands outside the city walls?

2. In lines 119–156 of Book 22, what courses of action does Hector consider and reject before fighting Achilles?

3. How does Athena deceive Hector? Why is Zeus unable to save Hector?

4. What is Hector's dying request? How does Achilles respond to it?

5. What does Achilles agree to do to allow Hector a proper burial?

Thinking Critically

6. The meeting of Hector and Achilles in Book 22 is the dramatic **climax** of the *Iliad.* At this suspenseful confrontation, Hector trembles and then runs away. How does Homer prepare you for Hector's flight by his revelation of the Trojan's thoughts and by his description of Achilles' advance? Does Hector's action diminish your respect for him, or can you sympathize with his reaction? Explain your response.

7. The Greeks greatly prized the quality they called *arete,* or personal honor. Do Achilles and Hector display this characteristic? Explain.

8. An **epic simile** is an extended simile in which an event of epic proportions is compared to something from every-day life that would be familiar to the audience. Re-read the description in Book 22 of the duel between Achilles and Hector, and identify all the epic similes Homer uses to describe their final clash. What effect do these Homeric similes create?

9. What aspects of Achilles' character are revealed in the scene with Priam in Book 24? How would your perception of Achilles have been affected if the *Iliad* had ended with Hector's death in Book 22?

Extending and Evaluating

10. Consider the role of the Olympian gods in these excerpts from the *Iliad.* List at least three incidents in the epic in which the Olympians direct or influence events. Do you think the mortal characters in the epic are mere puppets manipulated by the Olympians, or does Homer portray mortals as exercising freedom of choice and action? Give reasons for your answer.

11. What is your evaluation of the oral style of the epic? Did you find Homer's use of formulas, stock epithets, repetition, and similes appealing? How effective do you think such a style would be in oral performance? Explain.

Literary Criticism

12. Some critics see the central **theme** of the *Iliad* as the idea that people must be generous with one another—that if people allow reason to guide their behavior, they might be able to live together in peace and harmony. Which portions of the epic support this view of its theme? Do you agree that it is a central theme of the work? Why or why not?

13. The eighteenth-century German critic Gotthold Lessing said that Homer, as a true poet, was primarily concerned with narration and that he instinctively substituted action for description. Do you think this is true of the excerpts you've read? Give examples from the text to support your answer.

North Carolina Competency Goal
1.03; 4.05; 5.03

INTERNET

Projects and Activities
Keyword:
LE5 WL-2

SKILLS FOCUS

Reading Skills
Evaluate historical context.

Writing Skills
Compare and contrast heroes.

Vocabulary Skills
Understand synonyms and antonyms.

WRITING

Comparing and Contrasting Heroes

Consider Achilles and Hector as ideal heroes in ancient Greece. Write a brief essay in which you **compare** and **contrast** Achilles and Hector as heroes. In your essay, consider these points:

- What special qualities does each hero exhibit?

- Are the heroes' limitations and weaknesses the same, or are they different? In what ways do they mirror one another?

- Is one hero more "human" than the other?

Cite evidence from the epic to support your findings. You may use a chart like the one below to organize your ideas.

	Achilles	Hector
Qualities		
Emotions		
Strengths		
Weaknesses		

Funeral of Patroclus, from a red-figure krater (detail) (c. 5th century B.C.E.).

Museo Archeologico Nazionale, Naples.

Vocabulary Development

Words with Greek and Latin Roots

Many English words we use today come from ancient Greek and Latin. These English words are built on a Greek or a Latin **root,** or base, which contains the core of the word's meaning.

The root –*cred*–, for example, comes from a Latin word meaning "believe." The English words *incredulous, discredit,* and *incredible* all contain this Latin root. These words also contain **affixes**—word parts added to the beginning (**prefixes**) or the end (**suffixes**) of a root to modify its meaning. For instance, adding the prefix *in–* (meaning "not") and the suffix –*ible* (meaning "capable of") to the root –*cred*– forms the word *incredible*—meaning "not capable of being believed."

Some common Greek or Latin roots and affixes are listed in the charts below and in the next column. Note that there can be some variation in the spelling of the roots and affixes when they appear in English words. With a little study you will be able to recognize and use these word parts to figure out the meanings of unfamiliar words.

Greek or Latin Affix	Meaning	Example
–ic	relating to, characteristic of	diplomatic
–ive –ous	full of, given to, marked by	talkative credulous
–fy	to cause to make	liquefy simplify
dis–	apart	distract
pro–	before	prologue
mis–	hate	misogyny
re–	again back	revive
trans–	across through	transmit
para–	beside beyond	parallel

Greek or Latin Root	Meaning	Example
–andro– –anthropo–	man	androgyny anthropology
–dem–	people	epidemic democracy
–fract– –frag–	break	infraction fragment
–mort–	death	immortal
–ten–	hold keep	detention tenacity
–vid– –vis–	look see	video visionary

PRACTICE

Each of the following words is made up of Greek or Latin roots and affixes. Use the two charts and your own knowledge to figure out each word's meaning. Then, check your definition by looking up the word in a dictionary. Explain how the root or affix in each word helped you discover its meaning.

1. misanthropic
2. providence
3. fracture
4. mortify
5. retentive
6. endemic

Vocabulary Skills
Understand and use words derived from Greek and Latin.

Sappho

(Late seventh century B.C.)

Sappho (saf′ō) was born on the Greek island of Lesbos around 600 B.C. She wrote nine books of lyric verses—more than five hundred poems—but only a few fragments survive. Nevertheless, she is considered a supreme Greek lyric poet of this period. In fact, Plato admiringly dubbed her "the tenth Muse":

> Some say nine Muses—but count again.
> Behold the tenth: Sappho of Lesbos.

This remark is fitting because in Greek mythology the Muses, the goddesses of artistic inspiration, are, like Sappho, women. The comment is also appropriate because few Greek poets, male or female, achieved Sappho's stature.

Most scholars believe that Sappho was an educated woman who at some point in her life was exiled to Sicily. She may have returned to Lesbos to become the head of a group of priestesses who worshiped Aphrodite, the Greek goddess of love and beauty. We know that Sappho married and had a daughter, Cleis (klā′əs). Sappho's love for her daughter is the subject of some of her most moving lyric poems. According to one legend, Sappho killed herself for the love of a ferryman by throwing herself from a cliff. Another source, however, suggests that she died of old age in her bed, tended by her daughter.

Sappho composed most of her poems in a style called *monody*—that is, the poems were meant to be sung by a single voice, rather than by a chorus. Although it is clear that Sappho wrote "occasional poetry"—poetry written for public occasions, such as marriage ceremonies—most of her verse is intensely

Mosaic of Sappho from a villa in Sparta (detail) (late 3rd century B.C.E.).
Archaeological Museum, Sparta.

private and personal. In most of the poems that survive, Sappho speaks to the women who were her companions and friends.

Sappho's poetry exists today in fragmentary form. Many of these fragments were found on papyrus strips carelessly thrown away or wadded up in the mummified bodies of crocodiles. In many cases, all that remains of an original poem is two or three lines. In addition, the poems were copied, recopied, and translated by many different people over the centuries. Nevertheless, the genius of Sappho's poetic expression shines through brightly in a handful of glittering fragments.

Lyric Poems of Sappho

Make the Connection

Lyric poets often write to express their feelings about the people closest to them. Think about the people you care most about. What are their outstanding personality traits? What feelings do they inspire in you? Think of a few words that describe each person and that express your feelings.

Literary Focus

Imagery

The power of lyric poetry lies in its immediacy and its ability to convey a strong emotion quickly and fully. Lyric poets achieve this power by using sensory **imagery**—that is, words and phrases that appeal to one or more of the five senses. Strong images trigger memories and emotional responses. For instance, the purple ribbon in "Don't Ask Me What to Wear" evokes for the speaker memories of her mother and of her youth. The reader is invited to share the speaker's wistfulness, if not her memories.

> **Imagery** is language that appeals to the senses.
>
> *For more on Imagery, see the Handbook of Literary and Historical Terms.*

Background

Greek lyric verse resulted from a move away from the epic tradition to a poetry that expressed more intimate and personal themes. The word *lyric* is derived from *lyre,* the stringed instrument on which poets, including Sappho, accompanied themselves. These poet-singers addressed a variety of themes and topics. Some other prominent masters of Greek lyric poetry included Archilochus (är·kil′ə·kəs), Alcaeus (al·sē′əs), Simonides (sī·män′ə·dēz′), and Pindar, all of whom flourished from the seventh to the fifth centuries B.C.

Woman playing a cithara from a white-ground *lekythos* (detail).
Ashmolean Museum, University of Oxford, England.

North Carolina Competency Goal
1.03; 4.05; 5.01; 5.03

INTERNET
More About Sappho
Keyword: LE5 WL-2

Literary Skills
Understand imagery.

Lyric Poems

Sappho
translated by **Mary Barnard**

You Are the Herdsman of Evening

You are the herdsman of evening

Hesperus,[1] you herd
homeward whatever
Dawn's light dispersed

You herd sheep—herd
goats—herd children
home to their mothers

---

1. **Hesperus** (hes′pər·əs): evening star.

Sleep, Darling

Sleep, darling

I have a small
daughter called
Cleis,[2] who is

5   like a golden
flower
     I wouldn't
take all Croesus'[3]
kingdom with love
thrown in, for her

---

2. **Cleis** (klā′əs).
3. **Croesus** (krē′səs): Lydian king
famous for his great wealth.

We Drink Your Health

We drink your health

Lucky bridegroom!
Now the wedding you
asked for is over

5   and your wife is the
girl you asked for;
she's a bride who is
charming to look at,
with eyes as soft as
10 honey, and a face

that Love has lighted
with his own beauty.
Aphrodite has surely

outdone herself in
15 doing honor to you!

You May Forget But

You may forget but

Let me tell you
this: someone in
some future time
will think of us

Sappho (19th century) by Gustave Moreau.

Victoria & Albert Museum, London.

Tonight I've Watched

Tonight I've watched

The moon and then
the Pleiades[4]
go down

The night is now
half-gone; youth
goes; I am

in bed alone

---

4. **Pleiades** (plē′ə·dēz′): star cluster in
   the constellation Taurus.

Don't Ask Me What to Wear

Don't ask me what to wear

I have no embroidered
headband from Sardis to
give you, Cleis, such as
5   I wore
        and my mother
always said that in her
day a purple ribbon
looped in the hair was thought
to be high style indeed

10   but we were dark:
            a girl
whose hair is yellower than
torchlight should wear no
headdress but fresh flowers

He is More than a Hero

He is a god in my eyes—
the man who is allowed
to sit beside you—he

who listens intimately
5   to the sweet murmur of
your voice, the enticing

laughter that makes my own
heart beat fast. If I meet
you suddenly, I can't

10   speak—my tongue is broken;
a thin flame runs under
my skin; seeing nothing,

hearing only my own ears
drumming, I drip with sweat;
15   trembling shakes my body

and I turn paler than
dry grass. At such times
death isn't far from me

Gold earrings with amphora-
shaped pendants (3rd century
B.C.E.). Greek.

Historical District Museum, Burgas, Bulgaria.

Response and Analysis

Thinking Critically

1. In "You Are the Herdsman of Evening," what inanimate object is **personified,** or treated as human? How is this comparison extended throughout the poem?

2. In "Sleep, Darling," what **image** does the speaker use to show how valuable her daughter is?

3. Whom do you imagine the speaker to be in "You May Forget But"? For what do you think he or she will be remembered?

4. What **image** dominates "Tonight I've Watched"? What tone does this image convey?

5. What contrasting images does the poet use in the last four lines of "Don't Ask Me What to Wear"? What is the effect of this contrast?

6. What emotions do you think the speaker is feeling in "He is More than a Hero"? What **images** reveal these emotions?

Extending and Evaluating

7. Were you able to relate to the emotions and situations expressed in Sappho's poems? Explain why it is—or is not—possible to identify with these poems from ancient Greece.

Lyre.
Museo della Civiltà Romana, Rome.

WRITING

Comparing Lyric Poems

The American poet H. D. (Hilda Doolittle) (1886–1961), who was at the center of the Imagist movement of the early twentieth century, was influenced by the imagery and symbolism of ancient Greek poetry. Read H. D.'s poem "Moonrise," and compare it with Sappho's lyrics. Consider both poets' use of the speaker, the kind of emotion that is expressed, and the images each poet uses. You might want to make a chart like the one below.

	Sappho	H. D.
Speaker		
Emotions		
Images		

Moonrise

H. D.

Will you glimmer on the sea?
will you fling your spear-head
on the shore?
what note shall we pitch?
5 we have a song,
on the bank we share our arrows;
the loosed string tells our note:

O flight,
bring her swiftly to our song.
10 She is great,
we measure her by the pine trees.

North Carolina Competency Goal
1.03; 4.05; 5.03

INTERNET
Projects and Activities
Keyword:
LE5 WL-2

SKILLS FOCUS

Literary Skills
Analyze imagery.

Writing Skills
Compare lyric poems.

Thucydides

(c. 460–c. 400 B.C.)

As a young man, Thucydides (thoo·sid'i·dez') enjoyed wealth and privilege, and he went on to become a leading participant in the brilliant flowering of culture during the late fifth century B.C. in Athens. He had a bright future ahead of him as a military officer and a statesman. All that changed, however, during the Peloponnesian War between Athens and Sparta, which broke out in 431 B.C.

The war, which involved nearly every Greek city-state, lasted twenty-seven years, ending with the bitter defeat of Athens. The conflict was personally catastrophic for Thucydides. In 424 B.C., he was placed in charge of a fleet in the northern Aegean Sea. His failure to relieve the town of Amphipolis, which was under siege by the Spartans, cost him his post. He was sentenced to twenty years of exile from Athens.

Even before his exile, Thucydides had conceived the idea of writing a history of the Peloponnesian War. Now it became his all-consuming passion. By seeking out information from *both* Athenians and Spartans and keeping his narrative focused on his chosen topic, he set standards for himself that have defined the historian's craft down to the present day.

Thucydides viewed human beings as caught up in endless, predictable conflicts of self-interest. An accurate chronicle of the war, he believed, could provide invaluable lessons for the future. Time has proved him correct: Even now, one of the basic texts at the U.S. Naval War College in Newport, Rhode Island, is Thucydides' *History of the Peloponnesian War.*

Bust of Thucydides.
Musée du Louvre, Paris.

In his description of warfare, Thucydides turned away from the vision of heroic glory presented in earlier Greek works such as Homer's *Iliad.* For Thucydides, warfare was brutal and destructive—in his own phrase, "a violent teacher." Thucydides' *History* is filled with a sense of tragic destiny not far removed from that of his contemporary, the dramatist Sophocles (see page 198). In fact, some critics read the *History* as a kind of tragic drama of the pride and fall of Athens.

Funeral Speech of Pericles
from History of the Peloponnesian War

Make the Connection

Ancient Athens is often called the cradle of democracy. What are some of the notable features of a democracy? As a class, discuss what the word *democracy* means to you.

Literary Focus

Persuasion

Persuasion is a kind of writing that tries to convince the reader or listener to think or act in a certain way. Examples of persuasion include political speeches, advertisements, and editorials. Persuasion often appeals to the emotions, but the particular kind of persuasive writing that appeals primarily to reason rather than to emotion is called **argument.**

> **Persuasion** is a kind of writing that tries to convince the reader to think or act in a certain way.
>
> *For more on Persuasion, see the Handbook of Literary and Historical Terms.*

Reading Skills

Recognizing Persuasive Techniques

Speakers and writers who want to convince an audience to think, feel, or act in a particular way often use several persuasive techniques. As you read the speech, watch for examples of these persuasive techniques: **logical appeals** (using facts or argument to support a position) and **emotional appeals** (passages that use words that arouse strong feelings).

Background

The greatest Athenian statesman of Thucydides' day was Pericles (per'ə·klēz'). The occasion for the speech reproduced here was the annual public funeral for the Athenian war dead—in this instance, for the first year of the Peloponnesian War. In Thucydides' day, **rhetoric**—the use of language, especially oratory, for persuasion—was considered the highest form of prose. It was common practice for historians to present history through the speeches of famous figures who would embody a particular viewpoint. Thus, Pericles' speech embodies not only his own opinions, but the views of Athenians in general.

North Carolina Competency Goal
1.03; 3.04; 4.05; 5.01; 5.03

Vocabulary Development

obscurity (əb·skyoor'ə·tē) *n.:* lack of fame.

reprobation (rep'rə·bā'shən) *n.:* disapproval.

commiserate (kə·miz'ər·āt') *v.:* feel pity for or sympathize with.

emulate (em'yoo·lāt') *v.:* imitate.

arduous (är'joo·əs) *adj.:* difficult.

INTERNET

Vocabulary Practice
•
More About Thucydides
Keyword: LE5 WL-2

Literary Skills
Understand persuasion.

Reading Skills
Recognize persuasive techniques.

Funeral Speech of Pericles
from **History of the Peloponnesian War**
Thucydides
translated by **Benjamin Jowett**

"Most of those who have spoken here before me have commended the lawgiver who added this oration to our other funeral customs; it seemed to them a worthy thing that such an honor should be given at their burial to the dead who have fallen on the field of battle. But I should have preferred that, when men's deeds have been brave, they should be honored in deed only, and with such an honor as this public funeral, which you are now witnessing. Then

(Above) *Dying Warrior,* from the east pediment of the Temple of Aphaia, Aegina (c. 490 B.C.E.).

Staatliche Antikensammlung, Munich.

the reputation of many would not have been imperiled on the eloquence or want of eloquence of one, and their virtues believed or not as he spoke well or ill. For it is difficult to say neither too little nor too much; and even moderation is apt not to give the impression of truthfulness. The friend of the dead who knows the facts is likely to think that the words of the speaker fall short of his knowledge and of his wishes; another who is not so well informed, when he hears of anything which surpasses his own powers, will be envious and will suspect exaggeration. Mankind are tolerant of the praises of others so long as each hearer thinks that he can do as well or nearly as well himself, but, when the speaker rises above him, jealousy is aroused and he begins to be incredulous. However, since our ancestors have set the seal of their approval upon the practice, I must obey, and to the utmost of my power shall endeavor to satisfy the wishes and beliefs of all who hear me. ❶

"I will speak first of our ancestors, for it is right and seemly that now, when we are lamenting the dead, a tribute should be paid to their memory. There has never been a time when they did not inhabit this land, which by their valor they have handed down from generation to generation, and we have received from them a free state. But if they were worthy of praise, still more were our fathers, who added to their inheritance, and after many a struggle transmitted to us their sons this great empire. And we ourselves assembled here today, who are still most of us in the vigor of life, have carried the work of improvement further, and have richly endowed our city with all things, so that she is sufficient for herself both in peace and war. Of the military exploits by which our various possessions were acquired, or of the energy with which we or our fathers drove back the tide of war, Hellenic or barbarian, I will not speak; for the tale would be long and is familiar to you. But before I praise the dead, I should like to point out by what principles of action we rose to power, and under what institutions and through what manner of life our empire became great. For I conceive that such thoughts are not unsuited to the occasion, and that this numerous assembly of citizens and strangers may profitably listen to them. ❷

"Our form of government does not enter into rivalry with the institutions of others. We do not copy our neighbors, but are an example to them. It is true that we are called a democracy, for the administration is in the hands of the many and not of the few. But while the law secures equal justice to all alike in their private disputes, the claim of excellence is also recognized; and when a citizen is in any way distinguished, he is preferred to the public service, not as a matter of privilege, but as the reward of merit. Neither is poverty a bar, but a man may benefit his country whatever be the <u>obscurity</u> of

❶
At the beginning of the speech, Pericles states that he'd prefer to praise the deceased through deeds rather than words.

? *According to Pericles, what are the drawbacks of giving a speech in honor of the dead?*

❷
Pericles begins by speaking of Athenian ancestors.

? *What aspects of these ancestors does Pericles praise?*

Vocabulary

obscurity (əb·skyoor′ə·tē) *n.:* lack of fame.

his condition. There is no exclusiveness in our public life, and in our private intercourse we are not suspicious of one another, nor angry with our neighbor if he does what he likes; we do not put on sour looks at him which, though harmless, are not pleasant. While we are thus unconstrained in our private intercourse, a spirit of reverence pervades our public acts; we are prevented from doing wrong by respect for the authorities and for the laws, having an especial regard to those which are ordained for the protection of the injured as well as to those unwritten laws which bring upon the transgressor of them the reprobation of the general sentiment. ❸

"And we have not forgotten to provide for our weary spirits many relaxations from toil; we have regular games and sacrifices throughout the year; our homes are beautiful and elegant; and the delight which we daily feel in all these things helps to banish melancholy. Because of the greatness of our city the fruits of the whole earth flow in upon us; so that we enjoy the goods of other countries as freely as of our own.

"Then, again, our military training is in many respects superior to that of our adversaries. Our city is thrown open to the world, and we never expel a foreigner or prevent him from seeing or learning anything of which the secret if revealed to an enemy might profit him. We rely not upon management or trickery, but upon our own hearts and hands. And in the matter of education, whereas they from early youth are always undergoing laborious exercises which are to make them brave, we live at ease, and yet are equally ready to face the perils which they face. And here is the proof. The Lacedaemonians[1] come into Attica[2] not by themselves, but with their whole confederacy following; we go alone into a neighbor's country; and although our opponents are fighting for their homes and we on a foreign soil, we have seldom any difficulty in overcoming them. Our enemies have never yet felt our united strength; the care of a navy divides our attention, and on land we are obliged to send our own citizens everywhere. But they, if they meet and defeat a part of our army, are as proud as if they had routed us all, and when defeated they pretend to have been vanquished by us all. ❹

"If then we prefer to meet danger with a light heart but without laborious training, and with a courage which is gained by habit and not enforced by law, are we not greatly the gainers? Since we do not anticipate the pain, although, when the hour comes, we can be as brave as those who never allow themselves to rest; and thus too our city is equally admirable in peace and in war. For we are lovers of the beautiful, yet simple in our tastes, and we cultivate the mind without loss of manliness. Wealth we employ, not for talk and ostentation,

❸
? *According to Pericles, what are the positive traits of Athenian democracy?*

1. **Lacedaemonians** (las′ə·di·mō′nē·ənz): Spartans.

2. **Attica** (at′i·kə): region of Greece surrounding Athens.

❹
After discussing the superiority of Athenian society, Pericles goes on to discuss the superior aspects of the military training in Athens.

? *What distinguishes Athenian military training from that of its adversaries?*

Vocabulary

reprobation (rep′rə·bā′shən) *n.*: disapproval.

but when there is a real use for it. To avow poverty with us is no disgrace; the true disgrace is in doing nothing to avoid it. An Athenian citizen does not neglect the state because he takes care of his own household; and even those of us who are engaged in business have a very fair idea of politics. We alone regard a man who takes no interest in public affairs, not as a harmless, but as a useless character; and if few of us are originators, we are all sound judges of a policy. ❺ The great impediment to action is, in our opinion, not discussion, but the want of that knowledge which is gained by discussion preparatory to action. For we have a peculiar power of thinking before we act and of acting too, whereas other men are courageous from ignorance but hesitate upon reflection. And they are surely to be esteemed the bravest spirits who, having the clearest sense both of the pains and pleasures of life, do not on that account shrink from danger. In doing good, again, we are unlike others; we make our friends by conferring, not by receiving favors. Now he who confers a favor is the firmer friend, because he would fain by kindness keep alive the memory of an obligation; but the recipient is colder in his feelings, because he knows that in requiting another's generosity he will not be winning gratitude but only paying a debt. We alone do good to our neighbors not upon a calculation of interest, but in the confidence of freedom and in a frank and fearless spirit. To sum up: I say that Athens is the school of Hellas,[3] and that the individual Athenian in his own person seems to have the power of adapting himself to the most varied forms of action with the utmost versatility and grace. This is no passing and idle word, but truth and fact; and the assertion is verified by the position to which these qualities have raised the state. For in the hour of trial Athens alone among her contemporaries is superior to the report of her. No enemy who comes against her is indignant at the reverses which he sustains at the hands of such a city; no subject complains that his masters are unworthy of him. And we shall assuredly not be without witnesses; there are mighty monuments of our power which will make us the wonder of this and of succeeding ages; we shall not need the praises of Homer or of any other panegyrist[4] whose poetry may please for the moment, although his representation of the facts will not bear the light of day. For we have compelled every land and every sea to open a path for our valor, and have everywhere planted eternal memorials of our friendship and of our enmity. Such is the city for whose sake these men nobly fought and died; they could not bear the thought that she might be taken from them; and every one of us who survive should gladly toil on her behalf. ❻

"I have dwelt upon the greatness of Athens because I want to show you that we are contending for a higher prize than those who enjoy none of these privileges, and to establish by manifest proof the merit of these men whom I am now commemorating. Their loftiest praise has been already spoken. For in magnifying the city I have magnified

3. **Hellas** (hel′əs): Greece. **Hellenes** (hel′ēnz′) are Greeks.

4. **panegyrist** (pan′ə·jir′ist) *n.*: someone who gives a formal speech or a written tribute of great praise.

them, and men like them whose virtues made her glorious. And of how few Hellenes can it be said as of them, that their deeds when weighed in the balance have been found equal to their fame! Methinks that a death such as theirs has been gives the true measure of a man's worth; it may be the first revelation of his virtues, but is at any rate their final seal. For even those who come short in other ways may justly plead the valor with which they have fought for their country; they have blotted out the evil with the good, and have benefited the state more by their public services than they have injured her by their private actions. None of these men were enervated by wealth or hesitated to resign the pleasures of life; none of them put off the evil day in the hope, natural to poverty, that a man, though poor, may one day become rich. But, deeming that the punishment of their enemies was sweeter than any of these things, and that they could fall in no nobler cause, they determined at the hazard of their lives to be honorably avenged, and to leave the rest. They resigned to hope their unknown chance of happiness; but in the face of death they resolved to rely upon themselves alone. And when the moment came they were minded to resist and suffer, rather than to fly and save their lives; they ran away from the word of dishonor, but on the battlefield their feet stood fast, and in an instant, at the height of their fortune, they passed away from the scene, not of their fear, but of their glory. ❼

"Such was the end of these men; they were worthy of Athens, and the living need not desire to have a more heroic spirit, although they may pray for a less fatal issue. The value of such a spirit is not to be expressed in words. Anyone can discourse to you forever about the advantages of a brave defense, which you know already. But instead of listening to him I would have you day by day fix your eyes upon the greatness of Athens, until you become filled with the love of her; and when you are impressed by the spectacle of her glory, reflect that this empire has been acquired by men who knew their duty and had the courage to do it, who in the hour of conflict had the fear of dishonor always present to them, and who, if ever they failed in an enterprise, would not allow their virtues to be lost to their country, but freely gave their lives to her as the fairest offering which they could present at her feast. The sacrifice which they collectively made was individually repaid to them; for they received again each one for himself a praise which grows not old, and the noblest of all sepulchers—I speak not of that in which their remains are laid, but of that in which their glory survives, and is proclaimed always and on every fitting occasion both in word and deed. For the whole earth is the sepulcher of famous men; not only are they commemorated by columns and inscriptions in their own country, but in foreign lands there dwells also an unwritten memorial of them, graven not on stone but in the hearts of men. Make them your examples, and, esteeming courage to be freedom and freedom to be happiness, do

❼
This paragraph marks a shift in the speech's focus from Athens as a whole to the good points of its individual citizens.

? *What is it about Athenian individuals that Pericles seems to admire most?*

View of the Parthenon from atop the Acropolis, Athens.

not weigh too nicely the perils of war. The unfortunate who has no hope of a change for the better has less reason to throw away his life than the prosperous who, if he survives, is always liable to a change for the worse, and to whom any accidental fall makes the most serious difference. To a man of spirit, cowardice and disaster coming together are far more bitter than death striking him unperceived at a time when he is full of courage and animated by the general hope. ❽

"Wherefore I do not now <u>commiserate</u> the parents of the dead who stand here; I would rather <u>comfort</u> them. You know that your life has been passed amid manifold vicissitudes;[5] and that they may be deemed fortunate who have gained most honor, whether an hon-

❽ According to Pericles, how can Athenian citizens make the memory of the war dead live on?

5. **vicissitudes** (vi·sis′ə·tōōds′) *n. pl.:* changes.

Vocabulary

commiserate (kə·miz′ər·āt′) *v.:* feel pity for or sympathize with.

orable death like theirs, or an honorable sorrow like yours, and whose days have been so ordered that the term of their happiness is likewise the term of their life. I know how hard it is to make you feel this, when the good fortune of others will too often remind you of the gladness which once lightened your hearts. And sorrow is felt at the want of those blessings, not which a man never knew, but which were a part of his life before they were taken from him. Some of you are of an age at which they may hope to have other children, and they ought to bear their sorrow better; not only will the children who may hereafter be born make them forget their own lost ones, but the city will be doubly a gainer. She will not be left desolate, and she will be safer. For a man's counsel cannot have equal weight or worth, when he alone has no children to risk in the general danger. To those of you who have passed their prime, I say: Congratulate yourselves that you have been happy during the greater part of your days; remember that your life of sorrow will not last long, and be comforted by the glory of those who are gone. For the love of honor alone is ever young, and not riches, as some say, but honor is the delight of men when they are old and useless. **9**

"To you who are the sons and brothers of the departed, I see that the struggle to <u>emulate</u> them will be an <u>arduous</u> one. For all men praise the dead, and, however preeminent your virtue may be, hardly will you be thought, I do not say to equal, but even to approach them. The living have their rivals and detractors, but when a man is out of the way, the honor and good will which he receives is unalloyed. And, if I am to speak of womanly virtues to those of you who will henceforth be widows, let me sum them up in one short admonition:[6] To a woman not to show more weakness than is natural to her sex is a great glory, and not to be talked about for good or for evil among men. **10**

"I have paid the required tribute, in obedience to the law, making use of such fitting words as I had. The tribute of deeds has been paid in part; for the dead have been honorably interred, and it remains only that their children should be maintained at the public charge until they are grown up: this is the solid prize with which, as with a garland, Athens crowns her sons living and dead, after a struggle like theirs. For where the rewards of virtue are greatest, there the noblest citizens are enlisted in the service of the state. And now, when you have duly lamented, everyone his own dead, you may depart." **11**

9
Pericles believes that the parents of the deceased should be comforted, but not pitied.

? *What consolation does Pericles offer to the parents of those who have died?*

6. admonition (ad′mə·nish′ən) *n.*: reprimand.

10
? *Why will the brothers and sons of the departed find it difficult to follow their relatives' example?*

11
? *How does the city-state of Athens reward the families of the war dead?*

Vocabulary

emulate (em′yoo·lāt′) *v.*: imitate.
arduous (är′joo·əs) *adj.*: difficult.

Response and Analysis

Reading Check

1. How does Pericles define a democracy?

2. How does Pericles contrast the Athenians' military training with that of the Spartans? What proof does he offer of the Athenians' superiority?

3. Why does Pericles feel that the parents of the dead should not be pitied? What advice does he give the widows?

Thinking Critically

4. Explain how Pericles gains the attention of his listeners in the introduction to his speech.

5. What do you think is Pericles' purpose in praising Athens and Athenian democracy? What is he trying to **persuade** his listeners to do or believe?

6. Identify at least one example of **argument,** or persuasion that appeals to reason. Then, identify an example of an appeal to emotion.

7. In Pericles' day, Athens was a "man's world" as far as public life was concerned. How do Pericles' words to the women reflect that aspect of Athenian culture?

8. Briefly summarize the values Pericles praises in his oration.

Extending and Evaluating

9. What aspects of Pericles' speech might appear in political speeches today? Would a speech like Pericles' inspire you and your peers? Explain.

WRITING

Comparing Democracies

In a brief essay, analyze the ways in which U.S. democracy reflects the ancient Greek ideal. Completing a chart like the one below may help you plan your essay.

Ideals	Athens	United States
freedom of speech		
promotion based on merit		

Vocabulary Development

Semantic Mapping

obscurity   commiserate   arduous
reprobation   emulate

Make a **semantic map** like the following one for each of the Vocabulary words above. First, locate the word in the speech to determine its meaning in context.

arduous
Definition: difficult
Synonyms: hard, strenuous
Example: Running a marathon is an arduous undertaking.

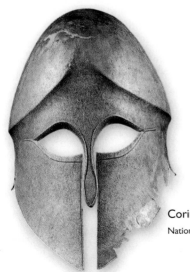

Corinthian bronze helmet (c. 330–c. 327 B.C.E.).
National Museum of History, Bulgaria (Inv. 548/63).

North Carolina Competency Goal
1.03; 4.05; 5.03; 6.01

INTERNET
Projects and Activities
Keyword: LE5 WL-2

SKILLS FOCUS

Literary Skills
Analyze persuasion.

Reading Skills
Recognize persuasive techniques.

Writing Skills
Compare democracies.

Vocabulary Skills
Make semantic maps.

Plato

(c. 429–c. 347 B.C.)

Plato was the preeminent philosopher of the Golden Age. As a young student of rhetoric from an aristocratic family, Plato's destiny was sealed when he met Socrates (469–399 B.C.). The older man was a teacher whose unorthodox style and uncompromising pursuit of the truth appealed to many prominent young men of Plato's time.

Most of what we know about Socrates comes from Plato's works, for the older philosopher left no writings of his own. Socrates was an eccentric. Pretending to be ignorant, he wandered the streets of Athens, a shabby and unkempt figure who questioned people about concepts such as virtue, truth, and wisdom. He never preached or offered his own solutions, but he would demonstrate by his ceaseless questioning that no argument was infallible. The technique of questioning that he developed is known as the **Socratic method.**

Socrates' pointed criticism of official authorities earned him a reputation as a public nuisance. The controversy over his teaching methods and his belief that an "unexamined life is not worth living" led to a vicious persecution. In 399 B.C., he was tried and executed on false charges of corrupting the minds of his young students.

Plato recorded much of Socrates' philosophy and many of his speeches in his *Dialogues.* Nearly all of Plato's thirty-four philosophical works are written in the form of such **dialogues,** in which two or more characters debate with the principal speaker and challenger, Socrates. Plato used the dialogues as a vehicle to present a comprehensive philosophical system known as **Platonism.** According to

Bust of Plato.
Museo Capitolino, Rome.

the Platonic system, ideas are the only reality, and people should rely on reason, not on their senses, to comprehend the world.

Around 387 B.C., Plato founded a school called the Academy, a center of philosophical learning. He wrote a number of famous works, including *The Republic,* which sets forth in brilliant detail his theory of an ideal state ruled by philosopher-kings. According to one story, when Plato was sixty years old, during a sea voyage, his ship was raided by pirates, and he was sold as a slave to a former student, who helped him return to Athens. Plato never left the city again.

from the Apology

Make the Connection

In this speech to the Athenian court, Socrates refuses to compromise his loyalty to the pursuit of truth, even at the cost of his life. How do you feel about people who refuse to compromise their beliefs? Are some beliefs worth dying for? Explain.

Literary Focus

Analogy

An **analogy** is a comparison of two things to show that they are alike in certain respects. We often use analogies to show how something unfamiliar is like something well known or widely experienced. For example, we might compare a biologist's microscope to a carpenter's hammer: Both are important tools used in a profession or trade. Socrates uses several analogies in the *Apology* to make his points clearer to his listeners and to strengthen his arguments.

> An **analogy** is a comparison of two things to show that they are alike in certain respects.
>
> *For more on Analogy, see the Handbook of Literary and Historical Terms.*

Reading Skills

Analyzing the Speaker's Philosophical Arguments

In his speech, Socrates argues that it is reasonable to hope that death is good, not evil. Look for any explicit or direct statements that express Socrates' **main idea.** Then, take note of the reasons, examples, and details that Socrates uses to support his argument and persuade his listeners.

Background

For the Greeks the term *apology* was not an expression of regret but rather a defense of a way of life or a belief system. At the conclusion of Socrates' speech, the jury of 501 Athenian citizens voted, found him guilty, and condemned him to death by poison.

Although the *Apology* is among Plato's *Dialogues,* it is itself a **monologue,** a lengthy speech given by one person. In Socrates' case, the monologue was his opportunity to explain himself and to honor the letter of the law. He even went so far as to suggest ironically that his services to Athens merited a pension. At this point, the jury reconfirmed the death penalty by an even larger majority. The selection that follows includes Socrates' final address to the court.

North Carolina Competency Goal
1.02; 1.03; 4.05; 5.01; 5.03; 6.01

Vocabulary Development

procured (prō·kyoord′) *v.*: secured; brought about by effort.

acquittal (ə·kwit′′l) *n.*: act of clearing a person of charges of wrongdoing.

censuring (sen′shər·iŋ) *v.* used as *n.*: expressing strong disapproval of.

intimation (in′tə·mā′shən) *n.*: hint.

reproved (ri·prōovd′) *v.*: expressed disapproval of.

INTERNET

Vocabulary Practice
•
More About Plato
Keyword: LE5 WL-2

SKILLS FOCUS

Literary Skills
Understand analogies.

Reading Skills
Analyze the speaker's philosophical arguments.

from the
Apology

from the Dialogues

Plato
translated by **Benjamin Jowett**

Not much time will be gained, O Athenians, in return for the evil name which you will get from the detractors of the city, who will say that you killed Socrates, a wise man; for they will call me wise, even although I am not wise, when they want to reproach you. If you had waited a little while, your desire would have been fulfilled in the course of nature. For I am far advanced in years, as you may perceive, and not far from death. I am speaking now not to all of you, but only to those who have condemned me to death. And I have another thing to say to them: You think that I was convicted because I had no words of the sort which would have procured my acquittal—I mean, if I had thought fit to leave nothing undone or unsaid. Not so; the deficiency which led to my conviction was not of words—certainly not. But I had not the boldness or impudence or inclination to address you as you would have liked me to do, weeping and wailing and lamenting, and saying and doing many things which you have been accustomed to hear from others, and which, as I maintain, are unworthy of me. I thought at the time that I ought not to do anything common or mean when in danger: nor do I now repent of the style of my defense; I would rather die having spoken after my manner, than speak in your manner and live. For neither in war nor yet at law ought I or any man to use every way of escaping death. Often in battle there can be no doubt that if a man will throw away his arms, and fall on his knees before his pursuers, he may escape death; and in other dangers there are other ways of escaping death, if a man is willing to say and do anything. The difficulty, my friends, is not to avoid death, but to avoid unrighteousness; for that runs faster than death. I am old and move slowly, and the slower runner has overtaken me, and my accusers are keen and quick, and the faster runner, who is unrighteousness, has over-

taken them. And now I depart hence condemned by you to suffer the penalty of death—they too go their ways condemned by the truth to suffer the penalty of villainy and wrong; and I must abide by my award—let them abide by theirs. I suppose that these things may be regarded as fated—and I think that they are well.

And now, O men who have condemned me, I would fain prophesy to you; for I am about to die, and in the hour of death men are gifted with prophetic power. And I prophesy to you who are my murderers, that immediately after my departure punishment far heavier than you have inflicted on me will surely await you. Me you have killed because you wanted to escape the accuser, and not to give an account of your lives. But that will not be as you suppose: far otherwise. For I say that there will be more accusers of you than there are now; accusers whom hitherto I have restrained: and as they are younger they will be more inconsiderate with you, and you will be more offended at them. If you think that by killing men you can prevent some one from censuring your evil lives, you are mistaken; that is not a way of escape which is either possible or honorable; the easiest and the noblest way is not to be disabling others, but to be improving yourselves. This is the prophecy which I utter before my departure to the judges who have condemned me.

Friends, who would have acquitted me, I would like also to talk with you about the thing which has come to pass, while the magistrates are busy, and before I go to the place at which I must die. Stay then a little, for we may as well talk with one another while there is time. You are my friends, and I should like to show you the meaning of this event which has happened to

The School of Athens (1510–1511) by Raphael.

Stanza della Segnatura, Vatican Palace, Vatican City.

Vocabulary

procured (prō·kyoord′) *v.*: secured; brought about by effort.

acquittal (ə·kwit′'l) *n.*: act of clearing a person of charges of wrongdoing.

censuring (sen′shər·iŋ) *v.* used as *n.*: expressing strong disapproval of.

me. O my judges—for you I may truly call judges—I should like to tell you of a wonderful circumstance. Hitherto the divine faculty of which the internal oracle[1] is the source has constantly been in the habit of opposing me even about trifles, if I was going to make a slip or error in any matter; and now as you see there has come upon me that which may be thought, and is generally believed to be, the last and worst evil. But the oracle made no sign of opposition, either when I was leaving my house in the morning, or when I was on my way to the court, or while I was speaking, at anything which I was going to say; and yet I have often been stopped in the middle of a speech, but now in nothing I either said or did touching the matter in hand has the oracle opposed me. What do I take to be the explanation of this silence? I will tell you. It is an intimation that what has happened to me is a good, and that those of us who think that death is an evil are in error. For the customary sign would surely have opposed me had I been going to evil and not to good.

Let us reflect in another way, and we shall see that there is great reason to hope that death is a good; for one of two things—either death is a state of nothingness and utter unconsciousness, or, as men say, there is a change and migration of the soul from this world to another. Now, if you suppose that there is no consciousness, but a sleep like the sleep of him who is undisturbed even by dreams, death will be an unspeakable gain. For if a person were to select the night in which his sleep was undisturbed even by dreams, and were to compare with this the other days and nights of his life, and then were to tell us how many days and nights he had passed in the course of his life better and more pleasantly than this one, I think that any man, I will not say a private man, but even the great king will not find many such days or nights, when compared with the others. Now, if death be of such a nature, I say that to die is gain; for eternity is then only a single night. But if

death is the journey to another place, and there, as men say, all the dead abide, what good, O my friends and judges, can be greater than this? If, indeed, when the pilgrim arrives in the world below, he is delivered from the professors of justice in this world, and finds the true judges who are said to give judgment there, Minos and Rhadamanthus and Aeacus and Triptolemus,[2] and other sons of God who were righteous in their own life, that pilgrimage will be worth making. What would not a man give if he might converse with Orpheus and Musaeus and Hesiod[3] and Homer? Nay, if this be true, let me die again and again. I myself, too, shall have a wonderful interest in there meeting and conversing with Palamedes,[4] and Ajax[5] the son of Telamon, and any other ancient hero who has suffered death through an unjust judgment; and there will be no small pleasure, as I think, in comparing my own sufferings with theirs. Above all, I shall then be able to continue my search into true and false knowledge; as in this world, so also in the next; and I shall find out who is wise, and who pretends to be wise, and is not. What would not a man give, O judges, to be able to examine the leader of the great Trojan expedition; or Odysseus[6]

---

2. **Minos** (mī′näs′): king of Crete. **Rhadamanthus** (rad′ə·man′thəs): brother of Minos. **Aeacus** (ē′ə·kəs): according to one legend, the father of Achilles. **Triptolemus** (trip·tōl′ə·məs): priest of Demeter. After death, all were made judges in Hades, the world of the dead.
3. **Orpheus** (ôr′fē·əs): famous musician and poet in Greek mythology. **Musaeus** (mŏŏ·zē′əs): Greek poet who lived around 1400 B.C. **Hesiod** (hē′sē·əd): Greek poet of the eighth century B.C.
4. **Palamedes** (pal′ə·mē′dēz): Greek hero who fought in the Trojan War. He was accused of treachery and stoned to death.
5. **Ajax:** Greek hero in the Trojan War. Convinced that the armor of Achilles was unjustly awarded to Odysseus rather than to himself, Ajax went mad.
6. **Odysseus** (ō·dis′ē·əs): cleverest of the Greek warriors; hero of Homer's *Odyssey*.

---

1. **internal oracle** *n.:* Socrates believed that he was constantly guided by a divine inner voice that warned him against evil acts and wrong choices.

Vocabulary

intimation (in′tə·mā′shən) *n.:* hint.

or Sisyphus,[7] or numberless others, men and women too! What infinite delight would there be in conversing with them and asking them questions! In another world they do not put a man to death for asking questions: assuredly not. For besides being happier than we are, they will be immortal, if what is said is true.

Wherefore, O judges, be of good cheer about death, and know of a certainty, that no evil can happen to a good man, either in life or after death. He and his are not neglected by the gods; nor has my own approaching end happened by mere chance. But I see clearly that the time had arrived when it was better for me to die and be released from trouble; wherefore the oracle gave no sign. For which reason, also, I am not angry with my condemners, or with my accusers; they have done me no harm, although they did not mean to do me any good; and for this I may gently blame them.

Still, I have a favor to ask of them. When my sons are grown up, I would ask you, O my friends, to punish them; and I would have you trouble them, as I have troubled you, if they seem to care about riches, or anything, more than about virtue; or if they pretend to be something when they are really nothing—then reprove them as I have <u>reproved</u> you, for not caring about that for which they ought to care, and thinking that they are something when they are really nothing. And if you do this, both I and my sons will have received justice at your hands.

The hour of departure has arrived, and we go our ways—I to die, and you to live. Which is better God only knows.

---

7. **Sisyphus** (sis′ə·fəs): After his death, Sisyphus was punished in Hades by eternally having to roll up a hill a huge stone that always rolled down just as it got to the top.

Vocabulary

reproved (ri·prōovd′) *v.*: expressed disapproval of.

Portrait statuette of Socrates (c. 1st century C.E.).
The British Museum, London.

All the Right Questions

INFORMATIONAL TEXT

Anita Hamilton

from *Time,* April 5, 2004

There's a buzz in the air at the El Diablo Coffee Co. in Seattle, and it's not just coming from the aroma of the shop's Cuban-style espresso drinks. On a recent Wednesday evening, as most patrons sat quietly reading books or tapping away on their laptop computers, about 15 people gathered in a circle discussing philosophy. "When is violence necessary?" asked one. "What is a well-lived life?" asked another, as the group enjoyed a well-caffeinated, intellectual high.

Known as a Socrates Cafe, the group at El Diablo is just one of 150 or so that meet in coffee shops, bookstores, libraries, churches and community centers across the country. Founded by Christopher Phillips, a former journalist and teacher, the cafes are designed to get people talking about philosophical issues. Using a kind of Socratic method, they encourage people to develop their views by posing questions, being open to challenges and considering alternative answers. Adhering to Socrates' belief that the unexamined life is not worth living, the cafes focus on exchanging ideas, not using them to pummel other participants. . . .

While a modern-day discussion group based on the teachings of a thinker from the 5th century B.C. may seem quaintly outdated, Socrates Cafes have found a surprisingly large and diverse following. Meetings have been held everywhere from a Navajo Nation reservation in Ganado, Ariz., to an airplane terminal in Providence, R.I. Ongoing groups have formed in prisons, senior centers and homeless shelters. . . .

For Phillips, the dialogue groups are about much more than good conversation. "It's grass-roots democracy," he says. "It's only in a group setting that people can hash out their ideas about how we should act not just as an individual but as a society.". . .

While Phillips believes the cafes can benefit anyone, one of his favorite groups is children. On a recent Thursday morning, he met with seven kids ranging in age from 6 to 16 at Children's Hospital in Oakland, Calif. Clad in multicolored hospital gowns and fuzzy slippers, the children were bashful about answering direct questions at first. But Phillips was undeterred. After making jokes about his own "uncool" haircut and lobbing out a couple of easy questions like "What's four plus three?" and "Do you like to draw?" he finally got his audience warmed up and eased them on to the heavier topic of truth, lies and secrets. "When is it not better to tell the truth?" Phillips asked his now rapt audience. "When is it good to lie?" Mariela, 10, who has severe asthma, replied, "When you're trying to help somebody escape from something like slavery."

Philosophy is important for kids of all ages, Phillips says later, because "it gives them this great chance to sculpt their moral code, to figure out clearly who they are and who they want to be. . . .The whole idea is not that we have to find a final answer; it's that we keep thinking about these things." One question at a time.

? According to the article, how do Socrates Cafes build on the philosophical ideas that Socrates developed?

Response and Analysis

Reading Check

1. In the second paragraph, what prophecy does Socrates make about those who voted to condemn him?

2. Why does Socrates say he is not angry with his accusers? For what does he "gently blame them"?

3. Why does Socrates say he is not afraid of death?

4. At the end of the speech, what favor does Socrates ask of his judges?

Thinking Critically

5. In the first paragraph, Socrates uses the **analogy** of two runners to argue that pleading for his life would be dishonorable. Explain what is being compared in this analogy. How does this comparison help to strengthen Socrates' argument?

6. Socrates was renowned for his sarcasm, or **verbal irony:** saying one thing but meaning another. What is ironic about this remark at the end of his speech: "In another world they do not put a man to death for asking questions"?

7. Socrates experienced bitter injustice in his own life. Yet he says that "no evil can happen to a good man, either in life or after death" (page 195). How do you explain this apparent contradiction?

8. What comments can you make about Socrates' character after reading this selection? Identify at least three words that can be used to describe him.

Extending and Evaluating

9. Socrates uses **analogies** when he argues that it is reasonable to hope that "death is a good" thing. Do you find Socrates' argument persuasive? Why or why not?

Literary Criticism

10. One of the Socratic dialogues of Plato explores the abstract idea of courage. In the *Apology,* however, we are presented with an actual example of courage. Why is an example more effective in conveying the idea of courage?

WRITING

Analyzing Problems and Solutions

Re-read the **Connection** on page 196 about modern-day Socratic discussion groups. In small groups, hold your own Socrates Café in which you discuss a problem that is facing your school. Remember that Socrates' technique of questioning, called the Socratic method, forced people to dig deeper into their thoughts and beliefs. Use questions to draw out, challenge, and clarify one another's ideas about the problem. Then, use the results of your discussion to write a brief essay in which you present and analyze the problem and offer what your group thinks is the best solution. Share your essay with the class, and discuss ways of implementing the solution you proposed.

▶ See "Analyzing Problems and Solutions" on pages 330–335 for help with this assignment.

North Carolina Competency Goal
1.02; 1.03; 2.01; 4.01; 4.05; 5.03; 6.01

INTERNET
Projects and Activities
Keyword: LE5 WL-2

Vocabulary Development

Synonyms

A **synonym** is a word that has the same or nearly the same meaning as another word. Choose the best synonym for each Vocabulary word below.

1. **procured:** a. sold b. obtained c. covered

2. **acquittal:** a. resignation b. repayment c. release

3. **censuring:** a. disapproving b. valuing c. exclaiming

4. **intimation:** a. hint b. declaration c. publication

5. **reproved:** a. persuaded b. rebuked c. ratified

SKILLS FOCUS

Literary Skills
Understand analogies.

Reading Skills
Analyze the speaker's philosophical arguments.

Writing Skills
Analyze problems and solutions

Vocabulary Skills
Understand synonyms.

Sophocles
(c. 496–406 B.C.)

The tragedies of Sophocles probe the depth of human suffering and despair as profoundly as the works of any writer in world literature. The playwright himself, in contrast to the misery he portrayed in his works, lived a long, comfortable, and happy life. He grew up in a well-to-do family in Athens, enjoyed a carefree childhood and education, and eventually became a distinguished public official as well as an outstanding dramatist.

Sophocles first achieved recognition in the theater at the age of twenty-eight, when he defeated Aeschylus—another great Greek playwright—in an annual dramatic competition. He went on to win twenty-four first prizes over the next six decades—the best record of any Greek playwright. He produced 123 plays, of which only seven survive today.

The artistic fulfillment of Sophocles' long life reflects the spirit of the age in which he lived. The first half of the fifth century B.C. in Athens was a time of political expansion and social optimism, following the great victories of the Greeks over the invading Persians at Marathon (490 B.C.) and Salamis (480 B.C.). In the second half of the century, the Athenians experienced tremendous intellectual and cultural developments. This was the brilliant era of the statesman Pericles, the historians Herodotus and Thucydides, and the philosopher Socrates. It was the age that raised the majestic temple called the Parthenon on the Acropolis high above the city and developed democracy as a political system. The age of Sophocles was indeed a time when anything seemed possible through human effort and reason.

Toward the end of Sophocles' life, however, this expansive spirit began to dwindle, largely

Bust of Sophocles.
Museo Archeologico Nazionale, Naples.

because of the costly investment of Athenian lives and resources in the long Peloponnesian War (431–404 B.C.). This conflict pitted Athens and its allies against the rival city of Sparta and various other allied city-states for twenty-seven years. Perhaps this conflict is one of the reasons that Sophocles' surviving plays—most of which were written after 440 B.C.—are so deeply troubling. They depict characters caught up in unsolvable dilemmas that test their faith in divine and human justice.

Introduction

Oedipus Rex

Oedipus Rex is considered one of the world's greatest tragedies. A **tragedy** is a serious drama featuring a main character, often of noble birth, who strives to achieve something and is ultimately defeated. The defeat of the hero may be caused by forces beyond his or her control, but often the main character's downfall is due to an inborn character flaw or weakness—the **tragic flaw**. In spite of defeat and even death, however, the tragic hero is ennobled by newly gained self-knowledge and wisdom.

The Greek Theater

By the second half of the fifth century B.C., drama in Greece was experiencing its Golden Age. In Athens, dramatic festivals—which had grown out of religious rituals—and contests were the center of cultural life. The Dionysia, an annual festival in honor of the god Dionysus, was a four-day extravaganza held in March or April. At the open-air Theater of Dionysus, some fifteen thousand spectators witnessed a variety of plays, both tragic and comic.

The Theater of Dionysus was carved out of a stone hillside and resembled a semicircle with steeply rising tiers of seats. At the bottom was the rounded orchestra, or performance area, where the chorus

Roman copy of Greek relief showing Menander, an Athenian dramatist of the 4th century B.C.E.

Museo Gregoriano Profano, Musei Vaticani, Vatican City.

sang and danced. Behind the orchestra was an open, practically bare stage, where the actors spoke their lines from behind huge masks. Male actors performed all the roles; by switching masks, one actor could play a number of roles—both male and female—in a single play.

The Oedipus Plays

Oedipus Rex is one of Sophocles' three "Theban plays"—three tragedies about King Oedipus (ed′i·pəs) of Thebes and his family. Sophocles composed these dramas over a thirty-six-year period, beginning with *Antigone* (442 B.C.), continuing with *Oedipus Rex* (c. 429 B.C.), and concluding with *Oedipus at Colonus* (406 B.C.).

The Story of Oedipus

Oedipus is the ill-fated king of Thebes whose mysterious past catches up with him and wreaks havoc on him and his family. The tale of King Oedipus would have been familiar to the Greek audience of the time and would have served as backstory to the play. Before the play begins, Oedipus has won the hand of Queen Jocasta, whose husband, King Laius, had been killed on the road by another traveler. Oedipus won Jocasta by solving a riddle posed by the Sphinx—a monster with the head of a woman, the body of a lion, and the wings of an eagle—who was terrorizing Thebes. What Oedipus did not know at the time—but discovers during the course of the play—is that he is the child of Laius and Jocasta. Seeking to avoid an awful prophecy that their son would one day kill his father and marry his mother, Jocasta and Laius had made arrangements to kill their baby son. They gave him to a shepherd, who was ordered to abandon the infant, his ankles pinned together, on the side of Mount Cithaeron. The shepherd pitied the baby, though, and so the infant was given to a Corinthian messenger, who in turn brought him to the king and queen of Corinth. The Corinthian royal couple named him Oedipus (meaning "swollen foot") and raised him as their own. Oedipus's discovery of his true identity as the murderer of his own father—for it was Oedipus who had unknowingly met King Laius on the road and killed him—and the spouse of his own mother is the central focus of *Oedipus Rex*.

The Structure and Themes of the Play

Oedipus Rex maintains a tight dramatic framework. All the action takes place in a single location and involves a small number of characters interacting with the central figure, Oedipus, who remains on stage for nearly the entire play. In addition, the Chorus—which serves simply as a nameless onlooker and commentator in other Greek tragedies—is transformed by Sophocles into a collective "actor" within the drama itself.

In this work what is left unsaid is often more powerful than what is explicitly expressed. Practically every line contains a possible double meaning or an ambiguity. This verbal irony reinforces the dramatic irony of the play, as the main characters—and even the Chorus—only gradually come to grips with what is understood by the audience at the very start.

The themes, or underlying messages, of *Oedipus Rex* include
- the quest for identity
- the nature of innocence and guilt
- the nature of moral responsibility
- the limitations of human will versus fate
- the abuse of power

The structure of most Greek tragedies presents a tight, formal arrangement of parts. These parts include the **prologue** (opening scene), the ***parados*** (the first of the Chorus's lyric songs, or choral odes), a regular alternation of scenes in **dialogue** and **choral odes,** and, finally, the ***exodos*** (concluding scene). These terms have been retained in this translation of *Oedipus Rex*.

(Foreground) Chorus, from *Oedipus the King*. Olivier Theatre/National Theatre, London; (background) theater, Epidauros (c. 3rd century B.C.E.).

Before You Read

Oedipus Rex

Make the Connection

Quickwrite

For the ancient Greeks the Oedipus myth was a striking example of how human fortunes can suffer unexpected, drastic reversals. Can you think of other examples of sharp reversals in literature or real life? Were the people involved responsible, or were they innocent victims? How do people explain and cope with such tragedies? Freewrite your answer.

Literary Focus

Dramatic Irony

Dramatic irony occurs when the reader or audience knows something important that a character in a story or drama does not know. The fundamental irony in *Oedipus Rex* stems from the audience's knowledge of Oedipus's true identity, while Oedipus is unaware of it. Sophocles creates variations on this central irony throughout the play, heightening the audience members' pity and horror.

INTERNET

Vocabulary Practice

•

More About Sophocles

Keyword: LE5 WL-2

Dramatic irony occurs when the reader or audience knows something important that a character in a story or drama does not know.

For more on Irony, see the Handbook of Literary and Historical Terms.

Background

During the early years of the Peloponnesian War, when *Oedipus Rex* was produced, Athens suffered from both political instability and a devastating plague. Thus, Sophocles opens his play with a situation that Athenians could identify with: The city of Thebes is beset by a terrible plague, with no end in sight. According to the oracle of Apollo, the plague will continue until the murderer of King Laius is caught and punished. Oedipus, casting himself in the role of the city's savior, vows to do everything in his power to apprehend the murderer and save his people. Little does he realize that his vow will relentlessly lead him to an encounter with himself, his past, and his darkest secrets.

Vocabulary Development

supplication (sup′lə·kā′shən) *n.*: humble request.

compunction (kəm·puŋk′shən) *n.*: feeling of remorse or guilt.

expedient (ek·spē′dē·ənt) *n.*: something that is useful or helpful.

decrepit (dē·krep′it) *adj.*: worn-out by old age.

disdain (dis·dān′) *n.*: scorn.

venerate (ven′ə·rāt′) *v.*: revere.

primal (prī′məl) *adj.*: original.

SKILLS FOCUS

Literary Skills
Understand dramatic irony.

(Opposite) Cycladic figure (c. 2500–c.1100 B.C.E.).

Oedipus Rex

Sophocles

translated by
Dudley Fitts *and*
Robert Fitzgerald

CHARACTERS

Oedipus (ed'i·pəs): King of Thebes.

A Priest

Creon (krē'än'): brother of Jocasta.

Teiresias (tī·rē'sē·əs): a blind seer.

Jocasta (jō·kas'tə): wife of Oedipus and widow of Laius (lā'yəs), former King of Thebes.

Messenger: from Corinth.

Shepherd of Laius

Second Messenger: from the palace.

Chorus of Theban Elders

Choragos (kō·rā'gəs): leader of the Chorus.

Antigone (an·tig'ə·nē') and **Ismene** (is·mē'nē): daughters of Oedipus and Jocasta.

Suppliants

Page

Servants and Attendants

Oedipus and the Sphinx, from a red-figure kylix (5th century B.C.E.).
Museo Gregoriano Etrusco, Musei Vaticani, Vatican City.

Part 1

SCENE

Before the palace of OEDIPUS, *King of Thebes. A central door and two lateral doors open onto a platform which runs the length of the facade. On the platform, right and left, are altars; and three steps lead down into the "orchestra," or chorus-ground. At the beginning of the action these steps are crowded by suppliants who have brought branches and chaplets of olive leaves and who lie in various attitudes of despair.* OEDIPUS *enters.*

PROLOGUE

Oedipus.

My children, generations of the living
In the line of Cadmus,° nursed at his ancient hearth:
Why have you strewn yourselves before these altars
In supplication, with your boughs and garlands?
5   The breath of incense rises from the city
With a sound of prayer and lamentation.

                                        Children,
I would not have you speak through messengers,
And therefore I have come myself to hear you—
I, Oedipus, who bear the famous name.

      (to a PRIEST) You, there, since you are eldest in the
10   company,
Speak for them all, tell me what preys upon you,
Whether you come in dread, or crave some blessing:
Tell me, and never doubt that I will help you
In every way I can; I should be heartless
15   Were I not moved to find you suppliant here.

Priest.

Great Oedipus, O powerful King of Thebes!
You see how all the ages of our people
Cling to your altar steps: here are boys
Who can barely stand alone, and here are priests
20   By weight of age, as I am a priest of God,
And young men chosen from those yet unmarried;
As for the others, all that multitude,
They wait with olive chaplets in the squares,
At the two shrines of Pallas, and where Apollo
Speaks in the glowing embers.
25   Your own eyes
Must tell you: Thebes is tossed on a murdering sea
And cannot lift her head from the death surge.
A rust consumes the buds and fruits of the earth;
The herds are sick; children die unborn,
30   And labor is vain. The god of plague and pyre
Raids like detestable lightning through the city,
And all the house of Cadmus is laid waste,
All emptied, and all darkened: Death alone
Battens upon the misery of Thebes.

35   You are not one of the immortal gods, we know;
Yet we have come to you to make our prayer

Vocabulary

supplication (sup′lə·kā′shən) *n.*: humble request.

---

2. Cadmus (kad′məs): in Greek mythology, a prince who kills a dragon and sows its teeth, which turn into an army of men who fight one another; with the five survivors of the battle, Cadmus founds Thebes.

1–6. Try to visualize the despairing postures of the suppliants as Oedipus addresses the people.
? *Together with the details of the incense and the sounds of lamentation, what mood does the scene suggest at the opening of the play?*

? **9.** *Do you think Oedipus is boasting here? Or is he merely being objective about his own status as the King of Thebes?*

As to the man surest in mortal ways
And wisest in the ways of God. You saved us
From the Sphinx, that flinty singer,° and the tribute
40 We paid to her so long; yet you were never
Better informed than we, nor could we teach you:
It was some god breathed in you to set us free.

Therefore, O mighty King, we turn to you:
Find us our safety, find us a remedy,
45 Whether by counsel of the gods or men.
A king of wisdom tested in the past
Can act in a time of troubles, and act well.
Noblest of men, restore
Life to your city! Think how all men call you
50 Liberator for your triumph long ago;
Ah, when your years of kingship are remembered,
Let them not say *We rose, but later fell*—
Keep the State from going down in the storm!
Once, years ago, with happy augury,
55 You brought us fortune; be the same again!
No man questions your power to rule the land:
But rule over men, not over a dead city!
Ships are only hulls, citadels are nothing,
When no life moves in the empty passageways.

Oedipus.
60 Poor children! You may be sure I know
All that you longed for in your coming here.
I know that you are deathly sick; and yet,
Sick as you are, not one is as sick as I.
Each of you suffers in himself alone
65 His anguish, not another's; but my spirit
Groans for the city, for myself, for you.

I was not sleeping, you are not waking me.
No, I have been in tears for a long while
And in my restless thought walked many ways.
70 In all my search, I found one helpful course,
And that I have taken: I have sent Creon,
Son of Menoeceus,° brother of the Queen,
To Delphi, Apollo's place of revelation,°
To learn there, if he can,
75 What act or pledge of mine may save the city.
I have counted the days, and now, this very day,
I am troubled, for he has overstayed his time.
What is he doing? He has been gone too long.
Yet whenever he comes back, I should do ill
80 To scant whatever duty God reveals.

39. Sphinx, that flinty singer: In Greek mythology the Sphinx is a winged monster that kills anyone who cannot answer her riddle: "What walks on four legs in the morning, two legs at noon, and three legs in the evening?" Oedipus gives the correct answer: "A man crawls as an infant, walks erect as a man, and uses a staff in old age." The Sphinx then kills herself.

? **35–59.** *What qualities or personality traits in Oedipus does the Priest single out as the ruler's special virtues?*

? **53.** *What familiar metaphor for a state or kingdom is suggested by this line? How does the Priest refer again to this metaphor in line 58?*

60. Notice that Oedipus repeatedly refers to the Thebans as "children."
? *What does this suggest about the way he sees himself and his role?*

72. Menoeceus (me·nē′sus).
73. Delphi (del′fī) **... revelation:** Delphi was the seat of the most famous oracle of the god Apollo.

Priest.

It is a timely promise. At this instant
They tell me Creon is here.

Oedipus. O Lord Apollo!

May his news be fair as his face is radiant!

Priest.

It could not be otherwise: he is crowned with bay,
The chaplet is thick with berries.

85 **Oedipus.** We shall soon know;

He is near enough to hear us now.

[*Enter* CREON.]

O Prince:

Brother: son of Menoeceus:
What answer do you bring us from the god?

Creon.

A strong one. I can tell you, great afflictions
90 Will turn out well, if they are taken well.

Oedipus.

What was the oracle? These vague words
Leave me still hanging between hope and fear.

Creon.

Is it your pleasure to hear me with all these
Gathered around us? I am prepared to speak,
But should we not go in?

95 **Oedipus.** Let them all hear it.

It is for them I suffer, more than for myself.

Creon.

Then I will tell you what I heard at Delphi.
In plain words
The god commands us to expel from the land of Thebes
100 An old defilement we are sheltering.
It is a deathly thing, beyond cure;
We must not let it feed upon us longer.

Oedipus.

What defilement? How shall we rid ourselves of it?

Creon.

By exile or death, blood for blood. It was
105 Murder that brought the plague-wind on the city.

Oedipus.

Murder of whom? Surely the god has named him?

"THE GOD COMMANDS US TO EXPEL FROM THE LAND OF THEBES AN OLD DEFILEMENT WE ARE SHELTERING."

93–96. These two short speeches about where to hold a discussion suggest a contrast between Oedipus's and Creon's attitudes toward the people.
? *What is this contrast?*

Creon.
My lord: long ago Laius was our king,
Before you came to govern us.

Oedipus.   I know;
I learned of him from others; I never saw him.

Creon.
110   He was murdered; and Apollo commands us now
To take revenge upon whoever killed him.

Oedipus.
Upon whom? Where are they? Where shall we find a clue
To solve that crime, after so many years?

Creon.
Here in this land, he said.
                                                    If we make enquiry,
115   We may touch things that otherwise escape us.

Oedipus.
Tell me: Was Laius murdered in his house,
Or in the fields, or in some foreign country?

Creon.
He said he planned to make a pilgrimage.
He did not come home again.

Oedipus.   And was there no one,
120   No witness, no companion, to tell what happened?

Creon.
They were all killed but one, and he got away
So frightened that he could remember one thing only.

Oedipus.
What was that one thing? One may be the key
To everything, if we resolve to use it.

Creon.
125   He said that a band of highwaymen attacked them,
Outnumbered them, and overwhelmed the King.

Oedipus.
Strange, that a highwayman should be so daring—
Unless some faction here bribed him to do it.

Creon.
We thought of that. But after Laius' death
130   New troubles arose and we had no avenger.

Oedipus.
What troubles could prevent your hunting down
the killers?

109. *What is dramatically ironic about Oedipus's line here?*

Preparations for a satiric drama. Red-figure volute krater (5th century B.C.E.).

Museo Archeologico Nazionale, Naples.

127. Notice that Oedipus refers to a single "highwayman" in this line, whereas Creon mentioned a "band of highwaymen" in line 125.

Do you think this is just a casual change from the plural to the singular? What might this slip on Oedipus's part (if it is a slip) suggest? Explain.

Creon.

> The riddling Sphinx's song
> Made us deaf to all mysteries but her own.

Oedipus.

> Then once more I must bring what is dark to light.
135 > It is most fitting that Apollo shows,
> As you do, this <u>compunction</u> for the dead.
> You shall see how I stand by you, as I should,
> To avenge the city and the city's god,
> And not as though it were for some distant friend,
140 > But for my own sake, to be rid of evil.
> Whoever killed King Laius might—who knows?—
> Decide at any moment to kill me as well.
> By avenging the murdered king I protect myself.
> Come, then, my children: leave the altar steps,
> Lift up your olive boughs!
145 >   One of you go
> And summon the people of Cadmus to gather here.
> I will do all that I can; you may tell them that.

> [*Exit a* PAGE.]

> So, with the help of God,
> We shall be saved—or else indeed we are lost.

Priest.

150 > Let us rise, children. It was for this we came,
> And now the King has promised it himself.
> Phoebus° has sent us an oracle; may he descend
> Himself to save us and drive out the plague.

[*Exeunt* OEDIPUS *and* CREON *into the palace by the central door. The* PRIEST *and the* SUPPLIANTS *disperse right and left. After a short pause the* CHORUS *enters the orchestra.*]

PARADOS°

Strophe 1

Chorus.

> What is God singing in his profound
155 > Delphi of gold and shadow?
> What oracle for Thebes, the sunwhipped city?

Vocabulary

compunction (kəm·puŋk′shən) *n.*: feeling of remorse or guilt.

134–145. These lines are dramatically ironic, because the audience knows that Oedipus himself is the murderer.

? *In addition to the dramatic irony, what does Oedipus's speculation about his own danger suggest about the nature of ancient Greek kingship?*

152. Phoebus (fē′bəs): name for Apollo as sun god; here, alluding to him as the god of prophecy.

Parados (par′ə·dōs′): entrance song of the Chorus. Song and speech alternate throughout the play. In this choral song the Chorus turns from one side of the orchestra to the other while singing the *strophe* (strō′fē). The Chorus moves in the opposite direction while singing the *antistrophe* (an·tis′trə·fē).

Fear unjoints me, the roots of my heart tremble.

Now I remember, O Healer,° your power, and wonder:
Will you send doom like a sudden cloud, or weave it
160 Like nightfall of the past?

Speak, speak to us, issue of holy sound:
Dearest to our expectancy: be tender!

Antistrophe 1

Let me pray to Athena, the immortal daughter of Zeus,
And to Artemis her sister
165 Who keeps her famous throne in the market ring,
And to Apollo, bowman at the far butts of heaven—
O gods, descend! Like three streams leap against
The fires of our grief, the fires of darkness;
Be swift to bring us rest!

170 As in the old time from the brilliant house
Of air you stepped to save us, come again!

170–171. The Chorus says that Apollo saved the city of Thebes once before. *To what previous crisis do you think they are alluding?*

Strophe 2

Now our afflictions have no end,
Now all our stricken host lies down
And no man fights off death with his mind;

175 The noble plowland bears no grain,
And groaning mothers cannot bear—
See, how our lives like birds take wing,
Like sparks that fly when a fire soars,
To the shore of the god of evening.

Antistrophe 2

180 The plague burns on, it is pitiless,
Though pallid children laden with death
Lie unwept in the stony ways,

And old gray women by every path
Flock to the strand about the altars

185 There to strike their breasts and cry
Worship of Phoebus in wailing prayers:
Be kind, God's golden child!

172–187. *How does the mood of Strophe 2 and Antistrophe 2 contrast with the mood of the first strophe and antistrophe? What images in the second pair of stanzas focus on death and decay?*

Strophe 3

There are no swords in this attack by fire,
No shields, but we are ringed with cries.
190 Send the besieger plunging from our homes
Into the vast sea room of the Atlantic
Or into the waves that foam eastward of Thrace°—

192. Thrace (thrās): region lying between the Aegean Sea, the Danube River, and the Black Sea.

For the day ravages what the night spares—

195 Destroy our enemy, lord of the thunder!
Let him be riven by lightning from heaven!

Antistrophe 3

Phoebus Apollo, stretch the sun's bowstring,
That golden cord, until it sing for us,
Flashing arrows in heaven!

Artemis, Huntress,

Race with flaring lights upon our mountains!

200 O scarlet god, O golden-banded brow,
O Theban Bacchus in a storm of Maenads,°

[*Enter* OEDIPUS, *center.*]

Whirl upon Death, that all the Undying hate!
Come with blinding torches, come in joy!

SCENE 1

Oedipus.

Is this your prayer? It may be answered. Come,
205 Listen to me, act as the crisis demands,
And you shall have relief from all these evils.

Until now I was a stranger to this tale,
As I had been a stranger to the crime.
Could I track down the murderer without a clue?
210 But now, friends,
As one who became a citizen after the murder,
I make this proclamation to all Thebans:
If any man knows by whose hand Laius, son of Labdacus,
Met his death, I direct that man to tell me everything.
215 No matter what he fears for having so long withheld it.
Let it stand as promised that no further trouble
Will come to him, but he may leave the land in safety.

Moreover: If anyone knows the murderer to be foreign,
Let him not keep silent: he shall have his reward from me.
220 However, if he does conceal it; if any man
Fearing for his friend or for himself disobeys this edict,
Hear what I propose to do:

I solemnly forbid the people of this country,
Where power and throne are mine, ever to receive that man
225 Or speak to him, no matter who he is, or let him
Join in sacrifice, lustration,° or in prayer.
I decree that he be driven from every house,

196–198. *What physical activity does the Chorus associate with Apollo? In the Chorus's imagination, is Apollo primarily a healer or a destroyer? Or is he both at once? Explain.*

201. Theban Bacchus (bak′əs): Bacchus, also known as Dionysus, is the god of revelry and brutality. He came to Thebes accompanied by female devotees who took part in frenzied celebrations of the god. Pentheus, the king of Thebes, mocked Bacchus and his followers and was punished by being torn limb from limb. **Maenads** (mē′nadz′): priestesses of Bacchus.

207–208. *What is unintentionally ironic about Oedipus's statement here?*

226. lustration (lus′trā′shən) *n.:* purification through ritual.

Being, as he is, corruption itself to us: the Delphic
Voice of Zeus has pronounced this revelation.
230 Thus I associate myself with the oracle
And take the side of the murdered king.

As for the criminal, I pray to God—
Whether it be a lurking thief, or one of a number—
I pray that that man's life be consumed in evil and
wretchedness.
235 And as for me, this curse applies no less
If it should turn out that the culprit is my guest here,
Sharing my hearth.
                    You have heard the penalty.
I lay it on you now to attend to this
For my sake, for Apollo's, for the sick
240 Sterile city that heaven has abandoned.
Suppose the oracle had given you no command:
Should this defilement go uncleansed forever?
You should have found the murderer: your king,
A noble king, had been destroyed!
                              Now I,
245 Having the power that he held before me,
Having his bed, begetting children there
Upon his wife, as he would have, had he lived—
Their son would have been my children's brother,
If Laius had had luck in fatherhood!
250 (But surely ill luck rushed upon his reign)—
I say I take the son's part, just as though
I were his son, to press the fight for him
And see it won! I'll find the hand that brought
Death to Labdacus' and Polydorus' child,°
255 Heir of Cadmus' and Agenor's line.°
And as for those who fail me,
May the gods deny them the fruit of the earth,
Fruit of the womb, and may they rot utterly!
Let them be wretched as we are wretched, and worse!

260 For you, for loyal Thebans, and for all
Who find my actions right, I pray the favor
Of justice, and of all the immortal gods.

Choragos.
Since I am under oath, my lord, I swear
I did not do the murder, I cannot name
265 The murderer. Might not the oracle
That has ordained the search tell where to find him?

Oedipus.
An honest question. But no man in the world

232–237. How does Sophocles deepen the irony of Oedipus's curse in these lines?

245–255. The irony in this long speech now reaches an almost unbearable intensity.
What tone of voice might an actor playing Oedipus use for these lines?

254. Labdacus (lab′də·kəs): king of Thebes and father of Laius. **Polydorus' child:** Polydorus (päl·i·dō′rəs) was the grandfather of Laius.
255. Agenor's line: Agenor (ə·jē′nôr), father of Cadmus, the founder of Thebes.

Oedipus with Chorus.
Douglas Campbell
performing as Oedipus
in Tyrone Guthrie's filmed
version of the play in the
classical Greek tradition.

The Granger Collection, New York.

Can make the gods do more than the gods will.

Choragos.
There is one last <u>expedient</u>—

Oedipus.   Tell me what it is.
270   Though it seem slight, you must not hold it back.

Choragos.
A lord clairvoyant° to the lord Apollo,
As we all know, is the skilled Teiresias.
One might learn much about this from him, Oedipus.

Oedipus.
I am not wasting time:
275   Creon spoke of this, and I have sent for him—
Twice, in fact; it is strange that he is not here.

Choragos.
The other matter—that old report—seems useless.

271. clairvoyant (kler·vȯi′ənt)
adj.: capable of perceiving
through intuition things that
cannot be seen.

Vocabulary

expedient (ek·spē′dē·ənt) *n.:* something that is useful or
helpful.

Oedipus.

Tell me. I am interested in all reports.

Choragos.

The King was said to have been killed by highwaymen.

Oedipus.

280   I know. But we have no witnesses to that.

Choragos.

If the killer can feel a particle of dread,
Your curse will bring him out of hiding!

Oedipus.   No.

The man who dared that act will fear no curse.

[*Enter the blind seer* TEIRESIAS, *led by a* PAGE.]

Choragos.

But there is one man who may detect the criminal.
285   This is Teiresias, this is the holy prophet
In whom, alone of all men, truth was born.

Oedipus.

Teiresias: seer: student of mysteries,
Of all that's taught and all that no man tells,
Secrets of Heaven and secrets of the earth:
290   Blind though you are, you know the city lies
Sick with plague; and from this plague, my lord,
We find that you alone can guard or save us.

Possibly you did not hear the messengers?
Apollo, when we sent to him,
295   Sent us back word that this great pestilence
Would lift, but only if we established clearly
The identity of those who murdered Laius.
They must be killed or exiled.
                        Can you use
Birdflight or any art of divination°
300   To purify yourself, and Thebes, and me
From this contagion? We are in your hands.
There is no fairer duty
Than that of helping others in distress.

Teiresias.

How dreadful knowledge of the truth can be
305   When there's no help in truth! I knew this well,
But made myself forget. I should not have come.

Oedipus.

What is troubling you? Why are your eyes so cold?

Calyx-krater vase, late Classical
period (340–330 B.C.E.) by the
Darius Painter.

Museum of Fine Arts, Boston. Gift of
Harry J. Denberg, Jerome M. Eisenberg,
and Benjamin Rowland, Jr., by exchange;
gift of Barbara and Lawrence Fleishman
and the Classical Department Curator's
Fund (1989.100).

299. Birdflight . . . divination:
prophets used the flight of
birds to interpret the future.

Teiresias.
> Let me go home. Bear your own fate, and I'll
> Bear mine. It is better so: trust what I say.

Oedipus.
310
> What you say is ungracious and unhelpful
> To your native country. Do not refuse to speak.

Teiresias.
> When it comes to speech, your own is neither temperate
> Nor opportune. I wish to be more prudent.

Oedipus.
> In God's name, we all beg you—

Teiresias.   You are all ignorant.
315
> No; I will never tell you what I know.
> Now it is my misery; then, it would be yours.

Oedipus.
> What! You do know something, and will not tell us?
> You would betray us all and wreck the State?

Teiresias.
> I do not intend to torture myself, or you.
320
> Why persist in asking? You will not persuade me.

Oedipus.
> What a wicked old man you are! You'd try a stone's
> Patience! Out with it! Have you no feeling at all?

Teiresias.
> You call me unfeeling. If you could only see
> The nature of your own feelings . . .

Oedipus.   Why,
325
> Who would not feel as I do? Who could endure
> Your arrogance toward the city?

Teiresias.   What does it matter!
> Whether I speak or not, it is bound to come.

Oedipus.
> Then, if "it" is bound to come, you are bound to tell me.

Teiresias.
> No, I will not go on. Rage as you please.

Oedipus.
> Rage? Why not!
>   And I'll tell you what I think:
330
> You planned it, you had it done, you all but
> Killed him with your own hands: if you had eyes,
> I'd say the crime was yours, and yours alone.

? 321–322. Is Oedipus's annoyed reaction here appropriate, or is Oedipus prematurely angry with Teiresias?

? 330–333. How do you react to Oedipus's accusation in these lines?

Teiresias.

335
    So? I charge you, then,
    Abide by the proclamation you have made:
    From this day forth
    Never speak again to these men or to me;
    You yourself are the pollution of this country.

Oedipus.

340
    You dare say that! Can you possibly think you have
    Some way of going free, after such insolence?

Teiresias.

    I have gone free. It is the truth sustains me.

Oedipus.

    Who taught you shamelessness? It was not your craft.

Teiresias.

    You did. You made me speak. I did not want to.

Oedipus.

    Speak what? Let me hear it again more clearly.

Teiresias.

345
    Was it not clear before? Are you tempting me?

Oedipus.

    I did not understand it. Say it again.

Teiresias.

    I say that you are the murderer whom you seek.

Oedipus.

    Now twice you have spat out infamy. You'll pay for it!

Teiresias.

    Would you care for more? Do you wish to be really angry?

Oedipus.

350
    Say what you will. Whatever you say is worthless.

Teiresias.

    I say you live in hideous shame with those
    Most dear to you. You cannot see the evil.

Oedipus.

    It seems you can go on mouthing like this forever.

Teiresias.

    I can, if there is power in truth.

Oedipus.   There is:

355
    But not for you, not for you,
    You sightless, witless, senseless, mad old man!

Teiresias.

    You are the madman. There is no one here

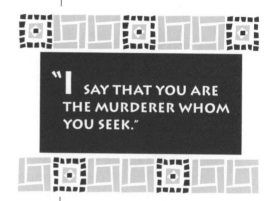

"I SAY THAT YOU ARE THE MURDERER WHOM YOU SEEK."

Who will not curse you soon, as you curse me.

Oedipus.
You child of endless night! You cannot hurt me
360   Or any other man who sees the sun.

Teiresias.
True: it is not from me your fate will come.
That lies within Apollo's competence,
As it is his concern.

Oedipus.   Tell me:
Are you speaking for Creon, or for yourself?

Teiresias.
365   Creon is no threat. You weave your own doom.

Oedipus.
Wealth, power, craft of statesmanship!
Kingly position, everywhere admired!
What savage envy is stored up against these,
If Creon, whom I trusted, Creon my friend,
370   For this great office which the city once
Put in my hands unsought—if for this power
Creon desires in secret to destroy me!

He has bought this decrepit fortuneteller, this
Collector of dirty pennies, this prophet fraud—
Why, he is no more clairvoyant than I am!
375   Tell us:
Has your mystic mummery° ever approached the truth?
When that hellcat the Sphinx was performing here,
What help were you to these people?
Her magic was not for the first man who came along:
380   It demanded a real exorcist. Your birds—
What good were they? or the gods, for the matter of that?
But I came by,
Oedipus, the simple man, who knows nothing—
I thought it out for myself, no birds helped me!
385   And this is the man you think you can destroy,
That you may be close to Creon when he's king!
Well, you and your friend Creon, it seems to me,
Will suffer most. If you were not an old man,
You would have paid already for your plot.

Choragos.
390   We cannot see that his words or yours
Have been spoken except in anger, Oedipus,

364. *Why should Oedipus suddenly connect Creon with Teiresias here? Look back at line 275 for a clue.*

376. mummery *n.:* pretentious or hypocritical rites.

383. This line contains a complex example of Sophoclean irony. As he mocks Teiresias, Oedipus tries deliberately to be ironic when he calls himself a "simple man, who knows nothing." *Explain how this line contains unintended dramatic irony.*

Vocabulary
decrepit (dē·krep′it) *adj.:* worn-out by old age.

And of anger we have no need. How can God's will
Be accomplished best? That is what most concerns us.

Teiresias.

    You are a king. But where argument's concerned
395   I am your man, as much a king as you.
    I am not your servant, but Apollo's.
    I have no need of Creon to speak for me.

    Listen to me. You mock my blindness, do you?
    But I say that you, with both your eyes, are blind:
400   You cannot see the wretchedness of your life,
    Nor in whose house you live, no, nor with whom.
    Who are your father and mother? Can you tell me?
    You do not even know the blind wrongs
    That you have done them, on earth and in the world below.
405   But the double lash of your parents' curse will whip you
    Out of this land some day, with only night
    Upon your precious eyes.
    Your cries then—where will they not be heard?
    What fastness of Cithaeron° will not echo them?
410   And that bridal-descant° of yours—you'll know it then,
    The song they sang when you came here to Thebes
    And found your misguided berthing.
    All this, and more, that you cannot guess at now,
    Will bring you to yourself among your children.
415   Be angry, then. Curse Creon. Curse my words.
    I tell you, no man that walks upon the earth
    Shall be rooted out more horribly than you.

Oedipus.

    Am I to bear this from him?—Damnation
    Take you! Out of this place! Out of my sight!

Teiresias.

420   I would not have come at all if you had not asked me.

Oedipus.

    Could I have told that you'd talk nonsense, that
    You'd come here to make a fool of yourself, and of me?

Teiresias.

    A fool? Your parents thought me sane enough.

Oedipus.

    My parents again!—Wait: who were my parents?

Teiresias.

425   This day will give you a father, and break your heart.

Oedipus.

    Your infantile riddles! Your damned abracadabra!°

390–393. Choragos speaks for the entire Chorus.

? *Do you agree with the Chorus's reaction to Oedipus here?*

409. Cithaeron (si·thērän): mountain in Boeotia (bē·ō′shə), where Oedipus was left to die as an infant.
410. descant (des′kant′) *n.*: melody.

426. abracadabra *n.*: silly talk.

Teiresias.

You were a great man once at solving riddles.

Oedipus.

Mock me with that if you like; you will find it true.

Teiresias.

It was true enough. It brought about your ruin.

Oedipus.

But if it saved this town?

430 **Teiresias** (*to the* PAGE). Boy, give me your hand.

Oedipus.

Yes, boy; lead him away.

                            —While you are here
We can do nothing. Go; leave us in peace.

Teiresias.

I will go when I have said what I have to say.
How can you hurt me? And I tell you again:
435 The man you have been looking for all this time,
The damned man, the murderer of Laius,
That man is in Thebes. To your mind he is foreign-born,
But it will soon be shown that he is a Theban,
A revelation that will fail to please.

                            A blind man,
Who has his eyes now; a penniless man, who is
440   rich now;
And he will go tapping the strange earth with his staff.
To the children with whom he lives now he will be
Brother and father—the very same; to her
Who bore him, son and husband—the very same
Who came to his father's bed, wet with his father's
445   blood.

Enough. Go think that over.
If later you find error in what I have said,
You may say that I have no skill in prophecy.

[Exit TEIRESIAS, led by his PAGE. OEDIPUS
goes into the palace.]

ODE° 1

Strophe 1

Chorus.

The Delphic stone of prophecies
450 Remembers ancient regicide°
And a still bloody hand.

427. *Explain Teiresias's mocking irony in this line. To what achievement of Oedipus does the prophet refer?*

Seer from the Stratford Festival production of *Oedipus Rex* (1954).

446–448. *What gestures might Teiresias make as he says these lines?*

Ode *n.:* song chanted by the Chorus. An ode separates one scene from the next.

450. regicide (rej′ə·sīd′) *n.:* murder of a monarch.

That killer's hour of flight has come.
He must be stronger than riderless
Coursers of untiring wind,
For the son of Zeus armed with his father's thunder
Leaps in lightning after him;
And the Furies° follow him, the sad Furies.

Antistrophe 1

Holy Parnassus'° peak of snow
Flashes and blinds that secret man,
That all shall hunt him down:
Though he may roam the forest shade
Like a bull gone wild from pasture
To rage through glooms of stone.
Doom comes down on him; flight will not avail him;
For the world's heart calls him desolate,
And the immortal Furies follow, forever follow.

Strophe 2

But now a wilder thing is heard
From the old man skilled at hearing Fate in the wingbeat
        of a bird.
Bewildered as a blown bird, my soul hovers and cannot
        find
Foothold in this debate, or any reason or rest of mind.
But no man ever brought—none can bring
Proof of strife between Thebes' royal house,
Labdacus' line, and the son of Polybus;
And never until now has any man brought word
Of Laius' dark death staining Oedipus the King.

Antistrophe 2

Divine Zeus and Apollo hold
Perfect intelligence alone of all tales ever told;
And well though this diviner works, he works in his
        own night;
No man can judge that rough unknown or trust in
        second sight,
For wisdom changes hands among the wise.
Shall I believe my great lord criminal
At a raging word that a blind old man let fall?
I saw him, when the carrion woman° faced him of old,
Prove his heroic mind! These evil words are lies.

455

460

465

470

475

480

455. To whom does the Chorus allude when they mention "the son of Zeus"? (The "Delphic stone" in line 449 and "Holy Parnassus' peak of snow" in line 458 are clues.)

457. Furies *n. pl.:* In Greek mythology, avenging spirits.

458. Parnassus (pär·nas′əs): In Greek mythology, the mountain where Apollo's oracle is located.

467–468. What does the Chorus mean by "wilder thing" in this line? Who is the "old man skilled at hearing Fate" who appeared in the previous scene?

483. carrion woman: Sphinx.

484. Why does the Chorus refuse to believe Teiresias's accusations against Oedipus?

SCENE 2

Creon.

485   Men of Thebes:
      I am told that heavy accusations
      Have been brought against me by King Oedipus.

      I am not the kind of man to bear this tamely.

      If in these present difficulties
490   He holds me accountable for any harm to him
      Through anything I have said or done—why, then,
      I do not value life in this dishonor.
      It is not as though this rumor touched upon
      Some private indiscretion. The matter is grave.
495   The fact is that I am being called disloyal
      To the State, to my fellow citizens, to my friends.

Choragos.

      He may have spoken in anger, not from his mind.

Creon.

      But did you not hear him say I was the one
      Who seduced the old prophet into lying?

Choragos.

500   The thing was said; I do not know how seriously.

Creon.

      But you were watching him! Were his eyes steady?
      Did he look like a man in his right mind?

Choragos.   I do not know,
      I cannot judge the behavior of great men.
      But here is the King himself.

      [*Enter* OEDIPUS.]

Oedipus.   So you dared come back.
505   Why? How brazen of you to come to my house,
      You murderer!
               Do you think I do not know
      That you plotted to kill me, plotted to steal my throne?
      Tell me, in God's name: am I a coward, a fool,
      That you should dream you could accomplish this?
510   A fool who could not see your slippery game?
      A coward, not to fight back when I saw it?
      You are the fool, Creon, are you not? hoping
      Without support or friends to get a throne?
      Thrones may be won or bought: you could do neither.

Creon.

515   Now listen to me. You have talked; let me talk, too.

486–487. What accusations does Creon refer to here?

503. Is the Chorus noncommittal here because they want to play the peacemaker, or are they "passing the buck," in your opinion?

Oedipus Rex rehearsal at the Coliseum, Rome.

You cannot judge unless you know the facts.

Oedipus.
You speak well: there is one fact; but I find it hard
To learn from the deadliest enemy I have.

Creon.
That above all I must dispute with you.

Oedipus.
520   That above all I will not hear you deny.

Creon.
If you think there is anything good in being stubborn
Against all reason, then I say you are wrong.

Oedipus.
If you think a man can sin against his own kind
And not be punished for it, I say you are mad.

Creon.
525   I agree. But tell me: what have I done to you?

Oedipus.
You advised me to send for that wizard, did you not?

Creon.
I did. I should do it again.

Oedipus.   Very well. Now tell me:
How long has it been since Laius—

Creon.   What of Laius?

Oedipus.
Since he vanished in that onset by the road?

Creon.
It was long ago, a long time.

530 **Oedipus.**   And this prophet,
Was he practicing here then?

Creon.   He was; and with honor, as now.

Oedipus.
Did he speak of me at that time?

Creon.   He never did;
At least, not when I was present.

Oedipus.   But . . . the inquiry?
I suppose you held one?

Creon.   We did, but we learned nothing.

Oedipus.
535   Why did the prophet not speak against me then?

Creon.
I do not know; and I am the kind of man
Who holds his tongue when he has no facts to go on.

Oedipus.
There's one fact that you know, and you could tell it.

Creon.
What fact is that? If I know it, you shall have it.

Oedipus.
540   If he were not involved with you, he could not say
That it was I who murdered Laius.

Creon.
If he says that, you are the one that knows it!—
But now it is my turn to question you.

Oedipus.
Put your questions. I am no murderer.

Creon.
First, then: You married my sister?

537. What tone of voice might the actor playing Creon use for this line?

545 Oedipus.   I married your sister.

Creon.
     And you rule the kingdom equally with her?

Oedipus.
     Everything that she wants she has from me.

Creon.
     And I am the third, equal to both of you?

Oedipus.
     That is why I call you a bad friend.

Creon.
550   No. Reason it out, as I have done.
     Think of this first: Would any sane man prefer
     Power, with all a king's anxieties,
     To that same power and the grace of sleep?
     Certainly not I.
555   I have never longed for the king's power—only his rights.
     Would any wise man differ from me in this?
     As matters stand, I have my way in everything
     With your consent, and no responsibilities.
     If I were king, I should be a slave to policy.

560   How could I desire a scepter more
     Than what is now mine—untroubled influence?
     No, I have not gone mad; I need no honors,
     Except those with the perquisites I have now.
     I am welcome everywhere; every man salutes me,
565   And those who want your favor seek my ear,
     Since I know how to manage what they ask.
     Should I exchange this ease for that anxiety?
     Besides, no sober mind is treasonable.
     I hate anarchy
570   And never would deal with any man who likes it.

     Test what I have said. Go to the priestess
     At Delphi, ask if I quoted her correctly.
     And as for this other thing: if I am found
     Guilty of treason with Teiresias,
575   Then sentence me to death! You have my word
     It is a sentence I should cast my vote for—
     But not without evidence!
                         You do wrong
     When you take good men for bad, bad men for good.
     A true friend thrown aside—why, life itself
     Is not more precious!
580   In time you will know this well:
     For time, and time alone, will show the just man,

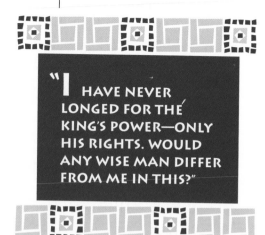

? 550–570. *What do you think of Creon's reasoning in these lines? Is his argument that he does not want to be king convincing, or is it sophistic—seemingly sound but actually logically faulty?*

Though scoundrels are discovered in a day.

Choragos.
This is well said, and a prudent man would ponder it.
Judgments too quickly formed are dangerous.

Oedipus.
585 But is he not quick in his duplicity?
And shall I not be quick to parry him?
Would you have me stand still, hold my peace, and let
This man win everything, through my inaction?

Creon.
And you want—what is it, then? To banish me?

Oedipus.
590 No, not exile. It is your death I want,
So that all the world may see what treason means.

Creon.
You will persist, then? You will not believe me?

Oedipus.
How can I believe you?

Creon.   Then you are a fool.

Oedipus.
To save myself?

Creon.   In justice, think of me.

Oedipus.
You are evil incarnate.

595 **Creon.**   But suppose that you are wrong?

Oedipus.
Still I must rule.

Creon.   But not if you rule badly.

Oedipus.
O city, city!

Creon.   It is my city, too!

Choragos.
Now my lords, be still. I see the Queen,
Jocasta, coming from her palace chambers;
600 And it is time she came, for the sake of you both.
This dreadful quarrel can be resolved through her.

[*Enter* JOCASTA.]

Jocasta.
Poor foolish men, what wicked din is this?

580–582. Explain the contrast that Creon draws between just men and scoundrels in these lines.

585–588. Whom does Oedipus address in these lines?

596. Why do you think Oedipus says that he must rule? Is it the tyrant in him or a belief in fate?

With Thebes sick to death, is it not shameful
That you should rake some private quarrel up?
(*to* OEDIPUS) Come into the house.

605   —And you, Creon, go now:
Let us have no more of this tumult over nothing.

Creon.

Nothing? No, sister: what your husband plans for me
Is one of two great evils: exile or death.

Oedipus.

He is right.

                 Why, woman, I have caught him squarely
Plotting against my life.

610 **Creon.**   No! Let me die
Accursed if ever I have wished you harm!

Jocasta.

Ah, believe it, Oedipus!
In the name of the gods, respect this oath of his
For my sake, for the sake of these people here!

Strophe 1

Choragos.

615 Open your mind to her, my lord. Be ruled by her, I beg you!

Oedipus.

What would you have me do?

Choragos.

Respect Creon's word. He has never spoken like a fool,
And now he has sworn an oath.

Oedipus.   You know what you ask?

Choragos.   I do.

Oedipus.   Speak on, then.

Choragos.

A friend so sworn should not be baited so,
620 In blind malice, and without final proof.

Oedipus.

You are aware, I hope, that what you say
Means death for me, or exile at the least.

Strophe 2

Choragos.

No, I swear by Helios,° first in Heaven!
        May I die friendless and accursed,
625 The worst of deaths, if ever I meant that!

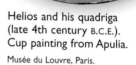

Helios and his quadriga
(late 4th century B.C.E.).
Cup painting from Apulia.

Musée du Louvre, Paris.

623. Helios (hē′lē·äs′): one
of the Titans; sun god often
confused with Apollo. He is
associated with truth.

It is the withering fields
    That hurt my sick heart:
Must we bear all these ills,
    And now your bad blood as well?

Oedipus.

630   Then let him go. And let me die, if I must,
    Or be driven by him in shame from the land of Thebes.
    It is your unhappiness, and not his talk,
    That touches me.
               As for him—
    Wherever he goes, hatred will follow him.

Creon.

635   Ugly in yielding, as you were ugly in rage!
    Natures like yours chiefly torment themselves.

Oedipus.

    Can you not go? Can you not leave me?

Creon.   I can.
    You do not know me; but the city knows me,
    And in its eyes I am just, if not in yours.

[Exit CREON.*]*

Antistrophe 1

Choragos.

    Lady Jocasta, did you not ask the King to go to
640   his chambers?

Jocasta.

    First tell me what has happened.

Choragos.

    There was suspicion without evidence; yet it rankled
    As even false charges will.

Jocasta.   On both sides?

Choragos.   On both.

Jocasta.   But what was said?

Choragos.

    Oh let it rest, let it be done with!
645   Have we not suffered enough?

Oedipus.

    You see to what your decency has brought you:
    You have made difficulties where my heart saw none.

630–633. Why does Oedipus yield to the Chorus's request not to punish Creon?

Antistrophe 2

Choragos.

Oedipus, it is not once only I have told you—
You must know I should count myself unwise
650   To the point of madness, should I now forsake you—
    You, under whose hand,
      In the storm of another time,
    Our dear land sailed out free.
      But now stand fast at the helm!

Jocasta.

655   In God's name, Oedipus, inform your wife as well:
Why are you so set in this hard anger?

Oedipus.

I will tell you, for none of these men deserves
My confidence as you do. It is Creon's work,
His treachery, his plotting against me.

Jocasta.

660   Go on, if you can make this clear to me.

Oedipus.

He charges me with the murder of Laius.

Jocasta.

Has he some knowledge? Or does he speak from hearsay?

Oedipus.

He would not commit himself to such a charge,
But he has brought in that damnable soothsayer
To tell his story.

665   **Jocasta.**   Set your mind at rest.
If it is a question of soothsayers, I tell you
That you will find no man whose craft gives knowledge
Of the unknowable.

      Here is my proof:

An oracle was reported to Laius once
670   (I will not say from Phoebus himself, but from
His appointed ministers, at any rate)
That his doom would be death at the hands of his
    own son—
His son, born of his flesh and of mine!

Now, you remember the story: Laius was killed
675   By marauding strangers where three highways meet;
But his child had not been three days in this world
Before the King had pierced the baby's ankles
And left him to die on a lonely mountainside.

? **661.** *Has Creon in fact charged Oedipus with the murder of Laius?*

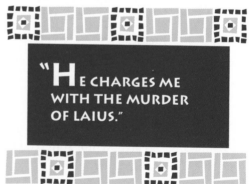

"HE CHARGES ME WITH THE MURDER OF LAIUS."

680 Thus, Apollo never caused that child
To kill his father, and it was not Laius' fate
To die at the hands of his son, as he had feared.
This is what prophets and prophecies are worth!
Have no dread of them.
                    It is God himself
Who can show us what he wills, in his own way.

Oedipus.
685 How strange a shadowy memory crossed my mind,
Just now while you were speaking; it chilled my heart.

Jocasta.
What do you mean? What memory do you speak of?

Oedipus.
If I understand you, Laius was killed
At a place where three roads meet.

Jocasta.   So it was said;
We have no later story.

690 **Oedipus.**   Where did it happen?

Jocasta.
Phocis,° it is called: at a place where the Theban Way
Divides into the roads toward Delphi and Daulis.°

Oedipus.
When?

Jocasta. We had the news not long before you came
And proved the right to your succession here.

Oedipus.
695 Ah, what net has God been weaving for me?

Jocasta.
Oedipus! Why does this trouble you?

Oedipus.   Do not ask me yet.
First, tell me how Laius looked, and tell me
How old he was.

Jocasta.   He was tall, his hair just touched
With white, his form was not unlike your own.

Oedipus.
700 I think that I myself may be accursed
By my own ignorant edict.

Jocasta.   You speak strangely.
It makes me tremble to look at you, my King.

Oedipus.
I am not sure that the blind man cannot see.

691. **Phocis** (fō′sis): country in which Mount Parnassus is located.
692. **Daulis** (dô′lis): in Phocis, east of Delphi.

695. What sudden change of tone might an actor playing Oedipus use in this line?

688–704. What might Oedipus begin to suspect as he starts to question Jocasta more carefully?

But I should know better if you were to tell me—

Jocasta.
705   Anything—though I dread to hear you ask it.

Oedipus.
Was the King lightly escorted, or did he ride
With a large company, as a ruler should?

Jocasta.
There were five men with him in all: one was a herald,
And a single chariot, which he was driving.

Oedipus.
Alas, that makes it plain enough!
710   But who—
Who told you how it happened?

Jocasta.   A household servant,
The only one to escape.

Oedipus.   And is he still
A servant of ours?

Jocasta.   No; for when he came back at last
And found you enthroned in the place of the dead king,
715   He came to me, touched my hand with his, and begged
That I would send him away to the frontier district
Where only the shepherds go—
As far away from the city as I could send him.
I granted his prayer; for although the man was a slave,
720   He had earned more than this favor at my hands.

Oedipus.
Can he be called back quickly?

Jocasta.   Easily.
But why?

Oedipus.   I have taken too much upon myself
Without inquiry; therefore I wish to consult him.

Jocasta.
Then he shall come.
                  But am I not one also
725   To whom you might confide these fears of yours?

Oedipus.
That is your right; it will not be denied you,
Now least of all; for I have reached a pitch
Of wild foreboding. Is there anyone
To whom I should sooner speak?

730   Polybus° of Corinth is my father.
My mother is a Dorian: Merope.°

713–720. *How did Jocasta behave toward the lone surviving witness to the attack on her husband?*

726–729. *How would you describe Oedipus's feelings toward Jocasta?*

730. Polybus (päl′i·bəs): king of Corinth.
731. Merope (mer′ə·pē): The Dorians are descended from Dorus, a son of Apollo.

(Left to right) Jocasta (Suzanne Bertish) and Oedipus (Alan Howard), from *Oedipus the King*. Olivier Theatre/National Theatre, London.

I grew up chief among the men of Corinth
Until a strange thing happened—
Not worth my passion, it may be, but strange.

735 At a feast, a drunken man maundering in his cups°
Cries out that I am not my father's son!

I contained myself that night, though I felt anger
And a sinking heart. The next day I visited
My father and mother, and questioned them. They stormed,
740 Calling it all the slanderous rant of a fool;
And this relieved me. Yet the suspicion
Remained always aching in my mind;
I knew there was talk; I could not rest;
And finally, saying nothing to my parents,
745 I went to the shrine at Delphi.
The god dismissed my question without reply;
He spoke of other things.
      Some were clear,
Full of wretchedness, dreadful, unbearable:
As, that I should lie with my own mother, breed

735. maundering
(môn′dər·iŋ) **in his cups:** talking aimlessly while under the influence of wine.

750   Children from whom all men would turn their eyes;
And that I should be my father's murderer.

I heard all this, and fled. And from that day
Corinth to me was only in the stars
Descending in that quarter of the sky,
755   As I wandered farther and farther on my way
To a land where I should never see the evil
Sung by the oracle. And I came to this country
Where, so you say, King Laius was killed.

I will tell you all that happened there, my lady.

760   There were three highways
Coming together at a place I passed;
And there a herald came towards me, and a chariot
Drawn by horses, with a man such as you describe

Seated in it. The groom leading the horses
765   Forced me off the road at his lord's command;
But as this charioteer lurched over towards me
I struck him in my rage. The old man saw me
And brought his double goad down upon my head
As I came abreast.
                He was paid back, and more!
770   Swinging my club in this right hand I knocked him
Out of his car, and he rolled on the ground.
                    I killed him.

I killed them all.
Now if that stranger and Laius were—kin,
Where is a man more miserable than I?
775   More hated by the gods? Citizen and alien alike
Must never shelter me or speak to me—
I must be shunned by all.
                  And I myself
Pronounced this malediction upon myself!

Think of it: I have touched you with these hands,
780   These hands that killed your husband. What defilement!
Am I all evil, then? It must be so,
Since I must flee from Thebes, yet never again
See my own countrymen, my own country,
For fear of joining my mother in marriage
And killing Polybus, my father.
785   Ah,
If I was created so, born to this fate,
Who could deny the savagery of God?

Oh holy majesty of heavenly powers!
May I never see that day! Never!

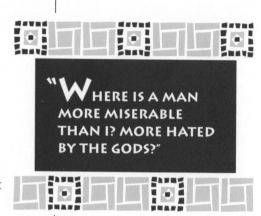

"WHERE IS A MAN MORE MISERABLE THAN I? MORE HATED BY THE GODS?"

773. *Why do you think Oedipus hesitates before the word* kin *in this line?*

785. Oedipus now suspects that he has unwittingly cursed himself as the true murderer of Laius.
However, given the fact that he still calls Polybus of Corinth his father in this line, what dreadful truth does he not yet suspect?

790   Rather let me vanish from the race of men
    Than know the abomination destined me!

Choragos.
    We too, my lord, have felt dismay at this.
    But there is hope: you have yet to hear the shepherd.

Oedipus.
    Indeed, I fear no other hope is left me.

Jocasta.
    What do you hope from him when he comes?

795 **Oedipus.**   This much:
    If his account of the murder tallies with yours,
    Then I am cleared.

Jocasta.   What was it that I said
    Of such importance?

Oedipus.   Why, "marauders," you said,
    Killed the King, according to this man's story.
800   If he maintains that still, if there were several,
    Clearly the guilt is not mine: I was alone.
    But if he says one man, single-handed, did it,
    Then the evidence all points to me.

Jocasta.
    You may be sure that he said there were several;
805   And can he call back that story now? He cannot.
    The whole city heard it as plainly as I.
    But suppose he alters some detail of it:
    He cannot ever show that Laius' death
    Fulfilled the oracle: for Apollo said
810   My child was doomed to kill him; and my child—
    Poor baby!—it was my child that died first.

    No. From now on, where oracles are concerned,
    I would not waste a second thought on any.

Oedipus.
    You may be right.
                But come: let someone go
815   For the shepherd at once. This matter must be settled.

Jocasta.
    I will send for him.
    I would not wish to cross you in anything,
    And surely not in this.—Let us go in.

                    [*Exeunt into the palace.*]

798–803. Jocasta referred to "marauding strangers" in the plural in line 675, and Oedipus now distinguishes between plural and singular.

? *Where was the issue of a single assailant versus several assailants hinted at earlier in the play?*

817. *What does the word* cross *mean in this line?*

ODE 2

Strophe 1

Chorus.

Let me be reverent in the ways of right,
820 Lowly the paths I journey on;
Let all my words and actions keep
The laws of the pure universe
From highest Heaven handed down.
For Heaven is their bright nurse,
825 Those generations of the realms of light;
Ah, never of mortal kind were they begot,
Nor are they slaves of memory, lost in sleep:
Their Father is greater than Time, and ages not.

Antistrophe 1

The tyrant is a child of Pride
830 Who drinks from his great sickening cup
Recklessness and vanity,
Until from his high crest headlong
He plummets to the dust of hope.
That strong man is not strong.
835 But let no fair ambition be denied;
May God protect the wrestler for the State
In government, in comely policy,
Who will fear God, and on His ordinance° wait.

838. ordinance (ôrd″n·əns) *n.*: decree or command.

Strophe 2

Haughtiness and the high hand of <u>disdain</u>
840 Tempt and outrage God's holy law;
And any mortal who dares hold
No immortal Power in awe
Will be caught up in a net of pain:
The price for which his levity is sold.
845 Let each man take due earnings, then,
And keep his hands from holy things,
And from blasphemy stand apart—
Else the crackling blast of heaven
Blows on his head, and on his desperate heart;
850 Though fools will honor impious men,
In their cities no tragic poet sings.

? **839–844.** *What fate does the Chorus predict for the haughty person?*

Vocabulary

disdain (dis·dān′) *n.*: scorn.

Antistrophe 2

Shall we lose faith in Delphi's obscurities,
We who have heard the world's core
Discredited, and the sacred wood
855   Of Zeus at Elis° praised no more?
The deeds and the strange prophecies
Must make a pattern yet to be understood.
Zeus, if indeed you are lord of all,
Throned in light over night and day,
860   Mirror this in your endless mind:
Our masters call the oracle
Words on the wind, and the Delphic vision blind!
Their hearts no longer know Apollo,
And reverence for the gods has died away.

855. Elis (ē′lis): city in the Peloponnesus.

856–857. *What does the Chorus insist will happen?*

Chorus, *Oedipus the King.*
from Olivier Theatre/National Theatre, London.

Response and Analysis

Part 1

Reading Check

1. What conflict or problem do the people of Thebes face as the play opens?

2. According to Ode 1, which god will inevitably punish the murderer of Laius? What misgivings disturb the Chorus's confidence, and how do they deal with these misgivings?

3. What argument does Jocasta use to persuade Oedipus to ignore the sooth-sayers and oracles? What minor detail in her argument motivates Oedipus to pursue a new line of inquiry?

4. Explain why Oedipus left Corinth. What chance remark caused him to question Polybus and Merope? What was he afraid of?

Thinking Critically

5. In line 35, the Priest says that the The-bans know that Oedipus is "not one of the immortal gods." How *do* the The-bans regard Oedipus? What reasons do they have for their opinion of him?

6. When Oedipus questions Creon about the murder of Laius, what **dramatic irony** does the playwright begin to develop?

7. Explain why it is **ironic** that the prophet Teiresias is blind. Why is Oedipus's angry and arrogant response to Teiresias also ironic?

8. In Ode 1, the Chorus expresses both confident optimism and nervous appre-hension. Explain how this indecision is a comment on the basic conflict of the play so far. What possible resolutions to the conflict can you predict?

9. What personality trait in Oedipus's character do you think drives him to in-sist that the Shepherd be summoned (line 814–815)? If you were Oedipus, would you pull back at this point, or would you insist on probing further to get at the truth?

Extending and Evaluating

10. Sophocles portrays Oedipus as a complex ruler with many conflicting character traits. Do you think a com-plex personality is likely to prove an advantage or a liability for a leader? Explain your answer.

WRITING

Analyzing the Odes

Each scene in *Oedipus Rex* is followed by an ode. Re-read the Parados, Ode 1, and Ode 2. What seems to be the function of each ode in response to the preceding scene? Is the function similar in each ode? Explain your answer in a brief essay.

North Carolina Competency Goal
1.03; 4.05; 5.03

SKILLS FOCUS

Literary Skills
Analyze dramatic irony.

Writing Skills
Analyze a play's odes.

Why do bees hum?

They've forgotten the words.

Oedipus Solves the Riddle of the Sphinx

(Front) Messenger from
Corinth (Simon Scott); (rear)
Jocasta (Suzanne Bertish) and
Oedipus (Alan Howard),
from *Oedipus the King*.
Olivier Theatre/National
Theatre, London.

Oedipus Rex

Part 2

Sophocles

translated by **Dudley Fitts and
Robert Fitzgerald**

SCENE 3

[*Enter* JOCASTA.]

Jocasta.

865   Princes of Thebes, it has occurred to me
To visit the altars of the gods, bearing
These branches as a suppliant, and this incense.
Our King is not himself: his noble soul

870 Is overwrought with fantasies of dread,
Else he would consider
The new prophecies in the light of the old.
He will listen to any voice that speaks disaster,
And my advice goes for nothing.

[*She approaches the altar, right.*]

                    To you, then, Apollo,
Lycian° lord, since you are nearest, I turn in prayer.
875 Receive these offerings, and grant us deliverance
From defilement. Our hearts are heavy with fear
When we see our leader distracted, as helpless sailors
Are terrified by the confusion of their helmsman.

[*Enter* MESSENGER.]

Messenger.
Friends, no doubt you can direct me:
880 Where shall I find the house of Oedipus,
Or, better still, where is the King himself?

Choragos.
It is this very place, stranger; he is inside.
This is his wife and mother of his children.

Messenger.
I wish her happiness in a happy house,
885 Blest in all the fulfillment of her marriage.

Jocasta.
I wish as much for you: your courtesy
Deserves a like good fortune. But now, tell me:
Why have you come? What have you to say to us?

Messenger.
Good news, my lady, for your house and your husband.

Jocasta.
What news? Who sent you here?

890 **Messenger.**   I am from Corinth.
The news I bring ought to mean joy for you,
Though it may be you will find some grief in it.

Jocasta.
What is it? How can it touch us in both ways?

Messenger.
The word is that the people of the Isthmus°
895 Intend to call Oedipus to be their king.

871. *What does Jocasta mean by "the new prophecies in the light of the old"? Explain what the new prophecies are. What were the old ones? What does Jocasta think of these prophecies?*

874. Lycian (lish'ē·ən): One of Apollo's names is Lycius, which has been explained variously as "wolf-god," "god of light," and "god of Lycia."

876–878. *Explain Jocasta's simile here. Who is being compared to whom?*

894. Isthmus: Corinth is located on a narrow strip of land connecting the Peloponnesus with eastern Greece.

Oedipus Rex. James Mason and Eleanor Stuart in a scene from the Stratford Festival production (1954).

Jocasta.
But old King Polybus—is he not reigning still?

Messenger.
No. Death holds him in his sepulcher.

Jocasta.
What are you saying? Polybus is dead?

Messenger.
If I am not telling the truth, may I die myself.

Jocasta.
(*to a* MAIDSERVANT) Go in, go quickly; tell this
to your master.

900

O riddlers of God's will, where are you now!
This was the man whom Oedipus, long ago,
Feared so, fled so, in dread of destroying him—
But it was another fate by which he died.

[*Enter* OEDIPUS, *center.*]

901–904. *What tone of voice might an actress playing Jocasta use here?*

Oedipus.

905   Dearest Jocasta, why have you sent for me?

Jocasta.

Listen to what this man says, and then tell me
What has become of the solemn prophecies.

Oedipus.

Who is this man? What is his news for me?

Jocasta.

He has come from Corinth to announce your
    father's death!

Oedipus.

910   Is it true, stranger? Tell me in your own words.

Messenger.

I cannot say it more clearly: the King is dead.

Oedipus.

Was it by treason? Or by an attack of illness?

Messenger.

A little thing brings old men to their rest.

Oedipus.

It was sickness, then?

Messenger.   Yes, and his many years.

Oedipus.

915   Ah!
Why should a man respect the Pythian hearth,° or
Give heed to the birds that jangle above his head?
They prophesied that I should kill Polybus,
Kill my own father; but he is dead and buried,
920   And I am here—I never touched him, never,
Unless he died of grief for my departure,
And thus, in a sense, through me. No. Polybus
Has packed the oracles off with him underground.
They are empty words.

Jocasta.   Had I not told you so?

Oedipus.

925   You had; it was my faint heart that betrayed me.

Jocasta.

From now on never think of those things again.

Oedipus.

And yet—must I not fear my mother's bed?

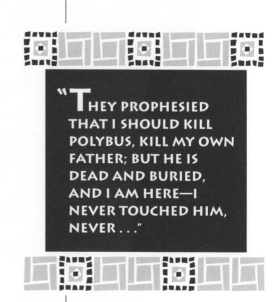

"THEY PROPHESIED THAT I SHOULD KILL POLYBUS, KILL MY OWN FATHER; BUT HE IS DEAD AND BURIED, AND I AM HERE—I NEVER TOUCHED HIM, NEVER . . ."

916. Pythian (pith′ē·ən) **hearth:** Delphi was also known as Pythia. The priestess of Apollo was called Pythia.

Jocasta.
Why should anyone in this world be afraid,
Since Fate rules us and nothing can be foreseen?
930   A man should live only for the present day.

Have no more fear of sleeping with your mother:
How many men, in dreams, have lain with their mothers!
No reasonable man is troubled by such things.

Oedipus.
That is true; only—
935   If only my mother were not still alive!
But she is alive. I cannot help my dread.

Jocasta.
Yet this news of your father's death is wonderful.

Oedipus.
Wonderful. But I fear the living woman.

Messenger.
Tell me, who is this woman that you fear?

Oedipus.
940   It is Merope, man; wife of King Polybus.

Messenger.
Merope? Why should you be afraid of her?

Oedipus.
An oracle of the gods, a dreadful saying.

Messenger.
Can you tell me about it or are you sworn to silence?

Oedipus.
I can tell you, and I will.
945   Apollo said through his prophet that I was the man
Who should marry his own mother, shed his
    father's blood
With his own hands. And so, for all these years
I have kept clear of Corinth, and no harm has come—
Though it would have been sweet to see my parents
    again.

Messenger.
950   And is this the fear that drove you out of Corinth?

Oedipus.
Would you have me kill my father?

Messenger.   As for that
You must be reassured by the news I gave you.

928–930. According to Jocasta, why should Oedipus not fear?

915–939. The Corinthian Messenger, who has been listening to the dialogue between Oedipus and Jocasta since line 915, now joins in for a crucial exchange that moves Oedipus several steps further toward the truth.
How might the actor playing the messenger behave in these lines?

Oedipus.
If you could reassure me, I would reward you.

Messenger.
I had that in mind, I will confess: I thought
955   I could count on you when you returned to Corinth.

Oedipus.
No: I will never go near my parents again.

Messenger.
Ah, son, you still do not know what you are doing—

Oedipus.
What do you mean? In the name of God tell me!

Messenger.
—If these are your reasons for not going home.

Oedipus.
960   I tell you, I fear the oracle may come true.

Messenger.
And guilt may come upon you through your parents?

Oedipus.
That is the dread that is always in my heart.

Messenger.
Can you not see that all your fears are groundless?

Oedipus.
How can you say that? They are my parents, surely?

Messenger.
Polybus was not your father.

Oedipus. 965   Not my father?

Messenger.
No more your father than the man speaking to you.

Oedipus.
But you are nothing to me!

Messenger.   Neither was he.

Oedipus.
Then why did he call me son?

Messenger.   I will tell you:
Long ago he had you from my hands, as a gift.

Oedipus.
970   Then how could he love me so, if I was not his?

Messenger.
He had no children, and his heart turned to you.

King Polybus Rescuing Oedipus,
from the manuscript of *Li livre
des ansienes estories*
(c. 1285 C.E.).

The British Library, London
(Add.15268, f.75v).

957–971. *What do
you imagine is Oedipus's
emotional state at this point:
one of growing relief, confusion, or despair?*

Oedipus.
What of you? Did you buy me? Did you find me
by chance?

Messenger.
I came upon you in the crooked pass of Cithaeron.

Oedipus.
And what were you doing there?

Messenger.   Tending my flocks.

Oedipus.
A wandering shepherd?

975   **Messenger.**   But your savior, son, that day.

Oedipus.
From what did you save me?

Messenger.   Your ankles should tell you that.

Oedipus.
Ah, stranger, why do you speak of that childhood pain?

Messenger.
I cut the bonds that tied your ankles together.

Oedipus.
I have had the mark as long as I can remember.

Messenger.
980   That was why you were given the name you bear.

Oedipus.
God! Was it my father or my mother who did it?
Tell me!

Messenger. I do not know. The man who gave you to me
Can tell you better than I.

Oedipus.
985   It was not you that found me, but another?

Messenger.
It was another shepherd gave you to me.

Oedipus.
Who was he? Can you tell me who he was?

Messenger.
I think he was said to be one of Laius' people.

Oedipus.
You mean the Laius who was king here years ago?

Messenger.
990   Yes; King Laius; and the man was one of his herdsmen.

980. This line refers to
the derivation of the name
Oedipus from words mean-
ing "swollen" and "foot."
The first part of Oedipus's
name, however, may also
be related to a Greek word
meaning "to know."
? *Why would this
etymology be ironically
appropriate?*

Oedipus.
Is he still alive? Can I see him?

Messenger.   These men here
Know best about such things.

Oedipus.   Does anyone here
Know this shepherd that he is talking about?
Have you seen him in the fields, or in the town?
995   If you have, tell me. It is time things were made plain.

Choragos.
I think the man he means is that same shepherd
You have already asked to see. Jocasta perhaps
Could tell you something.

Oedipus.   Do you know anything
About him, Lady? Is he the man we have summoned?
Is that the man this shepherd means?

1000   **Jocasta.**   Why think of him?
Forget this herdsman. Forget it all.
This talk is a waste of time.

Oedipus.   How can you say that,
When the clues to my true birth are in my hands?

Jocasta.
For God's love, let us have no more questioning!
1005   Is your life nothing to you?
My own is pain enough for me to bear.

Oedipus.
You need not worry. Suppose my mother a slave,
And born of slaves: no baseness can touch you.

Jocasta.
Listen to me, I beg you: do not do this thing!

Oedipus.
1010   I will not listen; the truth must be made known.

Jocasta.
Everything that I say is for your own good!

Oedipus.   My own good
Snaps my patience, then; I want none of it.

Jocasta.
You are fatally wrong! May you never learn who you are!

Oedipus.
Go, one of you, and bring the shepherd here.
1015   Let us leave this woman to brag of her royal name.

938–1000. Now it is Jocasta's turn to rejoin the dialogue after a long silence since line 937.

? *In these lines, what gestures or facial expressions might an actress playing Jocasta use to register her reactions to the revelations of the Corinthian Messenger?*

? **1004–1006.** *Why do you think Jocasta wants the questioning to end?*

? **1015.** *What does Oedipus assume about Jocasta in this bitter remark? Why is this assumption ironic?*

Jocasta.

    Ah, miserable!
    That is the only word I have for you now.
    That is the only word I can ever have.

                [*Exit into the palace.*]

Choragos.

    Why has she left us, Oedipus? Why has she gone
1020   In such a passion of sorrow? I fear this silence:
    Something dreadful may come of it.

Oedipus.   Let it come!

    However base my birth, I must know about it.
    The Queen, like a woman, is perhaps ashamed
    To think of my low origin. But I
1025   Am a child of Luck; I cannot be dishonored.
    Luck is my mother; the passing months, my brothers,
    Have seen me rich and poor.
                  If this is so,
    How could I wish that I were someone else?
    How could I not be glad to know my birth?

> **1024–1027.** *In these lines, what metaphors does Oedipus use to describe his parentage and family relationships?*

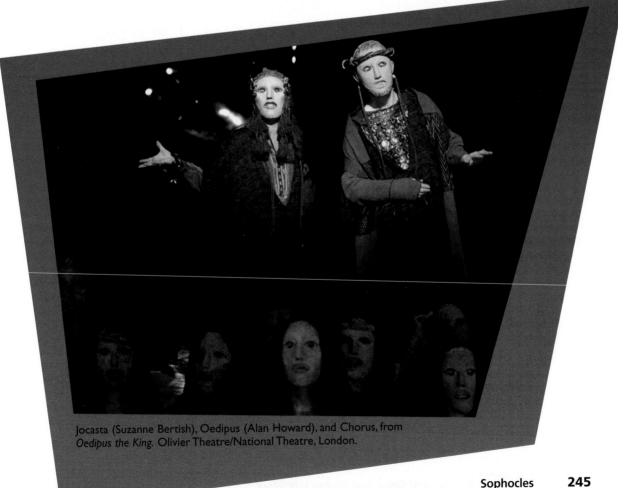

Jocasta (Suzanne Bertish), Oedipus (Alan Howard), and Chorus, from *Oedipus the King.* Olivier Theatre/National Theatre, London.

ODE 2

Strophe

Chorus.

1030 If ever the coming time were known
To my heart's pondering,
Cithaeron, now by Heaven I see the torches
At the festival of the next full moon,
And see the dance, and hear the choir sing

1035 A grace to your gentle shade:
Mountain where Oedipus was found,
O mountain guard of a noble race!
May the god who heals us lend his aid,
And let that glory come to pass

1040 For our king's cradling-ground.

Antistrophe

Of the nymphs that flower beyond the years,
Who bore you, royal child,
To Pan° of the hills or the timberline Apollo,
Cold in delight where the upland clears,

1045 Or Hermes for whom Cyllene's° heights are piled?
Or flushed as evening cloud,
Great Dionysus, roamer of mountains,
He—was it he who found you there,
And caught you up in his own proud

1050 Arms from the sweet god-ravisher°
Who laughed by the Muses' fountains?°

SCENE 4

Oedipus.

Sirs: though I do not know the man,
I think I see him coming, this shepherd we want:
He is old, like our friend here, and the men

1055 Bringing him seem to be servants of my house.
But you can tell, if you have ever seen him.

[*Enter* SHEPHERD *escorted by servants.*]

Choragos.

I know him, he was Laius' man. You can trust him.

Oedipus.

Tell me first, you from Corinth: is this the shepherd
We were discussing?

1043. Pan: son of Hermes; part goat, part man; associated with woodlands, forests, and mountains. Shepherds loved the music he played on his reed pipes.
1045. Cyllene (sə·lē′nē): mountain where Hermes was born.

> **1041–1051.** What fantasy does the Chorus briefly indulge about Oedipus's infancy in these lines? How does the mood of the ode deepen the irony of the play at this point?

1050. god-ravisher: the presumed mother of Oedipus.
1051. Muses' fountains: The Muses were born at a spring on the slopes of Mount Olympus.

Messenger.   This is the very man.

Oedipus.
(*to* SHEPHERD) Come here. No, look at me. You must
1060   answer
Everything I ask.—You belonged to Laius?

Shepherd.
Yes: born his slave, brought up in his house.

Oedipus.
Tell me: what kind of work did you do for him?

Shepherd.
I was a shepherd of his, most of my life.

Oedipus.
1065   Where mainly did you go for pasturage?

Shepherd.
Sometimes Cithaeron, sometimes the hills nearby.

Oedipus.
Do you remember ever seeing this man out there?

Shepherd.
What would he be doing there? This man?

Oedipus.
This man standing here. Have you ever seen him before?

Shepherd.
1070   No. At least, not to my recollection.

Messenger.
And that is not strange, my lord. But I'll refresh
His memory: he must remember when we two
Spent three whole seasons together, March to
    September,
On Cithaeron or thereabouts. He had two flocks;
1075   I had one. Each autumn I'd drive mine home
And he would go back with his to Laius' sheepfold.—
Is this not true, just as I have described it?

Shepherd.
True, yes; but it was all so long ago.

Messenger.
Well, then: do you remember, back in those days,
1080   That you gave me a baby to bring up as my own?

Shepherd.
What if I did? What are you trying to say?

1060. How would an actor playing Oedipus indicate his reaction to a movement or gesture by the Shepherd as he speaks this line? What tone of voice might the actor use?

"WELL, THEN: DO YOU REMEMBER, BACK IN THOSE DAYS, THAT YOU GAVE ME A BABY TO BRING UP AS MY OWN?"

Messenger.
King Oedipus was once that little child.

Shepherd.
Damn you, hold your tongue!

Oedipus.   No more of that!
It is your tongue needs watching, not this man's.

Shepherd.
1085   My King, my Master, what is it I have done wrong?

Oedipus.
You have not answered his question about the boy.

Shepherd.
He does not know . . . He is only making trouble . . .

Oedipus.
Come, speak plainly, or it will go hard with you.

Shepherd.
In God's name, do not torture an old man!

Oedipus.
1090   Come here, one of you; bind his arms behind him.

Shepherd.
Unhappy king! What more do you wish to learn?

Oedipus.
Did you give this man the child he speaks of?

Shepherd.   I did.
And I would to God I had died that very day.

Oedipus.
You will die now unless you speak the truth.

Shepherd.
1095   Yet if I speak the truth, I am worse than dead.

Oedipus.
Very well; since you insist upon delaying—

Shepherd.
No! I have told you already that I gave him the boy.

Oedipus.
Where did you get him? From your house? From somewhere else?

Shepherd.
Not from mine, no. A man gave him to me.

Oedipus.
1100   Is that man here? Do you know whose slave he was?

1083. Why do you think the Shepherd bursts in so angrily here?

1091. Who else in the play so far has called Oedipus "unhappy" because of his desire to learn more?

Shepherd.
For God's love, my King, do not ask me any more!

Oedipus.
You are a dead man if I have to ask you again.

Shepherd.
Then . . . Then the child was from the palace of Laius.

Oedipus.
A slave child? or a child of his own line?

Shepherd.
1105   Ah, I am on the brink of dreadful speech!

Oedipus.
And I of dreadful hearing. Yet I must hear.

Shepherd.
If you must be told, then . . .
              They said it was Laius' child;
But it is your wife who can tell you about that.

Oedipus.
My wife!—Did she give it to you?

Shepherd.   My lord, she did.

Oedipus.
Do you know why?

1110 **Shepherd.**   I was told to get rid of it.

Oedipus.
An unspeakable mother!

Shepherd.   There had been prophecies . . .

Oedipus.
Tell me.

Shepherd. It was said that the boy would kill his
    own father.

Oedipus.
Then why did you give him over to this old man?

Shepherd.
I pitied the baby, my King,
1115 And I thought that this man would take him far away
To his own country.
           He saved him—but for what a fate!
For if you are what this man says you are,
No man living is more wretched than Oedipus.

Oedipus.
Ah God!

(Top rear) Oedipus (Alan Howard); (front center) Old Shepherd (Peter Gordon); from *Oedipus the King.* Olivier Theatre/National Theatre, London.

? **1111.** *Who is the "mother"? Explain why you think Oedipus uses the adjective "unspeakable" to describe her here.*

Oedipus Rex. Scene from the stage production (1954) by Tyrone Guthrie.

It was true!

      All the prophecies!

1120   —Now,

O Light, may I look on you for the last time!
I, Oedipus,
Oedipus, damned in his birth, in his marriage damned,
Damned in the blood he shed with his own hand!

[*He rushes into the palace.*]

ODE 4

Strophe 1

Chorus.

1125   Alas for the seed of men.

    What measure shall I give these generations
    That breathe on the void and are void
    And exist and do not exist?

> **?** **1124.** *What do you predict Oedipus will do as he rushes offstage after this speech?*

Who bears more weight of joy
1130 Than mass of sunlight shifting in images,
Or who shall make his thought stay on
That down time drifts away?

Your splendor is all fallen.

O naked brow of wrath and tears,
1135 O change of Oedipus!
I who saw your days call no man blest—
Your great days like ghosts gone.

Antistrophe 1

That mind was a strong bow.

Deep, how deep you drew it then, hard archer,°
1140 At a dim fearful range,
And brought dear glory down!

You overcame the stranger—
The virgin with her hooking lion claws°—
And though death sang, stood like a tower
1145 To make pale Thebes take heart.

Fortress against our sorrow!

True king, giver of laws,
Majestic Oedipus!
No prince in Thebes had ever such renown,
1150 No prince won such grace of power.

Strophe 2

And now of all men ever known
Most pitiful is this man's story:
His fortunes are most changed, his state
Fallen to a low slave's
1155 Ground under bitter fate.

O Oedipus, most royal one!
The great door that expelled you to the light
Gave at night—ah, gave night to your glory:
As to the father, to the fathering son.

1160 All understood too late.

How could that queen whom Laius won,
The garden that he harrowed at his height,
Be silent when that act was done?

Antistrophe 2

But all eyes fail before time's eye,

1139. **hard archer:** Apollo.

1143. **virgin . . . claws:** The Sphinx was depicted as having the paws of a lion.

1165   All actions come to justice there.
    Though never willed, though far down the deep past,
    Your bed, your dread sirings,
    Are brought to book at last.
    Child by Laius doomed to die,
1170   Then doomed to lose that fortunate little death,
    Would God you never took breath in this air
    That with my wailing lips I take to cry:

    For I weep the world's outcast.

    I was blind, and now I can tell why:
1175   Asleep, for you had given ease of breath
    To Thebes, while the false years went by.

EXODOS°

[*Enter, from the palace,* SECOND MESSENGER.]

Second Messenger.
    Elders of Thebes, most honored in this land,
    What horrors are yours to see and hear, what weight
    Of sorrow to be endured, if, true to your birth,
1180   You venerate the line of Labdacus!
    I think neither Istros nor Phasis,° those great rivers,
    Could purify this place of the corruption
    It shelters now, or soon must bring to light—
    Evil not done unconsciously, but willed.

1185   The greatest griefs are those we cause ourselves.

Choragos.
    Surely, friend, we have grief enough already;
    What new sorrow do you mean?

Second Messenger.   The Queen is dead.

Choragos.
    Jocasta? Dead? But at whose hand?

Second Messenger.   Her own.
    The full horror of what happened you cannot know,
1190   For you did not see it; but I, who did, will tell you
    As clearly as I can how she met her death.

    When she had left us,
    In passionate silence, passing through the court,
    She ran to her apartment in the house,

Exodos (eks′ə·dəs): the final
scene.

1181. Istros (is′trəs) **nor
Phasis** (fā′sis).

? **1184.** *What distinction
does the Second Mes-
senger draw in this line? How
is this contrast important to
the action of the play as a
whole?*

Vocabulary

venerate (ven′ə·rāt′) *v.:* revere.

1195   Her hair clutched by the fingers of both hands.
    She closed the doors behind her; then, by that bed
    Where long ago the fatal son was conceived—
    That son who should bring about his father's death—
    We heard her call upon Laius, dead so many years,
1200   And heard her wail for the double fruit of her marriage,
    A husband by her husband, children by her child.

    Exactly how she died I do not know:
    For Oedipus burst in moaning and would not let us
    Keep vigil to the end: it was by him
1205   As he stormed about the room that our eyes were caught.
    From one to another of us he went, begging a sword,
    Cursing the wife who was not his wife, the mother
    Whose womb had carried his own children and himself.
    I do not know: it was none of us aided him,
1210   But surely one of the gods was in control!
    For with a dreadful cry
    He hurled his weight, as though wrenched out of himself,
    At the twin doors: the bolts gave, and he rushed in.
    And there we saw her hanging, her body swaying
1215   From the cruel cord she had noosed about her neck,
    A great sob broke from him, heartbreaking to hear,
    As he loosed the rope and lowered her to the ground.

    I would blot out from my mind what happened next!
    For the King ripped from her gown the golden brooches
1220   That were her ornament, and raised them, and plunged
      them down
    Straight into his own eyeballs, crying, "No more,
    No more shall you look on the misery about me,
    The horrors of my own doing! Too long you have known
    The faces of those whom I should never have seen,
1225   Too long been blind to those for whom I was searching!
    From this hour, go in darkness!" And as he spoke,
    He struck at his eyes—not once, but many times;
    And the blood spattered his beard,
    Bursting from his ruined sockets like red hail.

1230   So from the unhappiness of two this evil has sprung,
    A curse on the man and woman alike. The old
    Happiness of the house of Labdacus
    Was happiness enough: where is it today?
    It is all wailing and ruin, disgrace, death—all
1235   The misery of mankind that has a name—
    And it is wholly and forever theirs.

Choragos.
    Is he in agony still? Is there no rest for him?

? **1201.** *Explain what the Messenger means by this apparently contradictory line.*

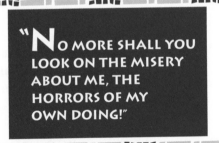

"**N**O MORE SHALL YOU LOOK ON THE MISERY ABOUT ME, THE HORRORS OF MY OWN DOING!"

Second Messenger.

     He is calling for someone to lead him to the gates
     So that all the children of Cadmus may look upon
     His father's murderer, his mother's—no,
1240   I cannot say it!

               And then he will leave Thebes,
     Self-exiled, in order that the curse
     Which he himself pronounced may depart from the house.
     He is weak, and there is none to lead him,
     So terrible is his suffering.

                    But you will see:
1245   Look, the doors are opening; in a moment
     You will see a thing that would crush a heart of stone.

[*The central door is opened;* OEDIPUS, *blinded, is led in.*]

Choragos.

     Dreadful indeed for men to see.
     Never have my own eyes
     Looked on a sight so full of fear.

1250   Oedipus!
     What madness came upon you, what daemon°
     Leaped on your life with heavier
     Punishment than a mortal man can bear?
     No: I cannot even
1255   Look at you, poor ruined one.
     And I would speak, question, ponder,
     If I were able. No.
     You make me shudder.

Oedipus.

     God.   God.
1260   Is there a sorrow greater?
     Where shall I find harbor in this world?
     My voice is hurled far on a dark wind.
     What has God done to me?

Choragos.

     Too terrible to think of, or to see.

Strophe 1

Oedipus.

1265   O cloud of night,
     Never to be turned away: night coming on,
     I cannot tell how: night like a shroud!
     My fair winds brought me here
                O God. Again
     The pain of the spikes where I had sight,

1246. *Describe the way you visualize the stage action and the entrance of Oedipus here.*

1251. daemon (dē′mən) *n.*: evil spirit.

1259–1263. *How would you read these lines?*

1270   The flooding pain
        Of memory, never to be gouged out.

Choragos.
        This is not strange.
        You suffer it all twice over, remorse in pain,
        Pain in remorse.

Antistrophe 1

Oedipus.
1275   Ah dear friend
        Are you faithful even yet, you alone?
        Are you still standing near me, will you stay here,
        Patient, to care for the blind?
                                    The blind man!
        Yet even blind I know who it is attends me,
1280   By the voice's tone—
        Though my new darkness hide the comforter.

Choragos.
        Oh fearful act!
        What god was it drove you to rake black
        Night across your eyes?

1265–1271. Do you read Oedipus's act of self-blinding as a punishment, as an attempt to "shut out" the truth, or as something else?

Oedipus Rex. Scene from the stage production (1954) by Tyrone Guthrie.

Strophe 2

Oedipus.

1285   Apollo. Apollo. Dear
Children, the god was Apollo.
He brought my sick, sick fate upon me.
But the blinding hand was my own!
How could I bear to see
1290   When all my sight was horror everywhere?

Choragos.

Everywhere; that is true.

Oedipus.

And now what is left?
Images? Love? A greeting even,
Sweet to the senses? Is there anything?
1295   Ah, no, friends: lead me away.
Lead me away from Thebes.
                        Lead the great wreck
And hell of Oedipus, whom the gods hate.

Choragos.

Your fate is clear, you are not blind to that.
Would God you had never found it out!

Antistrophe 2

Oedipus.

1300   Death take the man who unbound
My feet on that hillside
And delivered me from death to life! What life?
If only I had died,
This weight of monstrous doom
1305   Could not have dragged me and my darlings down.

Choragos.

I would have wished the same.

Oedipus.

Oh never to have come here
With my father's blood upon me! Never
To have been the man they call his mother's husband!
1310   Oh accursed! Oh child of evil,
To have entered that wretched bed—
                      the selfsame one!
More primal than sin itself, this fell to me.

Vocabulary

primal (prī′məl) *adj.*: original.

> **1285–1290.** *According to Oedipus, who is responsible for his blindness?*

Choragos.

    I do not know how I can answer you.
    You were better dead than alive and blind.

Oedipus.

1315   Do not counsel me any more. This punishment
    That I have laid upon myself is just.
    If I had eyes,
    I do not know how I could bear the sight
    Of my father, when I came to the house of Death,
1320   Or my mother: for I have sinned against them both
    So vilely that I could not make my peace
    By strangling my own life.
              Or do you think my children,
    Born as they were born, would be sweet to my eyes?
    Ah never, never! Nor this town with its high walls,
    Nor the holy images of the gods.
1325   For I,
    Thrice miserable!—Oedipus, noblest of all the line
    Of Cadmus, have condemned myself to enjoy
    These things no more, by my own malediction
    Expelling that man whom the gods declared
1330   To be a defilement in the house of Laius.
    After exposing the rankness of my own guilt,
    How could I look men frankly in the eyes?
    No, I swear it,
    If I could have stifled my hearing at its source,
1335   I would have done it and made all this body
    A tight cell of misery, blank to light and sound:
    So I should have been safe in a dark agony
    Beyond all recollection.
                Ah Cithaeron!
    Why did you shelter me? When I was cast upon you,
1340   Why did I not die? Then I should never
    Have shown the world my execrable birth.

    Ah Polybus! Corinth, city that I believed
    The ancient seat of my ancestors: how fair
    I seemed, your child! And all the while this evil
    Was cancerous within me!
1345   For I am sick
    In my daily life, sick in my origin.

    O three roads, dark ravine, woodland and way
    Where three roads met: you, drinking my father's blood,
    My own blood, spilled by my own hand: can you remember
1350   The unspeakable things I did there, and the things
    I went on from there to do?
             O marriage, marriage!

1328. What is the "malediction" (curse) to which Oedipus refers in this line?

1334–1338. What gesture might an actor playing Oedipus make as he speaks these lines?

The act that engendered me, and again the act
Performed by the son in the same bed—

                         Ah, the net
Of incest, mingling fathers, brothers, sons,
1355   With brides, wives, mothers: the last evil
That can be known by men: no tongue can say
How evil!

             No. For the love of God, conceal me
Somewhere far from Thebes; or kill me; or hurl me
Into the sea, away from men's eyes forever.

1360   Come, lead me. You need not fear to touch me.
Of all men, I alone can bear this guilt.

[*Enter* CREON.]

Choragos.
     We are not the ones to decide; but Creon here
     May fitly judge of what you ask. He only
     Is left to protect the city in your place.

Oedipus.
1365   Alas, how can I speak to him? What right have I
     To beg his courtesy whom I have deeply wronged?

Creon.
     I have not come to mock you, Oedipus,
     Or to reproach you, either.
     (*to* ATTENDANTS)   —You, standing there:
     If you have lost all respect for man's dignity,
1370   At least respect the flame of Lord Helios:
     Do not allow this pollution to show itself
     Openly here, an affront to the earth
     And Heaven's rain and the light of day. No, take him
     Into the house as quickly as you can.
1375   For it is proper
     That only the close kindred see his grief.

Oedipus.
     I pray you in God's name, since your courtesy
     Ignores my dark expectation, visiting
     With mercy this man of all men most execrable:
1380   Give me what I ask—for your good, not for mine.

Creon.
     And what is it that you would have me do?

Oedipus.
     Drive me out of this country as quickly as may be
     To a place where no human voice can ever greet me.

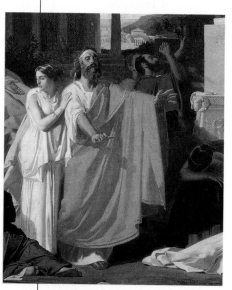

*Oedipus with Antigone After
Plucking Out His Eyes* (c. 19th
century) by Ernest Hillemacher.
Musée des Beaux-Arts, Orléans.

1365–1366. *Explain
why Oedipus feels that
he can hardly face speaking
to Creon.*

1367–1373. *Do you
think that Creon's com-
ment about Oedipus as an
example of "pollution" con-
tradicts his earlier statement
that he has not come to
"mock" or "reproach"
Oedipus? Or can you reconcile these two statements?
Explain.*

Creon.

      I should have done that before now—only,
1385   God's will had not been wholly revealed to me.

Oedipus.

      But his command is plain: the parricide°
      Must be destroyed. I am that evil man.

Creon. That is the sense of it, yes; but as things are,
      We had best discover clearly what is to be done.

Oedipus.

1390   You would learn more about a man like me?

Creon.

      You are ready now to listen to the god.

Oedipus.

      I will listen. But it is to you
      That I must turn for help. I beg you, hear me.

      The woman in there—
1395   Give her whatever funeral you think proper:
      She is your sister.
               —But let me go, Creon!
      Let me purge my father's Thebes of the pollution
      Of my living here, and go out to the wild hills,
      To Cithaeron, that has won such fame with me,
1400   The tomb my mother and father appointed for me,
      And let me die there, as they willed I should.
      And yet I know
      Death will not ever come to me through sickness
      Or in any natural way: I have been preserved
1405   For some unthinkable fate. But let that be.

      As for my sons, you need not care for them.
      They are men, they will find some way to live.
      But my poor daughters, who have shared my table,
      Who never before have been parted from their father—
1410   Take care of them, Creon; do this for me.
      And will you let me touch them with my hands
      A last time, and let us weep together?
      Be kind, my lord,
      Great prince, be kind!
               Could I but touch them,
1415   They would be mine again, as when I had my eyes.

    [*Enter* ANTIGONE *and* ISMENE, *attended.*]
      Ah, God!
      Is it my dearest children I hear weeping?
      Has Creon pitied me and sent my daughters?

1386. parricide (par′ə·sīd′)
n.: one who murders his or
her parent.

? 1396–1410. *What
does Oedipus request
of Creon?*

? 1416. *Antigone and
Ismene have no lines.
How could you best make
use of their presence on the
stage?*

Creon.

> Yes, Oedipus: I knew that they were dear to you
1420 > In the old days, and know you must love them still.

Oedipus.

> May God bless you for this—and be a friendlier
> Guardian to you than he has been to me!
>
> Children, where are you?
> Come quickly to my hands: they are your brother's—
1425 > Hands that have brought your father's once clear eyes
> To this way of seeing—
> > > > Ah dearest ones,
> I had neither sight nor knowledge then, your father
> By the woman who was the source of his own life!
> And I weep for you—having no strength to see you—,
1430 > I weep for you when I think of the bitterness
> That men will visit upon you all your lives.
> What homes, what festivals can you attend
> Without being forced to depart again in tears?
> And when you come to marriageable age,
1435 > Where is the man, my daughters, who would dare
> Risk the bane that lies on all my children?
> Is there any evil wanting? Your father killed
> His father; sowed the womb of her who bore him;
> Engendered you at the fount of his own existence!
> That is what they will say of you.
1440 > > > > > Then, whom
> Can you ever marry? There are no bridegrooms for you,
> And your lives must wither away in sterile dreaming.
>
> O Creon, son of Menoeceus!
> You are the only father my daughters have,
1445 > Since we, their parents, are both of us gone forever.
> They are your own blood: you will not let them
> Fall into beggary and loneliness;
> You will keep them from the miseries that are mine!
> Take pity on them; see, they are only children,
1450 > Friendless except for you. Promise me this,
> Great Prince, and give me your hand in token of it.
>
> [CREON *clasps his right hand.*]
> Children:
> I could say much, if you could understand me,
> But as it is, I have only this prayer for you:
1455 > Live where you can, be as happy as you can—
> Happier, please God, than God has made your father!

1426–1440. Why is Oedipus convinced that his daughters' futures will be all suffering? Why must they pay for his sins?

(Front center) Oedipus (Alan Howard), from *Oedipus the King*. Olivier Theatre/National Theatre, London.

Creon.
Enough. You have wept enough. Now go within.

Oedipus.
I must; but it is hard.

Creon.   Time eases all things.

Oedipus.
But you must promise—

Creon.   Say what you desire.

Oedipus.
Send me from Thebes!

1460 **Creon.**   God grant that I may!

Oedipus.
But since God hates me . . .

Creon.   No, he will grant your wish.

Oedipus.
You promise?

Creon.   I cannot speak beyond my knowledge.

Oedipus.
Then lead me in.

Creon.   Come now, and leave your children.

Oedipus.
No! Do not take them from me!

Creon.   Think no longer
1465   That you are in command here, but rather think
How, when you were, you served your own destruction.

[*Exeunt into the house all but the* CHORUS; *the*
CHORAGOS *chants directly to the audience:*]

Choragos.
Men of Thebes: look upon Oedipus.

This is the king who solved the famous riddle
And towered up, most powerful of men.
1470   No mortal eyes but looked on him with envy,
Yet in the end ruin swept over him.

Let every man in mankind's frailty
Consider his last day; and let none
Presume on his good fortune until he find
1475   Life, at his death, a memory without pain.

? **1462.** *Explain the irony of Creon's line, given all that has happened in the play.*

? **1465–1466.** *What is Creon saying to Oedipus here?*

? **1467–1475.** *What moral lesson does the Chorus draw from the action of the play?*

Tragedy and the Tragic Hero

The Greek philosopher Aristotle (c. 384–c. 322 B.C.) pays special attention to tragedy in his treatise *Poetics*. He explains that tragic dramas should be tightly unified constructions based on a single action and featuring a single **protagonist,** or hero. Tragedies generally deal with characters who are neither exceptionally virtuous nor exceptionally evil. According to Aristotle, the hero should have "a character between these two extremes—that of a man [or a woman] who is not preeminently good and just, yet whose misfortune is brought about not by vice or depravity, but by some error of judgment or frailty." This weakness is known as **hamartia** (hä′mär·tē′ə), which is often translated as "tragic flaw." Typically, this flaw takes the form of excessive pride or arrogance, called **hubris** (hyōo′bris).

As a tragedy unfolds, according to Aristotle, the tragic hero goes through one or more reversals of fortune leading up to a final recognition of a truth that has remained hidden from him. In the process he experiences profound suffering. Aristotle supplements his theory by observing that as the members of an audience witness this deep suffering, their emotions of pity and fear lead them to experience a feeling of **catharsis** (kə·thär′sis), or purgation, that leaves them with a new sense of self-awareness and renewal. Paradoxically, then, the experience of watching a tragedy and being purged of upsetting emotions brings a kind of pleasure to the spectator.

? In his analysis of tragedy in *Poetics,* Aristotle cites Sophocles' play *Oedipus Rex* several times as a supreme example of tragic drama. Were you moved to pity and fear by this tale of Oedipus's suffering? Did you also feel a final sense of renewal through the experience? Explain how the play affected you.

The Tragic Actor (detail). Wall painting from the Herculaneum.

Museo Archeologico Nazionale, Naples.

Response and Analysis

Part 2 and the Play as a Whole

Reading Check

1. What news does the Corinthian Messenger announce?

2. After Oedipus threatens him with torture, what crucial facts does the Shepherd disclose?

3. According to the Chorus in lines 1151–1155, how have Oedipus's fortunes changed?

4. Summarize the news announced by the Second Messenger. What actions by Oedipus and Jocasta does he describe?

Thinking Critically

5. In lines 891–892, the Corinthian Messenger indicates that his news may cause both joy and grief. Explain how this comment turns out to be a classic example of **irony** as the scene unfolds.

6. In lines 1000–1002, what conclusion has Jocasta evidently reached? How has she reached it?

7. Explain how lines 1105–1106 might be considered the **climax,** or turning point, of the play.

8. In lines 1317–1322, Oedipus says that he has sinned so vilely against both his parents that he could not bear to see them even in the house of Death. Yet we know that Oedipus acted in ignorance. Would Oedipus be judged guilty today? Judging from his portrayal of Oedipus's reaction to the discovery of his deeds, how do you think Sophocles felt about Oedipus's crimes?

9. In your opinion, has Sophocles succeeded in maintaining **suspense** right up to the end of the play? Explain.

10. The actual Greek title of the play is *Oedipus Tyrannos.* The term *tyrant* in ancient Greek did not mean a cruel despot, however; it referred more to a powerful, self-made ruler. Identify Oedipus's positive qualities as a ruler as well as his negative traits. In what ways is Oedipus an admirable ruler? In what ways is he a flawed ruler—even a tyrant?

11. The **plot** of *Oedipus Rex* builds with great force to a **climax** when Oedipus discovers the truth about his identity and his past actions. Why do you think the play does not simply end with the revelation of the truth and Oedipus's self-blinding? Explain what dramatic function is served by the final meeting between Oedipus and Creon.

12. Compare the first song of the Chorus in the Parodos with its lament in Ode 4. How has the attitude of the Chorus changed during the course of the drama? Whose point of view do you think the Chorus reflects: the author's, the audience's, or one or more of the characters'? Explain.

13. Based on your reading of *Oedipus Rex,* can you understand why the experience of an audience observing the suffering of a character in a **tragedy** may be, in fact, exhilarating and uplifting? Explain.

Extending and Evaluating

14. Consider the Chorus's closing speech in lines 1467–1475, in which it speaks sadly of Oedipus's pride and stature. What do you think these lines mean? Do you think it is possible to live a life that will be "a memory without pain"?

15. Sophocles' play raises some very difficult questions regarding guilt and responsibility for unintentional crimes. Can you think of any other examples of unforgivable acts committed in ways that make the assignment of responsibility almost impossible?

North Carolina Competency Goal
1.03; 4.05; 5.03

INTERNET

Projects and Activities
Keyword:
LE5 WL-2

SKILLS FOCUS

Literary Skills
Analyze dramatic irony.

Writing Skills
Analyze a tragic hero.

Listening and Speaking Skills
Perform a dramatic dialogue.

Vocabulary Skills
Create word information charts.

Literary Criticism

16. In Greek drama the most violent actions, such as Jocasta's suicide and Oedipus's self-blinding, often occur off-stage and are reported by messengers. Could one argue that the secondhand reporting of violence might, in fact, make a more chilling impression on an audience than an actual presentation of the violent actions themselves? Explain.

17. Some critics say that it is difficult to determine where Sophocles stands on the issue of free will versus determination. What evidence from the play suggests that Sophocles saw human beings' actions as determined by forces beyond their control, such as the gods and fate? What evidence do you find to suggest that Sophocles saw people as having the free will to create their own destinies?

WRITING
Analyzing Oedipus as a Tragic Hero

Read Aristotle's theory of tragedy as it is explained in the **Critical Comment** on page 263. Does Oedipus fit the description of the tragic hero? Do you agree or disagree that Oedipus's misfortune and downfall are brought about by "some error of judgment or frailty," or is your interpretation different? Write a three- to four-paragraph essay in which you analyze Oedipus as a tragic hero. Use evidence from the play, including direct quotations, to support your ideas. Include line numbers for quotations and for passages you are referring to.

LISTENING AND SPEAKING
Performing a Dramatic Dialogue

At the end of *Oedipus Rex*, several issues are left unresolved. Will Creon agree to exile Oedipus from Thebes? What will happen to Oedipus's children? Will the plague be lifted? Write a short dramatic dialogue as a sequel to the play. Try to incorporate the Chorus into your sequel. After you have written your dramatic dialogue, perform it for the class. Use facial expressions, gestures, and tone of voice to create distinct impressions. After your performance, compare your sequel's plot with the plot line of Sophocles' play, *Oedipus at Colonus,* which continues the story of Oedipus.

Vocabulary Development
Word Information Charts

| supplication | expedient | disdain | primal |
| compunction | decrepit | venerate | |

The chart below organizes some basic information about the word *supplication*. Using a dictionary, make similar charts for the rest of the Vocabulary words listed above.

supplication
Meaning: humble prayer
Origin: Latin, "to kneel down; pray"
Synonym and/or Antonym: request (synonym)
Example: The people of Thebes stood before Oedipus in <u>supplication</u>.

Grammar Link

Getting Along: Subject-Verb Agreement

Verbs and their subjects should share the same number; they should both be singular or both be plural. Otherwise, your reader may have trouble determining who is doing what. Here are some situations that require careful attention to subject-verb agreement:

The subject and verb are separated by a phrase or clause. If the subject does not immediately precede the verb, make sure that the verb agrees with the subject rather than a noun that happens to come before it.

> The <u>people</u> of the afflicted city <u>ask</u> Oedipus to save them from famine and sickness.

The subject is an indefinite pronoun. Most indefinite pronouns are singular (*anybody, anyone, each, either, everyone, everything, neither, no one, somebody, someone*). Some are plural (*both, many, several*). A few can be either singular or plural depending on how they are used (*all, any, more, most, none, some*).

> SINGULAR <u>None</u> of Thebes <u>seems</u> safe.

> PLURAL <u>None</u> of the citizens <u>know</u> what to do.

The subject is compound. If two or more subjects are joined by *and,* the verb is usually plural. If two or more subjects are joined by *or* or *nor,* the verb agrees with the subject closest to it.

> PLURAL <u>Creon and Oedipus</u> <u>discuss</u> the calamity.

> SINGULAR Neither <u>Creon</u> nor <u>Oedipus</u> <u>realizes</u> that Oedipus killed Laius.

> PLURAL Oedipus wonders whether one man <u>or</u> several <u>assailants</u> <u>are</u> to blame.

> SINGULAR Neither the chorus <u>members</u> nor their <u>leader</u> <u>expects</u> anything but the best.

The subject is followed by a parenthetical phrase such as *along with, as well as,* or *in addition to.* Although these phrases carry the same meaning as *and,* in formal usage a singular subject followed by a parenthetical phrase remains singular.

> <u>Teiresias</u>, as well as the oracle of Apollo, <u>knows</u> who is guilty.

North Carolina Competency Goal
1.03; 4.05; 5.03

SKILLS FOCUS

Grammar Skills
Understand subject-verb agreement.

PRACTICE

On a separate sheet of paper, correct any problems with subject-verb agreement in the following sentences. If the subject and verb agree, write *correct.*

1. On first meeting, Teiresias and Oedipus exchanges angry words.
2. To Oedipus, anyone trying to discover the facts seem threatening.
3. The people of Thebes, after further revelations, discover the truth.
4. Neither Teiresias nor Creon were wrong to accuse Oedipus.
5. Laius's murder, as well as Jocasta's suicide, wrack Oedipus with guilt.

Apply to Your Writing

Look through a writing assignment you are working on now or have already completed. Can you find any verbs that do not agree with their subjects? Revise to correct problems with subject-verb agreement.

▶ **For more help, see Agreement of Subject and Verb, 2a–i, in the Language Handbook.**

Roman Literature

Every moment think steadily, as a Roman and as a man, to do what thou hast in hand with perfect and simple dignity and feeling of affection and freedom and justice, and to give thyself relief from all other thoughts. And thou wilt give thyself relief, if thou doest every act of thy life as if it were the last, laying aside all carelessness and passionate aversion from the commands of reason, and all hypocrisy and self-love and discontent with the portion which has been given to thee. Thou seest how few the things are which, if a man lays hold of, he is able to live a life which flows in quiet and is like the existence of the gods; for the gods on their part will require nothing from him who observes these things.

— Marcus Aurelius from the *Meditations of Marcus Aurelius*, translated by George Long

Bust of Marcus Aurelius
(C. A.D. 161–c. A.D. 180).

267

Virgil

(70–19 B.C.)

Virgil writing the *Aeneid,* flanked by Clio, the Muse of history, and Melpomene, the Muse of tragedy (detail). Mosaic from Sousse, Tunisia. (late 4th century C.E.).
Bardo Museum, Tunisia.

Publius Vergilius Maro, known as Virgil (vʉr′jəl), lived most of his life under the shadow of political turmoil. During his youth and early adult years, various political factions struggled for control of Rome in a series of bloody civil wars. Only when Virgil was nearly forty did Julius Caesar's great-nephew Octavian finally restore order by becoming Rome's sole ruler. The reign of Octavian, who used the name *Augustus* (meaning "of good omen"), ushered in one of the longest eras of peace and order in the history of Rome. It was during this time that Virgil composed his epic history of the founding of Rome—the *Aeneid.*

Born near the northern town of Mantua, Virgil had deep roots in the Italian countryside. His father was a farmer who found the means to provide his son with a good education. This was the first opportunity for the shy young Virgil to experience the sophisticated life of the city. In Rome, like youths of nobler birth, Virgil studied subjects such as Greek law, philosophy, and literature. He tried working in the court system but found it too nerve-racking. With the outbreak of another war, Virgil retired to his country home. There he began to write pastoral poetry, or poetry that idealizes rural life.

During the war, the land owned by Virgil's family was confiscated. It was returned later through the influence of Octavian's counselor, who had taken an interest in Virgil's work. With the publication of the pastoral *Eclogues,* Virgil's reputation was fully established, and he turned away from the pastoral form to write the *Aeneid,* the epic story of Aeneas. He worked slowly and methodically on the *Aeneid* during the last ten years of his life. In a letter he complained that the project was driving him "almost out of his mind."

When the poem was nearly complete, Virgil became ill during a voyage to Greece. With his dying breath he begged his friends to burn the manuscript, since he was not satisfied with it. Fortunately, the emperor Augustus, who recognized the value of Virgil's poem both as literature and as favorable propaganda for his own rule, refused to comply with the poet's last wish and preserved the *Aeneid* for future generations.

Introduction

The Aeneid

At some point early in his career, Virgil resolved to devote his poetic powers to composing a great national epic of Rome that would put recent Roman achievements on a par with those of the Greeks. In writing a long epic about the wanderings of a Trojan refugee, Aeneas, Virgil consciously imitated the great Greek bard Homer (see page 120). Indeed, the first six books of the *Aeneid* contain many episodes and scenes inspired by Homer's *Odyssey,* while the last six books are roughly modeled on scenes from the *Iliad.*

The Story of Aeneas

Aeneas's travels begin with his exile after the fall of Troy. The ghost of his dead wife, Creusa, tells him to sail to Italy, where he will found a new empire. Over the course of six years, Aeneas travels by sea, often blown off course. At one point he lands in Carthage, where he and Queen Dido fall in love. They plan to marry, but the gods push Aeneas on toward Italy, where he is destined to establish the Roman culture.

In Cumae on the Italian coast, Aeneas consults the Sibyl, a priestess who sends him to the Underworld. There he meets the ghost of his father, Anchises. Aeneas is shown a long line of Roman leaders who will be descended from him, culminating with Augustus, Virgil's own patron. The concluding books of the epic describe the conquests and battles that Aeneas must undergo to establish a settlement for his people.

A New Kind of Epic Hero

In writing his epic of Rome's founding, Virgil consciously imitated Homer to some degree, but he thoroughly transformed the elements he borrowed from his Greek epic model. Most important, Virgil broke new ground by refashioning the portrayals of the Homeric heroes, adjusting them to fit a concept of the ideal Roman character. It is significant, for example, that the first time Virgil presents his hero in Book 1, Aeneas is weeping in frustration and envying the dead who fell at Troy. Virgil's Aeneas is no super-

Relief of soldiers and Roman officers of the Praetorian Guard (detail) (early 2nd century C.E.).

Musée du Louvre, Paris.

human, larger-than-life hero; instead, he is complex and three-dimensional. He is courageous and valiant, but also deeply sensitive and often divided by the conflict between duty and passion. The *Aeneid* marks the passing of an older heroic ideal and its replacement with a more complex, down-to-earth hero sharply constricted by adverse fate and human limitations.

Virgil's Influence

Among the great classical writers, Virgil has been one of the greatest influences in Western literature, not only because of the magnificent works he created but also because his work is representative of the time in which he lived and the values admired by his culture. The Age of Augustus, which Virgil celebrated in his works, was one of the high points of Roman civilization.

One reason for Virgil's remarkable impact on later literature was his appeal to Christian authors and educators. Virgil created his national epic shortly before the birth of Christ and the founding of Christianity, whose history would be affected by the Roman Empire for the next four centuries. Christianity condemned many pagan authors as unsuitable reading, but the moral virtues of duty, moderation, and piety that Virgil emphasized made him acceptable to Christians, and his poems were used as school texts. The *Aeneid* became a model that inspired the works of Dante Alighieri (see page 645), Edmund Spenser, John Milton, and other writers of the Middle Ages and the Renaissance.

The Procession of the Trojan Horse (1773) by Giovanni Battista Tiepolo.

The Granger Collection, New York.

Before You Read

from the Aeneid

Make the Connection

Quickwrite ✏️

In what ways do the lives of great leaders show a mixture of achievements and setbacks? Do you think less of leaders who show weakness or encounter failure? Think of one or two great leaders, either living or dead, and freewrite about triumph and tragedy in their lives.

Literary Focus

Conflict

Conflict is a struggle or clash between opposing characters, forces, or emotions. In an **external conflict** a character struggles against an outside force, such as society as a whole or a natural force. An **internal conflict** is a struggle between opposing needs, desires, or emotions *within* a single character. Look for examples of both kinds of conflict in the *Aeneid*.

> **Conflict** is a struggle or clash between opposing forces.
>
> *For more on Conflict, see the Handbook of Literary and Historical Terms.*

Reading Skills 📖

Analyzing Motivation

A character's **motivation** consists of the reasons that compel his or her actions. Writers reveal motivation through a combination of a character's desires and the circumstances in which the character

is placed. As you read, note specific words and actions that reveal the innermost needs and desires of Aeneas and the other main characters in Virgil's epic. Then, use these clues to make some inferences, or educated guesses, about the characters' motivations.

Background

Like Homer before him, Virgil starts his epic not at the beginning, but at a point in the middle of the story: *in medias res,* literally, "in the middle of things." Book 1 opens with Aeneas's shipwreck at Carthage (on the shores of North Africa) and his encounter with Queen Dido. At the start of Book 2, a great banquet is in progress in Carthage, and Queen Dido asks Aeneas to describe the fall of Troy. The banquet hall is hushed as Aeneas tells of the Greek siege of Troy. In this lengthy flashback, Aeneas will speak firsthand of the infamous Trojan horse; the death of King Priam; and his own encounters with Helen of Troy, his mother (the goddess Venus), and the ghost of his wife, Creusa.

North Carolina Competency Goal
1.03; 4.05; 5.01; 5.03; 6.01

go.
hrw
.com

INTERNET

Vocabulary Practice
•
More About Virgil
Keyword:
LE5 WL-2

Vocabulary Development

undulating (un′jə·lāt′iŋ) *v.* used as *adj.*: moving in a wavelike manner.

predatory (pred′ə·tôr′ē) *adj.*: relating to hunting and feeding on other animals.

futile (fyo͞ot′'l) *adj.*: useless.

omnipotent (äm·nip′ə·tənt) *adj.*: all-powerful.

tenuous (ten′yo͞o·əs) *adj.*: insubstantial; flimsy.

SKILLS FOCUS

Literary Skills
Understand conflict.

Reading Skills
Analyze motivation.

from the
AENEID

from BOOK 2: THE FALL OF TROY

Virgil *translated by* **Robert Fitzgerald**

CHARACTERS IN THE AENEID

Aeneas (i·nē′əs): ancestor of the Roman rulers; son of the goddess Venus and Anchises, the king of Dardanus.

Anchises (an·kī′sēz′): father of Aeneas; ally of Priam, the king of Troy.

Ascanius (as·kā′nē·əs): son of Aeneas and Creusa, also called Iulus.

Creusa (krē·yōō′sə): Priam's daughter; wife of Aeneas; first to tell Aeneas to journey to Italy.

Dido (dī′dō): queen of Carthage; lover of Aeneas who kills herself when he leaves her for Italy.

The Sibyl (sib′əl): priestess of Apollo who leads Aeneas through the Underworld.

Aeneas and Anchises (1618–1619) by Gian Lorenzo Bernini.

Galleria Borghese, Rome.

"Knowing their strength broken in warfare, turned
Back by the fates, and years—so many years—
Already slipped away, the Danaan° captains
By the divine handicraft of Pallas° built
5 A horse of timber, tall as a hill,
And sheathed its ribs with planking of cut pine.
This they gave out to be an offering
For a safe return by sea, and the word went round.
But on the sly they shut inside a company
10 Chosen from their picked soldiery by lot,
Crowding the vaulted caverns in the dark—
The horse's belly—with men fully armed.

3. Danaan (dān′ə·ən): name for the Greeks.
4. Pallas (pal′əs): name for the goddess Athena, here called Minerva.

4–12. In these lines Aeneas describes the Trojan horse, which has become a term that means "a cunning stratagem, or trick."
? *What do the Greeks claim the Trojan horse's purpose is? What is its actual purpose?*

(Opposite) *Episode of the Aeneid: The Trojan Horse,* from the Master of the Aeneid series (c. 1530–c. 1540) France. Limoges.

The Cleveland Museum of Art, 2004. Andrew R. and Martha Holden Jennings Fund (1974.40).

Virgil   **273**

Offshore there's a long island, Tenedos,°
Famous and rich while Priam's kingdom lasted,
15   A treacherous anchorage now, and nothing more.
They crossed to this and hid their ships behind it
On the bare shore beyond. We thought they'd gone,
Sailing home to Mycenae° before the wind,
So Teucer's town° is freed of her long anguish,
20   Gates thrown wide! And out we go in joy
To see the Dorian° campsites, all deserted,
The beach they left behind. Here the Dolopians°
Pitched their tents, here cruel Achilles lodged,
There lay the ships, and there, formed up in ranks,
25   They came inland to fight us. Of our men
One group stood marveling, gaping up to see
The dire gift of the cold unbedded goddess,°
The sheer mass of the horse.
                       Thymoetes° shouts
It should be hauled inside the walls and moored
30   High on the citadel—whether by treason
Or just because Troy's fate went that way now.
Capys° opposed him; so did the wiser heads:
'Into the sea with it,' they said, 'or burn it,
Build up a bonfire under it.
35   This trick of the Greeks, a gift no one can trust,
Or cut it open, search the hollow belly!'

Contrary notions pulled the crowd apart.
Next thing we knew, in front of everyone,
Laocoon with a great company
40   Came furiously running from the Height,
And still far off cried out: 'O my poor people,
Men of Troy, what madness has come over you?
Can you believe the enemy truly gone?
A gift from the Danaans, and no ruse?
45   Is that Ulysses'° way, as you have known him?
Achaeans° must be hiding in this timber,
Or it was built to butt against our walls,
Peer over them into our houses, pelt
The city from the sky. Some crookedness
50   Is in this thing. Have no faith in the horse!
Whatever it is, even when Greeks bring gifts
I fear them, gifts and all.'
                    He broke off then
And rifled his big spear with all his might
Against the horse's flank, the curve of belly.
55   It stuck there trembling, and the rounded hull
Reverberated groaning at the blow.

13. Tenedos (ten′ə·däs′): island sacred to Apollo.

18. Mycenae (mī·sē′nē): capital of the kingdom ruled by Agamemnon.
19. Teucer's town: Teucer (tū′sər) was a former king of Troy.
21. Dorian (dôr′ē·ən): one of the peoples of Greece.
22. Dolopians (dôl·ō′pē·ənz): people from Thessaly.

27. cold . . . goddess: Minerva.

28. Thymoetes (thī·mō′tēz).

32. Capys (ka′pəs): Aeneas's comrade.

38–52. What warning does Laocoon issue to his fellow Trojans?

45. Ulysses (yoo·lis′ēz′): Roman name for the Greek hero Odysseus.
46. Achaeans (ə·kē′ənz): name for the Greeks.

52–67. What striking images in these lines help you visualize the scene?

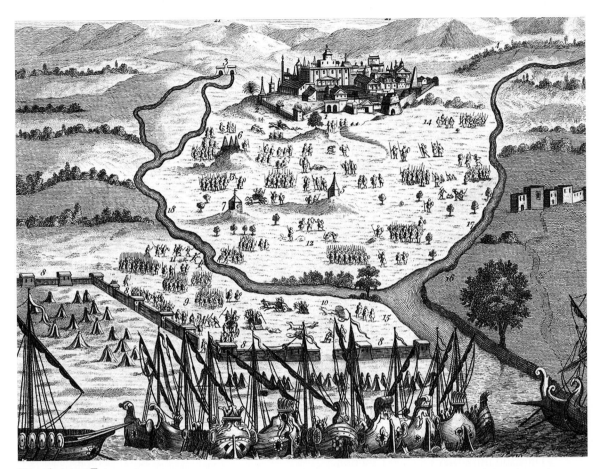

Map of ancient Troy.

If the gods' will had not been sinister,
If our own minds had not been crazed,
He would have made us foul that Argive° den
60   With bloody steel, and Troy would stand today—
O citadel of Priam, towering still!
But now look: hillmen, shepherds of Dardania,°
Raising a shout, dragged in before the king
An unknown fellow° with hands tied behind—
65   This all as he himself had planned,
Volunteering, letting them come across him,
So he could open Troy to the Achaeans.
Sure of himself this man was, braced for it
Either way, to work his trick or die.
70   From every quarter Trojans run to see him,
Ring the prisoner round, and make a game
Of jeering at him. Be instructed now
In Greek deceptive arts: one barefaced deed
Can tell you of them all.

59. Argive (är′gīv′): name for the Greeks.

62. Dardania (där·dā′nē·ə): Troy. The founder of the city was Dardanus.
64. unknown fellow: Sinon.

The spy Sinon puts on a convincing performance to persuade the Trojans that he has escaped from the Greeks after being betrayed and condemned to death. Having gained the Trojans' confidence, he easily makes them believe that the Greeks have abandoned the siege of the city, leaving the strange wooden horse behind to appease the angry gods.

75 And now another sign, more fearful still,
    Broke on our blind miserable people,
    Filling us all with dread. Laocoon,
    Acting as Neptune's priest that day by lot,
    Was on the point of putting to the knife
80 A massive bull before the appointed altar,
    When ah—look there!
    From Tenedos, on the calm sea, twin snakes—
    I shiver to recall it—endlessly
    Coiling, uncoiling, swam abreast for shore,
85 Their underbellies showing as their crests
    Reared red as blood above the swell; behind
    They glided with great <u>undulating</u> backs.
    Now came the sound of thrashed seawater foaming;
    Now they were on dry land, and we could see
90 Their burning eyes, fiery and suffused with blood,
    Their tongues a-flicker out of hissing maws.
    We scattered, pale with fright. But straight ahead
    They slid until they reached Laocoon.
    Each snake enveloped one of his two boys,
95 Twining about and feeding on the body.
    Next they ensnared the man as he ran up
    With weapons: coils like cables looped and bound him
    Twice round the middle; twice about his throat
    They whipped their back-scales, and their heads towered,
100 While with both hands he fought to break the knots,
    Drenched in slime, his headbands black with venom,
    Sending to heaven his appalling cries
    Like a slashed bull escaping from an altar,
    The fumbled axe shrugged off. The pair of snakes
105 Now flowed away and made for the highest shrines,
    The citadel of pitiless Minerva,
    Where coiling they took cover at her feet
    Under the rondure° of her shield. New terrors
    Ran in the shaken crowd: the word went round
110 Laocoon had paid, and rightfully,

92–115. As Laocoon is about to sacrifice a bull, snakes arrive and kill him as well as his sons.

? *For what reason do the Trojans believe that Laocoon was killed (see lines 109–112)?*

108. rondure (rän′jər′) *n:* circle.

Vocabulary

undulating (un′jə·lāt′iŋ) *v.* used as *adj.:* moving in a wavelike manner.

For profanation of the sacred hulk
With his offending spear hurled at its flank.
'The offering must be hauled to its true home,'
They clamored. 'Votive prayers to the goddess
Must be said there!'

115   So we breached the walls
And laid the city open. Everyone
Pitched in to get the figure underpinned
With rollers, hempen lines around the neck.
Deadly, pregnant with enemies, the horse

120 Crawled upward to the breach. And boys and girls
Sang hymns around the towrope as for joy
They touched it. Rolling on, it cast a shadow
Over the city's heart. O Fatherland,
O Ilium,° home of gods! Defensive wall

125 Renowned in war for Dardanus's people!
There on the very threshold of the breach
It jarred to a halt four times, four times the arms
In the belly thrown together made a sound—
Yet on we strove unmindful, deaf and blind,

130 To place the monster on our blessed height.
Then, even then, Cassandra's lips unsealed
The doom to come: lips by a god's command
Never believed or heeded by the Trojans.
So pitiably we, for whom that day

135 Would be the last, made all our temples green
With leafy festal boughs throughout the city.

As heaven turned, Night from the Ocean stream
Came on, profound in gloom on earth and sky
And Myrmidons° in hiding. In their homes

140 The Teucrians lay silent, wearied out,
And sleep enfolded them. The Argive fleet,
Drawn up in line abreast, left Tenedos
Through the aloof moon's friendly stillnesses
And made for the familiar shore. Flame signals

145 Shone from the command ship. Sinon, favored
By what the gods unjustly had decreed,
Stole out to tap the pine walls and set free
The Danaans in the belly. Opened wide,
The horse emitted men; gladly they dropped

150 Out of the cavern, captains first, Thessandrus,
Sthenelus and the man of iron, Ulysses;
Hand over hand upon the rope, Acamas, Thoas,
Neoptolemus and Prince Machaon,°
Menelaus and then the master builder,

155 Epeos,° who designed the horse decoy.

116–123. *How do the Trojans respond when the horse arrives in the city?*

124. **Ilium** (il′ē·əm): another name for Troy.

139. **Myrmidons** (mur′mə·dänz′): followers of Achilles.

150–153. **Thessandrus** (thə·san′drəs); **Sthenelus** (sthen′ə·ləs); **Acamas** (ak′ə·məs); **Thoas** (thō′əs); **Machaon** (ma·kā′on).
155. **Epeos** (e·pē′əs).

Into the darkened city, buried deep
In sleep and wine, they made their way,
Cut the few sentries down,
Let in their fellow soldiers at the gate,
160 And joined their combat companies as planned.

That time of night it was when the first sleep,
Gift of the gods, begins for ill mankind,
Arriving gradually, delicious rest.
In sleep, in dream, Hector appeared to me,
165 Gaunt with sorrow, streaming tears, all torn—
As by the violent car on his death day—
And black with bloody dust,
His puffed-out feet cut by the rawhide thongs.
Ah god, the look of him! How changed
170 From that proud Hector who returned to Troy
Wearing Achilles' armor, or that one
Who pitched the torches on Danaan ships;
His beard all filth, his hair matted with blood,
Showing the wounds, the many wounds, received
175 Outside his father's city walls. I seemed
Myself to weep and call upon the man
In grieving speech, brought from the depth of me:
'Light of Dardania, best hope of Troy,
What kept you from us for so long, and where?
180 From what far place, O Hector, have you come,
Long, long awaited? After so many deaths
Of friends and brothers, after a world of pain
For all our folk and all our town, at last,
Boneweary, we behold you! What has happened
185 To ravage your serene face? Why these wounds?'

He wasted no reply on my poor questions
But heaved a great sigh from his chest and said:
'Ai! Give up and go, child of the goddess,°
Save yourself, out of these flames. The enemy
190 Holds the city walls, and from her height
Troy falls in ruin. Fatherland and Priam
Have their due; if by one hand our towers
Could be defended, by this hand, my own,
They would have been. Her holy things, her gods
195 Of hearth and household° Troy commends to you.
Accept them as companions of your days;
Go find for them the great walls that one day
You'll dedicate, when you have roamed the sea.'

164–175. Hector appears to Aeneas in a dream during the first night the Trojan horse is allowed into the city.

? *How is Hector's appearance in Aeneas's vision different from his appearance when he was living?*

? **188–198.** *What advice does Hector offer to Aeneas in the vision? What does he predict will happen to Troy?*

188. child of the goddess: Aeneas is the son of Venus.

194–195. gods...household: Romans had household and domestic gods called lares (lā′rēz′) and penates (pē·nā′tēz′).

As he said this, he brought out from the sanctuary
200 Chaplets and Vesta, Lady of the Hearth,
With her eternal fire.
                              While I dreamed,
The turmoil rose, with anguish, in the city.
More and more, although Anchises' house
Lay in seclusion, muffled among trees,
205 The din at the grim onset grew; and now
I shook off sleep, I climbed to the roof top
To cup my ears and listen. And the sound
Was like the sound a grassfire makes in grain,
Whipped by a Southwind, or a torrent foaming
210 Out of a mountainside to strew in ruin
Fields, happy crops, the yield of plowing teams,
Or woodlands borne off in the flood; in wonder
The shepherd listens on a rocky peak.
I knew then what our trust had won for us,
215 Knew the Danaan fraud: Deiphobus'°
Great house in flames, already caving in
Under the overpowering god of fire;
Ucalegon's° already caught nearby;
The glare lighting the straits beyond Sigeum;°
220 The cries of men, the wild calls of the trumpets.

To arm was my first maddened impulse—not
That anyone had a fighting chance in arms;
Only I burned to gather up some force
For combat, and to man some high redoubt.°
225 So fury drove me, and it came to me
That meeting death was beautiful in arms.
Then here, eluding the Achaean spears,
Came Panthus, Othrys'° son, priest of Apollo,
Carrying holy things, our conquered gods,
230 And pulling a small grandchild along; he ran
Despairing to my doorway.
                                    'Where's the crux,
Panthus,' I said. 'What strongpoint shall we hold?'
Before I could say more, he groaned and answered:
'The last day for Dardania has come,
235 The hour not to be fought off any longer.
Trojans we have been; Ilium has been;
The glory of the Teucrians is no more;
Black Jupiter has passed it on to Argos.°
Greeks are the masters in our burning city.
240 Tall as a cliff, set in the heart of town,
Their horse pours out armed men. The conqueror,

207–212. In these lines, Virgil uses an **epic simile**, or lengthy comparison.
❓ *What does Virgil compare the battle to in these lines?*

215. Deiphobus (dē′ə·fō′bəs).

218. Ucalegon (yo͞o·kal′ə·gän).
219. Sigeum (si·jē′əm).

224. redoubt (ri·dout′) *n:* defense.

228. Panthus (pan′thəs); **Othrys** (ôth′ris).

234–248. As Aeneas prepares to enter the fray, he is visited by Panthus.
❓ *What details in Panthus's description indicate that Troy is in a hopeless situation?*

238. Argos (är′gäs′): town in the Peloponnesus.

Gloating Sinon, brews new conflagrations.°
Troops hold the gates—as many thousand men
As ever came from great Mycenae; others
245   Block the lanes with crossed spears; glittering
In a combat line, swordblades are drawn for slaughter.
Even the first guards at the gates can barely
Offer battle, or blindly make a stand.'

Impelled by these words, by the powers of heaven,
250   Into the flames I go, into the fight,
Where the harsh Fury, and the din and shouting,
Skyward rising, calls. Crossing my path
In moonlight, five fell in with me, companions:
Ripheus, and Epytus, a great soldier,
255   Hypanis, Dymas, cleaving to my side
With young Coroebus, Mygdon's° son. It happened
That in those very days this man had come
To Troy, aflame with passion for Cassandra,
Bringing to Priam and the Phrygians°
260   A son-in-law's right hand. Unlucky one,

242. conflagrations
(kän′flə·grā′shənz) *n.pl.:* fires.

249–252. In spite of
Panthus's words, Aeneas
rushes off to fight the
Greeks.
[?] *What does Aeneas's
response to Panthus
tell you about Aeneas's
character?*

254–256. Ripheus (rif′o͞os);
Epytus (e′pi·təs); **Hypanis**
(hī′pan·əs); **Dymas** (dī′məs);
Mygdon (mig′dän).
259. Phrygians (frij′ē·ənz):
people of Phrygia, a country in
Asia Minor where Troy was
located.

Siege of Troy II,
The Wooden Horse
(15th century C.E.)
by Biagio di Antonio.

Fitzwilliam Museum, University
of Cambridge, England.

To have been deaf to what his bride foretold!
Now when I saw them grouped, on edge for battle,
I took it all in and said briefly,

                       'Soldiers,
Brave as you are to no end, if you crave
265   To face the last fight with me, and no doubt of it,
How matters stand for us each one can see.
The gods by whom this kingdom stood are gone,
Gone from the shrines and altars. You defend
A city lost in flames. Come, let us die,
270   We'll make a rush into the thick of it.
The conquered have one safety: hope for none.'

The desperate odds doubled their fighting spirit:
From that time on, like <u>predatory</u> wolves
In fog and darkness, when a savage hunger

263–279. Aeneas
assumes leadership of a
small band of Trojan
soldiers.

? *What does Aeneas
emphasize as he speaks
to the soldiers? What effect
do his words have on them?*

Vocabulary

predatory (pred′ə·tôr´ē) *adj.*: relating to hunting and
    feeding on other animals.

275	Drives them blindly on, and cubs in lairs
	Lie waiting with dry famished jaws—just so
	Through arrow flights and enemies we ran
	Toward our sure death, straight for the city's heart,
	Cavernous black night over and around us.
280	Who can describe the havoc of that night
	Or tell the deaths, or tally wounds with tears?
	The ancient city falls, after dominion
	Many long years. In windrows° on the streets,
	In homes, on solemn porches of the gods,
285	Dead bodies lie. And not alone the Trojans
	Pay the price with their heart's blood; at times
	Manhood returns to fire even the conquered
	And Danaan conquerors fall. Grief everywhere,
	Everywhere terror, and all shapes of death.

283. windrows *n. pl.*: rows of hay or grain that have been raked together.

Aeneas and his small band of friends overcome a detachment of Greek soldiers and put on their armor and insignia. Thus disguised, they are able to cut down a number of the invaders.

290	When gods are contrary
	They stand by no one. Here before us came
	Cassandra, Priam's virgin daughter, dragged
	By her long hair out of Minerva's shrine,
	Lifting her brilliant eyes in vain to heaven—
295	Her eyes alone, as her white hands were bound.
	Coroebus, infuriated, could not bear it,
	But plunged into the midst to find his death.
	We all went after him, our swords at play,
	But here, here first, from the temple gable's height,
300	We met a hail of missiles from our friends,
	Pitiful execution, by their error,
	Who thought us Greek from our Greek plumes and shields.
	Then with a groan of anger, seeing the virgin
	Wrested from them, Danaans from all sides
305	Rallied and attacked us: fiery Ajax,
	Atreus'° sons, Dolopians in a mass—
	As, when a cyclone breaks, conflicting winds
	Will come together, Westwind, Southwind, Eastwind
	Riding high out of the Dawnland; forests
310	Bend and roar, and raging all in spume
	Nereus with his trident churns the deep.
	Then some whom we had taken by surprise
	Under cover of night throughout the city
	And driven off, came back again: they knew
315	Our shields and arms for liars now, our speech
	Alien to their own. They overwhelmed us.

? 300–302. *Why do Aeneas's fellow Trojans attack him?*

306. Atreus (ā′trē·əs): father of Agamemnon and Menelaus.

One by one the remaining Trojan warriors are killed in a hail of missiles from their own side. Aeneas is drawn by the cry of battle to King Priam's castle, where a great massacre is about to take place.

Mars gone berserk, Danaans
In a rush to scale the roof; the gate besieged
By a tortoise shell of overlapping shields.
320 Ladders clung to the wall, and men strove upward
Before the very doorposts, on the rungs,
Left hand putting the shield up, and the right
Reaching for the cornice. The defenders
Wrenched out upperworks and rooftiles: these
325 For missiles, as they saw the end, preparing
To fight back even on the edge of death.
And gilded beams, ancestral ornaments,
They rolled down on the heads below. In hall
Others with swords drawn held the entrance way,
330 Packed there, waiting. Now we plucked up heart
To help the royal house, to give our men
A respite, and to add our strength to theirs,
Though all were beaten. And we had for entrance
A rear door, secret, giving on a passage
335 Between the palace halls; in other days
Andromache,° poor lady, often used it,
Going alone to see her husband's parents
Or taking Astyanax° to his grandfather.
I climbed high on the roof, where hopeless men
340 Were picking up and throwing <u>futile</u> missiles.
Here was a tower like a promontory°
Rising toward the stars above the roof:
All Troy, the Danaan ships, the Achaean camp,
Were visible from this. Now close beside it
345 With crowbars, where the flooring made loose joints,
We pried it from its bed and pushed it over.
Down with a rending crash in sudden ruin
Wide over the Danaan lines it fell;
But fresh troops moved up, and the rain of stones
350 With every kind of missile never ceased.

Just at the outer doors of the vestibule
Sprang Pyrrhus, all in bronze and glittering,
As a serpent, hidden swollen underground

Vocabulary
futile (fyōōt′'l) *adj.:* useless.

By a cold winter, writhes into the light,
355 On vile grass fed, his old skin cast away,
     Renewed and glossy, rolling slippery coils,
     With lifted underbelly rearing sunward
     And triple tongue a-flicker. Close beside him
     Giant Periphas and Automedon,°
360 His armorbearer, once Achilles' driver,
     Besieged the place with all the young of Scyros,°
     Hurling their torches at the palace roof.
     Pyrrhus shouldering forward with an axe
     Broke down the stony threshold, forced apart
365 Hinges and brazen doorjambs, and chopped through
     One panel of the door, splitting the oak,
     To make a window, a great breach. And there
     Before their eyes the inner halls lay open,
     The courts of Priam and the ancient kings,
370 With men-at-arms ranked in the vestibule.
     From the interior came sounds of weeping,
     Pitiful commotion, wails of women
     High-pitched, rising in the formal chambers
     To ring against the silent golden stars;
375 And, through the palace, mothers wild with fright
     Ran to and fro or clung to doors and kissed them.
     Pyrrhus with his father's brawn stormed on,
     No bolts or bars or men availed to stop him:
     Under his battering the double doors
380 Were torn out of their sockets and fell inward.
     Sheer force cleared the way: the Greeks broke through
     Into the vestibule, cut down the guards,
     And made the wide hall seethe with men-at-arms—
     A tumult greater than when dikes are burst
385 And a foaming river, swirling out in flood,
     Whelms every parapet and races on
     Through fields and over all the lowland plains,
     Bearing off pens and cattle. I myself
     Saw Neoptolemus furious with blood
390 In the entrance way, and saw the two Atridae;°
     Hecuba I saw, and her hundred daughters,
     Priam before the altars, with his blood
     Drenching the fires that he himself had blessed.
     Those fifty bridal chambers, hope of a line
395 So flourishing; those doorways high and proud,
     Adorned with takings of barbaric gold,
     Were all brought low: fire had them, or the Greeks.
     What was the fate of Priam, you may ask.
     Seeing his city captive, seeing his own

359. Periphas (pʉr′ə·fəs); **Automedon** (ô·tä′mə·dən).
361. Scyros (sī′rəs): island in the Aegean Sea.

? 363–380. Describe Pyrrhus's actions. How is he like his father, Achilles?

390. Atridae (ə·trī′dē): Agamemnon and Menelaus.

? 398–404. How does Priam respond when his palace is invaded?

400 Royal portals rent apart, his enemies
In the inner rooms, the old man uselessly
Put on his shoulders, shaking with old age,
Armor unused for years, belted a sword on,
And made for the massed enemy to die.

405 Under the open sky in a central court
Stood a big altar; near it, a laurel tree
Of great age, leaning over, in deep shade
Embowered the Penates.° At this altar
Hecuba and her daughters, like white doves

410 Blown in a black storm, clung together,
Enfolding holy images in their arms.
Now, seeing Priam in a young man's gear,
She called out:

      'My poor husband, what mad thought
Drove you to buckle on these weapons?

415 Where are you trying to go? The time is past
For help like this, for this kind of defending,
Even if my own Hector could be here.
Come to me now: the altar will protect us,
Or else you'll die with us.'

           She drew him close,

420 Heavy with years, and made a place for him
To rest on the consecrated stone.

           Now see
Polites, one of Priam's sons, escaped
From Pyrrhus' butchery and on the run
Through enemies and spears, down colonnades,

425 Through empty courtyards, wounded. Close behind
Comes Pyrrhus burning for the death-stroke: has him,
Catches him now, and lunges with the spear.
The boy has reached his parents, and before them
Goes down, pouring out his life with blood.

430 Now Priam, in the very midst of death,
Would neither hold his peace nor spare his anger.

'For what you've done, for what you've dared,' he said,
'If there is care in heaven for atrocity,
May the gods render fitting thanks, reward you

435 As you deserve. You forced me to look on
At the destruction of my son: defiled
A father's eyes with death. That great Achilles
You claim to be the son of—and you lie—
Was not like you to Priam, his enemy;

440 To me who threw myself upon his mercy
He showed compunction, gave me back for burial

408. Penates (pē·nā′tēz′):
Roman household gods.

Bronze helmet with scene of
the sack of Troy.

Museo Archaeologico Nazionale, Naples.

432–443. Pyrrhus slays
Priam's son Polites in front
of him after a lengthy
pursuit.
  *Priam respected Achilles,
Pyrrhus's father, even
though Achilles was an
enemy. Why does Priam
say Pyrrhus is unworthy of
his father?*

The bloodless corpse of Hector, and returned me
To my own realm.'
                         The old man threw his spear
With feeble impact; blocked by the ringing bronze,
445 It hung there harmless from the jutting boss.°
Then Pyrrhus answered:
                         'You'll report the news
To Pelides,° my father; don't forget
My sad behavior, the degeneracy
Of Neoptolemus. Now die.'
                         With this,
450 To the altar step itself he dragged him trembling,
Slipping in the pooled blood of his son,
And took him by the hair with his left hand.
The sword flashed in his right; up to the hilt
He thrust it in his body.
                         That was the end
455 Of Priam's age, the doom that took him off,
With Troy in flames before his eyes, his towers
Headlong fallen—he that in other days
Had ruled in pride so many lands and peoples,
The power of Asia.
                         On the distant shore
460 The vast trunk headless lies without a name.

For the first time that night, inhuman shuddering
Took me, head to foot, I stood unmanned,
And my dear father's image came to mind
As our king, just his age, mortally wounded,
465 Gasped his life away before my eyes.
Creusa came to mind, too, left alone;
The house plundered; danger to little Iulus.
I looked around to take stock of my men,
But all had left me, utterly played out,
470 Giving their beaten bodies to the fire
Or plunging from the roof.
                         It came to this,
That I stood there alone. And then I saw
Lurking beyond the doorsill of the Vesta,
In hiding, silent, in that place reserved,
475 The daughter of Tyndareus.° Glare of fires
Lighted my steps this way and that, my eyes
Glancing over the whole scene, everywhere.
That woman, terrified of the Trojans' hate
For the city overthrown, terrified too
480 Of Danaan vengeance, her abandoned husband's
Anger after years—Helen, that Fury

445. boss *n.*: here, an architectural protuberance.

447. Pelides (pē′li·dēz): Achilles, son of Peleus.

? **449–460.** *Describe how King Priam dies.*

475. daughter of Tyndareus (tin·der′ē·əs): Helen.

Helen on the Walls of Troy
(c. 1895) by Gustave Moreau.
Musée du Louvre, Paris.

Both to her own homeland and Troy, had gone
To earth, a hated thing, before the altars.
Now fires blazed up in my own spirit—
485 A passion to avenge my fallen town
And punish Helen's whorishness.
                    'Shall this one
Look untouched on Sparta and Mycenae
After her triumph, going like a queen,
And see her home and husband, kin and children,
490 With Trojan girls for escort, Phrygian slaves?
Must Priam perish by the sword for this?
Troy burn, for this? Dardania's littoral°
Be soaked in blood, so many times, for this?
Not by my leave. I know
495 No glory comes of punishing a woman,
The feat can bring no honor. Still, I'll be
Approved for snuffing out a monstrous life,
For a just sentence carried out. My heart
Will teem with joy in this avenging fire,
500 And the ashes of my kin will be appeased.'

472–500. *As Aeneas contemplates what has happened to his homeland, what does he think may be a proper way to avenge the destruction of Troy?*

492. littoral (lit′ə·rəl) *n.:* here, shoreline.

So ran my thoughts. I turned wildly upon her,
But at that moment, clear, before my eyes—
Never before so clear—in a pure light
Stepping before me, radiant through the night,
505 My loving mother came: immortal, tall,
And lovely as the lords of heaven know her.
Catching me by the hand, she held me back,
Then with her rose-red mouth reproved me:

                                              'Son,

Why let such suffering goad you on to fury
510 Past control? Where is your thoughtfulness
For me, for us? Will you not first revisit
The place you left your father, worn and old,
Or find out if your wife, Creusa, lives,
And the young boy, Ascanius—all these
515 Cut off by Greek troops foraging everywhere?
Had I not cared for them, fire would by now
Have taken them, their blood glutted the sword.
You must not hold the woman of Laconia,°
That hated face, the cause of this, nor Paris.
520 The harsh will of the gods it is, the gods,
That overthrows the splendor of this place
And brings Troy from her height into the dust.
Look over there: I'll tear away the cloud
That curtains you, and films your mortal sight,
525 The fog around you.—Have no fear of doing
Your mother's will, or balk at obeying her.—
Look: where you see high masonry thrown down,
Stone torn from stone, with billowing smoke and dust,
Neptune is shaking from their beds the walls
530 That his great trident pried up, undermining,
Toppling the whole city down. And look:
Juno in all her savagery holds
The Scaean Gates,° and raging in steel armor
Calls her allied army from the ships.
535 Up on the citadel—turn, look—Pallas Tritonia°
Couched in a stormcloud, lightening, with her Gorgon!°
The Father° himself empowers the Danaans,
Urges assaulting gods on the defenders.
Away, child; put an end to toiling so.
540 I shall be near, to see you safely home.'

She hid herself in the deep gloom of night,
And now the dire forms appeared to me
Of great immortals, enemies of Troy.
I knew the end then: Ilium was going down
545 In fire, the Troy of Neptune going down,

508–522. Venus appears to Aeneas and asks him not to hold Helen responsible for the fall of Troy.

? *What does Venus say is the reason for Troy's fall? What does this tell you about Roman beliefs?*

518. **woman of Laconia** (lə·kō′nē·ə): Helen.

? **539–540.** *What does Venus offer to do for Aeneas?*

533. **Scaean** (skē′ən) **Gates:** northwest entry to Troy.

535. **Pallas Tritonia** (trə·tō′nē·ə): name for Minerva; she was supposed to have been born near Lake Tritonis in Libya.

536. **Gorgon** (gôr′gən): Medusa, a terrifying monster slain by Perseus; her head was given to the goddess Minerva, who carried it upon her father's shield.

537. **Father:** Jupiter (the Roman name for Zeus).

As in high mountains when the countrymen
Have notched an ancient ash, then make their axes
Ring with might and main, chopping away
To fell the tree—ever on the point of falling,
550 Shaken through all its foliage, and the treetop
Nodding; bit by bit the strokes prevail
Until it gives a final groan at last
And crashes down in ruin from the height.

Now I descended where the goddess guided,
555 Clear of the flames, and clear of enemies,
For both retired; so gained my father's door,
My ancient home.

*Arriving home, Aeneas finds his father, Anchises, resolved to
die in the carnage of Troy. Unable to persuade him to flee,
Aeneas swears, despite his wife's piteous pleas, that he will join
his father in death. Then he looks at his son and sees an omen
that changes his mind.*

She went on, and her wailing filled the house,
But then a sudden portent came, a marvel:
560 Amid his parents' hands and their sad faces
A point on Iulus' head seemed to cast light,
A tongue of flame that touched but did not burn him,
Licking his fine hair, playing round his temples.
We, in panic, beat at the flaming hair
565 And put the sacred fire out with water;
Father Anchises lifted his eyes to heaven
And lifted up his hands, his voice, in joy:

'Omnipotent Jupiter, if prayers affect you,
Look down upon us, that is all I ask,
570 If by devotion to the gods we earn it,
Grant us a new sign, and confirm this portent!'
The old man barely finished when it thundered
A loud crack on the left. Out of the sky
Through depths of night a star fell trailing flame
575 And glided on, turning the night to day.
We watched it pass above the roof and go
To hide its glare, its trace, in Ida's° wood;
But still, behind, the luminous furrow shone
And wide zones fumed with sulphur.

Goddess appearing to Aeneas.
Illustration from Virgil's *Aeneid.*

Biblioteca Apostolica Vaticana, Musei Vaticani,
Vatican City.

559–588. *What is
the initial portent, or
omen, that startles Aeneas?
What does Anchises think is
the meaning of the omen?*

577. Ida (ī′də): mountain
near Troy, the setting for the
Judgment of Paris.

Vocabulary

omnipotent (äm·nip′ə·tənt) *adj.:* all-powerful.

Now indeed

580 My father, overcome, addressed the gods,
And rose in worship of the blessed star.

'Now, now, no more delay. I'll follow you.
Where you conduct me, there I'll be.

Gods of my fathers,

Preserve this house, preserve my grandson. Yours
585 This portent was. Troy's life is in your power.
I yield. I go as your companion, son.'
Then he was still. We heard the blazing town
Crackle more loudly, felt the scorching heat.

'Then come, dear father. Arms around my neck:
590 I'll take you on my shoulders, no great weight.
Whatever happens, both will face one danger,
Find one safety. Iulus will come with me,
My wife at a good interval behind.
Servants, give your attention to what I say.
595 At the gate inland there's a funeral mound
And an old shrine of Ceres the Bereft;°
Near it an ancient cypress, kept alive
For many years by our fathers' piety.

589–599. *What does Aeneas say each family member is to do?*

596. Ceres the Bereft: mother of Proserpina (prō·sʉr′pi·nə), who was fated to spend part of the year in the Underworld.

The Judgment of Paris and Destruction of Troy (detail)
(16th century) by Matthias Gerung.
Musée du Louvre, Paris.

By various routes we'll come to that one place.
600 Father, carry our hearthgods, our Penates.
It would be wrong for me to handle them—
Just come from such hard fighting, bloody work—
Until I wash myself in running water.'

When I had said this, over my breadth of shoulder
605 And bent neck, I spread out a lion skin
For tawny cloak and stooped to take his weight.
Then little Iulus put his hand in mine
And came with shorter steps beside his father.
My wife fell in behind. Through shadowed places
610 On we went, and I, lately unmoved
By any spears thrown, and squads of Greeks,
Felt terror now at every eddy of wind,
Alarm at every sound, alert and worried
Alike for my companion and my burden.

604–614. What accounts for Aeneas's feeling of terror as he is leaving Troy?

615 I had got near the gate, and now I thought
We had made it all the way, when suddenly
A noise of running feet came near at hand,
And peering through the gloom ahead, my father
Cried out:
     'Run, boy; here they come; I see
Flame light on shields, bronze shining.'
620   I took fright,
And some unfriendly power, I know not what,
Stole all my addled wits—for as I turned
Aside from the known way, entering a maze
Of pathless places on the run—
                  Alas,
625 Creusa, taken from us by grim fate, did she
Linger, or stray, or sink in weariness?
There is no telling. Never would she be
Restored to us. Never did I look back
Or think to look for her, lost as she was,
630 Until we reached the funeral mound and shrine
Of venerable Ceres. Here at last
All came together, but she was not there;
She alone failed her friends, her child, her husband.
Out of my mind, whom did I not accuse,
635 What man or god? What crueler loss had I
Beheld, that night the city fell? Ascanius,
My father, and the Teucrian Penates,
I left in my friends' charge, and hid them well
In a hollow valley.
               I turned back alone
640 Into the city, cinching my bright harness.

624–649. As he is departing, Aeneas realizes that his wife, Creusa, has been lost. What does Aeneas do when he finds his wife has not been following him?

Nothing for it but to run the risks
Again, go back again, comb all of Troy,
And put my life in danger as before:
First by the town wall, then the gate, all gloom,
645 Through which I had come out—and so on backward,
Tracing my own footsteps through the night;
And everywhere my heart misgave me: even
Stillness had its terror. Then to our house,
Thinking she might, just might, have wandered there.
650 Danaans had got in and filled the place,
And at that instant fire they had set,
Consuming it, went roofward in a blast;
Flames leaped and seethed in heat to the night sky.
I pressed on, to see Priam's hall and tower.
655 In the bare colonnades of Juno's shrine
Two chosen guards, Phoenix° and hard Ulysses,
Kept watch over the plunder. Piled up here
Were treasures of old Troy from every quarter,
Torn out of burning temples: altar tables,
660 Robes, and golden bowls. Drawn up around them,
Boys and frightened mothers stood in line.
I even dared to call out in the night;
I filled the streets with calling; in my grief
Time after time I groaned and called Creusa,
665 Frantic, in endless quest from door to door.
Then to my vision her sad wraith° appeared—
Creusa's ghost, larger than life, before me.
Chilled to the marrow, I could feel the hair
On my head rise, the voice clot in my throat;
670 But she spoke out to ease me of my fear:

'What's to be gained by giving way to grief
So madly, my sweet husband? Nothing here
Has come to pass except as heaven willed.
You may not take Creusa with you now;
675 It was not so ordained, nor does the lord
Of high Olympus give you leave. For you
Long exile waits, and long sea miles to plow.
You shall make landfall on Hesperia°
Where Lydian Tiber° flows, with gentle pace,
680 Between rich farmlands, and the years will bear
Glad peace, a kingdom, and a queen for you.
Dismiss these tears for your beloved Creusa.
I shall not see the proud homelands of Myrmidons
Or of Dolopians, or go to serve
685 Greek ladies, Dardan lady that I am
And daughter-in-law of Venus the divine.

641–667. *What does Aeneas's frantic search for his wife reveal about his character? What does he discover about his wife's fate?*

656. Phoenix (fē′niks).

666. wraith (rāth) *n.:* ghost.

676–681. *What does Creusa say the future holds for Aeneas?*

678. Hesperia (hes·pir′ē·ə):
name given to Italy by Aeneas.
679. Lydian (lid′ē·ən) **Tiber:**
The Etruscans were supposed
to have come from Lydia, a
region in Asia Minor.

No: the great mother of the gods detains me
Here on these shores. Farewell now; cherish still
Your son and mine.'

                     With this she left me weeping,

690   Wishing that I could say so many things,
And faded on the <u>tenuous</u> air. Three times
I tried to put my arms around her neck,
Three times enfolded nothing, as the wraith
Slipped through my fingers, bodiless as wind,
Or like a flitting dream.

695   So in the end
As night waned I rejoined my company.
And there to my astonishment I found
New refugees in a great crowd: men and women
Gathered for exile, young—pitiful people

700   Coming from every quarter, minds made up,
With their belongings, for whatever lands
I'd lead them to by sea.

                     The morning star
Now rose on Ida's ridges, bringing day.
Greeks had secured the city gates. No help

705   Or hope of help existed.
So I resigned myself, picked up my father,
And turned my face toward the mountain range."

695–702. After seeing his wife in a vision, Aeneas returns to his father and the others who are leaving Troy.

? *What has changed about Aeneas's company since he has been away?*

Vocabulary

tenuous (ten′yo͞o·əs) *adj.:* insubstantial; flimsy.

Aeneas Fleeing Troy (c. 16th century) by Girolamo Genga.

Pinacoteca Nazionale, Siena.

Some of the most destructive wars in the ancient world were the Punic Wars, fought from 264–146 B.C., between Rome and the powerful African city called Carthage. Western civilization today would be very different if Carthage, instead of Rome, had been the victor in those wars. Legend has it that the wars were the result of a curse placed on Rome by Queen Dido of Carthage, who had been abandoned by Aeneas, the founder of Rome.

The most fearful Carthaginian general was a man named Hannibal Barca. In 218 B.C., Hannibal embarked on one of the most daring maneuvers in military history. He marched his army and a fleet of elephants over the Alps and

INFORMATIONAL TEXT

for years led a series of attacks on Rome from its northern borders. So fearful was Hannibal that even after his death Romans would use the cry "Hannibal ad portas!" ("Hannibal is at the gates!") to frighten children who misbehaved.

Eventually the Romans conquered Carthage. Their subsequent destruction of the city led to a term still used in the military: a "Carthaginian solution."

Here is a historian's account of the end of Carthage.

from Hannibal Crosses the Alps

John Prevas

The city burned for seventeen days, and even after it no longer contained life the Romans weren't finished. Once the fires had cooled, soldiers worked amidst the rubble and the thousands of incinerated human remains to obliterate any physical trace of what had once been known as "the jewel of the Mediter-ranean." First the city was set afire and then it was taken apart, stone by stone. Its inhabitants were killed or enslaved, though some managed to escape into the vastness of North Africa, their subsequent fates among the indigenous tribes unknown. The Romans even leveled the hill in the center of the city upon which the citadel had stood, to make nature's one-time gift to their enemy a less formidable height. Salt was sown in the ground and all traces of the city's civilization, including records, destroyed. Then the Romans' task was finally finished.

The phrase "Carthaginian solution" has endured into the 20th century, meaning not only the total annihilation of one's enemy but the sources of his strength as well. Dwight D. Eisenhower pondered the phrase in 1945 as Allied armies advanced on Nazi Germany; however, in that case the post-war arrange-ment became far less drastic. In 146 B.C. the "solution" was implemented. The Roman Republic not only defeated its greatest enemy but wiped all traces of its civilization off the face of the earth. It was as though the Romans needed to erase a trauma from their own collective consciousness: a time when Carthage lay not at their feet but at their throats.

A Carthaginian had once descended from the Alps into Italy, and for fifteen years his army remained, undefeated. He massacred thousands of soldiers of the Republic, seem-ingly at will in some of history's great battles, and laid waste to the peninsula. At one point the citizens of Rome cowered behind their gates, humiliated, while the invader stood outside the city's walls, challenging them to give battle. There were three separate wars between Carthage and Rome that spanned more than a century; however, as the Greek-born historian Polybius wrote, "All that happened to the Romans and the Carthaginians was brought about by one man: Hannibal.". . .

Few images in history have managed to capture and hold the imagination over the centuries quite like that of this bold North African. Perched upon a monstrous elephant, Hannibal Barca led his army of mercenaries over the highest and most dangerous passes of the Alps to challenge the Roman Republic for mastery of the ancient world. . . .

Why Hannibal ever undertook to cross the Alps can only be explained within the context of the power struggle which was then unfolding around the Mediterranean. During this period Rome had not yet become the glorious city of the Caesars and the ruler of a vast empire. It was a struggling young republic seeking to establish a prominent place for itself in the hierarchy of the ancient world.

Carthage, on the other hand, was already a powerful force in the Mediterranean and had been so for several centuries before Rome. The Carthaginians . . . had built for themselves a city of unrivaled splendor on the shores of North Africa near the site of modern day Tunis. The city was a marvel of architecture and engineering and it afforded its people a state of luxury unimaginable to most others in the ancient world. By the third century B.C.

Hannibal Crosses the Alps (1866). Woodcut after a drawing by Heinrich Leutemann.

Carthage had reached the height of its power as the largest and wealthiest city in the western Mediterranean. Yet there was a dark side to this commercial empire, which manifested itself in incomprehensible acts of cruelty. They crucified lions for their amusement and their generals for failure; and modern archaeologists have verified the assertions made by ancient historians: the Carthaginians threw infant children into a massive furnace.

? What does the writer suggest as a reason for the Romans' utter destruction of Carthage? During the time of Hannibal, how did Carthage compare with Rome?

Response and Analysis

Reading Check

1. Why do the Trojans assume that the Greeks have sailed for home?
2. What is Priam's fate? How is Helen saved from Aeneas's fury?
3. What signs convince Aeneas and Anchises to leave Troy?
4. What is Creusa's parting message to Aeneas?

Thinking Critically

5. What are Aeneas's main **motivations** in the story?
6. What strengths make Aeneas a leader? What weaknesses does Virgil reveal about him?
7. The narrative in Book 2 clearly portrays Aeneas's **external conflicts** with the Greeks. He experiences **internal conflict** when he witnesses Priam's death. Find at least two other examples in the narrative of **internal conflict**. What is the outcome of each?
8. Virgil's epic boasts several strong female characters. How do Cassandra, Hecuba, Venus, and Creusa each play an important role?
9. Like Homer, Virgil uses **epic similes,** or extended comparisons in which epic events are likened to everyday events in order to make them more accessible and interesting to the reader. Identify two examples of epic similes used by Virgil, and explain what makes these extended comparisons vivid and exciting.

Extending and Evaluating

10. If you were a Trojan refugee, would you accept Aeneas as a leader and follow him? Why or why not? You may wish to consult your Quickwrite notes.

Literary Criticism

11. In Latin the epithet *pius* (variously translated as "responsible," "dutiful," "conscientious") is repeatedly attached to the name of Aeneas throughout the epic. Some critics have noted that although Aeneas's faithfulness and sense of duty give him the self-mastery and commitment to overcome his external enemies, these same qualities also put him in conflict with himself. How does Aeneas's sense of duty to country, family, and destiny make him a complicated—and conflicted—hero? Use specific examples from the epic in your response.

WRITING

Comparing Heroes

In a brief essay, compare and contrast Aeneas with a hero you know from literature, film, or real life. Consider the following points of comparison:

- the values that motivate them
- the heroes' intellectual and physical powers
- their acceptance of aid from others
- their attitudes toward violence
- their display of leadership

Vocabulary Development
Etymologies

undulating	omnipotent
predatory	tenuous
futile	

Use a dictionary to research the origin, or etymology, of each Vocabulary word listed above. Use a chart like the one below, which shows the etymology of *undulating,* to organize your findings.

Word	Language of Origin	Original Word
undulating	Latin (L)	*unda,* meaning "a wave"

Catullus

(c. 84–c. 54 B.C.)

After 60 B.C., the maneuverings for power by Julius Caesar and his principal rival, Pompey, threatened to bring an end to the Roman Republic and to drag Rome into civil war. Most writers at this time were chiefly concerned with politics and public debate. One voice, the personal, lyric voice of Gaius Valerius Catullus (kə·tul'əs), stood out among them. Catullus turned away from the models of the Roman epics, which focused on war and politics. Instead, he found inspiration in the lyric poetry of the ancient Greeks, particularly the love lyrics of Sappho. Despite the personal nature of his poetry, Catullus won many admirers, including Julius Caesar himself. Ironically, Catullus's only attempt at public satire was a number of poems that showed his opposition to the ambitions of Julius Caesar.

As a young man, Catullus left the home of his prosperous family in Verona and headed for Rome. He soon joined the fashionable social and literary circles of the capital. His love affair with a wealthy Roman woman named Clodia (klō'dē·ə) is the subject of a long series of poems that explore the range of his feelings for her. Around 57 B.C., when he was disillusioned with love, Catullus left Rome to travel and to visit the tomb of his brother who had recently died. During his travels, he wrote much about his feelings of love and loss.

Catullus occupies an important place in the history of Latin poetry, not only for the excellence of his lyrics, but also for his experimentation with form. He popularized the use of the elegiac couplet—a pair of lines consisting of a hexameter (six metrical feet) and a pentameter (five metrical feet). This meter later became standard for an entire genre of Latin poetry called the love elegy.

Centuries later, Catullus became one of the most popular of the Roman poets rediscovered in the Renaissance. Leading European writers such as the Italian poet Petrarch (see page 680) and the English poet and playwright Ben Jonson imitated the lyrics of Catullus. Since the era of the Renaissance, Catullus's short "book" of 116 poems has been universally admired for its passion, sophistication, and charm.

Black bird perched on a vase (27 B.C.E.–396 C.E.). Roman wall painting.

Casa degli Uccelli, Pompeii, Italy.

Before You Read

Lyric Poems of Catullus

Make the Connection

Quickwrite

Have you ever felt strong but conflicting emotions for another person? For instance, have you ever had a friend or a relative whom you loved one day and were angry with the next? Jot down a list of all the feelings you had for this person. Were these feelings confusing or contradictory? How did you express and resolve these feelings?

Literary Focus

Hyperbole

Hyperbole is a figure of speech that uses exaggeration or overstatement for emphasis, often for comic effect. For example, when a friend tells you that she heard a joke so funny that she nearly died of laughter, she is using hyperbole. You believe the joke was very funny, but you know your friend did not—and could not—die from it. As you read these lyrics by Catullus, note where the speaker uses hyperbole to express strong emotion.

Background

Many of Catullus's poems are addressed to a Roman woman named Clodia with whom he had a passionate affair. She was ten years older than the poet and was married to a prominent Roman politician. Clodia's brother, Publius Clodius, was a notorious troublemaker in Roman politics and the bitter enemy of the famous orator Cicero. Clodia herself seems to have been both beautiful and faithless.

In his poems, Catullus calls Clodia by the name Lesbia, a reference to the great Greek lyric poet Sappho (see page 174), who lived on the island of Lesbos and whose love poetry Catullus admired. Catullus's poems to and about Lesbia cover a broad range of emotions—from hope at the beginning of their relationship to anger and disappointment at the end. At its best, Catullus's poetry is direct, strikingly vivid, and intensely personal.

North Carolina Competency Goal
1.02; 1.03;
4.05; 5.01;
5.03; 6.01

Hyperbole is a figure of speech that uses exaggeration or overstatement for emphasis.

For more on Hyperbole, see the Handbook of Literary and Historical Terms.

INTERNET
More About Catullus
Keyword:
LE5 WL-2

SKILLS FOCUS

Literary Skills
Understand hyperbole.

Young woman writing (detail) (late 1st century C.E.).
Wall painting from Pompeii.
Museo Archaeologico Nazionale, Naples.

Lyric Poems

Catullus

translated by **Reney Myers, Robert J. Ormsby,** *and* **Peter Whigham**

Wretched Catullus, Leave off Playing the Fool

Wretched Catullus, leave off playing the fool:
Give up as lost what is forever past.
But once, bright, golden suns beamed down and cast
A happiness on you when she would rule
5   Your steps and lead you into joyous play.
How much you loved her! More than any man
Can ever love. With her, what joy began!
That sunny world seemed yours in every way.
Yet now she does not want you, and alas,
10   You must not chase her nor live wretchedly,
Thus make your heart as hard as it can be.
So goodbye, baby! Catullus now will pass
You up, won't need you, nor will entertain
A thought of you nor seek your company.
15   Oh wicked thing, I'm tough as I can be!
Now who'll invite you? Where will you obtain
Praise of your beauty? Who'll make sorrows blisses?
Who'll love you now? Or bite your lips in kisses?
Not Catullus! He's determined to abstain.

—*translated by* Reney Myers *and* Robert J. Ormsby

Lesbia Says She'd Rather Marry Me

Lesbia says she'd rather marry me
than anyone,
         though Jupiter himself came asking
or so she says,
         but what a woman tells her lover in desire
should be written out on air & running water.

—*translated by* Peter Whigham

Flora, or Spring, gathering flowers (detail) (c. 1st century C.E.). Wall painting from the villa of Varano in Stabiae.

Museo Archaeologico Nazionale, Naples.

If Ever Anyone Anywhere

If ever anyone anywhere, Lesbia, is looking
    for what he knows will not happen
and then unexpectedly it happens
    the soul is astonished,
5 as we are now in each other,
    an event dearer than gold,
for you have restored yourself, Lesbia, desired
restored yourself, longed for, unlooked for,
    brought yourself back
10 to me. White day in the calendar!
    Who happier than I?
What more can life offer
than the longed for unlooked for event
   when it happens?

          —*translated by* Peter Whigham

I Hate and I Love

I hate and I love. And if you ask me how,
I do not know: I only feel it, and I'm torn in two.

          —*translated by* Peter Whigham

Response and Analysis

Thinking Critically

1. Describe the contrast between the first part (lines 1–11) and the second part (lines 12–19) of "Wretched Catullus, Leave off Playing the Fool." Is the speaker's "toughness" in the second part convincing? Give reasons for your answer.

2. What does the last line of "Lesbia Says She'ld Rather Marry Me" imply about Lesbia's sincerity? Describe the **tone,** or attitude, of the speaker of this poem. Is it bitter, accepting, or indifferent? Explain.

3. In the final lines of "If Ever Anyone Anywhere," Catullus uses the technique of the rhetorical question. A **rhetorical question** is one to which the speaker expects no answer, either because the answer is obvious or because the question is posed simply for emphasis or to make a point. How effective is this technique in the poem's context, in your opinion?

4. "I Hate and I Love" is a brief statement of ambivalence—the experience of feeling two strong, contradictory emotions at once. How is the speaker's tone in this poem different from that in "Lesbia Says She'ld Rather Marry Me"?

5. What examples of **hyperbole,** or deliberate overstatement, can you find in Catullus's poetry? What effect does the use of hyperbole have in each case?

Literary Criticism

6. One critic has suggested that the Romans may have considered Catullus's poetry frivolous or even trivial. How do you feel about Catullus's poetry? Do you think the expression of personal feelings is a valid and important use of literature? You may want to refer to your Quickwrite response.

WRITING

Comparing Lyric Poems

In a brief essay, compare and contrast one of Catullus's love lyrics with a lyric written by Sappho (see page 176). In your essay, be sure to include a discussion of how the speaker in each poem conveys emotion through imagery, figures of speech, and the careful control of tone.

North Carolina Competency Goal
1.02; 1.03; 4.05; 5.01; 5.03; 6.01

go.hrw.com

INTERNET

Projects and Activities
Keyword: LE5 WL-2

SKILLS FOCUS

Literary Skills
Analyze hyperbole.

Writing Skills
Compare lyric poems.

"I just love your poetry!"

Horace

(65–8 B.C.)

Quintus Horatius Flaccus, better known as Horace, lived during the Augustan Age, one of the most creative periods of Roman civilization. Horace, who was to become one of the greatest of Roman poets, had humble beginnings: His father was a freed slave. Nevertheless, his father was determined to give his son a first-rate education. Thus, as a boy, Horace was sent to study rhetoric and philosophy both in Rome and in Athens, Greece—a great privilege usually reserved only for the sons of the wealthiest upper classes.

As a young man, Horace made the mistake of fighting with Brutus on the losing side of the civil war that followed Julius Caesar's assassination in 44 B.C. Though his small land-holdings were confiscated after the war, Horace proved to be a survivor. He started to write poetry in order to make a place for himself in Roman society. His poetic gifts, combined with a sense of humor that prevented him from taking himself too seriously, made Horace a favorite of the rich literary patrons who surrounded the new emperor, Augustus. Horace remained at the center of sophisticated Roman literary society for the rest of his comfortable life.

Horace tended to moralize, and some critics feel that his poetry is not very profound. His poems are known more for their style than for

Fresco of Horace in the Duomo, Orvieto (1500–1503) by Luca Signorelli.

their substance. He wrote on a wide variety of subjects, both light and serious. He is best known for his humorous *Satires* and his poetic *Odes*. His work about the poet's craft, *The Art of Poetry*, had a profound effect on poets and critics during the Age of Rationalism in the seventeenth and eighteenth centuries in Europe.

Carpe Diem

Make the Connection

Before you read this poem, think about this common saying: "Seize the day." Do you believe in "seizing the day"—that is, living every day to its fullest, as though it were your last—or do you think it's wiser to postpone enjoyment in order to assure greater rewards in the future? Discuss your opinions with a partner or small group.

Literary Focus

Tone

Tone is the attitude a writer takes toward the reader, a subject, or a character. Tone is conveyed through the writer's choice of words and details. A tone can be described as satirical, tender, comic, awed, ironic, passionate, wistful, sad, or by any number of other adjectives. As you read this poem, pay attention to the tone. What does Horace think about "seizing the day"?

> **Tone** is the attitude a writer takes toward the reader, a subject, or a character.
>
> *For more on Tone, see the Handbook of Literary and Historical Terms.*

Background

Horace's greatest literary achievement is his collection called *Odes*. An **ode** is a complex lyric poem devoted to a serious subject. Before Horace, the typical ode was written for ceremonial or public occasions. Horace perfected a more personal and reflective type of ode.

"Carpe Diem" is an ode expressing a message that can be put in the form of a **maxim,** or a wise and concise saying. The Latin phrase *carpe diem* translates as "seize the day" and means "Enjoy life fully while you can." This philosophy of life appears throughout world literature in all times and cultures.

North Carolina Competency Goal
1.03; 4.05; 5.01; 5.03

INTERNET

More About Horace
Keyword:
LE5 WL-2

Twig with peaches (1st century C.E.).
Fresco from the Herculaneum, Naples.

Museo Archeologico Nazionale, Naples.

Literary Skills
Understand tone.

Carpe Diem

Horace
translated by **Thomas Hawkins**

Strive not, Leuconoe,° to know what end
The gods above to me or thee will send:
Nor with astrologers consult at all,
That thou mayst better know what can befall;

5   Whether thou liv'st more winters, or thy last
Be this, which Tyrrhen waves° 'gainst rocks do cast.
Be wise! Drink free, and in so short a space
Do not protracted hopes of life embrace:
Whilst we are talking, envious time doth slide;

10 This day's thine own; the next may be denied.

1. Leuconoe (lyōō·kō′nō·ē): intimate friend of the poet.

6. Tyrrhen (tir′ēn) **waves:** reference to the Tyrrhenian Sea, a part of the Mediterranean, southwest of Italy.

North Carolina Competency Goal
4.01; 5.01

Response and Analysis

Thinking Critically

1. In lines 1–6, what does the speaker advise Leuconoe *not* to do?

2. Describe the **tone** of the last four lines of "Carpe Diem." Would you say that it is enthusiastic and high-spirited, urging Leuconoe to go out and have a good time? Or is it thoughtful or even melancholy, encouraging Leuconoe to make the best use of time and not take life for granted? Explain.

3. *Carpe diem* is a recurring theme throughout world literature. Is Horace's idea of *carpe diem* best expressed by the saying "Eat, drink, and be merry," or is Horace expressing a deeper view of the theme?

Extending and Evaluating

4. What was the strongest impression you had after reading this poem? Did you agree or disagree with its message?

5. Do you think that Horace's advice in this poem is valuable today, or are there some situations in which you would reject the speaker's philosophy? Explain.

WRITING
Writing an Advice Column

Imagine that you are a writer of a newspaper advice column. Adopt the philosophy that Horace promotes in "Carpe Diem" in one of your responses to a reader needing personal advice. For example, your advice to a shy and timid person who is afraid of taking risks might be to "seize the day." In your response, summarize the reader's problem, give your advice, and explain why you think the philosophy expressed in "Carpe Diem" offers the best approach to dealing with the reader's problem.

INTERNET

Projects and Activities
Keyword:
LE5 WL-2

Literary Skills
Analyze tone.

Writing Skills
Write an advice column.

Introducing **Cultural Points** *of* **View**

Beginnings and Endings

You will be reading the three selections listed above in this Cultural Points of View feature on beginnings and endings—cultural stories about cycles of creation and destruction. In the top corner of the pages in this feature, you'll find a globe. Smaller versions of the globe appear next to the questions on page 313 that focus on beginnings and endings. At the end of the feature (page 320), you'll compare the three selections.

Examining the Theme: Beginnings and Endings

It is likely that the very first stories human beings told were **origin myths**—stories that explain how aspects of existence, such as animals, geographical features, and even the world itself, came to be. Many questions people had about their lives were answered by their origin myths: How was the world created? Why do people die? Is there life after death? Why are suffering and evil allowed to exist in the world?

The striking parallels between myths from widely different cultures tell us that certain themes, characters, events, and images are central to the human experience. They are **archetypes,** or basic models to which specific cultural details are added. Archetypes are so basic to human understanding that they reappear throughout time periods and cultures.

Make the Connection

Traditional stories, such as myths, epics, legends, and folk tales, help to define a culture and give it a sense of place in the universe. Think of some stories you know from your own culture of origin. If you don't know any traditional stories, think about stories or anecdotes your family tells about itself and its members. How do these stories serve to unite members of a culture or of a family?

Reading Skills

Comparing Universal Themes Across Texts

As you read the following selections, **compare** and **contrast** the accounts of creation and destruction. Be aware of recurring patterns, or archetypes, and jot them down. In many myths about beginnings and endings, there is an inherent moral—some lesson about how people should best live in the world and how they should conduct themselves. Look for these implied lessons in the following selections.

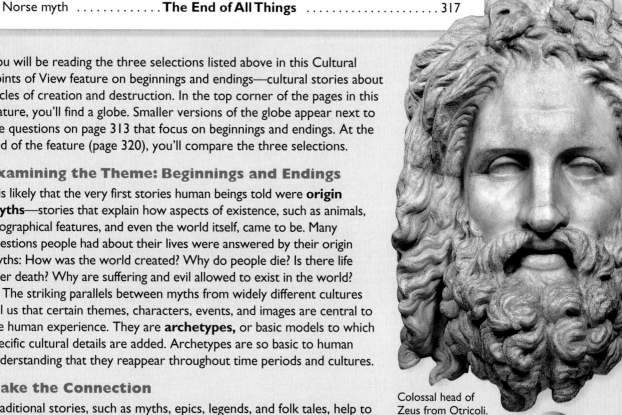

Colossal head of Zeus from Otricoli.

Museo Pio Clementino, Musei Vaticani, Vatican City.

SKILLS FOCUS

Pages 305–320 cover

Literary Skills
Analyze cultural points of view on a topic.

Reading Skills
Compare universal themes and archetypes across texts.

North Carolina Competency Goal
5.01

Ovid
(43 B.C.–A.D. 17)

Portrait of Ovid. Fresco in the Duomo by Luca Signorelli. Orvieto Cathedral.

Like his older contemporary, the poet Horace, Publius Ovidius Naso—better known as Ovid (äv′id)—thrived in Rome's high society. But unlike Horace, who moved in a circle that enjoyed the approval of the emperor Augustus, Ovid was attracted to Rome's more freewheeling "fast" set, a clique that included the emperor's unruly granddaughter, Julia. Ovid's poetry—much of which celebrated women—was considered witty and elegant, but not very serious. However, it caused the emperor Augustus a great deal of outrage, because Augustus—whose own rise to power was accomplished with much underhandedness and bloodshed—decided late in life that Rome was becoming dangerously immoral. He worried that Ovid's poetry encouraged infidelity in married women. Worse, he feared that his own granddaughter, Julia, had fallen under Ovid's immoral influence.

In an effort to fend off Rome's decline—and a family scandal—the emperor accused Ovid of irreverence toward the state and sent him into exile. Ovid, whose only true crime may have been the possession of knowledge about Julia's promiscuous behavior, was forced to leave Rome for a remote town on the Black Sea. Thus, the exiled Latin poet and lover of the Latin language ironically lived out his life among foreigners.

Among Ovid's most famous surviving works are his daring *Ars Amatoria* (The art of love), a poem that graphically outlines the techniques of amorous conquest, and its tongue-in-cheek sequel, *Remedia Amoris* (The cures of love). These works reinforced the impression of Ovid as a spokesman for decadence and pleasure-seeking. In spite of this reputation, however, Ovid's works present a balanced view of both the creative and the destructive forces of human passion. These two sides of Ovid's literary concern also underlie his greatest poetic masterpiece, *Metamorphoses* (met′ə·môr′fə·sēz′). Ovid's popularity experienced a revival hundreds of years later, during the Middle Ages, when he enjoyed the reputation of a wise professor of love. His teachings contributed greatly to the development of the medieval concept of courtly love.

Before You Read

from Metamorphoses

Cultural Points *of* View

The concept of **metamorphosis,** or transformation, is a universal theme in literature, and it serves to unify Ovid's great mythological poem. How does the process of metamorphosis occur in every life—even your own?

Literary Focus
Archetype

An **archetype** is a recurring pattern or model that serves as the basis for different, but related, versions of a character, plot, image, or theme. Archetypes such as the monster-slaying hero or the journey to the underworld are common across cultures. Archetypal stories seem to engage and satisfy the most basic human needs and longings.

One of the most universal archetypes is the story of how the world came to be. Every culture has its own version; in Ovid's poem you'll read the ancient Romans' account.

An **archetype** is the basic pattern or model of a character, a plot, a setting, or an object that recurs in storytelling.

For more on Archetype, see the Handbook of Literary and Historical Terms.

Background

Metamorphoses had a tremendous influence on later European literature, providing countless source stories for writers such as Chaucer, Boccaccio, and Shakespeare. In fact, Ovid's brief verse narratives about the transformations—seldom longer than two or three pages each—resemble short stories. Every narrative moves swiftly to establish the characters, the setting, and a central conflict, which then, more often than not, leads directly to the metamorphosis that is the heart of the story.

In *Metamorphoses,* Ovid uses the same verse form, the dactylic hexameter, that Homer and Virgil employ in their epics. Traditionally the Greeks and Romans associated this meter, consisting of six stressed syllables per line, with epics. Ovid's use of this meter suggests that he intended his huge collection of tales to be read as a grand epic. Unlike the epics of Homer and Virgil, however, *Metamorphoses* does not feature a central hero. Instead, it presents the whole range of Greco-Roman mythology— roughly two hundred poems in all—woven together in a continuous narrative sequence from the creation of the world to the assassination of Julius Caesar in 44 B.C.

North Carolina Competency Goal
1.03; 4.05; 5.01; 5.03

INTERNET
More About Ovid
Keyword:
LE5 WL-2

Literary Skills
Understand archetypes.

from Metamorphoses

Ovid

translated by **Rolfe Humphries**

My intention is to tell of bodies changed
To different forms; the gods, who made the changes,
Will help me—or I hope so—with a poem
That runs from the world's beginning to our own days.

The Creation

5 Before the ocean was, or earth, or heaven,
Nature was all alike, a shapelessness,
Chaos, so-called, all rude and lumpy matter,
Nothing but bulk, inert, in whose confusion
Discordant atoms warred: there was no sun
10 To light the universe; there was no moon
With slender silver crescents filling slowly;
No earth hung balanced in surrounding air;
No sea reached far along the fringe of shore.
Land, to be sure, there was, and air, and ocean,
15 But land on which no man could stand, and water
No man could swim in, air no man could breathe,
Air without light, substance forever changing,
Forever at war: within a single body
Heat fought with cold, wet fought with dry, the hard
20 Fought with the soft, things having weight contended
With weightless things.
       Till God, or kindlier Nature,
Settled all argument, and separated
Heaven from earth, water from land, our air
From the high stratosphere, a liberation
25 So things evolved, and out of blind confusion
Found each its place, bound in eternal order.
The force of fire, that weightless element,
Leaped up and claimed the highest place in heaven;
Below it, air; and under them the earth
30 Sank with its grosser portions; and the water,
Lowest of all, held up, held in, the land.

Whatever god it was, who out of chaos
Brought order to the universe, and gave it
Division, subdivision, he molded earth,
35 In the beginning, into a great globe,

Celestial and terrestrial map
of the Southern Hemisphere
(c. 18th century).

Even on every side, and bade the waters
To spread and rise, under the rushing winds,
Surrounding earth; he added ponds and marshes,
He banked the river-channels, and the waters
40 Feed earth or run to sea, and that great flood
Washes on shores, not banks. He made the plains
Spread wide, the valleys settle, and the forest
Be dressed in leaves; he made the rocky mountains
Rise to full height, and as the vault of Heaven
45 Has two zones, left and right, and one between them
Hotter than these, the Lord of all Creation

Marked on the earth the same design and pattern.
The torrid zone too hot for men to live in,
The north and south too cold, but in the middle
50 Varying climate, temperature and season.
Above all things the air, lighter than earth,
Lighter than water, heavier than fire,
Towers and spreads; there mist and cloud assemble,
And fearful thunder and lightning and cold winds,
55 But these, by the Creator's order, held
No general dominion; even as it is,
These brothers brawl and quarrel; though each one
Has his own quarter, still, they come near tearing
The universe apart. Eurus is monarch
60 Of the lands of dawn, the realms of Araby,
The Persian ridges under the rays of morning.
Zephyrus holds the west that glows at sunset,
Boreas, who makes men shiver, holds the north,
Warm Auster governs in the misty southland,
65 And over them all presides the weightless ether,
Pure without taint of earth.
                    These boundaries given,
Behold, the stars, long hidden under darkness,
Broke through and shone, all over the spangled heaven,
Their home forever, and the gods lived there,
70 And shining fish were given the waves for dwelling
And beasts the earth, and birds the moving air.

But something else was needed, a finer being,
More capable of mind, a sage, a ruler,
So Man was born, it may be, in God's image,

Mosaic band featuring aquatic
and other animals from Pompeii
(detail) (1st century C.E.).
Museo Archeologico Nazionale, Naples.

75　Or Earth, perhaps, so newly separated
　　From the old fire of Heaven, still retained
　　Some seed of the celestial force which fashioned
　　Gods out of living clay and running water.
　　All other animals look downward; Man,
80　Alone, erect, can raise his face toward Heaven.

The Four Ages

　　The Golden Age was first, a time that cherished
　　Of its own will, justice and right; no law,
　　No punishment, was called for; fearfulness
　　Was quite unknown, and the bronze tablets held
85　No legal threatening; no suppliant throng
　　Studied a judge's face; there were no judges,
　　There did not need to be. Trees had not yet
　　Been cut and hollowed, to visit other shores.
　　Men were content at home, and had no towns
90　With moats and walls around them; and no trumpets
　　Blared out alarums; things like swords and helmets
　　Had not been heard of. No one needed soldiers.
　　People were unaggressive, and unanxious;
　　The years went by in peace. And Earth, untroubled,
95　Unharried by hoe or plowshare, brought forth all
　　That men had need for, and those men were happy,
　　Gathering berries from the mountainsides,
　　Cherries, or blackcaps, and the edible acorns.
　　Spring was forever, with a west wind blowing
100　Softly across the flowers no man had planted,
　　And Earth, unplowed, brought forth rich grain; the field,
　　Unfallowed, whitened with wheat, and there were rivers

Mosaic band featuring aquatic
and other animals from Pompeii
(detail) (1st century C.E.).
Museo Archeologico Nazionale, Naples.

Of milk, and rivers of honey, and golden nectar
Dripped from the dark-green oak-trees.

After Saturn°

105　Was driven to the shadowy land of death,
　　And the world was under Jove, the Age of Silver
　　Came in, lower than gold, better than bronze.
　　Jove made the springtime shorter, added winter,
　　Summer, and autumn, the seasons as we know them.
110　That was the first time when the burnt air glowed
　　White-hot, or icicles hung down in winter.
　　And men built houses for themselves; the caverns,
　　The woodland thickets, and the bark-bound shelters
　　No longer served; and the seeds of grain were planted
115　In the long furrows, and the oxen struggled
　　Groaning and laboring under the heavy yoke.
　　Then came the Age of Bronze, and dispositions
　　Took on aggressive instincts, quick to arm,
　　Yet not entirely evil. And last of all
120　The Iron Age succeeded, whose base vein
　　Let loose all evil: modesty and truth
　　And righteousness fled earth, and in their place
　　Came trickery and slyness, plotting, swindling,
　　Violence and the damned desire of having.
125　Men spread their sails to winds unknown to sailors,
　　The pines came down their mountainsides, to revel
　　And leap in the deep waters, and the ground,
　　Free, once, to everyone, like air and sunshine,
　　Was stepped off by surveyors. The rich earth,
130　Good giver of all the bounty of the harvest,
　　Was asked for more; they dug into her vitals,
　　Pried out the wealth a kinder lord had hidden
　　In Stygian shadow,° all that precious metal,
　　The root of evil. They found the guilt of iron,
135　And gold, more guilty still. And War came forth
　　That uses both to fight with; bloody hands
　　Brandished the clashing weapons. Men lived on plunder.
　　Guest was not safe from host, nor brother from brother,
　　A man would kill his wife, a wife her husband,
140　Stepmothers, dire and dreadful, stirred their brews
　　With poisonous aconite, and sons would hustle
　　Fathers to death, and Piety lay vanquished,
　　And the maiden Justice, last of all immortals,
　　Fled from the bloody earth.

104. Saturn: Roman god of the seasonal cycle, loosely associated with Cronus the Titan, who was overthrown by his son Zeus (Jove, or Jupiter).

133. Stygian (stij′ē·ən) **shadow:** the netherworld, through which the river Styx is said to flow.

Bronze sculpture of Mars.
Museo Archeologico, Florence.

Response and Analysis

Reading Check

1. What was nature like before the creation? After the creation, what warring pairs of elements threatened to tear the universe apart?

2. According to "The Creation," how do human beings differ from animals?

3. Identify the Four Ages. What are the characteristics of each age?

Thinking Critically

4. Ovid's poetic treatment of the process of creation bears a number of striking similarities to the biblical account in Genesis (see page 53). What are some of these similarities?

5. During the Golden Age, only one of the four seasons exists. What is this season, and why is it appropriate?

6. What, if anything, causes each of the stages of decline in the Four Ages? Does a human action precede each stage of degeneration, or is the decline beyond human control? Explain.

7. What **archetypes,** or very old patterns of storytelling, can you identify in these tales by Ovid?

Extending and Evaluating

8. An **allegory** is a poem or story in which characters, settings, or events stand for something else, often abstract qualities or ideas. Allegories about the decline of civilization usually accept the premise that there was once a Golden Age—that human civilization long ago was indeed closer to a paradise than it is now. In an allegorical sense, was there ever a time of perfect harmony, or innocence, in human history—and has civilization been in decline ever since? Explain. Are we living in the "Iron Age" today?

WRITING

Writing a Myth

Create your own brief myth that explains the development of American culture from some point in the past to the present. Where your myth begins is up to you. You could, for example, choose to begin with the Pilgrims' landing at Plymouth Rock in 1620 or with the American Revolution of 1776. Or you could begin thousands of years before these events. Like Ovid, you may want to designate a certain number of "ages" or "stages" for your myth. For each age, list a few notable characteristics or events, or provide a description that helps to distinguish that era from the others.

Comparing Interpretations of Myths

The characters, settings, and events in an allegory may stand for other people or events, or for abstract qualities or ideas. In a brief essay, discuss how "The Creation" and "The Four Ages" might be interpreted as contrasting allegorical stories. How does "The Creation" suggest an optimistic point of view about the inevitability of progress? How does "The Four Ages" suggest a pessimistic viewpoint about the inevitability of decline? In your essay, be sure to support your points with specific references to the stories. A chart like the one below might help you to organize your ideas.

	Creation	Four Ages
Characterization of humans		
Characterization of gods		

North Carolina Competency Goal
5.01

INTERNET

Projects and Activities

Keyword:
LE5 WL-2

SKILLS FOCUS

Literary Skills
Analyze archetypes.

Writing Skills
Write a myth.
Compare interpretations of myths.

Connected Readings

You have just read two sections from Ovid's *Metamorphoses* that deal with the archetypal themes of beginnings and endings. As you read each of the following selections, ask yourself how their themes of beginnings and endings are similar to or different from those you encountered in Ovid's work. After you have read these selections, answer the questions on page 320, which ask you to compare the views on beginnings and endings.

Cultural Points *of* View

Before You Read

The Popol Vuh (pō′pəl vu′) or The Book of Counsel, is the Quiché (kē·chā′) Mayan book of creation. Called the Mayan Bible by poet Carlos Fuentes, the Popol Vuh is one of the most important sources of pre-Columbian myth in Central America.

The Quiché Mayans settled in the highlands of Guatemala around the ninth century A.D. Their great work, the Popol Vuh, tells the story of their origins and destiny. The Quiché Mayan people believed that the Popol Vuh was a gift from the gods and that it could help people see through the obvious and become aware of mysteries and secrets that were otherwise beyond the range of normal human insight.

The Quiché Mayan creation myth, "The Wooden People," comes from the first part of the Popol Vuh. This episode is the third creation story in a sequence of four. At this point in the mythic cycle, the gods have failed in two attempts to create suitable human beings. The first two attempts

resulted in the creation of the animal kingdom and a being made of mud that disintegrated almost as soon as it was formed. Now the gods have made beings out of a more substantial material: wood. These wooden creatures, called manikins ("little men") by the translator, become the world's first people.

War captain in a ceremonial procession, from the Mayan fresco series at Bonampak (detail).
Museo Nacional de Antropología, Mexico City.

MYTH

The Wooden People

from the Popol Vuh
A Quiché Mayan Myth
translated by Dennis Tedlock

This was the peopling of the face of the earth:

They came into being, they multiplied, they had daughters, they had sons, these manikins, woodcarvings. But there was nothing in their hearts and nothing in their minds, no memory of their mason and builder. They just went and walked wherever they wanted. Now they did not remember the Heart of Sky.[1]

And so they fell, just an experiment and just a cut-out for humankind. They were talking at first but their faces were dry. They were not yet developed in the legs and arms. They had no blood, no lymph. They had no sweat, no fat. Their complexions were dry, their faces were crusty. They flailed their legs and arms, their bodies were deformed.

And so they accomplished nothing before the Maker, Modeler[2] who gave them birth, gave them heart. They became the first numerous people here on the face of the earth.

Again there comes a humiliation, destruction, and demolition. The manikins, woodcarvings were killed when the Heart of Sky devised a flood for them. A great flood was made; it came down on the heads of the manikins, woodcarvings.

The man's body was carved from the wood of the coral tree by the Maker, Modeler. And as for the woman, the Maker, Modeler needed the pith of reeds for the woman's body. They were not competent, nor did they speak before the builder and sculptor who made them and brought them forth, and so they were killed, done in by a flood:

There came a rain of resin from the sky.

There came the one named Gouger of Faces: he gouged out their eyeballs.

There came Sudden Bloodletter: he snapped off their heads.

There came Crunching Jaguar: he ate their flesh.

There came Tearing Jaguar: he tore them open.

They were pounded down to the bones and tendons, smashed and pulverized even to the bones. Their faces were smashed because they were incompetent before their mother and their father, the Heart of Sky, named Hurricane. The earth was blackened because of this; the black rainstorm began, rain all day and rain all night. Into their houses came the animals, small and great. Their faces were crushed by things of wood and stone. Everything spoke: their water jars, their tortilla griddles, their plates, their cooking pots, their dogs, their grinding stones,

---

1. **Heart of Sky:** father god of the Quiché Mayans.
2. **Maker, Modeler:** Quiché Mayan god of creation.

The Wooden People **315**

each and every thing crushed their faces. Their dogs and turkeys told them:

"You caused us pain, you ate us, but now it is *you* whom *we* shall eat." And this is the grinding stone:

"We were undone because of you.

> Every day, every day,
> in the dark, in the dawn, forever.
> r-r-rip, r-r-rip,
> r-r-rub, r-r-rub,
> right in our faces, because of you.

This was the service we gave you at first, when you were still people, but today you will learn of our power. We shall pound and we shall grind your flesh," their grinding stones told them.

And this is what their dogs said, when they spoke in their turn:

"Why is it you can't seem to give us our food? We just watch and you just keep us down, and you throw us around. You keep a stick ready when you eat, just so you can hit us. We don't talk, so we've received nothing from you. How could you not have known? You *did* know that we were wasting away there, behind you.

"So, this very day you will taste the teeth in our mouths. We shall eat you," their dogs told them, and their faces were crushed.

And then their tortilla griddles and cooking pots spoke to them in turn:

"Pain! That's all you've done for us. Our mouths are sooty, our faces are sooty. By setting us on the fire all the time, you burn us. Since *we* felt no pain, *you* try it. We shall burn you," all their cooking pots said, crushing their faces.

The stones, their hearthstones were shooting out, coming right out of the fire, going for their heads, causing them pain. Now they run for it, helter-skelter.

They want to climb up on the houses, but they fall as the houses collapse.

They want to climb the trees; they're thrown off by the trees.

They want to get inside caves, but the caves slam shut in their faces.

Such was the scattering of the human work, the human design. The people were ground down, overthrown. The mouths and faces of all of them were destroyed and crushed. And it used to be said that the monkeys in the forests today are a sign of this. They were left as a sign because wood alone was used for their flesh by the builder and sculptor.

So this is why monkeys look like people: they are a sign of a previous human work, human design—mere manikins, mere woodcarvings.

Mayan bowl with spider monkeys and cacao pods.
Museo Nacional de Guatemala, Tikal Tomb 1, Vessel 239894.

Connected Readings

Cultural Points of View

Before You Read

In Western culture the myths of the Greeks and Romans have had a dominant effect on culture and the arts, but Norse myths are also a strong cultural influence. (Some of our days of the week are named for Norse deities.) Norse myths come from ancient Scandinavia and Germany. In Norse mythology the gods created humans and rule over them. But the Norse gods—unlike their Greek and Roman counterparts—are neither all-powerful nor immortal, and they are bound by their fate to be destroyed in Ragnarok (rag′nə·räk′), a vast, final battle against giants and various monsters.

There are three separate levels in the universe of Norse mythology. At the first level, there is Asgard (äs′gärd′), the world of the gods. At the middle level, there is Midgard (mid′gärd′), where humans, dwarfs, and giants dwell. At the bottom level, there is Niflheim (niv′əl·hām′), the world of the dead. All three levels are held together by the roots and branches of a mighty ash tree.

MYTH

The End of All Things

Barbara Leonie Picard

The Norsemen believed that, as Odin[1] had foreseen, the gods were doomed one day to perish, and this is how they told that it would come to pass.

First would there be three winters more terrible than any that had ever gone before, with snow and ice and biting winds and no power in the sun; and no summers to divide this cruel season and make it bearable, but only one long wintertime with never a respite. And at the end of that winter, Skoll,[2] the wolf who had ever pursued the sun, would leap upon it and devour it, and likewise would Hati[3] with the moon. And the stars which had been sparks from Muspellheim[4] would flicker and go out, so that there would be darkness in the world.

The mountains would shake and tremble, and the rocks would be torn from the earth; and the sea would wash over the fields and the forests as Iormungand,[5] the Midgard-Serpent, raised himself out of the water to advance on the land. And at that moment all chains would be sundered and all prisoners released; Fenris Wolf[6] would break free from Gleipnir,[7] and Loki[8] rise up from his prison under the ground. Out of fiery Muspellheim would come Surt the giant with his flaming sword; and out of her house would come Hel,[9] with Garm[10] the hound at her side, to join with her father, Loki. And all the frost and storm giants would gather together to follow them.

---

1. **Odin** (ō′din): king of the gods; god of war.
2. **Skoll** (skōl).
3. **Hati** (hä′tē).
4. **Muspellheim** (mus′pel·hām): realm of fire. Muspell was guarded by a giant named Surt.

---

5. **Iormungand** (yôr′mən·gand): offspring of Loki and a giantess.
6. **Fenris** (fen′ris) **Wolf:** son of Loki, the trickster.
7. **Gleipnir** (glāp′nēr): silken rope forged by the dwarfs.
8. **Loki** (lō′kē): god of fire; trickster and sky traveler.
9. **Hel** (hel): goddess of the Underworld.
10. **Garm** (gärm).

Raging Wotan (Odin) Rides to the Rock! (1911) by Arthur Rackham.
Illustration from *The Rhinegold and the Valkyrie.*

From Bifrost,[11] Heimdall,[12] with his sharp eyes, would see them come, and know that the moment which the gods had feared was at hand, and he would blow his horn to summon them to defend the universe. Then the Aesir[13] and the Vanir[14] would put on their armor, and the spirits of the dead warriors that were feasting in Valhall[15] take up their swords, and with Odin at their head in his golden helmet, ride forth to give battle to the enemies of good.

And in the mighty conflict which would follow, all the earth, all Asgard, even Niflheim itself, would shake with the clang and cry of war. Odin would fight against huge Fenris Wolf, and hard would be the struggle they would have. Thor,[16] with Miolnir,[17] would kill the Midgard-Serpent, as had ever been his wish to do; but he would not long survive his victory, for he would fall dead from the dying monster's poisonous breath.

Tyr[18] and Hel's hound, Garm, would rush at each other and close to fight, and with his good left hand, brave Tyr would hew down the mighty beast; but in its last struggles it would tear the god to pieces, and so would they perish both.

Surt with his flaming sword would bear down on Frey,[19] but Frey had given his own sword to Skirnir,[20] and as Loki had foretold, bitterly would he regret it, for he would have no more than the antler of a deer with which to defend himself. Yet would he not perish without a struggle.

As they had met and fought once before, over Freya's necklace,[21] so Loki and Heimdall would come together in battle once again, and Loki would laugh as he strove with his one-time friend. And in the same moment, each would strike the other a deadly blow, and both alike fall dead.

Though Odin would fight long and bravely with Fenris Wolf, in the end that mighty monster would be too strong for him, and the wolf with his gaping jaws would devour the father of the gods, and then perish at the hands of Vidar[22] the silent.

Then fire from Muspellheim would sweep over all, and thus would everything be destroyed; and it would indeed be the end of all things.

But the Norsemen believed that one day, out of the sea that had engulfed it, and out of the ruins, the world would grow again, fresh and green and beautiful; with fair people dwelling on it, born from Lifthrasir and Lif,[23] the only man and woman to escape the fire. And they believed that out of the ashes of old Asgard would arise another home for the gods, where would live in joy and peace the younger gods, who had not perished; the two sons of Odin, Vidar the silent god, and Vali[24] the son of Rind. And with them would be Magni,[25] the strong son of Thor, mightier even than his father; while out from the house of Hel, at last, would come Balder, and Hod, his brother. And everywhere would be happiness.

11. **Bifrost** (bēf′räst′): rainbow bridge connecting Asgard with Midgard.
12. **Heimdall** (hām′däl′): watchman of the rainbow bridge.
13. **Aesir** (a′sir′): warrior gods.
14. **Vanir** (vä′nir): nature gods who live in Asgard.
15. **Valhall (Valhalla)** (val·hal′): huge hall in Asgard where slain warriors are brought and feasted.
16. **Thor** (thôr): lord of thunder.
17. **Miolnir** (myul′nər): Thor's hammer.
18. **Tyr** (tir): bravest of the Aesir gods.
19. **Frey** (frā): god of plenty.
20. **Skirnir** (skir′nir): Frey's messenger.

21. **Freya's** (frā′əz) **necklace:** In one of the myths, the necklace of Freya (goddess of love and beauty) is stolen by Loki.
22. **Vidar** (vē′där): a son of Odin.
23. **Lifthrasir** (lift′rä·sēr); **Lif** (lif).
24. **Vali** (vä′lē): son of Odin and the goddess Rind.
25. **Magni** (mag′nē).

Analyzing Cultural Points *of* View

Beginnings and Endings

The questions on this page ask you to analyze the theme of beginnings and endings in the three preceding selections.

Ovid . . . . *from* **Metamorphoses**
Mayan myth . . . . **The Wooden People** *from the* Popol Vuh
Norse myth . . . . **The End of All Things**

Comparing a Theme Across Cultures: Beginnings and Endings

1. Compare the competence of the creators in *Metamorphoses* and in "The Wooden People." What can you infer about the view of Quiché Mayans, who depict their gods as failing in several attempts to create humans?

2. Compare the destructive forces of weather in *Metamorphoses* and "The Wooden People." How do modern views of natural forces differ from those held by ancient cultures?

3. Explain how the violent ending in "The End of All Things" is necessary for a new beginning to emerge. In what ways does rebirth also come out of destruction in Ovid's *Metamorphoses*? Explain.

4. Compare the idea of a Golden Age in *Metamorphoses* with the new beginning that comes after the final battle in "The End of All Things." Do you think that the new beginning, with happiness everywhere, will last? Explain your answer.

5. What do you think are some of the implied social or moral lessons in each of these myths? How might each of these myths be used in a culture to model proper behavior or warn against improper behavior?

WRITING

Expressing an Opinion

The mythologist David Adams Leeming says, "Great myths are never merely silly or superstitious tales. Great myths give us insights into the nature of our world." Write a brief essay in which you either agree or disagree with Leeming's statement. Use evidence from the myths you have just read to support your opinion.

North Carolina Competency Goal
3.01; 3.02;
3.03; 4.02;
5.01; 5.03

SKILLS FOCUS

Pages 305–320 cover

Literary Skills
Analyze and compare cultural points of view on a topic.

Reading Skills
Compare universal themes and archetypes across texts.

Writing Skills
Express an opinion.

Tacitus

(c. A.D. 56–c. A.D. 117)

If Publius Cornelius Tacitus (tas′ə·təs) had lived in another age, he might have become a great statesman. He was an exceptionally skilled orator, and he served Rome in a variety of public offices. He spent a good part of his life, however, under the tyrannical rule of unusually cruel and corrupt emperors. He grew up, for example, during the reign of Nero (nir′ō), who ruled A.D. 54–68, and spent most of his adult years under the reign of the sadistic Domitian (də·mish′ən), who ruled A.D. 81–96.

Tacitus's firsthand observations of the injustice and cruelty of the Roman emperors of his time drove him to take up the pen. Nearly all of Tacitus's writing shows a spirit of defiance. His first published work, *Agricola,* was a defense of his father-in-law, a public official who had been treated unjustly.

Tacitus is best known for his two historical works, of which only fragments have survived. The *Annals* depicts the troubled reigns of Tiberius, Caligula, Claudius, and Nero, which took place between the years A.D. 14 and A.D. 68. The *Histories* continues the chronicle up to the death of Domitian in A.D. 96. Tacitus also wrote an important treatise on rhetoric, or the art of persuasive speaking, called *Dialogues on the Orators.*

Modern readers expect histories to be complete, accurate, and objective—that is, written without directly revealing the writer's bias or point of view. Objective writing allows the reader to form his or her own opinions and conclusions. The notion of objective historical writing dates back to the earliest Greek historians, particularly Thucydides (see page 180). But Tacitus seems to have felt differently.

Bronze bust of the emperor Nero (c. 75 C.E.).
Musée du Louvre, Paris.

He often allowed his emotions and personal convictions to appear in his narrative. His contempt for the emperors' abuses of power and for those Romans who hypocritically flattered the rulers is clear.

Tacitus thought history should be used for moral purposes. He believed that the evil deeds of powerful people should not be forgotten after their deaths; he also believed that good deeds should be recorded and praised. Whether or not Tacitus exaggerated or distorted details to suit his own purposes, as some of his critics have claimed, he contributed perhaps more than any other source to the shaping of our picture of the early Roman Empire.

The Burning of Rome

Make the Connection

Quickwrite

Why do you think it would be important for a historian to distinguish between fact and opinion? Is it even possible to write objectively about history? Jot down your thoughts.

Literary Focus

Style

Style is the way a writer expresses his or her thoughts through language. All writers have some notion about how they can best convey their ideas. As a result, they make decisions about which words to use, how long or short the sentences and paragraphs should be, and what images and figures of speech are appropriate. Style is often viewed separately from content, but many times the style of a literary work is what makes the content memorable.

> **Style** is the way a writer expresses his or her thoughts through language.
>
> *For more on Style, see the Handbook of Literary and Historical Terms.*

Reading Skills

Making Inferences About an Author's Beliefs

At the top of a sheet of paper, write "Tacitus believes that . . ." Then, write the numbers 1–4 below this heading. As you read, list some of the things Tacitus believes about human nature and the ways in which historical events unfold. Some of Tacitus's beliefs may be stated directly, while others are only hinted at. You might have to make **infer-**

Literary Skills
Understand style.

Reading Skills
Make inferences about an author's beliefs.

ences, or educated guesses, to figure out some of these beliefs. When you are finished, place a checkmark next to the belief you think is most central to Tacitus's narrative.

Tacitus believes that. . . .
1.
2.
3.
4.

Background

This selection, from Book XV of the *Annals,* describes a disastrous fire in Rome in A.D. 64. Nero, whose actions lie at the center of Tacitus's account, became emperor of Rome in A.D. 54 as a teenager. Over time, he became steadily more vain, corrupt, and violent. In addition to revealing Tacitus's bitterness at Nero's irresponsibility, this account also records the Romans' reaction toward the new religion of Christianity.

Vocabulary Development

calamitous (kə·lam′ə·təs) *adj.:* disastrous.

inextricable (in·eks′tri·kə·bəl) *adj.:* unable to be disentangled.

propitiate (prō·pish′ē·āt′) *v.:* pacify; satisfy.

bounty (boun′tē) *n.:* reward; generosity.

avowal (ə·vou′əl) *n.:* acknowledgment.

The Burning of Rome

from **The Annals**

Tacitus
translated by **George Gilbert Ramsay**

The Burning of Rome (18th century) by Hubert Robert.

Musée des Beaux-Arts André Malraux, Le Havre.

And now came a calamitous fire—whether it was accidental or purposely contrived by the Emperor remains uncertain for on this point authorities are divided—more violent and destructive than any that ever befell our city. It began in that part of the Circus[1] which adjoins the Palatine and Caelian hills.[2] Breaking out in shops full of inflammable merchandise, it took hold and gathered strength at once; and being fanned by the wind soon embraced the entire length of the Circus, where there were no mansions with protective walls, no temple-enclosures, nor anything else to arrest its course. Furiously the destroying flames swept on, first over the level ground, then up the heights, then again plunging into the hollows, with a rapidity which outstripped all efforts to cope with them, the ancient city lending itself to their progress by its narrow tortuous streets and its misshapen blocks of buildings. The shrieks of panic-stricken women; the weakness of the aged, and the help-lessness of the young; the efforts of some to save themselves, of others to help their neighbors; the hurrying of those who dragged their sick along, the lingering of those who waited for them—all made up a scene of inextricable confusion.

Many persons, while looking behind them, were enveloped from the front or from the side; or having escaped to the nearest place of safety, found this, too, in possession of the flames, and even places which they had thought beyond their reach in the same plight with the rest. At last, not knowing where to turn, or what to avoid, they poured into the roads or threw themselves down in the fields: some having lost their all, not having even food for the day; others, though with means of escape open to them, preferred to perish for love of the dear ones whom they could not save. And none dared to check the flames; for there were many who threatened and forced back those who would extinguish them, while others openly flung in torches, saying that *they had their*

orders;—whether it really was so, or only that they wanted to plunder undisturbed.

At this moment Nero was at Antium.[3] He did not return to the city until the flames were approaching the mansion which he had built to connect the Palatine with the Gardens of Maecenas;[4] nor could they be stopped until the whole Palatine, including the palace and everything around it, had been consumed. Nero assigned the Campus Martius[5] and the Agrippa[6] monuments for the relief of the fugitive and houseless multitude. He threw open his own gardens also, and put up temporary buildings for the accommodation of the destitute; he brought up provisions from Ostia and the neighboring towns; and he reduced the price of corn to three sesterces[7] the peck. But popular as these measures were, they aroused no gratitude; for a rumor had got abroad that at the moment when the city was in flames Nero had mounted upon a stage in his own house, and by way of likening modern calamities to ancient, had sung the tale of the sack of Troy.

Not until the sixth day was the fire got under, at the foot of the Esquiline hill,[8] by demolishing

---

3. **Antium** (an′shē·əm): seaside town about thirty-two miles south of Rome, and Nero's birthplace. It is now called Anzio.
4. **Gardens of Maecenas** (mī·sē′nəs): luxurious plea-sure palace built by Maecenas, an intimate supporter of the emperor Augustus and an important patron of literary men, including Horace and Virgil.
5. **Campus Martius** (mär′shəs): Field of Mars, an area of central Rome, originally the site of a temple of Mars. It was later expanded to include a great many buildings, including baths, temples, and gardens constructed for Agrippa around 25 B.C.
6. **Agrippa** (ə·grip′ə): Marcus Vipsanius Agrippa (63–12 B.C.), a Roman military leader.
7. **sesterces** (ses·tər′sēz) *n. pl.*: silver pieces, each worth about five cents.
8. **Esquiline** (es′kwə·līn′) **hill:** one of the seven hills of ancient Rome.

Vocabulary

calamitous (kə·lam′ə·təs) *adj.*: disastrous.

inextricable (in·eks′tri·kə·bəl) *adj.*: unable to be disen-tangled.

---

1. **Circus:** Circus Maximus, a great arena used for chariot races.
2. **Palatine** (pal′ə·tīn′) **and Caelian** (sē′lē·ən) **hills:** two of the seven hills of ancient Rome.

a vast extent of buildings, so as to present nothing but the ground, and as it were the open sky, to its continued fury. But scarcely had the alarm subsided, or the populace recovered from their despair, when it burst out again in the more open parts of the city; and though here the loss of life was less, the destruction of temples and porticoes of pleasance was still more complete. And the scandal attending this new fire was the greater that it broke out in property owned by Tigellinus,[9] in the Aemilian[10] quarter; the general belief being that Nero had the ambition to build a new city to be called after his own name. For of the fourteen regions into which Rome was divided only four remained intact. Three were burnt to the ground; in the other seven, nothing remained save a few fragments of ruined and half-burnt houses.

To count up the number of mansions, of tenements, and of temples that were destroyed would be no easy matter. Among the oldest of the sacred buildings burnt was that dedicated by Servius Tullius to the Moon, and the Great Altar and fane[11] raised by Evander to the Present Hercules. The temple vowed by Romulus[12] to Jupiter, the Stayer of Flight; the Royal Palace of Numa;[13] the Temple of Vesta,[14] with the Household Gods[15] of the Roman people, were all destroyed; added to these were the treasures won in numerous battles, and masterpieces of Greek art, as well as ancient and genuine monuments of Roman genius which were remembered by the older generation amid all the splendor of the restored city, and which could never be replaced.

Some noted that the nineteenth of July, the day on which the fire began, was also the day on which the Senonian Gauls[16] had taken and burnt the city; others were so curious in their calculations as to discover that the two burnings were separated from one another by exactly the same number of years, of months, and of days.

Nero profited by the ruin of his country to erect a palace in which the marvels were not to be gold and jewels, the usual and commonplace objects of luxury, so much as lawns and lakes and mock-wildernesses, with woods on one side and open glades and vistas on the other. His engineers and masters-of-works were Severus and Celer; men who had the ingenuity and the impudence to fool away the resources of the Empire in the attempt to provide by Art what Nature had pronounced impossible.

For these men undertook to dig a navigable canal, along the rocky shore and over the hills, all the way from Lake Avernus[17] to the mouths of the Tiber.[18] There was no other water for supplying such a canal than that of the Pontine marshes;[19] and even if practicable, the labor would have been prodigious, and no object served. But Nero had a thirst for the incredible, and traces of his vain attempt to excavate the heights adjoining Lake Avernus are to be seen to this day.

The parts of the city unoccupied by Nero's palace were not built over without divisions, or indiscriminately, as after the Gallic fire, but in blocks of regular dimensions, with broad streets between. A limit was placed to the height of houses; open spaces were left; and colonnades were added to protect the fronts of tenements, Nero undertaking to build these at his own cost, and to hand over the building sites, cleared of

---

9. **Tigellinus** (tĭj′ə·lĭ′nəs): Nero's worthless friend, who joined and encouraged the emperor in his cruelties and debaucheries.
10. **Aemilian** (i·mē′li·ən).
11. **fane** (fān) *n.:* sanctuary or temple.
12. **Romulus** (räm′yoo·ləs): legendary founder of Rome.
13. **Numa:** Numa Pompilius (nooʹmə päm·pil′ē·əs): second king of Rome. He succeeded Romulus.
14. **Vesta** (ves′tə): goddess of the hearth.
15. **Household Gods:** Lares (lā′rez′) and Penates (pē·nā′tēz′), minor deities that presided over family and home.

16. **Senonian Gauls** (sə·nō′ni·ən gôlz): barbarians from northern Italy who captured and burned Rome about 390 B.C.
17. **Lake Avernus** (ə·vʉr′nəs): small lake near Cumae, in the center of an extinct volcano.
18. **Tiber:** The Tiber River runs through Rome.
19. **Pontine** (pän′tēn′) **marshes:** swampy region between Rome and Naples.

Roman Forum.

rubbish, to the proprietors. He offered premiums also, in proportion to the rank and means of owners, on condition of mansions or tenements being completed within a given time; and he assigned the marshes at Ostia for the reception of the rubbish, which was taken down the Tiber in the same vessels which had brought up the corn. Certain parts of the houses were to be built without beams, and of solid stone, Gabian or Alban, those stones being impervious to fire. Then as water had often been improperly intercepted by individuals, inspectors were appointed to secure a more abundant supply, and over a larger area, for public use; owners were required to keep appliances for quenching fire in some open place; party walls were forbidden, and every house had to be enclosed within walls of its own.

These useful provisions added greatly to the appearance of the new city; and yet there were not wanting persons who thought that the plan of the old city was more conducive to health, as the narrow streets and high roofs were a protection against the rays of the sun, which now beat down with double fierceness upon broad and shadeless thoroughfares.

Such were the measures suggested by human counsels; after which means were taken to <u>propitiate</u> the Gods. The Sibylline books[20] were consulted, and prayers were offered, as

---

20. **Sibylline** (sib′əl·īn′) **books:** nine ancient books, supposedly written by the sybil, or prophetess; these books reveal the destiny of Rome.

Vocabulary

propitiate (prō·pish′ē·āt′) v.: pacify; satisfy.

prescribed by them, to Vulcan,[21] to Ceres,[22] and to Proserpine.[23] Juno[24] was supplicated by the matrons, in the Capitol first, and afterwards at the nearest point upon the sea, from which water was drawn to sprinkle the temple and image of the Goddess; banquets to the Goddesses and all-night festivals were celebrated by married women.

But neither human aid, nor imperial bounty, nor atoning-offerings to the Gods, could remove the sinister suspicion that the fire had been brought about by Nero's order. To put an end therefore to this rumor, he shifted the charge onto others, and inflicted the most cruel tortures upon a body of men detested for their abominations, and popularly known by the name of Christians. This name came from one Christus, who was put to death in the reign of Tiberius by the Procurator Pontius Pilate; but though checked for the time, the detestable superstition broke out again, not in Judaea only, where the mischief began, but even in Rome, where every horrible and shameful iniquity, from every quarter of the world, pours in and finds a welcome.

First those who acknowledged themselves of this persuasion were arrested; and upon their testimony a vast number were condemned, not so much on the charge of incendiarism as for their hatred of the human race. Their death was turned into a diversion. They were clothed in the skins of wild beasts, and torn to pieces by dogs; they were fastened to crosses, or set up to be burned, so as to serve the purpose of lamps when daylight failed. Nero gave up his own gardens for this spectacle; he provided also Circensian games,[25] during which he mingled

with the populace, or took his stand upon a chariot, in the garb of a charioteer. But guilty as these men were and worthy of direst punishment, the fact that they were being sacrificed for no public good, but only to glut the cruelty of one man, aroused a feeling of pity on their behalf.

Meanwhile Italy was ransacked for contributions. The provinces and allied peoples were rifled, as well as the states which are called 'free.' Even the Gods had to submit to being plundered. The temples in the city were despoiled, and emptied of the gold consecrated at triumphs, or vowed by past generations of Romans in times of panic or prosperity. As for Asia and Achaia,[26] not offerings only, but the very images of the Gods were carried off by Acratus and Secundus Carrinas, who were sent out to those provinces for the purpose. The former was a freedman ready for any kind of villainy; the latter was a man whose lips were tinged with Greek learning, but who had no real culture in his heart.

We are told that Seneca[27] craved leave to withdraw to a remote country retreat to avoid the odium of such sacrilege; on this being denied him, he pretended to be suffering from some muscular ailment, and shut himself up in his own chamber. Other accounts say that Nero ordered poison to be administered to him by one of his own freedmen, called Cleonicus; but that Seneca escaped the trap, either by the man's avowal, or by his own precaution in adopting a simple diet of natural fruits, and slaking his thirst from running water.

---

21. **Vulcan** (vul′kən): god of fire and metalworking.
22. **Ceres** (sir′ēz′): goddess of grain and harvest.
23. **Proserpine** (prō·sur′pi·nē′): wife of Pluto, king of Hades.
24. **Juno** (jōo′nō): queen of the gods and goddess of marriage.
25. **Circensian** (sur·ken′si·ən) **games:** games held in the Circus, or arena.

26. **Asia and Achaia** (ə·kā′ə): Asia Minor and Greece.
27. **Seneca** (sen′i·kə): Nero's minister of state, a Stoic philosopher. He retired from office in A.D. 62. He was forced to commit suicide as the result of a court intrigue in A.D. 65.

Vocabulary

bounty (boun′tē) *n.*: reward; generosity.
avowal (ə·vou′əl) *n.*: acknowledgment.

Response and Analysis

Reading Check

1. According to Tacitus, why was nothing done to stop the burning of Rome?

2. When a second fire broke out, what rumor about the emperor was circulated? What steps did Nero take to squelch the rumor?

3. How did Nero pay for the rebuilding of Rome?

Thinking Critically

4. Cite specific passages in which Tacitus makes a subjective judgment on a person or occurrence. What evidence does he offer to support his opinions?

5. Locate the details describing Nero. What impression do these details create? Which details might have led another historian to a different conclusion?

6. Consider Tacitus's description of the first outbreak of the fire (page 324). Judging from his use of language, tone, and imagery, how would you describe Tacitus's **style**? For example, is it concise, impassioned, or detached? Support your answer with examples from the account.

7. Tacitus's famous passage about the Christians is one of the earliest historical references to Christianity by a non-Christian writer. How does Tacitus show that he is prejudiced against the Christians? On what grounds does he express anger about their persecution?

Extending and Evaluating

8. If you were editor in chief of a major daily newspaper and Tacitus applied for a job as a reporter, would you give him the job? Why or why not? You may want to consult your Quickwrite notes.

9. In your opinion, which of Tacitus's beliefs is most central to his approach to personalities and events in this account? (Refer to the list you created while reading.)

Literary Criticism

10. The burning of Rome was an actual event, but as many critics point out, it is difficult to distinguish between fact and fiction in Tacitus's account. What prejudices and personal biases does Tacitus reveal—and how does he reveal them? How does he try to sway readers' emotions through **loaded language**—language that has strong connotations and appeals to emotion rather than to reason? Use specific examples from the text in your response.

WRITING

Rewriting an Account

You are a historical "authority" who believes the fire was accidental and that Nero did his best to relieve the people's hardship and to rebuild the city. Write a short account of the fire, changing the tone toward the emperor from negative to positive.

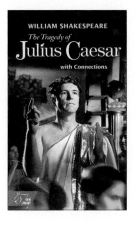

DRAMA

"Et tu, Brutè?"

Is there anything worse than being betrayed by the people you trust? Betrayal lies at the center of William Shakespeare's *The Tragedy of Julius Caesar*. The play is based on a biography of Julius Caesar that was written by the Greek author Plutarch. Caesar is an ambitious Roman general viewed by a group of Romans as a tyrant who is threatening the freedom of Rome. Using this pretext, the group comes up with a plot to assassinate Caesar. They even manage to convince Caesar's friend Brutus that the assassination would be in Rome's best interest.

This title is available in the HRW Library.

DRAMA

A Question of Loyalty

What would you do if you were forced to choose between a family member and the law? In *Antigone* (translated by Dudley Fitts and Robert Fitzgerald), one of the dramas that Sophocles composed for his trilogy of Theban plays, Oedipus's daughter Antigone is forced to make such a decision. Creon, the king of Thebes, passes a law forbidding the burial of Antigone's brother Polyneices. The law further states that anyone who buries Polyneices will face the penalty of death. Will Antigone follow the letter of the law or the law of her own conscience?

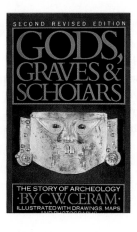

NONFICTION

Daring, Digging, and Discovering

C. W. Ceram brings the high drama and adventure of archaeology to life in his book *Gods, Graves and Scholars: The Story of Archeology*. This compelling presentation of archaeology's rich history juxtaposes the major discoveries made about ancient civilizations with the personal stories of the detectives who sought to uncover the buried secrets of the past. Along the way you will read about the doomed city of Pompeii, the treasures of ancient Troy, and the mysterious Rosetta stone of Egypt.

ADDITIONAL READING

- Homer continues the story he began in the *Iliad* with his second great epic, the *Odyssey,* translated by Robert Fagles. In this ultimate adventure story, Homer recounts the Greek warrior Odysseus's harrowing journey home following the end of the Trojan War.

- *Omeros,* which means "Homer" in Greek, is Derek Walcott's epic poem inspired by the works of Homer. Starring a contemporary version of Odysseus, the poem explores the universal experience of human suffering.

- Millions of readers made their first discovery of the rousing adventures of the Greek and Roman (and Norse) gods and heroes in the pages of Edith Hamilton's *Mythology,* still one of the most popular collections of classical myths ever published. Hamilton's straightforward retellings of the great myths are infused with her lifelong respect and love for classical literature.

Analyzing Problems and Solutions

Problem-solution essays, or proposals that call for definite action, are written every day—by newspaper columnists, politicians, or concerned citizens. Is there a problem in your school or neighborhood that you would really like to fix? To do this, you will first have to analyze the problem. When you understand the problem, you can evaluate possible solutions, choose the one that works best, and persuade others to accept your solution.

Prewriting

Choose a Topic

Problems, Problems, Problems Make a list of school or community problems that need solutions. Try to focus on problems that significantly affect a number of people. Here are some ways to find out what's on people's minds:

- take a poll of class members and their families
- read the letters to the editor and editorials in local newspapers
- interview your principal, a local official, or a community leader
- attend a parents' meeting or the meeting of another citizens' group

Decide which problem is most important to you. Be realistic, though, and choose a manageable problem that really could be solved through community effort.

Analyze the Problem

Face the Facts Before you can persuade others to work on a problem, you must convince them that the problem is serious and affects them. One of the best ways to analyze a problem is to provide answers to the *5W-How?* questions, as a student did on the chart on page 331.

SKILLS
FOCUS

North Carolina Competency Goal
6.01

Problem: Budget Cuts to School Art Programs

Who is affected by the problem?	students, teachers, parents, future employers
What has already been done about the problem?	letter-writing campaign to state legislators to restore funds for art education
Why is the problem occurring?	state budget deficits and prioritizing of funds for reading and math education
When did the problem begin?	with the economic slowdown and the decrease in federal government spending
Where is this problem occurring?	in public schools across the nation
How does the problem affect me?	school art classes have been eliminated

Look for Solutions While researching and interviewing, you should also be looking for possible solutions and deciding whether you think any of them could work in your particular situation. Do you have a better solution to offer? Look at the following proposed solutions to the problem of cuts in arts funding and one student's choice of a solution:

Solution 1: Political action—including letter-writing and e-mail campaigns, demonstrations, and teacher strikes—to get funding restored

Solution 2: Integration of art education into the language arts and social studies curricula

My Solution: Have students form after-school art clubs with help from local artists and community

Build Your Case

The Support You Need To convince your audience that your solution is the best, you must give strong **reasons** and back up those reasons with **evidence,** such as facts, statistics, examples, and expert opinions.

State Your Thesis Develop a thesis statement that presents the problem and your solution: "If there is no public money for school art programs, students and communities will have to work together to create after-school art-education programs run by volunteers."

PRACTICE & APPLY 1 Use the preceding instruction to select a topic for a problem-solution essay, analyze the problem, decide on the best solution, and gather evidence to support that solution.

TIP Since your ultimate aim is to persuade, consider using these rhetorical devices:

- logical appeals to readers' intelligence and reasoning powers
- emotionally loaded language to appeal to readers' feelings
- ethical appeals to readers' sense of right and wrong

North Carolina Competency Goal 6.01

SKILLS FOCUS

Writing Skills
Identify a problem and a solution.
Develop a thesis statement.

Writing

Writing a Problem-Solution Essay

A Writer's Framework

Introduction

- Capture your readers' attention with an interesting anecdote or example.
- Provide background information, if necessary.
- Include a thesis statement that identifies the problem and the best solution.

Body

- Analyze the problem and evaluate solutions.
- Give reasons and evidence to support your solution.
- Address any objections or counterarguments.

Conclusion

- Remind readers why your solution is the best.
- Issue a call to action, asking readers to work to solve the problem.
- Restate your thesis in a compelling way.

A Writer's Model

Keep Art Alive!

INTRODUCTION

How would you feel if you returned to school in the fall to discover that your favorite class had been dropped and your teacher laid off? What a shock and what a loss! This is exactly what happened to sixteen-year-old Letitia Adams of Walnut Creek, California. Letitia is upset not only because she will no longer be learning art, a subject she loves, but also because she saw her art class as a stepping stone to a career in commercial art. Now that opportunity seems to be lost.

Attention-grabbing anecdote

Students like Letitia are the losers in an educational system crippled by budget deficits. Yet, there is a way to ensure that the needs of such students are met. If there is no public money available for art instruction, Letitia and others like her can work with their schools and communities to create their own after-school art programs.

Thesis statement in last sentence

BODY
Analysis of problem

The cancellation of art and other programs not considered essential in public schools is a result of economic realities and political decisions. A sluggish economy and increased government spending in other areas have strained state budgets severely. At the same time, federal legislation requires the states to test students regularly in language arts and mathematics. The result at the local level is that the need to prepare students for these important tests is taking time and money away from programs like art education.

(continued)

No one can deny that it's important for students to master reading and mathematics, but the argument that art programs have little educational value has been soundly disproved. Educational researcher Alma Rodriguez says there is a large body of evidence showing that individuals learn in a variety of ways and that success in subjects like art often improves performance in other subjects.

How can we keep art education alive in our schools? Getting the art budget restored would be the ideal solution. However, that would require massive and time-consuming political action, and it assumes that states will somehow magically find the funds that currently are in such short supply. Even if political action were eventually effective, it wouldn't come in time for students who have *currently* lost their art classes.

Since today's students are the ones who lose out, it is they who must take action. They can set up their own art clubs after school, with the more accomplished artists tutoring those students who are just learning. They can ask retired art teachers, local working artists, and college art majors to volunteer their time to visit classes and share their knowledge. They can ask community members and local merchants to donate supplies. They can even organize community events like art exhibitions to raise money.

Although an after-school art program run by volunteers cannot take the place of formal instruction by a trained art teacher, it is a creative, short-term solution that can give students like Letitia Adams not only artistic opportunities but also valuable experience in community organization. Not only students, but also their schools and communities, can benefit from this kind of cooperation.

Counterargument addressed

Evidence: expert opinion

Best-solution reason, with logical appeal

Call to action

CONCLUSION Restatement of thesis

PRACTICE & APPLY 2 Using the framework and Writer's Model on these pages as your guide, write the first draft of your problem-solution essay.

INTERNET
More Writer's Models
Keyword:
LE5 WL-2

Revising

Self-evaluation

Review Your Work Read your essay through at least twice. Use the rubric on page 334 to help you determine where your essay needs revision.

Rubric: Writing a Problem-Solution Essay

Evaluation Questions	▶ Tips	▶ Revision Techniques
❶ Does the introduction clearly present a problem and offer a solution?	▶ **Underline** the problem and the solution you propose.	▶ **Add** a sentence that clearly identifies the problem. **Add** a sentence that clearly proposes a solution to the problem.
❷ Does the body of your essay explain the background of the problem?	▶ **Circle** background information on the problem, such as the causes and effects.	▶ **Add** more facts that give information about the problem.
❸ Do you propose a specific solution and explain why it is the best one?	▶ **Highlight** the best solution, and underline the reasons or evidence given to support it.	▶ **Elaborate** with more reasons or evidence supporting your solution.
❹ Have you restated your thesis in a conclusion that strengthens your call to action?	▶ **Put a star** next to the sentence that restates the thesis. Circle any language or details that strengthen your case.	▶ **Rewrite** the conclusion so that it restates the thesis more powerfully. Try adding details or appealing to emotion.

ANALYZING THE REVISION PROCESS

Study the revisions below, and answer the questions that follow.

> *Although*
> ~~It is clear that~~ an after-school art program run by volunteers cannot take the place of
> *formal*   ,   *creative, short-term*
> ~~professional~~ instruction by a trained art teacher. ~~However,~~ it is a ~~practical~~ solution that
>   *also*
> can give students like Letitia Adams not only artistic opportunities but ~~other~~
>   *in community organization*
> valuable experience.

Responding to the Revision Process

1. What is the effect of combining the two sentences into one?

2. What does the writer achieve by adding the details to the last part of the sentence?

3. Is there anything else you would do to strengthen the conclusion of the essay? Explain.

PRACTICE & APPLY ❸   Using the guidelines on these pages, revise the content, form, and style of your problem-solution essay.

Publishing

Proofread and Publish Your Essay

Last Pass It is a good idea to put your revised essay aside for a time and then take it up again when your mind is clear. Proofread it thoroughly, looking for errors in grammar, usage, and mechanics. Make use of your computer's spelling and grammar checks, but don't rely on them alone. Evaluate all suggested corrections, making your own decisions on what you will correct and how.

Reach Out You cannot solve the problem you have written about unless you involve others. Try one or more of the following ideas to get the word out, or try an idea of your own.

- Submit your essay to the opinion page of your school or local newspaper.

- Invite students, parents, teachers, and community members to a meeting to hear a rousing call-to-action speech based on your essay.

- Use your essay to write a letter to an individual or organization whose support could make your solution a reality.

Reflect on Your Essay

Think It Over Now that you have written a problem-solution essay, think back over the process you went through and what you learned from doing it. Answering the following questions may help you the next time you analyze a problem and propose a solution:

- Who was your audience for this essay? How did you tailor your essay to that particular audience?

- What was your best source of information about the problem? Explain your response.

- What additional support could you have offered for your proposed solution?

- What feedback did you get from your audience? How would you apply that feedback in your next problem-solution essay?

PRACTICE & APPLY 4 First, proofread your essay. Then, choose one of the options above to publish your essay for an audience. Finally, answer the reflection questions.

North Carolina Competency Goal
6.01

Writing Skills
Revise and proofread content and style.

Presenting and Evaluating a Persuasive Speech

In a democratic country like the United States, persuasive speeches are critical to the political process at all levels. You'll hear persuasive speeches at school board meetings, at a state conference on environmental issues, and on the congressional campaign trail. In this workshop you will present a persuasive argument as well as analyze the effectiveness of another persuasive speaker.

Preparing a Persuasive Speech

What Matters Most Persuasion doesn't focus on a neutral topic like "College Counselors at Our High School." It centers on a controversial, or arguable, issue like "More College Counselors Are Needed at Our High School." In addition to being controversial, the issue you choose for a persuasive speech must be one that both you and your potential audience care about.

Getting to the Point The purpose of a persuasive speech is to convince the audience to think or act in a certain way. Before you start gathering details and organizing your speech, make sure you're clear about the issue and your position on it. Here is an example of a clear **position statement:**

> Our high school needs two more college counselors in order to meet the needs of juniors and seniors who are planning to go to college.

Staking a Claim It's not easy to persuade other people to do or believe something they're opposed to. You have to give them strong reasons to do so.

- **Logical appeals** and evidence influence thinking and rational judgment by supporting the position with facts, statistics, examples, or expert opinions.

- **Emotional appeals** arouse feelings with emotional language and stories that tug at the heart.

- **Ethical appeals** invoke a sense of right or wrong.

The Organizational Angle Most persuasive arguments are organized in one of two ways—deductively or inductively.

- The **deductive** approach moves from the general to the specific and works well with a neutral or favorable audience. Start with your position statement, and then explain your reasons.

North Carolina Competency Goal
3.01; 3.02; 3.04; 4.04

- The **inductive** approach moves from the specific to general and works well with an audience opposed to your idea. Begin with your reasons, and conclude with your position statement.

Whether you organize your argument deductively or inductively, you'll have to think about the order of your reasons. Since audiences are more likely to remember the last thing they hear, end with your most important—and most dramatic—reason.

The Right Words The **rhetorical devices** listed below can give you the power to convince others—think of these devices as the three R's of persuasion. Try to incorporate them into your speech.

- **Repetition**—repeating words or groups of words
- **Rhetorical questions**—questions asked for effect, not response ("Can we afford to simply wait for things to change?")
- **Restatement**—repeating an idea using different language

Delivering Your Speech

Take It Seriously If you want your listeners to take you and your issue seriously, you must take your speech seriously. Write your speech out completely, and practice it several times. Use formal language, without slang or colloquialisms, to create a serious tone. On the final version of your speech, underline words and phrases you want to stress. Note where you want to increase volume, shift your tone, or pause.

TIP If you can find a tape recorder, record and play back your speech to critique it. Stand in front of a mirror as you practice your expressions, gestures, and eye contact.

Analyzing a Persuasive Speech

The Ears of a Critic When analyzing a persuasive speech, you need to pay attention to the kinds of appeals the speaker is using—logical, emotional, and ethical. With logical appeals, you need to evaluate the evidence to determine whether it is factual and true. Also be on the alert for **fallacious reasoning** and **propaganda,** such as the following examples.

- **Overgeneralization:** A generalization based on too little evidence or evidence that ignores exceptions.
- **False Causality:** An incorrect assumption that one event caused, rather than just preceded, another.
- **Bandwagon Effect:** An attempt to obtain agreement by claiming that everyone else agrees.
- **Attack** *Ad Hominem:* A criticism of a person rather than the issue itself.

PRACTICE & APPLY First, use the instructions in this workshop to prepare and deliver a persuasive speech. Then, analyze a persuasive speech given by one of your classmates or someone on television.

King Minos held Daedalus, an Athenian architect, and Daedalus's son, Icarus, prisoner on the island of Crete. The story of Daedalus and Icarus is one of the many Greek myths that the Roman poet Ovid retells in his long poem *Metamorphoses*. The word *metamorphoses* means "transformations," and the changes that Ovid's characters undergo are both physical and psychological. In the contemporary poem "Icarus's Flight," the American poet Stephen Dobyns offers a modern view of Icarus's choice.

DIRECTIONS: Read the following two poems. Then, read each multiple-choice question that follows, and write the letter of the best response.

from Metamorphoses

from Book 8: The Story of Daedalus and Icarus

Ovid
translated by Rolfe Humphries

Homesick for homeland, Daedalus hated Crete
And his long exile there, but the sea held him.
"Though Minos blocks escape by land or water,"
Daedalus said, "surely the sky is open,
5   And that's the way we'll go. Minos' dominion
Does not include the air." He turned his thinking
Toward unknown arts, changing the laws of nature.
He laid out feathers in order, first the smallest,
A little larger next it, and so continued,
10 The way that pan-pipes rise in gradual sequence.
He fastened them with twine and wax, at middle,
At bottom, so, and bent them, gently curving,
So that they looked like wings of birds, most surely.
And Icarus, his son, stood by and watched him,
15 Not knowing he was dealing with his downfall,
Stood by and watched, and raised his shiny face
To let a feather, light as down, fall on it,
Or stuck his thumb into the yellow wax,
Fooling around, the way a boy will, always,
20 Whenever a father tries to get some work done.

North Carolina Competency Goal
1.03; 4.05;
5.02; 5.03

SKILLS FOCUS

Pages 338–341 cover
Literary Skills
Compare and contrast poems.

Still, it was done at last, and the father hovered,
Poised, in the moving air, and taught his son:
"I warn you, Icarus, fly a middle course:
Don't go too low, or water will weigh the wings down;
25   Don't go too high, or the sun's fire will burn them.
Keep to the middle way. And one more thing,
No fancy steering by star or constellation,
Follow my lead!" That was the flying lesson,
And now to fit the wings to the boy's shoulders.
30   Between the work and warning the father found
His cheeks were wet with tears, and his hands trembled.
He kissed his son (*Good-bye,* if he had known it),
Rose on his wings, flew on ahead, as fearful
As any bird launching the little nestlings
35   Out of high nest into thin air. *Keep on,*
Keep on, he signals, *follow me!* He guides him
In flight—O fatal art!—and the wings move
And the father looks back to see the son's wings moving.
Far off, far down, some fisherman is watching
40   As the rod dips and trembles over the water,
Some shepherd rests his weight upon his crook,
Some ploughman on the handles of the ploughshare,
And all look up, in absolute amazement,
At those air-borne above. They must be gods!
45   They were over Samos, Juno's sacred island,
Delos and Paros toward the left, Lebinthus
Visible to the right, and another island,
Calymne, rich in honey. And the boy
Thought *This is wonderful!* and left his father,
50   Soared higher, higher, drawn to the vast heaven,
Nearer the sun, and the wax that held the wings
Melted in that fierce heat, and the bare arms
Beat up and down in air, and lacking oarage
Took hold of nothing. *Father!* he cried, and *Father!*
55   Until the blue sea hushed him, the dark water
Men call the Icarian now. And Daedalus,
Father no more, called "Icarus, where are you!
Where are you, Icarus? Tell me where to find you!"
And saw the wings on the waves, and cursed his talents,
60   Buried the body in a tomb, and the land
Was named for Icarus.

Icarus's Flight

Stephen Dobyns

What else could the boy have done? Wasn't
flight both an escape and a great uplifting?
And so he flew. But how could he appreciate
his freedom without knowing the exact point

5   where freedom stopped? So he flew upward
and the sun dissolved the wax and he fell.
But at last in his anticipated plummeting
he grasped the confines of what had been

his liberty. You say he flew too far?
10 He flew just far enough. He flew precisely
to the point of wisdom. Would it
have been better to flutter ignorantly

from petal to petal within some garden
forever? As a result, flight for him was not
15 upward escape, but descent, with his wings
disintegrating around him. Should it matter

that neither shepherd nor farmer with his plow
watched him fall? He now had his answer,
laws to uphold him in his downward plunge.
20 Cushion enough for what he wanted.

---

1. According to Ovid, Daedalus plans to escape his imprisonment on the island of Crete by —
    A   bribing his guards
    B   leading a revolt against King Minos
    C   swimming to the nearest island
    D   building wings and flying to freedom

2. In *Metamorphoses,* what does Daedalus's interest in "unknown arts" (line 7) suggest about his character?
    F   He is without conscience and is willing to do evil.
    G   He is a daring and original individual.
    H   He rarely takes risks.
    J   He is more divine than human.

Collection 2: Skills Review

3. In Ovid's poem, how does Icarus fail to follow his father's advice?

   A He refuses to leave Crete.

   B He flies too near the sun.

   C He flies too close to his father.

   D He enjoys his flight.

4. Ovid's Icarus might **symbolize** —

   F respect for authority

   G the triumph of ambition

   H the daring exuberance of youth

   J the wisdom of the young

5. In Dobyns's poem, what does Icarus learn as a result of his flight?

   A The penalty for disobedience

   B Respect for the sun

   C The limits of his freedom

   D The rewards of daring

6. In Dobyns's poem the attitude of the speaker toward Icarus is —

   F tragic regret

   G sober admiration

   H puzzled curiosity

   J deep disappointment

7. What contemporary attitude toward risk taking may Dobyns be reflecting in his portrayal of Icarus?

   A Limits imposed by others should not be accepted without question.

   B Taking unnecessary risks is shortsighted and destructive.

   C Daring action is its own reward.

   D Risks and benefits must always be carefully calculated.

8. Ovid's and Dobyns's poems are different in that —

   F in Ovid's poem, Icarus is rescued before he drowns

   G in Dobyns's poem, Icarus regrets his choice to fly so near the sun

   H in Ovid's poem, only Daedalus's experience is explored

   J in Dobyns's poem, only Icarus's experience is explored

Essay Question

Both Ovid and Stephen Dobyns retell the fascinating myth of a young man who ignores the message of moderation and pays the ultimate price. Although Icarus plunges to his death in both poems, the authors present different views about his death. In a brief essay, compare and contrast these views. Explore how each poem presents Icarus's reasons for flying so near the sun and the consequences of his choice. Consider not only the attitudes expressed directly in the poems, but also those implied in the details of character, action, and word choice.

Collection 2: Skills Review
Vocabulary Skills

Synonyms

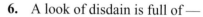

DIRECTIONS: Words that have similar meanings are called **synonyms**. For example, *futile* and *useless* are synonyms. In the sentences below, choose the word or group of words whose meaning is most similar to the meaning of the underlined word.

1. To <u>revere</u> a person is to —
   - **A** insult him or her
   - **B** defeat him or her
   - **C** respect him or her
   - **D** contradict him or her

2. An <u>expedient</u> plan is —
   - **F** exciting
   - **G** practical
   - **H** progressive
   - **J** complex

3. An <u>avowal</u> is the same as —
   - **A** an admission
   - **B** a pardon
   - **C** a prediction
   - **D** a dismissal

4. If you are in an <u>inextricable</u> situation, you are —
   - **F** fortunate
   - **G** expendable
   - **H** amused
   - **J** trapped

5. An <u>omnipotent</u> ruler is —
   - **A** bipartisan
   - **B** magnificent
   - **C** ignorant
   - **D** all-powerful

6. A look of <u>disdain</u> is full of —
   - **F** envy
   - **G** admiration
   - **H** scorn
   - **J** delight

7. A <u>calamitous</u> event is —
   - **A** disastrous
   - **B** enjoyable
   - **C** brief
   - **D** fortunate

8. <u>Reprobation</u> is the same as —
   - **F** liberation
   - **G** affirmation
   - **H** revenge
   - **J** disapproval

9. An <u>arduous</u> task is —
   - **A** rewarding
   - **B** difficult
   - **C** desirable
   - **D** thankless

10. An <u>intimation</u> is —
    - **F** a hint
    - **G** an injury
    - **H** a report
    - **J** an attitude

SKILLS FOCUS

Vocabulary Skills
Understand and identify synonyms.

Collection 2: Skills Review

Writing Skills

Test Practice DIRECTIONS: Read the following paragraph from a draft of a student's problem-solution essay. Then, answer the questions below it.

(1) Even though the health hazards of smoking have been scientifically proven, young people continue to take up the habit. (2) Teenagers are beginning to smoke at ever-younger ages. (3) The reasons for this increase are not entirely clear. (4) Some people blame the tobacco industry for deliberately targeting young people in their advertising. (5) Others say that laws forbidding the sale of cigarettes to minors are not vigorously enforced. (6) Antismoking education in the schools has been criticized as ineffective. (7) Attempts to scare students with pictures of diseased lungs or with statistics linking smoking to early death have not had the desired effect. (8) Antismoking campaigns have been more successful with adults. (9) Since existing efforts to solve the problem are failing, what is needed is a new approach.

1. Which sentence can be deleted to improve the paragraph's organization?
   A   Sentence 1
   B   Sentence 4
   C   Sentence 7
   D   Sentence 8

2. What function would this paragraph serve in a multiparagraph essay?
   F   It presents a variety of solutions to a problem.
   G   It identifies the problem and explores its causes.
   H   It argues forcefully for one solution.
   J   It presents a compelling call to action.

3. Which sentence could be improved by the addition of specific facts and statistics?
   A   Sentence 2
   B   Sentence 3
   C   Sentence 4
   D   Sentence 9

4. Which of these transitions, if added to sentence 7, would help clarify the relationship between sentences 6 and 7?
   F   On the other hand,
   G   In addition,
   H   For example,
   J   As a result,

5. Which sentence could be added to the end of the paragraph to state a thesis that proposes a specific solution?
   A   Research has shown that antismoking approaches that work with adults do not necessarily work with young people.
   B   The presentation of medical facts and statistics alone will not persuade young people to avoid tobacco.
   C   An approach that takes into account the unique psychology and culture of young people is what is needed.
   D   Peer-run workshops have the best chance of reducing the numbers of young people who take up smoking.

North Carolina Competency Goal
2.01; 4.03; 6.01

Writing Skills
Analyze a problem-solution essay.

Literature of India, China, and Japan

2500 B.C.–A.D. 1800s

The Search for Truth and Enlightenment

Only be willing to search for poetry, and there will be poetry:

My soul, a tiny speck, is my tutor.

Evening sun and fragrant grass are common things,

But, with understanding, they can become glorious verse.

—"Expression of feelings, VII" by Yüan Mei

INTERNET

Collection Resources
Keyword:
LE5 WL-3

(Opposite) Taoist immortal flies through the clouds (c. 1750). Manuscript page from *A Keepsake from the Cloud Gallery*. Qing dynasty.

The British Library, London (Add. 22689, f. 30).

India, China, and Japan

5000 B.C. | **1500 B.C.** | **1000 B.C.** | **500 B.C.**

c. 2500 B.C. The Indus Valley civilization arises in the Indus River valley

c. 2000 B.C. Indus Valley people use extensive irrigation and drainage systems

1766–1122 B.C. Art of writing develops in China during the Shang dynasty

c. 1500–c. 500 B.C. Vedic period in India

c. 1500 B.C. Invasions of Indo-European-speaking nomads coincide with decline of Indus Valley civilization; Hinduism begins to develop in India

c. 1111–c. 255 B.C. Feudal system develops in China during the Chou dynasty

Great Wall of China.

c. 1000 B.C. First ancestors of today's Japanese population arrive in Japan; earliest hymns from the Rig-Veda are written down

c. 900–500 B.C. Later Vedas, Upanishads, and Brahmanas are compiled

c. 551–479 B.C. The Chinese sage Confucius teaches ethical principles known as Confucianism, recorded in his *Analects*

c. 500s B.C. Teachings of Laotzu give rise to Tao-ism in China; *The Book of Songs* is compiled in China

400s B.C. Written form of Sanskrit is developed

c. 400 B.C.– A.D. 1000 Classical period of Indian epic and wisdom literature

221–206 B.C. Ch'in dynasty unifies China; Great Wall is built

206 B.C.–A.D. 220 Han dynasty in China; Confucianism becomes official state doctrine; Buddhist teachings are brought from India

c. 150 B.C. The Chinese invent paper

LITERARY, POLITICAL, AND SOCIAL EVENTS IN THE WORLD

5000 B.C. | **1500 B.C.** | **1000 B.C.** | **500 B.C.**

c. 4500 B.C. Sumer is settled in Mesopotamia

c. 3500–c. 3000 B.C. Egyptians invent hieroglyphic writing

c. 3000–c. 2500 B.C. Cuneiform tablets are inscribed with Sumerian writings

c. 1792 B.C. Babylon reaches its cultural and artistic peak under Hammurabi

c. 1354 B.C. Assyrians rise to power in Mesopotamia

c. 1300 B.C. The *Epic of Gilgamesh* is written down by Babylonians in Mesopotamia

c. 1100–c. 1000 B.C. Dorians conquer Greece; period known as the Greek Dark Ages begins

c. 1000 B.C. The Torah is assembled

c. 950–c. 750 B.C. The Book of Ruth is written

c. 753 B.C. Rome is founded

c. 700 B.C. Homer composes the *Iliad*

400s B.C. Classical era of Greek drama: Aeschylus, Sophocles, and Euripides write tragedies

c. 387 B.C. Plato founds the Academy in Athens

c. 6 B.C.–c. A.D. 30 The lifetime of Jesus of Nazareth

Relief portrait of Homer with Clio, muse of history. Detail from the *Sarcophagus of the Muses* (c. 150 B.C.E).

Musée du Louvre, Paris.

2500 B.C.—A.D. 1800s

INDIA, CHINA, AND JAPAN

A.D. 1	500	1000	1500–on
C. A.D. 1–C. A.D. 200 The Bhagavad-Gita is written down in India	**618–907** T'ang dynasty, called China's golden age	**1084–c. 1150** The lifetime of Chinese poet Li Ch'ing-chao	**1633** Shogun closes Japan to foreigners
C. A.D. 320–467 Gupta dynasty rules in India	**700s** Li Po and Tu Fu compose Chinese poetry	**c. 1200s** Zen sect of Buddhism develops in Japan	**1644–1694** The lifetime of Matsuo Bashō, one of the earliest Japanese poets to write haiku
C. A.D. 400 Buddhism and Chinese writings are introduced to Japan	**794–1185** Japan's Heian era witnesses a cultural flowering and the rise of feudalism; the aristocrats of Japan's Heian court compose tanka	**c. 1215–1279** Mongol leader Genghis Khan conquers China; his grandson Kubla Khan establishes the Yuan dynasty	**c. 1715–1763** Ts'ao Hsueh-ch'in writes *Dream of the Red Chamber*, one of China's most famous novels
A.D. 400s The great Sanskrit writer Kalidasa composes poetry and drama			**1853** Commodore Matthew Perry ends Japanese isolationist policy

Portrait of Genghis Khan.
National Palace Museum, Taipei, Taiwan.

1900 Boxer Rebellion ignites revolutionary spark in China

A.D. 1	500	1000	1500–on
A.D. 161–180 Marcus Aurelius reigns in Rome	**c. 650** Official text of the Koran is established	**c. 1210–c. 1260** The lifetime of Sundiata, hero of Mali's great oral epic *Sundiata*	**1660** Restoration comedies become popular in England
C. A.D. 300–1200 Rise and fall of the Empire of Ghana	**700s** Anglo-Saxon epic *Beowulf* is written down	**1307** Dante Alighieri begins writing the *Divine Comedy*	**1700s** The novel becomes popular in England
C. A.D. 313 Christianity is proclaimed the official religion of the Roman Empire	**900** *The Thousand and One Nights*, the famous collection of Arabian tales, is begun	**1347–1352** Black Death ravages Europe	**1775–1783** American Revolution
		1492 Columbus reaches the Americas	**1800s** Western European nations divide Africa into colonies

Landing of Columbus in America. Color engraving.

Cultural and Historical

A Family of Languages

3000 B.C.–1500 B.C.

In 1786, a British linguist named Sir William Jones suggested that many of the languages spoken in Europe and Asia derive from a single language, which linguists today have identified as Proto-Indo-European. Although there are no written records of this language, linguistic research shows it to be the basis of languages ranging from Greek and Latin to English, German, Bengali, Farsi, and Spanish. The people who used this language probably originated somewhere in Europe and then, after 3000 B.C., migrated into India and Persia (now called Iran). As a result, both Sanskrit—the ancient literary language of India—and Old Persian are offshoots of what we call the Indo-European family of languages. Today, almost half the world's people speak languages that can be traced back to Indo-European roots.

Portrait of Laotzu (c. 604–531 B.C.E.).
The Granger Collection, NY.

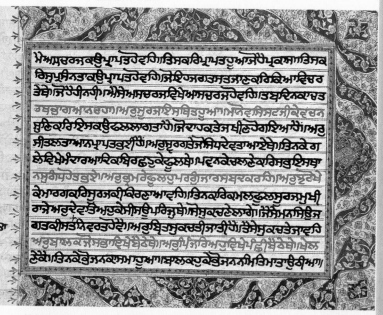

"Nirvanaprakarama" ("Exposition of the Greeting").
Musée Conde, Chantilly, France (Ms. 205/1203, fol. 49).

Milestones 2500 B.C.–A.D. 1800s

Philosophy and Religion

500s B.C.–A.D. 500s

Three major systems of thought have dominated Eastern philosophy and religion for more than twenty-five centuries and continue to influence the spiritual lives of people throughout the world today. **Confucianism,** founded in China by Confucius (551–479 B.C.), teaches that order, discipline, and social stability are the foundations for a good life. Confucius's teachings were collected by disciples and became the official state doctrine of China. The philosophy of **Taoism,** founded by Chinese philosopher Laotzu (sixth century B.C.), advises people to put aside desires and devote themselves to contemplating Tao, the source of unity in the natural world. **Buddhism,** based on the teachings of Siddhartha Gautama (563–483 B.C.), arose first in India but later migrated to China and Japan. Buddhism calls on people to renounce their desires and search for enlightenment—the direct, intuitive experience of divine truth.

The Samurai

1100s–1800s

Like the knights of medieval Europe, Japan's samurai warriors are romantic, larger-than-life figures who still capture the popular imagination. The samurai were members of an aristocratic warrior class in feudal Japan. They lived according to bushido, a code of honor and conduct that called for self-sacrifice and absolute loyalty to a feudal lord, or daimyo. Samurai were so highly regarded that at one time they were allowed to kill anyone lower in rank who offended them. Although the samurai class was abolished in the nineteenth century, its influence on Japanese culture persists to this day.

Illustration of samurai warriors.

India, China, and Japan
2500 B.C.–A.D. 1800s

PREVIEW

Think About ...

India, China, and Japan all boast rich, diverse, and long-lasting literary traditions. India is known for its sacred hymns, epics, dramas, and court poems, most of which reflect the beliefs of India's dominant religion, Hinduism.

Perhaps no culture has produced as much superb poetry as China, where poetry is revered as the highest art form. Influenced by Confucianism, Taoism, and Buddhism, Chinese poetry tends to focus on the contemplation of nature and the search for inner harmony. The Chinese are also known for their philosophical and historical writings.

Japanese poetry is distinguished by such forms as tanka and haiku. Japan is also famous for its unique dramatic forms, such as Noh plays, as well as for its prose tradition.

As you read about the history and literature of India, China, and Japan, look for answers to the following questions:

- How have the Hindu concepts of dharma, karma, the caste system, and reincarnation influenced Indian literature and culture?

- What are the central beliefs of Confucianism, Taoism, and Buddhism?

- What historical and cultural developments have influenced Japanese literature?

SKILLS FOCUS

Collection introduction (pages 350–364) covers

Literary Skills
Evaluate the philosophical, historical, and cultural influences of the historical period.

Indian Literature

We are not sure who the first settlers of India were, but we do know that an advanced civilization flourished in northern India between 2500 and 1500 B.C. Scholars call it the **Indus Valley** civilization, after the river that runs through the region. Artifacts from this sophisticated civilization show striking similarities to the art of later Hindu culture in India.

Leaf from a *Chandana Malayagiri Varta* series (1754).
Rajasthan. Marwar/Jodhpur.

The Aryans and the Vedic Period

The death blow to the Indus Valley civilization came around 1500 B.C., with a wave of migrations from the northwest. The newcomers, now called Aryans, were aggressive nomadic, or wandering, warriors and herders, who had superior copper and bronze weapons. The language they spoke gave rise to Old Persian, an ancient language spoken in what is now Iran, and Sanskrit, an ancient Indian language. All of these languages descended from an older parent language known as Proto-Indo-European.

The first literary period in India is known as the **Vedic** period; it lasted from approximately 1500 B.C. to approximately 500 B.C. This

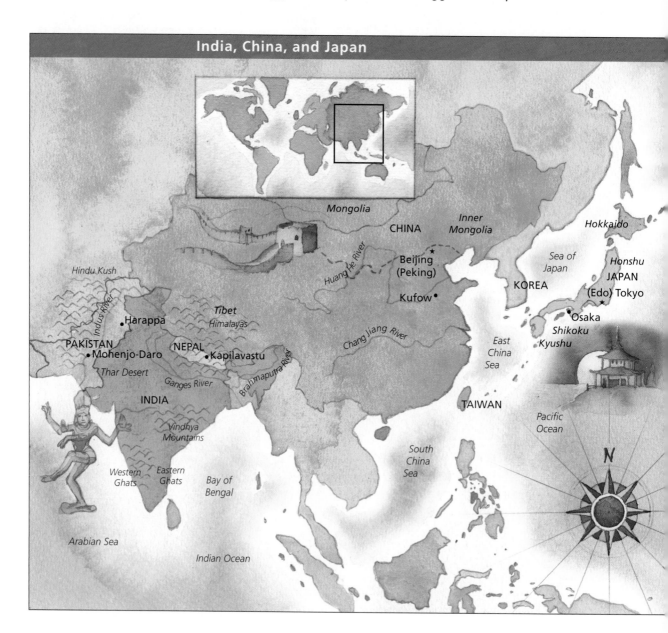

India, China, and Japan

period is named for the **Vedas** (vā′dəz), a collection of hymns and other texts that formed the cornerstone of Aryan culture. Many Hindus believe that these sacred hymns were revealed to humans directly by the gods.

The Classical Period: The Legacy of Sanskrit

After the Vedic period ended, Indian literature entered its classical period, which lasted until about A.D. 1000. The main literary language of northern India during this period was an Indo-European language, Sanskrit. The main languages of southern India come from an independent family of languages with ancient roots in the Indian subcontinent: the Dravidian (drə·vid′ē·ən) languages, such as Tamil (tam′əl) and Kannada (kä′nə·də).

One of the most fascinating facts about Sanskrit is that by 600 B.C., it had become a "frozen" literary language. While everyday speech changed and evolved, the written form of Sanskrit remained in a fixed state for centuries, its grammar and syntax virtually unaffected by time. An analogy would be if we today wrote everything in Old English, the language used in Anglo-Saxon literary works such as *Beowulf.*

Sanskrit (the name means "perfect speech") is one of the most important legacies of ancient Indian civilization. It is considered a sacred language, spoken by the gods. As such, Sanskrit was seen as the only appropriate form of expression for the noblest literary works, such as epics, court poems, and dramas.

Like the ancient Greeks, the Indians produced two great epics— the *Mahabharata* (mə·hä′bä′rə·tə) (see page 370) and the *Ramayana* (rä·mä′yə·nə) (see page 388). These works had been part of India's oral tradition for centuries, but they were finally written down in a more or less fixed form during the classical period.

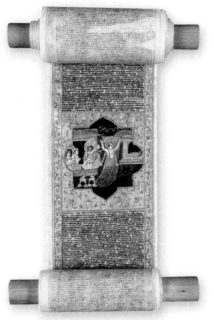

Text of the *Sri Bhagavata Purána.*
The British Library, London.

Hinduism: Unity in Diversity

It is impossible to understand the Indian literary tradition—which claims more texts than the ancient Greek and Roman traditions combined—without speaking of the religion followed by the majority of India's more than one billion people: **Hinduism.**

Hinduism evolved from the beliefs of the Aryans of the Vedic period. More than a religion, Hinduism is a way of life, with a seemingly endless variety of beliefs, rituals, and gods. It has no written doctrines or set of rules and no single prophet or religious leader, like Christ or Mohammad. Its pantheon, or assembly of gods, consists of innumerable deities by some counts. Three deities, called the Trimurti ("Three Forms") stand out in the ancient Hindu pantheon: Brahma (brä′mə) the Creator, Vishnu (vish′no͞o) the Protector, and Shiva (shē·və) the Destroyer/Preserver. In Hinduism

Relief of Hindu gods and goddesses from the Sri Murugan Temple.

today, the mother goddess, Shakti, consort of Shiva, is also a central deity. She may take several forms, including that of Kali, who presides over the cycles of creation and destruction.

Despite the enormous number of cults and sects in Hinduism, many Hindus believe that all the gods—indeed, everything in the universe—are aspects of a single essence, or immortal spirit. This belief in the ultimate oneness of existence serves as a counterweight to the diversity of India's enormous population and its many different classes of people and methods of worship.

Lessons of Indian Literature: Following One's Dharma

The two great Hindu epics, the *Mahabharata* and the *Ramayana*, vividly illustrate the teachings of Hinduism, particularly the concepts of dharma, karma, and reincarnation. **Dharma** (där′mə) comes from a Sanskrit verb meaning "to hold." The English word closest in meaning to *dharma* is "religion." Dharma also encompasses such concepts as duty, righteousness, ethics, morality, law, and order.

According to Hindu belief, everyone is born with a unique dharma, which unfolds through a person's lifetime according to his or her choices. Most of the lessons of dharma—what to do or not do in a given situation—must be determined by the individual on a moment-by-moment basis. There are times when even the most righteous person, such as the god Krishna in the *Mahabharata,* must lie or act in other unrighteous ways in order to be in accordance with his or her dharma. Ultimately, dharma requires that a person fulfill the duties of his or her station in life, however lofty or humble it might be.

The Caste System, Karma, and Reincarnation

A person's dharma is determined in part by his or her **caste** (kast), or social class. In the Hindu tradition, people are not created equal. Rather, they are categorized at birth into one of four ranks of society, generally based on occupation. (There are literally thousands of sub-castes.) Hindu religious law uses the word *varna* (vur′nə), meaning "color" or "rank," to refer to the order of the various castes. The origin of the varnas goes back at least to the Rig-Veda (see page 366). According to one Vedic hymn, the varnas resulted from the sacrifice of the primal, or first, man. His body was divided into the four varnas: From his head came the **Brahmans** (brä′mənz), the scholars, priests, and teachers; from his torso came the **Kshatriyas** (kə·shat′rē·yəz), the rulers and warriors; from his thighs came the **Vaisyas** (vīs′yəz), the merchants, farmers, and artisans; and from his feet came the **Sudras** (soo′drəz), those who do menial work. Excluded from society altogether are the so-called untouchables, whose tasks include disposing of dead animals and cleaning up human waste. In Hindu tradition, untouchables are believed to pollute others simply by touch or by sight.

Many Hindus believe in the concepts of karma and reincarnation. *Karma* is a Sanskrit word meaning "action." **Reincarnation,** also known as the "transmigration of souls," is the rebirth of a deceased person's soul in another body. One's actions, or karma, in this life influence one's rebirth and future life. A person with good karma will be reborn into a higher caste. When a soul is sufficiently purified, it is united with Brahman, the ultimate spiritual reality.

Buddhism: The Search for Spiritual Peace

During the close of the Vedic period, another major religion, **Buddhism,** came into being. Buddhism was founded by **Siddhartha Gautama** (sid·där′tə gou′tə·mə) (563–483 B.C.), a young prince who gave up a life of wealth and privilege to search for spiritual peace. (*Buddha* means "Enlightened One," a title given to Siddhartha by his followers.) Buddha came to believe that life is an endless cycle of suffering caused by the desire for earthly goods. The way to master this desire is to practice **yoga** (from a Sanskrit word meaning "union"), a spiritual practice that combines asceticism, or self-denial, with meditation, breathing practices, specific postures, and ethical, nonviolent behavior. Buddhism rejects the social stratification of the Hindu caste system.

By the twelfth century A.D., Buddhism had nearly disappeared in India, but it has had a lasting influence on Hinduism. Many Hindus practice some form of vegetarianism, in accordance with Buddhist teachings, and the contemplative life preached by Buddha remains a key aspect of Hinduism.

> *When doubts haunt me, when disappointments stare me in the face, and I see not one ray of light on the horizon, I turn to the* Bhagavad-Gita, *and find a verse to comfort me; and I immediately begin to smile in the midst of overwhelming sorrow.*
>
> —Mohandas Gandhi

Amida Buddha (late 12th century). Japanese sculpture, from the Kamakura period.

The Minneapolis Institute of Arts. The John R. Van Derlip Fund (78.20).

Islam in India

Islam was brought to western India by Arab traders in the eighth century A.D. By 1236, the first Muslim kingdom in India was established in Delhi. Muslim expansion continued in India for centuries, with countless Islamic and Hindu dynasties and empires fighting for dominance. Muslim conquests eventually led to the establishment of the Mughal (or Mogul) Empire, which lasted from 1526 to 1858. Yet, just as the Muslims were not absorbed into Hinduism, neither was India overwhelmed by Islamic culture and religion. Eventually, in 1947, as tensions built between the two groups, India was partitioned into two states: Pakistan for Muslims, and India for Hindus.

A CLOSER LOOK: CULTURAL INFLUENCES

Mughal Masterpieces

"A sublime monument to love." "Paintings of court life so dazzling it could not be imagined." These words describe two of the fabulous works of art produced during the Mughal Empire, which dominated India from 1526 to 1858. The Mughals, who migrated from Turkestan, spread Islamic culture throughout India. The result was a fascinating fusion of Indian and Middle Eastern artistic styles.

Art and architecture flourished under the Mughal emperor Shah Jahan, who ruled from 1628 to 1658. To memorialize his beloved wife Mumtaz Mahal, who had died in childbirth, Jahan built the Taj Mahal in the city of Agra. The Taj, which took over twenty thousand workers and more than twenty years to complete, consists of a tomb and a mosque that seem to float over a reflecting pool, surrounded by gardens that evoke the Islamic vision of Paradise. The Taj has a beautiful dome flanked by four graceful minarets; the dome is inlaid with precious gems and decorated with quotes from the Koran.

Taj Mahal and
reflecting pool.

INFORMATIONAL TEXT

Another masterpiece commissioned by Shah Jahan is the *Padshahnama*, or *Chronicle of the King of the World*, a collection of forty-four exquisite miniature paintings that chronicle the years of Shah Jahan's reign.

No storyteller could depict the splendor of Shah Jahan's court as rendered in the *Padshahnama*. Here we see weddings and executions, hunts, elephant fights, and court rituals; we see jeweled turbans, Agra carpets, silken canopies, elephants in gold carrying harem ladies, and horses with gold and silver bridles. The paintings are done in such fine detail that we see the horrified expressions of the witnesses to an execution—as well as flies buzzing around the severed head.

Chinese Literature

Chinese civilization has existed for nearly four thousand years—longer than any other world culture. The art of writing, using a unique "alphabet" of more than three thousand characters, developed in the second millennium (2000–1000) B.C. in China, and with it came the beginning of a literary tradition that continues to this day.

Chinese History: Dynastic Rule

China's history is characterized by periods of stability enforced by a strong central authority, followed by struggles between warring local princes and rival families trying to overthrow a ruling family, or dynasty.

The **Shang** (shän) dynasty, which came to power in China around 1766 B.C. and continued until 1122 B.C., is the first period of family rule for which there is historical evidence. It was during the Shang reign that the unique system of Chinese writing began to develop. Unlike our modest alphabet of twenty-six letters representing a limited number of sounds, the thousands of characters in the Chinese alphabet represent complete words or units of meaning.

The **Chou** (jō), the longest-lasting dynasty in Chinese history, overthrew the Shang and held power until about 256 B.C. The Chou established a structure of imperial rule that became the model of government for China until the early twentieth century. The emperor, usually the oldest son of the ruling family, controlled a vast territory by creating a network of local government officials whose advancement depended on their loyalty to the imperial family.

In 221 B.C., the **Ch'in** dynasty overpowered the Chou. (Some believe the name *China* derives from *Ch'in.*) The Ch'in rulers connected and fortified their empire by building roads and constructing a fifteen-hundred-mile defensive wall, now known as the Great Wall of China, across their northern border.

The **Han** (hän), **T'ang** (täŋ), and **Sung** (so͞oŋ) dynasties that followed were periods of expansion and greater contact with the outside world. Literature, the arts, technology, and trade flourished; yet each dynasty in turn eventually succumbed to corruption and infighting.

Portrait of Emperor K'ang-hsi, (reigned 1661–1722) Ch'ing dynasty.

Figure sitting on a riverbank, from the *Album of Eight Landscape Paintings* by Shen Chou (c. 1427–1509 C.E.). Ming dynasty.

Outside Influences

The **Mongols,** a warlike, semi-nomadic people from northeastern Asia, conquered imperial China in the late twelfth century A.D. The Mongols were overthrown and Chinese rule was restored in 1368 with the rise of the **Ming** dynasty. The Ming and later dynasties sought to reassert Chinese culture by limiting contact with foreign influences.

Despite centuries of Chinese efforts to limit outside influence, the expanding nations of nineteenth-century Europe (Great Britain, France, Germany, and Russia) forced the imperial authority to grant them large areas of Chinese territory, which the colonial powers ran for their own economic advantage.

Twentieth-century China witnessed civil war and the installation of a harsh Communist regime. But even the last five decades of Communist rule have run true to the age-old pattern of Chinese political history. Periods of stability have followed times of unrest; revolutionary fervor has given way to greater ideological flexibility; periodic demands for more democracy have been brutally crushed by a totalitarian central government.

Chinese Religion and Philosophy

Chinese literature, and indeed all of Chinese culture, has been profoundly influenced by three great schools of thought that originated in the sixth and fifth centuries B.C.: the philosophies of **Confucianism** and **Taoism** and the religion of **Buddhism,** which was founded in India.

Confucius (551–479 B.C.) was the first great Chinese teacher, and since his time the profession of teaching has commanded great respect in China. (The name *Confucius* is a Latinized version of the Chinese name *K'ung Fu-tzu.*) Confucius lived at a time of great political and social disorder; he was interested not in theology or the afterlife but in formulating principles for living a good life on earth. The teachings of Confucius are practical and conservative; they emphasize ethical values such as honesty, loyalty, respect for one's elders, love of learning, and moral restraint. Confucius did not write

> *Learning without thought is labor lost; thought without learning is perilous.*
>
> —from *The Confucian Analects*

A CLOSER LOOK: CULTURAL INFLUENCES

Teaching to the Test

INFORMATIONAL TEXT

If you think you have problems with standardized tests, consider the situation of a boy preparing for the civil service exams in imperial China more than 1,400 years ago. (Girls didn't have to worry about examinations, since they could not take civil service jobs. They hoped to marry and have sons who would excel in the examinations.)

Most boys wanted to work in the civil service, since it was considered the most honorable walk of life. To qualify, they had to take a series of extremely difficult examinations beginning after years of study. Those who passed were set for life as civil servants. This examination system lasted for almost fourteen hundred years; it was abolished in 1904 because the Chinese realized that education based on the memorization of classic texts was blocking the spread of new learning.

Boys began training for the examinations at home at the age of three. By the time they were eight, when their formal schooling began, they had learned a thousand basic Chinese ideograms, or written characters. By the age of fifteen, when their classical education was completed, they had memorized texts amounting to 431,286 characters. This meant they had memorized at the rate of two hundred characters a day for six years. Chinese education was based entirely on the texts of Confucius and books of poetry, documents, and rites. Students also learned to compose essays and formal poetry, since writing such pieces was part of the examinations.

The examiners tried to make the tests as difficult as possible. One test item asked where in the lengthy *Analects* the three particles *yeh, chi,* and *i* occur in sequence. When the question baffled the candidates, the examiners exclaimed, "We have outwitted them!"

An Ancient Chinese Public Examination (detail).

Bibliothèque Nationale de France, Paris.

down his teachings, but after his death they were recorded and compiled by his disciples in books now called the *Analects* (see page 408). The *Analects* formed the basis of Chinese education for centuries.

The next great teacher to influence Chinese thinking was **Laotzu** (lou′ dzu′), whose name is sometimes spelled Lao-tzu or Lao-tze. He was born around 570 B.C., and though little is known of his personal life, the values expressed in his book *Tao Te Ching* (see page 414) have greatly influenced Chinese thought and expression. Unlike Confucius, Laotzu was a mystic who believed that less government is better. Above all, the Taoist (dou′ist) philosophy founded by Laotzu regards nature as the great teacher. Taoists urge people to seek wisdom by turning their backs on the world and contemplating Tao, the mysterious force that governs and unifies all of nature.

Confucianism and Taoism were enriched by the arrival of a third powerful system of belief, Buddhism, brought from India during the Han dynasty. Buddhist thought stresses the importance of ridding oneself of earthly desires and seeking ultimate peace and enlightenment through detachment. The Buddhist emphasis on living ethically and transcending material concerns appealed to both Confucians and Taoists.

Bowl with yin-yang motif
(c. Qing dynasty, 1644–1911).
Musée des Arts Asiatiques-Guimet,
Paris.

The Balance of Opposites

Over their long history, the Chinese have endured and risen up from chaos and disaster again and again. This ability to endure might be traced to a perception of life as a process of continual change, in which opposing forces, such as heaven and earth or light and dark, balance one another. These opposites are symbolized by the yin and the yang. Yin, the passive, feminine force, counterbalances yang, the active, masculine force; and each contains a "seed" of the other, as represented in the traditional yin-yang symbol (see left). The yin-yang philosophy offers people hope during difficult times, since it teaches that evil contains the seed of good.

Chinese Literature

A reverence for literature and learning is an important aspect of Chinese culture. The volume of Chinese literature dwarfs that of all other literatures of the world; it has been estimated that more than half of all the books ever written are Chinese. Extensive knowledge of classic Chinese texts and the ability to write poetry were requirements for employment in the imperial bureaucracy, for centuries the main avenue to power and prestige for ambitious young men in China.

South wind and clear sky, from *36 Views of Mount Fuji* (c. 1823) by Katsusika Hokusai. Edo period.

Japanese Literature

Although Japan borrowed much from Chinese culture, including the Chinese system of writing, Japanese culture evolved its own character and style over time. The distinctiveness of Japanese culture grew out of the unique social arrangements and worldview of a people who, living on a starkly beautiful chain of mountainous islands, were largely isolated from their neighbors.

Japan's early political structure was based on clan, or family, divisions. Each clan consisted of a well-defined hierarchy of classes, with aristocrats, warriors, and priests at the top and peasants and workers at the bottom. Without any central authority, the clans constantly fought one another. Finally, in the fourth century A.D., one family, the **Yamato,** grew powerful enough to subdue the others.

The Yamato admired Chinese culture, political organization, and philosophy and took steps to introduce them to Japan. The Yamato prince **Shotoku** (shō·tō·kōo) actually imposed the Chinese imperial system on Japan during his reign (A.D. 593–622), creating an emperor, an imperial bureaucracy, and a grand capital city. In Japan, however, unlike in China, the emperor was largely a figurehead.

FAST FACTS

Philosophical Views

- The main tenets of Hinduism are dharma, karma, and reincarnation.

- Buddha teaches that life is an endless cycle of suffering caused by the desire for material goods.

- Confucius sets forth a philosophy emphasizing practical values.

- Taoism emphasizes the contemplation of Tao, the force that rules nature.

The Feudal Era: Warlords and Samurai

In the eighth century A.D., ambitious aristocrats began to amass huge private estates in the countryside, beyond the reach of the imperial authority. These lords surrounded themselves with professional warriors, called samurai (sam′ə·rī′). The samurai lived by a strict code of conduct, which was somewhat like the chivalric code of the knights of medieval Europe. Unlike chivalry, however, the samurai code was based more on absolute loyalty to one's overlord and on the concept of personal honor than on religious ideals.

In the latter part of the twelfth century, a strongman named Yoritomo seized control of the empire and had himself declared shogun, or general. Over the next four centuries a series of shoguns ruled Japan, but none could subdue the feuding warlords, who kept the country in a state of constant warfare.

The Downfall of Feudalism

Finally, in the late 1500s, a powerful shogun crushed the warring feudal lords, and the **Tokugawa shogunate,** or shogun-ruled regime, began to rule all of Japan from a new capital at Edo, later called Tokyo. At about this time, the Western world was seeking contact with Japan. These contacts alarmed the shogunate, which feared revolt at home or invasion from abroad. By 1633, Japan had become a closed society: All foreigners were expelled, Japanese Christians were persecuted, and the Japanese were forbidden to leave the country under penalty of death.

The Japanese maintained this policy of isolation for two centuries. Then, in 1853, Commodore Matthew Perry of the United States Navy steamed into Tokyo Bay, demanding that Japan open its doors to the West. Treaties were negotiated, and Japan began to trade with the Western powers. As feared, outside influences did cause change in Japan. The shogunate ended in 1868, and Japan, under a new and more powerful emperor, rapidly acquired the latest technological knowledge, introduced universal education, and created an impressive industrial economy.

Statue traditionally identified as Minamoto no Yoritomo, from the Kamakura period (c. 13th century).
Collection of the Tokyo National Museum.

Shintoism and Zen Buddhism

Followers of **Shintoism,** the ancient religion of Japan, revere divine spirits called kami, which reside in natural places and objects. Ancestors and the emperor were also regarded as divine. The native Shinto tradition easily accommodated the various strains of Buddhism adopted by the Japanese from the Chinese and the Koreans beginning in the fifth and sixth centuries A.D.

Although **Buddhism** originated in India, it was developed by Chinese monks and scholars and evolved into a number of schools or sects quite distinct from their Indian counterparts. Although followers of all schools of Buddhism sought spiritual freedom and inner tranquility, the various sects recommended different paths to this goal. **Zen Buddhism,** for example, imported from China in about 1200, challenged the intellectualism of older sects and advocated meditation, concentration, and self-discipline as the way to enlightenment. Zen priests and institutions helped develop the tea ceremony, landscape gardening, and military arts such as judo.

Japanese Literature: Pride in Poetry

Although originally inspired by Chinese models and preceded by a long oral tradition, Japanese literature came into its own after the fifth century A.D., when the Japanese adopted the Chinese system of writing, modifying it to fit their own needs.

As in China, composing poetry has always been a highly respected activity in Japan. From the beginnings of imperial government to the present day, poetry writing has been encouraged by official competition and rewarded by publication in anthologies. **Tanka,** a form that emerged in the eighth century A.D., is characterized by brief lyrical bursts of feeling and highly condensed language (see page 440). The tendency toward compression in Japanese poetry reached a peak in **haiku** (hī′kōō′), a form developed in the seventeenth century (see page 446).

Two Great Women Writers

The greatest flowering of classical Japanese prose occurred during the **Heian** (hā′än) **period** (A.D. 794–1185), when a leisurely life at court made it possible for two well-educated women to chronicle the hothouse atmosphere in which they lived. In the long and detailed *The Tale of Genji,* considered by many scholars to be the world's first true novel, the aristocrat Lady Murasaki Shikibu, a lady-in-waiting to the empress, traces the amorous life of a gifted and charming prince. Murasaki's novel has been widely translated, and today she is as highly

Japanese poetry has as its subject the human heart. It may seem to be of no practical use and just as well left uncomposed, but when one knows poetry well, one understands also without explanation the reasons governing order and disorder in the world.

—Kamo Mabuchi

regarded in Japan as William Shakespeare is in English-speaking countries. Another tenth-century court lady, Sei Shōnagon, immortalized the Heian age in her witty and revealing journal about court life, *The Pillow Book* (see page 456).

Japanese Drama

The most distinctive form of Japanese drama is called **Noh** (nō), which means "talent" or "skill." The purpose of the philosophical Noh dramas is to invoke a moment of wisdom in the tradition of Zen Buddhism. **Kabuki** (kä·bōō′kē), on the other hand, is a more theatrical kind of play involving dancing and singing, which was popular with a more general audience. Kabuki drama uses stock characters and stylized situations.

(Top) Noh mask of a young monk (c. 1370), from the Muromachi period.

Noh Theatre Collection, Kongo School, Kyoto.

(Bottom) Kabuki actors onstage for a performance of *Yoshitsume*.

REVIEW

Talk About . . .

Turn back to the Think About questions at the beginning of this introduction (page 350). Write down your responses; then, get together with classmates to compare and discuss your views.

Reading Check

1. Why is Sanskrit considered a "frozen language"?
2. Name one difference between Hinduism and Buddhism.
3. Summarize the philosophies of Confucianism and Taoism.

4. What does the traditional Chinese yin-yang symbol represent?
5. What caused Japan to become a closed society? When did it "open" again?

Literature of India, China, and Japan:

The Search for Truth and Enlightenment

Indian Literature

Find a wise teacher, honor him,
ask him your questions, serve him;
someone who has seen the truth
will guide you on the path to wisdom.

—*from the* Bhagavad-Gita,
translated by Stephen Mitchell

Reception Scene (detail)
(c. early 18th century). Mughal school.

Brooklyn Museum of Art, New York. A. Augustus
Healy Fund (41.1175).

365

Rig-Veda
(c. 1000 B.C.)

The Rig-Veda (rig′vā′də) is a collection of more than one thousand hymns revered as sacred texts of the Hindu religion. The original hymns are in an archaic form of Sanskrit, an ancient Indo-European language brought to India by the Aryans, who migrated from the west around 1500 B.C.

The Rig-Veda—the name means "hymns of supreme sacred knowledge"—is one of four Vedas, the most sacred books of Hinduism. In fact, the Rig-Veda is considered the most important book of Vedic scripture. The hymns began as part of sacred rituals in the lives of the Aryan people but survived to become a cornerstone of Hinduism. Because the Hindus regarded the Rig-Veda as being divinely inspired, or "heard" directly from the gods, they thought it only fitting that later generations also "hear" the hymns. Thus, even after Sanskrit became a written language, the hymns were transmitted orally by Vedic priests.

Generations of Brahmans (brä′mənz), or Hindu priests, learned the Vedic hymns according to a strict method of memorization. Today we can appreciate how effective this method was by comparing written versions of the Rig-Veda made by different scribes at different times: The hymns appear in practically the same words in each manuscript.

The Vedas reveal a great deal about early Indo-European civilizations. We know that the Aryans who came to India were nomads, people with no permanent home. According to the Vedic hymns, the Aryans eventually settled down and became farmers who raised crops and livestock, built simple huts, wore woven wool clothing, made iron tools, and developed communities. The hymns also tell us that the Aryan settlers had their share of social problems, including drunkenness, gambling, and fighting. Above all, the hymns reveal that the Aryans were a highly poetic people who worshiped the forces of nature.

The Aryans laid the foundation for a powerful religious faith: Hinduism. Hindu worship today generally departs a great deal from the rituals outlined in the ancient Vedic texts. On occasions such as weddings and funerals, however, Brahman priests in modern India still solemnly chant hymns from the Vedas.

Victoria & Albert Museum, London.

Page with a lady holding a blossom from the *Small Clive Album* (18th century). Mughal school.

Night
from the **Rig-Veda**

Make the Connection
Quickwrite ✎
In many literary works, as well as in everyday life, night is often associated with danger or evil. The ancient Aryans, however, believed that night also had some beneficial and beautiful aspects. What qualities do you associate with night? Freewrite your response.

Literary Focus
Hymn
A **hymn** is a lyric poem, or song, addressed to a divine being. Through hymns, people praise the power and wisdom of their deities. Hymns may also be requests for divine aid or mercy. Usually intended to be sung during ceremonies or religious worship, most hymns are formal and dignified in tone. The hymn "Night" achieves two purposes: It sings the praises of the goddess of night and enlists her help in protecting the singer's community.

> A **hymn** is a lyric poem, or song, addressed to a divine being.
>
> *For more on Hymn, see the Handbook of Literary and Historical Terms.*

Background
The Rig-Veda contains not only the oldest Vedic hymns but also the most lyrical ones. In their beauty and simplicity, these hymns have been compared to the psalms of the Hebrew Bible.

In Vedic literature a god was assigned to nearly every aspect of nature. For example, the god Surya was associated with the sun and the god Agni was associated with fire. The hymns were songs of praise for the beauty and wonders of nature. They were also prayers for protection and cooperation from natural forces. "Night," like many of the Vedic hymns, reveals that the ancient nomads who sang these songs both loved and feared the natural world around them.

Of the ten books of the Rig-Veda, "Night" is the only hymn dedicated to Ratri (rä′trē), the goddess of night. Night was thought to be a sister of Dawn, a bright goddess. Instead of being depicted as simply dark, Night is also described as a bright deity whose eyes, the stars, drive away the darkness.

INTERNET
More About the Rig-Vega
Keyword:
LE5 WL-3

SKILLS FOCUS

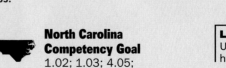
North Carolina Competency Goal
1.02; 1.03; 4.05; 5.01; 5.03; 6.01

Literary Skills
Understand hymns.

Night

from the Rig-Veda

translated by Wendy Doniger O'Flaherty

1. The goddess Night has drawn near, looking about on
   many sides with her eyes. She has put on all her glories.

2. The immortal goddess has filled the wide space, the
   depths and the heights. She stems the tide of darkness
   with her light.

3. The goddess has drawn near, pushing aside her sister
   the twilight. Darkness, too, will give way.

4. As you came near to us today, we turned homeward to
   rest, as birds go to their home in a tree.

5. People who live in villages have gone home to rest,
   and animals with feet, and animals with wings, even the
   ever-searching hawks.

6. Ward off the she-wolf and the wolf; ward off the thief.
   O night full of waves, be easy for us to cross over.

7. Darkness—palpable, black, and painted—has come
   upon me. O Dawn, banish it like a debt.

8. I have driven this hymn to you as the herdsman drives
   cows. Choose and accept it, O Night, daughter of the
   sky, like a song of praise to a conqueror.

Krishna gazes longingly at
Radha (detail) from the
Lumbagraon Gita Govinda
series (c. 1820–1825).
Punjab Hills, Kangra.

Brooklyn Museum of Art, Designated
Purchase Fund (72.43).

Response and Analysis

Thinking Critically

1. What positive or beneficial qualities of night are suggested in this **hymn**? How do these qualities compare with the features of night you listed in your Quickwrite?

2. **Personification** is a figure of speech in which a nonhuman thing is referred to as though it were human. In this hymn, Night is referred to as "she," as if it were a woman. What other details personify Night?

3. A **simile** is a figure of speech that makes a comparison between two unlike things using a word such as *like, as,* or *than.* Find at least three similes in this hymn. Explain what is being compared in each.

4. In a **metaphor,** two unlike things are compared directly, without the use of a comparative word such as *like.* What is being compared in the metaphor in the second part of verse 2 of the hymn?

5. **Apostrophe** is a figure of speech in which a speaker directly addresses an absent person, aspect of nature, or abstract quality as though it were present ("O mighty wind . . ."). The use of apostrophe is common in songs and hymns addressed to a deity. Which lines of this hymn contain examples of apostrophe, and who is being addressed in each? What is the effect of the apostrophes?

Extending and Evaluating

6. Although this hymn is set in an ancient world very different from ours, many of its details seem timeless. Which aspects of this poem seem contemporary and relevant to you? Which would probably not mean much to a modern reader?

WRITING

Comparing and Contrasting Two Hymns

In a two- or three-paragraph essay, compare and contrast the hymn "Night" from the Rig-Veda with the New Kingdom Egyptian hymn "The Great Hymn to the Aten" (see page 38). In your essay you may wish to consider the following points of each hymn:

- **subject**
- **purpose** (to praise the deity; to ask for divine help or mercy, etc.)
- **imagery** and **figures of speech** (similes, metaphors, personification, apostrophe, epithets, etc.)
- **tone** (dignified, informal, etc.)

Explore any other similarities or differences that you can find in the two hymns. In your concluding paragraph, speculate on the similarities and differences, as revealed in the hymns, between the views of the New Kingdom Egyptians and those of the ancient Aryans regarding their deities.

North Carolina Competency Goal
1.02; 1.03; 5.01; 5.03; 6.01

INTERNET

Projects and Activities
Keyword:
LE5 WL-3

SKILLS FOCUS

Literary Skills
Analyze hymns.

Writing Skills
Compare and contrast hymns.

Bhagavad-Gita

(c. 300 B.C.–c. A.D. 300)

The *Mahabharata* (mə·hä′bä′rə·tə), meaning "great story of Bharata's descendants," is one of the two great epics of ancient India. It tells about two rival families descended from a legendary king named Bharata: the Kauravas (kou′rä·vəz) and the Pandavas (pän′də·vəz). The central conflict of the epic is the rivalry between two sets of cousins over the kingdom of Kurukshetra (koo·roo·kshä′trə). The quarrel between the two families is ignited by Duryodhana (door·yō′də·nə), the eldest of the Kaurava branch of the family, who becomes jealous when his father gives a piece of the Kaurava kingdom to his cousins the Pandavas. In retaliation, Duryodhana challenges Yudhistira (yoo·dē′stē·rə), the eldest of the Pandava brothers, to a game of chance. By the end of the game, Yudhistira has lost all his wealth as well as his freedom and that of his brothers. Duryodhana then sentences the Pandavas to twelve years of exile in the forest.

The Bhagavad-Gita (bug′ə·vəd gē′tä)—literally "Song of the Lord"—is a long episode that interrupts the action of the *Mahabharata* at a point when the five Pandava brothers have returned from exile and are seeking to regain their share of the kingdom. Duryodhana decides to destroy the Pandavas, whom he regards as dangerous rivals. The armies of each side then mass for battle.

The Gita episode that follows consists of a dialogue between the Pandava brother Arjuna and his charioteer, Krishna, just before the great battle begins. The hero Arjuna sits weeping because he does not want to spill the blood of his relatives, the Kauravas. Krishna urges Arjuna to overcome his doubts and fight.

Krishna plays a double role in the epic. He is both Arjuna's human brother-in-law and, unbeknownst to the hero, the incarnation of Vishnu (vish′noo), one of the most important gods in the Hindu pantheon.

The Bhagavad-Gita is divided into eighteen sections, or "teachings," that deal with the nature of the body and the soul, the relationship of human beings to the divine, and ways to attain "the pure calm of infinity."

This ancient poem played a major role in shaping the philosophy of Mohandas Gandhi (1869–1948), who guided India to independence from Britain in 1947. Gandhi's philosophy of nonviolent protest profoundly influenced Martin Luther King, Jr., one of the leaders of the civil rights movement of the 1950s and 1960s. The teachings of the ancient Bhagavad-Gita have thus indirectly but critically affected modern American society.

Page with Krishna and Arjuna leaving for the battle (18th century). Kangra school.

Museum fuer Indische Kunst, Staatliche Museen zu Berlin.

Philosophy and Spiritual Discipline
from the **Bhagavad-Gita**

Make the Connection

How often do people experience a conflict between what they want to do (desire) and what they have to do (duty)? Think of one or two examples from your own experience or that of someone you know. How was the conflict resolved?

Literary Focus
Paradox

A **paradox** is an apparent contradiction that is actually true. For example, in this selection, Krishna states a paradox when he tells Arjuna, "Our bodies are known to end, / but the embodied self is enduring, / indestructible, and immeasurable. . . ." In Hinduism the "embodied self" is the spirit that inhabits the living body. The spirit endures; the body does not. As you read Krishna's words in the Bhagavad-Gita, you will find many such paradoxes.

> A **paradox** is an apparent contradiction that is actually true.
>
> *For more on Paradox, see the Handbook of Literary and Historical Terms.*

Reading Skills
Identifying the Speaker's Purpose

In this dialogue, Krishna is the principal speaker. As you read, clearly identify Krishna's purpose in talking to Arjuna. What does Krishna hope to accomplish? How does he use arguments to accomplish his purpose? To what qualities in Arjuna is Krishna trying to appeal?

Background

In this selection from the Bhagavad-Gita, Krishna urges the warrior Arjuna to fulfill his dharma, or sacred duty. Krishna argues that since it is the fate of every soul to be reincarnated, or assume another bodily form after death, Arjuna need not feel guilty about killing his enemies. The wise warrior should fulfill his dharma as a faithful Hindu and member of the warrior caste; he should not concern himself with worldly matters and should not care about pleasure or pain, profit or loss, success or failure. The narrator who reports this conversation between Krishna and Arjuna is Sanjaya, an attendant to Arjuna's blind uncle, King Dhritarashtra.

North Carolina Competency Goal
1.03; 4.05; 5.01; 5.03

Vocabulary Development

immutable (i·myoot′ə·bəl) *adj.*: unable to be changed.

manifest (man′ə·fest′) *adj.*: revealed.

impartial (im·pär′shəl) *adj.*: not favoring one thing over another.

mundane (mun·dān′) *adj.*: pertaining to the world.

lucid (loo′sid) *adj.*: rational.

INTERNET

Vocabulary Practice
•
More About the Bhagavad-Gita
Keyword: LE5 WL-3

Literary Skills
Understand paradox.

Reading Skills
Identify the speaker's purpose.

Philosophy and Spiritual Discipline

from the Bhagavad-Gita

translated by **Barbara Stoler Miller**

PRINCIPAL CHARACTERS IN THE BHAGAVAD-GITA

Sanjaya (sän·jī′ä): attendant to King Dhritarashtra.

Arjuna (är′jōō·nə): the third of the five Pandava brothers.

Krishna (krish′nə): Arjuna's charioteer, who is really a god.

Bhishma (bēsh′mə): great-uncle to the Pandava brothers.

Drona (drō′nə): Arjuna's teacher in archery.

Dhritarashtra (drē·tə·räsh′trə): Arjuna's uncle and father of the Pandavas' enemies, the Kauravas.

Sanjaya

1 Arjuna sat dejected,
   filled with pity,
   his sad eyes blurred by tears.
   Krishna gave him counsel.

Lord Krishna

2 Why this cowardice
   in time of crisis,
      Arjuna?
   The coward is
      ignoble, shameful,
   foreign to the ways
      of heaven.

2–3. One of the main tenets of Hinduism is the importance of fulfilling one's dharma, or sacred duty.

[?] *After reading Lord Krishna's words to Arjuna in these two stanzas, what can you infer about Arjuna's dharma?*

3 Don't yield to impotence![1]
   It is unnatural in you!
   Banish this petty weakness from your heart.
   Rise to the fight, Arjuna!

Arjuna

4 Krishna, how can I fight
   against Bhishma and Drona
   with arrows
   when they deserve my worship?

5 It is better in this world
   to beg for scraps of food
   than to eat meals
   smeared with the blood
   of elders I killed
   at the height of their power
   while their goals
   were still desires.

6 We don't know which weight
   is worse to bear—
   our conquering them
   or their conquering us.
   We will not want to live
   if we kill
   the sons of Dhritarashtra
   assembled before us.

7 The flaw of pity
   blights[2] my very being;
   conflicting sacred duties
   confound my reason.
   I ask you to tell me
   decisively—Which is better?
   I am your pupil.
   Teach me what I seek!

---

1. **impotence** (im′pə·təns) *n*.: weakness.
2. **blights** *v*.: damages.

Illustration of the musical mode of Megha Raga. Manuscript page from a *Ragamala* series (c. 1760). Mughal school.
The British Library, London.

8 I see nothing
that could drive away
the grief
that withers my senses;
even if I won kingdoms
of unrivaled wealth
on earth
and sovereignty over gods.

Sanjaya

9 Arjuna told this
to Krishna—then saying,
"I shall not fight,"
he fell silent.

10 Mocking him gently,
Krishna gave this counsel
as Arjuna sat dejected,
between the two armies.

Lord Krishna

11 You grieve for those beyond grief,
and you speak words of insight;
but learned men do not grieve
for the dead or the living.

12 Never have I not existed,
nor you, nor these kings;
and never in the future
shall we cease to exist.

13 Just as the embodied self
enters childhood, youth,
    and old age,
so does it enter another
    body;
this does not confound a
    steadfast man.

> **12.** Paraphrase Krishna's words here. What does he mean when he says, "Never have I not existed" and "never in the future / shall we cease to exist"? To what Hindu tenet, or belief, do his words refer?

14 Contacts with matter make us feel
heat and cold, pleasure and pain.
Arjuna, you must learn to endure
fleeting things—they come and go!

15 When these cannot torment a man,
when suffering and joy are equal
for him and he has courage,
he is fit for immortality.

16 Nothing of nonbeing comes to be,
nor does being cease to exist;
the boundary between these two
is seen by men who see reality.

17 Indestructible is the presence
that pervades all this;
no one can destroy
this unchanging reality.

18 Our bodies are known to end,
but the embodied self is enduring,
indestructible, and immeasurable;
therefore, Arjuna, fight the battle!

19 He who thinks this self a killer
and he who thinks it killed,
both fail to understand;
it does not kill, nor is it killed.

20 It is not born,
it does not die;
having been,
it will never not be;
unborn, enduring,
constant, and
    primordial,
it is not killed
when the body is killed.

> **18–20.** Keep in mind that Arjuna is hesitant to kill his elders, especially those he admires.
>
> **?** Why is the concept of reincarnation important in Krishna's argument that Arjuna fight against Bhishma and Drona?

21 Arjuna, when a man knows the self
to be indestructible, enduring, unborn,
unchanging, how does he kill
or cause anyone to kill?

22 As a man discards
worn-out clothes
to put on new
and different ones,
so the embodied self
discards
its worn-out bodies
to take on other new ones.

23 Weapons do not cut it,
fire does not burn it,
waters do not wet it,
wind does not wither it.

24 It cannot be cut or burned;
it cannot be wet or withered;
it is enduring, all-pervasive,
fixed, immovable, and timeless.

25 It is called unmanifest,
inconceivable, and immutable;
since you know that to be so,
you should not grieve!

26 If you think of its birth
and death as ever-recurring,
then too, Great Warrior,
you have no cause to grieve!

27 Death is certain for anyone born,
and birth is certain for the dead;
since the cycle is inevitable,
you have no cause to grieve!

28 Creatures are unmanifest in origin,
manifest in the midst of life,
and unmanifest again in the end.
Since this is so, why do you lament?

29 Rarely someone
sees it,
rarely another
speaks it,
rarely anyone
hears it—
even hearing it,
no one really knows it.

30 The self embodied in the body
of every being is indestructible;
you have no cause to grieve
for all these creatures, Arjuna!

31 Look to your own duty;
do not tremble before it;
nothing is better for a warrior
than a battle of sacred duty.

32 The doors of heaven open
for warriors who rejoice
to have a battle like this
thrust on them by chance.

33 If you fail to wage this war
of sacred duty,
you will abandon your own duty
and fame only to gain evil.

34 People will tell
of your undying shame,
and for a man of honor
shame is worse than death.

? 33–36. *What consequences will Arjuna face if he does not follow his duty by fighting?*

35 The great chariot warriors will think
you deserted in fear of battle;
you will be despised
by those who held you in esteem.

36 Your enemies will slander you,
scorning your skill
in so many unspeakable ways—
could any suffering be worse?

37 If you are killed, you win heaven;
if you triumph, you enjoy the earth;
therefore, Arjuna, stand up
and resolve to fight the battle!

38 Impartial to joy and suffering,
gain and loss, victory and defeat,
arm yourself for the battle,
lest you fall into evil.

39 Understanding is defined in terms of
      philosophy;
now hear it in spiritual discipline.
Armed with this understanding, Arjuna,
you will escape the bondage of action.

Vocabulary

immutable (i·my$\overline{oo}$t′ə·bəl) *adj.*: unable to be changed.
manifest (man′ə·fest′) *adj.*: revealed.
impartial (im·pär′shəl) *adj.*: not favoring one thing over
    another.

40 No effort in this world
   is lost or wasted;
   a fragment of sacred duty
   saves you from great fear.

41 This understanding is unique
   in its inner core of resolve;
   diffuse and pointless are the ways
   irresolute[3] men understand.

42 Undiscerning men who
        delight
   in the tenets of ritual lore
   utter florid speech,
        proclaiming,
   "There is nothing else!"

> **42–44.** How does Krishna characterize the men he calls "undiscerning"?

43 Driven by desire, they strive after heaven
   and contrive to win powers and delights,
   but their intricate ritual language
   bears only the fruit of action in rebirth.

44 Obsessed with powers and delights,
   their reason lost in words,
   they do not find in contemplation
   this understanding of inner resolve.

45 Arjuna, the realm of sacred lore
   is nature—beyond its triad of qualities,
   dualities, and mundane rewards,
   be forever lucid, alive to your self.

46 For the discerning priest,
   all of sacred lore
   has no more value than a well
   when water flows everywhere.

47 Be intent on action,
   not on the fruits of action;
   avoid attraction to the fruits
   and attachment to inaction!

48 Perform actions, firm in discipline,
   relinquishing attachment;
   be impartial to failure and success—
   this equanimity is called discipline.

---

3. **irresolute** (i·rez′ə·lōōt′) *adj.*: unable to make decisions

49 Arjuna, action is far inferior
   to the discipline of understanding;
   so seek refuge in understanding—pitiful
   are men drawn by fruits of action.

50 Disciplined by understanding,
   one abandons both good and
        evil deeds;
   so arm yourself for discipline—
   discipline is skill in actions.

> **50–51.** According to these stanzas, how does one acquire wisdom in one's actions?

51 Wise men disciplined by understanding
   relinquish the fruit born of action;
   freed from these bonds of rebirth,
   they reach a place beyond decay.

52 When your understanding passes beyond
   the swamp of delusion,
   you will be indifferent to all
   that is heard in sacred lore.

53 When your understanding turns
   from sacred lore to stand fixed,
   immovable in contemplation,
   then you will reach discipline.

Arjuna

54 Krishna, what defines a man
   deep in contemplation whose insight
   and thought are sure? How would he speak?
   How would he sit? How would he move?

Lord Krishna

55 When he gives up desires in his mind,
   is content with the self within himself,
   then he is said to be a man
   whose insight is sure, Arjuna.

56 When suffering does not disturb his mind,
   when his craving for pleasures has vanished,
   when attraction, fear, and anger are gone,
   he is called a sage whose thought is sure.

Vocabulary

mundane (mun·dān′) *adj.*: pertaining to the world.
lucid (lōō′sid) *adj.*: rational.

Arjuna and Krishna (detail) (c. 1761–1763). Manuscript page from *Razmnama*, a Persian translation of the *Mahabharata*.

The British Library, London. (Add. 5639, f.140v).

57 When he shows no preference
in fortune or misfortune
and neither exults nor hates,
his insight is sure.

58 When, like a tortoise retracting
its limbs, he withdraws his senses
completely from sensuous objects,
his insight is sure.

58. An **analogy** is a comparison of two seemingly dissimilar things that actually are similar in some respects.

? *In what way does Krishna say a wise man is similar to a "tortoise retracting its limbs"?*

59 Sensuous objects fade
when the embodied self abstains
    from food;
the taste lingers, but it too fades
in the vision of higher truth.

60 Even when a man of wisdom
tries to control them, Arjuna,
the bewildering senses
attack his mind with violence.

61 Controlling them all,
    with discipline he should focus
        on me;
    when his senses are under control,
    his insight is sure.

62 Brooding about sensuous objects
    makes attachment to them grow;
    from attachment desire arises,
    from desire anger is born.

63 From anger comes confusion;
    from confusion memory lapses;
    from broken memory understanding is lost;
    from loss of understanding, he is ruined.

64 But a man of inner strength
    whose senses experience objects
    without attraction and hatred,
    in self-control, finds serenity.

65 In serenity, all his sorrows
    dissolve;
    his reason becomes
        serene,
    his understanding sure.

64–65. *According to these stanzas, what is the result of giving up the desire for earthly things?*

66 Without discipline,
    he has no understanding or inner power;
    without inner power, he has no peace;
    and without peace where is joy?

67 If his mind submits to the play
    of the senses,

they drive away insight,
as wind drives a ship on water.

68 So, Great Warrior, when
        withdrawal
    of the senses
    from sense objects is
        complete,
    discernment is firm.

68. A **paradox** is a statement that appears contradictory but is actually true. *According to the arguments Krishna is using, how can "withdrawal of the senses" lead to discernment, or clear perception? (How can a person perceive without access to senses?)*

69 When it is night for all
        creatures,
    a master of restraint is
        awake;
    when they are awake, it is night
    for the sage who sees reality.

70 As the mountainous depths
    of the ocean
    are unmoved when waters
    rush into it,
    so the man unmoved
    when desires enter him
    attains a peace that eludes
    the man of many desires.

70. *How is someone who has renounced desires similar to ocean depths?*

71 When he renounces all desires
    and acts without craving,
    possessiveness,
    or individuality, he finds peace.

72 This is the place of the infinite spirit;
    achieving it, one is freed from delusion;
    abiding in it even at the time of death,
    one finds the pure calm of infinity.

Arjuna and His Charioteer, Lord Krsna Con. Darhwal school, India.

The great Indian leader Mohandas K. Gandhi was profoundly influenced by the Bhagavad-Gita, a book that taught him to free himself from money, property, ambition, and other material concerns. The following article explains why Gandhi is considered a "person of the century," someone who had a profound and lasting influence on the twentieth century—and beyond.

Person of the Century: Mohandas Gandhi (1869–1948)

INFORMATIONAL TEXT

Johanna McGeary

from *Time*, December 31, 1999

The Mahatma, the Great Soul, endures in the best part of our minds, where our ideals are kept: the embodiment of human rights and the creed of nonviolence. Mohandas Karamchand Gandhi is something else, an eccentric of complex, contradictory and exhausting character most of us hardly know. . . .

While studying in England to be a lawyer, he first read the Bible and the Bhagavad-Gita, the Hindu religious poem that became his "spiritual dictionary." For Gandhi, the epic was a clarion call to the soul to undertake the battle of righteousness. It taught him to renounce personal desires not by withdrawal from the world but by devotion to the service of his fellow man. In the Christian New Testament he found the stirrings of passive resistance in the words of the Sermon on the Mount.

Those credos came together in the two principles that ruled his public life: what he called Satyagraha, the force of truth and love; and the ancient Hindu ideal of ahimsa, or nonviolence to all living things. He first put those principles to political work in South Africa, where he had gone to practice law and

Mohandas Gandhi speaking in front of Rungda House, Bombay (August 29, 1931).

tasted raw discrimination. Traveling to Johannesburg in a first-class train compartment, he was ordered to move to the

(continued)

"colored" cars in the rear. When he refused, he was hauled off the train and left to spend a freezing night in the station. The next day he was humiliated and cuffed by the white driver of a stagecoach. The experience steeled his resolve to fight for social justice.

In 1906, confronting a government move to fingerprint all Indians, Gandhi countered with a new idea—"passive resistance," securing political rights through personal suffering and the power of truth and love. "Indians," he wrote, "will stagger humanity without shedding a drop of blood." He failed to provoke legal changes, and Indians gained little more than a newfound self-respect. But Gandhi understood the universal application of his crusade. Even his principal adversary, the Afrikaner leader Jan Smuts, recognized the power of his idea: "Men like him redeem us from a sense of commonplace and futility."

. . . Gandhi is that rare great man held in universal esteem, a figure lifted from history to moral icon. The fundamental message of his transcendent personality persists. He stamped his ideas on history, igniting three of the century's great revolutions—against colonialism, racism, violence. His concept of nonviolent resistance liberated one nation and sped the end of colonial empires around the world. His marches and fasts fired the imagination of oppressed people everywhere. . . . He shines as a conscience for the world. The saint and the politician go hand in hand, proclaiming the power of love, peace and freedom.

? What generalization about Gandhi is the writer making in this article? What details about Gandhi does she use to support her generalization?

Sunrise at the Shore Temple (built c. 700) in Mahabalipuram, India.

Response and Analysis

Reading Check

1. In stanzas 30–31, what argument does Krishna use to persuade Arjuna to fight? According to stanzas 33–36, what are the dangers to Arjuna's reputation if he fails to fight?

2. In stanzas 47–48, what outlook toward failure and success does Krishna recommend? On what should Arjuna be "intent," and on what should he *not* be intent?

3. In stanza 67, what does Krishna say happens to a man who gives in to his senses? In stanza 71, what does he say happens when a man gives up all desires?

Thinking Critically

4. From stanzas 4–8, what can you infer about Arjuna's values? How have these values contributed to his dilemma?

5. In the *Mahabharata,* the hero Yudhistira, Arjuna's brother, says that the highest duty is to refrain from injuring others. In the Bhagavad-Gita, however, Krishna tells Arjuna that it is his sacred duty to fight. How do stanzas 18–21 help to resolve this **paradox,** or apparent contradiction?

6. **Parallelism** is the use of words or phrases with the same grammatical structure. What is the effect of the parallelism in stanza 29?

7. What do you think is the most important teaching or lesson in Krishna's advice to Arjuna? Explain your choice.

Extending and Evaluating

8. The Bhagavad-Gita presents the Hindu idea of "relinquishing attachment"— that is, acting in accordance with duty without desire for or fear of a specific outcome. How might the concept of nonattachment help a person overcome a conflict between duty and desire?

WRITING

Persuading Arjuna with Cause and Effect

Do you think that Arjuna should fight or refuse to fight? Write a persuasive essay, directed toward Arjuna, in which you try to convince him to take the action that you think is right. First, identify the causes of Arjuna's conflict; then, analyze the effects that will occur if Arjuna does not take the course of action you advise. If you agree that he should fight, you may wish to put Krishna's arguments about dharma, reincarnation, and the renunciation of desire in your own words in order to persuade Arjuna. If you think that Arjuna should not fight, you need to come up with your own persuasive appeals—convincing logical, emotional, and ethical arguments. End your essay with a final, powerful call to action.

▶ See "Persuading with Cause and Effect," pages 472–477, for help with this assignment.

Vocabulary Development
Sentence Sense

immutable   mundane

manifest   lucid

impartial

On a separate sheet of paper, use each Vocabulary word listed above in an original sentence based on the characters and events in "Philosophy and Spiritual Discipline."

North Carolina Competency Goal
2.01; 4.01; 6.01

INTERNET

Projects and Activities
Keyword:
LE5 WL-3

SKILLS FOCUS

Literary Skills
Analyze paradox.

Reading Skills
Analyze the speaker's purpose.

Writing Skills
Write a persuasive essay.

Vocabulary Skills
Write sentences using vocabulary words.

Panchatantra

(c. 100 B.C.–c. A.D. 500)

The *Panchatantra* is an anonymous collection of tales written in Sanskrit, dating from between 100 B.C. and A.D. 500. The *Panchatantra* consists of fables, tales meant to teach moral lessons, organized into five sections. (The word *Panchatantra* means "five books.") The ambitious goal of the *Panchatantra* is stated in its introduction: "This work . . . has traveled the world, aiming at the awakening of intelligence in the young."

The stories in the *Panchatantra* are a combination of prose and poetry, with prose used for telling the tales and poetry for summing up the morals. Whereas earlier Indian works involve a religious element, the *Panchatantra* is a practical guide to surviving and thriving in the everyday world. Like many subsequent story collections, such as *The Thousand and One Nights* (see page 546), Giovanni Boccaccio's *Decameron* (see page 669), and Geoffrey Chaucer's *Canterbury Tales,* the *Panchatantra* contains a frame story that serves as an introduction and gives the tales a thematic unity.

In the frame story, Vishnusharman, a Brahman priest, is given the task of teaching three simple-minded princes about *niti* (ni′tē), which is loosely translated as "the wise conduct of life." A person with *niti* can get the better of evil or unscrupulous rivals or plotters by turning the tables on them—a useful talent in statecraft.

Teaching the princes is not an easy task, since the requirements for *niti* are physical and financial security, steadfastness, fulfilling friendships, and intelligence. The Brahman meets the challenge by instructing the princes to memorize the stories contained in the five books of the *Panchatantra,* which he claims to have written. Each book consists of fables and witty sayings that focus on a particular theme: losing friends, winning friends, losing profits and possessions, declaring war or establishing peace, and acting rashly.

The stories of the *Panchatantra* were translated into Middle Persian in the sixth century A.D. During the Middle Ages the book was translated into Arabic, Greek, Hebrew, Latin, German, and Italian. Since then, many of the stories have become world classics. The *Panchatantra* has appeared in some two hundred versions in more than fifty different languages and has influenced the literatures of many lands.

Elephant (c. 1820). Watercolor on paper.
Victoria & Albert Museum, London.

Before You Read

The Mice That Set Elephants Free
from the **Panchatantra**

Make the Connection
Quickwrite ✏

How do you or people you know go about making new friends? What approaches seem to work best? What thoughts and actions stand in the way of meeting new people and forming friendships? Freewrite your ideas.

Literary Focus
Fable

A **fable** is a brief story in prose or verse that teaches a moral or gives a practical lesson about life. The characters in most fables are animals that behave and speak like human beings. Occasionally the characters—whether humans or humanlike animals—represent abstract qualities, such as virtue or laziness.

> A **fable** is a brief story in prose or verse that teaches a moral or practical lesson.
>
> *For more on Fable, see the Handbook of Literary and Historical Terms.*

Background

The theme of Book II of the *Panchatantra*, from which this selection is taken, is the "winning of friends." "The Mice That Set Elephants Free" illustrates two of the main literary elements of the *Panchatantra* as a whole. One of these is the use of the **frame story,** or story-within-a-story. The narrator of the story is Spot, a deer who speaks to Slow the turtle. Like the elephant king of his story, Spot has been attacked by hunters. Spot's friends, including Slow the turtle, Swift the crow, and Gold the mouse, emphasize and exemplify the theme of reciprocal friendship, or give-and-take.

Another prominent literary element in the *Panchatantra* is the intermingling of prose and **epigrams**—brief, clever verses that often contain a moral. Epigrams are an effective device for summarizing the message of a fable. The frequent use of epigrams gives the *Panchatantra* much of its special flavor and appeal.

A buck. Mughal, (c. 1800).

North Carolina Competency Goal
1.03; 4.05; 5.01; 5.03; 6.01

go.hrw.com

INTERNET
More About the Panchatantra
Keyword:
LE5 WL-3

SKILLS FOCUS

Literary Skills
Understand fable.

The Mice That Set Elephants Free

from the Panchatantra

translated by **Arthur W. Ryder**

A deer named Spot arrived, panting with thirst and quivering for fear of hunters' arrows. On seeing him approach, Swift flew into a tree, Gold crept into a grass-clump, and Slow sought an asylum in the water. But Spot stood near the bank, trembling for his safety.

Then Swift flew into the air, inspected the terrain for the distance of a league, then settled on his tree again, and called to Slow: "Slow, my dear fellow, come out, come out! No evil threatens you here. I have inspected the forest minutely. There is only this deer who has come to the lake for water." Thereupon all three gathered as before.

Then, out of friendly feeling toward a guest, Slow said to the deer: "My good fellow, drink and bathe. Our water is of excellent quality, and cool." And Spot thought, after meditating on this invitation: "Not the slightest danger threatens me from these. And this because a turtle has no capacity for mischief when out of water, while mouse and crow feed only on what is dead. So I will make one of their company." And he joined them.

Then Slow bade him welcome and did the honors, saying: "I trust your circumstances are happy. Pray tell us how you happened into this neck of the woods." And Spot replied: "I am weary of a life without love. I have been hard pressed on every side by mounted grooms and dogs and hunters. But fear lent speed, I left them all behind, and came here to drink. Now I am desirous of your friendship."

Upon hearing this, Slow said: "We are little of body. It is unnatural for you to make friends with us. One should make friends with those capable of returning favors." But Spot rejoined:

> "Better with the learnèd dwell,
> Even though it be in hell

(Inset and border) *Captive Elephants* (detail) (c. 1600). India.
Williams College Museum of Art, Gift of Wendy Findlay (83.7).

> Than with vulgar spirits roam
> Palaces that gods call home.

"And since you know that one little of body may be of no little consequence, why these self-depreciatory remarks? Yet after all, such speech is becoming to the excellent. I therefore insist that you make friends with me today. There is a good old saying:

Make friends, make friends, however
strong
Or weak they be:
Recall the captive elephants
That mice set free."

"How was that?" asked Slow. And Spot told
the story of

The Mice That Set Elephants Free

There was once a region where people,
houses, and temples had fallen into decay. So
the mice, who were old settlers there, occupied
the chinks in the floors of stately dwellings with
sons, grandsons (both in the male and female
line), and further descendants as they were
born, until their holes formed a dense tangle.
They found uncommon happiness in a variety
of festivals, dramatic performances (with plots
of their own invention), wedding-feasts, eating-
parties, drinking-bouts, and similar diversions.
And so the time passed.

But into this scene burst an elephant-king,
whose retinue numbered thousands. He, with
his herd, had started for the lake upon information that there was water there. As he marched
through the mouse community, he crushed
faces, eyes, heads, and necks of such mice as he
encountered.

Then the survivors held a convention. "We
are being killed," they said, "by these lumbering
elephants—curse them! If they come this way
again, there will not be mice enough for seed.
Besides:

An elephant will kill you, if
He touch; a serpent if he sniff;
King's laughter has a deadly sting;
A rascal kills by honoring.

Therefore let us devise a remedy effective in this
crisis."

When they had done so, a certain number
went to the lake, bowed before the elephant-
king, and said respectfully: "O King, not far
from here is our community, inherited from a
long line of ancestors. There we have prospered
through a long succession of sons and grandsons. Now you gentlemen, while coming here to
water, have destroyed us by the thousand. Furthermore, if you travel that way again, there will
not be enough of us for seed. If then you feel
compassion toward us, pray travel another
path. Consider the fact that even creatures of
our size will some day prove of some service."

And the elephant-king turned over in his
mind what he had heard, decided that the statement of the mice was entirely logical, and
granted their request.

Now in the course of time a certain king
commanded his elephant-trappers to trap elephants. And they constructed a so-called water-
trap, caught the king with his herd, three days
later dragged him out with a great tackle made
of ropes and things, and tied him to stout trees
in that very bit of forest.

When the trappers had gone, the elephant-
king reflected thus: "In what manner, or
through whose assistance, shall I be delivered?"
Then it occurred to him: "We have no means of
deliverance except those mice."

So the king sent the mice an exact description of his disastrous position in the trap
through one of his personal retinue, an
elephant-cow who had not ventured into the
trap, and who had previous information of
the mouse community.

When the mice learned the matter, they
gathered by the thousand, eager to return the
favor shown them, and visited the elephant
herd. And seeing king and herd fettered, they
gnawed the guy-ropes where they stood, then
swarmed up the branches, and by cutting the
ropes aloft, set their friends free.

"And that is why I say:
Make friends, make friends, however
strong, ...

and the rest of it."

Response and Analysis

Reading Check

1. What conflict disturbs the mice after they have settled in at home? How do they deal with this conflict?

2. What crisis befalls the elephant-king?

3. How do the mice help the elephant-king?

Thinking Critically

4. What is Spot the deer's purpose in telling the tale of the mice and the elephants to Slow, Swift, and Gold? Explain how Spot's situation in the frame story parallels that of the elephants in the inner tale.

5. The assigning of human characteristics to animals or inanimate objects is called **anthropomorphism** (an′thrə·pō′môr′fiz′əm). In the frame story, what human traits do Spot, Swift, and Slow exhibit? In the tale itself, what human characteristics are attributed to the mice and the elephant-king? Explain how both the frame story and the tale itself would have been different if the characters had been people instead of humanlike animals.

6. What argument do the mice use to persuade the elephant-king to travel another path? Why do you think the elephant-king decides that this argument is "entirely logical"?

7. What lesson about friendship can be learned from this **fable**?

8. Elephants and mice differ greatly in size. What do you think this contrast adds to the force of the fable's underlying **moral,** or message?

9. An **epigram** is a brief, clever, and usually memorable statement. What additional lesson does the first four-line epigram in the fable convey?

Extending and Evaluating

10. Do you think "The Mice That Set Elephants Free" has any relevance to modern readers? How might the moral of the fable be applied today to such fields as business and law?

WRITING

Writing a Fable

"The Mice That Set Elephants Free" is taken from Book II of the *Panchatantra*, which features tales under the heading "The Winning of Friends." Make a list of behaviors that might help someone win a friend. Choose the one that you think is most conducive or favorable to forming a friendship. Then think of a brief fable of your own that would illustrate that behavior and its effects. Try to write at least one **epigram** to include in your tale. Look back at your Quickwrite notes for ideas.

North Carolina Competency Goal
1.02; 1.03; 4.05; 5.03; 6.01

INTERNET
Projects and Activities
Keyword:
LE5 WL-3

SKILLS FOCUS

Literary Skills
Analyze a fable.

Writing Skills
Write a fable.

"Fairuz at the Pond with the King of Elephants" (detail), from the *Kalila wa Dimna* manuscript (c. 1354).

The Bodleian Library, Oxford.
(Pococoke 400, f. 99r).

Vocabulary Development

Indo-European Word Families and Roots

English is one of many languages in both Europe and Asia that are part of the Indo-European family of languages. These languages derive from an ancient unrecorded language that linguists call Proto-Indo-European. Almost all English words can ultimately be traced back to this ancient language, which also gave rise to languages as diverse as Sanskrit, Greek, Latin, German, Welsh, Farsi, Spanish, and French, among others. Take a look at the following words for *mother* in several languages in the Indo-European word family and see the similarities between them:

Sanskrit	Greek	Latin	Old English	German	Spanish
matar	meter	mater	modor	mutter	madre

Many words in English have been traced back to their Indo-European roots; you will often see the abbreviation "IE" in the etymology, or word history, given in many dictionary entries. Some common Indo-European roots are listed in the chart below. Note that the spelling of the roots when they appear in English words may vary.

Indo-European Roots				
English	**Root Word**	**Meaning of Root**	**Meaning of Word**	**Related Words**
diagnosis	–gnō–	to know	identification of a disease	ignore, recognize
domestic	–dem–	house	having to do with household affairs	domain, dome
malice	–mel–	bad	ill will	dismal, malevolent
obstacle	–stā–	to stand	something that stands in the way	constant, statue
tenacious	–ten–	to stretch	holding persistently	contend, tendon

North Carolina Competency Goal
1.03; 4.05; 5.03; 6.01

PRACTICE

Make a chart like the one above for the following words. The root and its meaning are given in parentheses for each word. Use a dictionary to find the meaning of each word. Then, find at least one word in the same family as each word listed.

opulent (–op–, "to produce") expedite (–ped–, "foot")

incandesce (–kand–, "to shine") proclivity (–klei–, "to lean")

auxiliary (–aug–, "to increase")

SKILLS FOCUS

Vocabulary Skills
Understand Indo-European roots.

Ramayana

(c. 200 B.C.–c. A.D. 200)

The *Ramayana* (rä·mä′yə·nə) is India's other great Hindu epic. Less massive than the *Mahabharata,* it is also, in many ways, closer to the type of epic familiar to Western readers. Like such epic heroes as Gilgamesh and Achilles, the main character Rama (rä′mə) is part man and part god; like Krishna in the *Mahabharata,* he is an incarnation of the Hindu god Vishnu (vish′nŏŏ). Although both Rama and his wife Sita (sē′tə) are semidivine figures, their story in the epic is a moving, human tale of love and jealousy, loss and recovery, separation and return.

The *Ramayana* is a long poem of some 25,000 couplets written in Sanskrit. The authorship of the *Ramayana* is attributed to a shadowy figure, the poet and sage Valmiki (väl·mē′kē).

The main plot of the epic begins with Prince Rama. After winning his bride Sita through a miraculous trial of strength, Rama is ready to inherit the throne. However, he is banished from his father's kingdom as the result of an evil court intrigue, and for many years he wanders in exile, accompanied by Sita and his loyal brother Lakshmana (läk′shmə·nə).

In the first half of the epic, Sita is abducted by the fierce Ravana (rä′və·nə), the many-headed king of the demons. She is brought to Ravana's island fortress, the kingdom of Lanka. During their quest to rescue Sita, Rama and Lakshmana ally themselves with the monkey king Hanuman (hän′ŏŏ·män′). Rama finally defeats Ravana, wins back his bride, and returns in triumph to his kingdom.

During her captivity, Sita has proved to be as faithful as she is beautiful and wise. But despite the fact that Sita has passed through an ordeal of fire to prove her purity, Rama harbors lingering doubts about her fidelity. In despair, Sita departs from the earth to assume her place as a goddess.

The image of Sita as a flesh-and-blood woman of saintly devotion and great physical endurance reflects the ideal portrait of many classic Indian heroines. Similarly, the loving description of the lush forests, cool hermitages, and other holy places gives us insight into the "geography" of Indian consciousness. The *Ramayana,* like all national epics, holds up a mirror to the culture from which it arose.

Rama, Sita, and Lakshmana (detail) (c. 1650). Manuscript page from the *Ramayana.*

The British Library, London. (Add Ms. 15296(1), f.70r).

Before You Read

Rama and Ravana in Battle

from the Ramayana

Make the Connection

Quickwrite

Thousands of years before the Star Wars and the Lord of the Rings films, the struggle between good and evil in the *Ramayana* was imagined as a battle on a cosmic scale, involving fantastic weapons that could destroy the universe. What is the appeal of such stories? Freewrite for a few minutes ideas for a science fiction or fantasy film that would present an epic struggle between good and evil.

Literary Focus

Conflict

Conflict is a struggle or clash between opposing characters, forces, or emotions. A conflict may be **external**—a character or group struggling against an outside character, group, or force. A conflict may also be **internal**—a struggle between opposing needs, responsibilities, desires, or emotions within a character. As you read, be sure to note examples of both types of conflicts in the selection.

> **Conflict** is a struggle or clash between opposing characters, forces, or emotions.
>
> *For more on Conflict, see the Handbook of Literary and Historical Terms.*

Reading Skills

Analyzing Sequence of Events

As you read this selection, make a list of the major events in the order in which they are presented. After you finish reading, put the events on a time line in chronological order, the order in which they actually happened.

Background

This description of the climactic battle between Rama and Ravana is from Book 6 of the *Ramayana*. R. K. Narayan's retelling of the narrative is based on a medieval version of the *Ramayana* by the south Indian poet Kamban, who drew upon Valmiki's Sanskrit original but wrote his version of the epic in the Tamil language. In this episode the magic weapons and supernatural forces make for an exciting narrative. More important, however, is the blurring of reality and illusion, as well as the presentation of a conflict going beyond the simple opposition of good and evil.

Vocabulary Development

dispel (di·spel′) *v.:* remove; drive away.

impervious (im·pʉr′vē·əs) *adj.:* unaffected by.

enterprise (ent′ər·prīz′) *n.:* undertaking.

vanquishing (van′kwish·iŋ) *v.* used as *n.:* conquering.

pristine (pris•tēn′) *adj.:* pure, unspoiled.

North Carolina Competency Goal
1.02; 1.03; 4.05; 5.01; 5.03; 6.01

INTERNET

Vocabulary Practice
•
More About the Ramayana
Keyword: LE5 WL-3

SKILLS FOCUS

Literary Skills
Understand external and internal conflict.

Reading Skills
Analyze sequence of events.

Battle scene at Lanka (detail) (c. 1652). Manuscript page from the *Ramayana*.
The British Library, London. (Add Ms. 15297(1), f.29).

Rama and Ravana in Battle

from the Ramayana

translated by R. K. Narayan

Every moment, news came to Ravana of fresh disasters in his camp. One by one, most of his commanders were lost. No one who went forth with battle cries was heard of again. Cries and shouts and the wailings of the widows of warriors came over the chants and songs of triumph that his courtiers arranged to keep up at a loud pitch in his assembly hall. Ravana became restless and abruptly left the hall and went up on a tower, from which he could obtain a full view of the city. He surveyed the scene below but could not stand it. One who had spent a lifetime in destruction now found the gory spectacle intolerable. Groans and wailings reached his ears with deadly clarity; and he noticed how the monkey hordes[1] reveled in their bloody handiwork. This was too much for him. He felt a terrific rage rising within him, mixed with some admiration for Rama's valor. He told himself, "The time has come for me to act by myself again."

He hurried down the steps of the tower, returned to his chamber, and prepared himself for the battle. He had a ritual bath and performed special prayers to gain the benediction of Shiva;[2] donned his battle dress, matchless armor, armlets, and crowns. He had on a protective armor for every inch of his body. He girt his swordbelt and attached to his body his accouterments[3] for protection and decoration.

When he emerged from his chamber, his heroic appearance was breathtaking. He summoned his chariot, which could be drawn by horses or move on its own if the horses were hurt or killed. People stood aside when he came out of the palace and entered his chariot. "This is my resolve," he said to himself: "Either that woman Sita, or my wife Mandodari,[4] will soon have cause to cry and roll in the dust in grief. Surely, before this day is done, one of them will be a widow."

The gods in heaven noticed Ravana's determined move and felt that Rama would need all the support they could muster. They requested Indra[5] to send down his special chariot for Rama's use. When the chariot appeared at his camp, Rama was deeply impressed with the magnitude and brilliance of the vehicle. "How has this come to be here?" he asked.

"Sir," the charioteer answered, "my name is Matali.[6] I have the honor of being the charioteer of Indra. Brahma, the four-faced god and creator of the Universe, and Shiva, whose power has emboldened Ravana now to challenge you, have commanded me to bring it here for your use. It can fly swifter than air over all obstacles, over any mountain, sea, or sky, and will help you to emerge victorious in this battle."

Rama reflected aloud, "It may be that the rakshasas[7] have created this illusion for me. It may be a trap. I don't know how to view it." Whereupon Matali spoke convincingly to

---

1. **monkey hordes:** tribe of spirits aiding Rama in his battle with Ravana.
2. **Shiva** (shē′və): god of destructive forces. Originally a storm god, he carries a trident.
3. **accouterments** (ə·ko͞ot′ər·mənts) *n. pl.*: soldier's equipment, not including clothes or arms.

---

4. **Mandodari** (mən·dō′də·rē).
5. **Indra** (in′drə): important Hindu god who appears in several forms. He is sometimes the god of war and at other times the chief of all the minor gods.
6. **Matali** (mə·tɑl·ē′).
7. **rakshasas** (räk′shə·səz) *n. pl.*: malevolent spirits capable of assuming various shapes.

dispel the doubt in Rama's mind. Rama, still hesitant, though partially convinced, looked at Hanuman[8] and Lakshmana[9] and asked, "What do you think of it?" Both answered, "We feel no doubt that this chariot is Indra's; it is not an illusory creation."

Rama fastened his sword, slung two quivers full of rare arrows over his shoulders, and climbed into the chariot.

The beat of war drums, the challenging cries of soldiers, the trumpets, and the rolling chariots speeding along to confront each other, created a deafening mixture of noise. While Ravana had instructed his charioteer to speed ahead, Rama very gently ordered his chariot-driver, "Ravana is in a rage; let him perform all the antics he desires and exhaust himself. Until then be calm; we don't have to hurry forward. Move slowly and calmly, and you must strictly follow my instructions; I will tell you when to drive faster."

Ravana's assistant and one of his staunchest supporters, Mahodara[10]—the giant among giants in his physical appearance—begged Ravana, "Let me not be a mere spectator when you confront Rama. Let me have the honor of grappling with him. Permit me to attack Rama."

"Rama is my sole concern," Ravana replied. "If you wish to engage yourself in a fight, you may fight his brother Lakshmana."

Noticing Mahodara's purpose, Rama steered his chariot across his path in order to prevent Mahodara from reaching Lakshmana. Whereupon Mahodara ordered his chariot-driver, "Now dash straight ahead, directly into Rama's chariot."

The charioteer, more practical-minded, advised him, "I would not go near Rama. Let us keep away." But Mahodara, obstinate and intoxicated with war fever, made straight for Rama. He wanted to have the honor of a direct encounter with Rama himself in spite of Ravana's advice;

and for this honor he paid a heavy price, as it was a moment's work for Rama to destroy him, and leave him lifeless and shapeless on the field. Noticing this, Ravana's anger mounted further. He commanded his driver, "You will not slacken now. Go." Many ominous signs were seen now—his bowstrings suddenly snapped; the mountains shook; thunders rumbled in the skies; tears flowed from the horses' eyes; elephants with decorated foreheads moved along dejectedly. Ravana, noticing them, hesitated only for a second, saying, "I don't care. This mere mortal Rama is of no account, and these omens do not concern me at all." Meanwhile, Rama paused for a moment to consider his next step; and suddenly turned towards the armies supporting Ravana, which stretched away to the horizon, and destroyed them. He felt that this might be one way of saving Ravana. With his armies gone, it was possible that Ravana might have a change of heart. But it had only the effect of spurring Ravana on; he plunged forward and kept coming nearer Rama and his own doom.

Rama's army cleared and made way for Ravana's chariot, unable to stand the force of his approach. Ravana blew his conch[11] and its shrill challenge reverberated through space. Following it another conch, called "Panchajanya,"[12] which belonged to Mahavishnu[13] (Rama's original form before his present incarnation), sounded of its own accord in answer to the challenge, agitating the universe with its vibrations. And then Matali picked up another conch, which was Indra's, and blew it. This was the signal indicating the commencement of the actual battle. Presently Ravana sent a shower of arrows on Rama; and Rama's followers, unable to bear the sight of his body being studded with arrows, averted their heads. Then the chariot horses of Ravana and Rama glared at each other in hostility, and the flags topping the chariots—

---

8. **Hanuman** (hun'oo·män'): monkey king; principal ally of Rama in his war with Ravana.
9. **Lakshmana** (läk'shmə·nə): half brother of Rama, considered the embodiment of loyalty.
10. **Mahodara** (mə·hō'də·rə).

11. **conch** (käŋk) *n.*: shell used as a trumpet.
12. **Panchajanya** (pän·chə·jän'yə).
13. **Mahavishnu** (mə·hä·vish'noo).

Vocabulary

dispel (di·spel') *v.*: remove; drive away.

Ravana's ensign of the Veena[14] and Rama's with the whole universe on it—clashed, and one heard the stringing and twanging of bowstrings on both sides, overpowering in volume all other sound. Then followed a shower of arrows from Rama's own bow. Ravana stood gazing at the chariot sent by Indra and swore, "These gods, instead of supporting me, have gone to the support of this petty human being. I will teach them a lesson. He is not fit to be killed with my arrows but I shall seize him and his chariot together and fling them into high heaven and dash them to destruction." Despite his oath, he still strung his bow and sent a shower of arrows at Rama, raining in thousands, but they were all invariably shattered and neutralized by the arrows from Rama's bow, which met arrow for arrow. Ultimately Ravana, instead of using one bow, used ten with his twenty arms, multiplying his attack tenfold; but Rama stood unhurt.

Ravana suddenly realized that he should change his tactics and ordered his charioteer to fly the chariot up in the skies. From there he attacked and destroyed a great many of the monkey army supporting Rama. Rama ordered Matali, "Go up in the air. Our young soldiers are being attacked from the sky. Follow Ravana, and don't slacken."

There followed an aerial pursuit at dizzying speed across the dome of the sky and rim of the earth. Ravana's arrows came down like rain; he was bent upon destroying everything in the world. But Rama's arrows diverted, broke, or neutralized Ravana's. Terror-stricken, the gods watched this pursuit. Presently Ravana's arrows struck Rama's horses and pierced the heart of Matali himself. The charioteer fell. Rama paused for a while in grief, undecided as to his next step. Then he recovered and resumed his offensive. At that moment the divine eagle Garuda[15] was seen perched on Rama's flagpost,

---

14. **ensign of the Veena:** banner with the image of an ancient stringed instrument.
15. **Garuda** (gə·rōō′də).

Ravana with chariot (detail) (c. late 16th century). Manuscript page from a Persian translation of the *Ramayana*.

Freer Gallery of Art, Smithsonian Institution, Washington, DC. Gift of Charles Lang Freer (F1907.271-297v).

and the gods who were watching felt that this could be an auspicious sign.

After circling the globe several times, the dueling chariots returned, and the fight continued over Lanka.[16] It was impossible to be very clear about the location of the battleground as the fight occurred here, there, and everywhere. Rama's arrows pierced Ravana's armor and made him wince. Ravana was so insensible to pain and impervious to attack that for him to wince was a good sign, and the gods hoped that this was a turn for the better. But at this moment, Ravana suddenly changed his tactics. Instead of merely shooting his arrows, which were powerful in themselves, he also invoked several supernatural forces to create strange effects: he was adept in the use of various asthras[17] which could be made dynamic with special incantations. At this point, the fight became one of attack with supernatural powers, and parrying of such an attack with other supernatural powers.

Ravana realized that the mere aiming of shafts with ten or twenty of his arms would be of no avail because the mortal whom he had so contemptuously thought of destroying with a slight effort was proving formidable, and his arrows were beginning to pierce and cause pain. Among the asthras sent by Ravana was one called "Danda,"[18] a special gift from Shiva, capable of pursuing and pulverizing its target. When it came flaming along, the gods were struck with fear. But Rama's arrow neutralized it.

Now Ravana said to himself, "These are all petty weapons. I should really get down to proper business." And he invoked the one called "Maya"[19]—a weapon which created illusions and confused the enemy.

With proper incantations and worship, he sent off this weapon and it created an illusion of reviving all the armies and its leaders—Kumbakarna[20] and Indrajit[21] and the others—and bringing them back to the battlefield. Presently Rama found all those who, he thought, were no more, coming on with battle cries and surrounding him. Every man in the enemy's army was again up in arms. They seemed to fall on Rama with victorious cries. This was very confusing and Rama asked Matali, whom he had by now revived, "What is happening now? How are all these coming back? They were dead." Matali explained, "In your original identity you are the creator of illusions in this universe. Please know that Ravana has created phantoms to confuse you. If you make up your mind, you can dispel them immediately." Matali's explanation was a great help. Rama at once invoked a weapon called "Gnana"[22]— which means "wisdom" or "perception." This was a very rare weapon, and he sent it forth. And all the terrifying armies who seemed to have come on in such a great mass suddenly evaporated into thin air.

Ravana then shot an asthra called "Thama,"[23] whose nature was to create total darkness in all the worlds. The arrows came with heads exposing frightening eyes and fangs, and fiery tongues. End to end the earth was enveloped in total darkness and the whole of creation was paralyzed. This asthra also created a deluge of rain on one side, a rain of stones on the other, a hailstorm showering down intermittently, and a tornado sweeping the earth. Ravana was sure that this would arrest Rama's enterprise. But Rama was able to meet it with what was named "Shivasthra."[24] He understood the nature of the phenomenon and the cause of it and chose the appropriate asthra for counteracting it.

---

16. **Lanka** (läŋ′kə): Ravana's kingdom.
17. **asthras** (ä′strəs) *n. pl.*: weapons endowed with supernatural powers.
18. **Danda** (dän′də).
19. **Maya** (mä′yä′).

20. **Kumbakarna** (kum·bə·kär′nə).
21. **Indrajit** (in·drə·jit′).
22. **Gnana** (gnä′nə).
23. **Thama** (tä′mə).
24. **Shivasthra** (ṣhi·vä′strə).

Vocabulary

impervious (im·pʉr′vē·əs) *adj.*: unaffected by.
enterprise (ent′ər·prīz′) *n.*: undertaking.

Rama is presented with the celestial weapons (detail) (c. late 16th century).
Manuscript page from a Persian translation of the *Ramayana*.

Ravana now shot off what he considered his deadliest weapon—a trident endowed with extraordinary destructive power, once gifted to Ravana by the gods. When it started on its journey there was real panic all round. It came on flaming toward Rama, its speed or course unaffected by the arrows he flung at it.

When Rama noticed his arrows falling down ineffectively while the trident sailed towards him, for a moment he lost heart. When it came quite near, he uttered a certain mantra[25] from the depth of his being and while he was breathing out that incantation, an esoteric syllable in perfect timing, the trident collapsed. Ravana, who had been so certain of <u>vanquishing</u> Rama with his trident, was astonished to see it fall down within an inch of him, and for a minute wondered if his adversary might not after all be a divine being although he looked like a mortal. Ravana thought to himself, "This is, perhaps, the highest God. Who could he be? Not Shiva, for Shiva is my supporter; he could not be Brahma,[26] who is four faced; could not be Vishnu, because of my immunity from the weapons of the whole trinity. Perhaps this man is the primordial being, the cause behind the whole universe. But whoever he may be, I will not stop my fight until I defeat and crush him or at least take him prisoner."

With this resolve, Ravana next sent a weapon which issued forth monstrous serpents vomiting fire and venom, with enormous fangs and red eyes. They came darting in from all directions. Rama now selected an asthra called "Garuda" (which meant "eagle"). Very soon thousands of eagles were aloft, and they picked off the serpents with their claws and beaks and destroyed them. Seeing this also fail, Ravana's anger was roused to a mad pitch and he blindly emptied a quiverful of arrows in Rama's direction. Rama's arrows met them half way and turned them round so that they went back and their sharp points embedded themselves in Ravana's own chest.

Ravana was weakening in spirit. He realized that he was at the end of his resources. All his learning and equipment in weaponry were of no avail and he had practically come to the end of his special gifts of destruction. While he was going down thus, Rama's own spirit was soaring up. The combatants were now near enough to grapple with each other and Rama realized that this was the best moment to cut off Ravana's heads.[27] He sent a crescent-shaped arrow which sliced off one of Ravana's heads and flung it far into the sea, and this process continued; but every time a head was cut off, Ravana had the benediction of having another one grown in its place. Rama's crescent-shaped weapon was continuously busy as Ravana's heads kept cropping up. Rama lopped off his arms but they grew again and every lopped-off arm hit Matali and the chariot and tried to cause destruction by itself, and the tongue in a new head wagged, uttered challenges, and cursed Rama. On the cast-off heads of Ravana devils and minor demons, who had all along been in terror of Ravana and had obeyed and pleased him, executed a dance of death and feasted on the flesh.

Ravana was now desperate. Rama's arrows embedded themselves in a hundred places on his body and weakened him. Presently he collapsed in a faint on the floor of his chariot. Noticing his state, his charioteer pulled back and drew the chariot aside. Matali whispered to Rama, "This is the time to finish off that demon. He is in a faint. Go on. Go on."

But Rama put away his bow and said, "It is not fair warfare to attack a man who is in a faint. I will wait. Let him recover," and waited.

When Ravana revived, he was angry with his charioteer for withdrawing and took out his sword, crying, "You have disgraced me. Those who look on will think I have retreated." But his charioteer explained how Rama suspended the fight and forebore to attack when he was in a faint. Somehow, Ravana appreciated his explanation and patted his back and resumed his attacks.

27. **Ravana's heads:** Ravana is usually depicted with ten heads and ten pairs of arms.

Vocabulary

vanquishing (vaŋ′kwish·iŋ) v. used as n.: conquering.

25. **mantra** (man′trə) n.: formula believed to have magical power, used in incantations.
26. **Brahma** (brä′mə): god of creation.

Rama kills Ravana (detail) (c. 1652). Manuscript page from the *Ramayana*.
The British Library, London. (Add. 15297(1), f.166).

Having exhausted his special weapons, in desperation Ravana began to throw on Rama all sorts of things such as staves,[28] cast-iron balls, heavy rocks, and oddments he could lay hands on. None of them touched Rama, but glanced off and fell ineffectually. Rama went on shooting his arrows. There seemed to be no end of this struggle in sight.

Now Rama had to pause to consider what final measure he should take to bring this campaign to an end. After much thought, he decided to use "Brahmasthra,"[29] a weapon specially designed by the Creator Brahma on a former occasion, when he had to provide one for Shiva to destroy Tripura,[30] the old monster who assumed the forms of flying mountains and settled down on habitations and cities, seeking to destroy the world. The Brahmasthra was a special gift to be used only when all other means had failed. Now Rama, with prayers and worship, invoked its

fullest power and sent it in Ravana's direction, aiming at his heart rather than his head; Ravana being vulnerable at heart. While he had prayed for indestructibility of his several heads and arms, he had forgotten to strengthen his heart, where the Brahmasthra entered and ended his career.

Rama watched him fall headlong from his chariot face down onto the earth, and that was the end of the great campaign. Now one noticed Ravana's face aglow with a new quality. Rama's arrows had burnt off the layers of dross, the anger, conceit, cruelty, lust, and egotism which had encrusted his real self, and now his personality came through in its <u>pristine</u> form—of one who was devout and capable of tremendous attainments.[31] His constant meditation on Rama, although as an adversary, now seemed to bear

---

28. **staves** *n. pl.*: staffs.
29. **Brahmasthra** (brä·mä′strə).
30. **Tripura** (trip′oo·rə).

31. **attainments** *n. pl.*: accomplishments.

Vocabulary

pristine (pris•tēn′) *adj.*: pure; unspoiled.

The funeral of Ravana (detail) (c. 1652). Manuscript page from the *Ramayana*.
The British Library, London. (Add. 15297(1), f.173).

fruit, as his face shone with serenity and peace. Rama noticed it from his chariot above and commanded Matali, "Set me down on the ground." When the chariot descended and came to rest on its wheels, Rama got down and commanded Matali, "I am grateful for your services to me. You may now take the chariot back to Indra."

Surrounded by his brother Lakshmana and Hanuman and all his other war chiefs, Rama approached Ravana's body, and stood gazing on it. He noted his crowns and jewelry scattered piecemeal on the ground. The decorations and the extraordinary workmanship of the armor on his chest were blood covered. Rama sighed as if to say, "What might he not have achieved but for the evil stirring within him!"

At this moment, as they readjusted Ravana's blood-stained body, Rama noticed to his great shock a scar on Ravana's back and said with a smile, "Perhaps this is not an episode of glory for me, as I seem to have killed an enemy who was turning his back and retreating. Perhaps I was wrong in shooting the Brahmasthra into him." He looked so concerned at this supposed lapse on his part that Vibishana,[32] Ravana's brother, came forward to explain. "What you have achieved is unique. I say so although it meant the death of my brother."

"But I have attacked a man who had turned his back," Rama said. "See that scar."

Vibishana explained, "It is an old scar. In ancient days, when he paraded his strength around the globe, once he tried to attack the divine elephants that guard the four directions. When he tried to catch them, he was gored in the back by one of the tuskers and that is the scar you see now; it is not a fresh one though fresh blood is flowing on it."

Rama accepted the explanation. "Honor him and cherish his memory so that his spirit may go to heaven, where he has his place. And now I will leave you to attend to his funeral arrangements, befitting his grandeur."

---

32. **Vibishana** (vi′bē·shä′nə).

Response and Analysis

Reading Check

1. What resolution does Ravana make after putting on his armor and summoning his chariot?

2. What support do the gods give Rama? What doubts does Rama have about the chariot, and who reassures him?

3. How does Mahodara disobey Ravana's orders? What is the result of this disobedience?

4. What kinds of weapons are used in the battle? How is Ravana finally killed?

5. What information does Vibishana reveal to show Rama that he did not kill Ravana while Ravana's back was turned?

Thinking Critically

6. How do the details in the first paragraph establish the main **external conflict** in the episode? What details show Ravana's **internal conflict**?

7. **Suspense** is the uncertainty or anxiety you feel about what will happen next in a story. How does the author of the epic create suspense in this episode? Refer to the chronological time line of events that you made.

8. What role do the gods play in this excerpt from the *Ramayana*?

9. What values does Rama, the hero of this epic, embody? How does Rama's treatment of the defeated Ravana emphasize these values?

Extending and Evaluating

10. How did the epic battles in this selection relate to your ideas for a fantasy film involving good versus evil? Are the battles between Rama and Ravana simply exciting action sequences, or do they make a comment about deeper issues? Explain. ✏️

WRITING
Comparing Two Indian Epics

In an essay, compare Arjuna's situation in the Bhagavad-Gita (see page 371) with Rama's final confrontation with Ravana. In your essay, consider the way the gods help each hero, the hero's "sacred duty" in each epic, the doubts each hero experiences, and the importance of self-discipline and self-control to each hero.

Vocabulary Development
Semantic Mapping

dispel	vanquishing
impervious	pristine
enterprise	

Make a **semantic map** like the following one for the Vocabulary words above. Be sure to use the words in the correct context.

dispel
Definition: "remove; drive away"
Synonyms: disperse, scatter
Example: The sun's warm rays will soon *dispel* the morning mist.

North Carolina Competency Goal
1.02; 1.03; 4.05; 5.03; 6.01

go.
hrw
.com

INTERNET
Projects and Activities
Keyword:
LE5 WL-3

SKILLS FOCUS

Literary Skills
Analyze external and internal conflict.

Reading Skills
Analyze sequence of events.

Writing Skills
Compare epics.

Vocabulary Skills
Make semantic maps.

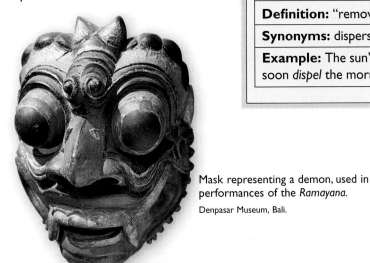

Mask representing a demon, used in performances of the *Ramayana*.
Denpasar Museum, Bali.

Grammar Link

Pointing to the Right Place: Agreement of Pronoun and Antecedent

A pronoun (*I, me, mine, he, his, her, its*) takes the place of one or more nouns or other pronouns. A pronoun usually refers to a nearby noun or pronoun called its antecedent. In the sentence *Sean washed his hands*, *Sean* is the antecedent of the pronoun *his*.

Pronouns should agree with their antecedents in **number** (singular or plural), **gender** (masculine, feminine, or neuter), and **person** (first, second, or third).

Rama and Ravana climb to their chariots. [plural number]

Rama's chariot can move without horses or a charioteer to guide it. [neuter gender]

You may see parallels between these fantastic vehicles and your own modern cars. [second person]

Lack of agreement between pronouns and antecedents confuses readers. Determining the number of **indefinite pronouns,** which do not refer to specific people or things, may be particularly difficult. Some indefinite pronouns are always singular (*anyone, each, either, everybody, neither, nothing, one, somebody, something*). Some are always plural (*both, few, many, several*). A few can be either singular or plural, depending on how they are used in the sentence (*all, any, more, most, none, some*).

SINGULAR	At first neither of the adversaries can harm his opponent.
PLURAL	Most of Rama's arrows hit their mark, but they scarcely make Ravana wince.
SINGULAR	Rama manages to turn most of Ravana's firepower back on itself.

North Carolina Competency Goal
1.03; 4.05; 5.03

Grammar Skills
Understand agreement of pronoun and antecedent.

The following sentences contain pronouns that do not agree with their antecedents. Rewrite each sentence to correct the error.

1. Ravana vows that one of the combatants' wives will mourn their husband.

2. Neither of the combatants is alone; both have allies to support him.

3. Rama defeats all of Ravana's asthras by opposing it with spiritual force.

4. Anyone seeing Ravana after his death would change their mind about the demon king.

Apply to Your Writing

Look through a writing assignment you are working on now or have already completed. Highlight each pronoun, and identify its antecedent. Make sure that pronouns and antecedents agree in number, gender, and person.

▶ **For more help, see Agreement of Pronoun and Antecedent, 2j–o, in the Language Handbook.**

Collection 3

Literature of India, China, and Japan:

The Search for Truth and Enlightenment

Chinese Literature

I built my hut in a zone of human habitation,
Yet near me there sounds no noise of horse or
      coach.
    Would you know how that is possible?
A heart that is distant creates a wilderness
      round it.
I pluck chrysanthemums under the
5   eastern hedge,
Then gaze long at the distant summer hills.
The mountain air is fresh at the dusk of day:
The flying birds two by two return.
In these things there lies a deep meaning;
Yet when we would express it, words
10   suddenly fail us.

—T'ao Ch'ien

Terra-cotta figurine depicting
a lady of the imperial court
(c. 7th century). T'ang dynasty.
Musée des Arts Asiatiques-Guimet, Paris.

401

ABOUT

The Book of Songs

(500s B.C.)

An Immortal Under Pines (c. 1635) by Ch'en Hung-shou. Detail of a hanging scroll, Ming dynasty.
National Palace Museum, Taiwan, Republic of China.

The *Book of Songs* is a collection of 305 of the earliest recorded poems in Chinese history. First compiled in the sixth century B.C., these poems were actually meant to be sung, although their melodies have long been lost. Regarded as the foundation of Chinese literature, *The Book of Songs* includes court songs that entertained the aristocracy, story songs that recounted legends from the Chou (jō) dynasty (1122–256 B.C.), and hymns that were sung in the temples, accompanied by dance. Many of the poems are brief folk songs or ballads. *The Book of Songs* provides a lyrical record of the people who lived in northern China and the feudal states surrounding the Yellow River during the early centuries of the Chou dynasty.

By the seventh century B.C., the *Songs* were so familiar that scholars began quoting lines or verses out of context, and often inaccurately, applying them to new situations. Eventually, many songs acquired interpretations probably never intended by the ancient singers.

Around 500 B.C., the Chinese philosopher Confucius (see page 407) reinterpreted many of the *Songs* to make them into models of his moral teachings. He felt that the *Songs* described a wide range of emotion and experience and that not to study them would be like closing one's eyes to the world.

The Book of Songs became one of the "Five Classics" of Confucianism—texts that embodied Confucian ideals in the five areas of metaphysics, politics, history, society, and poetry. As an expression of the Confucian poetic vision, *The Book of Songs* became part of the basic educational curriculum in China when Confucianism was adopted as the official state

doctrine during the Han dynasty (206 B.C.–A.D. 220). Each poem was accompanied by an official interpretation that explained the poem's relationship to the moral and social fabric of the period in which it was written. Until recent times, Chinese schoolchildren studied *The Book of Songs* as both poetry and moral lessons and were required to memorize all 305 songs.

Today, however, scholars are laying aside such traditional interpretations to see *The Book of Songs* simply as a classic work of literature that expresses a people's humanity. In the *Songs,* the people of Chou still sing to us across time, revealing the inner and outer worlds they lived in and, in the process, establishing the strong lyrical tradition that has shaped Chinese poetry.

Before You Read

from The Book of Songs

Make the Connection

The speakers in both of these poems are far from their homes. When you miss your family or friends, how do you express your feelings? Do you write a letter, send an e-mail, get on the telephone? How could you express your feelings if you couldn't directly communicate with the people you missed?

Literary Focus

Repetition

Repetition is a literary device that consists of repeated sounds, words, phrases, or other elements in prose and poetry. Writers use repetition to unify a work, build rhythm, and add emphasis to particular feelings and ideas. In folk songs and ballads, repetition often appears in the form of a recurring word or group of words called a **refrain**. For example, the refrain "For I'm weary with hunting, and fain would lie down" appears at the end of several stanzas in the Scottish ballad "Lord Randall." Refrains are not always repeated word for word; many refrains repeat with slight variations from stanza to stanza.

> **Repetition** is the intentional repeating of a sound, a word, a phrase, a line, or an idea in order to create a rhythmic effect, build suspense, or add emphasis.
>
> *For more on Repetition, see the Handbook of Literary and Historical Terms.*

Background

These two selections from *The Book of Songs* come from a collection of 160 folk songs attributed to the feudal states of the Chou empire. Among the earliest of the *Songs,* these folk songs have apparently been revised and refined since they were written centuries ago.

Like many selections in *The Book of Songs,* these folk songs tend to have strong, regular rhythms that echo the gongs, drums, bronze bells, and stone chimes of early Chinese music. These compact lyrics also feature repeated words and phrases, although there are often subtle changes in the repetition. The folk songs are best known, however, for their direct outpourings of ordinary human feeling, especially on the themes of separation, hardship, and love. The predominant theme of *The Book of Songs,* Confucius said, is "to keep the heart right."

North Carolina Competency Goal
1.03; 4.05; 5.01; 5.03

INTERNET
More About The Book of Songs
Keyword:
LE5 WL-3

SKILLS FOCUS

Literary Skills
Understand repetition.

Gilt-bronze lamp (c. 100 B.C.E.).

Heibei Provincial Museum. Photograph by Wang Yugui, courtesy of the Cultural Relics Bureau, Beijing and The Metropolitan Museum of Art, New York.

403

According to Chinese tradition, Song 103 expresses the feelings of a young princess of the state of Wei (wā). She is separated from her family by an unhappy marriage to the lord of Hsü, (shōō), the ruler of a small, nearby state. When she tries to return to her people, the men of Hsü detain her against her will.

from **The Book of Songs**

translated by **Arthur Waley**

O Oriole, Yellow Bird

103

O oriole, yellow bird,
Do not settle on the corn,
Do not peck at my millet.°
The people of this land
5 Are not minded to nurture me.
I must go back, go home
To my own land and kin.

O oriole, yellow bird,
Do not settle on the mulberries,
10 Do not peck my sorghum.°
With the people of this land
One can make no covenant.
I must go back, go home
To where my brothers are.

15 O oriole, yellow bird,
Do not settle on the oaks,
Do not peck my wine-millet.
With the people of this land
One can come to no understanding.
20 I must go back, go home
To where my own men° are.

---

3. **millet** (mil'it) *n.:* in Asia, cereal grass with small grain used for food.
10. **sorghum** (sôr'gəm) *n.:* tropical grass grown for its food products, such as syrup or grain.
21. **men:** here, the speaker's adult kinsmen, such as her father and uncles.

Auspicious Grain (14th century). Hanging scroll from the Yuan dynasty.
National Palace Museum, Taiwan, Republic of China.

Song 130 probably expresses the lament of a Chinese peasant, one who represents the common man forced to take up arms for a warlord. The Book of Songs *contains some of history's earliest antiwar songs.*

What Plant Is Not Faded?

130

What plant is not faded?
What day do we not march?
What man is not taken
To defend the four bounds?

5 What plant is not wilting?
What man is not taken from his wife?
Alas for us soldiers,
Treated as though we were not fellow-men!

Are we buffaloes, are we tigers
10 That our home should be these desolate wilds?
Alas for us soldiers,
Neither by day nor night can we rest!

The fox bumps and drags
Through the tall, thick grass.
15 Inch by inch move our barrows
As we push them along the track.

Terra-cotta warrior statues from the tomb of Chin Shih huang-ti at Xi'an, China.

The Book of Songs **405**

Response and Analysis

Thinking Critically

1. To whom is Song 103 addressed? What are the speaker's complaints about "the people of this land"?

2. In Song 103, why does the speaker tell the oriole of her desire to go home?

3. The first five sentences of Song 130 are all questions. What is the significance of the speaker's many questions? What feelings do they evoke?

4. Point out three lines in Song 130 that state the speaker's concerns. Paraphrase these concerns in your own words.

5. Choose an example of **repetition** in each poem. What emotion is expressed by the repeated phrase?

Extending and Evaluating

6. In what ways do these poems remind you of songs you know? Could they be set to music and still be relevant today? Why or why not?

WRITING

Comparing and Contrasting Two Folk Songs

In a two- to three-paragraph essay, compare and contrast Song 130 ("What Plant Is Not Faded?") with the classic folk song "Where Have All the Flowers Gone?" by Pete Seeger, to the right. End your essay with a comment about the qualities Seeger's song shares with the selections from *The Book of Songs* you have just read. Make a generalization about the relevance of these ancient Chinese poems.

North Carolina Competency Goal
1.03; 4.05; 5.03

INTERNET
Projects and Activities
Keyword:
LE5 WL-3

SKILLS FOCUS

Literary Skills
Analyze repetition.

Writing Skills
Compare and contrast two folk songs.

Where Have All the Flowers Gone?
Pete Seeger

Where have all the flowers gone,
    Long time passing?
Where have all the flowers gone,
    Long time ago.
5 Where have all the flowers gone?
The girls have picked them every one.
When will they ever learn?
When will they ever learn?

Where have all the young men gone,
10   Long time passing?
Where have all the young men gone,
    Long time ago.
Where have all the young men gone?
Gone for soldiers every one.
15 When will they ever learn?
When will they ever learn?

Where have all the soldiers gone,
    Long time passing?
Where have all the soldiers gone,
20   Long time ago.
Where have all the soldiers gone?
Gone to graveyards every one.
When will they ever learn?
When will they ever learn?

25 Where have all the graveyards gone,
    Long time passing?
Where have all the graveyards gone,
    Long time ago.
Where have all the graveyards gone?
30 Gone to flowers every one.
When will they ever learn?
When will they ever learn?

Confucius
(551–479 B.C.)

His family name was K'ung, and he is
known in Chinese history by the title
K'ung Fu-tzu (koͅoͅŋ foͅoͅd·zoͅoͅʹ), meaning
"Master K'ung." In the West he is known as
Confucius (kən·fyoͅoͅʹshəs).

Confucius grew up in a poor family of
possibly noble heritage. He lived an ordinary
life that was marked by an extraordinary love
of learning. When he married at the age of
nineteen, Confucius had already distinguished
himself as a young scholar. By the time he
died in 479 B.C., at the age of seventy-three,
this largely self-educated man had become the
most learned teacher in China.

Confucius was the first person in recorded
Chinese history to believe in education for all
and to regard teaching as a life's work. He gave
private lessons to young men, training them in
the moral character he saw as proper and
necessary to the ruling classes. But he longed
for a more public position in government that
would allow him to reform society according
to the ancient "Way of Goodness," a traditional code of personal ethics and honor that
contemporary rulers had discarded in favor of
personal gain. For a decade or more, Confucius
traveled from state to state seeking a ruler
who would put this traditional moral code into
practice. But his notions were out of step with
the rulers' ways of oppression and violence.
Finally, at the age of sixty-seven, Confucius
returned home to teach a small band of
followers in the practice of the Way.

Confucius left no writings. The only written
record of his teachings was put together by his
followers long after his death. This record of

Confucius (1734). Ink rubbing from a Chinese stele
found at Xi'an.

The Granger Collection, New York.

conversations with Confucius, the Master, is
known in English as the *Analects,* which means
"selected sayings" or "selections from a group
of works." The *Analects* is divided into twenty
books. Only six or seven of them may be
Confucius's actual teachings. The other books
were probably added by later disciples of the
Confucian school. Generations after Confucius's death, Confucian thought took hold in
China and profoundly influenced all of East
Asia, including Japan and Korea. In traditional
China the *Analects* was essential reading for
every educated person for more than two
thousand years.

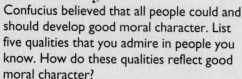

Before You Read

from the Analects

Make the Connection

Quickwrite

Confucius believed that all people could and should develop good moral character. List five qualities that you admire in people you know. How do these qualities reflect good moral character?

Literary Focus

Maxim

A **maxim** is a brief, direct statement that expresses a basic rule of human conduct or a general truth about human behavior. The statement "Success is getting what you want; happiness is wanting what you get" is a maxim. Familiar sayings such as "Honesty is the best policy" are also maxims. A maxim provides a simple and direct way to capture a profound, complex truth about conduct and behavior.

> A **maxim** is a concise and direct statement of a rule of conduct or proper behavior.
>
> *For more on Maxim, see the Hand-book of Literary and Historical Terms.*

North Carolina Competency Goal
1.02; 1.03;
4.05; 5.01;
5.03; 6.01

Literary Skills
Understand maxims.

Background

The sayings in the *Analects* range from brief statements to more extended dialogues between Confucius and his students. The sayings express ideas based on Chinese traditions. Confucius declared that he was not really a creator but a transmitter of ideas, a man who was not born with special wisdom but only with a love of past tradition. He believed that studying ancient teachings enabled people to join the continuous chain of minds stretching from the past to the present.

In the *Analects,* Confucius, called "the Master," speaks about the inner goodness people should cultivate. The true self of every person—marked by unselfishness, courage, and honor—is a reflection of *chung-yung,* usually translated as "the Golden Mean," an ideal of universal moral and social harmony. The *Analects* instructs the individual on how to achieve "moderation in all things" through moral education, the building of a harmonious family life, and the development of virtues such as loyalty, obedience, and a sense of justice.

Throughout the *Analects,* Confucius also emphasizes "filial piety," the carrying out of basic obligations to one's living and dead ancestors. (The word *filial* comes from a Latin word meaning "of a son or daughter," and *piety* refers to devotion; thus, "filial piety" refers to the proper behavior of a child toward a parent or ancestor.) In addition, he stresses the importance of social and religious rituals. He believed a person's inner virtues can be fully realized only through concrete acts of "ritual propriety," or proper behavior, toward other human beings.

from the *Analects*

Confucius
translated by **Arthur Waley**

The Master said, "He who rules by moral force is like the polestar,[1] which remains in its place while all the lesser stars do homage to it." (II, 1)

The Master said, "If out of the three hundred *Songs*[2] I had to take one phrase to cover all my teaching, I would say 'Let there be no evil in your thoughts.' " (II, 2)

The Master said, "At fifteen I set my heart upon learning. At thirty, I had planted my feet firm upon the ground. At forty, I no longer suffered from perplexities. At fifty, I knew what were the biddings of Heaven. At sixty, I heard them with docile ear. At seventy, I could follow the dictates of my own heart; for what I desired no longer overstepped the boundaries of right." (II, 4)

Tzu-yu[3] asked about the treatment of parents. The Master said, "Filial sons nowadays are people who see to it that their parents get enough to eat. But even dogs and horses are cared for to that extent. If there is no feeling of respect, wherein lies the difference?" (II, 7)

The Master said, "Yu,[4] shall I teach you what knowledge is? When you know a thing, to recognize that you know it, and when you do not know a thing, to recognize that you do not know it. That is knowledge." (II, 17)

---

1. **polestar** *n.:* North Star, toward which the Earth's axis points; also, a directing principle.
2. **Songs:** *The Book of Songs.*
3. **Tzu-yu** (dzo͞o′yo͞o′): one of Confucius's principal disciples, often credited with sayings of his own.
4. **Yu** (yō): disciple of humble birth.

Washing the Buddha by Wu Pin. Detail of a scroll from the *Album of a Record of Yearly Observances.*

National Palace Museum, Taiwan, Republic of China.

A *Long Scroll of Buddhist Images* (detail of a handscroll) (c. 1180) by Chang Sheng-wen. Song dynasty.
National Palace Museum, Taiwan, Republic of China.

The Master said, "He who seeks only coarse food to eat, water to drink, and bent arm for pillow, will without looking for it find happiness to boot. Any thought of accepting wealth and rank by means that I know to be wrong is as remote from me as the clouds that float above." (VII, 15)

The Duke of She[5] asked Tzu-lu[6] about Master K'ung (Confucius). Tzu-lu did not reply. The Master said, "Why did you not say 'This is the character of the man: so intent upon enlightening the eager that he forgets his hunger, and so happy in doing so that he forgets the bitterness of his lot and does not realize that old age is at hand.' That is what he is." (VII, 18)

Tzu-kung[7] asked about government. The Master said, "Sufficient food, sufficient weapons, and the confidence of the common people."

Tzu-kung said, "Suppose you had no choice but to dispense with one of these three, which would you forgo?" The Master said, "Weapons." Tzu-kung said, "Suppose you were forced to dispense with one of the two that were left, which would you forgo?" The Master said, "Food. For from of old, death has been the lot of all men; but a people that no longer trusts its rulers is lost indeed." (XII, 7)

Someone said, "What about the saying 'Meet resentment with inner power'?" The Master said, "In that case, how is one to meet inner power? Rather, meet resentment with upright dealing and meet inner power with inner power." (XIV, 36)

The Master said, "A gentleman is distressed by his own lack of capacity; he is never distressed at the failure of others to recognize his merits." (XV, 18)

Tzu-kung asked saying, "Is there any single saying that one can act upon all day and every day?" The Master said, "Perhaps the saying about consideration: 'Never do to others what you would not like them to do to you.'" (XV, 23)

---

5. **Duke of She** (shu): adventurer and self-styled nobleman, a contemporary of Confucius.
6. **Tzu-lu** (dzoo′loo′): disciple of Confucius, known for his outgoing personality.
7. **Tzu-kung** (dzoo′goon): disciple of Confucius, who also served as a government official.

Response and Analysis

Reading Check

1. According to the Master, Confucius, what simple rule of conduct can be acted upon every day?

2. To the Master's way of thinking, what is wrong with the "filial sons" of his day?

Thinking Critically

3. In Book II, Analect 7, Confucius speaks of filial piety (honoring one's parents) as more than just a form of good behavior. Why do you think he emphasizes such conduct in his teachings?

4. Which of the Master's sayings is most like the Bible's golden rule: "Do unto others as you would have them do unto you"? What is the main difference between Confucius's saying and the golden rule?

5. One of the **maxims** in the *Analects* states, "A gentleman is distressed by his own lack of capacity; he is never distressed at the failure of others to recognize his merits." Paraphrase this maxim in your own words. Do you agree or disagree with it? Why?

6. How do Confucius's teachings compare with your own views of moral conduct? Review your Quickwrite response.

Extending and Evaluating

7. Many people still quote traditional sayings that state rules of conduct, such as "Look before you leap" or "A penny saved is a penny earned." Why do you think such maxims have stood the test of time?

WRITING

Comparing and Contrasting Maxims

One of the most popular American writers of maxims is Benjamin Franklin (1706–1790). Franklin wrote humorous and wise sayings, many of which were taken from other languages, folk sayings, and the words of other writers. Some of his sayings are:

- Glass, china, and reputation are easily cracked and never well mended.

- Nothing brings more pain than too much pleasure; nothing more bondage than too much liberty.

- He that composes himself is wiser than he that composes books.

Find some of Franklin's other maxims, and compare them with those you have just read by Confucius. What are the similarities and differences in the two writers' views of good conduct? Do both believe in the Golden Mean? Write your ideas in a two-paragraph essay. Be sure to support your ideas with specific examples from each writer's works.

North Carolina Competency Goal
1.02; 1.03; 4.05; 5.03; 6.01

INTERNET

Projects and Activities
Keyword: LE5 WL-3

SKILLS FOCUS

Literary Skills
Analyze maxims.

Writing Skills
Compare and contrast maxims.

Nobleman's badge depicting four-clawed, dragonlike beast (17th century). Ming dynasty.

Taoist Writers

Portrait of Laotzu (detail) from Chinese Taoist fresco *Lord of the Southern Dipper.*

The Granger Collection, New York.

Laotzu

(c. 571 B.C.–?)

According to Chinese legend, Laotzu (lou′dzoo′) was born as an old, bearded, white-haired man, who was thereafter called "The Old Philosopher" or "The Old Boy" and lived to the age of 160. As the story suggests, Laotzu is a shadowy figure, more of a legend than a historical reality.

Laotzu is the reputed founder of the Chinese philosophy of Taoism (dou′iz′əm). Broadly defined, Taoism consists of the joyful acceptance of life and a willingness to yield to the natural world, becoming one with it.

In defining the essence of his philosophy, Laotzu said, "He who knows does not speak. He who speaks does not know." The Chinese poet Po Chü-i (bō joo′ē′) underscored the irony of this statement when he wrote:

"He who talks doesn't know,
    he who knows doesn't talk":
that is what Lao-tzu told us,
    in a book of five thousand words.
If he was the one who knew,
    how could he have been such a
        blabbermouth?

Chuang-tzu

(fourth century B.C.)

The Chinese philosopher Chuang-tzu (joo·än′dzoo′) was the most important early interpreter of Taoism. What little we know about him comes from *Chuang-tzu,* a book of fictional stories written by others that contains his teachings. In these stories, Chuang-tzu appears as a quirky character who cares little for public approval or material possessions.

Lieh-tzu

(fourth century B.C.)

Though some scholars doubt that he existed, most experts believe there was a real Lieh-tzu (lē′ə·dzoo), a Taoist teacher who had philosophical differences with his forebears Laotzu and Chuang-tzu. Lieh-tzu argued that a sequence of causes predetermines everything that happens, including one's choice of action. Since no one can change the unchangeable Way, or Tao, people should pursue their own self-interests.

Liu An

(172–122 B.C.)

Liu An (lē·oo′ än) was not only a Taoist scholar but also the grandson of the founder of the Han dynasty (206 B.C.–A.D. 220). Liu An's royal title was the Prince of Huai-nan (hwī′nän′). The prince surrounded himself with a circle of philosophers, and under his patronage they produced essays on metaphysics, cosmology, politics, and conduct.

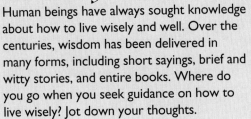

Before You Read

Taoist Writings

Make the Connection

Quickwrite

Human beings have always sought knowledge about how to live wisely and well. Over the centuries, wisdom has been delivered in many forms, including short sayings, brief and witty stories, and entire books. Where do you go when you seek guidance on how to live wisely? Jot down your thoughts.

Literary Focus

Paradox

A **paradox** is a seemingly contradictory statement that is actually true. For example, in the New Testament, Saint Paul uses a paradox when he states, "For when I am weak, then I am strong" (2 Corinthians). The statement challenges us to find an underlying truth that resolves the apparent contradiction. Saint Paul means that when he is weak in worldly terms, he is strong spiritually. Laotzu and other Taoist writers use paradox to focus attention on important Taoist insights. Reconciling paradoxes is key to understanding Taoist philosophy.

> A **paradox** is a seeming contradiction that expresses an underlying truth.
>
> *For more on Paradox, see the Handbook of Literary and Historical Terms.*

Background

The *Tao Te Ching* (dou de jin) is a brief collection of sayings and poetry that teach the nature of Taoism. Laotzu wrote the *Tao Te Ching* after leaving China during the decline of the Chou dynasty. In the *Tao Te Ching*, or "Classic of the Way of Power," Laotzu intended to provide guidance to rulers who wished to govern wisely. The *Tao Te Ching* has been translated more often than any other book in history except the Bible.

At the heart of the *Tao Te Ching* is a central figure, "the Master." According to the translator of this version, the master is a man or a woman "whose life is in perfect harmony with the way things are" and who has become one with "the Tao, the Truth, the Life." According to Laotzu, water symbolizes, or stands for, a model of Tao, for the fluid nature of water best expresses the nature of Tao.

In the centuries following the writing of the *Tao Te Ching*, various Chinese thinkers and teachers have interpreted and reinterpreted Laotzu's philosophy. Many of these writers use **anecdotes,** or brief stories, to convey their different approaches to Taoist philosophy. Chuang-tzu, for example, tends to point directly to the Tao, or the Way, which he sees at work in the universe. Lieh-tzu, on the other hand, emphasizes the folly of those who don't see beyond the obvious to the underlying patterns that govern all action.

North Carolina Competency Goal
1.02; 1.03; 4.05; 5.01; 5.03; 6.01

SKILLS FOCUS

Literary Skills
Understand paradox.

from the Tao Te Ching

Laotzu

translated by **Stephen Mitchell**

2

When people see some things as beautiful,
other things become ugly.
When people see some things as good,
other things become bad.

Being and non-being create each other.
Difficult and easy support each other.
Long and short define each other.
High and low depend on each other.
Before and after follow each other.

Therefore the Master
acts without doing anything
and teaches without saying anything.
Things arise and she lets them come;
things disappear and she lets them go.
She has but doesn't possess,
acts but doesn't expect.
When her work is done, she forgets it.
That is why it lasts forever.

8

The supreme good is like water,
which nourishes all things without trying to.
It is content with the low places that people
    disdain.
Thus it is like the Tao.

In dwelling, live close to the ground.
In thinking, keep to the simple.
In conflict, be fair and generous.
In governing, don't try to control.
In work, do what you enjoy.
In family life, be completely present.

When you are content to be simply yourself
and don't compare or compete,
everybody will respect you.

29

Do you want to improve the world?
I don't think it can be done.

The world is sacred.
It can't be improved.
If you tamper with it, you'll ruin it.
If you treat it like an object, you'll lose it.

There is a time for being ahead,
a time for being behind;
a time for being in motion,
a time for being at rest;
a time for being vigorous,
a time for being exhausted;
a time for being safe,
a time for being in danger.

The Master sees things as they are,
without trying to control them.
She lets them go their own way,
and resides at the center of the circle.

The Jingting Mountains and Waterfall in Autumn
(detail of hanging scroll) (1671) by Tao-chi.
Qing dynasty.

Musée des Arts Asiatiques-Guimet, Paris.

Taoist Anecdotes

translated by **Moss Roberts**

Wagging My Tail in the Mud

The hermit poet Chuang-tzu was angling° in the River Pu. The king of Ch'u sent two noblemen to invite Chuang to come before him. "We were hoping you would take on certain affairs of state," they said. Holding his pole steady and without looking at them, Chuang-tzu said, "I hear Ch'u has a sacred tortoise that has been dead three thousand years, and the king has it enshrined in a cushioned box in the ancestral hall. Do you think the tortoise would be happier wagging its tail in the mud than having his shell honored?" "Of course," replied the two noblemen. "Then begone," said Chuang-tzu. "I mean to keep wagging my tail in the mud."

—*Chuang-tzu*

The Butterfly

Chuang-tzu said, "Once upon a time I dreamed myself a butterfly, floating like petals in the air, happy to be doing as I pleased, no longer aware of myself! But soon enough I awoke and then, frantically clutching myself, Chuang-tzu was I! I wonder: Was Chuang-tzu dreaming himself the butterfly, or was the butterfly dreaming itself Chuang-tzu? Of course, if you take Chuang-tzu and the butterfly together, then there's a difference between them. But that difference is only due to their changing material forms."

—*Chuang-tzu*

The Missing Axe

A man whose axe was missing suspected his neighbor's son. The boy walked like a thief, looked like a thief, and spoke like a thief. But the man found his axe while he was digging in the valley, and the next time he saw his neighbor's son, the boy walked, looked, and spoke like any other child.

—*Lieh-tzu*

The Lost Horse

A man who lived on the northern frontier of China was skilled in interpreting events. One day for no reason, his horse ran away to the nomads across the border. Everyone tried to console him, but his father said, "What makes you so sure this isn't a blessing?" Some months later his horse returned, bringing a splendid nomad stallion. Everyone congratulated him, but his father said, "What makes you so sure this isn't a disaster?" Their household was richer by a fine horse, which the son loved to ride. One day he fell and broke his hip. Everyone tried to console him, but his father said, "What makes you so sure this isn't a blessing?"

A year later the nomads came in force across the border, and every able-bodied man took his bow and went into battle. The Chinese frontiersmen lost nine of every ten men. Only because the son was lame did the father and son survive to take care of each other. Truly, blessing turns to disaster, and disaster to blessing: the changes have no end, nor can the mystery be fathomed.

—*Liu An*

° **angling** *v.:* fishing.

Tomb figure of an equestrienne on a horse. China, Tang dynasty.

Response and Analysis

Thinking Critically

1. In passage 2 from the *Tao Te Ching*, what is the Master's approach to acting and teaching? What happens when she forgets her work?

2. In passage 2, point out one **paradox**, or apparent contradiction. What truth about life does Laotzu reveal in these lines?

3. In passage 8, in what two ways is water like the Tao? What must one do to gain people's respect?

4. In passage 29, how does Laotzu advise readers to approach the world? How is the Master used as an example of this approach?

5. In passage 29, what does Laotzu mean when he says the world cannot be improved? How does the rest of the passage support this idea?

6. How does Chuang-tzu defy society's expectations in "Wagging My Tail in the Mud"?

7. What does "Wagging My Tail in the Mud" reveal about Chuang-tzu's character? How does the tale reflect Taoist beliefs about the need to be true to oneself?

8. What is Chuang-tzu's purpose in imagining himself a butterfly in "The Butterfly"?

9. What does Lieh-tzu's tale "The Missing Axe" teach about how people tend to judge others?

10. What point is being made in "The Lost Horse" about distinguishing good and bad fortune?

Extending and Evaluating

11. What did you find wise or helpful in the Taoist texts? Which of these Taoist passages would you add to your list of sources of wisdom? What similarities do these Taoist passages share with the sources of wisdom you discussed in your Quickwrite notes?

WRITING

Comparing and Contrasting Two Passages

Lines 7–14 of passage 29 from the *Tao Te Ching* are similar in theme and form to the biblical poem "To Every Thing There Is a Season," below, from Chapter 3 of Ecclesiastes. In a two- or three-paragraph essay, compare and contrast the two selections. In your essay, consider similarities and differences in style and message.

To Every Thing There Is a Season
King James Bible

To every thing there is a season.
And a time to every purpose under the
    heaven:
A time to be born, and a time to die;
A time to plant, and a time to pluck
    up that which is planted;
5 A time to kill, and a time to heal;
A time to break down, and a time to
    build up;
A time to weep, and a time to laugh;
A time to mourn, and a time to dance;
A time to cast away stones, and a time
    to gather stones together;
10 A time to embrace, and a time to
    refrain from embracing;
A time to get, and a time to lose;
A time to keep, and a time to cast
    away;
A time to rend, and a time to sew;
A time to keep silence, and a time to
    speak;
15 A time to love, and a time to hate;
A time of war, and a time of peace.
        —Ecclesiastes 3:1–8

North Carolina Competency Goal
1.03; 4.05; 5.03; 6.01

go.hrw.com

INTERNET

Projects and Activities
Keyword:
LE5 WL-3

SKILLS FOCUS

Literary Skills
Analyze paradox.

Writing Skills
Compare and contrast two passages.

Observers of the Natural World

You will be reading the selections listed above in this Cultural Points of View feature. In the top corner of each page in this feature, you'll find a globe. Smaller versions of the globe appear next to the questions on page 429 that focus on the natural world. At the end of the feature (page 434), you'll compare the various points of view expressed in the selections.

Examining the Theme: Observers of the Natural World

The poets of China's T'ang dynasty period (A.D. 618–907) have been among the most successful writers in evoking both the beauty of nature and its personal meaning for them. These poets' ability to blend precise descriptions of nature with philosophical insights finds a parallel in writings from all over the world, especially in modern and contemporary writers who contemplate humanity's relationship with the natural world.

Make the Connection

Quickwrite

Recall a time when you were in a natural setting, such as a meadow or the seashore. Use specific words and phrases to create strong images of what you saw, heard, smelled, touched, or tasted.

Reading Skills

Comparing Universal Themes Across Texts

To examine how different writers approach a universal theme, it is helpful to take careful notes as you read each work. To organize your notes, you may want to make a chart with headings such as *details of setting, sensory images, symbolic levels of meaning,* and *overall attitude toward the subject.* When you have read all the selections, you can compare your notes.

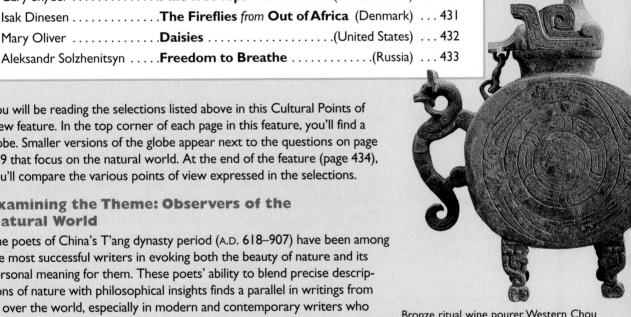

Bronze ritual wine pourer. Western Chou dynasty (c. 1027–771 B.C.E.).

National Museum, Beijing.

SKILLS FOCUS

Pages 419–434 cover

Literary Skills
Understand cultural points of view on a topic.

Reading Skills
Compare universal themes across texts.

North Carolina Competency Goal
1.02; 1.03; 4.05; 5.03; 6.01

T'ang Dynasty Poets

Li Po Chanting in Stroll
by Liang Kai (detail)
(13th century).
Southern Song dynasty.
Collection of the Tokyo
National Museum.

Li Po

(A.D. 701–762)

Along with his friend Tu Fu, Li Po (lē bō) embodies the highest poetic achievements of the T'ang dynasty, an age of great prosperity and cultural achievement. A free-spirited wanderer, Li Po nevertheless wrote traditional lyric poetry, characterized by a sense of playfulness, fantasy, and grace.

Although Li Po was probably born in central Asia, he grew up in the province of Szechwan (se'chwän') in southwestern China. He was a well-educated youth from a good family, but as a young man, he chose to live as a wandering vagabond.

As he traveled throughout China, Li Po wrote poetry and made friends with government officials, fellow poets, and even hermits. He also married and lived with his wife's family for a short time before resuming life as a wanderer.

His journeys served to spread his fame as a poet. He even abandoned his nomadic life at one point to become an imperial court poet. Sometime afterward, Li Po entered the service of a rebel prince. When the prince's bid for power failed, Li Po barely escaped a sentence of exile. Three years later the poet died suddenly. A romantic Chinese legend claims that he drowned one night as he leaned from his boat to embrace the watery reflection of the moon.

Tu Fu

(A.D. 712–770)

Tu Fu (dōō fōō) was born into a noble family of scholar-officials. As a youth, he was confident of securing one of the coveted imperial appointments but was bitterly disappointed when he failed the qualifying writing examinations.

Although Tu Fu passed the imperial examinations later in life, he never achieved his youthful dream of becoming an advisor to the emperor. Tu Fu's family connections and modest wealth, however, assured him of relative comfort until 755, when a violent rebellion ended the glory days of the T'ang dynasty. After that, Tu Fu was often in search of work, and his remaining years were marked by loss, hardship, and poor health.

The uncertain course of Tu Fu's life is reflected in his poetry, which is often tinged with bitterness and melancholy. As a young man, he wrote mainly about the beauty of nature and his own sorrows, but as he grew older, he turned to more humanitarian or social themes. He became sensitive to the sufferings of others and, after the bloody rebellion of 755, wrote many poems about the folly of war.

Tu Fu wrote in an elegant, innovative style that influenced Chinese poets for centuries. To the Chinese, "Li Po is the people's poet. Tu Fu is the poet's poet."

Portrait of Tu Fu. Rubbing of a stone carving of the Ching dynasty.

Succession of portals in the Palace of the Forbidden City, China.

Po Chü-i

(A.D. 772–846)

A lifelong poet, Po Chü-i grew up in Shensi province as the son of a minor government official. Po Chü-i passed the imperial literary examination at the exceptionally young age of twenty-eight. In the course of his lifetime, he was in and out of government positions, sometimes banished to the provinces and then later recalled to the capital. No doubt his government career was limited by his willingness to satirize government policies in his poems. Much of his poetry, however, is lighthearted and deals with his personal experiences and feelings, which he expresses in simple, straightforward language. It was even said of Po Chü-i that he read his poetry to an old woman and then revised anything she did not understand. After retiring from government service in 833, the poet suffered a stroke that left him paralyzed. He ended his days in a Buddhist monastery.

Han-shan

(late eighth century?)

Han-shan is the name of the author of a collection of T'ang dynasty poems. The poet appears to have taken the name "han-shan," or "cold mountain," from the place in the mountains of southeast China where he lived alone for most of his life. His real name and the time and place of his birth and death are unknown. In fact, his poems are the main source of information about him. The poems, which he carved into trees and walls, reveal Han-shan to be a devout Zen Buddhist who renounced family life and all worldly affairs to seek enlightenment in the solitude of nature. His best-known poems describe the beauty and ruggedness of his mountain retreat, but they also have a symbolic, spiritual dimension, representing the struggle for true knowledge and peace.

Before You Read

T'ang Dynasty Poems

Cultural Points of View

Quickwrite

Is there a particular place or time of year that brings out strong feelings in you? Perhaps you have a special place that you love to spend time in or a certain season that makes you feel happy, thoughtful, peaceful, sad, or restless. Write a brief description of this place or time of year, and reflect on your feelings about it.

Literary Focus

Mood

Every work of literature creates a feeling or mood in the reader. A poem's **mood**, or atmosphere, may be cheerful or gloomy, defiant or accepting, calm or agitated. The poet creates the mood with descriptive details and evocative language that call up specific images or feelings. In some poems a single mood dominates the whole work; in others there is a sudden or subtle shift of mood as the poem unfolds.

Background

Classical Chinese poetry is almost exclusively lyrical and often focuses on the contemplation of nature and the search for harmony between inner and outer forces. The very essence of Chinese poetry is the exploration of passing feelings and impressions and the appreciation of the interplay of opposites. Life is seen as a process of continual change, with opposing forces seeking to balance one another. Thus, Chinese poets muse about the changing seasons, phases of the moon, and the path to inner peace. They paint vivid word pictures of natural scenes, often in moments of solitude, using lean, spare imagery. This minimalist, or simplified, approach requires the reader to respond to subtle word associations and multiple layers of meaning.

INTERNET

More About Tu Fu
•
More About Po Chü-i
Keyword:
LE5 WL-3

Mood is the feeling or atmosphere the writer creates with words and images.

For more on Mood, see the Handbook of Literary and Historical Terms.

SKILLS FOCUS

Literary Skills
Understand mood.

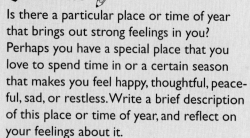

A cherry tree blossoms in spring at the Yang Ming Shan Park, Taipei, Taiwan, Republic of China.

Spring Thoughts

Li Po

translated by **Elling O. Eide**

When the grass in Yen is still jade thread,
The mulberries of Ch'in are drooping green boughs.
The days when your mind is filled with returning,
Those are the times when my heart is breaking.
But the spring wind and I have been strangers,
What is it doing in my gauze bedcurtains?

Conversation Among Mountains

Li Po

translated by **David Young**

You ask why I live
in these green mountains

I smile
can't answer

5 I am completely at peace

a peach blossom
sails past
on the current

there are worlds
10 beyond this one

The Poet Lin Bu Wandering in the Moonlight by Du Chin
(detail of hanging scroll) (late 15th century). Ming dynasty.
The Cleveland Museum of Art. John L. Severance Fund, (1954.582).

Taking Leave of a Friend

Li Po
translated by **David Young**

Here at the city wall
green mountains to the north
white water winding east
we part

5   one tumbleweed
ten thousand miles to go

high clouds
wandering thoughts

sunset
10   old friendship

you wave, moving off
your horse
whinnies
twice

Swallows and Apricot Blossoms, after Ts'ui Po.
Hanging scroll from the Ming dynasty (1368–1644).
National Palace Museum, Taiwan, Republic of China.

424

Loneliness

Tu Fu
translated by **Kenneth Rexroth**

A hawk hovers in air.
Two white gulls float on the stream.
Soaring with the wind, it is easy
To drop and seize
Birds who foolishly drift with the current.
Where the dew sparkles in the grass,
The spider's web waits for its prey.
The processes of nature resemble the business of men.
I stand alone with ten thousand sorrows.

Dreaming of Li Po

Tu Fu
translated by **David Hinton**

Death at least gives separation repose.°
Without death, its grief can only sharpen.
You wander out in malarial° southlands,
and I hear nothing of you, exiled

5   old friend. Knowing I think of you
always now, you visit my dreams, my heart
frightened it is no living spirit
I dream. Endless miles—you come

so far from the Yangtze's° sunlit maples
10 night shrouds the passes when you return.
And snared as you are in their net,
with what bird's wings could you fly?

Filling my room to the roof-beams, the moon
sinks. You nearly linger in its light,
15 but the waters deepen in long swells,
unfed dragons—take good care old friend.

---

1. **repose** *n.:* rest.
3. **malarial** *adj.:* plagued by malaria, a disease
transmitted by mosquitoes.
9. **Yangtze:** river in China.

Night in the House by the River

Tu Fu
translated by **Kenneth Rexroth**

It is late in the year;
Yin and Yang° struggle
In the brief sunlight.
On the desert mountains
5　Frost and snow
Gleam in the freezing night.
Past midnight,
Drums and bugles ring out,
Violent, cutting the heart.
10　Over the Triple Gorge the Milky Way
Pulsates between the stars.
The bitter cries of thousands of households
Can be heard above the noise of battle.
Everywhere the workers sing wild songs.
15　The great heroes and generals of old time
Are yellow dust forever now.
Such are the affairs of men.
Poetry and letters
Persist in silence and solitude.

2. Yin and Yang: opposing forces. Yin is the passive, feminine force, Yang is the active, masculine force (see page 360).

Autumn Colors on the Ch'iao and Hua Mountains (1296) by Chao Meng-fu. Handscroll from the Yuan dynasty.

National Palace Museum, Taiwan, Republic of China.

Madly Singing in the Mountains

Po Chü-i
translated by **Arthur Waley**

There is no one among men that has not a special failing;
And my failing consists in writing verses.
I have broken away from the thousand ties of life;
But this infirmity still remains behind.
5   Each time that I look at a fine landscape,
Each time that I meet a loved friend,
I raise my voice and recite a stanza of poetry
And marvel as though a God had crossed my path.
Ever since the day I was banished to Hsün-yang
10   Half my time I have lived among the hills.
And often, when I have finished a new poem,
Alone I climb the road to the Eastern Rock.
I lean my body on the banks of white Stone;
I pull down with my hands a green cassia° branch.
15   My mad singing startles the valleys and hills;
The apes and birds all come to peep.
Fearing to become a laughing-stock to the world.
I choose a place that is unfrequented by men.

14. cassia (kash′ə) *n.*: tree common in Southeast Asia.

I climb the road to Cold Mountain

Han-shan
translated by **Burton Watson**

I climb the road to Cold Mountain,
The road to Cold Mountain that never ends.
The valleys are long and strewn with stones;
The streams broad and banked with thick grass.
Moss is slippery, though no rain has fallen;
Pines sigh, but it isn't the wind.
Who can break from the snares of the world
And sit with me among the white clouds?

Here is a tree older than the forest itself

Han-shan
translated by **Burton Watson**

Here is a tree older than the forest itself;
The years of its life defy reckoning.
Its roots have seen the upheavals of hill and valley,
Its leaves have known the changes of
               wind and frost.
The world laughs at its shoddy exterior
And cares nothing for the fine grain
               of the wood inside.
Stripped free of flesh and hide,
All that remains is the core of truth.

Forest Chamber Grotto at Chü-ch'ü (detail of hanging scroll) (after 1368) by Wang Meng. Ming dynasty.
National Palace Museum, Taiwan, Republic of China.

Response and Analysis

Thinking Critically

1. How does the coming of spring make the speaker of "Spring Thoughts" feel? Why does he feel this way? How do the setting and mood compare with the place you wrote about in your Quickwrite notes?

2. How does the **mood** of "Conversation Among Mountains" contrast with that of "Spring Thoughts"? What lines help explain the speaker's mood in the first poem?

3. In "Taking Leave of a Friend," what details of **setting** help you understand the speaker's feelings about his friend's departure?

4. How do the images of the hawk and the spider's web reveal the speaker's attitude in "Loneliness"? What does the speaker mean when he says, "The processes of nature resemble the business of men"?

5. What disturbs the natural world and the poet's solitude in "Night in the House by the River"?

6. In Tu Fu's time a poem was expected to represent only one **mood,** tone, and setting. Tu Fu broke with tradition and often shifted moods, tones, and images within a poem. Find at least one shift in one of Tu Fu's poems you have read. How does this shift affect the meaning of the poem?

7. How do you think the speaker of "Madly Singing in the Mountains" truly feels about his "special failing"?

8. What might the "Cold Mountain" **setting** in Han-shan's poem "I climb the road . . ." symbolize, or stand for? How does the speaker feel about his remoteness from the busy world below?

9. What might the tree in Han-shan's poem "Here is a tree . . ." stand for? How would you summarize the poem's **theme,** or comment on life?

WRITING

Writing a Lyric Poem

All the T'ang dynasty poets you have just read have observed some aspect of the natural world, described it in powerful images, and responded to what they experienced. Try writing your own lyric poem in the tradition of these great writers. Write about a place or a time of year that has special meaning to you; you may want to go back to your Quickwrite notes or simply brainstorm some new ideas of your own. Make your poem rich in sensory images (images that appeal to the five senses), and be sure that you convey a mood that will be obvious to your reader: peacefulness, sorrow, joy. Share your finished poem with others.

Huang Shan (Yellow Mountains), southern Anhui province, China.

North Carolina Competency Goal
1.02; 1.03; 4.05; 5.03; 6.01

INTERNET

Projects and Activities

Keyword: LE5 WL-3

SKILLS FOCUS

Literary Skills
Analyze mood.

Writing Skills
Write a lyric poem.

Connected Readings

You have just read poems by various T'ang dynasty poets and considered their points of view on nature. The next four selections you will read also make strong statements about nature. As you read, ask yourself how the viewpoints presented in these selections are similar to and how they are different from those of the T'ang dynasty poems. After you read, you'll find questions on page 434 asking you to compare all the selections you've read.

Cultural Points *of* View

Before You Read

A native of the American West, Gary Snyder (1930–) is usually grouped with the Beat generation of poets, who made their mark in the 1950s. A follower of Zen Buddhism and a student of Asian literature and languages, Snyder has been strongly influenced by Chinese and Japanese poetry and by Native American ecological values. A committed environmentalist, Snyder has inter-spersed his career as a poet, lecturer, and activist with stints as a logger, trail builder, and forest lookout.

In "Pine Tree Tops," Snyder, like the Chinese and Japanese poets he admires, carefully observes a natural scene and then subtly muses on both the influence of human beings on nature and the influence of nature on human beings.

POEM

Pine Tree Tops

Gary Snyder

In the blue night
frost haze, the sky glows
with the moon
pine tree tops
bend snow-blue, fade
into sky, frost, starlight.
The creak of boots.
Rabbit tracks, deer tracks,
what do we know.

Cultural Points *of* View

Before You Read

Isak Dinesen, the pen name of Karen Blixen, was born in Denmark in 1885 and died in 1962. In 1914, she and her husband Baron Blixen moved to East Africa, where they established a coffee plantation. After she and her husband were divorced in 1921, Baroness Blixen continued to manage the plantation for ten years until coffee prices collapsed. When she was finally forced to sell the farm, she reluctantly returned to Denmark. In an effort to support herself, Blixen began writing. Her first book, *Seven Gothic Tales* (1934), was written in English and was well received by readers in the United States. Yet it was the publication of *Out of Africa* (1937), her memoir of her years in Kenya, that cemented her reputation. The book, later made into a film, evokes the African landscape, animals, and people in lyrical prose of great beauty and delicacy.

In "The Fireflies," a selection from *Out of Africa,* Dinesen paints a word picture of a June night in the African highlands so vivid that readers easily see what she sees and feel what she feels.

MEMOIR

The Fireflies *from* Out of Africa

Isak Dinesen

Here in the highlands, when the long rains are over, and in the first week of June nights begin to be cold, we get the fireflies in the woods.

On an evening you will see two or three of them, adventurous lonely stars floating in the clear air, rising and lowering, as if upon waves, or as if curtseying. To that rhythm of their flight they lighten and put out their diminutive lamps. You may catch the insect and make it shine upon the palm of your hand, giving out a strange light, a mysterious message, it turns the flesh pale green in a small circle round it. The next night there are hundreds and hundreds in the woods.

For some reason they keep within a certain height, four or five feet, above the ground. It is impossible then not to imagine that a whole crowd of children of six or seven years, are running through the dark forest carrying candles, little sticks dipped in a magic fire, joyously jumping up and down, and gambolling as they run, and swinging their small pale torches merrily. The woods are filled with a wild frolicsome life, and it is all perfectly silent.

Cultural Points *of* View

Before You Read

Mary Oliver was born in Cleveland, Ohio, in 1935 and has spent her life writing poetry and teaching others about its power and mystery. She won a Pulitzer Prize in 1984 for her collection *American Primitive* and a National Book Award in 1992 for *New and Selected Poems*. Nature, and her response to it, is the subject of much of Oliver's poetry, but her approach to nature is marked by humility and wonder. In poems like "Daisies," she seeks intimate sensory experiences rather than insights or answers from her encounters with nature. She seemingly wishes to participate without disturbing and enjoy without interpreting.

POEM

Daisies

Mary Oliver

It is possible, I suppose, that sometime
    we will learn everything
there is to learn: what the world is, for example,
    and what it means. I think this as I am crossing
5 from one field to another, in summer, and the
    mockingbird is mocking me, as one who either
knows enough already or knows enough to be
    perfectly content not knowing. Song being born
of quest he knows this: he must turn silent
10   were he suddenly assaulted with answers. Instead

oh hear his wild, caustic, tender warbling ceaselessly
    unanswered. At my feet the white-petalled daisies display
the small suns of their centerpiece, their—if you don't
    mind my saying so—their hearts. Of course
15 I could be wrong, perhaps their hearts are pale and
    narrow and hidden in the roots. What do I know.
But this: it is heaven itself to take what is given,
    to see what is plain; what the sun
lights up willingly; for example—I think this
20   as I reach down, not to pick but merely to touch—
the suitability of the field for the daisies, and the
    daisies for the field.

Cultural Points *of* View

Before You Read

Born in 1918, Aleksandr Solzhenitsyn fought bravely for the Soviet Union in World War II, but in a letter to a friend, he dared to criticize the tyrannical rule of the Soviet premier Joseph Stalin. For this offense, Solzhenitsyn was sent to prison and labor camps for eight years. After Stalin died in 1953, he was released but had to spend three more years in exile in central Asia. There Solzhenitsyn wrote his novel *One Day in the Life of Ivan Denisovich* (1962) about a man unjustly imprisoned for a political crime.

While the anti-Stalinist Nikita Khrushchev was in power, Solzhenitsyn's works were in favor, but when Khrushchev was ousted in 1964, his works were banned. When Solzhenitsyn managed to get his exposé of the Soviet penal system, *The Gulag Archipelago* (1974), published in Paris, the author was charged with treason and exiled from Russia. Eventually, he settled in the United States until 1994, when he returned to Russia, after the collapse of the Soviet Union.

In this prose poem "Freedom to Breathe," a former prisoner expresses what it means to him to stand under a blossoming apple tree and breathe as a free man. **Prose poetry** is prose that uses poetic devices, such as rhythm, imagery, and figurative language, to express a single idea or emotion.

PROSE POEM

Freedom to Breathe

Aleksandr Solzhenitsyn
translated by **Michael Glenny**

A shower fell in the night and now dark clouds drift across the sky, occasionally sprinkling a fine film of rain.

I stand under an apple tree in blossom and I breathe. Not only the apple tree but the grass round it glistens with moisture; words cannot describe the sweet fragrance that pervades the air. I inhale as deeply as I can, and the aroma invades my whole being; I breathe with my eyes open, I breathe with my eyes closed—I cannot say which gives me the greater pleasure.

This, I believe, is the single most precious freedom that prison takes away from us: the freedom to breathe freely, as I now can. No food on earth, no wine, not even a woman's kiss is sweeter to me than this air steeped in the fragrance of flowers, of moisture and freshness.

No matter that this is only a tiny garden, hemmed in by five-story houses like cages in a zoo. I cease to hear the motorcycles backfiring, radios whining, the burble of loudspeakers. As long as there is fresh air to breathe under an apple tree after a shower, we may survive a little longer.

Analyzing Cultural Points of View

Observers of the Natural World

The questions on this page ask you to analyze the views on nature expressed in the preceding four selections and in the T'ang dynasty poems.

Gary Snyder . . . . **Pine Tree Tops**

Isak Dinesen . . . . **The Fireflies**

Mary Oliver . . . . **Daisies**

Aleksandr Solzhenitsyn . . . . **Freedom to Breathe**

North Carolina Competency Goal
4.02; 5.01; 5.03

Comparing a Theme Across Cultures

1. What similarities and differences can you find between Gary Snyder's "Pine Tree Tops" and the poems of one of the T'ang dynasty poets? Review your reading notes, and consider imagery, word choice, line length, and each writer's attitudes toward nature. Ask yourself what each poet seems to suggest as the ideal relationship between human beings and nature and what emotions nature evokes in each poet.

2. Although *Out of Africa* is a prose work, Isak Dinesen uses the techniques of poetry to bring the African night alive. Analyze the poetic techniques she uses in "The Fireflies" to re-create her experience. Explore her use of setting, concrete details, sensory images, figurative language, rhythm, and other sound devices.

3. In "Daisies" the speaker wanders and muses about knowing and not knowing and asking and answering. What kinds of questions and answers do you think the speaker is referring to, and what conclusion does she come to about the importance of knowing or having answers? In her view, what is the best way to respond to nature? Cite specific lines from the poem to support your answers.

4. The narrator of "Freedom to Breathe" has a unique perspective on what is an unremarkable experience for most people—breathing the spring air. How did Solzhenitsyn's personal history make it possible for him to capture the extraordinary nature of an ordinary experience? What do you think is the **theme,** or message, of this prose poem?

INTERNET

Interactive Reading Workshop

Keyword: LE5 WL-3

WRITING

Comparing Universal Themes

Lyric poets from every corner of the world and in every era have reflected on such universal themes as the attraction of solitude versus the lure of involvement with the world, the impact of nature on the human psyche, and the nature of truth or art. Write an essay comparing and contrasting how two lyric poets of your choice have approached one of these universal themes. Be sure to consider the setting, imagery, mood, symbolism, and overall message of the poems you are comparing.

SKILLS FOCUS

Pages 419–434 cover

Literary Skills
Analyze and compare cultural points of view on a topic.

Reading Skills
Compare universal themes across texts.

Writing Skills
Compare universal themes.

Li Ch'ing-chao

(c. A.D. 1084–1151)

Li Ch'ing-chao (lē chiŋ′jɑu′) has long been regarded as China's greatest female poet of any period. A gifted and versatile writer, Li Ch'ing-chao was also one of the most liberated women of her day.

Li Ch'ing-chao grew up in a literary-minded family of noted scholars and officials. Her mother wrote poetry, and her father belonged to a powerful literary circle. Because of her father's position as an imperial scholar-officer, Li Ch'ing-chao was brought up in court society and was trained in the arts and classical literature. This was an unusual upbringing for a woman in the Sung dynasty.

When Li Ch'ing-chao was seventeen, she competed with a friend of her father's in writing poetry. She also dared to criticize the friend's views in her poems. In doing so, she violated the Confucian code of conduct for aristocratic women. But instead of being punished for her immodesty, Li Ch'ing-chao gained admiration for her talents.

At the age of eighteen, Li Ch'ing-chao married the son of a powerful government minister from a prominent family. It was a happy marriage in which Li Ch'ing-chao and her husband wrote poems to each other and shared common interests in literature and the arts. Over time, they amassed one of the largest art collections in China.

In 1129, Li Ch'ing-chao's whole world collapsed when her husband died, possibly of typhoid, just before the imperial capital was invaded by barbarians from the north. During the next few years, Li Ch'ing-chao fled for her life, following the Sung court's retreat south of the Yangtze (yaŋk′sē) River.

Woman with chignon (detail). Tang dynasty (c. 618–902 C.E.).

Musée des Arts Asiatiques-Guimet, Paris.

In her later years as a widow, Li Ch'ing-chao remained a target of court intrigue. She lost many of her possessions and lived the last years of her life in misery.

Only about fifty poems remain of the six volumes of lyric poetry Li Ch'ing-chao wrote in her lifetime. Many of her poems celebrate her happy marriage or express her loneliness when her husband was away. The aim of her poetry, she said, was to capture a single moment in time.

Before You Read

Peonies

Make the Connection

The Chinese view the peony, a large fragrant flower, as a symbol of female beauty and love, as well as a sign of spring. Seen as the queen of flowers, it is often used as a symbol of the emperor's favorite lady. Do you have any special symbols—a particular animal, such as a dolphin or wolf, for example, or an object, such as a star or a leaf—that have deep personal meaning for you? Explain.

Literary Focus

Personification

Personification is a figure of speech in which a nonhuman thing or quality is described as if it were human. The phrase "Mother Earth," for example, personifies our planet by associating it with the nurturing qualities of a human mother. In traditional Chinese poetry, elements in nature, such as the wind or clouds, are often given human qualities.

> **Personification** is the assignment of human characteristics to something that is not human.
>
> *For more on Personification, see the Handbook of Literary and Historical Terms.*

Background

Li Ch'ing-chao composed many poems in the *tz'u* (tsə), or "lyric meter," form. This form requires that the poet supply words to pre-established musical patterns. Chinese poets, in fact, never say they "write a tz'u." Instead, they "fill in a tz'u," keeping to the precise patterns of well-known Chinese songs.

Originally, the tz'u were lyrics written to songs from central Asia and sung by popular musical entertainers. Later, the elite poets of China wrote tz'u by following the songs' different metrical patterns, including the number and length of lines and specific rhyme schemes. Along with the title of their tz'u, Chinese poets often included the original tune title to indicate the metrical pattern they followed. Later tz'u were usually not intended to be sung.

Li Ch'ing-chao is regarded as the greatest writer of tz'u poetry in any period of Chinese literature. Her poem "Peonies" reflects the special poetic qualities of ambiguity, delicacy, and indirectness that distinguish tz'u from other forms of Chinese verse.

North Carolina Competency Goal
1.03; 4.05; 5.01; 5.03

SKILLS FOCUS

Literary Skills
Understand personification.

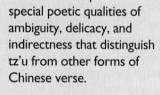

Woman playing the pan flute. Detail of terra-cotta figurine from the Tang dynasty (618–907).

Musée des Arts Asiatiques-Guimet, Paris.

Peonies from the *Album of Paintings of Flowers, Fruits, Birds and Animals* (c. 1774) by Jiang Yu. Qing dynasty.

School of Oriental & African Studies Library, University of London.

Peonies

Li Ch'ing-chao
translated by **Kenneth Rexroth**
and Ling Chung

You open the low curtains of the women's quarter in the
    palace.
And carefully the carved railings guard you.
You stand alone in the middle of the balcony in the end of
    Spring.
Your flowerlike face is clear and bright as flowing water.
5   Gentle, modest, your natural innocence is apparent to all.
All flowers have withered except you.
In the morning breeze, in glittering dew,
You make your morning toilet
And become still more splendid and bewitching.
10   The wind envies you as you laugh at the moon.
The God of Spring falls in love with you forever.
Over the east side of the city the sun rises
And shines on the ponds and the gardens
And teahouses of the courtesans in the south side.
15   The perfumed carriages run home.
The banquet tables are cleared of scattered flowers and silks.
Who will succeed you when you have become perfumed dust?
The Palace of Brilliant Light° was not more beautiful,
As the sun rises through the branches of your blossoms.
20   I pledge my love to you in a gold cup.
As the painted candles gutter and die,
I for one do not welcome the yellow twilight.

18. Palace of Brilliant Light: allusion to the emperor's palace, whose golden staircases and inlaid-pearl walls glowed in the dark with a brilliant light.

Response and Analysis

Thinking Critically

1. What do the opening lines of the poem tell about the place and time in which the poem is set? Who do you think the "you" being addressed is? Who is the speaker?

2. What does the **personification** of the peonies reveal about the poet's feelings toward nature?

3. Describe the **mood** that is suggested in the first and middle parts of "Peonies." What contrasting mood is expressed in the last part of the poem? Which particular lines express the change in mood?

4. Is "Peonies" simply a celebration of something very beautiful (a flower or woman), or does it express deeper concerns? Before you answer, consider the meaning implied in lines 6 and 17.

Extending and Evaluating

5. In this poem, springtime evokes somber thoughts as well as feelings of delight. In what sense can springtime be both a happy and a melancholy season?

WRITING

Composing Song Lyrics

"Peonies" was originally composed to fit a popular melody. Choose a song that you like, and write new lyrics for it. Write about any subject, but make sure that the words you write fit the rhythmic pattern and the rhyme scheme of the song you have selected. You may want to perform or record your song for the class when you have finished it.

Literary Focus

Ambiguity

Ambiguity is the expression of an idea in language that suggests more than one meaning. Li Ch'ing-chao uses ambiguity throughout "Peonies" as when she says, "I for one do not welcome the yellow twilight." Is the speaker referring to the time just after sunset, or to a developing darkness in human affairs? Or does she intend "twilight" to mean a gradual decline in a woman's youth and beauty—perhaps her own? The poet's ambiguity deliberately leads us into several streams of thought, all of which make sense in the context of the poem, and all of which may be true.

Analyze the poet's use of ambiguity in "Peonies." Consider the following: lines that suggest the speaker is addressing a flower and lines that suggest the speaker is addressing a woman; the identity of the "you" who is being addressed in the poem; the possible identity of the poem's speaker (the "I" in lines 20–22).

North Carolina Competency Goal
1.03; 5.03

INTERNET

Projects and Activities
Keyword:
LE5 WL-3

SKILLS FOCUS

Literary Skills
Analyze personification and ambiguity.

Writing Skills
Compose song lyrics.

Cinnabar-lacquered table depicting scholars playing chess under a pine tree (18th century).

Literature of India, China, and Japan:

The Search for Truth and Enlightenment

Japanese Literature

Poetry has its seeds in man's heart.... Man's activities are various and whatever they see or hear touches their hearts and is expressed in poetry. When we hear the notes of the nightingale among the blossoms, when we hear the frog in the water, we know that every living being is capable of song. Poetry, without effort, can move heaven and earth, can touch the gods and spirits . . . it turns the hearts of man and woman to each other and it soothes the soul of the fierce warrior.

—Ki no Tsurayuki
from the Kokinshū

Portrait of Ushiwakamaru (detail of hanging scroll) (19th century) by Kano Osanobu. Edo period.

Museum of the Imperial Collections, Tokyo. Photographs through courtesy of the International Society for Educational Information, Inc.

Introduction

Tanka

Invented more than a thousand years ago, tanka may be the most beloved form of Japanese poetry. Even today, the emperor of Japan holds an annual tanka-writing competition to celebrate the New Year.

The Origin of Tanka

Tanka, meaning "short songs," are brief lyrical poems. The traditional tanka consists of exactly thirty-one syllables, divided among five lines. Within this set form, the great tanka poets manage to compress an entire world of beauty and emotion.

The earliest known tanka appeared in a collection of poems called the *Manyōshū* (män·yō'shoo), or *Collection of Ten Thousand Leaves.* This anthology, which contains a variety of poetic forms, is still widely quoted and praised. Most of the tanka in the *Manyōshū* describe nature, the impermanence of life, and the joys and sorrows of solitude and love.

When the *Manyōshū* appeared, Japanese poets were just beginning to break away from the powerful influence of Chinese literary tradition. At first, Japanese was exclusively a spoken language, and the earliest Japanese poets had to write their poems using Chinese characters. Between the fifth and eighth centuries A.D., a system for writing Japanese was developed, adapting Chinese characters to describe Japanese sounds. These phonetic characters came to be known as *kana* (kä'nä), meaning "borrowed names."

By the time the *Manyōshū* was compiled, Japanese poets had begun to appreciate the lyrical power of their own language. Historically, the Japanese view the *Manyōshū* as the beginning of a written literature that they could call entirely their own.

Thirty-Six Poets (detail of a two-panel screen) (19th century) by Sakai Hoitsu. Edo period.

Freer Gallery of Art, Smithsonian Institution, Washington, DC. Purchase (F1970.22).

Tanka and Medieval Court Life

Tanka continued to thrive throughout the medieval period. During the Heian (hä'än) period (794–1185), writing tanka was a common ritual of court life, playing a key role in courtship. A prince would dash off a tanka and send it to his loved one, who would reply with a poem of her own.

In 905, a second great tanka anthology, the *Kokinshū* (kō·kēn'shoo), appeared. The more than a thousand poems in the *Kokinshū* embody the beauty, precision, and economy of words that have come to be associated with Japanese poetry.

Tanka Poets

The Poetess Ono no Komachi (detail) (c. 1820).
Edo period.

Spencer Museum of Art, The University of Kansas, Lawrence.
William Bridges Thayer Memorial (0000.1561).

Lady Ise
(late ninth to mid-tenth centuries)

Lady Ise was born in the late ninth century into a highly educated family of scholars and poets. Her father served as governor of various provinces, including Ise. It was during his tenure there that his beautiful and accomplished daughter entered court service, where she became a lady-in-waiting to the emperor's consort and later an intimate of the emperor himself. Lady Ise's poems not only appeared in the imperial anthologies but were collected in an anthology of her work alone.

Oshikochi Mitsune
(late ninth century)

Oshikochi Mitsune (ō′shē·kō′chē mē·tsōō′·nā) was among the greatest poets of the ninth-century Heian era in Japan. He was one of the editors of the *Kokinshū,* the second great anthology of tanka verse; some of his tanka appear in that landmark anthology. His poems are often melancholy, but never sentimental.

Ki no Tsurayuki
(884–946)

Another editor of the *Kokinshū,* Ki no Tsurayuki (kē′ nō tsōō·rä·yōō′kē), born in 884, became a high court official as well as an accomplished writer and calligrapher. In addition to tanka, he also wrote a travel diary that interwove poetry and prose. In Tsurayuki's time, most cultured Japanese men wrote in Chinese. Generally, only women, as well as men who could not afford a classical education, wrote in Japanese. Since Tsurayuki preferred to write in Japanese but wanted to avoid ridicule, he wrote his diary under a woman's name.

Ono no Komachi
(mid-ninth century)

Ono no Komachi (ō′nō nō kō·mä′chē) is probably the most revered of the poets whose tanka appeared in the *Kokinshū.* Her great physical beauty and the emotional power of her verse made her a celebrated figure in mid–ninth century Japan. More than three centuries after her death, a Noh dramatist, Kan'ami Kiyotsugu, wrote a play about her, and she was the subject of many popular legends, due primarily to the intensity and passion of her poems.

Saigyo
(1118–1190)

Saigyo (sä′ē·gyō), sometimes referred to as Priest Saigyo, was among the most accomplished of the twelfth-century writers of tanka, and he has remained one of Japan's best-loved poets. He abandoned his position as a royal bodyguard at the age of twenty-three to become a priest. He wrote tanka during his years of wandering through the Japanese countryside.

Tanka

Make the Connection

Quickwrite ✏️

Many tanka describe a scene of momentary beauty or a single emotion, such as love or loneliness. Suppose you wanted to create an image—a drawing, painting, or photograph—to convey a scene or emotion that is meaningful to you. Freewrite for a few minutes, describing the content of your image and what it conveys.

Literary Focus

Tanka

The **tanka** form is a five-line Japanese poem that contains exactly thirty-one syllables. Three of the poem's lines have seven syllables each, and the other two have five syllables each. When translated into English, the traditional tanka syllable structure is usually abandoned in order to capture the essence of the Japanese original.

All tanka evoke strong images and emotions, and the best are subtle and indirect. In the art of tanka, what the poet does *not* say is as important as what he or she *does* say. It is up to the reader to connect what is stated directly with what is implied.

> **Tanka** are five-line Japanese poems that evoke a strong image or emotion by indirect means.
>
> *For more on Tanka, see the Handbook of Literary and Historical Terms.*

Background

The poems of the great tanka poets are so familiar in Japan that they are the basis of a popular "poem-card" game traditionally played at the New Year. In this game one player reads the first half of a poem from the thirteenth-century anthology *The Verses of a Hundred Poets*. The other players must choose the correct ending of the poem from among the hundred cards spread on the floor.

The tanka collected here were composed by five different poets over a period of four centuries, yet they share similar themes and techniques. Because all of these tanka are translations, they necessarily differ from the originals—not only in syllable structure but also in rhythm and cadence. In other ways, however, the translations reflect the tradition of Japanese tanka. They are unrhymed, for example, and many include striking similes and metaphors. They also utilize the repetition of sounds for musical effect—an important feature of Japanese poetry that can only partially be achieved in English.

In the tanka you are about to read, you will find examples of both **alliteration** (repeated consonant sounds, as in "seven scarlet blossoms") and **assonance** (repeated vowel sounds, as in "breezes stirred the green leaves"). The Japanese language lends itself especially to assonance, for Japanese has fewer vowel sounds than English. Thus, it is easy to create words or phrases that repeat the same vowel sound. In classical tanka, assonance was used to create certain moods or ideas. The vowel sound *a*, for example, was linked with the idea of brilliance or clarity, while the vowel sound *o* evoked a sense of gloominess or obscurity, as in the phrase *oboro-zuki,* which means "pale, clouded moon."

North Carolina Competency Goal
1.02; 1.03; 4.05; 5.01; 5.03; 6.01

SKILLS FOCUS

Literary Skills
Understand tanka.

TANKA

A flower of waves

A flower of waves
blossoms in the distance
and ripples shoreward
as though a breeze had quickened
the sea and set it blooming.

> —Lady Ise
> *translated by* Etsuko Terasaki
> with Irma Brandeis

The sight of the flowers

The sight of the flowers
        has worked a change in my heart,
but I will take care
        to show nothing in my face—
lest someone should find it out.

> —Oshikochi Mitsune
> *translated by* Steven D. Carter

Though I go to you

Though I go to you
        ceaselessly along dream paths,
the sum of those trysts°
        is less than a single glimpse
                granted in the waking world.

> —Ono no Komachi
> *translated by* Helen Craig McCullough

Doesn't he realize

Doesn't he realize
that I am not
like the swaying kelp
in the surf,
where the seaweed gatherer
can come as often as he wants.

> —Ono no Komachi
> *translated by* Kenneth Rexroth
> and Ikuko Atsumi

Flowers (detail of a two-panel screen)
(c. 18th century) by Watanbe Shiko. Edo period.

Freer Gallery of Art, Smithsonian Institution, Washington, DC.
Gift of Charles Lang Freer, (F1903.238).

° **trysts** *n.pl.:* secret meetings.

Earthly Paradise of Wuling (detail of handscroll painting) (c. 1780) by Tani Bunchō. Edo period.
The British Museum, London (1980.2-25.04).

Unseen by men's eyes

Unseen by men's eyes,
the colored leaves have scattered
    deep in the mountains:
truly we may say brocade
    worn in the darkness of night!

> —Ki no Tsurayuki
> *translated by*
> Helen Craig McCullough

Now that the blossoms

Now that the blossoms
    have all fallen at my house
I can only hope
    that it will seem like home—
a place to come to again.

> —Ki no Tsurayuki
> *translated by* Steven D. Carter

One lone pine tree

One lone pine tree
growing in the hollow—
and I thought
I was the only one
without a friend

> —Saigyo
> *translated by* Hiroaki Sato
> and Burton Watson

Drops of dew

Drops of dew
strung on strands
of spider web—
such are the trappings
that deck out this world

> —Saigyo
> *translated by* Hiroaki Sato
> and Burton Watson

Response and Analysis

Thinking Critically

1. What is the **metaphor,** or comparison of unlike things, at the heart of Lady Ise's tanka? Although her emotions are not stated directly, what do you think she feels about the scene she is describing?

2. The meaning of Mitsune's tanka is particularly subtle, or difficult to pin down. Assuming that the poem is set in the spring, how might the "sight of the flowers" cause a change of heart in the speaker? The speaker wishes to hide his feelings from "someone." Who might that person be?

3. Who do you think the "you" is in "Though I go to you" by Ono no Komachi? How would you paraphrase the speaker's message to that person? What emotion is this tanka expressing?

4. How does the speaker in "Doesn't he realize" use an **image** from nature to make a point about her feelings? What is she indirectly communicating about her character?

5. What **imagery** and details of **setting** does Tsurayuki use in each of his tanka to evoke a season? What emotions do his images and word choices convey?

6. What **mood** does each of Saigyo's tanka convey? What **images** convey each mood?

7. What **sound effects** does the translator of "Drops of dew" use to make the tanka pleasing to the ear?

Poem cards (c. 1805) by Shinsai Ga. Edo period.

Spencer Museum of Art, The University of Kansas, Lawrence. William Bridges Thayer Memorial (0000.1453).

Extending and Evaluating

8. Make a generalization about the **themes,** or comments on life, of tanka based on the eight poems you have just read. What is your conclusion? For instance, what do the poems say about the relationship between people and nature?

WRITING

Writing a Tanka with a Partner

As a class, play a variation of the traditional Japanese "poem-card" game (see page 442). On a three-by-five-inch note card, write the first three lines of a tanka. Then, exchange your card with a partner, who will complete the tanka by writing the last two lines on another card. (Take some time to revise your work so that you are both satisfied with the complete tanka.) Identify the two "halves" of the tanka by writing the same number on the back of each card. Then, along with the rest of the class, spread out all the cards tanka-side up and see if you can correctly guess which tanka halves go together. (The person with the most correct answers wins the tanka competition.) You may want to look back at your Quickwrite description of a scene or emotion to get ideas for the subject matter and imagery of your tanka.

North Carolina Competency Goal
1.02; 1.03; 4.02; 4.05; 5.01; 5.03; 6.01

INTERNET

Projects and Activities

Keyword: LE5 WL-3

SKILLS FOCUS

Literary Skills
Analyze tanka.

Writing Skills
Write a tanka with a partner.

Introduction
Haiku

A **haiku** is a brief, unrhymed poem three lines long. In Japanese each haiku has seventeen syllables: The first and last lines have five syllables each and the middle line has seven. This strict, compressed form challenges haiku poets to convey their feelings and observations in a few vivid images.

The Challenges of Haiku

Since the Japanese language differs so much from English, translators must make accommodations in order to capture the spirit of the original. In many cases translated haiku have more than seventeen syllables and sometimes more than three lines. Another challenge for translators is that Japanese haiku leave so much unsaid. As a result, the same haiku can be translated in numerous ways, each with subtle differences. Consider these three versions of a well-known haiku by Bashō. The first is a fairly literal translation by Harold G. Henderson:

> Old pond:
>   frog jump-in
>   water-sound.

Harry Behn's translation retains the seventeen-syllable structure of the original Japanese:

>   An old silent pond . . .
> A frog jumps into the pond,
>   splash! Silence again.

A looser translation by Asatarō Miyamori captures the image but abandons the three-line form:

> The ancient pond!
> A frog plunged—splash!

Some haiku contain allusions to Zen philosophy and Japanese history and customs. These references might be lost on non-Japanese readers, yet the images and feelings conveyed by most haiku can be understood and appreciated by readers from any time and culture.

The Colorful Realm of Living Beings (detail of hanging scroll) (c. 1757–1767). Edo period.
Museum of the Imperial Collections, Tokyo.

Haiku Poets

Matsuo Bashō
(1644–1694)

Examples of short verses similar to haiku can be found in Japanese literature as early as the thirteenth and fourteenth centuries. However, the art of haiku was not perfected until the seventeenth century, when the greatest of the classical haiku poets, Bashō (ba'shō), wrote and taught.

Bashō was the son of a samurai and spent his youth in the service of a local lord. He began writing verse when he was nine and soon showed remarkable promise. Before he was thirty, he had won acclaim as a poet and had started his own poetry school.

Two factors shaped Bashō's poetry: his devotion to Zen Buddhism and his travels. In 1684, at the age of forty, Bashō set out on the first of his many journeys through Japan. Traveling alone, he endured great discomfort and loneliness. Yet some of his best haiku were composed on these lonely journeys.

Uejima Onitsura
(1660–1738)

Onitsura was one of Bashō's greatest admirers and, like the master, he came from a samurai background and started writing poetry at a young age. Although Onitsura admired Bashō's poetry, he did not imitate Bashō's style. Onitsura's poems are generally more exuberant than Bashō's and somewhat less philosophical.

Taniguchi Buson
(1715–1783)

Buson was a younger contemporary of Onitsura who soon established his own poetic style. His haiku are generally regarded as second only to Bashō's. Buson was also an accomplished painter, and his poems reflect his fascination with light and color.

Kobayashi Issa
(1762–1826)

Issa is one of the most beloved of Japan's haiku masters. His life was extraordinarily sad. His mother died when he was just an infant, and his relationship with his stepmother was so troubled that his father sent him away from home to study when he was just fourteen. His first wife bore him five children, but all of them died in infancy, and then his wife fell ill and died. Possibly because of these many sorrows, Issa's poems are taut with barely suppressed emotion, though they are rarely sentimental.

Seated statue of Bashō (17th century) by Ran-Koo. Edo period.

Musée Historique des Tissus, Lyon, France.

Haiku

Make the Connection

Quickwrite

Many haiku describe subtle changes in nature, such as the passage of day to night or night to day, the changing of the seasons, or the cycle of plant growth and decay. Form a mental picture of one such natural change and then freewrite about it. Include the sights, sounds, smells, tastes, and textures you associate with the scene.

Literary Focus

Haiku

The traditional Japanese **haiku** consists of three unrhymed lines with a total of seventeen syllables. With so few words to work with, haiku poets must rely on strong imagery, often from nature, to capture a scene and suggest an emotional response to it. **Imagery** is imaginative language that appeals to the senses—sight, hearing, smell, touch, and taste. For example, a haiku poet might use the words "a toppling mountain of water" to convey a rough, overpowering sea or "trails of bright foam" to suggest the playfulness of waves on a shore.

North Carolina Competency Goal
1.02; 1.03; 4.05; 5.01; 5.03; 6.01

Background

The thirteen haiku that follow were written by four different poets over a span of two centuries. In spite of this diversity, the poems have a great deal in common. All are highly condensed and combine two or three vivid images, sometimes in surprising ways. Many present a scene from nature, but the mood of the poems varies widely. Some are melancholy or meditative; others are joyous or appreciative of nature's beauty.

The first five selections are by Bashō. In all of them, Bashō finds beauty and significance in seemingly ordinary or insignificant objects or events. His insight is inspired by the Buddhist belief that, through contemplation, anyone can find significance in even the humblest of things. Although haiku tends not to contain figures of speech, such as similes and metaphors, it is rich in images that appeal to all the senses. In most haiku the poet master presents the sensory images without comment and allows readers to draw their own conclusions about their meaning.

go.hrw.com

INTERNET

More About Haiku
Keyword: LE5 WL-3

Haiku is a three-line, unrhymed Japanese verse form that uses imagery to convey a scene or suggest an emotion.

For more on Haiku, see the Handbook of Literary and Historical Terms.

SKILLS FOCUS

Literary Skills
Understand haiku.

Haiku

Matsuo Bashō

After bells had rung

After bells had rung
    and were silent . . .
    flowers chimed
a peal of fragrance

A cuckoo calls

A cuckoo calls
    and suddenly . . .
    the bamboo grove
lighted by moonbeams

Moonlit flower-field . . .

Moonlit flower-field . . .
    daylight gives it
    back again
to a cotton farm

How still it is!

How still it is!
    cicadas
    buzzing in sun
drilling into rock . . .

Under a helmet

Under a helmet
    hung in a shrine,
    a cricket
chirps his last command

        —translated by Peter Beilenson
    and Harry Behn

The Colorful Realm of Living Beings (detail) (c. 1757–1767).
Hanging scroll from the Edo period.

Museum of the Imperial Collections (Sannomaru Shozakan). Museum
of the Imperial Collections, Tokyo. Photographs through courtesy
of the International Society for Educational Information, Inc.

Uejima Onitsura

We cover fragile bones

We cover fragile bones
   in our festive best
   to view
immortal flowers

A drift of ashes

A drift of ashes
   from a burned field,
   a wailing
wind sighing away . . .

      —*translated by* Peter Beilenson
       and Harry Behn

Kobayashi Issa

A snowy mountain

A snowy mountain
   echoes in the
   jeweled eyes
of a dragonfly

Everything I touch

Everything I touch
   with tenderness,
   alas
pricks like a bramble°

      —*translated by* Peter Beilenson
       and Harry Behn

Taniguchi Buson

Such a moon—

Such a moon—
the thief
pauses to sing.

      —*translated by* Lucien Stryk
       and Takashi Ikemoto

Avoiding fishnet

Avoiding fishnet
and fishing lines,
moon on the water.

      —*translated by* Tony Barnstone

Calmly Fuji stands

Calmly Fuji stands
   high above
   the new leaves' waves
that bury the earth

A red moon goes down

A red moon goes down
   late in the west . . .
   shadows flow eastward
and vanish

      —*translated by* Peter Beilenson
       and Harry Behn

(Opposite) *Mount Fuji and Tea Fields* (1928) by
Matsuoka Eikyu. Detail of hanging scroll.
Shōwa period.

Museum of the Imperial Collections, Tokyo.
Photographs through courtesy of the International
Society for Educational Information, Inc.

° **bramble** *n.*: prickly plant.

Versed in Traffic Control

INFORMATIONAL TEXT

Maggie Farley

from *Los Angeles Times,* May 18, 2002

Aaron Naparstek knows the exact moment when the car horns pushed him over the edge and turned him into a vigilante poet.

It wasn't just the constant noise outside his Brooklyn apartment window when he was trying to work from home. It wasn't just the sonic blasts from tractor-trailers that set off car alarms up and down the block. It was the sheer futility of it—that New Yorkers believe beeping their horns actually can dissolve a traffic jam, the way some people think that the more times they push an elevator button, the sooner the car will arrive.

While working on his health-care Web site—which includes, among other things, meditations for stress relief—the noise made him irritable. He couldn't concentrate. He got to the point where he could distinguish different taxi models just by the sounds of their horns. Then, one day, a guy in a blue sedan just made him snap.

"He was *leaning* on his horn," Naparstek said. "It wasn't just, 'Toot, toot.' It was: 'Nnnnnnnnnnnnnnnnnnnnnnnnnnnnnnnnnnn.'"

Naparstek decided that, if the sedan was still honking by the time he got to the refrigerator and back to the window, it deserved an egg on the windshield. The first one hit the trunk. The second hit the roof. "Clearly, I'd gone insane," Naparstek said. "But I was thinking, 'I want windshield.'"

As the egg splattered right on target, the honker got out of his car and ranted at Naparstek, threatening to come back and kill him while he slept. And while the driver made his death threats, the line of cars that were stacked up for blocks all started to honk their horns.

Naparstek realized that, while fleetingly cathartic, the egg-throwing had added to the problem. So he tried a nonviolent approach. Prompted by his Zen meditation training, Naparstek wrote a flurry of haiku—three-line stanzas in the classic Japanese 5-7-5 syllable form—and taped them on lampposts along Clinton Street. He dubbed them "honku."

You from New Jersey
Honking in front of my house
In your SUV.

Smoking cigarettes
Blasting Hot97
Futilely honking.

(Above) Aaron Naparstek.
www.honku.org.

Drivers couldn't read his poetry from the street, so Naparstek wasn't expecting much of a response. But then other honku started to appear—ones he hadn't written. Soon the lampposts were papered with 17-syllable verses, some printed out, some scrawled spontaneously under his.

We walk happily
You honk in snarled traffic
Who gets there first? Us!!

Gazing at windows
I think of the children's sleep
Broken by the noise.

From 17 syllables, a community movement was born. In the tree-lined neighborhood of million-dollar brownstones, dog-walkers and mothers pushing strollers could be seen wandering away from the lampposts, counting syllables on their fingers as they composed their own honku. Over the weeks, emboldened pedestrians began to chastise ill-mannered drivers. Neighbors clustered at corners and shared strategies. By the end of April, the honku-generated buzz brought five police officers to Clinton Street to hand out $125 tickets for noise violations. The local councilman deputized Naparstek as an official "traffic calmer."

"It may be," mused Naparstek, "the country's only example where police and politicians responded to poetry." . . .

? Describe the tone of this article. What seems to be the writer's attitude toward Aaron Naparstek's honku project? Does the writer succeed in making clear how honku is both similar to and different from traditional haiku? Explain.

Response and Analysis

Thinking Critically

1. What are some of the **images** from nature that Bashō includes in his haiku? What **moods** do these natural images create?

2. Based on the five haiku by Bashō, what would you say is Bashō's general attitude toward nature?

3. Traditionally, the Japanese put on their best clothing to go view the blossoming cherry trees in spring. With that in mind, how do you interpret Onitsura's "We cover fragile bones"? How would you describe his **tone,** or attitude, toward his subject?

4. What **mood** do the images in Onitsura's "A drift of ashes" create? What word choices help create that mood?

5. What two **images** from nature does Issa combine in "A snowy mountain"? What connection do you think he is suggesting between these two things?

6. How does Issa's "Everything I touch" differ from the other haiku reprinted here? What **mood** does it convey?

7. Buson uses the moon as an **image** in three of his haiku. What might the moon **symbolize,** or represent, in these poems?

8. What **mood** or experience do you think Buson is praising in "Calmly Fuji stands"?

North Carolina Competency Goal
1.02; 1.03; 2.01; 4.01; 4.02; 5.01; 5.03; 6.01

INTERNET

Projects and Activities

Keyword: LE5 WL-3

SKILLS FOCUS

Literary Skills
Analyze haiku.

Writing Skills
Write a haiku.

WRITING

Writing a Haiku

Bashō is a master at creating striking sensory images, and he sometimes combines these images in unexpected ways. For example, image and sound are surprisingly juxtaposed, or combined, in "flowers chimed / a peal of fragrance." This is an example of a particular kind of figurative language called **synesthesia** (sin′əs•thē′zhə), in which an image that appeals to one sense (such as taste) is conveyed in terms of an image that appeals to a different sense (such as sound), as in a phrase like "sweet laughter."

Look through the haiku you have just read for images that appeal to sight, sound, smell, taste, or touch. Then, try writing your own haiku, using at least two sensory images. You may want to look back at your Quickwrite notes for ideas. Remember that your haiku should be only three lines long and need not rhyme. Try also to imitate the haiku masters in *suggesting* a mood or meaning, rather than spelling one out. You might even try experimenting with synesthesia in your haiku. Revise your haiku until it is as spare and compressed as you can make it. Then, read it aloud to the class.

Mount Fuji and Sakura tree, Japan.

Sei Shōnagon

(c. 965–?)

Seated Lady at Her Toilette (detail). School of Hokusai, Edo period (1825–1850).

Seattle Art Museum. Eugene Fuller Memorial Collection (39.193).

One of the liveliest female voices in Japanese literature is more than a thousand years old: Sei Shōnagon (sā'ē shō'nä·gōn'), who served as a lady in waiting to the empress Sadako (sä'dä·kō) in the late tenth century during the middle of the famous Heian period in Japan (A.D. 794–1185).

We know very little about Shōnagon's life. She was born around 965 into the Kiyowara (kē·yō·wä'rä) clan. Her father, a minor government official, had earned a modest reputation as a poet. Around 990, Shōnagon went to Kyoto, where she served in the royal court for about ten years. What became of her after she left court remains a mystery.

The little knowledge we have of Shōnagon's life comes from her writings. During her ten years in Kyoto, Shōnagon jotted down various ideas and impressions and tucked the papers away in her room. Part diary, part random notes, these writings came to be known as the *Notes of the Pillow*. In Shōnagon's day, "pillows" were made of wood, and some had drawers in which letters or journals could be stored. Men and women at court may have amused themselves by scribbling their thoughts in a notebook in the evenings and hiding the notes in these "pillow books."

From Lady Shōnagon's diary, we learn that the Japanese calendar dictated everything from coronations to cutting toenails; that royal cats had a higher rank than some governors; that aristocratic women wore their hair ankle-length and colored their teeth black; and that those same women lived most of their lives behind decorative screens, even though they were, like Shōnagon, often highly educated, talented, and influential.

Lady Shōnagon wrote prose so clear and expressive that it is still held up as a model to Japanese schoolchildren. It is therefore hard to imagine that she did not intend *The Pillow Book* to be published. Nevertheless, she claimed to be dismayed after her book was discovered:

> 66 I wrote these notes at home, when I had a good deal of time to myself and thought no one would notice what I was doing. Everything that I have seen and felt is included. Since much of it might appear malicious and even harmful to people, I was careful to keep my book hidden. But now it has become public, which is the last thing I expected. . . . 99

Some scholars claim that this passage was added long after Shōnagon died. Despite centuries of exhaustive research, many mysteries surround Shōnagon's life and her manuscript. The witty Shōnagon probably would have enjoyed that irony.

Before You Read

from The Pillow Book

Make the Connection

According to Lady Shōnagon, *The Pillow Book* was intended to be a private journal, yet it was discovered and eventually published. How would you feel if someone read and made public a letter or diary of yours that you meant to keep private?

Literary Focus

Style

Style refers to the particular way in which writers use words and sentences to express their ideas. **Diction,** or word choice, is one important element of style. A writer's diction can be described as plain or fancy, abstract or concrete. Another aspect of style is **syntax,** or the way sentences are constructed. A writer's sentences can be long or short, simple or complex. **Tone,** or the attitude a writer takes toward his or her subject, is another important aspect of style. Tone can be described with an adjective: sarcastic, amused, tender, thoughtful, melancholy. Lady Shōnagon's writing contains a variety of tones, but always present is her wit: a verbal cleverness combined with keen perception.

INTERNET

Vocabulary Practice

Keyword: LE5 WL-3

> **Style** is the unique manner in which writers use language to express their ideas.
>
> *For more on Style, see the Handbook of Literary and Historical Terms.*

Reading Skills

Analyzing Style

The Pillow Book contains vivid sketches of people and places, snatches of poetry, and 164 lists. We learn a great deal about Shōnagon herself through what she chooses to write about, what she says about her subjects, and the style in which she writes. As you read Shōnagon's lists of likes and dislikes, jot down lines that especially reveal Shōnagon's personality. What key elements of her writing style help you to form an opinion of her?

Background

In Japan, forms of personal writing such as the diary have been a major literary genre for centuries. *The Pillow Book* is more a collection of inspired jottings than a diary. Every phrase is stamped with Shōnagon's personality. She was quick to praise an elegant turn of phrase or a beautiful kimono, but, like most aristocrats of her time, she had little interest in working people, whom she considered rough and ill-mannered.

Vocabulary Development

wisps *n.:* thin strands.

incantations (in'kan·tā'shənz) *n. pl.:* chants or songs with magical qualities.

insignificant (in'sig·nif'i·kənt) *adj.:* unimportant.

stealthily (stelth'·ə·lē) *adv.:* in a sly way.

convulsed (kən·vulst') *v.* used as *adj.:* shaken uncontrollably, as with laughter or weeping.

North Carolina Competency Goal
1.03; 4.03; 4.05; 5.01; 5.03

SKILLS FOCUS

Literary Skills
Understand style and tone.

Reading Skills
Analyze style.

from
The Pillow Book

Sei Shōnagon
translated by **Ivan Morris**

Pillow with fan and floral decoration, Kakiemon type. Edo period (late 17th century).

Cleveland Museum of Art. Severance and Greta Millikin Collection (1964.275).

In Spring It Is the Dawn

In spring it is the dawn that is most beautiful. As the light creeps over the hills, their outlines are dyed a faint red and wisps of purplish cloud trail over them.

In summer the nights. Not only when the moon shines, but on dark nights too, as the fireflies flit to and fro, and even when it rains, how beautiful it is!

In autumn the evenings, when the glittering sun sinks close to the edge of the hills and the crows fly back to their nests in threes and fours and twos; more charming still is a file[1] of wild geese, like specks in the distant sky. When the sun has set, one's heart is moved by the sound of the wind and the hum of the insects.

In winter the early mornings. It is beautiful indeed when snow has fallen during the night, but splendid too when the ground is white with frost; or even when there is no snow or frost, but it is simply very cold and the attendants hurry from room to room stirring up the fires and bringing charcoal, how well this fits the season's mood! But as noon approaches and the cold wears off, no one bothers to keep the braziers[2] alight, and soon nothing remains but piles of white ashes.

from Hateful Things

One is in a hurry to leave, but one's visitor keeps chattering away. If it is someone of no importance, one can get rid of him by saying, "You must tell me all about it next time"; but, should it be the sort of visitor whose presence commands one's best behavior, the situation is hateful indeed.

One finds that a hair has got caught in the stone on which one is rubbing one's inkstick, or again that gravel is lodged in the inkstick, making a nasty, grating sound.

---

1. file (fīl) *n.:* single line or row.

2. braziers (brā′zhərz) *n. pl.:* metal pans used to hold burning coals.

Vocabulary

wisps *n.:* thin strands.

Someone has suddenly fallen ill and one summons the exorcist.[3] Since he is not at home, one has to send messengers to look for him. After one has had a long fretful wait, the exorcist finally arrives, and with a sigh of relief one asks him to start his incantations. But perhaps he has been exorcizing too many evil spirits recently; for hardly has he installed himself and begun praying when his voice becomes drowsy. Oh, how hateful!

A man who has nothing in particular to recommend him discusses all sorts of subjects at random as though he knew everything.

Things That Cannot Be Compared

Summer and winter. Night and day. Rain and sunshine. Youth and age. A person's laughter and his anger. Black and white. Love and hatred. The little indigo plant[4] and the great philodendron. Rain and mist.

When one has stopped loving somebody, one feels that he has become someone else, even though he is still the same person.

In a garden full of evergreens the crows are all asleep. Then, towards the middle of the night, the crows in one of the trees suddenly wake up in a great flurry and start flapping about. Their unrest spreads to the other trees, and soon all the birds have been startled from their sleep and are cawing in alarm. How different from the same crows in daytime!

Embarrassing Things

While entertaining a visitor, one hears some servants chatting without any restraint in one of the back rooms. It is embarrassing to know that one's visitor can overhear. But how to stop them?

A man whom one loves gets drunk and keeps repeating himself.

To have spoken about someone not knowing that he could overhear. This is embarrassing even if it be a servant or some other completely insignificant person.

To hear one's servants making merry. This is equally annoying if one is on a journey and staying in cramped quarters or at home and hears the servants in a neighboring room.

Parents, convinced that their ugly child is adorable, pet him and repeat the things he has said, imitating his voice.

An ignoramus[5] who in the presence of some learned person puts on a knowing air and converses about men of old.

A man recites his own poems (not especially good ones) and tells one about the praise they have received—most embarrassing.

Lying awake at night, one says something to one's companion, who simply goes on sleeping.

In the presence of a skilled musician, someone plays a zither[6] just for his own pleasure and without tuning it.

A son-in-law who has long since stopped visiting his wife runs into his father-in-law in a public place.

Masahiro Really Is a Laughing-Stock

Masahiro really is a laughing-stock. I wonder what it is like for his parents and friends. If people see him with a decent-looking servant, they always call for the fellow and laughingly ask how he can wait upon such a master and what he thinks of him. There are skilled dyers and weavers in Masahiro's household, and when it comes to dress, whether it be the color of his

---

3. **exorcist** (eks′ôr·sist) *n.:* person who casts out evil spirits through ritual prayers.
4. **indigo** (in′di·gō′) **plant** *n.:* plant that yields a deep blue dye. Dyeing was an important art form of the aristocratic women of the Heian period.

5. **ignoramus** (ig′nə·rā′məs) *n.:* one who is stupid and inexperienced.
6. **zither** (zith′ər) *n.:* The instrument being referred to here is a *koto*, a Japanese instrument with thirteen strings.

Vocabulary

incantations (in′kan·tā′shənz) *n. pl.:* chants or songs with magical qualities.
insignificant (in′sig·nif′i·kənt) *adj.:* unimportant.

Tosa-style fan decorated with a court scene depicting a party of noblemen. Edo period (17th century).

under-robe or the style of his cloak, he is more elegant than most men; yet the only effect of his elegance is to make people say, "What a shame someone else isn't wearing these things!"

And how strangely he expresses himself! Once, when he was due to report for night duty at the Palace, he ordered that the clothes and other things he would need should be brought from his house. "Send *two* servants," he said. One man came and said that he could easily carry everything. "You're an odd fellow," said Masahiro. "How can one man bring the things of two people? After all, can you put two measures in a one-measure jar?" No one had the slightest idea what he meant; but there was loud laughter.

On another occasion a messenger brought Masahiro a letter from someone, asking for an immediate reply. "You hateful fellow!" said Masahiro. "Has someone been putting peas on the stove?[7] And who's stolen the ink and brush I had in this residence? Very odd! I could understand people taking rice or wine . . ." And again everyone laughed.

When the Empress Dowager was ill, Masahiro was sent from the Palace to inquire after her. When he came back, people asked which of her gentlemen-in-waiting had been present. He named a few people, four or five in all. "Was no one else there?" "Well, there were some others," replied Masahiro, "but they had all left." It is amazing that we could still laugh at him—so accustomed were we to hearing his foolishness.

One day when I was alone he came up to me and said, "My dear lady, I have something I must tell you at once—something that I've just heard." "And what may that be?" I asked. He approached my curtain.[8] "I heard someone who instead of saying, 'Bring your body closer,' used the phrase

---

7. **peas on the stove:** In Shōnagon's time, the image of peas popping in a stove was used to describe people in a hurry, but Masahiro's use of the expression is peculiar.

8. **curtain:** Masahiro is speaking to Shōnagon through a curtain. In feudal Japan, women of high society spent much of their time behind wooden screens hung with heavy curtains. The screens protected the women from being seen by men and strangers.

Woman Visiting a Shrine (detail) (c. 1800) by Suzuki Harunobu. Edo period.

'Bring up your five parts.'"[9] And again I burst into laughter.

On the middle night during the period of official appointments Masahiro was responsible for filling the lamps with oil. He rested his foot on the cloth under the pedestal of one of the lamps, and since the cloth happened to have been freshly oiled, his foot stuck to it. As soon as he started to walk off, the lamp fell over and, as he hurried along with the cloth stuck to his foot, the lamp dragged after him, making a terrible clatter.

---

9. **five parts:** Buddhist term referring to the knees, elbows, and head. When a person bowed and touched all "five parts" to the ground, it implied utmost respect.

One day when he thought he was alone in the Table Room, neither of the First Secretaries having reported for duty, Masahiro took a dish of beans that was lying there and went behind the Little Screen.[10] Suddenly someone pulled aside the screen—and there was Masahiro, <u>stealthily</u> munching away at the beans. Everyone who saw him was <u>convulsed</u> with laughter.[11]

Pleasing Things

Finding a large number of tales that one has not read before. Or acquiring the second volume of a tale whose first volume one has enjoyed. But often it is a disappointment.

Someone has torn up a letter and thrown it away. Picking up the pieces, one finds that many of them can be fitted together.

One has had an upsetting dream and wonders what it can mean. In great anxiety one consults a dream-interpreter, who informs one that it has no special significance.

A person of quality is holding forth about something in the past or about a recent event that is being widely discussed. Several people are gathered round him, but it is oneself that he keeps looking at as he talks.

A person who is very dear to one has fallen ill. One is miserably worried about him even if he lives in the capital and far more so if he is in some remote part of the country. What a pleasure to be told that he has recovered!

---

10. **Little Screen:** In the royal palace in Kyoto, this separated the Imperial Dining Room from the Imperial Washing Room. It had a cat painted on one side and birds and bamboo on the other.

11. **saw him . . . laughter** Eating was a private business in Heian Japan—most aristocrats ate alone. Thus, Masahiro's behavior would seem strange and ludicrous to Shōnagon and other court members— almost like being caught without his clothes on.

Vocabulary

stealthily (stelth′·ə·lē) *adv.:* in a sly way.
convulsed (kən·vulst′) *v.* used as *adj.:* shaken uncontrollably, as with laughter or weeping.

I am most pleased when I hear someone I love being praised or being mentioned approvingly by an important person.

A poem that someone has composed for a special occasion or written to another person in reply is widely praised and copied by people in their notebooks. Though this is something that has never yet happened to me, I can imagine how pleasing it must be.

A person with whom one is not especially intimate refers to an old poem or story that is unfamiliar. Then one hears it being mentioned by someone else and one has the pleasure of recognizing it. Still later, when one comes across it in a book, one thinks, "Ah, this is it!" and feels delighted with the person who first brought it up.

I feel very pleased when I have acquired some Michinoku paper, or some white, decorated paper, or even plain paper if it is nice and white.

A person in whose company one feels awkward asks one to supply the opening or closing line of a poem. If one happens to recall it, one is very pleased. Yet often on such occasions one completely forgets something that one would normally know.

I look for an object that I need at once, and I find it. Or again, there is a book that I must see immediately; I turn everything upside down, and there it is. What a joy!

When one is competing in an object match[12] (it does not matter what kind), how can one help being pleased at winning?

I greatly enjoy taking in someone who is pleased with himself and who

has a self-confident look, especially if he is a man. It is amusing to observe him as he alertly waits for my next repartee;[13] but it is also interesting if he tries to put me off my guard by adopting an air of calm indifference as if there were not a thought in his head.

I realize that it is very sinful of me, but I cannot help being pleased when someone I dislike has a bad experience.

It is a great pleasure when the ornamental comb that one has ordered turns out to be pretty.

I am more pleased when something nice happens to a person I love than when it happens to myself.

Entering the Empress's room and finding that ladies-in-waiting are crowded round her in a tight group, I go next to a pillar which is some distance from where she is sitting. What a delight it is when Her Majesty summons me to her side so that all the others have to make way!

---

13. **repartee** (rep′är·tē′) *n.*: sharp and clever reply.

---

12. **object match:** kind of game in which teams of players competed to solve riddles about objects, such as flowers, seashells, birds, insects, and fans.

Writing box in black lacquer with gold and silver *makie*, including *takamakie*. Edo period (18th century).

The British Museum, London.

Response and Analysis

Reading Check

1. Point out two passages from "Things That Cannot Be Compared" and "In Spring It Is the Dawn" that highlight Lady Shōnagon's appreciation of the natural world.

2. What three actions does Shōnagon offer as proof that Masahiro "really is a laughing-stock"?

3. In "Embarrassing Things," what conduct does Shōnagon find embarrassing in servants?

Thinking Critically

4. In "Pleasing Things," what role do reading and writing seem to play in Shōnagon's life? Cite four examples to support your view.

5. What is Shōnagon's attitude toward people of very high rank? Give two examples to support your opinion.

6. Give three examples of Shōnagon's writing **style**—one example of her diction, one of her syntax, and one of her **tone**. What words would you use to describe her style?

7. What kind of person do you think Shōnagon was, based on inferences you have drawn from the excerpts you have read? What aspects of her writing **style** lead you to these inferences?

WRITING

Making Your Own List

The Pillow Book is full of lists of everything from "Things That Fall from the Sky" to "Depressing Things" and "Things That Should Be Large." Create your own list of things that are connected in some way that has a personal meaning to you. For example, you could make a list of habits that annoy you, things that look better in the dark, jobs you'd never want to take, or situations that embarrass you. Show your personality and opinions through your own personal style, and don't be afraid to be funny, sarcastic, or serious.

North Carolina Competency Goal
1.03; 4.05; 5.03; 6.01

INTERNET

Projects and Activities
Keyword:
LE5 WL-3

SKILLS FOCUS

Literary Skills
Analyze style and tone.

Reading Skills
Analyze style.

Writing Skills
Make a list.

Vocabulary Skills
Answer questions about vocabulary words.

Vocabulary Development
In Your Own Words

Answer the questions below about the Vocabulary words in boldface. Make sure your answers show that you understand the meaning of each Vocabulary word.

1. Why might **incantations** sometimes be heard at the bedside of the sick?

2. When might you be likely to see **wisps** of smoke coming from a chimney?

3. If an audience is **convulsed** in laughter, what kind of play are they probably watching?

4. Why might a thief act **stealthily**?

5. What might happen if a speaker includes too many **insignificant** details in a speech?

Zen Parables

Zen is difficult to describe. It is a sect of Buddhism, but it is less a religion than a form of Buddhist meditative practice. It has no holy book, no ornate church or temple, no complicated ritual. Zen monks do not preach sermons about right and wrong behavior. Zen focuses on the inner self, rather than on the outer self that acts in the world. Yet for eight hundred years, Zen has strongly appealed to Japanese warriors as well as to monks, politicians, and artists. Today, it is also practiced by people in the East and the West from all walks of life and different religions who wish to find inner peace, relieve stress, and focus on essential priorities.

The Philosophy of Zen

The object of Zen is to free the mind from everyday, conventional logic through meditation. Followers of Zen believe that meditation empties the mind and suppresses the ego, leading to a clearer understanding of one's own nature. According to one legend, Bodhidharma, a famous Zen monk, gazed at a blank wall for nine years before achieving inner enlightenment.

Monks and Warriors

Originating in India and spreading to China, Zen Buddhism was introduced to Japan in 1191. Zen monasteries were soon founded in Kamakura and Kyoto. During the Kamakura period (1185–1333), the samurai, feudal warriors who served the aristocracy, were attracted to Zen because of its discipline and simplicity. They applied Zen principles to martial arts such as archery and fencing.

Virtually every aspect of Japanese culture has been influenced by Zen. Because monks

Japanese painting of a Zen monk.

drank bitter green tea in order to stay awake during meditation, tea drinking grew into an intricate and symbol-laden ritual. The arts also felt the impact of Zen, as manifested in the conciseness of haiku poetry (see page 448). Nearly every art form of classical Japan—painting, poetry, dance, architecture, drama, and even gardening—has been shaped to some degree by Zen, with its emphasis on simplicity, self-discipline, and meditation. Even the expressions of everyday Japanese speech reflect Zen values.

Zen Parables

Make the Connection

Quickwrite ✎

As a class, compile a list of familiar stories that teach a lesson—perhaps the stories are from the Bible or another religious text, or they may be folk tales you have read or heard from members of your family. What lessons do the stories teach? How did you figure out the lessons? Do any of the stories share the same message?

Literary Focus

Parable

Parables are brief stories that teach a moral, or lesson, about life. They are often allegorical, having both literal and symbolic levels of meaning. The most famous parables in Western literature are those told by Christ in the New Testament (see page 83). Christ presents moral lessons in short tales about everyday events such as a stray sheep or a spendthrift son. Behind the simple story is a wise lesson about the right way to live. Many Zen stories are also deceptively simple tales that contain profound truths.

North Carolina Competency Goal
1.03; 4.05;
5.01; 5.03;
6.01

> A **parable** is a short, allegorical story that teaches a moral or religious lesson about life.
>
> *For more on Parables, see the Handbook of Literary and Historical Terms.*

Literary Skills
Understand parable.

Background

Zen parables were originally used to teach aspiring monks about Buddhism. The relationship between a Zen monk and his teacher is an extraordinary one. Instead of imparting knowledge in a clear and logical way, the Zen master at first deliberately tries to confuse his students, a tactic that forces them to abandon preconceived ideas. This technique prepares the students to understand the sometimes paradoxical, or contradictory, nature of truth.

For example, to unsettle his students, a master may assume a fierce expression and a cold demeanor. He may ask a pupil a question and then interrupt him halfway through the answer. He may pose what appears to be a ridiculous question, such as "What did your face look like before you were born?" He may command students to perform seemingly impossible tasks like "Pull a bird out of your sleeve." He may also answer a serious question with an absurd response. If a pupil asks, "What is the nature of the Buddha?" his master might reply, "Pass me that fan!" or "Pork dumpling!"

Zen masters behave in these ways in part to make students wary of language and conventional ways of thinking. Words, according to Zen philosophy, can be dangerous, for they prevent people from experiencing the world directly as it actually is.

ZEN PARABLES

translated by **Paul Reps**

Carved statue of a Luohan. Yuan dynasty
(c. 1271–1368).

Victoria & Albert Museum, London (A.29-1931).

Muddy Road

Tanzan and Ekido[1] were once traveling together down a muddy road. A heavy rain was still falling.

Coming around a bend, they met a lovely girl in a silk kimono[2] and sash, unable to cross the intersection.

"Come on, girl," said Tanzan at once. Lifting her in his arms, he carried her over the mud.

Ekido did not speak again until that night when they reached a lodging temple. Then he no longer could restrain himself. "We monks don't go near females," he told Tanzan, "especially not young and lovely ones. It is dangerous. Why did you do that?"

"I left the girl there," said Tanzan. "Are you still carrying her?"

---

1. **Tanzan** (tän′zän′) **and Ekido** (e·kē′dō).
2. **kimono** *n.:* wide-sleeved robe, fastened with a sash; part of the traditional costume for men and women in Japan.

Dragon and Tiger by Choo Kyoshi. Detail of a multi-panel screen. Edo period (19th century).

A Parable

Buddha told a parable in a sutra:[3]

A man traveling across a field encountered a tiger. He fled, the tiger after him. Coming to a precipice, he caught hold of the root of a wild vine and swung himself down over the edge. The tiger sniffed at him from above. Trembling, the man looked down to where, far below, another tiger was waiting to eat him. Only the vine sustained him.

Two mice, one white and one black, little by little started to gnaw away the vine. The man saw a luscious strawberry near him. Grasping the vine with one hand, he plucked the strawberry with the other. How sweet it tasted!

---

3. **sutra** (sōō′trə) *n.*: one of a collection of stories that describe the teachings of the Buddha.

The Thief Who Became a Disciple

One evening as Shichiri Kojun[4] was reciting sutras a thief with a sharp sword entered, demanding either his money or his life.

Shichiri told him: "Do not disturb me. You can find the money in that drawer." Then he resumed his recitation.

A little while afterwards he stopped and called: "Don't take it all. I need some to pay taxes with tomorrow."

The intruder gathered up most of the money and started to leave. "Thank a person when you receive a gift," Shichiri added. The man thanked him and made off.

A few days afterwards the fellow was caught and confessed, among others, the offense against Shichiri. When Shichiri was called as a witness he said: "This man is no thief, at least as far as I am concerned. I gave him the money and he thanked me for it."

After he had finished his prison term, the man went to Shichiri and became his disciple.

The Taste of Banzo's Sword

Matajuro Yagyu[5] was the son of a famous swordsman. His father, believing that his son's work was too mediocre to anticipate mastership, disowned him.

So Matajuro went to Mount Futara[6] and there found the famous swordsman Banzo.[7] But Banzo confirmed the father's judgment. "You wish to learn swordsmanship under my guidance?" asked Banzo. "You cannot fulfill the requirements."

"But if I work hard, how many years will it take me to become a master?" persisted the youth.

"The rest of your life," replied Banzo.

"I cannot wait that long," explained Matajuro. "I am willing to pass through any hardship if only you will teach me. If I become your devoted servant, how long might it be?"

---

4. **Shichiri Kojun** (shē·chē′rē kō′jən).
5. **Matajuro Yagyu** (mä·tä·jōō′rō yäg′ōō).
6. **Mount Futara** (fōō·tä′rä).
7. **Banzo** (bän′zō).

Combat of Samurai Warriors by Utagawa Hiroshige. Edo period (19th century).

Musée des Arts Asiatiques-Guimet, Paris.

"Oh, maybe ten years," Banzo relented.

"My father is getting old, and soon I must take care of him," continued Matajuro. "If I work far more intensively, how long would it take me?"

"Oh, maybe thirty years," said Banzo.

"Why is that?" asked Matajuro. "First you say ten and now thirty years. I will undergo any hardship to master this art in the shortest time!"

"Well," said Banzo, "in that case you will have to remain with me for seventy years. A man in such a hurry as you are to get results seldom learns quickly."

"Very well," declared the youth, understanding at last that he was being rebuked for impatience, "I agree."

Matajuro was told never to speak of fencing and never to touch a sword. He cooked for his master, washed the dishes, made his bed, cleaned the yard, cared for the garden, all without a word of swordsmanship.

Three years passed. Still Matajuro labored on. Thinking of his future, he was sad. He had not even begun to learn the art to which he had devoted his life.

But one day Banzo crept up behind him and gave him a terrific blow with a wooden sword.

The following day, when Matajuro was cooking rice, Banzo again sprang upon him unexpectedly.

After that, day and night, Matajuro had to defend himself from unexpected thrusts. Not a moment passed in any day that he did not have to think of the taste of Banzo's sword.

He learned so rapidly he brought smiles to the face of his master. Matajuro became the greatest swordsman in the land.

Zen Garden's Calming Effect Due to Subliminal Image?

Hillary Mayell

National Geographic News, September 25, 2002

It's the kind of thing you simply have to experience for yourself. Otherwise, the Zen rock garden of the Ryoanji Temple in Kyoto, Japan, a United Nations World Heritage site, simply defies the imagination.

The garden, after all, has no plants—no flowers, no trees, not even any weeds.

It's a 30- by 10-meter (roughly 98- by 32-foot) rectangle surrounded by earthen walls on three sides and a wooden veranda[1] on the fourth. Inside the rectangle is a vista of white pebbles and 15 rocks. And it is world famous for the peace and serenity anyone and everyone who visits it feels.

Visual-imaging scientists in Japan say they've figured out what it is about the garden that engenders[2] this serenity. The secret: The more than 500-year-old garden is harboring a subliminal[3] message in the form of a tree.

Zen, Meditation, and Rock Gardens

The Ryoanji Temple (Temple of the Peaceful Dragon) is a Zen place of worship and meditation first built sometime during the 1450s. It burned when most of Kyoto was leveled by fire during the Onin Wars, and was rebuilt in 1486. The rock garden, which fronts the abbot's[4] quarters, was laid out around this time as a place for the monks to meditate.

Thought by many to be the quintessence[5] of Zen art, the garden is in the dry landscape style called Karesansui ("withered landscape").

The garden's 15 rocks are of various sizes, placed in five separate groupings. The white gravel that surrounds them is raked every day; perfect circles around the rocks, perfectly straight lines in the rest of the space. The rocks are arranged so that no matter where a visitor stands, only 14 can be seen. It is said that only when you attain spiritual enlightenment as a result of Zen meditation will you see the 15th stone.

Over the centuries, various explanations for the garden's layout have been given: That the white gravel represents the ocean and the rocks the islands of Japan; that they represent a mother tiger and her cubs, swimming in the river of the white sand toward a fearful dragon; or that the rocks represent the Chinese symbol for "heart" or "mind."

Unconscious Eye

However, it's the empty space created by the placement of the rocks and the void created by the white gravel that has long intrigued visitors.

Now the mystery may have been resolved.

Gert van Tonder, a postdoctoral fellow of the Japanese Society for the Promotion of Science

---

1. **veranda** (və·ran**′**də) *n.:* porch with a roof.
2. **engenders** (en·jen**′**dərz) *v.:* causes.
3. **subliminal** (sub·lim**′**ə·nəl) *adj.:* meant to affect one's subconscious.
4. **abbot** (ab**′**ət) *n.:* head of a monastery.
5. **quintessence** (kwin·tes**′**əns) *n.:* perfect example of a thing.

Rock garden at Ryoanji Temple, Kyoto.

at Kyoto University, and Michael J. Lyons, a senior scientist at ATR Media Information Labs in Kyoto, applied a shape-analysis technique that can reveal hidden structural features to the garden's empty space.

Earlier studies of how humans and other primates process visual images suggest that we have an unconscious sensitivity to the medial axis of shapes, said van Tonder.

"Imagine starting two fires in a field of dry grass," he said. "Where the fires meet, at points equidistant between the two starting locations, is the medial axis."

His analysis indicates that the same unconscious sensitivity is able to discern the image of a trunk and branches of a tree within the Zen garden's pattern of rocks and stones. Viewed from the veranda, the image is apparent to the subconscious but is invisible to the eye.

The authors conclude in a report published in the September 26 issue of the journal *Nature* that the unconscious perception of this pattern is the source of the garden's calming effect.

If the rocks were to be rearranged, the invisible tree structure is lost, they say.

Van Tonder believes the garden's designer intended to create the subliminal feature—demonstrating an understanding of the physics of the human eye and subconscious hundreds of years ago.

? According to the article, what might be the "secret" behind the calming effect of the Zen garden at Ryoanji Temple? How does the writer of this article use details to help you understand the layout of the Zen garden?

Response and Analysis

Reading Check

1. Who are Tanzan and Ekido? For what does Ekido criticize Tanzan in "Muddy Road"?

2. Name all the dangers that the man in "A Parable" faces.

3. In "The Thief Who Became a Disciple," what does Shichiri testify in court?

4. In "The Taste of Banzo's Sword," why does Matajuro become sad working with the master Banzo?

Thinking Critically

5. In "Muddy Road," what does Tanzan mean when he asks Ekido if he is still carrying the girl?

6. In "A Parable," what might the precipice, the tigers, and the mice **symbolize,** or stand for? What is the significance of the man eating the strawberry? What lesson about life do you think this **parable** teaches?

7. Why do you think the thief becomes the disciple of Shichiri Kojun? What values does this **parable** teach?

8. Describe Banzo's unconventional teaching methods. What do you think he is teaching Matajuro about the art of swordsmanship?

Extending and Evaluating

9. Are any of the lessons in these Zen parables similar to lessons in stories that you know? Review the list you made for your Quickwrite response.

WRITING

Writing a Parable

Many Zen parables contain a **paradox,** or apparent contradiction that is actually true. Think about how a seeming contradiction can ultimately prove true. Then, write a brief parable of your own about one of the following paradoxical situations:

- a competition that is won through losing
- a person who becomes rich by giving something away
- an enemy who becomes a friend when he or she is trusted
- a difficult task that becomes easy once a person stops trying so hard
- a scary situation that changes when a person stops feeling fear

LISTENING AND SPEAKING

Acting Out a Parable

Pair off with another student, and adapt one of the Zen parables you've just read to a modern setting and situation without losing its moral. For instance, you could adapt "The Taste of Banzo's Sword" by making Banzo a basketball coach who teaches his students by throwing balls at them when they least expect it. Then, with your partner, create a script for your dramatization, and act out your parable for the class.

NONFICTION
"The gospel of selfless action"

In *The Bhagavad Gita According to Gandhi,* the great spiritual leader Mohandas Gandhi presents his renowned translation and interpretation of these sacred Hindu texts. The verses of the Bhagavad-Gita were especially meaningful for Gandhi; he even used a section of the Gita as the focal point for his regular meditation practice. Gandhi's commentary on the Gita is illustrated with examples from his own life that help to convey the profound spiritual lessons contained in this ancient text.

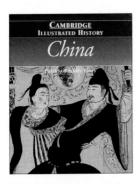

NONFICTION
Delving into China's Past

Patricia Buckley Ebrey provides a sweeping overview of Chinese civilization in the *Cambridge Illustrated History of China.* Ebrey covers important events ranging from the origins of Confucianism to the Cultural Revolution while discussing the country's succession of dynasties. An array of striking photographs brings more than eight thousand years of history to life.

FICTION
A Search for Meaning

Hermann Hesse's novel *Siddhartha* focuses on one individual's unforgettable struggle to achieve enlightenment. Siddhartha is a young man who appears to have all the trappings of success and happiness: He is handsome, strong, intelligent, and loved by everyone. Yet Siddhartha is profoundly unhappy because he longs to achieve ultimate self-realization. When Siddhartha leaves his family and the comforts of home in order to join a group of ascetics (people who practice extreme self-denial), he embarks on the first stage of his journey to enlightenment.

ADDITIONAL READING

- R. K. Narayan's adaptation of the *Ramayana* is a prose version of the great epic that is an integral part of India's culture. In addition to offering a compelling story about the war between good and evil, the *Ramayana* contains insightful life lessons.

- If you'd like to read more of the beautiful poems composed during China's T'ang and Sung dynasties, take a look at *One Hundred Poems from the Chinese,* by Kenneth Rexroth. The first section consists of thirty-five poems written by Tu Fu, while the second section contains the works of various other poets.

- Harold G. Henderson's *An Introduction to Haiku: An Anthology of Poems and Poets from Bashō to Shiki* conveys the stark beauty of haiku through a representative selection of poems as well as a description of the characteristics of this deceptively simple poetic form.

Persuading with Cause and Effect

Writing Assignment
Write an essay in which you examine the causes and effects of a situation and persuade your readers to take action to change it.

When you look around your school, your neighborhood, or your town or city, you probably see situations that prompt you to say: "Something's wrong here. This has got to change." In order to change a set of circumstances, however, you need to understand its **causes,** how the situation came about, and its **effects,** the results or consequences of the situation remaining as it is. You can then use your cause-and-effect analysis to persuade others to join you in taking action that will improve the situation.

Prewriting

North Carolina Competency Goal
2.02; 6.01

SKILLS FOCUS

Writing Skills
Write a persuasive cause-and-effect essay.

Choose a Situation

Time for Change To choose a topic for a **persuasive cause-and effect essay,** think about situations you and others have complained about recently. What are people talking about in the cafeteria or writing about in letters to the editor? Make a list of problems you've observed, and then choose a situation that you and your audience can do something about.

Analyze the Causes and Effects

How Did It Happen and Why Does It Matter? The situation you have chosen to write about is probably part of a larger chain of causes and effects—meaning that the current situation was caused by an earlier action, decision, or inaction. Ask yourself, "What was the *cause* of this situation in the first place?" Then, turn your attention to the *effects* of the present situation. If you believe the effects are negative, you will want your readers to think the situation needs to be changed.

You may want to use a flowchart like the one below to help with your analysis. It tracks the causes and effects of uncontrolled reproduction of pets.

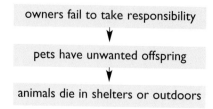

owners fail to take responsibility
↓
pets have unwanted offspring
↓
animals die in shelters or outdoors

State Your Opinion

Have Your Say Make your feelings about the situation you have chosen clear by forming a strong **opinion statement** that you can use early in your essay. Describe what you think needs to be changed, and suggest ways to make that change happen.

Gather Evidence

Proof Positive To persuade your readers to accept your opinion, provide credible and relevant **evidence** that supports your analysis of the causes and effects of the situation you want to change. Here are some important kinds of evidence you can use: expert opinions, quotations, facts and statistics, anecdotes, and case studies (individual examples used as the basis for generalizations).

Call for Action

What Can Be Done? After explaining the causes and effects of the situation, recommend a specific action for your readers to take. Address any **counterclaims,** or objections to your proposal, that your audience might have. Provide evidence to back up your counterarguments and support the effectiveness of your call to action.

 PRACTICE & APPLY 1 Use the preceding instruction to choose and analyze a situation for a persuasive cause-and-effect essay.

TIP When you want to persuade others to share your beliefs, you can strengthen your explanations and evidence with any one or more of these **rhetorical devices:** appeals to the mind with logical reasoning, appeals to the heart with emotionally charged language, and appeals to the conscience with ethical arguments about right and wrong.

 **North Carolina Competency Goal** 2.02; 2.03; 6.01; 6.02

SKILLS FOCUS

Writing Skills
Choose and analyze a situation for a persuasive cause-and-effect essay.

Writing

Persuading with Cause and Effect

A Writer's Framework

Introduction

- Begin with a striking statement or anecdote.

- Provide background information on the situation if necessary.

- Include a clear opinion statement that tells how you feel and hints at the call to action you will make.

Body

- Explain the causes and effects of the situation.

- Use persuasive appeals— logical, emotional, and ethical.

- Support your analysis with evidence—facts, statistics, anecdotes, expert opinions, case studies.

Conclusion

- Propose a specific course of action.

- Address any counterclaims readers may have.

- Restate your opinion and the need for change.

- End with a motivating appeal for effective action.

Be a Responsible Pet Owner!

The local animal shelters are teeming with dogs and cats that have no home and no prospect of ever having one. Dogs and cats are also roaming local streets, woods, and parks looking for shelter. These animals were bred to be our household companions, but many are waiting in cramped cages to be put to sleep or struggling to survive outdoors. Helpless cats and dogs are needlessly suffering because pet owners are failing to act responsibly.

Why are there so many unwanted cats and dogs? The answer is clear: Too many owners permit their pets to have puppies and kittens that the owners are not prepared to care for. The more responsible owners take these young animals to shelters. The less responsible ones abandon them outdoors, where they fight to stay alive and produce more homeless animals like themselves.

Animals born as a result of pet owners' irresponsibility face a bleak future. Each year an estimated four to six million animals are put to death in shelters. Although the staff of most shelters are dedicated to the well-being of animals, they simply cannot find good homes for all the animals in their custody. At the same time, former pets that roam outdoors fare no better. They may live longer than the shelter animals, but their existence is harsh and dangerous. As veterinarian Angela Gutierrez reports: "Stray cats and dogs contract and spread diseases, sustain injuries in fights with other animals, get hit by cars, and generally suffer from hunger and exposure."

Ecologists tell us that in addition to suffering, roaming dogs and cats endanger native wildlife. For example, a recent study shows that cats on the hunt have a devastating effect on bird populations, especially when birds are nesting or fledging. When a cat pounces on a bird too young to fly, the cat is only following its instincts. However, the cat is forced to hunt birds as a result of human choices.

There is a solution to the growing population of homeless cats and dogs. Pet owners can have their cats and dogs spayed and neutered. Owners need not be concerned that preventing their animals from reproducing will harm their pets in any way. On the contrary, veterinary research shows that spaying and neutering prevents diseases of the reproductive organs, resulting in better health and longer lives for these animals. Animals cannot decide what is best for them, but pet owners can. There is too much unavoidable suffering in the world to fail to take this practical step to reduce the number of suffering animals.

SKILLS FOCUS

Writing Skills
Write the first draft
of a persuasive
cause-and-effect essay.

PRACTICE & APPLY 2 Using the framework and Writer's Model on these pages as your guide, write the first draft of your persuasive cause-and-effect essay.

Revising

Self-Evaluation

Look Again Before you share your draft with others, read through it at least twice. Use the rubric below to help you evaluate your essay's content and organization.

Rubric: Persuading with Cause and Effect		
Evaluation Questions	▶ **Tips**	▶ **Revision Techniques**
❶ Does the introduction state an opinion about a problematic situation and hint at how it could be changed?	▶ **Highlight** the opinion statement. **Underline** the hint on how the situation might be changed.	▶ **Add** an opinion statement that tells how you feel about the situation and hints at how it could be changed.
❷ Does the body of the essay explain the causes and effects of the situation?	▶ **Circle** the situation. **Bracket** the cause. **Double bracket** the effects.	▶ **Add** an explanation of the situation's causes. **Elaborate** with explanations of the situation's effects.
❸ Does the essay include a variety of supporting evidence?	▶ Put a **check** by and **label** each kind of evidence.	▶ **Add** a variety of evidence— facts, statistics, expert opinions, and so on.
❹ Does the essay use logical, emotional, or ethical appeals?	▶ **Draw a box around** and **label** any logical, emotional, or ethical appeals.	▶ **Add** logical, emotional, or ethical appeals.
❺ Does the conclusion address counterclaims and end with a strong call to action?	▶ **Draw wavy lines** under the call to action and sentences that address counterclaims.	▶ **Add** sentences that address counterclaims. **Reword** to include a specific call to action and a final, strong appeal.

go. hrw .com

INTERNET

More Writer's Models
Keyword:
LE5 WL-3

North Carolina Competency Goal
2.02; 6.01; 6.02

When you are revising your essay, consider adding words that help explain the situation, its cause, and its negative effects. These words include *because, due to, as a result of,* and *consequently.*

ANALYZING THE REVISION PROCESS

Study the revisions below, and answer the questions that follow.

The local animal shelters are teeming with dogs and cats that have no home and no prospect of ever having one. Dogs and cats are also ~~inhabiting~~ *roaming* local streets, woods, and parks ˄*looking for shelter.* These animals were bred to be our household companions, but many are waiting in cramped cages to be ~~euthanized~~ *put to sleep* or struggling to survive outdoors, ˄ ~~where they often get hurt or killed.~~ Helpless cats and dogs are needlessly suffering and ˄*because* pet owners are failing to act responsibly.

Responding to the Revision Process

1. How is the tone of the introduction affected by substituting "put to sleep" for "euthanized" in sentence 3?

2. How does replacing "and" with "because" improve the last sentence?

PRACTICE & APPLY 3 Using the guidelines on these pages, revise the content and organization of your persuasive cause-and-effect essay.

FUN AT THE OFFICE #773
Removing Periods and Inserting Commas

Cartoon by Jim Sizemore. www.CartoonStock.com

Publishing

Proofread and Publish Your Essay

Final Touches Appearance counts. An essay with errors in grammar, usage, spelling, or mechanics will not impress your readers. Be sure to take time to proofread your work carefully and correct any errors you find. You may even want to read your essay aloud to yourself or a classmate to detect any errors in grammar or awkward phrasing. Make use of a dictionary, a grammar handbook, and your computer spelling and grammar checks, but don't rely on any one of these aids alone.

Spread the Word Now that you've written about a situation that you believe needs to be changed, you will want to get your message out to as many people as possible. Here are some ways to publish your essay:

- Send your essay to people in positions of authority or influence in your school, neighborhood, or local government. These are the people who shape opinions and have the power to bring about change.

- Use your essay as the basis of a persuasive speech, and deliver the speech to an audience that can have a direct impact on the situation you want to change. For information about **adapting your essay for a persuasive speech,** see page 478.

Reflect on Your Essay

North Carolina Competency Goal
2.02; 6.01

Looking Back Now that you have considered the causes and effects of a situation in need of reform, think over your experience. Review your thought processes and the skills you applied in your analysis. Then, answer these questions:

- What brought the situation to your attention in the first place?

- How did you discover the cause of the situation? Explain your research process.

- How effective was your call to action? Can you think of any way you might have made an even stronger appeal?

PRACTICE & APPLY 4 First, proofread your essay. Then, choose one of the options above to publish your essay for an audience. Finally, answer the reflection questions.

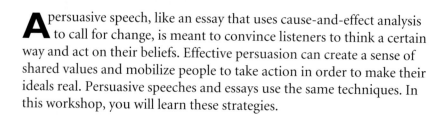
Giving a Persuasive Speech

Speaking Assignment

Adapt your persuasive cause-and-effect essay to a persuasive speech, and deliver it to your class.

A persuasive speech, like an essay that uses cause-and-effect analysis to call for change, is meant to convince listeners to think a certain way and act on their beliefs. Effective persuasion can create a sense of shared values and mobilize people to take action in order to make their ideals real. Persuasive speeches and essays use the same techniques. In this workshop, you will learn these strategies.

Adapt Your Essay

For the Ear Not the Eye To adapt your cause-and-effect essay for oral presentation, put yourself in the place of your audience. Remember that listeners cannot re-read or review what you have already said. You have essentially one chance to make your case. Therefore, keep your vocabulary, sentence structure, and logic relatively simple, but maintain the formal tone you used in your essay.

Start Strong You must grab your audience's attention from the moment you start speaking. Adapt and elaborate the **introduction** of your essay in order to make a dramatic opening impression. For example, add details to an anecdote, repeat a memorable quotation, or emphasize an expert opinion. Don't forget to clearly express your opinion before getting into the details of your case.

Make Your Case The middle and longest part of your speech will be devoted to persuading your audience to agree with your opinion statement and take whatever action you propose. You will have to present convincing **evidence** to support your analysis. Keep the following suggestions in mind as you review the body of your essay:

- Remember that you have a limited amount of time to present your case. Therefore, you will probably have to simplify or omit some of the explanation or evidence that you included in your essay. Concentrate on valid, compelling evidence and **logical reasoning** that is relevant to the lives and experiences of your listeners.

- Choose the most effective **rhetorical devices**—emotional, logical, and ethical appeals—from your essay. Make your choices on the basis of your audience's values and interests. For example, if you are addressing an audience of animal lovers, you can speak emotionally about the suffering of unwanted pets. However, to communicate effectively with a committee of scientists or elected officials, you might use logical appeals that speak to professional ethics and civic duty.

SKILLS FOCUS

Listening and Speaking Skills
Give a persuasive speech.

North Carolina Competency Goal
2.02

End Effectively Conclude your speech by summarizing the points you have made. Include a clear call to action. Then, end with a stirring final sentence. Speak slowly so that your words have maximum impact. Consider using literary devices such as alliteration, repetition, and parallel structure to make your last sentence memorable.

Answer Before You're Asked Public speakers—from heads of corporations to students running for class president—know that one of the most effective strategies for convincing others is to anticipate and answer their **concerns** and **counterclaims.** If the audience for your speech is different from the one for your essay, consider whether the new audience will have different concerns or raise different objections. If so, adjust your speech to respond to their **counterarguments.**

Interview an Authority If you think your speech needs more evidence to be persuasive, consider interviewing an authority or someone with firsthand experience of the situation you are exploring. Arrange a time to talk to the person, and prepare by making a list of relevant questions. Your questions should reveal that you are knowledgeable about the subject. Take careful notes during the interview, or obtain the interviewee's permission to tape the session. Ask your questions in a respectful manner, and at the end of the interview, express appreciation. Review your notes and decide what you will add to your speech. Finally, evaluate the effectiveness of your interview process, asking yourself what you might do better next time.

Order Your Ideas Maintain the same basic organization in your speech as in your essay. Use connecting and ordering expressions to help show the relationships between the ideas in your speech.

Present Your Speech

On Your Toes To present a formal speech, you must stand up and speak from memory. Speakers who read from a text often lose their audience's interest. Write out the text of your speech word for word, and memorize it. Plan the verbal and nonverbal techniques you will use at various points in your speech, and annotate your text. **Verbal techniques** include variations in the tone, pitch, and volume of your voice. **Nonverbal techniques** include gestures, pauses, and eye contact. You may also wish to prepare and use visual aids, such as charts, graphs, and photos, to support your points. Rehearse your speech using a mirror, an audio or video recorder, or a willing friend as a trial audience.

INTERNET

Speeches
Keyword:
LE5 WL-3

 **PRACTICE & APPLY 5** Use the instruction in this workshop to adapt your persuasive cause-and-effect essay into a persuasive speech. Then, practice and deliver your speech.

Test Practice

Some themes are of such deep concern to human beings that writers from widely different cultures and time periods keep exploring them. The eighth-century Chinese poet Tu Fu and the nineteenth-century English poet Percy Bysshe Shelley both wrote poems about fallen glory. In "Jade Flower Palace," Tu Fu's speaker gazes at the remains of a once-grand palace, while in "Ozymandias," Shelley's speaker contemplates the meaning of a shattered statue of a once-mighty ruler.

DIRECTIONS: Read the following two poems. Then, read each multiple-choice question that follows, and write the letter of the best response.

Jade Flower Palace

Tu Fu

translated by **Kenneth Rexroth**

The stream swirls. The wind moans in
The pines. Gray rats scurry over
Broken tiles. What prince, long ago,
Built this palace, standing in
5   Ruins beside the cliffs? There are
Green ghost fires in the black rooms.
The shattered pavements are all
Washed away. Ten thousand organ
Pipes whistle and roar. The storm
10   Scatters the red autumn leaves.
His dancing girls are yellow dust.
Their painted cheeks have crumbled
Away. His gold chariots
And courtiers are gone. Only
15   A stone horse is left of his
Glory. I sit on the grass and
Start a poem, but the pathos of
It overcomes me. The future
Slips imperceptibly away.
20   Who can say what the years will bring?

North Carolina Competency Goal
1.03; 4.05; 5.02; 5.03

SKILLS FOCUS

Literary Skills
Compare and contrast literary works.

Ozymandias

Percy Bysshe Shelley

I met a traveler from an antique land
Who said: Two vast and trunkless legs° of stone
Stand in the desert . . . Near them, on the sand,
Half sunk, a shattered visage° lies, whose frown,
5   And wrinkled lip, and sneer of cold command,
Tell that its sculptor well those passions read
Which yet survive, stamped on these lifeless things,
The hand that mocked them, and the heart° that fed;
And on the pedestal these words appear:
10   "My name is Ozymandias, king of kings,
Look on my works, ye Mighty, and despair!"
Nothing beside remains. Round the decay
Of that colossal wreck, boundless and bare
The long and level sands stretch far away.

---

2. **trunkless legs:** that is, the legs without the rest of the
body.
4. **visage** *n.:* face.
8. **hand . . . heart:** the hand of the sculptor who, with his art,
criticized the passions to which Ozymandias gave himself
wholeheartedly.

Collection 3: Skills Review

1. Which of the following scenes is a detail of the setting of "Jade Flower Palace"?

   A sand dunes

   B green meadows

   C abandoned cars

   D a stone horse

2. What kind of mood does the setting of "Jade Flower Palace" create?

   F melancholy

   G angry

   H triumphant

   J hopeful

3. Why does the speaker in Tu Fu's poem fail to write a poem after gazing at the palace ruins?

   A He is distracted by an approaching storm.

   B He is overcome by the beauty of his surroundings.

   C He falls into a daydream about the past.

   D He is saddened by the realization that time alters all.

4. What overall attitude toward time does the speaker of Tu Fu's poem express?

   F He sees time as an ally.

   G He fears time's destructive power.

   H He is indifferent to the changes wrought by time.

   J He sees time as a healing power.

5. What does the traveler in "Ozymandias" find in the desert sand?

   A the remains of a decayed ship

   B the legs and head of a statue of a man

   C a sculptor of stone monuments

   D the ruins of an ancient city

6. Which of the following images from Shelley's poem gives a clue to the kind of ruler Ozymandias was?

   F "Two vast and trunkless legs"

   G "a shattered visage"

   H "sneer of cold command"

   J "that colossal wreck"

7. How does the sculptor in Shelley's poem feel about the ruler whose statue he has carved?

   A He admires the ruler's power.

   B He fears the ruler's anger.

   C He desires the ruler's approval.

   D He dislikes the ruler's arrogance.

Collection 3: Skills Review

8. In "Ozymandias" what is ironic about the words on the pedestal: "My name is Ozymandias, king of kings, / Look on my works, ye Mighty, and despair!"?

   F Nothing remains of Ozymandias's works but ruins.

   G The traveler who reports this felt happiness, not despair, when he read the words.

   H The words on the pedestal are barely recognizable.

   J Ozymandias ruled a poor, tiny kingdom and was never a "king of kings."

9. What is similar about the settings of the two poems?

   A Both poems are set in desert landscapes.

   B Both settings contain crumbling buildings.

   C Both settings are deserted and isolated.

   D Both poems are set in the recent past.

10. Which of the following theme statements applies to both "Jade Flower Palace" and "Ozymandias"?

   F Time destroys all human achievements.

   G Art is the only human endeavor that can defeat time.

   H Only the works of the powerful can avoid the ravages of time.

   J Memory is the only recourse in the face of time's destructiveness.

Essay Question

Although the themes of "Jade Flower Palace" and "Ozymandias" are similar, there are differences between the two poems in setting, mood, and tone. Write an essay in which you consider these similarities and differences. Pay special attention to each poet's use of imagery and concrete details. In the final paragraph, explain which poem comes closer to your ideas and feelings about the passage of time and the value of human striving.

Collection 3: Skills Review
Vocabulary Skills

Words with Multiple Meanings

DIRECTIONS: Choose the answer in which the underlined word is used in the same way as it is used in the lines from "Rama and Ravana in Battle."

1. ". . . wailings of the widows of warriors came over the chants and songs of triumph that his courtiers arranged to keep up at a loud <u>pitch</u>. . ."

   A The log cabin's walls were filled with <u>pitch</u> to stop up the gaps.

   B He threw a wild <u>pitch</u> in the last baseball game.

   C I need to learn how to <u>pitch</u> a tent before I go camping.

   D The chorus sang at a soft <u>pitch</u> throughout the concert.

2. "He felt a <u>terrific</u> rage rising within him, mixed with some admiration for Rama's valor."

   F We had a <u>terrific</u> time at the amusement park this weekend.

   G That dress looks <u>terrific</u> on you!

   H The tornado swept through the town with <u>terrific</u> force.

   J Her performance in the school play was <u>terrific</u>.

3. "He summoned his chariot, which could be <u>drawn</u> by horses. . . ."

   A I have <u>drawn</u> portraits many times.

   B The carriage was <u>drawn</u> through Central Park.

   C His face looks <u>drawn</u> and pinched lately.

   D I have <u>drawn</u> myself a bath.

4. "Following it another conch, . . . which belonged to Mahavishnu (Rama's original form before his <u>present</u> incarnation) . . ."

   F I used to be the secretary of the club before my <u>present</u> role as treasurer.

   G She bought me a lovely <u>present</u> for my birthday.

   H He was <u>present</u> in class on the day of the test.

   J I have to <u>present</u> my paper to the contest judges.

5. "Presently he collapsed in a faint. . . . Noticing his <u>state</u>, his charioteer pulled back and drew the chariot aside."

   A The separation of church and <u>state</u> is often a controversial topic.

   B You must <u>state</u> your beliefs clearly at the beginning of your paper.

   C Ever since the dance, she has been in a <u>state</u> of bliss.

   D His report was on the Secretary of <u>State</u>.

North Carolina Competency Goal
6.01

Vocabulary Skills
Understand multiple-meaning words.

Collection 3: Skills Review

Writing Skills

Test Practice DIRECTIONS: Read the following paragraph from a draft of a student's persuasive cause-and-effect essay. Then, answer the questions below it.

(1) The number and variety of migrating songbirds are diminishing every year. (2) This sharp population decline is due mainly to the loss of habitat for feeding and breeding. (3) Pesticide poisoning has also contributed to the declining numbers of birds. (4) Not only are the tropical rain forests—where migrating birds spend the winter—fast disappearing, but there is also less and less open land at every point on migration routes. (5) As a result, birds have fewer and fewer places to rest and refuel on their long north-south travels. (6) The trend need not continue. (7) Open space can be maintained for birds, even in crowded cities and sprawling suburbs. (8) What is needed is more land set aside for parks, including green strips along streams, roads, and railroad beds.

1. The function of Sentence 2 in the paragraph is to—
    A describe the effects of the situation
    B give an opinion on the situation
    C explain the cause of the situation
    D state a call to action

2. Which sentence could be added to support the argument made in Sentence 7?
    F Birds cannot thrive in close proximity to humans.
    G Birds need huge tracts of open land in order to find food.
    H Central Park in New York City, for example, has long been a haven for migrating birds.
    J Overdevelopment threatens the quality of life for all urban residents.

3. Which sentence should be deleted to improve the paragraph's coherence?
    A 2
    B 3
    C 5
    D 7

4. Which of the following sentences uses a word or phrase to clarify the cause-and-effect relationship between ideas?
    F 4
    G 5
    H 6
    J 7

5. Which sentence could be added to address a reader's counterclaim that human needs would be neglected by taking care of the needs of birds?
    A More homes and offices must be built to keep up with the growing human population.
    B Since humans are destroying bird habitat, it is they who must restore it.
    C The decline of bird populations is a threat to human survival.
    D More parks would benefit people as well as birds because people need open space for their health and well-being.

North Carolina Competency Goal
2.01; 2.02; 6.01

Writing Skills
Answer questions about a cause-and-effect essay.

Literature of Africa and the Middle East

700 B.C.–A.D. 1800s

The Power of the Word

The tyranny of silence shall be broken—

New shining words by us, the poets, spoken;

Whereas a diver threads dull pearls upon a string

We choose the words which soar—

and give them wing.

—Qulzum

INTERNET

Collection Resources

Keyword: LE5 WL-4

(Opposite) Grand Mosque of Djene.

Africa and

500 B.C.	A.D. 1	250	500

c. 500–c. 330 B.C. Zoroastrianism thrives in Persia

c. 430 B.C. Greek scholar Herodotus writes the *Histories,* focusing on the Greco-Persian wars

c. 1st century B.C. Bantu speakers move from the Cameroon Highlands south and east through Africa

c. A.D. 124 Apuleius, writer of *The Golden Ass,* the only complete surviving Latin novel, is born in Algeria

c. A.D. 200 Christianity is introduced into northern Africa by way of the Roman Empire

c. A.D. 300–c. 1200 Rise and fall of the empire of Old Ghana

c. A.D. 320–c. 340 King 'Ēzānā converts to Christianity

c. A.D. 330 The kingdom of Kush falls to Aksum

A.D. 354–430 Lifetime of Saint Augustine, bishop of Hippo (modern-day Algeria) and author of the *Confessions*

500s–1500s Classical period of Arabic literature

622 Muhammad makes his pilgrimage to Medina; the Islamic era begins

642 Muslims from Arabia conquer Egypt

c. 650 Official text of the Koran is established

c. 700–c. 1300 East Africa has a golden age of trade

Journey of the Prophet Muhammad (c. 1425). Leaf from an illustrated manuscript of Majma al-Tawarikh.
The Metropolitan Museum of Art, Cora Timken Burnett Collection of Persian Miniatures and Other Persian Art Objects, Bequest of Cora Timken Burnett, 1956. (57.51.9). Photograph ©2004 The Metropolitan Museum of Art.

500 B.C.	A.D. 1	250	500

c. 400s B.C. Written form of Sanskrit is developed

380–343 B.C. Last Egyptian dynasty

221–206 B.C. Ch'in dynasty unifies China; Great Wall is built

c. 100 B.C.–c. A.D. 500 The *Panchatantra* is written in India

27 B.C. Roman Empire is established

c. A.D. 50–c. 150 The books of the Christian New Testament are written

c. A.D. 70 Romans destroy Jerusalem

A.D. 161–180 Marcus Aurelius is Roman emperor

c. A.D. 320–467 Gupta dynasty rules in India

c. A.D. 400 Buddhism and Chinese writings are introduced to Japan

A.D. 400s The great Sanskrit writer Kalidasa writes poetry and drama in India

593–622 Japanese prince Shotoku encourages the adoption of Chinese culture

c. 600–c. 1200 Rival Indian rulers fight for power

c. 700 The Anglo-Saxon epic *Beowulf* is written down

Helmet from Sutton Hoo (7th century A.D.).
The British Museum, London (1939.10-10.93).

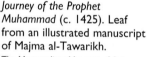

the Middle East 700 B.C.–A.D. 1800s

AND THE MIDDLE EAST

750	1000	1250	1500–on
813 School of astronomy is founded in Baghdad	**1000s** Islam is practiced in Mali	**c. 1326–c. 1389** Lifetime of Sufi poet Hafiz	**c. 1670s** Ashanti Empire is formed in Africa
819–999 Persian prose style is created during the Samanid dynasty	**1048–1131** Lifetime of Omar Khayyám, writer of the *Rubáiyát*	**c. 1352** Arab geographer Ibn Battūtah explores the Sahara	**early 1800s** Rise of the Zulu nation in southern Africa
900 *The Thousand and One Nights,* the famous collection of Arabian tales, is begun	**1187** Muslims defeat Christian invaders and take Jerusalem	**c. 1450–c. 1500** Decline of Old Zimbabwe	**late 1800s–early 1900s** Western European nations divide Africa into colonies
	c. 1200–c. 1500 Swahili language and culture thrive in East Africa	**c. 1468** The reign of Sonni 'Alī in Songhai begins	
		1483 Portuguese explorers arrive in the Congo	

Illustration of Sindbad the Sailor carrying a sea monster from *One Thousand and One Nights* (18th century).

c. 1210–c. 1260 Lifetime of Sundiata, hero of Old Mali's great epic *Sundiata*

1213 Saadi, the Persian poet, is born

Ashanti weight.

750	1000	1250	1500–on
794–1185 Japan's Heian era witnesses a cultural flowering and the rise of feudalism; the aristocrats of Japan's Heian court compose tanka	**1066** Norman Conquest of England	**1347–1352** Black Death ravages Europe	**c. 1658** John Milton begins writing *Paradise Lost*
800 Charlemagne is crowned first emperor of the Holy Roman Empire	**c. 1100** The French epic the *Song of Roland* is written	**1368–1644** Ming dynasty in China	**1775–1783** American Revolution
900s Beginnings of medieval drama	**1192** The shogun becomes the supreme power in Japan	**1387** Geoffrey Chaucer begins writing *The Canterbury Tales*	**1853** Commodore Perry ends Japanese isolationist policy
	c. 1200 The *Nibelungenlied,* the national epic of Germany, is written	**c. 1455** Gutenberg Bible is printed	**1900** Boxer Rebellion erupts in China
		1492 Columbus reaches the Americas	

Cultural and Historical

The Golden Age of Africa,
A.D. 300–1600

For about 1,300 years, Africa enjoyed a long golden age. From A.D. 300 to about 1600, sculpture, music, metalwork, textiles, and oral literature flourished in Africa's large and small kingdoms—Aksum, Old Ghana, Old Mali, Songhai, Luba, Malawi, Swahili, Old Zimbabwe, and Zulu. Two of the great African oral epics originated from kingdoms in western Africa: *The Dausi,* from the Soninke people of the kingdom of Old Ghana, and *Sundiata,* from the Mandingo people of Old Mali.

Sculpture of a Kota reliquary figure known as Mbulu Ngulu. From Gabon, Africa (c. 1800–1900).

Rise of a New World Religion,
A.D. 622

Around the year 622, one of the most important and powerful religious movements in human history began. In that year, Muhammad, a native of Mecca on the Arabian peninsula, received revelations that led to the formation of a new, unifying religion called Islam, meaning "submission." Muhammad is seen as the great prophet of Islam, and his revelations, believed to be the

Masjid an-Nabawi in Medina, Saudi Arabia.

direct word of the one God, Allah, were collected and recorded in the Islamic holy book, the Koran. The followers of Islam, called Muslims, are called to live disciplined lives, to devote themselves to community and charity, and to observe Islamic laws as revealed in the Koran. Enormously popular, especially among the poor and powerless, Islam swept the Middle East and parts of Africa and the Far East and eventually spread as far west as Spain. Today there are over one billion followers of Islam all over the world.

A Respect for Learning, 800s–1200s

There has always been a strong literary tradition in Arabic culture. Poetry in particular has long been respected—an attitude that is reflected in the Arabic word for poet, *sha'er*, which means "he who knows."

Perhaps Arabic culture's greatest gift to the West was its enormous achievement of translating into Arabic numerous Greek and Roman works of literature, medicine, astronomy, mathematics, and philosophy. Under the Abbasid rulers, scholars were sent all over the empire searching for manuscripts to translate. Because of this great effort in translation, the Arabs preserved works of learning that would otherwise have been lost to the world forever; untold thousands of those ancient Greek and Roman texts were neglected during the so-called Dark Ages in Europe. In addition to their conservation of classical texts, the Arabs made their own original, lasting contributions to literature, philosophy, mathematics, and science.

The Divan of Khata'i.

Arthur M. Sackler Gallery, Smithsonian Institution, Washington, DC: Smithsonian Unrestricted Trust Funds, Smithsonian Collections Acquisition Program and Dr. Arthur M. Sackler (S1986.53).

Africa and the Middle East
700 B.C.–A.D. 1800s

PREVIEW

Think About ...

Africa's rich literary tradition, which stretches back to ancient kingdoms, has thrived as a largely oral tradition. The literary traditions of the Middle East include Arabic sacred and secular writings and the powerful poetic expressions of the Persians.

As you read about the development of African, Arabic, and Persian literature, look for answers to the following questions:

- What were some of the achievements made during Africa's Golden Age?

- Why is much of African literature part of an oral rather than a written tradition?

- How did the new religion, Islam, change Arabic and Persian culture and literature?

- What benefits did Europe derive from Arabic culture?

- What kinds of literature flourished in Persia under the influence of the Islamic empire?

North Carolina Competency Goal
1.02; 1.03;
4.02; 4.05;
5.01; 5.03

Collection introduction (pages 492–502) covers

Literary Skills
Evaluate the philosophical, historical, and cultural influences of this historical period.

African Literature

African literature is as old as the pyramids, for written literature on the African continent really began with the ancient Egyptians. Yet ancient Egypt was not the only civilization in Africa. Egypt fell into decline toward the end of its New Kingdom period (about 1000 B.C.), losing much of its status as a world power. As Egyptian power was waning, the kingdom of Kush, at the southern end of the Nile, was gaining strength and prominence. For centuries the Egyptians had struggled to contain the Kushites' power. Then, around 710 B.C., Kushite kings succeeded in conquering and ruling Egypt. Like Egypt, Kush was ruled by a royal family. An important difference, however, was that the Kushite royal families traced their

Brass plaque showing the
Oba of Benin with attendants.
Edo peoples (16th century).

The British Museum, London
(Ethno 1898.1-15.38).

lineage through the female line, meaning that more women ruled in
Kush than in any other ancient civilization. The Kushite kingdom
flourished long after Egypt's demise, and its capital city Meroë
thrived as a major producer of iron well into the second century A.D.

In addition to Kush, smaller civilizations grew up around the edges
of the Sahara. These groups farmed and raised livestock in the fertile
grasslands surrounding the desert. Among them were the Fasa of
northern Sudan, who had a well-developed oral literary tradition.
The Fasa's deeds are recalled today in fragments of the Soninke oral
epic *The Dausi*, which reached its present form in the sixteenth
century but probably existed at least three centuries earlier.

Africa's Golden Age

In the third century A.D., a rich kingdom called Aksum (äk'soom') arose in what is now Ethiopia in eastern Africa. Aksum flourished at the center of a trade route that extended from Rome to India. The culture fell into decline in the sixth century A.D., but not before it developed its own writing system, which evolved into several modern scripts still used in Ethiopia today.

Drought drove many migrants south and west. In western Africa, a series of great civilizations arose. The first of these, the kingdom of Old Ghana, was formed by the Soninke after A.D. 300 and lasted for more than a hundred years. The Soninke kings became rich from trading gold for salt. In the eleventh century, though, Ghana was invaded, and the kings began to lose their power. By about A.D. 1235, the Malinke people took over and created the empire of Old Mali, which was then succeeded by the empire of Songhai, among others. The legendary city of Timbuktu was a center of trade and culture in both the Mali and Songhai empires.

Bamana antelope headpiece (Tji Wara) (20th century).
North Carolina Museum of Art.

Houses in Timbuktu.

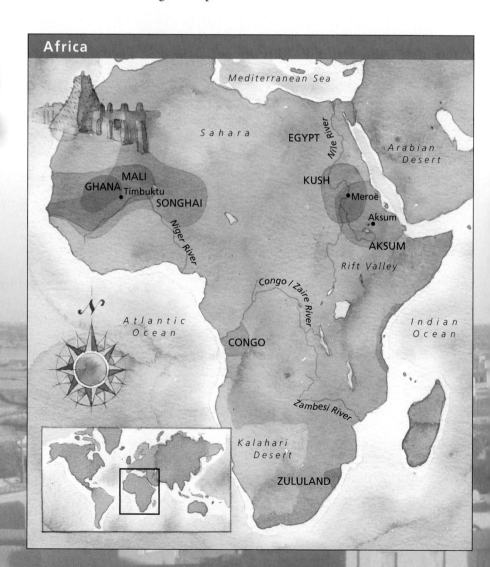

Africa

Mediterranean Sea
Sahara
EGYPT
Nile River
Arabian Desert
MALI
GHANA
Timbuktu
SONGHAI
KUSH
•Meroë
•Aksum
AKSUM
Niger River
Rift Valley
Congo / Zaire River
Atlantic Ocean
CONGO
Indian Ocean
Zambesi River
Kalahari Desert
ZULULAND

During the fourth century A.D., the Roman Empire proclaimed Christianity its state religion and took control of the entire northern coast of Africa. This early Christian influence spread east to Aksum, eventually leading to the foundation of the Ethiopian Orthodox Church, still one of the largest religious groups in Ethiopia.

Around A.D. 700, Islam was introduced into Africa, and with it, the Arabic writing system. By 1235, Islam was the state religion of Old Mali, and other eastern African nations were also largely Muslim.

This period between A.D. 300 and 1600 marked Africa's Golden Age. During this time, sculpture, music, metalwork, textiles, and literature flourished. From Africa's Golden Age came several oral epics, including the Malian epic *Sundiata* (see page 520), as well as praise poems, fables, proverbs, ritual dramas, and other forms of African oral literature.

Africa's Oral Tradition

Although many African cultures used writing systems for record keeping and other practical purposes, African literature before the twentieth century is primarily an oral tradition. One reason involves the tonal quality of many African languages, in which words change meaning depending on the tone in which they are spoken. For example, in a Bantu language spoken in Cameroon, one word can mean "payment" if spoken in a high tone and "crossroads" if spoken in a low tone. (Though English is not tonal, we can get some idea of tonality if we think of the way we say "uh-huh" for "yes," "uh-uh" for "no," and "uh-oh" to indicate problems.) Another

Elders. Dogon griot, Mali.
© Jason Lauré.

Sculpture depicting the head of Queen Mother, Queen Idia (16th century).

Museum of Mankind, Gift of Sir William Ingram, The British Museum, London (Ethno 1897.10-11).

reason the African literary tradition is largely oral is simply that the oral tradition has been so strongly developed and vital in African cultures: Bards, storytellers, town criers, and oral historians have been part of everyday life in African cultures for hundreds of years. In West Africa, for example, the traditional keepers of oral literature were the **griots** (grē′ōz), historians and storytellers who can be thought of as "living libraries." Today, a griot may be a professional storyteller, a singer, or an entertainer, but in the past griots had important roles in memorizing and transmitting their nations' histories, laws, and literature.

The literary forms of Africa are many and varied, yet they share certain features. Striking images of nature, poignant insights into the human condition, and subtle ironies speak clearly to modern readers, transcending barriers of time and culture.

Arabic and Persian Literature

The Persian king Darius with his dignitaries. From a 14th-century Armenian copy of the oldest 5th-century *Romance of Alexander*.

Mechitarista Congregation, Venice.

Sometime around 1500 B.C., tribes of people known as Aryans were part of a massive migration of people who moved west out of central Asia, settling in India. Later, around 700 B.C., other Aryan groups settled in what is now Iran. One of these Aryan groups was called Persian, from the Greek name for the part of Iran in which they settled. Under two great leaders—Cyrus the Great (died 529 B.C.) and Darius I (520–486 B.C.)—the Persians built the largest empire the world had yet seen, stretching at its peak from northern India to North Africa.

When the Aryan settlers arrived in the Middle East, they worshiped many gods. That changed when a prophet from eastern Iran named Zarathustra (Zoroaster in Greek) revolutionized religious belief in the Persian Empire by introducing **Zoroastrianism** (zō′rō•as′trē•ən•iz′əm). Followers of Zoroastrianism believed in two gods—one good and one evil—who were locked in an ongoing struggle in which good would ultimately be triumphant. As the Persians conquered their neighbors, they spread Zoroastrianism.

In 331 B.C., the Macedonian king **Alexander the Great** conquered the Persian Empire, but the Persians fought fiercely—first against the Greeks, then against the Romans—to preserve their culture. The struggle would continue until the seventh century A.D., when another people, the Arabs, swept through the region, bringing with them a new religion: Islam.

Ascent of the Prophet
to heaven, from the
Falnameh of Ja'far
al-Sadiq attributed to
Aqa Mirak.

Courtesy of the Arthur M.
Sackler Gallery, Smithsonian
Institution, Washington, DC:
Smithsonian Unrestricted
Trust Funds, Smithsonian
collections Acquisition
Program & Dr. Arthur M.
Sackler (S1986.253).

The Birth of Islam

The early Arabs were largely sheltered from world events on the Arabian peninsula, which they called "the Arab island." Although some lived in coastal cities or desert settlements under local leadership, most lived in fiercely independent, nomadic communities. Into this vast landscape of scattered tribes came a man who preached a unifying faith called Islam.

   Islam was founded by a man named **Muhammad** (c. A.D. 570–632), a native of Mecca, a city plagued by poverty. Muhammad was so upset by the plight of the poor that he often retreated to the hills to seek spiritual guidance. It was during one of these meditations, followers of Islam believe, that Muhammad was visited by the angel Gabriel, who revealed to him the word of Allah, the one God. Later, Muhammad shared this and subsequent revelations with his followers, who recorded them in the holiest book of Islam, the **Koran** (also written as Qur'an), which means "recitation."

Islam contains many elements similar to the older religions of Judaism and Christianity. For example, the Hebrew laws from the time of Moses are fundamental to the teachings of Islam, and like Christians, **Muslims**—the followers of Islam—believe in a hierarchy of angels and a day of judgment. Islam also teaches that the all-powerful God acted through prophets and believers, from Abraham to Jesus, and that Muhammad was the last in this long line of prophets. One of the main requirements of Islam is that believers submit their will to Allah. In fact, the word *Islam* means "submission."

The Rise of the Islamic Empire

Islam, which stresses community and charity, held a strong appeal for Mecca's poor, and Muhammad quickly made scores of converts. However, powerful men in Mecca sought to silence Muhammad, and he had to flee north to Medina, where he officially founded his min-

Schematic view of Medina (16th century).

Museum of Islamic Art, Cairo, Egypt.

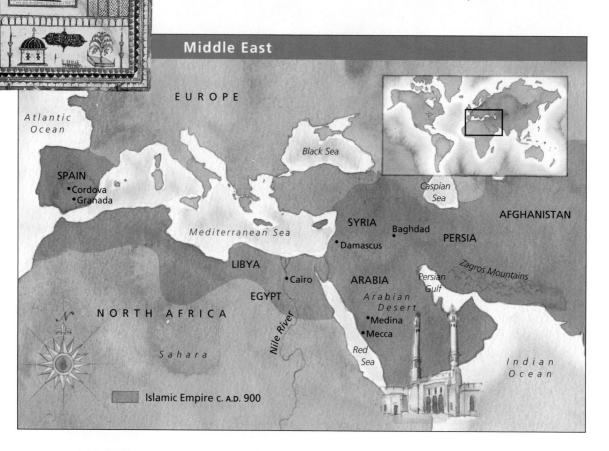

Middle East

EUROPE

Atlantic Ocean

Black Sea

SPAIN
•Cordova
•Granada

Caspian Sea

AFGHANISTAN

SYRIA
Baghdad
•
•Damascus

PERSIA

Mediterranean Sea

Zagros Mountains

LIBYA

•Cairo

ARABIA

Persian Gulf

EGYPT

Arabian Desert

NORTH AFRICA

•Medina
•Mecca

Nile River

Sahara

Red Sea

Indian Ocean

☐ Islamic Empire c. A.D. 900

istry in 622. The Meccans continued their attacks against Muhammad and his followers in Medina but were continually defeated. In 630, Muhammad returned to Mecca in triumph. Several years after Muhammad's death, Arab armies overthrew Persia. In the 640s, the Islamic faith also spread to many parts of Africa and the Far East and today claims around one billion followers worldwide.

A CLOSER LOOK: CULTURAL INFLUENCES

Where Nasrudin Goes, Laughter Follows

Heads up, everyone—here comes Mulla Nasrudin, philosopher and advisor to kings, wrapped in his patched cloak, plodding along on his donkey. As Nasrudin fans the world over know, wherever the Mulla goes, laughter is sure to follow.

Mulla made a business of riding his donkey across the border to the neighboring country daily, loading the panniers [baskets] with straw. The border inspector, suspecting Mulla to be a smuggler, examined his panniers thoroughly every time but failed to find anything. Years later when Mulla retired, he happened to meet the old inspector.

"Now that you have retired, Mulla, tell me whatever it was you smuggled so successfully."

"Donkeys," answered Mulla.

In one sense, no one yet has been able to catch Nasrudin. Persian stories about Mulla ("master") Nasrudin date from at least the thirteenth century, and having traveled like Nasrudin himself, they are told today throughout the Middle East.

The comical Mulla has cut across many cultural boundaries, perhaps because, as the Sufi storytellers knew, "fools" have always been sources of wisdom.

A friend visiting Mulla from another town brought him a duck for a gift. Mulla broiled the duck and shared it with his friend. For a time Mulla kept having visitors who claimed

they were friends of the friends of the friend who brought him the duck and asked him for a duck meal.

The last stranger who showed up claimed, "I am the friend of the friend of the friend of the friend of the friend who brought you the duck."

Inviting the stranger in, Mulla offered him a bowl of hot water.

"And what is this?" the guest inquired.

"This is the soup of the soup of the soup of the soup of the duck which my friend brought me as a gift," said Mulla.

Arab Traders by Hariri. Illuminated manuscript from *Maqamal* (c. 1237).
Bibliotheque Nationale, Paris.

A Cultural Explosion

Following Muhammad's death, Islamic political and spiritual leadership was placed in the hands of a caliph (kā′lif), or "successor." The seat of the caliph's power was the caliphate. In A.D. 750, a powerful Muslim leader named Abbas and his followers, the **Abbasids,** founded a caliphate in Baghdad (the capital of modern Iraq). Here, Arabic influences mixed freely with Persian traditions, producing a splendid marriage of cultures. Although most Persians converted to Islam, Persian literary, intellectual, and administrative practices were maintained. Well before Europe opened its first university, the House of Wisdom was established in Baghdad. The **Abbasid Caliphate** sparked a cultural explosion that swept across the empire. Classical Arabic civilization reached a peak between the ninth and thirteenth centuries.

After Europe emerged from the Dark Ages, it benefited from this great Arabic cultural legacy. In addition to developing the Arabic system of numerals, Arab thinkers made great contributions in algebra, chemistry, astronomy, music theory, and philosophy. Perhaps the greatest legacy of Arabic culture, however, came from the Arabs' translation of ancient Greek and Roman manuscripts, which otherwise might have been lost forever.

Astrolabe (14th century).
National Museum, Damascus, Syria.

Arabic Literature: Sacred and Secular

The Arabs have a long oral literary tradition. In pre-Islamic Arabia, Souk Ozak (sook′ ō•zäk′), or Ozak Market, was one center of oral tradition. There, once a year, poets gathered to compete in contests. Whether with Arab proverbs—the most ancient form of Arabic literature—or with verses from the Koran, the streets of Arab cities and

Kadiomin Mosque,
Baghdad, Iraq.

towns still buzz with the poetry of the Arabic tongue. While Christians traditionally use bells to call the faithful to worship, Muslims use the human voice. Throughout the day, Arabic communities echo with calls to communal prayer.

The Arabs have a long written tradition as well. The *Hadith,* which means "traditions of the prophet," is a vast collection of sayings and actions attributed to Muhammad. Together with the Koran, the *Hadith* provided a foundation for the development of a thriving Arabic literary tradition.

Poetry also was highly valued from the beginnings of Arabic literature and continued to be respected throughout the Islamic period. The Arabic word for poet is *sha'er,* literally "he who knows." Not all poets were men, however. One type of verse, a lament for the deceased, was composed exclusively by women. In pre-Islamic Medina, a woman named al-Khansa wrote strikingly poignant verse about the death of a beloved brother (see page 538). Later, in the classical era, many Arabic poets created sensual love lyrics that overflowed with courtly love conventions similar to those found in later medieval European poetry.

Much Arabic prose was sacred, dealing with interpretations of the Koran, but influential secular prose was written as well. The travel writings of Ibn Battūta gave birth to the modern science of sociology, and the Arab historical tradition influenced European writers. Arabic prose writers also aimed to entertain: *The Thousand and One Nights* (see page 546), composed in Baghdad from the ninth through the sixteenth centuries, still delights modern readers with its fanciful tales of Sindbad the sailor and other characters.

FAST FACTS

Historical Highlights

- The kingdom of Kush conquers Egypt around A.D. 710 and maintains its rule over Egypt for over fifty years.

- From the third to the sixth century A.D., Aksum flourishes at the center of a trade route that extends from Rome to India.

- The establishment of a stable Islamic empire in the seventh century makes possible a great flowering of Arabic literature, science, and philosophy.

Persian Poetry and Prose

Under the enormous momentum of its initial conquests, the Islamic empire made hundreds of thousands of converts, not only to Islam but also to the Arabic language. But eventually the cultures and languages of many of the conquered peoples made a comeback. Remote reaches of the empire produced their own ruling dynasties. In Iran, for example, the **Samanid** dynasty held considerable power from A.D. 875 to 999. Although it upheld Islamic law, this family of rulers, descended from Persians, encouraged the use of Persian forms for artistic pursuits. The first great poet

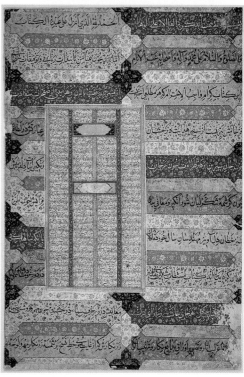

Page from a manuscript of the *Shahname.*
Francis Bartlett Donation of 1912 and Picture Fund. Courtesy, Museum of Fine Arts, Boston (14/692).

Literature of Africa and the Middle East **501**

- The strong communal nature and tonal languages of many African cultures encourage and sustain an oral literature, which is created and transmitted by local story-tellers and bards.

- Notable Persian poets include Dakiki, who emphasizes Persian history in his work, and Omar Khayyám, who writes in the traditional Persian form known as the *rubá'i.*

of this Persian revival under Samanid patronage was Dakiki (died 975). His work emphasized Persian history, including Zoroastrian ideas. Later, Ferdowsi (c. 940–1020) used Dakiki's material in the composition of the Persian epic *Shahname,* or *Book of Kings.*

The poet Omar Khayyám (c. 1048–1131) wrote in a traditional Persian form, the rubá'i. The form was not considered "high art" by Khayyám's contemporaries, but Edward FitzGerald's nineteenth-century English translation of the *Rubáiyát* (see page 554) made Khayyám the most famous Persian poet in the West.

Some of the greatest works of Persian poetry are a product of **Sufism,** a sect of Islam that attracted many Persian followers. A mystical sect, Sufism teaches that a direct, personal experience with Allah can be achieved through intuition. The Sufis developed a popular poetic form called the ghazal, a type of ode. The Sufi poet Hafiz (1326–1389) was a master of this form. Rumi (1207–1273), another Sufi mystic (see page 558), wrote the *Masnavi,* the premiere collection of Sufi poetry.

Most Persian prose works were in the fields of philosophy and history. Animal fables, however, were also a great favorite among Persian audiences. The Sufis produced Persian prose in the form of sayings, anecdotes, and teaching tales. The *Gulistan* by Saadi (see page 563), a thirteenth-century Sufi sage, stands as a masterpiece of Persian prose.

REVIEW

Talk About . . .

Turn back to the Think About questions at the beginning of this introduction (page 492). Write down your responses, and get together with classmates to compare and discuss your views.

Reading Check

1. When was Africa's Golden Age, and what arts flourished during that period?
2. Identify two important reasons why the literary traditions of Africa have remained largely oral.

3. What was the origin of the religion of Islam, and what are some of its key beliefs?
4. What were the cultural contributions of the Abbasid Caliphate?
5. How did Persian culture make a comeback during the Samanid dynasty?

Collection 4

**Literature of Africa
and the Middle East:
The Power of the Word**

African Literature

I teach kings the history of their ancestors
so that the lives of the ancients might serve
them as an example, for the world is old, but
the future springs from the past.

—from *Sundiata*

Relief plaque (detail) depicting three chiefs
making offerings to the Oba (16th century).
Museum of Mankind, London.

The African Oral Tradition

The stories, poems, proverbs, epics, and other products of Africa's oral traditions weave a social fabric, binding communities together and preserving cultural values and traditional beliefs. The selection of works presented here from the literary traditions of various African cultures reveals the wisdom, humor, and vitality of African oral literature.

"Elephant-Hunter, Take Your Bow!" is a traditional hunting song of the Gabon Pygmy, from west-central Africa, on the Gulf of Guinea. Common to many oral traditions is the ancient belief that words have magical powers and can be used to control events and bring about specific outcomes. By singing this song, Gabon Pygmy hunters believed that they could cast a spell over the elephant, ensuring a successful hunt.

"Why We Tell Stories About Spider" is a West African trickster tale. The **trickster,** a universal or **archetypal** figure in the myths and folk tales of many cultures, uses cunning to get the better of others—especially those who are bigger and stronger than he or she. Throughout Africa, the trickster character is often an animal, especially a spider (called Anaanu in this story, Anansi in others), a tortoise, or a hare. This story is also, as the title suggests, an example of one of the most ancient and common types of traditional tale—the etiological (ē′tē·ə·läj′i·kəl) tale, which explains how and why certain things came to be.

"The Five Helpers," from the Togolese people of western Africa, on the Gulf of Guinea, is an example of a **dilemma tale,** or enigma tale. Dilemma tales are a form of moral tale that ends with a question, inviting the audience to share their judgments.

Ashanti mask depicting a trophy head.
Reproduced by permission of the Trustees of the Wallace Collection, London (OA1683).

Dilemma tales are truly interactive, for they require audiences to think about right and wrong behavior and to participate in debate and argumentation.

"Talk" is a humorous tale from the Ashanti, who come from a region in central Ghana in western Africa. It is an example of a **chain tale** or **cumulative tale**—a formulaic story in which every incident that came before is repeated as each new incident is added. (The song "The Twelve Days of Christmas" may be a familiar example.) The story is really a single, extended joke. Like a tall tale, "Talk" stretches reality beyond belief.

The African Oral Tradition

Make the Connection

Quickwrite

Words can inspire, heal, and encourage. They can also wound, deceive, and ruin reputations. Can you think of a speech that impressed you, advice that influenced you, or criticism that hurt your feelings? Jot down a few ideas about the power of words in your life.

Literary Focus

Oral Tradition

Literature of the **oral tradition** refers to works that are not written down but instead are passed from generation to generation through word of mouth. Proverbs, myths, folk tales, fables, and epics in all cultures come from oral traditions.

Oral literature in Africa tends to be part of a traditional repertoire familiar to the listeners. The audience often joins in the oral performance when repeated lines, or **refrains,** occur. In fact, the performance of African oral literature almost always involves spirited audience participation. Songs and tales often use the call-and-response format,

in which the leader calls out a line or phrase and the audience responds with an answering line or phrase. Listeners may also join in singing songs, making comments and catcalls, shouting the proverbs that accompany the tales, or even giving the performer advice.

As Africa changes and becomes more urbanized, storytelling is developing in new ways. Professional entertainers have begun to replace traditional storytellers and to introduce new styles of performance.

> Literature of the **oral tradition** is not written down but is passed from generation to generation by word of mouth. Folk tales, proverbs, myths, and epics are among the many types of literature that belong to the oral tradition.
>
> *For more on Oral Tradition, see the Handbook of Literary and Historical Terms.*

Reading Skills

Understanding Cultural Characteristics

Although the selections that appear here are in written form, keep in mind not only that the literature is in translation but also that it reflects its oral origins. African oral literature features such devices as repetition and parallel structure, which create rhythm, build suspense, and serve as memory aids for griots and other storytellers.

In Africa, storytelling is a performance art, an interactive experience that creates bonds among community members. Try reading each selection aloud, imagining the interactions of storyteller and audience.

Ashanti stool from Ghana.
Private collection.

North Carolina Competency Goal
1.02; 1.03; 4.05; 5.01; 5.03; 6.01

Literary Skills
Understand oral tradition.

Reading Skills
Understand cultural characteristics.

*This ritual hunting song consists of several stanzas and a **refrain**, lines that are repeated at the end of each stanza. In performance, the song leader would sing the main stanzas and the other hunters would join in the refrain.*

The song calls for imitating the actions of the elephant and of the hunters. It also reveals a reverential attitude toward nature and the spirits of the forest. Many African songs and ritual poems are accompanied by instruments and often by dance or rhythmic movements that act out what the words say. In reading the words, try to imagine how the singers might have used dance or movements to dramatize the song and to emphasize its words.

Elephant-Hunter, Take Your Bow!

A Gabon Pygmy Song
translated by **C. M. Bowra**

On the weeping forest, under the wing of the evening,
The night, all black, has gone to rest happy;
In the sky the stars have fled trembling,
Fireflies which shine vaguely and put out their lights;
5   On high the moon is dark, its white light is put out.
The spirits are wandering.
Elephant-hunter, take your bow!
Elephant-hunter, take your bow!

In the frightened forest the tree sleeps, the leaves are dead,
10   The monkeys have closed their eyes, hanging from branches on high.
The antelopes slip past with silent steps,
Eat the fresh grass, prick their ears attentively,
Lift their heads and listen frightened.
The cicada is silent and stops his grinding song.
15   Elephant-hunter, take your bow!
Elephant-hunter, take your bow!

In the forest lashed by the great rain,
Father elephant walks heavily, *baou, baou,*
Careless, without fear, sure of his strength,
20   Father elephant, whom no one can vanquish;
Among the trees which he breaks he stops and starts again.
He eats, roars, overturns trees and seeks his mate.
Father elephant, you have been heard from afar.

Elephant-hunter, take your bow!
25 *Elephant-hunter, take your bow!*

In the forest where no one passes but you,
Hunter, lift up your heart, leap, and walk.
Meat is in front of you, the huge piece of meat,
The meat which walks like a hill,
30 The meat which makes glad the heart,
The meat that will roast on the hearth,
The meat into which the teeth sink,
The fine red meat and the blood that is drunk smoking.
Elephant-hunter, take your bow!
35 *Elephant-hunter, take your bow!*

Trickster tales are among the most common type of African folk tale. The trickster is a universal character type—or **archetype**—*that appears in virtually all world folk traditions. The African trickster may remind you of certain characters in African American folklore, like Brer Rabbit, who use wit and deceit to fool others. While the trickster's actions may be entertaining, they can result in serious consequences. Thus, the trickster often is presented as having a dual nature— cleverness and cunning on the one hand and treachery and destructiveness on the other. Which characteristics are revealed in the following tale of Anaanu, the Spider?*

Why We Tell Stories About Spider

A West African Trickster Tale

translated by **Jack Berry**

In the olden days stories were told about God, not about Anaanu, the Spider. One day, Anaanu felt a very strong desire to have stories told about him. So he went to God and said, "Dear God, I want to have your stories told about me."

And God said, "My dear Anaanu, to have stories told about you is a very heavy responsibility. If you want it, I will let you have it, but first you must prove to me that you are fit to have it. I want you to bring me three things: first, a swarm of bees; second, a live python; third, a live leopard, the King of the Forest himself. If you can bring me these three things, I will allow the stories that are told about me to be told about you instead."

Anaanu went away and sat down and thought. For three whole days he sat and thought. Then he got up, smiling, and took a huge calabash° with a lid. He put some honey in this calabash, set it on his head, and he walked into the forest. He came to a place where a swarm of bees was hovering around some branches. Then he took

the calabash off his head, opened the lid, and started saying loudly to himself while looking into the calabash, "They can fill it; they can't fill it; they can fill it; they can't fill it."

The bees heard him and asked, "Anaanu, what are you talking about?"

And Anaanu said, "Oh, it would be nothing if it were not for that foolish friend of mine. We had an argument. I said that, despite the honey in the calabash, there is still enough space for the makers of the honey to go into the calabash. But he said you are too many, that you cannot go inside the space that is left. I say you can fill it; he says you can't."

Then the leader of the bees said, "Ho! That is easily proved. We can go inside." So he flew into the calabash. And all the bees flew in after him. As soon as they were all inside, Anaanu clapped the lid onto the calabash, very tightly, and took the calabash to God. He said, "I have brought you the

---

° **calabash** (kal′ə·bash′) *n.:* here, the hollowed-out shell of a gourd.

first thing, the swarm of bees." And God looked inside the calabash and said, "Well done, Anaanu, but where are the python and the leopard?"

Anaanu went away into the forest and cut a long stick from a branch of a tree. He scraped all the bark off this stick so that it became a long white pole. Then he went deeper into the forest, carrying the pole and shouting to himself, "It is longer than he; it is not longer than he; it is longer than he; it is not longer than he."

Now the python, who was very proud of his length, for which he was feared throughout the forest, was lying down curled up and resting. When he saw Anaanu, he said, "What are you talking about, Anaanu?"

And Anaanu said, "Oh, it is nothing but an argument that I had with a very ignorant and foolish friend of mine. Do you know that when I told him that you are longer than this stick, from the black mark to the other end, he refused to believe me, and said the stick is longer than you? I say you are longer; he says you are not."

The python growled and said, "What! There is nobody in this world longer than I. As for that stick, bah! I shall soon show you who is longer."

So saying, Python stretched himself beside the stick, putting his head on the black mark. Anaanu said, "To be sure I get the correct length by which you exceed the stick, let me tie you closely to the stick so you won't wiggle and seem shorter." So Anaanu tied Python firmly to the stick. But as soon as Anaanu had finished doing so, he lifted the stick onto his shoulder and

said, "Now, my friend, we will go on a little journey." Then he took the python to God and said, "I have brought you the second thing, the python."

And God looked at the long pole with its burden and said, "Well done, Anaanu, but you still have to bring me Leopard, the King of the Forest himself."

Anaanu went away and dug a deep pit in the forest, on Leopard's path, and covered the pit with sticks and leaves. Leopard, who was going hunting for his food, soon came along the trail and fell into the pit. He was trapped and couldn't get out. Anaanu soon appeared, as if by chance, and said, "Eh, is this King Leopard himself? Well, well, well! But if I am kind enough to bring my family to help me get you out of this pit, you will reward us by eating us all."

But Leopard replied, "How can you talk like that, Anaanu? How could I do such a thing after you have saved my life? I promise that, if you get me out of this pit, no leopard will ever eat a spider again."

And Anaanu said, "All right, I believe you. I will call my family to help get you out of this pit." So Anaanu brought his family and also a heavy stick and a lot of rope. He threw the stick into the pit and jumped in after it. And he told Leopard, "Since you are so heavy, we will have to hoist you out with this stick and some ropes." So Leopard took hold of the stick between his four paws. Anaanu tied first his two front paws to the stick and then his two hind paws, all very firmly. Then his family hoisted them both out of the pit. But as soon as they came out, Anaanu jumped off and grabbed the tail end of the pole. He told Leopard, "Now we will go and visit someone you know." So saying, he dragged the stick with its load to God and said, "I have brought you Leopard, the King of the Forest himself." And God looked at Anaanu and said, "You have done very well, Anaanu. You have achieved the impossible. You deserve to have stories told about you. So from today I decree that the stories that were once told about me shall be told about you."

And that is why stories are told about Anaanu, the spider.

*African **dilemma tales** are moral tales intended for listeners to discuss and debate. They are open-ended stories that invite the audience to respond to a question. There is no "right" answer; the point of such tales is to encourage the audience to weigh the values of actions and to judge proper ways of behaving within society. Even when these stories have fantastic or supernatural elements, they are almost always about family and community relationships, and their underlying messages speak to the problems of real life. After you read the following tale, ask yourself, "How would I answer the closing question?"*

Wooden figurine from Sierra Leone
(c. 19th century). Mende tribe.
University of Pennsylvania Museum of Archaeology
& Anthropology Philadelphia (37-22-279).

The Five Helpers

A Grumshi Dilemma Tale (Togo)
retold by **A. W. Cardinall**

There was once a beautiful girl, the daughter of a chief. She was finer to look upon than any other girl that men could see. But there was no one whom she would agree to marry.

Men came from all countries, but she would not have them. And all the land heard the news of this girl, that though she was of marriageable age, she would take no one.

There was also a snake, a large python who dwelt in a vast lake nearby the river. When he heard about this girl, he decided that he would marry her. So he changed himself into a man and came to the village.

As soon as the maiden saw the young man she was delighted, and said she would marry him at once. Everyone was pleased, and that night they took the young man and the girl on to the roof of the house, for the houses in that village had flat roofs, and there they left them.

Now during the night, the snake licked the girl all over and swallowed her, and changing again into his snake form, he made off to the great lake.

Next morning people came to the house and called to the girl and her man to come down. There was no answer, and the chief told the people to climb up and see what was the matter. This they did, and reported that both the girl and the man were missing.

The chief was very angry, and at once ordered all the people to follow the girl and her lover. But they could find no tracks. So they called for a man who could smell everything. He at once smelled the trail of the girl and followed it down to the great water. There he could go no further. The people, urged on by the anger of the chief, then called on a man famous through all the country for his thirst. They told him to drink up the lake. This he did. But still there was no sign of the man or the girl. Then the people called a man famous for his capacity for work and told him to take out all the mud from the lake. This he did, and thereby revealed a hole. But it was so deep that no one could reach the bottom. Then they remembered that there was a man with an arm that could stretch over all the Dagomba Island. They told him to put his arm in the hole and pull. Out came the great python, which was immediately killed. And when they had cut open its stomach, they found the girl inside, but she was dead. Then the people remembered a man who had the power of medicine, and was able to raise the dead. He came at once and restored the girl to life. Now which of those five men did best?

What if speech were given to inanimate objects and to living things other than human beings? This tale comically explores such a possibility, reflecting the lively humor and sense of the absurd that are common in folk tales told by the various peoples of West Africa. As you read, enjoy the effect of the repetition in this tale, and note how the storyteller combines realistic details with fantastic events.

Talk

An Ashanti Tale (Ghana)

retold by **Harold Courlander**

A farmer went out to his field one morning to dig up some yams. While he was digging, one of the yams said to him: "Well, at last you're here. You never weeded me, but now you come around with your digging stick. Go away and leave me alone!"

The farmer turned around and looked at his cow in amazement. The cow was chewing her cud and looking at him.

"Did you say something?" he asked.

The cow kept on chewing and said nothing, but the man's dog spoke up.

"It wasn't the cow who spoke to you," the dog said. "It was the yam. The yam says leave him alone."

The man became angry, because his dog had never talked before, and he didn't like his tone besides. So he took his knife and cut a branch from a palm tree to whip his dog. Just then the palm tree said, "Put that branch down!"

The man was getting very upset about the way things were going, and he started to throw the palm branch away, but the palm branch said, "Man, put me down softly!"

He put the branch down gently on a stone, and the stone said, "Hey, take that thing off me!"

This was enough, and the frightened farmer started to run for his village. On the way he met a fisherman going the other way with a fish trap on his head.

"What's the hurry?" the fisherman asked.

"My yam said, 'Leave me alone!' Then the dog said, 'Listen to what the yam says!' When I went to whip the dog with a palm branch the tree said, 'Put that branch down!' Then the palm branch said, 'Do it softly!' Then the stone said, 'Take that thing off me!'"

"Is that all?" the man with the fish trap asked. "Is that so frightening?"

"Well," the man's fish trap said, "did he take it off the stone?"

Jewelry worn as insignia by senior officials of the court of the Ashanti kings (18th–19th centuries).
The British Museum, London.

"Wah!" the fisherman shouted. He threw the fish trap on the ground and began to run with the farmer, and on the trail they met a weaver with a bundle of cloth on his head.

"Where are you going in such a rush?" he asked them.

"My yam said, 'Leave me alone!'" the farmer said. "The dog said, 'Listen to what the yam says!' The tree said, 'Put that branch down!' The branch said, 'Do it softly!' And the stone said, 'Take that thing off me!'"

"And then," the fisherman continued, "the fish trap said, 'Did he take it off?'"

"That's nothing to get excited about," the weaver said, "no reason at all."

"Oh, yes it is," his bundle of cloth said. "If it happened to you you'd run too!"

"Wah!" the weaver shouted. He threw his bundle on the trail and started running with the other men.

They came panting to the ford in the river and found a man bathing.

"Are you chasing a gazelle?" he asked them.

The first man said breathlessly: "My yam talked at me, and it said, 'Leave me alone!' And my dog said, 'Listen to your yam!' And when I cut myself a branch the tree said, 'Put that branch down!' And the branch said, 'Do it softly!' And the stone said, 'Take that thing off me!'"

The fisherman panted, "And my trap said, 'Did he?'"

The weaver wheezed, "And my bundle of cloth said, 'You'd run too!'"

"Is that why you're running?" the man in the river asked.

"Well, wouldn't you run if you were in their position?" the river said.

The man jumped out of the water and began to run with the others. They ran down the main street of the village to the house of the chief. The chief's servants brought his stool out, and he came and sat on it to listen to their complaints. The men began to recite their troubles.

"I went out to my garden to dig yams," the farmer said, waving his arms. "Then everything began to talk! My yam said, 'Leave me alone!' My dog said, 'Pay attention to your yam!' The tree said, 'Put that branch down!' The branch said, 'Do it softly!' And the stone said, 'Take it off me!'"

"And my fish trap said, 'Well, did he take it off?'" the fisherman said.

"And my cloth said, 'You'd run too!'" the weaver said.

"And the river said the same," the bather said hoarsely, his eyes bulging.

The chief listened to them patiently, but he couldn't refrain from scowling.

"Now this is really a wild story," he said at last. "You'd better all go back to your work before I punish you for disturbing the peace."

So the men went away, and the chief shook his head and mumbled to himself, "Nonsense like that upsets the community."

"Fantastic, isn't it?" his stool said. "Imagine, a talking yam!"

Ashanti chair.
Private collection.

Response and Analysis

Reading Check

1. In "Why We Tell Stories About Spider," what three tasks must Anaanu perform?
2. In "The Five Helpers," what does each of the five helpers do?
3. What is the final joke of "Talk"?

Thinking Critically

4. **Personification** is a figure of speech in which an object or animal is given human feelings, thoughts, or attitudes. Find examples of personification in "Elephant-Hunter, Take Your Bow!" What feelings are attributed to nature? Do you think these feelings reflect those of the hunters? Explain.

5. Tales are often considered to be the creation of tricksters, who use speech deceptively. How does Spider earn the right to have stories told about him?

6. "The Five Helpers" concludes with a question that invites discussion. What do you think is the value of debating a question to which there is no correct answer?

7. Explain why the title of "Talk" is or is not appropriate.

8. African songs and tales reflect the social lives of communities and their people's values and experiences. What have these selections revealed to you about the concerns, values, and traditions of the people who created them? Provide details from the selections in your response.

Extending and Evaluating

9. The power of words is summed up in this saying: "The pen is mightier than the sword." Compare that saying with this one: "Sticks and stones may break my bones, but words will never hurt me." Do you agree or disagree with these sentiments? Compile a list of expressions or sayings about the importance or unimportance of words, and explain why you agree or disagree with the statements. Refer to your Quickwrite notes for ideas.

LISTENING AND SPEAKING

Telling a Tale

Try your hand at storytelling. First, choose a story to tell; you may tell one of the African stories you have just read or find a story from any culture of your choice in a book of myths or folk tales. Then, practice reading the story with expression, changing your tone of voice for each character. Learn the story well enough that you won't have to keep looking at the page; you should be able to make some eye contact with your audience and even use a few actions or gestures at appropriate points in the tale. Present your story to the class.

North Carolina Competency Goal
1.02; 1.03; 4.05; 5.03; 6.01

INTERNET
Projects and Activities
Keyword: LE5 WL-4

Bracelet with spider relief from Benin, Nigeria.
Antenna Gallery, Dakar, Senegal.

Literary Skills
Analyze oral tradition.

Reading Skills
Understand cultural characteristics.

Listening and Speaking Skills
Present a tale.

The African Oral Tradition 513

Before You Read

African Proverbs

Make the Connection

Quickwrite 🖉

Proverbs are memorable not only because they are so brief (usually no more than a sentence) but also because, like poetry, they compress sometimes complicated ideas into a few thoughtfully crafted words. As a class, brainstorm as many proverbs as you can, like these: "It's no use crying over spilled milk," "A penny saved is a penny earned," "The early bird gets the worm," and so on. Then, choose a proverb that is particularly meaningful to you and briefly describe how you have experienced the truth of that proverb in your own life.

Literary Focus

Proverb

A **proverb** is a concise saying that expresses a common human truth or experience. Proverbs are usually intended to convey accumulated cultural wisdom and experience, advising people about common human failings, such as greed, stupidity, procrastination, and gullibility. Proverbs are often witty and full of wordplay, incorporating such literary elements as **metaphor** ("An ounce of prevention is worth a pound of cure"), **alliteration** ("He who laughs last laughs best"), **parallelism** ("Where there's a will, there's a way"), and **rhyme** ("When the cat's away, the mice will play").

North Carolina Competency Goal
1.02; 1.03; 4.05; 5.01; 5.03; 6.01

Background

In cultures that value oral literature, proverbs function as the distilled essence of a people's values and knowledge. For many African cultures, proverbs are far more than quaint old sayings; they are tools of argument and debate. Proverbs are used to settle legal disputes, resolve ethical problems, and teach children the philosophy of their people. They represent a poetic form that uses few words to achieve great depth of meaning. Because proverbs often contain puns, rhymes, and clever allusions, they also provide sheer entertainment and enjoyment.

Speakers who know and use proverbs have power within the community; their eloquence makes others want to listen to them, and their ability to apply the proverbs to appropriate circumstances demonstrates an understanding of social and political realities. More than one modern African leader has turned to the wisdom of proverbs in order to affirm decisions and to gain popular support and respect.

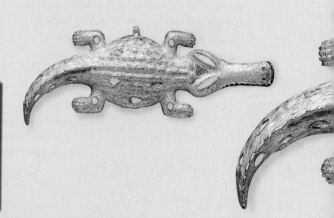

> A **proverb** is a short saying that expresses a common truth or experience.
>
> *For more on Proverb, see the Handbook of Literary and Historical Terms.*

Literary Skills
Understand proverbs.

African Proverbs

compiled by **Charlotte** *and* **Wolf Leslau**

Leopard figurine.
The British Museum, London.

Rain beats a leopard's skin, but it does not wash out the spots.

Only when you have crossed the river, can you say the crocodile has a lump on his snout.

Hunger is felt by a slave and hunger is felt by a king.

What is bad luck for one man is good luck for another.

—Ashanti

He who asks questions, cannot avoid the answers.

Rain does not fall on one roof alone.

—Cameroon

What is said over the dead lion's body, could not be said to him alive.

Great events may stem from words of no importance.

The friends of our friends are our friends.

No matter how long the night, the day is sure to come.

—Zaire

Ashanti gold crocodile (c. 1900).
Gold of Africa Museum. Cape Town, South Africa.

Restless feet may walk into a snake pit.

You cannot build a house for last year's summer.

A blade won't cut another blade; a cheat won't cheat another cheat.

Where there is no shame, there is no honor.

—Ethiopia

The fool is thirsty in the midst of water.

What one hopes for is always better than what one has.

As the wound inflames the finger, so thought inflames the mind.

—Ethiopia (the Oromo)

One camel does not make fun of the other camel's hump.

When a needle falls into a deep well, many people will look into the well, but few will be ready to go down after it.

—Guinea

If you climb up a tree, you must climb down the same tree.

Quarrels end, but words once spoken never die.

—*Sierra Leone*

He who is unable to dance says that the yard is stony.

A man who continually laments is not heeded.

There is no cure that does not cost.

—*Kenya*

If you are building a house and a nail breaks, do you stop building, or do you change the nail?

Proverbs are the daughters of experience.

—*Burundi*

The day on which one starts out is not the time to start one's preparations.

He who is being carried does not realize how far the town is.

When the mouse laughs at the cat, there is a hole nearby.

Before healing others, heal thyself.

Time destroys all things.

—*Nigeria*

If you speak, speak to him who understands you.

When you know who his friend is, you know who he is.

If your son laughs when you scold him, you ought to cry, for you have lost him; if he cries, you may laugh, for you have a worthy heir.

An intelligent enemy is better than a stupid friend.

—*Senegal*

Dogon village huts in the Bandiagara Gorge, Mali.

Don't be so much in love that you can't tell when the rain comes.

An eel that was not caught is as big as your thigh.

Cross the river in a crowd and the crocodile won't eat you.

—*Madagascar*

When the man is away, the monkey eats up the maize and enters the hut.

Do not call to a dog with a whip in your hand.

Even an ant may harm an elephant.

—*Zululand*

A proverb is the horse of conversation: when the conversation lags, a proverb revives it.

A wise man who knows his proverbs can reconcile difficulties.

He who does not mend his clothes will soon have none.

Familiarity breeds contempt; distance breeds respect.

—*Niger*

Response and Analysis

Reading Check

1. Which proverb from Nigeria tells you that the Nigerian culture probably values self-sufficiency?

2. How is the proverb from Nigeria "Time destroys all things" both similar to and different from the familiar saying "Time heals all wounds"?

3. Which Zululand proverb is similar to the common expression "When the cat's away, the mice will play"?

4. Which other African proverbs that you've just read are similar to sayings you know?

Thinking Critically

5. Sometimes two countries or cultural groups have proverbs with similar meanings but different wording and imagery. From among the African proverbs you've just read, find an example of two proverbs from different cultures that have similar meanings expressed in different ways.

6. **Parallelism,** or the repetition of certain words and phrases in a similar structure or order, is a common device used in proverbs. Find three examples of parallelism in the proverbs you've just read. What does the use of parallelism achieve?

7. Another common literary element found in proverbs is **alliteration,** or the repetition of consonant sounds. Identify three proverbs that use alliteration. What does the use of alliteration add to the proverb?

Extending and Evaluating

8. Which proverbs did you like best? Did you like them for their humor, for their moral messages, for their clever comparisons—or for some other characteristic? Compare your favorite African proverb with the proverb you wrote about in your Quickwrite. Explain how your preferences reflect your own values, principles, and sense of humor.

WRITING

Writing a Fable

Proverbs are similar to the morals that appear at the conclusions of many popular fables. (For example, the proverb "Look before you leap" is the moral at the end of Aesop's fable "The Fox and the Goat.") Working with a partner or small group, write a brief fable that could illustrate an African proverb of your choice. Act out the fable, and challenge the rest of the class to guess which proverb best fits as the "moral" of your fable.

North Carolina Competency Goal
1.02; 1.03; 4.05; 5.03; 6.01

INTERNET

Projects and Activities

Keyword: LE5 WL-4

SKILLS FOCUS

Literary Skills
Analyze proverbs.

Writing Skills
Write a fable.

Sundiata: An Epic of Old Mali

Sundiata, like most ancient epics, began as an **oral epic,** also known as a **primary epic.** When epics are eventually written and translated into foreign languages, they undergo changes since translators find it difficult to carry over some original poetic elements into foreign languages. But the narrative, or storytelling, elements of epics *do* carry over into writing, and they survive translation easily. The best-preserved, best-known African epic is *Sundiata,* from the Mandingo people of western Africa. This epic is known to several West African cultures, and it exists in various versions, all passed on by griots, the oral historians of Africa.

Sundiata: Fact and Legend

Like most of the world's epics, *Sundiata* is a fascinating blend of fact and legend. Sundiata Keita, the story's hero, really existed. He was a powerful leader who, in 1235, defeated the Sosso nation of western Africa and reestablished the Mandingo empire of Old Mali. Under Sundiata, Mali expanded from the Atlantic coast to the northern border of present-day Nigeria, including the lands today called Guinea, Gambia, Senegal, Mali, and western Niger. Arts and trade flourished during his reign, and the empire he founded lasted more than 250 years. Sundiata's empire finally fell to the Songhai, under Askia the Great, in 1493.

Even though *Sundiata* is based on fact, it is not a historical document. Rather, over time, the story of Sundiata has become a **legend**—a story about extraordinary deeds that has been passed on from one generation to the next. Like many legends, the story of Sundiata is based on fact that has become greatly embellished over time.

Bambara marka (ceremonial mask) from Mali.

Sundiata in Written Form

The epic of Sundiata was first recorded in Guinea during the 1950s, when it was told by the griot Djeli Mamoudou Kouyaté (djä′lē mä′mo͞o·do͞o ko͞o·yä′tä) to folklorist D. T. Niane. No one knows how many centuries old this version of the epic is. Niane edited the epic as he heard it and translated it from Mandingo into French. His version was later translated into English. Because the epic is now "twice removed" from its original source, it has lost many of the features of the original language: its meter, assonance, and alliteration. However, it still contains some of the original songs, repetition, and proverbs that accompanied the oral performance.

Before You Read

from Sundiata: An Epic of Old Mali

Make the Connection
Quickwrite ✏

Whom do you consider heroic? Think of a relative, friend, or someone you've read about whom you consider a hero. In a paragraph, explain which qualities make this person heroic.

Literary Focus
Epic

An **epic** is a long narrative work that relates the deeds of a larger-than-life hero who embodies the values of his or her society. Epics blend history, legend, and myth and are often told orally for generations before finally being written down.

Sundiata, the heroic main character, or **protagonist,** is like other epic heroes in that he has an unusual childhood and shows signs of greatness even in his early years. As he grows up, he endures many trials. He undertakes a long journey into exile and back before emerging as a leader of his people. He proves himself greater than the powerful foe, or **antagonist,** who opposes him: the evil sorcerer-king Soumaoro Kanté.

The supernatural plays a major role in the epic: Sundiata, his mother, his sister, and his enemies all possess superhuman powers. His story is told in a formal, elevated style from the **omniscient** ("all-knowing") **point of view** of a griot, or storyteller. This omniscient narrator does not take part in the action yet knows everything that is happening. The events of the epic, including its many detailed battle scenes, have a larger-than-life significance: They represent a mighty conflict between good and evil. All these aspects of *Sundiata* reflect patterns common to epics throughout the world.

> An **epic** is a long narrative work that relates the deeds of a larger-than-life hero who embodies the values of his or her society.
>
> *For more on Epic, see the Handbook of Literary and Historical Terms.*

Reading Skills
Making Inferences from Details

When you pay attention to details in a story, you notice the little things—the way a character walks or the way a character relates to his or her family. Such details may seem unimportant at first, but they can provide greater insight into the story as you read further. In order to gain this insight, you make **inferences,** or educated guesses, about what the story is conveying through the details.

As you read these excerpts from *Sundiata*, keep track of the details to see what they might reveal about the main characters and about the values of the Mandingo culture.

Vocabulary Development

affront (ə·frunt′) *n.:* intentional insult.

efface (ə·fās′) *v.:* erase.

nascent (nas′ənt) *adj.:* starting to grow.

deployed (dē·ploid′) *v.:* stationed military troops.

impregnable (im·preg′nə·bəl) *adj.:* incapable of being captured.

implored (im·plôrd′) *v.:* begged earnestly for.

razing (rāz′iŋ) *v.* used as *n.:* tearing down completely.

North Carolina Competency Goal
1.02; 1.03; 2.01; 3.04; 4.03; 4.05; 5.01; 5.03; 6.01

go.hrw.com

INTERNET
Vocabulary Practice
Keyword: LE5 WL-4

SKILLS FOCUS

Literary Skills
Understand characteristics of an epic.

Reading Skills
Make inferences from details.

The setting and characters in Sundiata *reveal the unique history and traditions of the culture from which the epic sprang. Mali in the thirteenth century was a powerful kingdom, enriched by alliances with many neighboring nations. Its civilization was complex and wealthy, its leaders well educated. But its king, Sundiata's father, died when Sundiata was still a child, leaving Mali vulnerable. An invasion by Mali's enemies, the Sossos, is the event that tests Sundiata's heroism.*

These excerpts from Sundiata *show the hero from his seemingly unpromising childhood to his mighty achievements in adulthood. As you read, note Sundiata's qualities as a leader and hero to his people.*

from
Sundiata
An Epic of Old Mali
D. T. Niane
translated by G. D. PICKETT

CHARACTERS IN THE EPIC

Maghan Sundiata (sōon·dyä′tä): the hero of the epic. He is also called Mari Djata and Sogolon Djata.

King Maghan Kon Fatta: Sundiata's father, the king of Mali.

Sogolon (sô·gô·lōn′) **Kedjou:** Sundiata's mother.

Balla Fasséké (bä′lä fä·sā′kä): Sundiata's griot.

Sassouma Bérété (sä·sōo′mä bä·rä′tä): the queen mother; the first wife of the king.

Dankaran Touman (dän′kä·rän tōo·män): Sassouma Bérété's son. He is King Maghan Kon Fatta's successor and Sundiata's half brother.

Soumaoro Kanté: the sorcerer-king of Sosso; Sundiata's nemesis.

Women prepare baobab leaves for use in cooking. Bassamba, Pays Tamberma, Togo.

Maghan Sundiata, also called Mari Djata, is the son of King Maghan Kon Fatta of Mali and his second wife, Sogolon Kedjou. A mysterious hunter has predicted that the boy will one day be a mightier leader than Alexander the Great, the legendary Macedonian conqueror. Few people believe this prophecy, however, because Mari Djata is already seven years old and has still not learned how to walk. He seems an unlikely candidate for emperor.

King Maghan Kon Fatta dies and his first wife, Sassouma Bérété, makes her own son the king. Always jealous of Mari Djata and his mother, Sassouma banishes them to the backyard of the palace, forcing them to live a life of poverty.

from The Lion's Awakening

Sogolon Kedjou and her children lived on the queen mother's leftovers, but she kept a little garden in the open ground behind the village. It was there that she passed her brightest moments looking after her onions and gnougous.[1] One day she happened to be short of condiments and went to the queen mother to beg a little baobab[2] leaf.

"Look you," said the malicious Sassouma, "I have a calabash[3] full. Help yourself, you poor woman. As for me, my son knew how to walk at seven and it was he who went and picked these baobab leaves. Take them then, since your son is

---

1. **gnougous** *n. pl.:* root vegetables.
2. **baobab** (bā′ō·bab′) *n.:* tropical tree whose leaves are used as a cooking herb.
3. **calabash** *n.:* hollowed-out gourd used as a bowl.

Granary in village of Sangha.

unequal to mine." Then she laughed derisively with that fierce laughter which cuts through your flesh and penetrates right to the bone.

Sogolon Kedjou was dumbfounded. She had never imagined that hate could be so strong in a human being. With a lump in her throat she left Sassouma's. Outside her hut Mari Djata, sitting on his useless legs, was blandly eating out of a calabash. Unable to contain herself any longer, Sogolon burst into sobs and seizing a piece of wood, hit her son.

"Oh son of misfortune, will you never walk? Through your fault I have just suffered the greatest <u>affront</u> of my life! What have I done, God, for you to punish me in this way?"

Mari Djata seized the piece of wood and, looking at his mother, said, "Mother, what's the matter?"

"Shut up, nothing can ever wash me clean of this insult."

"But what then?"

"Sassouma has just humiliated me over a matter of a baobab leaf. At your age her own son could walk and used to bring his mother baobab leaves."

"Cheer up, Mother, cheer up."

"No. It's too much. I can't."

"Very well then, I am going to walk today," said Mari Djata. "Go and tell my father's smiths to make me the heaviest possible iron rod. Mother, do you want just the leaves of the baobab or would you rather I brought you the whole tree?"

Vocabulary

affront (ə·frunt′) *n.:* intentional insult.

"Ah, my son, to wipe out this insult I want the tree and its roots at my feet outside my hut."

Balla Fasséké, who was present, ran to the master smith, Farakourou, to order an iron rod.

Sogolon had sat down in front of her hut. She was weeping softly and holding her head between her two hands. Mari Djata went calmly back to his calabash of rice and began eating again as if nothing had happened. From time to time he looked up discreetly at his mother who was murmuring in a low voice, "I want the whole tree, in front of my hut, the whole tree."

All of a sudden a voice burst into laughter behind the hut. It was the wicked Sassouma telling one of her serving women about the scene of humiliation and she was laughing loudly so that Sogolon could hear. Sogolon fled into the hut and hid her face under the blankets so as not to have before her eyes this heedless boy, who was more preoccupied with eating than with anything else. With her head buried in the bedclothes Sogolon wept and her body shook violently. Her daughter, Sogolon Djamarou, had come and sat down beside her and she said, "Mother, Mother, don't cry. Why are you crying?"

Mari Djata had finished eating and, dragging himself along on his legs, he came and sat under the wall of the hut for the sun was scorching. What was he thinking about? He alone knew.

The royal forges were situated outside the walls and over a hundred smiths worked there. The bows, spears, arrows and shields of Niani's warriors came from there. When Balla Fasséké came to order the iron rod, Farakourou said to him, "The great day has arrived then?"

"Yes. Today is a day like any other, but it will see what no other day has seen."

The master of the forges, Farakourou, was the son of the old Nounfaïri, and he was a soothsayer like his father. In his workshops there was an enormous iron bar wrought by his father Nounfaïri. Everybody wondered what this bar was destined to be used for. Farakourou called six of his apprentices and told them to carry the iron bar to Sogolon's house.

When the smiths put the gigantic iron bar down in front of the hut the noise was so frightening that Sogolon, who was lying down, jumped up with a start. Then Balla Fasséké,[4] son of Gnankouman Doua, spoke.

"Here is the great day, Mari Djata. I am speaking to you, Maghan, son of Sogolon. The waters of the Niger can efface the stain from the body, but they cannot wipe out an insult. Arise, young lion, roar, and may the bush know that from henceforth it has a master."

The apprentice smiths were still there, Sogolon had come out and everyone was watching Mari Djata. He crept on all fours and came to the iron bar. Supporting himself on his knees and one hand, with the other hand he picked up the iron bar without any effort and stood it up vertically. Now he was resting on nothing but his knees and held the bar with both his hands. A deathly silence had gripped all those present. Sogolon Djata closed his eyes, held tight, the muscles in his arms tensed. With a violent jerk he threw his weight on to it and his knees left the ground. Sogolon Kedjou was all eyes and watched her son's legs which were trembling as though from an electric shock. Djata was sweating and the sweat ran from his brow. In a great effort he straightened up and was on his feet at one go—but the great bar of iron was twisted and had taken the form of a bow!

Then Balla Fasséké sang out the "Hymn to the Bow," striking up with his powerful voice:

"Take your bow, Simbon,
Take your bow and let us go.
Take your bow, Sogolon Djata."

When Sogolon saw her son standing she stood dumb for a moment, then suddenly she sang

---

4. **Balla Fasséké:** Before he died, the king had named Balla Fasséké as Mari Djata's griot. As griots traditionally served kings, this appointment indicated King Maghan Kon Fatta's faith in the prophecy that Sundiata would one day become king. Here, Balla Fasséké is playing the role of the town crier for Sundiata.

Vocabulary

efface (ə·fās′) v.: erase.

these words of thanks to God who had given her son the use of his legs:

> "Oh day, what a beautiful day,
> Oh day, day of joy;
> Allah[5] Almighty, you never created a
>   finer day.
> So my son is going to walk!"

Standing in the position of a soldier at ease, Sogolon Djata, supported by his enormous rod, was sweating great beads of sweat. Balla Fasséké's song had alerted the whole palace and people came running from all over to see what had happened, and each stood bewildered before Sogolon's son. The queen mother had rushed there and when she saw Mari Djata standing up she trembled from head to foot. After recovering his breath Sogolon's son dropped the bar and the crowd stood to one side. His first steps were those of a giant. Balla Fasséké fell into step and pointing his finger at Djata, he cried:

> "Room, room, make room!
> The lion has walked;
> Hide antelopes,
> Get out of his way."

Behind Niani there was a young baobab tree and it was there that the children of the town came to pick leaves for their mothers. With all his might the son of Sogolon tore up the tree and put it on his shoulders and went back to his mother. He threw the tree in front of the hut and said, "Mother, here are some baobab leaves for you. From henceforth it will be outside your hut that the women of Niani will come to stock up."

Sogolon Djata walked. From that day forward the queen mother had no more peace of mind. But what can one do against destiny? Nothing. Man, under the influence of certain illusions, thinks he can alter the course which God has mapped out, but everything he does falls into a higher order which he barely understands. That is why Sassouma's efforts were vain against Sogolon's son, everything she did lay in the child's destiny. Scorned the day before and the object of

Staff detail: Seated male figure from Mali (16th–20th centuries).
The Metropolitan Museum of Art, Edith Perry Chapman Fund, 1975 (1975.306).

---

5. **Allah:** Arabic name for God.

Bambara oryx mask.

public ridicule, now Sogolon's son was as popular as he had been despised. The multitude loves and fears strength. All Niani talked of nothing but Djata; the mothers urged their sons to become hunting companions of Djata and to share his games, as if they wanted their offspring to profit from the nascent glory of the buffalo-woman's son. The words of Doua on the name-giving day[6] came back to men's minds and Sogolon was now surrounded with much respect; in conversation people were fond of contrasting Sogolon's modesty with the pride and malice of Sassouma Bérété. It was because the former had been an exemplary wife and mother that God had granted strength to her son's legs for, it was said, the more

---

6. **The words . . . name-giving day:** Doua, King Maghan's griot, had repeated the hunter's prophecy at the infant Sundiata's ceremonial naming.

a wife loves and respects her husband and the more she suffers for her child, the more valorous will the child be one day. Each is the child of his mother; the child is worth no more than the mother is worth. It was not astonishing that the king Dankaran Touman was so colorless, for his mother had never shown the slightest respect to her husband and never, in the presence of the late king, did she show that humility which every wife should show before her husband. People recalled her scenes of jealousy and the spiteful remarks she circulated about her co-wife and her child. And people would conclude gravely, "Nobody knows God's mystery. The snake has no legs yet it is as swift as any other animal that has four."

While still a child, Sundiata becomes a great hunter. He becomes friends with Manding Bory, the son of his father's third wife. When an attempt to kill Sundiata fails, the jealous Sassouma and her son Dankaran Touman drive Sundiata into exile. The hero and his family find refuge in the kingdom of Mema.

As Sundiata grows to manhood, the evil Soumaoro Kanté, sorcerer-king of a neighboring kingdom, gains power and conquers many nations. When Sundiata hears that Soumaoro has invaded Mali, he decides to challenge the sorcerer-king and gain control of his rightful kingdom. Sundiata thus makes his way to Sosso, Soumaoro's capital city, to meet Soumaoro face to face. Sundiata fights and wins several battles along the way and becomes a popular leader. Many new soldiers gladly join his ranks.

from **Krina**

Sundiata went and pitched camp at Dayala in the valley of the Niger. Now it was he who was blocking Soumaoro's road to the south. Up till that time, Sundiata and Soumaoro had fought each other without a declaration of war. One does not wage war without saying why it is

Vocabulary

nascent (nas′ənt) *adj.*: starting to grow.

being waged. Those fighting should make a declaration of their grievances to begin with. Just as a sorcerer ought not to attack someone without taking him to task for some evil deed, so a king should not wage war without saying why he is taking up arms.

Soumaoro advanced as far as Krina, near the village of Dayala on the Niger and decided to assert his rights before joining battle. Soumaoro knew that Sundiata also was a sorcerer, so, instead of sending an embassy, he committed his words to one of his owls. The night bird came and perched on the roof of Djata's tent and spoke. The son of Sogolon in his turn sent his owl to Soumaoro. Here is the dialogue of the sorcerer-kings:

"Stop, young man. Henceforth I am the king of Mali. If you want peace, return to where you came from," said Soumaoro.

"I am coming back, Soumaoro, to recapture my kingdom. If you want peace you will make amends to my allies and return to Sosso where you are the king."

"I am king of Mali by force of arms. My rights have been established by conquest."

"Then I will take Mali from you by force of arms and chase you from my kingdom."

"Know, then, that I am the wild yam of the rocks;[7] nothing will make me leave Mali."

"Know, also that I have in my camp seven master smiths who will shatter the rocks. Then, yam, I will eat you."

"I am the poisonous mushroom that makes the fearless vomit."

"As for me, I am the ravenous cock, the poison does not matter to me."

"Behave yourself, little boy, or you will burn your foot, for I am the red-hot cinder."

"But me, I am the rain that extinguishes the cinder; I am the boisterous torrent that will carry you off."

"I am the mighty silk-cotton tree that looks from on high on the tops of other trees."

"And I, I am the strangling creeper that climbs to the top of the forest giant."

"Enough of this argument. You shall not have Mali."

"Know that there is not room for two kings on the same skin, Soumaoro; you will let me have your place."

"Very well, since you want war I will wage war against you, but I would have you know that I have killed nine kings whose heads adorn my room. What a pity, indeed, that your head should take its place beside those of your fellow madcaps."

"Prepare yourself, Soumaoro, for it will be long before the calamity that is going to crash down upon you and yours comes to an end."

Balla Fasséké, Sundiata's griot, and Nana Triban, Sundiata's half sister, have been imprisoned in Soumaoro's palace, but they finally escape. They join Sundiata on the eve of the battle of Krina. Fakoli Koroma, Soumaoro's nephew, also arrives at the camp. Because Soumaoro kidnapped his wife, Fakoli has vowed revenge. Nana Triban and Fakoli pledge their loyalty to Sundiata, and Nana Triban tells Sundiata that the way to ensure Soumaoro's defeat is to touch him with a cock's spur. On the morning of the battle, Sundiata and Manding Bory, his half brother, devise a plan to strip Soumaoro of his power.

"Brother," said Manding Bory, "have you got the bow ready?"

"Yes," replied Sundiata. "Look."

He unhooked his bow from the wall, along with the deadly arrow. It was not an iron arrow at all, but was made of wood and pointed with the spur of a white cock. The cock's spur was the Tana of Soumaoro,[8] the secret which Nana

---

7. **the wild yam of the rocks:** When the vines of these yams grow in boulder-strewn areas, their underground tubers anchor them among the rocks and make them very difficult to uproot.

8. **the Tana of Soumaoro:** The cock's spur (the spiny projection on the leg of a rooster) is Soumaoro's Tana—that is, the taboo, or prohibition, imposed on him by his ancestors. In breaking this taboo, Soumaoro will incur the wrath of his ancestors, who will then withdraw the magic powers that have made him invincible.

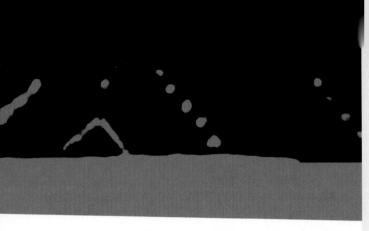

Triban had managed to draw out of the king of Sosso.

"Brother," said Nana Triban, "Soumaoro now knows that I have fled from Sosso. Try to get near him for he will avoid you the whole battle long."

These words of Nana Triban left Djata worried, but Balla Fasséké, who had just come into the tent, said to Sundiata that the soothsayer had seen the end of Soumaoro in a dream.

The sun had risen on the other side of the river and already lit the whole plain. Sundiata's troops <u>deployed</u> from the edge of the river across the plain, but Soumaoro's army was so big that other sofas[9] remaining in Krina had ascended the ramparts to see the battle. Soumaoro was already distinguishable in the distance by his tall headdress, and the wings of his enormous army brushed the river on one side and the hills on the other. As at Neguéboria,[10] Sundiata did not deploy all his forces. The bowmen of Wagadou[11] and the Djallonkés stood at the rear ready to spill out on the left towards the hills as the battle spread. Fakoli Koroma and Kamandjan[12] were in the front line with Sundiata and his cavalry.

With his powerful voice Sundiata cried "An gnewa."[13] The order was repeated from tribe to tribe and the army started off. Soumaoro stood on the right with his cavalry.

Djata and his cavalry charged with great dash but they were stopped by the horsemen of Diaghan and a struggle to the death began. Tabon Wana[14] and the archers of Wagadou stretched out their lines towards the hills and the battle spread over the entire plain, while an unrelenting sun climbed in the sky. The horses of Mema were extremely agile, and they reared forward with their forehooves raised and swooped down on the horsemen of Diaghan, who rolled on the ground trampled under the horses' hooves. Presently the men of Diaghan gave ground and fell back towards the rear. The enemy center was broken.

It was then that Manding Bory galloped up to announce to Sundiata that Soumaoro, having thrown in all his reserve, had swept down on Fakoli and his smiths. Obviously Soumaoro was bent on punishing his nephew. Already

---

9. **sofas** *n. pl.:* warriors.
10. **Neguéboria:** earlier battle fought and won by Sundiata.
11. **Wagadou:** name for Old Ghana.
12. **Kamandjan:** king of Sibi; one of Sundiata's childhood friends.

---

13. *An gnewa:* Forward.
14. **Tabon Wana:** king of Tabon; also called Fran Kamara.

Vocabulary

deployed (dē·ploid′) *v.:* stationed military troops.

Container (Aduno Koro) with figures from Mali (16th–19th centuries).
The Metropolitan Museum of Art, The Michael C. Rockefeller Memorial Collection. Bequest of Nelson A. Rockefeller, 1979 (1979.206.255).

overwhelmed by the numbers, Fakoli's men were beginning to give ground. The battle was not yet won.

His eyes red with anger, Sundiata pulled his cavalry over to the left in the direction of the hills where Fakoli was valiantly enduring his uncle's blows. But wherever the son of the buffalo passed, death rejoiced. Sundiata's presence restored the balance momentarily, but Soumaoro's sofas were too numerous all the same. Sogolon's son looked for Soumaoro and caught sight of him in the middle of the fray. Sundiata struck out right and left and the Sossos scrambled out of his way. The king of Sosso, who did not want Sundiata to get near him, retreated far behind his men, but Sundiata followed him with his eyes. He stopped and bent his bow. The arrow flew and grazed Soumaoro on the shoulder. The cock's spur no more than scratched him, but the effect was immediate and Soumaoro felt his powers leave him. His eyes met Sundiata's. Now trembling like a man in the grip of a fever, the vanquished Soumaoro looked up towards the sun. A great black bird flew over above the fray and he understood. It was a bird of misfortune.

"The bird of Krina," he muttered.

The king of Sosso let out a great cry and, turning his horse's head, he took to flight. The Sossos saw the king and fled in their turn. It was a rout![15] Death hovered over the great plain and blood poured out of a thousand wounds. Who can tell how many Sossos perished at Krina? The rout was complete and Sundiata then dashed off in pursuit of Soumaoro.

Sundiata and Fakoli pursue Soumaoro, who has fled with his son Sosso Balla. They succeed in capturing Sosso Balla, but Soumaoro escapes into a cave. He is never heard from again. Sundiata heads for the nearby village of Koulikoro, where he waits for his army.

The victory of Krina was dazzling. The remains of Soumaoro's army went to shut themselves up in Sosso. But the empire of Sosso was done for. From everywhere around kings sent their submission to Sundiata. The king of Guidimakhan sent a richly furnished embassy to Djata and at the same time gave his daughter in marriage to the victor. Embassies flocked to Koulikoro, but when Djata had been joined by all the army he marched on Sosso. Soumaoro's city, Sosso, the impregnable city, the city of smiths skilled in wielding the spear.

In the absence of the king and his son, Noumounkeba, a tribal chief, directed the de-

---

15. **rout** *n.*: defeat.

Vocabulary

impregnable (im·preg′nə·bəl) *adj.*: incapable of being captured.

fense of the city. He had quickly amassed all that he could find in the way of provisions from the surrounding countryside.

Sosso was a magnificent city. In the open plain her triple rampart with awe-inspiring towers reached into the sky. The city comprised a hundred and eighty-eight fortresses and the palace of Soumaoro loomed above the whole city like a gigantic tower. Sosso had but one gate; colossal and made of iron, the work of the sons of fire. Noumounkeba hoped to tie Sundiata down outside of Sosso, for he had enough provisions to hold out for a year.

The sun was beginning to set when Sogolon Djata appeared before Sosso the Magnificent. From the top of a hill, Djata and his general staff gazed upon the fearsome city of the sorcerer-king. The army encamped in the plain opposite the great gate of the city and fires were lit in the camp. Djata resolved to take Sosso in the course of a morning. He fed his men a double ration and the tam-tams[16] beat all night to stir up the victors of Krina.

At daybreak the towers of the ramparts were black with sofas. Others were positioned on the ramparts themselves. They were the archers. The Mandingoes[17] were masters in the art of storming a town. In the front line Sundiata placed the sofas of Mali, while those who held the ladders were in the second line protected by the shields of the spearmen. The main body of the army was to attack the city gate. When all was ready, Djata gave the order to attack. The drums resounded, the horns blared and like a tide the Mandingo front line moved off, giving mighty shouts. With their shields raised above their heads the Mandingoes advanced up to the foot of the wall, then the Sossos began to rain large stones down on the assailants. From the rear, the bowmen of Wagadou shot arrows at the ramparts. The attack spread and the town was assaulted at all points. Sundiata had a murderous reserve; they were the bowmen

whom the king of the Bobos had sent shortly before Krina. The archers of Bobo are the best in the world. On one knee the archers fired flaming arrows over the ramparts. Within the walls the thatched huts took fire and the smoke swirled up. The ladders stood against the curtain wall and the first Mandingo sofas were already at the top. Seized by panic through seeing the town on fire, the Sossos hesitated a moment. The huge tower surmounting the gate surrendered, for Fakoli's smiths had made themselves masters of it. They got into the city where the screams of women and children brought the Sossos' panic to a head. They opened the gates to the main body of the army.

Then began the massacre. Women and children in the midst of fleeing Sossos implored mercy of the victors. Djata and his cavalry were now in front of the awesome tower palace of Soumaoro. Noumounkeba, conscious that he was lost, came out to fight. With his sword held aloft he bore down on Djata, but the latter dodged him and, catching hold of the Sosso's braced arm, forced him to his knees whilst the sword dropped to the ground. He did not kill him but delivered him into the hands of Manding Bory.

Soumaoro's palace was now at Sundiata's mercy. While everywhere the Sossos were begging for quarter,[18] Sundiata, preceded by Balla Fasséké, entered Soumaoro's tower. The griot knew every nook and cranny of the palace from his captivity and he led Sundiata to Soumaoro's magic chamber.

When Balla Fasséké opened the door to the room it was found to have changed its appearance since Soumaoro had been touched by the fatal arrow. The inmates of the chamber had lost their power. The snake in the pitcher was in the throes of death, the owls from the perch were flapping pitifully about on the ground. Every-

18. **quarter** *n.*: mercy.

16. **tam-tams** *n. pl.*: small drums.
17. **Mandingoes**: inhabitants of Old Mali.

thing was dying in the sorcerer's abode. It was all up with the power of Soumaoro. Sundiata had all Soumaoro's fetishes[19] taken down and before the palace were gathered together all Soumaoro's wives, all princesses taken from their families by force. The prisoners, their hands tied behind their backs, were already herded together. Just as he had wished, Sundiata had taken Sosso in the course of a morning. When everything was outside of the town and all that there was to take had been taken out, Sundiata gave the order to complete its destruction. The last houses were set fire to and prisoners were employed in the razing of the walls. Thus, as Djata intended, Sosso was destroyed to its very foundations.

Yes, Sosso was razed to the ground. It has disappeared, the proud city of Soumaoro. A ghastly wilderness extends over the places where kings came and humbled themselves before the sorcerer-king. All traces of the houses have vanished and of Soumaoro's seven-story palace there remains nothing more. A field of desolation, Sosso is now a spot where guinea fowl and young partridges come to take their dust baths.

Many years have rolled by and many times the moon has traversed the heaven since these places lost their inhabitants. The bourein,[20] the tree of desolation, spreads out its thorny undergrowth and insolently grows in Soumaoro's capital. Sosso the Proud is nothing but a memory in the mouths of griots. The hyenas come to wail there at night, the hare and the hind come and feed on the site of the palace of Soumaoro, the king who wore robes of human skin.

Sosso vanished from the earth and it was Sundiata, the son of the buffalo, who gave these places over to solitude. After the destruction of Soumaoro's capital the world knew no other master but Sundiata.

---

19. **fetishes** *n. pl.:* objects believed to have magical powers.
20. **bourein** *n.:* dwarf shrub.

Vocabulary

razing (rāz′iŋ) *v.* used as *n.:* tearing down completely.

Seated male figure with lance from Mali (15th–20th centuries).

The Metropolitan Museum of Art. Gift of the Kronos Collection, in honor of Martin Lerner, 1983 (1983.600a,b).

For years, westerners have been under the mistaken impression that Africa had only an oral tradition with little or no written literary heritage. This view is challenged, however, by the discovery of thousands of medieval manuscripts in Mali that shed light on Africa's written tradition. These manuscripts also reveal that Timbuktu, in particular, was a cultural and literary center during the Middle Ages.

When Timbuktu Was the Paris of Islamic Intellectuals in Africa

INFORMATIONAL TEXT

Lila Azam Zanganeh
from *The New York Times*, April 24, 2004

In popular imagination, the word *Timbuktu* is a trip of three syllables to the ends of the earth. Today this West African city is a slumbering and decrepit citadel at the southern edge of the Sahara, in Mali, one of the poorest countries in the world.

Yet it is here that some of the most astonishing developments in African intellectual history have been occurring. In recent years, thousands of medieval manuscripts that include poetry by women, legal reflections and innovative scientific treatises have come to light, reshaping ideas about African and Islamic civilizations. . . .

"The manuscripts reveal that black Africa had literacy and intellectualism—thus going beyond the mere notion of Africa as a continent of 'song and dance,'" John O. Hunwick, a scholar who has uncovered some of the writings, said in a recent interview.

. . . These manuscripts, some dating to the 14th century and written mostly in Arabic, show that medieval Timbuktu was a religious and cultural hub as well as a commercial crossroads on the trans-Saharan caravan route. Situated at the strategic point where the Sahara touches on the River Niger, it was the gateway for African goods bound for the merchants of the Mediterranean, the courts of Europe and the larger Islamic world.

When the Renaissance was barely stirring in Europe, Timbuktu was already the center of a prolific written tradition. By the end of the 15th century, Timbuktu's 50,000 residents thrived on the commerce of gold, salt and slaves, and hundreds of students and scholars convened at the city's Sankoré mosque. There were countless Koranic schools and as many as 80 large private libraries. Wandering scholars were drawn to Timbuktu's manuscripts all the way from North Africa, Arabia and even Persia.

The bulk of these texts have remained buried for years in Timbuktu's mud homes. Many owners are the descendants of the skilled craftsman class, and the manuscripts often represent a family heritage passed on from generation to generation.

Mr. Hunwick, a professor of history and religion at Northwestern University who has spent 40 years doing research on Africa, came across piles of manuscripts in the musty trunks of a family library in 1999. They were part of a private collection of several thousand

Koran manuscript (12th century) from a library in Bouj Beha, 150 miles from Timbuktu.

manuscripts, some more than 600 years old. While most were written in Arabic, others used Arabic letters to transcribe local tongues like Fulani and Songhay. Mr. Hunwick said he was awe-struck.

The collection was in the possession of descendants of Mahmoud Kati, a 16th-century scholar who, along with others, jotted intricate notes in the margins of his books. Occasionally Kati commented on the texts, but mostly his notes strayed to other topics, from weddings and funerals to floods and droughts. Of a meteor shower in August 1583, he wrote: "In the year 991 in God's month of Rajab the Goodly, after half the night had passed stars flew around the sky as if fire had been kindled in the whole sky—east, west, north and south. It became a mighty flame lighting up the earth, and people were extremely disturbed about that. It continued until after dawn."

As early as 1967, Unesco recommended the creation of a manuscript conservation center in Timbuktu. Six years later, with financing from Kuwait, the Malian government opened the Ahmed Baba Center in the city, and it has been collecting manuscripts, acquiring more than 18,000 works so far.

"These amount to about 10 to 15 percent of the written potential in Timbuktu and its region," said Ali Ould Sidi, the chief of the city's small but active cultural affairs office. Some scholars believe there are up to one million manuscripts in Mali, about 100,000 of which are in the Timbuktu region. These texts—possibly the most ancient to survive in sub-Saharan Africa—offer a window into the ways black Muslim scholars thought and imagined the world around them over centuries.

? What was the role of Timbuktu in medieval times? In what ways does the discovery of the Timbuktu manuscripts change the accepted view of Africa's literary tradition?

Response and Analysis

Reading Check

1. How are Mari Djata (Sundiata) and his family mistreated after his father dies?

2. How does Mari Djata avenge his mother's humiliation at the hands of the jealous Sassouma?

3. What is the outcome of the **conflict** between Sundiata and the sorcerer-king Soumaoro?

4. What does Sosso look like before the battle of Krina? What does it look like afterward?

Thinking Critically

5. The incident in which Mari Djata (Sundiata) begins to walk reveals a great deal about his **character.** From that incident, what can you **infer** about Sundiata's sense of justice? What does the incident reveal about his physical strength and determination?

6. Three brief songs occur in the excerpt from "The Lion's Awakening." What events do these songs accompany? What purpose do you think these songs serve in the narrative?

7. An exchange of boasts before battle, like Sundiata and Soumaoro's dialogue (see page 527), occurs frequently in epics. Scholars think that *Sundiata* was often performed for the Mandingo army before battles. What effect do you think the boastful exchange might have had on such an audience?

8. Why do you think Sundiata chose to destroy the city of Sosso rather than make it part of his kingdom?

9. An **epic,** with its blend of history and legend, reflects a society's values. Based on your reading of these excerpts from *Sundiata,* what values do you think were honored by the Mandingo culture? Can you tell what kinds of behaviors the culture despised?

10. How does Sundiata compare with the heroic person you wrote about in your Quickwrite? What qualities, if any, do the two heroic figures share? How are they different from one another?

Extending and Evaluating

11. *Sundiata,* like many epics, glorifies war. War is depicted as colorful, exciting, and glorious. Explain how modern views of war are similar to those expressed in *Sundiata* and how they are different. (Consider the media of modern culture, such as television, movies, and video games.)

WRITING

Recording an Oral History

Begin an oral history of your own family, school, or community. Interview someone about a historical event, large or small, that the person witnessed. Perhaps the person you interview will remember details about a famous leader or celebrity. He or she may have participated in a war or some large group effort or witnessed a natural disaster. Ask the person to recall details about the event. Write up your interview, and share it with the class.

Vocabulary Development
Summarizing the Story

affront	impregnable
efface	implored
nascent	razing
deployed	

Using the Vocabulary words listed above, write a summary of the excerpts from *Sundiata*. Not every sentence you write must contain a Vocabulary word. You may use any word more than once.

North Carolina Competency Goal
1.02; 1.03; 2.01; 4.01; 5.01; 5.03; 6.01

go.hrw.com

INTERNET

Projects and Activities
Keyword:
LE5 WL-4

SKILLS FOCUS

Literary Skills
Analyze characteristics of an epic.

Reading Skills
Make inferences from details.

Writing Skills
Record an oral history.

Vocabulary Skills
Summarize the story using vocabulary words.

Vocabulary Development

Using Context Clues

You can often guess the meaning of an unfamiliar word by examining its **context**—the words, phrases, and sentences that surround it. There are several main types of context clues:

1. Synonyms. The sentence or passage may contain a word or phrase that is similar in meaning to the word you do not know.

"Through your fault I have just suffered the greatest affront of my life!"

"...nothing can ever wash me clean of this insult."

—from *Sundiata*

Insult is a synonym for *affront*.

2. Antonyms. The sentence may contain a word or phrase that means the opposite of the word you do not know.

"Scorned the day before and the object of public ridicule, now Sogolon's son was as popular as he had been despised."

—from *Sundiata*

Despised, which is the opposite of *popular,* means "hated."

3. Definitions. The sentence may contain a direct definition of the unknown word.

Griots are African storytellers.

"African storytellers" is the definition of *griots*.

4. Restatements. The unknown word's meaning may be clarified by a restatement that is signaled by dashes, parentheses, or phrases such as *that is* or *in other words*.

Sosso was razed. In other words, it was completely destroyed.

Razed is a synonym for *destroyed*.

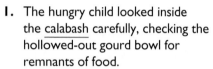

PRACTICE

In the following sentences, words from *Sundiata* are underlined. (In the text, these words are footnoted.) Identify the context clues that help you determine the meaning of each underlined word. Then, identify which type of context clues they are.

1. The hungry child looked inside the calabash carefully, checking the hollowed-out gourd bowl for remnants of food.

2. The Sossos begged for quarter, not more pain and suffering.

3. The gnougous (root vegetables) were a common part of the diet of the people of Old Mali.

4. The baobab is a tropical tree with edible fruit and leaves that can be used as an herb for cooking.

North Carolina Competency Goal
6.01

SKILLS FOCUS

Vocabulary Skills
Understand and analyze context clues.

Senior Dogon men.

Grammar Link

From Time to Time: Keeping Verb Tenses Consistent

The **tense** of a verb indicates when an action or state of being takes place. Sometimes you have to shift tenses within a paragraph or even a sentence, but unnecessary shifts in tense can be awkward and confusing. The following necessary shifts from *Sundiata* indicate the difference between the narrator describing past events and the narrator making a general comment about these events:

NECESSARY SHIFTS   Sundiata and Soumaoro <u>had fought</u> each other without a declaration of war. One <u>does not wage</u> war without saying why <u>it is being waged</u>.

Unless you have a good reason for switching tenses, stick to one consistent tense.

INCONSISTENT   Sundiata <u>is</u> an epic hero because he <u>embodied</u> the values of Mali's culture.

CONSISTENT   Sundiata <u>is</u> an epic hero because he <u>embodies</u> the values of Mali's culture.

Use the present tense when writing about what happens in a work of literature. The consistent example above shows the use of the **literary present.**

If two events occurred at different times in the past, use different tenses to show which event happened first.

UNCLEAR   By the time I <u>finished</u> the epic, I <u>will come</u> to admire Sundiata's sense of justice.

CLEAR   By the time I <u>finished</u> the epic, I <u>had come</u> to admire Sundiata's sense of justice. [This sentence makes clear that I admired Sundiata's sense of justice before I finished reading the epic.]

PRACTICE

Check the following sentences for consistency of verb tense. If the tenses are consistent, write *OK.* If the tenses are inconsistent, rewrite the sentence using the correct verb tense. Some sentences may contain more than one error.

1. Griots perform African epics like *Sundiata* for many years before the epics were finally written down.

2. While it enlivened an oral performance of the epic, repetition can be problematic when reading a translated version of *Sundiata.*

3. As the excerpt reaches its conclusion, Sundiata ordered his men to destroy Sosso.

4. *Sundiata* is a riveting story that entertains readers and teaches them about Mali's culture at the same time.

Apply to Your Writing

Review a writing assignment you are working on now or have already completed. Note the tense of each verb. Are there any unnecessary shifts in tense? Correct any shifts to make verb tenses clear and consistent.

▶ **For more help, see Tenses and Their Uses, 3b–c, in the Language Handbook.**

Collection 4

Literature of Africa and the Middle East:

The Power of the Word

Arabic and Persian Literature

Dates

We grow to the sound of the wind
Playing his flutes in our hair,

Palm tree daughters,
Brown flesh Bedouin,
5 Fed with light
By our gold father;

We are loved of the free-tented,
The sons of space, the hall-forgetters,
The wide-handed, the bright-sworded
10 Masters of horses.

Who has rested in the shade of our palms
Shall hear us murmur ever above his
    sleep.

—Kisa'i of Merv, *from* The Book of the
    Thousand Nights and One Night,
    translated by E. Powys Mathers

Detail of *Horseman and Groom* attributed
to Qadami Qazvin (c. 1560).

Courtesy of the Arthur M. Sackler Museum, Harvard
University Art Museums, Gift of John Goelet, formerly
in the collection of Louis J. Cartier (1958.62.2).

al-Khansa

(c. A.D. 575–c. 644)

Her full name was Tumadir bint Amr, but this Arabian poet is best known by her nickname, al-Khansa, which means "the snub-nosed." Only a few facts about her have survived the centuries since she lived. She was born around A.D. 575 and belonged to the Sulyam tribe and the Sharid clan. She was married to a kinsman and bore six children. Around 630, when she was in her mid-fifties, al-Khansa's community accepted the then-new religion of Islam. She was among the converts and may even have been part of the tribal delegation that went to the town of Medina to offer submission directly to Muhammad. The exact date of her death is unknown, but she lived into old age, dying around 644 or possibly even as late as 660.

Only a thousand or so lines of al-Khansa's poetry remain, but those fragments are enough to assure her place in Arabic literature. Her work is technically brilliant, emotionally rich, and highly eloquent. Among her poems is "On Her Brother," an **elegy,** or poem composed to lament the death of a loved one. Even in al-Khansa's day, the elegy was an ancient form, but she gave it a new degree of refinement. Her poem is richly textured with pride and sorrow that resonate through time. The poem conveys a sense of the characters of both the subject and the poet.

As a poet, al-Khansa enjoyed respect and high status in her community. Pre-Islamic clans such as hers felt themselves blessed when one of their members proved to have the poetic gift. They believed that through poetry the memory of their accomplishments could endure beyond their lifetimes. A gifted person like al-Khansa thus helped ensure the

Young woman giving her dog a drink.
Free Library of Philadelphia, Pennsylvania.

immortality of the community. Her poems have not only kept her name and the name of her brother alive but also have preserved the history and glory of her clan.

On Her Brother

Make the Connection

Quickwrite

To the pre-Islamic Arabs, immortality meant being remembered by the living after death. Do you agree that this is a form of immortality? In what other ways can people be "immortalized"? Write down your thoughts.

Literary Focus

Elegy

An **elegy** is usually a poem that memorializes the death of a person or laments a permanent loss. Elegies may express sorrow over the passing of a particular individual, or they may be meditations on the inevitable passing of youth, life, and beauty. Most elegies are formal in language and structure and melancholy or somber in tone.

> An **elegy** is a formal poem that mourns the death of a person or laments something that is lost.
>
> *For more on Elegy, see the Handbook of Literary and Historical Terms.*

Background

Although al-Khansa died a Muslim, her poetry belongs to the pre-Islamic era. Pre-Islamic Arab society, in general, did not believe in an afterlife. For these Arabs, the only possible immortality was an enduring reputation. Since the people of al-Khansa's time had no tradition of historical writing, they depended on poets like her to preserve the memory of esteemed members of the community and their deeds.

Much of al-Khansa's poetry was inspired by her brother Sakhr, a tribal leader who was killed in an ambush by enemy warriors as he returned from a successful battle. Al-Khansa seems to have loved him especially because he had always respected her independence. The deeds for which al-Khansa praises her brother reflect the heroic Arabian character of the sixth and seventh centuries A.D. Daring horsemanship was highly prized, and men proved their skills in frequent raids and battles.

Of the approximately one thousand lines of al-Khansa's poetry that survive, over nine hundred mourn the death of her brother.

Two warriors on horseback in combat. School of Tabriz (c. 1480). Topkapi Palace Museum, Istanbul, Turkey.

North Carolina Competency Goal
1.03; 4.05; 5.01; 5.03; 6.01

SKILLS FOCUS

Literary Skills
Understand elegy.

On Her Brother

al-Khansa

translated by **Willis Barnstone**

My brother was not a camel driver,
a coward, shallow-hearted like a beast.

His sword glittered like a pool
under roaming night clouds.

5   He ran faster
than any of his men.

What good is life—even if he were
happy—since he ran out of time?

10   Each man whose family was happy in him
will visit his grave.

You saw a knight
on a horse running with its tail floating

in the wind, a brown warrior wrapped
in a coat of thin iron.

15   When they overtook him they shouted
like shepherds at daybreak.

Response and Analysis

North Carolina Competency Goal
1.02; 1.03; 4.05; 5.03; 6.01

Thinking Critically

1. What **figures of speech,** or imaginative comparisons, does al-Khansa use to express her opinion of her brother's worth?

2. Which lines in al-Khansa's **elegy** reveal her sorrow? What feelings besides sorrow does she express? Give examples.

3. People in al-Khansa's culture expected poets to confer immortality on their subjects. For what does al-Khansa memorialize her brother? Do you think she succeeded in "immortalizing" him?

4. Do you think it was al-Khansa's main purpose in her **elegy** to meditate on the nature of death or preserve the memory of her brother or both? Explain.

Extending and Evaluating

5. If you wished to ensure immortality for someone you know who died, how would you do it? You may want to review your Quickwrite notes.

6. What human needs do you think are met by creating a memorial such as an elegy?

WRITING

Composing an Elegy

Write a brief elegy in memory of someone who died whose loss you keenly felt. You need not write about someone you knew personally. You might choose someone famous (like Martin Luther King, Jr.) whose memory you want to celebrate even though you never met him or her in person. Use figures of speech and descriptive language to describe the character of the person who died and to express your sadness.

LISTENING AND SPEAKING

Reciting an Elegy

With a small group, organize a memorial service for the person you wrote about in your elegy. Read your elegy aloud, and select other fitting memorials to the person, such as music, photographs, and artwork by and about the person you are honoring.

INTERNET

Projects and Activities
Keyword:
LE5 WL-4

SKILLS FOCUS

Literary Skills
Analyze elegy.

Writing Skills
Compose an elegy.

Listening and Speaking Skills
Recite an elegy.

ABOUT THE
Koran
(c. A.D. 651–652)

Page from the Koran: Sura 79, verses 40–46; Sura 80, verses 1–19 (mid-14th century).

Freer Gallery of Art, Smithsonian Institution, Washington, DC: Purchase. (F1930.59).

To the more than one billion Muslims worldwide, the Koran (kə•ran') is the word of Allah, the Arabic name for God. According to Muslim belief, the Koran comes from tablets kept in heaven, dictated by the angel Gabriel to the prophet Muhammad.

Muhammad was born into a prominent family in the Arabian city of Mecca around A.D. 570. Despite his family's high social position, Muhammad's childhood was filled with hardship and sorrow. By the age of six, he was an orphan. Nevertheless, by adulthood he had managed to become a worldly and successful merchant.

When he was about forty, this prosperous businessman, possibly troubled by civil unrest in Mecca, began to meditate at night in a hillside cave near his home. It was here that, according to Islamic belief, the angel Gabriel appeared to Muhammad and announced: "You are the messenger of God." Muhammad experienced numerous visions, or revelations, in the years that followed, and he dedicated his life to preaching the oneness of God and rejecting the beliefs that many Arabs held in his day.

Muhammad recognized the similarities between the messages he had received and the doctrines of Christianity and Judaism. However, more than these religions, Muhammad's preaching emphasized the power of divine judgment and the need for pious submission to the will of Allah. Hence, the name given to Muhammad's religion, Islam, means "submission." One who accepts Islam is a Muslim—"one who submits to God."

According to tradition, Muhammad could neither read nor write, so his followers memorized his utterances or jotted them down on whatever they could find—a leaf, a scrap of leather, a rock. After Muhammad died, his followers feared that his words would be lost forever if they did not gather all the versions and record them in a single authoritative Arabic text. Within twenty years, a group of scribes had accomplished this goal and had ordered the destruction of all other versions of Muhammad's revelations. They called this scripture the Koran (also written as Qur'an), an Arabic word meaning "recitation," and decreed it the official scripture of Islam.

Before You Read

from the Koran

Make the Connection

The possibility of compassion and mercy is a central theme in the Koran, as it is in the sacred literature of many other religions. Discuss the meanings of the words *compassion* and *mercy*. How do you see these two principles operating in every-day life? Give examples of circumstances you know of in which compassion or mercy was either shown or withheld.

Literary Focus
Antithesis

Didactic literature, or literature intended to instruct, often makes use of certain techniques, such as antithesis, to help readers remember important ideas. **Antithesis** is a form of parallelism in which sharply contrasting ideas are expressed in grammatically balanced sentences. For example, the English poet Alexander Pope wrote, "To err is human; to forgive, divine." The statement emphasizes the contrast between humans who are weak and prone to mistakes and a divine God who is both all-powerful and forgiving.

Antithesis is a contrast of ideas expressed in a grammatically balanced statement.

For more on Antithesis, see the Hand-book of Literary and Historical Terms.

North Carolina Competency Goal
1.03; 4.05; 5.01; 5.03

INTERNET

More About the Koran
Keyword:
LE5 WL-4

SKILLS FOCUS

Literary Skills
Understand antithesis.

Background

Because of the Koran's divine authority, as well as the grace and power of its language, orthodox Muslims consider it perfect and unalterable. When readers recite the Koran on public occasions, precise rules govern their tone and pronunciation. In addition, Muslims consider that translation can lead to distortion and can only approximate the words of Allah. Although the Koran appears in Turkish, Urdu, English, and many other languages, these translations are considered paraphrases and cannot be used in rituals or ceremonies.

The central theme of the Koran is that there is only one all-powerful God—Allah—who created the world. This God is merciful and compassionate, but he is also the God of Judgment Day. The proper response to Allah is to submit to his will, be generous to the poor, and lead an upright life. Every individual has a choice between following the good, which leads to an afterlife of eternal bliss, or giving in to evil, which leads to eternal damnation.

Muslim scholars have devoted their lives to a study of the Koran, interpreting classical Arabic words and writing commentaries on various passages of the holy book. Their work not only ensures that Muslims understand Allah's revelation but also confirms the Koran as the perfect model of Arabic grammar and diction.

The Koran consists of 114 suras, or chapters. Every sura but the ninth begins with these words: "In the name of Allah, the Compassionate, the Merciful."

from the Koran

translated by **N. J. Dawood**

THE EXORDIUM

*IN THE NAME OF ALLAH
THE COMPASSIONATE
THE MERCIFUL*

*Praise be to Allah, Lord of the Creation,
The Compassionate, the Merciful,
King of Judgment-day!
You alone we worship, and to You alone
we pray for help.
Guide us to the straight path
The path of those whom You have favored,
Not of those who have incurred Your wrath,
Nor of those who have gone astray.*

THE CESSATION

*In the Name of Allah,
the Compassionate, the Merciful*

When the sun ceases to shine; when the stars
fall down and the mountains are blown away;
when camels big with young are left untended
and the wild beasts are brought together;
when the seas are set alight and men's souls
are reunited; when the infant girl, buried
alive, is asked for what crime she was slain;
when the records of men's deeds are laid open
and the heaven is stripped bare; when Hell
burns fiercely and Paradise is brought near:
then each soul shall know what it has done.

I swear by the turning planets and by the
stars that rise and set; by the fall of night and
the first breath of morning: this is the word of
a gracious and mighty messenger, held in
honor by the Lord of the Throne, obeyed in
heaven, faithful to his trust.

No, your compatriot is not mad. He saw
him[1] on the clear horizon. He does not grudge

Koran stand from Turkestan (8th–14th centuries).
The Metropolitan Museum of Art, Rogers Fund, 1910 (10.218).

---

1. **He saw him:** reference to the Prophet's vision of
   Gabriel.

the secrets of the unseen; nor is this the utterance of an accursed devil.

Whither then are you going?

This is an admonition to all men: to those among you that have the will to be upright. Yet you cannot will, except by the will of Allah, Lord of the Creation.

DAYLIGHT

*In the Name of Allah,
the Compassionate, the Merciful*

By the light of day, and by the fall of night, your Lord has not forsaken you, nor does He abhor you.

The life to come holds a richer prize for you than this present life. You shall be gratified with what your Lord will give you.

Did He not find you an orphan and give you shelter?

Did He not find you in error and guide you?

Did He not find you poor and enrich you?

Therefore do not wrong the orphan, nor chide away the beggar. But proclaim the goodness of your Lord.

COMFORT

*In the Name of Allah,
the Compassionate, the Merciful*

Have We[2] not lifted up your heart and relieved you of the burden which weighed down your back?

Have We not given you high renown?

Every hardship is followed by ease. Every hardship is followed by ease.

When your task is ended resume your toil, and seek your Lord with all fervor.

---

2. **We:** Allah.

Sharjah Mosque, United Arab Emirates.

Response and Analysis

Reading Check

1. In "The Exordium," what does the speaker ask Allah to do?
2. What does "The Cessation" say souls will learn when the earth ends?
3. According to "Daylight," what three things should a person do to show gratitude for God's goodness?
4. What reassuring words does "Comfort" offer?

Thinking Critically

5. In "The Exordium," Muhammad prays for guidance to "the path of those whom You have favored, / Not of those who have incurred Your wrath." The righteous, described in the first clause, stand in **antithesis** to the sinful, described in the second clause. Find and explain other examples of antitheses in these excerpts.
6. Many of the sentences in "Daylight" and "Comfort" are written as questions. How does the use of questions reinforce the lessons being taught in these passages?
7. Which of the images in these excerpts do you find most striking and memorable? What impact do you think these images are intended to have on readers or listeners?

Extending and Evaluating

8. In "The Cessation," Muhammad urges his followers to be "upright." In "Daylight," he instructs them not to "wrong the orphan, nor chide away the beggar." How might modern Muslims apply these teachings to their daily lives?

WRITING

Composing a Sermon

Create a brief **sermon**—a speech about moral behavior—to deliver to your classmates. Begin by choosing for your theme a particular moral lesson, such as the necessity of taking personal responsibility, the importance of respecting others' beliefs, or the need to resolve conflicts peacefully. Decide next how you want to persuade or motivate your audience. For example, do you want to threaten punishment, appeal to their sense of fairness, or promise rewards? Write a draft of your sermon, using the technique of antithesis to emphasize your important points and make them easy to remember. When you are satisfied with your written sermon, practice delivering it at home so that you can present it to the rest of the class.

North Carolina Competency Goal
1.03; 4.05; 5.03

INTERNET
Projects and Activities
Keyword:
LE5 WL-4

SKILLS FOCUS

Literary Skills
Analyze antithesis.

Writing Skills
Compose a sermon.

Scene in a mosque, from the *Falnameh* of Ja'far al-Sadiq attributed to Aqa Mirak.

Musee d'Art et d'Histoire, Geneva (1971-107/35).

The Koran   545

The Thousand and One Nights

(c. 850–c. 1500)

Ever since the writer Antoine Galland translated *The Thousand and One Nights*—or *The Arabian Nights' Entertainment*—into French in the early eighteenth century, this collection of tales has been the best known and most widely read work of Arabic literature in the West. The often fantastic adventures of Ali Baba, Aladdin, and Sindbad are known throughout the world today.

The Thousand and One Nights probably developed over several centuries. The original stories came from many oral and written sources, including such collections as the Indian *Panchatantra* (see page 383) and tales brought by travelers from China, India, and every part of the Middle East. Scholars have identified sources for many of the stories, but the true origins of many others remain unknown because they exist in more than one version and in more than one language.

The earliest references to *The Thousand and One Nights* appear in manuscripts from as early as the ninth century A.D. Kept alive by Arab storytellers throughout the Middle Ages, the collection grew and changed. By the mid-sixteenth century, the stories had been put into the form we know today by an unknown Egyptian compiler. The group of tales was first published in Arabic in 1548.

The tales in the collection are loosely held together by an element that was common in medieval literature—a **frame story**. In the frame story, a sultan, Shahriyar, is enraged at his wife's unfaithfulness and orders her executed. He then takes a new wife each day but has her killed at dawn the next day because he believes that no woman can ever be faithful. The supply of potential wives is running low when the sultan takes Scheherazade

Scheherazade amusing the sultan Shahriyar with the tales for a thousand and one nights, from the *Arabian Nights* (19th century).
The Granger Collection, New York.

(shə·her′ə·zäd′) as his wife.

Scheherazade is a spellbinding storyteller. She is also extremely clever. Each night she entertains the sultan with a new tale but delays revealing the ending until the following night. The captivated sultan keeps postponing her execution in order to hear the ends of her stories. After one thousand and one nights of tales, he abandons his plan to kill Scheherazade, and the couple remain happily married.

The Fisherman and the Jinnee

Make the Connection

People often talk about the power of stories. Scheherazade's stories were so powerful that they kept her alive for one thousand and one nights. What kinds of powers do stories have? Can you think of a time when a story had a powerful effect on you or someone you know? In a small group, discuss the many ways stories can affect our lives.

Literary Focus

Moral

In discussing what stories can accomplish, you may have mentioned their ability to teach a lesson, or **moral,** about how to live wisely and well. Folk and fairy tales, fables, and parables are all types of literature that incorporate morals in order to teach as well as entertain their audience.

> A **moral** is the lesson about life that folk and fairy tales and other forms of literature teach.
>
> For more on Moral, see the Handbook of Literary and Historical Terms.

Persian plate showing a knight with a falcon (13th century).
Louvre, Paris.

Reading Skills

Inferring a Message

The moral or lesson of a literary work is sometimes stated directly in a saying or proverb at the beginning or end of the story. More often, the reader has to **infer,** or figure out, the message by interpreting clues in the text. Details of plot and character, when put together and interpreted correctly, will reveal the writer's message. Here are some questions you can ask yourself to help you infer a message or moral:

• What does the main character want?

• What means does the main character use to get what he or she wants?

• What effect do the character's actions have on attaining the goal?

North Carolina Competency Goal
1.03; 4.05; 5.01; 5.03

Vocabulary Development

invoking (in·vōk′iŋ) v. used as adj.: calling upon.

prodigious (prō·dij′əs) adj.: very large; huge.

inverted (in·vʉrt′ed) v. used as adj.: turned upside down.

adjured (ə·joord′) v.: commanded as under oath.

resolutely (rez′ə·loot′lē) adv.: firmly; determinedly.

perfidious (pər·fid′ē·əs) adj.: wicked; unfaithful.

INTERNET

Vocabulary Practice
•
More About The Thousand and One Nights
Keyword: LE5 WL-4

Literary Skills
Understand moral.

Reading Skills
Infer a message.

547

Fisherman and the Jinnie from *Arabian Nights* (1898) by H. J. Ford.
The Granger Collection, NY.

The Fisherman and the Jinnee

from Tales from The Thousand and One Nights

translated by **N. J. Dawood**

Once upon a time there was a poor fisherman who had a wife and three children to support.

He used to cast his net four times a day. It chanced that one day he went down to the sea at noon and, reaching the shore, set down his basket, rolled up his shirt-sleeves, and cast his net far out into the water. After he had waited for it to sink, he pulled on the cords with all his might; but the net was so heavy that he could not draw it in. So he tied the rope ends to a wooden stake on the beach and, putting off his clothes, dived into the water and set to work to bring it up. When he had carried it ashore, however, he found in it a dead donkey.

"By Allah, this is a strange catch!" cried the fisherman, disgusted at the sight. After he had freed the net and wrung it out, he waded into the water and cast it again, <u>invoking</u> Allah's help. But when he tried to draw it in he found it even heavier than before. Thinking that he had caught some enormous fish, he fastened the ropes to the stake and, diving in again, brought up the net. This time he found a large earthen vessel filled with mud and sand.

Angrily the fisherman threw away the vessel, cleaned his net, and cast it for the third time. He waited patiently, and when he felt the net grow heavy he hauled it in, only to find it filled with bones and broken glass. In despair, he lifted his eyes to heaven and cried: "Allah knows that I cast my net only four times a day. I have already cast it for the third time and caught no fish at all. Surely He will not fail me again!"

Vocabulary
invoking (in·vōk′iŋ) *v.* used as *adj.*: calling upon.

With this the fisherman hurled his net far out into the sea, and waited for it to sink to the bottom. When at length he brought it to land he found in it a bottle made of yellow copper. The mouth was stopped with lead and bore the seal of our master Solomon son of David. The fisherman rejoiced, and said: "I will sell this in the market of the coppersmiths. It must be worth ten pieces of gold." He shook the bottle and, finding it heavy, thought to himself: "I will first break the seal and find out what is inside."

The fisherman removed the lead with his knife and again shook the bottle; but scarcely had he done so, when there burst from it a great column of smoke which spread along the shore and rose so high that it almost touched the heavens. Taking shape, the smoke resolved itself into a jinnee[1] of such prodigious stature that his head reached the clouds, while his feet were planted on the sand. His head was a huge dome and his mouth as wide as a cavern, with teeth ragged like broken rocks. His legs towered like the masts of a ship, his nostrils were two inverted bowls, and his eyes, blazing like torches, made his aspect fierce and menacing.

The sight of this jinnee struck terror to the fisherman's heart; his limbs quivered, his teeth chattered together, and he stood rooted to the ground with parched tongue and staring eyes.

"There is no god but Allah and Solomon is His Prophet!"[2] cried the jinnee. Then, addressing himself to the fisherman, he said: "I pray you, mighty Prophet, do not kill me! I swear never again to defy your will or violate your laws!"

"Blasphemous giant," cried the fisherman, "do you presume to call Solomon the Prophet of Allah? Solomon has been dead these eighteen hundred years, and we are now approaching the end of Time. But what is your history, pray, and how came you to be imprisoned in this bottle?"

On hearing these words the jinnee replied sarcastically: "Well, then; there is no god but Allah! Fisherman, I bring you good news."

"What news?" asked the old man.

"News of your death, horrible and prompt!" replied the jinnee.

"Then may heaven's wrath be upon you, ungrateful wretch!" cried the fisherman. "Why do you wish my death, and what have I done to deserve it? Have I not brought you up from the depths of the sea and released you from your imprisonment?"

But the jinnee answered: "Choose the manner of your death and the way that I shall kill you. Come, waste no time!"

"But what crime have I committed?" cried the fisherman.

"Listen to my story, and you shall know," replied the jinnee.

"Be brief, then, I pray you," said the fisherman, "for you have wrung my soul with terror."

"Know," began the giant, "that I am one of the rebel jinn who, together with Sakhr the Jinnee, mutinied against Solomon son of David. Solomon sent against me his Vizier,[3] Asaf ben Berakhya, who vanquished me despite my supernatural power and led me captive before his master. Invoking the name of Allah, Solomon adjured me to embrace his faith and pledge him absolute obedience. I refused, and he imprisoned me in this bottle, upon which he set a seal of lead bearing the Name of the Most High. Then he sent for several of his faithful jinn, who carried me away and cast me into the middle of the sea. In the ocean depths I vowed: 'I will bestow eternal riches on him who sets me free!' But a hundred years passed away and no one freed me. In the second hundred years of my imprisonment I said: 'For him who frees me I will open up the buried treasures of the

---

1. **jinnee** *n.:* evil supernatural being in Arabic mythology; commonly spelled genie in English.
2. **There is . . . Allah and Solomon is His Prophet:** Allah is the Arabic name for God. Solomon was the king of Israel (c. 960 B.C.), who was known for his matchless wisdom.

---

3. **Vizier** *n.:* high-ranking official in Muslim countries; originally a Muslim ruler's chief representative, who interacted with the ruler's subjects.

Vocabulary

prodigious (prō·dij′əs) *adj.:* very large; huge.
inverted (in·vurt′ed) *v.* used as *adj.:* turned upside down.
adjured (ə·joord′) *v.:* commanded as under oath.

Fisherman and the Jinnie from *Arabian Nights* (detail)
(1907) by Edmund Dulac.

earth!' And yet no one freed me. Whereupon I flew into a rage and swore: 'I will kill the man who sets me free, allowing him only to choose the manner of his death!' Now it was you who set me free; therefore prepare to die and choose the way that I shall kill you."

"O wretched luck, that it should have fallen to my lot to free you!" exclaimed the fisherman. "Spare me, mighty jinnee, and Allah will spare you; kill me, and so shall Allah destroy you!"

"You have freed me," repeated the jinnee. "Therefore you must die."

"Chief of the jinn," cried the fisherman, "will you thus requite[4] good with evil?"

"Enough of this talk!" roared the jinnee. "Kill you I must."

At this point the fisherman thought to himself: "Though I am but a man and he is a jinnee, my cunning may yet overreach his malice." Then, turning to his adversary, he said: "Before you kill me, I beg you in the Name of the Most High engraved on Solomon's seal to answer me one question truthfully."

The jinnee trembled at the mention of the

---

4. **requite** (ri·kwīt') *v.*: repay.

Name, and, when he had promised to answer truthfully, the fisherman asked: "How could this bottle, which is scarcely large enough to hold your hand or foot, ever contain your entire body?"

"Do you dare doubt that?" roared the jinnee indignantly.

"I will never believe it," replied the fisherman, "until I see you enter this bottle with my own eyes!"

Upon this the jinnee trembled from head to foot and dissolved into a column of smoke, which gradually wound itself into the bottle and disappeared inside. At once the fisherman snatched up the leaden stopper and thrust it into the mouth of the bottle. Then he called out to the jinnee: "Choose the manner of your death and the way that I shall kill you! By Allah, I will throw you back into the sea, and keep watch on this shore to warn all men of your treachery!"

When he heard the fisherman's words, the jinnee struggled desperately to escape from the bottle, but was prevented by the magic seal. He now altered his tone and, assuming a submissive air, assured the fisherman that he had been jesting with him and implored him to let him out. But the fisherman paid no heed to the jinnee's entreaties,[5] and <u>resolutely</u> carried the bottle down to the sea.

"What are you doing with me?" whimpered the jinnee helplessly.

"I am going to throw you back into the sea!" replied the fisherman. "You have lain in the depths eighteen hundred years, and there you shall remain till the Last Judgement! Did I not beg you to spare me so that Allah might spare you? But you took no pity on me, and He has now delivered you into my hands."

"Let me out," cried the jinnee in despair, "and I will give you fabulous riches!"

"<u>Perfidious</u> jinnee," retorted the fisherman, "you justly deserve the fate of the King in the tale of 'Yunan and the Doctor.'"

"What tale is that?" asked the jinnee.

---

5. **entreaties** (en·trēt'ēz) *n. pl.*: requests.

Vocabulary

resolutely (rez'ə·lōōt'lē) *adv.*: firmly; determinedly.
perfidious (pər·fid'ē·əs) *adj.*: wicked; unfaithful.

Response and Analysis

Reading Check

1. What does the fisherman draw from the sea the fourth time he casts his net? What does the fisherman do with his catch?

2. How does the fisherman try to persuade the jinnee not to kill him?

3. How does the fisherman finally manage to trick the jinnee?

4. What is the jinnee's last offer to the fisherman? Why do you think he makes such a promise?

Thinking Critically

5. Were you able to **infer** any message, or **moral,** in this story? Think about the character of the fisherman, how the jinnee comes to him, and how he ultimately outsmarts the jinnee.

6. Which details in this story obviously come from Islamic culture? Do you think it is necessary to know something about Islam in order to enjoy this story? Explain.

Extending and Evaluating

7. At what point do you think Scheherazade would have ended her recital of "The Fisherman and the Jinnee" in order to hold the sultan's interest?

Literary Criticism

8. Some Arab scholars have dismissed *The Thousand and One Nights* as mere popular entertainment. They have argued that the tales are not great literature because the stories have crude and simplistic plots and no depth in characterization or theme. What do you think about such an assessment of the value of the kinds of stories found in *The Thousand and One Nights*?

WRITING

Writing a Folk Tale

Try your hand at writing a brief folk tale of your own, perhaps following the pattern of "The Fisherman and the Jinnee," in which a person is looking for one thing but finds something completely unexpected—and troublesome. Your story can be humorous or serious, but it should have a solid plot structure, fantastic and imaginative details, and a basic moral or message. You may wish to illustrate your folk tale or read it aloud to the class.

Vocabulary Development
Yes or No?

Be sure you can justify your answers to these questions about the Vocabulary words in boldface.

1. Have you ever found yourself **invoking** the help of an enemy?

2. Are **inverted** letters easy to read?

3. Would you **resolutely** deny false rumors about your actions?

4. Are the heroes in fairy tales usually **perfidious**?

5. Are witnesses **adjured** to tell the truth when testifying?

6. Are giants **prodigious**?

North Carolina Competency Goal
1.03; 4.05; 5.03

go.hrw.com

INTERNET

Projects and Activities

Keyword:
LE5 WL-4

SKILLS FOCUS

Literary Skills
Analyze a moral.

Reading Skills
Infer a message.

Writing Skills
Write a folk tale.

Vocabulary Skills
Answer questions about vocabulary words.

Omar Khayyám

(A.D. 1048–1131)

The poet Ghiyasoddin Abolfat'h Omar ebn Ebrahim is known as Omar Khayyám (kī·yäm′), which means "Omar the tentmaker." Khayyám, however, was not a tentmaker but a scholar whose knowledge extended to an amazing variety of disciplines. Not only was he thoroughly familiar with the works of Greek philosophers, but he also understood the sciences of his day, including medicine and astronomy. In addition, he was an excellent mathematician.

While still in his twenties, Khayyám wrote a scholarly paper on algebra in which he showed how to solve a kind of problem no one had ever been able to solve before. Another paper, on elementary geometry, helped advance the knowledge of numbers. He was also one of a group of astronomers who revised the Islamic calendar. The calendar that Khayyám and his colleagues produced was unmatched in accuracy until the Gregorian calendar was developed in the West almost five hundred years later.

Impressive as these achievements are, westerners know of Khayyám today not for his work in science but for writing a number of four-line verses of poetry called *rubá'i* (rōō·bä·ī′), a Persian poetic form. The poet behind the verses is a somewhat mysterious figure. It was not until the 1940s that researchers determined the dates of Khayyám's birth and death. It is known that he was born in Nishapur (now in Iran), then a major center of trade in the northeastern Persian province of Khorasan. None of his poetry came to light until well after his death. And though hundreds of four-line verses have been attributed to Khayyám,

Detail of *Two Lovers Landing on the Island of Terrestrial Bliss* from Haft Awrang (Seven Thrones) (c. 1556–1565).

Courtesy of the Freer Gallery of Art, Smithsonian Institution, Washington, DC. (F46.12).

scholars have so far been able to confirm his authorship of only a few of them.

In Persia, Khayyám's poetry enjoyed only modest popularity. References to his poetry appear in works by contemporaries, but Khayyám himself apparently considered his verses and epigrams minor in comparison to his scientific writing. In the 1850s, however, an English poet and translator named Edward FitzGerald (1809–1883) was struck by the poetic beauty of the *rubáiyát* (the plural form of *rubá'i*) and began translating them into English. It was FitzGerald's translations that brought Khayyám worldwide fame as a poet over seven hundred years after he died. In fact, FitzGerald's translation of the *Rubáiyát of Omar Khayyám* has been called the most famous translation of a literary work into English.

Before You Read

from the Rubáiyát

Make the Connection
Quickwrite ✐

Khayyám's *Rubáiyát* expresses the theme that life is good and to be enjoyed fully. The poet argues that it is foolish to postpone pleasure until another day because that day may never come. You have encountered this *carpe diem* ("seize the day") philosophy in other literary works from other cultures. Do you agree with this view of life? Jot down your reasons for agreeing or disagreeing.

Literary Focus
Rubá'i

Rubá'i—rubáiyát (rōō'bī·yät') in the plural—is the Persian word for **quatrain**, or four-line verse. In English translation, the standard form for *rubáiyát* is that the first, second, and last lines rhyme. The third line usually does not rhyme with the other three. The *rubá'i* is an ancient literary form that Persian poets used to express their thoughts on diverse subjects. Because a *rubá'i* is so short and its rhyme scheme so restrictive, it often makes use of metaphor and imagery to express its meaning.

> A *rubá'i* is a four-line verse form that originated in Persian poetry.
>
> *For more on* Rubá'i, *see the Handbook of Literary and Historical Terms.*

Background

Khayyám's birthplace, the region of Khorasan, or "the land of the sun," is now divided between Iran, Turkmenistan, and Afghanistan. In the poet's day, it lay at the crossroads of trade and travel between Asia and Europe. Merchants and travelers from all over the world passed through this cosmopolitan region, enriching the native Persian culture with artistic and philosophical influences from China, India, and classical Greece.

But during Khayyám's lifetime, Khorasan was repeatedly attacked and then ruled by a Turkic people called the Seljuks (sel'jōōks'). The Seljuk Turks brought with them an authoritarian and religiously orthodox rule. They prohibited wine and other sensual pleasures that Khayyám clearly enjoyed. His verse, with its focus on the sweetness and pleasures of life, gently challenged the repressiveness of Seljuk rule.

There are other translations of Khayyám's work, but none has gained the popularity or fame of FitzGerald's, which remains in print to this day. Yet FitzGerald's translations are not always literally true to the originals. FitzGerald considered himself a "free translator" who focused on what he felt to be the meaning and spirit of the poetry. He wanted English readers to respond to the *rubáiyát* as he imagined readers of the originals might have responded. Therefore, he used contemporary images that were more familiar to British readers whenever the original imagery struck him as too obscure or culturally specific.

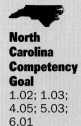

North Carolina Competency Goal
1.02; 1.03; 4.05; 5.03; 6.01

INTERNET
More About Omar Khayyám
Keyword:
LE5 WL-4

SKILLS FOCUS

Literary Skills
Understand *rubá'i.*

from the Rubáiyát

Omar Khayyám
translated by Edward FitzGerald

1

Wake! For the Sun, who scattered into flight
The Stars before him from the Field of Night,
    Drives Night along with them from Heav'n
        and strikes
The Sultán's Turret with a Shaft of Light.

7

Come, fill the Cup, and in the fire of Spring
Your Winter-garment of Repentance fling:
    The Bird of Time has but a little way
To flutter—and the Bird is on the Wing.

12

A Book of Verses underneath the Bough,
A Jug of Wine, a Loaf of Bread—and Thou
    Beside me singing in the Wilderness—
Oh, Wilderness were Paradise enow![1]

13

Some for the Glories of This World; and some
Sigh for the Prophet's[2] Paradise to come;
    Ah, take the Cash, and let the Credit go,
Nor heed the rumble of a distant Drum!

17

Think, in this battered Caravanserai[3]
Whose Portals are alternate Night and Day,
    How Sultán after Sultán with his Pomp
Abode his destined Hour, and went his way.

19

I sometimes think that never blows so red
The Rose as where some buried Caesar bled;
    That every Hyacinth[4] the Garden wears
Dropped in her Lap from some once lovely Head.

24

Ah, make the most of what we yet may spend,
Before we too into the Dust descend;
    Dust into Dust, and under Dust to lie
Sans[5] Wine, sans Song, sans Singer, and—sans End!

27

Myself when young did eagerly frequent
Doctor and Saint, and heard great argument
    About it and about: but evermore
Came out by the same door where in I went.

28

With them the seed of Wisdom did I sow,
And with mine own hand wrought to make
        it grow;
    And this was all the Harvest that I reaped—
"I came like Water, and like Wind I go."

71

The Moving Finger writes; and, having writ,
Moves on: nor all your Piety nor Wit
    Shall lure it back to cancel half a Line,
Nor all your Tears wash out a Word of it.

---

1. **enow** (ē·nou′) *adj.:* enough (archaic).
2. **Prophet's:** Muhammad's.
3. **caravanserai** (kar′ə·van′sə·rī′) *n.:* inn providing services for caravans.

---

4. **hyacinth** (hī′ə·sinth′) *n.:* In classical mythology, the hyacinth sprang up from the blood of Hyacinthus after he was accidentally killed by Apollo. In the *Odyssey,* locks of hair are compared to clusters of hyacinth.
5. **sans** (sanz) *prep.:* without (French).

(Opposite) *Ladies Preparing for a Picnic* (detail) (c. 1575) from a *Khamesh* of Amir Khusraw. Shiraz.
Bodleian Library, University of Oxford, MS Elliott (189, f. 192a).

72

And that inverted Bowl they call the Sky,
Whereunder crawling cooped we live and die,
   Lift not your hands to *It* for help—for It
As impotently moves as you or I.

96

Yet Ah, that Spring should vanish with the Rose!
That Youth's sweet-scented manuscript
         should close!
   The Nightingale that in the branches sang,
Ah whence, and whither flown again, who knows!

99

Ah Love! could you and I with Him conspire
To grasp this sorry Scheme of Things entire,
   Would not we shatter it to bits—and then
Remold it nearer to the Heart's Desire!

100

Yon rising Moon that looks for us again—
How oft hereafter will she wax and wane;
   How oft hereafter rising look for us
Through this same Garden—and for *one* in vain!

101

And when like her, O Sákí,[6] you shall pass
Among the Guests Star-scattered on the Grass,
   And in your joyous errand reach the spot
Where I made One—turn down an empty Glass!

TAMÁM[7]

---

6. **Sákí** (sä′kē): wine bearer (Persian).
7. **Tamám:** finished, complete (Persian).

Detail of *Standing Figure* attributed to Muhammadi
(mid-16th century).

Response and Analysis

Thinking Critically

1. In verse 12, what does the speaker say would be "Paradise enow" for him? What do all these things have in common?

2. In verse 99, the speaker says that he and his love would like to remold the "sorry Scheme of Things" closer to their desire. What kind of a world do you think they would create?

3. How does the speaker's tone change in the course of verse 99?

4. The theme of *carpe diem* ("seize the day") also appears in the Gilgamesh epic (see page 23) and in Horace's "Carpe Diem" (see page 304). Do the three works all express this idea in the same way, or do the attitudes differ? Which work's ideas are closest to your own? Review your Quickwrite response. ✏

5. Verse 24 is a particularly good example of a **rubá'i,** a four-line poem that expresses an idea in a brief, witty style—often with a twist at the end. What is the speaker in verse 24 saying about life and death? How does the ending of the poem provide a clever twist?

6. In verse 71, what is the "Moving Finger"? State the meaning of the verse in your own words. What does it imply about how one should live life?

Extending and Evaluating

7. Khayyám's *Rubáiyát* has been consistently in print since FitzGerald's first translation in the 1850s. Why do you think there has been a continuing audience for this book? Do you think it will remain popular in the twenty-first century? Why or why not?

WRITING

Interpreting a Poet's Philosophy

A hedonist makes pleasure-seeking the goal of life. A pessimist expects the worst of people and of events. Khayyám has been called both a hedonist and a pessimist. Do you think it is possible to be both at the same time? In an essay of three or four paragraphs, cite passages from the *Rubáiyát* that support your point of view of Khayyám as a hedonist, a pessimist, or both. Organize your ideas by jotting down evidence on a two-column chart like the one below.

Hedonist	Pessimist
rubá'i no. ideas / phrases	rubá'i no. ideas / phrases

North Carolina Competency Goal
1.02; 1.03; 4.05; 5.03; 6.01

INTERNET

Projects and Activities
Keyword: LE5 WL-4

SKILLS FOCUS

Literary Skills
Analyze rubá'i.

Writing Skills
Interpret a poet's philosophy.

Las Mesquita, Córdoba, Spain.

Rumi

(A.D. 1207–1273)

Jalal ad-Din ar-Rumi, known as Rumi (rōo′mē), was born in Balkh, in the province of Khorasan, now divided between modern Afghanistan, Turkmenistan, and Iran. His father was a famous teacher and mystic—one who believes that God's truth comes not through learning or through the senses but through flashes of enlightenment.

Rumi grew up to practice Sufism (sōo′fiz′əm), a mystical form of Islam. Sufis stress the importance of understanding God through personal intuition. By 1240, Rumi's fame as a Sufi teacher had spread throughout the region, and he had gathered about him a group of followers, or disciples.

The turning point in Rumi's life, however, was his relationship with the wandering holy man Shams ad-Dīn ("Sun of Religion"), whom he met in 1244. To Rumi, Shams seemed a nearly perfect example of beauty and truth, and the two mystics became inseparable. However, one night in 1247 Shams mysteriously disappeared. Researchers have established that the holy man was murdered and quickly buried near a well that is still in Konya, a city in Turkey. It is believed that followers of Rumi— perhaps with the consent of Rumi's own sons—committed the murder because they were jealous of Shams's relationship with their master. Assuming Shams had abandoned him, Rumi turned to poetry for consolation and wrote a collection of lyrics and odes, the *Divan-i-Shams-i-Tabrizi*. Rumi signed Shams's name to the poems in honor of his beloved friend and in keeping with the Sufi belief that he and Shams were one in spirit.

Portrait of Rumi.

Rumi's prose work fills three volumes, but he is most famous for a volume of poetry titled the *Masnavi*. This didactic epic of 26,000 couplets—pairs of rhyming lines—written in informal, colloquial language, defines Sufi teachings. Interspersed with the teachings are quotations from the Koran, stories of the life and teachings of Muhammad, legends of pre-Islamic poets and prophets, Arabic versions of Sanskrit beast fables, and Near Eastern folk tales. It has been said that Rumi's *Masnavi* is for Iranians "second in importance only to the Koran."

Unmarked Boxes

Make the Connection

Quickwrite 🖊

This poem begins with a statement of a comforting belief: "Don't grieve. Anything you lose comes round / in another form." In other words, the things we think we lose—the carefree pleasures of early childhood, for example—are replaced by other pleasures, such as the privilege of getting a driver's license. What do you think of Rumi's idea? List some things that you have lost and gained throughout life.

Literary Focus

Analogy

An **analogy** is a kind of comparison that explains something unfamiliar by describing it in terms of something familiar. For example, someone might draw an analogy between a helicopter ride and an exciting fairground ride, such as a roller coaster. You might then understand that a helicopter lurches and dips, and you would know the feeling in your stomach that accompanies such a ride. Analogies can help to describe ideas and objects as well as experiences.

An **analogy** is a comparison of two things to show that they are alike in certain respects.

For more on Analogy, see the Handbook of Literary and Historical Terms.

Background

The poet Rumi belonged to the branch of Islamic mysticism known as Sufism. The Sufis believe in the doctrine of *Vahdat-ol-Vojood,* or "the unity of all things." To Sufis, this means that all things profane (that is, impure or not holy) are, in fact, holy. Although this may sound contradictory, it is simply a way of saying that God is present in everything. For example, a rose, a profane organism, may embody God's perfect beauty and therefore be sacred for what it represents. Sufi belief also suggests that all things and beings in the visible world are different only in form, for they are essentially one in God. Finally, the doctrine implies that God is at once present and absent—present because God resides in all beings, but absent because we do not directly perceive God through our five senses.

North Carolina Competency Goal
1.02; 1.03;
4.05; 5.03;
6.01

Ceiling of the Mihrab,
Great Mosque of Córdoba, Spain.

INTERNET
More About Rumi
Keyword:
LE5 WL-4

Literary Skills
Understand
analogy.

559

Unmarked Boxes

Rumi

translated by **John Moyne**
and **Coleman Barks**

Don't grieve. Anything you lose comes round
in another form. The child weaned from
   mother's milk
now drinks wine and honey mixed.

God's joy moves from unmarked box to
   unmarked box,
from cell to cell. As rainwater, down into
5   flowerbed.
As roses, up from ground.
Now it looks like a plate of rice and fish,
now a cliff covered with vines,
now a horse being saddled.
10   It hides within these,
till one day it cracks them open.

Part of the self leaves the body when we sleep
and changes shape. You might say, "Last night
I was a cypress tree, a small bed of tulips,
a field of grapevines." Then the phantasm
15   goes away.
You're back in the room.
I don't want to make anyone fearful.
Hear what's behind what I say.

Fa'ilatun fa'ilatun fa'ilatun fa'ilat.°
20   There's the light gold of wheat in the sun
and the gold of bread made from that wheat.
I have neither. I'm only talking about them.

as a town in the desert looks up
at stars on a clear night.

---

19. Fa'ilatun ... fa'ilat: This line is composed of
phrases used to indicate various types of poetic
"feet." It is the equivalent of "iamb, iamb, iamb,
trochee."

Detail of *A Prince Enthroned* from a copy of the fifth book
of *The Nathnawi* by Rumi (c. 1530).

Courtesy of the Arthur M. Sackler Gallery, Smithsonian Institution,
Washington, DC: Smithsonian Unrestricted Trust Funds, Smithsonian
collections Acquisition Program & Dr. Arthur M. Sackler (s1986/85).

CONNECTION *to* UNMARKED BOXES

According to legend, one day Rumi heard the chiming hammer of a goldsmith and was inspired to begin a whirling dance. This dance was to become the principal ritual of the Turkish religious order Mevlevi, also known as the whirling dervishes (dervish means "holy one"). Part of the larger branch of Sufism, the Mevlevi are called whirling dervishes because they seek union with God by twirling in circles.

INFORMATIONAL TEXT

Perfect Circles

Kimberly Gdula

from *Dance Spirit,* September 1, 2001

"Wherever you turn, there is the face of God." (Qur'an 2:115)

Marveled for their ability to whirl interminably, dervishes—referred to as *semazens* in the Mevlevi religious order—take this teaching to heart. In fact, it is representative of both the inspiration and training behind every turner's magical display because, without God, the tradition of whirling would not exist. "Turning itself is one part of a larger education of the heart and the whole human being," says Kabir Helminski, a Mevlevi sheikh. . . .

Within the confines of a religious retreat, an initial 40 days of training is required. But turners commonly take a year or more to prepare for their first public appearance. . . .

Training begins with instruction of the proper beginning form, the alif. This entails crossed arms with hands resting on opposite shoulders—a position held while the dervish bows in surrender. But it is the turning position, learned next, that actually teaches abandonment of fear and resistance. "Not until someone is reasonably comfortable in the [turning] form," says Helminski, "can they go to further stages of surrender."

Here's how it's done: Your left leg serves as the axis on which you turn, while your right leg is lifted up the back of your left calf with your right foot crossing behind your left knee before it is placed back in the spot from which it was lifted. Each movement is a 360 degree revolution. From the moment you start spinning, your right arm extends upward with the right hand turned so your palm faces up (receiving) and your left arm [is] held parallel to the floor, the palm of your left hand facing down (bestowing). Helminski explains, "It's as if a spiritual energy is being received, passing

(continued)

Whirling dervishes in the Divan Edebiyati Monastery and Museum in Turkey.

through the heart and brought into this world as a service."

As for focus, turners keep a steady gaze on the left hand, though they also take notice of what's going on around them. . . . "The movement is, in a way, a feedback mechanism to show you if your concentration is right. If not, you'll lose your balance or lose the beauty of the form." The ease with which turners stop abruptly would seem an ultimate gauge of concentration, but Helminski stresses that dizziness and nausea are rare because the intense concentration enables wobble-free execution. . . .

Dervishes typically whirl for 40 minutes during a ceremony called Semi, during which four continuous segments of turning are interrupted only briefly by sudden, cued stops between them. Helminski says this reminds turners "to remember their servanthood and to keep a balance between sobriety and ecstasy" and that it's not intended as a break from the movement. "If they needed to turn for an hour, they could, without stopping," he says. . . .

? What details tell you that this article was written for a magazine for dancers? How might the article have been different if it had been written for general readers?

Response and Analysis

INTERNET

Projects and Activities

Keyword:
LE5 WL-4

Literary Skills
Analyze analogies.

Writing Skills
Write a poem.

Thinking Critically

1. What, according to the speaker, does God's joy look like?

2. What does the speaker mean by "unmarked boxes"? Explain in your own words what the line "God's joy moves from unmarked box to unmarked box" might mean.

3. The first stanza suggests that nothing is ever lost; rather, things only change form. Which of the images in stanza 2 best expresses this idea? Can you think of other examples that illustrate the same idea?

4. In stanza 3, what kind of sleep is Rumi referring to? Explain.

5. How has the poet used **analogy** to explain the idea that "anything you lose comes round / in another form"? List the analogies the poet makes. How do these things compare with the things you wrote about in your Quickwrite? ✏

Extending and Evaluating

6. Do you think this poem has relevance only to those who share Sufi beliefs, or does it also speak to people with different points of view? Explain.

WRITING

Writing a Poem

Rumi points out the joy that can come from such everyday sights as a plate of rice and fish, a vine-covered cliff, or a horse being saddled. List some joyous moments that you have experienced. What **images** best capture your moments of joy? Use the images you've chosen to write a poem on the topic of recapturing the experience of joy. If you prefer, collect some favorite images from magazines and other sources and create a collage of joyous moments.

North Carolina Competency Goal
1.02; 1.03; 2.01; 4.01; 4.05; 5.03; 6.01

Saadi

(c. A.D. 1213–c. 1291)

The poet Musharrif Oddin Muslih Oddin was known as Saadi (sä′dē), which means "fortunate" in Persian. He spent much of his life as a wandering dervish, or holy man, moving from place to place, studying and practicing Sufism, a mystical branch of Islam (see page 564). He had neither a home nor personal belongings, yet he somehow produced two of the great classics of Persian literature—the *Bustan* (*The orchard*) and the *Gulistan* (*The rose garden*).

Scholars know only a few facts about Saadi's life. He was born in Shiraz (in present-day Iran) and attended college at the Nizamiya Academy in Baghdad, where he received a classical Islamic education. A devout Sufi, he chose poverty and rootlessness as a way of life, wandering great distances. His books mention journeys to Central Asia and India, and it is believed that he made several religious pilgrimages to Mecca. On these journeys, he may have studied under the famous mystic Suhrawardi and met the poet Jalal ad-Din ar-Rumi, author of the *Masnavi* (see page 558).

During Saadi's lifetime, the Middle East was in almost constant turmoil. Mongol armies swept in from the eastern plains, and crusaders from western Europe, intent on claiming lands around Jerusalem for Christianity, made war on the Islamic peoples of the region. On a journey to North Africa, Saadi was captured by crusaders and held in Tripoli (now part of Libya), where he was forced to labor as a ditchdigger. According to one story, he married the daughter of the man who paid his ransom, but the marriage was unhappy. Eventually, Saadi left his wife and made his way back to Shiraz, where he enjoyed the patronage of the royal ruler

Mystical Conversation between Sufic Sheikhs.
Indian School (17th century).
Institute of Oriental Studies, St. Petersburg, Russia.

Sa'd bin Zangi (sä′d bēn zän·jē′), whose first name he adopted as his own.

Saadi's work is greatly beloved by the Iranian people, and his place in Persian literature is firmly established. His stories and sayings seem simple and use plain language, but they express Sufi wisdom in a way that wins admiration from scholars and general readers alike. Because his work had such wide appeal, Saadi has ensured the continuation of Sufi beliefs.

Anecdotes and Sayings of Saadi

Make the Connection

Quickwrite

What familiar "wise" sayings do you know? Do you ever say, "If you can't stand the heat, get out of the kitchen" or "No pain, no gain"? Have you ever considered where these sayings come from and whether they are really wise or helpful? Brainstorm a list of such sayings with your classmates and discuss their meanings and usefulness.

Literary Focus

Anecdote

Much of literature can be understood on more than one level. On the surface, a story or saying may have an obvious meaning. However, many "simple" pieces of literature have an underlying meaning. An **anecdote,** for example, is a short, simple story usually involving a single incident, but it can illustrate a complicated idea about human behavior. In the same way, a saying may have a broader meaning than is first apparent. For instance, the saying "Don't cry over spilled milk" applies to more than just milk. It is about not regretting anything unfortunate that cannot be changed.

North Carolina Competency Goal
1.02; 1.03; 4.05; 5.03; 6.01

Background

Saadi's writings are notable for two reasons. First, their simple, direct language makes them an ideal beginner's textbook for learning the Persian language. Second, although they consist primarily of only simple sayings and anecdotes, they are considered some of the finest expressions of Sufi thought.

For Sufis, Sufism is not only a religion or a philosophy but also a way of life. Sufis are not attached to possessions or places, and they are not driven by concerns of time, money, or worldly achievement. They concentrate instead on the development of the human mind and on reaching a higher plane of understanding than can be gained through the senses alone. Sufi mystics believe that higher knowledge can only be attained through a gradual process of thought and practice. Sufi mystics would traditionally withdraw from the material world and devote themselves to a harsh, homeless existence. As they wandered, they would beg for a living and meditate on God's love. It is in their writings that mystics such as Saadi reach out to share their knowledge with the world at large.

go.hrw.com

INTERNET

More About Saadi
Keyword:
LE5 WL-4

An **anecdote** is a brief story that focuses on a single incident, often to make a point or teach a lesson.

For more on Anecdote, see the Handbook of Literary and Historical Terms.

SKILLS FOCUS

Literary Skills
Understand anecdote.

Mosque lamp with the name of the emir Shaiku (c. 1355). Mamluk dynasty.
Museum of Islamic Art, Cairo.

Anecdotes and Sayings of Saadi

Saadi
translated by **Idries Shah**

The Pearl
A raindrop, dripping from a cloud,
Was ashamed when it saw the sea.
"Who am I where there is a sea?" it said.
When it saw itself with the eye of humility,
A shell nurtured it in its embrace.

Learning
None learned the art of archery from me
Who did not make me, in the end, the target.

Conceit
He who has self-conceit in his head—
Do not imagine that he will ever hear the truth.

To Know One's Faults
In the eyes of the wise, the seeker of combat with
an elephant is not really brave.
    Brave is he who says nothing unbecoming
      in wrath.
    A lout abused a man who patiently said:
    "O you of bright prospects: I am worse even
      than you say.
    I know all my faults, while you do not know
      them."

Relative
A Lamp has no rays at all in the face of the sun;
And a high minaret[1] even in the foothills of a
    mountain looks low.

Illustration of dervishes in an Arabic book
(17th century).

---

1. **minaret** (min′ə·ret′) *n.:* tower attached to a
mosque from which worshipers are called to prayer.

The Sick Man

Throughout the long night a man wept
At the bedside of a sick man.
When day dawned the visitor was dead—
And the patient was alive.

The Thief and the Blanket

A thief entered the house of a Sufi, and found nothing there. As he was leaving, the dervish[2] perceived his disappointment and threw him the blanket in which he was sleeping, so that he should not go away empty-handed.

The Destiny of a Wolf-Cub

The destiny of a wolf-cub is to become a wolf, even if it is reared among the sons of men.

The Straight Path

I have never seen a man lost who was on a straight path.

A Tree Freshly Rooted

A tree, freshly rooted, may be pulled up by one man on his own. Give it time, and it will not be moved, even with a crane.

The Dervish Under a Vow of Solitude

A dervish under a vow of solitude sat in a desert as a king passed with his retinue.[3] Being in a special state of mind he took no notice, not even raising his head as the procession passed.

The king, emotionally overcome by his regal pretensions, was angry and said: "These wearers of the patchwork robe are as impassive as animals, possessing neither politeness nor due humility."

His vizier[4] approached the dervish, saying: "O dervish! The Sultan of the whole of the Earth has just passed by you. Why did you not pay the required homage?"

The dervish answered: "Let the Sultan look for homage from those who seek to benefit from his goodwill. Tell him, too, that kings are created for the protection of their subjects. Subjects are not created for the service of kings."

If You Cannot Stand a Sting

If you cannot stand a sting, do not put your finger in a scorpion's nest.

Ambition

Ten dervishes can sleep beneath one blanket; but two kings cannot reign in one land. A devoted man will eat half his bread, and give the other half to dervishes. A ruler may have a realm, but yet plot to overcome the world.

The Dervish in Hell

One night a king dreamt that he saw a king in paradise and a dervish in hell.

The dreamer exclaimed: "What is the meaning of this? I should have thought that the positions would be reversed."

A voice answered: "The king is in heaven because he respected dervishes. The dervish is in hell because he compromised with kings."

Heedless Man

Whoever gives advice to a heedless man is himself in need of advice.

The Fool and the Donkey

A foolish man was raving at a donkey. It took no notice. A wiser man who was watching said: "Idiot! The donkey will never learn *your* language —better that you should observe silence and instead master the tongue of the donkey."

---

2. **dervish** *n.:* member of any Muslim sect who lives a life of poverty and chastity. Some dervishes practice a whirling dance as a form of worship.
3. **retinue** (ret'n·oo') *n.:* servants or followers.
4. **vizier** (vi·zir') *n.:* high-ranking official in Muslim countries.

(Opposite) Persian painting of a camel composed of figures (c. 1580–1590).

Response and Analysis

Thinking Critically

1. In "Learning," what does the speaker suggest about the wisdom of teaching the art of archery? To what might this **aphorism,** or saying, apply besides archery?

2. In "Conceit," why will a person who is conceited never "hear the truth"? What advice does this saying imply?

3. In "To Know One's Faults," who is brave in the eyes of the wise?

4. What is **ironic,** or unexpected, about the outcome of "The Sick Man"? What do you think is the message of this **anecdote?**

5. Bearing in mind that a simple saying may have more than one interpretation, what do you think is the underlying meaning of "The Straight Path"?

6. What does "A Tree Freshly Rooted" imply about the advantages of allowing something to "take root"? When might pulling up something freshly rooted be advantageous?

7. What appears to be the moral of the **anecdote** "The Dervish in Hell"? What simple incident is used to illustrate the moral?

Extending and Evaluating

8. The Sufis use the sayings and anecdotes of Saadi and others as teaching tools, urging people to meditate upon the deeper meanings contained in them. Do you think the sayings and stories of Saadi may be helpful to people today? How do these sayings and anecdotes compare in effectiveness with the sayings you listed in your Quickwrite response?

WRITING

Comparing a Sufi Anecdote with a Zen Parable

Like Sufism, Zen (see page 463) is a system of belief that tries to express complex ideas in simple ways. Read the Zen parable "The Thief Who Became a Disciple" (see page 466). Then, compare and contrast that parable with the anecdote "The Thief and the Blanket" by Saadi. Discuss how the two are alike and different on the surface, as well as how they are alike and different in their underlying meanings.

Writing an Extended Definition

Saadi's anecdotes are brief stories that teach basic truths about life. But what is truth? In an essay, write an extended definition of *truth*. Start by looking up the definition of *truth* in a dictionary. Then, think of ways to expand that definition to cover its more subtle shades of meaning. You may get ideas for your essay from things you have witnessed, experiences in your own life, or stories you have read about in newspapers or magazines.

▶ Use "Writing an Extended Definition," pages 570–575, for help with this assignment.

Illustration of dervishes in an Arabic book (detail) (17th century).

FICTION
"We Have Fallen Apart."

Chinua Achebe's first novel, *Things Fall Apart*, presents a candid portrait of the traditions and beliefs that form the heart of a nineteenth-century village in Nigeria. Okonkwo, the central character, is a proud and fearsome man highly regarded by his community. Okonkwo's ultimate fall from grace mirrors the decline of traditional village life under the influence of European colonization.

This title is available in the HRW Library.

WISDOM LITERATURE
A Spiritual Celebration

During the thirteenth century, the Sufi mystic Rumi composed spiritual verses about love and transcendence that still inspire people today. *The Illustrated Rumi: A Treasury of Wisdom from the Poet of the Soul* (translated by Philip Dunn, Manuela Dunn Mascetti, and R. A. Nicholson) is a splendid introduction to the work of this bestselling poet. In this translation, Rumi's enlightening poems and stories are set against a backdrop of rare Sufi and Islamic artwork.

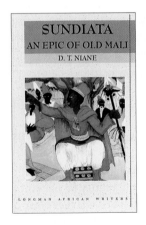

EPIC
Sundiata the Invincible

Sundiata: An Epic of Old Mali is a dramatic tale that dates back to the thirteenth century. The epic conveys the richness of Mali's history and culture as it describes the destiny of the hero Sundiata, who transforms Mali into a powerful empire. Thanks to a French-speaking scholar and an English translator (D. T. Niane and G. D. Pickett, respectively)—to say nothing of generations of griots, or oral storytellers, who have passed this story down—we can read this accessible translation of the complete epic adventure today.

ADDITIONAL READING

- *Tales of the Dervishes: Teaching Stories of the Sufi Masters over the Past Thousand Years*, by Idries Shah, is an intriguing collection of thought-provoking tales. As the title of the book indicates, Sufi masters used these tales to provide their disciples with a greater understanding of life.

- Jerome W. Clinton's translation of *The Tragedy of Sohráb and Rostám, from the Persian National Epic, the Shahname of Abol-Qasem Ferdowsi* is a rousing version of the tragic battle between the hero Rostám and his son Sohráb. The *Shahname,* also known as the *Book of Kings,* is a record of Persian history that dates back to the eleventh century A.D.

- Harold Courlander presents a rich anthology of African proverbs, legends, creation myths, poetry, and tales in *A Treasury of African Folklore.* This collection encompasses not only motifs unique to Africa but also the universal themes and concerns common to all world cultures: crime and punishment, love and duty, sacrifice and honor.

Writing an Extended Definition

Writing Assignment
Write an essay in which you provide an extended definition of a word whose meaning cannot be fully understood from a brief dictionary definition.

Sometimes a dictionary definition is all you need to understand or explain a word or an idea. Some words and concepts, however, may need a more extended definition or explanation for their meaning to be completely clear. An **extended definition** fleshes out a dictionary definition by elaborating on the word's meaning. As a student, you may be asked to provide extended definitions on essay tests in many subject areas as well as in class discussions.

Prewriting

North Carolina Competency Goal
6.01

SKILLS FOCUS

Writing Skills
Write an extended definition.

Choose a Word to Define

What Does It Mean? Make a list of words you have heard or read recently whose meanings were not clear to you. These may include unfamiliar technical words, such as *genome,* that you want to be able to understand and use. Or you may want to explain your personal understanding of more abstract terms like *friendship* or *work ethic.* When selecting a word to define in your essay, consider your readers and choose a term that they too are likely to be curious about.

Define Your Term

Start with the Basics Looking up the word you have chosen in a dictionary is a good way to begin gathering ideas for an extended definition. A dictionary definition can help you determine two important pieces of information: the class or category to which the term belongs (for example, the word *love* is part of a larger class of abstract concepts) and characteristics that distinguish the term from others in its class or category.

Elaborate on the Meaning

Beyond a Dictionary After considering the short dictionary definition, you can begin to extend that definition, or elaborate on it, by finding examples, descriptions, comparisons and contrasts, opinions, quotations, and personal experiences that help explain aspects of the word's meaning.

A graphic organizer called a definition map can help you expand your definition. A **definition map** gives a clear visual image of how an extended definition can be constructed. You can reconfigure the map in any way that helps you understand the different aspects of the word you are defining. Below is a definition map for the term *wisdom,* which is defined in the Writer's Model on page 572. Notice that the map defines *wisdom* not only by listing its characteristics but also by listing what wisdom is *not.*

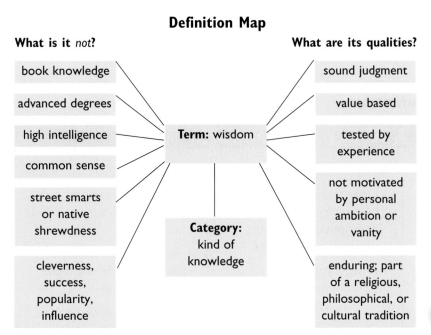

Definition Map

What is it *not*?

- book knowledge
- advanced degrees
- high intelligence
- common sense
- street smarts or native shrewdness
- cleverness, success, popularity, influence

Term: wisdom

Category: kind of knowledge

What are its qualities?

- sound judgment
- value based
- tested by experience
- not motivated by personal ambition or vanity
- enduring; part of a religious, philosophical, or cultural tradition

Develop Your Thesis

What's Your Point of View? After you have enough ideas to elaborate on your definition, ask yourself what main point, or **thesis,** you want to make about the word you are defining. One way of developing a thesis is to show that a term can mean something quite different from what most people think it means. Another way to develop a thesis is to show how a term differs from its dictionary definition. For example, the author of the Writer's Model on page 572 begins her essay with a dictionary definition of *wisdom*—"knowledge of what is right, true, and lasting"—and goes on to explain that wisdom is more than just knowing what is right; it is living what one knows.

Organize Your Ideas

Put It in Order Now you must decide on the most logical and effective order in which to present your ideas. If you are defining an abstract quality, such as *patriotism,* you may want to present the various aspects of the term in the order of their importance, starting with either the least or the most important. Other possible arrangements include

TIP If you need more information about your term, you may have to do formal or informal research or both. **Formal research** is investigation of primary and secondary sources—for example, historical documents and letters, literature, textbooks, encyclopedias, and newspaper and periodical articles. **Informal research** is gathering information by talking to people or observing aspects of popular culture—for example, song lyrics, advertisements, television shows, and movies. You will have to decide, depending on your subject and thesis, which form of research will give you the best results.

moving from the dictionary definition to a more personal definition based on your own experience, beliefs, and values. You could also move from a negative definition to a more positive one or vice versa.

Use the preceding instruction to choose a word and elaborate on its definition.

North Carolina Competency Goal
6.01; 6.02

Writing

Writing an Extended Definition

A Writer's Framework

Introduction

- Grab the reader's attention with a striking example, quotation, or question.
- Provide a dictionary or common definition.
- Provide a clear thesis that explains your take on the definition.

Body

- Offer support for your thesis by providing examples, descriptions, anecdotes, opinions, comparisons.
- Present your support in a logical order.

Conclusion

- Give an overview or summary of your extended definition.
- Remind readers what is unique or different about your definition.
- Explain the importance or relevance of your definition to others besides yourself.

A Writer's Model

What Is Wisdom?

INTRODUCTION
Attention-grabbing opener
Dictionary definition

"Wise guy." "Wisecrack." "Wise up." What does the word *wise* mean in all these expressions? Who is wise, and what is wisdom? A dictionary might define *wisdom* as "knowledge of what is right, true, and lasting." However, none of these expressions has much to do with those qualities. On the contrary, they seem to have more to do with being sarcastic and street-smart than being honest and knowledgeable. This contradiction leads me to the conclusion that wisdom is a type of knowledge that is neither widely recognized nor widely practiced.

Thesis statement

BODY
Paragraph 1: what wisdom is not

In fact, it seems easier to say what wisdom is *not* than what it is. For example, is the knowledge of people who have read many books or earned advanced degrees wisdom? No—the highly educated, especially

(continued)

in this age of specialization, are often experts only in their own narrow fields. What about those who score in the highest percentiles on intelligence tests—do they possess wisdom? Since some criminals have very high IQs, intelligence alone does not guarantee wisdom. Then there is that much talked-about quality called common sense. Is it wisdom? No—common sense, along with street smarts or native shrewdness, is more about getting by or getting ahead than about knowing what is right, true, and lasting.

What then is wisdom? In my opinion, the idea of experience must be added to the dictionary definition of wisdom as moral knowledge. Wisdom is more than just knowledge. It is lived experience to which sound, value-based judgment has been applied. True wisdom is not a recipe for worldly success or public admiration. I think the best evidence for the presence of wisdom is inner and outer harmony. A wise person knows something about himself or herself, the world, and the ideal relationship between the two.

In summary, wisdom is not only moral knowledge but also experience, insight, and inspiration that helps people, here and now, live a meaningful life based on enduring values. Wisdom has never been easily recognized or readily put into practice, but perhaps it has never been so difficult to discern as in our information age, in which knowledge is so accessible, but the truth is so elusive.

Supporting details: examples

Paragraph 2: what wisdom is

Logical order: from dictionary definition to personal definition

Supporting details: descriptions of characteristics

CONCLUSION

Summary of personal definition

Explanation of definition's importance

PRACTICE & APPLY 2 Using the framework and Writer's Model on these pages as your guide, write the first draft of your extended definition essay.

INTERNET

More Writer's Models

Keyword: LE5 WL-4

Revising

Self-Evaluation

Take Another Look Read your draft once to look for organizational weaknesses and confusing or incompletely developed ideas. Read it a second time to focus on style and word choice. Be sure to use appropriate connecting words and phrases that help readers follow the progression of your ideas.

TIP Working with a peer to refine your essay can be very helpful. Another reader may see things you missed and tell you when something is not clear or does not make sense.

Rubric: Writing an Extended Definition

▶ Evaluation Questions	▶ Tips	▶ Revision Techniques
❶ Does the introduction provide an attention-grabbing opener and briefly define the term?	▶ **Bracket** the attention-grabbing opener. **Circle** the brief definition.	▶ **Add** an attention grabber. If necessary, add a brief definition.
❷ Is necessary background information provided and a clear thesis presented?	▶ **Underline** background information. **Draw a wavy line** under the thesis.	▶ **Add** any necessary background information. **Add** to or **elaborate** on your thesis.
❸ Do the body paragraphs develop the thesis with a variety of appropriate support?	▶ **Put a check mark** next to each supporting detail. **Label** each kind of support.	▶ **Elaborate** your support by adding more relevant details. **Delete** any details that do not support your thesis.
❹ Is the support offered in an order that makes sense and is easy to follow?	▶ In the margin, **print** the name of your ordering principle.	▶ **Rearrange** supporting details in the most logical order.
❺ Does the conclusion summarize the definition and explain its importance?	▶ **Highlight** the summary definition and **double underline** the explanation of the definition's importance.	▶ **Add** a summary of your definition and an explanation of its importance.

ANALYZING THE REVISION PROCESS

Study the revisions below, and answer the questions that follow.

> *In summary,*   *only*
> ⌄Wisdom is not⌄moral knowledge but also experience,
>
> insight, and inspiration that helps people, here and now, live a
>
> meaningful life based on enduring values. Wisdom has never
>
>   *, but*
> been easily recognized or readily put into practice.⌄Perhaps it
>
> has never been so difficult to discern as in our information
>
>   *the truth*
> age, in which knowledge is so accessible, but ~~true value~~ is so
>
> elusive.

 Using the guidelines on these pages, revise the content and form of your extended definition.

Publishing

Proofread and Publish Your Essay

Fit to Print If there are spelling, grammar, or punctuation errors in a dictionary, users may wonder if the definitions are accurate. The same is true for an extended definition essay. So proofread your essay to make sure it is error free.

Spread the News Now that you have finished proofreading your extended definition, it's time to think of ways to share your work. Here are some ideas:

- Compile an online *Dictionary of Hard-to-Define Terms.* Enter your definitions on different Web pages, and create links between terms in the same categories.

- Use publishing software to design and print a class *Dictionary of Extended Definitions.*

Reflect on Your Essay

Thinking Back What have you learned from the process of writing an extended definition? Record your reflections by jotting down answers to the following questions:

- What did you learn about the usefulness and limitations of dictionary definitions?

- What was your best source of information about the word you were defining? Explain your research process.

PRACTICE & APPLY First, proofread your essay. Then, choose one of the options above to share your essay. Finally, discuss your answers to the reflection questions.

North Carolina Competency Goal
1.03; 4.05; 5.02; 5.03

Pages 576–579 cover

Literary Skills
Compare and contrast myths.

Test Practice

Almost every culture has a story that explains the origin of death. In many such stories, death comes into the world through the actions of a **trickster,** a universal figure in world myths and folk tales, especially those from Africa and North America. Tricksters are ambivalent figures who upset the world order and leave trouble and chaos behind them, whether intentionally or not. Tricksters are not necessarily evil. In fact, they often possess positive traits, such as cleverness, curiosity, and creativity. Their actions often serve to teach us a lesson.

The myth "Coyote and the Origin of Death" comes from the American Indian Caddo people, and "The Origin of Death" is from Africa's Khoikhoi people. Like many folk tales, these stories feature animal characters as tricksters.

DIRECTIONS: Read the following selections. Then, read each multiple-choice question that follows, and write the letter of the best response.

Coyote and the Origin of Death

A Caddo Myth
retold by Richard Erdoes *and* Alfonso Ortiz

In the beginning of this world, there was no such thing as death. Everybody continued to live until there were so many people that the earth had no room for any more. The chiefs held a council to determine what to do. One man rose and said he thought it would be a good plan to have the people die and be gone for a little while, and then return.

As soon as he sat down, Coyote jumped up and said he thought people ought to die forever. He pointed out that this little world is not large enough to hold all of the people, and that if the people who died came back to life, there would not be food enough for all.

All the other men objected. They said that they did not want their friends and relatives to die and be gone forever, for then they would grieve and worry and there would be no happiness in the world. Everyone except Coyote decided to have people die and be gone for a little while, and then come back to life again.

The medicine men built a large grass house facing the east. When they had completed it, they called the men of the tribe together and told them that people who died would be restored to life in the medicine house. The chief medicine man explained that they would sing a song calling the spirit of the dead to the grass house. When the spirit came, they would restore it to life. All the people were glad, because they were anxious for the dead to come and live with them again.

When the first man died, the medicine men assembled in the grass house and sang. In about ten days a whirlwind blew from the west and circled about the grass house. Coyote saw it, and as the whirlwind was about to enter the house, he closed the door. The spirit of the whirlwind, finding the door closed, whirled on by. In this way Coyote made death eternal, and from that time on, people grieved over their dead and were unhappy.

Now whenever anyone meets a whirlwind or hears the wind whistle, he says: "Someone is wandering about." Ever since Coyote closed the door, the spirits of the dead have wandered over the earth trying to find some place to go, until at last they discovered the road to the spirit land.

Coyote ran away and never came back, for when he saw what he had done, he was afraid. Ever after that, he has run from one place to another, always looking back first over one shoulder and then over the other to see if anyone is pursuing him. And ever since then he has been starving, for no one will give him anything to eat.

The Origin of Death

A Khoikhoi Myth
retold by **Paul Radin**

The Moon, it is said, once sent an insect to men, saying, "Go to men and tell them, 'As I die, and dying live; so you shall also die, and dying live.'"

The insect started with the message, but, while on his way, was overtaken by the hare, who asked, "On what errand are you bound?"

The insect answered, "I am sent by the Moon to men, to tell them that as she dies and dying lives, so shall they also die and dying live."

The hare said, "As you are an awkward runner, let me go." With these words he ran off, and when he reached men, he said, "I am sent by the Moon to tell you, 'As I die and dying perish, in the same manner you also shall die and come wholly to an end.'"

The hare then returned to the Moon and told her what he had said to men. The Moon reproached him angrily, saying, "Do you dare tell the people a thing which I have not said?"

With these words the Moon took up a piece of wood and struck the hare on the nose. Since that day the hare's nose has been split, but men believe what Hare had told them.

1. In "Coyote and the Origin of Death," the reason the council considers the idea of death is that the earth —
   A is becoming overcrowded
   B suffers from ecological damage
   C has a number of people who cannot get along together
   D is overrun with greed

2. In "Coyote and the Origin of Death," the majority of voters at the council support —
   F permanent death
   G temporary death
   H no death
   J permanent death for some and temporary death for others

3. In "Coyote and the Origin of Death," permanent death enters the world because —
   A the council votes for it
   B the people listen to coyote
   C coyote closes a door
   D one chief takes a foolish gamble

4. In "Coyote and the Origin of Death," the character Coyote —
   F sets out to do evil
   G is himself tricked into causing eternal death
   H makes sure the council gets what it wants
   J gets the outcome he wants

5. In "The Origin of Death," who makes people believe death is permanent?
   A the Moon
   B the hare
   C the insect
   D the coyote

6. In "The Origin of Death," the trickster makes people believe death is permanent by —

F killing the insect

G killing the hare

H twisting the Moon's words

J twisting the hare's words

7. "The Origin of Death" explains not only the origin of death but also —

A the hare's appearance

B why people dislike insects

C why the moon is visible at night

D why the earth is overpopulated

8. The tricksters in "Coyote and the Origin of Death" and "The Origin of Death" are similar in that they both —

F try to destroy humankind

G change the nature of life and death forever

H become outcasts

J intend to bring evil into the world

Essay Question

"Coyote and the Origin of Death" and "The Origin of Death" possess certain similarities and differences. Think about the elements these two tales share as well as the differences that set them apart. Write an essay in which you compare and contrast the two stories. As you write, keep the following elements in mind: the characterization of each story's trickster, the condition of the world in each story before and after the deception, and the lesson each story conveys.

Collection 4: Skills Review

Vocabulary Skills

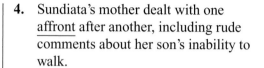

Context Clues

DIRECTIONS: Choose the answer that gives the best definition of the underlined word.

1. Though Sosso seemed <u>impregnable</u>, Sundiata's army was able to capture the city when it attacked.

   Impregnable means —

   A impressionable
   B impenetrable
   C combustible
   D vulnerable

2. Since the <u>razing</u> of Soumaoro's palace, few people remember the glorious building that once stood in Sosso.

   Razing means —

   F emptying
   G maintaining
   H designing
   J destroying

3. Once Sundiata's warriors were <u>deployed</u> near the river, they were in an ideal strategic position to attack their enemies.

   Deployed means —

   A deceived
   B found
   C depleted
   D stationed

4. Sundiata's mother dealt with one <u>affront</u> after another, including rude comments about her son's inability to walk.

   Affront means —

   F insult
   G assault
   H rumor
   J obstacle

5. The townspeople were stunned by the fortitude Sundiata possessed when he was a youth; his strength should have been only <u>nascent</u> at his age.

   Nascent means —

   A discernible
   B forming
   C secondary
   D unimpressive

6. The warriors <u>implored</u> Sundiata to have mercy on them, but he was unmoved by their pleas.

   Implored means —

   F bribed
   G connived
   H advised
   J begged

North Carolina Competency Goal
6.01

Vocabulary Skills
Use context clues to determine the meanings of words.

Collection 4: Skills Review

Writing Skills

Test Practice DIRECTIONS: Read the following paragraph from a draft of a student's extended definition essay. Then, answer the questions below it.

(1) Where is the wisdom of the ages to be found? (2) Cultures, old and new, have passed on their ideas of the good, the true, and the lasting in both spoken and written form. (3) Proverbs are sources of wisdom found in many cultures. (4) These sayings not only reveal the values of the people who created them but also give a picture of daily life. (5) The vast storehouse of wisdom that has been written down spans time and space. (6) The anecdotes and sayings of Saadi, a thirteenth-century Persian Sufi master, are examples of how the wisdom of a particular religion and culture has been passed on in written form. (7) Others include the Hebrew Bible, the Koran, and the New Testament. (8) The wisdom of the ages is available to everyone through books and the Internet.

1. Which of the following sentences functions as the topic sentence for the paragraph?
   A Sentence 1
   B Sentence 2
   C Sentence 7
   D Sentence 8

2. What is the main form of support used in this paragraph?
   F anecdotes
   G comparisons
   H expert opinions
   J examples

3. Which sentence could be deleted to improve the paragraph's coherence?
   A Sentence 2
   B Sentence 3
   C Sentence 5
   D Sentence 7

4. Which of the following revisions of sentence 3 improves the organization of the paragraph and makes it easier to follow?
   F Proverbs, or wise sayings, are an example of how wisdom can be passed on orally.
   G You probably use proverbs all the time without knowing it.
   H Proverbs are similar to axioms.
   J Proverbs are effective because they are brief and memorable.

5. In an essay providing an extended definition of *wisdom,* this paragraph would be most effective as —
   A an attention-grabbing opener
   B a brief definition of the term
   C an elaboration of the term's meaning through examples
   D an overview of the extended definition

North Carolina Competency Goal
2.01; 6.01; 6.02

SKILLS FOCUS

Writing Skills
Answer questions about an extended definition essay.

European Literature from the Middle Ages to the Enlightenment

500–1800

A Time of Transition

O, wonder!

How many goodly creatures are there here!

How beauteous mankind is! O brave new world

That has such people in't!

—William Shakespeare, *The Tempest,*
Act V, Scene 1

(Opposite) *Departure of Marco Polo* (detail) (c. 1338).
Bodleian Library, Oxford, England.

INTERNET

Collection
Resources
Keyword:
LE5 WL-5

Literature from the Middle

1000	1100	1200	1300
c. 900s–c. 1000s Feudalism emerges in western Europe	**c. 1100** The French epic poem *The Song of Roland* is written	**c. 1200** *The Nibelungenlied,* the epic poem of Germany, is begun	**1300s** The beginning of the Renaissance in Italy
1054 The Christian Church is divided into two branches: the Roman Catholic Church and the Eastern Orthodox churches	**c. 1150** Paper is first mass-produced in Spain	**c. 1225–1274** Lifetime of Thomas Aquinas, the highly regarded theologian and philosopher of the Roman Catholic Church	**c. 1307** Dante Alighieri begins work on *The Divine Comedy*
1066 Duke of Normandy invades England	**c. 1180** French poet Chrétien de Troyes, writer of *Perceval,* dies	**c. 1232** Pope Gregory IX begins the Inquisition	**1347–1352** The Black Death wipes out about one quarter of Europe's population
1096 The Crusades to free Jerusalem begin		**1270** The end of the Crusades	**1353** Giovanni Boccaccio completes work on the *Decameron*
			c. 1387 Geoffrey Chaucer begins writing *The Canterbury Tales*

Doctor Angelicus. Portrait of Thomas Aquinas (c. 1475) by Joos Ghent.
Musée du Louvre, Paris.

1000	1100	1200	1300
900 *The Thousand and One Nights,* the famous collection of Arabian tales, is begun	**c. 1100** The Zagwe dynasty revives Ethiopia	**1200s** Zen Buddhism begins to influence Japanese culture	**1300s** Zimbabwe emerges as a major commercial empire in Africa
960–1279 Under the Sung dynasty, Neo-Confucianism becomes the official state doctrine of China	**1131** Omar Khayyám, Persian astronomer and writer of the *Rubáiyát,* dies	**1213** Saadi, the author of the *Gulistan,* is born	**1325** Aztecs begin to establish themselves in Mexico
1000–1500 In Africa, large kingdoms such as Luba and the Kongo are established	**1192** Minamoto Yoritomo becomes the first shogun of Japan, establishing a military government	**c. 1235** In Africa the empire of old Mali is established	**1368–1644** The Ming dynasty rules China
c. 1010 Lady Murasaki Shikibu completes the world's first novel, *The Tale of Genji,* in Japan		**1275** In China, Kublai Khan receives a visit from Marco Polo	
		1279–1368 The Mongols gain control of all of China	

Seated figure, probably Tonatiuh, the sun god. Aztec.
Museum für Voelkerkunde, Basel, Switzerland.

Ages to the Enlightenment 500–1800

1400	1500	1600	1700
1431 Joan of Arc is burned at the stake in France by the English	**1513** Niccolò Machiavelli writes *The Prince* in Italy	**1605–1615** Miguel de Cervantes publishes parts I and II of *Don Quixote* in Spain	**1755** Samuel Johnson's *A Dictionary of the English Language* is published
c. 1455 In Germany, Johann Gutenberg completes work on the Gutenberg Bible	**1517** Martin Luther's ninety-five theses pave the way to the Protestant Reformation	**1660** In England, the monarchy is restored with Charles II	**1759** Voltaire publishes *Candide* in France
1485 *Le Morte d'Arthur* by Sir Thomas Malory is published	**1564** William Shakespeare is born	**1667** John Milton publishes the first of two versions of his epic poem *Paradise Lost* in England	**1760** George III, who would go on to lose the American Colonies, becomes king of England
1492 Columbus reaches the Americas	**1572** Montaigne begins to compose the *Essais* in France	**1668–1694** The French poet Jean de La Fontaine publishes the *Fables*	**1775** The beginning of the American Revolution
	1590–1609 Edmund Spenser writes *The Faerie Queene* in England	**1689** The Bill of Rights is passed by the English Parliament	**1789–1799** The French Revolution ends absolute monarchy in France

Portrait of William Shakespeare. Oil on canvas by an unknown artist (1546–1616). The Granger Collection, New York.

1400	1500	1600	1700
1400s Portuguese explorers are present on Africa's west coast; the fall of the Mali empire	**1500s** Regional lords battle for dominance in Japan	**1600s** Japanese Noh form fully develops after centuries of refinement	**1700s** Europeans explore the African interior
c. 1438 Establishment of the Incan empire in Peru	**1521** Cortés conquers the Aztecs in Mexico	**c. 1603** In Japan, Okuni founds the first Kabuki theater company	**1799** In Egypt the Rosetta stone is discovered
1453 The Ottomans overthrow the Byzantine Empire by capturing Constantinople		**c. 1632–c. 1649** In India the Taj Mahal is built	**1800s** Rise and fall of the Zulu nation in Africa
1498 The Portuguese arrive in India		**1644–1694** Lifetime of Matsuo Bashō, master of the haiku	
		1691 *Reply to Sister Philotea* is published by Sor Juana Inés de la Cruz	

Siege of Constantinople (detail). (c. 16th century). Fresco. Moldovita Monastery, Romania.

Cultural and Historical

The Growth of Literacy
500s–1400s

In the early Middle Ages, Latin was used to record and transmit knowledge. Since only members of the clergy could read and write Latin, the Church controlled the flow of information. By the late Middle Ages, though, a growth in literacy among the population led to a new feeling of intellectual independence; more people could read and be educated. Gradually, the use of vernacular, or native, languages grew, and Latin eventually lost its role as the language of the educated elite.

By the Renaissance the opening of schools and universities encouraged the growth of literacy and made education available to the middle class. The most important factor in spreading literacy was the printing press. Johann Gutenberg

is generally reputed to be the first European to have printed a book using movable type: a Latin Bible (c. 1455). The printing press led to the standardization of European vernacular languages. The invention of the printing press also paved the way for the development of newspapers and magazines—reading material for a general public.

Printing press from the beginning of the 16th century. Engraving after a miniature.
Bibliothèque Nationale, Paris.

Chivalry and Courtly Love
c. 1000–c. 1300

During the Middle Ages two important concepts that helped to define the era developed: the ideals of chivalry and courtly love. Chivalry began as a military code of behavior. Medieval manuals instructed a knight to serve God; to be loyal to his lord; to be honorable; to be fair to his opponents; and to show humility, kindness, and generosity. Chivalric ideals were expressed in medieval romances—long poems about the adventures of knights.

The concept of courtly love emerged in the late eleventh century as part of the evolution of chivalric ideals. It became an important element of the medieval romance. The code of courtly love called for a knight to dedicate his services to a beautiful lady of noble birth, who served as his inspiration and ideal. Since the lady was above him in social rank and usually had an aristocratic husband, the knight could never hope to marry her and had to content himself with worshiping her from afar.

Euryalus Sends His First Letter to Lucretia (detail). Unknown artist.
J. Paul Getty Museum. Los Angeles, California (MS. 68, FOL. 30).

Milestones 500–1800

The Scientific Method
c. 1300s–c. 1700s

The recovery of the Greek and Roman classics introduced medieval people to a method of looking at the world that was independent of the dogmatic approach approved by the Church. This secular worldview grew as Europe entered the Renaissance and began to emphasize human values and perceptions. Advances in physics and astronomy during the late Renaissance led to Galileo's creation of a sound scientific method that called for observation, hypothesis, experimentation, and measurement. During the Enlightenment period, scientists used reason to uncover universal truths, and they developed precision instruments with which to measure and quantify their discoveries. The principal scientific achievement of the age was Sir Isaac Newton's discovery of the law of universal gravity.

Telescope, triangle, magnet compass, and pendulum clock belonging to Galileo Galilei (detail) (c. 1564–1642).
Museo di Storia della Scienza, Florence, Italy.

Europe from the Middle Ages to the Enlightenment

500–1800

PREVIEW

Think About ...

Literary developments in Europe following the classical era are often divided into three major periods: the Middle Ages (A.D. 500–1500), the Renaissance (c. 1300–1600s), and the Enlightenment (1650–1800). The dates for these periods are approximate, and there is considerable overlap of themes and genres in the literature of all three periods. Many important literary works emerged, including epics, romances, sonnets, prose fiction, satires, and drama. As you read about the history and literature of these periods, look for answers to the following questions:

- How was literature influenced by the two great institutions of the Middle Ages: the Church and feudalism?

- How was humanism reflected in science, philosophy, and the arts during the Renaissance?

- Why did satire become such an important genre during the Enlightenment, or Age of Reason?

**North Carolina
Competency Goal**
1.02; 1.03; 4.02;
4.05; 5.01; 5.03

Collection
introduction
(pages 588–604)
covers
Literary Skills
Evaluate the
philosophical,
cultural,
and historical
influences of
the time period.

The Literature of the Middle Ages

The period between A.D. 500 and 1500 in Europe is called the **Middle Ages,** or the medieval (mē′dē•ē′vəl) period. The Middle Ages lies between the era of classical Greek and Roman culture and the later rebirth of those values in the Renaissance. Once perceived as a static, or unchanging, interval in history, the medieval period was in fact a dynamic time in which new political, economic, and cultural institutions emerged.

Grape harvest (detail) (15th century) by Limbourg Brothers. Calendar miniature.

Musée Condé, Chantilly, France.

The Collapse of the Roman Empire

At the height of its glory in the second century A.D., the Roman Empire commanded all of the territory around the Mediterranean as far east as modern-day Iran and as far north as Britain. But the central government could not defend its frontiers or maintain contact with isolated outposts. The Roman Empire eventually broke into two large parts: the Eastern Roman, or Byzantine (biz′ən•tēn′), Empire and the Western Roman Empire.

The **Byzantine Empire,** with its seat of government at Byzantium (now Istanbul), ruled Egypt, the eastern Mediterranean, Asia Minor, and the Balkans. Throughout the Middle Ages, classical knowledge and culture lost in the west were preserved by the Byzantine Empire.

In the early fifth century A.D., the **Western Roman Empire** was invaded by Germanic peoples who contributed to the later development of the mainstays of medieval European culture: knighthood, the feudal system, and the code of chivalry. The date usually given for the fall of Rome is A.D. 476, when the city was overrun by the forces of the German chief, Odoacer.

The Age of Faith: The Christian Church

In A.D. 330, the emperor **Constantine,** who had converted to Christianity, renamed Byzantium Constantinople. His efforts to Christianize the empire had far-reaching effects on medieval Europe. In 451, the pope became the undisputed religious authority of the Church. When the Roman Empire fell apart, the Christian Church maintained and enlarged its own authority. The Church was able to assert its independence from princes and kings and to build a government of its own.

The Church exerted its authority through its monopoly on knowledge. Because Latin was the language in which knowledge was preserved and transmitted, and because the clergy were among the elite who could read and write Latin, the Church maintained firm control over education.

Although the writings of the Church focused on religion and philosophy, monasteries—communities of monks and other clerics—often maintained chronicles, or records of events. Many chronicles focused on local events, weather conditions, the state of crops, and day-to-day happenings. These records are an invaluable aid to understanding everyday life in the era.

The Rise of Charlemagne

In 768, **Charlemagne** (shär′lə•mān′) became king of the Franks, a Germanic people, and in 800, he became the first emperor of the new Holy Roman Empire. Although he could not read or write, Charlemagne encouraged scholarship, education, and innovation in architecture. Charlemagne's reign opened a new era of learning.

Charlemagne departing for Spanish Crusade with Roland and Archbishop Turpin of Reims (13th century). From the Charlemagne Lancet window at Chartres Cathedral.

Chartres, France.

He ordered classical Greek and Roman manuscripts to be collected, encouraged the development of a new system for writing Latin, and invited scholars to open schools. Charlemagne's splendid court was copied in other parts of Europe. The arts and architecture began to flourish, and many great cathedrals were raised to glorify God. After Charlemagne's death in 814, his kingdom, which covered all of France and much of what is now Italy and eastern Europe, was eventually split up and was later invaded by Vikings.

The Temperate and the Intemperate by Master of the Dresden Prayer Book.

J. Paul Getty Museum, Los Angeles, California (91.MS.81.recto).

Feudalism: A System of Allegiance

Following Charlemagne's death, power in Europe fell into the hands of numerous nobles, who ruled local areas by a system called **feudalism** (fyōod″l•iz′əm). Feudalism was an economic, social, and military system in which **vassals** (vas′əlz), or tenants, pledged their loyalty to a lord, exchanging work on his land or military service for his protection. Usually the lord himself was a vassal to a more powerful overlord, who in turn served as a vassal to a prince or king. Thus, the feudal system was like a pyramid. At the bottom were the **serfs,** or peasants, who worked their lord's land, had few rights, and were totally subject to the lord's will. At the top was the king, who recognized only God as his sovereign. Loyalty to one's lord and to one's peers was the vital element that held the feudal system together.

Medieval Literature: Epic Deeds

Throughout the early Middle Ages, minstrels sang or chanted accounts of the fabulous deeds of legendary heroes. A number of these stories about epic heroes are still enjoyed today. The eighth-century Anglo-Saxon poem *Beowulf,* for example, tells the story of Beowulf, a warrior who defeats the ferocious monster Grendel and kills a terrible dragon. *The Nibelungenlied,* the national epic of Germany (see page 636), was composed in the early 1200s out of much older tales. It relates the heroic exploits of Siegfried, who possesses phenomenal strength and courage. The Norse and Icelandic sagas of Snorri Sturluson and others were tales about historical kings, pre-Christian Norse deities, and legendary heroes. In general, the medieval epics glorify physical strength, courage, and loyalty by celebrating warriors who defeat evil and restore order to their societies.

People of the Middle Ages existed under mental, moral, and physical circumstances so different from our own as to constitute almost a foreign civilization.

—Barbara Tuchman, *A Distant Mirror*

Medieval Oral Literature and Drama

From the twelfth to the fifteenth centuries, French poets called trouvères (troo•verz′) composed and sang the popular ***chansons de geste*** ("songs of heroic deeds"). The Christian epic *The Song of Roland* (see page 606) survives as a fine example of this form.

Since the majority of people during the Middle Ages were illiterate, most literature was presented orally. Common people entertained themselves with folk tales, legends, and beast fables. **Ballads,** or narrative songs, were also popular; they told the kind of sensational stories that make the headlines in today's tabloids—stories about murder, love, and revenge.

Literary entertainment was also presented visually, as in the case of drama. Medieval drama developed from Catholic Church services. Three kinds of religious plays were popular during the Middle Ages. The **miracle plays,** which dramatized the lives of the saints and the Virgin Mary, were performed on saints' days, while the **mystery plays**—which enacted biblical events, particularly the mystery of Christ's redemption of sinners—were performed on the same days as church festivals. **Morality plays** dramatized the content of the religious sermons that were so familiar to medieval audiences. The characters in such morality plays as *Everyman* were allegorical; they stood for abstract concepts and bore names like Truth, Mercy, and Good Deeds.

The Romance and Courtly Love

In time the rough realities of feudalism were refined by the code of chivalry. **Chivalry,** a term derived from *chevalier,* the French word for "knight," was basically a military code of behavior. A knight was supposed to be fair to his opponents, loyal to his lord, and honorable in all things. He was also supposed to show Christian humility to his peers, kindness to those beneath him, and generosity to all. Of course, not all knights could live up to this code or even tried to. Many were, after all, mercenary soldiers available to the highest bidder. But unquestionably, chivalry helped to civilize the competitive, often brutal world of the Middle Ages.

Chivalric ideals were expressed in the **romances.** These were long poems about knightly adventures that were recited by traveling poets. The stories were later written down, both in verse and in prose.

The **Arthurian romances** were among the most popular of the medieval romances. The stories of Arthur, a legendary Celtic king, and his knights of the Round Table first spread throughout England and Wales and then migrated to the continent. Chrétien de Troyes (see page 623) was one of the most famous of the medieval romance poets.

Panel depicting Saint Jerome (detail) (1476), from the Demidoff Altarpiece by Carlo Crivelli.

Szépmüveszéti Museum, Budapest.

A new element of **courtly love** served to distinguish the romances from the earlier epics. The knight's glorious deeds were performed not in the service of king or country but on behalf of a beautiful, fair, and noble lady, who was above him in status and usually married—and therefore unattainable. Sometimes she was a person the knight had only glimpsed from a distance or heard about.

Praise for an unattainable courtly lady was already a popular theme in medieval poetry. During the eleventh century in southern France, poet-musicians called **troubadours** (troō′bə•dôrz′) had begun to write light, graceful lyrics based on the theme of courtly love.

Also in France, the Breton *lais* (*lai* means "song") were influenced by the ideals of courtly love. The *lais* were short stories with supernatural or fairy-tale elements, written in verse and sung to the accompaniment of the lyre or the lute. A number of *lais* were collected in French by Marie de France (see page 617), who lived at the English court not long after the Normans of France had conquered England.

Scribe dedicating *La Teseida* to an unknown young woman (detail) from *La Teseida* (1340–1341) by Giovanni Boccaccio.

Österreichische Nationalbibliothek, Vienna.

A CLOSER LOOK: CULTURAL INFLUENCES

From the Middle Ages to Middle-Earth

INFORMATIONAL TEXT

A deadly dragon, a cursed golden ring, elves and dwarfs, the forces of good on a dangerous quest to defeat the powers of evil—these are all images that could have sprung from the pages of medieval legends, epics, and sagas. They are also elements in what are probably the most popular fantasies of contemporary times: *The Hobbit* and *The Lord of the Rings* trilogy. The writer of these fantasies, J.R.R. Tolkien (1892–1973), was a distinguished professor who taught Old English and Middle English at Oxford University in England. He loved the literature of the Middle Ages, particularly the Germanic and Norse myths and Icelandic sagas that he had read as a young man.

While Tolkien was teaching at Oxford, he was also at work creating his own mythical world, complete with its own languages and geography. He set his tales in a place he called Middle-earth, a name which recalls the Norse realm Midgard—the human world

between the heavens and the underworld. Tolkien took pains to point out that Middle-earth was not another planet but our own world in a much earlier time. In his first story about Middle-earth, *The Hobbit* (1937), Tolkien gave his characters names from the Norse myths: Gandalf, Thorin, Bombur, Durin. The story features the villainous dragon Smaug, killed by a man named Bard—recalling the medieval saga of the Germanic hero Siegfried, who slays the dragon Fafnir.

The Hobbit was followed by the three-volume fantasy epic *The Lord of the Rings* (1954–1955). The trilogy focuses on the hobbit Frodo and the fellowship of heroic companions from all races of Middle-earth who aid him in his quest to destroy the One Ring of the Dark Lord, Sauron. As in the Germanic sagas, the ring is an agent of destruction and a curse to those who come into contact with it. Tolkien said that the ring stands for the evils of industrialization, which made possible the devastation of two world wars.

Frodo (Elijah Wood), Gollum (Andy Serkis), and Sam (Sean Astin) in *The Lord of the Rings: The Return of the King* (2003).

593

The Late Middle Ages

The late Middle Ages, from about 1300 to about 1500, was a time of enormous upheaval that dealt severe blows to the two great medieval institutions, the feudal system and the Church. One blow to the system of landownership was the growth of towns and cities. The **Crusades** (1096–1270), a series of military expeditions undertaken by Christian forces to seize the Holy Land from the Muslims, had opened up trade routes to the East. These routes allowed an influx of new goods that enhanced the financial status of the merchant class and accelerated the development of towns and cities.

A dramatic climate change in the 1300s, later called the Little Ice Age, brought bitterly cold weather and reduced crop yields. Soon after, the **Black Death,** or bubonic plague, wiped out entire European villages. As a result, there were few serfs to work the fields, and the serfs who remained demanded more freedoms. Technology created change, too, for the development of gunpowder meant that a cannon could decide the outcome of a feudal battle in a matter of hours. Thus the system of feudalism was gradually undermined as the Middle Ages came to a close.

The power of the Church was challenged by charges of corruption and internal arguments, or schisms (siz'əmz). The Church's role as biblical interpreter became less important, since with the growth of literacy came a new intellectual independence. Also, with the development of the printing press, critics and reformers were able to write, print, and circulate literary satires that ridiculed the Church's corrupt practices.

Crusaders Led by Bishop (detail)
(14th century). France.

The British Library, London
(Egerton.1500.f.46).

The Rise of Vernacular Languages

The most significant development in literature during the late Middle Ages was the rising use of the **vernacular,** or native, languages instead of Latin, the language of the educated elite. This development signaled that great changes were taking place all over Europe: an emerging sense of nationalism, the increase of educated readers, the availability of printed material, and the recognition and acceptance of such local oral literatures as stories and songs. The use of vernacular in works such as Dante's *Divine Comedy* (see page 646) established it as acceptable in literature.

Effects of Good Government in the City (1338–1340) by Ambrogio Lorenzetti.

Palazzo Pubblico, Siena, Italy.

The Literature of the Renaissance

The word *renaissance* means "rebirth." The Renaissance is a name given to a period of change and growth, from roughly 1300 to the 1600s, when Europeans began to discover anew the Greek and Roman classics. The Renaissance began in Italy in the fourteenth century and then moved north and west until it reached England in the sixteenth century. During this time, which marks the beginning of the modern world in Europe, people began to explore the scope of human potential as never before.

Voyages to New Worlds

Since the times of the Crusades in the eleventh and twelfth centuries, Europe had been trading with the East. The rapidly increasing demand for exotic Eastern spices, cloth, and wood created new wealth for traders and merchants. Commercial centers prospered, especially the Italian city-states that were trade links to the Near East and Africa.

The Astronomer (1668) by Johannes Vermeer.
Musée du Louvre, Paris.

The Turkish conquest of Constantinople in 1453 temporarily blocked the overland route to the East. The need for new trade routes led to great voyages of discovery and exploration. The Spanish and the Portuguese were eager to find their own way to the East. In 1492, the Italian explorer Christopher Columbus attempted to reach the East by sailing west across the Atlantic. Instead of reaching Asia, he landed in the Americas. Commissioned by Portugal to open an eastern route to Asia, Vasco da Gama reached India in 1498, and within five years Indian merchandise was flowing into Portugal. In 1519, the Portuguese navigator Ferdinand Magellan—in search of a western trade route for Spain—sailed around South America and into a vast ocean that he called the Pacific. These voyages of discovery brought great prosperity and stirred people's imaginations, even as the indigenous peoples of the so-called New World often suffered greatly from their contact with the Europeans.

The Renaissance's primary concern with the world of here and now stimulated experimentation rather than logic, observation rather than inherited precepts.

—Julian Mates and Eugene Cantelupe, *Renaissance Culture*

Humanism: An Emphasis on the Individual

A literary and intellectual movement known as **humanism** spread throughout Europe. The humanists' interest in *human* values distinguishes them from medieval philosophers, whose system of thought was fundamentally centered around God and questions of religion.

Humanists revived the study of classical Greek and Roman art, literature, history, and philosophy. In doing so, the humanists nurtured **classicism** in the arts—the application of Greco-Roman principles such as reason, balance, and moderation.

The Arts in the Renaissance

Wealthy Italian merchant families used the riches they earned from trade to support the exploration of human thought and imagination. They became patrons of the arts, financing the works of writers, musicians, philosophers, and other artists and thinkers.

The works of Renaissance artists clearly expressed the belief that humankind is the measure of all things. In the 1300s, the Italian painter Giotto (jŏt′tŏ) (c. 1266–1337) developed a new style of painting that emphasized natural-looking forms instead of flat, stylized figures. The paintings and sculptures of Michelangelo (1475–1564) demonstrated a fascination with the shape, substance, and power of the human body.

View of the Vatican from the Tiber River, Italy.

Codex Atlanticus (detail)
by Leonardo da Vinci
(1452–1519).

Biblioteca Ambrosiana, Milan, Italy
(fol. 386r).

Perhaps the most imaginative and gifted figure of the Renaissance was Leonardo da Vinci (1452–1519). In addition to being a great artist, da Vinci was an inventor, an architect, a musician, and a scientist, with an interest in meteorology and geology. He studied the moon's effect on the tides, theorized about the formation of fossils, initiated the science of hydraulics, and studied human anatomy. He also believed that humans were capable of flight, and he designed several flying devices.

A New Spirit of Inquiry

Da Vinci's detailed observations—all carefully recorded in his notebooks—were fundamental to his work. This method of inquiry was different from the medieval method of relying on information approved by the Church. As scientists developed their skills of observation, they questioned accepted teachings. Nicolaus Copernicus (1473–1543), a Polish astronomer who taught in Italy, challenged the views of Ptolemy, an ancient astronomer who had claimed that the sun revolved around the earth. Copernicus argued that the earth rotated on an axis and revolved around the sun. His ideas contradicted the Church's teaching that the earth was the hub of the universe and that humans were the focus of God's attention.

A century later the Italian astronomer Galileo (1564–1642) wrote a book defending Copernicus's theory. The Church's Inquisitors—officials who examined supposed heretics—forced him to recant, or withdraw his statements. But legend has it that as Galileo rose from his knees after his recantation, he whispered, "But it does move!"

One Italian statesman, Niccolò Machiavelli (1469–1527), turned the new humanist spirit of inquiry and observation toward the political landscape of the Italian city-states. In *The Prince*, Machiavelli advised rulers to be calculating and coldblooded. Because he saw that conflict among the various city-states kept Italy in chaos, he argued that the state needed a powerful central authority to keep order. Machiavelli's name has come to be associated with the philosophy that "the end justifies the means."

> *In taking a state the conqueror must arrange to commit all his cruelties at once, so as not to have to recur to them every day, and so as to be able to reassure people and win them over by benefiting them. Whoever acts otherwise . . . is always obliged to stand with knife in hand, and can never depend on his subjects. . . .*
>
> —Machiavelli, *The Prince*

The Rise of Printing

The imaginative fervor that had begun in Italy and spread throughout Europe was fueled by the technology of printing. Around 1455, Johann Gutenberg (c. 1400–1468) produced Europe's first printed book, the Gutenberg Bible. The new print technology met strong resistance from the Church. Throughout Europe, Church leaders imposed strong restrictions on the printing and sales of books, and more than one printer was burned at the stake as a heretic. Yet the new technology hastened the spread of literacy among ordinary people. During the Middle Ages, books had belonged to a privileged few, and most people could not read. But during the sixteenth century, books became cheap and plentiful, and information that had once belonged to the few was now available to many. Within several short decades, Gutenberg's invention transformed Europe.

Page 280 recto with prologue to the Book of Job from the Gutenberg Bible (1455–1456), printed by Johannes Gutenberg.

Staatsbibliothek zu Berlin. Berlin, Germany.

The Church Loses Power

In northern Europe, humanism had taken the form of a widespread effort to reform the corrupt Church and to loosen its hold on people's minds. Critics questioned the sale of indulgences—the practice of "forgiving" sins in exchange for money—and demanded that the wealthy Church practice the poverty it preached. Some reformers directly undermined the authority of the Church. John Wycliffe (c. 1330–1384), for example, coordinated the translation of the Bible into English and sent teachers, called Poor Preachers, to read it in the churches. Wycliffe taught that people had a direct relationship to God and did not need priests to act as go-betweens.

Desiderius Erasmus (c. 1466–1536), a Dutch priest and scholar, was a sharp critic of the Church and an effective advocate of reform. His scholarly study paved the way for the radical reforms of Martin Luther (1483–1546), a German monk who, in 1517, officially began the Reformation when he made public a list of complaints against Church practices. These complaints, called the Ninety-five Theses, were condemned by Pope Leo. The pope ordered Luther to recant, but Luther refused, and the reform movement, called **Protestantism,** gathered force. Reformers appeared in Scandinavia, Scotland, Switzerland, and the Netherlands; among them was the theologian John Calvin (1509–1564), whose teachings became the basis of Puritanism in England and America.

Renaissance Literature

A key figure on the literary scene was the Italian poet Petrarch (1304–1374), who was perhaps the first person to use the term *Renaissance* to describe the time in which he lived. He popularized sonnets, which became a widely used lyric form (see page 678). He and his contemporary Giovanni Boccaccio (1313–1375) were among the first writers to use the vernacular—that is, the language spoken by the people (in this case, Italian)—rather than Latin, the traditional language of literature. Boccaccio is best known for the *Decameron,* a collection of stories that show skillful development of narrative and realistic detail (see page 668).

Prose fiction was moving in the direction of what we know today as the novel. In France, François Rabelais (c. 1494–1553) wrote a series of stories called *Gargantua and Pantagruel* that developed plotlines over a long series of events. In Spain, Miguel de Cervantes (1547–1616) wrote what many consider to be the first novel in the Western hemisphere, which is about a would-be knight named Don Quixote (see page 688).

To poets, particularly French poets, the humanist spirit demanded imitation of classical Greek and Roman forms. This style is called **neoclassicism.** Pierre de Ronsard (1524–1585) is famous for the poems he modeled after those of classical poets, as well as for his sonnets (see page 683).

The Renaissance also saw the revival of drama, especially in Spain and England. Nowhere was the spirit of the English Renaissance better expressed than in the plays of William Shakespeare (1564–1616). Shakespeare's skill in language and characterization has earned him a place with the greatest writers of all time.

Statue of Cervantes' *Don Quixote*. Madrid, Spain.

The Literature of the Enlightenment

Vast political and social changes marked the period known as the **Age of Enlightenment,** or, as it is sometimes called, the **Age of Reason.** During the seventeenth and eighteenth centuries, many people came to believe that they could arrive at truth solely through human reason. Through rational, logical thinking, human beings could probe the secrets of the universe and understand the true relationship between themselves and God.

A Time of Contrasts

In the seventeenth and eighteenth centuries, exotic goods from the East and immense quantities of gold and silver from the Americas enriched the monarchs of Europe—especially absolute monarchs like France's Louis XIV (1638–1715), who dubbed himself the Sun King and built a magnificent palace at Versailles.

Aristocrats led elegant lives. They lived in ornate homes lavishly decorated and surrounded by vast formal gardens and parks. The wealthy enhanced their reputations by becoming patrons of the arts,

FAST FACTS

Historical Highlights

- During the Crusades (1096–1270), the Holy Land is seized from the Muslims.

- The Black Death wipes out many villages in the four-teenth century.

- Copernicus challenges the belief that the sun revolves around the earth. In 1630, Galileo defends this theory but is forced to recant.

- Luther's Ninety-five Theses launch the Reformation in 1517.

- The power of the monarchy is challenged in the French Revolution (1789–1799).

particularly of music, which filled their leisure hours. The German composer Johann Sebastian Bach (1685–1750) and the Austrian composers Joseph Haydn (1732–1809) and Wolfgang Amadeus Mozart (1756–1791) were favorites of Europe's royal courts.

By contrast, the lower classes lived in great poverty. They flocked to the cities in search of work. They lived in slums and suffered from malnutrition. Epidemic illnesses ravaged the cities. The crime rate was high, and the wooden thatch-roofed houses in which poor people lived were especially vulnerable to fire. The restlessness of the poor during this time foreshadowed social upheavals to come.

Science: A Clockwork Universe

Enthusiasm for scientific investigation spurred the creation of societies to promote research, like the Royal Society of London for the Promotion of Natural Knowledge and the Academy of Sciences in France. The most influential scientific developments occurred in mathematics. René Descartes (1596–1650) believed that the deductive method used in mathematics was the way to discover universal truths. In *Mathematical Principles of Natural Philosophy* (1687), Sir Isaac Newton (1642–1727) describes a clockwork universe governed by absolute laws that can be expressed mathematically.

The philosophy put forth by Descartes, Newton, and others came to be called **rationalism.** Rationalism's influence reached beyond science. It supported the idea that unchanging laws govern politics and morality. The philosopher Thomas Hobbes (1588–1679) advanced the social theory that people choose what is in their best interest. Hobbes argued that people's common interests lead them to make a "social contract." They accept their sovereign's power over them in exchange for protection against their own greedy, evil nature.

Pitt and Napoleon Divide the World (c. 1809) by James Gillray.

Social Theory: The Spark of Revolution

The movement toward democratic government was championed by the British philosopher John Locke (1632–1704). He was an **empiricist**—someone who believes that experience rather than logic is the only reliable source of knowledge. Locke proposed that at birth the mind is a blank slate (a tabula rasa) on which experience is recorded. He also believed people had natural rights that rulers were supposed to protect. In Locke's view, revolution was not only a right but also an obligation. His political theories inspired Thomas Paine, Thomas Jefferson, and Benjamin Franklin in America.

In France, Jean Jacques Rousseau (1712–1778) wrote that humanity is naturally good but is corrupted by the environment, by education, and by government. He believed that governments must be subject to the will of the people.

Literature: An Age of Satire

The literature of the seventeenth and eighteenth centuries was strongly influenced by new social and scientific ideas. Satire was a popular literary form. Jean de La Fontaine (1621–1695) wrote shrewdly satiric fables (see page 704). Molière (1622–1673) wrote satiric dramas exposing the greed, hypocrisy, and faults of French

FAST FACTS

Philosophical Views
- The system of feudalism is based on the loyalty of vassals to a lord.
- The power of the Church is challenged by schisms and by reformers.
- Humanism emphasizes human individuality and potential.

A CLOSER LOOK: CULTURAL INFLUENCES

Drama During the Enlightenment

INFORMATIONAL TEXT

Even today, there is probably not a season on Broadway that does not feature one of the satiric comedies of the great French dramatist Molière (mōl·yer′) (1622–1673). Given that Molière's primary target was French society, it is not surprising that he had to fight state and religious authorities for the right to stage his plays. When his play *Tartuffe* was banned by the authorities, Molière said, " 'Tis a mighty stroke at any vice to make it the laughing stock of everybody; for men will easily suffer reproof; but they can by no means endure mockery. They will consent to be wicked but not ridiculous."

Of all the forms of imaginative expression, drama has probably always been the one most closely monitored by the authorities. For centuries in England, many respectable people considered theaters to be sinful. After the Puritans took over the Parliament in England in 1642, one of the first things they did after beheading the king was to close the theaters. The stages in England remained dark until 1660, when a new government invited Charles II, the exiled son of the murdered king, to return to England from France. As it happened, Charles had developed a

Scene from *Tartuffe* by Molière. (1850).
Victoria & Albert Museum, London.

passion for the theater in France, and so on his return and restoration to the throne, he immediately reopened the old theaters. Thus was born the period in England known as the Restoration.

• Mainstays of medieval
European culture are
knighthood, the feudal
system, and the code
of chivalry.

• Medieval literature
reflects the ideals of
heroism in epics.
Chivalric ideals are
expressed in
romances.

• Renaissance reform-
ers undermine the
authority of the
Church by translating
the Bible into the
vernacular.

• In the Enlightenment,
satire becomes a
weapon against vice
and folly.

society. Perhaps the most scathing satire was produced by Irish-born writer Jonathan Swift (1667–1745). *Gulliver's Travels* and "A Modest Proposal" reflect Swift's bitter outrage at the corruption he saw.

Possibly the most famous literary figure of the age was the French philosopher and rational skeptic Voltaire (1694–1778). In *Candide* (see page 709), Voltaire continually challenges Rousseau's optimistic assertion that humans are "naturally" good. Voltaire maintained that art should be used to change society, and his satires were directed at people who abused privilege and power.

Revolutions Ignited

The new ideas of the Enlightenment took on concrete form as masses of people, desiring a better life, challenged the power of the monarchies. In England the civil war that began in 1642 climaxed with the beheading of Charles I. The American Revolution and the French Revolution, more than a century later, were both fought for the rights of individuals.

The French Revolution failed to establish the ideal government that the philosophers envisioned. The American Revolution, how-ever, succeeded in establishing a stable, representational government with a Constitution and Bill of Rights created by people whose ideas were shaped by the science, the philosophy, and the art of the Age of Enlightenment.

REVIEW

Talk About . . .

Turn back to the Think About questions at the beginning of this introduction (page 588). Write down your responses, and get together with classmates to compare and discuss your views.

Reading Check

1. In what way were the Christian Church and feudalism the two pillars of the Middle Ages?
2. How was the power of the Church threatened and undermined during the Middle Ages and the Renaissance?

3. What is humanism, and what role did it play during the Renaissance?
4. What were the major ideas that caused people to revolt against monarchies during the Enlightenment?
5. What literary forms developed in the Middle Ages, the Renaissance, and the Age of Enlightenment?

European Literature from the Middle Ages to the Enlightenment:

A Time of Transition

Literature of the Middle Ages

Now it is the effect of love that a true lover cannot be degraded with any avarice. Love causes a rough and uncouth man to be distinguished for his handsomeness; it can endow a man even of the humblest birth with nobility of character; it blesses the proud with humility; and the man in love becomes accustomed to performing many services gracefully for everyone. O what a wonderful thing is love, which makes a man shine with so many virtues and teaches everyone, no matter who he is, so many good traits of character!

—Andreas Capellanus,
from The Art of Courtly Love

Boar and bear hunt from the *Devonshire Hunting Tapestries* (detail) (15th century) from the Netherlands.
Victoria & Albert Museum, London.

ABOUT

The Song of Roland

(c. 1100)

France

Portrait of Charlemagne (early 16th century) by Albrecht Dürer.

Germanisches Nationalmuseum, Nuremberg, Germany.

The *Song of Roland* is the earliest surviving example of the Old French *chansons de geste* (shän·sôn' də zhest'), or "songs of deeds," composed from the twelfth to the fifteenth centuries. These epic poems focus on the heroic deeds of Charlemagne, the king of the Franks from A.D. 768 to 814, and other feudal lords. *The Song of Roland* shares many characteristics with classical epic poems, such as the *Iliad* and the *Aeneid* (see pages 120 and 269): long speeches, detailed descriptions of battles, supernatural elements, and the repetition of key phrases.

Roland in History

The Song of Roland is based on historical events. In Charlemagne's time, Spain was ruled by Arab Muslims. Charlemagne agreed to help one of two Muslim rivals who were battling for control of Spain. But Charlemagne's campaign in Spain was a disaster, and in 778, his army was forced to retreat. As they crossed back into France, the rear guard of his army was overrun by the Basques (bäskz), a people who live in the Pyrenees mountain chain that divides France and Spain. One of the commanders of Charlemagne's rear guard during this battle at Roncesvalles was a man named Roland.

The National Epic of France

By the eleventh century, Europe was in the midst of the Crusades, the "holy wars" to wrest Jerusalem from the Muslims. Anti-Muslim feeling ran high in Europe. As the world had changed, so too had the story of Roland and the battle of Roncesvalles. The story evolved into a national epic about the religious conflict between Chris-

tians and Muslims in the eleventh century. The Basques were transformed into Arabs—referred to in the poem as "Saracens," "pagans," and "idol worshipers." Roland, who had played only a minor role in history, became a legendary hero, a nephew of Charlemagne, and a model Christian knight.

In the selection included here, Roland, his noble friend Oliver, and their small force are trapped in a pass in the Pyrenees as a result of the treachery of Ganelon, Roland's stepfather. Ganelon is envious of Roland's reputation as a warrior and furious because Roland has recommended him for dangerous duty as Charlemagne's ambassador to the Saracen king Marsilion. Ganelon has encouraged King Marsilion to attack the rear guard of Charlemagne's army, pitting 400,000 Saracens against 20,000 Franks. He has also persuaded Charlemagne to place Roland in command of the rear guard, the portion of the army in greatest danger. In this translation, Charlemagne, which means "Charles the Great," is referred to simply as Charles.

Before You Read

from The Song of Roland

Make the Connection

Quickwrite ✏️

Roland, the hero of *The Song of Roland,* acts according to his concept of honor. What does the word *honor* mean to you? In general, what do you think it means in society today? Jot down three actions or decisions you or people you know (or have read about) have made that you consider honorable.

Literary Focus

Climax

Climax is the point of greatest emotional intensity or suspense in a plot, when the conflict reaches its peak and the outcome of the story is finally determined. In a lengthy work like *The Song of Roland,* there may be several climactic moments, though the greatest climax usually occurs near the end of the narrative. Some critics refer to a climactic moment as a **turning point, or crisis.** At the turning point, something happens that seals the hero's fate, and his or her fortunes begin to improve or decline afterward as the plot moves toward its resolution, or ending.

As you read these excerpts from *The Song of Roland,* keep in mind that although you are not getting the full plot of the epic, you are reading the main portions of the epic's most famous episode. What is the climactic moment in this excerpt? How does it function as a turning point in the narrative?

> **Climax** is the point in a plot that creates the greatest emotional intensity or suspense.
>
> *For more on Climax, see the Handbook of Literary and Historical Terms.*

Reading Skills

Drawing Inferences About Character

When you draw an **inference** about character, you use clues in the text, as well as your own knowledge and experience, to figure out what a character is like. As you read, pay attention to clues that hint at Roland's character: what he says, what others say to him and about him, and what he does. In what ways is he a hero? Which of his character traits might be considered flaws?

Background

The Song of Roland is an **epic,** a long narrative poem that relates the great deeds of a larger-than-life figure. The **epic hero,** Roland, embodies the values of the society he represents. Roland is the ideal medieval knight: a heroic fighter, a loyal follower of his king, a trusted friend, and a devout Christian.

The narrative unit of *The Song of Roland* is a special kind of stanza known as a *laisse,* or verse paragraph. Each *laisse* moves the action ahead yet remains self-contained. Note that most lines end with punctuation and that every stanza ends with a sense of anticipation—a kind of mini-climax.

Vocabulary Development

exulting (eg·zult′iŋ) *v.* used as *adv.:* rejoicing greatly.

siege (sēj) *n.:* sustained attempt to obtain control.

feigned (fānd) *v.:* pretended.

fostered (fôs′tərd) *v.:* brought up in a nurturing way.

North Carolina Competency Goal
1.03; 2.01; 3.04; 4.05; 5.01; 5.03; 6.01

go.hrw.com

INTERNET

More About The Song of Roland
•
Vocabulary Practice

Keyword: LE5 WL-5

SKILLS FOCUS

Literary Skills
Understand climax.

Reading Skills
Draw inferences about character.

from The Song of Roland

translated by **Frederick Goldin**

*Roland's companion Oliver has seen the advancing
Saracen army and knows that the small French rear guard
is outnumbered. He begs Roland to blow on his magical
horn, the olifant, in order to summon more troops from
Charles's (Charlemagne's) army, but Roland refuses,
saying that he will lose his reputation and bring shame
on the French if he calls for help. Roland believes that he
and the other French fighters are more than equal to the
Saracens. Oliver continues to urge Roland to call for help,
to no avail. Finally, Roland, Oliver, Archbishop Turpin,
and the other French fighters clash with the Saracens in
the mountain pass. For a time the French hold their own.*

110

The battle is fearful and full of grief.
Oliver and Roland strike like good men,
the Archbishop, more than a thousand blows,
and the Twelve Peers° do not hang back, they strike!

5 the French fight side by side, all as one man.
The pagans die by hundreds, by thousands:
whoever does not flee finds no refuge from death,
like it or not, there he ends all his days.
And there the men of France lose their greatest arms;

10 they will not see their fathers, their kin again,
or Charlemagne, who looks for them in the passes.
Tremendous torment now comes forth in France,
a mighty whirlwind, tempests of wind and thunder,
rains and hailstones, great and immeasurable,

15 bolts of lightning hurtling and hurtling down:
it is, in truth, a trembling of the earth.
From Saint Michael-in-Peril° to the Saints,
from Besançon° to the port of Wissant,
there is no house whose veil of walls does not crumble.

20 A great darkness at noon falls on the land,
there is no light but when the heavens crack.
No man sees this who is not terrified,
and many say: "The Last Day! Judgment Day!
The end! The end of the world is upon us!"

25 They do not know, they do not speak the truth:
it is the worldwide grief for the death of Roland.

4. Twelve Peers: noblemen chosen as Charles's select band of leaders.

17. Saint Michael-in-Peril: sanctuary on the coast of Normandy.

18. Besançon (bə·zän·sōn′): city in east central France; part of the original kingdom of Burgundy.

Les Grandes Chroniques de France (15th century).

Russia National Library, St. Petersburg, Russia.

Charlemagne's Twelve Peers fight fiercely against the Saracens, but they are greatly outnumbered. At last it becomes apparent even to Roland that the battle cannot be won, and he finally decides to use his horn, the olifant, to call Charlemagne's army for relief. But Oliver, angered that Roland's pride prevented him from blowing the horn earlier, when it could have done some good, stops Roland with harsh words, pointing out that it truly would be a disgrace to sound the horn now, when all hope has been lost.

130

And Roland says: "We are in a rough battle.
I'll sound the olifant, Charles will hear it."
Said Oliver: "No good vassal would do it.
30 When I urged it, friend, you did not think it right.
If Charles were here, we'd come out with no losses.
Those men down there—no blame can fall on them."
Oliver said: "Now by this beard of mine,
If I can see my noble sister, Aude,°
35 once more, you will never lie in her arms!"

131

And Roland said: "Why are you angry at me?"
Oliver answers: "Companion, it is your doing.
I will tell you what makes a vassal good:
    it is judgment, it is never madness;
restraint is worth more than the raw nerve of a fool.
40 Frenchmen are dead because of your wildness.
And what service will Charles ever have from us?
If you had trusted me, my lord would be here,
we would have fought this battle through to the end,
Marsilion would be dead, or our prisoner.
45 Roland, your prowess—had we never seen it!
    And now, dear friend, we've seen the last of it.
No more aid from us now for Charlemagne,
a man without equal till Judgment Day,
you will die here, and your death will shame France.
We kept faith, you and I, we were companions;
    and everything we were will end today.
50 We part before evening, and it will be hard."

34. Aude (ō′dā): Roland's betrothed.

Olifant (A.D. 1100).

Maria Antoinette Evans Fund, 57.581. Courtesy, Museum of Fine Arts, Boston. Reproduced with permission. © 1999 Museum of Fine Arts, Boston.

132

Turpin the Archbishop hears their bitter words,
digs hard into his horse with golden spurs
and rides to them; begins to set them right:
"You, Lord Roland, and you, Lord Oliver,
55 I beg you in God's name do not quarrel.
To sound the horn could not help us now, true,
but still it is far better that you do it:
let the King come, he can avenge us then—
these men of Spain must not go home exulting!
60 Our French will come, they'll get down on their feet,
and find us here—we'll be dead, cut to pieces.
They will lift us into coffins on the backs of mules,
and weep for us, in rage and pain and grief,
and bury us in the courts of churches;
65 and we will not be eaten by wolves or pigs or dogs."
Roland replies, "Lord, you have spoken well."

133

Roland has put the olifant to his mouth,
he sets it well, sounds it with all his strength.
The hills are high, and that voice ranges far,
70 they heard it echo thirty great leagues away.
King Charles heard it, and all his faithful men.
And the King says: "Our men are in a battle."
And Ganelon disputed him and said:
"Had someone else said that, I'd call him liar!"

134

75 And now the mighty effort of Roland the Count:
he sounds his olifant; his pain is great,
and from his mouth the bright blood comes leaping out,
and the temple bursts in his forehead.
That horn, in Roland's hands, has a mighty voice:
80 King Charles hears it drawing through the passes.
Naimon° heard it, the Franks listen to it.
And the King said: "I hear Count Roland's horn;
he'd never sound it unless he had a battle."
Says Ganelon: "Now no more talk of battles!
85 You are old now, your hair is white as snow,
the things you say make you sound like a child.
You know Roland and that wild pride of his—

Roland blows the horn at Roncevaux, from *Le Chanson de Roland* (13th century) by French School.

Private collection.

81. Naimon: duke and advisor to Charlemagne.

Vocabulary

exulting (eg·zult′iŋ) v. used as *adv.:* rejoicing greatly.

what a wonder God has suffered it so long!
Remember? he took Noples° without your command:

90   the Saracens rode out, to break the siege;
they fought with him, the great vassal Roland.
Afterwards he used the streams to wash the blood
from the meadows: so that nothing would show.
He blasts his horn all day to catch a rabbit,

95   he's strutting now before his peers and bragging—
who under heaven would dare meet him on the field?
So now: ride on! Why do you keep on stopping?
The Land of Fathers lies far ahead of us."

89. **Noples:** in Spain.

*Roland sounds his horn again. Charles commands his army
to ride to Roland's aid, but it is too late to save Roland and
his peers, who have been defeated by the Saracens. Before
he dies, Oliver asks forgiveness of Roland.*

168

Now Roland feels that death is very near.

100   His brain comes spilling out through his two ears;
prays to God for his peers: let them be called;
and for himself, to the angel Gabriel;
took the olifant: there must be no reproach!
took Durendal° his sword in his other hand,

105   and farther than a crossbow's farthest shot
he walks toward Spain, into a fallow land,
and climbs a hill: there beneath two fine trees
stand four great blocks of stone, all are of marble;
and he fell back, to earth, on the green grass,

110   has fainted there, for death is very near.

104. Durendal (dü'ren·däl):
Roland's unbreakable sword;
said to be the sword that had
belonged to the Trojan hero
Hector.

169

High are the hills, and high, high are the trees;
there stand four blocks of stone, gleaming of marble.
Count Roland falls fainting on the green grass,
and is watched, all this time, by a Saracen:

115   who has feigned death and lies now with the others,
has smeared blood on his face and on his body;
and quickly now gets to his feet and runs—
a handsome man, strong, brave, and so crazed with pride
that he does something mad and dies for it:

Vocabulary

siege (sēj) *n.:* sustained attempt to obtain control.
feigned (fānd) *v.:* pretended.

The Battle of Roncevaux
and the death of Roland,
miniature from *The History
of the Emperors*.

Bibliothèque de l'Arsenal, Paris, France.

120 laid hands on Roland, and on the arms of Roland,
and cried: "Conquered! Charles's nephew conquered!
I'll carry this sword home to Arabia!"
As he draws it, the Count begins to come round.

170

Now Roland feels *someone taking his sword!*
125 opened his eyes, and had one word for him:
"I don't know you, you aren't one of ours";
grasps that olifant that he will never lose,
strikes on the helm beset with gems in gold,
shatters the steel, and the head, and the bones,
130 sent his two eyes flying out of his head,
dumped him over stretched out at his feet dead;
and said: "You nobody! how could you dare
lay hands on me—rightly or wrongly: how?
Who'll hear of this and not call you a fool?
135 Ah! the bell-mouth of the olifant is smashed,
the crystal and the gold fallen away."

171

Now Roland the Count feels his sight is gone;
gets on his feet, draws on his final strength,
the color on his face lost now for good.
140 Before him stands a rock; and on that dark rock
in rage and bitterness he strikes ten blows:
the steel blade grates, it will not break, it stands unmarked.
"Ah!" said the Count, "Blessed Mary, your help!
Ah Durendal, good sword, your unlucky day,

Charlemagne in tent (detail)
(c. 1215) from the Shrine of
Charlemagne.

Cathedral Treasury, Cathedral
(Palatine Chapel), Aachen, Germany.

145   for I am lost and cannot keep you in my care.
The battles I have won, fighting with you,
the mighty lands that holding you I conquered,
that Charles rules now, our King, whose beard is white!
Now you fall to another: it must not be
    a man who'd run before another man!
150   For a long while a good vassal held you:
there'll never be the like in France's holy land."

173

Roland the Count strikes down on a dark rock,
and the rock breaks, breaks more than I can tell,
and the blade grates, but Durendal will not break,
155   the sword leaped up, rebounded toward the sky.
The Count, when he sees that sword will not be broken,
softly, in his own presence, speaks the lament:
"Ah Durendal, beautiful, and most sacred,
the holy relics in this golden pommel!
160   Saint Peter's tooth and blood of Saint Basile,°
a lock of hair of my lord Saint Denis,°
and a fragment of blessed Mary's robe:
your power must not fall to the pagans,
you must be served by Christian warriors.
165   May no coward ever come to hold you!
It was with you I conquered those great lands
that Charles has in his keeping, whose beard is white,
the Emperor's lands, that make him rich and strong."

160. Saint Peter: one of
Jesus's disciples who was the
first pope of the Catholic
church. **Saint Basile** (ba·sēl′):
fourth-century religious writer
and monastery administrator;
fought for orthodoxy within
the Catholic Church.

161. Saint Denis (də·nē′):
third-century apostle to the
Gauls, who was martyred;
patron saint of France.

174

Now Roland feels death coming over him,
170 death descending from his temples to his heart.
He came running underneath a pine tree
and there stretched out, face down, on the green grass,
lays beneath him his sword and the olifant.
He turned his head toward the Saracen hosts,
175 and this is why: with all his heart he wants
King Charles the Great and all his men to say,
he died, that noble Count, a conqueror;
makes confession, beats his breast often, so feebly,
offers his glove, for all his sins, to God.

176

180 Count Roland lay stretched out beneath a pine;
he turned his face toward the land of Spain,
began to remember many things now:
how many lands, brave man, he had conquered;
and he remembered: sweet France, the men of his line,
185 remembered Charles, his lord, who fostered him:
cannot keep, remembering, from weeping, sighing;
but would not be unmindful of himself:
he confesses his sins, prays God for mercy:
"Loyal Father, you who never failed us,
190 who resurrected Saint Lazarus° from the dead,
and saved your servant Daniel° from the lions:
now save the soul of me from every peril
for the sins I committed while I still lived."
Then he held out his right glove to his Lord:
195 Saint Gabriel° took the glove from his hand.
He held his head bowed down upon his arm,
he is gone, his two hands joined, to his end.
Then God sent him his angel Cherubim°
and Saint Michael,° angel of the sea's Peril;
200 and with these two there came Saint Gabriel:
they bear Count Roland's soul to Paradise.

190. Saint Lazarus: story of this miracle appears in John 11:1–44.

191. Daniel: story is told in Daniel 6:16–27.

195. Saint Gabriel: one of the seven archangels; messenger of good news.

198. Cherubim (cher′yōō·bim′): one of the heavenly beings at God's throne.

199. Saint Michael: one of the archangels.

Vocabulary

fostered (fôs′tərd) v.: brought up in a nurturing way.

Response and Analysis

Reading Check

1. What explanation is given for the great darkness that engulfs the land during the battle?

2. As the battle proceeds, it becomes clear that the French will be defeated. What does Roland want to do? How does Oliver respond?

3. What does Charles think the sound of Roland's horn means?

Thinking Critically

4. Roland's code of chivalry puts great emphasis on personal honor. Compare Roland's notion of honor with the concepts you wrote about in your Quickwrite response. What similarities, if any, are there?

5. What **inference** can you draw about the characters of Roland and Oliver from their disagreement?

6. A **foil** is a character who sets off another character by contrast. How does Oliver serve as a foil to Roland?

7. **Repetition** is an important feature in the *chansons de geste*. Identify at least two examples of repetition in the poem, and explain what effect the repetition achieves.

8. As an **epic hero,** Roland represents the values of his society. List at least three values of medieval European culture that this epic appears to celebrate.

9. Explain how Roland dies in the **climax** of the selection. Do you think Roland would have preferred this death to one from a Saracen sword? Why or why not?

Extending and Evaluating

10. If Roland were a contemporary war hero, do you think his death would be mourned as a defeat or celebrated as a victory? Explain.

WRITING

Comparing Epic Heroes

Write a short essay comparing Roland and the *Iliad*'s Achilles (see page 123) as epic heroes. Consider the strengths and flaws of each hero and how their codes of honor differ. In what sense is each character a tragic hero—an exemplary individual who is nevertheless defeated by his own mistakes and weaknesses? Use a chart like the following to organize your ideas.

	Roland	Achilles
Codes of honor		
Positive character traits		
Negative character traits		
Conclusion		

Vocabulary Development
Match It Up

Match each Vocabulary word from the column on the left with the word or phrase that is closest to it in meaning in the column on the right.

1. exulting   a. reared

2. siege   b. made a false show

3. feigned   c. expressing jubilation

4. fostered   d. prolonged effort to overcome resistance

Marie de France

(twelfth century)

France

Marie de France is considered one of the finest writers of the Middle Ages, and yet all we know for certain about her comes from this reference in one of her works: "Marie is my name, I am of France." Scholars do believe that Marie was born in France, probably of noble birth because she was quite well educated. At some point she probably went to England and wrote for the French-speaking court of Henry II. In addition to her native French, she knew Latin and English and was familiar with the Greek and Roman classics as well as with contemporary French works.

Marie wrote three separate works in French between 1160 and 1215. The first, the *Lais,* is a group of twelve short verse narratives. The second is the *Fables,* a collection of fables translated from English into Old French. The third, *St. Patrick's Purgatory,* is a translation from Latin into French of the life of a saint.

Marie drew the inspiration for her *lais* from tales of Celtic origin—tales told by traveling minstrels (jongleurs) from the province of Brittany in France. The *lais* may have been performed in Breton, the Celtic language spoken in Brittany. The minstrels accompanied themselves on an instrument called a rote, a kind of lyre or harp. None of these original tales have survived.

Marie's *lais* differed from much of the romantic literature of her day. The typical literature of the Middle Ages, such as *The Song of Roland* (see page 607) and *Perceval* (see page 624), was dominated by masculine ideas about war, love, and chivalry and focused on the knight's responsibility to society. The educated classes, bored with these larger-than-life portraits of heroes and military events in medieval epics, wanted stories that were more personal. Marie provided for their needs with her stories about knights and their ladies, human misfortune, unhappy and restricting marriages, and heroes and heroines trapped by life's circumstances.

Illumination of Tristan and Iseult.
Österreichische Nationalbibliothek, Vienna.
cod.2537fol.103r

Chevrefoil

Make the Connection

Quickwrite

Think of all the love stories you have read, seen on television or at the movies, or heard about. Are they happy or tragic? Do the lovers die or do they live "happily ever after"? Jot down some notes about the features of these love stories.

Literary Focus

Extended Metaphor

A **metaphor** is a figure of speech that makes a connection between two seemingly unlike things without using such connective words as *like, as, than,* or *resembles.* An **extended metaphor** is developed over several lines of writing or even through an entire work. As you read "Chevrefoil," note how the union of the honeysuckle and the hazel tree is used as an extended metaphor for the love of Tristan and Iseult (i·sōōlt′).

> An **extended metaphor** is a metaphor that is developed over several lines of writing or through an entire work.
>
> *For more on Extended Metaphor, see the Handbook of Literary and Historical Terms.*

North Carolina Competency Goal
1.02; 1.03; 4.05; 5.01; 5.03; 6.01

Background

Because medieval marriages were arranged by parents, romantic love was not part of marriage. As a result, an elaborate system known as courtly love evolved in upper-class society. In the courtly love tradition a young lover typically idealizes a married woman of noble background. He suffers when they are apart and longs to be united with her.

"Chevrefoil" (shev′rə·fwäl′), which means "honeysuckle," concerns the forbidden love of Tristan and Iseult. According to this famous Celtic story, Tristan is sent to Ireland to bring Iseult, a beautiful princess, to Cornwall, England, where she is to wed Tristan's uncle, King Mark. However, on the way to Cornwall, Tristan and Iseult accidentally drink a magic potion that causes them to fall in love. King Mark marries Iseult, but when he discovers the love between his nephew and his wife, he sends Tristan into exile. Many adventures befall the lovers from that time on, and eventually they die on the same day.

In "Chevrefoil," Marie de France focuses on a single moment in the story of Tristan and Iseult. Because the details of the entire narrative would have been familiar to her readers, Marie is free to concentrate on a scene that summarizes the sorrow and fatefulness of the famous love story.

SKILLS FOCUS

Literary Skills
Understand extended metaphor.

(Opposite) *Tristan and Isolde with the Potion* (c. 1916) by John William Waterhouse.
Collection of Fred and Sherry Ross. www.Artrenewal.org. Port Reading, New Jersey.

Chevrefoil

Marie de France
translated by **Robert Hanning**
and **Joan Ferrante**

I should like very much
to tell you the truth
about the *lai* men call *Chevrefoil*—
why it was composed and where it
    came from.
5 Many have told and recited it to me
and I have found it in writing,
about Tristan and the queen
and their love that was so true,
that brought them much suffering
10 and caused them to die the same day.
King Mark was annoyed,
angry at his nephew Tristan;
he exiled Tristan from his land
because of the queen whom he loved.
15 Tristan returned to his own country,
South Wales, where he was born,
he stayed a whole year;
he couldn't come back.
Afterward he began to expose himself
20 to death and destruction.
Don't be surprised at this:
for one who loves very faithfully
is sad and troubled
when he cannot satisfy his desires.
25 Tristan was sad and worried,
so he set out from his land.
He traveled straight to Cornwall,
where the queen lived,
and entered the forest all alone—
30 he didn't want anyone to see him;
he came out only in the evening
when it was time to find shelter.
He took lodging that night,

with peasants, poor people.
35 He asked them for news
    of the king—what he was doing.
    They told him they had heard
    that the barons had been summoned by ban.°
    They were to come to Tintagel°
40 where the king wanted to hold his court;
    at Pentecost° they would all be there,
    there'd be much joy and pleasure,
    and the queen would be there too.
    Tristan heard and was very happy;
45 she would not be able to go there
    without his seeing her pass.
    The day the king set out,
    Tristan also came to the woods
    by the road he knew
50 their assembly must take.
    He cut a hazel tree in half,
    then he squared° it.
    When he had prepared the wood,
    he wrote his name on it with his knife.
55 If the queen noticed it—
    and she should be on the watch for it,
    for it had happened before
    and she had noticed it then—
    she'd know when she saw it,
60 that the piece of wood had come from her love.
    This was the message of the writing
    that he had sent to her:
    he had been there a long time,
    had waited and remained
65 to find out and to discover
    how he could see her,
    for he could not live without her.
    With the two of them it was just
    as it is with the honeysuckle
70 that attaches itself to the hazel tree:
    when it has wound and attached
    and worked itself around the trunk,
    the two can survive together;
    but if someone tries to separate them,
75 the hazel dies quickly
    and the honeysuckle with it.

38. ban *n.:* official proclamation.
39. Tintagel (tin·taj′əl): cape in northwestern Cornwall where, according to legend, King Arthur was born.
41. Pentecost (pen′tə·kôst′): seventh Sunday after Easter; Whitsunday.

52. squared *v.:* cut to a square or rectangular shape.

The love potion, intended for Isolde the Fair and King Mark of Cornwall, but drunk by Tristan and Isolde the Fair (19th century), from *The Story of Tristan and Isolde*. Stained-glass window from the Music Room, Harden Grange, near Bingley, Yorkshire, England.

Bradford Art Galleries and Museums, West Yorkshire, United Kingdom.

"Sweet love, so it is with us:
You cannot live without me, nor I without you."
The queen rode along;
80 she looked at the hillside
and saw the piece of wood; she knew what it was,
she recognized all the letters.
The knights who were accompanying her,
who were riding with her,
85 she ordered to stop:
she wanted to dismount and rest.
They obeyed her command.
She went far away from her people
and called her girl
90 Brenguein, who was loyal to her.
She went a short distance from the road;
and in the woods she found him
whom she loved more than any living thing.
They took great joy in each other.
95 He spoke to her as much as he desired,
she told him whatever she liked.
Then she assured him
that he would be reconciled with the king—
for it weighed on him
100 that he had sent Tristan away;
he'd done it because of the accusation.
Then she departed, she left her love,
but when it came to the separation,
they began to weep.
105 Tristan went to Wales,
to wait until his uncle sent for him.
For the joy that he'd felt
from his love when he saw her,
by means of the stick he inscribed
110 as the queen had instructed,
and in order to remember the words,
Tristan, who played the harp well,
composed a new *lai* about it.
I shall name it briefly:
115 in English they call it *Goat's Leaf*
the French call it *Chevrefoil.*
I have given you the truth
about the *lai* that I have told here.

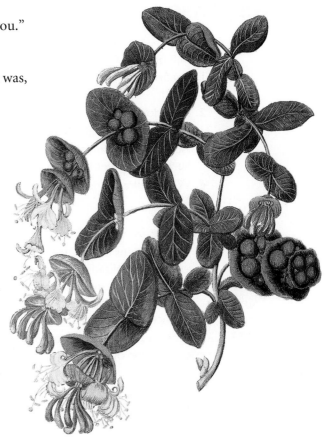

Honeysuckle (detail) (1613).
Engraving for Basilius Besler's
Florilegium, from Nuremburg.

The Granger Collection, New York.

Response and Analysis

Reading Check

1. According to the speaker, what is the "truth"—the source—of this *lai*?

2. How does Tristan learn that Iseult will be traveling through the forest?

3. How does Tristan let Iseult know that he wants to meet her?

4. What assurance does Iseult give Tristan?

Thinking Critically

5. The traditions of courtly love call for a knight's idealization of a married woman and for suffering when the lovers are separated. How are these characteristics handled in "Chevrefoil"?

6. An **extended metaphor** creates a comparison over several lines or even throughout an entire poem. Explain the extended metaphor that compares the survival of Tristan and Iseult's love to that of the honeysuckle and the hazel tree.

7. A **conflict** is a struggle or clash between opposing characters, forces, or emotions. What do you consider the main conflict to be in "Chevrefoil"?

Extending and Evaluating

8. In what ways might Tristan and Iseult behave differently in the modern world? In what ways have the constraints of society changed? Do similar constraints still exist? Explain.

9. Do you consider Marie de France's characters realistic? Does she provide insight into the psychology of her lovers? Explain.

Literary Criticism

10. Marie de France often organizes a *lai* around a central **symbol,** or thing that stands both for itself and for something else. The translators Robert Hanning and Joan Ferrante have said that these symbols "provide valuable insight into the nature of love." In your opinion, has Marie de France chosen an effective symbol in the attachment of the honeysuckle to the hazel tree? Give reasons for your response.

WRITING

Analyzing a Story's Appeal

Many writers throughout the centuries have retold or alluded to the story of the tragic lovers Tristan and Iseult. Write a brief essay exploring why this tale of forbidden love has had such a lasting appeal. You might want to consider the comment by a character in Shakespeare's *A Midsummer Night's Dream,* who says, "The course of true love never did run smooth." In your essay, mention other tragic love stories that you are familiar with. You might want to look back at your Quickwrite notes for ideas.

North Carolina Competency Goal
1.02; 1.03; 4.02; 4.05; 5.03; 6.01

INTERNET

Projects and Activities
Keyword: LE5 WL-5

SKILLS FOCUS

Literary Skills
Analyze extended metaphor.

Writing Skills
Analyze a story's appeal.

Chrétien de Troyes
(c. 1135–c. 1190)
France

King Arthur (c. 1490) from Tapestry of the Nine Worthies.

Historisches Museum, Basel, Switzerland.

The work of Chrétien de Troyes (krā·tyan də trwä′) is important for several reasons. He created a new type of poetic narrative, the **Arthurian romance.** He also introduced the legend of the Grail into the Arthurian romances, and he influenced the techniques and themes of Arthurian literature that was to come.

Although he was one of the most famous medieval court poets, we have little definite knowledge of Chrétien's life. He probably was born at Troyes, a city in northeastern France, and trained for a position in the Church. His education most likely included study of the classics, since early in his career he wrote verse adaptations of works by the Roman poet Ovid (see page 306). He soon became fascinated, however, by Celtic stories of King Arthur and his knights. He wrote five Arthurian romances, including one about the love of Lancelot and Guinevere. *Perceval, ou le conte du graal* (*Perceval, or The Story of the Grail*), like most other Arthurian romances, focuses not on King Arthur but on the adventures of other knights of the Round Table. Probably composed between 1180 and 1190, *Perceval* was dedicated to Philippe d'Alsace, a count of Flanders. The poem is divided into two parts. The first part presents the young Perceval's instruction in chivalry; the second part focuses on the quests of the knight Gauvain (Gawain). In Perceval, Chrétien presented a new kind of medieval hero, a knight less interested in worldly glory than in such Christian values as penitence and charity. This hero's quest is not for the love of a lady but for spiritual perfection. He performs his great deeds for the love of God. Unfortunately, the outcome of Perceval's spiritual quest is never resolved; Chrétien died before he could complete his poem.

Perceval is the earliest known version of the legend of the Holy Grail. The excerpt included here contains a celebrated episode from the poem: the procession of the Grail. In Chrétien's story the Grail, a holy object, is described as some sort of dish used to carry a single communion wafer, an important element in Christian ritual. In later Arthurian romances the Grail is Christ's chalice at the Last Supper, the same cup that is later used to collect drops of Christ's blood at the Crucifixion. Many knights of Arthur's Round Table try—and fail—to find this holy object, which can be obtained only by a person who is absolutely pure.

Chrétien wrote his romance in what was then the standard form for French narrative verse: **couplets,** or lines of rhymed verse, that contain eight syllables. He is quite skillful in his handling of dialogue. This verse translation by Ruth Harwood Cline follows the characteristics of the original text.

Before You Read

The Grail
from **Perceval**

Make the Connection
Quickwrite

Consider this quotation from the poem: ". . . one can be too talkative, / but also one can be too still." Recall an experience in which your decision to be silent rather than to speak up turned out to be a mistake. Jot down what you learned.

Literary Focus
Romance

A medieval **romance** is a verse narrative about the adventures of kings, queens, knights, and ladies. These adventures take place in idealized settings and often include mysterious supernatural events. Knights in the romances are bound by the codes of chivalry and courtly love.

Arthurian romances are stories of King Arthur and his knights of the Round Table. Some Arthurian romances, like *Perceval*, highlight Christian values above the ideals of chivalry and courtly love. Perceval's devotion is to God, and he embodies Christian virtues, such as charity and humility, more than chivalric values. His quest for the Grail is a spiritual quest, not a quest for fame.

> A **romance** is a medieval verse narrative chronicling the adventures of a brave knight or other hero who performs glorious deeds for the love of a beautiful lady or some other ideal.
>
> *For more on Romance, see the Handbook of Literary and Historical Terms.*

Background

Although Perceval is the son of a great knight, his mother has kept him from knowing anything about knighthood because she does not want her son to die young, as her husband and two other sons have. After meeting five wandering knights, though, Perceval gets a thirst for adventure and sets off for King Arthur's court. After he defeats an opponent called the Red Knight and takes his armor and weapons, Perceval meets a nobleman, Gornemant, who teaches him how to fight. After conferring knighthood on Perceval, Gornemant advises him to show mercy to knights and avoid asking too many questions.

Worried about his mother, whom he regrets having deserted, Perceval decides to return home. He has just left the castle of Belrepeire, where he has fallen in love with the lady Blancheflor. As the excerpt opens, he comes to a river that he cannot cross. In this section of the romance, Perceval is referred to only as "the youth" or "the young man."

Vocabulary Development

elated (ē·lāt′id) *v.* used as *adj.*: very happy.

forged (fôrjd) *v.*: made a metal object by heating and hammering.

tempered (tem′pərd) *v.*: strengthened by heating and sudden cooling.

juxtaposed (juks′tə·pōzd′) *v.* used as *adj.*: placed side by side.

undeterred (un·dē·tʉrd′) *adj.* used as *adv.*: unobstructed; without restriction.

North Carolina Competency Goal
1.02; 1.03; 4.05; 5.01; 5.03; 6.01

go. hrw .com

INTERNET

Vocabulary Practice
•
More About Chrétien de Troyes
Keyword: LE5 WL-5

SKILLS FOCUS

Literary Skills
Understand romance.

The Grail

from Perceval

Chrétien de Troyes
translated by **Ruth Harwood Cline**

The youth began his journey from
the castle, and the daytime whole
he did not meet one living soul:
no creature from the wide earth's span,
5   no Christian woman, Christian man
who could direct him on his way.
The young man did not cease to pray
the sovereign father, God, Our Lord,
if He were willing, to accord
10   that he would find his mother still
alive and well. He reached a hill
and saw a river at its base.
So rapid was the current's pace,
so deep the water, that he dared
15   not enter it, and he declared,
"Oh God Almighty! It would seem,
if I could get across this stream,
I'd find my mother, if she's living."
He rode the bank with some misgiving
20   and reached a cliff, but at that place
the water met the cliff's sheer face
and kept the youth from going through.
A little boat came into view;
it headed down the river, floating
25   and carrying two men out boating.
The young knight halted there and waited.
He watched the way they navigated
and thought that they would pass the place
he waited by the cliff's sheer face.
30   They stayed in mid-stream, where they
        stopped
and took the anchor, which they dropped.
The man afore, a fisher, took
a fish to bait his line and hook;

King Arthur and the Knights of the Round Table
arriving at castle (detail) (c. 1183) from a French
manuscript by Chrétien de Troyes.

Biblioteca Nazionale, Turin, Italy.

Galahad being introduced to the company of the Round Table (c. 1370–1380), from an Italian manuscript.

Bibliothèque Nationale de France, Paris (Ms.Fr. 343, fol.3).

in size the little fish he chose
35   was larger than a minnow grows.
The knight, completely at a loss,
not knowing how to get across,
first greeted them, then asked the pair,
"Please, gentlemen, nearby is there
40   a bridge to reach the other side?"
To which the fisherman replied,
"No, brother, for besides this boat,
the one in which we are afloat,
which can't bear five men's weight as
       charge,
45   there is no other boat as large
for twenty miles each way and more,
and you can't cross on horseback, for
there is no ferry, bridge, nor ford."
"Tell me," he answered, "by Our Lord,
50   where I may find a place to stay."

The fisherman said, "I should say
you'll need a roof tonight and more,
so I will lodge you at my door.
First find the place this rock is breached°
55   and ride uphill, until you've reached
the summit of the cliff," he said.
"Between the wood and river bed
you'll see, down in the valley wide,
the manor house where I reside."
60   The knight rode up the cliff until
he reached the summit of the hill.
He looked around him from that stand
but saw no more than sky and land.
He cried, "What have I come to see?
65   Stupidity and trickery!
May God dishonor and disgrace

---

54. the ... breached: opening in the cliff wall.

the man who sent me to this place!
He had the long way round in mind,
when he told me that I would find
70   a manor when I reached the peak.
Oh, fisherman, why did you speak?
For if you said it out of spite,
you tricked me badly!" He caught sight
of a tower starting to appear
75   down in a valley he was near,
and as the tower came into view,
if people were to search, he knew,
as far as Beirut,° they would not
find any finer tower or spot.
80   The tower was dark gray stone, and square,
and flanked by lesser towers, a pair.
Before the tower the hall was laid;
before the hall was the arcade.°
On toward the tower the young man rode
85   in haste and called the man who showed
the way to him a worthy guide.
No longer saying he had lied,
he praised the fisherman, <u>elated</u>
to find his lodgings as he stated.
90   The youth went toward the gate and found
the drawbridge lowered to the ground.
He rode across the drawbridge span.
Four squires awaited the young man.
Two squires came up to help him doff
95   his arms and took his armor off.
The third squire led his horse away
to give him fodder, oats, and hay.
The fourth brought a silk cloak, new-made,
and led him to the hall's arcade,
100   which was so fine, you may be sure
you'd not find, even if you were
to search as far as Limoges,° one
as splendid in comparison.
The young man paused in the arcade,
105   until the castle's master made
two squires escort him to the hall.
The young man entered with them all

and found the hall was square inside:
it was as long as it was wide;
110   and in the center of its span
he saw a handsome nobleman°
with grayed hair, sitting on a bed.
The nobleman wore on his head
a mulberry-black sable cap
115   and wore a dark silk robe and wrap.
He leaned back in his weakened state
and let his elbow take his weight.
Between four columns, burning bright,
a fire of dry logs cast its light.
120   In order to enjoy its heat,
four hundred men could find a seat
around the outsized fire, and not
one man would take a chilly spot.
The solid fireplace columns could
125   support the massive chimney hood,
which was of bronze, built high and wide.
The squires, one squire on either side,
appeared before their lord foremost
and brought the youth before his host.
130   He saw the young man, whom he greeted.
"My friend," the nobleman entreated,
"don't think me rude not to arise;
I hope that you will realize
that I cannot do so with ease."
135   "Don't even mention it, sir, please,
I do not mind," replied the boy,
"may Heaven give me health and joy."
The lord rose higher on the bed,
as best he could, with pain, and said,
140   "My friend, come nearer, do not be
embarrassed or disturbed by me,
for I command you to come near.
Come to my side and sit down here."
The nobleman began to say,
145   "From where, sir, did you come today?"
He said, "This morning, sir, I came

---

111. **a handsome nobleman:** The castle's lord is
generally known as the Fisher King. He suffers
from a mysterious malady.

Vocabulary

elated (ē·lāt′id) *v.* used as *adj.*: very happy.

---

78. **Beirut** (bā·rōōt′): capital of Lebanon; seaport on
the Mediterranean.
83. **arcade** (är·kād′) *n.*: passage with arched roof or
line of arches.
102. **Limoges** (lē·mōzh′): city in west central France.

The Attainment: The Vision of the Holy Grail to Sir Galahad, Sir Bors and Sir Percival
(19th century) by Sir Edward Burne-Jones.

Birmingham Museums & Art Gallery (24.5.03-31.8.03).

from Belrepeire,° for that's its name."
"So help me God," the lord replied,
"you must have had a long day's ride:
150 to start before the light of morn
before the watchman blew his horn."
"Sir, I assure you, by that time
the morning bells had rung for prime,"°
the young man made the observation.
155 While they were still in conversation,
a squire entered through the door
and carried in a sword he wore
hung from his neck and which thereto
he gave the rich man, who withdrew
160 the sword halfway and checked the blade

to see where it was forged and made,
which had been written on the sword.
The blade was wrought, observed the lord,
of such fine steel, it would not break
165 save with its bearer's life at stake
on one occasion, one alone,
a peril that was only known
to him who forged and tempered it.
The squire said, "Sir, if you permit,
170 your lovely blonde niece sent this gift,
and you will never see or lift
a sword that's lighter for its strength,
considering its breadth and length.

---

147. Belrepeire (bel·rə·pār′): castle of Perceval's lady,
Blancheflor; before meeting the Fisher King, Perceval
defended Belrepeire, which was under siege.

153. prime *n*.: in the Catholic liturgy the first hour of
daylight.

Vocabulary

forged (fôrjd) *v*.: made a metal object by heating and
hammering.

tempered (tem′pərd) *v*.: strengthened by heating and
sudden cooling.

Please give the sword to whom you choose,
175 but if it goes to one who'll use
the sword that he is given well,
you'll greatly please the demoiselle.°
The forger of the sword you see
has never made more swords than three,
180 and he is going to die before
he ever forges any more.
No sword will be quite like this sword."
Immediately the noble lord
bestowed it on the newcomer,
185 who realized that its hangings were
a treasure and of worth untold.
The pommel° of the sword was gold,
the best Arabian or Grecian;
the sheath's embroidery gold Venetian.

----

177. **demoiselle** (dem′wä·zel′) *n.:* damsel; young lady.
187. **pommel** (päm′əl) *n.:* knob on the hilt of a sword
or dagger.

190 Upon the youth the castle's lord
bestowed the richly mounted sword
and said to him, "This sword, dear brother,
was destined for you and none other.
I wish it to be yours henceforth.
195 Gird on the sword and draw it forth."
He thanked the lord, and then the knight
made sure the belt was not too tight,
and girded on the sword, and took
the bare blade out for a brief look.
200 Then in the sheath it was replaced:
it looked well hanging at his waist
and even better in his fist.
It seemed as if it would assist
the youth in any time of need
205 to do a brave and knightly deed.
Beside the brightly burning fire
the youth turned round and saw a squire,
who had his armor in his care,

among the squires standing there.
210 He told this squire to hold the sword
and took his seat beside the lord,
who honored him as best he might.
The candles cast as bright a light
as could be found in any manor.
215 They chatted in a casual manner.
Out of a room a squire came, clasping
a lance of purest white: while grasping
the center of the lance, the squire
walked through the hall between the fire
220 and two men sitting on the bed.
All saw him bear, with measured tread,
the pure white lance. From its white tip
a drop of crimson blood would drip
and run along the white shaft and
225 drip down upon the squire's hand,
and then another drop would flow.
The knight who came not long ago
beheld this marvel, but preferred
not to inquire why it occurred,
230 for he recalled the admonition
the lord made part of his tuition,°
since he had taken pains to stress
the dangers of loquaciousness.°
The young man thought his questions
    might
235 make people think him impolite,
and that's why he did not inquire.
Two more squires entered, and each squire
held candelabra, wrought of fine
pure gold with niello° work design.
240 The squires with candelabra fair
were an extremely handsome pair.
At least ten lighted candles blazed
in every holder that they raised.
The squires were followed by a maiden
245 who bore a grail, with both hands laden.
The bearer was of noble mien,°

well dressed, and lovely, and serene,
and when she entered with the grail,
the candles suddenly grew pale,
250 the grail cast such a brilliant light,
as stars grow dimmer in the night
when sun or moonrise makes them fade.
A maiden after her conveyed
a silver platter past the bed.
255 The grail, which had been borne ahead,
was made of purest, finest gold
and set with gems; a manifold
display of jewels of every kind,
the costliest that one could find
260 in any place on land or sea,
the rarest jewels there could be,
let not the slightest doubt be cast.
The jewels in the grail surpassed
all other gems in radiance.
265 They went the same way as the lance:
they passed before the lord's bedside
to another room and went inside.
The young man saw the maids' procession
and did not dare to ask a question
270 about the grail or whom they served;
the wise lord's warning he observed,
for he had taken it to heart.
I fear he was not very smart;
I have heard warnings people give:
275 that one can be too talkative,
but also one can be too still.
But whether it was good or ill,
I do not know, he did not ask.
The squires who were assigned the task
280 of bringing in the water and
the cloths obeyed the lord's command.
The men who usually were assigned
performed these tasks before they dined.
They washed their hands in water, warmed,
285 and then two squires, so I'm informed,
brought in the ivory tabletop,
made of one piece: they had to stop
and hold it for a while before
the lord and youth, until two more
290 squires entered, each one with a trestle.°
The trestles had two very special,

---

231. the lord made part of his tuition: Perceval was instructed by the knight Gornemant not to talk too much so that people will not realize how uneducated he is.

233. loquaciousness (lō·kwā′shəs·nis) *n.*: talkativeness.

239. niello (nē·el′ō) *n.*: method of decorating with inlaid metals.

246. mien (mēn) *n.*: appearance.

---

290. trestle (tres′əl) *n.*: frame used to support a tabletop.

rare properties, which they contained
since they were built, and which remained
in them forever: they were wrought
295 of ebony, a wood that's thought
to have two virtues: it will not
ignite and burn and will not rot;
these dangers cause no harm nor loss.
They laid the tabletop across
300 the trestles, and the cloth above.
What shall I say? To tell you of
the cloth is far beyond my scope.
No legate,° cardinal, or pope
has eaten from a whiter one.
305 The first course was of venison,
a peppered haunch, cooked in its fat,
accompanied by a clear wine that
was served in golden cups, a pleasant,
delicious drink. While they were present
310 a squire carved up the venison.
He set the peppered haunch upon
a silver platter, carved the meat,
and served the slices they would eat
by placing them on hunks of bread.
315 Again the grail passed by the bed,
and still the youth remained reserved
about the grail and whom they served.
He did not ask, because he had
been told so kindly it was bad
320 to talk too much, and he had taken
these words to heart. He was mistaken;
though he remembered, he was still
much longer than was suitable.
At every course, and in plain sight,
325 the grail was carried past the knight,
who did not ask whom they were serving,
although he wished to know, observing
in silence that he ought to learn
about it prior to his return.
330 So he would ask: before he spoke
he'd wait until the morning broke,
and he would ask a squire to tell,
once he had told the lord farewell
and all the others in his train.
335 He put the matter off again
and turned his thoughts toward drink and
food.

They brought, and in no stingy mood,
the foods and different types of wine,
which were delicious, rich and fine.
340 The squires were able to provide
the lord and young knight at his side
with every course a count, king, queen,
and emperor eat by routine.
At dinner's end, the two men stayed
345 awake and talked, while squires made
the beds and brought them fruit: they ate
the rarest fruits: the nutmeg, date,
fig, clove, and pomegranate red.
With Alexandrian gingerbread,
350 electuaries° at the end,
restoratives, a tonic blend,
and pliris archonticum°
for settling his stomachum.
Then various liqueurs were poured
355 for them to sample afterward:
straight piment,° which did not contain
sweet honey or a single grain
of pepper, wine of mulberries,
clear syrups, other delicacies.
360 The youth's astonishment persisted;
he did not know such things existed.
"Now, my dear friend," the great lord said,
"the time has come to go to bed.
I'll seek my room—don't think it queer—
365 and you will have your bed out here
and may lie down at any hour.
I do not have the slightest power
over my body anymore
and must be carried to my door."
370 Four nimble servants, strongly set,
came in and seized the coverlet
by its four corners (it was spread
beneath the lord, who lay in bed)
and carried him away to rest.
375 The others helped the youthful guest.
As he required, and when he chose,

---

303. legate (leg′it) *n.:* ambassador.

350. electuaries (ē·lek′cho͞o·er′ēz) *n. pl.:* medicinal pastes
formed by combining honey or syrup with drugs.

352. pliris archonticum (plē′ris är·kon′tē·kəm): kind of
electuary.

356. piment *n.:* wine usually flavored with honey and
spice.

they took his clothing off, and hose,°
and put him in a bed with white,
smooth linen sheets; he slept all night
380 at peace until the morning broke.
But when the youthful knight awoke,
he was the last to rise and found
that there was no one else around.
Exasperated and alone,
385 he had to get up on his own.
He made the best of it, arose
and awkwardly drew on his hose
without a bit of help or aid.
He saw his armor had been laid
390 at night against the dais'° head
a little distance from his bed.
When he had armed himself at last,
he walked around the great hall past
the rooms and knocked at every door
395 which opened wide the night before,
but it was useless: juxtaposed,
the doors were tightly locked and closed.
He shouted, called, and knocked outside,
but no one opened or replied.
400 At last the young man ceased to call,
walked to the doorway of the hall,
which opened up, and passed through
          there,
and went on down the castle stair.
His horse was saddled in advance.
405 The young man saw his shield and lance
were leaned against the castle wall
upon the side that faced the hall.
He mounted, searched the castle whole,
but did not find one living soul,
410 one servant, or one squire around.

He hurried toward the gate and found
the men had let the drawbridge down,
so that the knight could leave the town
at any hour he wished to go.
415 His hosts had dropped the drawbridge so
the youth could cross it undeterred.
The squires were sent, the youth inferred,
out to the wood, where they were set
to checking every trap and net.
420 The drawbridge lay across the stream.
He would not wait and formed a scheme
of searching through the woods as well
to see if anyone could tell
about the lance, why it was bleeding,
425 about the grail, whom they were feeding,
and where they carried it in state.
The youth rode through the castle gate
and out upon the drawbridge plank.
Before he reached the other bank,
430 the young man started realizing
the forefeet of his horse were rising.
His horse made one great leap indeed.
Had he not jumped well, man and steed
would have been hurt. His rider swerved
435 to see what happened and observed
the drawbridge had been lifted high.
He shouted, hearing no reply.
"Whoever raised the bridge," said he,
"where are you? Come and talk to me!
440 Say something to me; come in view.
There's something I would ask of you,
some things I wanted to inquire,
some information I desire."
His words were wasted, vain and fond;°
445 no one was willing to respond.

444. fond *adj.:* foolish.

Vocabulary

juxtaposed (juks′tə·pōzd′) *v.* used as *adj.:* placed side
   by side.
undeterred (un·dē·turd′) *adj.* used as *adv.:* unobstructed; without restriction.

377. hose *n.:* tightfitting, stockinglike outer garments worn by men during medieval times.
390. dais (dā′is) *n.:* raised platform.

Response and Analysis

Reading Check

1. Why is Perceval unable to cross the river?
2. What is special about the sword the castle's lord gives to Perceval?
3. What objects are carried in the procession through the hall?
4. How does Perceval plan to find out about the Grail?
5. When Perceval awakes and finds everyone gone, what does he conclude?

Thinking Critically

6. Perceval, following Gornemant's advice not to speak, refrains from asking questions about the strange things he sees during the Grail procession. What comments does the narrator make about Perceval's failure to speak up, and what do these comments reveal about the narrator's judgment of Perceval's behavior? What might the narrator's observations **foreshadow** about the future consequences of Perceval's silence?

7. Medieval **romances** often include mysterious and fantastic events. How is this aspect developed in the *Perceval* excerpt? Are these supernatural elements essential to the plot of the story, or do they merely serve to build atmosphere? Explain.

8. Explain what you think is the meaning of the mysterious Grail procession. What might be the significance of the lance and the Grail?

Extending and Evaluating

9. In medieval tales, heroes often have to pass various kinds of tests. What test does Perceval undergo in this episode? Do you think he passes it? Why or why not?

10. What **moral,** or lesson about life, is implied by the fact that Perceval fails to speak up during the Grail procession and then cannot get answers to his questions the next morning? How does Perceval's failure to ask questions tie in with the experience you wrote about in your Quickwrite?

Literary Criticism

11. One view of *Perceval* is that it represents a conflict between the ideals of Arthurian chivalry and the religious ideals inspired by the quest for the Grail. Considering what you have seen of the conventions of courtly love and chivalry in other works, do you think that the two sets of ideals are incompatible? Explain.

WRITING

Writing a News Report

Later in the story, after leaving the castle, Perceval learns that had he asked about the lance and the Grail, the lord of the castle would have been healed. Perceval vows to find the Grail, but since the poem was left unfinished, the outcome of his quest is unclear. Write a newspaper article or television news script that reports on the final outcome of Perceval's quest. Write in a contemporary journalistic style, using the *5W-How?* method, which answers the questions *who? what? when? where? why?* and *how?* Your report may be serious or humorous.

North Carolina Competency Goal
1.02; 1.03; 4.05; 5.03; 6.01

INTERNET

Projects and Activities
Keyword: LE5 WL-5

SKILLS FOCUS

Literary Skills
Analyze romance.

Writing Skills
Write a newspaper or television report.

Vocabulary Skills
Summarize a narrative using vocabulary words.

Vocabulary Development
Summarizing the Narrative

tempered   juxtaposed

elated   undeterred

forged

Using the Vocabulary words listed above, write a summary of the excerpt from *Perceval.* Not every sentence you write must contain a Vocabulary word. You may use a word more than once.

Grammar Link

Avoiding Misplaced and Dangling Modifiers

Modifiers make sentences lively and specific. Putting a modifier in the wrong place, however, or in a position where it modifies nothing, can make your sentence a riddle or, even worse, an unintended joke. A **misplaced modifier** accidentally modifies the wrong word, usually because the word it is intended to modify is too far away. To avoid this problem, place the modifier as close as possible to the word it should modify.

MISPLACED Perceval is a young knight of the famous King Arthur who doubts his abilities. [Perceval, not King Arthur, doubts his abilities.]

CLEAR Perceval, who doubts his abilities, is a young knight of the famous King Arthur.

While a misplaced modifier modifies the wrong word, a **dangling modifier** does not logically modify *any* word in the sentence. A modifying word, phrase, or clause at the beginning of a sentence should modify the noun or pronoun that comes directly after it. If the modifier does not, you can fix the problem by (1) placing the correct noun or pronoun immediately after the opening modifier, (2) adding words to the modifier to make its meaning clear, or (3) rewriting the entire sentence.

DANGLING Peering from the cliff, the nobleman's castle is not visible at first. [Was the *castle* peering from the cliff?]

CLEAR Peering from the cliff, Perceval cannot see the nobleman's castle at first.

Grammar Skills
Avoid using misplaced and dangling modifiers.

"How about some little pads and pencils?"

PRACTICE

Correct any misplaced or dangling modifiers in the following sentences. You may need to add or change words or rewrite sentences.

1. Cursing, the mysterious fisherman who gives directions perplexes Perceval.

2. Seeing the castle at last, a warm reception has been prepared for Perceval.

3. Perceval marvels at the sumptuous banquet on the table laid out before him.

4. Warned not to speak out of turn, the Grail passes through the hall several times without comment.

5. Perceval resolves at dinner first thing in the morning to ask a squire about the Grail.

Apply to Your Writing

Review a writing assignment you are working on now or have already completed. Revise any sentences to correct misplaced or dangling modifiers. Pay special attention to sentences that begin with a modifying word, phrase, or clause.

▶ **For more help, see Placement of Modifiers, 5g–h, in the Language Handbook.**

The Nibelungenlied

(c. 1200)

Germany

Siegfried Slaying the Dragon (1880) by Konrad Dielitz.

The Nibelungenlied (nē′bə·loon′ən·lēt′), the national epic of Germany, is a gripping tale of love, revenge, and murder. Like *The Song of Roland*, *The Nibelungenlied* consists of materials pieced together from many oral and written sources, both historical and legendary, that were familiar to medieval audiences. The unknown author of the epic transformed these materials into a single, unified work. This author is thought to have lived somewhere near the Danube River in what is now Austria. Scholars generally agree that he composed the poem sometime between the years 1195 and 1205.

A Treasure and a Curse

The title of the epic literally means "song of the Nibelungs." In German myth and literature the Nibelungs were an evil family that possessed an accursed treasure, which included a hoard of gold and a magic ring. The hero of *The Nibelungenlied* is Siegfried (sig′frēd), a prince who lives on the lower Rhine in western Europe. As the epic opens, Siegfried has taken the treasure of the Nibelungs. As a result, he is placed under a curse. Along with the treasure, Siegfried also comes into possession of a cloak that makes its wearer invisible. Armed with these new powers, Siegfried kills a dragon and bathes in its blood. The blood hardens his skin, thereafter protecting him from all wounds. As he bathes, however, a linden leaf falls between his shoulders so that the dragon's blood fails to touch one small spot. Thus, Siegfried is forever vulnerable in that one spot—just as the Greek hero Achilles was vulnerable in his heel.

The Epic's Structure

The Nibelungenlied was originally written as a long narrative poem divided into two parts. In the first half of the epic, Siegfried woos and weds the beautiful Princess Kriemhild (krēm′hilt′), the sister of Gunther (goon′tər), king of Burgundy, an area in what is now southern France. Gunther, in turn, woos a warrior princess of Iceland, Brunhild (broon′hilt′). However, he cannot win her without Siegfried's secret help.

By helping Gunther win Brunhild, Siegfried sows the seeds of his own downfall, for Brunhild later discovers that she had been tricked into marriage, and has Siegfried killed. Kriemhild later takes her own revenge for Siegfried's death, but ultimately she too is killed.

How Siegfried Was Slain

from The Nibelungenlied

Make the Connection

Quickwrite

Betrayal is a key concept in *The Nibelungenlied*. During the Middle Ages, loyalty was one of the supreme virtues and disloyalty one of the greatest wrongs. Think about the issues of loyalty and betrayal. What do they mean to you? Jot down your thoughts.

Literary Focus

Foreshadowing

Foreshadowing is the use of clues in a narrative to hint at what is going to happen later in the plot. To arouse the reader's curiosity and build suspense, a writer often plants clues early. If you have read the excerpts from the *Iliad,* you will recall that Athena appears to Achilles and promises that he will be repaid for Agamemnon's arrogance (see lines 249–251, page 133). Her speech foreshadows Agamemnon's offer of compensation and its payment later in the epic.

As you read the selection from *The Nibelungenlied,* look for clues that point to the outcome of the narrative. Which clues help to build suspense?

> **Foreshadowing** is the use of clues in a narrative to suggest what is to come.
>
> *For more on Foreshadowing, see the Handbook of Literary and Historical Terms.*

North Carolina Competency Goal

1.02; 1.03; 2.01; 3.04; 4.05; 5.01; 5.03; 6.01

INTERNET

Vocabulary Practice
•
Interactive Reading Model

Keyword: LE5 WL-5

SKILLS FOCUS

Literary Skills
Understand foreshadowing.

Reading Skills
Make predictions.

Reading Skills

Making Predictions

When you read, you make **inferences** based on clues in the text and your own knowledge and experience. A **prediction** is a special type of inference—an educated guess about what is to come later. Predictions are not always accurate. As a careful reader, you should compare the predictions you make with what actually happens to determine if you have missed or misread any clues.

As you read, identify clues that suggest or foreshadow what will happen later in the narrative. Then, make predictions based on these clues. Modify your predictions as necessary, and note the details that cause you to change your predictions.

Vocabulary Development

instigation (in′stə·gā′shən) *n.:* urging on to an evil act.

sinister (sin′is·tər) *adj.:* threatening harm or evil.

intrepid (in·trep′id) *adj.:* fearless; extremely brave.

versatile (vʉr′sə·təl) *adj.:* able to do many things.

thwarted (thwôrt·ed) *v.* used as *adj.:* hindered; blocked.

sumptuous (sump′chōō·əs) *adj.:* lavish.

(Opposite) A praying knight in armor (14th century). Stained-glass window.

Castle Armory, Kreuzenstein, Austria.

How Siegfried Was Slain

from **The Nibelungenlied**
translated by **A. T. Hatto**

Characters

Siegfried (sig′frēd): prince of the lower Rhine.

Kriemhild (krēm′hilt′): Siegfried's wife and the sister of King Gunther.

Gunther (gŏon′tər): king of Burgundy.

Hagen (hä′gən): Gunther's chief vassal, or subject.

In order to win Brunhild, a warrior princess of Iceland, Gunther must defeat her in three contests of strength and skill. Using his cloak of invisibility, Siegfried helps Gunther accomplish all three feats. Brunhild yields to Gunther and becomes his bride. Years later, Kriemhild reveals to Brunhild how Siegfried had tricked her. Brunhild enlists Gunther and his vassal Hagen in a plot to kill Siegfried.

As the selection begins, Siegfried is leaving Kriemhild to take part in a hunt. Hagen has tricked Kriemhild into revealing the secret of Siegfried's vulnerable spot.

The fearless warriors Gunther and Hagen treacherously proclaimed a hunt in the forest where they wished to chase the boar, the bear, and the bison—and what could be more daring? Siegfried rode with their party in magnificent style. They took all manner of food with them; and it was while drinking from a cool stream that the hero was to lose his life at the instigation of Brunhild, King Gunther's queen.

Bold Siegfried went to Kriemhild while his and his companions' hunting gear was being

Vocabulary

instigation (in′stə·gā′shən) *n.:* urging on to an evil act.

Hunt in Honour of Emperor Charles V at Torgau Castle by Lucas Cranach the Elder (1472–1553). Museo del Prado, Madrid.

loaded onto the sumpters[1] in readiness to cross the Rhine, and she could not have been more afflicted. "God grant that I may see you well again, my lady," he said, kissing his dear wife, "and that your eyes may see me, too. Pass the time pleasantly with your relations who are so kind to you, since I cannot stay with you at home."

Kriemhild thought of what she had told Hagen, but she dared not mention it and began to lament that she had ever been born. "I dreamt last night—and an ill-omened dream it was—" said lord Siegfried's noble queen, weeping with unrestrained passion, "that two boars chased you over the heath and the flowers were dyed with blood! How can I help weeping so? I stand in great dread of some attempt against your life.—What if we have offended any men who have the power to vent their malice on us? Stay away, my lord, I urge you."

"I shall return in a few days' time, my darling. I know of no people here who bear me any hatred. Your kinsmen without exception wish me well, nor have I deserved otherwise of them."

"It is not so, lord Siegfried. I fear you will come to grief. Last night I had a sinister dream of how two mountains fell upon you and hid you from my sight! I shall suffer cruelly if you go away and leave me." But he clasped the noble woman in his arms and after kissing and caressing her fair person very tenderly, took his leave and went forthwith. Alas, she was never to see him alive again.

They rode away deep into the forest in pursuit of their sport. Gunther and his men were accompanied by numbers of brave knights, but Gernot and Giselher stayed at home. Ahead of the hunt many horses had crossed the Rhine laden with their bread, wine, meat, fish, and

---

1. **sumpters** *n. pl.*: pack animals.

Vocabulary

sinister (sin′is·tər) *adj.*: threatening harm or evil.

various other provisions such as a King of Gunther's wealth is bound to have with him.

The proud and <u>intrepid</u> hunters were told to set up their lodges on a spacious isle in the river on which they were to hunt, at the skirt of the greenwood over towards the spot where the game would have to break cover. Siegfried, too, had arrived there, and this was reported to the King. Thereupon the sportsmen everywhere manned their relays.

"Who is going to guide us through the forest to our quarry, brave warriors?" asked mighty Siegfried.

"Shall we split up before we start hunting here?" asked Hagen. "Then my lords and I could tell who are the best hunters on this foray into the woods. Let us share the huntsmen and hounds between us and each take the direction he likes—and then all honor to him that hunts best!" At this, the hunters quickly dispersed.

"I do not need any hounds," said lord Siegfried, "except for one tracker so well fleshed that he recognizes the tracks which the game leave through the wood: then we shall not fail to find our quarry."

An old huntsman took a good sleuthhound and quickly led the lord to where there was game in abundance. The party chased everything that was roused from its lair, as good hunting men still do today. Bold Siegfried of the Netherlands killed every beast that his hound started, for his hunter was so swift that nothing could elude him. Thus, <u>versatile</u> as he was, Siegfried outshone all the others in that hunt.

The very first kill was when he brought down a strong young tusker,[2] after which he soon chanced on an enormous lion. When his hound had roused it he laid a keen arrow to his bow and shot it so that it dropped in its tracks at the third bound. Siegfried's fellow huntsmen acclaimed him for this shot. Next, in swift succession, he killed a wisent, an elk, four mighty aurochs,[3] and a fierce and monstrous buck—so well mounted was he that nothing, be it hart or hind, could

evade him. His hound then came upon a great boar, and, as this turned to flee, the champion hunter at once blocked his path, bringing him to bay; and when in a trice the beast sprang at the hero in a fury, Siegfried slew him with his sword, a feat no other hunter could have performed with such ease. After the felling of this boar, the tracker was returned to his leash and Siegfried's splendid bag was made known to the Burgundians.

"If it is not asking too much, lord Siegfried," said his companions of the chase, "do leave some of the game alive for us. You are emptying the hills and woods for us today." At this the brave knight had to smile.

There now arose a great shouting of men and clamor of hounds on all sides, and the tumult grew so great that the hills and the forest re-echoed with it—the huntsmen had unleashed no fewer than four and twenty packs! Thus, many beasts had to lose their lives there, since each of these hunters was hoping to bring it about that *he* should be given the high honors of the chase. But when mighty Siegfried appeared beside the campfire there was no chance of that.

The hunt was over, yet not entirely so. Those who wished to go to the fire brought the hides of innumerable beasts, and game in plenty—what loads of it they carried back to the kitchen to the royal retainers! And now the noble King had it announced to those fine hunters that he wished to take his repast, and there was one great blast of the horn to tell them that he was back in camp.

At this, one of Siegfried's huntsmen said: "Sir, I have heard a horn blast telling us to return to our lodges.—I shall answer it." There was much blowing to summon the companions.

"Let us quit the forest, too," said lord Siegfried. His mount carried him at an even pace, and the others hastened away with him but with the noise of their going they started a savage bear, a very fierce beast.

---

2. **tusker** *n.*: wild boar.
3. **wisent** (vē′zənt) *n.* … **aurochs** (ô′räks′) *n.pl.*: terms for European bison and wild oxen.

"I shall give our party some good entertainment," he said over his shoulder. "Loose the hound, for I can see a bear which will have to come back to our lodges with us. It will not be able to save itself unless it runs very fast." The hound was unleashed, and the bear made off at speed. Siegfried meant to ride it down but soon found that his way was blocked and his intention thwarted, while the mighty beast fancied it would escape from its pursuer. But the proud knight leapt from his horse and started to chase it on foot, and the animal, quite off its guard, failed to elude him. And so he quickly caught and bound it, without having wounded it at all—nor could the beast use either claws or teeth on the man. Siegfried tied it to his saddle, mounted his horse, and in his high-spirited fashion led it to the campfire in order to amuse the good knights.

And in what magnificent style Siegfried rode! He bore a great spear, stout of shaft and broad of head; his handsome sword reached down to his spurs; and the fine horn which this lord carried was of the reddest gold. Nor have I ever heard tell of a better hunting outfit: he wore a surcoat of costly black silk and a splendid hat of sable, and you should have seen the gorgeous silken tassels on his quiver, which was covered in panther skin for the sake of its fragrant odor![4] He also bore a bow so strong that apart from Siegfried any who wished to span it would have had to use a rack. His hunting suit was all of otter skin, varied throughout its length with furs of other kinds from whose shining hair clasps of gold gleamed out on either side of this daring lord of the hunt. The handsome sword that he wore was Balmung,[5] a weapon so keen and with such excellent edges that it never failed to bite when swung against a helmet. No wonder this splendid hunter was proud and gay. And (since I am bound to tell you all) know that his quiver was full of good arrows with gold mountings and heads a span in width, so that

any beast they pierced must inevitably soon die.

Thus the noble knight rode along, the very image of a hunting man. Gunther's attendants saw him coming and ran to meet him to take his horse—tied to whose saddle he led a mighty bear! On dismounting, he loosed the bonds from its muzzle and paws, whereupon all the hounds that saw it instantly gave tongue. The beast made for the forest and the people were seized with panic. Affrighted by the tumult, the bear strayed into the kitchen—and how the cooks scuttled from their fire at its approach! Many caldrons were sent flying and many fires were scattered, while heaps of good food lay among the ashes. Lords and retainers leapt from their seats, the bear became infuriated, and the King ordered all the hounds on their leashes to be loosed—and if all had ended well they would have had a jolly day! Bows and spears were no longer left idle, for the brave ones ran towards the bear, yet there were so many hounds in the way that none dared shoot. With the whole mountain thundering with peoples' cries the bear took to flight before the hounds and none could keep up with it but Siegfried, who ran it down and then dispatched it with his sword. The bear was later carried to the campfire, and all who had witnessed this feat declared that Siegfried was a very powerful man.

The proud companions were then summoned to table. There were a great many seated in that meadow. Piles of sumptuous dishes were set before the noble huntsmen, but the butlers who were to pour their wine were very slow to appear. Yet knights could not be better cared for than they and if only no treachery had been lurking in their minds those warriors would have been above reproach.

"Seeing that we are being treated to such a variety of dishes from the kitchen," said lord Siegfried, "I fail to understand why the butlers bring us no wine. Unless we hunters are better looked after, I'll not be a companion of the

---

4. **odor:** It was believed that a panther's hide gave off a pleasant scent that attracted other animals.
5. **Balmung** (bäl'muŋ): In medieval epics, weapons often have names.

Vocabulary

thwarted (thwôrt·ed) v. used as adj.: hindered; blocked.
sumptuous (sump'choo·əs) adj.: lavish.

hunt. I thought I had deserved better attention."

"We shall be very glad to make amends to you for our present lack," answered the perfidious King from his table. "This is Hagen's fault—he wants us to die of thirst."

"My very dear lord," replied Hagen of Troneck, "I thought the day's hunting would be away in the Spessart[6] and so I sent the wine there. If we go without drink today I shall take good care that it does not happen again."

"Damn those fellows!" said lord Siegfried. "It was arranged that they were to bring along seven panniers[7] of spiced wine and mead[8] for me. Since that proved impossible, we should have been placed nearer the Rhine."

"You brave and noble knights," said Hagen of Troneck, "I know a cool spring nearby—do not be offended!—let us go there."—A proposal which (as it turned out) was to bring many knights into jeopardy.

Siegfried was tormented by thirst and ordered the board to be removed all the sooner in his eagerness to go to that spring at the foot of the hills. And now the knights put their treacherous plot into execution.

Word was given for the game which Siegfried had killed to be conveyed back to Worms[9] on wagons, and all who saw it gave him great credit for it.

Hagen of Troneck broke his faith with Siegfried most grievously, for as they were leaving to go to the spreading lime tree he said: "I have often been told that no one can keep up with Lady Kriemhild's lord when he cares to show his speed. I wish he would show it us now."

"You can easily put it to the test by racing me to the brook," replied gallant Siegfried of the Netherlands. "Then those who see it shall declare the winner."

Knight receives a ring from his lady, from the Manness Scroll.

Heidelberg, Germany.

"I accept your challenge," said Hagen.

"Then I will lie down in the grass at your feet, as a handicap," replied brave Siegfried, much to Gunther's satisfaction. "And I will tell you what more I shall do. I will carry all my equipment with me, my spear and my shield and all my hunting clothes." And he quickly strapped on his quiver and sword. The two men took off their outer clothing and stood there in their white vests. Then they ran through the clover like a pair of wild panthers. Siegfried appeared first at the brook.

Gunther's magnificent guest who excelled so many men in all things quickly unstrapped his sword, took off his quiver, and after leaning his great spear against a branch of the lime, stood

---

6. **Spessart** (spes′ərt): mountain range in southern Germany.
7. **panniers** (pan′yərz) *n. pl.:* large baskets for carrying loads on the back.
8. **mead** (mēd) *n.:* alcoholic drink made from honey and water, sometimes mixed with spices, fruit, or malt.
9. **Worms** (vôrmz): city on the Rhine.

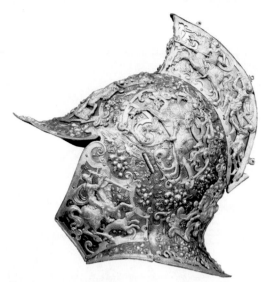

Steel helmet embossed with copper gilt openwork appliqués (Parade burgonet) (1599) from Augsburg.
The Granger Collection, New York.

his sword, and, had he succeeded in doing so, Hagen would have had his pay. But finding no sword, the gravely wounded man had nothing but his shield. Snatching this from the bank he ran at Hagen, and King Gunther's vassal was unable to elude him. Siegfried was wounded to death, yet he struck so powerfully that he sent many precious stones whirling from the shield as it smashed to pieces. Gunther's noble guest would dearly have loved to avenge himself. Hagen fell reeling under the weight of the blow and the riverside echoed loudly. Had Siegfried had his sword in his hand it would have been the end of Hagen, so enraged was the wounded man, as indeed he had good cause to be.

The hero's face had lost its color and he was no longer able to stand. His strength had ebbed away, for in the field of his bright countenance he now displayed Death's token. Soon many fair ladies would be weeping for him.

The lady Kriemhild's lord fell among the flowers, where you could see the blood surging from his wound. Then—and he had cause—he rebuked those who had plotted his foul murder. "You vile cowards," he said as he lay dying. "What good has my service done me now that you have slain me? I was always loyal to you, but now I have paid for it. Alas, you have wronged your kinsmen so that all who are born in days to come will be dishonored by your deed. You have cooled your anger on me beyond all measure. You will be held in contempt and stand apart from all good warriors."

The knights all ran to where he lay wounded to death. It was a sad day for many of them. Those who were at all loyal-hearted mourned for him, and this, as a gay and valiant knight, he had well deserved.

The King of Burgundy too lamented Siegfried's death.

"There is no need for the doer of the deed to weep when the damage is

beside the rushing brook. Then he laid down his shield near the flowing water, and although he was very thirsty he most courteously refrained from drinking until the King had drunk. Gunther thanked him very ill for this.

The stream was cool, sweet, and clear. Gunther stooped to its running waters and after drinking stood up and stepped aside. Siegfried in turn would have liked to do the same, but he paid for his good manners. For now Hagen carried Siegfried's sword and bow beyond his reach, ran back for the spear, and searched for the sign[10] on the brave man's tunic. Then, as Siegfried bent over the brook and drank, Hagen hurled the spear at the cross, so that the hero's heart's blood leapt from the wound and splashed against Hagen's clothes. No warrior will ever do a darker deed. Leaving the spear fixed in Siegfried's heart, he fled in wild desperation, as he had never fled before from any man.

When lord Siegfried felt the great wound, maddened with rage he bounded back from the stream with the long shaft jutting from his heart. He was hoping to find either his bow or

---

10. **sign:** Kriemhild had unwittingly told Hagen that Siegfried was vulnerable in only one spot, between his shoulder blades. Hagen suggested that she sew a cross on Siegfried's clothing so that Hagen would know where to shield him in battle.

Sword of Justice (1693) from Germany

Bequeathed by Mrs. H. E. Tilling. The British Museum, London (1961,2-2,15).

done," said the dying man. "He should be held up to scorn. It would have been better left undone."

"I do not know what you are grieving for," said Hagen fiercely. "All our cares and sorrows are over and done with. We shall not find many who will dare oppose us now. I am glad I have put an end to his supremacy."

"You may well exult," said Siegfried. "But had I known your murderous bent I should easily have guarded my life from you. I am sorry for none so much as my wife, the lady Kriemhild. May God have mercy on me for ever having got a son who in years to come will suffer the reproach that his kinsmen were murderers. If I had the strength I would have good reason to complain. But if you feel at all inclined to do a loyal deed for anyone, noble King," continued the mortally wounded man, "let me commend my dear sweetheart to your mercy. Let her profit from being your sister. By the virtue of all princes, stand by her loyally! No lady was ever more greatly wronged through her dear friend. As to my father and his vassals, they will have long to wait for me."

The flowers everywhere were drenched with blood. Siegfried was at grips with Death, yet not for long, since Death's sword ever was too sharp. And now the warrior who had been so brave and gay could speak no more.

When those lords saw that the hero was dead they laid him on a shield that shone red with gold, and they plotted ways and means of concealing the fact that Hagen had done the deed. "A disaster has befallen us," many of them said. "You must all hush it up and declare with one voice that Siegfried rode off hunting alone and was killed by robbers as he was passing through the forest."

"I shall take him home," said Hagen of Troneck. "It is all one to me if the woman who made Brunhild so unhappy should come to know of it. It will trouble me very little, however much she weeps."

The Death of Siegfried (1924) by Max Slevogt.

Response and Analysis

Reading Check

1. How does Siegfried show his skill as a hunter?

2. How do Hagen and Gunther manage to lure Siegfried alone to the stream?

3. How does Hagen kill Siegfried?

4. How do the hunters plan to conceal the true facts of Siegfried's murder?

Thinking Critically

5. Why do you think King Gunther and his vassal Hagen are willing to carry out Brunhild's revenge on Siegfried? Consider the chivalric code and its emphasis upon loyalty.

6. **Foreshadowing** is the use of clues to hint at what is going to happen later in the plot. What clues at the beginning of the selection help you predict what will happen? How did these clues affect your reading of the story?

7. The bear that Siegfried has captured causes comic disorder before Siegfried dispatches it. What does this humorous scene reveal about Siegfried? Why is this lighthearted mood **ironic**?

8. What is the author's attitude toward the murder of Siegfried? How can you tell?

9. Discuss the various levels of deception in this episode. How do the various characters react to these deceptions? How do their reactions compare to your own feelings about betrayal and loyalty? Look back at your Quickwrite notes for ideas.

WRITING

Analyzing a Foil

A **foil** is a literary character who provides a contrast to another character. Writers often use foils to emphasize certain traits in their heroes. Write a brief essay in which you analyze Hagen as a foil to Siegfried. Which of Siegfried's qualities are highlighted by the contrast to Hagen? Before you write, you may wish to organize your thoughts in a chart like the following one.

	Siegfried	Hagen
Appearance		
Physical strength		
Courage		
Moral sense		
Personality		

Vocabulary Development
Choosing the Right Word

instigation	versatile
sinister	thwarted
intrepid	sumptuous

Answer the following questions with the correct Vocabulary word from the list above.

1. Which word describes a hero?

2. Which word describes someone with multiple talents?

3. Which word describes a lavish meal?

4. Which word means "frustrated"?

5. Which word means "ominous"?

6. Which word describes the act of stirring up a rebellion?

Dante Alighieri
(1265–1321)
Italy

Dante Alighieri (dän′tä ä′lē·gyä′rē) was born in Florence to an old and moderately distinguished family. Little is known about his early life, but one event from his youth stands out. At the age of nine, Dante attended a party at the house of a gentleman named Folco Portinari. There he met and fell in love with Portinari's daughter Beatrice, who was a year younger than Dante. He met Beatrice again nine years later. A misunderstanding developed between them, and before it could be mended, Beatrice died. Dante was heartbroken. He recorded the story of his love for her in the *Vita Nuova (New Life),* a spiritual autobiography containing both prose and verse. Dante later married Gemma Donati (a marriage arranged since their childhoods), but his feelings for Beatrice dominated his emotional and spiritual life for as long as he lived.

From an early age, Dante wrote poetry and associated himself with the literary people of Florence, but his life was not limited to the pursuit of the arts. His era was a time of political turbulence, and Florence was torn by civil war three times during his residence there. He may have participated in the fighting at least once himself. Certainly Dante became deeply involved in the political life of the city, and as an elected official, he sought to end Florence's civil strife, going so far on one occasion as to exile his best friend and some of his wife's relatives because of their part in the conflict. Dante was strongly opposed to the involvement of the pope and the Church in political conflicts. He favored the renewal of a Roman empire to take care of worldly concerns so that the Church could focus solely on spiritual matters.

Dante Writing The Divine Comedy (14th century) by Italian School.
Biblioteca Marciana, Venice, Italy.

In 1301, while Dante was out of Florence on an official mission, the city was seized by his political enemies, and in his absence he was sentenced to die. He never returned to his beloved city and lived the rest of his life in exile. Where he lived and whether he saw his wife and children again after leaving Florence are not known. What is known is that he died in Ravenna, where he is buried, and that during his exile he completed his great poetic achievement, *The Divine Comedy,* which shows the influence of his political beliefs and experiences.

Dante and the Divine Comedy by Domenico di Michelino (1417–1491).

Duomo, Florence, Italy.

Introduction

The Divine Comedy

The Divine Comedy, written between 1308 and 1321, tells of an imaginary journey that takes the Italian poet Dante through Hell, Purgatory, and Paradise. This journey is symbolic of the spiritual quest for salvation. It involves recognizing sin (the journey through Hell), rejecting sin and awaiting redemption (the time in Purgatory), and finally achieving salvation through faith in divine revelation (seeing the light of God in Paradise). During his journey, especially through Hell, Dante encounters historical figures from ancient Rome, characters from classical Greek mythology, and political enemies from his own era. Because of the range of people and experiences on which Dante reflects in *The Divine Comedy,* the work provides a portrait of almost every aspect of medieval life.

Form, Number, and Symbol

Dante constructed his poem in accordance with a special scheme of numbers. The poem contains one hundred **cantos,** or chapters, because the number one hundred is the square of the number ten, regarded in the Middle Ages as the perfect number. The work begins with an introductory canto, and it is then divided equally into three sections of thirty-three cantos each. The whole poem is composed in **tercets** (tur′sits), three-line stanzas, and uses a rhyme scheme called **terza rima** (tert′sə rē′mə). In terza rima the middle line of one tercet rhymes with the first and third lines of the next tercet, creating a strong interlocking pattern of sound and meaning. The English translation by John Ciardi, which you will read, follows the terza rima rhyme scheme used by Dante.

The number three is important in *The Divine Comedy* because of its relation to the Christian Trinity, which is the union of three divine figures—Father, Son, and Holy Spirit—in one God. The poem is divided into three parts: the *Inferno,* the *Purgatorio,* and the *Paradiso.* Dante's spiritual journey takes place over three days, beginning in Hell on Good Friday, the day of Christ's crucifixion, and ending symbolically in Paradise on Easter Sunday. Finally, the entire action of the poem takes place under the guidance of three women: the Virgin Mary, the mother of Christ; Saint Lucia, Dante's patron saint; and Beatrice, who appears toward the end of Dante's journey through Purgatory and leads him into Paradise.

The Role of Virgil

For much of his journey through the *Inferno* and *Purgatorio,* Dante is guided by Virgil, the Roman poet who wrote the *Aeneid* and died nineteen years before the birth of Christ (see page 268). Virgil explains and instructs, and the clarity of his mind is constantly contrasted with Dante's own confusion.

Dante speaks of Virgil with reverence. Yet Dante's Christian beliefs require that Virgil, who had never been baptized, be consigned to the first circle of Hell, along with other "virtuous pagans" from the classical eras of Greece and Rome. Dante's attitude toward Virgil reflects the split between his Christian beliefs and the emerging humanist ideals of the Renaissance. The classical poets Homer, Horace, and Ovid, as well as philosophers and scientists of the pre-Christian age, are all in Hell, yet Dante feels honored when they call him one of their own. For Dante, Virgil is the ultimate symbol of what human reason can achieve without faith. Dante saw reason as limited, however; it is only through faith that Dante can grasp the truth of Paradise.

Beatrice—Dante's Spiritual Guide

Beatrice is Dante's symbol of love and faith. She sends Virgil to guide Dante through Hell and Purgatory. It is she alone who can guide Dante toward salvation and Paradise. The entire journey is expected to turn Dante forever from error, or sin. It is a journey toward truth and grace that is made possible by the love of the woman who first gave Dante a glimpse of spiritual perfection.

Style and Language

Dante's poem avoids the lofty language that was the style reserved in his day for literary epics and tragedies. His language is sparse, direct, and idiomatic, much like the ordinary Italian speech of his time. It was a stroke of genius to use everyday language, or the vernacular, in a poem of such encyclopedic proportions. *The Divine Comedy* is regarded as the finest poetry ever written in Italian. Moreover, the work ranges widely across all levels of imagination and reality.

Before You Read

from the Inferno
from The Divine Comedy

Make the Connection

In your opinion, what are the greatest wrongs that people can commit? Murder? Betrayal? Revenge? If punishments could be made to fit crimes, what would be the appropriate punishment for each of these wrongdoings? Discuss briefly.

Literary Focus
Allegory

An **allegory** is a work in which characters, settings, and events stand for abstract or moral concepts. An allegory can be read on more than one level. The parables in the New Testament, such as "The Prodigal Son" (see page 83), convey lessons about life through allegory by using characters, objects, and events to stand for abstract concepts. In Ovid's *Metamorphoses* (see page 307), the myth "The Four Ages" is sometimes read as an allegory for the decline of civilization.

North Carolina Competency Goal
1.03; 4.05; 5.01; 5.03

go.hrw.com

INTERNET

More About Dante Alighieri
•
Vocabulary Practice

Keyword: LE5 WL-5

An **allegory** is a work in which characters, settings, and events stand for abstract or moral concepts.

For more on Allegory, see the Handbook of Literary and Historical Terms.

SKILLS FOCUS

Literary Skills
Understand allegory.

Reading Skills
Make generalizations.

Reading Skills
Making Generalizations

A **generalization** is a broad conclusion drawn from explicit, or obvious, examples in the text. A generalization is often built on a series of inferences based on specific instances or details. As you read the *Inferno,* pay attention to where different types of sinners have been placed in Hell. What does this arrangement of Hell reveal about Dante's system of morality—his standards of right and wrong?

Background

The first book of *The Divine Comedy,* the *Inferno,* is the best-known and most dramatic of the poem's three parts. Dante travels through the nine levels of Hell—the Inferno—descending slowly farther and farther away from God until he ultimately meets Satan. At each level, Dante meets suffering souls tormented for eternity in ways that fit the sins they committed while alive.

Vocabulary Development

despicable (di·spik'ə·bəl) *adj.:* hateful; abominable.

reprimand (rep'rə·mand') *n.:* rebuke; scolding.

writhes (rīᵗhz) *v.:* squirms in agony; contorts the body.

dexterously (deks'tər·əs·lē) *adv.:* nimbly.

clambered (klam'bərd) *v.:* climbed with difficulty.

(Opposite) Dante running from the three beasts, from Canto I of the *Inferno* (1824–1827). Illustration by William Blake.

National Gallery of Victoria, Melbourne, Australia.

from the Inferno

from The Divine Comedy

Dante Alighieri
translated by John Ciardi

Canto 1

The Dark Wood of Error

Midway in his allotted threescore years and ten, Dante comes to himself with a start and realizes that he has strayed from the True Way into the Dark Wood of Error (Worldliness). As soon as he has realized his loss, Dante lifts his eyes and sees the first light of the sunrise (the Sun is the Symbol of Divine Illumination) lighting the shoulders of a little hill (The Mount of Joy). It is the Easter Season, the time of resurrection, and the sun is in its equinoctial rebirth. This juxtaposition of joyous symbols fills Dante with hope and he sets out at once to climb directly up the Mount of Joy, but almost immediately his way is blocked by the Three Beasts of Worldliness: The Leopard of Malice and Fraud, The Lion of Violence and Ambition, *and* The She-Wolf of Incontinence.

These beasts, and especially the She-Wolf, drive him back despairing into the darkness of error. But just as all seems lost, a figure appears to him. It is the shade of Virgil, Dante's symbol of Human Reason.

Virgil explains that he has been sent to lead Dante from error. There can, however, be no direct ascent past the beasts: the man who would escape them must go a longer and harder way. First he must descend through Hell (The Recognition of Sin), then he must ascend through Purgatory (The Renunciation of Sin), and only then may he reach the pinnacle of joy and come to the Light of God. Virgil offers to guide Dante, but only as far as Human Reason can go. Another guide (Beatrice, symbol of Divine Love) *must take over for the final ascent, for Human Reason is self-limited. Dante submits himself joyously to Virgil's guidance and they set off.*

The Inscription Over the Gate (1824–1827)
by William Blake.

Tate Gallery, London.

Midway in our life's journey,° I went astray
 from the straight road and woke to find myself
3   alone in a dark wood. How shall I say

what wood that was! I never
 saw so drear,
 so rank, so arduous a
 wilderness!
Its very memory gives a
6   shape to fear.

Death could scarce be more
 bitter than that place!
But since it came to good,
 I will recount
9   all that I found revealed there by God's grace.

1–12. In *The Divine Comedy* the dark wood symbolizes worldliness and sin.

❓ How has Dante ended up in the dark wood? What images in these lines convey the horror and confusion that Dante feels in this fearsome place?

---

 1. **Midway . . . journey:** Dante sets the action in 1300, when he was thirty-five.

How I came to it I cannot rightly say,
 so drugged and loose with sleep had I become
12   when I first wandered there from the True Way.

But at the far end of that valley of evil
 whose maze had sapped my very heart with fear
15   I found myself before a little hill

and lifted up my eyes. Its shoulders glowed
 already with the sweet rays of that planet°
18   whose virtue leads men straight on every road,

and the shining strengthened me against the fright
 whose agony had wracked the lake of my heart
21   through all the terrors of that piteous night.

Just as a swimmer, who with his last breath
 flounders ashore from perilous seas, might turn
24   to memorize the wide water of his death—

so did I turn, my soul still fugitive
 from death's surviving image, to stare down
27   that pass that none had ever left alive.

And there I lay to rest from my heart's race
 till calm and breath returned to me. Then rose
30   and pushed up that dead slope at such a pace

each footfall rose above the last. And lo!
 almost at the beginning of the rise
33   I faced a spotted Leopard, all tremor and flow

and gaudy pelt. And it would
   not pass, but stood
 so blocking my every turn
   that time and again
 I was on the verge of turning
36   back to the wood.

This fell at the first widening of the dawn
 as the sun was climbing Aries with those stars
39   that rode with him to light the new creation.°

❓ **33–60.** What three beasts does Dante encounter? What do they force him to do?

---

17. **planet:** the sun, which was thought to be a planet by Ptolemaic astronomers in the ancient world.

37–39. **This fell . . . creation:** Dante awakens in the dark wood just before dawn on Good Friday. His spiritual rebirth begins in the Easter season, the time of the Resurrection of Christ.

Thus the holy hour and the sweet season
 of commemoration did much to arm my fear
42 of that bright murderous beast with their good omen.

Yet not so much but what I shook with dread
 at sight of a great Lion that broke upon me
45 raging with hunger, its enormous head

held high as if to strike a mortal terror
 into the very air. And down his track,
48 a She-Wolf drove upon me, a starved horror

ravening and wasted beyond all belief.
 She seemed a rack for avarice, gaunt and craving.
51 Oh many the souls she has brought to endless grief!

She brought such heaviness upon my spirit
 at sight of her savagery and desperation,
54 I died from every hope of that high summit.

And like a miser—eager in acquisition
 but desperate in self-reproach when Fortune's wheel
57 turns to the hour of his loss—all tears and attrition

I wavered back; and still the beast pursued,
 forcing herself against me bit by bit
60 till I slid back into the sunless wood.

And as I fell to my soul's ruin, a presence
 gathered before me on the discolored air,
63 the figure of one who seemed hoarse from long silence.

At sight of him in that friendless waste I cried:
 "Have pity on me, whatever thing you are,
66 whether shade or living man." And it replied:

"Not man, though man I once was, and my blood
 was Lombard, both my parents Mantuan.
69 I was born, though late, *sub Julio,*° and bred

in Rome under Augustus in the noon
 of the false and lying gods. I was a poet
72 and sang of old Anchises' noble son°

who came to Rome after the burning of Troy.
 But you—why do *you* return to these distresses
75 instead of climbing that shining Mount of Joy

---

69. *sub Julio:* in the reign of Julius Caesar.
72. Anchises' (an·kī′sēz′) **noble son:** Aeneas, hero
 of the *Aeneid;* according to legend, he was the
 founder of Rome.

---

which is the seat and first cause of man's bliss?"
 "And are you then that Virgil and that fountain
78 of purest speech?" My voice grew tremulous:

"Glory and light of poets!
 now may that zeal
and love's apprenticeship
 that I poured out
on your heroic verses
81 serve me well!

For you are my true master
 and first author,
the sole maker from
 whom I drew the breath
of that sweet style whose
 measures have brought
84 me honor.

See there, immortal sage, the beast I flee.
 For my soul's salvation, I beg you, guard me from her,
87 for she has struck a mortal tremor through me."

And he replied, seeing my soul in tears:
 "He must go by another way who would escape
90 this wilderness, for that mad beast that fleers

before you there, suffers no man to pass.
 She tracks down all, kills all, and knows no glut,
93 but, feeding, she grows hungrier than she was.

She mates with any beast, and will mate with more
 before the Greyhound comes to hunt her down.
96 He will not feed on lands nor loot, but honor

and love and wisdom will make straight his way.
 He will rise between Feltro and Feltro,° and in him
99 shall be the resurrection and new day

of that sad Italy for which Nisus died,
 and Turnus, and Euryalus, and the maid Camilla.°
102 He shall hunt her through every nation of sick pride

79–87. Keep in mind that Virgil, whom Dante much admired, is the writer of the *Aeneid,* the epic poem that depicts the founding of Rome. Dante sees Virgil as a symbol of human reason.

? *Why is Virgil an appropriate symbol of human reason?*

---

98. Feltro and Feltro: Can Grande della Scala
 (1290–1329) was an Italian leader born in
 Verona, which is situated between Feltre and
 Montefeltro.
100–101. Nisus . . . Turnus . . . Euryalus . . . Camilla:
 When Aeneas led the Trojans into Italy, these
 figures were killed in a war between the Trojans
 and the Latins.

till she is driven back forever to Hell
    whence Envy first released her on the world.
105   Therefore, for your own good, I think it well

you follow me and I will be your guide
    and lead you forth through an eternal place.
108   There you shall see the ancient spirits tried

in endless pain, and hear their lamentation
    as each bemoans the second death of souls.°
111   Next you shall see upon a burning mountain°

souls in fire and yet content in
    fire,
    knowing that whensoever it
    may be
they yet will mount into the
114   blessed choir.

> **105–114.** Virgil offers to lead Dante into Hell and Purgatory.
>
> **?** Why does Virgil counsel Dante to follow him?

---

110. second death of souls: damnation.
111. burning mountain: the mountain Purgatory.

To which, if it is still your
    wish to climb,
    a worthier spirit shall be
    sent to guide you.
With her shall I leave you,
117   for the King of Time,

who reigns on high, forbids
    me to come there
since, living, I rebelled
    against his law.
120   He rules the waters and the land and air

and there holds court, his city and his throne.
    Oh blessed are they he chooses!" And I to him:
123   "Poet, by that God to you unknown,

lead me this way. Beyond this present ill
    and worse to dread, lead me to Peter's gate
126   and be my guide through the sad halls of Hell."

And he then: "Follow." And he moved ahead
in silence, and I followed where he led.

> **115–119.** Virgil explains that he cannot lead Dante into Heaven because he is forbidden to go there.
>
> **?** Why might "a worthier spirit" be allowed to lead Dante into Heaven whereas Virgil cannot?

Canto 3

The Vestibule of Hell

The Opportunists

The Poets pass the Gate of Hell and are immediately assailed by cries of anguish. Dante sees the first of the souls in torment. They are The Opportunists, *those souls who in life were neither for good nor evil but only for themselves. Mixed with them are those outcasts who took no sides in the Rebellion of the Angels. They are neither in Hell nor out of it. Eternally unclassified, they race round and round pursuing a wavering banner that runs forever before them through the dirty air; and as they run they are pursued by swarms of wasps and hornets, who sting them and produce a constant flow of blood and putrid matter which trickles down the bodies of the sinners and is feasted upon by loathsome worms and maggots who coat the ground.*

The law of Dante's Hell is the law of symbolic retribution. As they sinned so are they punished. They took no sides, therefore they are given no place. As they pursued the ever-shifting illusion of their own advantage, changing their courses with every changing wind, so they pursue eternally an elusive, ever-shifting banner. As their sin was a darkness, so they move in darkness. As their own guilty conscience pursued them, so they are pursued by swarms of wasps and hornets. And as their actions were a moral filth, so they run eternally through the filth of worms and maggots which they themselves feed.

Dante recognizes several, among them Pope Celestine V, *but without delaying to speak to any of these souls, the Poets move on to* Acheron, *the first of the rivers of Hell. Here the newly-arrived souls of the damned gather and wait for monstrous* Charon *to ferry them over to punishment. Charon recognizes Dante as a living man and angrily refuses him passage. Virgil forces Charon to serve them, but Dante swoons with terror, and does not reawaken until he is on the other side.*

i qua & a turbo fpirit · Ein
tung; inuenitur aliquod co
duob; contigue renicatur o
n contraria feparata inueniat.

notabile nos admonet uix fidem · ut in
tantes infernum nung; funt in pretio
euitur · Et ideo by pmo thebaidos dicit
Gratius istam portam ee irremeabile · ex

Detail of Hell with a commentary (14th century) by Fra Guidone de Pisa,
from an Italian manuscript of the *Divine Comedy*.

Musée Condé, Chantilly, France (Folio 50R. MS. 597).

I AM THE WAY INTO THE CITY OF WOE.
I AM THE WAY TO A FORSAKEN PEOPLE.
3   I AM THE WAY INTO ETERNAL SORROW.

SACRED JUSTICE MOVED MY ARCHITECT.
I WAS RAISED HERE BY DIVINE OMNIPOTENCE,
6   PRIMORDIAL LOVE AND ULTIMATE INTELLECT.

ONLY THOSE ELEMENTS TIME CANNOT WEAR
WERE MADE BEFORE ME, AND BEYOND TIME I STAND.°
9   ABANDON ALL HOPE YE WHO ENTER HERE.°

These mysteries I read cut
    into stone
      above a gate. And turning I
      said: "Master,
    what is the meaning of
12   this harsh inscription?"

And he then as initiate to novice:°
    "Here must you put by all
      division of spirit
15   and gather your soul against all cowardice.

> **1–18.** Virgil advises Dante that he cannot have any "division of spirit" if he wishes to withstand the experience of Hell.
>
> **?** *What do you think is the meaning of "division of spirit" in line 14?*

8. **BEYOND TIME I STAND:** punishment of sin is endless.
9. **YE WHO ENTER HERE:** the damned.
13. **as initiate to novice:** as one who has been instructed to one who has not.

This is the place I told you to expect.
    Here you shall pass among the fallen people,
18   souls who have lost the good of intellect."

So saying, he put forth his hand to me,
    and with a gentle and encouraging smile
21   he led me through the gate of mystery.

Here sighs and cries and wails coiled and recoiled
    on the starless air, spilling my soul to tears.
    A confusion of tongues and monstrous accents
24   toiled

in pain and anger. Voices hoarse and shrill
    and sounds of blows, all intermingled, raised
27   tumult and pandemonium that still

whirls on the air forever dirty with it
    as if a whirlwind sucked at sand. And I,
30   holding my head in horror, cried: "Sweet Spirit,

what souls are these who run through this black haze?"
    And he to me: "These are
      the nearly soulless
    whose lives concluded
33   neither blame nor praise.

> **?** **32–36.** *What two kinds of souls are found together here, according to Virgil?*

They are mixed here with that despicable corps
   of angels who were neither for God nor Satan,
36   but only for themselves. The High Creator

scourged them from Heaven for its perfect beauty,
   and Hell will not receive them since the wicked
39   might feel some glory over them." And I:

"Master, what gnaws at them so hideously
   their lamentation stuns the very air?"
42   "They have no hope of death," he answered me,

"and in their blind and
   unattaining state
their miserable lives have
   sunk so low
45   that they must envy every other fate.

> **42–45.** Why would the souls of the uncommitted be envious of death?

No word of them survives their living season.
   Mercy and Justice deny them even a name.
48   Let us not speak of them: look, and pass on."

I saw a banner there upon the mist.
   Circling and circling, it seemed to scorn all pause.
51   So it ran on, and still behind it pressed

a never-ending rout of souls in pain.
   I had not thought death had undone so many
54   as passed before me in that mournful train.

And some I knew among them; last of all
   I recognized the shadow of that soul
57   who, in his cowardice, made the Great Denial.°

At once I understood for certain: these
   were of that retrograde and faithless crew
60   hateful to God and to His enemies.

These wretches never born and never dead
   ran naked in a swarm of wasps and hornets
63   that goaded them the more the more they fled,

and made their faces stream with bloody gouts
   of pus and tears that dribbled to their feet
   to be swallowed there by loathsome worms
66   and maggots.

56–57. I . . . Great Denial: This reference is generally believed to be to Pope Celestine V. Fearing that his own soul would be corrupted by worldliness, he abdicated in favor of Pope Boniface VIII, who became a political enemy of Dante's and represented the secularization of the Church.

Then looking onward I made
   out a throng
assembled on the beach of a
   wide river,
whereupon I turned to him:
69   "Master, I long

to know what souls these are,
   and what strange usage
makes them as eager to cross
   as they seem to be
in this infected light." At
72   which the Sage:

> **67–78.** In response to Dante's question about the souls gathered on the beach, Virgil tells Dante that he will learn about them when they reach Acheron.
>
> **?** Why does Dante turn his eyes downward and feel ashamed after Virgil's response?

"All this shall be made known to you when we stand
   on the joyless beach of Acheron."° And I
75   cast down my eyes, sensing a reprimand

in what he said, and so walked at his side
   in silence and ashamed until we came
78   through the dead cavern to that sunless tide.

There, steering toward us in an ancient ferry
   came an old man° with a white bush of hair,
81   bellowing: "Woe to you depraved souls! Bury

here and forever all hope of Paradise:
   I come to lead you to the other shore,
84   into eternal dark, into fire and ice.

And you who are living yet, I say begone
   from these who are dead." But when he saw
   me stand
87   against his violence he began again:

"By other windings and by other steerage
   shall you cross to that other shore. Not here!
   Not here!
90   A lighter craft than mine must give you passage."

---

74. Acheron (ak′ər·än′): in Greek mythology, the river of woe in the Underworld; dead souls are ferried across the river to Hades.

80. an old man: in Greek mythology, Charon, (ker′ən), the ferryman who carries the dead to Hades.

Vocabulary

despicable (di·spik′ə·bəl) *adj.*: hateful; abominable.

reprimand (rep′rə·mand′) *n.*: rebuke; scolding.

And my Guide to him: "Charon, bite back your spleen:
  this has been willed where what is willed must be,
93 and is not yours to ask what it may mean."

The steersman of that marsh
  of ruined souls,
who wore a wheel of flame
  around each eye,
stifled the rage that shook
96 his woolly jowls.

94–99. Charon is described as having flames around each eye, a harsh voice, and a deep rage within him.

? What effect does Charon have on the spirits he leads to shore? How do you know?

But those unmanned and
  naked spirits there
turned pale with fear and
  their teeth began to chatter
99 at sound of his crude bellow. In despair

they blasphemed God, their parents, their time on
  earth, the race of Adam, and the day and the
  hour and the place and the seed and the womb
102 that gave them birth.

But all together they drew to that grim shore
  where all must come who lose the fear of God.
105 Weeping and cursing they come for evermore,

and demon Charon with eyes like burning coals
  herds them in, and with a whistling oar
108 flails on the stragglers to his wake of souls.

As leaves in autumn loosen and stream down
  until the branch stands bare above its tatters
111 spread on the rustling ground, so one by one

the evil seed of Adam in its Fall
  cast themselves, at his signal, from the shore
114 and streamed away like birds who hear their call.

So they are gone over that shadowy water,
  and always before they reach the other shore
117 a new noise stirs on this, and new throngs gather.

"My son," the courteous Master said to me,
  "all who die in the shadow of God's wrath
120 converge to this from every clime and country.

And all pass over eagerly, for here
  Divine Justice transforms and spurs them so
123 their dread turns wish: they yearn for what they fear.°

_____
122–123. **Divine Justice ... fear:** The damned have actually chosen Hell. They have free will and the power to sin or not to sin.

Scene from Dante's _Inferno_ (detail) (15th century) by Guiniforte delli Bargigi, Italy.
Bibliothèque Nationale, Paris, France (Ms. 2017, f.245).

No soul in Grace comes ever to this crossing;
  therefore if Charon rages at your presence
126 you will understand the reason for his cursing."

When he had spoken, all the twilight country
  shook so violently, the terror of it
129 bathes me with sweat even in memory:

the tear-soaked ground gave
  out a sigh of wind
that spewed itself in flame
  on a red sky,
and all my shattered senses
132 left me. Blind,

132–134. Dante faints at the conclusion of this canto.

? What causes Dante to swoon?

like one whom sleep comes over in a swoon,
I stumbled into darkness and went down.

Paolo and Francesca da Rimini (detail) (1867)
by Dante Gabriel Rossetti.

National Gallery of Victoria, Melbourne, Australia (Felton Bequest).

Canto 5

Circle Two   *The Carnal*

The Poets leave Limbo and enter the Second Circle.
*Here begin the torments of Hell proper, and here,
blocking the way, sits* Minos, *the dread and semibestial judge of the damned who assigns to each
soul its eternal torment. He orders the Poets back;
but Virgil silences him as he earlier silenced
Charon, and the Poets move on.*

*They find themselves on a dark ledge swept by a
great whirlwind, which spins within it the souls of
the* Carnal, *those who betrayed reason to their
appetites. Their sin was to abandon themselves to
the tempest of their passions: so they are swept forever in the tempest of Hell, forever denied the light
of reason and of God. Virgil identifies many among
them.* Semiramis *is there, and* Dido, Cleopatra,
Helen, Achilles, Paris, *and* Tristan. *Dante sees*
Paolo *and* Francesca *swept together, and in the
name of love he calls to them to tell their sad story.
They pause from their eternal flight to come to him,
and Francesca tells their history while Paolo weeps
at her side. Dante is so stricken by compassion at
their tragic tale that he swoons once again.*

So we went down to the second ledge° alone;
   a smaller circle of so much greater pain
3   the voice of the damned rose in a bestial moan.

There Minos° sits, grinning,
    grotesque, and hale.
   He examines each lost
    soul as it arrives
   and delivers his verdict
6   with his coiling tail.

> **? 4–12.** *How does
> a condemned
> soul learn which circle
> of Hell he or she will
> be placed in?*

That is to say, when the ill-fated soul
   appears before him it confesses all,
9   and that grim sorter of the dark and foul

decides which place in Hell shall be its end,
   then wraps his twitching tail about himself
12   one coil for each degree it must descend.

The soul descends and others take its place:
   each crowds in its turn to judgment, each confesses,
15   each hears its doom and falls away through space.

"O you who come into this camp of woe,"
   cried Minos when he saw me turn away
   without awaiting his judgment, "watch where
18   you go

once you have entered here, and to whom you turn!
   Do not be misled by that wide and easy passage!"
21   And my Guide to him: "That is not your concern;

it is his fate to enter every door.
   This has been willed where what is willed must be,
24   and is not yours to question. Say no more."

Now the choir of anguish, like a wound,
   strikes through the tortured air. Now I have come
27   to Hell's full lamentation, sound beyond sound.

I came to a place stripped bare of every light
   and roaring on the naked dark like seas
30   wracked by a war of winds. Their hellish flight

---

1. **second ledge:** In keeping with a concept borrowed from Aristotle, Dante places the sins of the
flesh in the upper circles of Hell, where punishment is mildest; the sins of anger in the middle circles; and the sins resulting from an abuse of reason
in the lowest circles, where the torment is greatest.
4. **Minos** (mī′näs′): semibestial judge of the damned;
Minos, the son of Europa and Zeus, is also one of
the judges of Hades in classical Greek mythology.

of storm and counterstorm
        through time foregone,
sweeps the souls of the
        damned before its charge.
Whirling and battering it
33   drives them on,

and when they pass the
        ruined gap of Hell
through which we had
        come, their shrieks begin anew.
36   There they blaspheme the power of God eternal.

And this, I learned, was the never ending flight
        of those who sinned in the flesh, the carnal and lusty
39   who betrayed reason to their appetite.

As the wings of wintering starlings bear them on
        in their great wheeling flights, just so the blast
42   wherries these evil souls through time foregone.

Here, there, up, down, they whirl and, whirling, strain
        with never a hope of hope to comfort them,
45   not of release, but even of less pain.

As cranes go over sounding their harsh cry,
        leaving the long streak of their flight in air,
48   so come these spirits, wailing as they fly.

And watching their shadows lashed by wind, I cried:
        "Master, what souls are these the very air
51   lashes with its black whips from side to side?"

"The first of these whose
        history you would know,"
he answered me, "was
        Empress of many tongues.
Mad sensuality corrupted
54   her so

that to hide the guilt of her
        debauchery
she licensed all depravity
        alike,
and lust and law were one
57   in her decree.

She is Semiramis° of whom the tale is told
        how she married Ninus and succeeded him
60   to the throne of that wide land the Sultans hold.

---

58. Semiramis (si·mir′ə·mis): legendary queen of
Assyria.

> **28–39.** Dante learns that the souls of people whose appetites determined their actions are swept into a whirlwind in Hell.
>
> **?** *Considering the reason that these souls are banished to Hell, what do you think the whirlwind symbolizes?*

> **58–67.** You may be familiar with another epic list or catalog (the convention Dante uses here) from reading the *Iliad* or the *Aeneid*. This list presents famous figures from legend and literature who were known for their sins of passion.
>
> **?** *What message does Dante intend to convey to the reader by presenting this epic list?*

The other is Dido;° faithless to the ashes
        of Sichaeus, she killed herself for love.
63   The next whom the eternal tempest lashes

is sense-drugged Cleopatra. See Helen there,
        from whom such ill arose. And great Achilles,°
66   who fought at last with love in the house of prayer.

And Paris. And Tristan."° As they whirled above
        he pointed out more than a thousand shades
69   of those torn from the mortal life by love.

I stood there while my Teacher one by one
        named the great knights and ladies of dim time;
72   and I was swept by pity and confusion.

At last I spoke: "Poet, I should be glad
        to speak a word with those two° swept together
75   so lightly on the wind and still so sad."

And he to me: "Watch them. When next they pass,
        call to them in the name of love that drives
        and damns them here. In that name they will
78   pause."

Thus, as soon as the wind in its wild course
        brought them around, I called: "O wearied souls!
81   if none forbid it, pause and speak to us."

As mating doves that love calls to their nest
        glide through the air with motionless raised wings,
84   borne by the sweet desire that fills each breast—

---

61. Dido (dī′dō): queen of Carthage who vowed to be
true to her dead husband, Sichaeus, but broke her
vow when she fell in love with Aeneas; after Aeneas
abandoned her, Dido threw herself on a funeral pyre.

65. Achilles: great Greek warrior who deserted his
army in order to marry Polyxena (pō·lik′sē·nə), a
Trojan princess; Achilles was killed by Paris, a
Trojan warrior, when he went to the temple for
the wedding.

67. Tristan: In medieval legend, Tristan fell in love
with Iseult (i·sōōlt′), a young princess betrothed
to his uncle, King Mark of Cornwall. Eventually
both lovers died on the same day (see page 618).

74. those two: Paolo (pä′ô·lô) and Francesca
(frän·ches′kä); Francesca da Rimini, a niece of
Dante's patron, had been murdered with her
lover, Paolo Malatesta, by her husband, Giovanni
(who was also Paolo's brother), when he found
the lovers together.

Just so those spirits turned on the torn sky
  from the band where Dido whirls across the air;
87 such was the power of pity in my cry.

"O living creature, gracious, kind, and good,
  going this pilgrimage through the sick night,
90 visiting us who stained the earth with blood,

were the King of Time our friend, we would pray
    His peace
  on you who have pitied us. As long as the wind
93 will let us pause, ask of us what you please.

The town where I was born lies by the shore
  where the Po descends into its ocean rest
96 with its attendant streams in one long murmur.

Love, which in gentlest hearts will soonest bloom
  seized my lover with passion for that sweet body
99 from which I was torn unshriven to my doom.

Love, which permits no loved one not to love,
  took me so strongly with delight in him
102 that we are one in Hell, as we were above.

Love led us to one death. In the depths of Hell
  Caina° waits for him who took our lives."
105 This was the piteous tale they stopped to tell.

And when I had heard those world-offended lovers
  I bowed my head. At last the Poet spoke:
  "What painful thoughts are these your lowered
108   brow covers?"

When at length I answered, I began: "Alas!
  What sweetest thoughts, what green and young
    desire
111 led these two lovers to this sorry pass."

Then turning to those spirits once again,
  I said: "Francesca, what you suffer here
114 melts me to tears of pity and of pain.

But tell me: in the time of your sweet sighs
  by what appearances found love the way
117 to lure you to his perilous paradise?"

---

104. Caina: level of Hell reserved for murderers of
kin; named for Cain, the son of Adam and Eve,
who killed his brother Abel.

And she: "The double grief of a lost bliss
  is to recall its happy hour in pain.
120 Your Guide and Teacher knows the truth of this.

But if there is indeed a soul in Hell
  to ask of the beginning of our love
123 out of his pity, I will weep and tell:

On a day for dalliance we read the rhyme
  of Lancelot,° how love had mastered him.
  We were alone with
126   innocence and dim time.

Pause after pause that high
    old story drew
  our eyes together while we
    blushed and paled;
129 but it was one soft passage overthrew

> **124–133.**
> What effect did
> reading about Lancelot
> have on Francesca and
> Paolo? What conse-
> quences do they suffer
> as a result?

our caution and our hearts. For when we read
  how her fond smile was kissed by such a lover,
132 he who is one with me alive and dead

breathed on my lips the tremor of his kiss.
  That book, and he who wrote it,° was a pander.
135 That day we read no further." As she said this,

the other spirit, who stood by her, wept
  so piteously, I felt my senses reel
138 and faint away with anguish. I was swept

by such a swoon as death is,
    and I fell,
as a corpse might fall, to the
    dead floor of Hell.

> **138–140.** Dante
> faints at the conclu-
> sion of this canto.
>
> What causes
> Dante to faint in
> this instance?

---

125. Lancelot: In the medieval legends of King
Arthur, Lancelot fell in love with Guinevere,
Arthur's queen, and their love led to the down-
fall of the knights of the Round Table.

134. he who wrote it: In an old French version of
the romance of Lancelot, it is the character
called Gallehaut who urges on the secret lovers
Lancelot and Guinevere. The Italian for Gallehaut is *Galeotto,* which is also the word meaning
"pander," that is, a go-between for lovers, one
who urges on the passions between secret
lovers. The book was thus a kind of "pander"
between Paolo and Francesca.

The centre of Hell; Lucifer in the ice of Giudecca (c.1438–1444).
Detail from *The Divine Comedy: Inferno* by Dante Alighieri. Sienna, Italy.
British Library, London.

Dante and Virgil continue to descend deeper and deeper into Hell, encountering increasingly horrible sins and their corresponding punishments. Near the end of Canto 32, Dante, having reached the frigid ninth circle of Hell, encounters two souls squeezed into the same icy hole. One sinner is chewing on the head of the other. Dante asks the first soul why he is devouring the other, offering to tell the sinner's story to the world. In Canto 33, Dante learns the gruesome history of Count Ugolino and Bishop Ruggieri, both Dante's contemporaries in thirteenth-century Italy.

Canto 34

Ninth Circle: Cocytus

Round Four: Judecca

The Center

Compound Fraud

The Treacherous to Their Masters

Satan

"*On march the banners of the King,*" Virgil begins as the Poets face the last depth. He is quoting a medieval hymn, and to it he adds the distortion and perversion of all that lies about him. "*On march the banners of the King—of Hell.*" And there before them, in an infernal parody of Godhead, they see Satan in the distance, his great wings beating like a windmill. It is their beating that is the source of the icy wind of Cocytus, the exhalation of all evil.

All about him in the ice are strewn the sinners of the last round, Judecca, *named for Judas Iscariot.* These are the Treacherous to Their Masters. *They lie completely sealed in the ice, twisted and distorted into every conceivable posture. It is impossible to speak to them, and the Poets move on to observe Satan.*

He is fixed into the ice at the center to which flow all the rivers of guilt; and as he beats his great wings as if to escape, their icy wind only freezes him more surely into the polluted ice. In a grotesque parody of the Trinity, he has three faces, each a different color, and in each mouth he clamps a sinner whom he rips eternally with his teeth. *Judas Iscariot is in the central mouth:* Brutus *and* Cassius *in the mouths on either side.*

Having seen all, the Poets now climb through the center, grappling hand over hand down the hairy flank of Satan himself—a last supremely symbolic action—and at last, when they have passed the center of all gravity, they emerge from Hell. A long climb from the earth's center to the Mount of Purgatory awaits them, and they push on without rest, ascending along the sides of the river Lethe, till they emerge once more to see the stars of Heaven, just before dawn on Easter Sunday.

The Judecca, Lucifer (19th century) by Gustave Doré.

"On march the banners of the
King of Hell,"°
my Master said. "Toward us.
Look straight ahead:
can you make him° out at

3   the core of the frozen shell?"

Like a whirling windmill seen
afar at twilight,
or when a mist has risen from the ground—

6   just such an engine rose upon my sight

1–12. Dante enters the last circle of Hell and sees the fearsome sight of Satan.

? *According to Dante, what is this final circle of Hell like?*

stirring up such a wild and bitter wind
I cowered for shelter at my Master's back,

9   there being no other windbreak I could find.

I stood now where the souls of the last class
(with fear my verses tell it) were covered wholly;

12   they shone below the ice like straws in glass.

Some lie stretched out; others are fixed in place
upright, some on their heads, some on their soles;

15   another, like a bow, bends foot to face.

When we had gone so far across the ice
that it pleased my Guide to show me the foul
creature

18   that once had worn the grace of Paradise,

---

1. **On march . . . Hell:** Virgil is deliberately distorting
    the words of a medieval hymn that was written to
    celebrate the Holy Cross.
3. **him:** Satan.

he made me stop, and, stepping aside, he said:
    "Now see the face of Dis!° This is the place
21   where you must arm your soul against all dread."

Do not ask, Reader, how my blood ran cold
    and my voice choked up
      with fear. I cannot write it:
    this is a terror that cannot
24   be told.

22–27. Why does Dante ask the reader to "imagine for yourself what I became"?

I did not die, and yet I lost life's breath:
    imagine for yourself what I became,
27   deprived at once of both my life and death.

The Emperor of the Universe of Pain
    jutted his upper chest above the ice;
30   and I am closer in size to the great mountain

the Titans° make around the central pit,
    than they to his arms. Now, starting from this part,
33   imagine the whole that corresponds to it!

If he was once as beautiful as now
    he is hideous, and still turned on his Maker,
36   well may he be the source of every woe!

With what a sense of awe I saw his head
    towering above me! for it had three faces:
39   one was in front, and it was fiery red;

the other two, as weirdly wonderful,
    merged with it from the middle of each shoulder
    to the point where all converged at the top of
42   the skull;

the right was something between white and bile;
    the left was about the color one observes
45   on those who live along the banks of the Nile.

Under each head two wings rose terribly,
    their span proportioned to so gross a bird:
48   I never saw such sails upon the sea.

---

20. Dis (dis): Satan; in Greek mythology, the god of the Underworld; also, the realm of the dead.
31. Titans (tīt′nz): in Greek mythology, a family of gods overthrown by Zeus and the Olympians and confined to Tartarus, the region below Hades.

They were not feathers—their texture and their form
    were like a bat's wings—and he beat them so
51   that three winds blew from him in one great storm:

it is these winds that freeze all Cocytus.°
    He wept from his six eyes, and down three chins
54   the tears ran mixed with bloody froth and pus.°

In every mouth he worked a broken sinner
    between his rake-like teeth.
      Thus he kept three
    in eternal pain at his eternal
57   dinner.

37–57. How many faces does Satan have, and what colors are they? What are his wings like? What is his "eternal dinner"?

For the one in front the biting seemed to play
    no part at all compared to the ripping: at times
60   the whole skin of his back was flayed away.

"That soul that suffers most," explained my Guide,
    "is Judas Iscariot,° he who kicks his legs
63   on the fiery chin and has his head inside.

Of the other two, who have their heads thrust forward,
    the one who dangles down from the black face
66   is Brutus:° note how he <u>writhes</u> without a word.

And there, with the huge and sinewy arms, is the soul
    of Cassius.°—But the night
    is coming on
    and we must go, for we
69   have seen the whole."

61–68. Who are the three sinners being chewed by Satan? What sin have these greatest of all sinners committed?

---

52. Cocytus (kō·sīt′əs): one of the six rivers of the Underworld.
54. bloody froth and pus: the grisly result of chewing sinners.
62. Judas Iscariot (jōō′dəs is·ker′ē·ət): disciple who betrayed Jesus.
66. Brutus: one of the Roman conspirators who assassinated Julius Caesar.
68. Cassius (kash′əs): Brutus's co-conspirator.

Vocabulary

writhes (rīthz) v.: squirms in agony; contorts the body.

Then, as he bade, I clasped his neck, and he,
   watching for a moment when the wings
72   were opened wide, reached over <u>dexterously</u>

and seized the shaggy coat of the king demon;
   then grappling matted hair and frozen crusts
75   from one tuft to another, <u>clambered</u> down.

When we had reached the joint where the great thigh
   merges into the swelling of the haunch,
78   my Guide and Master, straining terribly,

turned his head to where his feet had been
   and began to grip the hair as if he were climbing;
81   so that I thought we moved toward Hell again.

"Hold fast!" my Guide said, and his breath came shrill
   with labor and exhaustion. "There is no way
   but by such stairs to rise
84   above such evil."

> **?** **84.** *What are the "stairs" to which Virgil refers?*

At last he climbed out
      through an opening
   in the central rock, and he seated me on the rim;
87   then joined me with a nimble backward spring.

I looked up, thinking to see Lucifer°
   as I had left him, and I saw instead
90   his legs projecting high into the air.

Now let all those whose dull minds are still vexed
   by failure to understand what point it was
   I had passed through, judge
93   if I was perplexed.

> **?** **93.** *What is Dante perplexed by?*

"Get up. Up on your feet," my Master said.
   "The sun already mounts to middle tierce,°
96   and a long road and hard climbing lie ahead."

It was no hall of state we had found there,
   but a natural animal pit hollowed from rock
99   with a broken floor and a close and sunless air.

"Before I tear myself from the Abyss,"
   I said when I had risen, "O my Master,
102   explain to me my error in all this:

---

88. Lucifer (lōō′sə·fər): Satan.
95. middle tierce: 7:30 A.M.

where is the ice? and Lucifer—how has he
   been turned from top to bottom: and how can
      the sun
105   have gone from night to day so suddenly?"

And he to me: "You imagine you are still
   on the other side of the center where I grasped
108   the shaggy flank of the Great Worm of Evil

which bores through the world—you *were* while
   I climbed down,
   but when I turned myself about, you passed
111   the point to which all gravities are drawn.

You are under the other hemisphere where you stand;
   the sky above us is the half opposed
114   to that which canopies the great dry land.

Under the midpoint of that
      other sky
   the Man° who was born
      sinless and who lived
   beyond all blemish, came to
117   suffer and die.

> **?** **115–117.** *Why do you think Dante mentions Christ at this point in the poem?*

You have your feet upon a little sphere
   which forms the other face of the Judecca.°
120   There it is evening when it is morning here.

And this gross Fiend and Image of all Evil
   who made a stairway for us with his hide
123   is pinched and prisoned in the ice-pack still.

On this side he plunged down from heaven's height,
   and the land that spread here once hid in the sea
126   and fled North to our hemisphere for fright;

and it may be that moved by that same fear,
   the one peak° that still rises on this side
129   fled upward leaving this great cavern here."

---

116. the Man: Christ.
119. Judecca: level of Hell named for Judas Iscariot, who betrayed Christ.
128. one peak: Mount of Purgatory.

Vocabulary

dexterously (deks′tər·əs·lē) *adv.*: nimbly.
clambered (klam′bərd) *v.*: climbed with difficulty.

The Poets Emerge from Hell (19th century) by Gustave Doré.

Down there, beginning at the further bound
    of Beelzebub's° dim tomb, there is a space
132   not known by sight, but only by the sound

of a little stream° descending through the hollow
    it has eroded from the massive stone
135   in its endlessly entwining lazy flow."

My Guide and I crossed over and began
    to mount that little known and lightless road
138   to ascend into the shining world again.

---

131. Beelzebub's: Beelzebub (bē·el′zə·bub′) is
    another name for Satan.
133. a little stream: Lethe (lē′thē), river of forgetful-
    ness in classical mythology.

He first, I second, without thought of rest
    we climbed the dark until we reached the point
141   where a round opening brought in sight the blest

and beauteous shining of the
    Heavenly cars.
And we walked out once
    more beneath the Stars.°

> **136–143.** Dante and Virgil emerge from Hell.
>
> **?** *What might the stars symbolize in these lines?*

---

143. Stars: Each of the three divisions of Dante's
poem ends with the symbolism of heavenly
stars. The time—just before dawn on Easter
Sunday—is also symbolic of hope.

Dante Alighieri   **663**

Dante's Allegory

Dante wrote *The Divine Comedy* as an **allegory,** a narrative that takes place on both a literal and a figurative, or symbolic, level. Dante begins the poem with an age-old metaphor that is so common it has become a cliché: the description of life as a journey. When Dante says, "Midway in our life's journey," we can readily understand that he has reached middle age. From "I went astray," we understand that he is no longer acting as he thinks he should. A "dark wood" could be a state of mental confusion. In thinking further about the poem, we may even decide that the *I* in this passage has an allegorical, or symbolic, meaning since the character of Dante could also be any one of us.

In an allegory, concrete details from the external world are used to represent mental states or spiritual truths. By choosing this form of expression, a writer may be able to communicate ideas that would otherwise be difficult to explain. A writer may also be able to make these truths highly dramatic. It would be one thing for Dante to say that he overcame the evil in his own heart. It is quite another thing for him to describe himself "grappling matted hair and frozen crusts" as he climbs on Satan's flank.

On a literal level in *The Divine Comedy,* the character of Dante travels through Hell, Purgatory, and Paradise before reaching God. On a symbolic level, however, his journey represents the progress of every individual soul toward God as well as the progress of people through personal and political hardships toward peace on earth. Throughout *The Divine Comedy,* Dante mentions people, places, ideas, and events that are firmly rooted in his own time. But far from being an outdated work that makes sense only in the context of the Middle Ages, *The Divine Comedy* has great relevance to us today. By writing an allegory, Dante gives his narrative significance that goes far beyond the specifics of particular people and events.

"Hon, what's an allegory?"

Drawing by Weber.
© The New Yorker
Collection 1991
Robert Weber from
cartoonbank.com.
All Rights Reserved.

Response and Analysis

Reading Check

1. What is Dante's state of mind at the beginning of the poem?

2. How does Virgil offer to help Dante?

3. Why does Charon refuse to allow Dante to cross Acheron?

4. What is Minos's role in the second circle of Hell?

5. According to Canto 34, what sinners are punished in the lowest, last circle of Hell? How are they punished?

6. According to Dante, what does Satan look like? What is Satan doing?

Thinking Critically

7. Dante says in line 12 of Canto 1 that he has wandered from the "True Way." If the "Dark Wood of Error" is a **symbol** of worldliness, what does the True Way represent? On an **allegorical** level, what might the three animals that try to force Dante back into the Dark Wood represent?

8. Dante is both the author of *The Divine Comedy* and a character in it. How does Dante feel when he learns Virgil's identity in Canto 1? Why is Virgil important to Dante as a poet?

9. The inscription on the gate of Hell tells the damned to abandon all hope. In what way does hopelessness torment the spirits of the damned in Canto 3?

10. In Canto 5, lines 82–87, Dante compares Paolo and Francesca to doves. Why do you suppose Dante uses such a sympathetic image for the lovers?

11. By including details about Paolo and Francesca's reading, what attitude do you think Dante is expressing toward courtly-love poetry?

12. In Canto 34, why does Dante regard Judas, Brutus, and Cassius as the worst sinners of all? How does Judas's sin differ from that of Brutus and Cassius?

13. In what way could Satan's three faces be explained as symbols?

Extending and Evaluating

14. Dante ranks human sins by his placement of different sinners in Hell. Does their punishment fit their crimes? Explain.

15. What importance does Dante place on reason? What generalization can you make about Dante's view of reason? Use evidence in the poem to make your generalization.

Literary Criticism

16. In his introduction to the *Inferno,* Archibald T. MacAllister states that Dante believed "that the mind must be moved in order to grasp what the senses present to it; therefore he combines sight, sound, hearing, smell and touch with fear, pity, anger, horror and other appropriate emotions to involve his reader to the point of seeming actually to experience his situations and not merely to read about them." Do you agree that Dante's use of images effectively draws readers into his story and makes them feel strong emotions? Explain, using specific examples from the selection.

North Carolina Competency Goal
1.03; 4.05; 5.03

INTERNET

Projects and Activities
Keyword: LE5 WL-5

SKILLS FOCUS

Literary Skills
Analyze allegory.

Reading Skills
Make generalizations.

WRITING

Making a Literary Judgment

Many readers are surprised to find that Dante describes the center of Hell as a frozen rather than a fiery place. The English Puritan writer John Milton in *Paradise Lost* pictures Hell as a gigantic furnace, as shown in the following lines from Book I:

> A dungeon horrible, on all sides round
> As one great furnace flamed, yet from
>   those flames
> No light, but rather darkness visible
> Served only to discover sights of woe,
> Regions of sorrow, doleful shades,
>   where peace
> And rest can never dwell, hope never
>   comes
> That comes to all; but torture without
>   end
> Still urges, and a fiery deluge, fed
> With everburning sulphur
>   unconsumed. . . .

Think of the qualities of both fire and ice. In your opinion, which is better suited to symbolically describe the place farthest from God, the center of Hell? Write a three-paragraph essay defending your position. Be sure to support your choice with at least three strong reasons.

North Carolina Competency Goal
1.03; 4.05;
5.03; 6.01

Vocabulary Development
Substituting Words

despicable   dexterously

reprimand   clambered

writhes

Substitute the correct Vocabulary word from the list above for each underlined word or phrase below.

1. Dante asked so many questions of Virgil that he risked a <u>rebuke</u>.

2. In the Ninth Circle, Brutus <u>squirms</u> in eternal pain.

3. In Hell, Dante sees the <u>contemptible</u> angels who were opportunists.

4. Virgil <u>climbed</u> down until he reached an opening in the central rock.

5. He moved <u>skillfully</u>.

The Styx by Gustave Doré.

666

Collection 5

European Literature from the Middle Ages to the Enlightenment:

A Time of Transition

Renaissance and Enlightenment Literature

What a piece of work is a man! how noble in reason! how infinite in faculties! in form and moving how express and admirable! in action how like an angel! in apprehension how like a god! the beauty of the world, the paragon of animals!

—William Shakespeare, *Hamlet*, Act II, Scene 2

Portrait of a Youth (detail) (c. 1480) by Sandro Botticelli.
Andrew W. Mellon Collection, National Gallery of Art, Washington, D.C. (1937.1.19).

667

Giovanni Boccaccio

(1313–1375)
Italy

Giovanni Boccaccio (bō·käch′ē·ō′) was born in the summer of 1313, perhaps in Florence or possibly in Certaldo, a small Tuscan town twenty miles outside Florence. The illegitimate son of an unknown Frenchwoman and a Florentine merchant banker, Boccaccio spent his boyhood with his father. At the age of fourteen, however, he was sent to Naples, where his father had arranged for him to be a clerk in one of his banks.

After finishing his apprenticeship at the bank, Boccaccio entered the University of Naples and earned a degree in law. But in 1340, Boccaccio's father suffered a financial setback, and he asked his son to return to Florence. There Boccaccio met Francesco Petrarch, the great Italian poet (see page 680), who became a lifelong friend and literary advisor. And there too he experienced the most catastrophic event of his lifetime: in 1348, the Black Death struck Florence. During this plague three out of four people in Florence died a gruesome death. The streets of the city were piled high with swollen, reeking corpses covered with black splotches.

Boccaccio used the plague as the backdrop for his masterpiece, the *Decameron*. Written in the vernacular—the everyday speech spoken by Italians then—instead of Latin, the *Decameron*'s one hundred tales deal with two great subjects: love and the corruption of the clergy. The stories are told by ten wealthy young Florentines, seven women and three men, who have retreated to a villa in the hills of Fiesole to escape the Black Death. Here, safe from the pestilence, they pass the time by telling one another stories. They stay ten days

Portrait of Boccaccio by Andrea del Castagno (1421–1457).

Galleria degli Uffizi, Florence, Italy.

(the word *decameron* comes from the Greek words for "ten" and "day"), and on each day the group hears ten stories.

Completed about 1353, the *Decameron* established Boccaccio's literary reputation. Boccaccio, however, did not consider the *Decameron* to be his best work. In fact, he considered it trifling and, in later life, shifted his attention to writing scholarly works in Latin. He made great strides in the humanistic study of the ancient Greek and Roman classics. Nevertheless, it is the *Decameron* that has survived the test of time. William Shakespeare, John Milton, and many other writers in English and other languages have used Boccaccio's work as both a model and a source.

Brother Onion

from the **Decameron**

Make the Connection

Quickwrite

Have you or someone you know ever had to improvise during a performance or a presentation when something didn't go as planned? Was someone able to "save the day" by thinking quickly and working around the problem? Write briefly about the experience. In a few sentences, describe the situation and the way you or the other person responded to it.

Literary Focus

Irony

In literature, differences between expectation and reality are known as **irony**. **Situational irony** occurs when what actually happens in a story is the opposite of what is expected or appropriate. **Dramatic irony** occurs when the audience or reader knows something important that a character in the story does *not* know. As you read this story from the *Decameron*, look for both kinds of irony. What effect on the story does each type of irony have?

> **Irony** is a contrast between what is expected and what actually happens.
>
> *For more on Irony, see the Handbook of Literary and Historical Terms.*

Reading Skills

Reading and Re-reading for Details

The first time you read something, you get the general gist of the text. When you re-read, however, you notice smaller—and often crucial—details. Try reading this story from the *Decameron* twice. The first time, read to find out what happens. The second time, re-read to discover details and clues that you may have missed before. Jot down some of these details. What do they reveal about the direction of the plot or the behavior of the characters?

Background

Many of the tales included in the *Decameron* were adapted from folk tales and fables that Boccaccio learned as a youth. To unify the tales, Boccaccio places them within a **frame story**—a story that binds together a group of different narratives. In Boccaccio's frame story, ten wealthy young Florentines entertain one another with stories while waiting out the plague. The stories they tell make up a picture of the European world of the time. The story you are about to read is the tenth tale told on the sixth day of the young Florentines' retreat.

North Carolina Competency Goal
1.03; 4.02; 4.03; 4.05; 5.01; 5.03; 6.01

INTERNET

More About Giovanni Boccaccio
•
Vocabulary Practice

Keyword: LE5 WL-5

Vocabulary Development

piety (pī′ə·tē) *n.*: religious devotion.

eloquence (el′ə·kwəns) *n.*: graceful and persuasive speech.

slanderous (slan′dər·əs) *adj.*: insulting to others.

amorous (am′ə·rəs) *adj.*: showing love or desire.

scorned (skôrnd) *v.*: rejected.

Literary Skills
Understand irony.

Reading Skills
Read and re-read for details.

Monk in meditation, from the sign of Pisces (15th century). Fresco.

Palazzo della Ragione, Padua, Italy.

Brother Onion

from the **Decameron**

Giovanni Boccaccio

translated by **Mark Musa** *and* **Peter Bondanella**

Brother Onion promises some peasants that he will show them a feather from the wings of the angel Gabriel; instead, able to find only some charcoal, he tells them that it is some of the charcoal used to roast Saint Lorenzo.

Certaldo, as you may have heard, is a fortified city in the Val d'Elsa, within our own territory, which, no matter how small it may be now, was inhabited at one time by noble and well-to-do people. Because it was such good grazing ground,

one of the brothers of Saint Anthony used to go there once each year to receive the alms[1] that people were stupid enough to give him. He was called Brother Onion, and he was perhaps received there as warmly for his name as for his <u>piety</u>, since

---

1. **alms** (ämz) *n.:* food, money, and other items given to the poor.

Vocabulary

piety (pī′ə·tē) *n.:* religious devotion.

that area of the country produced onions which were famous throughout Tuscany.

Brother Onion was short, redheaded, with a cheerful face, and he was the nicest scoundrel in the world; and besides the fact that he had no education, he was such a skillful and quick talker that whoever did not know him would not only have taken him for a great master of eloquence but would have considered him to be Cicero[2] himself or perhaps Quintilian;[3] and he was a godfather, a friend, or an acquaintance of almost everyone in the district.

Now, as was his custom, he went there for one of his regular visits in the month of August; and one Sunday morning, when all the good men and women of the surrounding villages were gathered together in the parish church for mass, Brother Onion stepped forward, when the time seemed right to him, and said:

"Ladies and gentlemen, as you know, it is your practice every year to send some of your grain and crops—some of you more and others less, according to your capacity and your piety—to the poor brothers of our blessed Messer Saint Anthony, so that the blessed Saint Anthony may keep your oxen, your donkeys, your pigs, and your sheep safe from all danger; furthermore, you are used to paying, especially those of you who are enrolled in our order, those small dues which are paid once a year. To collect these contributions, I have been sent by my superior, that is, by Messer Abbot; and so, with God's blessing, after three o'clock this afternoon, when you hear the bells ring, you will come here to the front of the church, where in my usual manner I shall preach my sermon and you will kiss the cross; moreover, since I know you all to be most devoted to my lord Messer Saint Anthony, as a special favor, I shall show you a most holy and beautiful relic[4] which I myself brought back from the Holy Land, overseas: it is one of the feathers of the angel Gabriel, precisely the one which was left in the Virgin Mary's bedchamber when he came to perform the Annunciation before her in Nazareth."[5]

He said this, and then he stopped talking and returned to the mass. When Brother Onion was making this announcement, there happened to be, among the many others in the church, two young men who were most clever: one called Giovanni del Bragoniera and the other Biagio Pizzini, both of whom, after laughing quite a bit over Brother Onion's relic, decided to play a trick on him and his feather—even though they were old and close friends of his. They found out that Brother Onion would be eating that day in the center of town with a friend; when they figured it was around the time for him to be at table, they took to the street and went to the inn where the friar was staying. The plan was this: Biagio would keep Brother Onion's servant occupied by talking to him while Giovanni would look for this feather, or whatever it was, among the friar's possessions and would steal it from him, and then they could see just how he would be able to explain its disappearance to the people later on.

Brother Onion had a servant, whom some called Guccio the Whaler, others Guccio the Dauber, and still others Guccio the Pig; he was such a crude individual that even Lippo Topo himself would not have been able to do him justice. Brother Onion would often joke about him with his friends, and say:

"My servant has nine qualities, and if any one

---

2. **Cicero** (106–43 B.C.): Roman statesman and orator who was known for his use of rhetoric. Many Italian Renaissance writers, including Boccaccio, modeled their writing on Cicero's style.
3. **Quintilian** (c. A.D. 35–c. 96): Roman rhetorician who influenced writers of the Middle Ages and Renaissance.
4. **relic** n.: body part or another object associated with a holy figure, regarded with reverence by believers.
5. **feathers of . . . before her in Nazareth:** According to the Bible, the angel Gabriel appeared to the Virgin Mary and announced that she would give birth to Jesus, the Son of God, an event called the Annunciation.

Vocabulary

eloquence (el′ə·kwəns) n.: graceful and persuasive speech.

of them had existed in Solomon,[6] Aristotle,[7] or Seneca,[8] it would have sufficed to spoil all of their virtue, their intelligence, and holiness. Just think, then, what kind of man he must be, having nine such qualities, but no virtue, intelligence, or holiness!"

And when he was asked what these nine qualities were, he would answer in rhymes:

"I'll tell you. He's lying, lazy, and dirty; negligent, disobedient, and slanderous; heedless, careless, and mannerless; besides this, he has other various little faults that are best left unmentioned. And what is most amusing about him is that wherever he goes, he wants to take a wife and set up housekeeping; and because he has a long, black, greasy beard, he thinks he is very handsome and attractive—in fact, he imagines that every woman who sees him falls in love with him, and if he were allowed to, he would run after them so fast that he would lose his pants. And it is true that he is of great assistance to me, for he never lets anyone speak in secret to me without wishing to hear his share of the conversation, and if it happens that I am asked a question about something, he is so afraid that I will not know how to reply that he immediately answers 'yes' or 'no' for me as he sees fit."

Brother Onion had left his servant back at the inn and had ordered him to make sure that no one touched his belongings, and especially his saddlebags, for the sacred objects were inside them. But Guccio the Dauber was happier to be in a kitchen than a nightingale was to be on the green branches of a tree, especially if he knew that some servant girl was also there. When he noticed the innkeeper's maid, . . . Guccio left Brother Onion's room unlocked and all his possessions unguarded as he swooped down into the kitchen just like a vulture pouncing on some carcass. Although it was still August, he took a seat near the fire and began to talk with the girl, whose name was Nuta, telling her that he was a gentleman by procuration, that he had a fantastic amount of florins (not counting those he had to give away to others), and that he knew how to do and say so many things—more than even his very master ever dreamed of doing and saying. And with absolutely no concern for his cowl,[9] which was covered with so much grease it would have seasoned all the soup kettles in Altopascio, or his torn and patched-up doublet,[10] covered with sweat stains all around his collar and under his arms and in more spots and colors than a piece of cloth from India or China ever had, or his shoes, which were all worn out, or his hose, which were rent, he spoke to her as if he were the lord of Châtillon, talking about how he wanted to fit her out in new clothes and take her away from all this drudgery to be in the service of someone else, and how he would give her the hope for a better life (even if he could not give her very much), and he told her many other things in this very amorous manner, but, like most of his undertakings that would blow away with the wind, this one too came to nothing.

And so, when the two young men found Guccio the Pig busy with Nuta (something which made them very happy since this meant that half of their task was done), without anyone to stop them, they entered Brother Onion's bedchamber, which they found open, and the first thing they picked up to search was the saddlebag in which the feather was kept; they opened it, and discovered a little box wrapped in silk, and when they

---

9. **cowl** (koul) *n.*: monk's hood.
10. **doublet** (dub′lit) *n.*: man's jacket.

Vocabulary

slanderous (slan′dər·əs) *adj.*: insulting to others.
amorous (am′ə·rəs) *adj.*: showing love or desire.

(Opposite) The angel Gabriel, from *The Annunciation* (15th century) by Fra Angelico.
Museo Diocesano, Cortona, Italy.

---

6. **Solomon** (c. 960 B.C.): king of Israel known for his wisdom. Rulers from other kingdoms traveled from afar to consult with him.
7. **Aristotle** (384–322 B.C.): Greek philosopher and Plato's greatest student. His extensive writings on the arts and sciences significantly influenced Western philosophy.
8. **Seneca** (c. 4 B.C.–A.D. 65): Roman philosopher and writer who served as an advisor to the Roman emperor Nero.

opened it, they found a feather inside, just like the kind that comes from a parrot's tail; and they realized that it had to be the one that Brother Onion promised the people of Certaldo. And it certainly would have been easy for him to make them believe his story, for in those times the luxurious customs of Egypt had not yet penetrated to any great degree into Tuscany, as they were later to do throughout all of Italy, much to its ruin; and if these feathers were known to just a few, those few certainly were not among the inhabitants of that area; on the contrary, as long as the crude customs of their forefathers endured there, not only had they never seen a parrot, but most of the people there had never heard of them.

The young men were happy to have discovered the feather. They took it out, and in order not to leave the little box empty, they filled the box with some charcoal that they found in a corner of the room.

They shut the lid and arranged everything just as they had found it, and unnoticed, they merrily departed with the feather and they waited to hear what Brother Onion would say when he found charcoal in place of the feather. The simple-minded men and women who were in church, having heard that they would be seeing one of the angel Gabriel's feathers after nones,[11] returned home when the mass was finished; one neighbor, one friend spread the news to another, and when everyone had finished eating, so many men and women rushed into town to see this feather that there was hardly enough space for all of them.

After a hearty meal and a short nap, Brother Onion got up a little after nones, and when he heard that a great crowd of peasants was gathering to see the feather, he ordered Guccio the Dauber to come along with him to ring the church bells and to bring the saddlebags with him. With great reluctance, he left Nuta and the kitchen and made his way there very slowly; he arrived there panting, for drinking a good deal of water had bloated his stomach. But on Brother Onion's order, he went to the door of the church and began to ring the bells loudly.

When all of the people were gathered together, Brother Onion began his sermon without noticing that any of his belongings had been tampered with, and he spoke of many things in a way that served his ends, and when he came to the moment of showing the angel Gabriel's feather, he first had the congregation recite the Confiteor[12] and had two candles lighted. First, he drew back his cowl, then he unwound the silk and took out the box; after pronouncing several words of praise about the angel Gabriel and his relic, he opened the box. When he saw it was full of charcoal, he did not suspect that Guccio Whale had done this to him, for he knew him too well to believe he was capable of such tricks, nor did he even blame him for not keeping others from doing this; he merely cursed himself silently for having made him guardian of his belongings when he knew him to be so negligent, disobedient, careless, and absent-minded—nevertheless, without changing expression, he raised his face and hands to heaven, and spoke so that all could hear him:

"O Lord, may thy power be praised forever!" Then, he closed the box and turned to the people, saying:

"Ladies and gentlemen, I will have you know that when I was very young, I was sent by my superior to those parts of the earth of the rising sun, and I was charged by express order to discover the special privileges of Porcelain which, although they cost nothing to seal, are much more useful to others than to ourselves; I set out on my way, leaving from Venice and passing through Greekburg, then riding through the kingdom of Garbo and on through Baldacca, and I came to Parione, whereupon, not without some thirst, I reached, after some time, Sardinia.

"But why do I go on listing all the countries that I visited? After passing the straits of St. George, I came to Truffia and Buffia—lands heavily populated with a great many people— and from there I came to Liarland, where I discovered many of our friars and those of other

---

11. **nones** (nōnz) *n.*: afternoon prayer.

12. **Confiteor** (kən·fit′ē·ər) *n.*: prayer recited at the beginning of a Mass.

orders who scorned a life of hardship for the love of God, who cared little about the troubles of others, following their own interests, and who spent no money other than that which had not yet been coined in those countries; and afterwards I came to the land of Abruzzi where men and women walk around on mountaintops in wooden shoes and dress their pigs in their own guts. And further on I discovered people who carry bread twisted around sticks and wine in goatskins; then I arrived at the mountains of Basques, where all the streams run downhill.

"To make a long story short, I traveled so far that I came to Parsnip, India, where I swear by the habit I wear on my back that I saw billhooks[13] fly, an incredible thing to one who has not witnessed it; but Maso del Saggio, whom I found there cracking nuts and selling the husks retail, was witness to the fact that I do not lie about this matter. But, not able to find there what I was seeking, and since to travel further would have meant going by sea, I turned back and came to the Holy Land, where cold bread in the summer costs four cents and you get the heat for nothing; and there I found the venerable father Messer Blamemenot Ifyouplease, the most worthy patriarch of Jerusalem, who, out of respect for the habit of Our Lord Messer Saint Anthony, which I have always worn, wanted me to see all the holy relics he had there with him; and they were so numerous that if I had counted them all, I would have finished up with a list several miles long; but in order not to disappoint you, let me tell you about some of them.

"First he showed me the finger of the Holy Spirit, as whole and as solid as it ever was, and the forelock of the seraphim[14] which appeared to Saint Francis, and one of the nails of the cherubim, and one of the ribs of the True-Word-Made-Fresh-at-the-Windows, and vestments of the holy Catholic faith, and some of the beams from the star which appeared to the three wise men in the East, and a phial of the sweat of Saint Michael when he fought the devil, and the jawbones from the death of Saint Lazarus, and many others.

"And since I freely gave him copies of the *Slopes of Montemorello* in the vernacular and several chapters of the *Caprezio,* which he had been hunting for some time, he gave me in return part of his holy relics, presenting me with one of the teeth of the Holy Cross, and a bit of the sound of the bells of the temple of Solomon, in a little phial, and the feather from the angel Gabriel which I already told you I have, and one of the wooden shoes of Saint Gherardo da Villamagna, which I gave, not long ago in Florence, to Gherardo de' Bonsi, who holds it in the greatest reverence; and he also gave me some of the charcoal upon which the most holy martyr Saint Lorenzo[15] was roasted alive. All these articles I most devoutly brought back with me, and I have them all.

"The truth is that my superior has never permitted me to show them until they were proven to be authentic, but now, because of certain miracles that were performed through them and letters received from the patriarch, he is now sure that they are authentic, and he has allowed me to display them to you. And, since I am afraid to trust them to anyone else, I always carry them with me. As a matter of fact, I carry the feather from the angel Gabriel in one little box, in order not to harm it, and the coals over which Saint Lorenzo was roasted in another, and both boxes are so much alike that I often mistake the one for the other, and this is what happened to me today; for while I thought that I had brought the box containing the feather here, instead I brought the one with the charcoal. But I do not consider this to be an error; on the contrary, it is the will of God, and he himself placed the box in my hands, reminding me in this way that the Feast of Saint

---

15. **Saint Lorenzo:** Roman clergyman who was roasted to death in A.D. 258 by command of the Roman emperor because of his Christian faith.

---

13. **billhooks** *n.:* pruning tools with curved blades.
14. **seraphim** (ser′ə·fim′) *n.:* an angel of the highest order.

Vocabulary

scorned (skôrnd) *v.:* rejected.

The Decameron (1916) by John William Waterhouse.
Lady Lever Art Gallery, Port Sunlight, Merseyside, United Kingdom.

Lorenzo is only two days away; and since God wished me to show you the charcoal in order to rekindle in your hearts the devotion that you owe to Saint Lorenzo, rather than the feather that I had wanted to show you instead, he made me take out these blessed charcoals that were once bathed in the sweat of that most holy body. And so, my blessed children, remove your cowls and come forward devoutly to behold them. But first, I want each of you to know that whoever makes the sign of the cross on himself with this charcoal will live for one year safe in the knowledge that he will not be cooked by fire without his feeling it."

And after he had said those words, he sang a hymn in praise of Saint Lorenzo, opened the box, and displayed the charcoal. The foolish throng gazed upon it in reverent admiration, and they crowded around him and gave him larger offerings than they ever had before, begging him to touch each one of them with the coals. And so, Brother Onion took these charcoals in his hand and on their white shirts and doublets and on the women's veils he made the largest crosses possible, remarking that, as he had proved many times, no matter how much the charcoals were consumed in making those crosses, afterwards they would always return to their former size no sooner than they were placed back in the little box.

And in this manner, and with great profit for himself, Brother Onion turned the entire population of Certaldo into crusaders and, by means of his quick wit, tricked those who had thought they had tricked him by stealing his feather. The two young men had been present during his sermon and had heard the new story he had invented and they laughed so hard that they thought their jaws would break, for they knew how farfetched his story was; and after the crowd broke up, they went up to him and got the greatest joy in the world out of telling him what they had done; then they gave him back his feather, which in the following year raked in for him no less than the charcoal had that day.

Response and Analysis

Reading Check

1. Why has Brother Onion been sent to Certaldo?

2. What does Brother Onion claim to possess?

3. How does Guccio help Giovanni and Biagio play their prank?

4. How does Brother Onion explain the "mix-up" to his audience?

Thinking Critically

5. **Irony** is a discrepancy between expectations and reality. What central irony is at play in this story? (Consider the identity and behavior of the main character.)

6. What does the reader know about Brother Onion's three-o'clock presentation that Brother Onion himself does not know? How did this **dramatic irony** affect your reading of the story?

7. After Brother Onion opens the box, he begins to tell a long story about his many travels. Why do you think he does this? What does his action reveal about his character?

8. What aspects of human nature do you think Boccaccio is **satirizing,** or ridiculing, in this story?

9. When you re-read the story, what new details did you notice? How did these details change your understanding of the story?

Extending and Evaluating

10. In your opinion, is Brother Onion's response to the prank admirable or contemptible? How does his response to the unexpected compare with your own, as described in your Quickwrite response?

WRITING
Analyzing Character

In a brief essay, analyze the characters of Brother Onion and Guccio. Point out the words and statements that describe their physical appearances and behaviors. What do these details suggest about their characters or natures?

LISTENING AND SPEAKING
A Storytelling Session

The ten storytellers in the frame story of Boccaccio's *Decameron* spin engaging, comical yarns while the Black Death rages around them. Imagine that you and your classmates are isolated along with Boccaccio's storytellers. What story will you tell to entertain your companions? Tell your story to the class. It can be a story you have made up yourself, a story you have read or heard, or even a lengthy joke. If you wish, record your storytelling session and critique one another's oral performances.

Vocabulary Development
Etymologies

piety   amorous

eloquence   scorned

slanderous

Use a good dictionary to research the origin, or etymology, of each Vocabulary word above. Organize your findings in a chart like this one.

Word	Language of Origin	Original Word
piety	Latin (L)	pius, meaning "dutiful conduct"

North Carolina Competency Goal
1.02; 1.03;
4.02; 4.05;
5.01; 5.03;
6.01

INTERNET

Projects and Activities
Keyword:
LE5 WL-5

SKILLS FOCUS

Literary Skills
Analyze irony.

Reading Skills
Read and re-read for details.

Writing Skills
Write a character analysis.

Listening and Speaking Skills
Tell a story.

Vocabulary Skills
Determine etymologies.

Introduction

The Sonnet in the Renaissance

A **sonnet** is a fourteen-line lyric poem. The word *sonnet* is derived from the Italian word *sonetto,* meaning "little sound" or "song." It is one of the most difficult forms for a poet to master because of its rigid structural requirements: It must conform to strict patterns of rhythm and rhyme.

The Petrarchan Sonnet

In Italy the sonnet form was perfected by Francesco Petrarca, known in English as Petrarch. The form he popularized is called the **Italian,** or **Petrarchan, sonnet.** The Petrarchan sonnet has two parts: an eight-line section, called the **octave,** followed by a six-line section, called the **sestet.** The octave rhymes *abbaabba,* and the sestet rhymes *cdecde, cdcdcd, ccdeed,* or *cdcdee.* The transition between the two parts, called the **volta,** or turn, is usually found in the ninth line—the beginning of the sestet—as in Petrarch's Sonnet 15, below. This structure makes the Italian sonnet the ideal form for a two-part statement: question-answer, problem-solution, or theme-comment.

Sonnet 15
Petrarch
translated by Joseph Auslander

Tears, bitter tears fall in a bitter rain,	*a*	
And my heart trembles with a storm of sighs	*b*	
When on your beauty bend my burning eyes,	*b*	
For whose sole sake the world seems flat and vain.	*a*	octave
5 But ah, when I can see that smile again,	*a*	
That chaste, sweet, delicate smile, then passion dies	*b*	
Withered in its own flaming agonies:	*b*	
Gazing upon you, passion is lost and pain.	*a*	
But all too soon my very soul is rocked	*c*	volta
10 When you depart and with your passing dear	*d*	
Pluck from my perilous heaven my stars, O Sweet!	*e*	
Then at the last, by Love's own keys unlocked,	*c*	sestet
My soul from out my body leaping clear	*d*	
On wings of meditation finds your feet.	*e*	

(Above and opposite) *The Stoning of St. Stephen* (detail) by Raphael (1483–1520).   Palazzo Ducale. Mantua, Italy.

In addition to its formal structural features, the Petrarchan sonnet is also known for its use of the **Petrarchan conceit**—a metaphor or simile that makes a striking and sometimes fanciful comparison, usually to describe the beauty of women or the pangs of love. In the typical Petrarchan sonnet the lover has "hair of spun gold," "teeth like pearls," and "lips of ruby." Although these conceits were probably fresh and inventive when they were first coined, they eventually became conventional and overused. By the 1600s, Shakespeare was ridiculing such conceits in his Sonnet 130 (see page 732).

The Shakespearean Sonnet

Petrarchan sonnets are difficult to write in English because of the demanding rhyme scheme; English does not include as many rhyming words as Italian. English poets created their own version of the sonnet, called the **English,** or **Shakespearean, sonnet.** Like the Petrarchan sonnet, the Shakespearean sonnet is fourteen lines long. However, instead of the octave-sestet arrangement, this sonnet form uses three four-line units, called **quatrains,** followed by a final **couplet.** The typical rhyme scheme of the Shakespearean sonnet is *abab cdcd efef gg*. The Shakespearean sonnet is written in a **meter,** or rhythmic pattern, called **iambic pentameter,** with each line consisting of five unstressed (˘) syllables alternating with five stressed (´) syllables. Shakespeare's Sonnet 73 is an example.

Sonnet 73
William Shakespeare

That time of year thou mayst in me behold	*a*
When yellow leaves, or none, or few, do hang	*b*
Upon those boughs which shake against the cold,	*a* quatrain
Bare ruined choirs where late the sweet birds sang.	*b*
5 In me thou see'st the twilight of such day	*c*
As after sunset fadeth in the west;	*d*
Which by and by black night doth take away,	*c* quatrain
Death's second self that seals up all in rest.	*d*
In me thou see'st the glowing of such fire	*e*
10 That on the ashes of his youth doth lie,	*f*
As the deathbed whereon it must expire,	*e* quatrain
Consumed with that which it was nourished by.	*f*
This thou perceiv'st, which makes thy love more strong,	*g* couplet
To love that well which thou must leave ere long.	*g*

Renaissance Sonnet Writers
Italy and France

Francesco Petrarch
(1304–1374)

The Italian poet Petrarch was a man of two worlds: the dying Middle Ages and the emerging Renaissance. Although Petrarch achieved great fame as a poet and scholar, he suffered considerably as he tried to balance his own worldly ambitions and desires with the religious values of medieval life.

Although Petrarch's love for a woman named Laura is legendary, a personal relationship never developed between them. In fact, the poet managed to see Laura only occasionally and from a distance. Torn by conflicting desires, Petrarch viewed his love for Laura and his hunger for fame as two golden chains holding him back from the love of God. Although he took religious vows in 1330, he was unable to commit himself to religious life. He devoted himself instead to the written word, and in 1341 was crowned poet laureate in Rome.

Petrarch's beloved Laura died of the plague in 1348, although she would live on in the poet's works. Her idealized image inspired the 317 sonnets contained in Petrarch's *Canzoniere* ("Song Book"). This first series of sonnets, written in Italian, set the fashion throughout the Renaissance for bittersweet love lyrics in various European languages.

Pierre de Ronsard
(1524–1585)

Pierre de Ronsard (rōn·sàr′) seemed destined from a very young age for a career in diplomacy, serving as a page in the court of the Scottish King James V. But when Ronsard was sixteen, an illness left him partially deaf, cutting short his diplomatic career. Rejecting a life as a

Francesco Petrarca, from murals from a hall in the Villa Carducci (1450). Legnaia, Italy.

Galleria degli Uffizi, Florence, Italy.

priest, he instead began studying the classics. In reading Greek and Latin poetry he discovered his true vocation as a poet.

With six other poets, Ronsard founded an influential group known as the *Pléiade*—a name derived from a cluster of seven stars called the Pleiades. The *Pléiade* maintained that vernacular French was worthy of more than just popular *lais* and *ballades*. The group used the vernacular in their odes, elegies, and satires, which were based on the works of classical Greek and Roman poets. Ronsard's four books of *Odes* (1550–1552), which he dedicated to the classical poets Pindar and Horace, were so successful that his own generation called him "the Prince of Poets."

Before You Read

Renaissance Sonnets

Make the Connection

Quickwrite ✎

Love is probably the most written-about emotion of all. How is love represented in today's culture? Do we tend to idealize love, like many writers of the past? Or is our view more practical—even cynical?

Consider some of the messages our culture expresses about love relationships (all types—romantic love, love between friends, love of family). Jot down a few of your thoughts about depictions of love, including examples drawn from movies, television programs, popular songs, and romance novels.

Literary Focus

Sonnet

The sonnets of the Renaissance follow not only strict formal conventions of **meter** and **rhyme scheme** but many stylistic conventions as well. Often poets choose not to express their emotions outright but instead disguise them in **figures of speech.** For example, **metaphors** are often used to compare a lovelorn speaker to a captive bird, a wounded stag, or a moth drawn to a flame. Likewise, **personification** is frequently used to cast strong feelings into human form—to embody love in the form of Cupid, for instance.

As these figures of speech suggest, the Renaissance sonnet serves as an expression of the poet's intense personal feelings, whether they are feelings of romantic love or regret in old age. Sometimes, as in "To Hélène," both emotions manage to make their way into the same poem.

> A **sonnet** is a formally structured fourteen-line lyric poem that may have one of several rhyme schemes and that often uses figures of speech to express intense feelings.
>
> *For more on Sonnet, see the Handbook of Literary and Historical Terms.*

Background

The sonnet became popular during the Renaissance, when people were writing more about worldly matters: science, politics, geographic exploration, romantic love. During the Middle Ages most lyric poems were written to praise God. But the sonnet of the Renaissance is secular, or nonreligious, and serves as an expression of a poet's intense personal feelings.

A major theme in secular Renaissance poetry is *carpe diem* (kär′pē dē′em), a Latin phrase meaning "seize the day"—that is, make the most of the present moment because life is short. *Carpe diem* implies that the best things in life, such as youth, love, and beauty, are only fleeting pleasures and should be enjoyed before they fade away. The sonnets presented here reveal a bittersweet mixture of love and sadness typical of much Renaissance poetry.

North Carolina Competency Goal
1.02; 1.03; 4.05; 5.01; 5.03; 6.01

INTERNET

More About Francesco Petrarch
•
More About Pierre de Ronsard
•
More About Sor Juana Inés de la Cruz

Keyword: LE5 WL-5

SKILLS FOCUS

Literary Skills
Understand sonnets.

In Sonnet 61, Petrarch blesses, or expresses gratitude for, all things connected with his first encounter with Laura, the woman he idealizes.

Sonnet 61

Francesco Petrarch
translated by **Joseph Auslander**

Blest be the day, and blest the month and year,
Season and hour and very moment blest,
The lovely land and place where first possessed
By two pure eyes I found me prisoner;
5   And blest the first sweet pain, the first most dear,
Which burned my heart when Love° came in as guest;
And blest the bow, the shafts which shook my breast,
And even the wounds which Love delivered there.
Blest be the words and voices which filled grove
10 And glen with echoes of my lady's name;
The sighs, the tears, the fierce despair of love;
And blest the sonnet-sources of my fame;
And blest that thought of thoughts which is her own,
Of her, her only, of herself alone!

6. Love: Cupid, the god of love, often depicted as a winged child with bow and arrow.

Portrait of Laura (14th century).
Biblioteca Medicea Laurenziana, Florence, Italy (Ms. Plut. 41, 1).

The Seignorial Life: The Reading (detail) (16th century). Tapestry by Loire Valley workshop.
Musée du Moyen Age (Cluny), Paris, France.

One of Ronsard's most famous sonnets, "To Hélène" is part of a collection of love poems dedicated to a court lady who may have rejected the then-aging poet.

To Hélène

Pierre de Ronsard
translated by **Robert Hollander**

When you are very old, in evening candlelight,
Moved closer to the coals and carding out your wool,°
You'll sing my songs and marvel that you were such a fool:
"O Ronsard did praise me when I was young and bright."

5   Then you'll have no handmaid to help you pass the night,
Spinning while your gossip leads her into lull,
Until you say my name and her rousèd eyes grow full
In wonder of your glory in what Ronsard did write.

When I am in the earth, poor ghost without his bones,
10   A sleeper in the shade of myrtle trees and stones,
Then you, beside the hearth, old and crouched and gray,
Will yearn for all that's lost, repenting your disdain.
Live it well, I pray you, today won't come again:
Gather up the roses before they fall away.

2. carding out your wool: combing strands of wool to untangle them before spinning threads.

Response and Analysis

Thinking Critically

1. What **metaphors,** or direct comparisons, does the speaker in Petrarch's Sonnet 61 use to describe his state of mind? Find two examples.

2. **Oxymoron** is a figure of speech that states an apparent contradiction, such as "deafening silence." Identify two oxymorons in Petrarch's Sonnet 61. What effect do these figures of speech produce?

3. What is the most important word in Petrarch's sonnet? How does the poet emphasize this word?

4. What argument does Ronsard develop in "To Hélène"? How do you think the real Hélène would have responded to this argument?

5. In your own words, restate the advice Ronsard gives Hélène in the last two lines of his poem. What can we conclude overall about the poet's feelings for her?

Extending and Evaluating

6. Suppose you were the recipient of either Sonnet 61 or "To Hélène." How would you respond? Would you be touched, irritated, amused? Explain your reaction.

7. Review your Quickwrite notes describing representations of love in today's culture. Which sonnet most closely resembles the description and examples you gave? Explain. ✏️

WRITING

Comparing and Contrasting Poems

Read "When You Are Old" by the Irish poet W. B. Yeats (1865–1939), written in imitation of Ronsard's sonnet "To Hélène."

North Carolina Competency Goal
1.02; 1.03; 4.05; 5.01; 5.03; 6.01

INTERNET
Projects and Activities
Keyword: LE5 WL-5

SKILLS FOCUS

Literary Skills
Analyze sonnets.

Writing Skills
Compare and contrast poems.

When You Are Old
W. B. Yeats

When you are old and gray and
    full of sleep,
And nodding by the fire, take
    down this book,
And slowly read, and dream of
    the soft look
Your eyes had once, and of their
    shadows deep;

5 How many loved your moments
    of glad grace,
And loved your beauty with love
    false or true;
But one man loved the pilgrim
    soul in you,
And loved the sorrows of your
    changing face.

And bending down beside the
    glowing bars,
10 Murmur, a little sadly, how Love
    fled
And paced upon the mountains
    overhead
And hid his face amid a crowd of
    stars.

Write a paragraph or two comparing and contrasting Yeats's poem with Ronsard's. Your essay should include answers to the following questions:

• To whom is each poem addressed, and in what way are the two persons similar?

• How does the speaker in each poem want the person addressed to think of him in the future?

• What does each speaker want the person he is addressing to do?

• In what ways are the speakers' intentions similar and different?

Sor Juana Inés de la Cruz's Sonnet 148 is written in the style of Petrarch and makes use of the common theme of carpe diem, or "Enjoy life fully while you can." Sor Juana (1651–1695), one of the most important writers in Mexican literature, served as a lady-in-waiting for several years at the Spanish court in Mexico City before becoming a Catholic nun.

Sonnet 148:
Better Death Than Suffer the Affronts of Growing Old

Sor Juana Inés de la Cruz
translated by **Margaret Sayers Peden**

In the gardens, Celia gazed upon a rose
that candid in its haughty ostentation,
and bright in tints of scarlet and rich crimson,
joyfully its fragile face exposed,

5   and said: "Enjoy the day, fear not the blows
of Fate in this too fleeting celebration,
the death that on the morrow claims its portion,
cannot take from you the joys this day bestows;

    though the perfume of life fade on the air,
10 and the hour of your passing too soon toll,
fear not the death that finds you young and fair:

    take the counsel that experience extols,
to die while beautiful is finer far
than to suffer the affront of growing old."

Sister Juana Inés de la Cruz (1750) (detail) by Miguel Cabrera.
Museo Nacional de Historia, Castillo de Chapultepec, Mexico City, D.F., Mexico.

WRITING

Comparing Sonnets

Write a brief essay in which you compare and contrast Sor Juana's Sonnet 148 with Ronsard's sonnet "To Hélène." To gather details for your comparison, fill out a chart like the one here. Then, write your essay using the block method: First, explain how Ronsard uses the following elements of poetry; then, identify how Sor Juana uses them. Remember to use specific quotations from the poems to support your ideas.

	Ronsard	Sor Juana
Speaker		
Person addressed		
Images		
Tone		
Message		
Sonnet form		

North Carolina Competency Goal
1.03; 4.05; 5.03

SKILLS FOCUS

Writing Skills
Compare sonnets.

Literary Focus

Enjambment

Enjambment (en·jam′mənt), the use of run-on lines, is the smooth continuation of a thought from one line of verse to the next. The term is from a French word meaning "to straddle," suggesting that the sentence or idea straddles, or links, two or more lines. Inexperienced readers tend to stop at the end of each line in a poem, usually at a rhyme, regardless of the punctuation. When read aloud in this way, many poems sound artificial, like nursery rhymes, and the rhyme interferes with the meaning of the lines. Readers with more experience know that if a thought continues for more than one line, they should read through to the end of the thought and not stop simply because there is a rhyme.

Enjambment takes the emphasis off the rhyme scheme so that the real meaning of a poem can come through. Otherwise the poem might become boring and singsong, a mere repetition of sounds and a strict reproduction of form rather than an expression of a poet's complex thoughts and feelings. Often, too, enjambment is used to create suspense: The first part of the thought may lead up to something that the second part in the next line may or may not carry through.

Try to get a sense of the flow of poetic lines by reading aloud the sonnets of Petrarch and Ronsard. Pay attention to the punctuation marks and the enjambment. Enjambment works to make a poem sound more like a real person speaking his or her thoughts. Read a sonnet for a classmate without paying attention to run-on lines; simply stop at the end of each line without paying attention to the punctuation. Then, have your partner read the same sonnet to you, this time reading the lines according to their punctuation and paying attention to run-on lines. How are your readings different? Which interpretation sounds more natural? Why?

Vincenz of Beauvais, from manuscript (1450).
Bibliothèque Nationale, Paris
(Ms. francais 6275, fol.50 v).

Miguel de Cervantes
(1547–1616)
Spain

Portrait of Miguel de Cervantes.
The Granger Collection, New York.

Miguel de Cervantes (sər·vän′tēz′) was born in Alcalá de Henares, a small town close to Madrid, Spain. Since Cervantes' family moved frequently in search of work, the author's formal education was probably minimal. However, records indicate that Cervantes attended a liberal arts school, where his first identified work, an elegy for a young queen, was published.

Seeing no prospects at home, Cervantes enlisted in the army. In 1571, he was wounded while fighting the Turkish naval forces in the Battle of Lepanto. Although Cervantes was feverishly ill at the time, he insisted on coming to the defense of the allied forces. The Turkish navy was defeated, but Cervantes was shot in the chest and left hand. His hand was permanently disabled, and Cervantes earned the nickname "el manco de Lepanto"—"the one-handed man of Lepanto."

On his way back to Spain, bearing letters of commendation for his bravery, Cervantes was captured and enslaved by Algerian pirates. Ironically, the letters caused his captors to set a higher ransom for him and keep him in captivity for a longer period of time. After five years, Cervantes' family finally managed to raise the ransom money.

When Cervantes returned to Spain, his attempts to obtain an official government post proved unsuccessful. Jobless and in debt, he tried writing plays and a pastoral romance, but he was unable to support himself as a writer and finally obtained work as a tax collector. In the ensuing years, Cervantes continually experienced financial difficulties and even spent time in jail for failure to pay his debts. It is said that during his time in jail, Cervantes came up with the story of Don Quixote, a senile, aged landowner who imagines that he is a chivalrous knight. Some of Cervantes' own real-life adventures would make their way into his masterpiece, *The Ingenious Gentleman Don Quixote of La Mancha,* which was published in January 1605 and has been translated into over sixty languages. Cervantes' novel immediately caused a sensation, and after the first edition was sold out, pirated (illegally printed) copies began to appear. It seemed that everyone in Spain, and soon everyone in Europe, was laughing at the droll adventures of the ridiculous knight, Don Quixote.

At the age of fifty-eight, Cervantes was a famous author, but he was still poor. As was common until the nineteenth century, authors were at the mercy of publishers and were seldom able to retain the copyrights on their books. Thus, *Don Quixote's* publisher, not Cervantes, reaped the lion's share of the book's profits, and Spain's greatest writer died in poverty on April 22, 1616. To his family Cervantes left only a little money and many debts. To the world he left a comic masterpiece that has earned him the title of "father of the modern novel."

Before You Read

from Don Quixote

Make the Connection
Quickwrite ✏️

Cervantes' novel resulted in a new word used to describe a person who is a well-intentioned but foolishly idealistic dreamer: *quixotic* (kwik·sät′ik). What quixotic heroes in popular culture—films, comic strips, television, books—can you think of? What traits do these heroes share? Jot down your thoughts.

North Carolina Competency Goal
1.02; 1.03; 2.01; 3.04; 4.05; 5.01; 5.03; 6.01

Literary Focus
Parody

A literary **parody** is an imitation of another work of literature for amusement or instruction. A parody uses exaggeration or absurd subject matter to make something serious seem laughable. In *Don Quixote*, Cervantes twists and distorts every aspect of the medieval romance and its chivalric knights. Quixote sees himself as one of the knights of old, but his armor is run-down, his horse is a nag, and his greatest enemies turn out to be windmills.

> **Parody** is the imitation of a work of literature for amusement or instruction.
>
> *For more on Parody, see the Handbook of Literary and Historical Terms.*

go.hrw.com

INTERNET

Vocabulary Practice
•
More About Miguel de Cervantes

Keyword: LE5 WL-5

SKILLS FOCUS

Literary Skills
Understand parody.

Reading Skills
Make inferences about an author's beliefs.

Reading Skills 📖
Making Inferences About an Author's Beliefs

"Within every joke lies a kernel of truth," an old saying goes. This saying can be applied to parodies too. A parody's humorous details often provide clues readers can use to make **inferences,** or educated guesses, about the author's own beliefs. On a sheet of paper, write the following sentence stem: *Cervantes believed that readers of medieval romances _____.* As you read, use the story's details to help you complete this inference—and to make several of your own.

Background

Medieval tales of chivalry and courtly romance were still devoured by readers in Cervantes' time. In these stories idealized knights fought villains, dragons, and monsters and embarked on quests in honor of their ladyloves. Such heroes stood for military values such as courage and loyalty, combined with Christian virtues such as piety and chastity. Yet *Don Quixote* is much more than a parody of the romances of Cervantes' day. It touchingly develops two of literature's most enduring themes: the struggle of the idealist in a materialistic world and the interplay of reality and human imagination.

Vocabulary Development

grandiloquent (gran·dil′ə·kwənt) *adj.*: pompous or overblown in speech or writing.

errant (er′ənt) *adj.*: rambling; wandering off course or beyond set limits (often used in the phrase *knight-errant*).

sonorous (sə·nôr′əs) *adj.*: having a full, rich sound; grand-sounding.

ameliorate (ə·mēl′yə·rāt′) *v.*: make better.

(Opposite) Statue of Don Quixote from Spain.

from

Don Quíxote

Miguel de Cervantes
translated by **Edith Grossman**

Don Quixote in His Study by George Cattermole (1800–1868).
Victoria & Albert Museum, London.

CHAPTER I

*Which describes the condition and profession of
the famous gentleman Don Quixote of La Mancha*

Somewhere in La Mancha, in a place whose
name I do not care to remember, a gentleman
lived not long ago, one of those who has a lance
and ancient shield on a shelf and keeps a skinny
nag and a greyhound for racing. An occasional
stew, beef more often than lamb, hash most nights,
eggs and abstinence on Saturdays, lentils on Fri-
days, sometimes squab as a treat on Sundays—
these consumed three-fourths of his income.[1]
The rest went for a light woolen tunic and velvet
breeches and hose of the same material for feast
days, while weekdays were honored with dun-
colored coarse cloth. He had a housekeeper past
forty, a niece not yet twenty, and a man-of-all-
work who did everything from saddling the
horse to pruning the trees. Our gentleman was

approximately fifty years old; his complexion was
weathered, his flesh scrawny, his face gaunt, and
he was a very early riser and a great lover of the
hunt. Some claim that his family name was Quixada, or Quexada, for there is a certain amount of
disagreement among the authors who write of
this matter, although reliable conjecture seems to
indicate that his name was Quexana. But this does
not matter very much to our story; in its telling
there is absolutely no deviation from the truth.

And so, let it be said that this aforementioned
gentleman spent his times of leisure—which
meant most of the year—reading books of
chivalry with so much devotion and enthusiasm
that he forgot almost completely about the hunt
and even about the administration of his estate;
and in his rash curiosity and folly he went so far
as to sell acres of arable land in order to buy books
of chivalry to read, and he brought as many of
them as he could into his house; and he thought
none was as fine as those composed by the worthy
Feliciano de Silva,[2] because the clarity of his prose

---

1. **An occasional stew . . . income:** Cervantes describes
   typical aspects of the ordinary life of the rural
   gentry. The indications of reduced circumstances
   include the foods eaten by Don Quixote: beef, for
   example, was less expensive than lamb.

2. **Feliciano de Silva:** the author of several novels of
   chivalry; the phrases cited by Cervantes are typical
   of the language in these books that drove Don
   Quixote mad.

and complexity of his language seemed to him more valuable than pearls, in particular when he read the declarations and missives of love, where he would often find written: *The reason for the unreason to which my reason turns so weakens my reason that with reason I complain of thy beauty.* And also when he read: *. . . the heavens on high divinely heighten thy divinity with the stars and make thee deserving of the deserts thy greatness deserves.*

With these words and phrases the poor gentleman lost his mind, and he spent sleepless nights trying to understand them and extract their meaning, which Aristotle himself, if he came back to life for only that purpose, would not have been able to decipher or understand. Our gentleman was not very happy with the wounds that Don Belianís gave and received, because he imagined that no matter how great the physicians and surgeons who cured him, he would still have his face and entire body covered with scars and marks. But, even so, he praised the author for having concluded his book with the promise of unending adventure, and he often felt the desire to take up his pen and give it the conclusion promised there; and no doubt he would have done so, and even published it, if other greater and more persistent thoughts had not prevented him from doing so. He often had discussions with the village priest—who was a learned man, a graduate of Sigüenza[3]—regarding who had been the greater knight, Palmerín of England or Amadís of Gaul; but Master Nicolás, the village barber, said that none was the equal of the Knight of Phoebus, and if any could be compared to him, it was Don Galaor, the brother of Amadís of Gaul, because he was moderate in everything: a knight who was not affected, not as weepy as his brother, and incomparable in questions of courage.

In short, our gentleman became so caught up in reading that he spent his nights reading from dusk till dawn and his days reading from sunrise to sunset, and so with too little sleep and too much reading his brains dried up, causing him to lose his mind. His fantasy filled with everything he had read in his books, enchantments as well as combats, battles, challenges, wounds, courtings, loves, torments, and other impossible foolishness, and he became so convinced in his imagination of the truth of all the countless <u>grandiloquent</u> and false inventions he read that for him no history in the world was truer. He would say that El Cid Ruy Díaz[4] had been a very good knight but could not compare to Amadís, the Knight of the Blazing Sword, who with a single backstroke cut two ferocious and colossal giants in half. He was fonder of Bernardo del Carpio[5] because at Roncesvalles[6] he had killed the enchanted Roland by availing himself of the tactic of Hercules when he crushed Antaeus, the son of Earth, in his arms. He spoke highly of the giant Morgante because, although he belonged to the race of giants, all of them haughty and lacking in courtesy, he alone was amiable and well-behaved. But, more than any of the others, he admired Reinaldos de Montalbán,[7] above all when he saw him emerge from his castle and rob anyone he met, and when he crossed the sea and stole the idol of Mohammed made all of gold, as recounted in his history. He would have traded his housekeeper, and even his niece, for the chance to strike a blow at the traitor Guenelon.[8]

The truth is that when his mind was completely gone, he had the strangest thought any lunatic in the world ever had, which was that it seemed reasonable and necessary to him, both for the sake of his honor and as a service to the nation,

---

4. **El Cid Ruy Díaz:** a historical figure (eleventh century) who has passed into legend and literature.
5. **Bernardo del Carpio:** a legendary hero, the subject of ballads as well as poems and plays.
6. **Roncesvalles:** the site in the Pyrenees, called Roncesvaux in French, where Charlemagne's army fought the Saracens in 778.
7. **Reinaldos de Montalbán:** a hero of the French *chansons de geste;* in some Spanish versions, he takes part in the battle of Roncesvalles.
8. **Guenelon:** the traitor responsible for the defeat of Charlemagne's army at Roncesvalles.

Vocabulary

grandiloquent (gran·dil′ə·kwənt) *adj.*: pompous or overblown in speech or writing.

---

3. **graduate of Sigüenza:** The allusion is ironic: Sigüenza was a minor university, and its graduates had the reputation of being not very well educated.

to become a knight errant and travel the world with his armor and his horse to seek adventures and engage in everything he had read that knights errant engaged in, righting all manner of wrongs and, by seizing the opportunity and placing himself in danger and ending those wrongs, winning eternal renown and everlasting fame. The poor man imagined himself already wearing the crown, won by the valor of his arm, of the empire of Trebizond at the very least; and so it was that with these exceedingly agreeable thoughts, and carried away by the extraordinary pleasure he took in them, he hastened to put into effect what he so fervently desired. And the first thing he did was to attempt to clean some armor that had belonged to his great-grandfathers and, stained with rust and covered with mildew, had spent many long years stored and forgotten in a corner. He did the best he could to clean and repair it, but he saw that it had a great defect, which was that instead of a full sallet helmet with an attached neckguard, there was only a simple headpiece; but he compensated for this with his industry, and out of pasteboard he fashioned a kind of half-helmet that, when attached to the headpiece, took on the appearance of a full sallet. It is true that in order to test if it was strong and could withstand a blow, he took out his sword and struck it twice, and with the first blow he undid in a moment what it had taken him a week to create; he could not help being disappointed at the ease with which he had hacked it to pieces, and to protect against that danger, he made another one, placing strips of iron on the inside so that he was satisfied with its strength; and not wanting to put it to the test again, he designated and accepted it as an extremely fine sallet.

Then he went to look at his nag, and though its hooves had more cracks than his master's pate and it showed more flaws than Gonnella's horse, that *tantum pellis et ossa fuit,*[9] it seemed to him that Alexander's Bucephalus and El Cid's

Babieca were not its equal. He spent four days thinking about the name he would give it; for— as he told himself—it was not seemly that the horse of so famous a knight, and a steed so intrinsically excellent, should not have a worthy name; he was looking for the precise name that would declare what the horse had been before its master became a knight errant and what it was now; for he was determined that if the master was changing his condition, the horse too would change its name to one that would win the fame and recognition its new position and profession deserved; and so, after many names that he shaped and discarded, subtracted from and added to, unmade and remade in his memory and imagination, he finally decided to call the horse *Rocinante,*[10] a name, in his opinion, that was noble, sonorous, and reflective of what it had been when it was a nag, before it was what it was now, which was the foremost nag in all the world.

Having given a name, and one so much to his liking, to his horse, he wanted to give one to himself, and he spent another eight days pondering this, and at last he called himself *Don Quixote,*[11] which is why, as has been noted, the authors of this absolutely true history determined that he undoubtedly must have been named Quixada and not Quexada, as others have claimed. In any event, recalling that the valiant Amadís had not been content with simply calling himself Amadís but had added the name of his kingdom and realm in order to bring it fame, and was known as Amadís of Gaul, he too, like a good knight,

---

9. **Gonnella's . . . ossa fuit:** Pietro Gonnella, the jester at the court of Ferrara, had a horse famous for being skinny. The Latin translates as "was nothing but skin and bones."

10. **Rocinante:** *Rocín* means "nag"; *ante* means "before," both temporally and spatially.

11. **Don Quixote:** *Quixote* means the section of armor that covers the thigh.

Vocabulary

errant (er′ənt) *adj.*: rambling; wandering off course or beyond set limits (often used in the phrase *knight-errant*).

sonorous (sə·nôr′əs) *adj.*: having a full, rich sound; grand-sounding.

(Opposite) *Sancho and Don Quixote* by Honoré Daumier (1808–1879).

Burrell Collection, Glasgow, Scotland.

Knights Jousting by Albrecht Dürer.
British Museum, London.

wanted to add the name of his birthplace to his own, and he called himself *Don Quixote of La Mancha*,[12] thereby, to his mind, clearly stating his lineage and country and honoring it by making it part of his title.

Having cleaned his armor and made a full helmet out of a simple headpiece, and having given a name to his horse and decided on one for himself, he realized that the only thing left for him to do was to find a lady to love; for the knight errant without a lady-love was a tree without leaves or fruit, a body without a soul. He said to himself:

"If I, because of my evil sins, or my good fortune, meet with a giant somewhere, as ordinarily befalls knights errant, and I unseat him with a single blow, or cut his body in half, or, in short, conquer and defeat him, would it not be good to have someone to whom I could send him so that he might enter and fall to his knees before my sweet lady, and say in the humble voice of surrender: 'I, lady, am the giant Caraculiambro, lord of the island Malindrania, defeated in single combat by the never sufficiently praised knight Don Quixote of La Mancha, who commanded me to appear before your ladyship, so that your highness might dispose of me as you chose'?"

Oh, how pleased our good knight was when he had made this speech, and even more pleased when he discovered the one he could call his lady! It is believed that in a nearby village there was a very attractive peasant girl with whom he had once been in love, although she, apparently, never knew or noticed. Her name was Aldonza Lorenzo,[13] and he thought it a good idea to call her the lady of his thoughts, and, searching for a name that would not differ significantly from his and would suggest and imply that of a princess and great lady, he decided to call her *Dulcinea of Toboso*,[14] because she came from Toboso, a name, to his mind, that was musical and beautiful and filled with significance, as were all the others he had given to himself and everything pertaining to him.

---

12. **La Mancha:** La Mancha was not one of the noble medieval kingdoms associated with knighthood.

13. **Aldonza Lorenzo:** Aldonza, considered to be a common, rustic name, had comic connotations.
14. *Dulcinea of Toboso:* Her name is based on the word *dulce* ("sweet").

from CHAPTER II

Which tells of the first sally that the ingenious Don Quixote made from his native land

And so, having completed these preparations, he did not wish to wait any longer to put his thought into effect, impelled by the great need in the world that he believed was caused by his delay, for there were evils to undo, wrongs to right, injustices to correct, abuses to ameliorate, and offenses to rectify. And one morning before dawn on a hot day in July, without informing a single person of his intentions, and without anyone seeing him, he armed himself with all his armor and mounted Rocinante, wearing his poorly constructed helmet, and he grasped his shield and took up his lance and through the side door of a corral he rode out into the countryside with great joy and delight at seeing how easily he had given a beginning to his virtuous desire. But as soon as he found himself in the countryside he was assailed by a thought so terrible it almost made him abandon the enterprise he had barely begun; he recalled that he had not been dubbed a knight, and according to the law of chivalry, he could not and must not take up arms against any knight; since this was the case, he would have to bear blank arms, like a novice knight without a device on his shield, until he had earned one through his own efforts. These thoughts made him waver in his purpose; but, his madness being stronger than any other faculty, he resolved to have himself dubbed a knight by the first person he met, in imitation of many others who had done the same, as he had read in the books that had brought him to this state. As for his arms being blank and white,[15] he planned to clean them so much that when the dubbing took place they would be whiter than ermine; he immediately grew serene and continued on his way, following only the path his horse wished to take, believing that the virtue of his adventures lay in doing this. . . .

Don Quixote gets himself "knighted" by a bewildered innkeeper, who marvels at such an
extraordinary variety of madness, but he is finally tricked by his friends and brought home, where he is treated as a lunatic. His family deprives him of the dangerous books, and they hope that the madness will pass.

from CHAPTER VII

Regarding the second sally of our good knight Don Quixote of La Mancha

So it was that he spent two very quiet weeks at home, showing no signs of wanting to repeat his initial lunacies, and during this time he had lively conversations with his two friends the priest and the barber, in which he said that what the world needed most were knights errant and that in him errant chivalry would be reborn. The priest at times contradicted him, and at other times he agreed, because if he did not maintain this ruse, he would not have been able to talk to him.

During this time, Don Quixote approached a farmer who was a neighbor of his, a good man—if that title can be given to someone who is poor—but without much in the way of brains. In short, he told him so much, and persuaded and promised him so much, that the poor peasant resolved to go off with him and serve as his squire. Among other things, Don Quixote said that he should prepare to go with him gladly, because it might happen that one day he would have an adventure that would gain him, in the blink of an eye, an ínsula,[16] and he would make him its governor. With these promises and others like them, Sancho Panza,[17] for that was the farmer's name, left his wife and children and agreed to be his neighbor's squire.

Then Don Quixote determined to find some money, and by selling one thing, and pawning

---

16. **ínsula:** a Latinate word for "island" that appeared frequently in novels of chivalry; Cervantes uses it throughout for comic effect.
17. **Sancho Panza:** *Panza* means "belly" or "paunch."

Vocabulary

ameliorate (ə·mēl′yə·rāt′) *v.*: make better.

---

15. **As for his arms . . . white:** The wordplay is based on the word *blanco*, which can mean both "blank" and "white."

another, and undervaluing everything, he managed to put together a reasonable sum. He also acquired a round shield, which he borrowed from a friend, and doing the best he could to repair his broken helmet, he informed his squire of the day and time he planned to start out so that Sancho could supply himself with whatever he thought he would need. He ordered him in particular to bring along saddlebags, and Sancho said he certainly would bring them and also planned to take along a donkey he thought very highly of because he wasn't one for walking any great distance. As for the donkey, Don Quixote had to stop and think about that for a while, wondering if he recalled any knight errant who had with him a squire riding on a donkey, and none came to mind, yet in spite of this he resolved to take Sancho along, intending to obtain a more honorable mount for him at the earliest opportunity by appropriating the horse of the first discourteous knight he happened to meet. He furnished himself with shirts and all the other things he could, following the advice the innkeeper had given him; and when this had been accomplished and completed, without Panza taking leave of his children and wife, or Don Quixote of his housekeeper and niece, they rode out of the village one night, and no one saw them, and they traveled so far that by dawn they were certain they would not be found even if anyone came looking for them.

Sancho Panza rode on his donkey like a patriarch, with his saddlebags, and his wineskin, and a great desire to see himself governor of the ínsula his master had promised him. Don Quixote happened to follow the same direction and route he had followed on his first sally, which was through the countryside of Montiel, and he rode there with less difficulty than he had the last time, because at that hour of the morning the sun's rays fell obliquely and did not tire them. Then Sancho Panza said to his master:

"Señor Knight Errant, be sure not to forget what your grace promised me about the ínsula; I'll know how to govern it no matter how big it is."

To which Don Quixote replied:

"You must know, friend Sancho Panza, that it was a very common custom of the knights errant of old to make their squires governors of the ínsulas or kingdoms they won, and I have resolved that so amiable a usage will not go unfulfilled on my account; on the contrary, I plan to improve upon it, for they sometimes, and perhaps most times, waited until their squires were old, and after they had had their fill of serving, and enduring difficult days, and nights that were even worse, they would grant them the title of count, or perhaps even marquis, of some valley or province of greater or smaller size; but if you live and I live, it well might be that before six days have passed I shall win a kingdom that has others allied to it, and that would be perfect for my crowning you king of one of them. And do not think this is any great thing; for events and eventualities befall knights in ways never seen or imagined, and I might well be able to give you even more than I have promised."

"If that happens," replied Sancho Panza, "and I become king through one of those miracles your grace has mentioned, then Juana Gutiérrez,[18] my missus, would be queen, and my children would be princes."

"Well, who can doubt it?" Don Quixote responded.

"I doubt it," Sancho Panza replied, "because in my opinion, even if God rained kingdoms down on earth, none of them would sit well on the head of Mari Gutiérrez. You should know, sir, that she isn't worth two *maravedís* as a queen; she'd do better as a countess, and even then she'd need God's help."

"Leave it to God, Sancho," said Don Quixote, "and He will give what suits her best; but do not lower your desire so much that you will be content with anything less than the title of captain general."

"I won't, Señor," Sancho replied, "especially when I have a master as distinguished as your grace, who will know how to give me everything that's right for me and that I can handle."

---

18. **Juana Gutiérrez:** Presumably through an oversight on the part of Cervantes, Sancho's wife has several other names, including Mari Gutiérrez, Juana Panza, Teresa Cascajo, and Teresa Panza.

Don Quixote on Horseback by Honoré Daumier (1808–1879).

Neue Pinakothek, Munich, Germany.

Peter O'Toole as Don Quixote hanging from windmill, from *Man of La Mancha* (1972). Detail from film still.

from CHAPTER VIII

Regarding the good fortune of the valorous Don Quixote in the fearful and never imagined adventure of the windmills, along with other events worthy of joyful remembrance

As they were talking, they saw thirty or forty of the windmills found in that countryside, and as soon as Don Quixote caught sight of them, he said to his squire:

"Good fortune is guiding our affairs better than we could have desired, for there you see, friend Sancho Panza, thirty or more enormous giants with whom I intend to do battle and whose lives I intend to take, and with the spoils we shall begin to grow rich, for this is righteous warfare, and it is a great service to God to remove so evil a breed from the face of the earth."

"What giants?" said Sancho Panza.

"Those you see over there," replied his master, "with the long arms; sometimes they are almost two leagues long."

"Look, your grace," Sancho responded, "those things that appear over there aren't giants but windmills, and what looks like their arms are the sails that are turned by the wind and make the grindstone move."

"It seems clear to me," replied Don Quixote, "that thou art not well-versed in the matter of adventures: these are giants; and if thou art afraid, move aside and start to pray whilst I enter with them in fierce and unequal combat."

And having said this, he spurred his horse, Rocinante, paying no attention to the shouts of his squire, Sancho, who warned him that, beyond any doubt, those things he was about to attack were windmills and not giants. But he was so convinced they were giants that he did not hear the shouts of his squire, Sancho, and could not see, though he was very close, what they really were; instead, he charged and called out:

"Flee not, cowards and base creatures, for it is a single knight who attacks you."

Just then a gust of wind began to blow, and the great sails began to move, and, seeing this, Don Quixote said:

"Even if you move more arms than the giant Briareus,[19] you will answer to me."

And saying this, and commending himself with all his heart to his lady Dulcinea, asking that she come to his aid at this critical moment, and well-protected by his shield, with his lance in its socket, he charged at Rocinante's full gallop and attacked the first mill he came to; and as he thrust his lance into the sail, the wind moved it with so much force that it broke the lance into pieces and picked up the horse and the knight, who then dropped to the ground and were very badly battered. Sancho Panza hurried to help as fast as his donkey could carry him, and when he reached them he discovered that Don Quixote could not move because he had taken so hard a fall with Rocinante.

"God save me!" said Sancho. "Didn't I tell your grace to watch what you were doing, that

---

19. **Briareus:** a monstrous giant in Greek mythology who had fifty heads and a hundred arms.

these were nothing but windmills, and only somebody whose head was full of them wouldn't know that?"

"Be quiet, Sancho my friend," replied Don Quixote. "Matters of war, more than any others, are subject to continual change; moreover, I think, and therefore it is true, that the same Frestón the Wise who stole my room and my books has turned these giants into windmills in order to deprive me of the glory of defeating them: such is the enmity he feels for me; but in the end, his evil arts will not prevail against the power of my virtuous sword."

"God's will be done," replied Sancho Panza.

He helped him to stand, and Don Quixote remounted Rocinante, whose back was almost broken. And, talking about their recent adventure, they continued on the road to Puerto Lápice,[20] because there, said Don Quixote, he could not fail to find many diverse adventures since it was a very heavily trafficked place; but he rode heavyhearted because he did not have his lance; and expressing this to his squire, he said:

"I remember reading that a Spanish knight named Diego Pérez de Vargas, whose sword broke in battle, tore a heavy bough or branch from an oak tree and with it did such great deeds that day, and thrashed so many Moors, that he was called Machuca, the Bruiser, and from that day forward he and his descendants were named Vargas y Machuca.[21] I have told you this because from the first oak that presents itself to me I intend to tear off another branch as good as the one I have in mind, and with it I shall do such great deeds that you will consider yourself fortunate for deserving to see them and for being a witness to things that can hardly be believed."

"It's in God's hands," said Sancho. "I believe everything your grace says, but sit a little straighter, it looks like you're tilting, it must be from the battering you took when you fell."

"That is true," replied Don Quixote, "and if I do not complain about the pain, it is because it is not the custom of knights errant to complain about any wound, even if their innards are spilling out because of it."

"If that's true, I have nothing to say," Sancho responded, "but God knows I'd be happy if your grace complained when something hurt you. As for me, I can say that I'll complain about the smallest pain I have, unless what you said about not complaining also applies to the squires of knights errant."

Don Quixote could not help laughing at his squire's simplemindedness; and so he declared that he could certainly complain however and whenever he wanted, with or without cause, for as yet he had not read anything to the contrary in the order of chivalry. Sancho said that it was time to eat. His master replied that he felt no need of food at the moment, but that Sancho could eat whenever he wished. With this permission, Sancho made himself as comfortable as he could on his donkey, and after taking out of the saddlebags what he had put into them, he rode behind his master at a leisurely pace, eating and, from time to time, tilting back the wineskin with so much gusto that the most self-indulgent tavern-keeper in Málaga might have envied him. And as he rode along in that manner, taking frequent drinks, he did not think about any promises his master had made to him, and he did not consider it work but sheer pleasure to go around seeking adventures, no matter how dangerous they might be.

In short, they spent the night under some trees, and from one of them Don Quixote tore off a dry branch to use as a lance and placed on it the iron head he had taken from the one that had broken. Don Quixote did not sleep at all that night but thought of his lady Dulcinea, in order to conform to what he had read in his books of knights spending many sleepless nights in groves and meadows, turning all their thoughts to memories of their ladies. Sancho Panza did not do the same; since his stomach was full, and not with chicory water, he slept the entire night, and if his master had not called him, the rays of the sun shining in his face and the song of numerous birds joyfully greeting the arrival of the new day would have done nothing to rouse him. When he woke he

---

20. **Puerto Lápice:** an entrance to the mountains of the Sierra Morena, between La Mancha and Andalucía.

21. **Machuca:** a historical figure of the thirteenth century.

made another pass at the wineskin and found it somewhat flatter than it had been the night before, and his heart grieved, for it seemed to him they were not likely to remedy the lack very soon. Don Quixote did not wish to eat breakfast because, as has been stated, he meant to live on sweet memories. They continued on the road to Puerto Lápice, and at about three in the afternoon it came into view.

"Here," said Don Quixote when he saw it, "we can, brother Sancho Panza, plunge our hands all the way up to the elbows into this thing they call adventures. But be advised that even if you see me in the greatest danger in the world, you are not to put a hand to your sword to defend me, unless you see that those who offend me are baseborn rabble, in which case you certainly can help me; but if they are gentlemen, under no circumstances

CONNECTION *to* DON QUIXOTE

Don Quixote

INFORMATIONAL TEXT

from an Interview with Edith Grossman

The NewsHour with Jim Lehrer, December 23, 2003

JEFFREY BROWN: Last year, a panel of 100 writers from around the world picked *Don Quixote* as the greatest novel of all time. Now translator Edith Grossman has produced a new English language version of Miguel Cervantes' Spanish classic from the early 1600s. Grossman has been known until now for her translations of contemporary Latin American authors. Don Quixote's tilting with windmills and other adventures, of course, have been the stuff of magazines, musicals, and the western imagination for 400 years. I talked with Edith Grossman recently in her New York apartment.

. . . So you have a major classic by any standard, and you have to sit down to translate it. It must be scary. . . .

EDITH GROSSMAN: Terrifying. Part of it is the weight of 400 years of scholarship. The other part is the immense responsibility involved in translating a book of this stature, and the influence that your translation will have on readers.

JEFFREY BROWN: What is it that makes it so compelling? I mean, why does it still have influence almost 400 years later?

EDITH GROSSMAN: Part of it has to do with the writing style of Cervantes, who was a brilliant writer. Another part of it has to do with the characters he created, who are truly modern in the sense that they are not at the end of the novel who they were at the beginning, but they change and grow and develop and have an impact on the world, and the world has an impact on them. And they interact with each other and with other people whom they meet.

JEFFREY BROWN: One of the things that you say in your preface is that the essential challenge in translation is discovering the voice to write the text in English: Taking the Spanish and finding the voice in English. What do you mean by that?

EDITH GROSSMAN: Ralph Manheim, who was a translator from Germany, once said that translators are like actors who say other people's lines, and speak as the author would speak if the author spoke English. And so what we try to do, what

is it licit or permissible for you, under the laws of chivalry, to help me until you are dubbed a knight."

"There's no doubt, Señor," replied Sancho, "that your grace will be strictly obeyed in this; besides, as far as I'm concerned, I'm a peaceful man and an enemy of getting involved in quarrels or disputes. It's certainly true that when it comes to defending my person I won't pay much attention to those laws, since laws both human and di-

vine permit each man to defend himself against anyone who tries to hurt him."

"I agree," Don Quixote responded, "but as for helping me against gentlemen, you have to hold your natural impulses in check."

"Then that's just what I'll do," replied Sancho, "and I'll keep that precept as faithfully as I keep the Sabbath on Sunday."

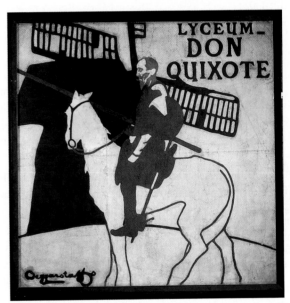

Lyceum-Don Quixote (1895) by the Beggarstaffs. Poster.
The Victoria & Albert Museum, London (E. 1208.1927).
Reproduced by permission of Elizabeth Banks.

translators try to do, is hear that voice and find the voice in English that matches it. . . . I'm trying to reach back as well to the authentic sound of the author.

And what I mean by sound and voice is that there is elevated diction, for example—the difference between Don Quixote's ordinary language and Sancho's ordinary language is enormous. Quixote is a very well-educated man, and Sancho Panza is illiterate, so their levels of language are different. Cervantes makes it very clear that they're different. And what I was trying to do was to re-create that difference in English. . . .

JEFFREY BROWN: Cervantes was, in a sense, winking at his readership of the time, correct?

EDITH GROSSMAN: In the sense that the novels of chivalry were the reality TV of their day. It was the most popular form in Spain, and everyone read novels of chivalry. It's what people did with their leisure time. And he simply destroyed the genre by laughing at it, by way of *Don Quixote*.

JEFFREY BROWN: What are you hoping that a new readership of *Don Quixote* will get from it?

EDITH GROSSMAN: Enormous pleasure, and the opportunity, if it's the first time they're reading the book, to experience a masterpiece. . . .

? In this interview, the translator Edith Grossman talks about trying to re-create the difference between Don Quixote's and Sancho Panza's speech. As you read the excerpt from *Don Quixote* on pages 689–701, could you detect this difference? Explain.

Response and Analysis

Reading Check

1. What kind of books does Don Quixote like to read? What effect do they have on his life?

2. Why does Sancho Panza become Don Quixote's squire?

3. How does Don Quixote explain his defeat by the windmill?

4. What natural human needs, which Don Quixote ignores, does Sancho Panza satisfy for himself?

Thinking Critically

5. How are Don Quixote's helmet, horse, and ladylove examples of a **parody** of a medieval romance?

6. A **foil** is a character used as a contrast to another character. In what ways is Sancho Panza a foil to Don Quixote? Identify behaviors suggesting that the two men are opposites.

7. Is Don Quixote's quest fundamentally different from or similar to the quests undertaken by heroes of epics or romances? Explain.

8. Clearly, Cervantes wants us to laugh at his protagonist as he prepares for his preposterous undertaking, but is Don Quixote presented as merely a fool, or is he also a true hero? What, if anything, makes him heroic?

Extending and Evaluating

9. What **inferences** can you make about the following topics?

   • Cervantes' beliefs about medieval romances

   • Cervantes' feelings toward Don Quixote himself

   Explain why you think each inference is sound.

10. Don Quixote's exploits have given us the term *quixotic* to describe any idealistic or impractical project. Do you know anybody whose behavior could be described as quixotic? Has your own behavior ever fallen into this category? Explain. You may wish to consult your Quickwrite notes.

WRITING

Writing a Parody

Imagine a modern-day Don Quixote who is fascinated by the heroes in contemporary movies, comic books, or TV shows. Write a parody in which your character takes on the role of a modern hero and goes to places such as the supermarket or the video store in search of adventure. What are your character's goals? What wrongs will he or she attempt to right?

Vocabulary Development
Question and Answer

Answer the following questions. Each response should demonstrate your knowledge of the underlined Vocabulary word.

1. Does a toy whistle make a sonorous sound?

2. What might a grandiloquent knight say to his ladylove?

3. Would an errant dog make a good pet?

4. How might you ameliorate a tense situation?

North Carolina Competency Goal
1.02; 1.03; 2.01; 4.01; 4.05; 5.03; 6.01

INTERNET

Projects and Activities

Keyword:
LE5 WL-5

SKILLS FOCUS

Literary Skills
Analyze parody.

Reading Skills
Make inferences about an author's beliefs.

Writing Skills
Write a parody.

Vocabulary Skills
Answer questions about vocabulary words.

Jean de La Fontaine
(1621–1695)
France

Jean de La Fontaine (zhän de la fōn·ten′) was said to be an impractical dreamer who was awkward in social situations. One story illustrates his lack of social graces at a boring dinner party. After making excuses that he needed to leave an hour early for another engagement, his hostess noted that it would take him only twenty minutes to reach his destination. He replied, "But you see, I prefer the longest way."

La Fontaine also seems to have chosen the longest route to a literary career. He was born in 1621 at Château-Thierry (sha′tō′tē·er′ē), where his father supervised forest areas and water management for the region. While in school, La Fontaine was first introduced to Greek and Latin, the languages of the classical writers he later came to admire. Rather than pursue classical studies, however, La Fontaine entered a seminary in Paris to study theology. But seminary discipline did not suit the dreamy, absent-minded young man, and at age twenty-two he returned to Château-Thierry to dabble in legal studies. Four years later, in accordance with his father's wishes, he married Marie Hericart, who was only fourteen years old at the time. La Fontaine had little interest in his marriage, however, and some time later the couple separated and he embarked on a literary career.

When he was thirty-three, La Fontaine published his first work, *The Eunuch,* an adaptation of a comedy by the Roman writer Terence. The play was a failure, but La Fontaine kept writing, and eventually his writing and his charm won him generous sums of money from powerful patrons, including ministers in the court of King Louis XIV. This patronage

Jean de La Fontaine by Hyacinthe Rigaud (1659–1743). Musée Jean de La Fontaine, Château-Thierry, France.

enabled La Fontaine to produce other works, the most successful being the *Fables.* Based in part on the animal fables of classical writers like Aesop and Phaedrus, the *Fables* appeared in a series of twelve books between the years 1668 and 1694 and won immediate popularity. Regarded by the French as tiny masterpieces, they are models of perfect style that are still memorized by French students today.

Before You Read

from Fables

Make the Connection

Quickwrite

Wile E. Coyote, the *Lion King* hyenas, the Big Bad Wolf—we love to hate them, but why? Partly because they remind us of ourselves, or, more specifically, of our own worst traits. In a similar way, we tend to see the noblest aspects of ourselves in the Road Runner, Simba, and the resourceful third Little Pig.

Make a list of animals (or animal characters) and the human traits we assign to them. For each animal, explain why we associate a certain characteristic with it. Why do you think we enjoy stories about animals who are like us?

Literary Focus

Moral

*The **moral** of the story is . . .* We hear these words from the earliest days of childhood but still never tire of a fable's "reveal"—of its concise, plainly stated lesson about life. There is something pleasing about being given the answer so freely, something satisfying about having the loose ends tied up in one sturdy little knot of wisdom. In La Fontaine's fables this "knot of wisdom" often takes the form of an **epigram,** or clever saying, that sums up a theme in a very compact rhyme, much like the refrain of a song.

Regardless of its *form* however, a moral's *content* is often familiar to us: It is often a lesson we have already learned from life itself. Nevertheless, there is comfort in hearing it articulated, for in doing so we are reassured that humanity has access—with the help of our best storytellers—to some of life's most important truths.

> A **moral** is a lesson about life that a story teaches.
>
> *For more on Moral, see the Handbook of Literary and Historical Terms.*

Background

The fables of La Fontaine are **beast fables**—brief stories in which animals take on the traits of people in order to teach practical lessons about life, especially to mock corrupt or thoughtless behavior. La Fontaine's fables seem lighthearted at first. They have a playful rhyme scheme and rhythm, and their characters are the kinds of animals that often appear in children's books. But these animals are not cute and cuddly; they demonstrate human characteristics in a way that is less than flattering to people, conjuring through their words and actions a world of deceit and cowardice. It's no surprise, then, that La Fontaine did not write the fables specifically for children. And yet the fables' didactic, or educational, nature makes them good teaching tools. La Fontaine himself believed that children "should not be left in ignorance"—that adults should "teach them what a lion is, a fox, and so on, and why a person is sometimes compared to a fox or a lion."

Fox in a Chicken Yard (1766) by Jean-Baptiste Huet, the Elder or Younger.

from *Fables*

Jean de La Fontaine *translated by* Elizur Wright, Jr.

The Cock and the Fox

Upon a tree there mounted guard
   A veteran cock, adroit and cunning,
   When to the roots a fox up running,
Spoke thus, in tones of kind regard:—
5   Our quarrel, brother, is at an end;
     Henceforth I hope to live your friend;
       For peace now reigns
       Throughout the animal domains.
   I bear the news:—come down, I pray,
10   And give me the embrace fraternal;

   And please, my brother, don't delay.
     So much the tidings do concern all,
   That I must spread them far today.
   Now you and yours can take your walks
15   Without a fear or thought of hawks.
And should you clash with them or others,
In us you'll find the best of brothers;—
For which you may, this joyful night,
   Your merry bonfires light.
20   But, first, let's seal the bliss

Jean de La Fontaine   **705**

With one fraternal kiss.
"Good friend," the cock replied, "upon my
  word,
A better thing I never heard;
    And doubly I rejoice
25   To hear it from your voice:
And really, there must be something in it,
    For yonder come two greyhounds,
        which, I flatter
Myself, are couriers on this very matter:
They come so fast, they'll be here in a
  minute.
    I'll down, and all of us will seal the
30   blessing
With general kissing and caressing."
    "Adieu,"° said Fox, "my errand's
        pressing:
I'll hurry on my way,
    And we'll rejoice some other day."
35 So off the fellow scampered, quick and light,
To gain the foxholes of a neighboring
    height—
Less happy in his stratagem than flight.
    The cock laughed sweetly in his sleeve—
'Tis doubly sweet deceiver to deceive.

---

32. Adieu (ə·dyo͞o′): French for "goodbye."

The Council Held by the Rats

Old Rodilard, a certain cat,
    Such havoc of the rats had made,
'Twas difficult to find a rat
    With nature's debt unpaid.°
5   The few that did remain,
    To leave their holes afraid,
From usual food abstain,
    Not eating half their fill.
    And wonder no one will,
10 That one who made on rats his revel,
With rats passed not for cat, but devil.
Now, on a day, this dread rat eater,
Who had a wife, went out to meet her;
And while he held his caterwauling,°

---

4. With nature's debt unpaid: remaining alive.
14. caterwauling v. used as n.: shrill howl
  characteristic of cats during mating.

15 The unkilled rats, their chapter calling,
Discussed the point, in grave debate,
How they might shun impending fate.
    Their dean, a prudent rat,
Thought best, and better soon than late,
20   To bell the fatal cat;
That, when he took his hunting round,
The rats, well cautioned by the sound,
Might hide in safety underground;
    Indeed he knew no other means.
25   And all the rest
        At once confessed
Their minds were with the dean's.
No better plan, they all believed,
Could possibly have been conceived.
30 No doubt the thing would work right well,
If any one would hang the bell.
    But, one by one, said every rat,
    I'm not so big a fool as that.
The plan, knocked up in this respect,
35 The council closed without effect.
And many a council I have seen,
Or reverend chapter with its dean,
    That, thus resolving wisely,
    Fell through like this precisely.

40   To argue or refute
            Wise counselors abound;
        The man to execute
            Is harder to be found.

*The Council Held
by the Rats* (1868)
by Gustave Doré.

Response and Analysis

Reading Check

1. What does the fox say to trick the cock? What is his real intention?
2. How does the cock get the better of the fox in the end?
3. What plan does the dean of rats devise to protect the rats from the cat?
4. Why are the rats unable to put their plan into effect?

Thinking Critically

5. How could the expression "my enemy's enemy is my best friend" apply to the story of the cock and the fox?
6. In the final **quatrain,** or four lines, of "The Council Held by the Rats," La Fontaine explicitly presents his **moral** in the form of an **epigram.** Restate the moral in your own words. What is the moral of "The Cock and the Fox"?
7. Consider the characters of the animals in the fables. What qualities do we typically associate with foxes and rats? How are these qualities apparent in the stories?
8. What human traits are ridiculed in these two beast fables?
9. La Fontaine's fables have been criticized for their cynical **tone,** or attitude. How would you describe the tone of these two fables? What do you think of their tone?

Extending and Evaluating

10. What is your reaction to the morals of La Fontaine's fables? Do you think they are too bitter and jaded, or do they confirm any of your own experiences? Explain.
11. For what reasons, other than entertainment, might human beings project human qualities onto animals—whether they be cartoon characters, pets, or inhabitants of the wild? Review your Quickwrite notes for ideas.

WRITING

Writing a Fable

Consider a lesson you have learned in the past, such as the virtue of being on time or the wisdom of not speaking in anger. Translate your experience into a fable with its own moral. (You might want to write the moral first.) Your fable may be written in either prose or verse, but it must feature animal characters who demonstrate human qualities, such as the characters in La Fontaine's fables.

North Carolina Competency Goal
1.02; 1.03; 4.05; 5.03; 6.01

The Hare and the Frogs. by Gustave Doré.

INTERNET

Projects and Activities
Keyword: LE5 WL-5

Literary Skills
Analyze moral.

Writing Skills
Write a fable.

Voltaire

(1694–1778)

France

François Marie Arouet, better known by his pseudonym, Voltaire, was a writer who believed in presenting the truth. He criticized the wastefulness of war, religious intolerance, and the unnecessary poverty and powerlessness of the average citizen. As a result of his frankness, he was imprisoned twice, exiled from Paris once, had his books and pamphlets banned by the French government, and was denied burial by the Parisian clergy when he died. Yet the spirit of his writing prevailed, and thirteen years after his death, the new postrevolutionary government brought back Voltaire's remains to Paris with great ceremony. Thousands of people lined the streets to see the funeral procession.

Voltaire was one of the main founders of modern historical writing. He found traditional approaches to writing history inadequate, preferring to write philosophical treatises on morals. These essays were not abstract—they focused on how people actually lived and worked according to their moral principles. His efforts were not well received, however, by the people in power. His most formidable work, *Essay on the Morals and the Spirit of the Nations from Charlemagne to Louis XIII*, was banned when it was published, and Voltaire was exiled.

Aside from his voluminous correspondence and hundreds of pamphlets on a variety of issues that arose in his time, Voltaire wrote in every literary genre. *La Henriade*, an epic poem about Henry IV, which he wrote during his first imprisonment, was regarded by some of his contemporaries as equal to the works of Homer and Virgil. Between *Oedipe*, written when he was eighteen, and *Irene*, written at age

Portrait of Voltaire (1718) by Catherine Lusurier.
Chateaux de Versailles et de Trianon, Versailles, France.

eighty-three, Voltaire wrote numerous plays, most of them great successes. His *Philosophic Dictionary* was perhaps the most widely read nonfiction book of his time. He wrote numerous romances, plays, and tales, of which *Candide* has proven to be the most enduring.

Voltaire had little patience for purely metaphysical speculation. Instead, he placed emphasis on modest but practical achievement. This philosophical stance is reflected in the last page of *Candide*: "Let us work without arguing . . . it's the only way to make life endurable."

Before You Read

from Candide

Make the Connection

Quickwrite ✏

If it were possible to live in the "best of all possible worlds" right here on earth, what would such a place be like? What kinds of things would you *not* find there? If someone told you that we already live in the "best of all possible worlds," how would you respond? Write a paragraph expressing your ideas.

Literary Focus

Satire

Satire is writing that ridicules human weakness, vice, or folly in order to bring about social reform. An expert satirist like Voltaire uses a variety of tools—from witty barbs to heavy bludgeons—to expose his subject to ridicule and flatten his opponents' sacred cows. As Voltaire exposes one absurdity after another, readers become convinced that they would be fools *not* to agree with his point of view. As you read this excerpt from *Candide,* look for Voltaire's outrageous exaggerations and deadpan understatements, for illogic dressed up as common sense, and for situations that are simply silly.

> **Satire** is writing that ridicules human weakness, vice, or folly in order to bring about social reform.
>
> *For more on Satire, see the Handbook of Literary and Historical Terms.*

Reading Skills

Appreciating a Writer's Style

An author's style is the *how* of the writing rather than the *what.* As you read this selection from *Candide,* ask yourself why Voltaire may have chosen to use certain words, phrases, or figures of speech. List some of the ones that in your opinion best represent Voltaire's humorous style.

Background

Candide is subtitled "Optimism" and tells a tale of the woes that befall a naive simpleton who is brought up to believe that this world is the best of all possible worlds. The plot takes the form of a quest: the young man's quest for union with his beloved. The tale is told with great verve and humor, and, like all pursuits of this kind, the journey involves much suffering but ends in wisdom.

North Carolina Competency Goal
1.03; 4.05; 5.01; 5.03

Vocabulary Development

candor (kan′dər) *n.:* honesty and frankness; fair, unbiased attitude.

pensive (pen′siv) *adj.:* thinking seriously.

vivacity (vī·vas′ə·tē) *n.:* liveliness.

prudent (prōō′dənt) *adj.:* careful in behavior; cautious.

discretion (di·skresh′ən) *n.:* prudence; quality of being cautious about one's behavior.

disconcert (dis′kən·surt′) *v.:* unsettle; confuse.

ingenious (in·jēn′yəs) *adj.:* original; clever.

INTERNET

More About Voltaire
•
Vocabulary Practice
Keyword:
LE5 WL-5

SKILLS FOCUS

Literary Skills
Understand satire.

Reading Skills
Appreciate a writer's style.

from Candide

Voltaire
translated by **Richard Aldington**

Chapter 1

How Candide was brought up in a noble castle, and how he was expelled from the same

In the castle of Baron Thunder-ten-tronckh in Westphalia[1] there lived a youth, endowed by Nature with the most gentle character. His face was the expression of his soul. His judgment was quite honest and he was extremely simple-minded; and this was the reason, I think, that he was named Candide. Old servants in the house suspected that he was the son of the Baron's sister and a decent honest gentleman of the neighborhood, whom this young lady would never marry because he could only prove seventy-one quarterings,[2] and the rest of his genealogical tree was lost, owing to the injuries of time.

The Baron was one of the most powerful lords in Westphalia, for his castle possessed a door and windows. His Great Hall was even decorated with a piece of tapestry. The dogs in his stable yards formed a pack of hounds when necessary; his grooms were his huntsmen; the village curate was his Grand Almoner.[3] They all called him "My Lord," and laughed heartily at his stories.

The Baroness weighed about three hundred and fifty pounds, was therefore greatly respected, and did the honors of the house with a dignity which rendered her still more respectable. Her daughter Cunegonde, aged seventeen, was rosy-cheeked, fresh, plump and tempting. The Baron's son appeared in every respect worthy of his father. The tutor Pangloss was the oracle of the house, and little Candide followed his lessons with all the candor of his age and character.

Pangloss taught metaphysico-theologo-cosmoloonigology.[4] He proved admirably that there is no effect without a cause and that in this best of all possible worlds, My Lord the Baron's castle was the best of castles and his wife the best of all possible Baronesses.

"'Tis demonstrated," said he, "that things cannot be otherwise; for, since everything is made for an end, everything is necessarily for the best end. Observe that noses were made to wear spectacles; and so we have spectacles. Legs were visibly instituted to be breeched, and we have breeches.

---

1. **Westphalia:** region in western Germany, noted for its hams. Voltaire considered it "vast, sad, sterile, detestable."
2. **quarterings** *n. pl.:* divisions on a coat of arms or family tree. Seventy-one quarterings would trace a person's genealogy back over 2,000 years.
3. **Grand Almoner:** member of a noble household responsible for distributing charity to the poor.

4. **metaphysico-theologo-cosmoloonigology:** The doctrine of philosophical optimism by Leibniz, a seventeenth-century German philosopher, which is evident in satirical statements such as "this is the best of all possible worlds." This doctrine is a frequent target of Voltaire's biting wit. Voltaire is satirizing Leibniz and his followers by embedding the word *loon* in this made-up field of philosophy.

Vocabulary

candor (kanʹdər) *n.:* honesty and frankness; fair, unbiased attitude.

The Stolen Kiss (c. 1780) by Jean-Honoré Fragonard.
Musée du Louvre, Paris.

Stones were formed to be quarried and to build castles; and My Lord has a very noble castle; the greatest Baron in the province should have the best house; and as pigs were made to be eaten, we eat pork all the year round; consequently, those who have asserted that all is well talk nonsense; they ought to have said that all is for the best."

Candide listened attentively and believed innocently; for he thought Miss Cunegonde extremely beautiful, although he was never bold enough to tell her so. He decided that after the happiness of being born Baron of Thunder-ten-tronckh, the second degree of happiness was to be Miss Cunegonde; the third, to see her every day; and the fourth, to listen to Doctor Pangloss, the greatest philosopher of the province and therefore of the whole world.

One day when Cunegonde was walking near the castle, in a little wood which was called The Park, she observed Doctor Pangloss in the bushes, giving a lesson in experimental physics to her mother's waiting-maid, a very pretty and docile brunette. Miss Cunegonde had a great inclination for science and watched breathlessly the reiterated experiments she witnessed; she observed clearly the Doctor's sufficient reason, the effects and the causes, and returned home very much excited, <u>pensive</u>, filled with the desire of learning; reflecting that she might be the sufficient reason of young Candide and that he might be hers.

On her way back to the castle she met Candide and blushed; Candide also blushed. She bade him good-morning in a hesitating voice; Candide replied without knowing what he was saying. Next day, when they left the table after dinner, Cunegonde and Candide found themselves behind a screen; Cunegonde dropped her

Vocabulary

pensive (pen′siv) *adj.*: thinking seriously.

handkerchief, Candide picked it up; she innocently held his hand; the young man innocently kissed the young lady's hand with remarkable vivacity, tenderness and grace; their lips met, their eyes sparkled, their knees trembled, their hands wandered. Baron Thunder-ten-tronckh passed near the screen, and, observing this cause and effect, expelled Candide from the castle by kicking him in the backside frequently and hard. Cunegonde swooned; when she recovered her senses, the Baroness slapped her in the face; and all was in consternation in the noblest and most agreeable of all possible castles.

After he is banished from the castle, Candide wanders aimlessly until he reaches a town nearby, where he is unwittingly recruited into the Bulgarian army and begins his training. He suffers much abuse at the hands of his fellow soldiers and is almost beaten to death, but he is pardoned by the king of Bulgaria at the last moment.

Some chapters later, after escaping the slaughter of the Seven Years' War, Candide encounters Pangloss in Holland. Pangloss informs Candide that his beloved Cunegonde has been disemboweled by the Bulgarians and that the Baron's castle and everyone in it is destroyed. While en route to Portugal, the two survive a shipwreck and arrive in Lisbon just in time for the great earthquake. There the Inquisition arrests them as heretics responsible for the devastation, and Candide is publicly flogged; Pangloss, however, is hanged and presumed dead. A "good old woman" then reunites Candide with Cunegonde, who describes how she survived the Bulgarians and came to be held by the Grand Inquisitor. Candide kills the Inquisitor and sails with Cunegonde for South America, where they hope to find "the best of all possible worlds" and lasting happiness. But Candide loses Cunegonde for the sake of the immediate happiness of the governor of Buenos Aires, and again the sweet-natured youth is forced to run, along with his new footman Cacambo. In their flight, Candide and Cacambo are nearly skewered and boiled by cannibals, the Oreillons, but Cacambo exhibits his clearheadedness by talking the savages out of their dinner plans.

Chapter 17
Arrival of Candide and his valet in the country of Eldorado and what they saw there

When they reached the frontiers of the Oreillons,[5] Cacambo said to Candide:
   "You see this hemisphere is no better than the other; take my advice, let us go back to Europe by the shortest road."

---

5. **Oreillons:** French, roughly meaning "Big Ears."

Vocabulary
vivacity (vĭ·vas′ə·tē) *n.:* liveliness.

*Pirara and Lake Amucu,
The Site of Eldorado*
by Charles Bentley
(1806–1854).

Yale Center for British Art,
Paul Mellon Collection, USA.

"How can we go back," said Candide, "and where can we go? If I go to my own country, the Bulgarians and the Abares[6] are murdering everybody; if I return to Portugal[7] I shall be burned; if we stay here, we run the risk of being spitted at any moment. But how can I make up my mind to leave that part of the world where Miss Cunegonde is living?"

"Let us go to Cayenne,"[8] said Cacambo, "we shall find Frenchmen there, for they go all over the world; they might help us. Perhaps God will have pity on us."

It was not easy to go to Cayenne. They knew roughly the direction to take, but mountains, rivers, precipices, brigands and savages were everywhere terrible obstacles. Their horses died of fatigue; their provisions were exhausted; for a whole month they lived on wild fruits and at last found themselves near a little river fringed

---

6. **Abares:** that is, the French, who fought against the "Bulgarians," or Prussians, in the Seven Years' War (1756–1763).
7. **Portugal:** Following the earthquake in Lisbon, Candide was persecuted by the Inquisition. He fears being burned as a heretic if he returns.

---

8. **Cayenne** (kī·en′): seaport in French Guiana in South America.

with coconut-trees which supported their lives and their hopes.

Cacambo, who always gave advice as <u>prudent</u> as the old woman's,[9] said to Candide:

"We can go no further, we have walked far enough; I can see an empty canoe in the bank, let us fill it with coconuts, get into the little boat and drift with the current; a river always leads to some inhabited place. If we do not find anything pleasant, we shall at least find something new."

"Come on then," said Candide, "and let us trust to Providence."

They drifted for some leagues between banks which were sometimes flowery, sometimes bare, sometimes flat, sometimes steep. The river continually became wider; finally it disappeared under an arch of frightful rocks which towered up to the very sky. The two travelers were bold enough to trust themselves to the current under this arch. The stream, narrowed between walls, carried them with horrible rapidity and noise. After twenty-four hours they saw daylight again; but their canoe was wrecked on reefs; they had to crawl from rock to rock for a whole league and at last they discovered an immense horizon, bordered by inaccessible mountains. The country was cultivated for pleasure as well as for necessity; everywhere the useful was agreeable. The roads were covered or rather ornamented with carriages of brilliant material and shape, carrying men and women of singular beauty, who were rapidly drawn along by large red sheep whose swiftness surpassed that of the finest horses of Andalusia, Tetuan and Mequinez.

"This country," said Candide, "is better than Westphalia."

He landed with Cacambo near the first village he came to. Several children of the village, dressed in torn gold brocade, were playing coits[10] outside the village. Our two men from the other world amused themselves by looking on; their coits were large round pieces, yellow, red, and green, which shone with peculiar luster. The travelers were curious enough to pick up some of them; they were of gold, emeralds, and rubies, the least of which would have been the greatest ornament in the Mogul's throne.

"No doubt," said Cacambo, "these children are the sons of the King of this country playing at coits."

At that moment the village schoolmaster appeared to call them into school.

"This," said Candide, "is the tutor of the Royal Family."

The little beggars immediately left their game, abandoning their coits and everything with which they had been playing. Candide picked them up, ran to the tutor, and presented them to him humbly, giving him to understand by signs that their Royal Highnesses had forgotten their gold and their precious stones. The village schoolmaster smiled, threw them on the ground, gazed for a moment at Candide's face with much surprise, and continued on his way.

The travelers did not fail to pick up the gold, the rubies, and the emeralds.

"Where are we?" cried Candide. "The children of the Kings must be well brought up, since they are taught to despise gold and precious stones."

Cacambo was as much surprised as Candide. At last they reached the first house in the village, which was built like a European palace. There were crowds of people round the door and still more inside; very pleasant music could be heard and there was a delicious smell of cooking. Cacambo went up to the door and heard them speaking Peruvian; it was his maternal tongue, for everyone knows that Cacambo was born in a village of Tucuman where nothing else is spoken.

"I will act as your interpreter," he said to Candide, "this is an inn, let us enter."

Immediately two boys and two girls of the inn, dressed in cloth of gold, whose hair was bound up with ribbons, invited them to sit down to the

---

9. **the old woman:** The old woman traveled with Candide and Cunegonde to the New World. She knew everything of life, having survived kidnapping by pirates, enslavement in Morocco, catching the plague in Algiers, and being disfigured by the Turks.

10. **coits** *n. pl.:* quoits, a game resembling horseshoes.

Vocabulary

prudent (prōō′dənt) *adj.:* careful in behavior; cautious.

table d'hôte.[11] They served four soups each garnished with two parrots, a boiled condor which weighed two hundred pounds, two roast monkeys of excellent flavor, three hundred colibris[12] in one dish and six hundred hummingbirds in another, exquisite ragouts and delicious pastries, all in dishes of a sort of rock-crystal. The boys and girls brought several sorts of drinks made of sugar-cane. Most of the guests were merchants and coachmen, all extremely polite, who asked Cacambo a few questions with the most delicate discretion and answered his in a satisfactory manner.

When the meal was over, Cacambo, like Candide, thought he could pay the reckoning by throwing on the table two of the large pieces of gold he had picked up; the host and hostess laughed until they had to hold their sides. At last they recovered themselves.

"Gentlemen," said the host, "we perceive you are strangers; we are not accustomed to seeing them. Forgive us if we began to laugh when you offered us in payment the stones from our highways. No doubt you have none of the money of this country, but you do not need any to dine here. All the hotels established for the utility of commerce are paid for by the government. You have been ill-entertained here because this is a poor village; but everywhere else you will be received as you deserve to be."

Cacambo explained to Candide all that the host had said, and Candide listened in the same admiration and disorder with which his friend Cacambo interpreted.

"What can this country be," they said to each other, "which is unknown to the rest of the world and where all nature is so different from ours? Probably it is the country where

Gold objects in an Aztec shop (16th century) from an account of Aztec crafts written by Bernardino.
Biblioteca Medicea Laurenziana, Florence, Italy
(Ms Palat. 218-220 Book IX).

everything is for the best; for there must be one country of that sort. And, in spite of what Dr. Pangloss said, I often noticed that everything went very ill in Westphalia."

Chapter 18
What they saw in the land of Eldorado

Cacambo informed the host of his curiosity, and the host said:

"I am a very ignorant man and am all the better for it; but we have here an old man who has retired from the court and who is the most learned and most communicative man in the kingdom."

---

11. **table d'hôte** (tä′bəl dōt′): complete meal served at a fixed price.
12. **colibris** *n. pl.:* hummingbirds with curved bills, once classified as a separate species.

Vocabulary

discretion (di·skresh′ən) *n.:* prudence; quality of being cautious about one's behavior.

And he at once took Cacambo to the old man. Candide now played only the second part and accompanied his valet.

They entered a very simple house, for the door was only of silver and the paneling of the apartments in gold, but so tastefully carved that the richest decorations did not surpass it. The antechamber indeed was only encrusted with rubies and emeralds; but the order with which everything was arranged atoned for this extreme simplicity.

The old man received the two strangers on a sofa padded with colibri feathers, and presented them with drinks in diamond cups; after which he satisfied their curiosity in these words:

"I am a hundred and seventy-two years old and I heard from my late father, the King's equerry,[13] the astonishing revolutions of Peru of which he had been an eyewitness. The kingdom where we now are is the ancient country of the Incas, who most imprudently left it to conquer part of the world and were at last destroyed by the Spaniards.

"The princes of their family who remained in their native country had more wisdom; with the consent of the nation, they ordered that no inhabitants should ever leave our little kingdom, and this it is that has preserved our innocence and our felicity. The Spaniards had some vague knowledge of this country, which they called Eldorado,[14] and about a hundred years ago an Englishman named Raleigh[15] came very near to it; but, since we are surrounded by inaccessible rocks and precipices, we have hitherto been exempt from the rapacity[16] of the nations of Europe who have an inconceivable lust for the pebbles and mud of our land and would kill us to the last man to get possession of them."

The conversation was long; it touched upon the form of the government, manners, women, public spectacles, and the arts. Finally Candide, who was always interested in metaphysics, asked through Cacambo whether the country had a religion. The old man blushed a little.

"How can you doubt it?" said he. "Do you think we are ingrates?"

Cacambo humbly asked what was the religion of Eldorado. The old man blushed again.

"Can there be two religions?" said he. "We have, I think, the religion of everyone else; we adore God from evening until morning."

"Do you adore only one god?" said Cacambo, who continued to act as the interpreter of Candide's doubts.

"Manifestly," said the old man, "there are not two or three or four. I must confess that the people of your world ask very extraordinary questions."

Candide continued to press the old man with questions; he wished to know how they prayed to God in Eldorado.

"We do not pray," said the good and respectable sage, "we have nothing to ask from him; he has given us everything necessary and we continually give him thanks."

Candide was curious to see the priests; and asked where they were. The good old man smiled.

"My friends," said he, "we are all priests; the King and all the heads of families solemnly sing praises every morning, accompanied by five or six thousand musicians."

"What! Have you no monks to teach, to dispute, to govern, to intrigue and to burn people who do not agree with them?"

"For that, we should have to become fools," said the old man; "here we are all of the same opinion and do not understand what you mean with your monks."

At all this Candide was in an ecstasy and said to himself:

"This is very different from Westphalia and the castle of His Lordship the Baron; if our friend Pangloss had seen Eldorado, he would not have said that the castle of Thunder-ten-tronckh was the best of all that exists on the earth; certainly, a man should travel."

---

13. **equerry** (ek′wər·ē) *n.:* officer in charge of horses.
14. **Eldorado** (el′də·rä′dō): legendary place of spectacular riches.
15. **Raleigh:** Sir Walter Raleigh's *Discovery of Guiana* (1595) helped spread the legend of Eldorado.
16. **rapacity** *n.:* greed.

Manco Capac, first Inca king, (mid-18th century).

Brooklyn Museum of Art, Brooklyn, New York.

After this long conversation the good old man ordered a carriage to be harnessed with six sheep and gave the two travelers twelve of his servants to take them to court.

"You will excuse me," he said, "if my age deprives me of the honor of accompanying you. The King will receive you in a manner which will not displease you and doubtless you will pardon the customs of the country if any of them <u>disconcert</u> you."

Candide and Cacambo entered the carriage; the six sheep galloped off and in less than four hours they reached the King's palace, which was situated at one end of the capital. The portal was two hundred and twenty feet high and a hundred feet wide; it is impossible to describe its material. Anyone can see the prodigious superiority it must have over the pebbles and sand we call *gold* and *gems.*

Twenty beautiful maidens of the guard received Candide and Cacambo as they alighted from the carriage, conducted them to the baths and dressed them in robes woven from the down of colibris; after which the principal male and female officers of the Crown led them to his Majesty's apartment through two files of a thousand musicians each, according to the usual custom. As they approached the throne room, Cacambo asked one of the chief officers how they should behave in his Majesty's presence; whether they should fall on their knees or flat on their faces, whether they should put their hands on their heads or on their backsides; whether they should lick the dust of the throne room; in a word, what was the ceremony?

"The custom," said the chief officer, "is to embrace the King and to kiss him on either cheek."

Vocabulary

disconcert (dis′kən·sʉrt′) *v.*: unsettle; confuse.

Candide and Cacambo threw their arms round his Majesty's neck; he received them with all imaginable favor and politely asked them to supper.

Meanwhile they were carried to see the town, the public buildings rising to the very skies, the marketplaces ornamented with thousands of columns, the fountains of pure water, the fountains of rose-water and of liquors distilled from sugar-cane, which played continually in the public squares paved with precious stones which emitted a perfume like that of cloves and cinnamon.

Candide asked to see the law courts; he was told there were none, and that nobody ever went to law. He asked if there were prisons and was told there were none. He was still more surprised and pleased by the palace of sciences, where he saw a gallery two thousand feet long, filled with instruments of mathematics and physics.

After they had explored all the afternoon about a thousandth part of the town, they were taken back to the King. Candide sat down to table with his Majesty, his valet Cacambo and several ladies. Never was better cheer, and never was anyone wittier at supper than his Majesty. Cacambo explained the King's witty remarks to Candide and even when translated they still appeared witty. Among all the things which amazed Candide, this did not amaze him the least.

They enjoyed this hospitality for a month. Candide repeatedly said to Cacambo:

"Once again, my friend, it is quite true that the castle where I was born cannot be compared with this country; but then Miss Cunegonde is not here and you probably have a mistress in Europe. If we remain here, we shall only be like everyone else; but if we return to our own world with only twelve sheep laden with Eldorado pebbles, we shall be richer than all the kings put together; we shall have no more Inquisitors[17] to fear and we can easily regain Miss Cunegonde."

Cacambo agreed with this; it is so pleasant to be on the move, to show off before friends, to make a parade of the things seen on one's travels, that these two happy men resolved to be so no longer and to ask his Majesty's permission to depart.

"You are doing a very silly thing," said the King. "I know my country is small; but when we are comfortable anywhere we should stay there; I certainly have not the right to detain foreigners, that is a tyranny which does not exist either in our manners or our laws; all men are free, leave when you please, but the way out is very difficult. It is impossible to ascend the rapid river by which you miraculously came here and which flows under arches of rock. The mountains which surround the whole of my kingdom are ten thousand feet high and as perpendicular as rocks; they are more than ten leagues broad and you can only get down from them by way of precipices. However, since you must go, I will give orders to the directors of machinery to make a machine which will carry you comfortably. When you have been taken to the other side of the mountains, nobody can proceed any farther with you; for my subjects have sworn never to pass this boundary and they are too wise to break their oath. Ask anything else of me you wish."

"We ask nothing of your Majesty," said Cacambo, "except a few sheep laden with provisions, pebbles, and the mud of this country."

The King laughed.

"I cannot understand," said he, "the taste you people of Europe have for our yellow mud; but take as much as you wish, and much good may it do you."

He immediately ordered his engineers to make a machine to hoist these two extraordinary men out of his kingdom.

Three thousand learned scientists worked at it; it was ready in a fortnight and only cost about twenty million pounds sterling in the money of that country. Candide and Cacambo were placed on the machine; there were two large red sheep saddled and bridled for them to ride on when they had passed the mountains, twenty sumpter[18] sheep laden with provisions, thirty

---

17. **Inquisitors:** members of the Roman Catholic tribunal charged with combating heresy.

18. **sumpter** *n.* used as *adj.*: used for carrying packs and other loads.

carrying presents of the most curious productions of the country and fifty laden with gold, precious stones and diamonds. The King embraced the two vagabonds tenderly.

Their departure was a splendid sight and so was the ingenious manner in which they and their sheep were hoisted on to the top of the mountains.

The scientists took leave of them after having landed them safely, and Candide's only desire and object was to go and present Miss Cunegonde with his sheep.

"We have sufficient to pay the governor of Buenos Aires," said he, "if Miss Cunegonde can be bought. Let us go to Cayenne, and take ship, and then we will see what kingdom we will buy."

Candide and Cacambo make their way to Surinam, where Candide comes upon a black man who has been enslaved and horribly mistreated. When Candide sees the evils of the slave trade

firsthand, he comes to a turning point and renounces Pangloss's philosophy of optimism. Cacambo, at the request of Candide, sets out for Buenos Aires to rescue Cunegonde. Candide resolves to head back to Europe on another ship, but in pursuing this goal is swindled out of a great deal of his fortune. He finally finds a scholarly but miserable man named Martin to accompany him on the sea voyage. With Martin to counsel him, Candide finds his way back to Europe, where little by little he loses the rest of his fortune from Eldorado. Eventually he is reunited with Cunegonde as well as Cacambo, Pangloss, and the old woman. Candide marries Cunegonde, even though she has by now grown horribly ugly. With their companions, they retire to a little farm, where they learn to work together to cultivate a garden in the hope of making life bearable.

Vocabulary

ingenious (in·jēn′yəs) *adj.*: original; clever.

The Farm (1750)
by Jean-Baptiste Oudry.
Musée du Louvre, Paris.

The Utopia as a Literary Genre

INFORMATIONAL TEXT

The word *utopia* (yōō·tō′pē·ə) is derived from Greek and means "no place." Sir Thomas More was the first to employ this word for a literary genre when he wrote his famous book *Utopia* (1516), an account of an imaginary republic. He fully intended a pun on the Greek word *eutopia,* which means "place (where all is) well."

The idea of an imaginary earthly paradise goes back to antiquity. Elements of it can be found in the Mesopotamian classic *Gilgamesh* (see page 23), as well as in Homer's descriptions of the Elysian Fields in the *Odyssey*. Plato's *Republic* was the first full-fledged description of a utopia, though of a distinctly Spartan and authoritarian type. Within medieval Christianity itself, and especially after St. Augustine, the attainment of a heavenly city was considered a perfectly reasonable objective.

The main impulse in utopian literature is to imagine a social and political order free of the cruelties and corruptions of the existing order. More's *Utopia,* for example, retains some of Plato's authoritarianism and incorporates the harsh moral codes of More's own time; but its welfare state is socialistic in character, with its abolition of private property and its free universal education, medicine, food, and the like. Voltaire's Eldorado, the city of gold where gold has no monetary value, is essentially in More's tradition.

Countless literary utopias were explored in the seventeenth and eighteenth centuries. Much later, H. G. Wells, the author of *A Modern Utopia,* among many other books of this type, became perhaps the most interesting writer of this genre in the twentieth century. The popularity of utopian literature has produced its opposite as well, the **dystopia,** or anti-utopia, which portrays an imaginary world of pure horror. Aldous Huxley's *Brave New World* and George Orwell's *Animal Farm* and *Nineteen Eighty-four* are examples of this countergenre. Much of science fiction, we might note, hovers

Illustration from a contemporary edition (c. 16th century) of *Utopia* by Thomas More.

Kunstbibliothek, Staatliche Museen zü Berlin.

between the utopian and the anti-utopian.

If, as Candide concludes, everything is well "only in Eldorado," why do you suppose he does not try to return there? In other words, what ironic point is Voltaire making by having his hero end up with an ugly wife on a little farm where he does nothing more earth-shattering than cultivate a garden?

Before it came to be known as a city of gold, El Dorado (meaning "The Gilded One" in Spanish) was first applied to an infamous South American ruler who was said to cover his entire body with gold dust during local ceremonies. This story spread, and in 1538, explorers went in search of the mysterious El Dorado, whom they never found. Over the years, as the search went on, the legend of El Dorado came to be associated with an entire region believed to be filled with gold. The quest for this mythical place has continued into the twenty-first century. The article below describes a recent search conducted by the Polish-Italian explorer Jacek Palkiewicz.

INFORMATIONAL TEXT

Explorer: Legendary El Dorado Pinpointed

Rossella Lorenzi

Discovery News, August 9, 2002

Boat in Amazon tributary.

The fabled treasure of El Dorado may lie in tunnels and caves at the bottom of a lake in the Peruvian Amazon, according to a Polish-Italian explorer who has returned from a three-week reconnaissance trip in search of the legendary city.

Called Paititi by the Incas and El Dorado by the Spaniards, the mythical city is thought to have been the last place of refuge for the Incas when they fled with their treasures ahead of the advancing Spanish conquerors in 1532.

According to Jacek Palkiewicz, best known for discovering the real source of the Amazon River in 1996, Paititi should lie 105 kilometers (65 miles) northeast of Cuzco—the ancient capital of the Inca empire—in the unexplored Madre de Dios River basin. "We are just a step away from the city. We have pinpointed a 1.5-square-mile plateau with a lake and pre-Incan stone buildings totally covered in vegetation. Terrestrial radar confirmed the existence of an underwater labyrinth of caverns and tunnels. An ideal place to hide the Inca treasure the conquerors didn't succeed in finding," Palkiewicz told Discovery News.

The place would coincide both with legend and ancient documents. While stories of a waterfall and a square lake leading to Paititi abound, a 17th-century document states that the city is "further the lands and the mountains, ten days towards the east of Cuzco."

Moreover, a 16th-century manuscript, recently discovered in the Roman Archives of the Society of Jesus, describes the Kingdom of Paititi as "a very wealthy city adorned with gold, silver and precious stones."

According to the document, the city was discovered and evangelized at the end of the 16th century by Jesuit missionaries. Palkiewicz believes the Vatican never revealed Paititi's location, fearing a gold rush and mass hysteria.

El Dorado has lured many explorers over the past five centuries: among them famed British army surveyor Colonel Percy Harrison Fawcett, who left in search of Paititi in 1925; and more recently, a 1972 Franco-American expedition led by Bob Nichols; and the 1997 exploration of Norwegian anthropologist Lars Hafksjold. They all vanished in the jungles.

The latest explorer to set off in search of the legend, Palkiewicz will begin a final, systematic search in October [2002]. With a budget of more than $1 million, the expedition will include scientists specializing in the study of caves and the help of state-of-the-art technology.

"I'm pretty sure we will come back with extraordinary news," he said.

But other experts are skeptical.

"The whole idea that the Incas fled Cuzco for the jungles, bearing these treasures en masse, has no real evidence behind it. The climate and the constant threat of very real diseases that the highlander Incas had no defense against . . . rule out that hypothesis. And the idea of a city under a lake, although quite romantic, seems quite unlikely," Boston anthropologist Gregory Deyermenjian, who has conducted various searches for Paititi since 1984, told Discovery News.

? In what ways is the El Dorado described in this article similar to the Eldorado that Candide and Cacambo visit?

Aerial view of the Tigre River, an Amazon River tributary that meanders through the Peruvian rainforest.

Response and Analysis

Reading Check

1. Who is Pangloss, and what does Candide learn from him?

2. Why does Candide get expelled from the Baron's castle?

3. Briefly describe the main characteristics of Eldorado. What value do the inhabitants place on gold and gems?

4. How do Candide and Cacambo leave Eldorado?

Thinking Critically

5. From Voltaire's description of Eldorado, what can you infer about his views on organized religion, government, and wealth?

6. How does Voltaire's Eldorado compare with the "best of all possible worlds" you described in your Quickwrite notes? 🖊

7. Satire relies on many elements of comedy, such as exaggeration, understatement, warped logic, and improbable situations. Using these four elements as headings, list as many examples of each element as you can find in the selection.

8. Is the humor of *Candide* intended merely to amuse, or does it have a more serious purpose? (Why, for example, do you think we find ourselves laughing *at* Voltaire's characters and never *with* them?) Explain. 📖

Extending and Evaluating

9. At a later point in the story, Candide finally sees the error of Pangloss's teachings and renounces optimism, defining it as "the mania of maintaining that everything is well when we are wretched." Do you agree with Candide's statement? Why or why not? State your own definition of optimism.

10. Voltaire wrote *Candide* more than 230 years ago. How well has its satire aged? What value might *Candide* hold for someone growing up today?

WRITING

Examining a Controversial Issue

In *Candide* Voltaire uses biting satire to imply, or suggest, his views on controversial issues ranging from religion and slavery to the military and economics.

Become a modern-day Voltaire, presenting an idea for social reform by writing a satirical editorial that examines a controversial issue—an issue that can be argued on both sides. Remember that satirists often try to make their arguments by showing the opposing view as absurd or inhumane—something a serious editorial on a controversial issue would never do. Remember too that satirists use outrageous exaggerations, deadpan understatements, warped logic, and ridiculous examples to hammer home their points. Make your position clear, but choose your issue carefully; it should be a topic that will make people think, not offend them.

➤ See "Examining a Controversial Issue in an Editorial" on pages 726–731 for help with this assignment.

Vocabulary Development
What's the Difference?

On a separate sheet of paper, explain the difference between each underlined Vocabulary word and its partner.

1. <u>candor</u> and *bluntness*

2. <u>pensive</u> and *preoccupied*

3. <u>vivacity</u> and *vigor*

4. <u>prudent</u> and *carefree*

5. <u>discretion</u> and *caution*

6. <u>disconcert</u> and *offend*

7. <u>ingenious</u> and *idiotic*

North Carolina Competency Goal
1.02; 1.03; 4.05; 5.03; 6.01

INTERNET

Projects and Activities

Keyword: LE5 WL-5

SKILLS FOCUS

Literary Skills
Analyze satire.

Reading Skills
Appreciate a writer's style.

Writing Skills
Examine a controversial issue.

Vocabulary Skills
Analyze differences between words.

Vocabulary Development

Etymology: The Story Behind a Word

An **etymology** traces a word's derivation, or origin. You can use a dictionary to find a derivation; it usually appears in brackets after the entry word's pronunciation and part-of-speech designation. The dictionary should contain a section that explains the organization, abbreviations, and symbols used in its etymologies. Some etymologies will also refer you to prefixes and root words related to the entry word. Let's look at the beginning of a dictionary entry for the word *ignorant*.

> **ig·no·rant** (igʹnə·rənt) *adj.* [OFr < L *ignorans*, prp. of *ignorare*, to have no knowledge of: see IGNORE]

When you look up *ignorant* in a dictionary, you find that it derives from ("<") the Latin ("L") word *ignorare*, meaning "to have no knowledge of," by way of Old French ("OFr"). The etymology also refers us to the English word *ignore*. When you look up *ignore*, you find that it originally comes from the Latin root *in–*, meaning "not," combined with the Indo-European root *gna–* or *gno–*, meaning "know."

> [Fr *ignorer* < L *ignorare*, to have no knowledge of < *in–*, not + base of *gnarus*, knowing < IE base *gnā–*, *gnō–*, KNOW]

One way to learn more about a word's origin is by filling out an etymology map. When you complete an etymology map, you will include a word's meanings, its related words, and a sentence using the word. See the etymology map for the word *ignorant* below.

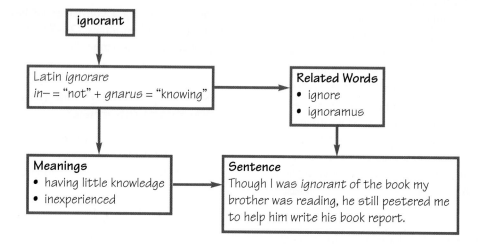

North Carolina Competency Goal
1.03; 4.05; 5.03; 6.01

SKILLS FOCUS

Vocabulary Skills
Determine etymologies.

PRACTICE

Now it's your turn. Use a dictionary to find out the etymology of the words below. Then, fill out an etymology map for each word.

1. philosopher
2. optimism
3. hemisphere
4. tyranny
5. ingenious

READ ON: FOR INDEPENDENT READING

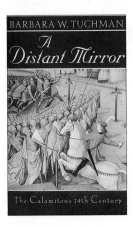

NONFICTION
A Turbulent Century

A Distant Mirror is Barbara W. Tuchman's riveting portrait of Europe in the fourteenth century, a time of war, massacres, crusades, and the scourge of the Black Death. Against this backdrop, Tuchman depicts everyday life during the Middle Ages. At the center of Tuchman's book is the French knight Enguerrand de Coucy VII, who serves as a point of reference for the narrative.

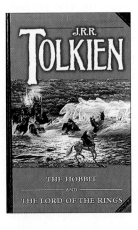

FICTION
The Ring of Power

Hobbits and orcs are just some of the unusual beings that fill J.R.R. Tolkien's epic trilogy, *The Lord of the Rings*. *The Fellowship of the Ring*, the first volume, recounts Frodo and his eight friends' perilous quest to destroy the One Ring, which wields terrible power. In the second volume, *The Two Towers*, Frodo and his faithful sidekick, Sam, are left to fend for themselves as they press on toward Mount Doom, the only place where the ring can be destroyed. In *The Return of the King*, Frodo faces his greatest challenges in his struggle to save Middle-earth.

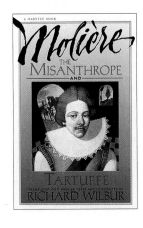

DRAMA
The Faces of Hypocrisy

Molière's plays *The Misanthrope* and *Tartuffe* (translated by Richard Wilbur) are seventeenth-century satires that take aim at hypocrisy. In *The Misanthrope* the title character is a recluse named Alceste, whose high ideals for behavior are sorely tested by the society he lives in. Religious hypocrisy is the focus of *Tartuffe,* which features the charming con artist Tartuffe, who wears many guises and takes advantage of the sanctimonious and wealthy character Orgon.

ADDITIONAL READING

- *The Canterbury Tales,* a medieval masterpiece by the English poet Geoffrey Chaucer, focuses on a motley cast of characters making a pilgrimage to the English town of Canterbury. The unforgettable tales are narrated by people representing a cross-section of medieval society.

- *The Tempest,* the last tragicomedy William Shakespeare ever wrote, is sometimes called a "summing up" play in which Shakespeare bids farewell to his art. The story features Prospero, the rightful duke of Milan, who was overthrown by his brother, Antonio, and banished from the kingdom. The drama, rich in atmosphere, poetry, and fantasy, centers on Prospero's efforts to regain the throne and punish those who conspired against him.

- In *Utopia,* the Renaissance author Sir Thomas More presents his vision of an ideal society, a republic in which all property is commonly owned and such necessities as medicine and food are free.

Examining a Controversial Issue in an Editorial

Writing Assignment
Examine a controversial issue, evaluate the pros and cons, take a position, and present your position in an editorial.

Have you ever found yourself arguing for—or against—something when a majority of the people you know had exactly the opposite opinion? If so, you know what it is like to take a position on a controversial issue—an issue that can be debated, or argued, on both sides. Writing an editorial in which you examine a controversial issue and put forth your own ideas is an excellent way to engage in the kind of dynamic airing of views that spurs creative solutions to problems and gets citizens involved in improving society.

Prewriting

Choose an Issue

What Do You Care About? Although controversy pervades our society, people tend to care most about issues that affect them directly. In choosing a controversial issue, then, it's best to start with topics that really matter to you. You may want to make a two-column list with a topic on the left and a question on the right like this one:

> **TIP** When choosing a controversial issue to examine, be sure it is one that can be validly argued. In other words, there should be supporting evidence for both sides, not merely a clash of preferences, such as whether it is better to travel by train or by bus.

Topic	Issue-Raising Question
• safety in school	• Should metal detectors be installed in all schools?
• traffic safety	• Should driver education courses be mandatory for all?

Examine the Issue

Learn All You Can Before you take a position on a controversial issue, you should carefully examine all the available facts and opposing arguments. You may find that a little research will change the way you view an issue. Then, when you are sure of where you stand on the issue, you can persuasively present your position to others.

To find out all you can about the issue you've chosen, first gather as much factual information as possible. Then, collect a variety of opinions on the best way to handle the issue. You may want to consult

North Carolina Competency Goal
3.01; 6.01

SKILLS FOCUS

Writing Skills
Examine a controversial issue in an editorial.

some or all of these sources: current articles and research from the Internet or a local library; government publications; editorials in school, local, or national newspapers; local and national television news programs; experts, such as physicians, educators, or police officers.

Look at Both Sides When you have collected sufficient facts and opinions about your topic, state the issue as a question or proposal. Then, make a two-column chart listing pros and cons. Such a chart will help you evaluate your data and determine where you stand on the issue.

Issue: Should Soda and Junk Food Be Sold in Schools?

Pro Arguments	Con Arguments
1. It is important for students to make their own nutritional choices.	1. Research shows that obesity is rising rapidly among children and imperiling their health.
2. Sales of soda and junk-food snacks create much-needed revenue for schools.	2. There are other ways for schools to raise funds that do not endanger students' health.

Take a Stand

Develop a Position Statement Write a brief, direct statement of where you stand on the issue. This is your **position statement,** or **thesis.** It will help you focus your arguments and choose an organization for your paper. For example, on the issue of junk food in schools, the writer of the model on page 728 wrote the following position statement: *Since the availability of fattening snack foods in schools threatens children's health, schools must resolve to put children first and remove these high-sugar, high-fat junk foods.*

Gather the Evidence No matter how persuasively you present your position on a controversial issue, there's no reason for people to agree with you unless you can support your position with evidence. Look over the research you've done, and make sure you've gathered enough evidence to support your reasons. Some of the best kinds of evidence are **statistics** (facts presented in the form of numerical information); **examples** (specific instances of an idea or situation); **expert opinions** (quotations or paraphrased statements made by experts); **analogies** (comparisons that show similarities between two otherwise unrelated facts or ideas); **case studies** (examples from scientific studies); and **anecdotes** (brief, personal stories that illustrate a point).

North Carolina Competency Goal
3.01; 6.01

PRACTICE & APPLY 1 Use the preceding instruction to select a controversial issue, examine its pros and cons, develop a position statement, and choose how you will persuade others to share your position.

Writing Skills
Assess, organize, and analyze information for an editorial on a controversial issue. Draft a thesis statement, and support it with evidence.

Writing

Writing an Editorial

A Writer's Framework

Introduction
- Get readers interested in the issue with a surprising fact, statistic, or quotation.
- Provide background information on the issue, if necessary.
- Include a statement that sums up your position.

Body
- Offer facts and arguments that support your position.
- Organize your support in a logical order, such as order of importance.
- Present and counter arguments against your position.

Conclusion
- Restate your position on the issue.
- Remind your readers why the issue is important or how it affects them.
- Issue a call for action or solidarity with your view.

A Writer's Model

Eating Away at Kids' Health

INTRODUCTION
Attention-grabbing statistic

Background information

Position statement

Between 13 and 15 percent of children and adolescents are overweight, according to the Centers for Disease Control and Prevention. This is an alarming statistic that indicates increasing health problems for young people, since scientific studies have shown that obesity increases the risk of developing diabetes, high blood pressure, heart disease, and other illnesses. At the same time that childhood obesity is increasing, schools are selling soda and other high-sugar and high-fat snacks right on school premises. These sales produce much-needed revenue for financially strapped schools, but is this a fair exchange? Since the availability of fattening snack foods in schools threatens children's health, schools must resolve to put children first and remove these high-sugar, high-fat junk foods.

BODY
Paragraph 2: Primary argument in support of position

Expert opinion

The health risks of eating too much fat or too much sugar are well documented. In fact, there is already a federal law that prohibits the sale of sugar-sweetened drinks in schools during lunch periods. There is no law, however, that prohibits the operation of soda and snack-food vending machines at other times in the school day. The law seems to suggest that consuming high-calorie snacks during the school day can do no harm as long as students have had a healthy lunch. A study published in the medical journal *The Lancet*, however, finds that the likelihood of

(continued)

"becoming obese among children increased 1.6 times for each additional can or glass of sugar-sweetened drink that they consumed every day."

In addition to obesity, there are other risks associated with the consumption of soda and other sweet snacks. These include caffeine dependence, which may increase distractibility and problems with alertness due to rapid shifts in blood sugar levels. Even though these side effects of caffeine and sugar may have no long-term harmful effects, they can affect students' ability to pay attention while in class. Since educating students is the primary mission of schools, can schools really justify any practice that interferes with students' readiness to learn?

Paragraph 3: Secondary arguments in support of position

The most common justification for the sale of junk food in schools is that it raises money for desirable educational and extracurricular activities. No one denies that aid to schools has been slashed, but imperiling students' health is no way to improve their education. Schools can and must find other ways to raise money—ways that do not take a toll on children's health.

Paragraph 4: Counterargument addressed

Since obesity is a proven threat to health and since excessive snacking can lead to obesity and attention problems in class, school officials and parents must recognize that there is no good argument for continuing to make unhealthy snacks available in school. Certainly schools cannot monitor what children eat after school and in their own homes, but by educating children about the dangers of junk foods and banning these foods from school premises, schools will be educating children on how to make good decisions about their health. Making non-nutritious, fattening foods readily available at school seriously undermines this goal and sends a confusing double message to children. Our children are our future, and we should not put them, their health, or their education at risk.

CONCLUSION

Restatement of position and call for action

PRACTICE & APPLY 2 Using the framework and Writer's Model on these pages as your guide, write the first draft of your editorial on a controversial issue.

INTERNET
More Writer's Models
Keyword:
LE5 WL-5

Revising

Peer Evaluation

Get Feedback from Others The best way to find out if your editorial is clear and persuasive is to read it to others and ask them for their reactions. Find out if they understand the importance of the issue you raised and if they are persuaded to share your view by the support you supplied. Use this feedback and the rubric that follows to determine where your editorial needs revision.

Rubric: Writing an Editorial

Evaluation Questions	▶ Tips	▶ Revision Techniques
❶ Does the introduction grab readers' attention and alert them to your position?	▶ **Underline** the attention-grabbing opener. **Bracket** your position statement.	▶ **Add** an attention-grabbing detail to the opening. **Add** a position statement.
❷ Does the body of your editorial offer convincing support for your position?	▶ **Circle** supporting evidence for your position, including facts and logical arguments.	▶ **Add** more factual evidence or logical arguments to support your position.
❸ Does the body of your editorial present and address counterarguments?	▶ **Highlight** opposing arguments and your response to them.	▶ **Include** one or more arguments against your position and counter them.
❹ Does your conclusion restate your position and call on readers to believe as you do?	▶ **Put a star** next to the restatement of your position. **Draw a wavy line** under your call for action.	▶ **Rewrite** the conclusion so that it restates your position and rallies your readers behind your view.

ANALYZING THE REVISION PROCESS
Study the revisions below, and answer the questions that follow.

, according to the Centers for Disease Control and Prevention
Between 13 and 15 percent of children and adolescents are overweight. ∧

This is an alarming statistic that indicates increasing health problems for

, since
young people. ∧ ~~S~~cientific studies have shown that obesity increases the risk

of developing diabetes, high blood pressure, heart disease, and other

that childhood obesity is increasing,
illnesses. At the same time, ∧ schools are selling soda and other high-sugar

and high-fat snacks right on school premises.

Responding to the Revision Process
1. How does the added information improve the opening sentence?
2. What is the effect of combining the second and third sentences?

 **PRACTICE & APPLY 3** Using the guidelines on these pages, evaluate and revise the logic, organization, and word choice of your editorial.

Publishing

Proofread and Publish Your Editorial

Final Polish Proofread your editorial carefully to make sure you have made no errors in grammar, spelling, punctuation, or capitalization. Pay particular attention to the spelling of proper names and the punctution of quoted material. Mistakes can damage your credibility with your readers, and they will be less likely to take your arguments seriously.

Spread the Word Since the purpose of an editorial, like all forms of persuasive writing, is to change minds and hearts, you will want to publish your ideas as widely as possible. Here are some options:

- Submit your editorial to school and local newspapers.

- Hand out copies of your editorial at parent-teacher meetings and meetings of any other citizens' groups involved in your issue.

- Adapt your editorial for oral presentation by creating a list of talking points. Give your speech to the school board or other interested political body.

Reflect on Your Editorial

Lessons Learned Think back on your experience of examining a controversial issue, taking a stand, and presenting your position in a convincing editorial. What did you learn from the experience? To help you reflect, answer the following questions:

- What new information did you learn about the issue as a result of your research?

- Should you have appealed more to reason and less to emotion, or vice versa?

- What useful strategies have you learned to persuade others to consider your point of view?

North Carolina Competency Goal
3.01; 6.01

SKILLS FOCUS

Writing Skills
Proofread for grammar, usage, and mechanics errors.

PRACTICE & APPLY 4 First, proofread your editorial. Then, choose one of the options above for gaining a wider audience. Finally, answer the reflection questions.

Collection 5: Skills Review
Comparing Literature

Test Practice Louise Labé (1525–1566), a well-educated Frenchwoman, died two years after Shakespeare was born; like him, though, she was well versed in the conventions of the sonnet. Labé wrote her sonnets in the Italian, or Petrarchan, style. A fourteen-line verse form originating in fourteenth-century Italy, the Petrarchan sonnet has a two-part structure, with a first part of eight lines (octet) and a second part of six lines (sestet). Shakespeare departed from the Petrarchan form, organizing his sonnets into three quatrains (four-line verses) followed by a couplet (two-line verse). Shakespeare also extended the subject matter and tone of the Italian sonnets. In Sonnet 130, for example, he challenges the language and sentiments of conventional love sonnets, mocking their conceits: stale, exaggerated figures of speech such as "your cheeks are like roses" and "your breath is sweet perfume to me." Louise Labé, in her own way, does the same in her Sonnet 23.

DIRECTIONS: Read the following two sonnets. Then, read each multiple-choice question that follows and write the letter of the best response.

Sonnet 130

William Shakespeare

My mistress' eyes are nothing like the sun,
Coral is far more red than her lips' red.
If snow be white, why then her breasts are dun,°
If hairs be wires, black wires grow on her head.
5 I have seen roses damasked,° red and white,
But no such roses see I in her cheeks.
And in some perfumes is there more delight
Than in the breath that from my mistress reeks,
I love to hear her speak, yet well I know
10 That music hath a far more pleasing sound.
I grant I never saw a goddess go,
My mistress, when she walks, treads on the ground.
    And yet, by Heaven, I think my love as rare
    As any she belied° with false compare.

---

  3. dun *adj.:* dull grayish brown.
  5. damasked *v.:* of more than one color.
14. belied *v.:* misrepresented.

North Carolina Competency Goal
1.03; 4.05;
5.01; 5.02;
5.03

Pages 732–735
cover
Literary Skills
Compare and contrast
sonnets.

Sonnet 23

Louise Labé

translated by **Willis Barnstone**

What good is it to me if long ago
you eloquently praised my golden hair,
compared my eyes and beauty to the flare
of two suns where, you say, love bent the bow,
5 sending the darts that needled you with grief?
Where are your tears that faded in the ground?
Your death? by which your constant love is bound
in oaths and honor now beyond belief?
Your brutal goal was to make *me* a slave
10 beneath the ruse° of being served by you.
Pardon me, friend, and for once hear me through:
I am outraged with anger and I rave.
Yet I am sure, wherever you have gone,
your martyrdom is hard as my black dawn.

---

10. ruse *n.:* trick.

Collection 5: Skills Review

Comparing Literature

1. How does Shakespeare depart from the conventional love sonnet in the first quatrain of Sonnet 130?
    A He abandons rhyme altogether.
    B He declares that his mistress does not meet any of the usual descriptions of beauty.
    C He avoids all figurative language and comparisons.
    D He concentrates on spiritual rather than physical beauty.

2. How would you describe the tone of the second and third quatrains of Sonnet 130?
    F Melancholy
    G Highly romantic
    H Gently mocking
    J Philosophical

3. Which of the following images or comparisons from Sonnet 130 contrasts with those of conventional love poetry?
    A "My mistress' eyes are nothing like the sun"
    B "If hairs be wires, black wires grow on her head"
    C "The breath that from my mistress reeks"
    D All of the above

4. What surprise does the final couplet of Sonnet 130 contain?
    F The speaker loves his mistress even though she is imperfect.
    G The speaker's mistress has left him for another man.
    H The mistress is actually very beautiful, like a goddess.
    J The mistress is falsely modest about her own beauty.

5. What is the attitude of the speaker of Sonnet 23 toward the flattery and oaths of her former lover?
    A She cherishes them as fond memories.
    B She is saddened by the loss of his true devotion.
    C She reproaches him angrily for his bad faith.
    D She misses his flattery now that he is dead.

6. In lines 9 and 10, the speaker of Sonnet 23 accuses her lover of —
    F making himself her slave
    G brutally betraying her
    H seeming to serve her only to get her in his power
    J being unfaithful to her with another woman

7. What is the "black dawn" the speaker describes in the last line of Sonnet 23?

   A Her realization that her lover is dead

   B Her angry recognition that she has been manipulated

   C Her sad certainty that she will never love again

   D Her positive resolve to get on with her life

8. Judging from the tone of Sonnet 23, what do you think was Louise Labé's personal experience of love?

   F She had little experience of love in her life.

   G She was disappointed and let down by those she loved.

   H She was blessed with true and lasting love.

   J She withheld her love and trust from those who loved her.

9. What attitude toward the conventional language of lovers and love poetry do both Shakespeare and Labé reveal in their sonnets?

   A Both poets distrust and mock the conventional speech of lovers and love poetry.

   B Both poets rely on the conventional language of love poetry in their sonnets.

   C Both poets express their admiration for conventional "love speech."

   D Both poets bitterly reject all talk of love.

10. What rhetorical device does Labé use in her sonnet that Shakespeare does not use in his?

   F A formal rhyme scheme

   G A closing couplet that sums up the speaker's attitude

   H Direct questions to the person being addressed

   J References to overused figures of speech

Essay Question

Both Shakespeare's Sonnet 130 and Louise Labé's Sonnet 23 are about love, but they differ from each other and from other more conventional love poems in what they have to say about that eternally interesting topic. In a brief essay, compare and contrast the two sonnets. Be sure to consider the speaker and the person addressed in each sonnet as well as the imagery, tone, and overall message. Pay particular attention to the final two lines of each sonnet, since these sum up the speaker's attitude toward love and the loved one.

Collection 5: Skills Review

Vocabulary Skills

Test Practice

Analogies

DIRECTIONS: For each item, choose the lettered pair of words that expresses a relationship *most* like the relationship between the pair of capitalized words.

1. SINISTER : WHOLESOME ::
   - **A** upright : respectable
   - **B** transparent : opaque
   - **C** colorful : tragic
   - **D** original : creative

2. AMOROUS : LOVER ::
   - **F** quarrelsome : diplomat
   - **G** graceful : dancer
   - **H** courteous : criminal
   - **J** attentive : stranger

3. PIETY : HOLINESS ::
   - **A** patriotism : politics
   - **B** commotion : peacefulness
   - **C** dedication : devotion
   - **D** contempt : pity

4. EXULTING : REJOICING ::
   - **F** domineering : submitting
   - **G** forgiving : condemning
   - **H** marching : retreating
   - **J** objecting : protesting

5. INSTIGATION : PROVOCATION ::
   - **A** defiance : agreement
   - **B** communication : quarrel
   - **C** demolition : discovery
   - **D** condemnation : accusation

6. DEXTEROUSLY : AWKWARDLY ::
   - **F** tenderly : gently
   - **G** deftly : skillfully
   - **H** courageously : cowardly
   - **J** tremendously : greatly

7. SIEGE : ARMY ::
   - **A** robbery : police
   - **B** exam : doctor
   - **C** trial : press
   - **D** navigation : architect

8. SLANDEROUS : LIES ::
   - **F** private : secrets
   - **G** spacious : cells
   - **H** timid : warriors
   - **J** tiresome : boxes

9. SCORNED : RIDICULED ::
   - **A** nurtured : discouraged
   - **B** tempted : seduced
   - **C** twisted : straightened
   - **D** complied : replied

10. ELOQUENCE : ORATOR ::
    - **F** tactfulness : athlete
    - **G** honesty : musician
    - **H** speed : sprinter
    - **J** gentleness : boxer

Collection 5: Skills Review

Writing Skills

DIRECTIONS: Read the following paragraph from a draft of a student's editorial on a controversial issue. Then, answer the questions below it.

(1) Food and beverage companies argue that childhood obesity is a complex problem with more than one cause. (2) Industry spokespersons claim there is no reliable evidence that the availability of snack food in schools is a major cause of the growing obesity rates among children. (3) They point to lack of exercise as a major cause of children's weight problems. (4) They suggest that schools spend the extra revenue they make from snack sales on athletic programs that will help kids stay fit. (5) Increased computer use and television viewing contribute to the declining rate of exercise among children. (6) Some parents assert that a ban on the sale of high-calorie snack foods in schools infringes on parents' rights to make decisions about their children's diet. (7) Some school officials argue that banning junk-food sales in school will make no overall difference in students' weight because such food is widely available outside school. (8) Students will simply buy what they want to eat outside, thus depriving schools of needed revenue to no good effect.

1. In an editorial in favor of banning junk-food sales in schools, this paragraph would serve as —
   A a restatement of the writer's position
   B a presentation of arguments for the ban
   C a presentation of arguments against the ban
   D an introduction to the issue

2. Which two sentences could be combined to make the paragraph more concise?
   F Sentences 1 and 2
   G Sentences 3 and 4
   H Sentences 4 and 5
   J Sentences 6 and 7

3. Which sentence could be deleted to improve the paragraph's coherence?
   A Sentence 3
   B Sentence 5

   C Sentence 6
   D Sentence 7

4. Which of these transitions could be added to the beginning of sentence 3?
   F For example,
   G Therefore,
   H However,
   J Instead,

5. Which of the following approaches could serve as a valid counterargument to a claim made in this paragraph?
   A Research that shows a link between junk-food consumption and childhood obesity
   B An argument that children should be given the responsibility to monitor their own diets
   C Research that shows the importance of exercise to control weight
   D An argument that schools should provide a choice of foods to students

North Carolina Competency Goal
2.01; 3.02; 3.04; 4.03; 6.01

SKILLS FOCUS

Writing Skills
Answer questions about an editorial on a controversial issue.

Collection 6

European Literature in the Nineteenth Century

1800–1900

Imagination and Reality

"If you wish to understand what revolution is, call it progress; and if you wish to understand what progress is, call it tomorrow."

—from *Les Misérables* by Victor Hugo

INTERNET

Collection Resources
Keyword:
LE5 WL-6

(Opposite) *Rue Saint-Honoré* (1897)
by Camille Pissarro.
Fundación Colección Thyssen-Bornemisza, Madrid.

Europe in the Nineteenth

1800

1798 William Wordsworth and Samuel Taylor Coleridge publish *Lyrical Ballads* in England

1802 Victor Hugo, author of *The Hunchback of Notre Dame* and *Les Misérables*, is born in France

1804 Napoleon crowns himself emperor in France

1808 In Germany, Johann Wolfgang von Goethe publishes Part 1 of *Faust*

Napoleon I, Emperor of France (c. 1819–1822) by Francois Le Villain.

1810

1815 At Waterloo, Napoleon is defeated by British, Dutch, and German forces and is subsequently sent into exile

1818 Mary Shelley publishes *Frankenstein* in England

1824 The first labor unions are permitted in Great Britain

1825

1825 The Decembrist uprising takes place in Russia

1831 The English naturalist Charles Darwin begins his voyage aboard the *Beagle*

1832 The Reform Bill of 1832 gives more power to the middle class by granting the right to vote to males who own property worth ten pounds or more in annual rent

1839 In England, the Custody Act allows divorced women to have access to their children

1840

1844 The symbolist poet Paul Verlaine is born in France

1845 Close to 1 million people die in Ireland as a result of the potato famine

1848 *The Communist Manifesto* by the German socialists Karl Marx and Friedrich Engels is published

Karl Marx (c. 1880).

1800

1801 British and Ottoman troops defeat the French in Egypt

1804 The island Santo Domingo is renamed Haiti

1808 The United States bans importation of slaves from Africa

1810

1811 Venezuela, led by Simón Bolívar, gains independence from Spain

1821 Mexico declares its independence from Spain

1822 The Rosetta stone is deciphered, making Egyptian hieroglyphs readable

1825

1835 The Great Trek begins as Boers journey to the African interior

1836 The Mexican army defeats Texans at the Alamo

1840

1842 The Treaty of Nanjing makes Hong Kong a British colony

Fall of the Alamo to Santa Anna's Mexican forces in Texas (1836). Hand-colored woodcut.

Century 1800–1900

1850–1893 The lifetime of the French short story writer Guy de Maupassant

1852 Charles Louis Napoléon Bonaparte is proclaimed Emperor Napoleon III in France

1857 *Les Fleurs du mal* (*The flowers of evil*) by Charles Baudelaire is published in France

1859 Charles Darwin publishes *On the Origin of Species by Means of Natural Selection* in England

1861 Serfs in Russia are freed

1865 *Alice's Adventures in Wonderland* by Lewis Carroll is published in England

1867 Second Reform Act gives most industrial working men the right to vote in England

1869 Leo Tolstoy publishes *War and Peace* in Russia

1879 Henrik Ibsen publishes *A Doll's House* in Norway

1880 The French writer Émile Zola sets down the literary principles of naturalism in his essay "Le Roman expérimental" ("The Experimental Novel")

1881 Czar Alexander II of Russia is assassinated after repeated attempts on his life

1889 Emmeline Pankhurst forms Women's Franchise League, arguing for British women's suffrage

1896 Anton Chekhov's *The Sea Gull* is first performed in St. Petersburg, Russia

1897 The Russian political leader Vladimir Lenin is exiled to Siberia for questionable political activities

Colonel Dvorketsky, chief of the police, conveying the assassinated Czar Alexander II to the Winter Palace (April 21, 1881). Magazine illustration.

1850–1864 Millions of Chinese die during the Taiping Rebellion

1853 Commodore Perry ends Japanese isolationist policy

1857–1859 In India, British soldiers put down the sepoy rebellion against their rule

1863 The Emancipation Proclamation declares slavery illegal in U.S. Confederate states

1867 Revolutionaries overthrow the shogun in Japan; the emperor is restored to power

1869 The Suez Canal is opened in Egypt; Mohandas Gandhi is born in India

1879 In South Africa, the Zulu War begins

1884 *The Adventures of Huckleberry Finn* by Mark Twain is published in the United States

1885 The Berlin Conference sets the ground rules for the division of Africa among European nations; the Indian National Congress, which lobbies for Indian self-rule, is formed

1886 The American Federation of Labor is founded

1895 Japan takes control of Taiwan from China

1898 The United States gains control of Guam, Puerto Rico, and the Philippines following the Spanish-American War

The Te Deum at Port Said, for the inauguration of the Suez Canal by the Empress Eugenie in 1869 by Eduoard Riou (1833–1890). Engraving by Jules Didier. Bibliothèque des arts décoratifs, Paris.

European Literature in the Nineteenth Century   **741**

Cultural and Historical

The Industrial Revolution

1800s

The early and mid-nineteenth century, sometimes called the age of progress, was a time of rapid advancements in science and technology that forever altered the lives of Europeans. Although such new inventions as the steam engine, telegraph, and electric light brought exciting changes and gave rise to a prosperous new middle class, not all of this progress was beneficial to everyone. With the invention of machines to do work once done at home, masses of people left the countryside and migrated to crowded cities to look for work. There, filthy slums developed, and adults and children labored in factories that were unsafe and inhumane. An impoverished lower class grew even as the middle and upper classes looked to material progress to improve life for all of humanity.

Ironworks (1875) by Adolph von Menzel.
Alte Nationalgalerie, Berlin.

The Age of Romanticism

1798–1832

Romanticism began as a revolt against the rational, classically influenced ideals of the Enlightenment. Whereas Enlightenment writers usually wrote about philosophical or political issues and generally followed strict rules governing form and language, the Romantics valued feeling, intuition, and imagination and wrote about

Milestones 1800–1900

The Stages of Life
(c. 1835) by Caspar
David Friedrich.

Museum der Bildenden
Künste, Leipzig, Germany.

The Rise of Realism

Late 1800s

The nineteenth century was marked by political revolutions that introduced liberal reforms. But by the last half of the century, it became clear that the reforms had not brought about an era of justice. Instead, the gap between rich and poor had widened. One outcome of this troubling development was the rise of realism in literature, a reaction against the ideals of Romanticism. The realists wanted to observe and record the truth about people's lives—to mirror what they saw as objective reality and eliminate sentimentality from literature. One branch of realism, naturalism, sought to eliminate subjectivity in literature. The naturalists wanted to dissect everyday life as dispassionately as scientists dissected laboratory specimens, revealing people as mere victims of forces beyond their control: heredity, fate, and their environment. The works of Charles Darwin on the theory of evolution and of Karl Marx and Friedrich Engels on the economics of capitalism added to the sense that the individual had little control over his or her own destiny.

After Dinner at Ornans (detail)
(1848) by Gustave Courbet.

Musée des Beaux-Arts, Lille, France.

ordinary people's lives, using everyday language. The Romantics found inspiration in nature, rural life, folklore, and fantasy and turned away from what they saw as the squalor of industrialization and urban life. Romantic writers placed supreme value on the individual and were passionately committed to individual freedom. Political revolutions and uprisings in Europe gave the Romantics hope that a new era of justice for common people was on the horizon.

Europe in the Nineteenth Century
1800–1900

PREVIEW

Think About ...

As the nineteenth century dawned, Europe was in a state of political upheaval. The American and French Revolutions, which began in the late eighteenth century, were followed by a series of popular revolts in various countries in the first half of the nineteenth century. Alongside these events came an explosion of science and technology known as the Industrial Revolution, a tumultuous period of progress that led not only to scientific advancements but also to increased pollution, urban expansion, and terrible working conditions. Against this backdrop two influential branches of literary thought emerged: Romanticism, which emphasized the importance of imagination and emotion, and realism, which emphasized the objective, factual observation of the lives of ordinary people.

As you read about the history and literature of Europe in the nineteenth century, look for answers to the following questions:

- How did the Romantics react to the social upheaval in Europe in the early nineteenth century?

- What impact did the Industrial Revolution have on people living in Europe?

- What are the most important characteristics of realism?

North Carolina Competency Goal
1.02; 1.03; 4.02; 4.05; 5.01; 5.03

SKILLS FOCUS

Collection introduction (pages 744–755) covers

Literary Skills
Evaluate the philosophical, historical, and cultural influences of the historical period.

European Literature in the Nineteenth Century

Some people think of literature as a quiet, peaceful pursuit. However, literature seems tame only in societies where freedom of speech is taken for granted. In recent history, writers helped to prepare the way for the anti-Communist revolution in Eastern Europe. More than two hundred years ago, the writings of the philosophers Voltaire and Jean Jacques Rousseau in France and John Locke in England created a new awareness of social injustice and lit the fuse for the revolutionary explosion in America and Europe.

The Balcony (1868) by Edouard Manet.

Musée d'Orsay, Paris, France.

A Revolt Against Reason?

In contrast to the eighteenth century, which had billed itself as the Age of Reason, the Romantic era is sometimes thought of as a time of revolt against reason. It is doubtful, though, whether the average eighteenth-century citizen was more rational than citizens and intellectuals before or since. In fact, the Romantic era produced such powerful thinkers as Germany's Arthur Schopenhauer, America's Ralph Waldo Emerson, Denmark's Søren Kierkegaard, and England's Samuel Taylor Coleridge. The Romantics did not reject reason. They did, however, elevate emotion, intuition, and imagination to a higher status.

Shock Waves of Revolution

News of revolt in the American Colonies reached Europe in 1775, arousing both fears and hopes. Monarchs and aristocrats were alarmed by the American Revolution, but the discontented middle class and peasantry of Europe were inspired by the Americans' struggle for liberty. When the **French Revolution** broke out in 1789, Europe changed overnight. On July 14, 1789, an angry mob stormed the Bastille prison in Paris. That date, now called Bastille Day, which the French celebrate just as Americans celebrate July 4, 1776, marked the beginning of a new era.

Revolutionary fever spread throughout Europe, horrifying most aristocrats and thrilling democratic idealists. During its early years, the French Revolution became a kind of tourist attraction. Intellectuals

The emblem of the revolution (liberté [liberty], egalité [equality] et fraternité [brotherhood]) with sapper and Jacobin (c. 1793).

The Storming of the Bastille on July 14, 1789 (1789).
Château et Trianons, Versailles, France.

and artists from across Europe and America visited France to see the new regime firsthand. Thomas Paine, the most powerful propagandist of the American Revolution, immigrated to France to participate in the uprising against the aristocracy. At the beginning of the new century, the French Revolution inspired Simón Bolívar's revolt against the Spanish empire in Latin America.

Nationalism, a doctrine that advocates national independence and places national interests above those of other countries, became an important force in nineteenth-century European politics. The emergence of nationalism is closely connected with the principles of the French Revolution. The revolutionaries glorified their country and called for liberty, equality, and fraternity.

The Reign of Terror and the Rise of Napoleon

Many Romantic thinkers were at first thrilled by the French Revolution. However, intoxication turned to despair, for in 1793, the revolutionaries executed King Louis XVI, and the French Revolution became the **Reign of Terror.** The guillotines (gil′ə·tēnz′) worked overtime as the extremists of the Revolution beheaded not only their opponents but also former allies with whom they now disagreed. In 1794, the radical leader of the Reign of Terror, Robespierre, was himself executed. The French Republic was in a state of confusion that did not ease until a young Corsican military officer, **Napoleon Bonaparte** (1769–1821), staged a coup, or forceful overthrow, in 1799.

Using aggressive military tactics, Napoleon soon became dictator of continental Europe. In 1815, Napoleon was finally defeated by a coalition of English, Prussian, and Russian forces at the Battle of Waterloo. He spent the rest of his life in exile. Opposition to Napoleon's conquests stirred up nationalism in European politics.

Napoleon Bonaparte Crossing the Alps by Jacques Louis David (1748–1825).
Malmaison Musée du Chateau, France.

The writers, artists, and thinkers of the 1790s reacted to these revolutionary events in different ways. Some retained their liberal ideals, while others, like British poet William Wordsworth, became increasingly disillusioned and ultimately conservative in their political views. Nevertheless, most of the members of that generation, and the generation that followed it, had enough ideals and views in common to be called by a single label: the **Romantics.**

The Fighting Temeraire *Tugged to Her Last Berth to Be Broken Up, 1838* (1839) by Joseph Mallord William Turner.

National Gallery of Art, London (NG524). Turner Bequest, 1856.

> *Bliss was it in that dawn to be alive, / but to be young was very heaven.*
>
> —William Wordsworth

What Is Romanticism?

Romanticism was a revolt against the restrictions imposed by the classical, aristocratic ideals of the eighteenth century. It was a liberation of the artist's imagination and style. Poets such as Wordsworth declared themselves free to write in the language of everyday speech about everyday people and events. The Romantics idealized nature and the lifestyles of people who lived close to nature, such as farmers and shepherds. This reverence for nature was in part a reaction to the increasingly urban and industrial character of Europe. For some Romantics, disillusionment with nineteenth-century life led to an interest in settings more exotic than the countryside. These writers and artists found inspiration in medieval ballads and courtly tales, as well as in myths, folk tales, and tales of the supernatural.

Another important characteristic of Romanticism is the belief in the importance of the individual. The Romantic individual was daring, rebellious, and free to express previously taboo emotions—to express, in Wordsworth's phrase, "the spontaneous overflow of powerful feelings." Poets such as Victor Hugo (see page 777), Paul

Verlaine, Arthur Rimbaud, and Charles Baudelaire (see pages 790 and 785) experimented with rhyme, meter, and subject matter, breaking rules that had been obeyed for generations. In music, the German composer Beethoven turned the highly structured classical sonata into an expansive form for the expression of powerful internal struggles.

The New Age Falters

As a new generation of Romantics grew up in the first half of the nineteenth century, it became clear that Europe was in turmoil. In France the monarchy was restored after Napoleon's downfall. The new monarchy, in turn, was replaced by the Second Republic in 1848. Unsuccessful popular revolts occurred in Italy, Austria, Poland, Hungary, and Belgium.

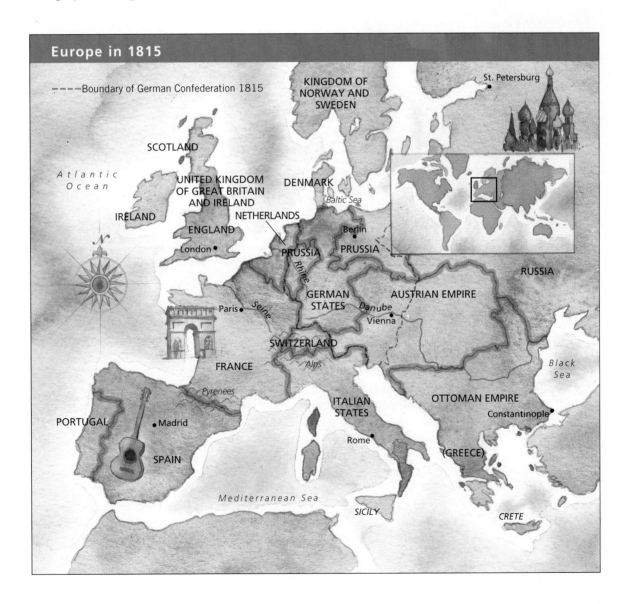

Europe in 1815

- - - Boundary of German Confederation 1815

The most famous of these unsuccessful revolts was the Decembrist uprising of 1825 in Russia, in which many intellectuals and writers, including Alexander Pushkin (see page 771), were implicated. The czar executed the military officers who had tried to establish a constitutional government, and a century of botched reforms and revolutions followed. The Russian serfs, or peasants, were finally freed in 1861, but the nation continued to be plagued by censorship, ignorance, poverty, and tyranny. Russian literature in the nineteenth century became a forum for reformist ideas, in which educated Russians were intensely interested.

In the Black Country
by Constantin Meunier (1831–1905).
Musée d'Orsay, Paris.

Progress, Pollution, and Poverty

The political events of the early and mid-nineteenth century—an era often labeled the age of progress—went hand in hand with the **Industrial Revolution.** This explosion of scientific knowledge led to many technological achievements, such as the steam engine, the electric dynamo (a machine that converts mechanical energy into electrical energy), and the processes for producing aluminum and steel. New inventions—the telegraph, the electric light, and the repeating rifle—were changing the world in exciting, sometimes frightening ways. Factories were built, and

A CLOSER LOOK: CULTURAL INFLUENCES

Preserving a National Heritage: The Brothers Grimm

INFORMATIONAL TEXT

During the first half of the nineteenth century, when European and American Romantic writers were turning to folklore and rural folk beliefs for artistic inspiration, two German brothers, Jakob (1785–1863) and Wilhelm (1786–1859) Grimm, undertook the enormous task of collecting German folklore. The brothers, who were both philologists, or linguists (people who study the origin, structure, and development of language), believed that folklore contained basic truths about the origin of civilization and that it recorded the "true" laws, customs, and proud heritage of the German people. By collecting and publishing the folklore of Germany before the oral tradition was lost, they believed that they could provide German readers with a sense of national pride and purpose.

The Grimms collected stories from their middle-class neighbors, mostly educated women who had been told the stories by their nursemaids and servants. The brothers were determined to present the stories in as close to their original forms as possible. But within their lifetimes, they revised their collection several times, hoping to appeal to an audience of middle-class Germans and their children. They often gave the tales a moralistic spin, and they also removed some of the more gruesome elements from the

steamboats and railroads, with their attendant noise and smoke, became part of the rural and urban landscapes. Farmworkers moved to cities to work in factories, but these cities, unprepared for the rapid population growth, offered them only slums to live in. In addition, during this great age of scientific progress and rapid change, Charles Darwin (1809–1882) developed a theory of evolution that upset people's ideas about who they were and where they had come from.

Many people prospered during the Industrial Revolution. A new middle class of manufacturers, bankers, and lawyers became the most significant force in European society. This dominant class was optimistic that material progress would improve life for all humanity. Few poor people shared this optimism, however. The economic theorist Karl Marx (1818–1883), whose ideas influenced Tolstoy (see page 803), and in the twentieth century led to the establishment of communist systems around the world, was a persuasive critic of the new social order. Most peasants lived in abject poverty. In the cities, people lived in slums, crowding into unsafe and unsanitary buildings. City streets were filthy, and working conditions in factories and mines were inhumane. Children and adults worked twelve-hour days, six days a week, with no safety standards or compensation for accidents. British children working in mines were used as draft animals, pulling carts full of coal. They rarely saw daylight.

Finches from the Galápagos Archipelago, from the *Journal of Researches into the Geology and Natural History of the Various Countries* (1890) by R. T. Pritchett.

John Murray, London. The British Library.

Princess and Frog Prince, from the *Frog Prince* (1874) by Walter Crane.

tales. (This practice of "cleaning up" the tales continues to this day, for as sanitized as they were, the Grimms' first edition of fairy tales is far more graphic than more modern retellings of the stories.)

Psychologists, educators, folklorists, and literary critics have long debated the Grimm brothers' contributions to folklore preservation. Some argue that the Grimms so altered the original form and purpose of the tales that they no longer accurately reflect the oral tradition the brothers were trying to preserve. While the Grimms certainly added their own values to the tales, they also preserved an important part of the German heritage. The Germans themselves responded enthusiastically to this attempt to capture a sense of collective pride: In Germany, *Grimms' Fairy Tales* has sold more than any other book except the Bible.

Many writers were troubled by these conditions. The liberal reforms begun during the revolutions of the late eighteenth century had not brought about an era of justice—in fact, the gap between rich and poor was wider than ever.

The Industrial Revolution fostered **colonialism**—the establishment of foreign colonies for economic advantage. As European nations became industrialized, they sought to obtain new markets and raw materials. Toward the end of the nineteenth century, European nations competed to establish their domination over other countries, particularly countries in Africa and Asia. Many Europeans emigrated to new lands and founded settlements. The practice of empire building by dominating less powerful countries and establishing colonies is known as **imperialism.**

The Realist Creed

Realism, a reaction against Romanticism, flourished during the last half of the nineteenth century. Like many other labels, *realism* is a bit misleading. The realists were not the first writers to describe the world as it is. The Romantics were also careful observers of the lives of ordinary people. In fact, some writers, such as Hugo and Pushkin, can be identified with both Romanticism and realism.

In France, under the leadership of the novelist Gustave Flaubert, the realists tried to make a science of their art by eliminating sentimentality from their tone and excessive decoration from their descriptions. Their aim was to observe and record the daily lives of ordinary people without distorting the truth. Unlike writers who emphasized the noble, uplifting aspects of human life, realists simply tried to mirror life, whether noble or ignoble, without making judgments. Of course, no artist can ever completely withhold judgment or feeling from his or her work, and good writing does much more than mirror reality. Flaubert's *Madame Bovary* is admired today not so much for its objectivity as for its perfect prose and its satire of the middle class.

Naturalism, a radical offshoot of realism, arose in France in the 1870s. Members of this movement, led by Émile Zola, considered free will an illusion, and they often portrayed their characters as helpless victims

Émile Zola (1868) by Edouard Manet.
Musée d'Orsay, Paris.

Avenue de l'Opera, Paris
(19th century). Sepia photograph.

of heredity, fate, and environment. Writers were no longer subjective in their choice of details; in fact, the naturalists attempted to abolish the boundary between scientist and artist, aiming to write in a detached, objective, and analytical style. The most talented naturalists, however, could not stay within the narrow ideology of their school. The French author Guy de Maupassant (see page 795) is sometimes called a naturalist, but his work is sharpened by irony and an unsurpassed gift for choosing the right details.

In poetry, **symbolism** became the major literary movement of the late nineteenth century. Symbolist poets avoided direct statements of meaning and instead used symbols to suggest meaning or mood. Charles Baudelaire is widely acknowledged to be the forerunner of this movement, and Arthur Rimbaud and Paul Verlaine are considered its most prominent practitioners.

The Sun (1916) by Edvard Munch.
University Collections, Oslo, Norway.

At the Rich Relative (1891) by Evgeniylosipovich Bukovetsky.
Tretyakov Gallery, Moscow.

The Realist, if he is an artist, will try not to show us a commonplace photograph of life, but to give us a more complete view of it, more striking, more convincing than reality itself.

—Guy de Maupassant

Realism in Russia

Several of the most important realists emerged from the fringes of Europe: Russia and Norway. When realism reached Russia, it acquired a softer tone and a grander vision. Ivan Turgenev, a Russian writer who had lived in Paris and had been influenced by Flaubert, Zola, and other French writers, examined the lives of serfs and nobles in *A Sportsman's Sketches* (1852), helping to create a clamor for emancipation. He wrote in ornate, lyrical prose brimming with sympathy and warmth. Other Russian novelists, including Leo Tolstoy and Fyodor Dostoevsky, learned a great deal from Turgenev. Realism flourished in Russia, fostering a powerful movement that called for the liberation of the serfs and, later, the entire society. Yet the primary aim of the Russian realists was not social reform but a desire to answer the ultimate questions of human life. In very different ways, Tolstoy and Dostoevsky repeatedly asked, "How should people live?" and "What are good and evil?"

Both Tolstoy and Dostoevsky wrote gigantic, sprawling novels filled with violence, love, and family crises and peopled with characters from a wide cross section of society. Compared with these two giants, the playwright and short story writer Anton Chekhov (see page 813) "painted" on a relatively small canvas. He found his subjects and themes in the common illusions and daily sufferings of unremarkable people. Like Tolstoy and Dostoevsky, however, Chekhov dealt with the meaning of life and death. His stories and plays are about people's attempts—usually frustrated—to find meaning and purpose in their lives.

Drama: The Stage as Living Room

The Norwegian realist playwright Henrik Ibsen utterly transformed nineteenth-century theater. Before Ibsen, audiences flocked to theaters to see sensational and contrived romantic costume dramas. Ibsen revolutionized the stage by treating it as a room in which the "fourth wall" had been removed, allowing audiences to eavesdrop on the everyday lives of ordinary people who could be their neighbors. Sets began to look like actual rooms in every detail; actors moved unaffectedly, like real people, and spoke natural, colloquial dialogue. Ibsen was one of the first playwrights to incorporate stage directions (*she smiles, moving to the window*) indicating how characters should act and speak. Most important, however, was Ibsen's focus on realistic human conflicts as outgrowths of social problems. In fact, Ibsen's dramas are sometimes referred to as "problem plays"—though his underlying messages about social problems never eclipse his rich, fully developed characterizations.

The Legacy of the Nineteenth Century

The great ideas of the nineteenth century—progress, social reform, evolution, psychology—became the foundations of contemporary thought. The literary styles of the nineteenth century—from effusive Romantic poetry to terse realist prose—still influence contemporary writing. Both realistic descriptions of life and powerful expressions of feeling are legacies of the schools of Romanticism and realism.

REVIEW

Talk About ...

Turn back to the Think About questions at the beginning of this introduction (page 744). Write down your responses, and get together with classmates to compare and discuss your views.

Reading Check

1. Name two effects the French Revolution had on the rest of Europe.
2. What criticisms of society did Karl Marx make during the Industrial Revolution?
3. What are the characteristics of symbolist poetry?
4. Name two ways writing of the realism movement from Russia and Norway differed from other writing in Europe at the time.
5. In what ways are Henrik Ibsen's dramas different from dramas that had been written before?

Johann Wolfgang von Goethe
(1749–1832)
Germany

Not only was Goethe (gö'tə) one of the greatest writers in German literature, he was also a universal genius who made important contributions to the fields of science, philosophy, and government. In addition, he was a skilled musician, painter, and athlete.

Goethe was born in Frankfurt to wealthy parents who had him tutored at home. He later said that his mother gave him "her happy nature and fondness for storytelling." (One enthusiastic visitor to his mother said, "Now I really understand how Goethe became Goethe.") After a false start as a law student, Goethe began studying the arts at Strasbourg, where he met Johann Gottfried von Herder, a leader of the *Sturm und Drang* ("Storm and Stress") movement that heralded the start of German Romanticism. Its members rebelled against the cool rationalism of the Enlightenment; instead, they emphasized the power of the imagination and spontaneous expression. Goethe's most notable contribution to the *Sturm und Drang* movement was his novel *The Sorrows of Young Werther* (1774), which made him internationally famous. Werther, the sensitive young man who suffers from a hopeless love, became a symbol of the Romantic hero.

In 1775, the young duke of Saxe-Weimar, Karl August, invited Goethe to stay at his court, and within a few years, Weimar blossomed into the cultural center of Germany. During his first ten years at Weimar, Goethe served as chief minister of state, instituting important political reforms; in addition, he studied music, biology, and painting. In 1786, he left to travel in Italy. This trip marked an important shift in his artistic development, as he became influenced by classical art and architecture.

Johann Wolfgang von Goethe (c. 19th century) by Heinrich Cristoph.

Goethe Museum, Frankfurt, Germany.

Goethe's life after his return from Italy was especially productive. He wrote a number of masterpieces during this period: love poems, prose plays, travel books, novels, narrative poetry, and several poetic dramas, most notably *Faust* (Part I in 1808; Part II in 1833), generally considered his greatest work.

Unlike some Romantic artists, Goethe did not advertise himself as a mystic, a hermit, or an adventurer. Instead, he thought of himself as an ordinary man—a public servant, a husband, and a father. But in his old age, Goethe became a living monument, receiving pilgrims who visited him from around the world. Even Napoleon, the supreme egotist, said after meeting Goethe, *"Voilà un homme!"* ("There is a man!").

Before You Read

from Faust, Part I

Make the Connection

Quickwrite ✏️

Should people accept their limitations gracefully, or is it better to strive to overcome restrictions in one's life? At what point could striving to exceed limitations become dangerous to oneself or others? Freewrite your ideas in a brief paragraph or two.

Literary Focus

Characterization

Characterization is the process by which an author reveals a character's personality. A writer can reveal a character in the following ways:

- Describe the character's appearance.
- Record what the character says.
- Reveal what the character thinks and feels.
- Show the character's actions.
- Show how other characters act toward the character.
- State directly what the character is like—kind, angry, timid, and so on.

The first five methods are examples of **indirect characterization,** meaning that the reader must use the author's clues along with personal judgment to infer a character's personality. The last method is called **direct characterization:** The writer simply states directly what a character is like.

> **Characterization** is the process by which an author reveals a character's personality.
>
> *For more on Characterization, see the Handbook of Literary and Historical Terms.*

Reading Skills

Evaluating a Character's Actions

Throughout *Faust,* the title character must make difficult decisions between two courses of action. As you read, jot down your opinion of Faust's character after he has decided to take a particular course of action. After you finish reading, look back at your notes and evaluate Faust's character based on your judgment of his actions.

Background

There really was a Dr. Faust: In Germany in the early sixteenth century, a man named Johannes Faustus gained a wide reputation as a skillful magician. People said this man sold his soul to the devil in exchange for knowledge of the magical arts. The English playwright Christopher Marlowe (1564–1593) wrote a popular play called *The Tragical History of Doctor Faustus* based on this man. In *Faust,* Goethe further embellishes the story behind this legendary figure.

Vocabulary Development

fervent (fur′vənt) *adj.:* very intense in feeling.

eschew (es·choo′) *v.:* shun; avoid.

prevaricate (pri·var′i·kāt′) *v.:* avoid the truth; lie.

pedant (ped′′nt) *n.:* teacher who emphasizes details or rules instead of genuine learning.

North Carolina Competency Goal
1.02; 1.03; 4.05; 5.03; 6.01

INTERNET

Vocabulary Practice
•
More About Johann Wolfgang von Goethe
Keyword: LE5 WL-6

Literary Skills
Understand characterization.

Reading Skills
Evaluate a character's actions.

Illustrations by Carl Vogel von
Vogelstein (1788–1868) from
Faust by Goethe.

Palazzo Pitti, Florence, Italy.

Faust

PART I

Johann Wolfgang von Goethe
translated by **Louis MacNeice**

Prologue in Heaven

[*Enter the* LORD *and the* HEAVENLY HOSTS, *with* MEPHISTOPHELES°
following. The THREE ARCHANGELS *step forward.*]

Raphael.
 The chanting sun, as ever, rivals
 The chanting of his brother spheres
 And marches round his destined circuit—
 A march that thunders in our ears.
5 His aspect cheers the Hosts of Heaven
 Though what his essence none can say;
 These inconceivable creations
 Keep the high state of their first day.°

Gabriel.
 And swift, with inconceivable swiftness,
10 The earth's full splendor rolls around,
 Celestial radiance alternating
 With a dread night too deep to sound;
 The sea against the rocks' deep bases
 Comes foaming up in far-flung force,
15 And rock and sea go whirling onward
 In the swift spheres' eternal course.

Michael.
 And storms in rivalry are raging
 From sea to land, from land to sea,
 In frenzy forge the world a girdle
20 From which no inmost part is free.
 The blight of lightning flaming yonder
 Marks where the thunderbolt will play;
 And yet Thine envoys, Lord, revere
 The gentle movement of Thy day.

Choir of Angels.
25 Thine aspect cheers the Hosts of Heaven
 Though what Thine essence none can say,
 And all Thy loftiest creations
 Keep the high state of their first day.

[MEPHISTOPHELES *steps forward.*]

Mephistopheles.
 Since you, O Lord, once more approach and ask
30 If business down with us be light or heavy—
 And in the past you've usually welcomed me—
 That's why you see me also at your levee.°
 Excuse me, I can't manage lofty words—
 Not though your whole court jeer and find me low;

Mephistopheles
(mef′ə•stäf′ə•lēz′): the devil.

? 1–24. *What words and images in Raphael's lines convey the orderly aspects of creation? What details in Gabriel's and Michael's lines convey the more chaotic state of earth?*

8. the high state of their first day: Unlike human beings, who have fallen from their original state of innocence, the sun, planets, and other "inconceivable creations" remain unfallen.

? 29–36. *How would you describe Mephistopheles' tone as he speaks to the Lord?*

32. levee (lev′ē) *n.:* reception.

35 My pathos certainly would make you laugh
Had you not left off laughing long ago.
Your suns and worlds mean nothing much to me;
How men torment themselves, that's all I see.
The little god of the world, one can't reshape, reshade him;
40 He is as strange today as that first day you made him.
His life would be not so bad, not quite,
Had you not granted him a gleam of Heaven's light;
He calls it Reason, uses it not the least
Except to be more beastly than any beast.
45 He seems to me—if your Honor does not mind—
Like a grasshopper—the long-legged kind—
That's always in flight and leaps as it flies along
And then in the grass strikes up its same old song.
I could only wish he confined himself to the grass!
50 He thrusts his nose into every filth, alas.

Lord.
Mephistopheles, have you no other news?
Do you always come here to accuse?
Is nothing ever right in your eyes on earth?

Mephistopheles.
No, Lord! I find things there as downright bad as ever.
55 I am sorry for men's days of dread and dearth;
Poor things, *my* wish to plague 'em isn't <u>fervent</u>.

Lord.
Do you know Faust?

Mephistopheles.
⠀⠀⠀⠀⠀The Doctor?°

Lord.
⠀⠀⠀⠀⠀⠀⠀⠀⠀Aye, my servant.

Mephistopheles.
Indeed! He serves you oddly enough, I think.
The fool has no earthly habits in meat and drink.
60 The ferment in him drives him wide and far,
That he is mad he too has almost guessed;
He demands of heaven each fairest star
And of earth each highest joy and best,
And all that is new and all that is far
65 Can bring no calm to the deep-sea swell of his breast.

Lord.
Now he may serve me only gropingly,
Soon I shall lead him into the light.

57. The Doctor: doctor of philosophy; Ph.D.

58–65. Pay attention to what Mephistopheles is saying about Faust's character. Ferment is the breakdown of organic compounds due to the chemical action of a substance like bacteria or yeast; it can also be a state of agitation or upheaval.

❓ *What do you think is the "ferment" in Faust that Mephistopheles refers to in these lines?*

Vocabulary

fervent (fûr′vənt) *adj.:* very intense in feeling.

The gardener knows when the sapling first turns green
That flowers and fruit will make the future bright.

Mephistopheles.

70   What do you wager? You will lose him yet,
Provided *you* give *me* permission
To steer him gently the course I set.

Lord.

So long as he walks the earth alive,
So long you may try what enters your head;
75   Men make mistakes as long as they strive.

Mephistopheles.

I thank you for that; as regards the dead,
The dead have never taken my fancy.
I favor cheeks that are full and rosy-red;
No corpse is welcome to my house;
80   I work as the cat does with the mouse.

Lord.

Very well; you have my full permission.
Divert this soul from its primal source
And carry it, if you can seize it,
Down with you upon your course—
85   And stand ashamed when you must needs admit:
A good man with his groping intuitions
Still knows the path that is true and fit.

Mephistopheles.

All right—but it won't last for long.
I'm not afraid my bet will turn out wrong.
90   And, if my aim prove true and strong,
Allow me to triumph wholeheartedly
Dust shall he eat—and greedily—
Like my cousin the Snake° renowned in tale and song.

Lord.

That too you are free to give a trial;
95   I have never hated the likes of you.
Of all the spirits of denial
The joker is the last that I eschew.
Man finds relaxation too attractive—
Too fond too soon of unconditional rest;
100 Which is why I am pleased to give him a companion
Who lures and thrusts and must, as devil, be active.
But ye, true sons of Heaven, it is your duty
To take your joy in the living wealth of beauty.

81–93. Mephistopheles and the Lord are having a disagreement in these lines.
? *What does the Lord think will be the outcome of Mephistopheles' plan? What does Mephistopheles believe the outcome will be?*

93. my cousin the Snake: In the Garden of Eden, the devil took on the shape of a serpent and tempted Eve to eat an apple from the Tree of Knowledge.

94–101. In these lines the Lord points out that "relaxation" appeals to people, perhaps too much.
? *Why does the Lord appreciate Mephistopheles' presence on earth?*

Vocabulary

eschew (es·chōō′) *v.*: shun; avoid.

The changing Essence which ever works and lives
105 Wall you around with love, serene, secure!
And that which floats in flickering appearance
Fix ye it firm in thoughts that must endure.

Choir of Angels.
Thine aspect cheers the Hosts of Heaven
Though what Thine essence none can say,
110 And all Thy loftiest creations
Keep the high state of their first day.

[*Heaven closes.*]

Mephistopheles (*alone*).
I like to see the Old One now and then
And try to keep relations on the level.
It's really decent of so great a person
115 To talk so humanely even to the Devil.

112–115. Even though they are rivals, Mephistopheles describes the Lord as humane and decent.
? *What do Mephistopheles' words reveal about the relationship between Mephistopheles and the Lord?*

The Fatal Hour: Fantastic Subject by Alexandre Evariste Fragonard (1780–1850).
Stair Sainty Matthiesen Gallery, New York.

Faust has become disappointed with the limitations of human knowledge. Although as a doctor of philosophy he has explored many areas of learning, he still has not found the meaning of life. He has even dabbled in the art of "white magic," but it has yielded him no more knowledge than his own reason. Despairing, Faust considers suicide, but when he hears the bells ringing in celebration of Easter, he is brought back to the world of simple enjoyment. He goes for a walk in the countryside, thinking that he, like other people, might be satisfied with an acceptance of his limitations. Returning to his study, he struggles with Mephistopheles, who attempts to persuade him to try the devil's way, the way of sensual pleasures, with no thought of the consequences. Faust falls into despair again. He curses love, hope, faith, and patience.

The Pact with the Devil

Mephistopheles.
Stop playing with your grief which battens°
Like a vulture on your life, your mind!
The worst of company would make you feel
That you are a man among mankind.
5   Not that it's really my proposition
To shove you among the common men;
Though I'm not one of the Upper Ten,°
If you would like a coalition
With me for your career through life,
10 I am quite ready to fit in,
I'm yours before you can say knife.
I am your comrade;
If you so crave,
I am your servant, I am your slave.

Faust.
15 And what have I to undertake in return?

Mephistopheles.
Oh it's early days to discuss what that is.

Faust.
No, no, the devil is an egoist
And ready to do nothing gratis°
Which is to benefit a stranger.
20 Tell me your terms and don't <u>prevaricate</u>!
A servant like you in the house is a danger.

Mephistopheles.
I will bind myself to your service in this world.
To be at your beck and never rest nor slack;

---

1. **battens** *v.*: feeds.

7. **the Upper Ten:** top level of society; short for "the upper ten thousand."

18. **gratis** (grat′is) *adv.*: for free.

Vocabulary
prevaricate (pri·var′i·kāt′) *v.*: avoid the truth; lie.

When we meet again on the other side,
25   In the same coin you shall pay me back.

Faust.
    The other side gives me little trouble;
    First batter this present world to rubble,
    Then the other may rise—if that's the plan.
    This earth is where my springs of joy have started,
30   And this sun shines on me when brokenhearted;
    If I can first from them be parted,
    Then let happen what will and can!
    I wish to hear no more about it—
    Whether there too men hate and love
35   Or whether in those spheres too, in the future,
    There is a Below or an Above.

Mephistopheles.
    With such an outlook you can risk it.
    Sign on the line! In these next days you will get
    Ravishing samples of my arts;
40   I am giving you what never man saw yet.

Faust.
    Poor devil, can *you* give anything ever?
    Was a human spirit in its high endeavor
    Even once understood by one of your breed?
    Have you got food which fails to feed?
45   Or red gold which, never at rest,
    Like mercury runs away through the hand?
    A game at which one never wins?
    A girl who, even when on my breast,
    Pledges herself to my neighbor with her eyes?
50   The divine and lovely delight of honor
    Which falls like a falling star and dies?
    Show me the fruits which, before they are plucked, decay
    And the trees which day after day renew their green!

Mephistopheles.
    Such a commission doesn't alarm me,
55   I have such treasures to purvey.
    But, my good friend, the time draws on when we
    Should be glad to feast at our ease on something good.

Faust.
    If ever I stretch myself on a bed of ease,
    Then I am finished! Is that understood?
60   If ever your flatteries can coax me
    To be pleased with myself, if ever you cast
    A spell of pleasure that can hoax me—
    Then let *that* day be my last!
    That's my wager!

14–25. Though Mephistopheles offers to be Faust's "servant" and "slave," Faust realizes that he will have to give Mephistopheles something in return.
? *What are the conditions of Mephistopheles' offer?*

41–53. In these lines, Faust recites a list of gifts he believes the devil could grant him.
? *What do all the gifts Faust mentions have in common? What does this tell you about Faust's expectations in dealing with the devil?*

Mephistopheles tempts Faust with enchanting visions. Lithograph by Theodor Hosemann after Peter Cornelius (1835).

Mephistopheles.

        Done!

Faust.

                Let's shake!

65   If ever I say to the passing moment
       "Linger a while! Thou art so fair!"
       Then you may cast me into fetters,
       I will gladly perish then and there!
       Then you may set the death bell tolling,
70   Then from my service you are free,
       The clock may stop, its hand may fall,
       And that be the end of time for me!

Mephistopheles.

       Think what you're saying, we shall not forget it.

Faust.

       And you are fully within your rights;
75   I have made no mad or outrageous claim.
       If I stay as I am, I am a slave—
       Whether yours or another's, it's all the same.

Mephistopheles.

       I shall this very day at the College Banquet
       Enter your service with no more ado,
80   But just one point—As a life-and-death insurance
       I must trouble you for a line or two.

Faust.

       So you, you <u>pedant</u>, you too like things in writing?

> **?** **58–73.** *What are the conditions of the agreement between Mephistopheles and Faust?*

Vocabulary

pedant (ped′'nt) *n.*: teacher who emphasizes details or
    rules instead of genuine learning.

Have you never known a man? Or a man's word? Never?
Is it not enough that my word of mouth
85   Puts all my days in bond forever?
Does not the world rage on in all its streams
And shall a promise hamper *me*?
Yet this illusion reigns within our hearts
And from it who would be gladly free?
90   Happy the man who can inwardly keep his word;
Whatever the cost, he will not be loath to pay!
But a parchment, duly inscribed and sealed,
Is a bogey from which all wince away.
The word dies on the tip of the pen
95   And wax and leather lord it then.
What do you, evil spirit, require?
Bronze, marble, parchment, paper?
Quill or chisel or pencil of slate?
You may choose whichever you desire.

Mephistopheles.

100   How can you so exaggerate
With such a hectic rhetoric?
Any little snippet is quite good—
And you sign it with one little drop of blood.

Faust.

If that is enough and is some use,
105   One may as well pander to your fad.

Mephistopheles.

Blood is a very special juice.

Faust.

Only do not fear that I shall break this contract.
What I promise is nothing more
Than what all my powers are striving for.
110   I have puffed myself up too much, it is only
Your sort that really fits my case.
The great Earth Spirit has despised me
And Nature shuts the door in my face.
The thread of thought is snapped asunder,
115   I have long loathed knowledge in all its fashions.
In the depths of sensuality
Let us now quench our glowing passions!
And at once make ready every wonder
Of unpenetrated sorcery!
120   Let us cast ourselves into the torrent of time,
Into the whirl of eventfulness,
Where disappointment and success,
Pleasure and pain may chop and change
As chop and change they will and can;

80–99. *What is Mephistopheles asking Faust to do as "insurance" for their agreement? What is Faust's argument against doing this?*

100–106. *How does Mephistopheles persuade Faust to agree to his request? What might be ironic about Mephistopheles' comment in line 106?*

116–141. *How will Faust and Mephistopheles satisfy Faust's passions?*

125   It is restless action makes the man.

Mephistopheles.
No limit is fixed for you, no bound;
If you'd like to nibble at everything
Or to seize upon something flying round—
Well, may you have a run for your money!
130   But seize your chance and don't be funny!

Faust.
I've told you, it is no question of happiness.
The most painful joy, enamored° hate, enlivening
Disgust—I devote myself to all excess.
My breast, now cured of its appetite for knowledge,
135   From now is open to all and every smart,
And what is allotted to the whole of mankind
That will I sample in my inmost heart,
Grasping the highest and lowest with my spirit,
Piling men's weal and woe upon my neck,
140   To extend myself to embrace all human selves
And to founder in the end, like them, a wreck.

Mephistopheles.
O believe *me,* who have been chewing
These iron rations many a thousand year,
No human being can digest
145   This stuff, from the cradle to the bier.°
This universe—believe a devil—
Was made for no one but a god!
He exists in eternal light
But *us* he has brought into the darkness
150   While *your* sole portion is day and night.

Faust.
I will all the same!

Mephistopheles.
                        That's very nice.
There's only one thing I find wrong;
Time is short, art is long.
You could do with a little artistic advice.
155   Confederate° with one of the poets
And let him flog his imagination
To heap all virtues on your head,
A head with such a reputation:
Lion's bravery,
160   Stag's velocity,
Fire of Italy,
Northern tenacity.
Let *him* find out the secret art
Of combining craft with a noble heart

132. enamored (en·am'ərd)
v. used as *adj.:* charmed; filled
with love.

145. bier (bir) *n.:* platform on
which a coffin or corpse is
placed.

? 153. *What is the
meaning of the state-
ment "Time is short, art
is long"?*

155. confederate
(kən'fed·ə·rāt) *v.:* meet with.

165 And of being in love like a young man,
Hotly, but working to a plan.
Such a person—*I'd* like to meet him;
"Mr. Microcosm"° is how I'd greet him.

Faust.
What am I then if fate must bar
170 My efforts to reach that crown of humanity
After which all my senses strive?

Mephistopheles.
You are in the end . . . what you are.
You can put on full-bottomed wigs with a million locks,
You can put on stilts instead of your socks,
175 You remain forever what you are.

Faust.
I feel my endeavors have not been worth a pin
When I raked together the treasures of the human mind,
If at the end I but sit down to find
No new force welling up within.
180 I have not a hair's breadth more of height,
I am no nearer the Infinite.

Mephistopheles.
My very good sir, you look at things
Just in the way that people do;
We must be cleverer than that
185 Or the joys of life will escape from you.
Hell! You have surely hands and feet,
Also a head and you-know-what;
The pleasures I gather on the wing,
Are they less mine? Of course they're not!
190 Suppose I can afford six stallions,
I can add that horsepower to my score
And dash along and be a proper man
As if my legs were twenty-four.
So goodbye to thinking! On your toes!
195 The world's before us. Quick! Here goes!
I tell you, a chap who's intellectual
Is like a beast on a blasted heath
Driven in circles by a demon
While a fine green meadow lies round beneath.

Faust.
200 How do we start?

Mephistopheles.
We just say go—and skip.
But please get ready for this pleasure trip.

[*Exit* FAUST.]

168. Mr. Microcosm: that is, man as the microcosm, or essence, of the world.

172–175. *What belief about humanity does Mephistopheles express in these lines?*

196–199. *What does Mephistopheles mean when he compares an intellectual to a tortured beast in these lines?*

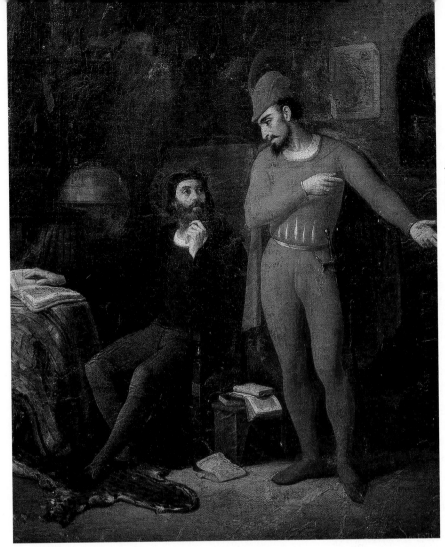

Mephistopheles Tempting Faust by Enrico Sartori (1831–1889).

Museo Civico, Cremona, Italy.

Only look down on knowledge and reason,
The highest gifts that men can prize,
Only allow the spirit of lies
205   To confirm you in magic and illusion,
And then I have you body and soul.
Fate has given this man a spirit
Which is always pressing onwards, beyond control,
And whose mad striving overleaps
210   All joys of the earth between pole and pole.
Him shall I drag through the wilds of life
And through the flats of meaninglessness,
I shall make him flounder and gape and stick
And to tease his insatiableness
215   Hang meat and drink in the air before his watering lips;
In vain he will pray to slake his inner thirst,
And even had he not sold himself to the devil
He would be equally accursed.

216–218. *Why does Mephistopheles think Faust would have been accursed even if Faust hadn't made a pact with him?*

Response and Analysis

Reading Check

1. What agreement do Mephistopheles and the Lord make about Faust?
2. What pact do Mephistopheles and Faust make?
3. What does Faust claim to be seeking?

Thinking Critically

4. What is Faust's initial attitude toward Mephistopheles? Why, then, does Faust agree to the bargain with Mephistopheles?
5. Compare and contrast the **characters** of Faust and Mephistopheles. How does Goethe reveal their characters? What words would you use to describe their character traits?
6. What is Romantic about the Lord's position in allowing Faust to be tested by Mephistopheles? How is Goethe's Romanticism shown in Faust's "mad striving" and refusal to rest? Explain how Faust might be considered a Romantic hero.

Extending and Evaluating

7. Modern scientists, who have unlocked many of nature's secrets, have gone far beyond what Faust could have imagined. What are the present dangers of the search for scientific knowledge and the human mastery of nature? In the modern world, do you see examples of the kind of boundless striving that characterizes Faust? Explain.

Literary Criticism

8. The scholar Victor Lange says that the Prologue to the play "is the key to everything that is to come." Do you agree or disagree? Explain.

WRITING
Evaluating a Character's Actions

Look at what you wrote for the Quickwrite and Reading Skills on page 757. Have any of your ideas changed since reading *Faust*? Do you think that Faust is justified in pursuing knowledge at the risk of his own soul? Do you think he should be punished for making such a dangerous bargain with the devil? What decision would you make if you were in Faust's shoes? Write a brief essay in which you evaluate Faust's decision.

Vocabulary Development
Question and Answer

Answer the following questions to test your understanding of the under-lined Vocabulary words.

1. What is the difference between *fervent* and *tranquil*?
2. How do you eschew cigarettes?
3. What is the opposite of *prevaricate*?
4. What aspects of learning does a pedant emphasize?

Doctor Faust by Rembrandt van Rijn (1606–1669). Etching.
Fondazione Magnani Rocca, Corte di Mamiano, Italy.

Alexander Pushkin
(1799–1837)
Russia

Alexander Sergejevitch Pushkin (1827) by Wassilj A. Tropinin.
Pushkin Museum, Moscow.

The Russians revere, re-read, and quote Pushkin as the English do Shakespeare. He was born in Moscow to an old aristocratic family that had lost most of its fortune. Pushkin had an African great-grandfather— Abram Hannibal, a general under Peter the Great—whose ancestry he cherished.

Through both his father's extensive library and his beloved nurse's old tales, Pushkin steeped himself in imaginative literature. He also developed an early interest in radical politics and began writing poetry. At fifteen, he published his first poem.

In 1820, Pushkin's radical political poetry and wild living resulted in his exile from a political post in St. Petersburg. Undaunted, Pushkin became such a master of verse, drama, and fiction that he is usually called the father of modern Russian literature. His early narrative poems made him famous in Russian literary circles, and although the settings and plots of these works were highly Romantic, their portrayals of Russian characters and customs struck a new note of verisimilitude, or trueness to life. He developed a new realism in characterization and a vigorous, simple, and natural language unlike any in Russian literature. He wrote prose works, such as *The Queen of Spades* (1834) and *The Negro of Peter the Great* (1837), that showed great mastery of character and style. His highest achievement, however, was in poetry, particularly the historical drama *Boris Godunov* (1825) and the verse novel *Eugene Onegin* (1833). His shorter poems reveal his gift for finding beauty in everyday things. All his work, like his life, exhibits a high-spirited, dashing casualness that reveals powerful feelings underneath. Peter Ilyich Tchaikovsky, one of several composers who adapted the poet's words to music, said that Pushkin's poems "sang themselves."

In 1831, Pushkin married a flirtatious beauty, Natalya Goncharova. She became involved with a French nobleman at the Russian court, Baron Georges d'Anthes, who pursued her so feverishly that he married her sister in order to get closer to her. Pushkin's patience with this situation apparently came to an end in January 1837. Under circumstances that remain partly mysterious today, he—like one of his own Romantic characters—entered into a duel with d'Anthes to defend his wife's honor. Pushkin was fatally wounded in the duel. At his death he was mourned as a national hero. Today he is viewed as a founder of Russian culture, equivalent in stature to Dante in Italy, Shakespeare in England, and Goethe in Germany.

I Have Visited Again

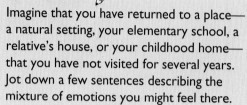

Make the Connection

Quickwrite

Imagine that you have returned to a place—a natural setting, your elementary school, a relative's house, or your childhood home—that you have not visited for several years. Jot down a few sentences describing the mixture of emotions you might feel there.

Literary Focus

Setting

The **setting** of a work is the place and time where it occurs. Writers may use setting to influence or reveal character, explore a theme, set a mood, create symbols, or develop ironic situations. Romantic writers often looked to nature and rural settings to explain complex feelings about themselves and to explore universal themes such as the passing of time, the stages of a human life, and the place of the individual in the world.

North Carolina Competency Goal
1.02; 1.03; 4.05; 5.01; 5.03; 6.01

> **Setting** is the time and place of a work.
>
> *For more on Setting, see the Hand-book of Literary and Historical Terms.*

Background

Exile was a major focus for Russian writers throughout the nineteenth and twentieth centuries for the simple and painful reason that many Russian writers were exiled for their political views. When he was eighteen, Pushkin began his first job, at the foreign office in St. Petersburg. While there, Pushkin wrote verses that were critical of the czar. Disturbed by the popularity of this politically liberal poetry, the government transferred Pushkin to southern Russia. For the rest of his life, Pushkin's every move was observed and reported on by the secret police. He was finally dismissed from the foreign service in 1824 and exiled to his mother's estate for two years. In "I Have Visited Again," a poem written late in his career, Pushkin tells of returning to the estate ten years after his exile there. He knew every corner of the estate so well, during the many different phases of his life and seasons of the year, that his descriptions of it are quite varied.

Notice the several layers of memory in the poem. The speaker remembers his years of exile; but during those years, he remembers other years still further back. He anticipates the future and also imagines that he will be remembered by his descendants. In effect, he describes three different settings.

SKILLS FOCUS

Literary Skills
Understand setting.

In the Woods of the Contess Mordvinov by Ivan Shishkin (1832–1898).

Tretyakov Gallery, Moscow.

I Have Visited Again

Alexander Pushkin
translated by **D. M. Thomas**

> . . . I have visited again
> That corner of the earth where I spent two
> Unnoticed, exiled years. Ten years have passed
> Since then, and many things have changed for me,
> 5   And I have changed too, obedient to life's law—
> But now that I am here again, the past
> Has flown out eagerly to embrace me, claim me,
> And it seems that only yesterday I wandered
> Within these groves.

Village in the Spring by Arnold Borisovich Lakhovsky (1880–1937).

Sotheby's, London, Lot 257, 14/12/95.

Here is the cottage, sadly

10 Declined now, where I lived with my poor old nurse.
She is no more. No more behind the wall
Do I hear her heavy footsteps as she moved
Slowly, painstakingly about her tasks.

Here are the wooded slopes where often I

15 Sat motionless, and looked down at the lake,
Recalling other shores and other waves . . .
It gleams between golden cornfields and green meadows,
A wide expanse; across its fathomless waters
A fisherman passes, dragging an ancient net.

20 Along the shelving banks, hamlets are scattered
—Behind them the mill, so crooked it can scarcely
Make its sails turn in the wind . . .

On the bounds

Of my ancestral acres, at the spot
Where a road, scarred by many rainfalls, climbs

25 The hill, three pine trees stand—one by itself,
The others close together. When I rode
On horseback past them in the moonlit night,
The friendly rustling murmur of their crowns
Would welcome me. Now, I have ridden out

30 Upon that road, and seen those trees again.

They have remained the same, make the same murmur—
But round their aging roots, where all before
Was barren, naked, a thicket of young pines
Has sprouted; like green children round the shadows

35 Of the two neighboring pines. But in the distance
Their solitary comrade stands, morose,
Like some old bachelor, and round its roots
All is barren as before.

I greet you, young

And unknown tribe of pine trees! I'll not see

40 Your mighty upward thrust of years to come
When you will overtop these friends of mine
And shield their ancient summits from the gaze
Of passers-by. But may my grandson hear
Your welcome murmur when, returning home

45 From lively company, and filled with gay
And pleasant thoughts, he passes you in the night,
And thinks perhaps of me . . .

Response and Analysis

Thinking Critically

1. Briefly describe the **mood,** or atmosphere, of the poem as a whole. Cite the lines and passages that, in your opinion, most strongly express that mood. What elements of the **setting** do they describe?

2. **Personification** is a form of figurative language in which an author describes a nonhuman thing or quality in human terms. What objects does the speaker personify in the poem? What comparison does he make between these objects and human beings?

3. In the first stanza, the speaker says that change is "life's law." How does the poem's **setting** demonstrate the law of change?

4. How would you state the **theme,** or central idea about life, of this poem? What role does the **setting** play in the development of this theme?

Literary Criticism

5. The Pushkin biographer Walter Vickery says that Pushkin's "view of the world is, in the final analysis, somewhat bleak and tragic." Do you think Vickery's statement is accurate with regard to this poem? Explain your answer, using specific examples from the poem.

WRITING

Using Setting to Convey Emotion

Use your Quickwrite notes to help you write a poem or prose paragraph about returning to a place after some years have passed. What has changed or stayed the same? How have your feelings about the place changed? What emotions does the **setting** trigger in you?

Comparing Poems

In a brief essay, compare "I Have Visited Again" with "Mutability" by the English Romantic poet Percy Bysshe Shelley. Consider what each poet says about the inevitability of change in nature and human lives. Compare the moods evoked by the imagery in both poems.

Mutability
Percy Bysshe Shelley

1

The flower that smiles today
　　　　Tomorrow dies;
All that we wish to stay
　　　　Tempts and then flies.
5　What is this world's delight?
Lightning that mocks the night,
　　Brief even as bright.
2
Virtue, how frail it is!
　　　　Friendship how rare!
10　Love, how it sells poor bliss
　　　　For proud despair!
But we, though soon they fall,
Survive their joy and all
　　Which ours we call.
3
15　Whilst skies are blue and bright,
　　　　Whilst flowers are gay,
Whilst eyes that change ere night
　　　　Make glad the day,
Whilst yet the calm hours creep,
20　Dream thou—and from thy sleep
　　Then wake to weep.

North Carolina Competency Goal
1.02; 1.03; 4.02; 4.05; 5.03; 6.01

INTERNET

Projects and Activities

Keyword: LE5 WL-6

SKILLS FOCUS

Literary Skills
Analyze setting.

Writing Skills
Use setting to convey emotion. Compare poems.

Vocabulary Development

Denotation and Connotation

A word's **denotation** is its strict dictionary definition. Denotations are objective, meaning that they are not derived from someone's opinions and experiences. A word's **connotations** are the feelings and associations that the word suggests. Connotations are subjective, meaning that they are based on individual thoughts and feelings that may change over time. Take, for example, the word *flown* in line 7 of Pushkin's "I Have Visited Again": "the past / Has flown out eagerly to embrace me." The denotation, or literal meaning, of *flown* is "rushed; came quickly."

Why is *flown* a better word to use in this line than *rushed* or *came quickly*? The word *rushed* and the phrase *came quickly* can be used in many different contexts, and they bring to mind a variety of images and associations. For example, you might rush to school if you think you're going to be late, or you might walk quickly toward someone who is calling your name. *Flown,* however, has a greater emotional impact. Its connotations include soaring through the air as well as a sense of joy and urgency—associations that enhance our response to the speaker's experience.

North Carolina Competency Goal
1.03; 4.05; 5.03; 6.01

Vocabulary Skills
Distinguish between the denotative and connotative meanings of words.

"'Born in conservation,' if you don't mind. 'Captivity' has negative connotations."

PRACTICE

In order to help you think about why Pushkin used each of the underlined words rather than a synonym in the lines from "I Have Visited Again" below, answer the following questions about connotations.

1. "And it seems that only yesterday I <u>wandered</u> / Within these groves." (lines 8–9)

What connotations does *wandered* have that *explored* does not? When you think of someone wandering, what images come to mind?

2. "Do I hear her heavy footsteps as she moved / Slowly, <u>painstakingly</u> about her tasks." (lines 12–13)

What connotations does *painstakingly* have that *carefully* does not? How do you think someone looks if she moves painstakingly?

3. "A wide expanse; across its <u>fathomless</u> waters / A fisherman passes" (lines 18–19)

What connotations does *fathomless* have that the phrase *too deep to measure* does not? Can you think of another meaning of *fathomless*?

4. "But round their aging roots, where all before / Was <u>barren</u>, naked, a thicket of young pines / Has sprouted" (lines 32–34)

What connotations does *barren* have that *unproductive* does not? How do you think a barren landscape might look?

5. "I greet you, young / And unknown <u>tribe</u> of pine trees!" (lines 38–39)

What connotations does *tribe* have that *group* does not? What does the image of a tribe of pine trees make you visualize?

Victor Hugo
(1802–1885)
France

Even people who knew nothing of Victor Hugo's work were awed by his physical presence. He was a man of legendary strength, energy, and appetite. He was also a man of enormous vanity, who said at one point that Paris should be renamed Hugo.

The son of one of Napoleon's officers, Hugo spent his childhood in Madrid, Naples, and Paris. In his schoolwork and in his personal writing, he soon revealed his talent, his perfectionism, and his amazing stamina. Within two years, between the ages of seventeen and nineteen, he wrote 272 articles for a journal he edited with his brother. He published his first collection of poetry in 1822, the year he married his childhood sweetheart, Adèle Foucher. By the time he was thirty-eight, he had published eight plays, seven volumes of poetry, and the novels *Han d'islande* (1823) and *The Hunchback of Notre Dame* (1831). At forty, as the most popular and respected author in France, Hugo was elected to the prestigious literary body called the French Academy.

In 1843, Hugo's first failure—a play called *Les Burgraves*—led directly to the collapse of Romanticism in the French theater. The same year also brought a personal tragedy: His favorite daughter and her husband were drowned in a boating accident. Hugo's grief, like everything else about him, was colossal. For the next ten years he published nothing. He wrote only for himself, to ease his grief.

As a distraction from the pain during these years, Hugo entered political life. But he was formally exiled as a political rebel in 1852. In his exile he was not forgotten; in fact, his banishment contributed to his already enormous popularity. In exile he wrote his famous protest

Victor Hugo by Leon Bonnat (1833–1922).
Victor Hugo House, Paris.

novel *Les Misérables* (1862), as well as many of his greatest poems. When Napoleon III fell from power in 1870, Hugo returned to France.

More than a million people attended Hugo's funeral, which was a tremendous spectacle. The funeral parade was miles long, led by entire regiments of cavalry, followed by carriages filled with the greatest dignitaries of Europe. The French people felt they were burying not just a writer but a national hero.

For Independent Reading

You may enjoy reading one of Hugo's famous novels:

- *Les Misérables*

Russia 1812

from The Expiation

Make the Connection

On a map or globe, find the distance from Moscow to Paris. Then in an encyclopedia, a geographical dictionary, or on the Internet, find out as much as you can about the terrain and climate of the territory between Moscow and Paris. With your classmates, discuss the hardships that an army retreating along this route in wintertime might face.

Literary Focus

Imagery and Figurative Language

Imagery is descriptive writing that appeals to our senses of sight, hearing, smell, touch, or taste and helps create an emotional response ("Soldiers plod barefoot through icy mud and snow"). **Figurative language** describes one thing in terms of another, usually very different thing and is not meant to be understood on a literal level. Examples of figurative language include simile and metaphor. A **simile** compares unlike things by using a connective word such as *like* or *as* ("My feet feel like chunks of ice"). A **metaphor** compares without using those connective words ("My feet are chunks of ice"). Figurative language often compresses a great deal of meaning in few words. As you read, consider how the details in Hugo's poem compare with the details you might find in a nonfiction account of the same event. How does Hugo's use of imagery and figurative language contribute to a sense of being there?

North Carolina Competency Goal
1.03; 4.05; 5.01; 5.03

INTERNET

More About Victor Hugo
Keyword:
LE5 WL-6

SKILLS FOCUS

Literary Skills
Understand imagery and figurative language.

> **Imagery** is descriptive writing that appeals to the senses. **Figurative language** describes one thing in terms of another thing.
>
> *For more on Imagery and Figurative Language, see the Handbook of Literary and Historical Terms.*

Background

"Russia 1812," which shows the influence of both Romanticism and realism, is excerpted from Hugo's poem *The Expiation* (1852). (Expiation is the act of making amends.) The subject of the excerpt is Napoleon Bonaparte's retreat from Moscow in 1812. The French army, known also as the Grand Army, had invaded Russia and reached Moscow on September 15 of that year. Expecting to find food and shelter in the city, Napoleon and his soldiers discovered instead that the Russians had evacuated Moscow, set it on fire, and taken all its supplies with them. On October 19, after a brief occupation, Napoleon ordered the Grand Army to retreat. The retreat across the frozen plains of Russia was devastating for the French. It has been said that the Russian winter, not the Russian army, defeated Napoleon. Of the 600,000 men who left for Russia, no more than one third returned.

Napoleon's Campaign in France
(1864) by Ernest Meissonier.
Musée d'Orsay, Paris.

Russia 1812

from The Expiation

Victor Hugo
translated by **Robert Lowell**

The snow fell, and its power was multiplied.
For the first time the Eagle° bowed its head—
dark days! Slowly the Emperor returned—
behind him Moscow! Its onion domes still burned.
5 The snow rained down in blizzards—rained and froze.

2. Eagle: Napoleon's nickname; also the emblem for
Napoleon's armies.

Past each white waste a further white waste rose.
None recognized the captains or the flags.
Yesterday the Grand Army, today its dregs!
No one could tell the vanguard from the flanks.
10 The snow! The hurt men struggled from the ranks,
hid in the bellies of dead horses, in stacks
of shattered caissons.° By the bivouacs,°
one saw the picket° dying at his post,
still standing in his saddle, white with frost,
15 the stone lips frozen to the bugle's mouth!
Bullets and grapeshot° mingled with the snow,
that hailed . . . The Guard, surprised at shivering, march
in a dream now; ice rimes° the gray mustache.
The snow falls, always snow! The driving mire
20 submerges; men, trapped in that white empire,
have no more bread and march on barefoot—gaps!
They were no longer living men and troops,
but a dream drifting in a fog, a mystery,
mourners parading under the black sky.
25 The solitude, vast, terrible to the eye,
was like a mute avenger everywhere,
as snowfall, floating through the quiet air,
buried the huge army in a huge shroud.
Could anyone leave this kingdom? A crowd—
30 each man, obsessed with dying, was alone.
Men slept—and died! The beaten mob sludged on,
ditching the guns to burn their carriages.
Two foes. The North, the Czar.° The North was worse.
In hollows where the snow was piling up,
35 one saw whole regiments fallen asleep.
Attila's dawn, Cannaes of Hannibal!°
The army marching to its funeral!
Litters, wounded, the dead, deserters—swarms,
crushing the bridges down to cross a stream.
40 They went to sleep ten thousand, woke up four.
Ney,° bringing up the former army's rear,
hacked his horse loose from three disputing Cossacks . . .
All night, the *qui vive?*° The alert! Attacks;
retreats! White ghosts would wrench away our guns,
45 or we would see dim, terrible squadrons,
circles of steel, whirlpools of savages,
rush sabering through the camp like dervishes.°
And in this way, whole armies died at night.

The Emperor was there, standing—he saw.
50 This oak already trembling from the axe,
watched his glories drop from him branch by branch:

12. **caissons** (kā′sənz) *n. pl.:* wagons used for transporting ammunition. **bivouacs** (biv′waks′) *n. pl.:* makeshift encampments.
13. **picket** *n.:* soldier stationed to guard a body of troops against a surprise attack.
16. **grapeshot** *n.:* cluster of small iron balls fired from a cannon.
18. **rimes** *v.:* frosts.

33. **Czar** (zär): ruler of Russia.
36. **Attila's** (ə•til′əz) . . . **Hannibal** (han′ə•bəl): Attila, leader of the barbaric Huns, was finally defeated when he attacked Gaul in A.D. 451. Hannibal, a Carthaginian general, destroyed the Roman army at Cannae, but it was his final victory.
41. **Ney** (nā): marshal in charge of the defense of the rear in the French army's retreat from Moscow.
43. *qui vive?* (kē vēv′): a sentry's challenge; literally, "who lives?"
47. **dervishes** *n. pl.:* Muslims dedicated to a life of poverty and chastity, who practice a whirling devotional dance.

chiefs, soldiers. Each one had his turn and chance—
they died! Some lived. These still believed his star,
and kept their watch. They loved the man of war,
55 this small man with his hands behind his back,
whose shadow, moving to and fro, was black
behind the lighted tent. Still believing, they
accused their destiny of *lèse-majesté.*°
His misfortune had mounted on their back.
60 The man of glory shook. Cold stupefied
him, then suddenly he felt terrified.
Being without belief, he turned to God:
"God of armies, is this the end?" he cried.
And then at last the expiation came,
65 as he heard someone call him by his name,
someone half-lost in shadow, who said, "No,
Napoleon." Napoleon understood,
restless, bareheaded, leaden, as he stood
before his butchered legions in the snow.

58. lèse-majesté
(lez′ma′zhes·tā′) *n.:* treason;
literally, "injured majesty."

Episode from Napoleon's Retreat from Russia in 1812
(19th century) by Theodore Gericault.

Musée des Beaux-Arts, Rouen, France.

The following article describes some of the remnants that archaeologists have found from the terrible winter of 1812 when Napoleon's Grand Army retreated across Russia's frozen winter landscape, at the cost of tens of thousands of human lives.

Baltic Soil Yields Evidence of a Bitter End to Napoleon's Army

INFORMATIONAL TEXT

Michael Wines
from *The New York Times,* September 14, 2002

When construction workers excavating an old Soviet military base for roads and apartments unearthed the first of their grisly discoveries last fall, the conclusion was obvious: here lay the handiwork of Stalinist death squads that spread terror throughout Lithuania in the 1940's and 1950's.

Then they found the buttons.

Scattered like pebbles among perhaps 2,000 contorted skeletons, the buttons were embossed with numbers, the last traces of military uniforms of the regiments of an earlier tyrant. What the workers had found, it soon became clear, were remains of the Grand Army of Napoleon, reduced to frozen, starving rabble after the retreat from its disastrous siege of Moscow in 1812.

Now, crammed between construction cranes and stacks of concrete brick a few miles north of downtown Vilnius, a corps of archaeologists and anatomists is mining a mass grave of Napoleon's soldiers, reconstructing the army's final days—and taking a remarkable measure of what it was like to be a man in Europe nearly two centuries ago.

"From a scientific perspective, it's an enormous database—a cross-section of the population of young males at the beginning of the 19th century," said Rimantas Jankauskas, a physical anthropologist at Vilnius University who is helping to lead the inquiry into the site. "They all died at one moment."

The evidence indicates that Napoleon's army died of starvation, exhaustion and cold—bitter, numbing cold that left many drawn into a fetal position to conserve heat.

Anthropologists suspect that as many as 7,000 soldiers and camp-followers are interred at this one site, in a booming residential and commercial development in Vilnius's suburbs.

It is but a fraction of the army's total remains: one Russian officer reported at the time that he had tallied 36,999 dead soldiers in Vilnius. Dr. Virgilijus Pugaciauskas, of the Institute of Lithuanian History, said the true number of soldiers buried here may approach 80,000—up to a fifth of the army that Napoleon had massed against the Russian empire.

Vilnius is where the army foundered. Marching through here in June 1812 toward Moscow, Napoleon had been greeted as a hero by Lithuanians who sought to throw off Russian occupation. Vilnius became a rear-guard headquarters for an army—half French, half from other European countries—that at its peak may have numbered 500,000.

But as historians have long noted, the army was short on provisions for both men and

Mass grave containing remains of Napoleon's soldiers discovered in Vilnius, Lithuania.

horses. When it was not fighting its way to Moscow, it had to loot even friendly villages to sustain itself. When Napoleon gave up his siege of Moscow in October 1812, the army retreated through territory laid waste to deny them sustenance.

Napoleon himself left the army on the evening of Dec. 5, leaving instructions to reorganize in Vilnius. But the troops that staggered into Vilnius were in no shape to regroup: frostbitten by minus-20-degree weather, clad in silks, kerchiefs and women's clothes in a fruitless battle against the cold, they lay down and began to die.

Contemporary reports tell of 7,500 bodies stacked in one hospital alone. Other accounts depict bodies strewn so high across Vilnius's central square that passage was blocked.

"Sire, I must tell you the truth," one commander wrote Napoleon from Vilnius. "The soldiers throw away their guns because they cannot hold them; both officers and soldiers think only of protecting themselves from the terrible cold."

Napoleon's commanders fled Vilnius on Dec. 10, hours ahead of approaching Russian forces. The Russians first tried to cremate the bodies; then, overcome by the smoke and stench, they dumped them into the French defensive trenches. The cleanup lasted until March.

It is one of those V-shaped trenches that construction workers first uncovered last fall. Archaeologists are probing the second leg of the V this month. The skeletons are taken to the university's medical school for study before being sent to a military cemetery for reburial. . . .

Workers are collecting the few scraps of uniforms—in one case, a nearly complete military hat—to be analyzed for parasites. DNA analysis may help resolve whether a strain of typhus borne by lice helped decimate the troops. . . .

? Based on the details mentioned in the article, what do you think Napoleon's army experienced as they retreated from Moscow in the winter of 1812? How does this compare with the experience Hugo describes in "Russia 1812"?

Response and Analysis

Reading Check

1. What two foes of Napoleon does the speaker mention? Which foe is more powerful?

2. What do the French soldiers do to stay alive?

3. Observing the destruction of his army, how does Napoleon feel?

Thinking Critically

4. To which senses does the poem's **imagery** appeal? What overall emotional effect does the imagery create?

5. Why do you think Hugo repeats the word *snow* so many times in the opening lines? What effect does this **repetition** have?

6. Explain what the **figures of speech** "circles of steel" and "whirlpools of savages" are describing. (Recall that armies perished as a result of their actions.)

7. In lines 50–52, what **metaphor** does Hugo use in his description of the French army? Explain the comparison in your own words.

8. What is **ironic** about the sentry's question, *"qui vive?"* ("who lives?"), in line 43?

9. Explain how Hugo's choice of words in the poem reveals his attitude toward Napoleon.

10. Re-read lines 67–69. What do you think Napoleon "understood"?

11. In what sense is the fate of the French army an "expiation"? Of what crime or error have the French been guilty?

Extending and Evaluating

12. "Russia 1812" contains many disturbing, graphic images of suffering. Think of a book, magazine article, movie, or television program that contains similar images. What purpose do such graphic portrayals serve today? Do you think people have become insensitive to suffering in literature and the media? Could most people still be affected by the imagery in Hugo's poem? Explain.

WRITING

Comparing Views of Nature

Compare and contrast Pushkin's and Hugo's views of nature, providing examples from "I Have Visited Again" (see page 772) and "Russia 1812." What roles does nature play in each poem? Do the poets view nature as benevolent or harmful? Explain.

Writing a Newspaper Account

Imagine that you are a reporter for either a French or Russian newspaper in 1812. Write a news story describing the French retreat from Moscow. Include specific details from the poem, but write them as a journalist would, not as a poet. Remember to slant your story according to your chosen nationality. Create a catchy headline, and if you like, accompany your story with an illustration or a map.

North Carolina Competency Goal
2.01; 4.01

INTERNET

Projects and Activities
Keyword:
LE5 WL-6

Literary Skills
Analyze imagery and figures of speech.

Writing Skills
Compare views of nature. Write a newspaper account.

Charles Baudelaire
(1821–1867)
France

Charles Baudelaire (1863) by Etienne Carjat.
The Granger Collection, New York.

One short book, *The Flowers of Evil*, made Charles Baudelaire (shärl bōd·ler′) the most influential poet of the nineteenth century. Baudelaire was the first "decadent"—an artist who rejected middle-class society and experienced firsthand the poverty and sordidness of Paris street life. Most of his poems are melancholy and deal with vice, poverty, drunkenness, or something that Baudelaire considered worse than all of them—boredom.

Baudelaire was born into a well-to-do family, and from the beginning he was a sensitive child. His father died when he was six, and his mother married someone the boy hated. His stepfather sent him to military school, but Baudelaire rebelled against the school's authorities. When he was eighteen, he moved to Paris, where he lived as a bohemian (an artist who lives in an unconventional way) in the Paris art community while he struggled to write.

The young Baudelaire inherited some money from his father's estate; living extravagantly, he managed to squander half the money in two years. He then fell into an intense period of dissipation, physical illness, and mental disturbance. He lived on the small allowance his mother gave him and devoted himself to art, declaring that writing was the only thing worth doing.

When Baudelaire was twenty-five, he discovered the American writer Edgar Allan Poe and became obsessed with him, identifying thoroughly with this troubled artist who appeared to be his spiritual and emotional twin. Twenty years of Baudelaire's life were devoted to translating Poe's works and championing his genius; he made Poe famous in France and Europe decades before Poe was appreciated in America. Thanks to Baudelaire, the symbolist poets, including Paul Verlaine and Stéphane Mallarmé, became fascinated by Poe and considered him their literary master.

In addition to translating Poe, Baudelaire wrote art criticism, but it was his own poetry that brought out the fullness of his perfectionism. Baudelaire struggled for many years writing and rewriting the poems in his only published work, *The Flowers of Evil*. The title of this collection reflects the nature of its poems, whose morbid, melancholy, and occasionally horrifying images are expressed with delicate skill and exquisite phrases. When the book was published in 1857, Baudelaire was fined for offending public morals, and six poems had to be cut out with scissors before the already printed edition could be offered for sale. This censorship may have contributed to the long downslide that marked Baudelaire's last ten years. During that time he wrote some important prose poems and some fragments but no poetic masterpieces to match his earlier success. At the age of forty-six, insane and paralyzed, he died in his mother's arms.

Invitation to the Voyage

Make the Connection

Quickwrite

What is your imaginary land of bliss—of ultimate happiness? In a few sentences, describe what it looks like, what you would do there, and who would accompany you on your voyage to that land.

Literary Focus

Refrain and Mood

A word, phrase, line, or group of lines that is repeated in a poem is called a **refrain.** Most often used in songs or in poems that have a songlike quality, refrains can help to unify the work, build rhythm, and add emphasis. Refrains can also help a writer create a **mood,** or specific emotional effect, such as happiness, despair, or fear. As you read "Invitation to the Voyage," consider what the refrain adds to the mood of the poem.

> **Refrain** is a repeated word, phrase, line, or group of lines.
> **Mood** is the overall emotion created by a literary work.
>
> *For more on Refrain and Mood, see the Handbook of Literary and Historical Terms.*

Background

Like the Romantic poets, Baudelaire wrote subjectively, casting the light of his own moods over his entire world. But he saw himself as an anti-Romantic, for he prized precise language and form and considered most Romantic poetry vague and formless. He found inspiration in alleys, sidewalks, and gutters rather than in hills, brooks, and rainbows. In French literature, Baudelaire's poetry is a bridge between the works of the Romantics and those of the symbolists, poets who used symbols to suggest rather than directly state meaning or mood.

"Invitation to the Voyage" is a rarity among Baudelaire's poems—its tone is mostly light and happy. Much of the poem was inspired by an interrupted sea voyage he took to India and his brief stay on a tropical island to overcome seasickness. But the final stanza describes Holland as Baudelaire imagined it to be from looking at Dutch landscape paintings. The speaker of the poem invites a woman to accompany him to this imaginary land of bliss. The real-life model for the woman was Marie Daubrun, an actress with whom Baudelaire was infatuated.

The two lines repeated at the end of each stanza—the **refrain**—have been quoted often. The great modern painter Henri Matisse used the second repeated line as the title for a major painting: In French, it is *Luxe, Calme, et Volupté.*

North Carolina Competency Goal
1.02; 1.03; 4.05; 5.01; 5.03; 6.01

INTERNET
More About Charles Baudelaire
Keyword: LE5 WL-6

SKILLS FOCUS

Literary Skills
Understand refrain and mood.

Sail Boats by Georges Pierre Seurat (1859–1891).

The Barnes Foundation, Merion, Pennsylvania.

Invitation to the Voyage

Charles Baudelaire
translated by **Richard Wilbur**

> My child, my sister,
> > dream
> How sweet all things would seem
> Were we in that kind land to live together,
> And there love slow and long,
> 5 There love and die among
> Those scenes that image you, that sumptuous weather.
> Drowned suns that glimmer there
> Through cloud-disheveled air
> Move me with such a mystery as appears
> 10 Within those other skies

Marine, Mer du Nord (1888) by Henri Le Sidaner.
Sotheby's, London.

Of your treacherous eyes
When I behold them shining through their tears.

There, there is nothing else but grace and measure,
Richness, quietness, and pleasure.

15   Furniture that wears
        The luster of the years
Softly would glow within our glowing chamber,
        Flowers of rarest bloom
        Proffering their perfume
20   Mixed with the vague fragrances of amber;
        Gold ceilings would there be,
        Mirrors deep as the sea,
The walls all in an Eastern splendor hung—
        Nothing but should address
25   The soul's loneliness,
Speaking her sweet and secret native tongue.

There, there is nothing else but grace and measure,
Richness, quietness, and pleasure.

        See, sheltered from the swells
30   There in the still canals
Those drowsy ships that dream of sailing forth;
        It is to satisfy
        Your least desire, they ply
Hither through all the waters of the earth.
35   The sun at close of day
        Clothes the fields of hay,
Then the canals, at last the town entire
        In hyacinth and gold;
        Slowly the land is rolled
40   Sleepward under a sea of gentle fire.

There, there is nothing else but grace and measure,
Richness, quietness, and pleasure.

Response and Analysis

Thinking Critically

1. In line 1, the speaker addresses his lover as "My child, my sister." How does this sentiment contrast with that of "treacherous eyes" in line 11?

2. Identify at least two lines or phrases in the poem that hint that the speaker's real life is not happy.

3. What does the first stanza reveal about Baudelaire's concept of love?

4. Lines 13–14 are repeated as a **refrain.** List as many other examples of repetition as you can find in the poem, including repetition of words, sounds, and images. How do these repetitions affect the **mood,** or atmosphere, of the poem?

5. The three stanzas of the poem support the idea presented in the **refrain.** The first stanza represents "pleasure," the second "richness," the third "quietness." How does the **imagery** of each stanza contribute to this interpretation?

WRITING

Describing an Imaginary Land

Using your Quickwrite notes as a starting point, describe your imaginary land of bliss. Use images that appeal to the senses of sight, hearing, touch, taste, or smell. Feel free to write your description in either poetry or prose. If you write a poem, try using a refrain.

Comparing Translations

In reading "Invitation to the Voyage," you are not just reading Baudelaire. You are also reading a translation from nineteenth-century French into contemporary English. You have just read a translation by Richard Wilbur (born 1921), one of the leading poets in the United States. The following excerpt is a translation by Francis Duke of the first stanza and the refrain of Baudelaire's poem.

from Invitation to Travel
Charles Baudelaire
translated by Francis Duke

My sister, my child,
How life would have smiled
At us two, together, down there,
In love at each breath,
5 In love until death,
In that land whose nature you share!
Whose sun, in their shrouds
Of scudding wet clouds
Arouse in my heart the same cheer,
10 The same charmed surprise,
As your fickle eyes
When sparkles dart forth through a
    tear!

There, beauty and harmony dwell
Where springs of voluptuousness
    well.

In a two- or three-paragraph essay, compare Duke's and Wilbur's translations. Consider the meaning and mood of each version; the diction, or word choice; the use of rhythm, rhyme, and other sound effects; and the naturalness of the language. Which title and version of the poem do you prefer? Why?

North Carolina Competency Goal
1.02; 1.03; 4.05; 5.03; 6.01

INTERNET

Projects and Activities

Keyword: LE5 WL-6

Literary Skills
Analyze refrain and mood.

Writing Skills
Describe an imaginary land. Compare translations.

Paul Verlaine
(1844–1896)

Arthur Rimbaud
(1854–1891)
France

Verlaine and Rimbaud, from *Le Coin de Table*
(detail) (1872) by Fantin-Latour.
The Granger Collection, New York.

The lives of Paul Verlaine (pôl ver·len′) and Arthur Rimbaud (àr·tür′ ram·bō′) were closely linked. These two symbolist poets shared a turbulent relationship, rebelled against conventional society, sought out experiences of squalor and degradation, died relatively young, and became legendary for their poetry.

Verlaine was one of France's leading poets during the second half of the nineteenth century, though he began his career as an insurance clerk. He hoped that his marriage to sixteen-year-old Mathilde would provide an anchor and help cure him of alcoholism. He wrote a number of moving poems to her, but soon he discovered Rimbaud and came under his influence. Verlaine abandoned Mathilde and went on a yearlong spree that ended when he shot and wounded Rimbaud in a quarrel. Verlaine was sent to prison; when he was released, he found that he had lost both his wife and his relationship with Rimbaud forever. From this point on, his life went downhill. He published *Romances sans paroles* in 1874 to almost no critical notice; however, it is now considered the first major symbolist work.

Like Verlaine, Rimbaud was a self-destructive genius. His father abandoned the family when Rimbaud was six, and he was raised in poverty by a strict mother. At fourteen, Rimbaud, experimenting with syntax and unusual imagery, was already writing first-rate poetry. In 1871, he sent some poems to Verlaine, who had already achieved some recognition for his anti-Romantic poetry. Rimbaud asked the older poet for his financial help and patronage, and Verlaine responded enthusiastically. Before long, Rimbaud was dominating Verlaine psychologically.

Rimbaud adopted an aesthetic doctrine that asserted the poet is a seer and a sufferer who must develop his art through self-induced delirium. After his relationship with Verlaine ended, he gave up poetry and began a career of full-time wandering, during which he served with and later deserted the Dutch army and worked as a gunrunner in Africa. Ironically, while living in a palm leaf hut in Africa, Rimbaud became a celebrity in Paris: Verlaine, who thought his former friend was dead, had published Rimbaud's earlier work, *Illuminations* (1886), with great success, though Rimbaud seemed unaware of it.

After a decade of wandering and suffering, Rimbaud returned to France, where he died of cancer. In a final letter to his sister, he laments, "Yes, our life is a misery, an endless misery! Why do we exist?"

Before You Read

The Sky Is Just Beyond the Roof
The Sleeper of the Valley

Make the Connection

Quickwrite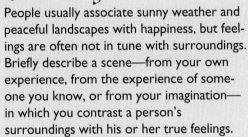

People usually associate sunny weather and peaceful landscapes with happiness, but feelings are often not in tune with surroundings. Briefly describe a scene—from your own experience, from the experience of someone you know, or from your imagination—in which you contrast a person's surroundings with his or her true feelings.

Literary Focus

Symbolist Poetry

Symbolist poetry began in France as a reaction to Romantic poetry. To symbolist poets, Romantic poetry was full of overly rich language, often stereotypical imagery, and empty wordiness. The symbolists, who believed that emotions were extremely difficult to express accurately, avoided making direct statements in poetry and instead tried to *suggest* meaning through the use of personal, precise, evocative images. The name of their literary movement came from their use of **symbols.** (A symbol is an object, place, event, or even person or animal that stands both for itself and for something beyond itself.) The symbolists also skillfully manipulated the sound of language to great poetic effect. In some ways, symbolism is akin to music in its ability to create mood.

Symbolist poetry emphasizes the use of highly personal symbols to suggest ideas, emotions, and moods.

For more on Symbolism, see the Handbook of Literary and Historical Terms.

Background

Both Verlaine and Rimbaud were symbolists who mastered the use of sensory imagery. Their visual images are compact and suggestive, like those of a painter who creates a broad landscape in a few brushstrokes. In addition, both poets have the knack of appealing to more than one sense with a single image or figure of speech.

"The Sky Is Just Beyond the Roof" is one of the poems Verlaine wrote while he was in prison for shooting Rimbaud. As you read the poem, imagine that the speaker is looking out the barred window of his cell, over the roof of the prison, at a clear blue sky that represents freedom. In the poem, Verlaine explores the theme of remorse for misspent youth.

"The Sleeper of the Valley" is one of Rimbaud's more accessible and straightforward poems. It describes a landscape with one human figure and ends with a surprising twist. The poem reflects Rimbaud's attitude toward military service.

North Carolina Competency Goal
1.03; 4.02; 4.05; 5.01; 5.03; 6.01

INTERNET

More About Paul Verlaine and Arthur Rimbaud

Keyword: LE5 WL-6

Literary Skills
Understand symbolism.

The Sky Is Just Beyond the Roof

Paul Verlaine
translated by **Bergen Applegate**

The sky is just beyond the roof
   So blue, so calm;
A treetop just beyond the roof
   Rocks its slow palm.

5   The chime in the sky that I see
   Distantly rings:
A bird on the tree that I see
   Plaintively° sings.

My God, my God, but life is there,
10   Tranquil and sweet;
This peaceful murmur that I hear
   Comes from the street!

What have you done, you who stand here,
   In tears and ruth?°
15   Say, what have you done, you who are here,
   With your lost youth?

8. plaintively *adv.:* mournfully.

14. ruth *n.:* remorse; sorrow.

Study of Sky and Trees (detail) by John Constable (1776–1837).
Victoria & Albert Museum, London.

792

Waterlilies in a Pond by Isaac Ilyitah Leviatan (1860–1900).

The Sleeper of the Valley

Arthur Rimbaud
translated by **Ludwig Lewisohn**

There's a green hollow where a river sings
Silvering the torn grass in its glittering flight,
And where the sun from the proud mountain flings
Fire—and the little valley brims with light.

5   A soldier young, with open mouth, bare head,
Sleeps with his neck in dewy watercress,°
Under the sky and on the grass his bed,
Pale in the deep green and the light's excess.

He sleeps amid the iris and his smile
10 Is like a sick child's slumbering for a while.
Nature, in thy warm lap his chilled limbs hide!

The perfume does not thrill him from his rest.
He sleeps in sunshine, hand upon his breast,
Tranquil—with two red holes in his right side.

6. watercress *n.:* white-flowered plant that generally grows in running water.

Response and Analysis

Thinking Critically

1. What emotion does line 9 in "The Sky Is Just Beyond the Roof" express?

2. The first three stanzas of "The Sky Is Just Beyond the Roof" are narrated from the **first-person point of view.** In your opinion, who is the "you" in the fourth stanza? Why is this person in tears?

3. Identify **images** that appeal to more than one sense in "The Sleeper of the Valley." What is the effect of this imagery?

4. **Irony** occurs when there is a discrepancy between appearance and reality. Explain how irony is created by the language and imagery in "The Sleeper of the Valley."

5. How do both poems use **imagery** to suggest the loss of youth?

6. What features of **symbolist poetry** do you see in these poems? How do the poems differ from the earlier Romantic poetry you have read, such as Pushkin's "I Have Visited Again" (see page 772)?

Extending and Evaluating

7. The beautiful imagery of both poems and the irony of "The Sleeper of the Valley" serve to enhance the impact of each situation that the poet is describing. How do the moods created by this imagery contrast with the settings of the poems? How does this contrast compare with the one you wrote about in your Quickwrite?

Literary Criticism

8. The Rimbaud biographer Enid Starkie says that in "The Sleeper of the Valley," "we find that quality of compassion which is a feature of Rimbaud's personality and work." What evidence of compassion do you find in the poem, if any? Explain your answer.

WRITING

Analyzing Diction

In "The Sky Is Just Beyond the Roof," Verlaine uses words such as *sky, roof, bird,* and *street.* In "The Sleeper of the Valley," Rimbaud uses words and phrases such as *silvering, dewy watercress, iris,* and *chilled limbs.* Write a brief essay comparing and contrasting the **diction,** or word choice, of Verlaine and Rimbaud. Which poet uses simpler, plainer words? Which poet uses more adjectives and adverbs? For each poem, analyze how the poet's diction affects the way we see the objects in the poem and the way we feel about them. Then, state why you think each poet might have chosen the kinds of descriptive words he did. Assume that the translations accurately reflect the differences in diction in the original French. You might want to use a chart like the one below to organize your ideas.

	"The Sky Is Just Beyond the Roof"	"The Sleeper of the Valley"
Use of simple, direct language (nouns and verbs)		
Adjectives and adverbs		
Effect of diction		

North Carolina Competency Goal
1.02; 1.03; 4.02; 4.05; 5.01; 5.03; 6.01

INTERNET

Projects and Activities

Keyword: LE5 WL-6

Literary Skills
Analyze symbolism.

Writing Skills
Analyze diction.

Guy de Maupassant
(1850–1893)
France

Guy de Maupassant (19th century).
The Granger Collection, New York.

Toward the end of his life, Guy de Maupassant (gē də mō·pä·sän′) captured the essence of his literary fame by saying, "It was I who brought back the short story and novelette into great vogue in France." Even more remarkable was that in a mere eleven years he had published six novels and nearly three hundred short stories.

Maupassant was born in rural Normandy, in northwestern France. His father was an amateur painter, one of the idle rich living off a paternal allowance, and his mother was a strong-willed woman who read Shakespeare in English, smoked, rode horses, and further startled the locals by wearing skirts that exposed her ankles. She instilled in Maupassant a love of storytelling and was a close friend of the famous French realist Gustave Flaubert (flō·ber′) (1821–1880), who would become Maupassant's mentor.

Tutored by his mother and a parish priest until he was about thirteen, Maupassant then entered a seminary where he studied the classics and remembered that "the boys were made to wash their feet but three times a year, the night before each vacation." In 1869, he began law studies in Paris, then quit to serve in the French army during the Franco-Prussian war. After the war, he became a government clerk and began weekly Sunday visits to Flaubert, who would criticize his writing and encourage him to "become original." Maupassant said, "He made me describe, in a few sentences, a being or an object in such a way as to particularize it clearly, to distinguish it from all the other beings or all the other objects of the same race or kind."

"Boule de Suif" ("Ball of Fat"), Maupassant's first published story written under his own name, was declared by Flaubert to be "a masterpiece." It made Maupassant an overnight sensation. Soon afterward, he quit his clerical job and began writing short stories and articles for newspapers. His stories are known for their clarity, telling detail, and occasional plot twists or surprise endings. They also reveal his knowledge of rural life in Normandy and both the fashionable and seedy side of life in Paris.

By 1891, Maupassant had begun to succumb to a physical and mental breakdown common in the final stages of syphilis. He died in a Paris asylum shortly before his forty-third birthday.

For Independent Reading

You may enjoy reading these popular stories by Maupassant:

- "The Necklace"
- "The Jewels"
- "Two Friends"

The Piece of String

Make the Connection

Have you ever been falsely accused of something? How did you react? Discuss with your classmates how someone who has been falsely accused of committing a crime might go about proving his or her innocence.

Literary Focus

Conflict

Conflict is a struggle or clash between opposing characters, forces, or emotions. In an **external conflict,** a character struggles against some outside force, such as another character, society, or an element of nature. An **internal conflict** is a struggle between opposing desires or needs within a character's own mind. In "The Piece of String," Maupassant dramatizes both types of conflict.

North Carolina Competency Goal
1.03; 4.05; 5.01; 5.03

> **Conflict** is a struggle or clash between opposing characters, forces, or emotions.
>
> *For more on Conflict, see the Handbook of Literary and Historical Terms.*

go.hrw.com

INTERNET

Vocabulary Practice
•
More About Guy de Maupassant

Keyword: LE5 WL-6

SKILLS FOCUS

Literary Skills
Understand external and internal conflict.

Reading Skills
Understand cause and effect.

Reading Skills

Understanding Cause and Effect

A **cause** makes something happen. An **effect** is what happens. In a story, ideas and events are often connected in a cause-and-effect relationship. As you read "The Piece of String," notice how a seemingly insignificant event can cause unexpected and disastrous effects.

Background

Maupassant wrote many of his works for newspapers that restricted story length to a few columns. This allowed him to develop an extremely concise style using a few details just precise enough to individualize characters and settings. His subject matter was influenced by French realists and naturalists who rebelled against Romantic sentimentality and the false beautification of rural life. (The naturalists went a step further in their objective descriptions of social conditions, often showing characters as helpless victims of fate, heredity, or environment.) The critic and translator Roger Colet notes, "The realities which Maupassant lays bare in his stories, with a zeal born perhaps of an anxious determination not to be deceived himself, are rarely pleasant."

Vocabulary Development

perpetually (pər·pech′o͞o·əl·ē) *adv.*: constantly.

penchant (pen′chənt) *n.*: fondness for.

pompous (päm′pəs) *adj.*: self-important.

indignation (in′dig·nā′shən) *n.*: anger resulting from injustice.

incredulity (in′krə·do͞o′lə·tē) *n.*: disbelief; doubt.

Peasants, Pigs, and a Village Under a Clear Sky (1888) by Paul Gauguin.
Coll. Lucille Ellis Simon, Los Angeles, California.

The Piece of String

Guy de Maupassant
translated by **Roger Colet**

On all the roads around Goderville the peasants and their wives were making their way toward the little town, for it was market day. The men were plodding along, their bodies leaning forward with every movement of their long bandy legs—legs deformed by hard work, by the pressure of the plow which also raises the left shoulder and twists the spine, by the spreading of the knees required to obtain a firm stance for reaping, and by all the slow, laborious tasks of country life. Their blue starched smocks, shining as if they were varnished, and decorated with a little pattern in white embroidery on the collar and cuffs, bellied out around their bony frames like balloons ready to fly away, with a head, two arms and two feet sticking out of each one.

Some were leading a cow or a calf by a rope, while their wives hurried the animal on by whipping its haunches with a leafy branch. The women carried large baskets on their arms from which protruded the heads of chickens or ducks. And they walked with a shorter, brisker step than their husbands, their gaunt, erect figures wrapped in skimpy little shawls pinned across their flat chests and their heads wrapped in tight-fitting white coifs topped with bonnets.

Then a cart went by, drawn at a trot by a small horse, with two men sitting side by side bumping up and down and a woman at the back holding on to the sides to lessen the jolts.

The square in Goderville was crowded with a confused mass of animals and human beings. The horns of the bullocks, the tall beaver hats of the well-to-do peasants, and the coifs of the peasant women stood out above the throng. And the high-pitched, shrill, yapping voices made a wild, continuous din, dominated now and then by a great deep-throated roar of laughter from a jovial countryman or the long lowing of a cow tied to the wall of a house.

Everywhere was the smell of cowsheds and milk and manure, of hay and sweat, that sharp, unpleasant odor of men and animals which is peculiar to people who work on the land.

Maître[1] Hauchecorne of Bréauté[2] had just arrived in Goderville and was making his way toward the market square when he caught sight of a small piece of string on the ground. Maître Hauchecorne, a thrifty man like all true Normans, reflected that anything which might come in useful was worth picking up, so he bent down—though with some difficulty, for he suffered from rheumatism. He picked up the piece of thin cord and was about to roll it up carefully when he noticed Maître Malandain,[3] the saddler, standing at his door watching him. They had had a quarrel some time before over a halter and they had remained on bad terms ever since, both of

them being the sort to nurse a grudge. Maître Hauchecorne felt a little shamefaced at being seen by his enemy like this, picking a bit of string up out of the muck. He hurriedly concealed his find, first under his smock, then in his trouser pocket; then he pretended to go on looking for something on the ground which he couldn't find, before continuing on his way to the square, leaning forward, bent double by his rheumatism.

He was promptly lost in the noisy slow-moving crowd, in which everyone was engaged in endless and excited bargaining. The peasants were prodding the cows, walking away and coming back in an agony of indecision, always afraid of being taken in and never daring to make up their minds, watching the vendor's eyes, and perpetually trying to spot the man's trick and the animal's defect.

After putting their big baskets down at their feet, the women had taken out their fowls, which now lay on the ground, tied by their legs, their eyes terrified and their combs scarlet. They listened to the offers they were made and either stuck to their price, hard-faced and impassive, or else, suddenly deciding to accept the lower figure offered, shouted after the customer who was slowly walking away: "All right, Maître Anthime,[4] it's yours."

Then, little by little, the crowd in the square thinned out, and as the Angelus[5] rang for noon, those who lived too far away to go home disappeared into the various inns.

At Jourdain's[6] the main room was crowded with people eating, while the vast courtyard was full of vehicles of all sorts—carts, gigs, wagons, tilburies, and indescribable shandrydans,[7] yellow with dung, broken down and patched

---

4. **Anthime** (än·tēm′).
5. **Angelus** (an′jə·ləs): church bell that rings three times a day, calling people to say a prayer beginning "The angel of the Lord . . ."
6. **Jourdain's** (zhôr·dänz′).
7. **tilburies . . . shandrydans:** two-wheeled carriages and rickety vehicles.

Vocabulary

perpetually (pər·pech′oo·əl·ē) *adv*.: constantly.

---

1. **Maître** (me′tr′): French word meaning something like "mister" (literally, "master").
2. **Hauchecorne** (ōsh′kôrn) . . . **Bréauté** (brā′ō·tā′).
3. **Malandain** (má′lăn·dăn′).

together, raising their shafts to heaven like a pair of arms, or else heads down and bottoms up.

Close to the people sitting at table, the bright fire blazing in the huge fireplace was scorching the backs of the row on the right. Three spits were turning, carrying chickens, pigeons, and legs of mutton; and a delicious smell of meat roasting and gravy trickling over browning flesh rose from the hearth, raising people's spirits and making their mouths water.

All the aristocracy of the plow took its meals at Maître Jourdain's. Innkeeper and horse dealer, he was a cunning rascal who had made his pile.

Dishes were brought in and emptied, as were the jugs of yellow cider. Everybody talked about the business he had done, what he had bought and sold. News and views were exchanged about the crops. The weather was good for the greens but rather damp for the wheat.

All of a sudden the roll of a drum sounded in the courtyard in front of the inn. Except for one or two who showed no interest, everybody jumped up and ran to the door or windows with his mouth still full and his napkin in his hand.

After finishing his roll on the drum, the town crier made the following pronouncement, speaking in a jerky manner and pausing in the wrong places: "Let it be known to the inhabitants of Goderville, and in general to all—persons present at the market that there was lost this morning, on the Beuzeville[8] road, between—nine and ten o'clock, a black leather wallet containing five hundred francs and some business documents. Anybody finding the same is asked to bring it immediately—to the town hall or to return it to Maître Fortuné Houlbrèque[9] of Manneville. There will be a reward of twenty francs."

Then the man went away. The dull roll of the drum and the faint voice of the town crier could be heard once again in the distance.

Everybody began talking about the incident, estimating Maître Houlbrèque's chances of recovering or not recovering his wallet.

The meal came to an end.

They were finishing their coffee when the

Portrait of an Old Man with a Stick (1889–1890) by Paul Gauguin.
Musée de la Ville de Paris, Musée du Petit-Palais, Paris.

police sergeant appeared at the door and asked: "Is Maître Hauchecorne of Bréauté here?"

Maître Hauchecorne, who was sitting at the far end of the table, replied: "Yes, here I am."

The sergeant went on: "Maître Hauchecorne, will you be good enough to come with me to the town hall? The Mayor would like to have a word with you."

The peasant, surprised and a little worried, tossed down his glass of brandy, stood up, and even more bent than in the morning, for the first few steps after a rest were especially difficult, set off after the sergeant, repeating: "Here I am, here I am."

---

8. **Beuzeville** (bôz·vēlʹ).
9. **Fortuné Houlbrèque** (fôr·tyu·nä'ōōl·brek').

The Mayor was waiting for him, sitting in an armchair. He was the local notary, a stout, solemn individual, with a penchant for pompous phrases.

"Maître Hauchecorne," he said, "you were seen this morning, on the Beuzeville road, picking up the wallet lost by Maître Houlbrèque of Manneville."

The peasant gazed in astonishment at the Mayor, already frightened by this suspicion which had fallen upon him, without understanding why.

"Me? I picked up the wallet?"

"Yes, you."

"Honest, I don't know nothing about it."

"You were seen."

"I were seen? Who seen me?"

"Monsieur[10] Malandain, the saddler."

Then the old man remembered, understood, and flushed with anger.

"So he seen me, did he, the bastard! He seen me pick up this bit of string, Mayor—look!"

And rummaging in his pocket, he pulled out the little piece of string.

But the Mayor shook his head incredulously. "You'll never persuade me, Maître Hauchecorne, that Monsieur Malandain, who is a man who can be trusted, mistook that piece of string for a wallet."

The peasant angrily raised his hand and spat on the floor as proof of his good faith, repeating: "But it's God's truth, honest it is! Not a word of it's a lie, so help me God!"

The Mayor went on: "After picking up the object you even went on hunting about in the mud for some time to see whether some coin might not have fallen out."

The old fellow was almost speechless with fear and indignation.

"Making up . . . making up . . . lies like that to damn an honest man! Making up lies like that!"

In spite of all his protestations, the Mayor did not believe him.

He was confronted with Maître Malandain, who repeated and maintained his statement. They hurled insults at each other for an hour. Maître Hauchecorne was searched, at his own request. Nothing was found on him.

Finally the Mayor, not knowing what to think, sent him away, warning him that he was going to report the matter to the public prosecutor and ask for instructions.

The news had spread. As he left the town hall, the old man was surrounded by people who questioned him with a curiosity which was sometimes serious, sometimes ironical, but in which there was no indignation. He started telling the story of the piece of string. Nobody believed him. Everybody laughed.

As he walked along, other people stopped him, and he stopped his acquaintances, repeating his story and his protestations over and over again, and showing his pockets turned inside out to prove that he had got nothing.

Everybody said: "Get along with you, you old rascal!"

And he lost his temper, irritated, angered, and upset because nobody would believe him. Not knowing what to do, he simply went on repeating his story.

Darkness fell. It was time to go home. He set off with three of his neighbors to whom he pointed out the place where he had picked up the piece of string; and all the way home he talked of nothing else.

In the evening he took a turn round the village of Bréauté in order to tell everybody his story. He met with nothing but incredulity.

He felt ill all night as a result.

The next day, about one o' clock in the afternoon, Marius Paumelle,[11] a laborer on Maître Breton's farm at Ymauville,[12] returned the wallet and its contents to Maître Houlbrèque of Manneville.

---

10. **Monsieur** (mə•syö′): French title of respect, meaning "Mister."

11. **Marius Paumelle** (má•rē•yo͞os′ pō•mel′).
12. **Ymauville** (ē•mō•vēl′).

Vocabulary

penchant (pen′chənt) *n.:* fondness for.
pompous (päm′pəs) *adj.:* self-important.
indignation (in′dig•nā′shən) *n.:* anger resulting from injustice.
incredulity (in′krə•do͞o′lə•tē) *n.:* disbelief; doubt.

The man claimed to have found the object on the road; but, as he could not read, he had taken it home and given it to his employer.

The news spread round the neighborhood and reached the ears of Maître Hauchecorne. He immediately went out and about repeating his story, this time with its sequel. He was triumphant.

"What really got my goat," he said, "wasn't so much the thing itself, if you see what I mean, but the lies. There's nothing worse than being blamed on account of a lie."

He talked about his adventure all day; he told the story to people he met on the road, to people drinking in the inn, to people coming out of church the following Sunday. He stopped total strangers and told it to them. His mind was at rest now, and yet something still bothered him without his knowing exactly what it was. People seemed to be amused as they listened to him. They didn't appear to be convinced. He had the impression that remarks were being made behind his back.

The following Tuesday he went to the Goderville market, simply because he felt an urge to tell his story.

Malandain, standing at his door, burst out laughing when he saw him go by. Why?

He accosted a farmer from Criquetot,[13] who didn't let him finish his story, but gave him a dig in the ribs and shouted at him: "Go on, you old rogue!" Then he turned on his heels.

Maître Hauchecorne was taken aback and felt increasingly uneasy. Why had he been called an old rogue?

Once he had sat down at table in Jourdain's inn, he started explaining the whole business all over again.

A horse dealer from Montivilliers[14] called out to him: "Get along with you, you old rascal! I know your little game with the bit of string."

Hauchecorne stammered: "But they found the wallet!"

The other man retorted: "Give over, Grandpa! Him as brings a thing back isn't always him as finds it. But mum's the word!"

The peasant was speechless. At last he understood. He was being accused of getting an accomplice to return the wallet.

He tried to protest, but the whole table burst out laughing.

He couldn't finish his meal and went off in the midst of jeers and laughter.

He returned home ashamed and indignant, choking with anger and embarrassment, all the more upset in that he was quite capable, with his Norman cunning, of doing what he was accused of having done, and even of boasting of it as a clever trick. He dimly realized that, since his duplicity was widely known, it was impossible to prove his innocence. And the injustice of the suspicion cut him to the quick.

Then he began telling the story all over again, making it longer every day, adding fresh arguments at every telling, more energetic protestations, more solemn oaths, which he thought out and prepared in his hours of solitude, for he could think of nothing else but the incident of the piece of string. The more complicated his defense became, and the more subtle his arguments, the less people believed him.

"Them's a liar's arguments," people used to say behind his back.

Realizing what was happening, he ate his heart out, exhausting himself in futile efforts.

He started visibly wasting away.

The local wags[15] now used to get him to tell the story of the piece of string to amuse them, as people get an old soldier to talk about his battles. His mind, seriously affected, began to give way.

Towards the end of December he took to his bed.

He died early in January, and in the delirium of his death agony he kept on protesting his innocence, repeating over and over again: "A bit of string . . . a little bit of string . . . look, Mayor, here it is . . ."

---

13. Criquetot (krēk•tō′).
14. Montivilliers (mōn•tē′vēl•yā′).

15. wags *n. pl.*: jokers.

Response and Analysis

Reading Check

1. What does Hauchecorne find on the ground?

2. What does the saddler Malandain claim he has seen Hauchecorne do?

3. What happens to the lost wallet?

Thinking Critically

4. Explain the sequence of **cause** and **effect** in the story. What is **ironic**, or unexpected, about it?

5. Do you think Malandain really believes Hauchecorne found the wallet? If not, why does he lie?

6. Do you think the story's **external conflict** is mainly a struggle between two people or between a person and a whole society? Explain.

7. How would you describe Hauchecorne's **internal conflict**? What does his futile attempt to resolve his conflict reveal about his **character**?

8. How does the description of peasants bargaining for cattle prepare you for the skepticism that Hauchecorne encounters after the wallet is returned?

9. Did you find the story's ending believable? Why or why not?

Literary Criticism

10. The Maupassant biographer Michael Lerner says, "His work has a universal value; his characters, though belonging by their dress, habits and way of life to their age, live on by the timeless features of their behavior." Briefly evaluate Lerner's comment with regard to these questions: Could Goderville represent any town in the world? Could the events in the story and the characters' reactions happen today? Explain your answers.

WRITING

Supporting an Opinion

The power of this story appeals to our sense of justice: We feel that a man should not be punished for a crime he didn't commit. Do you think Hauchecorne helped bring about his own downfall, or is he a victim of fate and social conditions? Explain your opinion, supporting it with specific details from the story.

Analyzing a Literary Element

In a three-paragraph essay, analyze Maupassant's use of a literary element that is prominent in the story: setting, character, irony, tone, or another element that stands out for you. Express the relationship between the literary element and the story's meaning or significance in a clear thesis statement like this: "In 'The Piece of String,' Guy de Maupassant uses the setting of a small market town in rural France to explore how the pressures of a closed and judgmental society can undermine and even destroy a weak individual."

▶ See "Analyzing Literature," pages 824–829, for help with this assignment.

Vocabulary Development
What's the Difference?

On a separate sheet of paper, answer each of the following questions about the underlined Vocabulary words.

1. What's the difference between *perpetually* and *intermittently*?

2. What's the difference between *penchant* and *compulsion*?

3. What's the difference between *pompous* and *humble*?

4. What's the difference between *indignation* and *annoyance*?

5. What's the difference between *incredulity* and *credulity*?

North Carolina Competency Goal
1.03; 4.05; 5.03; 6.01

INTERNET
Projects and Activities
Keyword:
LE5 WL-6

SKILLS FOCUS

Literary Skills
Analyze external and internal conflict.

Reading Skills
Analyze cause and effect.

Writing Skills
Express an opinion. Analyze a literary element.

Vocabulary Skills
Answer questions about vocabulary words.

Leo Tolstoy
(1828–1910)
Russia

Leo Tolstoy (1909) by Alexander Viktorowitsch Morawow.

Tretyakov Gallery, Moscow.

Leo Tolstoy's father was a count and his mother a princess, but both had died before Tolstoy was ten, and he and his siblings were raised by relatives. At nineteen, he inherited his parents' estate of Yasnaya Polyana, which included more than three hundred serfs—workers who were the property of landowners. The young Tolstoy failed in an attempt to modernize farming techniques for his serfs, then proceeded to live somewhat aimlessly and incur heavy gambling debts. In 1852, Tolstoy joined the Russian army and fought in the Caucasus against Chechen tribesmen. By 1855, he was in the Crimean War commanding a gun battery at Sevastopol. These army experiences inspired him to write a number of war stories and sketches including *The Raid* (1853), *Sevastopol in May* (1855), and the incomparable short novel *Hadji Murad* (published posthumously in 1912). Years later Tolstoy noted, "I didn't become a general in the army, but I did in literature."

In 1862, Tolstoy married Sonya Bers, a resolute woman who would bear him thirteen children and manage their estate. She also recopied his nearly indecipherable manuscript for *War and Peace* (1869) seven times.

By age fifty, Tolstoy had reached a moral and spiritual crisis. His writings became fervent attacks on the government, church, and private ownership (all three of which he felt operated by threat of force). He repudiated his two greatest novels: *War and Peace*, which dramatizes Russian life during the Napoleonic wars, and *Anna Karenina* (1877), a tragic story of love, adultery, separation, and suicide. (Tolstoy even called Shakespeare's works "trivial and immoral.") Aspiring to be holy and to do good,

Tolstoy found his best models in Russia's self-sufficient Christian peasants. He tried to live the simple life he preached and also became a pacifist. (Mohandas Gandhi called himself, in a letter to Tolstoy, "a humble follower of your doctrine.") Sonya was appalled, and after bitter quarreling, she obtained Tolstoy's substantial royalties to support the family. At eighty-two, he decided to lead a poor, reclusive life and fled his home in secret, at night, with his doctor and youngest daughter. At a tiny, remote railroad station, the fugitives disembarked, and Tolstoy, ill with a high fever, was taken to the stationmaster's house. There, amid a mob scene of reporters and family who had eventually tracked him down, he died of pneumonia.

For Independent Reading

The following story by Tolstoy is one of his most popular:

- "How Much Land Does a Man Need?"

The Long Exile

Make the Connection

Quickwrite

Imagine that you have been wrongly convicted of a murder and sent to a distant prison. Years later you discover the identity of the actual murderer. Jot down a few notes on how you think you would react.

Literary Focus

Theme

North Carolina Competency Goal
1.02; 1.03; 4.02; 4.03; 4.05; 5.01; 5.03; 6.01

Theme is the central insight about life in a work of literature. A theme is not the same as the subject or topic of a work, which can usually be expressed in a word or phrase: *ambition, alienation, regret.* You should be able to state the theme of a story in a sentence or two that gives a generalization about life. Instead of stating that the theme of a story is revenge, for example, you might say, "Seeking revenge only further harms the person who has been wronged."

Most themes are **implied**—that is, a reader must determine the theme based on details given in the story. Two important clues to consider in determining theme are how the main character has changed and how the conflict has been resolved.

go.hrw.com

INTERNET

Vocabulary Practice
•
More About Leo Tolstoy
Keyword: LE5 WL-6

> **Theme** is the central insight about life in a work of literature.
>
> *For more on Theme, see the Handbook of Literary and Historical Terms.*

SKILLS FOCUS

Literary Skills
Understand theme.

Reading Skills
Draw conclusions.

Reading Skills

Drawing Conclusions

In order to determine a story's theme, you may have to draw conclusions about such things as a character's psychology and motivations or what certain details in the story are leading up to. You might have to keep monitoring and revising your conclusions as new information is presented. As you read "The Long Exile," what conclusions do you draw about Aksenof's character? Does his ultimate decision about Makar surprise you? Why or why not?

Background

The alternate title for "The Long Exile" is "God Sees the Truth, but Bides His Time." Tolstoy composed it for his *Primer,* a schoolbook for peasant children, and meant it to briefly, clearly, and dramatically illustrate particular moral conduct. Of the *Primer* he said, "I've put more work and love into it than into anything else I've done, and I know that this is the one important work of my life."

Vocabulary Development

turbulent (tur′byə·lənt) *adj.:* disorderly; unruly.

condemned (kən·demd′) *v.:* judged guilty.

submissiveness (səb·mis′iv·nis) *n.:* obedience; lack of resistance.

melancholy (mel′ən·käl′ē) *n.:* sadness.

endure (en·door′) *v.:* withstand; undergo.

The Peasants (1914) by Zinaida Serebriakova.
Russian State Museum, St. Petersburg.

The Long Exile

Leo Tolstoy

translated by

Nathan Haskell Dole

Once upon a time there lived in the city of Vladimir a young tradesman named Aksenof. He had two shops and a house.

Aksenof had a ruddy complexion and curly hair; he was a very jolly fellow and a good singer. When he was young he used to drink too much, and when he was tipsy he was <u>turbulent</u>; but after his marriage he ceased drinking, and only occasionally had a spree.

One summer Aksenof was going to Nizhni to the great Fair. As he was about to bid his family good-by, his wife said to him:—

"Ivan Dmitrievitch, do not start today; I dreamed that some misfortune befell you."

Aksenof laughed at her, and said:—

"Are you still afraid that I shall go on a spree at the Fair?"

His wife said:—

"I myself know not what I am afraid of, but I had such a bad dream; you seemed to be coming home from town, and you took off your hat, and I looked, and your head was all gray."

Aksenof laughed.

Vocabulary

turbulent (tʉr′byə·lənt) *adj.*: disorderly; unruly.

"That means good luck. See, I am going now. I will bring you some rich remembrances."

And he bade his family farewell and set off.

When he had gone half his journey, he fell in with a tradesman who was an acquaintance of his, and the two stopped at the same tavern for the night. They took tea together, and went to sleep in adjoining rooms.

Aksenof did not care to sleep long; he awoke in the middle of the night, and in order that he might get a good start while it was cool he aroused his driver and bade him harness up, went down into the smoky hut, settled his account with the landlord, and started on his way.

After he had driven forty versts,[1] he again stopped to get something to eat; he rested in the vestibule of the inn, and when it was noon, he went to the doorstep and ordered the samovar[2] got ready; then he took out his guitar and began to play.

Suddenly a troïka[3] with a bell dashed up to the inn, and from the equipage[4] leaped an official with two soldiers; he came directly up to Aksenof, and asked:—

"Who are you? Where did you come from?"

Aksenof answered without hesitation, and asked him if he would not like to have a glass of tea with him.

But the official kept on with his questions:—

"Where did you spend last night? Were you alone or with a merchant? Have you seen the merchant this morning? Why did you leave so early this morning?"

Aksenof wondered why he was questioned so closely; but he told everything just as it was, and asked:—

"Why do you put so many questions to me? I am not a thief or a murderer. I am on my own business; there is nothing to question me about."

Then the official called up the soldiers,

---

1. **versts** *n. pl.:* former Russian units used to measure length; one unit equals approximately two thirds of a mile.
2. **samovar** *n.:* urn used in Russia to boil water to make tea.
3. **troïka** *n.:* Russian carriage led by a team of three horses positioned side by side.
4. **equipage** *n.:* horse and carriage.

and said:—

"I am the police inspector, and I have made these inquiries of you because the merchant with whom you spent last night has been stabbed. Show me your things, and you men search him."

They went into the tavern, brought in the trunk and bag, and began to open and search them. Suddenly the police inspector pulled out from the bag a knife, and demanded:—

"Whose knife is this?"

Aksenof looked, and saw a knife covered with blood taken from his bag, and he was frightened.

"And whose blood is that on the knife?"

Aksenof tried to answer, but he could not articulate his words:—

"I . . . I . . . don't . . . know . . . I . . . That knife . . . it is . . . not mine. . . ."

Then the police inspector said:—

"This morning the merchant was found stabbed to death in his bed. No one except you could have done it. The tavern was locked on the inside, and there was no one in the tavern except yourself. And here is the bloody knife in your bag, and your guilt is evident in your face. Tell me how you killed him and how much money you took from him."

Aksenof swore that he had not done it, that he had not seen the merchant after he had drunk tea with him, that the only money that he had with him—eight thousand rubles—was his own, and that the knife was not his.

But his voice trembled, his face was pale, and he was all quivering with fright, like a guilty person.

The police inspector called the soldiers, and commanded them to bind Aksenof, and take him to the wagon.

When they took him to the wagon with his feet tied, Aksenof crossed himself and burst into tears.

They confiscated Aksenof's things and his money, and took him to the next city, and threw him into prison.

They sent to Vladimir to make inquiries about Aksenof's character, and all the merchants and citizens of Vladimir declared that Aksenof, when he was young, used to drink and was wild, but that now he was a worthy man. Then he was

The Last Tavern at the City Gates (1868) by Vasili Grigorevich Perov.
Tretyakov Gallery, Moscow.

brought up for judgment.

He was sentenced for having killed the merchant and for having robbed him of twenty thousand rubles.

Aksenof's wife was dumfounded by the event, and did not know what to think. Her children were still small, and there was one at the breast. She took them all with her and journeyed to the city where her husband was imprisoned.

At first they would not grant her admittance, but afterward she got permission from the nachalniks[5] and was taken to her husband.

When she saw him in his prison garb, in chains, together with murderers, she fell to the floor, and it was a long time before she recovered from her swoon. Then she placed her children around her, sat down amid them, and began to tell him about their domestic affairs, and to ask him about everything that had happened to him.

He told her the whole story.

She asked:—

"What is to be done now?"

He said:—

"We must petition the Tsar.[6] It is impossible that an innocent man should be <u>condemned</u>."

The wife said that she had already sent in a petition to the Tsar, but that the petition had not been granted. Aksenof said nothing, but was evidently very much downcast.

Then his wife said:—

"You see the dream I had, when I dreamed that you had become gray-headed, meant something, after all. Already your hair has begun to turn gray with trouble. You ought to have stayed at home that time."

And she began to tear her hair, and she said:—

"Vanya, my dearest husband, tell your wife the truth: Did you commit that crime?"

Aksenof said:—

"So you, too, have no faith in me!"

---

6. Tsar (zär) *n.:* emperor in the period before the Russian Revolution in 1917.

Vocabulary

condemned (kən·demd′) *v.:* judged guilty.

---

5. nachalniks *n. pl.:* chiefs; commanders.

And he wrung his hands and wept.

Then a soldier came and said that it was time for the wife and children to go. And Aksenof for the last time bade his family farewell.

When his wife was gone, Aksenof began to think over all that they had said. When he remembered that his wife had also distrusted him, and had asked him if he had murdered the merchant, he said to himself:—

"It is evident that no one but God can know the truth of the matter, and He is the only one to ask for mercy, and He is the only one from whom to expect it."

And from that time Aksenof ceased to send in petitions, ceased to hope, and only prayed to God. Aksenof was sentenced to be knouted,[7] and then to exile with hard labor.

And so it was done.

He was flogged with the knout, and then, when the wounds from the knout were healed, he was sent with other exiles to Siberia.

Aksenof lived twenty-six years in the mines. The hair on his head had become white as snow, and his beard had grown long, thin, and gray. All his gayety had vanished. He was bent, his gait was slow, he spoke little, he never laughed, and he spent much of his time in prayer.

Aksenof had learned while in prison to make boots, and with the money that he earned he bought the "Book of Martyrs," and used to read it when it was light enough in prison, and on holidays he would go to the prison church, read the Gospels, and sing in the choir, for his voice was still strong and good.

The authorities liked Aksenof for his submissiveness, and his prison associates respected him and called him "Grandfather" and the "man of God." Whenever they had petitions to be presented, Aksenof was always chosen to carry them to the authorities; and when quarrels arose among the prisoners, they always came to Aksenof as umpire.

Aksenof never received any letters from home, and he knew not whether his wife and children were alive.

One time some new convicts came to the prison. In the evening all the old convicts gathered around the newcomers, and began to ply them with questions as to the cities or villages from which this one or that one had come, and what their crimes were.

At this time Aksenof also was sitting on his bunk, near the strangers, and, with bowed head, was listening to what was said.

One of the new convicts was a tall, healthy-looking old man of sixty years, with a close-cropped gray beard. He was telling why he had been arrested. He said:—

"And so, brothers, I was sent here for nothing. I unharnessed a horse from a postboy's sledge, and they caught me with it, and insisted that I was stealing it. But I said, 'I only wanted to go a little faster, so I whipped up the horse. And, besides, the driver was a friend of mine. It's all right,' I said. 'No,' said they; 'you were stealing it.' But they did not know what and where I had stolen. I have done things which long ago would have sent me here, but I was not found out; and now they have sent me here without any justice in it. But what's the use of grumbling? I have been in Siberia before. They did not keep me here very long, though." . . .

"Where did you come from?" asked one of the convicts.

"Well, we came from the city of Vladimir; we are citizens of that place. My name is Makar, and my father's name was Semyon."

Aksenof raised his head and asked:—

"Tell me, Semyonuitch, have you ever heard of the Aksenofs, merchants in Vladimir city? Are they alive?"

"Indeed, I have heard of them! They are rich merchants, though their father is in Siberia. It seems he was just like any of the rest of us sinners. And now tell me, grandfather, what you were sent here for?"

Aksenof did not like to speak of his misfortunes; he sighed, and said:—

---

7. **knouted** (nout'id) *v.*: lashed with a leather whip called a knout.

Vocabulary

submissiveness (səb·mis'iv·nis) *n.*: obedience; lack of resistance.

Christ Pantocrator. Silver, gilt, and enamel Russian icon.

"Twenty-six years ago I was condemned to hard labor on account of my sins."

Makar Semyonof said:—

"But what was your crime?"

Aksenof replied, "So I must have deserved this."

But he would not give any further particulars; the other convicts, however, related why Aksenof had been sent to Siberia. They told how on the road someone had killed a merchant, and put the knife into Aksenof's luggage, and how he had been unjustly punished for this.

When Makar heard this, he glanced at Aksenof, slapped himself on the knees, and said:—

"Well, now, this is wonderful! This is really wonderful! You have been growing old, grandfather!"

They began to ask him what he thought was wonderful, and where he had seen Aksenof. But Makar did not answer; he only repeated:—

"A miracle, boys! how wonderful that we should meet again here!"

And when he said these words, it came over Aksenof that perhaps this man might know who had killed the merchant. And he said:—

"Did you ever hear of that crime, Semyonuitch, or did you ever see me before?"

"Of course I heard of it! The country was full of it. But it happened a long time ago. And I have forgotten what I heard," said Makar.

"Perhaps you heard who killed the merchant?" asked Aksenof.

Makar laughed, and said:—

"Why, of course the man who had the knife in his bag killed him. It would have been impossible

A House for Uncle (1880) by Koniev.

Photographed at the exhibition in Karl-Marx-Stadt (Chemnitz), State Art Collection.

for any one to put the knife in your things and not have been caught doing it. For how could the knife have been put into your bag? Was it not standing close by your head? And you would have heard it, wouldn't you?"

As soon as Aksenof heard these words he felt convinced that this was the very man who had killed the tradesman. He stood up and walked away. All that night he was unable to sleep. Deep <u>melancholy</u> came upon him, and he began to call back the past in his imagination.

He imagined his wife as she had been when for the last time she had accompanied him to the Fair. She seemed to stand before him exactly as if she were alive, and he saw her face and her eyes, and he seemed to hear her words and her laugh.

Then his imagination brought up his children before him; one a boy in a little fur coat, and the other at his mother's breast.

And he imagined himself as he was at that time, young and happy. He remembered how he had sat on the steps of the tavern when they arrested him, and how he had played on his guitar, and how his soul was full of joy at that time.

And he remembered the place of execution where they had flogged him, and the executioner, and the people standing around, and the chains and the convicts, and all his twenty-six years of prison life, and he remembered his old age.

And such melancholy came upon Aksenof that he was tempted to put an end to himself.

"And all on account of this criminal!" said Aksenof to himself.

And then he began to feel such anger against Makar Semyonof that he almost lost himself, and was crazy with desire to pay off the load of vengeance. He repeated prayers all night, but could not recover his calm. When day came, he walked by Makar and did not look at him.

Thus passed two weeks. At night Aksenof was not able to sleep, and such melancholy had come over him that he did not know what to do.

One time during the night, as he happened to be passing through the prison, he saw that the soil was disturbed under one of the bunks. He stopped to examine it. Suddenly Makar crept from under the bunk, and looked at Aksenof with a startled face.

Aksenof was about to pass on so as not to see him, but Makar seized his arm, and told him how he had been digging a passage under the wall, and how every day he carried the dirt out in his boot-legs and emptied it in the street when they went out to work. He said:—

"If you only keep quiet, old man, I will get you out too. But if you tell on me, they will flog me; but afterward I will make it hot for you. I will kill you."

When Aksenof saw the man who had injured him, he trembled all over with rage, twitched away his arm, and said:—

"I have no reason to make my escape, and to kill me would do no harm; you killed me long

Vocabulary

melancholy (mel′ən·käl′ē) *n.:* sadness.

ago. But as to telling on you or not, I shall do as God sees fit to have me."

On the next day, when they took the convicts out to work, the soldiers discovered where Makar Semyonof had been digging in the ground; they began to make a search, and found the hole. The chief came into the prison and asked everyone, "Who was digging that hole?"

All denied it. Those who knew did not name Makar, because they were aware that he would be flogged half to death for such an attempt.

Then the chief came to Aksenof. He knew that Aksenof was a truthful man, and he said:—

"Old man, you are truthful; tell me before God who did this."

Makar Semyonof was standing near, in great excitement, and he looked at the nachalnik, but he dared not look at Aksenof.

Aksenof's hands and lips trembled, and it was some time before he could speak a word. He said to himself:—

"If I shield him . . . but why should I forgive him when he has been my ruin? Let him pay for my sufferings! But shall I tell on him? They will surely flog him. But what difference does it make what I think of him? Will it be any the easier for me?"

Once more the chief demanded:—

"Well, old man, tell the truth! Who dug the hole?"

Aksenof glanced at Makar Semyonof, and then said:—

"I cannot tell, your honor. God does not bid me tell. I will not tell. Do with me as you please; I am in your power."

In spite of all the chief's efforts, Aksenof would say nothing more. And so they failed to find out who dug the hole.

On the next night, as Aksenof was lying on his bunk, and was almost asleep, he heard someone come along and sit down at his feet.

He peered through the darkness and saw that it was Makar. Aksenof asked:—

"What do you wish of me? What are you doing here?"

Makar Semyonof remained silent. Aksenof arose, and said:—

"What do you want? Go away, or else I will call the guard."

Makar Semyonof bent close to Aksenof, and said in a whisper:—

"Ivan Dmitrievitch, forgive me!"

Aksenof said:—

"What have I to forgive you?"

"I killed the merchant and put the knife in your bag. And I was going to kill you too, but there was a noise in the yard; I thrust the knife in your bag, and slipped out of the window."

Aksenof said nothing, and he did not know what to say. Makar got down from the bunk, knelt on the ground, and said:—

"Ivan Dmitrievitch, forgive me, forgive me for God's sake. I will confess that I killed the merchant—they will pardon you. You will be able to go home."

Aksenof said:—

"It is easy for you to say that, but how could I endure it? Where should I go now? . . . My wife is dead! my children have forgotten me. . . . I have nowhere to go." . . .

Makar did not rise; he beat his head on the ground, and said:—

"Ivan Dmitritch, forgive me! When they flogged me with the knout, it was easier to bear than it is now to look at you. . . . And you had pity on me after all this . . . you did not tell on me. . . . Forgive me for Christ's sake! Forgive me, though I am a cursed villain!"

And the man began to sob.

When Aksenof heard Makar Semyonof sobbing, he himself burst into tears, and said:—

"God will forgive you; maybe I am a hundred times worse than you are!"

And suddenly he felt a wonderful peace in his soul. And he ceased to mourn for his home, and had no desire to leave the prison, but only thought of his last hour.

Makar Semyonof would not listen to Aksenof, and confessed his crime.

When the orders came to let Aksenof go home, he was dead.

Vocabulary

endure (en·door′) v.: withstand; undergo.

Response and Analysis

Reading Check

1. What is Aksenof convicted of?
2. Who really killed the merchant?

Thinking Critically

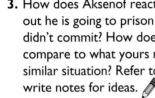

North Carolina Competency Goal
1.02; 1.03;
4.02; 4.05;
5.01; 5.03;
6.01

3. How does Aksenof react when he finds out he is going to prison for a crime he didn't commit? How does his reaction compare to what yours might be in a similar situation? Refer to your Quick-write notes for ideas.

4. After his wife's visit, what are Aksenof's thoughts and feelings about his situation? What conclusions can you draw about his **character** at this point?

5. Why do you think that Aksenof never receives any letters from his family?

INTERNET
Projects and Activities
Keyword:
LE5 WL-6

6. What is **ironic,** or unexpected, about the attitudes that the authorities and inmates come to have toward Aksenof?

7. How is Makar's statement "I was sent here for nothing" an example of ironic **foreshadowing,** or a hint as to what will happen?

8. How does Aksenof infer the identity of the real murderer?

9. What does Makar reveal about his **character** when he visits Aksenof?

10. How would you state the **theme** of the story? What conclusions did you draw while reading the story that led you to understand the theme?

Literary Skills
Analyze theme.

Reading Skills
Draw conclusions.

Writing Skills
Compare two stories.

Vocabulary Skills
Write sentences about the story using vocabulary words.

WRITING

Comparing Stories

Both "The Long Exile" and "The Piece of String" (page 796) address injustice. Write an essay comparing the two stories. In your comparison, point out similarities and differences in mood, plot, setting, cause and effect, characterization, conflict, resolution, and theme. Use a chart like the one below to organize your thoughts.

	"The Long Exile"	"The Piece of String"
Mood		
Plot		
Setting		
Cause and Effect		
Characterization		
Conflict		
Resolution		
Theme		

Vocabulary Development
Sentence Sense

turbulent   melancholy

condemned   endure

submissiveness

On a separate sheet of paper, use each Vocabulary word listed above in an original sentence based on the characters and events in "The Long Exile."

Anton Chekhov

(1860–1904)

Russia

Anton Chekhov (c. late 19th–early 20th century).

To say that Anton Chekhov was a prolific writer is an understatement: He published more than a thousand stories, as well as five major plays. Born in the small seaport of Taganrog in southern Russia, he was the grandson of a serf (who amassed enough money to buy his family's freedom) and the son of an unsuccessful shopkeeper. A natural mimic, Chekhov honed his impersonation skills for his classmates, and by age thirteen he was a regular at the local theater, where he was even allowed backstage to meet the actors.

When Chekhov was sixteen, his father's business failed. The family regrouped in Moscow, where Chekhov enrolled in a five-year university course as a medical student and began publishing comic sketches for humor magazines to help support the family. His writing attracted the attention of the editor for the popular magazine *Fragments*. While writing for *Fragments*, he was forced to limit his stories to one hundred lines. Chekhov complained, but according to his biographer, Ronald Hingley, "It was now that he first began to develop the extreme economy of expression which eventually became an outstanding quality of his style."

In 1884, Chekhov received his medical degree and started his practice while also continuing to write, but his fiction now included more serious stories. By 1887, he had begun to write one-act comedies. He later dismissed these plays as unimportant "vaudevilles," but theatergoers loved them. And Chekhov realized that if his talent for serious writing ever dried up, they could be a seemingly inexhaustible source of revenue. Nevertheless, he turned to more serious treatments of human emotions for his full-length plays, which include

The Sea Gull (1896), *Uncle Vanya* (1897), *The Three Sisters* (1901), and *The Cherry Orchard* (1904). Each new play was a greater triumph than the last.

During this time Chekhov had bought a large country estate for his family and married Olga Knipper, an actress in *The Sea Gull*. He had left medicine for writing but continued to treat poor patients free of charge. He further showed his compassion by organizing famine relief, providing money to build schools, and aiding destitute writers—an ironic contrast to the many characters in his plays who are weak-willed, selfish, and fraught with inertia. At age forty-four, Chekhov died of tuberculosis at a spa in Germany, and in a final irony, his body was sent home in a rail car marked "Fresh Oysters."

For Independent Reading

Chekhov's most popular stories and plays include the following titles:

- "The Bet"
- *The Bear*
- *The Marriage Proposal*

A Problem

Make the Connection

Suppose you are a parent whose son or daughter has been arrested for shoplifting. Would you insist that he or she be prosecuted, or would you try to get the charges dropped, perhaps paying for the stolen items if possible? What, if anything, would your ideas about family honor and reputation have to do with your response?

Literary Focus

Irony

Irony is a contrast between expectations and reality. **Verbal irony** occurs when a writer or speaker says one thing but really means the opposite. **Situational irony** occurs when what actually happens in a story is the opposite of what is expected or appropriate. **Dramatic irony** occurs when the reader knows something important that a character in a story does not know. Chekhov uses irony in "A Problem" to help suggest meaning without stating it.

what the character does and says, as well as the opinions and reactions of other characters. As you read "A Problem," try to make inferences about the main character Sasha.

Background

What does the term *Chekhovian* mean? It refers to a quiet, wry understanding of the melancholy of everyday life. Chekhov's style is understated, muted, and gloomily comic. His major stories and plays were innovative because they emphasized character and mood rather than plot. He is so successful in conveying mood that the critic D. S. Mirsky called his stories "biographies of a mood." Traditional plot structure, which relies on action and complications, is rarely found in his works. His typical characters are sensitive and intelligent but also idle, foolish, self-deceiving, and alienated—yearning for a fulfillment that never arrives. Yet these characters, though foolish, are often pathetically touching at the same time.

North Carolina Competency Goal
1.03; 2.01; 3.04; 4.02; 4.05; 5.01; 5.03

INTERNET

Vocabulary Practice
•
More About Anton Chekhov
Keyword: LE5 WL-6

> **Irony** is a contrast or discrepancy between expectations and reality.
>
> *For more on Irony, see the Handbook of Literary and Historical Terms.*

Reading Skills

Making Inferences About Character

When you make an **inference** about a character, you make an intelligent guess about what the character is like, what the character is thinking or feeling, or what the character may do in the future. Your inference should be based on specific evidence in the story:

SKILLS FOCUS

Literary Skills
Understand irony.

Reading Skills
Make inferences about character.

Vocabulary Development

reprehensible (rep′ri·hen′sə·bəl) *adj.*: deserving of criticism or blame.

dissipated (dis′ə·pāt′id) *adj.*: wasted by excessive drinking and gambling.

suavely (swäv′lē) *adv.*: smoothly.

edifying (ed′i·fī′iŋ) *v.* used as *adj.*: morally instructive.

petrified (pe′trə·fīd′) *adj.*: paralyzed with shock or fear.

Five Portraits (1901) by Vilhelm Hammershøis.
Thielska Galleriet, Stockholm, Sweden (nr117).

A Problem

Anton Chekhov
translated by **Constance Garnett**

The strictest measures were taken that the Uskovs' family secret might not leak out and become generally known. Half of the servants were sent off to the theater or the circus; the other half were sitting in the kitchen and not allowed to leave it. Orders were given that no one was to be admitted. The wife of the Colonel, her sister, and the governess, though they had been initiated into the secret, kept up a pretense of knowing nothing; they sat in the dining room and did not show themselves in the drawing room or the hall.

Sasha Uskov, the young man of twenty-five who was the cause of all the commotion, had arrived some time before, and by the advice of kind-hearted Ivan Markovitch, his uncle, who was taking his part, he sat meekly in the hall by the door leading to the study, and prepared himself to make an open, candid explanation.

The other side of the door, in the study, a

family council was being held. The subject under discussion was an exceedingly disagreeable and delicate one. Sasha Uskov had cashed at one of the banks a false promissory note,[1] and it had become due for payment three days before, and now his two paternal uncles and Ivan Markovitch, the brother of his dead mother, were deciding the question whether they should pay the money and save the family honor, or wash their hands of it and leave the case to go for trial.

To outsiders who have no personal interest in the matter such questions seem simple; for those who are so unfortunate as to have to decide them in earnest they are extremely difficult. The uncles had been talking for a long time, but the problem seemed no nearer decision.

"My friends!" said the uncle who was a colonel, and there was a note of exhaustion and bitterness in his voice. "Who says that family honor is a mere convention? I don't say that at all. I am only warning you against a false view; I am pointing out the possibility of an unpardonable mistake. How can you fail to see it? I am not speaking Chinese; I am speaking Russian!"

"My dear fellow, we do understand," Ivan Markovitch protested mildly.

"How can you understand if you say that I don't believe in family honor? I repeat once more; fa-mil-y ho-nor false-ly un-der-stood is a prejudice! Falsely understood! That's what I say: whatever may be the motives for screening a scoundrel, whoever he may be, and helping him to escape punishment, it is contrary to law and unworthy of a gentleman. It's not saving the family honor; it's civic cowardice! Take the army, for instance. . . . The honor of the army is more precious to us than any other honor, yet we don't screen our guilty members, but condemn them. And does the honor of the army suffer in consequence? Quite the opposite!"

The other paternal uncle, an official in the Treasury, a taciturn,[2] dull-witted, and rheumatic man, sat silent, or spoke only of the fact that the Uskovs' name would get into the newspapers if the case went for trial. His opinion was that the case ought to be hushed up from the first and not become public property; but, apart from publicity in the newspapers, he advanced no other argument in support of this opinion.

The maternal uncle, kind-hearted Ivan Markovitch, spoke smoothly, softly, and with a tremor in his voice. He began with saying that youth has its rights and its peculiar temptations. Which of us has not been young, and who has not been led astray? To say nothing of ordinary mortals, even great men have not escaped errors and mistakes in their youth. Take, for instance, the biography of great writers. Did not every one of them gamble, drink, and draw down upon himself the anger of right-thinking people in his young days? If Sasha's error bordered upon crime, they must remember that Sasha had received practically no education; he had been expelled from the high school in the fifth class; he had lost his parents in early childhood, and so had been left at the tenderest age without guidance and good, benevolent influences. He was nervous, excitable, had no firm ground under his feet, and, above all, he had been unlucky. Even if he were guilty, anyway he deserved indulgence and the sympathy of all compassionate souls. He ought, of course, to be punished, but he was punished as it was by his conscience and the agonies he was enduring now while awaiting the sentence of his relations. The comparison with the army made by the Colonel was delightful, and did credit to his lofty intelligence; his appeal to their feeling of public duty spoke for the chivalry of his soul, but they must not forget that in each individual the citizen is closely linked with the Christian. . . .

"Shall we be false to civic duty," Ivan Markovitch exclaimed passionately, "if instead of punishing an erring boy we hold out to him a helping hand?"

Ivan Markovitch talked further of family honor. He had not the honor to belong to the Uskov family himself, but he knew their distinguished family went back to the thirteenth century; he did not forget for a minute, either, that his precious, beloved sister had been the

1. **promissory note:** written promise to pay a certain sum of money on demand; IOU.
2. **taciturn** (tas′ə·tʉrn′) *adj.:* silent.

Roulette by Edvard Munch (1863–1944).
Munch Museum, Oslo, Norway.

wife of one of the representatives of that name. In short, the family was dear to him for many reasons, and he refused to admit the idea that, for the sake of a paltry fifteen hundred rubles,[3] a blot should be cast on the escutcheon[4] that was beyond all price. If all the motives he had brought forward were not sufficiently convincing, he, Ivan Markovitch, in conclusion, begged his listeners to ask themselves what was meant by crime? Crime is an immoral act founded upon ill-will. But is the will of man free? Philosophy has not yet given a positive answer to that question. Different views were held by the learned. The latest school of Lombroso,[5] for

---

3. **rubles** *n. pl.:* money used in Russia.
4. **a blot . . . escutcheon** (e·skuch′ən): disgrace to a reputation.
5. **Lombroso:** Cesare Lombroso (1836–1909), Italian physician and criminologist, who believed that criminals are a distinct human type with specific physical and mental deviations and that criminal behavior is the result of hereditary factors.

instance, denies the freedom of the will, and considers every crime as the product of the purely anatomical peculiarities of the individual.

"Ivan Markovitch," said the Colonel, in a voice of entreaty, "we are talking seriously about an important matter, and you bring in Lombroso, you clever fellow. Think a little, what are you saying all this for? Can you imagine that all your thunderings and rhetoric will furnish an answer to the question?"

Sasha Uskov sat at the door and listened. He felt neither terror, shame, nor depression, but only weariness and inward emptiness. It seemed to him that it made absolutely no difference to him whether they forgave him or not; he had come here to hear his sentence and to explain himself simply because kind-hearted Ivan Markovitch had begged him to do so. He was not afraid of the future. It made no difference to him where he was: here in the hall, in prison, or in Siberia.

"If Siberia, then let it be Siberia, damn it all!"

He was sick of life and found it insufferably hard. He was inextricably involved in debt; he had not a farthing[6] in his pocket; his family had become detestable to him; he would have to part from his friends and his women sooner or later, as they had begun to be too contemptuous of his sponging on them. The future looked black.

Sasha was indifferent, and was only disturbed by one circumstance; the other side of the door they were calling him a scoundrel and a criminal. Every minute he was on the point of jumping up, bursting into the study, and shouting in answer to the detestable metallic voice of the Colonel:

"You are lying!"

"Criminal" is a dreadful word—that is what murderers, thieves, robbers are; in fact, wicked and morally hopeless people. And Sasha was very far from being all that. . . . It was true he owed a great deal and did not pay his debts. But debt is not a crime, and it is unusual for a man not to be in debt. The Colonel and Ivan Markovitch were both in debt. . . .

"What have I done wrong besides?" Sasha wondered.

He had discounted a forged note. But all the young men he knew did the same. Handrikov and Von Burst always forged IOU's from their parents or friends when their allowances were not paid at the regular time, and then when they got their money from home they redeemed them before they became due. Sasha had done the same, but had not redeemed the IOU because he had not got the money which Handrikov had promised to lend him. He was not to blame; it was the fault of circumstances. It was true that the use of another person's signature was considered reprehensible; but, still, it was not a crime but a generally accepted dodge, an ugly formality which injured no one and was quite harmless, for in forging the Colonel's signature Sasha had had no intention of causing anybody damage or loss.

"No, it doesn't mean that I am a criminal . . ." thought Sasha. "And it's not in my character to

bring myself to commit a crime. I am soft, emotional. . . . When I have the money I help the poor. . . ."

Sasha was musing after this fashion while they went on talking the other side of the door.

"But, my friends, this is endless," the Colonel declared, getting excited. "Suppose we were to forgive him and pay the money. You know he would not give up leading a dissipated life, squandering money, making debts, going to our tailors and ordering suits in our names! Can you guarantee that this will be his last prank? As far as I am concerned, I have no faith whatever in his reforming!"

The official of the Treasury muttered something in reply; after him Ivan Markovitch began talking blandly and suavely again. The Colonel moved his chair impatiently and drowned the other's words with his detestable metallic voice. At last the door opened and Ivan Markovitch came out of the study; there were patches of red on his cleanshaven face.

"Come along," he said, taking Sasha by the hand. "Come and speak frankly from your heart. Without pride, my dear boy, humbly and from your heart."

Sasha went into the study. The official of the Treasury was sitting down; the Colonel was standing before the table with one hand in his pocket and one knee on a chair. It was smoky and stifling in the study. Sasha did not look at the official or the Colonel; he felt suddenly ashamed and uncomfortable. He looked uneasily at Ivan Markovitch and muttered:

"I'll pay it . . . I'll give it back. . . ."

"What did you expect when you discounted the IOU?" he heard a metallic voice.

"I . . . Handrikov promised to lend me the money before now."

Sasha could say no more. He went out of the

---

6. **farthing** *n.*: coin of little value.

Vocabulary

reprehensible (rep′ri·hen′sə·bəl) *adj.*: deserving of criticism or blame.

dissipated (dis′ə·pāt′id) *adj.*: wasted by excessive drinking and gambling.

suavely (swäv′lē) *adv.*: smoothly.

Interior with the Artist's Brothers (c. 1830) by Wilhelm Bendz.
The Granger Collection, New York.

study and sat down again on the chair near the door. He would have been glad to go away altogether at once, but he was choking with hatred and he awfully wanted to remain, to tear the Colonel to pieces, to say something rude to him. He sat trying to think of something violent and effective to say to his hated uncle, and at that moment a woman's figure, shrouded in the twilight, appeared at the drawing room door. It was the Colonel's wife. She beckoned Sasha to her, and, wringing her hands, said, weeping:

"*Alexandre,* I know you don't like me, but . . . listen to me; listen, I beg you. . . . But, my dear, how can this have happened? Why, it's awful, awful! For goodness' sake, beg them, defend yourself, entreat them."

Sasha looked at her quivering shoulders, at the big tears that were rolling down her cheeks, heard behind his back the hollow, nervous voices of worried and exhausted people, and shrugged his shoulders. He had not in the least expected that his aristocratic relations would raise such a tempest over a paltry fifteen hundred rubles! He could not understand her tears nor the quiver of their voices.

An hour later he heard that the Colonel was getting the best of it; the uncles were finally inclining to let the case go for trial.

"The matter's settled," said the Colonel, sighing. "Enough."

After this decision all the uncles, even the emphatic Colonel, became noticeably depressed. A silence followed.

"Merciful Heavens!" sighed Ivan Markovitch. "My poor sister!"

And he began saying in a subdued voice that most likely his sister, Sasha's mother, was present unseen in the study at that moment. He felt in his soul how the unhappy, saintly woman was weeping, grieving, and begging for her boy. For the sake of her peace beyond the grave, they ought to spare Sasha.

The sound of a muffled sob was heard. Ivan Markovitch was weeping and muttering something which it was impossible to catch through the door. The Colonel got up and paced from corner to corner. The long conversation began over again.

But then the clock in the drawing room struck two. The family council was over. To avoid seeing the person who had moved him to such wrath, the Colonel went from the study, not into the hall, but into the vestibule[7]. . . . Ivan Markovitch came out into the hall. . . . He was agitated and rubbing his hands joyfully. His tear-stained eyes looked good-humored and his mouth was twisted into a smile.

"Capital," he said to Sasha. "Thank God! You can go home, my dear, and sleep tranquilly. We have decided to pay the sum, but on condition that you repent and come with me tomorrow into the country and set to work."

A minute later Ivan Markovitch and Sasha in their greatcoats and caps were going down the stairs. The uncle was muttering something edifying. Sasha did not listen, but felt as though some uneasy weight were gradually slipping off his shoulders. They had forgiven him; he was free! A gust of joy sprang up within him and sent a sweet chill to his heart. He longed to breathe, to move swiftly, to live! Glancing at the street lamps and the black sky, he remembered that Von Burst was celebrating his name day that evening at the "Bear," and again a rush of joy flooded his soul. . . .

"I am going!" he decided.

But then he remembered he had not a farthing, that the companions he was going to would despise him at once for his empty pockets. He must get hold of some money, come what may!

"Uncle, lend me a hundred rubles," he said to Ivan Markovitch.

His uncle, surprised, looked into his face and backed against a lamppost.

"Give it to me," said Sasha, shifting impatiently from one foot to the other and beginning to pant. "Uncle, I entreat you, give me a hundred rubles."

His face worked; he trembled, and seemed on the point of attacking his uncle. . . .

"Won't you?" he kept asking, seeing that his uncle was still amazed and did not understand. "Listen. If you don't, I'll give myself up tomorrow! I won't let you pay the IOU! I'll present another false note tomorrow!"

Petrified, muttering something incoherent in his horror, Ivan Markovitch took a hundred-ruble note out of his pocketbook and gave it to Sasha. The young man took it and walked rapidly away from him. . . .

Taking a sledge,[8] Sasha grew calmer, and felt a rush of joy within him again. The "rights of youth" of which kind-hearted Ivan Markovitch had spoken at the family council woke up and asserted themselves. Sasha pictured the drinking party before him, and, among the bottles, the women, and his friends, the thought flashed through his mind:

"Now I see that I am a criminal; yes, I am a criminal."

---

7. **vestibule** *n.:* small entrance hall or room.

8. **sledge** *n.:* horse-drawn sled or sleigh used for transportation over snow or ice.

Vocabulary

edifying (ed′i·fi′iŋ) *v.* used as *adj.:* morally instructive.
petrified (pe′trə·fīd′) *adj.:* paralyzed with shock or fear.

Response and Analysis

Reading Check

1. What decision does the family finally make about Sasha?

2. What request does Sasha make of Ivan at the end of the story?

Thinking Critically

3. What **dramatic irony** can you see in the suggestion that Sasha is being punished by his conscience?

4. What do you think is Chekhov's attitude toward Sasha? Is his **tone** judgmental, sarcastic, or compassionate? Explain your answer by providing examples from the story.

5. How would you describe the **mood** of the story? How do the family crisis and Sasha's attitude toward it contribute to the mood?

6. Based on what they say in the story, what **inferences** can you make about the characters of Ivan Markovitch and the Colonel?

7. How is the final scene between Ivan and Sasha an example of **situational irony**?

8. Explain why Sasha's opinion of himself changes at the end of the story. Do you agree with what he says about himself in the last line of the story? Why or why not?

9. Did the final scene come as a surprise to you, or had you **inferred** what would become of Sasha at the story's conclusion? Explain.

Literary Criticism

10. The critic Anatole France said, "Russian fiction is largely the account of the undoing of human life, rather than of its shaping." Do you think France's statement applies to "A Problem"? Why or why not?

WRITING

Interpreting the Story's Title

In a brief essay, interpret the meaning or significance of the title "A Problem." Use these questions to guide your essay:

- To what serious moral problem does the title refer?
- What other serious family problem is presented in the story?
- In what sense is the forged promissory note the least serious problem?

Vocabulary Development
Synonyms

A **synonym** is a word that has the same or nearly the same meaning as another word. Choose the best synonym for each Vocabulary word below.

1. **reprehensible:** a. hideous b. blameless c. guilty

2. **dissipated:** a. wasted b. excessive c. remote

3. **suavely:** a. elegantly b. abruptly c. blandly

4. **edifying:** a. obscene b. instructive c. uplifting

5. **petrified:** a. stunned b. ancient c. lively

North Carolina Competency Goal
1.03; 4.05; 5.03; 6.01

INTERNET
Projects and Activities
Keyword: LE5 WL-6

Literary Skills
Analyze irony.

Reading Skills
Make inferences about character.

Writing Skills
Interpret a story's title.

Vocabulary Skills
Identify synonyms.

Grammar Link

Make Your Meaning Clear: Avoiding Sentence Fragments and Run-on Sentences

Writing well requires knowing where one sentence ends and another begins. The following **sentence fragment** looks like a sentence but does not express a complete thought:

FRAGMENT Listening to the family council through the door.

This fragment leaves you wondering, "Who is listening to the family council through the door?" Although sentence fragments are acceptable in informal writing and dialogue, avoid using them in formal writing. Instead, correct fragments by making them complete sentences.

COMPLETE   Sasha remains in the hallway, listening
SENTENCE   to the family council through the door.

While a fragment does not express a complete thought, a **run-on sentence** runs together two complete thoughts as if they were one. (Run-on sentences are not just long, wordy sentences; they are two sentences in one.) There are two types of run-ons: A **fused sentence** has no punctuation at all between the complete thoughts, and a **comma splice** separates the thoughts with only a comma. You can correct both kinds of run-on sentences by using a stronger type of punctuation, such as a period or semicolon.

FUSED   The men debate in the study the
SENTENCE   women remain in the dining room.

CORRECT   The men debate in the study. The
             women remain in the dining room.

COMMA   Ivan Markovitch advocates mercy,
SPLICE   the Colonel, however, demands
             justice.

CORRECT   Ivan Markovitch advocates mercy; the
             Colonel, however, demands justice.

North Carolina Competency Goal
1.03; 4.05; 5.03

SKILLS FOCUS

Grammar Skills
Understand sentence fragments and run-on sentences.

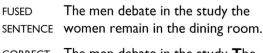

PRACTICE

Identify each of the following items as containing a **sentence fragment** (SF), a **fused sentence** (FS), or a **comma splice** (CS). Then, revise each item by completing, combining, or separating sentences.

1. The taciturn uncle merely wants to avoid a scandal, Ivan Markovitch, on the other hand, wants to protect Sasha.

2. Sasha tries to justify his actions. Arguing to himself that debt is not a crime.

3. Sasha says little in his own defense only afterward does he try to think of something.

4. Just as Ivan Markovitch appeals to the theories of Lombroso. Sasha believes that crime is bred into one's character.

5. Sasha does not seem to realize what his uncle has done for him, instead, the young man asks Ivan Markovitch for more money.

Apply to Your Writing

Review a writing assignment you are working on now or have already completed. Have you included any fragments or run-on sentences? Revise them to make sentences complete and separate.

▶ **For more help, see Sentence Fragments, 9d, and Run-on Sentences, 9e, in the Language Handbook.**

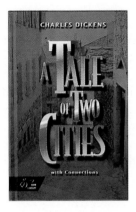

FICTION
A Tale of Vengeance and Redemption

Charles Dickens brings the dissension and passion of the French Revolution to life in his dramatic work *A Tale of Two Cities.* The novel opens with an unflinching account of growing social unrest and brutality in France and England during the year 1775. Dickens relates the events that connect the Manette, Defarge, and Evrémonde families, who are representative of the society that they inhabit in the midst of this turmoil. Ultimately, the least likely character receives redemption when he makes an unforgettable sacrifice that gives someone else a new chance at life.

This title is available in the HRW Library.

FICTION
Everyman

Leo Tolstoy's *The Death of Ivan Ilych and Other Stories* (translated by Aylmer Maude and J. D. Duff) is a collection of stories that revolve around the desires and emotions that are common to all people. The characters in the stories grapple with weighty issues such as death, greed, vanity, and hypocrisy. In the story "The Death of Ivan Ilych," a middle-class family man is suddenly faced with his impending death and must cope with the feelings of fear and denial that threaten to overwhelm him.

DRAMA
An Independent Woman

When Henrik Ibsen's play *A Doll's House* (translated by Michael Meyer) was published in 1879, it proved highly controversial. The play addressed the subject of marital conflict and the independence of women at a time when it was the status quo for middle-class women to be wholly dependent on their husbands. The play's main character is Nora Helmer, who has secretly been repaying a debt she incurred to save the life of her husband, Torvald. At that time, women could not legally borrow money, and Nora's creditor threatens to inform Torvald of her secret. Nora is faced with a dilemma that eventually forces her to see her marriage clearly for the first time.

ADDITIONAL READING

- *Les Misérables,* translated by Lee Fahnestock and Norman MacAfee, is Victor Hugo's literary masterpiece that takes an unsentimental look at the Parisian underworld. At the center of the story is the plight of Jean Valjean, who is hunted by Inspector Javert for stealing a loaf of bread in order to feed his family.

- The distinguished scholar and translator Paul Schmidt presents vibrant translations in the collection *The Plays of Anton Chekhov.* This book includes major works, such as *The Cherry Orchard, Uncle Vanya,* and *The Three Sisters,* that established Chekhov as a master playwright.

- In *Citizens: A Chronicle of the French Revolution,* Simon Schama presents a detailed account of the French Revolution. Schama's book offers a fresh interpretation of the causes of the revolution.

Analyzing Literature

When you read a story, you usually have an emotional response to it. You like it or dislike it or are moved, confused, or troubled by it. There is a whole range of personal reactions you can have to any literary work, but after your initial response, you might begin to wonder how the work produced these effects on you and what the author's purpose for writing was. To answer such questions, you must analyze the work. In a **literary analysis,** you examine the story's parts or literary elements to figure out how they work together to produce an overall effect and meaning.

Prewriting

Choose a Story

A Story with Depth Since you will be putting a lot of time and thought into analyzing a story, choose one that really engages you and has some quality that you particularly appreciate—an unpredictable plot, strong characterization, or a compelling theme. If the story seems predictable or unoriginal to you, there will be little to delve into or analyze. Here are some ways you can find a good story with depth:

- Look for stories by an author you already know and admire or by an author who has received critical acclaim or won major literary awards. Perhaps you are interested in writers from a particular culture or time period.

- Ask your friends, parents, or teachers to recommend a story that they enjoyed.

- Look through short story collections at your school or local library. You might focus on stories that have won awards or been praised by critics.

- Look for stories you have seen dramatized on film or television.

Analyze Literary Elements

Read and Re-read After you've chosen a story, read it once to get an overall impression. Then, read it again, making notes and paying closer attention to the literary elements of character, plot, and setting and how these work together to convey the theme. To analyze these elements, ask yourself the questions on the next page.

**SKILLS
FOCUS**

Writing Skills
Write a literary analysis of a short story.

**North Carolina
Competency Goal**
3.03; 6.01

- **Character:** Who are the major characters? What motivates them? How does the writer bring them to life? Do any of them change? How?

- **Plot:** What conflict or problem do the characters face? Is the conflict resolved? How? If not, why not?

- **Setting:** Where and when does the story take place? Does the setting influence the characters, plot, or theme? Does it affect the tone or mood of the story? If so, how?

- **Theme:** What generalization about life or human nature does the interaction of the characters, plot, and setting suggest? Can you relate this theme to your own life?

Write a Thesis Statement

Choose Your Focus Since there are many elements at work in any story, choose the one you think is most important. Is the story primarily effective and memorable for its characters, for its strong sense of place (setting), or for its insights into human life (theme)? Next, think about how the writer has made that element the focus—how that element helps to express the meaning or significance of the story. When you identify the relationship between the main element and others in the story, draft a thesis statement that expresses that relationship. Here is a student's thesis statement for Chekhov's story "A Problem":

> In "A Problem," Anton Chekhov establishes an ironic tone that gradually reveals his theme: People are not always what they appear to be, and events do not turn out as expected.

North Carolina Competency Goal
3.03; 6.01

Support Your Thesis

Go Back to the Text When you are drafting your essay, develop your thesis with **key points** and support these with direct **evidence** from the story. You can present your evidence in these forms:

- **Direct quotations**—exact words from the story set within quotation marks

- **Paraphrase**—a restatement of the author's ideas in your own words

- **Summary**—a condensation of plot events or of the author's most important ideas

TIP Use the **literary present** tense whenever you summarize the plot of a story or refer to an author's relationship with his or her work; for example, "Chekhov often **uses** irony in his stories."

Writing Skills
Assess, organize, and analyze information for a literary analysis. Draft a thesis statement, and support it with evidence.

PRACTICE & APPLY 1 Choose a short story and analyze its literary elements. Choose an element to focus on, and develop key points about it. Write a thesis statement, and select and organize evidence to support it.

Writing

Analyzing a Short Story

A Writer's Framework

Introduction	Body	Conclusion
• Grab the reader's attention by relating an anecdote or asking questions.	• Discuss one key point in each paragraph.	• Restate your thesis in a new way.
• Identify the story's title and author.	• Support each key point with evidence from the text.	• Summarize your key points.
• State your thesis, presenting the main element and key points.	• Elaborate on each key point with supporting evidence.	• End with a thoughtful comment that connects your analysis to real life.

A Writer's Model

Is It Only the Young Who Are Foolish?

INTRODUCTION
Attention-grabbing questions

What would you do if a relative who had done something illegal asked you to help him out of trouble? Would you save him from punishment or make him face the consequences of his actions? Most of all, what would your attitude be toward this person? In a short story exploring this situation, there are a variety of attitudes, or tones, the author could take toward his characters and their situation, ranging from sympathy to contempt. In "A Problem," Anton Chekhov establishes an ironic tone that gradually reveals his theme: People are not always what they appear to be, and events do not turn out as expected.

Title and author
Thesis statement

BODY
Key point: characterization
Evidence: examples of ironic characters

As we read Chekhov's story, we begin to see that the characters' actions often do not correspond to their words or their images of themselves. For example, the Colonel, who sees himself as the hard-headed guardian of civic duty, ends up agreeing to bail out his irresponsible nephew when told that the young man's dead mother's spirit may be in the room, suffering. Then there is the response of Sasha, the accused forger, who convinces himself that he has done nothing seriously wrong and is good at heart. Chekhov describes Sasha thinking,

Direct quotation

"'Criminal' is a dreadful word—that is what murderers, thieves, robbers are. . . . It was true he owed a great deal and did not pay his debts. But debt is not a crime. . . ." He even says to himself, "And it's not in my character to bring myself to commit a crime. I am soft, emotional. . . ." Even though Sasha has committed a crime by forging a promissory note,

Elaboration

he doesn't believe himself capable of a real crime. He and the Colonel

(continued)

are presented in ironic terms because they are not the people they think they are or would like to be.

Events in the story also take ironic or surprising turns. In addition to the Colonel's unexpectedly agreeing to bail out Sasha, the soft-hearted Sasha flies into a fury at the Colonel and cannot defend himself out loud after mentally preparing an elaborate defense in private. It is sensitive and compassionate Ivan Markovitch, however, whose expectations are most violently overturned. Convinced that a little forgiving indulgence is all that is needed to reform Sasha, Markovitch is amazed and helpless when the culprit demands a loan from him minutes after being reprieved.

What is Chekhov telling us about human nature by building all these ironies into his characterization and into the sequence of events in his story? The examples above suggest that he sees human beings as rather weak and self-deceiving. We try to think well of ourselves but often do not act according to our self-evaluations. The twists in Chekhov's plot suggest that he sees life as unpredictable and out of the control of those who would like to shape events as they see fit. His ironic tone gently reminds us of our own less than heroic tendencies and of life's capacity to defeat and disappoint us.

Key point: sequence of events

Evidence: examples of ironic plot twists

CONCLUSION
Restatement of thesis

Summary of key points

Comment relating analysis to life

PRACTICE & APPLY 2 Using the framework and Writer's Model on these pages as your guide, write the first draft of your analysis of a short story.

INTERNET
More Writer's Models
Keyword:
LE5 WL-6

North Carolina Competency Goal
3.03; 6.01; 6.02

Writing Skills
Write the first draft of your analysis.

Revising

Self-Evaluation

Look Again Use the chart on the next page to help you evaluate and revise the content and organization of your short story analysis. Ask yourself the questions on the left. If you need help answering the questions, follow the tips in the middle column. When you need to revise, use the techniques in the right-hand column.

Rubric: Analyzing a Short Story

Evaluation Questions	▶ Tips	▶ Revision Techniques
❶ Does the introduction grab the reader's attention and name the title and author of the story?	▶ **Put a check mark** by the sentences that capture the reader's attention. **Highlight** the title and author.	▶ **Add** sentences that will grab the reader's interest. **Add** the story's title or author to the introduction.
❷ Does the thesis statement identify the main element and the key points you are going to make about it?	▶ **Draw a wavy line** under the main element. **Put a star** beside each key point.	▶ **Add** an identification of the main element or the key points you will make about it in your thesis statement.
❸ Does each body paragraph discuss one key point?	▶ **Number** each key point. Be sure that each paragraph covers only one key point.	▶ **Rearrange** key points so that only one is discussed in each body paragraph.
❹ Are the key points supported with sufficient evidence from the text? Did you elaborate on this evidence?	▶ **Underline** the supporting evidence for each key point, and **double-underline** the elaboration.	▶ **Add** evidence to support each key point. **Elaborate** by explaining how evidence supports each key point.
❺ Does the conclusion restate the thesis and summarize the key points? Does it end with a thoughtful comment?	▶ **Highlight** the restated thesis. **Bracket** the summary of the key points, and **double-bracket** the final comment.	▶ **Add** a restatement of the thesis and a summary of key points. **Add** a final comment relating the analysis to life.

ANALYZING THE REVISION PROCESS
Study the revisions below, and answer the questions that follow.

As we read Chekhov's story, we begin to see that the characters'

actions often do not correspond to their words or their images of

themselves. *For example,* The Colonel, who sees himself as the hardheaded guardian

of civic duty, ends up agreeing to bail out his irresponsible nephew when

told that the young man's dead mother's spirit may be in the room,

Then there is the response of suffering. Sasha, the accused forger, who convinces himself that he has

done nothing seriously wrong and is good at heart.

Responding to the Revision Process

1. How does the addition of the connecting phrase at the beginning of the second sentence help clarify the organization?

2. How does the addition of the phrase at the beginning of the last sentence improve the sentence?

 **PRACTICE & APPLY** 3 Using the guidelines on these pages, revise the content and organization of your literary analysis.

SKILLS FOCUS

Writing Skills
Revise for content and style.

Publishing

Proofread and Publish Your Analysis

Look Closely Before you share your literary analysis, proofread it carefully. Any departure from the standard rules of grammar, spelling, usage, or mechanics could damage your credibility with your audience. Make sure to spell all proper names correctly.

Share Your Work When you are sure your analysis is error free, print it and make it available to others. Here are some publishing possibilities:

- Work with other students to create a class collection of short story analyses. Ask your school librarian to add the collection to the school library stacks and catalog it in the library database.

- Deliver your short story analysis as an oral response to literature. For more on **presenting a literary analysis,** see page 830.

North Carolina Competency Goal
3.03; 6.01; 6.02

Reflect on Your Essay

Take Stock Think back on your experience of writing a literary analysis. These questions will help guide your thinking:

- Why did you choose to analyze this particular story? Would you use the same process the next time you analyze a story? Why or why not?

- How did your feelings or understanding of the story change as a result of studying it in depth? Explain your answer.

 **PRACTICE & APPLY** 4 First, proofread your analysis. Then, choose one of the options above to publish your work. Finally, use the questions to reflect upon what you learned in writing this analysis.

SKILLS FOCUS

Writing Skills
Proofread for grammar, usage, and mechanics errors.

Presenting a Literary Analysis

Speaking Assignment
Adapt your written literary analysis into an oral response to literature, and deliver it to your class.

Writing a literary analysis is not the only way to share your ideas about a literary work. You can address a group of listeners rather than asking your audience to read your written analysis. Although you will communicate essentially the same ideas, you will use different techniques to reach an audience of listeners. This workshop will help you adapt your written analysis for an oral response to literature.

Adapt Your Analysis

Less Is More Listeners generally cannot absorb as much information as quickly as readers can. Even if you do not have a set time limit for your oral presentation, keep it short and focus on a limited number of important points and evidence. You will lose your audience if you overwhelm them with too much information.

Streamline Your Content Adapt your written thesis statement by shortening or simplifying it if necessary. You might also want to summarize your key points at the beginning to prepare your listeners for the elaboration you will be providing later in your presentation. Be alert for long, complex sentences in your written analysis; you may want to break them down to shorter, simpler sentences in your speech. Be sure, though, to use transitional words and phrases to orient your listeners and provide a smooth flow to your ideas.

Give Evidence Although you want to be concise, you must support each key point you make with sufficient and accurate evidence. Make it clear when you are quoting from the text you are analyzing, and try to choose short quotations that readers can understand after one hearing; longer quotations will be harder for listeners to follow. If you quote or paraphrase ideas from a secondary source, be sure you identify the title and author of the work you are citing. Do not overwhelm your listeners with evidence; the few quotations or paraphrases that most strongly support your thesis will do.

Use Rhetorical Devices To make your presentation more listener-friendly, try the following techniques:

- Use **rhetorical questions,** or questions with debatable answers that are asked more for effect than for a correct response. For example, a student analyzing Chekhov's story "A Problem" might ask, "Who has the bigger problem, Sasha or his relatives?"

- Use **parallel structure,** or the same grammatical form, for similar ideas. For example, "The Colonel wishes to save civic honor, Ivan Markovitch wishes to save Sasha, and Sasha wishes to save himself." The rhythm and repetition of parallel structure, or parallelism, unify

North Carolina Competency Goal
3.03

SKILLS FOCUS

Listening and Speaking Skills
Present an oral response to a literary work. Use effective rhetorical techniques.

ideas, heighten the emotional effect of words, and make your ideas more memorable.

Put Your Ideas in Order Just as in your written analysis, your oral presentation can follow **chronological order** or **order of importance.** Help your listeners by giving them word clues to your organizing principle, such as *first, next,* and *finally* for chronological order and *most important* and *least important* for order of importance.

Make Note Cards Write notes on note cards to remind yourself of important points. Number these cards in the order in which you want to present the ideas. You can glance at these cards as you speak to remind yourself of what you want to say and to keep your ideas in order. The note card below is based on the Writer's Model on page 826.

The note card below is based on the Writer's Model on page 826.

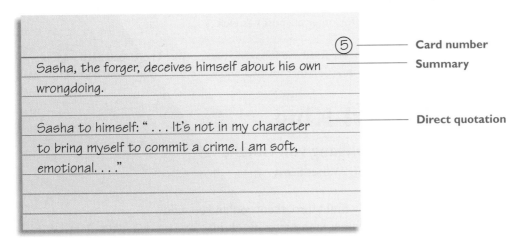

Card number

Summary

Direct quotation

⑤

Sasha, the forger, deceives himself about his own wrongdoing.

Sasha to himself: " . . . It's not in my character to bring myself to commit a crime. I am soft, emotional. . . ."

the clarity with which speakers pronounce their words.

> **TIP** **Enunciation** is the clarity with which speakers pronounce their words. Poor enunciation makes listeners strain, giving them the impression the speaker does not care about them or the ideas in the presentation. Practice your enunciation before you present your analysis.

Rehearse and Present Your Analysis

Practice Makes Perfect In order to make a successful presentation, you will not only have to know what you are going to say and when you are going to say it, but you will also have to focus on *how* you speak. This means practicing, or rehearsing, your delivery in order to fine-tune such verbal details as **emphasis, pacing,** and **enunciation** and such nonverbal details as **gestures, facial expressions,** and **posture.** Try these rehearsal strategies:

- Videotape or audiotape your presentation, and play it back, noting ways you could improve your delivery. Practice and then record again. Repeat this process until you are comfortable with your performance.

- Give your presentation to a group of friends or family members, and ask for feedback. Revise your performance based on the feedback, and then present it to another group for their responses.

> **TIP** **Gestures** are body movements that emphasize emotions or ideas. Good speakers use natural gestures, such as nodding their heads, shrugging, and emphasizing points with hand movements.

North Carolina Competency Goal 3.03

Listening and Speaking Skills
Practice and present your literary analysis.

PRACTICE & APPLY 5 Use the instruction in this workshop to adapt the literary analysis you wrote for the Writer's Workshop for an oral presentation. Rehearse and then present your oral response to literature to your classmates.

Test Practice

The folklore of many cultures contains stories of spirits, fairies, or other beings from the supernatural realm who attempt to steal or entice young children away from their earthly homes. These old myths fired the imagination of poets with Romantic leanings like the German writer Johann Wolfgang von Goethe (1749–1832) and the Irish poet William Butler Yeats (1865–1939). While the original stories may have been designed to remind listeners of the power of the supernatural and even frighten them a bit, Goethe and Yeats used these folk beliefs in their poetry for other purposes as well.

DIRECTIONS: Read the following two poems. Then, read each multiple-choice question that follows, and write the letter of the best response.

The Erl-King

Johann Wolfgang von Goethe
translated by Sir Walter Scott

O who rides by night thro' the woodland so wild?
It is the fond father embracing his child;
And close the boy nestles within his loved arm.
To hold himself fast, and to keep himself warm.

5 "O father, see yonder! see yonder!" he says;
"My boy, upon what dost thou fearfully gaze?"
"O, 'tis the Erl-King with his crown and his shroud."
"No, my son, it is but a dark wreath of the cloud."

   (The Erl-King speaks)
"O come and go with me, thou loveliest child;
10 By many a gay sport shall thy time be beguiled;
My mother keeps for thee full many a fair toy,
And many a fine flower shall she pluck for my boy."

"O father, my father, and did you not hear
The Erl-King whisper so low in my ear?"
15 "Be still, my heart's darling—my child, be at ease;
It was but the wild blast as it sung thro' the trees."

   Erl-King
"O wilt thou go with me, thou loveliest boy?
My daughter shall tend thee with care and with joy;

North Carolina Competency Goal
1.03; 4.05;
5.02; 5.03

Pages 832–835 cover

Literary Skills
Compare and contrast literature.

20 She shall bear thee so lightly thro' wet and thro' wild,
And press thee, and kiss thee, and sing to my child."

"O father, my father, and saw you not plain
The Erl-King's pale daughter glide past thro' the rain?"
"O yes, my loved treasure, I knew it full soon;
It was the gray willow that danced to the moon."

Erl-King

25 "O come and go with me, no longer delay,
Or else, silly child, I will drag thee away."
"O father! O father! now, now, keep your hold,
The Erl-King has seized me—his grasp is so cold!"

Sore trembled the father; he spurr'd thro' the wild,
30 Clasping close to his bosom his shuddering child;
He reaches his dwelling in doubt and in dread,
But, clasp'd to his bosom, the infant was dead.

The Stolen Child

William Butler Yeats

Where dips the rocky highland
Of Sleuth Wood in the lake,
There lies a leafy island
Where flapping herons wake
5 The drowsy water-rats;
There we've hid our faery vats,
Full of berries
And of reddest stolen cherries.
Come away, O human child!
10 *To the waters and the wild*
With a faery, hand in hand,
For the world's more full of weeping
than you can understand.

Where the wave of moonlight glosses
The dim grey sands with light,
15 Far off by furthest Rosses
We foot it all the night,

Weaving olden dances,
Mingling hands and mingling glances
Till the moon has taken flight;
20 To and fro we leap
And chase the frothy bubbles,
While the world is full of troubles
And is anxious in its sleep.
Come away, O human child!
25 *To the waters and the wild*
With a faery, hand in hand,
For the world's more full of weeping
than you can understand.

Where the wandering water gushes
From the hills above Glen-Car,
30 In pools among the rushes
That scarce could bathe a star,
We seek for slumbering trout

And whispering in their ears
Give them unquiet dreams;
35 Leaning softly out
From ferns that drop their tears
Over the young streams.
Come away, O human child!
To the waters and the wild
40 *With a faery, hand in hand,*
For the world's more full of weeping
than you can understand.

Away with us he's going,
The solemn-eyed:
He'll hear no more the lowing
45 Of the calves on the warm hillside
Or the kettle on the hob
Sing peace into his breast,
Or see the brown mice bob
Round and round the oatmeal-chest.
50 *For he comes, the human child,*
To the waters and the wild
With a faery, hand in hand,
From a world more full of weeping
than he can understand.

---

1. In the second stanza of "The Erl-King," how does the boy react to the sight of the Erl-King?

A The boy is curious about him.

B The boy fears him.

C The boy doubts what he sees.

D The boy laughs at the sight.

2. In the third and fifth stanzas, how does the Erl-King try to persuade the boy to go away with him?

F The king promises him much joy, affection, and toys.

G The king threatens to harm the boy's father.

H The king promises to bring along the boy's mother.

J The king has his daughter speak lovingly to the boy.

3. How does the Erl-King's tone change in lines 25–26?

A The king begins to plead with the boy.

B The king ignores the boy and instead speaks to the father.

C The king promises the child immortality.

D The king threatens to force the boy to come with him.

4. The Erl-King most likely symbolizes, or stands for —

F death

G rebellion

H hope

J desperation

5. Which of the following statements best expresses the theme of "The Erl-King"?

  A Death comes to all and should be welcomed with open arms.

  B All humans are vulnerable to death's grasp, even the most innocent.

  C Love and devotion are the best defenses against death.

  D Death is a release from the troubles of life.

6. The speaker in "The Stolen Child" is —

  F a human child

  G an impartial observer

  H a fairy spirit

  J a dairy farmer

7. In "The Stolen Child," what motivation is offered to the child to "come away"?

  A To escape the sorrows of the human world

  B To become a ruler in the fairy kingdom

  C To seek riches in the fairy realm

  D To win the love of a fairy princess

8. Which word would *not* be used to describe the fairies and their world in "The Stolen Child"?

  F Mischievous

  G Carefree

  H Nocturnal

  J Anxious

9. The endings of "The Erl-King" and "The Stolen Child" are similar in that —

  A the child willingly departs with the supernatural figure

  B the child manages to remain in the human world

  C the fate of the child is unclear

  D the child leaves the human world

10. The imagery in both poems is associated with —

  F winter

  G sunlight

  H nature

  J fatherhood

Essay Question

Goethe and Yeats use the folk myth of the stolen child to explore what lies beyond our human world and what may become of us after death. In a brief essay, compare and contrast the supernatural figures in the two poems and the ways they interact with the child they seek to carry away to their world. Pay particular attention to the imagery and descriptive details used to describe the human world and the world of the supernatural. Which realm appears more attractive? Are the attractions real or illusory? Compare and contrast also the mood, or atmosphere, of the two poems, and discuss whether the endings seem happy, tragic, or something less clear and definitive.

Collection 6: Skills Review

Vocabulary Skills

Synonyms

DIRECTIONS: In the sentences below, choose the word or group of words whose meaning is most similar to the meaning of the underlined word.

1. To <u>eschew</u> a concept is to —
   A   question it
   B   avoid it
   C   implement it
   D   ridicule it

2. Someone who is <u>pompous</u> is —
   F   arrogant
   G   cheerful
   H   incompetent
   J   high ranking

3. <u>Incredulity</u> is the same as —
   A   simplicity
   B   vigilance
   C   insincerity
   D   doubt

4. A <u>turbulent</u> time could be described as —
   F   chaotic
   G   prosperous
   H   religious
   J   joyful

5. <u>Submissiveness</u> is the same as —
   A   restlessness
   B   bitterness
   C   obedience
   D   indifference

6. <u>Melancholy</u> is the same as —
   F   confusion
   G   sadness
   H   fearfulness
   J   perseverance

7. If you <u>endure</u> something you —
   A   desert it
   B   understand it
   C   fear it
   D   put up with it

8. If something is <u>reprehensible</u>, it is —
   F   deserving of blame
   G   fascinating
   H   worthy of admiration
   J   ugly

9. Someone who acts <u>suavely</u> acts —
   A   cautiously
   B   crudely
   C   smoothly
   D   violently

10. If you are <u>petrified</u>, you are —
    F   diligent
    G   protected
    H   ignorant
    J   afraid

SKILLS FOCUS

Vocabulary Skills
Understand and identify synonyms.

Collection 6: Skills Review

Writing Skills

Test Practice DIRECTIONS: Read the following paragraph from a draft of a student's analysis of a short story. Then, answer the questions that follow.

(1) As its title suggests, Anton Chekhov's short story "A Problem" is built around a conflict. (2) The characters have a problem, and much of the plot involves a debate over what to do about it. (3) The problem is that a wayward young nephew, Sasha, has forged an IOU and will be arrested if the family does not pay his debt. (4) Sasha's uncle the Colonel maintains that civic honor bars the family from shielding the criminal. (5) Another uncle fears a public scandal and wants to hush up the incident to protect the family from embarrassing publicity. (6) The women of the household pretend to know nothing about what is going on and so do not join the discussion. (7) The "maternal uncle, kind-hearted Ivan Markovitch" wants Sasha to be forgiven and protected from the consequences of his youthful follies. (8) The culprit himself has little control over his fate and must wait for the decision of his elders.

1. What function does the first sentence in this literary analysis serve?
    A   It summarizes the key points.
    B   It provides evidence for the thesis.
    C   It states what the paragraph will be about.
    D   It elaborates on the evidence.

2. Which reference from the text of the story could be added to support the ideas in sentence 4?
    F   The Colonel proclaims, "Whatever may be the motives for screening a scoundrel . . . it is contrary to law and unworthy of a gentleman. It's not saving the family honor; it's civic cowardice!"
    G   He says, "If Siberia, then let it be Siberia. . . ."
    H   "To outsiders who have no personal interest in the matter such questions seem simple; for those who are so unfortunate as to have to decide . . . they are extremely difficult."
    J   He asks, "Shall we be false to civic duty . . . if instead of punishing an erring boy we hold out to him a helping hand?"

3. Which sentence could be deleted to improve the paragraph's organization?
    A   Sentence 3
    B   Sentence 4
    C   Sentence 6
    D   Sentence 7

4. What is missing from this paragraph that will have to be covered in subsequent paragraphs to complete the analysis?
    F   Further exploration of Chekhov's purpose for writing
    G   Elaboration on the characterization of the uncles
    H   Views of other family members on Sasha's fate
    J   Identification and evaluation of the resolution of the conflict

North Carolina Competency Goal
2.01; 4.03; 6.01

SKILLS FOCUS

Writing Skills
Analyze a short story.

Modern and Contemporary World Literature

1900–Present

A World Without Borders

Thus I have understood and felt that world literature is no longer an abstract anthology, nor a generalization invented by literary historians; it is rather a certain common body and a common spirit, a living heartfelt unity reflecting the growing unity of mankind.

—Aleksandr Solzhenitsyn
from Nobel Prize
Acceptance Speech, 1970

(Opposite) *La Grande Famille* (1947)
by René Magritte.

Private Collection.

go.hrw.com

INTERNET

Collection Resources
Keyword:
LE5 WL-7

Modern and Contemporary

1900

1904 Chilean poet Pablo Neruda is born; Russian writer Anton Chekhov dies

1909 Swedish writer Selma Lagerlöf is first woman awarded Nobel Prize in literature

1910

1914 *Dubliners,* by James Joyce, is published

1915 Franz Kafka's *The Metamorphosis* is published

1919 Primo Levi is born in Italy

1922 *The Waste Land,* by T. S. Eliot, is published

1924 E. M. Forster's *A Passage to India* is published

Isak Dinesen on her farm in Kenya, 1930.
The Granger Collection, New York.

1925

1926 Poet Rainer Maria Rilke dies

1928 Elie Wiesel is born in Romania; Gabriel García Márquez is born in Colombia

1933 *Blood Wedding,* a play by Federico García Lorca, is produced; Octavio Paz publishes *Forest Moon,* his first volume of poetry

1935

1935 R. K. Narayan's debut novel, *Swami and Friends,* is published

1937 *Out of Africa,* by Isak Dinesen, is published

1942 Albert Camus publishes "The Myth of Sisyphus"

1945 Poet Gabriela Mistral of Chile is awarded the Nobel Prize in literature

1949 Jamaica Kincaid, author of *Annie John,* is born in Antigua

MODERN AND CONTEMPORARY POLITICAL AND

1900

1900 Boxer Rebellion ignites revolutionary spark in China

1902 Great Britain defeats the Boers of South Africa in the Boer War

1905 The Treaty of Portsmouth brings an end to the Russo-Japanese War

1906 The All-India Muslim League is formed

1910

1910 South Africa gains independence from Great Britain

1912 Chinese Nationalists declare China a republic

1914 Austrian Archduke Francis Ferdinand is assassinated; World War I begins

1918 World War I ends

1920 Mohandas Gandhi becomes leader of the Indian National Congress

1925

1928 Chiang Kai-shek, leader of the National-ists, helps unite China under one government; in England the right to vote is given to all women over age twenty-one

1929 The New York Stock Exchange crashes, causing economic depression around the world

1933 In Germany, Adolf Hitler is appointed chancellor

1935

1936–1939 The Spanish Civil War

1939 World War II begins when Germany invades Poland

1941 Japan attacks U.S. bases at Pearl Harbor

1945 Germany surren-ders; the United States drops atomic bombs on Hiroshima and Nagasaki in Japan; World War II ends

1947 India is partitioned

World Literature 1900–Present

1950

1953 Winston Churchill is awarded the Nobel Prize in literature

1956–1957 Naguib Mahfouz publishes *The Cairo Trilogy—Palace Walk, Palace of Desire,* and *Sugar Street*

1958 *Things Fall Apart,* by Nigerian writer Chinua Achebe, is published; Elie Wiesel publishes *Night*

1960

1962 Aleksandr Solzhenitsyn's novel *One Day in the Life of Ivan Denisovich* is published

1963 Anita Desai publishes *Cry, the Peacock,* her first novel

1967 Gabriel García Márquez publishes *One Hundred Years of Solitude*

1972 Japanese author Yasunari Kawabata dies

1975

1980 Polish writer Czeslaw Milosz is awarded the Nobel Prize in literature

1984 Argentine writer Julio Cortázar dies

Nadine Gordimer at the Nobel Prize ceremony, December 10, 1991, Stockholm, Sweden.

1985–on

1986 Argentine writer Jorge Luis Borges dies

1988 Egyptian writer Naguib Mahfouz is awarded the Nobel Prize in literature

1991 Nadine Gordimer of South Africa is awarded the Nobel Prize in literature

2001 Trinidadian writer V. S. Naipaul is awarded the Nobel Prize in literature

SOCIAL EVENTS

1950

1950 India puts its constitution into effect

1950–1953 The Korean War

1950s–1960s Most colonies in Africa gain independence from Europe

1958 China launches the Great Leap Forward

1960

1961 The Berlin Wall is built

1967 The Six-Day War (also called the June War) takes place in the Middle East

1969 American astronauts are the first to walk on the moon

1975

1975 The Vietnam War ends; Portugal is the last European country to give up its African colonies

1979 Margaret Thatcher becomes first female prime minister of the United Kingdom; United States and China establish diplomatic relations; in Rhodesia (now Zimbabwe), black Africans gain control of the government from the white minority

1985–on

1989 Berlin Wall is dismantled; China's military kills and wounds thousands of people protesting against the Chinese government

1994 In South Africa, Nelson Mandela is elected president

1997 Britain returns Hong Kong to China

2001 Terrorists hijack planes and destroy the twin towers of the World Trade Center, in New York City, and part of the Pentagon in Washington, D.C.

Edwin E. "Buzz" Aldrin, Jr., on the moon. July 20, 1969.

Cultural and Historical

Modernism and Postmodernism

Modernism, a literary movement that flourished during the first half of the twentieth century, arose from a sense that the art forms of the past could not adequately capture human experience and the reality of the modern world. Influenced by breakthroughs in psychology and innovations in other art forms, modernism emphasizes subjective perceptions and uses new and experimental techniques to capture the sense of fragmentation and the uncertainty associated with modern life. The term *modernism* encompasses a number of separate movements, including surrealism, absurdism, expressionism, and futurism.

Postmodernism, which appeared after World War II, may be viewed as an extension of modernism, continuing its preoccupation with alienation, despair, and concepts of personal identity. Postmodernism takes the modernist experiment with fragmentation, discontinuity, and ambiguity to new levels, seeing opportunities for synthesis and "reinvention" in everything that has come before. In postmodernism the art forms of all times and cultures become the raw material for new and unexpected artistic expressions— sometimes playful and sometimes shocking.

Edgar Warpol: The Man with Suitcases (1967–1968) by Tadeusz Kantor.

Muzeum Sztuki w Lodzi, Lodz.

Globalization

Globalization refers to the process of increasing interdependence of businesses, technologies, services, and labor throughout the world in the last quarter century. Advances in telecommunication and the rise of the Internet have led to an increase in travel and communication among economies that were formerly completely separated. As the trend toward globalization

Milestones 1900–Present

continues in the twenty-first century, it is transforming social, political, and economic activities and leading to worldwide systems of interconnection. Boundaries between local matters and global developments have become more fluid, putting many nations in greater contact than ever before.

The Information Age

The term *information age* generally refers to the period beginning in the late twentieth century when publications and computer networks made information easily accessible and created an "information revolution." We are bombarded constantly with electronically processed information—on TV, on the Internet, on electronic billboards, and in magazines and newspapers. New techniques of encoding and distributing digital information are speeding up the spread of information throughout society. However, there is a technology gap known as the "digital divide" in telecommunication and information: Many people throughout the world still lack information resources and ready access to telephones, computers, and the Internet.

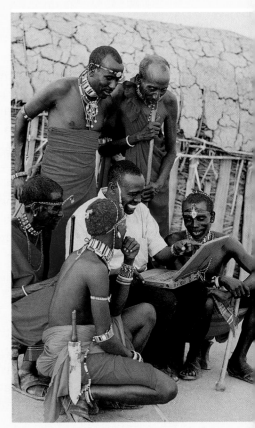

Masai family looking at laptop computer.

Modern and Contemporary World Literature
1900–Present

Think About ...

In an age of stunning technological advances, widespread warfare, and global communication, humans have gained an increased awareness of the impact they have on their world. Modern and contemporary writers have found a multitude of ways to address the complex issues that define our rapidly changing age.

As you read about the historical and philosophical contexts of modern and contemporary world literature, look for answers to the following questions:

- What are the most prominent movements associated with modern and contemporary world literature?

- How does world literature since 1900 reflect a preoccupation with self-identity, the fragmentation of individual experience, and the individual's sense of alienation?

- Name several major writers who have emerged in the past century in Latin American, African, Middle Eastern, European, and Asian literature.

North Carolina Competency Goal
1.02; 1.03; 4.02; 4.05; 5.01; 5.03

SKILLS FOCUS

Collection introduction (pages 844–855) covers
Literary Skills
Evaluate the philosophical, political, and social influences of the historical period.

World literature since 1900 has spanned many forms: poetry, fiction, drama, memoir, journalism, and a number of genres that resist classification. World writers continue to raise new and compelling questions as they present their responses to such external issues as war, racial strife, human rights, political freedom, poverty, and individual expression. In our time, world literature continues to reflect a mosaic of experiences—both universal and deeply personal.

World War I: The Great War

A defining event of the modern period was **World War I** (1914–1918). The Great War, as it was called—the war that was to end all wars—resulted in widespread disillusion and disaffection that changed the way many people—especially artists—viewed the world. A major cause of the First World War was intense competition among the European powers for overseas colonies and markets. Germany, Turkey, and Bulgaria joined Austria-Hungary to fight the

The City (1919) by Fernand Léger.

Philadelphia Museum of Art, Philadelphia, Pennsylvania A. E. Gallatin Collection, 1952.

Allies, who included Great Britain, France, Russia, Italy, and the United States. The conflict was a brutal exercise in trench warfare, made even more devastating by the latest advances in military technology—such as poison gas and machine guns. For many, shocked by the extent of the carnage and the loss of millions of lives, the war marked the end of the optimistic nineteenth-century belief that human history was a record of slow but certain progress.

The peace that followed World War I was short-lived. In 1929, an economic downturn known as the **Great Depression** devastated economies throughout the world. The aftermath of war and the dire economic circumstances led to instability, rebellion, and violence in

> *Nonviolence is the first article of my faith. It is also the last article of my creed.*
>
> —Speech,
> March 23, 1922,
> Mohandas K. Gandhi

German soldier trapped in a trench in Stalingrad as the Soviet army advances (1943).

some parts of the world. The **Russian Revolution** (1917), for example, ended the monarchy and established Communist rule. In the Far East, Japan invaded China and other neighboring countries. In Europe, fascist dictators such as Hitler in Germany, Mussolini in Italy, and Franco in Spain rose to power, planting the seeds for further destruction in World War II.

World War II

World War II began in 1939, when Nazi Germany invaded Poland. The main opponents in the war were the **Axis powers**—Germany, Italy, and Japan—and the **Allies:** Great Britain, France, the Soviet Union, China, the United States, and others.

In May 1945, Germany surrendered to the Allies. After the American president Harry Truman ordered the atomic bombings of two Japanese cities, Hiroshima and Nagasaki, in August, the war finally ended. The world now became aware of the complete devastation humanity could wreak. In Hiroshima and Nagasaki, over 300,000 people had been burned or irradiated to death by the nuclear bombs. The Nazi plan to exterminate all European Jews and others they considered "undesirable" was also revealed in all its horror. In the death camps of Auschwitz and Treblinka in German-occupied Poland, and camps elsewhere, the Nazis systematically killed over twelve million people. The death toll of World War II included more than twelve million soldiers and twenty million civilians.

Nagasaki (August 10, 1945) by Yosuke Yamahata.
©Shogo Yamahata.

The Cold War: The Beginning of the Nuclear Age

The end of World War II marked the beginning of the nuclear age. A **Cold War** developed between the United States and the Soviet Union, the world's "superpowers." Until the period of glasnost ("openness" in Russian) in the mid-1980s, the United States and the Soviet Union were involved in a stupendous arms race. At the height of the Cold War, both sides had stockpiled enough nuclear weapons to kill every man, woman, and child on the planet twelve times.

The Emergence of Modern States

Perhaps more significant in the long run than the Cold War was the decline of the Western imperial powers and the independence of their former colonies. At the beginning of the twentieth century, the colonies of the European empires spanned the globe. But Europe's long period of exploration, conquest, and colonization was coming to an end. By the middle of the century, colonial empires were being dismantled as many European countries that began the century as world powers found their once seemingly limitless resources dwindling. This decline of European imperialism resulted in the emergence of dozens of newly independent states in Africa and Asia, as well as the political redefinition of older nations there and in Europe and Latin America. These nations and others began to assert their own identities and reclaim their former territories. Literary and cultural critics often refer to this time as the **postcolonial** period.

Former colonies in Asia, Africa, and elsewhere found that self-determination is seldom achieved without conflict. War has broken out several times in the Middle East over the establishment of the Jewish state of Israel in former British Palestine. Korea and Vietnam, once freed from foreign rule, were torn apart by internal factions struggling to impose their own rule.

Science, Technology, and the Information Age

Since 1900, amazing developments in science and technology have changed almost every aspect of human life. From televisions, automobiles, airplanes, and computers to space technology, the Internet, and medical advances, the world has experienced a historically unprecedented

Mission commander Robert L. Gibson (in red) clasps the hand of Vladimir N. Dezhurov, the *Mir-18* commander, after the U.S. shuttle *Atlantis* docks with Russia's space station. June 29, 1995.

acceleration in the quality and pace of life. But technological progress has also led to damaging effects: the massacres in the trenches of World War I, the horrors of the Holocaust in World War II, the destructive power of the atom bomb, environmental pollution, and the ongoing threat posed by weapons of mass destruction, such as nuclear and biochemical weapons.

Advances in science and technology have propelled us into the **information age,** a term that generally refers to the period beginning in the last quarter of the twentieth century, when computers revolutionized everyday life by making information quickly accessible to countless millions, bringing the global community closer together than ever before. The trend toward **globalization** binds nations together in new political, economic, and social networks.

Technological advances have not fulfilled their early promise of wiping out poverty and disease from the world: The less-industrialized nations in the developing world still suffer from the effects of poverty, such as malnutrition and homelessness, and diseases that have been controlled or eradicated in industrialized nations still claim countless lives.

Artistic Responses to the Modern World

The world changed radically after World War I. Traditional values came under attack, and art forms of the past were seen as inadequate to express the experiences and the reality of the modern world. Writers, painters, filmmakers, musicians, dancers, and other creative artists felt free to experiment boldly with new themes and styles.

A determination to break new ground was apparent in the fine arts. Pablo Picasso and Georges Braque, who were influenced by African sculpture and by geometrical concepts, developed a style called

disCONNEXION (2002–2003) by Danwen Xing. C-Print, from series (D_01).

Courtesy of Danwen Xing, SCALO, and Meredith Palmer Gallery, Ltd., New York, NY.

Guernica (1937) by Pablo Picasso.

Museo Nacional Centro de Arte Reina Sofia, Madrid.

cubism, which reduced objects and figures to their basic geometric forms. Other art movements such as expressionism, surrealism, dadaism, and futurism changed art for generations. Artists became less interested in objective representation and more concerned with subjective, emotional reactions to their subjects. In 1937, Picasso painted *Guernica* (see page 848), a large mural created in reaction to the brutal German bombing of the village of Guernica during the Spanish Civil War. Shortly after he completed the mural, the German Gestapo (secret police) began harassing Picasso at his studio in Nazi-occupied Paris. One officer, noticing a photograph of *Guernica* lying on a table, asked, "Did you do that?" "No," Picasso replied, "you did."

Modernism in Literature

A broad movement called **modernism** flourished between 1890 and 1940. Modernist literature, heavily influenced by the psychoanalytic theories of Sigmund Freud (1856–1939) and other pioneers of modern psychology, reflects the fragmentation and uncertainty that writers perceived all around them. Emphasizing psychological exploration over direct social commentary, modernism plays with juxtapositions, symbols, and allusions and exploits the multiple meanings of language. The tone and point of view of much modernist literature is deeply ironic. Some modernists, like James Joyce, turned to experimental techniques such as **stream of consciousness**— a style that uses interior monologue to mimic the free associations of thought. Other writers, such as Franz Kafka (see page 868), use absurd situations and nightmarish settings to express anomie: the sense of disconnectedness and alienation felt by the individual in modern society.

Poets such as T. S. Eliot and Rainer Maria Rilke (see page 856) broke with traditional forms to express their own personal visions.

> *Perfection of means and confusion of goals seem, in my opinion, to characterize our age.*
> —Albert Einstein,
> *Out of My Later Years*

The Anxiety of Waiting by Giorgio de Chirico (1888–1978).
Fondazione Magnani Rocca, Corte di Mamiano, Italy.

In *The Waste Land* (1922), Eliot laments the spiritual desolation of a modern, industrialized city. Many other modernist poets abandoned traditional forms, using free verse and experimenting with punctuation and with the physical appearance of the poem on the page.

Responses to War

In the period of disenchantment following the two world wars, literature increasingly focused on themes of alienation, uncertainty, and despair. Erich Maria Remarque's *All Quiet on the Western Front* (1929) and Ernest Hemingway's *A Farewell to Arms* (1929) are two novels, written from opposite sides of the battle line, that reveal the tragedy of World War I. Elie Wiesel wrote *Night* (see page 913), a memoir of his imprisonment in Auschwitz, the most infamous Nazi death camp, during World War II. In *Survival in Auschwitz* (1947), Primo Levi also tells of his experiences in Auschwitz (see page 905).

After World War II, some writers began searching for a philosophy that would allow them to understand and accept the apparent senselessness of existence. The French intellectual and writer Jean-Paul Sartre was central in bringing this new view of the world—existentialism—into the arts. **Existentialism** takes its name from the belief that a person's physical existence precedes his or her "essence," or meaning. There are no preexisting meanings, values, or guidelines for human beings; each person must create his or her own meaning, or essence, in life by accepting the responsibility for informed choice and moral commitment. In "The Myth of Sisyphus" (see page 899), Albert Camus—an existentialist who refused to be labeled as such—presents

Indestructible Object
(or *Object to Be Destroyed*)
(1964) by Man Ray.
Replica of 1923 original.

The Museum of Modern Art, New York.

Infantry, Near Nijmegen, Holland
by Captain David Alex Colville.

Beaverbrook Collection of War Art
© Canadian War Museum (CWM)
(An1971026 1-2079).

Student performance of Samuel Beckett's *The Endgame* at the Playhouse Theatre on the campus of the University of California, c. 1986.

an absurd situation that nevertheless illustrates his view: No matter how futile life might seem, we each have the choice to make something meaningful out of it.

Theater of the absurd was drama's response to the fragmented modern world. To reflect a world in which human existence is seemingly meaningless and human behavior is irrational and incoherent, playwrights such as Eugène Ionesco, Samuel Beckett, and Harold Pinter created dramas with characters who speak only in banalities and with plots that go nowhere.

Postmodernism: Dissolving Boundaries

In the post–World War II world, modernism found its continuation and extension in **postmodernism.** Postmodernism provides an ironic commentary on the literature of the past. It questions traditional forms, character devices, settings, and plot structures. It dissolves the boundaries between various art forms, between high and low culture, and between genres. Postmodernist writers are self-aware and often ironic in their approach, playing with narrative structure, point of view—even language itself—in an effort to upset preconceived notions of reality versus illusion and objectivity versus subjectivity. Intellectual playfulness is a hallmark of postmodernism, which often challenges readers to create their own meaning.

White Walls (2002) by Robin Rhode. 28 c-prints, 9 x 11¾ inches (22.86 x 29.85 cm) each.

Courtesy of the artist and Perry Rubenstein Gallery, New York.

Cultural Identity and Literature

The theme of cultural identity is prevalent among postcolonial writers, especially those from less-industrialized nations. These writers have seen their local cultures uprooted by colonialism or foreign influences, and they have had to ask themselves whether their role as artists is to celebrate their native traditions, imitate foreign models, or create entirely new modes of expression.

The Argentine writer Jorge Luis Borges (see page 933), one of the central figures in the Latin American literary "Boom" that followed World War II, wrote fiction that blends fantastic events with philosophical inquiry. Like other postmodernists, Borges ignores the traditional elements of fiction. The Chilean poet Pablo Neruda (see page 937) was greatly influenced by the mod-

Dialectics of the Revolution (formerly: *The Destruction of the Old Order*) by José Clemente Orozco (1883–1949).

Escuela Nacional Preparatoria San Ildefonso, Mexico City, D.F., Mexico.
© Clemente Orozco Valladares

A CLOSER LOOK: CULTURAL INFLUENCES

The Gold Standard: The Nobel Prize in Literature

INFORMATIONAL TEXT

One writer refused it. One government forced a writer to decline it. Some writers never write again after they receive it. For many writers it is the culmination of a lifetime dream. What is it? It is the Nobel Prize in literature, the "gold standard" in literary prizes.

Nobel Prizes are awarded yearly by the Swedish Academy—in chemistry, physics, medicine, economics, literature, and peace. The substantial monetary awards that go with the prizes were provided by Swedish industrialist Alfred Nobel (1833–1896) in his will. Nobel stipulated that the prizes were to go to people whose work "conferred the greatest benefit on mankind"; ironically, Nobel made his fortune manufacturing dynamite.

Controversy has always surrounded the Nobel Prize. In 1901, when the French poet Sully Prudhomme got the prize instead of the towering Russian writer Leo Tolstoy, forty-two writers and artists protested the choice. One writer, however, has refused the award: The French philosopher Jean-Paul Sartre would not accept the 1964 prize, saying that any writer who wished to remain free should not be transformed by an institution. On the other hand, one writer was prevented from receiving the prize: The Russian novelist and poet Boris Pasternak was cruelly forced to refuse the 1958 prize by the Soviet government.

For years the literature prize was given almost exclusively to Europeans, but eventually

ernist movement, but his epic work, *Alturas de Macchu-Picchu* (*Heights of Macchu-Picchu*), reconciles the poet with his country's ancient Indian heritage.

The 1960s saw the development of **magic realism,** a literary style which seamlessly blends elements of the real world with the world of fantasy. Magic realists such as Colombia's Gabriel García Márquez (see page 956) were influenced by **surrealism,** which encouraged the free association of ideas as a means of exploring the unconscious mind. In the work of Julio Cortázar (see page 946), nightmarish fantasies occur in the midst of everyday reality.

In the early 1930s in Paris, a literary and cultural movement known as **negritude** originated among African students from the colonies. Its goal was to instill pride in the African heritage and culture, rather than encourage assimilation. Some African writers embraced negritude as a necessary response to years of imperialism, while others, like Chinua Achebe (see page 995) and Wole Soyinka (see page 1002), felt that negritude tended to idealize Africa's pre-colonial past. They felt that African literature must instead examine that past more critically.

African writers have also debated the question of which language to write in: that of the colonizer—in many cases, the only common language for the descendants of various tribes—or their native tongues.

writers throughout the world began to receive the awards. The first American winner was Sinclair Lewis, in 1930; the first Latin American winner was Gabriela Mistral, in 1945. It was not until 1968 that an Asian won the award (Japan's Yasunari Kawabata), and the first African winner, Wole Soyinka, was named in 1986.

A superstition surrounds the prize. The American writer John Steinbeck, the 1962 winner, said that he was always afraid of the award because people never seemed to write anymore after they received it. "I wouldn't have accepted it," he said, "if I hadn't thought I could beat the rap." Six years later, Steinbeck died, having published nothing more since receiving the prize.

Gao Xingjian receiving his Nobel Prize. Stockholm, December 10, 2000.

A great writer is, so to speak, a second government in his country. And for that reason no regime has ever loved great writers, only minor ones.

—Aleksandr Solzhenitsyn,
The First Circle

Instead of using experimental techniques and unconventional narrative strategies, some contemporary writers still present pictures of their societies realistically. The works of R. K. Narayan (see page 1053), Yasunari Kawabata (see page 1046), and Zhang Jie (see page 1061) explore interpersonal relationships and social issues in realistic settings.

The Rise of the Women's Movement

Since 1900, women writers have struggled to establish a cultural identity, for until the early twentieth century, most women had virtually no political voice and little representation in literature. In 1948, Simone de Beauvoir's groundbreaking work *The Second Sex* appeared in France. De Beauvoir calls for equal opportunity for women. Another landmark work, *The Feminine Mystique* (1963), by the American writer Betty Friedan, helped to radicalize the atmosphere of the 1960s. The international women's movement has seen the emergence of many gifted women writers who have helped define its politics and culture.

World Literature: Unity and Diversity

The most striking feature of contemporary world literature is its **pluralism**—the existence of many distinctive and diverse groups in

(Top) Nelson Mandela being sworn in as the first democratically elected president of South Africa. May 10, 1994; (bottom right) Wangari Maathai of Kenya, winner of the 2004 Nobel Peace Prize, watering a tree she has just planted. October 11, 2004; (bottom left) Shirin Ebadi of Iran receiving her Nobel Peace Prize. Oslo, December 10, 2003.

various geographical areas. Pluralism is reflected in multiple literary styles, but certain trends can be identified in this huge body of literature: the importance of the individual; the artist's subjective perceptions; and the interaction of the individual with the larger culture. The past is reexamined, and painful collisions between cultures and between traditional and modern beliefs are portrayed unflinchingly.

At the same time, world literature reflects a "world without borders." Like technology, business, economics, popular culture, and other aspects of contemporary life, literature is becoming increasingly globalized. More works are being translated into other languages more quickly than ever before, and the emergence of such technologies as the Internet has helped bring writers and readers all over the world together. Asian writers incorporate elements of Latin American magic realism into their works, while Middle Eastern poets find inspiration in the works of long-dead European writers.

In literature, as in history, many different stories are proceeding at once. The sweeping changes of the twentieth century do not fit easily into the straightforward literary structure of the past. Very few people could have foreseen the reunification of East and West Germany in 1989, the dissolution of the Soviet Union and the end of the Cold War, the "ethnic cleansing" that erupted during the Yugoslav wars in the 1990s, the worldwide devastation of the AIDS (acquired immune deficiency syndrome) pandemic, or the terrorist attacks on American soil on September 11, 2001. We know only that challenges to our understanding and imagination remain. "The only certain thing about the future," the historian Eric Hobsbawm writes in *The Age of Empire,* "is that it will surprise even those who have seen furthest into it."

R E V I E W

Talk About ...

Turn back to the Think About questions at the beginning of this introduction (page 844). Write down your responses, and get together with a classmate to compare and discuss your views.

Reading Check

1. What are some of the advantages of technological progress since 1900? What are some negative side effects?

2. How did writers respond to the two world wars?

3. How did modernism affect developments in the arts and literature?

4. Briefly describe the philosophy of existentialism.

5. What does the term *postcolonial* refer to? How does it apply to literature?

Rainer Maria Rilke

(1875–1926)

Austria/Czech Republic

The German-language poet Rainer Maria Rilke (rī′nər mä·rē′ä ril′kə) believed that the monotonous routines of everyday life caused people to develop a "husk" around themselves—a barrier that prevented them from being receptive to new ideas. To prevent his own "husk" from forming, Rilke spent his life on the road—wandering from country to country, stopping briefly wherever admirers provided food and shelter.

Rilke was born to a German-speaking family in Prague, now the capital of the Czech Republic, when the area was still part of the Austro-Hungarian Empire. During childhood he was torn between his mother, who dressed him as a girl, and his father, who sent him to military academies. In 1892, Rilke's wealthy uncle came to the rescue, offering to pay for his nephew's studies in philosophy, art, and German literature. Rilke liked these subjects and continued to study them in Munich, Germany. In 1901, Rilke married the German sculptor Clara Westhoff. He soon discovered that married life did not suit him, and he separated from his wife in order to travel and write.

One of the greatest influences on Rilke and his work was the French sculptor Auguste Rodin (rô·dan′), with whom Rilke worked. Rodin taught the young poet that art was hard work, not merely an outpouring of emotion.

After leaving Rodin, Rilke revised much of his earlier verse and composed some of his finest poetry. Soon after this burst of creativity, however, Rilke entered a dry period. Seeking inspiration, he visited northern Africa and then went to live in the Italian city of Trieste. There he began a series of philosophical poems, the *Duino Elegies* (1923). The project was inter-

Portrait of Rainer Maria Rilke (1916) by Loulou Albert-Lazard.

Marbach, Schiller-Nationalmuseum.

rupted by World War I, in which he served briefly in the Austrian military. After the war Rilke settled in Switzerland, completed the *Duino Elegies,* and wrote his complex work *The Sonnets to Orpheus* (1923) (see page 859). Plagued by ill health since the war, Rilke died of a blood disease when he was only fifty-one. By this time his poems, with their meticulously chiseled images, had already established him as one of the most original poets of the twentieth century.

Black Cat
Sonnet 5 *from* The Sonnets to Orpheus I

Make the Connection

Quickwrite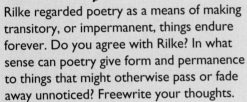

Rilke regarded poetry as a means of making transitory, or impermanent, things endure forever. Do you agree with Rilke? In what sense can poetry give form and permanence to things that might otherwise pass or fade away unnoticed? Freewrite your thoughts.

Literary Focus

Figures of Speech

A **figure of speech** (also called **figurative language**) describes one thing in terms of another, very different thing. If you say, "My feet are chunks of ice," you are using a figure of speech called a **metaphor,** which compares two unlike things directly, without using a specific word of comparison. Your feet are not literally chunks of ice, but the metaphor helps us understand that they are very cold. Often metaphors are implied and not stated directly at all: "I was standing on two chunks of ice." Another figure of speech, the **simile,** compares two unlike things by using a specific word of comparison, such as *like* or *as:* "My feet are *like* two chunks of ice."

Background

Rilke once confided to the sculptor Auguste Rodin that he was suffering from writer's block. Rodin advised him to go to the zoo and look at an animal until he could "see" it, adding that it might take as long as two or three weeks to accomplish this goal. Rilke took this strange advice to heart. He went to the zoo, concentrated on a panther, and then wrote the first of his *Dinggedichte* (diŋ′gə·diHt·ə), or "thing poems," of which "Black Cat" is an example.

The Sonnets to Orpheus, according to Rilke, "were no intended or expected work; they appeared, often *many* in one day (the first part of the book was written in about three days), completely unexpectedly. . . . I could do nothing but submit, purely and obediently, to the dictation of this inner impulse." Rilke dedicated these sonnets to the memory of an acquaintance's young daughter, Vera Knoop, a beautiful and spirited dancer and musician who contracted a glandular disease as a child that killed her when she was only in her late teens.

North Carolina Competency Goal
1.02; 1.03; 4.05; 5.01; 5.03; 6.01

INTERNET

More About Rainer Maria Rilke
Keyword: LE5 WL-7

Literary Skills
Understand figures of speech.

Figures of speech describe one thing in terms of something else. Two common figures of speech are the metaphor and the similie. A **metaphor** makes a comparison without the use of a specific word of comparison. A **simile** includes a word of comparison, such as *like* or *as.*

For more on Figures of Speech, see the Handbook of Literary and Historical Terms.

What Rilke most admired about Rodin's sculptures was their
ability to capture not only the outward appearance of a person, an
animal, or an object, but also the inner vitality and spirit of the
subject. Each of Rilke's "thing poems," like Rodin's sculptures, seeks
to convey both external reality and the "inward nature of things."

Black Cat

Rainer Maria Rilke

translated by Stephen Mitchell

A ghost, though invisible, still is like a place
your sight can knock on, echoing; but here
within this thick black pelt, your strongest gaze
will be absorbed and utterly disappear:

5   just as a raving madman, when nothing else
can ease him, charges into his dark night
howling, pounds on the padded wall, and feels
the rage being taken in and pacified.

She seems to hide all looks that have ever fallen
10   into her, so that, like an audience,
she can look them over, menacing and sullen,
and curl to sleep with them. But all at once

as if awakened, she turns her face to yours;
and with a shock, you see yourself, tiny,
15   inside the golden amber of her eyeballs
suspended, like a prehistoric fly.°

15–16. amber . . . prehistoric fly: Flies and other small creatures from millions of years ago are sometimes found perfectly preserved in amber, or fossilized tree sap. The color amber takes its name from the translucent yellow or brownish yellow color of this sap.

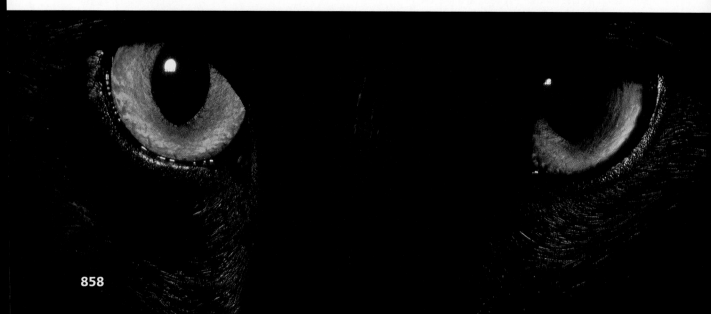

In Greek mythology, Orpheus is the greatest musician in the world, able to charm animals, trees, and even rivers. When his beloved wife, Eurydice, dies, Orpheus puts his lyre on his back and travels down to the Underworld, intent on using his music to win her release. Hades, the ruler of the Underworld, is so deeply affected by Orpheus's music that he agrees to release Eurydice from death, on one condition: that Orpheus walk ahead and not look back at her as they return from the Underworld. But Orpheus can't help himself. Filled with anxiety and doubt, he looks back—and Eurydice instantly vanishes.

There are many stories about what happens to Orpheus later. According to one story, he wanders the world desolate and is torn to pieces by a band of frenzied women called the Maenads. It is said that his head is buried on the island of Lesbos, home of the great Greek poet Sappho.

Sonnet 5

from The Sonnets to Orpheus I

Rainer Maria Rilke
translated by Stephen Mitchell

Orpheus (c. 1903–1910)
by Odilon Redon.
The Cleveland Museum of Art (1926.25).

Erect no gravestone to his memory; just
let the rose blossom each year for his sake.
For it *is* Orpheus. Wherever he has passed
through this or that. We do not need to look

5   for other names. When there is poetry,
it is Orpheus singing. He lightly comes and goes.
Isn't it enough if sometimes he can stay
with us a few days longer than a rose?

Though he himself is afraid to disappear,
10   he *has* to vanish: don't you understand?
The moment his word steps out beyond our life here,

he moves where you will never find his trace.
The lyre's strings do not constrict his hands.
And it is in overstepping that he obeys.

Early in the twentieth century an aspiring young poet named Franz Xaver Kappus wrote to Rilke for advice. The two corresponded for several years. After Rilke died, Kappus published Rilke's letters in Letters to a Young Poet *(1929). The following excerpt is from Rilke's first letter to Kappus.*

from Letters to a Young Poet

INFORMATIONAL TEXT

Rainer Maria Rilke

You ask whether your verses are any good. You ask me. You have asked others before this. You send them to magazines. You compare them with other poems, and you are upset when certain editors reject your work. Now (since you have said you want my advice) I beg you to stop doing that sort of thing. You are looking outside, and that is what you should most avoid right now. No one can advise or help you—no one. There is only one thing you should do. Go into yourself. Find out the reason that commands you to write; see whether it has spread its roots into the very depths of your heart; confess to yourself whether you would have to die if you were forbidden to write. This most of all: ask yourself in the most silent hour of your night: *must* I write? Dig into yourself for a deep answer. And if this answer rings out in assent, if you meet this solemn question with a strong, simple *"I must,"* then build your life in accordance with this necessity; your whole life, even into its humblest and most indifferent hour, must become a sign and witness to this impulse. Then come close to Nature. Then, as if no one had ever tried before, try to say what you see and feel and love and lose. Don't write love poems; avoid those forms that are too facile and ordinary: they are the hardest to work with, and it takes a great, fully ripened power to create something individual where good, even glorious, traditions exist in abundance. So rescue yourself from these general themes and write about what your everyday life offers you; describe your sorrows and desires, the thoughts that pass through your mind and your belief in some kind of beauty—describe all these with heartfelt, silent, humble sincerity and, when you express yourself, use the Things around you, the images from your dreams, and the objects that you remember. If your everyday life seems poor, don't blame *it;* blame yourself; admit to yourself that you are not enough of a poet to call forth its riches; because for the creator there is no poverty and no poor, indifferent place. And even if you found yourself in some prison, whose walls let in none of the world's sounds—wouldn't you still have your childhood, that jewel beyond all price, that treasure house of memories? Turn your attention to it. Try to raise up the sunken feelings of this enormous past; your personality will grow stronger, your solitude will expand and become a place where you can live in the twilight, where the noise of other people passes by, far in the distance.—And if out of this turning-within, out of this immersion in your own world, *poems* come, then you will not think of asking anyone whether they are good or not.

? According to Rilke's letter, what is the most important question a writer must ask himself or herself?

Response and Analysis

Thinking Critically

1. According to the first stanza of "Black Cat," why is it easier to see a ghost than the black cat?

2. There is an extended **simile** in the second stanza of "Black Cat." What is the poet comparing the raving madman pounding on the walls of his padded cell to? Identify two other similes in this poem, and explain what they reveal about the cat's inner nature.

3. In the last stanza of "Black Cat," the speaker invites us to see ourselves (and him) reflected in the cat's eyes as though we are a fly suspended in amber. What does this **simile** reveal about the inner nature of the cat? What might it reveal about the way the speaker views himself or humanity in general?

4. In Sonnet 5, which lines show that the speaker identifies Orpheus with poetry?

5. According to the first stanza in Sonnet 5, the speaker suggests that a rose would be a fitting memorial to Orpheus. A rose changes from a bud to a flower and then quickly dies, only to bloom again. How, then, is a rose a better memorial to Orpheus than something more permanent, like a gravestone?

6. What is Rilke suggesting about the role of the poet—or any artist—when he says that Orpheus is obedient only in "overstepping," or going beyond limits? What force or principle does Orpheus obey?

Extending and Evaluating

7. Both "Black Cat" and Sonnet 5 contain images of permanence and impermanence—of things that stay the same and things that change. Look back at your Quickwrite notes. Do you think that in these two poems, Rilke has demonstrated that poetry has the power to make transitory things endure? Explain.

WRITING

Writing a "Thing Poem"

Choose an animal you are familiar with or one you feel a strong connection to. Find a way to observe the animal closely—even if only through photographs or film. Then, like Rilke, write a "thing poem" in which you try to capture the essential spirit of the animal by describing its outward appearance. Use figurative language and powerful imagery to describe the animal and convey your sense of its inner nature.

Detail of poster advertising *Orpheus of the Lyre* (1959) by Jean Cocteau.

North Carolina Competency Goal
1.02; 1.03; 4.05; 5.03; 6.01

INTERNET

Projects and Activities
Keyword:
LE5 WL-7

SKILLS FOCUS

Literary Skills
Analyze figures of speech.

Writing Skills
Write a "thing poem."

Luigi Pirandello
(1867–1936)
Italy

The life of the Italian writer Luigi Pirandello was filled with dramatic reversals. These twists of fate played an important role in shaping his philosophical outlook and literary voice. Born in Sicily, Pirandello studied at the University of Rome and at the University of Bonn in Germany, where he earned a doctorate in philology, the study of language. Marriage to the daughter of a wealthy merchant afforded Pirandello the freedom to write, and during the 1890s, he produced several volumes of verse and short stories.

After 1900, however, Pirandello experienced a series of misfortunes. The sulfur mine on which his wife's wealth depended was destroyed by a landslide. Pirandello's wife succumbed to mental illness and was institutionalized. And beyond these personal tragedies, in 1915, Italy became involved in the bloody conflict of World War I.

During this period, Pirandello began to focus his writing on psychological themes. Pirandello's play *Right You Are (If You Think You Are)* (1917) embodies his conviction that truth is relative and that there is no such thing as objective reality. This outlook reached its most forceful expression in Pirandello's landmark plays, *Six Characters in Search of an Author* (1921) and *Henry IV* (1922). These plays brought Pirandello international fame and had a major influence on the evolution of twentieth-century drama, most notably in the theater of the absurd of the 1940s and 1950s.

Like many other pioneers of modern European drama—such as Eugène Ionesco, Samuel Beckett, and Bertolt Brecht—Pirandello deliberately drew attention to the form and structure of his plays. In *Six Characters in Search*

of an Author, for example, he created a "theater within the theater." The theme of illusion versus reality was a major focus of Pirandello's work. He summed up his world view in a comment he made in 1920: "I think that life is a very sad piece of buffoonery; because we have in ourselves, without being able to know why, wherefore or whence, the need to deceive ourselves constantly by creating a reality (one for each and never the same for all), which from time to time is discovered to be vain and illusory."

Pirandello was awarded the Nobel Prize in literature in 1934.

Before You Read

War

Make the Connection
Quickwrite ✏️
You are a parent whose son or daughter was sent off to fight in a war. You have recently learned that your child died in battle. What, if anything, helps you to make sense of things and cope with your grief? Write a brief journal entry about your loss.

Literary Focus
Epiphany
In literature the term *epiphany* (from a Greek word meaning "manifestation" or "showing forth") refers to a moment of sudden insight or revelation experienced by a character. An epiphany usually occurs at or near the end of a story, taking the form of a sudden remark, symbol, or action that reveals character and sums up or clarifies the meaning of a complex experience. Sometimes the character who has the epiphany is aware that he or she has achieved a new insight. At other times the epiphany is obvious only to the reader, who suddenly becomes aware of a character's true nature or desires.

> An **epiphany** is a sudden remark, symbol, or moment that provides a startling new insight.
>
> *For more on Epiphany, see the Handbook of Literary and Historical Terms.*

Reading Skills 📖
Drawing Conclusions
When you draw a conclusion, you use specific statements or other evidence to make an inference with broader implications. For example, from details in the first two paragraphs of "War" you might conclude that Pirandello's story will involve characters under great stress and will focus on a serious theme. As you read, jot down any words or phrases that help you draw conclusions about Pirandello's views of war and human nature in general.

Background
The war that looms so large in this story is World War I (1914–1918), which was fought mainly in Europe. The causes of the conflict included nationalism and imperialistic ambitions in the world's major powers and the complex alliances they formed to further their interests. Italy entered the war in 1915 on the side of the Allies, which included Britain, France, and Russia. (The United States remained neutral for the first few years of the war but entered the conflict on the Allied side in April 1917.) The war cost an estimated ten million soldiers' lives before an armistice was finally declared on November 11, 1918.

North Carolina Competency Goal
1.03; 4.03; 4.05; 5.01; 5.03

Vocabulary Development

plight (plīt) *n.*: unfortunate condition.

pettiness (pet'ē·nis) *n.*: insignificance.

disillusion (dis'i·lōō'zhən) *n.*: disenchantment; disappointment.

stoically (stō'i·kəl·lē) *adv.*: calmly; without emotion.

incongruous (in·käŋ'grōō·əs) *adj.*: not fitting; out of place.

INTERNET
Vocabulary Practice
•
More About Luigi Pirandello
Keyword: LE5 WL-7

SKILLS FOCUS

Literary Skills
Understand epiphany.

Reading Skills
Draw conclusions.

WAR

Luigi Pirandello
translated by **Samuel Putnam**

The passengers who had left Rome by the night express had had to stop until dawn at the small station of Fabriano in order to continue their journey by the small old-fashioned "local" joining the main line with Sulmona.

At dawn, in a stuffy and smoky second-class carriage in which five people had already spent the night, a bulky woman in deep mourning, was hoisted in—almost like a shapeless bundle. Behind her—puffing and moaning, followed her husband—a tiny man, thin and weakly, his face death-white, his eyes small and bright and looking shy and uneasy.

Having at last taken a seat he politely thanked the passengers who had helped his wife and who had made room for her; then he turned round to the woman trying to pull down the collar of her coat and politely enquired:

"Are you all right, dear?"

The wife, instead of answering, pulled up her collar again to her eyes, so as to hide her face.

"Nasty world," muttered the husband with a sad smile.

And he felt it his duty to explain to his traveling companions that the poor woman was to be pitied for the war was taking away from her her only son, a boy of twenty to whom both had devoted their entire life, even breaking up their home at Sulmona to follow him to Rome where he had to go as a student, then allowing him to volunteer for war with an assurance, however, that at least for six months he would not be sent to the front[1] and now, all of a sudden, receiving a wire saying that he was due to leave in three days' time and asking them to go and see him off.

The woman under the big coat was twisting and wriggling, at times growling like a wild animal, feeling certain that all those explanations would not have aroused even a shadow of sympathy from those people who—most likely—were in the same plight as herself. One of them, who had been listening with particular attention, said:

"You should thank God that your son is only leaving now for the front. Mine has been sent there the first day of the war. He has already come back twice wounded and been sent back again to the front."

"What about me? I have two sons and three nephews at the front," said another passenger.

"Maybe, but in our case it is our *only* son," ventured the husband.

"What difference can it make? You may spoil your only son with excessive attentions, but you cannot love him more than you would all your other children if you had any. Paternal love is not like bread that can be broken into pieces and split amongst the children in equal shares. A father gives *all* his love to each one of his children without discrimination, whether it be one or ten, and if I am suffering now for my two sons, I am not suffering half for each of them but double. . . ."

"True . . . true . . ." sighed the embarrassed husband, "but suppose (of course we all hope it will never be your case) a father has two sons at the front and he loses one of them, there is still one left to console him . . . while . . ."

"Yes," answered the other, getting cross, "a son left to console him but also a son left for whom he must survive, while in the case of the father of an only son if the son dies the father can die too and put an end to his distress. Which of the two positions is the worse? Don't you see how my case would be worse than yours?"

---

1. **front** *n.:* combat zone in a war.

Vocabulary

plight (plīt) *n.:* unfortunate condition.

Armored Train in Action (1915)
by Gino Severini.

"Nonsense," interrupted another traveler, a fat, red-faced man with bloodshot eyes of the palest gray.

He was panting. From his bulging eyes seemed to spurt inner violence of an uncontrolled vitality which his weakened body could hardly contain.

"Nonsense," he repeated, trying to cover his mouth with his hand so as to hide the two missing front teeth. "Nonsense. Do we give life to our children for our own benefit?"

The other travelers stared at him in distress. The one who had had his son at the front since the first day of the war sighed: "You are right. Our children do not belong to us, they belong to the Country. . . ."

"Bosh,"[2] retorted the fat traveler. "Do we think of the Country when we give life to our children? Our sons are born because . . . well, because they must be born and when they come to life they take our own life with them. This is the truth. We belong to them but they never belong to us. And when they reach twenty they are exactly what we were at their age. We too had a father and mother, but there were so many other things as well . . . girls, cigarettes, illusions, new ties . . . and the Country, of course, whose call we would have answered—when we were twenty—even if father

---

2. **bosh** *interj.:* nonsense.

and mother had said no. Now, at our age, the love of our Country is still great, of course, but stronger than it is the love for our children. Is there any one of us here who wouldn't gladly take his son's place at the front if he could?"

There was a silence all round, everybody nodding as to approve.

"Why then," continued the fat man, "shouldn't we consider the feelings of our children when they are twenty? Isn't it natural that at their age they should consider the love for their Country (I am speaking of decent boys, of course) even greater than the love for us? Isn't it natural that it should be so, as after all they must look upon us as upon old boys who cannot move any more and must stay at home? If Country exists, if Country is a natural necessity like bread, of which each of us must eat in order not to die of hunger, somebody must go to defend it. And our sons go, when they are twenty, and they don't want tears, because if they die, they die inflamed and happy (I am speaking, of course, of decent boys). Now, if one dies young and happy, without having the ugly sides of life, the boredom of it, the pettiness, the bitterness of disillusion . . . what more can we ask for him? Everyone should stop crying: everyone should laugh, as I do . . . or at least thank God— as I do—because my son, before dying, sent me a message saying that he was dying satisfied at having ended his life in the best way he could have wished. That is why, as you see, I do not even wear mourning. . . ."

He shook his light fawn coat as to show it; his livid lip over his missing teeth was trembling, his eyes were watery and motionless, and soon after, he ended with a shrill laugh which might well have been a sob.

"Quite so . . . quite so . . ." agreed the others.

The woman who, bundled in a corner under her coat, had been sitting and listening had—for the last three months—tried to find in the words of her husband and her friends something to console her in her deep sorrow, something that might show her how a mother should resign herself to send her son not even to death but to a probable danger of life. Yet not a word had she found amongst the many which had been said . . . and

her grief had been greater in seeing that nobody—as she thought—could share her feelings.

But now the words of the traveler amazed and almost stunned her. She suddenly realized that it wasn't the others who were wrong and could not understand her but herself who could not rise up to the same height of those fathers and mothers willing to resign themselves, without crying, not only to the departure of their sons but even to their death.

She lifted her head, she bent over from her corner trying to listen with great attention to the details which the fat man was giving to his companions about the way his son had fallen as a hero, for his King and his Country, happy and without regrets. It seemed to her that she had stumbled into a world she had never dreamt of, a world so far unknown to her and she was so pleased to hear everyone joining in congratulating that brave father who could so stoically speak of his child's death.

Then suddenly, just as if she had heard nothing of what had been said and almost as if waking up from a dream, she turned to the old man, asking him:

"Then . . . is your son really dead?"

Everybody stared at her. The old man, too, turned to look at her, fixing his great, bulging, horribly watery light gray eyes, deep in her face. For some little time he tried to answer, but words failed him. He looked and looked at her, almost as if only then—at that silly, incongruous question— he had suddenly realized at last that his son was really dead . . . gone forever . . . forever. His face contracted, became horribly distorted, then he snatched in haste a handkerchief from his pocket and, to the amazement of everyone, broke into harrowing, heart-rending, uncontrollable sobs.

Vocabulary

pettiness (pet′ē·nis) *n.*: insignificance.
disillusion (dis′i·lōō′zhən) *n.*: disenchantment; disappointment.
stoically (stō′i·kəl·lē) *adv.*: calmly; without emotion.
incongruous (in·kän′grōō·əs) *adj.*: not fitting; out of place.

Response and Analysis

Reading Check

1. Where and when do the story's characters meet?

2. Why are the woman and her husband in mourning?

3. Which character argues that parents should be comforted by a son's heroic death in combat?

4. What question does the woman ask the fat man? How does he react?

Thinking Critically

5. How would you describe the overall **mood,** or atmosphere, of this story? What details in the story support your view?

6. How does the fat man's account of his son's heroic death affect the woman whose only son is about to go to war?

7. Explain the **epiphany** that the fat man experiences after the woman asks her "silly" question. What do you think his surprising reaction reveals about the way he has dealt with his son's death? Could this moment be a turning point in his life? Explain.

8. Consider Pirandello's approach to the characters and the situation in the story. What conclusion might you draw about the author's attitude toward war?

9. Review your Quickwrite notes. After reading this story, have your views changed at all? Explain. ✏️

Extending and Evaluating

10. Pirandello once said that his art was full of "bitter compassion for all those who deceive themselves." How does this remark apply to this story, in your opinion? Use specific references to the text to explain your answer.

WRITING

Write a Dialogue

What thoughts do you think the husband and wife take away with them after the story ends? Write a brief dialogue in which they react to the events in the railway carriage.

DATE DENARO PER LA VITTORIA:
LA VITTORIA È LA PACE

BANCA ITALIANA DI SCONTO

Civico Museo d'Arte Contemporanea, Milan, Italy.

Give Money for Victory: Victory Is Peace.
Poster by Banca Italiana.

North Carolina Competency Goal
1.02; 1.03; 4.05; 5.03; 6.01

SKILLS FOCUS

Literary Skills
Analyze epiphany.

Reading Skills
Draw conclusions.

Writing Skills
Write a dialogue.

Vocabulary Skills
Make semantic maps.

Vocabulary Development
Semantic Mapping

plight	stoically
pettiness	incongruous
disillusion	

Make a **semantic map** like the following one for the Vocabulary words above. Locate each word in the story to determine its meaning in context.

plight
Definition: unfortunate, awkward, or dangerous situation
Synonym: predicament
Example: The refugees' desperate plight caused a groundswell of sympathy.

Franz Kafka
(1883–1924)
Austria/Czech Republic

Franz Kafka once wrote that literature should be an ax that smashes through the "frozen sea" inside every person. For Kafka, the "frozen sea" meant the feelings of alienation and despair he and many others experienced in the unstable years of the early twentieth century. These emotions were given powerful expression in Kafka's grotesque tales. In *The Metamorphosis* (1915), a man wakes up to find himself transformed into a giant insect. The main character in *The Trial* (1925) is arrested, tried by a mysterious court, convicted, and executed without ever knowing his crime. In *The Castle* (1926), the narrator is forbidden to communicate with the man who rules a castle and controls every aspect of his existence. In these and other works, Kafka demonstrates his mastery of **surrealism**—a literary and artistic style in which reality is presented in a distorted or absurd way to suggest the irrational world of dreams and nightmares.

Like many of his characters, Kafka was lonely and insecure. His insecurities stemmed partly from social tensions in his native city of Prague. Now the capital of the Czech Republic, Prague was under Austrian control for most of Kafka's life. Kafka, a member of the German-speaking minority, was educated in Prague's elite German-language academy and became part of a group of Jewish intellectuals known as the Prague Circle. As a Jew, he was keenly aware of his outsider status among the mainly Catholic Czech population.

Kafka had a distant and troubled relationship with his father, a stern man who treated his sensitive son with indifference and even contempt. Kafka expressed his dislike and fear, as well as his yearning for his father's approval, in "Letter to His Father," a one-hundred-page document that was never actually sent to his father.

Kafka was rarely satisfied with his literary efforts, and before his death from tuberculosis, he asked his friend and editor Max Brod (1884–1968) to burn his manuscripts. Fortunately for future readers, Brod ignored the request and published the manuscripts. Kafka's works have had an enormous influence on modern literature. His writings have given rise to the term *Kafkaesque*, used to describe a situation of baffling, nightmarish complexity and absurdity.

For Independent Reading

You might enjoy reading this novella by Kafka:
• *The Metamorphosis*

The Hunger Artist

Make the Connection
Quickwrite

Extraordinary achievement takes great effort and dedication. Artists and athletes, for example, often go to extreme lengths to attain their goals and win the attention and admiration of others. Can you think of situations in which this pursuit of perfection or recognition has gone too far? Jot down your thoughts.

Literary Focus
Theme

Every literary work has something to say about life. The central idea or insight into human experience in a literary work is its **theme.** The theme of a work is not the same as its subject. A literary work may have love as its subject, but what it says *about* love is its theme. One writer may express the idea that love denied can turn to hate; another may see love as the only antidote to despair. A theme is not necessarily the same as a moral or lesson, but it is a comment on life's meaning.

> The **theme** is the main idea or message about life in a literary work.
>
> *For more on Theme, see the Handbook of Literary and Historical Terms.*

Reading Skills
Analyzing Details

Although some writers directly state their themes in their works, most imply or suggest them through the details, or pieces of information, they include. It is up to the reader to study these individual details about the characters, plot, and setting and put them together to arrive at the overall message or theme. As you read, jot down words and phrases that help you understand what the main character is like, what he wants, and what forces in his environment prevent him from getting what he wants. When you have finished reading, share your notes with other students and discuss what main point about life Kafka seems to be making in this story.

North Carolina Competency Goal
1.02; 1.03; 4.03; 4.05; 5.01; 5.03; 6.01

Vocabulary Development

duress (doo·res') *n.:* pressure; force.

nocturnal (näk·tur'nəl) *adj.:* of or pertaining to the night.

cache (kash) *n.:* hiding place for goods or valuables.

itinerant (ī·tin'ər·ənt) *adj.:* traveling; moving from place to place.

emaciated (ē·mā'shē·āt'id) *v.* used as *adj.:* extremely thin; wasted away.

INTERNET

Vocabulary Practice
•
More About Franz Kafka

Keyword: LE5 WL-7

Literary Skills
Understand theme.

Reading Skills
Analyze details.

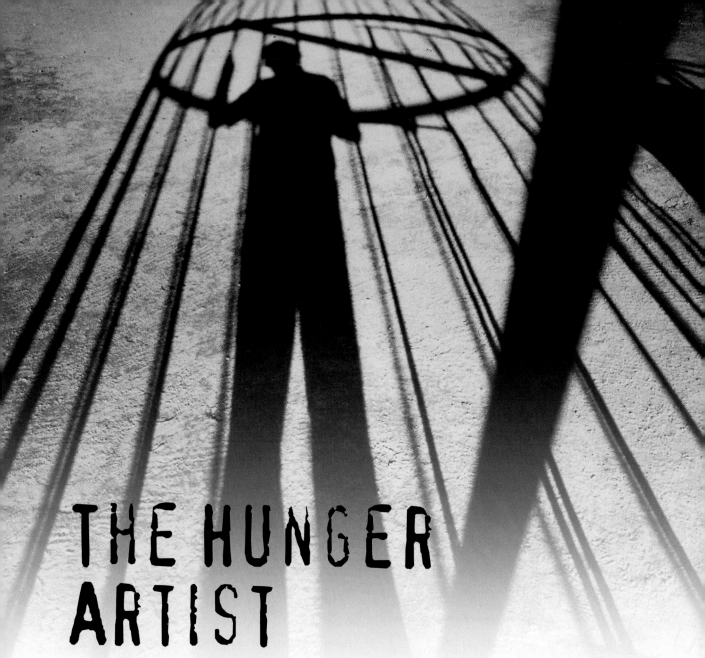

THE HUNGER ARTIST

Franz Kafka

translated by **Joachim Neugroschel**

In the past few decades, the interest in hunger artists has greatly declined. While staging such performances under one's own management used to pay off quite handsomely, today this is utterly impossible. Those were different times. Back then the whole town would focus on the hunger artist; the involvement grew hunger-day by hunger-day; everybody wanted to see the hunger artist at least once daily. Later on, holders of season tickets would spend days on end sitting in front of the small barred cage; and viewings also took place at night, their effect being heightened by torchlight.

In good weather the cage was brought outdoors, and now it was especially children to whom the hunger artist was shown. Though for grown-ups it was often mere fun, in which they took part because it was the latest fad, the children gaped with open mouths, holding one another's hands for safety's sake, as the hunger artist, pale, in a black leotard, with intensely protruding ribs, rejecting even a chair, sat on straw spread on the ground. He would sometimes nod politely, answer questions with a forced smile, perhaps stick his arm through the bars to let people feel how skinny he was; but then he would retreat entirely into himself, ignoring everyone, not even heeding the crucial striking of the clock, which was the only piece of furniture in the cage; rather, he would stare into space with almost closed eyes, now and then taking a sip of water from a tiny glass in order to moisten his lips.

Aside from the ever-changing spectators, there were permanent watchmen chosen by the public—usually butchers, strangely enough, who, always three at a time, had the job of observing the hunger artist day and night, to make sure he consumed no food on the sly. However, this was a pure formality, introduced to reassure the masses; for insiders knew that during the hunger period the hunger artist would never, under any circumstance, not even under duress, have eaten the tiniest crumb; it would have reflected on his artistic honor.

Granted, not every watchman was capable of grasping this; some of the nocturnal watch groups were very lax in their watching: they would deliberately assemble in a remote corner, absorbed in a game of cards, with the obvious intention of granting the hunger artist some respite for a bit of refreshment that they assumed he could produce from some private cache. Nothing was more tormenting for the hunger artist than such watchmen: they made him feel wretched, they made hungering dreadfully difficult for him. At times he would overcome his weakness and sing during their shift, sing as long as he could keep it up, to show these people how unfair their suspicions were. But his singing didn't help much; they were merely astonished at his skillfulness in eating even while singing.

The hunger artist greatly preferred the watchmen who sat right at the bars and who, not content with the dim nocturnal illumination in the hall, would target him with the flashlights supplied by the impresario.[1] The harsh glare never bothered the hunger artist: he couldn't sleep anyway and, no matter what the illumination or the time, he could doze a little, even in the overcrowded, boisterous hall. He was quite prepared to spend a completely sleepless night with these watchmen; he was prepared to joke with them, tell them stories about his itinerant life, then listen to their stories—anything to keep them awake, to continue showing them that there was nothing edible in the cage and that he hungered as none of them could hunger.

He was happiest, however, when morning then came: a lavish breakfast was brought in at his expense, and the watchmen tore into it with the appetites of healthy men forced to stay up all night. Now there were people who viewed this breakfast as an attempt at unduly influencing the watchmen, but they were overstepping the line; and when asked whether they would care to test the issue by working the night shift and then having no breakfast, they retreated into themselves, but they clung to their suspicions all the same.

Of course, these were part of the inevitable suspicions aroused by the profession of hungering. After all, no one could spend every day and night uninterruptedly watching the hunger artist; so no one could tell on the basis of personal experience whether the hungering had been truly uninterrupted and flawless. Only the hunger

---

1. **impresario** (im′prə·sä′rē·ō) *n.*: entertainment manager.

Vocabulary

duress (dŏŏ·res′) *n.*: pressure; force.
nocturnal (näk·tʉr′nəl) *adj.*: of or pertaining to the night.
cache (kash) *n.*: hiding place for goods or valuables.
itinerant (ī·tin′ər·ənt) *adj.*: traveling; moving from place to place.

artist himself could know this, and only he could simultaneously be the spectator completely satisfied with his hungering.

Yet there was another reason why he was never satisfied. Perhaps it was not mere hunger that left him so thoroughly <u>emaciated</u> that some people, much to their regret, had to avoid his demonstrations because they could not bear the sight of him; perhaps he was so emaciated because of dissatisfaction with himself. You see, he alone knew, and no insider realized, how easy it was to hunger. It was the easiest thing in the world. Nor did he make any bones about it. But people refused to believe him; at best some regarded him as modest, but mostly they considered him a publicity hound or even a swindler, for whom hunger was easy because he knew how to make it easy for himself and who then had the gall to practically admit it.

That was what he had to put up with, and in the course of time he had grown accustomed to it all; however, this dissatisfaction gnawed away at him mentally, and never after any hunger period—this had to be granted to his credit—had he voluntarily left the cage. The impresario had set forty days as the maximum length of hungering; he never let the period extend beyond that, even in the major cities, and for good reason. Experience taught that a city's interest could be increasingly prodded by forty days of more and more intense promotion; but then the novelty wore off and there was a notable slackening of demand. There were, of course, minor differences between various towns and between various countries. But as a rule of thumb, forty days was the maximum term.

Then, on the fortieth day, they opened the door of the cage, which was wreathed with flowers; an enthusiastic audience filled the amphitheater, a military band played, two doctors entered the cage to take the hunger artist's necessary measurements, the results were announced through a megaphone, and finally, two young ladies, happy that they of all people had the winning tickets, came to assist the hunger artist out of the cage and down the few steps to a small table, where meticulously selected invalid fare was served. At this point the hunger artist always resisted. True, he willingly slipped his bony arms into the helpfully extended hands of the ladies, who were bending down to him, but he refused to stand up. Why stop now after precisely forty days? He could have endured it longer, infinitely longer; why stop now of all times when he was in his best—indeed, not yet in his best hungering form? Why did they want to deprive him of the fame he would garner for continuing to hunger and not only becoming the greatest hunger artist of all time—which, no doubt, he already was—but outdoing himself beyond human imagining, for he felt no limits to his ability to hunger?

Why did this throng,[2] which claimed to admire him, have so little patience with him; if he could endure further hungering, why couldn't they endure it? Besides, he was tired, he felt comfortable sitting in the straw, and now he was supposed to stand up full-length and go to the meal, the very thought of which triggered nausea, which he arduously repressed out of sheer consideration for the two ladies. And he gazed up into the eyes of the seemingly so friendly, yet actually so brutal ladies and he shook his overweight head on his feeble neck.

But then, what always happened happened. The impresario came, raised his arms wordlessly (the music drowned out all speech) over the hunger artist as if inviting heaven to have a look at its creature here on the straw—this pitiful martyr, which, to be sure, the hunger artist was, though in an entirely different sense. The impresario then put his arm around the hunger artist's narrow waist, with exaggerated caution aimed at making people appreciate what a feeble thing he was dealing with here. Then, not without secretly shaking him a bit, so that the hunger artist's legs and torso uncontrollably reeled and tottered to and fro, the impresario handed him over to the ladies, who had meanwhile turned deathly pale.

---

2. **throng** *n.:* crowd.

Vocabulary

emaciated (ē·mā′shē·āt′id) *v.* used as *adj.:* extremely thin; wasted away.

Now the hunger artist put up with everything; his head lolled on his chest, looking as if it had rolled there and were kept there in some inscrutable way; his body was hollowed out; his knees squeezed hard together in a self-preservation cramp, while his feet scraped along the ground as if it were not the real ground—they were still hunting for the real ground. And the full, albeit very meager weight of the body rested on one lady, who, panting and peering about for help (this was not how she had envisioned her honorary assistance), craned her neck as far away as possible to at least keep her face from touching the hunger artist. But this effort failed, and her more fortunate if trembling colleague, rather than coming to her aid, contented herself with carrying the hunger artist's hand—that small bundle of bones; the one lady therefore burst into tears amid the audience's delighted laughter and she had to be replaced by an attendant, who had been ready for a long time.

Next came the meal, a wee bit of which the impresario managed to feed the drowsing, almost comatose hunger artist while chattering merrily in order to divert attention from his client's condition; then the audience was hailed with a toast, which the hunger artist had supposedly whispered to the impresario, and the orchestra underscored it all with a resounding flourish. The crowd now scattered, and no one had any right to be dissatisfied with the show; no one, only the hunger artist himself—always only he himself.

And thus, aside from short, regular breaks, he lived for many years, in apparent glory, honored by the world, but usually in a dismal mood, which grew more and more dismal because no one could take it seriously. And how could they comfort him anyway? What more could he desire? And if ever some good-natured person happened to pity him and tried to explain that his melancholy was probably caused by his hungering, the hunger artist, especially if his hunger period was well advanced, might fly into a rage and, to everyone's alarm, begin shaking the bars of his cage like a wild beast. However, the impresario had a method of punishment that he liked to inflict for such outbursts. He apologized for the hunger artist in front of the public and admitted that his behavior was excusable only because of the irritability provoked by his hunger, which well-fed people could not readily comprehend.

In this connection, the impresario went on to discuss, and offer the same explanation for, the hunger artist's statement that he could hunger a lot longer than he did hunger. The impresario praised the lofty aspirations, the goodwill, the great self-denial implicit in those words; but then he sought to refute that statement simply with photographs, which were also hawked[3] and which showed the hunger artist on a fortieth day, in bed, debilitated, at death's door.

---

3. **hawked** *v.:* sold.

Walking Man II (1960)
by Alberto Giacometti.

National Gallery of Art, Washington, D.C.
Gift of Enid A. Haupt (1977.47.7).

This familiar yet always nerve-wracking perversion of the truth was too much for the hunger artist. The result of an untimely halt to the hungering was being cited as the cause! Fighting against this incomprehension, this world of incomprehension, was impossible. Time and again, poised at the bars, he had listened to the impresario eagerly and in good faith; but the instant the photographs appeared, he would always let go of the bars and sink back into the straw with a sigh, and the reassured spectators could once again view him from up close.

Several years later, when the witnesses of such scenes thought back to them, they often could not understand themselves. For meanwhile, as mentioned above, public interest had shifted; the change had come almost overnight. There may have been underlying reasons, but who cared about digging them out? In any case: one day, the pampered hunger artist was deserted by the pleasure-hunting crowds, who now preferred other exhibitions. For one last time the impresario hustled him across half of Europe to see if the old interest might not be surviving here and there, but it was all to no avail. It was as if everyone had connived[4] to develop a downright loathing of hunger exhibitions. In reality, of course, the change could not have been so sudden, and people now belatedly remembered early signs that had been insufficiently noticed, insufficiently stifled amid the raptures of success; but it was too late for countermeasures. Granted, the demand for hungering was certain to revive some day; but this was no consolation for the living.

What should the hunger artist do now? This man, who had been cheered by thousands of people, could not display himself in sideshows at small fairs; and as for starting a new profession, the hunger artist was not merely too old, he was, more than anything, all too fanatically devoted to hungering. And so he dismissed the impresario, his companion in an unparalleled career, and quickly signed up with a large circus; to spare his own vulnerability, he avoided reading the terms of the contract.

---

4. **connived** (kə·nīvd') *v*.: cooperated secretly.

A large circus, with its constant turnover of huge numbers of people and animals and apparatuses, can find use for anyone at any time, even a hunger artist, provided his demands are reasonable. And besides, in this case they hired not just the hunger artist but also his long-famous name. Given the peculiar nature of this art, which did not decrease with increasing age, one could not even say that an artist, past his prime and no longer at the summit of his artistry, had sought refuge in a quiet circus job. On the contrary, the hunger artist guaranteed that he could hunger just as well as ever, which was entirely credible. Indeed, he claimed that if they left him to his own devices, which they promised unhesitatingly, he could now outdo himself and truly astonish the world—a statement that, to be sure, drew a smile from the professionals, who were mindful of the current mood, which, in his eagerness, the hunger artist had readily forgotten.

At bottom, however, the hunger artist did not lose his sense of the actual circumstances and he took it as par for the course that he and his cage would be placed not as a star attraction at the center of the ring, but as a quite easily accessible sideshow near the animal cages. Big, gaudily painted posters framed his cage, announcing what was to be seen there. During intermissions, when the spectators thronged to view the animals, they almost inevitably had to pass the hunger artist and halt there for a moment or two. They might have stayed on a bit, but any calm and lengthy viewing was made impossible by the people shoving them from behind in the narrow corridor, unable to understand this stop on the way to the animals that they were so eager to see. That was also the reason why the hunger artist grew terrified of these visits, though, of course, he longed for them as the purpose of his life. At first he could hardly wait for intermission and he ecstatically looked forward to the flood of spectators; but then only too soon, when even the most obstinate, almost conscious self-deception could not hold out against experience, he was forced to realize that most of these people were intent on visiting the animals.

The Circus (1913) by Charles Cottet.
Musée d'Orsay, Paris.

And this distant view of the spectators remained the finest one. For when they reached him, he was promptly inundated by the raging, shouting, and cursing of the two continuously forming groups: the faction (it soon became the more unpleasant one for the hunger artist) that wanted to view him comfortably, not out of sympathy but out of caprice[5] and defiance; and the faction that only wanted to get to the animals. Once the large cluster was past, it was followed by the stragglers; but, while nothing prevented them from halting for as long as they

---

5. **caprice** (kə·prēs′) *n.:* sudden wish; whim.

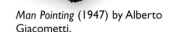

Man Pointing (1947) by Alberto Giacometti.

The Museum of Modern Art, New York.
Gift of Mrs. John D. Rockefeller III (678.1954).

liked, they hurried by with barely a sidelong glance in order to reach the animals in time. Nor was it an all-too-frequent stroke of luck for a father to come along with his children, point at the hunger artist, explain the whole business in detail, and tell about earlier years, when he had attended similar but incomparably grander demonstrations. The children, inadequately prepared by school and by life, were completely at sea (what did hungering mean to them?); yet the glow of their inquiring eyes hinted that new and more merciful times were imminent.

Perhaps, the hunger artist might then say to himself that it would all be slightly better if he weren't so close to the animal cages. This made it too easy for people to choose, not to mention that he was deeply pained and constantly depressed by the emanations[6] from the cages, the restlessness of the beasts at night, the raw meat carried past him to the predators, the roars during the feedings. But he did not have the nerve to file a complaint with the managers; after all, it was the animals who drew the swarm of visitors, one of whom might now and then be intrigued by the hunger artist. And who could tell where they might dump him if he reminded them of his existence, thereby letting them know that he was, strictly speaking, merely an impediment[7] on the way to the animal cages.

A smaller impediment, to be sure, a smaller and smaller impediment. People became habituated[8] to the bizarre notion that nowadays someone might ask them to pay attention to a hunger artist; and that habituation passed judgment on him. He could hunger for all he was worth, and hunger he did; but nothing could save him now, people hurried by, ignoring him. Try explaining the art of hungering to someone! If a person doesn't feel it, then you can't make him understand. The lovely posters became dirty and illegible; they were torn down, no one thought of replacing them. Initially, each completed hunger-day had been carefully marked on the small notice board; but then the figure had long since remained the same, for after the first few weeks the staff had grown tired of even this minor task. And so the hunger artist kept on hungering, as he had once dreamed of doing; but no one counted the days, no one, not even the hunger artist himself, knew how long he had been hungering, and his heart grew

---

6. **emanations** *n. pl.:* things that come forth or are given off; here, sounds or odors.

7. **impediment** *n.:* obstacle.
8. **habituated** (hə·bich′o͞o·āt′id) *v.* used as *adj.:* used to.

heavy. And if once in a while some idle passerby happened to stop, make fun of the old number, and talk about a hoax, it was in its way the stupidest lie that indifference and inborn malice could come up with. For it was not the hunger artist who was cheating: he labored honestly, but the world was cheating him of his reward.

However, many more days wore by, and that too came to an end. One day a supervisor noticed the cage, and he asked the attendants why this perfectly useful cage with the rotten straw inside it was being left vacant. No one knew why, until somebody, with the help of the notice board, recalled the hunger artist. Poking sticks into the straw, they found the hunger artist.

"Are you still hungering?" asked the supervisor. "When are you finally going to quit?"

"Forgive me, everyone," whispered the hunger artist.

But the supervisor, holding his ear to the bars, was the only person who could understand him. "Certainly," said the supervisor, tapping his forehead in order to inform the staff of the hunger artist's condition. "We forgive you."

"I always wanted you people to admire my hungering," said the hunger artist.

"We do admire it," said the supervisor obligingly.

"But you shouldn't admire it," said the hunger artist.

"Well, then we won't admire it," said the supervisor. "Why shouldn't we admire it?"

"Because I have to hunger, I can't help it," said the hunger artist.

"Wow!" said the supervisor. "Why can't you help it?"

"Because," said the hunger artist, lifting his head slightly, pursing his lips as if for a kiss, and whispering right into the supervisor's ear so that nothing would be lost. "Because I couldn't find any food that I liked. Had I found some, believe me, I wouldn't have made any fuss, I would have stuffed myself like you and everyone else."

Those were his last words but his broken eyes contained the firm, though no longer proud conviction that he was hungering on.

"Clean the place up!" said the supervisor, and they buried the hunger artist together with the straw.

A young panther was then put into the cage. It was a tangible relief for even the most obtuse[9] person to see this wild beast tossing about in the long-desolate cage. The panther lacked for nothing. The guards, without a second thought, brought him the food he liked. Nor did he even seem to miss his freedom; this noble body, so well equipped with all it needed that it was ready to burst, even appeared to be carrying freedom around with it. Freedom seemed to be lodged somewhere in his teeth; and his joy in life poured so fervently from his maw[10] that it wasn't easy for the spectators to hold their ground. But they pulled themselves together, thronged around the cage, and refused to move on.

---

9. **obtuse** *adj.:* dense; slow-witted.
10. **maw** *n.:* mouth and jaws of a flesh-eating animal.

In the fall of 2003, the American magician David Blaine fasted for forty-four days in a transparent plastic box above the Thames River in London. He lost fifty-six pounds and was hospitalized immediately after the fast ended. In the following article, Helen Schary Motro comments on the meaning of Blaine's stunt and compares it with politically motivated hunger strikes and with the fasting of Kafka's hunger artist.

An Ignoble[1] Fast

INFORMATIONAL TEXT

Helen Schary Motro

from *The Christian Science Monitor,* September 26, 2003

The great patriot, pacifist, and father of Indian independence, Mahatma Gandhi, proved that self-sacrifice may be a more potent weapon than force. By the simple tactic of hunger strikes, he brought sea change to India. His numerous fasts over three decades pressured the British toward Indian self-rule, improved the status of the Untouchables caste, and protested against Muslim-Hindu civil violence.

Gandhi's weapon remains a vital one, employed by underdogs worldwide to bring attention to their plight and press for their cause. It is undertaken foremost by prisoners, whose only weapon is their own bodies. In Turkey this year at least 64 maximum-security prisoners died as a result of fasting; in China a journalist began fasting in June to protest a 10-year sentence for "subverting the state's authority." . . .

Even as these desperate individuals decline sustenance in a dangerous effort to be noticed and achieve justice, in London, American stuntman David Blaine is busy fasting not for principle—but for money and fame. He'll receive £5 million for a publicity stunt currently creating an uproar in the English capital. Since Sept. 5, Mr. Blaine has been suspended in a transparent box over the Thames River on view to all Londoners, vowing to imbibe nothing but water for 44 days.

He has boasted that his stunt was inspired by a short story by Franz Kafka. In the mordant,[2] unforgettable "A Hunger Artist," published in 1924, Kafka recounts with pathos[3] and enigma the tale of a man whose career was public fasting. Even at the height of the hunger artist's fame, his impresario limited the fast to 40 days, claiming that was the outside limit of public interest. Kafka's story, however, is about the artist at the sorry nadir[4] of his career. Whereas his fasts had once attracted enormous crowds, "the interest in professional fasting has markedly diminished," and he is compelled to resort to a shabby cage in the rear of a circus. In the end, there are no witnesses to his last self-imposed limitless fast, from which he dies.

Blaine's vapid[5] stunt, filmed live on British television, is snarling traffic and attracting an

---

1. **ignoble** (ig·nō′bəl) *adj.:* not noble; dishonorable.

2. **mordant** (môr′dənt) *adj.:* sharp; biting.
3. **pathos** (pā′thäs′) *n.:* quality that arouses compassion.
4. **nadir** (nā′dər) *n.:* low point.
5. **vapid** (vap′id) *adj.:* lacking good taste.

Illusionist David Blaine inside a glass box suspended near Tower Bridge in London on September 6, 2003.

escalating throng of daily hecklers, even embroiling Paul McCartney in a shoving match at the scene. It has little in common with the tragic overtones of Kafka, whose wasted protagonist truly perished from neglect by a fickle world. . . .

Whereas Kafka's story created a character full of pathos, the author's real criticism was aimed at the spectators—symbols of humankind's triviality, callousness, and fickleness.

Today's crowd is smart enough not to fall for Blaine's tasteless stunt. Instead, their disdain is feeding Blaine his due.

Kafka wrote his story before Gandhi conceived of the hunger strike as the potent political tactic of the powerless. The tool of committed ideologues[6] should not be billed as cheap entertainment. Perhaps that's what the angry London public is inchoately[7] trying to tell Blaine. He should get out of his box and have breakfast—leaving hunger strikes to nobler causes.

> **?** How does the author of this article feel about David Blaine's fast? What loaded words does she use to express her opinion? What do you think was her purpose in writing this article?

6. **ideologues** (id′ē·ə·lôgz′) *n. pl.:* supporters of a body of ideas.
7. **inchoately** (in·kō′it·lē) *adv.:* in a disorganized way.

Response and Analysis

Reading Check

1. Describe the "performance" of the hunger artist.

2. What do the night watchmen think of the hunger artist? How do the children respond to him?

3. How does the response of the public to the hunger artist change over the years?

4. What happens to the hunger artist at the end of the story?

Thinking Critically

5. What is the impresario's **motivation** for employing the hunger artist? How would you describe the way the audience's interest in the hunger artist changes throughout the course of the story?

6. What limit does the impresario place on the performance of the hunger artist? How do his interests differ from those of the hunger artist himself?

7. Several times in the story the hunger artist is described as dissatisfied with himself. What details in the story suggest what the hunger artist truly desires?

8. Describe what happens to the hunger artist when he signs up with the circus. What is the worst aspect of this experience for him? Why?

9. At the end of the story, how does the hunger artist explain his inability to eat? What might his ultimate fate **symbolize,** or stand for?

Extending and Evaluating

10. In what ways is the hunger artist like athletes, artists, and other performers today who push the limits, dedicate themselves to their goals, and achieve the extraordinary? In what ways is he different? Refer to your Quickwrite notes.

WRITING
Analyzing a Theme

Kafka identifies his main character as an artist. What generalization might Kafka be making about artistic endeavor? In a brief essay, analyze the story as a commentary on the **theme** of the artist in society. Consider the hunger artist's sense of "artistic honor," the changing interests of the public, the hunger artist's torment over the fact that people do not understand his achievement, the hunger artist's final fate, and the statements the hunger artist makes about his "hungering." Use specific quotations and examples from the story to support your points.

Vocabulary Development
True or False?

Identify each of the following statements as true or false, and briefly explain your answer. The underlined words are Vocabulary words.

1. Confessions obtained under <u>duress</u> are always valid.

2. Dogs are <u>nocturnal</u> animals.

3. Thieves might have a good reason to use a <u>cache</u>.

4. <u>Itinerant</u> laborers tend to stay in one place for many years.

5. Gluttons are usually <u>emaciated</u>.

Isak Dinesen

(1885–1962)

Denmark

When the American author Ernest Hemingway accepted the 1954 Nobel Prize in literature, he remarked that the award should instead have gone to the Danish writer Karen Blixen, who wrote under the name Isak Dinesen. Hemingway, who loved Africa and set several of his works there, was especially impressed with Dinesen's *Out of Africa,* an autobiographical account of her years in British East Africa, now Kenya. Although Dinesen is often regarded as the European author who best captured the beauty of the African landscape, she wrote equally accomplished works about northern Europe and the Danish upper class.

Born into a family of wealthy aristocrats in coastal Denmark, Dinesen's spirit of adventure was often at odds with her sheltered upbringing. After her father died and the cousin she loved refused to marry her, she defiantly set sail for Africa to marry the cousin's twin brother, Bror Blixen-Finecke. In 1914, the couple established a coffee plantation in what is now Kenya. Blixen was a wayward, faithless husband who often left Dinesen on her own. After the couple divorced in 1921, Dinesen ran the six-thousand-acre farm by herself for ten years.

Many of Dinesen's stories celebrate the power of women. In *Out of Africa,* Dinesen says that she often visited the Somali women on her property to listen to their stories. "It was a trait common to all these tales," Dinesen wrote, "that the heroine, chaste or not, would get the better of the male characters and come out of the tale triumphant. . . . Within this enclosed women's world . . . I felt the presence . . . of a Millennium when women were to reign supreme in the world."

In 1931, the price of coffee plummeted and Dinesen's plantation went bankrupt. In the same year her lover, the British pilot Denys Finch-Hatton, was killed in a plane crash. These events led Dinesen to return to Denmark and devote herself to writing. Three years later she published *Seven Gothic Tales,* stories about mysterious events and persecuted heroines set in Europe hundreds of years ago. Dinesen's international reputation was cemented with *Out of Africa,* which was published simultaneously in Denmark and Britain in 1937.

For Independent Reading

You may enjoy reading Dinesen's popular works:

- *Out of Africa*
- "Babette's Feast"

The Ring

Make the Connection

Do you think marriage requires completely open communication, or are there areas of privacy that each individual needs to maintain and protect? Is it ever right for someone to keep secrets from a husband or wife? If so, under what circumstances?

Literary Focus

Static and Dynamic Characters

Characters can be categorized in several different ways. For example, characters are sometimes identified as either flat or round. A flat character is one-dimensional and undeveloped, while a round character, as the name implies, is three-dimensional and developed, exhibiting the complexities of a real person. Another way to look at characters is to identify them as either static or dynamic. In old fairy tales and in simple stories that teach moral lessons, the characters are usually **static**—they do not change in the course of the story. In more complex stories the main character, or protagonist, is usually **dynamic**—that is, he or she changes in some important way as a result of the story's events. Often the change is the result of some understanding reached by the character—perhaps a discovery about himself or herself or about human nature in general.

A **static character** remains the same throughout a story. A **dynamic character** changes in the course of a story.

For more on Static and Dynamic Characters, see Character in the Handbook of Literary and Historical Terms.

Reading Skills

Understanding Cause and Effect

The plot of a story is made up of a series of **causes** and **effects:** Events take place and cause something else to happen. When you analyze a character in a story and try to understand how and why the character has changed, you ask yourself, "What caused this change in the character?" and "How has this event affected the character?" As you examine cause and effect in this story, look for clues dropped by the writer—in even the smallest details.

Background

At the time this story takes place, Denmark, the setting, was not yet a democracy. The nobility lived in a grand style while the rest of the population lived in poverty, sometimes turning to crimes such as poaching—trespassing on a landowner's property to hunt or fish—in order to feed themselves and their families. Such crimes were harshly punished: Livestock thieves often faced death if they were caught. Some members of the upper class advocated social, political, and economic reforms to benefit the poor. Many others found such ideas dangerous.

Vocabulary Development

solicitously (sə·lis′ə·təs·lē) *adv.*: in a caring or concerned way.

void (void) *n.*: empty space.

scrutinized (skrōōt′′n·īzd′) *v.*: looked at closely and carefully.

ample (am′pəl) *adj.*: roomy; large.

apparition (ap′ə·rish′ən) *n.*: ghost or ghostlike figure that appears unexpectedly.

Our English Coasts (1852) by William Holman Hunt.
The Granger Collection, New York.

The Ring

Isak Dinesen

On a summer morning a hundred and fifty years ago a young Danish squire and his wife went out for a walk on their land. They had been married a week. It had not been easy for them to get married, for the wife's family was higher in rank and wealthier than the husband's. But the two young people, now twenty-four and nineteen years old, had been set on their purpose for ten years; in the end her haughty parents had had to give in to them.

They were wonderfully happy. The stolen meetings and secret, tearful love letters were now things of the past. To God and man they were one; they could walk arm in arm in broad daylight and drive in the same carriage, and they would walk and drive so till the end of their days.

Their distant paradise had descended to earth and had proved, surprisingly, to be filled with the things of everyday life: with jesting and railleries, with breakfasts and suppers, with dogs, haymaking, and sheep. Sigismund, the young husband, had promised himself that from now there should be no stone in his bride's path, nor should any shadow fall across it. Lovisa,[1] the wife, felt that now, every day and for the first time in her young life, she moved and breathed in perfect freedom because she could never have any secret from her husband.

To Lovisa—whom her husband called Lise[2]—the rustic atmosphere of her new life was a matter of wonder and delight. Her husband's fear that the existence he could offer her might not be good enough for her filled her heart with laughter. It was not a long time since she had played with dolls; as now she dressed her own hair, looked over her linen press and arranged her flowers, she again lived through an enchanting and cherished experience: one was doing everything gravely and <u>solicitously</u>, and all the time one knew one was playing.

It was a lovely July morning. Little woolly clouds drifted high up in the sky, the air was full of sweet scents. Lise had on a white muslin frock and a large Italian straw hat. She and her husband took a path through the park; it wound on across the meadows, between small groves and groups of trees, to the sheep field. Sigismund was going to show his wife his sheep. For this reason she had not brought her small white dog, Bijou,[3] with her, for he would yap at the lambs and frighten them, or he would annoy the sheep dogs. Sigismund prided himself on his sheep; he had studied sheep breeding in Mecklenburg[4] and England, and had brought back with him Cotswold rams[5] by which to improve his Danish

stock. While they walked he explained to Lise the great possibilities and difficulties of the plan.

She thought: "How clever he is, what a lot of things he knows!" and at the same time: "What an absurd person he is, with his sheep! What a baby he is! I am a hundred years older than he."

But when they arrived at the sheepfold the old sheepmaster Mathias met them with the sad news that one of the English lambs was dead and two were sick. Lise saw that her husband was grieved by the tidings; while he questioned Mathias on the matter she kept silent and only gently pressed his arm. A couple of boys were sent off to fetch the sick lambs, while the master and servant went into the details of the case. It took some time.

Lise began to gaze about her and to think of other things. Twice her own thoughts made her blush deeply and happily, like a red rose, then slowly her blush died away, and the two men were still talking about sheep. A little while after, their conversation caught her attention. It had turned to a sheep thief.

This thief during the last months had broken into the sheepfolds of the neighborhood like a wolf, had killed and dragged away his prey like a wolf, and like a wolf had left no trace after him. Three nights ago the shepherd and his son on an estate ten miles away had caught him in the act. The thief had killed the man and knocked the boy senseless, and had managed to escape. There were men sent out to all sides to catch him, but nobody had seen him.

Lise wanted to hear more about the horrible event, and for her benefit old Mathias went through it once more. There had been a long fight in the sheep house, in many places the earthen floor was soaked with blood. In the fight the thief's left arm was broken; all the same, he had climbed a tall fence with a lamb on his back. Mathias added that he would like to string up the murderer with these two hands of his, and Lise nodded her head at him gravely in approval.

---

1. **Lovisa** (lō·vē′sə).
2. **Lise** (lē′sə).
3. **Bijou** (bē′zhōō′): French for "jewel."
4. **Mecklenburg:** agricultural region in northern Germany.
5. **Cotswold rams:** males of a kind of sheep originally bred in the Cotswold Hills of southwestern England.

Vocabulary

solicitously (sə·lis′ə·təs·lē) *adv.*: in a caring or concerned way.

The Lake in the Woods (1891) by Peder Monsted.

She remembered Red Riding Hood's wolf, and felt a pleasant little thrill running down her spine.

Sigismund had his own lambs in his mind, but he was too happy in himself to wish anything in the universe ill. After a minute he said: "Poor devil."

Lise said: "How can you pity such a terrible man? Indeed Grandmamma was right when she said that you were a revolutionary and a danger to society!" The thought of Grandmamma, and of the tears of past days, again turned her mind away from the gruesome tale she had just heard.

The boys brought the sick lambs and the men began to examine them carefully, lifting them up and trying to set them on their legs; they squeezed them here and there and made the little creatures whimper. Lise shrank from the show and her husband noticed her distress.

"You go home, my darling," he said, "this will take some time. But just walk ahead slowly, and I shall catch up with you."

So she was turned away by an impatient husband to whom his sheep meant more than his wife. If any experience could be sweeter than to be dragged out by him to look at those same sheep, it would be this. She dropped her large summer hat with its blue ribbons on the grass and told him to carry it back for her, for she wanted to feel the summer air on her forehead and in her hair. She walked on very slowly, as he had told her to do, for she wished to obey him in everything. As she walked she felt a great new happiness in being altogether alone, even without Bijou. She could not remember that she had ever before in all her life been altogether alone. The landscape around her was still, as if full of promise, and it was hers. Even the swallows cruising in the air were hers, for they belonged to him,[6] and he was hers.

She followed the curving edge of the grove and after a minute or two found that she was out of sight to the men by the sheep house. What could

---

6. **him:** Sigismund. In Denmark at the time of the story, birds and other wild animals on an estate were the owner's property, and anyone who hunted or caught them without permission would be prosecuted.

now, she wondered, be sweeter than to walk along the path in the long flowering meadow grass, slowly, slowly, and to let her husband overtake her there? It would be sweeter still, she reflected, to steal into the grove and to be gone, to have vanished from the surface of the earth from him when, tired of the sheep and longing for her company, he should turn the bend of the path to catch up with her.

An idea struck her; she stood still to think it over.

A few days ago her husband had gone for a ride and she had not wanted to go with him, but had strolled about with Bijou in order to explore her domain. Bijou then, gamboling, had led her straight into the grove. As she had followed him, gently forcing her way into the shrubbery, she had suddenly come upon a glade in the midst of it, a narrow space like a small alcove with hangings of thick green and golden brocade, big enough to hold two or three people in it. She had felt at that moment that she had come into the very heart of her new home. If today she could find the spot again she would stand perfectly still there, hidden from all the world. Sigismund would look for her in all directions; he would be unable to understand what had become of her and for a minute, for a short minute—or, perhaps, if she was firm and cruel enough, for five—he would realize what a <u>void</u>, what an unendurably sad and horrible place the universe would be when she was no longer in it. She gravely <u>scrutinized</u> the grove to find the right entrance to her hiding place, then went in.

She took great care to make no noise at all, therefore advanced exceedingly slowly. When a twig caught the flounces of her <u>ample</u> skirt she loosened it softly from the muslin, so as not to crack it. Once a branch took hold of one of her long golden curls; she stood still, with her arms lifted, to free it. A little way into the grove the soil became moist; her light steps no longer made any sound upon it. With one hand she held her small handkerchief to her lips, as if to emphasize the secretness of her course. She found the spot she sought and bent down to divide the foliage and make a door to her sylvan closet. At this, the hem

of her dress caught her foot and she stopped to loosen it. As she rose she looked into the face of a man who was already in the shelter.

He stood up erect, two steps off. He must have watched her as she made her way straight toward him.

She took him in in one single glance. His face was bruised and scratched, his hands and wrists stained with dark filth. He was dressed in rags, barefooted, with tatters wound round his naked ankles. His arms hung down to his sides, his right hand clasped the hilt of a knife. He was about her own age. The man and the woman looked at each other.

This meeting in the wood from beginning to end passed without a word; what happened could only be rendered by pantomime. To the two actors in the pantomime it was timeless; according to a clock it lasted four minutes.

She had never in her life been exposed to danger. It did not occur to her to sum up her position, or to work out the length of time it would take to call her husband or Mathias, whom at this moment she could hear shouting to his dogs. She beheld the man before her as she would have beheld a forest ghost: the <u>apparition</u> itself, not the sequels of it, changes the world to the human who faces it.

Although she did not take her eyes off the face before her, she sensed that the alcove had been turned into a covert.[7] On the ground a couple of sacks formed a couch; there were some gnawed bones by it. A fire must have been made here in the night, for there were cinders strewn on the forest floor.

After a while she realized that he was observing her just as she was observing him. He was no

---

7. **covert** *n.:* covered shelter.

Vocabulary

void (void) *n.:* empty space.

scrutinized (skroot′n·īzd′) *v.:* looked at closely and carefully.

ample (am′pəl) *adj.:* roomy; large.

apparition (ap′ə·rish′ən) *n.:* ghost or ghostlike figure that appears unexpectedly.

The Forest Palace (1918) by Johannes S. Kjarval.

Listasafn Islands, National Gallery of Iceland. Inv. no. LÎ 162. Purchased in 1919.

longer just run to earth and crouching for a spring, but he was wondering, trying to know. At that she seemed to see herself with the eyes of the wild animal at bay in his dark hiding place: her silently approaching white figure, which might mean death.

He moved his right arm till it hung down straight before him between his legs. Without lifting the hand he bent the wrist and slowly raised the point of the knife till it pointed at her throat. The gesture was mad, unbelievable. He did not smile as he made it, but his nostrils distended, the corners of his mouth quivered a little. Then slowly he put the knife back in the sheath by his belt.

She had no object of value about her, only the wedding ring which her husband had set on her finger in church, a week ago. She drew it off, and in this movement dropped her handkerchief. She reached out her hand with the ring toward him.

She did not bargain for her life. She was fearless by nature, and the horror with which he inspired her was not fear of what he might do to her. She commanded him, she besought him to vanish as he had come, to take a dreadful figure out of her life, so that it should never have been there. In the dumb movement her young form had the grave authoritativeness of a priestess conjuring down some monstrous being by a sacred sign.

He slowly reached out his hand to hers, his finger touched hers, and her hand was steady at the touch. But he did not take the ring. As she let it go it dropped to the ground as her handkerchief had done.

For a second the eyes of both followed it. It rolled a few inches toward him and stopped before his bare foot. In a hardly perceivable movement he kicked it away and again looked into her face. They remained like that, she knew not how long, but she felt that during that time something happened, things were changed.

He bent down and picked up her handkerchief. All the time gazing at her, he again drew his knife and wrapped the tiny bit of cambric round the blade. This was difficult for him to do because his left arm was broken. While he did it his face under the dirt and suntan slowly grew whiter till it was almost phosphorescent. Fumbling with both hands, he once more stuck the knife into the sheath. Either the sheath was too big and had never fitted the knife, or the blade was much worn—it went in. For two or three more seconds his gaze rested on her face; then he lifted his own face a little, the strange radiance still upon it, and closed his eyes.

The movement was definitive and unconditional. In this one motion he did what she had begged him to do: he vanished and was gone. She was free.

She took a step backward, the immovable, blind face before her, then bent as she had done to enter the hiding place, and glided away as noiselessly as she had come. Once outside the grove she stood still and looked round for the meadow path, found it and began to walk home.

Her husband had not yet rounded the edge of the grove. Now he saw her and helloed to her gaily; he came up quickly and joined her.

The path here was so narrow that he kept half behind her and did not touch her. He began to explain to her what had been the matter with the lambs. She walked a step before him and thought: All is over.

After a while he noticed her silence, came up beside her to look at her face and asked, "What is the matter?"

She searched her mind for something to say, and at last said: "I have lost my ring."

"What ring?" he asked her.

She answered, "My wedding ring."

As she heard her own voice pronounce the words she conceived their meaning.

Her wedding ring. "With this ring"—dropped by one and kicked away by another—"with this ring I thee wed."[8] With this lost ring she had wedded herself to something. To what? To poverty, persecution, total loneliness. To the sorrows and the sinfulness of this earth. "And what therefore God has joined together let man not put asunder."

"I will find you another ring," her husband said. "You and I are the same as we were on our wedding day; it will do as well. We are husband and wife today, too, as much as yesterday, I suppose."

Her face was so still that he did not know if she had heard what he said. It touched him that she should take the loss of his ring so to heart. He took her hand and kissed it. It was cold, not quite the same hand as he had last kissed. He stopped to make her stop with him.

"Do you remember where you had the ring on last?" he asked.

"No," she answered.

"Have you any idea," he asked, "where you may have lost it?"

"No," she answered. "I have no idea at all."

---

8. **with this ring . . . I thee wed:** quotation from the vows exchanged at a wedding ceremony.

Response and Analysis

Reading Check

1. Identify and explain the **causes** and **effects** of the following events in the story:
   - Lise's husband sends her home while he stays with the lambs.
   - Lise goes into the secluded grove.
   - Lise does not tell her husband the truth at the end.

Thinking Critically

2. Why do you think Lise feels at the beginning of the story that never having secrets from her husband allows her to move and breathe in "perfect freedom"?

3. Identify the **dynamic character** in this story. How would you describe the way that character has changed by the end of the story? Did you predict this change when you began reading the story? Explain.

4. Explain why Lise offers her wedding ring to the murderer. What might the ring **symbolize,** or represent, in Lise's life? What change in Lise's life does the loss of the ring represent?

5. Why is it **ironic** that Sigismund is touched that his wife "should take the loss of his ring so to heart"?

Extending and Evaluating

6. What do you think Lise and Sigismund's married life will be like from now on? Use evidence from the story to support your position.

7. Consider the biblical account of the Fall of Adam and Eve (see page 56). Explain how "The Ring" could be seen as a modern version of this story of the loss of innocence.

WRITING
Analyzing a Character

In an essay, analyze the character of Lise, focusing on the change that occurs when she encounters the murderer in the glade. In describing her character before and after this encounter, remember to consider her actions, the things she says, the way other characters respond to her, and the writer's direct comments about Lise and the events in the glade. Include your answers to these questions: Why does Lise decide to enter the glade? Why doesn't she speak to the man? Why does she offer the murderer her wedding ring? Why doesn't she tell her husband about the man in the glade?

North Carolina Competency Goal
1.03; 4.05; 5.03; 6.01

Vocabulary Development
Which Word?

solicitously	ample
void	apparition
scrutinized	

Which one of the Vocabulary words above could be used to name or describe the following things or actions?

1. a ghost
2. the blackness of outer space
3. the way a kind person treats other people
4. a large, loose-fitting blouse
5. looked closely at a piece of evidence

INTERNET

Projects and Activities

Keyword: LE5 WL-7

SKILLS FOCUS

Literary Skills
Analyze static and dynamic characters.

Reading Skills
Understand cause and effect.

Writing Skills
Analyze a character.

Vocabulary Skills
Answer questions about vocabulary words.

Anna Akhmatova
(1889–1966)
Russia

Anna Akhmatova (1914) by N. I. Altman.
The Granger Collection, New York.

Anna Akhmatova (uk·mät′ə·və) wrote more than seven hundred poems during her long career, but for most of her life she was forbidden to publish by the Soviet government. She was even afraid to write down her poems for fear they'd be used as evidence against her, so she memorized them and whispered them to friends, who recorded them for her. Today she is considered one of Russia's greatest poets.

Anna Andreyevna Gorenko grew up just outside St. Petersburg and began writing poetry at age eleven. Concerned that her poems would somehow embarrass the family, her father insisted that she take a pen name, so she chose her great-grandmother's name—Akhmatova. At twenty-one, she joined a group of young poets and married their leader, Nikolay Gumilyov, though they divorced later.

Although her first two books of lyric poems were widely praised, after the Russian Revolution in 1917 government officials condemned Akhmatova's writing as "bourgeois and aristocratic." (*Bourgeois* was a term of contempt used to refer to property-owning classes, regarded by the Communists as exploiters of the workers.) Many intellectuals fled the Soviet Union at this time, but Akhmatova chose to remain in her homeland. In 1921, her ex-husband was executed for conspiracy to overthrow the government, and Akhmatova too came under suspicion. In 1922, she was blacklisted by the Communist Party and forbidden to publish. In 1935, Akhmatova's only son, Lev, was imprisoned. Each day for seventeen months, Akhmatova stood in line with other women outside the Leningrad prison, hoping for news of loved ones inside. Upon discovering who Akhmatova was, one of the women asked her to describe the daily vigil held in front of the prison. The result was what many critics consider Akhmatova's masterpiece, the fifteen-part poem *Requiem* (1964). Although Akhmatova wrote it between 1935 and 1940, it was not published in Russia in its entirety until the late 1980s.

In 1940, Akhmatova was allowed to publish a book of early poems, but it was quickly banned. In 1946, she was condemned by Soviet leaders for writing "empty poetry lacking in ideas and alien to our people" and was subsequently expelled from the Union of Soviet Writers. After her son was arrested again in 1949, Akhmatova wrote several poems praising Stalin and communism in an effort to expedite his release.

After Stalin died in 1953, Akhmatova's poems began to appear in Russian magazines. Akhmatova also wrote literary criticism and translated the works of writers such as Victor Hugo and Rabindranath Tagore. She died in a convalescent home near Moscow at the age of seventy-six.

Before You Read

"Everything Is Plundered..."
and Before spring there are days like these

Make the Connection
Quickwrite 🖊

You are a magazine photo editor, and you've just been given two assignments. Your first assignment is to put together a photo essay that shows the horror and destruction of war. Your second assignment is to create a photo essay using nature photos to evoke feelings of peace and stability. In two columns (headed *War* and *Nature*), jot down your ideas for the images you'd choose.

Literary Focus
Imagery

Imagery is language that appeals to all five senses—sight, hearing, smell, touch, and taste. A poem's imagery puts you in the speaker's shoes—observing what the speaker sees, smelling what's in the air. Without imagery, language becomes abstract, pale, and colorless. In a review of her second book of poetry, Anna Akhmatova's first husband wrote, "The most outstanding factor in Akhmatova's poetry is her style: she almost never explains, she demonstrates...." As you read these two poems, see how Akhmatova uses imagery to convey her ideas and to evoke feelings.

> **Imagery** is language that appeals to the senses of sight, hearing, smell, touch, and taste.
>
> *For more on Imagery, see the Handbook of Literary and Historical Terms.*

Landscape with a Green House (1908) by Wassily Kandinsky.
Hermitage, St. Petersburg, Russia.

Background

In 1912, Anna Akhmatova and her husband, Nikolay Gumilyov, helped found a movement called **Acmeism** (ak′mē·iz′əm), or **Adamism,** in reaction to what they saw as the vagueness and mysticism of Symbolism (see page 791), which was extremely popular in St. Petersburg at the time. Rejecting Symbolism's ornate style and ambiguity, the Acmeists called for clarity of ideas and language achieved through carefully chosen words and a focus on the real world. The poet Joseph Brodsky called Akhmatova "a traditional poet, in the highest sense of the word" and compared her poems, in their apparent "simplicity," to those of the American poet Robert Frost.

go. hrw .com

INTERNET
More About
Anna Akhmatova
Keyword:
LE5 WL-7

SKILLS FOCUS

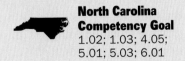

North Carolina Competency Goal
1.02; 1.03; 4.05; 5.01; 5.03; 6.01

Literary Skills
Understand imagery.

The New Planet (1921) by Konstantin Yuon.
Tretyakov Gallery, Moscow, Russia.

"Everything Is Plundered ..."

Anna Akhmatova

translated by **Stanley Kunitz**

Everything is plundered, betrayed, sold,
Death's great black wing scrapes the air,
Misery gnaws to the bone.
Why then do we not despair?

5 By day, from the surrounding woods,
cherries blow summer into town;
at night the deep transparent skies
glitter with new galaxies.

And the miraculous comes so close
10 to the ruined, dirty houses—
something not known to anyone at all,
but wild in our breast for centuries.

Before spring there are days like these

Anna Akhmatova

translated by **Judith Hemschemeyer**

Before spring there are days like these:
Under the dense snow the meadow rests,
The trees merrily, drily rustle,
And the warm wind is tender and supple.
And the body marvels at its lightness,
And you don't recognize your own house,
And that song you were tired of before,
You sing like a new one, with deep emotion.

Response and Analysis

Thinking Critically

1. What **mood,** or emotional effect, is produced by the imagery in stanza 1 of "Everything Is Plundered . . ."? Compare the images Akhmatova uses in this poem with those on your Quickwrite list (see page 891).

2. A **metaphor** is a figure of speech that compares two unlike things by saying that one thing *is* another. Explain the two implied metaphors in lines 2 and 3 of "Everything Is Plundered . . .".

3. What do you think the speaker means by "the miraculous" (line 9)? The dash at the end of line 10 tells you that lines 11 and 12 explain or give further information about what "the miraculous" means. **Paraphrase** this stanza in your own words.

4. The speaker poses a question in line 4 of "Everything Is Plundered . . .". How does the rest of the poem answer that question?

5. How would you state the **theme,** or central message, of "Everything Is Plundered . . ."? How is this theme supported by the poem's **imagery**? Refer to the text to support your view.

6. What **mood** is produced by the imagery in "Before spring . . ."? Find specific words and phrases that create that mood.

7. What do you think the speaker means by line 6 of "Before spring . . ."? What feeling or emotion does this line suggest?

8. Translators are challenged to find just the right word to convey meaning, to suggest connotations, and to re-create a poem's sound effects. Analyze the sound effects in one of Akhmatova's poems. Consider each of the following devices:

   - **assonance,** the repetition of vowel sounds (*gray lake*)

   - **alliteration,** the repetition of consonant sounds (*red robin*)

   - **near/slant rhyme,** the use of sounds that are similar but not exactly the same at the ends of lines (*dove, wove*)

   - **repetition** of words and sentence structures

WRITING

Comparing Two Poems

In a brief essay, **compare and contrast** the two poems by Akhmatova. In your comparison, consider how images of nature are used in the two poems to convey meaning. How are the themes, or messages, of the poems alike? How are they different? What is simple and straightforward about each poem, and what is elusive, or hard to understand? Support your points with specific references to the text of both poems. You might analyze the following elements point by point in your comparison:

Literary Element	"Everything Is Plundered . . ."	"Before spring . . ."
Imagery		
Structure		
Theme		
Mood		
Figurative language		

North Carolina Competency Goal
1.02; 1.03; 4.02; 4.05; 5.03; 6.01

INTERNET

Projects and Activities

Keyword: LE5 WL-7

SKILLS FOCUS

Literary Skills
Analyze imagery.

Writing Skills
Compare two poems.

Federico García Lorca

(1898–1936)

Spain

On the evening of July 19, 1936, the Chilean poet Pablo Neruda (nə·rōo′də) (see page 937), then living in Spain, went to meet his friend Federico García Lorca (fe′de·rē′kô gär·sē′ə lôr′kə). Neruda waited and waited, but Lorca never appeared. He had been kidnapped by Fascist supporters of the Spanish dictator Francisco Franco. The kidnappers took Lorca to a Granada cemetery, forced him to dig his own grave, and then shot him. The murder shocked the world, especially because the thirty-eight-year-old writer had never taken an active role in politics. Viewed as a martyr, he became known as the "Poet of the Blood," and his poems about sorrow and death took on additional significance.

Granada, the site of Lorca's brutal murder, was also the city near which he grew up. Born into a well-to-do farming family, Lorca valued the simple pleasures of rural life and also learned to love music, poetry, and all the arts. In 1919, Lorca went to Madrid to study at the city's university. Among the talented artists he met there were Juan Ramón Jiménez, already a distinguished poet, and Salvador Dali, the experimental painter whose surrealism would influence Lorca's poetry and plays.

His most famous plays are tragedies dealing with thwarted womanhood. *Blood Wedding* (1933) is the story of a bride who runs away with a previous lover and is then murdered by her husband. This play, together with *Yerma* (1934) and *The House of Bernarda Alba* (1936), is among Lorca's finest dramatic works.

Shortly before his death, Lorca published *Lament for the Death of a Bullfighter* (1935), considered the greatest elegy in modern Spanish poetry and a moving premonition of his own death. Lorca was at the height of his celebrity when he was murdered by the Fascists. As Pablo Neruda later mourned, "Who could have believed there were monsters on this earth, in his own Granada, capable of such an inconceivable crime?"

Before You Read

The Guitar

Make the Connection

Music can evoke all kinds of feelings, from sadness to joy, from excitement to serenity. Some of us even have a favorite musical instrument—oboe, piano, violin, electric guitar—whose sounds touch us in a unique way. Describe the sounds your favorite musical instrument makes. What feelings and images do these sounds bring to mind?

Literary Focus

Free Verse

Free verse is poetry that is free of the traditional rules governing meter, rhyme scheme, and form. Free verse is written to imitate the rhythms of ordinary conversation. Although it does not have a regular meter or rhyme scheme, free verse does include poetic devices such as imagery, rhyming sounds, onomatopoeia, alliteration, assonance (repeated vowel sounds), and other kinds of repetition. Because there is no fixed meter to determine where each line should end, the free-verse poet must decide how to break the poem into lines. Poets use line breaks to shape meaning, build emphasis, and create rhythm. "The Guitar" was originally written in Spanish; notice that the translator uses free verse in translating the poem from Spanish to English.

> **Free verse** is poetry that is free of traditional rules governing meter, rhyme scheme, and form.
>
> *For more on Free Verse, see the Handbook of Literary and Historical Terms.*

Background

Lorca often drew inspiration from Andalusia, the area of southern Spain where he grew up. Andalusia's mixture of Arab and Spanish culture and its rich tradition of Romany folk music includes *cante jondo,* literally "deep song." Highly emotional and rhythmic, *cante jondo* is often played as accompaniment to flamenco, a passionate style of dance performed by colorfully dressed dancers. Many of Lorca's poems, including "The Guitar," evoke the strong feelings associated with *cante jondo.*

The guitar, which is usually used to play *cante jondo,* has long been associated with Spain. It was developed, probably in the sixteenth century, from the *vihuela,* a guitar-shaped instrument played by medieval Spanish minstrels. Later modifications resulted in what is now known as the classical or Spanish guitar. The work of the great Spanish guitarist Andrés Segovia (1893–1987) helped popularize this instrument in the twentieth century.

Flamenco performers singing in the Zambra La Rocio cave in Granada, Spain.

North Carolina Competency Goal
1.03; 4.05; 5.01; 5.03

go.hrw.com

INTERNET

More About Federico García Lorca
Keyword: LE5 WL-7

SKILLS FOCUS

Literary Skills
Understand free verse.

Federico García Lorca **895**

Guitar and Newspaper
(1925) by Juan Gris.
Galerie Daniel Malingue, Paris.

The Guitar

Federico García Lorca

translated by **Rachel Benson** *and* **Robert O'Brien**

The cry of the guitar
begins.
The crystals of dawn are
breaking.
5　The cry of the guitar
begins.
It's useless to stop it.
It's impossible to
stop it.
10　Its cry monotonous
as the weeping of water,
as the weeping of wind
over the snowfall.
It's impossible to

15　stop it.
It cries for
distant things.
Sand of the scalding South
seeking white camellias.°
20　It mourns the arrow without target,
evening without morning, and the first
bird dead upon the branch.
Oh, guitar!
Heart wounded by five swords.

---

19. camellias (kə·mēl′yəz): blooms of an
　　evergreen shrub that grows in mild
　　climates. Camellia bushes would not
　　thrive in a hot, sandy place.

Response and Analysis

Thinking Critically

1. What word is used to name the sound of the guitar in line 1? Identify the point where this word is repeated in the poem. Why is this word important?

2. What sounds in nature is the sound of the guitar compared to?

3. What three things does the guitar mourn?

4. What part of the body is the guitar compared to in the last line? What do you think the "five swords" are?

5. How would you describe the overriding emotion associated with the guitar and its sounds? What **images** in the poem suggest this emotion?

6. In saying that it is "impossible to stop" the guitar, what might the speaker be suggesting?

7. This poem is written in **free verse,** yet it creates a haunting rhythm. Find examples of **repetition** in the poem that help create that rhythm. (Look for repetition of sentence structures and words.) Find examples of **assonance,** or repeated vowel sounds, that help create the poem's music.

WRITING

Comparing Translations

In a brief essay, compare Robert Bly's translation of "The Guitar" (on the right) with the translation by Benson and O'Brien that you have just read. Focus on **word choice, imagery,** and **sounds.** You can construct your comparison either by analyzing each translation separately or by discussing the literary elements in sequence, explaining how each translation deals with those elements. Here are outlines for the two essay structures:

Outline A

Translation 1
- word choice
- imagery
- sounds

Translation 2
- word choice
- imagery
- sounds

Outline B

Word choice
- translation 1
- translation 2

Imagery
- translation 1
- translation 2

Sounds
- translation 1
- translation 2

The Guitar
Federico García Lorca
translated by Robert Bly

    The crying of the guitar
starts.
The goblets
of the dawn break.
5 The crying of the guitar
starts.
No use to stop it.
It is impossible
to stop it.
10 It cries repeating itself
as the water cries,
as the wind cries
over the snow.
It is impossible
15 to stop it.
It is crying for things
far off.
The warm sand of the South
that asks for white camellias.
20 For the arrow with nothing to hit,
the evening with no dawn coming,
and the first bird of all dead
on the branch.
Guitar!
25 Heart wounded, gravely,
by five swords.

North Carolina Competency Goal
1.03; 5.03

INTERNET
Projects and Activities
Keyword:
LE5 WL-7

Literary Skills
Analyze free verse.

Writing Skills
Compare translations.

Albert Camus

(1913–1960)
Algeria/France

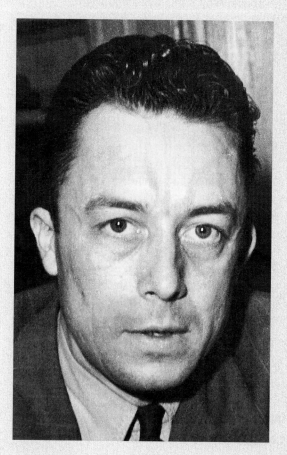

Albert Camus (ka·moo′) believed that every person asks *why?* at some point in his or her life. We wonder why we are here, what we should be doing, and what life itself means. **Existentialism,** a philosophy that arose in response to the confusion many people felt in the early decades of the twentieth century, attempted to answer these questions by claiming that neither the universe nor human life has any inherent, or essential, meaning. Camus reacted against this attitude by creating his own brand of humanistic existentialism. He believed that although existence probably has no ultimate meaning, human beings have the capacity—and the need—to create meaningful lives for themselves. Camus suggested that instead of giving up, each person must try to create his or her own meaning in life by making choices and acting on them.

Of French and Spanish descent, Camus grew up in Algeria when it was still a French colony. After studying philosophy at the University of Algiers, Camus became active in Algeria's French-language theater. He also worked for a French-language newspaper and published two essay collections. In these essays and in his later work, Camus articulated his philosophy of moral commitment, which earned him the title *le Juste,* "the just man."

In 1942, Camus published *The Stranger* and "The Myth of Sisyphus," which explore the quest for moral purpose in a meaningless world. The protagonist of *The Stranger* refuses to tell white lies in order to fit into polite society. He also refuses to believe in any religion or in human love. He nevertheless discovers, while in prison awaiting execution, a passion for the simple fact of life itself. In "The Myth of Sisyphus," Camus reinterprets a classical myth to show that although life may be futile, a person can find value in the struggle to reach even an impossible moral goal. In Camus's view, Sisyphus, condemned by the gods to endlessly roll a boulder uphill, is happy because he has found meaning in his impossible task. By extension, Camus implies that life is our "rock"— what matters most is that we do something with it. Camus won the Nobel Prize in literature in 1957.

Before You Read

The Myth of Sisyphus

Make the Connection

Something that is absurd is not sensible or reasonable; it is so far removed from reality and rationality as to be ridiculous, even laughable. What would an "absurd hero" be? What might such a hero do, and what might the outcome of his or her actions be?

Literary Focus

Allusion

Writers often include **allusions** in their work—references to areas of culture, such as literature, history, art, philosophy, politics, religion, and myth. They expect readers to recognize these cultural references and hope that the associations made will deepen readers' understanding and appreciation of the writer's ideas. Beginning with the title of his essay, "The Myth of Sisyphus," Albert Camus makes frequent references to characters, events, and places from Greek mythology. From these allusions Camus builds his meaning.

> An **allusion** is a reference in a literary work to an area of culture or field of knowledge.
>
> *For more on Allusion, see the Handbook of Literary and Historical Terms.*

Reading Skills

Using Prior Knowledge

When you read a literary work rich in allusions, it is helpful to sort out what you already know from what you need to find out. You may find it helpful to create and fill out a chart like this one as you read:

Allusion	What I Know	What I Need to Find Out
Pluto	God of the Underworld	Relationship to Sisyphus

You can find the meanings of allusions in a variety of ways: reading footnotes, looking for context clues, and consulting print and online reference sources.

Background

Camus based his essay on the classical myth of Sisyphus (sis'ə·fəs), a clever but arrogant human who loves life and dares to defy the gods. After his death, Sisyphus even manages to escape from Pluto's dark Underworld and return to life, a crime that deeply offends Jupiter, king of the gods. To punish Sisyphus, Jupiter condemns him to roll a huge rock up a steep hill for all eternity. As soon as Sisyphus reaches the top of the hill, he has to stand by and watch while the rock rolls back down. Then he has to return to the bottom of the hill and roll the rock to the top again, and again, and again, with no end to his toil.

Vocabulary Development

levity (lev'i·tē) *n.:* lack of seriousness; disrespectful lightness or improper gaiety.

benediction (ben'ə·dik'shən) *n.:* blessing; gift.

chastise (chas·tīz') *v.:* punish; criticize harshly.

absurd (ab·sʉrd') *adj.:* so unreasonable as to be ridiculous; meaningless.

fidelity (fə·del'ə·tē) *n.:* loyalty.

North Carolina Competency Goal
1.03; 4.05; 5.01; 5.03

INTERNET

Vocabulary Practice
•
More About Albert Camus

Keyword: LE5 WL-7

SKILLS FOCUS

Literary Skills
Understand allusion.

Reading Skills
Use prior knowledge.

899

The Myth of Sisyphus

Albert Camus
translated by **Justin O'Brien**

The gods had condemned Sisyphus to ceaselessly rolling a rock to the top of a mountain, whence the stone would fall back of its own weight. They had thought with some reason that there is no more dreadful punishment than futile and hopeless labor.

If one believes Homer, Sisyphus was the wisest and most prudent of mortals. According to another tradition, however, he was disposed to practice the profession of highwayman.[1] I see no contradiction in this. Opinions differ as to the reasons why he became the futile laborer of the underworld. To begin with, he is accused of a certain levity in regard to the gods. He stole their secrets. Aegina, the daughter of Aesopus, was carried off by Jupiter. The father was shocked by that disappearance and complained to Sisyphus. He, who knew of the abduction, offered to tell about it on condition that Aesopus would give water to the citadel of Corinth.[2] To the celestial thunderbolts he preferred the benediction of water. He was punished for this in the underworld. Homer tells us also that Sisyphus had put Death in chains. Pluto could not endure the sight of his deserted, silent empire. He dispatched the god of war, who liberated Death from the hands of her conqueror.

It is said also that Sisyphus, being near to death, rashly wanted to test his wife's love. He ordered her to cast his unburied body into the middle of the public square. Sisyphus woke up in the underworld. And there, annoyed by an obedience so contrary to human love, he obtained from Pluto permission to return to earth in order to chastise his wife. But when he had seen again the face of this world, enjoyed water and sun, warm stones and the sea, he no longer wanted to go back to the infernal darkness. Recalls, signs of anger, warnings were of no avail. Many years more he lived facing the curve of the gulf, the sparkling sea, and the smiles of earth. A decree of the gods was necessary. Mercury came and seized the impudent man by the collar and, snatching him from his joys, led him forcibly back to the underworld, where his rock was ready for him.

You have already grasped that Sisyphus is the absurd hero. He *is*, as much through his passions as through his torture. His scorn of the gods, his hatred of death, and his passion for life won him that unspeakable penalty in which the whole being is exerted toward accomplishing nothing. This is the price that must be paid for the passions of this earth. Nothing is told us about Sisyphus in the underworld. Myths are made for the imagination to breathe life into them. As for this myth, one sees merely the whole effort of a body straining to raise the huge stone, to roll it and push it up a slope a hundred times over; one sees the face screwed up, the cheek tight against the stone, the shoulder bracing the clay-covered mass, the foot wedging it, the fresh start with arms outstretched, the wholly human security of two earth-clotted hands. At the very end of his long effort measured by skyless space and time without depth, the purpose is achieved. Then Sisyphus watches the stone rush down in a few moments toward that lower world whence he will have to push it up again toward the summit. He goes back down to the plain.

It is during that return, that pause, that Sisyphus interests me. A face that toils so close to stones is already stone itself! I see that man going

---

1. **highwayman** *n.:* robber on a highway.
2. **Corinth** (kôr′inth): ancient city in Greece.

Vocabulary

levity (lev′i·tē) *n.:* lack of seriousness; disrespectful lightness or improper gaiety.
benediction (ben′ə·dik′shən) *n.:* blessing; gift.
chastise (chas·tīz′) *v.:* punish; criticize harshly.
absurd (ab·surd′) *adj.:* so unreasonable as to be ridiculous; meaningless.

Sisyphus (1992) by William Wolff.

back down with a heavy yet measured step toward the torment of which he will never know the end. That hour like a breathing space which returns as surely as his suffering, that is the hour of consciousness. At each of those moments when he leaves the heights and gradually sinks toward the lairs of the gods, he is superior to his fate. He is stronger than his rock.

If this myth is tragic, that is because its hero is conscious. Where would his torture be, indeed, if at every step the hope of succeeding upheld him? The workman of today works every day in his life at the same tasks, and this fate is no less absurd. But it is tragic only at the rare moments when it becomes conscious. Sisyphus, proletarian[3] of the gods, powerless and rebellious, knows the whole extent of his wretched condition: It is what he

---

3. **proletarian** (prō′lə·ter′ē·ən) *n.:* member of the working class.

thinks of during his descent. The lucidity that was to constitute his torture at the same time crowns his victory. There is no fate that cannot be surmounted by scorn.

If the descent is thus sometimes performed in sorrow, it can also take place in joy. This word is not too much. Again I fancy Sisyphus returning toward his rock, and the sorrow was in the beginning. When the images of earth cling too tightly to memory, when the call of happiness becomes too insistent, it happens that melancholy rises in man's heart: This is the rock's victory, this is the rock itself. The boundless grief is too heavy to bear. These are our nights of Gethsemane.[4] But crushing truths perish from being acknowledged. Thus, Oedipus[5] at the outset obeys fate without knowing it. But from the moment he knows, his tragedy begins. Yet at the same moment, blind and desperate, he realizes that the only bond linking him to the world is the cool hand of a girl. Then a tremendous remark rings out: "Despite so many ordeals, my advanced age and the nobility of my soul make me conclude that all is well." Sophocles' Oedipus, like Dostoevsky's Kirilov,[6] thus gives the recipe for the absurd victory. Ancient wisdom confirms modern heroism.

One does not discover the absurd without being tempted to write a manual of happiness. "What! by such narrow ways—?" There is but one world, however. Happiness and the absurd are two sons of the same earth. They are inseparable. It would be a mistake to say that happiness necessarily springs from the absurd discovery. It happens as well that the feeling of the absurd springs from happiness. "I conclude that all is well," says Oedipus, and that remark is sacred. It echoes in the wild and limited universe of man. It teaches that all is not, has not been, exhausted. It drives out of this world a god who had come into it with dissatisfaction and a preference for futile sufferings. It makes of fate a human matter, which must be settled among men.

All Sisyphus' silent joy is contained therein. His fate belongs to him. His rock is his thing. Likewise, the absurd man, when he contemplates his torment, silences all the idols. In the universe suddenly restored to its silence, the myriad wondering little voices of the earth rise up. Unconscious, secret calls, invitations from all the faces, they are the necessary reverse and price of victory. There is no sun without shadow, and it is essential to know the night. The absurd man says yes and his effort will henceforth be unceasing. If there is a personal fate, there is no higher destiny, or at least there is but one which he concludes is inevitable and despicable. For the rest, he knows himself to be the master of his days. At that subtle moment when man glances backward over his life, Sisyphus returning toward his rock, in that slight pivoting he contemplates that series of unrelated actions which becomes his fate, created by him, combined under his memory's eye, and soon sealed by his death. Thus, convinced of the wholly human origin of all that is human, a blind man eager to see who knows that the night has no end, he is still on the go. The rock is still rolling.

I leave Sisyphus at the foot of the mountain! One always finds one's burden again. But Sisyphus teaches the higher <u>fidelity</u> that negates the gods and raises rocks. He too concludes that all is well. This universe henceforth without a master seems to him neither sterile nor futile. Each atom of that stone, each mineral flake of that night-filled mountain, in itself forms a world. The struggle itself toward the heights is enough to fill a man's heart. One must imagine Sisyphus happy.

---

4. **Gethsemane** (geth·sem′ə·nē): garden east of Jerusalem, where Jesus suffered intensely as he contemplated his possible death.
5. **Oedipus** (ed′i·pəs): character in Greek mythology who unknowingly kills his father and marries his mother. In *Oedipus at Colonus,* the last of three plays written by the Greek dramatist Sophocles (c. 496–406 B.C.) about this tragic hero, Oedipus has blinded himself and is led by the hand by his daughter Antigone.
6. **Kirilov** (kē·rē′luf): character in Dostoevsky's 1872 novel *The Possessed.*

Vocabulary
fidelity (fə·del′ə·tē) *n.:* loyalty.

Response and Analysis

Reading Check

1. What is Sisyphus condemned to do by the gods?

2. What happens when Sisyphus is allowed to return to earth after his death?

3. What kind of hero does Camus claim Sisyphus is?

Thinking Critically

4. How does Sisyphus behave toward the gods? What does this behavior tell you about Sisyphus's **character**?

5. What part of Sisyphus's labor most interests Camus? How does Sisyphus overcome the absurdity, or meaninglessness, of his task?

6. Why do you think Camus includes **allusions** to Gethsemane and Oedipus in his essay? How do these references relate to Sisyphus's plight and add to the meaning of the essay?

7. What other **allusions** does Camus include in the essay? What does each one mean, and how do you know? You may want to check your reading notes.

8. The story of Sisyphus has given us the word *Sisyphean* (sis′ə·fē′ən), an adjective used to describe a task that seems hopeless, unproductive, and without end. Does Camus view Sisyphus's task as hopeless and unproductive? Explain.

9. What lessons on facing life's absurdities does Camus draw from the story of Sisyphus? Can you imagine Sisyphus as happy? Give reasons for your answer.

Extending and Evaluating

10. Camus's writing has been called epigrammatic, meaning he writes in **epigrams,** brief statements packed with meaning. Find one sentence in "The Myth of Sisyphus" that has particular meaning for you, and explain its significance.

WRITING

Responding to the Text

According to Camus, "the workman of today works every day in his life at the same tasks, and this fate is no less absurd" than Sisyphus's meaningless and repetitive labor. Imagine yourself as one of the workers Camus describes. In a brief journal entry, discuss the ways Camus's philosophy might help you face life with hope and joy in spite of the obstacles and absurdities you may face.

Vocabulary Development
Analogies

levity	absurd
benediction	fidelity
chastise	

In an **analogy** the words in one pair relate to each other in the same way as the words in a second pair. Complete each of the following analogies with a Vocabulary word from the list above.

1. PRAISE : BLAME :: _____ : curse

2. SHOUT : WHISPER :: _____ : reward

3. CAREFUL : CAUTIOUS :: _____ : ridiculous

4. DISDAIN : DISLIKE :: _____ : loyalty

5. SELFISHNESS : GENEROSITY :: _____ : seriousness

North Carolina Competency Goal
1.03; 4.05; 5.03; 6.01

INTERNET
Projects and Activities
Keyword:
LE5 WL-7

SKILLS FOCUS

Literary Skills
Analyze allusion.

Reading Skills
Use prior knowledge.

Writing Skills
Respond to the text.

Vocabulary Skills
Complete word analogies.

Primo Levi
(1919–1987)
Italy

Primo Levi (prē′mō lä′vē) was a highly versatile writer, producing distinguished novels, essays, and short stories as well as poetry and literary translations. But it is as an author of memoirs that Levi is best known. A **memoir** is a type of autobiography that usually focuses on a particular period or series of events. In Levi's case, the historical significance of the events he chronicled was overwhelming: the atrocities of the Holocaust.

Levi studied chemistry at the University of Turin in northern Italy. In 1938, the Fascist regime in Italy barred Jews from receiving academic degrees. Nevertheless, Levi graduated with honors in 1941. Soon after graduation he joined a resistance group. In late 1943, he was denounced as a Jew, imprisoned in a detention center, and then deported to Auschwitz, a Nazi extermination camp in southern Poland.

"From our transport of 650 people, only fifteen men and nine women survived," Levi later recalled. After enduring eleven months in the death camp, Levi was freed by the Soviets. His struggles to survive did not end then, though: It took him eight months of difficult travel to return to Italy.

Levi recorded his prison experiences soon after the end of World War II in his memoir *If This Is a Man* (1947), translated into English under the title *Survival in Auschwitz*. Levi stated that he had two goals in writing the book: to bear witness and to free himself of the weight of his own experiences. Some years later, in 1963, Levi published a second memoir, *The Reawakening,* dealing with his arduous journey home from Auschwitz to Turin.

Critics disagree about the fundamental tone of Levi's work. To some readers, Levi seems basically hopeful about the human spirit and humanity's prospects. To others, Levi's relatively detached, objective style and tone signal a pessimistic outlook. Biographers have speculated that toward the end of his life, Levi was haunted by "survivor's guilt" and by the notion that only the selfish and the cruel could muster the energy and cunning to survive the Nazi death camps. His final book, *The Drowned and the Saved* (1986), an examination of the ultimate meaning of the Nazis' atrocities, struck some critics as particularly pessimistic. Perhaps Levi felt that his efforts to bear witness to evil were being increasingly marginalized in a world where atrocities have become disturbingly common.

A Good Day
from Survival in Auschwitz

Make the Connection

Quickwrite

How reliable do you think a **memoir**—an autobiographical account of a particular period or series of events—can be in presenting information about a historical event? What information and ideas can a historical memoir offer that cannot be found in a more objective source, such as a history textbook or an encyclopedia article? Write your thoughts in a paragraph.

Literary Focus

Tone

Tone is a writer's attitude toward a character, a subject, or the reader. In "A Good Day," Levi's tone is **ironic**—that is, there is a contrast between what is said and what is meant, or between what appears to be true and what really *is* true. As you read, consider Levi's use of irony to describe the horrendous plight of the prisoners at Auschwitz, beginning with the title of the selection. Look for examples of the writer's direct observations about the meaning of his experiences.

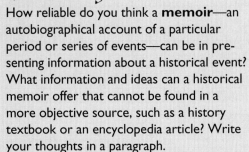

> **Tone** is a writer's attitude toward a character, a subject, or the reader.
>
> *For more on Tone, see the Handbook of Literary and Historical Terms.*

Reading Skills

Making Generalizations

A **generalization** is a type of inference in which a broad conclusion is drawn from explicit examples in the text. For example, after reading the beginning paragraphs of "A

Good Day," you might make the generalization "Levi believes that having a purpose is a universal human need, no matter how simple or basic the purpose is." As you read this memoir, take notes in the form of a double-entry journal. On the left, list ideas that Levi states explicitly. On the right, record generalizations about Levi's outlook that you think logically follow from his views.

Background

Beginning in the 1930s, the Nazis secretly transported Jews and other "undesirables," such as Romanies, homosexuals, political dissidents, and people with disabilities, to concentration camps such as Dachau and Buchenwald in Germany. After 1940, the Nazis established extermination camps such as Auschwitz and Treblinka in Poland. In all, about twelve million people were killed, nearly six million of them Jews. Primo Levi wrote *Survival in Auschwitz* just after World War II ended, when the full horror of the Nazi extermination camps was still not widely known.

Vocabulary Development

tenacious (tə·nā′shəs) *adj.*: persistent; tough.

opaque (ō·pāk′) *adj.*: not allowing light to penetrate.

debilitating (dē·bil′ə·tāt′iŋ) *v.* used as *adj.*: weakening.

imperceptible (im′pər·sep′tə·bəl) *adj.*: not plain or distinct.

rancid (ran′sid) *adj.*: spoiled.

derision (di·rizh′ən) *n.*: ridicule; scorn.

North Carolina Competency Goal
1.02; 1.03; 4.05; 5.01; 5.03; 6.01

INTERNET
Vocabulary Practice
Keyword: LE5 WL-7

SKILLS FOCUS

Literary Skills
Understand tone.

Reading Skills
Make generalizations.

A Good Day

from **Survival in Auschwitz**

Primo Levi

translated by **Stuart Woolf**

The conviction that life has a purpose is rooted in every fiber of man, it is a property of the human substance. Free men give many names to this purpose, and think and talk a lot about its nature. But for us the question is simpler.

Today, in this place, our only purpose is to reach the spring. At the moment we care about nothing else. Behind this aim there is not at the moment any other aim. In the morning while we wait endlessly lined up in the roll-call square for the time to leave for work, while every breath of wind penetrates our clothes and runs in violent shivers over our defenseless bodies, and everything is grey around us, and we are grey; in the morning, when it is still dark, we all look at the sky in the east to spot the first signs of a milder season, and the rising of the sun is commented on every day: today a little earlier than yesterday, today a little warmer than yesterday, in two months, in a month, the cold will call a truce and we will have one enemy less.

Today the sun rose bright and clear for the first time from the horizon of mud. It is a Polish sun, cold, white and distant and only warms the skin, but when it dissolved the last mists a murmur ran through our colorless numbers, and when even I felt its lukewarmth through my clothes I understood how men can worship the sun.

"*Das Schlimmste ist vorüber,*" said Ziegler, turning his pointed shoulders to the sun: the worst is over. Next to us there is a group of Greeks, those admirable and terrible Jews of Salonica,[1] tenacious, thieving, wise, ferocious and united, so determined to live, such pitiless opponents in the struggle for life; those Greeks who have conquered in the kitchens and in the yards, and whom even the Germans respect and the Poles fear. They are in their third year of camp, and nobody knows better than them what the camp means. They now stand closely in a circle, shoulder to shoulder, and sing one of their interminable chants.

Felicio the Greek knows me. "*L'année prochaine à la maison!*"[2] he shouts at me, and adds: "*à la maison par la Cheminée!*"[3] Felicio has been at Birkenau. And they continue to sing and beat their feet in time and grow drunk on songs.

When we finally left by the main entrance of the camp, the sun was quite high and the sky serene. At midday one could see the mountains; to the west, the steeple of Auschwitz (a steeple here!), and all around the barrage balloons.[4] The smoke from the Buna lay still in the cold air, and a row of low hills could be seen, green with forests: and our hearts tighten because we all know that Birkenau is there, that our women finished there, and that soon we too will finish there; but we are not used to seeing it.

For the first time we are aware that on both sides of the road, even here, the meadows are

---

1. **Salonica:** seaport in northern Greece (usually spelled *Salonika*). During World War II, its Jewish population was deported to concentration camps.

2. *L'année prochaine à la maison:* French for "Next year I'll be back home!"
3. *à la maison par la Cheminée:* French for "at home by the fireside."
4. **barrage balloons** *n. pl.:* anchored balloons with cables or nets attached, used to capture low-flying aircraft.

Vocabulary

tenacious (tə·nā′shəs) *adj.:* persistent; tough.

1943 A.D. (1943) by
Ben Shahn.

Courtesy of the Syracuse
University Art Collection.
Gift of William Pearson Tolley
(1960.034). Art © Estate of
Ben Shahn/Licensed by VAGA,
New York, NY.

green; because, without a sun, a meadow is as if it were not green.

The Buna is not: the Buna is desperately and essentially <u>opaque</u> and grey. This huge entanglement of iron, concrete, mud and smoke is the negation of beauty. Its roads and buildings are named like us, by numbers or letters, not by weird and sinister names. Within its bounds not a blade of grass grows, and the soil is impregnated with the poisonous saps of coal and petroleum, and the only things alive are machines and slaves—and the former are more alive than the latter.

The Buna is as large as a city; besides the managers and German technicians, forty thousand foreigners work there, and fifteen to twenty languages are spoken. All the foreigners live in different Lagers[5] which surround the Buna: the Lager of the English prisoners-of-war, the Lager of the Ukranian women, the Lager of the French volunteers and others we do not know. Our Lager (*Judenlager, Vernichtungslager, Kazett*) by itself provides ten thousand workers who come from all the nations of Europe. We are the slaves of the slaves, whom all can give orders to, and our name is the number which we carry tattooed on our arm and sewn on our jacket.

---

5. Lagers *n. pl.:* camps.

Vocabulary

opaque (ō·pāk′) *adj.:* not allowing light to penetrate.

The Carbide Tower, which rises in the middle of Buna and whose top is rarely visible in the fog, was built by us. Its bricks were called *Ziegel, briques, tegula, cegli, kamenny, mattoni, téglak,* and they were cemented by hate; hate and discord, like the Tower of Babel, and it is this that we call it: —*Babelturm, Bobelturm;* and in it we hate the insane dream of grandeur of our masters, their contempt for God and men, for us men.

And today just as in the old fable, we all feel, and the Germans themselves feel, that a curse— not transcendent and divine, but inherent and historical—hangs over the insolent building based on the confusion of languages and erected in defiance of heaven like a stone oath.

As will be told, the Buna factory, on which the Germans were busy for four years and for which countless of us suffered and died, never produced a pound of synthetic rubber.

But today the eternal puddles, on which a rainbow veil of petroleum trembles, reflect the serene sun. Pipes, rails, boilers, still cold from the freezing of the night, are dripping with dew. The earth dug up from the pits, the piles of coal, the blocks of concrete, exhale in light vapors the humidity of the winter.

Today is a good day. We look around like blind people who have recovered their sight, and we look at each other. We have never seen each other in sunlight: someone smiles. If it was not for the hunger!

For human nature is such that grief and pain—even simultaneously suffered—do not add up as a whole in our consciousness, but hide, the lesser behind the greater, according to a definite law of perspective. It is providential[6] and is our means of surviving in the camp. And this is the reason why so often in free life one hears it said that man is never content. In fact it is not a question of a human incapacity for a state of absolute happiness, but of an ever-insufficient knowledge of the complex nature of the state of unhappiness; so that the single name of the major cause is given to all its causes, which are composite and set out in an order of urgency. And if the most immediate cause of stress comes to an end, you are grievously amazed to see that another one lies behind; and in reality a whole series of others.

So that as soon as the cold, which throughout the winter had seemed our only enemy, had ceased, we became aware of our hunger; and repeating the same error, we now say: "If it was not for the hunger! . . ."

But how could one imagine not being hungry? The Lager *is* hunger: we ourselves are hunger, living hunger.

On the other side of the road a steam-shovel is working. Its mouth, hanging from its cables, opens wide its steel jaws, balances a moment as if uncertain in its choice, then rushes upon the soft, clayey soil and snaps it up voraciously, while a satisfied snort of thick white smoke rises from the control cabin. Then it rises, turns half around, vomits backwards its mouthful and begins again.

Leaning on our shovels, we stop to watch, fascinated. At every bite of its mouth our mouths also open, our Adam's apples dance up and down, wretchedly visible under the flaccid skin. We are unable to tear ourselves away from the sight of the steam-shovel's meal.

Sigi is seventeen years old and is hungrier than everybody, although he is given a little soup every evening by his probably not disinterested protector. He had begun to speak of his home in Vienna and of his mother, but then he slipped on to the subject of food and now he talks endlessly about some marriage luncheon and remembers with genuine regret that he failed to finish his third plate of bean soup. And everyone tells him to keep quiet, but within ten minutes Béla is describing his Hungarian countryside and the fields of maize and a recipe to make meat-pies with corncobs and lard and spices and . . . and he is cursed, sworn at and a third one begins to describe . . .

How weak our flesh is! I am perfectly well aware how vain these fantasies of hunger are, but dancing before my eyes I see the spaghetti which we had just cooked, Vanda, Luciana,

---

6. **providential** (prӓv′ə·den′shəl) *adj.:* fortunate; of or like something occurring through divine intervention.

Stars of Twilight (1995) by Samuel Bak.
Courtesy of Pucker Gallery, Boston.

Franco and I, at the sorting-camp when we suddenly heard the news that we would leave for here the following day; and we were eating it (it was so good, yellow, filling), and we stopped, fools, stupid as we were—if we had only known! And if it happened again . . . Absurd. If there is one thing sure in this world it is certainly this: that it will not happen to us a second time.

Fischer, the newest arrival, pulls out of his pocket a bundle, tied together with the painstaking exactitude of the Hungarians, and inside there is a half-ration of bread: half the bread of this morning. It is notorious that only the High Numbers keep their bread in their pockets; none of us old ones are able to preserve our bread for an hour. Various theories circulate to justify this

incapacity of ours: bread eaten a little at a time is not wholly assimilated; the nervous tension needed to preserve the bread without touching it when one is hungry is in the highest degree harmful and debilitating; bread which is turning stale soon loses its alimentary[7] value, so that the sooner it is eaten, the more nutritious it is; Alberto says that hunger and bread in one's pocket are terms of opposite sign which automatically cancel each other out and cannot exist in the same individual; and the majority affirm justly that, in the end, one's stomach is the securest safe

7. **alimentary** (al′ə·men′tə·rē) *adj.:* nourishing.

Vocabulary

debilitating (dē·bil′ə·tāt′iŋ) *v.* used as *adj.:* weakening.

against thefts and extortions.[8] "*Moi, on m'a jamais volé mon pain!*"[9] David snarls, hitting his concave stomach: but he is unable to take his eyes off Fischer who chews slowly and methodically, "lucky" enough to still have half-a-ration at ten in the morning: "*Sacré veinard, va!*"[10]

But it is not only because of the sun that today is a happy day: at midday a surprise awaits us. Besides the normal morning ration, we discover in the hut a wonderful pot of over eleven gallons, one of those from the Factory Kitchen, almost full. Templer looks at us, triumphant; this "organization" is his work.

Templer is the official organizer of the Kommando: he has an astonishing nose for the soup of civilians, like bees for flowers. Our Kapo, who is not a bad Kapo, leaves him a free hand, and with reason: Templer slinks off, following imperceptible tracks like a bloodhound, and returns with the priceless news that the Methanol Polish workers, one mile from here, have abandoned ten gallons of soup that tasted rancid, or that a wagonload of turnips is to be found unguarded on the siding next to the Factory Kitchen.

Today there are ninety pints and we are fifteen, Kapo and *Vorarbeiter*[11] included. This means six pints each: we will have two at midday as well as the normal ration, and will come back to the hut in turns for the other four during the afternoon, besides being granted an extra five minutes' suspension of work to fill ourselves up.

What more could one want? Even our work seems light, with the prospect of four hot, dense pints waiting for us in the hut. The Kapo comes to us periodically and calls: "*Wer hat noch zu fressen?*"[12] He does not say it from derision or to sneer, but because this way of eating on our feet, furiously, burning our mouths and throats, without time to breathe, really is "*fressen*," the way of eating of animals, and certainly not "*essen*," the human way of eating, seated in front of a table, religiously. "*Fressen*" is exactly the word, and is used currently among us.

Meister Nogalla watches and closes an eye at our absences from work. Meister Nogalla also has a hungry look about him, and if it was not for the social conventions, perhaps he would not despise a couple of pints of our warm broth.

Templer's turn comes. By plebiscitary[13] consensus, he has been allowed ten pints, taken from the bottom of the pot. For Templer is not only a good organizer, but an exceptional soup-eater, and is uniquely able to empty his bowels at his own desire and in anticipation of a large meal, which contributes to his amazing gastric capacity.

Of this gift of his, he is justly proud, and everybody, even Meister Nogalla, knows about it. Accompanied by the gratitude of all, Templer the benefactor enters the latrine for a few moments and comes out beaming and ready, and amidst the general benevolence prepares to enjoy the fruits of his work:

"*Nu, Templer, hast du Platz genug für die Suppe gemacht?*"[14]

At sunset, the siren of the *Feierabend*[15] sounds, the end of work; and as we are all satiated, at least for a few hours, no quarrels arise, we feel good, the Kapo feels no urge to hit us, and we are able to think of our mothers and wives, which usually does not happen. For a few hours we can be unhappy in the manner of free men.

---

8. **extortions** (ek·stôr′shənz) *n. pl.:* acts of getting money or goods through threats or force.
9. *Moi, on m'a jamais volé mon pain:* French for "As for me, no one's ever stolen *my* bread!"
10. *Sacré veinard, va:* French for "Lucky devil!"
11. *Vorarbeiter:* German for "foreman."
12. *Wer hat noch zu fressen:* German for "Who hasn't eaten yet?"
13. **plebiscitary** (plə·bis′ə·ter′ē) *adj.:* of or based on a vote.
14. *Nu, Templer, hast du Platz genug für die Suppe gemacht:* German for "So now, Templer, have you made enough room for the soup?"
15. *Feierabend:* German for "end of the workday."

Vocabulary

imperceptible (im′pər·sep′tə·bəl) *adj.:* not plain or distinct.

rancid (ran′sid) *adj.:* spoiled.

derision (di·rizh′ən) *n.:* ridicule; scorn.

Response and Analysis

Reading Check

1. What is the men's "only purpose" as the selection opens?

2. Why do the men's "hearts tighten" as they gaze at Birkenau?

3. What is the Buna?

4. What surprise awaits the men at midday?

Thinking Critically

5. What meaning does the **allusion,** or reference, to the biblical Tower of Babel on page 908 add to the description of the Carbide Tower of Buna?

6. How does Levi create an ironic **tone** in his descriptions of the setting—the rising of the sun, the Buna factory, the steam shovel—and of the actions of the prisoners?

7. What **generalization** does Levi make about human happiness and unhappiness? Give examples of how Levi supports this generalization in the selection. How does the generalization help you grasp the full meaning of the final, ironic sentence—"For a few hours we can be unhappy in the manner of free men"?

8. Review your Quickwrite notes. What details, insights, or ideas did you get from Levi's memoir that you would not have found in, for example, a history textbook?

Extending and Evaluating

9. Like many other Holocaust survivors, Levi felt the need to serve as a witness and to tell his story so that such events would never be repeated in human history. Do you think memoirs like this one are effective antidotes to inhumanity? Do you think they can help stop something similar from happening again? Explain.

WRITING

Identifying Main Idea and Details

The **main idea** of a text deals not only with the subject matter of the text but also with the author's feelings or beliefs about the topic. A main idea may be directly stated or implied. **Supporting details** include examples, facts, quotations, and other evidence used to reinforce the main idea. In a brief essay, summarize the main idea of Levi's work and provide at least three supporting details in your own words.

Vocabulary Development
Synonyms

A **synonym** is a word that has the same or nearly the same meaning as another word. Choose the best synonym for each Vocabulary word in boldface below.

1. **tenacious:** a. fragile b. astute c. persistent

2. **rancid:** a. acidic b. spoiled c. candid

3. **derision:** a. hilarity b. scorn c. rigor

4. **imperceptible:** a. clear b. glad c. indistinct

5. **opaque:** a. dense b. agile c. forceful

6. **debilitating:** a. destructive b. mercurial c. weakening

North Carolina Competency Goal
1.02; 1.03; 4.05; 5.03; 6.01

go. hrw .com

INTERNET

Projects and Activities
Keyword: LE5 WL-7

SKILLS FOCUS

Literary Skills
Analyze tone.

Reading Skills
Make generalizations.

Writing Skills
Identify main idea and details.

Vocabulary Skills
Identify synonyms.

NOBEL PRIZE WINNER

Elie Wiesel
(1928–   )
Romania/United States

"If the Greeks invented tragedy, the Romans the epistle, and the Renaissance the sonnet, our generation invented a new literature, that of testimony," Elie Wiesel (el'ē vē·zel') once remarked. Nearly everything that Wiesel has written or said publicly since surviving the Holocaust has been a testimony, an effort to tell the world about the horrors of the Nazi death camps and to prevent such atrocities from happening again.

Wiesel grew up in the close-knit Jewish community of Sighet, a village in Romania's Carpathian Mountains. His world was centered on religious studies and family life. But this secure existence was brought to an abrupt end with the arrival of the Nazis in Sighet in 1944. All the Jewish inhabitants of the village were deported to extermination or concentration camps in Poland. Wiesel, then fifteen years old, was separated from his mother and sister immediately upon arrival in Auschwitz. He never saw them again.

In late 1944, Allied armies approached Germany. The outlying concentration camps were evacuated by the SS (*Schutzstaffel*), special Nazi police forces in charge of the camps. The SS troops forced prisoners to clean up the camps to destroy evidence of the troops' crimes. They then forced the surviving prisoners to march to camps inside Germany to prevent their liberation. Many inmates perished during these long journeys, known as death marches. Wiesel and his father were forced to take part in such a march, which took them to the "death train" that Wiesel describes in this excerpt from the final chapters of *Night*. In the spring of 1945, just before the war ended, the young Wiesel also lost his father.

Alone and ill, one of Europe's millions of displaced persons, Wiesel settled in Paris after the war. He wrote the first version of his autobiography in Yiddish in 1955. The manuscript was later revised and shortened and was eventually published as *Night*, now considered one of the most powerful accounts of the Nazi atrocities.

Since writing *Night*, Wiesel has produced many works about the Holocaust, the systematic mass murder of European Jews by the Nazis. In 1986, Wiesel was awarded the Nobel Peace Prize. In his acceptance speech he explained why he has never stopped reminding the world of the Holocaust: "We must always take sides. Neutrality helps the oppressor, never the victim. Silence encourages the tormentor, never the tormented."

Before You Read

from Night

Make the Connection

Elie Wiesel says we must always speak out against oppression: "Silence encourages the tormentor, never the tormented." Think about events that took place during the Holocaust as well as other examples of oppression taking place in the world today. Why do you think these events occur?

Literary Focus

Memoir

A **memoir** is a type of autobiography, an author's written account of his or her own life. Usually more tightly focused than an autobiography, a memoir concentrates on a particular period or series of events, often ones of historical importance. Authors' purposes in writing memoirs vary. Some writers want to show how historical events affect individuals' lives; some want to make political or philosophical points; some aim to set the record straight.

> A **memoir** is an autobiographical written account of an important period or series of events in a writer's life.
>
> *For more on Memoir, see the Handbook of Literary and Historical Terms.*

Reading Skills

Interpreting Real-World Events

When you read about real-world events in a memoir, try to distinguish subjective writing from objective reporting. **Subjective writing,** which presents the writer's firsthand experiences and interpretations of events, is often biased—in other words, it reveals the writer's personal feelings and beliefs.

Objective reporting, on the other hand, is meant to be factual and impersonal. As you read this extract from Wiesel's memoir, take notes on the objective facts that Wiesel presents. Note other details that convey Wiesel's subjective responses to the horrific events he lived through.

Background

Perhaps the single most horrifying image of World War II is the Nazi concentration camp. Thousands died even in concentration camps never intended for extermination, such as Bergen-Belsen (including Anne Frank, who died there of typhus in March 1945). In the death camps, Jews and other prisoners were shot by firing squads, executed in gas chambers, tortured in medical experiments, worked to death as slave laborers, or killed by starvation and disease. Their bodies were then burned in ditches or ovenlike structures called crematoria. By the spring of 1945—the final days of the war—the camps had exacted a terrible toll in human lives: About twelve million people had perished, including Wiesel's father, who died just before Buchenwald was liberated on April 11, 1945. In May, Nazi Germany collapsed, the SS guards fled, and the camps ceased to operate.

North Carolina Competency Goal
1.03; 4.03; 4.05; 5.01; 5.03

INTERNET

Vocabulary Practice

•

More About Elie Wiesel

Keyword: LE5 WL-7

Vocabulary Development

appeasing (ə·pēz′iŋ) *v.* used as *n.*: relieving; quieting.

livid (liv′id) *adj.*: grayish blue, as if bruised.

apathy (ap′ə·thē) *n.*: lack of interest or feeling; indifference.

inert (in·urt′) *adj.*: lacking the power to move or act.

SKILLS FOCUS

Literary Skills
Understand memoir.

Reading Skills
Interpret real-world events.

Ovens (1980) by Mindy Weisel.

Jean Albano Gallery, Chicago.

from Night

Elie Wiesel

translated by **Stella Rodway**

We stayed at Gleiwitz[1] for three days. Three days without food or drink. We were not allowed to leave the barracks. SS men guarded the door.

I was hungry and thirsty. I must have been very dirty and exhausted, to judge from the appearance of the others. The bread we had brought

1. **Gleiwitz** (glī**′**vits′): Nazi concentration camp in south-western Poland. Gleiwitz was a "subcamp" of Auschwitz.

from Buna[2] had long since been devoured. And who knew when we would be given another ration?

The front was following us. We could hear new gun shots again, very close. But we had neither the strength nor the courage to believe that the Nazis would not have time to evacuate us, and that the Russians would soon be here.

We heard that we were going to be deported into the center of Germany.

On the third day, at dawn, we were driven out of the barracks. We all threw blankets over our shoulders, like prayer shawls. We were directed toward a gate which divided the camp into two. A group of SS officers were standing there. A rumor ran through our ranks—a selection![3]

The SS officers did the selecting. The weak, to the left; those who could walk well, to the right.

My father was sent to the left. I ran after him. An SS officer shouted at my back:

"Come back here!"

I slipped in among the others. Several SS rushed to bring me back, creating such confusion that many of the people from the left were able to come back to the right—and among them, my father and myself. However, there were some shots and some dead.

We were all made to leave the camp. After half an hour's marching we arrived right in the middle of a field divided by rails. We had to wait for the train to arrive.

The snow fell thickly. We were forbidden to sit down or even to move.

The snow began to form a thick layer over our blankets. They brought us bread—the usual ration. We threw ourselves upon it. Someone had the idea of appeasing his thirst by eating the snow. Soon the others were imitating him. As we were not allowed to bend down, everyone took out his spoon and ate the accumulated snow off his neighbor's back. A mouthful of bread and a spoonful of snow. The SS who were watching laughed at this spectacle.

Hours went by. Our eyes grew weary of scouring the horizon for the liberating train. It did not arrive until much later in the evening. An infinitely long train, composed of cattle wagons, with no roofs. The SS pushed us in, a hundred to a carriage, we were so thin! Our embarkation completed, the convoy set out.

Pressed up against the others in an effort to keep out the cold, head empty and heavy at the same time, brain a whirlpool of decaying memories. Indifference deadened the spirit. Here or elsewhere—what difference did it make? To die today or tomorrow, or later? The night was long and never ending.

When at last a gray glimmer of light appeared on the horizon, it revealed a tangle of human shapes, heads sunk upon shoulders, crouched, piled one on top of the other, like a field of dust-covered tombstones in the first light of the dawn. I tried to distinguish those who were still alive from those who had gone. But there was no difference. My gaze was held for a long time by one who lay with his eyes open, staring into the void. His livid face was covered with a layer of frost and snow.

My father was huddled near me, wrapped in his blanket, his shoulders covered with snow. And was he dead, too? I called him. No answer. I would have cried out if I could have done so. He did not move.

My mind was invaded suddenly by this realization—there was no more reason to live, no more reason to struggle.

---

2. **Buna** (bo͞o′nə): synthetic-rubber plant built at Auschwitz. Many inmates at Auschwitz were forced to labor in the plant until they died from exhaustion or were too weak to work, whereupon they were sent to the gas chambers.
3. **selection** *n.*: Nazi process of choosing which inmates would live or die, usually based on their ability to work. At this point in Wiesel's narrative, the selection is based on prisoners' ability to continue marching.

Vocabulary

appeasing (ə·pēz′iŋ) *v.* used as *n.*: relieving; quieting.
livid (liv′id) *adj.*: grayish blue, as if bruised.

The train stopped in the middle of a deserted field. The suddenness of the halt woke some of those who were asleep. They straightened themselves up, throwing startled looks around them.

Outside, the SS went by, shouting:

"Throw out all the dead! All corpses outside!"

The living rejoiced. There would be more room. Volunteers set to work. They felt those who were still crouching.

"Here's one! Take him!"

They undressed him, the survivors avidly sharing out his clothes, then two "gravediggers" took him, one by the head one by the feet, and threw him out of the wagon like a sack of flour.

From all directions came cries:

"Come on! Here's one! This man next to me. He doesn't move."

I woke from my apathy just at the moment when two men came up to my father. I threw myself on top of his body. He was cold. I slapped him. I rubbed his hands, crying:

"Father! Father! Wake up. They're trying to throw you out of the carriage. . . ."

His body remained inert.

The two gravediggers seized me by the collar.

"Leave him. You can see perfectly well that he's dead."

"No!" I cried. "He isn't dead! Not yet!"

I set to work to slap him as hard as I could. After a moment my father's eyelids moved slightly over his glazed eyes. He was breathing weakly.

"You see," I cried.

The two men moved away.

Twenty bodies were thrown out of our wagon. Then the train resumed its journey, leaving behind it a few hundred naked dead, deprived of burial, in the deep snow of a field in Poland.

We were given no food. We lived on snow; it took the place of bread. The days were like nights, and the nights left the dregs of the darkness in our souls. The train was traveling slowly, often stopping for several hours and then setting off again. It never ceased snowing. All through these days and nights we stayed crouching, one on top of the other, never speaking a word. We were no more than frozen bodies. Our eyes closed, we waited merely for the next stop, so that we could unload our dead.

Ten days, ten nights of traveling. Sometimes we would pass through German townships. Very early in the morning, usually. The workmen were going to work. They stopped and stared after us, but otherwise showed no surprise.

One day when we had stopped, a workman took a piece of bread out of his bag and threw it into a wagon. There was a stampede. Dozens of starving men fought each other to the death for a few crumbs. The German workmen took a lively interest in this spectacle.

Some years later, I watched the same kind of scene at Aden.[4] The passengers on our boat were amusing themselves by throwing coins to the "natives," who were diving in to get them. An attractive, aristocratic Parisienne[5] was deriving special pleasure from the game. I suddenly noticed that two children were engaged in a death struggle, trying to strangle each other. I turned to the lady.

"Please," I begged, "don't throw any more money in!"

"Why not?" she said. "I like to give charity. . . ."

In the wagon where the bread had fallen, a real battle had broken out. Men threw themselves on top of each other, stamping on each other, tearing at each other, biting each other. Wild beasts of prey, with animal hatred in their eyes; an extraordinary vitality had seized them, sharpening their teeth and nails.

A crowd of workmen and curious spectators had collected along the train. They had probably

---

4. **Aden** (äd'n): seaport of a former British colony (now Yemen), located in the southern Arabian peninsula on the Gulf of Aden.
5. **Parisienne:** girl or woman born or living in Paris.

Vocabulary

apathy (ap'ə·thē) *n.:* lack of interest or feeling; indifference.

inert (in·urt') *adj.:* lacking the power to move or act.

Prisoners stand in uniform during a roll call at the Buchenwald concentration camp (c. 1938–1940). Buchenwald, Germany.

United States Holocaust Memorial Museum (USHMM #10105).

never seen a train with such a cargo. Soon, nearly everywhere, pieces of bread were being dropped into the wagons. The audience stared at these skeletons of men, fighting one another to the death for a mouthful.

A piece fell into our wagon. I decided that I would not move. Anyway, I knew that I would never have the strength to fight with a dozen savage men! Not far away I noticed an old man dragging himself along on all fours. He was trying to disengage himself from the struggle. He held one hand to his heart. I thought at first he had received a blow in the chest. Then I understood; he had a bit of bread under his shirt. With remarkable speed he drew it out and put it in his mouth. His eyes gleamed; a smile, like a grimace, lit up his dead face. And was immediately extinguished. A shadow had just loomed up near him. The shadow threw itself upon him. Felled to the ground, stunned with blows, the old man cried:

"Meir. Meir, my boy! Don't you recognize me? I'm your father . . . you're hurting me . . . you're killing your father! I've got some bread . . . for you too . . . for you too. . . ."

He collapsed. His fist was still clenched around a small piece. He tried to carry it to his mouth. But the other one threw himself upon him and snatched it. The old man again whispered something, let out a rattle, and died amid the general indifference. His son searched him, took the bread, and began to devour it. He was not able to get very far. Two men had seen and hurled themselves upon him. Others joined in. When they withdrew, next to me were two corpses, side by side, the father and the son.

I was fifteen years old.

In our wagon, there was a friend of my father's called Meir Katz. He worked as a gardener at Buna and used to bring us a few green vegetables occasionally. Being less undernourished than the rest of us, he had stood up to imprisonment better. Because he was relatively more vigorous, he had been put in charge of the wagon.

On the third night of our journey I woke up suddenly and felt two hands on my throat, trying to strangle me. I just had the time to shout, "Father!"

Nothing but this word. I felt myself suffocating. But my father had woken up and seized my

Elie Wiesel   **917**

attacker. Too weak to overcome him, he had the idea of calling Meir Katz.

"Come here! Come quickly! There's someone strangling my son."

A few moments later I was free. I still do not know why the man wanted to strangle me.

After a few days, Meir Katz spoke to my father:

"Chlomo, I'm getting weak. I'm losing my strength. I can't hold on. . . ."

"Don't let yourself go under," my father said, trying to encourage him. "You must resist. Don't lose faith in yourself."

But Meir Katz groaned heavily in reply.

"I can't go on any longer, Chlomo! What can I do? I can't carry on. . . ."

My father took his arm. And Meir Katz, the strong man, the most robust of us all, wept. His son had been taken from him at the time of the first selection, but it was now that he wept. It was now that he cracked up. He was finished, at the end of his tether.

On the last day of our journey a terrible wind arose; it snowed without ceasing. We felt that the end was near—the real end. We could never hold out in this icy wind, in these gusts.

Someone got up and shouted:

"We mustn't stay sitting down at a time like this. We shall freeze to death! Let's all get up and move a bit. . . ."

We all got up. We held our damp blankets more tightly around us. And we forced ourselves

CONNECTION *to* NIGHT

The following excerpt is from a newspaper article about a Holocaust survivor reunion that took place at the U.S. Holocaust Museum in 2003. The article focuses on Noemi Ban, a Hungarian survivor in her eighties.

INFORMATIONAL TEXT

Holocaust Survivors Bring Memories

Lisa Pollak

from *The Baltimore Sun,* November 4, 2003

The earrings look like miniature flowers, with opal petals and delicate gold stems. Years ago, they belonged to a Jewish woman who lived in Hungary. But as the threat of Hitler's armies loomed, the woman's mother made a suggestion: Her daughter should give the treasured earrings to her brother, who was leaving Europe to make a life in the United States.

The woman did as her mother suggested. When the Nazis invaded Hungary in 1944, the earrings were safe, but her family was not. Her husband was sent away to do forced labor, and the others were deported to Auschwitz. Of the five family members taken there, four never returned: the woman, her mother, 12-year-old daughter and 6-month-old son all perished. Only her oldest child, 21-year-old Noemi, survived. . . .

The war had been over for years before Noemi learned that her mother's earrings survived it. After liberation in 1945, she'd gone home to Hungary and found that her father was alive. So was her boyfriend, Earnest, who quickly became her husband. Only in 1957, after her family had fled Hungary for the United States, did her uncle in New York show her what he had saved.

to move a few steps, to turn around where we were.

Suddenly a cry rose up from the wagon, the cry of a wounded animal. Someone had just died.

Others, feeling that they too were about to die, imitated his cry. And their cries seemed to come from beyond the grave. Soon everyone was crying out. Wailing, groaning, cries of distress hurled into the wind and the snow.

The contagion spread to the other carriages. Hundreds of cries rose up simultaneously. Not knowing against whom we cried. Not knowing why. The death rattle of a whole convoy who felt the end upon them. We were all going to die here. All limits had been passed. No one had

any strength left. And again the night would be long.

Meir Katz groaned:

"Why don't they shoot us all right away?"

That same evening, we reached our destination.

It was late at night. The guards came to unload us. The dead were abandoned in the train. Only those who could still stand were able to get out.

Meir Katz stayed in the train. The last day had been the most murderous. A hundred of us had got into the wagon. A dozen of us got out—among them, my father and I.

We had arrived at Buchenwald.

. . . [F]or years now, Noemi, an award-winning teacher, has told her stories in front of audiences, and her experiences fill a book called *Sharing Is Healing,* a Holocaust memoir written to be accessible for young readers.

In that book, she writes of the day she arrived at Auschwitz. How she and her family emerged from the fetid train car and lined up in pairs to be inspected by SS soldiers. She stood next to her mother, who held baby Gabor, as they waited in a long line, at the end of which a soldier waved a whip right and left. Some prisoners were going one way, some another.

Finally, it was her family's turn.

"We were standing in front of the Nazi soldier. He looked at us. With fear in our hearts we looked at him. The SS soldier raised the horsewhip and signaled my grandma, my mother, my sister and my little brother to his left. Another look at me and he sent me to his right. It took not more than a few seconds, and I was separated from my dear ones.

"We couldn't talk to each other. But when I looked back, I did see my dear mother bending toward me with my little brother in her arms. Then I saw her eyes, her beautiful loving eyes. Those eyes told me, 'I love you, take care!' This was the last time I ever saw them. I never saw them again."

For all the painful memories being shared [at the reunion], the day in some ways felt as joyous and hopeful as any family reunion. But as Nobel Peace Prize winner Elie Wiesel reminded his fellow survivors that afternoon, their joy is never completely devoid of sorrow. "Close your eyes, and see the invisible faces of those we have left behind," Wiesel urged. "Your presence and our presence here today is our answer to their silent question. . . . We have kept our promise. We have not forgotten you."

In the darkened tent, it was hard to see Noemi's earrings, but it was impossible to miss the tears in her eyes.

? Where has this reporter mixed subjective writing—expression of her feelings—with objective, factual reporting? What do you think was her purpose in writing this article?

Response and Analysis

Reading Check

1. What was the purpose of the selection process that took place before the prisoners left the camp?

2. When the SS instruct the prisoners to throw out their dead, how do the living respond?

3. What does Wiesel do when some of the prisoners try to lift a person lying next to him? Who is this person?

4. How does the bread thrown into the cars cause a number of deaths? Why doesn't Wiesel join in the struggle over the bread?

5. What role does Meir Katz play during the train journey?

Thinking Critically

6. Wiesel says about dying, "Here or elsewhere—what difference did it make? To die today or tomorrow, or later?" Judging from this comment, how would you describe Wiesel's state of mind at the time?

7. What details in this account show that Wiesel has not allowed sentiment to overshadow his **objective** reporting of events? What details reveal Wiesel's **subjective** responses to these horrific experiences?

8. At one point, Wiesel notes, "I tried to distinguish those who were still alive from those who had gone. But there was no difference." What point do you think Wiesel is trying to make?

9. Review the selection, and note every time the word *night* (or a related word) is used. Is Wiesel speaking of a literal or figurative night—or both? Is *Night* an appropriate title for his memoir? Explain.

10. What do you think Wiesel's main purpose was in writing *Night*? Find details in the text to support your response.

Extending and Evaluating

11. For years, Wiesel was torn by conflicting emotions: the desire to bear witness to what had happened in the death camps and the fear that any attempt to put his experiences into words would show disrespect for the dead. Do you think Wiesel ultimately resolved this problem in *Night*? Explain.

WRITING

Interpreting a Real-World Event

In a brief essay, describe how Wiesel's account affected your own views on the events of the Holocaust. Begin your essay with a generalization about the Holocaust, and then use details from Wiesel's memoir to support that generalization. Show how Wiesel uses both **objective** and **subjective** writing to recount his experiences. End your essay by discussing how Wiesel's writing affected your interpretations of this real-world event.

Vocabulary Development
Analyzing Context Clues

Explain why the context clues are wrong in each sentence below. The words in boldface are Vocabulary words from the story.

1. Tom knew he had succeeded in **appeasing** Janet when she turned on him in a fury.

2. After her morning jog, her face was **livid** and rosy.

3. My feeling of **apathy** spurred me to join four new clubs.

4. This chemical is **inert**: It has the ability to change quickly.

Czeslaw Milosz

(1911–2004)
Poland/United States

Czeslaw Milosz (ches'wäf mē'wôsh) first experienced the savagery of war as a small child during World War I. He and his mother traveled through Russia with his father, an engineer recruited by the czar's army to build bridges near battle zones. When the family returned home to Lithuania after the war, their town had become part of the new Polish state.

Milosz was working in Warsaw in 1939 when the Soviet Union and Nazi Germany invaded Poland. In August 1944, during the Nazi occupation, the Poles in Warsaw staged a bloody uprising, in which over 150,000 people perished. At one point during the German assault on the city, Milosz was pinned to the ground as machine guns blasted the street around him; he recalls seeing cobblestones leap upright like porcupine quills. His wife rushed back to their house shortly before it was destroyed by artillery fire and stuffed his writings into a briefcase. Surviving by a miracle each day, said Milosz, "left you with an uncomfortable feeling: 'Why me and not someone else?'"

Milosz obtained a law degree in 1934. He remained in Warsaw throughout the six-year Nazi occupation and began to study English. Milosz joined the Polish resistance movement and wrote anti-Nazi poetry, which was published by underground presses and read at secret gatherings.

After the war, Milosz accepted a diplomatic post at the Polish embassy in Washington, D.C., but found himself becoming increasingly disillusioned with Poland's Communist government. In 1951, while serving as cultural attaché in Paris, Milosz defected; he spent the next ten years in France. In 1961, he moved to the United States (he became a U.S. citizen in 1970) and taught Slavic languages and literature at the University of California at Berkeley.

In 1980, Milosz received the Nobel Prize in literature. In his acceptance speech he expressed his belief that poetry must bear witness to "the demoniac [demonic] doings of history": "Those who are alive receive a mandate from those who are silent forever. They can fulfill their duties only by trying to reconstruct precisely things as they were and by wresting the past from fictions and legends."

Song of a Citizen

Make the Connection

How do people survive and cope with cataclysmic events—war, natural catastrophes, acts of terrorism? What ideas, feelings, images, or memories have helped you or people you know deal with and make sense of tragic events in the news or in their own lives?

Literary Focus

Dramatic Monologue

A **dramatic monologue** is a poem in which a speaker addresses one or more silent listeners. The speaker may be thinking aloud, mulling over a problem, or coming to an important decision. From the speaker's words the reader learns the speaker's identity, situation, and character. The speaker may also reveal the identity of the characters he or she is addressing, as well as the setting of the monologue. The speaker may be the poet; more often, though, the speaker is an invented character disclosing information he or she doesn't consciously intend to reveal.

North Carolina Competency Goal
1.03; 4.05;
5.01; 5.03

> A **dramatic monologue** is a poem in which a speaker addresses one or more silent listeners.
>
> *For more on Dramatic Monologue, see the Handbook of Literary and Historical Terms.*

Background

As a university student in the early 1930s, Milosz cofounded a leftist literary group called Zagary, whose members later became known as the Catastrophists because their writings prophesied cosmic devastation. The Nazi occupation of Warsaw, which lasted from 1939 to 1945, seemed to fulfill the Catastrophists' dire forecasts: Most of the city lay in ashes, and hundreds of thousands of people died or were deported to concentration camps.

During the occupation of Warsaw, Milosz wrote a number of anti-Nazi poems. In the poem cycle "The Voices of Poor People" (1943), which includes "Song of a Citizen," Milosz reflects bitterly on the destruction of Warsaw and engages in "a search for a means of how to deal directly with the Nazi occupation," in Milosz's words. The poem cycle circulated among members of Poland's underground resistance movement but was not published until after the war. Many years later Milosz heard that a typewritten copy had been found in a suitcase left behind on a train whose passengers had been rounded up and taken away to die at Auschwitz. The suitcase also contained a traveling magician's cape and top hat.

SKILLS FOCUS

Literary Skills
Understand dramatic monologue.

Photographer taking a posed photo amid World War II ruins, November 1946. Warsaw, Poland.

Song of a Citizen

Czeslaw Milosz

A stone from the depths that has witnessed the seas drying up
and a million white fish leaping in agony,
I, poor man, see a multitude of white-bellied nations
without freedom. I see the crab feeding on their flesh.

5   I have seen the fall of States and the perdition° of tribes,
the flight of kings and emperors, the power of tyrants.
I can say now, in this hour,
that I—am, while everything expires,
that it is better to be a live dog than a dead lion,°
10 as the Scripture says.

5.   perdition (pər·dish′ən)
n.: ruin.

9.   it... lion: allusion to Ecclesiastes 9:4: "But whoever is joined with all the living has hope, for a living dog is better than a dead lion."

A poor man, sitting on a cold chair, pressing my eyelids,
I sigh and think of a starry sky,
of non-Euclidean space,° of amoebas and their pseudopodia,°
of tall mounds of termites.

15 When walking, I am asleep, when sleeping, I dream reality,
pursued and covered with sweat, I run.
On city squares lifted up by the glaring dawn,
beneath marble remnants of blasted-down gates,
I deal in vodka and gold.
20 And yet so often I was near,
I reached into the heart of metal, the soul of
    earth, of fire, of water.
And the unknown unveiled its face
as a night reveals itself, serene, mirrored by tide.
Lustrous copper-leaved gardens greeted me
25 that disappear as soon as you touch them.

And so near, just outside the window—the
    greenhouse of the worlds
where a tiny beetle and a spider are equal to planets,
where a wandering atom flares up like Saturn,
and, close by, harvesters drink from a cold jug
30 in scorching summer.

This I wanted and nothing more. In my later years
like old Goethe° to stand before the face of the earth,
and recognize it and reconcile it
with my work built up, a forest citadel
35 on a river of shifting lights and brief shadows.

This I wanted and nothing more. So who
is guilty? Who deprived me
of my youth and my ripe years, who seasoned
my best years with horror? Who,
40 who ever is to blame, who, O God?

And I can think only about the starry sky,
about the tall mounds of termites.

Warsaw, Poland, April 3, 1946.

13. non-Euclidean space:
space that cannot be measured
by the simple geometric rules
defined by the Greek mathematician Euclid (c. 300 B.C.).
pseudopodia *n. pl.:* footlike
projections used for moving
and for taking in food.

32. Goethe (gö′tə): Johann
Wolfgang von Goethe
(1749–1832), a German writer
who sought the meaning of
life. See page 756.

Response and Analysis

Reading Check

1. What things does the speaker say he sees or has seen in the first two stanzas?

2. What is the speaker thinking about in lines 11–14? What is he thinking about at the very end of the poem?

3. What does the speaker say is "just outside the window" (line 26)?

4. What does the speaker say he wanted for his later years?

Thinking Critically

5. Identify details that reveal the **setting** of the poem. What is the main impression you get of the setting?

6. Whom do you think the speaker is addressing in this **dramatic monologue**? Give evidence for your answer.

7. What details provide clues to the speaker's **character**? What kind of person does he seem to be?

8. Several phrases or sentences are repeated in the poem. Identify these phrases or sentences, and explain why you think Milosz chooses to emphasize them.

9. Identify **images** in the poem that relate to science and nature. What point might Milosz be making about the relationship between science, nature, and our perception of the world around us?

10. At the end of the poem, the speaker asks three questions that are really a single question. Phrase this question in your own words. How would you answer this question?

11. Look up the definition of *citizen* in a dictionary. Why do you think Milosz called this poem "Song of a Citizen"? How is this song different from the kind of song you might expect a citizen to sing?

Extending and Evaluating

12. Speaking of the Nazi occupation of Poland, Milosz has said that there's "no question of anyone surviving that period in Poland with a clear conscience. There had to be many occasions in which not turning away would have meant heroically choosing to die." What situations in the world today might require such a choice? Do you agree with the speaker's statement in line 9, that "it is better to be a live dog than a dead lion"—that personal survival is more important than taking action against injustice or cruelty? Explain.

WRITING

Responding to a Writer's Ideas

In his *History of Polish Literature*, Milosz questions the poet's role during wartime. He asks, "if the screams of the tortured are audible in the poet's room, is not his activity an offense to human suffering? And if the next hour may bring his death and the destruction of his manuscript, should the poet engage in such a pasttime?" In a brief essay, discuss possible answers to Milosz's questions. In your essay, consider also this question: What larger purpose can poetry, or art in general, serve "in the midst of an all-pervading savagery"?

North Carolina Competency Goal
1.03; 4.05; 5.03

INTERNET

Projects and Activities
Keyword:
LE5 WL-7

Literary Skills
Analyze dramatic monologue.

Writing Skills
Respond to a writer's ideas.

Wislawa Szymborska

(1923–   )

Poland

When Wislawa Szymborska (vēs·wä'vä shēm·bor'skä) won the Nobel Prize in 1996, few people outside of her native Poland had heard of her. The resulting interest in Szymborska has finally brought her poetry to the world's attention—and dramatically altered the life of this intensely private writer, who has never sought the limelight. Szymborska has been acclaimed for her ability to turn philosophical musings about subjects such as war, love, and suffering into poems that are complex yet clear; the Swedish Academy described her as "the Mozart of poetry." She herself says, "I would like everything I write to be clear [and] intelligible, and I worry a lot if something proves incomprehensible to a reader."

Szymborska's direct and accessible style may be a response to the chaos and tragedy she witnessed as a Pole during the twentieth century. As many as six million Poles, including three million Jews, died during the German occupation in World War II. In 1944–1945, the Soviets liberated Poland from the Nazis but imposed their own form of repression, Communism, which endured for over forty years. The Communists instituted a policy of "socialist realism" in the arts, forcing artists to glorify the Communist system in their work. Szymborska's early poetry, which she has since renounced, conformed to this directive. However, with *Calling Out to Yeti* (1957), Szymborska began to challenge conformity. As a contributor to the influential review *Zycie Literackie* (Literary life) from the 1950s until 1981, she acquired a reputation as a serious poet. Her work during this period, such as the collections *Salt* (1962) and *Could Have* (1972), contains poems notable for their irony and precise language. Unlike many central and Eastern European poets, who regard their work as political, Szymborska considers her work to be primarily personal.

According to Szymborska, all poets engage in a dialogue with the statement *I don't know.* In her Nobel Prize acceptance speech she asserted that "each poem marks an effort to answer this statement, but as soon as the final period hits the page, the poet begins to hesitate, starts to realize that this particular answer was pure makeshift, absolutely inadequate. . . . So the poets keep on trying."

In Praise of Feeling Bad About Yourself

Make the Connection

Popular books, magazines, talk shows, and Web sites abound with advice about boosting our self-esteem and feeling good about ourselves. Yet the title of this poem suggests that there may be some merit in feeling bad about ourselves. What could feeling bad about yourself mean? Under what circumstances, if any, do you think people *should* feel bad about themselves?

Literary Focus

Irony

Irony is a contrast between expectation and reality, between what appears to be true and what actually is true. Writers often use irony to surprise us, to force us to see things in a new way, to jolt us out of our complacency. Irony can be amusing, but it can also be bitter and disturbing. In modern and postmodern literature, irony has been a dominant element, a way of expressing the contradictions and complexities of modern life.

> **Irony** is a contrast between expectation and reality, between what appears to be true and what actually is true.
>
> *For more on Irony, see the Handbook of Literary and Historical Terms.*

Background

The irony that pervades contemporary Eastern European literature might be partly explained by the horrors people endured during World War II and the long years of repression under Stalinist Russia that followed. During those years, idealism was trampled under the jackboots of Hitler's storm troopers and suffocated in the concentration camps of Europe and the gulags (forced labor camps) of Soviet Russia. The poem that follows was written by a Pole who saw her country become a bloody battleground, brutalized by Germans and Russians alike. The Germans built two of the most infamous concentration camps, Auschwitz and Treblinka, in Poland, and there they murdered and starved millions of people. In 1940, the Soviets murdered more than four thousand Polish army officers in the Katyn Forest. In 1944, the Soviets stood by and allowed the retreating Germans to destroy not only the forces of Polish resistance in Warsaw but the city itself.

It is not surprising, therefore, that Szymborska refuses to romanticize the human condition. Instead, she comments on human weaknesses and follies, creating verse that is at once wise and darkly ironic.

North Carolina Competency Goal
1.02; 1.03; 4.02; 4.05; 5.01; 5.03; 6.01

Literary Skills
Understand irony.

In Praise of Feeling Bad About Yourself

Wislawa Szymborska

translated by **Stanislaw Barańczak**
and **Clare Cavanagh**

The buzzard never says it is to blame.
The panther wouldn't know what scruples mean.
When the piranha strikes, it feels no shame.
If snakes had hands, they'd claim their hands were clean.

5   A jackal doesn't understand remorse.
Lions and lice don't waver in their course.
Why should they, when they know they're right?

Though hearts of killer whales may weigh a ton,
in every other way they're light.

10   On this third planet of the sun
among the signs of bestiality
a clear conscience is Number One.

Seated Youth (1917) by Wilhelm Lehmbruck.
National Gallery of Art, Washington, D.C.

Response and Analysis

Thinking Critically

1. What animals does the speaker mention in the first two stanzas? What characteristics do all these creatures have in common?

2. A **paradox** is an apparent contradiction that contains a truth. What paradox do you find in the third stanza, in the description of the heart of the killer whale? (How can a heart that weighs a ton be light?)

3. How would you **paraphrase**—or restate in your own words—the final stanza?

4. Think about why Szymborska gave this poem its title. What exactly does "feeling bad about yourself" mean, and why does the poet write "in praise of" it? How does the title capture the central **irony** of this poem?

5. How might Szymborska's ideas in this poem apply to humanity in general? to each of us as individuals?

WRITING

Comparing Translations

In a short essay, compare the poem you just read with the following translation of the same poem. Focus on differences or similarities in **diction** (word choice), **imagery,** and **rhythm.** At the end of your essay, state which translation you think is the better one and explain why. You can organize your essay in one of two ways: You can focus first on one poem and then on the other, or you can focus on the elements themselves.

Organization A
Translation 1
- diction
- imagery
- rhythm

Translation 2
- diction
- imagery
- rhythm

Organization B
Diction
- translation 1
- translation 2

Imagery
- translation 1
- translation 2

Rhythm
- translation 1
- translation 2

In Praise of Self-Deprecation

Wislawa Szymborska
translated by Magnus J. Krynski *and* Robert A. Maguire

The buzzard has nothing to fault
    himself with.
Scruples are alien to the black
    panther.
Piranhas do not doubt the rightness
    of their actions.
The rattlesnake approves of himself
    without reservations.

5 The self-critical jackal does not exist.
The locust, alligator, trichina, horsefly
live as they live and are glad of it.

The killer-whale's heart weighs one
    hundred kilos
but in other respects it is light.

10 There is nothing more animal-like
than a clear conscience
on the third planet of the Sun.

North Carolina Competency Goal
1.03; 4.05; 5.03

INTERNET
Projects and Activities
Keyword:
LE5 WL-7

Literary Skills
Analyze irony.

Writing Skills
Compare translations.

Gabriela Mistral
(1889–1957)
Chile

Gabriela Mistral (gä′brē·ā′lä mēs·träl′) was born Lucila Godoy Alcayaga in 1889 in Vicuña, Chile, high in the Andes Mountains. Her father, a schoolteacher and traveling entertainer, left the family when Lucila was only three. To support herself and her mother, Mistral began teaching at the age of fifteen. She continued to work as an educator throughout her life, serving at one point as the advisor to the Mexican minister of education. Her career as a poet was launched in 1914 when she won a writing contest in Santiago, Chile, under the pen name Gabriela Mistral. Her entry, a collection titled *Sonnets of Death,* had been inspired by the suicide of her fiancé several years earlier.

After winning the contest, Mistral moved rapidly to the forefront of Latin American poetry. She held a number of diplomatic and literary posts. In 1945, she became both the first female poet and the first Latin American to win the Nobel Prize.

Mistral's works, which include several volumes of children's verse, explore such themes as love, death, childhood, poverty, and motherhood. Mistral's poems convert one woman's particular experiences of love and loss into universal human expressions.

Before You Read

Time

North Carolina Competency Goal
1.02; 1.03; 4.05; 5.01; 5.03; 6.01

Literary Skills
Understand simile.

Make the Connection
Quickwrite
Gabriela Mistral divides time into four parts—daybreak, morning, afternoon, and night. Before you read the poem, write each of these words on a sheet of paper. To what object or action might you compare each time of day? Jot down your ideas.

Literary Focus
Simile
Similes, comparisons between two apparently unlike things, include a word of comparison such as *like, as, than,* or *resembles: The light shimmered on the water like sparkling confetti.*

(In fact, the English word *simile* comes from a Latin word meaning "like.") Poets often use similes to describe something abstract and difficult to define, such as beauty or death.

> A **simile** is a figure of speech that makes a comparison between two seemingly unlike things by using a connective word such as *like, as, than,* or *resembles.*
>
> For more on Simile, see the *Handbook of Literary and Historical Terms.*

Time

Gabriela Mistral
translated by Doris Dana

DAYBREAK

My heart swells that the Universe
like a fiery cascade may enter.
The new day comes. Its coming
leaves me breathless.
5 I sing. Like a cavern brimming
I sing my new day.

For grace lost and recovered
I stand humble. Not giving. Receiving.
Until the Gorgon[1] night,
10 vanquished, flees.

MORNING

She has returned! She has returned!
Each morning the same and new.
Awaited every yesterday,
she must return this morning.

5 Mornings of empty hands
that promised and betrayed.
Behold this new morning unfold,
leap like a deer from the East,
awake, happy and new,
10 alert, eager and rich with deeds.

Brother, raise up your head
fallen to your breast. Receive her.
Be worthy of her who leaps up,
soars and darts like a halcyon,[2]
15 golden halcyon plunging earthward singing
Alleluia, alleluia, alleluia![3]

AFTERNOON

I feel my heart melt like wax
in this sweetness:
slow oil, not wine,
my veins,
I feel my life fleeting
silent and sweet as a gazelle.

NIGHT

Mountain ranges dissolve,
cattle wander astray,
the sun returns to its forge,
all the world slips away.

5 Orchard and garden are fading,
the farmhouse already immersed.
My mountains submerge their crests
and their living cry.

All creatures are sliding aslant
10 down toward forgetfulness and sleep.
You and I, also, my baby,
tumble down toward night's keep.

---

1. **Gorgon:** In Greek mythology, a hideous woman with snakes for hair who turns people who look at her into stone. Here the word means "terrifying."
2. **halcyon** (hal′sē·ən) *n.*: kingfisher; according to legend, a bird that has a calming effect on the ocean during the winter solstice.
3. **alleluia** (al′ə·loo′yə) *interj.*: hallelujah; expression of praise.

Response and Analysis

Thinking Critically

1. Identify two **similes** in "Daybreak" and two in "Morning." Explain what is being compared in each figure of speech. What effect do these comparisons achieve?

2. **Personification** is a comparison in which something nonhuman is referred to as human. What is being personified in "Morning"? What do you think was Mistral's purpose in using personification?

3. Each of the four parts of the poem has a distinctive **mood**. Describe the mood in each section of the poem, and explain whether you think the mood expressed fits the time of day being described.

4. "Daybreak" and "Afternoon" are characterized by a kind of stillness, while "Morning" is full of movement—a sense of excitement and expectancy. What kind of movement characterizes "Night"? What words and phrases help create this sense?

5. Review the comparisons you generated for the Quickwrite activity (page 930). Are any of them similar to the ones Mistral uses in this poem? Which of Mistral's comparisons seems the most unexpected or unusual to you?

6. When Mistral won the Nobel Prize in literature in 1945, she was introduced as the "spiritual queen of Latin America." Where in "Time" do you see language that is associated with sacred or spiritual concerns? How does this language affect the poem's meaning and power?

Literary Criticism

7. Mistral's writing has been praised for possessing "a voice of its own, authentic and consciously realized. The affirmation within the poetry of the intimate 'I' . . . makes it profoundly human, and it is this human quality that gives it its universal value." Do you think the "I" who speaks in "Time" creates an identification with all people, or do you think the "I" speaks only for a particular individual? Explain.

WRITING

Writing a Poem

"Time" presents the abstract concept of time in terms of the times of day, but there may be other ways to represent the concept of time: the seasons or months of a year, the days of the week, the cycle of a school year, the stages of a human lifetime. Write your own poem called "Time," choosing a pattern and structure that work for you. Like Mistral, you may choose to divide your poem into parts.

Statue of Gabriela Mistral. Monte Grande, Chile.
Photograph courtesy of Maritza M. Osuna.

North Carolina Competency Goal
1.02; 1.03; 4.05; 5.03; 6.01

go.hrw.com

INTERNET
Projects and Activities
Keyword: LE5 WL-7

SKILLS FOCUS

Literary Skills
Analyze simile.

Writing Skills
Write a poem.

Jorge Luis Borges

(1899–1986)

Argentina

Jorge Luis Borges (hôr′he lōō·ēs′ bôr′hes) seems to have been destined to become a writer. In addition to possessing great natural gifts, Borges was exposed to a number of important literary influences throughout his childhood in Argentina. Borges considered the hours he spent reading in his father's vast library particularly important in his life. He also believed that his father gave him an appreciation for poetry by making him aware of the power and symbolism of words.

English was the first language that Borges learned to read, and he eagerly read the English-language works in his father's vast collection. Borges's favorites included the adventure stories of Robert Louis Stevenson, Edgar Allan Poe's tales of horror, and the fairy tales in *The Thousand and One Nights* (see page 547). Ironically, Borges read an English translation of *Don Quixote* (see page 688) before reading the original Spanish version of the classic. When he finally read the work in Spanish, he thought it sounded like a bad translation!

Borges learned a number of other languages as a result of a fateful family trip to Europe in 1914. While they were traveling, World War I broke out, and the family took refuge in neutral Switzerland. While attending school there, Borges learned French and Latin. He also learned German on his own. After reading German translations of Walt Whitman's poems, Borges was inspired to try his hand at writing poetry.

After the war the Borges family moved to Spain, where Borges encountered a group of poets who promoted an avant-garde style of poetry known as Ultraism, which emphasizes the use of metaphor. Borges became a strong proponent of this movement. When he returned to Argentina, he published his first poetry collection, *Fervor de Buenos Aires, poemas* (Fervor of Buenos Aires, poems), which was clearly influenced by Ultraism.

Although Borges considered himself primarily a poet, in the 1940s he started writing the experimental prose he is famous for. The stories he wrote include extraordinary elements such as transparent tigers, characters with doubles, wizards who conjure visions in a bowl of ink, and encyclopedias capable of setting events in motion. In *The Garden of the Forking Paths* (1941) and *El Aleph* (1945), Borges disregarded typical elements of fiction, such as plot and character. In these works he combines fantasy and reality to create a world of riddles, mystery, and philosophical inquiry.

Borges began using one of his characteristic images during the 1940s—the labyrinth, or maze. Borges viewed the labyrinth as a metaphor for the twists and turns we encounter throughout the journey of life. One such twist in Borges's own life was his complete loss of sight in the 1950s. In spite of his blindness, however, Borges continued to write, producing critically acclaimed works that cemented his international reputation as a master of experimental fantastic fiction.

Before You Read

Borges and I

Make the Connection
Quickwrite

Writers and artists often feel that they lead two separate lives—an imaginative life that is expressed in the works they create and an ordinary life that involves mundane activities such as doing laundry or paying bills. Think of a writer, artist, or performer whose work you have seen, read, or heard about. Explain how the public's perception of that person's life differs from his or her actual life. (For example, Stephen King is known for his horror stories but lives a relatively peaceful life in New England.) In what sense does every human being lead a "double life"?

Literary Focus
First-Person Point of View

Borges tells this story from the **first-person point of view.** The first-person narrator is the "I" character who tells the story. Generally, when we read a story with a first-person narrator, we feel as if we are listening to a friend or as if we are reading someone's letters or diary. In this unusual story the first-person narrator and the "other man" he is talking about are different aspects of the same person.

North Carolina Competency Goal
1.03; 4.03; 4.05; 5.01; 5.03; 6.01

INTERNET
More About Jorge Luis Borges
Keyword: LE5 WL-7

SKILLS FOCUS

Literary Skills
Understand first-person point of view.

Reading Skills
Draw conclusions.

Reading Skills
Drawing Conclusions

When you read a selection, you can **draw conclusions** about the characters and events mentioned in the text. From the details that the author provides you can draw reasonable conclusions about different aspects of a story, such as a character's true motivation. As you read "Borges and I," take note of any conclusions, or judgments, you are able to make about the narrator.

Background

Borges was interested in philosophical issues, such as the nature of reality and the interplay between the imagined and the real. He was especially interested in the way art affects our perceptions of the world. He believed that reality consists not only of what we have actually seen and done but also of what we have read and what our reading has led us to imagine.

Borges calls the following story a parable and describes it as "my personal rendering of the old Jekyll-and-Hyde theme, save that in their case the opposition is between good and evil and in my version the opposites are the spectator and the spectacle."

> In a story told from the **first-person point of view,** the narrator is a character in the story and we are limited to knowing only what that character sees and knows.
>
> *For more on Point of View, see the Handbook of Literary and Historical Terms.*

Borges and I

Jorge Luis Borges

translated by **Andrew Hurley**

Portrait d'Edward James (1937) by René Magritte.
Museum Boymans van Beuningen, Rotterdam, the Netherlands.

It's Borges, the other one, that things happen to. I walk through Buenos Aires and I pause—mechanically now, perhaps—to gaze at the arch of an entryway and its inner door; news of Borges reaches me by mail, or I see his name on a list of academics or in some biographical dictionary. My taste runs to hourglasses, maps, seventeenth-century typefaces, etymologies, the taste of coffee, and the prose of Robert Louis Stevenson;[1] Borges shares those preferences, but in a vain sort of way that turns them into the accoutrements of an actor. It would be an exaggeration to say that our relationship is hostile—I live, I allow myself to live, so that Borges can spin out his literature, and that literature is my justification. I willingly admit that he has written a number of sound pages, but those pages will not save *me*, perhaps because the good in them no longer belongs to any individual, not even to that other man, but rather to language itself, or to tradition. Beyond that, I am doomed—utterly and inevitably—to oblivion, and fleeting moments will be all of me that survives in that other man. Little by little, I have been turning everything over to him, though I know the perverse way he has of distorting and magnifying everything. Spinoza[2] believed that all things wish to go on being what they are—stone wishes eternally to be stone, and tiger, to be tiger. I shall endure in Borges, not in myself (if, indeed, I am anybody at all), but I recognize myself less in his books than in many others', or in the tedious strumming of a guitar. Years ago I tried to free myself from him, and I moved on from the mythologies of the slums and outskirts of the city to games with time and infinity, but those games belong to Borges now, and I shall have to think up other things. So my life is a point-counterpoint, a kind of fugue, and a falling away—and everything winds up being lost to me, and everything falls into oblivion, or into the hands of the other man.

I am not sure which of us it is that's writing this page.

---

1. **Robert Louis Stevenson:** (1850–1894), Scottish writer of adventure novels, poems, and essays.
2. **Spinoza:** Baruch Spinoza (1632–1677), a Dutch philosopher.

Response and Analysis

Reading Check

1. According to the narrator, to whom do things happen?
2. What interests does the narrator have?
3. What does the narrator refer to as the justification for his life?
4. What does the narrator say his fate is?
5. What is it that the narrator does not know at the end?

Thinking Critically

6. What distinction does the narrator make between "Borges" and "I"?
7. What does the narrator mean when he says that "Borges" displays his interests "in a vain sort of way"? What does this comment tell you about the narrator? Refer to the list of conclusions you made about the narrator while you were reading.
8. What is the narrator implying about Borges's writing when he makes the statement "I allow myself to live, so that Borges can spin out his literature"?
9. According to the narrator, the work that "Borges" writes belongs not to him but "to language itself, or to tradition." What do you think this statement means?
10. The narrator claims that "[i]t would be an exaggeration to say that our relationship is hostile." Do you agree with this statement? How do you think the narrator really feels about the "other" Borges?

Extending and Evaluating

11. Do you think that most people can feel like two different people at the same time, like the narrator and "Borges"? If so, when and why might someone experience this feeling? Be sure to consult your Quickwrite notes (see page 934) when writing your response.

Literary Criticism

12. "Borges and I" is one example of the experimental prose Borges is known for. This kind of writing can be categorized as **metafiction,** or fiction that self-consciously draws attention to its fictional qualities. Examples of metafiction include stories in which the author is a character or in which a character knows he or she is in a work of fiction, as well as stories about a person writing or reading a story. Although "Borges and I" contains some of these elements of metafiction, it simultaneously ignores traditional elements of fiction, such as plot and setting. Do you think that this selection suffers because of the absence of these elements? Do you think it qualifies as fiction? Explain.

WRITING

Writing a Diary Entry

Think about the different sides of your personality. What part of your personality is emphasized at school? at home? when you are alone? Write a short diary entry following the model of "Borges and I." The "I" character is your private side that others often do not see. The character with your name is the public part of your personality. You may have the "I" character comment on the daily activities of the other character.

You may find it helpful to fill out a chart like this one before you begin writing:

Qualities I Show in Public	The Way I Really Am

go.hrw.com

INTERNET

Projects and Activities
Keyword:
LE5 WL-7

SKILLS FOCUS

Literary Skills
Analyze first-person point of view.

Reading Skills
Draw conclusions.

Writing Skills
Write a diary entry.

Pablo Neruda

(1904–1973)

Chile

NOBEL PRIZE WINNER

"❝I have lived singing and defending them," Pablo Neruda (pä′blô nə·rōō′də) said of the Chilean people. Neruda had two passions in life: poetry and politics.

Born Neftalí Ricardo Reyes Basoalto, Neruda grew up in Temuco, a frontier town in the south of Chile. Neruda's early passion for literature was nourished by the poet Gabriela Mistral (see page 930), who was at that time the head of a local girls' school. The Russian novels she gave him from the school library served as inspirations on a par with the Latin American literature he studied in school.

As a teenager, Neruda published articles and his first poem in a local paper. In 1920, when he began writing for a literary magazine, he took the pen name Pablo Neruda, after the nineteenth-century Czech poet Jan Neruda. Neruda was only twenty years old when he published *Veinte poemas de amor y una canción desesperada* (Twenty love poems and a song of despair) (1924), a collection of love poems that became hugely popular, eventually selling two million copies worldwide.

In the 1940s, Neruda became increasingly involved in politics, and his poetry reflected this shift. *Canto general* (1950), a collection regarded as his masterpiece, includes both historical and mythological explorations of Latin America and harsh criticism of mid–twentieth century Chile. Among the approximately 250 poems is *Alturas de Macchu-Picchu* (The heights of Macchu Picchu), a masterly series of meditations on the centuries of oppression in Chile.

Neruda was passionate about government service and human rights activism—concerns that often put his life in danger. He had first become seriously involved with politics when he worked in the diplomatic service from 1927 to 1935. As consul in Argentina, and later in Spain, Neruda became close friends with the poet Federico García Lorca (see page 894). Lorca's murder by Fascist forces during the Spanish Civil War (1936–1939) inspired Neruda to join the Communist party in 1945. He later became a senator. Because of his opposition to the government, however, he decided to leave Chile in 1949.

Neruda returned to his homeland in 1952 and began writing *Odas elementales* (Elemental odes) (1954), which marked a movement toward a simpler style and a celebration of ordinary objects. Then, in 1959, with *Cien sonetos de amor* (One hundred love sonnets), Neruda returned to his earlier themes of love and relationships. In 1971, Neruda was awarded the Nobel Prize in literature. In his acceptance speech he commented on the poet's need to stay connected to humanity and to the concerns of everyday life: "There is no insurmountable solitude. All paths lead to the same goal: to convey to others what we are. And we must pass through solitude and difficulty, isolation and silence in order to reach forth to the enchanted place where we can dance our clumsy dance and sing our sorrowful song—but in this dance or in this song there are fulfilled the most ancient rites of our conscience in the awareness of being human and of believing in a common destiny."

Before You Read

Sonnets 49 *and* 71

Make the Connection

Quickwrite ✏️

Think about what the word *love* meant to you five years ago. It probably means something different to you today. What does love mean to a child, to a mature adult, and to an elderly person? How do one's views of love change with age and experience? Jot down your thoughts.

Literary Focus

Figures of Speech

A **figure of speech** is a word or phrase that describes one thing in terms of another, very different thing. Figures of speech are not literally true, but they can help us see the world in imaginative ways. Two of the most common figures of speech are metaphor and personification. A **metaphor** is a comparison of two unlike things that does not include a word of comparison such as *like* or *as*. **Personification** occurs when a thing or quality is talked about as if it were human. Look for examples of metaphor and personification as you read Neruda's sonnets.

INTERNET

More About Pablo Neruda

Keyword: LE5 WL-7

> A **figure of speech** is a word or phrase that describes one thing in terms of another, different thing.
>
> *For more on Figures of Speech, see the Handbook of Literary and Historical Terms.*

Literary Skills
Understand figures of speech.

North Carolina Competency Goal
1.02; 1.03; 4.05; 5.01; 5.03; 6.01

Background

Pablo Neruda's early love poems present a speaker who pursues and adores women yet considers them mainly in terms of what they can do for him: provide a temporary refuge from loneliness. *One Hundred Love Sonnets,* the book in which the following two sonnets appear, was written more than thirty-five years after Neruda's first poems. Most of these sonnets celebrate a different kind of love: the joys of a stable, monogamous relationship. They are, in fact, written to Matilde Urrutia, Neruda's third wife. Neruda wrote these sonnets while living with Matilde in a house that overlooked the Pacific at Isla Negra, a small fishing village in Chile. The couple filled their small home with simple, beautiful things that readers might recognize in Neruda's poetry: shells, driftwood, wave-polished stones, ship and church bells, glistening pieces of glass. In the book's dedication, Neruda addresses Matilde:

> My beloved wife, . . . I made these sonnets out of wood; I gave them the sound of that opaque pure substance, and that is how they should reach your ears. Walking in forests or on beaches, along hidden lakes, in latitudes sprinkled with ashes, you and I have picked up pieces of pure bark, pieces of wood subject to the comings and goings of water and the weather. Out of such softened relics . . . I built up these lumber piles of love, and with fourteen boards each I built little houses, so that your eyes, which I adore and sing to, might live in them.

Sonnets

Pablo Neruda
translated by **Stephen Tapscott**

Sonnet 49

It's today: all of yesterday dropped away
among the fingers of the light and the
   sleeping eyes.
Tomorrow will come on its green footsteps;
no one can stop the river of the dawn.

5   No one can stop the river of your hands,
your eyes and their sleepiness, my dearest.
You are the trembling of time, which passes
between the vertical light and the
   darkening sky.

The sky folds its wings over you,
10 lifting you, carrying you to my arms
with its punctual, mysterious courtesy.

That's why I sing to the day and to the moon,
to the sea, to time, to all the planets,
to your daily voice, to your nocturnal skin.

Sonnet 71

Love crosses its islands, from grief to grief,
it sets its roots, watered with tears,
and no one—no one—can escape the
   heart's progress
as it runs, silent and carnivorous.

You and I searched for a wide valley, for
5   another planet
where the salt wouldn't touch your hair,
where sorrows couldn't grow because of
   anything I did,
where bread could live and not grow old.

A planet entwined with vistas and foliage,
10 a plain, a rock, hard and unoccupied:
we wanted to build a strong nest

with our own hands, without hurt or harm
   or speech,
but love was not like that: love was a
   lunatic city
with crowds of people blanching° on
   their porches.

----
14. blanching *v.* used as *adj.:* turning pale.

Offering by Antoni Tapies.
Museo d'Arte Moderna Ca'Pesaro, Venice, Italy.

Response and Analysis

Thinking Critically

1. How would you describe the speaker's view of love in Sonnet 49?

2. Identify at least two examples of **personification** and two examples of **metaphor** in Sonnet 49. In these **figures of speech,** what recurring images of the natural world seem important to Neruda? What do these images reveal about the speaker's feelings toward his beloved?

3. In Sonnet 71, what hopes did the speaker and his beloved have for their life together? What do they find out about love?

4. Does Sonnet 71 present a negative view of love, or is the speaker revealing a side of love that has both positive and negative aspects? Explain, citing specific **images** from the poem.

5. These sonnets follow the form, though not the rhyme scheme, of the **Italian,** or **Petrarchan, sonnet** (see page 678). Some of Neruda's sonnets do contain the abrupt turns of thought found in the classic sonnet. Identify the change, or turn, in each of the sonnets you have read.

6. Do you think the views of love presented in each of the two sonnets contradict each other? Why or why not?

Literary Criticism

7. The critic and writer Stephen Dobyns notes that in Chile in the 1960s, Neruda's first collection of love poetry was still being "discussed, wondered over, and dreamt with. Despite having been written in the twenties, it seemed of the moment. . . . My wife and her friends felt no doubt about what the poems meant. They had no need for critics. The poems were being spoken directly to them." Do you feel that the two sonnets you've just read speak directly to you, a student today? Do they reflect contemporary views of romantic love, or are they dated and irrelevant? You may want to consult your Quickwrite notes.

WRITING

Comparing Sonnets

Review one of the Renaissance sonnets you studied in Collection 5 and, in a brief essay, compare and contrast it with one of Neruda's sonnets. In your essay, explore these points:

- the form of each sonnet (Petrarchan or Shakespearean)
- the speaker's intention in each sonnet
- things you learn about the person to whom the sonnet is addressed
- the theme of each sonnet
- the poet's use of figures of speech
- differences between the views of love presented in the two sonnets

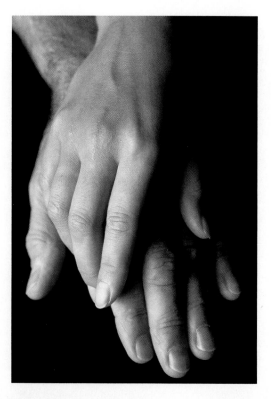

North Carolina Competency Goal
1.02; 1.03; 4.05; 5.03; 6.01

INTERNET

Projects and Activities
Keyword: LE5 WL-7

SKILLS FOCUS

Literary Skills
Analyze figures of speech.

Writing Skills
Compare sonnets.

Octavio Paz
(1914–1998)
Mexico

Octavio Paz (ôk·tä′vyô päs) was born in Mexico City into a family he called "typically Mexican"—part Spanish, part Indian, and not very wealthy. Paz grew up in his grandfather's home, which he remembered as an old house that was falling apart, but that had a huge overgrown garden and one large room full of books. Paz read all the books in his grandfather's library.

Paz's poetic talents were recognized when he was very young. His first volume of poetry, *Forest Moon* (1933), was published just after he graduated from the National University of Mexico. By 1937, when his next volume was published, he was well on his way to literary celebrity. Diplomatic appointments took Paz to Paris, East Asia, and India. An enthusiastic scholar, Paz studied the literature and history of every nation he visited. Paz's poetry often reveals the influence of European modernist and Asian verse, but his subjects and imagery are rooted in the sand, stones, and soil of the Mexican landscape. Paz uses these simple images to explore abstract philosophical concepts, such as the nature of truth and reality. For example, his longest poem, *Sun Stone* (1957), about the carved stone disc that the ancient Aztecs used as their calendar, deals with the concepts of time as a cycle and the interrelatedness of all things. In spite of his fame as a poet, though, Paz is perhaps best known for his literary essays, such as those collected in *The Labyrinth of Solitude,* which focuses on the character of the Mexican people.

In accepting the 1990 Nobel Prize in literature, Octavio Paz recalled his early years as a writer. He claimed that he had no idea then why he wrote his poems—he only knew that he felt a deep need to write them. Only later did he come to understand that his poems were his passage to the present, his way of connecting himself to his country and to the modern world. Indeed, as one of the most influential poets and essayists in the world, Octavio Paz truly became a man of his century.

Wind, Water, Stone/Viento, Agua, Piedra.
A Tree Within

Make the Connection

Quickwrite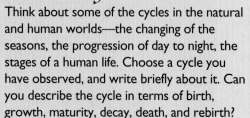

Think about some of the cycles in the natural and human worlds—the changing of the seasons, the progression of day to night, the stages of a human life. Choose a cycle you have observed, and write briefly about it. Can you describe the cycle in terms of birth, growth, maturity, decay, death, and rebirth?

Literary Focus

Personification

Poets frequently use **personification** to give human characteristics to nonhuman things. For example, if a poet writes, "The breeze sighs in the trees," the writer is personifying the breeze, since breezes don't really sigh; only human beings do. Another example appears in the image "the lonely night." Here, the night is being personified, or given feelings, which it really doesn't have. Personification is an important element in these two poems by Octavio Paz.

North Carolina Competency Goal
1.02; 1.03;
4.05; 5.01;
5.03; 6.01

> **Personification** is a figure of speech in which something non-human is given human characteristics.
>
> *For more on Personification, see the Handbook of Literary and Historical Terms.*

Background

The cycles of Mexico's social and political history and of its natural history have inspired many of Paz's poems, including "Wind, Water, Stone." Much of Mexico is dry, rocky, and sparsely forested. The effects of wind and water are easily visible in this desertlike landscape, as certain areas are worn down and others built up.

Mexico's periods of great civilization have followed similar patterns of breaking down and building up again. During the Classic period, from about A.D. 250 until the 900s, the Maya civilization thrived. Then came the Toltec empire, which was at its peak from 900 to about 1200. Finally the great Aztec empire arose. Centered at Tenochtitlán (now Mexico City), whose name means "stone rising in water," the Aztec empire fell to Spanish conquerors early in the sixteenth century. Paz singled out the Spaniards' conquest of the Indians as the moment when the true Mexico was isolated and overshadowed by a foreign culture. Mexico remained a colony of Spain until 1821, when Mexicans revolted and won their independence.

SKILLS FOCUS

Literary Skills
Understand personification.

(Opposite) *Fossils, Mistaken, Point* (1999)
by Melville McLean.
Courtesy Alexandre Gallery, New York.

Wind, Water, Stone

Octavio Paz
translated by **Eliot Weinberger**

for Roger Caillois

Water hollows stone,
wind scatters water,
stone stops the wind.
Water, wind, stone.

5 Wind carves stone,
stone's a cup of water,
water escapes and is wind.
Stone, wind, water.

Wind sings in its whirling,
10 water murmurs going by,
unmoving stone keeps still.
Wind, water, stone.

Each is another and no other:
crossing and vanishing
15 through their empty names:
water, stone, wind.

Viento, Agua, Piedra.

Octavio Paz

A Roger Caillois

El agua horada la piedra,
el viento dispersa el agua,
la piedra detiene al viento.
Agua, viento, piedra.

5 El viento esculpe la piedra,
la piedra es copa del agua,
el agua escapa y es viento.
Piedra, viento, agua.

El viento en sus giros canta,
10 el agua al andar murmura,
la piedra inmóvil se calla.
Viento, agua, piedra.

Uno es otro y es ninguno:
entre sus nombres vacíos
15 pasan y se desvanecen
agua, piedra, viento.

Roots (1943) by Frida Kahlo.

A Tree Within

Octavio Paz
translated by **Eliot Weinberger**

A tree grew inside my head.
A tree grew in.
Its roots are veins,
its branches nerves,
5   thoughts its tangled foliage.
Your glance sets it on fire,
and its fruits of shade
are blood oranges
and pomegranates of flame.
                      Day breaks
10   in the body's night.
There, within, inside my head,
the tree speaks.
            Come closer—can you hear it?

Response and Analysis

Thinking Critically

1. To what natural processes do lines 1, 5, and 7 of "Wind, Water, Stone" refer?

2. Given what you learned about the meaning of the name *Tenochtitlán* in the Background (see page 942), do you think the stone in this poem stands for something more than a stone? Explain your answer.

3. How are the wind, water, and stone **personified** in stanzas 2 and 3?

4. What does "Wind, Water, Stone" suggest about the relationship of all things in nature? What does the last stanza suggest about the ability of natural things to endure?

5. In what sense may "Wind, Water, Stone" actually be about human beings or human civilizations?

6. Read both the English and the Spanish versions of "Wind, Water, Stone" aloud. In what ways are the rhythms and sounds of each version similar? In what ways are they different?

7. In lines 1–2 of "A Tree Within," what does the emphasis on the tree's inward growth suggest about the tree's symbolic, or broader, meaning?

8. Like metaphor, **personification** compares or equates unlike things. What unlike things are equated in lines 3–5 of "A Tree Within"?

9. How is the tree inside the speaker's head transformed in line 6? What do you think this transformation represents?

10. What **imagery** is used to emphasize the transformation that takes place in "A Tree Within"?

11. What do you think the tree will say to the speaker and his companion (lines 11–12)?

Extending and Evaluating

12. Does everything that exists pass through stages of birth, growth, maturity, decay, death, rebirth, and so on? Do you see human life and human civilizations as moving only upward or downward, or as moving in cycles that are constantly repeated? Explain your answer. You may wish to refer to your Quickwrite notes.

WRITING

Personifying Nature

Write a poem or paragraph in which you personify an element of nature, such as a tree, a flower, an animal, the sun, the moon, the stars, or the sea. You may want to fill out a chart like the one below before you begin writing.

Subject: Sunset

Detail	Human Quality
appearance	dressed in a dusky-rose gown
actions	lingered like a long-lost friend
feelings	sadly sank below the horizon

North Carolina Competency Goal
1.02; 1.03; 4.05; 5.03; 6.01

INTERNET

Projects and Activities

Keyword: LE5 WL-7

Literary Skills
Analyze personification.

Writing Skills
Personify nature.

Julio Cortázar
(1914–1984)
Argentina

Julio Cortázar believed that fantasy and reality, the rational and the irrational, exist on intersecting planes. This philosophy surely stemmed in part from the fact that Cortázar himself had his feet in two very different worlds—Latin America and Europe.

Born in Belgium to Argentine parents, Cortázar was raised in a suburb of Buenos Aires, Argentina, by his mother and an aunt after his father left the family. Throughout his childhood, Cortázar read voraciously. (He especially loved the works of the French science fiction writer Jules Verne, whose novel *Around the World in Eighty Days* Cortázar later used as the basis for his own work *Around the Day in Eighty Worlds*.) After high school, he gave up his university studies in order to take a teaching job to support his family. During this time he began to write stories, but he didn't publish his first collection, *Bestiary,* until November 1951.

That month marked a turning point in Cortázar's life: Dissatisfied with the regime of the Argentine dictator Juan Perón, he accepted a French-government grant to study in Paris. He worked as a freelance translator for the United Nations and various publishers there until his death from leukemia in 1984. Though he lived in exile most of his life, mainly in France—he became a French citizen in 1981—Cortázar always thought of himself as Argentine.

Cortázar's works are playful and experimental. In 1963, his masterpiece, *Hopscotch,* was published to great acclaim, and it paved the way for American appreciation of other Latin American novels. Named for a child's game, this dizzying and demanding novel even includes instructions for the different ways it can be read.

Cortázar's literary style, heavily influenced by French surrealism and the writings of Edgar Allan Poe (whose books Cortázar translated into Spanish), often contains elements of the fantastic and absurd, blending imagination with reality in seamless ways. For example, in his story "We Love Glenda So Much," a movie star's obsessed fans decide to murder her rather than tolerate any chance that her future performances will be less than perfect. The critic Daniel Stern writes of Cortázar's stories, "It is as if Cortázar is showing us that it is essential for us to reimagine the reality in which we live and which we can no longer take for granted."

For Independent Reading

You may enjoy the following stories by Cortázar:

- "House Taken Over"
- "Axolotl"

The Night Face Up

Make the Connection

Although dreams are sometimes difficult to remember, an especially vivid one can be impossible to forget. Have you ever had a dream that was so detailed and clear that it seemed real? What elements of the dream made it so memorable?

Literary Focus

Suspense

Plot-driven stories always contain a certain degree of **suspense:** They generate in us a sense of uncertainty or anxiety about what will happen next. But suspense is not created by plot elements alone. Atmosphere, vivid details, and pacing all contribute to our mounting anticipation. As you read "The Night Face Up," pay attention to the many ways in which Cortázar builds suspense.

> **Suspense** is the uncertainty or anxiety we feel about what is going to happen in a story.
>
> *For more on Suspense, see the Hand-book of Literary and Historical Terms.*

Reading Skills

Making Predictions

In a story filled with suspenseful moments, you might feel an urge to flip to the end to find out what happens. But a careful reader can make **predictions,** or educated guesses about what will happen, based on a story's details. When you reach particularly suspenseful points in "The Night Face Up," take a minute to jot down what you think will happen. After you finish the story, see if your predictions are accurate.

Background

The "war of the blossom" cited in Cortázar's editorial footnote at the beginning of this story probably refers to the Aztec holy war called *xochiyaoyotl,* the "flowered war," a ritual hunt held by the Aztecs during relatively peaceful times as a way of keeping up the supply of prisoners for use in human sacrifice.

Human sacrifice was an important practice of the Aztec culture, which flourished in the fifteenth century. Aztecs looked upon the practice as a religious necessity, a sacred ritual to be enacted with one purpose in mind: to feed the sun so that it would continue to travel across the sky and keep the world alive. Every year, on altars at the summits of temple pyramids, hundreds of people—usually slaves or prisoners of war—met their deaths as a presiding priest cut open their chests and removed their hearts in offerings to the sun god.

North Carolina Competency Goal
1.03; 4.05; 5.01; 5.03

Vocabulary Development

solace (säl′is) *n.:* comfort in times of trouble.

habitual (hə·bich′o͞o·əl) *adj.:* done repeatedly by habit.

beneficent (bə·nef′ə·sənt) *adj.:* kind; helpful.

translucent (trans·lo͞o′sənt) *adj.:* allowing some light to pass through.

INTERNET

Vocabulary Practice

Keyword: LE5 WL-7

SKILLS FOCUS

Literary Skills Understand suspense.

Reading Skills Make predictions.

THE NIGHT FACE UP

Julio Cortázar
translated by Paul Blackburn

*And at certain periods they went out to hunt
enemies; they called it the war of the blossom.**

Halfway down the long hotel vestibule,[1] he
thought that probably he was going to be
late, and hurried on into the street to get out his
motorcycle from the corner where the next-door
superintendent let him keep it. On the jewelry
store at the corner he read that it was ten to nine;
he had time to spare. The sun filtered through
the tall downtown buildings, and he—because
for himself, for just going along thinking, he did
not have a name—he swung onto the machine,
savoring the idea of the ride. The motor whirred
between his legs, and a cool wind whipped his
pantslegs.

He let the ministries[2] zip past (the pink, the
white), and a series of stores on the main street,
their windows flashing. Now he was beginning
the most pleasant part of the run, the real ride: a
long street bordered with trees, very little traffic,
with spacious villas whose gardens rambled all
the way down to the sidewalks, which were
barely indicated by low hedges. A bit inattentive
perhaps, but tooling along on the right side of
the street, he allowed himself to be carried away
by the freshness, by the weightless contraction
of this hardly begun day. This involuntary relaxation, possibly, kept him from preventing
the accident. When he saw that the woman
standing on the corner had rushed into the
crosswalk while he still had the green light, it
was already somewhat too late for a simple solution. He braked hard with foot and hand,
wrenching himself to the left; he heard the
woman scream, and at the collision his vision
went. It was like falling asleep all at once.

He came to abruptly. Four or five young men
were getting him out from under the cycle. He
felt the taste of salt and blood, one knee hurt, and
when they hoisted him up he yelped, he couldn't
bear the pressure on his right arm. Voices which
did not seem to belong to the faces hanging
above him encouraged him cheerfully with jokes
and assurances. His single solace was to hear
someone else confirm that the lights indeed had
been in his favor. He asked about the woman,
trying to keep down the nausea which was edg-
ing up into his throat. While they carried him
face up to a nearby pharmacy, he learned that
the cause of the accident had gotten only a few
scrapes on the legs. "Nah, you barely got her
at all, but when ya hit, the impact made the
machine jump and flop on its side…" Opinions,
recollections of other smashups, take it easy,
work him in shoulders first, there, that's fine, and
someone in a dustcoat giving him a swallow of
something soothing in the shadowy interior of
the small local pharmacy.

Within five minutes the police ambulance
arrived, and they lifted him onto a cushioned
stretcher. It was a relief for him to be able to lie
out flat. Completely lucid, but realizing that he
was suffering the effects of a terrible shock, he
gave his information to the officer riding in the
ambulance with him. The arm almost didn't
hurt; blood dripped down from a cut over the
eyebrow all over his face. He licked his lips once
or twice to drink it. He felt pretty good, it had
been an accident, tough luck; stay quiet a few
weeks, nothing worse. The guard said that the
motorcycle didn't seem badly racked up. "Why
should it," he replied. "It all landed on top of
me." They both laughed, and when they got to
the hospital, the guard shook his hand and
wished him luck. Now the nausea was coming
back little by little; meanwhile they were pushing
him on a wheeled stretcher toward a pavilion
further back, rolling along under trees full of
birds, he shut his eyes and wished he were asleep
or chloroformed. But they kept him for a good
while in a room with that hospital smell, filling

---

*   The war of the blossom was the name the Aztecs
    gave to a ritual war in which they took prisoners for
    sacrifice. It is metaphysics to say that the gods see
    men as flowers, to be so uprooted, trampled, cut
    down.—Ed. [Cortázar's note]

1. **vestibule** (ves**'**tə·byōōl') *n.:* entrance hall or lobby.
2. **ministries** *n. pl.:* buildings that are headquarters of
    government departments.

Vocabulary

solace (säl**'**is) *n.:* comfort in times of trouble.

out a form, getting his clothes off, and dressing him in a stiff, grayish smock. They moved his arm carefully, it didn't hurt him. The nurses were constantly making wisecracks, and if it hadn't been for the stomach contractions he would have felt fine, almost happy.

They got him over to X-ray, and twenty minutes later, with the still-damp negative lying on his chest like a black tombstone, they pushed him into surgery. Someone tall and thin in white came over and began to look at the X-rays. A woman's hands were arranging his head, he felt that they were moving him from one stretcher to another. The man in white came over to him again, smiling, something gleamed in his right hand. He patted his cheek and made a sign to someone stationed behind.

It was unusual as a dream because it was full of smells, and he never dreamt smells. First a marshy smell, there to the left of the trail the swamps began already, the quaking bogs from which no one ever returned. But the reek lifted, and instead there came a dark, fresh composite fragrance, like the night under which he moved, in flight from the Aztecs. And it was all so natural, he had to run from the Aztecs who had set out on their manhunt, and his sole chance was to find a place to hide in the deepest part of the forest, taking care not to lose the narrow trail which only they, the Motecas, knew.

What tormented him the most was the odor, as though, notwithstanding the absolute acceptance of the dream, there was something which resisted that which was not <u>habitual</u>, which until that point had not participated in the game. "It smells of war," he thought, his hand going instinctively to the stone knife which was tucked at an angle into his girdle of woven wool. An unexpected sound made him crouch suddenly stock-still and shaking. To be afraid was nothing strange, there was plenty of fear in his dreams. He waited, covered by the branches of a shrub and the starless night. Far off, probably on the other side of the big lake, they'd be lighting the bivouac[3] fires; that part of the sky had a reddish

glare. The sound was not repeated. It had been like a broken limb. Maybe an animal that, like himself, was escaping from the smell of war. He stood erect slowly, sniffing the air. Not a sound could be heard, but the fear was still following, as was the smell, that cloying incense of the war of the blossom. He had to press forward, to stay out of the bogs and get to the heart of the forest. Groping uncertainly through the dark, stooping every other moment to touch the packed earth of the trail, he took a few steps. He would have liked to have broken into a run, but the gurgling fens[4] lapped on either side of him. On the path and in darkness, he took his bearings. Then he caught a horrible blast of that foul smell he was most afraid of, and leaped forward desperately.

"You're going to fall off the bed," said the patient next to him. "Stop bouncing around, old buddy."

He opened his eyes and it was afternoon, the sun already low in the oversized windows of the long ward. While trying to smile at his neighbor, he detached himself almost physically from the final scene of the nightmare. His arm, in a plaster cast, hung suspended from an apparatus with weights and pulleys. He felt thirsty, as though he'd been running for miles, but they didn't want to give him much water, barely enough to moisten his lips and make a mouthful. The fever was winning slowly and he would have been able to sleep again, but he was enjoying the pleasure of keeping awake, eyes half-closed, listening to the other patients' conversation, answering a question from time to time. He saw a little white pushcart come up beside the bed, a blond nurse rubbed the front of his thigh with alcohol and stuck him with a fat needle connected to a tube which ran up to a bottle filled with a milky, opalescent liquid. A young intern arrived with some metal and leather apparatus which he adjusted to fit onto the good arm to check something or other. Night fell, and the fever went

---

3. **bivouac** (biv′wak′) *n.* used as *adj.:* A bivouac is a temporary camp for soldiers.

4. **fens** *n. pl.:* marshy lowland areas; swamps.

Vocabulary

habitual (hə·bich′o͞o·əl) *adj.:* done repeatedly by habit.

along dragging him down softly to a state in which things seemed embossed as through opera glasses,[5] they were real and soft and, at the same time, vaguely distasteful; like sitting in a boring movie and thinking that, well, still, it'd be worse out in the street, and staying.

A cup of a marvelous golden broth came, smelling of leeks, celery, and parsley. A small hunk of bread, more precious than a whole banquet, found itself crumbling little by little. His arm hardly hurt him at all, and only in the eyebrow where they'd taken stitches a quick, hot pain sizzled occasionally. When the big windows across the way turned to smudges of dark blue, he thought it would not be difficult for him to sleep. Still on his back so a little un-comfortable, running his tongue out over his hot, too-dry lips, he tasted the broth still, and with a sigh of bliss, he let himself drift off.

First there was a confu-sion, as of one drawing all his sensations, for that moment blunted or muddled, into himself. He realized that he was running in pitch dark-ness, although, above, the sky crisscrossed with treetops was less black than the rest. "The trail," he thought. "I've gotten off the trail." His feet sank into a bed of leaves and mud, and then he couldn't take a step that the branches of shrubs did not whiplash against his ribs and legs. Out of breath, knowing despite the darkness and silence that he was surrounded, he crouched down to listen. Maybe the trail was very near, with the first daylight he would be able to see it again. Nothing now could help him to find it. The hand that had unconsciously gripped the haft of the dagger climbed like a fen scorpion up to his neck where the protecting amulet[6] hung. Barely moving his lips, he mumbled the supplication of the corn which brings about the <u>beneficent</u> moons, and the prayer to Her Very Highness, to the distributor of all Motecan possessions. At the same time he felt his ankles sinking deeper into the mud, and the waiting in the dark-ness of the obscure grove of live oak grew intolerable to him. The war of the blossom had started at the beginning of the moon and had been going on for three days and three nights now. If he managed to hide in the depths of the forest, getting off the trail further up past the marsh country, perhaps the warriors wouldn't follow his track. He thought of the many pris-oners they'd already taken. But the number didn't count, only the consecrated period. The hunt would con-tinue until the priests gave the sign to return. Everything had its number and its limit, and it was within the sacred period, and he on the other side from the hunters.

He heard the cries and leaped up, knife in hand. As if the sky were aflame on the horizon, he saw torches moving among the branches, very

---

5. **opera glasses** *n.:* small binocular telescope for use in a theater.

(Above) Mask of Tezcatlipoca, the smoking mirror. Turquoise and lignite mosaic set over a human skull. Aztec.

---

6. **amulet** (am'yoo·lit) *n.:* object worn as a charm or protection to ward off evil or bad luck.

Vocabulary

beneficent (bə·nef'ə·sənt) *adj.:* kind; helpful.

near him. The smell of war was unbearable, and when the first enemy jumped him, leaped at his throat, he felt an almost-pleasure in sinking the stone blade flat to the haft into his chest. The lights were already around him, the happy cries. He managed to cut the air once or twice, then a rope snared him from behind.

"It's the fever," the man in the next bed said. "The same thing happened to me when they operated on my duodenum.[7] Take some water, you'll see, you'll sleep all right."

Laid next to the night from which he came back, the tepid shadow of the ward seemed delicious to him. A violet lamp kept watch high on the far wall like a guardian eye. You could hear coughing, deep breathing, once in a while a conversation in whispers. Everything was pleasant and secure, without the chase, no . . . But he didn't want to go on thinking about the nightmare. There were lots of things to amuse himself with. He began to look at the cast on his arm, and the pulleys that held it so comfortably in the air. They'd left a bottle of mineral water on the night table beside him. He put the neck of the bottle to his mouth and drank it like a precious liqueur. He could now make out the different shapes in the ward, the thirty beds, the closets with glass doors. He guessed that his fever was down, his face felt cool. The cut over the eyebrow barely hurt at all, like a recollection. He saw himself leaving the hotel again, wheeling out the cycle. Who'd have thought that it would end like this? He tried to fix the moment of the accident exactly, and it got him very angry to notice that there was a void there, an emptiness he could not manage to fill. Between the impact and the moment that they picked him up off the pavement, the passing out or what went on, there was nothing he could see. And at the same time he had the feeling that this void, this nothingness, had lasted an eternity. No, not even time, more as if, in this void, he had passed across something, or had run back immense distances. The shock, the brutal dashing against the pavement. Anyway, he had felt an immense relief in coming out of the black pit while the people were lifting him off the ground.

With pain in the broken arm, blood from the split eyebrow, contusion on the knee; with all that, a relief in returning to daylight, to the day, and to feel sustained and attended. That was weird. Someday he'd ask the doctor at the office about that. Now sleep began to take over again, to pull him slowly down. The pillow was so soft, and the coolness of the mineral water in his fevered throat. The violet light of the lamp up there was beginning to get dimmer and dimmer.

As he was sleeping on his back, the position in which he came to did not surprise him, but on the other hand the damp smell, the smell of oozing rock, blocked his throat and forced him to understand. Open the eyes and look in all directions, hopeless. He was surrounded by an absolute darkness. Tried to get up and felt ropes pinning his wrists and ankles. He was staked to the ground on a floor of dank, icy stone slabs. The cold bit into his naked back, his legs. Dully, he tried to touch the amulet with his chin and found they had stripped him of it. Now he was lost, no prayer could save him from the final . . . From afar off, as though filtering through the rock of the dungeon, he heard the great kettledrums of the feast. They had carried him to the temple, he was in the underground cells of Teocalli[8] itself, awaiting his turn.

He heard a yell, a hoarse yell that rocked off the walls. Another yell, ending in a moan. It was he who was screaming in the darkness, he was screaming because he was alive, his whole body with that cry fended off what was coming, the inevitable end. He thought of his friends filling up the other dungeons, and of those already walking up the stairs of the sacrifice. He uttered another choked cry, he could barely open his mouth, his jaws were twisted back as if with a rope and a stick, and once in a while they would open slowly with an endless exertion, as if they were made of rubber. The creaking of the wooden latches jolted

---

7. **duodenum** (do͞o′ō·dē′nəm) *n.:* part of the small intestine that connects with the stomach.

8. **Teocalli** (tē′ō·kal′ē) *n.:* four-sided pyramid, surmounted by a temple, that was used by the Aztecs for worship and sacrifice.

(Opposite) El Castillo. Mayan pyramid. Chichén Itzá, Mexico.

him like a whip. Rent, writhing, he fought to rid himself of the cords sinking into his flesh. His right arm, the strongest, strained until the pain became unbearable and he had to give up. He watched the double door open, and the smell of the torches reached him before the light did. Barely girdled by the ceremonial loincloths, the priests' acolytes[9] moved in his direction, looking at him with contempt. Lights reflected off the sweaty torsos and off the black hair dressed with feathers. The cords went slack, and in their place the grappling of hot hands, hard as bronze; he felt himself lifted, still face up, and jerked along by the four acolytes who carried him down the passageway. The torch-bearers went ahead, indistinctly lighting up the corridor with its dripping walls and a ceiling so low that the acolytes had to duck their heads. Now they were taking him out, taking him out, it was the end. Face up, under a mile of living rock which, for a succession of moments, was lit up by a glimmer of torchlight. When the stars came out up there instead of the roof and the great terraced steps rose before him, on fire with cries and dances, it would be the end. The passage was never going to end, but now it was beginning to end, he would see suddenly the open sky full of stars, but not yet, they trundled him along endlessly in the reddish shadow, hauling him roughly along and he did not want that, but how to stop it if they had torn off the amulet, his real heart, the life-center.

In a single jump he came out into the hospital night, to the high, gentle, bare ceiling, to the soft shadow wrapping him round. He thought he must have cried out, but his neighbors were peacefully snoring. The water in the bottle on the night table was somewhat bubbly, a <u>translucent</u> shape against the dark azure shadow of the windows. He panted, looking for some relief for his lungs, oblivion for those images still glued to his eyelids. Each time he shut his eyes he saw them take shape instantly, and he sat up, completely wrung out, but savoring at the same time the surety that now he was awake, that the night nurse would answer if he rang, that soon it would be daybreak, with the good, deep sleep he usually had at that hour, no images, no

nothing . . . It was difficult to keep his eyes open, the drowsiness was more powerful than he. He made one last effort, he sketched a gesture toward the bottle of water with his good hand and did not manage to reach it, his fingers closed again on a black emptiness, and the passageway went on endlessly, rock after rock, with momentary ruddy flares, and face up he choked out a dull moan because the roof was about to end, it rose, was opening like a mouth of shadow, and the acolytes straightened up, and from on high a waning moon fell on a face whose eyes wanted not to see it, were closing and opening desperately, trying to pass to the other side, to find again the bare, protecting ceiling of the ward. And every time they opened, it was night and the moon, while they climbed the great terraced steps, his head hanging down backward now, and up at the top were the bonfires, red columns of perfumed smoke, and suddenly he saw the red stone, shiny with the blood dripping off it, and the spinning arcs cut by the feet of the victim whom they pulled off to throw him rolling down the north steps. With a last hope he shut his lids tightly, moaning to wake up. For a second he thought he had gotten there, because once more he was immobile in the bed, except that his head was hanging down off it, swinging. But he smelled death, and when he opened his eyes he saw the blood-soaked figure of the executioner-priest coming toward him with the stone knife in his hand. He managed to close his eyelids again, although he knew now he was not going to wake up, that he was awake, that the marvelous dream had been the other, absurd as all dreams are—a dream in which he was going through the strange avenues of an astonishing city, with green and red lights that burned without fire or smoke, on an enormous metal insect that whirred away between his legs. In the infinite lie of the dream, they had also picked him off the ground, someone had approached him also with a knife in his hand, approached him who was lying face up, face up with his eyes closed between the bonfires on the steps.

Vocabulary

translucent (trans·loo′sənt) *adj.:* allowing some light to pass through.

---

9. **acolytes** (ak′ə·līts′) *n. pl.:* helpers or assistants, often in a religious context.

Response and Analysis

Reading Check

1. How did the motorcycle accident happen? Who was to blame for it?

2. What are the two principal **settings** in the story? Identify the point at which the first transition between settings occurs. Then, identify the final transition.

3. What happens to the Aztecs' prisoner? to the motorcycle-accident victim?

Thinking Critically

4. Look back at the **predictions** you made as you read "The Night Face Up." Which details from the story helped you make accurate predictions? Which details threw you off?

5. What might be Cortázar's purpose in starting his story with a quotation about "the war of the blossom," and including an editorial footnote?

6. How does the author use specific concrete details, such as the lamp and the surgical scalpel, to build **suspense**? In what other ways does Cortázar build suspense?

7. Find three examples of **similes** (comparisons using connective words) in the story. Identify as many comparisons between the two parallel parts of the story as you can. In what sense can the entire story be regarded as an **extended simile**—that is, an extended comparison between two different things?

8. Find passages in the story where the words *face up* appear. Now that you have read the story, what do you think the title means?

9. What is the "infinite lie of the dream," as revealed at the end of the story?

WRITING

Interpreting the Story

Consider the following possible explanations for the parallel events of the story:

- A modern-day motorcycle rider, who subconsciously feels like a sacrificial victim while recuperating from an accident in the hospital, dreams that he is a prisoner of the Aztecs.

- A modern-day motorcycle rider's accident and hospital stay are actually a dream of the Aztecs' prisoner.

- Two different people, occupying the same space in different time periods, are thrown into each other's realities by their respective traumatic experiences.

- A modern-day motorcycle rider, near death after a serious accident, is remembering a past life; the Aztecs' prisoner, soon to be a victim of ritual human sacrifice, is having premonitions of a future life.

- The story is an exploration of the consciousness of one human mind at the moment of death, when—according to a traditional expression—one's entire life passes before one's eyes.

Choose one of the explanations above, or develop a convincing explanation of your own, and support it in a well-organized essay, using evidence from the story.

Vocabulary Development
Sentence Sense

solace   beneficent

habitual   translucent

Use each of the Vocabulary words above in an original sentence based on "The Night Face Up."

North Carolina Competency Goal
1.03; 4.05; 5.03; 6.01

INTERNET
Projects and Activities
Keyword: LE5 WL-7

SKILLS FOCUS

Literary Skills
Analyze suspense.

Reading Skills
Make predictions.

Writing Skills
Interpret the story.

Vocabulary Skills
Write sentences about the story using vocabulary words.

Gabriel García Márquez

(1928–   )

Colombia

Gabriel García Márquez recalls reading Franz Kafka's novella *The Metamorphosis* as a nineteen-year-old and suddenly realizing that the story's strangeness reminded him of tales his grandmother used to tell him. The surrealistic fiction of Kafka (see page 868) and the imaginative stories told by ordinary Latin Americans were to become major influences on the development of García Márquez's literary style.

In his 1982 acceptance speech for the Nobel Prize in literature, García Márquez condemned the way Latin Americans ignore their own heritage and accept the hand-me-downs of European history and culture. He told the audience an anecdote about a statue that stands in the main square of a Central American capital city. The statue is meant to represent the nation's president, but it is in fact a likeness of one of Napoleon's commanders that was purchased from a warehouse of secondhand sculpture in Paris. It is this kind of wholesale borrowing from the traditions of Europe that García Márquez dislikes. He wants Latin Americans to write from their own experience—in which the mundane activities of day-to-day life are often guided by supernatural beliefs.

García Márquez spent the first eight years of his life with his grandparents in the small village of Aracataca, just off Colombia's northern Caribbean coast. He lovingly re-created this village, calling it Macondo, in his first short novel, *Leaf Storm* (1955), and later in his masterpiece, *One Hundred Years of Solitude* (1967). Although Macondo is little more than a railway station nestled in a swampy wilderness, it seems that anything that could possibly happen anywhere happens there—from the merely strange to the downright supernatural.

With the English publication of *One Hundred Years of Solitude* in 1970, García Márquez came to international attention. So did his distinctive technique—a literary style now known as **magic realism.** Magic realism, a style born in Latin America but now imitated by writers (and filmmakers) the world over, combines incredible events with realistic details and relates them all in a matter-of-fact tone. The term *magic realism (lo real maravilloso)* was coined in 1949 by the Cuban writer Alejo Carpentier, who used the phrase to describe a blurring of the lines that separate the real from the imagined. In many of García Márquez's works, as well as those of a number of other Latin American authors of his era, the reader is never quite certain where reality ends and fantasy begins. Myth, imagination, religion, supernatural events, and fantasy combine in such works to tear down the boundaries of our rigid concept of "reality."

Tuesday Siesta

Make the Connection

Some people—in spite of poverty, in spite of tragedy, even in spite of shame—can maintain dignity. What, to you, is the meaning of dignity?

Literary Focus

Setting

The setting—the time and place of a literary work—is often as important to the story's meaning as the characters and the plot are. The setting is usually revealed through descriptive details and imagery that create a specific emotional effect, or **mood.** In a well-crafted story the characters, action, and setting all work together to convey the **theme,** or overall meaning.

> **Setting** is the time and place of a story.
>
> *For more on Setting, see the Handbook of Literary and Historical Terms.*

Reading Skills

Making Inferences from Details

The meaning of a literary work is rarely spelled out for the reader. Instead, the reader must put together many individual details of setting, character, and plot to figure out the writer's overall message. This requires **making inferences**—that is, making educated guesses based on specific details. As you read the following story, make notes of telling details, paying particular attention to any similar or repeated details that may suggest a pattern of meaning.

Background

García Márquez began his writing career in the newspaper industry, and he always considered himself to be at heart a journalist. This background accounts for the keenly observed, realistic details in even his most fanciful fiction.

The realistic story "Tuesday Siesta" is based on a haunting scene García Márquez witnessed during his childhood, when he saw the mother and sister of a young thief who had been killed walking through town to place flowers on his grave. This sight left such a deep impression on the young García Márquez that it became the seed of "Tuesday Siesta": "That vision pursued me for many years, like a single dream that the entire town watched through its windows as it passed, until I managed to exorcise it in a story."

In Spain and some Latin American countries, a *siesta* is an early afternoon period of rest for everyone; even shops and businesses close down.

North Carolina Competency Goal
1.03; 2.01; 3.04; 4.02; 4.03; 4.05; 5.03

Vocabulary Development

symmetrical (si·me′tri·kəl) *adj.:* evenly matched; corresponding in form.

interminable (in·tur′mi·nə·bəl) *adj.:* endless.

permeated (pur′mē·āt′id) *v.:* spread throughout.

inscrutable (in·skrōōt′ə·bəl) *adj.:* hard to understand; unknowable.

INTERNET

Vocabulary Practice
•
More About Gabriel García Márquez

Keyword: LE5 WL-7

SKILLS FOCUS

Literary Skills
Understand setting.

Reading Skills
Make inferences from details.

Gabriel García Márquez **957**

Tuesday Siesta

Gabriel García Márquez
translated by **J. S. Bernstein**

The train emerged from the quivering tunnel of sandy rocks, began to cross the symmetrical, interminable banana plantations, and the air became humid and they couldn't feel the sea breeze any more. A stifling blast of smoke came in the car window. On the narrow road parallel to the railway there were oxcarts loaded with green bunches of bananas. Beyond the road, in uncultivated spaces set at odd intervals there were offices with electric fans, red-brick buildings, and residences with chairs and little white tables on the terraces among dusty palm trees and rosebushes. It was eleven in the morning, and the heat had not yet begun.

"You'd better close the window," the woman said. "Your hair will get full of soot."

The girl tried to, but the shade wouldn't move because of the rust.

They were the only passengers in the lone third-class car. Since the smoke of the locomotive kept coming through the window, the girl left her seat and put down the only things they had with them: a plastic sack with some things to eat and a bouquet of flowers wrapped in newspaper. She sat on the opposite seat, away from the window, facing her mother. They were both in severe and poor mourning clothes.

The girl was twelve years old, and it was the first time she'd ever been on a train. The woman seemed too old to be her mother, because of the blue veins on her eyelids and her small, soft, and shapeless body, in a dress cut like a cassock.[1] She was riding with her spinal column braced firmly against the back of the seat, and held a peeling patent-leather handbag in her lap with both hands. She bore the conscientious serenity of someone accustomed to poverty.

By twelve the heat had begun. The train stopped for ten minutes to take on water at a station where there was no town. Outside, in the mysterious silence of the plantations, the shadows seemed clean. But the still air inside the car smelled like untanned leather. The train did not pick up speed. It stopped at two identical towns with wooden houses painted bright colors. The woman's head nodded and she sank into sleep. The girl took off her shoes. Then she went to the washroom to put the bouquet of flowers in some water.

When she came back to her seat, her mother was waiting to eat. She gave her a piece of cheese, half a corn-meal pancake, and a cookie, and took an equal portion out of the plastic sack for herself. While they ate, the train crossed an iron bridge very slowly and passed a town just like the ones before, except that in this one there was a crowd in the plaza. A band was playing a lively tune under the oppressive sun. At the other side of town the plantations ended in a plain which was cracked from the drought.

The woman stopped eating.

"Put on your shoes," she said.

The girl looked outside. She saw nothing but the deserted plain, where the train began to pick up speed again, but she put the last piece of cookie into the sack and quickly put on her shoes. The woman gave her a comb.

"Comb your hair," she said.

The train whistle began to blow while the girl was combing her hair. The woman dried the sweat from her neck and wiped the oil from her

---

1. **cassock** (kas′ək) *n.*: long garment usually worn by members of the clergy.

Vocabulary

symmetrical (si·me′tri·kəl) *adj.*: evenly matched; corresponding in form.

interminable (in·tur′mi·nə·bəl) *adj.*: endless.

Mujeres by Rufino Tamayo.
Picture Collection of the National Bank of Mexico.

face with her fingers. When the girl stopped combing, the train was passing the outlying houses of a town larger but sadder than the earlier ones.

"If you feel like doing anything, do it now," said the woman. "Later, don't take a drink anywhere even if you're dying of thirst. Above all, no crying."

The girl nodded her head. A dry, burning wind came in the window, together with the locomotive's whistle and the clatter of the old cars. The woman folded the plastic bag with the rest of the food and put it in the handbag. For a moment a complete picture of the town, on that bright August Tuesday, shone in the window. The girl wrapped the flowers in the soaking-wet newspapers, moved a little farther away from the window, and stared at her mother. She received

a pleasant expression in return. The train began to whistle and slowed down. A moment later it stopped.

There was no one at the station. On the other side of the street, on the sidewalk shaded by the almond trees, only the pool hall was open. The town was floating in the heat. The woman and the girl got off the train and crossed the abandoned station—the tile split apart by the grass growing up between—and over to the shady side of the street.

It was almost two. At that hour, weighted down by drowsiness, the town was taking a siesta. The stores, the town offices, the public school were closed at eleven, and didn't reopen until a little before four, when the train went back. Only the hotel across from the station, with its bar and

Gabriel García Márquez   959

pool hall, and the telegraph office at one side of the plaza stayed open. The houses, most of them built on the banana company's model, had their doors locked from inside and their blinds drawn. In some of them it was so hot that the residents ate lunch in the patio. Others leaned a chair against the wall, in the shade of the almond trees, and took their siesta right out in the street.

Keeping to the protective shade of the almond trees, the woman and the girl entered the town without disturbing the siesta. They went directly to the parish house. The woman scratched the metal grating on the door with her fingernail, waited a moment, and scratched again. An electric fan was humming inside. They did not hear the steps. They hardly heard the slight creaking of a door, and immediately a cautious voice, right next to the metal grating: "Who is it?" The woman tried to see through the grating.

"I need the priest," she said.

"He's sleeping now."

"It's an emergency," the woman insisted.

Her voice showed a calm determination.

The door was opened a little way, noiselessly, and a plump, older woman appeared, with very pale skin and hair the color of iron. Her eyes seemed too small behind her thick eyeglasses.

"Come in," she said, and opened the door all the way.

They entered a room permeated with an old smell of flowers. The woman of the house led them to a wooden bench and signaled them to sit down. The girl did so, but her mother remained standing, absent-mindedly, with both hands clutching the handbag. No noise could be heard above the electric fan.

The woman of the house reappeared at the door at the far end of the room. "He says you should come back after three," she said in a very low voice. "He just lay down five minutes ago."

"The train leaves at three-thirty," said the woman.

It was a brief and self-assured reply, but her voice remained pleasant, full of undertones. The woman of the house smiled for the first time.

"All right," she said.

When the far door closed again, the woman sat down next to her daughter. The narrow waiting room was poor, neat, and clean. On the other side of the wooden railing which divided the room, there was a worktable, a plain one with an oilcloth cover, and on top of the table a primitive typewriter next to a vase of flowers. The parish records were beyond. You could see that it was an office kept in order by a spinster.[2]

The far door opened and this time the priest appeared, cleaning his glasses with a handkerchief. Only when he put them on was it evident

---

2. **spinster** *n.*: unmarried older woman.

Vocabulary

permeated (pʉr′mē·āt′id) *v.*: spread throughout.

that he was the brother of the woman who had opened the door.

"How can I help you?" he asked.

"The keys to the cemetery," said the woman.

The girl was seated with the flowers in her lap and her feet crossed under the bench. The priest looked at her, then looked at the woman, and then through the wire mesh of the window at the bright, cloudless sky.

"In this heat," he said. "You could have waited until the sun went down."

The woman moved her head silently. The priest crossed to the other side of the railing, took out of the cabinet a notebook covered in oilcloth, a wooden penholder, and an inkwell, and sat down at the table. There was more than enough hair on his hands to account for what was missing on his head.

"Which grave are you going to visit?" he asked.

"Carlos Centeno's," said the woman.

"Who?"

"Carlos Centeno," the woman repeated.

The priest still did not understand.

"He's the thief who was killed here last week," said the woman in the same tone of voice. "I am his mother."

The priest scrutinized her. She stared at him with quiet self-control, and the Father blushed. He lowered his head and began to write. As he filled the page, he asked the woman to identify herself, and she replied unhesitatingly, with precise details, as if she were reading them. The Father began to sweat. The girl unhooked the buckle of her left shoe, slipped her heel out of it, and rested it on the bench rail. She did the same with the right one.

It had all started the Monday of the previous week, at three in the morning, a few blocks from there. Rebecca, a lonely widow who lived in a house full of odds and ends, heard above the sound of the drizzling rain someone trying to force the front door from the outside. She got up, rummaged around in her closet for an ancient revolver that no one had fired since the days of Colonel Aureliano Buendía, and went into the living room without turning on the lights. Orienting herself not so much by the noise at the

lock as by a terror developed in her by twenty-eight years of loneliness, she fixed in her imagination not only the spot where the door was but also the exact height of the lock. She clutched the weapon with both hands, closed her eyes, and squeezed the trigger. It was the first time in her life that she had fired a gun. Immediately after the explosion, she could hear nothing except the murmur of the drizzle on the galvanized[3] roof. Then she heard a little metallic bump on the cement porch, and a very low voice, pleasant but terribly exhausted: "Ah, Mother." The man they found dead in front of the house in the morning, his nose blown to bits, wore a flannel shirt with colored stripes, everyday pants with a rope for a belt, and was barefoot. No one in town knew him.

"So his name was Carlos Centeno," murmured the Father when he finished writing.

"Centeno Ayala," said the woman. "He was my only boy."

The priest went back to the cabinet. Two big rusty keys hung on the inside of the door; the girl imagined, as her mother had when she was a girl and as the priest himself must have imagined at some time, that they were Saint Peter's keys. He took them down, put them on the open notebook on the railing, and pointed with his forefinger to a place on the page he had just written, looking at the woman.

"Sign here."

The woman scribbled her name, holding the handbag under her arm. The girl picked up the flowers, came to the railing shuffling her feet, and watched her mother attentively.

The priest sighed.

"Didn't you ever try to get him on the right track?"

The woman answered when she finished signing.

"He was a very good man."

The priest looked first at the woman and then at the girl, and realized with a kind of pious amazement that they were not about to cry. The woman continued in the same tone:

---

3. **galvanized** *v.* used as *adj.:* metal-plated.

Day of the Dead altar decorations (c. 1985–1995).
Acatlán, Oaxaca, Mexico.

"I told him never to steal anything that anyone needed to eat, and he minded me. On the other hand, before, when he used to box, he used to spend three days in bed, exhausted from being punched."

"All his teeth had to be pulled out," interrupted the girl.

"That's right," the woman agreed. "Every mouthful I ate those days tasted of the beatings my son got on Saturday nights."

"God's will is <u>inscrutable</u>," said the Father.

But he said it without much conviction, partly because experience had made him a little skeptical and partly because of the heat. He suggested that they cover their heads to guard against sunstroke. Yawning, and now almost completely asleep, he gave them instructions about how to find Carlos Centeno's grave. When they came back, they didn't have to knock. They

should put the key under the door; and in the same place, if they could, they should put an offering for the Church. The woman listened to his directions with great attention, but thanked him without smiling.

The Father had noticed that there was someone looking inside, his nose pressed against the metal grating, even before he opened the door to the street. Outside was a group of children. When the door was opened wide, the children scattered. Ordinarily, at that hour there was no one in the street. Now there were not only children. There were groups of people under the almond trees. The Father scanned the street swimming in the heat and then he understood. Softly, he closed the door again.

"Wait a moment," he said without looking at the woman.

His sister appeared at the far door with a black jacket over her nightshirt and her hair down over her shoulders. She looked silently at the Father.

"What was it?" he asked.

"The people have noticed," murmured his sister.

"You'd better go out by the door to the patio," said the Father.

"It's the same there," said his sister. "Everybody is at the windows."

The woman seemed not to have understood until then. She tried to look into the street through the metal grating. Then she took the bouquet of flowers from the girl and began to move toward the door. The girl followed her.

"Wait until the sun goes down," said the Father.

"You'll melt," said his sister, motionless at the back of the room. "Wait and I'll lend you a parasol."

"Thank you," replied the woman. "We're all right this way."

She took the girl by the hand and went into the street.

Vocabulary

inscrutable (in·skrōōt′ə·bəl) *adj.:* hard to understand; unknowable.

Response and Analysis

Reading Check

1. Where do the woman and girl go when they leave the train?

2. What does the woman want from the priest?

Thinking Critically

3. List some details of **setting** that create a picture of the mother and daughter's destination. What emotional effect do these details create?

4. The mother tells the daughter not to take a drink and, above all, not to cry when they go into the town. From these details, what can you **infer** about the mother's character and the reason for her journey?

5. What can you **infer** about the thief from the details of his crime and from what his mother says about him? Why do you think he was stealing?

6. Why do the priest and his sister want the mother and daughter to leave by the patio door or wait until sundown?

7. What does the mother's decision to leave at once through the front door reveal about her character?

8. Describe the author's attitude toward the mother in the story. Do you think the author's attitude extends to poor people in general? What would you say is the **theme,** or meaning about life, revealed in the story?

WRITING

Writing a Sequel

When the mother and daughter first arrive in the town, it is the siesta period. All activity has ceased as the townspeople seek to escape the heat. However, when the mother and daughter are about to leave the priest's house, the town has awakened. What do you think will happen when the two go out into the street? Write a follow-up to the story: Describe what happens when the mother and daughter head for the cemetery. In your story, be sure to stay true to the characters of the woman and the girl as García Márquez has revealed them in "Tuesday Siesta."

North Carolina Competency Goal
1.03; 4.02; 4.05; 5.03; 6.01

Vocabulary Development
Question and Answer Charts

symmetrical   permeated

interminable   inscrutable

Make up two questions about each Vocabulary word above, and organize your answers in a chart like the one below. After you have completed charts for all the words, invite another group or classmate to answer your questions.

symmetrical	
Question	**Answer**
What is an example of something that is symmetrical?	Butterfly wings are an example of something symmetrical.

INTERNET

Projects and Activities
Keyword:
LE5 WL-7

SKILLS FOCUS

Literary Skills
Analyze setting.

Reading Skills
Make inferences from details.

Writing Skills
Create a sequel.

Vocabulary Skills
Make question and answer charts.

Gabriel García Márquez   **963**

Luisa Valenzuela

(1938–)

Argentina

The daughter of an accomplished writer, Luisa Valenzuela grew up surrounded by the giants of Argentina's literary world. "That is why," she says, "my ambition was to be a painter." As dazzled as she was by her mother's writing, Valenzuela wanted to blaze her own path, breaking new ground in her own way. Even though she did eventually become a writer, most critics agree that her literary efforts *have* been groundbreaking.

After publishing her first story at age seventeen and graduating from the University of Buenos Aires, Valenzuela moved to Paris. There, while writing programs for French television, she also completed her first novel, *Something to Smile About* (1966). After spending time in New York City and Barcelona, Spain, Valenzuela returned to her native Argentina.

The year was 1974, and the mood in Buenos Aires was one of fear and oppression. Destabilized by the death of its president, Juan Perón, Argentina was rapidly falling under the control of a fascist military dictatorship. Working under the threat of censorship, suppression, and violence, Valenzuela believed that it was her responsibility as a writer to witness and record the atrocities of the day. "I wrote them [her stories] in cafes," she says, "reacting to the generalized paranoia and fear, and thinking that I should write in illegible handwriting so that no one could read over my shoulder. . . . Writing about it, unfortunately, does not stop the horror." The novel and stories she produced during this period, collected in *Strange Things Happen Here* (1979), lay bare the horrors of life in a fascist dictatorship in bold language and unflinching detail—two qualities that would become trademarks of Valenzuela's fiction.

An invitation to become a writer in residence at Columbia University in New York City gave Valenzuela a welcome reason to leave Argentina. "Exile can be devastating," she says, "but the perspective and separation refine the marksmanship." This principle proved true with Valenzuela's next novel, *The Lizard's Tail* (1983), considered by many to be her most important work. In this story about the rise and fall of a politician-sorcerer, Valenzuela pushes beyond conventional forms and themes, using a surreal, stream-of-consciousness style to explore power, politics, and magic.

An heir to the legacy of the great magic realists of Latin America (such as Gabriel García Márquez and Julio Cortázar), Valenzuela resists being labeled one herself. "Magical realism was a beautiful resting place," she says, "but the thing is to go forward." And go forward she has, producing dozens of works that explore difficult topics—including violence, political oppression, and gender discrimination—in an impressionistic style characterized by "dazzling ellipses, bizarre fantasy and baroque textures." It seems that Valenzuela has become a kind of painter after all.

The Censors

Make the Connection

Many people have strong feelings about censorship. Some feel that in a free country, there should be no censorship; people should be free to speak, write, read, and view what they please, as long as they do not disturb the rights of others. Others feel that censorship is necessary, that certain views, ideas, and works (for example, books, movies, art) are objectionable and not fit for society. What are your thoughts about censorship? Are there times or circumstances in which censorship is valid? Who should decide what will be censored? What should the limits of censorship be?

Literary Focus

Irony and Theme

Irony takes place when something happens that is the opposite of what is expected. In literature, this is known as **situational irony**, which sometimes creates humor—think of the wolf's unfortunate fate in "The Three Little Pigs." At other times, authors use situational irony to shock readers into thinking differently about something—to convey a certain **theme,** or central insight. As you begin reading "The Censors," ask yourself what the story is about. When you finish, ask yourself again. How has your answer changed?

> **Irony** is a contrast between what is expected and what actually happens. **Theme** is the central insight about human experience conveyed in a work of literature.
>
> *For more on Irony and Theme, see the Handbook of Literary and Historical Terms.*

Reading Skills

Determining the Author's Purpose

Luisa Valenzuela wrote "The Censors" in Argentina during a period of extreme violence and political repression. Writing, she says, helped her to understand the horrors she witnessed around her. As you read, ask yourself what other purposes Valenzuela might have had in writing this story.

Background

Under many dictatorial governments, spreading ideas that undermine the government's authority is illegal. In such states, officials are hired to read mail and other writing and to destroy whatever they deem "dangerous." The writers themselves—and the recipients—may also be punished. Speaking about her own writing in Argentina, Valenzuela recalls that one "could not show the product even to one's most intimate friends, for fear of endangering them."

Vocabulary Development

irreproachable (ir′i·prō′chə·bəl) *adj.*: innocent.

sabotage (sab′ə·täzh′) *v.*: damage.

staidness (stād′nəs) *n.*: soberness.

subversive (səb·vur′siv) *adj.*: seeking to overthrow a government or other established system.

North Carolina Competency Goal
1.03; 4.02; 4.05; 5.01; 5.03

INTERNET
Vocabulary Practice
Keyword: LE5 WL-7

SKILLS FOCUS

Literary Skills
Understand irony and theme.

Reading Skills
Determine the author's purpose.

Luisa Valenzuela   **965**

The Censors

Luisa Valenzuela

translated by **David Unger**

Poor Juan! One day they caught him with his guard down before he could even realize that what he had taken to be a stroke of luck was really one of fate's dirty tricks. These things happen the minute you're careless, as one often is. Juancito let happiness—a feeling you can't trust—get the better of him when he received from a confidential source Mariana's new address in Paris and knew that she hadn't forgotten him. Without thinking twice, he sat down at his table and wrote her a letter. *The* letter. The same one that now keeps his mind off his job during the day and won't let him sleep at night (what had he scrawled, what had he put on that sheet of paper he sent to Mariana?).

Juan knows there won't be a problem with the letter's contents, that it's <u>irreproachable</u>, harmless. But what about the rest? He knows that they examine, sniff, feel, and read between the lines of each and every letter, and check its tiniest comma and most accidental stain. He knows that all letters pass from hand to hand and go through all sorts of tests in the huge censorship offices and that, in the end, very few continue on their way. Usually it takes months, even years, if there aren't any snags; all this time the freedom, maybe even the life, of both sender and receiver is in jeopardy. And that's why Juan's so troubled: thinking that something might happen to Mariana because of his letter. Of all people, Mariana, who must finally feel safe there where she always dreamt about living. But he knows that the *Censor's Secret Command* operates all over the world and cashes in on the discount in air fares; there's nothing to stop them from going as far as that obscure Paris neighborhood, kidnapping Mariana, and returning to their cozy homes, certain of having fulfilled their noble mission.

Well, you've got to beat them to the punch, do what every one tries to do: <u>sabotage</u> the machinery, throw sand in its gears, that is to say get to the bottom of the problem to try to stop it.

This was Juan's sound plan when he, along with many others, applied for a censor's job—not because he had a calling like others or needed a job: no, he applied simply to intercept his own letter, an idea none too original but comforting. He was hired immediately, for each day more and more censors are needed and no one would bother to check on his references.

Ulterior motives couldn't be overlooked by the *Censorship Division,* but they needn't be too strict with those who applied. They knew how hard it would be for the poor guys to find the letter they wanted and even if they did, what's a letter or two compared to all the others that the new censor would snap up? That's how Juan managed to join the *Post Office's Censorship Division,* with a certain goal in mind.

The building had a festive air on the outside that contrasted with its inner <u>staidness</u>. Little by little, Juan was absorbed by his job, and he felt at peace since he was doing everything he could to retrieve his letter to Mariana. He didn't even worry when, in his first month, he was sent to *Section K* where envelopes are very carefully screened for explosives.

It's true that on the third day a fellow worker had his right hand blown off by a letter, but the division chief claimed it was sheer negligence on the victim's part. Juan and the other employees

---

Vocabulary

irreproachable (ir′i·prō′chə·bəl) *adj.*: innocent.
sabotage (sab′ə·täzh′) *v.*: damage.
staidness (stād′nəs) *n.*: soberness.

Luisa Valenzuela 967

Soon his work became so absorbing that his noble mission blurred in his mind. Day after day he crossed out whole paragraphs in red ink, pitilessly chucking many letters into the censored basket. These were horrible days when he was shocked by the subtle and conniving ways employed by people to pass on <u>subversive</u> messages; his instincts were so sharp that he found behind a simple "the weather's unsettled" or "prices continue to soar" the wavering hand of someone secretly scheming to overthrow the Government.

His zeal brought him swift promotion. We don't know if this made him happy. Very few letters reached him in *Section B*—only a handful passed the other hurdles—so he read them over and over again, passed them under a magnifying glass, searched for microdots with an electron microscope, and tuned his sense of smell so that he was beat by the time he made it home. He'd barely manage to warm up his soup, eat some fruit, and fall into bed, satisfied with having done his duty. Only his darling mother worried, but she couldn't get him back on the right track. She'd say, though it wasn't always true: Lola called, she's at the bar with the girls, they miss you, they're waiting for you. Or else she'd leave a bottle of red wine on the table. But Juan wouldn't indulge: any distraction could make him lose his edge and the perfect censor had to be alert, keen, attentive, and sharp to nab cheats. He had a truly patriotic task, both self-sacrificing and uplifting.

His basket for censored letters became the best fed as well as the most cunning in the whole *Censorship Division*. He was about to congratulate himself for having finally discovered his true mission, when his letter to Mariana reached his hands. Naturally, he censored it without regret. And just as naturally, he couldn't stop them from executing him the following morning, one more victim of his devotion to his work.

were allowed to go back to their work, though feeling less secure. After work, one of them tried to organize a strike to demand higher wages for unhealthy work, but Juan didn't join in; after thinking it over, he reported the man to his superiors and thus he got promoted.

You don't form a habit by doing something once, he told himself as he left his boss's office. And when he was transferred to *Section J,* where letters are carefully checked for poison dust, he felt he had climbed a rung in the ladder.

By working hard, he quickly reached *Section E* where the job became more interesting, for he could now read and analyze the letters' contents. Here he could even hope to get hold of his letter to Mariana, which, judging by the time that had elapsed, would have gone through the other sections and was probably floating around in this one.

<hr />

Vocabulary

subversive (səb·vʉrʹsiv) *adj.*: seeking to overthrow a
    government or other established system.

Response and Analysis

Reading Check

1. What does Juan do "without thinking twice" at the beginning of the story?

2. Why does Juan apply for a censor's job?

3. How does Juan earn his first promotion at work?

4. What does Juan do "naturally" at the end of the story?

Thinking Critically

5. How—and why—does Juan's purpose change in the course of the story? Explain how this change is the story's central **irony.**

6. **Foreshadowing** is the use of clues to hint at what will happen later. Find two examples of foreshadowing in this story. Did they help you predict the ending? Explain.

7. **Verbal irony** occurs when words are used to imply an opposite meaning (as when someone says, "Oh, great!" in response to an unfortunate occurrence). Find several examples of verbal irony in the story, and explain how they contribute to its overall tone and message.

8. In a sentence, express what you think is the story's **theme.** Start your sentence with the word *censorship.*

9. Why do you think the author called her story "The Censors" instead of "The Censor"?

10. As a writer in Argentina during the 1970s, Luisa Valenzuela lived in fear of censorship. She decided to leave Argentina, she says, "in order not to fall into self-censorship." Judging from this information, what **purpose** do you think Valenzuela had in writing this story? Do you think she had more than one purpose? Explain.

Extending and Evaluating

11. What is funny about this story? (Think about the writer's use of both exaggeration and understatement, as well as the story's central irony.) Would the story have been more effective or less effective if it had been written in a serious, realistic way? Explain.

WRITING

Writing a Letter to the Editor

Imagine that you have just read "The Censors" in a magazine you subscribe to. Write a letter to the editor, either praising or criticizing the story for the stand it takes on censorship. Include your own views on censorship, and cite quotations or passages from the story that you agree or disagree with.

Vocabulary Development
Summarizing the Story

irreproachable	staidness
sabotage	subversive

On a separate sheet of paper, write a summary of "The Censors" that includes each of the Vocabulary words above.

North Carolina Competency Goal
1.03; 4.05; 5.03; 6.01

go. hrw .com

INTERNET

Projects and Activities
Keyword: LE5 WL-7

SKILLS FOCUS

Literary Skills
Analyze irony and theme.

Reading Skills
Identify the author's purpose.

Writing Skills
Write a letter.

Vocabulary Skills
Summarize the story using vocabulary words.

Vocabulary Development

Understanding Idioms and Jargon

For translators, two particularly challenging types of language to translate are idioms and jargon. Rather than translating idioms or jargon literally, translators must look for expressions in English that convey the same meaning as do the expressions in the original language.

An **idiom** is an expression specific to a particular language; its meaning cannot be understood by a mere literal definition of its individual words. We use idioms so often in everyday speech that we take their meanings for granted, forgetting how little literal sense they make: *jump through hoops, eat crow, cut your losses, fall head over heels in love, pull yourself up by your bootstraps,* and countless others.

Idioms usually cannot be translated directly into another language. For example, the Spanish idiom *costar un ojo de la cara* literally means "cost you an eye from your face"—a colorful way of saying that something costs a lot of money. An English translator would not translate the phrase literally, since the expression doesn't make much sense in English. The translator would probably try to maintain the colloquial tone of the original Spanish, however, and might substitute the similar English idiom "costs an arm and a leg" for the Spanish idiom. Like many idioms, *"costar un ojo de la cara"* and "costs an arm and a leg" both imply a comparison: The cost of something that is desired by someone is prohibitively expensive; paying that price would be like sacrificing parts of one's own body.

When the narrator of "The Censors" says that the inspectors at the post office "read between the lines" of every letter, the narrator means that the inspectors read each letter carefully for meanings that may not be immediately obvious, not that the censors actually read between lines of text. Other idioms in "The Censors" include *stroke of luck* ("fortunate occurrence"), *beat them to the*

punch ("do something before others do"), *get to the bottom of* ("find out the real cause of"), and *on the right track* ("doing something correctly").

Jargon is the specialized vocabulary used by people in particular professions or areas of study. Lawyers and doctors have their own jargon, as do software developers, educators, chefs, musicians, baseball players, and comic book collectors, among many others. "The Censors" contains bureaucratic jargon that reflects the totalitarian nature of the government of Valenzuela's fictional Latin American nation: *Censorship Division, Section K, screened,* and *censored basket.* Like idioms, jargon presents a challenge for translators, who must look for the best word or phrase to convey the meaning of the original term.

"*Now, now, Ruffy, if you'll spare me the threats I'll spare you the legal jargon.*"

PRACTICE

1. With a small group, survey your classmates, family, or neighbors. Ask them to think of as many idioms as they can, in English or other languages they know. Prepare a dictionary of common idioms to share with the class.

2. With a small group, select a profession or area of expertise and collect jargon that is associated with the area you selected. Then, present the terms you learned to the rest of the class.

North Carolina Competency Goal
1.03; 4.05; 5.03; 6.01

SKILLS FOCUS

Vocabulary Skills
Understand idioms and jargon.

Introducing **Cultural Points** *of* **View**

Mightier Than the Sword: The Role of the Writer

You will be reading the four selections listed above in this Cultural Points of View feature on the role of the writer. In the top corner of the pages in this feature, you'll find a globe icon. Smaller versions of this globe icon appear next to the questions on page 978 that focus on the role of the writer. At the end of the feature (page 984), you'll compare the various points of view expressed in the selections.

Gabriel García Márquez in Mexico City. May 29, 2004.

Examining the Issue: The Role of the Writer

For many writers, the purpose of their art is twofold: to preserve a record of human experience and to bring about change in society. A writer might attempt to encourage social change by broadening readers' experiences of life or making readers more sensitive to the sorrows and joys experienced by people in different socioeconomic or cultural groups. Some writings have actually sent ripples through society and produced political changes.

Make the Connection

Quickwrite 🖉

What do you think the role of writers can—or should—be in people's lives? What can writers do to bring about social change? When have you been affected by a writer's ideas? Jot down your thoughts.

SKILLS FOCUS

Reading Skills 📖

Comparing Main Ideas Across Texts

After you read each of the following selections, take some time to write down the main idea it presents about the topic of the writer's role in society. Note passages that seem to express key points or important generalizations. Then, try out several statements of your own in which you sum up what you think is the text's major idea. What are the common points presented in each selection?

Pages 971–984 cover

Literary Skills
Analyze cultural points of view on a topic.

Reading Skills
Compare main ideas across texts.

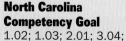

North Carolina Competency Goal
1.02; 1.03; 2.01; 3.04; 4.03; 4.05; 5.03; 6.01

Isabel Allende

(1942–   )

Chile

From earliest childhood, Isabel Allende (ä·yen′dä) loved making up imaginative tales. By the age of seventeen, she was already earning a living as a journalist in Santiago, the capital of her homeland, Chile. But her story-teller's urge to embellish reality was strong. "I could never be objective," she recalls. "I exaggerated and twisted reality. I would put myself in the middle of every feature."

Allende—who was born in Lima, Peru, where her Chilean diplomat father was stationed—read and traveled widely in her youth. Her parents divorced when she was very young, and much of her childhood was spent with her mother and maternal grandparents in Santiago.

Allende was close to her uncle, Salvador Allende, who became president of Chile in 1970. In September 1973, after Allende had instituted many controversial socialist reforms, a bloody military coup, or overthrow, ended the life of the democratically elected president. Chile, which had a long history of democracy, was thrown into chaos. After more than a year of living under the repressive, violent new Chilean government, Isabel, with her husband, went into exile in Venezuela.

In 1981, Allende learned that her beloved grandfather, who was almost one hundred years old and still living in Chile, was near death. Because she could not return to Chile to visit him, she found solace in writing recollections of her early family life—recollections that she ultimately transformed into the magic-realist fiction of *The House of the Spirits* (1982), her first novel and an international bestseller. Other works followed, including *The Stories of Eva Luna* (1991); *Daughter of Fortune* (1999) and *Portrait in Sepia* (2001), which deal with characters from *The House of the Spirits;* and two adventures for young adults, *City of the Beasts* (2002) and *Kingdom of the Golden Dragon* (2004).

In 1994, Allende published *Paula,* a tribute to her daughter, who died of a rare hereditary disease after lying in a coma for a year. Her later memoir, *My Invented Country* (2003), explores the impact of two September elevenths: September 11, 1973, when her uncle Salvador Allende was killed, and September 11, 2001, when terrorists attacked her adopted country, the United States.

Allende, who lives in California, continues to write.

Before You Read

from Writing As an Act of Hope

Cultural Points *of* View

It might surprise you to realize that writers in different countries writing under different political systems often have very similar answers to the question *Why write?* Allende opens with a straightforward statement that suggests the most important reason for writing. She spent years in exile from her native country, Chile, because it was dangerous to return home. Other writers in this textbook have endured the same kind of exile—shut out from their own countries because of their words and ideas.

How many possible answers can you think of to the question *Why write?*

Literary Focus
Essay

An **essay** is a short piece of nonfiction that discusses a particular topic in a limited, focused way. A **traditional** or **formal essay,** which is often written to inform or persuade readers, is usually factual in content, serious and even impersonal in tone, and tightly and logically organized. Allende's essay is an example of a **personal** or **informal essay,** which is usually conversational in tone and full of personal opinions. Informal essays can ramble and even stray from their topic, so they often reveal as much about the writer as they do about the topic—which is one reason they can be entertaining to read.

> An **essay** is a short piece of nonfiction that examines a subject in a limited way.
>
> *For more on Essay, see the Handbook of Literary and Historical Terms.*

Reading Skills
Understanding Text Structures: Comparison and Contrast

Expository, or informational, text is structured differently from narrative text. The easiest way to discern the structure of a text is to look for signal or transitional words. For example, such transitional expressions as *different from, the same as, but, although,* and *on the other hand* indicate that a writer is presenting information in a comparison-and-contrast structure. You **compare** when you look at the features of two things and note how they are alike or different. When you **contrast,** on the other hand, you look at two things and note how they are different.

Throughout her essay, Allende uses contrast—that is, she supports a point she is making by describing two situations that are very different. As you read, take note of the dramatic contrasts that Allende creates in order to illustrate her points.

Vocabulary Development

cataclysms (kat′ə·kliz′əmz) *n. pl.:* violent upheavals that cause sudden changes.

labyrinth (lab′ə·rinth′) *n.:* maze; a complex, puzzling arrangement.

pathological (path′ə·läj′i·kəl) *adj.:* diseased.

discourse (dis′kôrs′) *n.:* conversation of ideas.

rancor (raŋ′kər) *n.:* anger; bitter hatred.

North Carolina Competency Goal
1.02; 3.04; 4.03

INTERNET
More About Isabel Allende
Keyword: LE5 WL-7

Literary Skills
Understand an essay.

Reading Skills
Understand text structures: comparison and contrast.

Isabel Allende   **973**

from

Writing As an Act of Hope

Isabel Allende

Maybe the most important reason for writing is to prevent the erosion of time, so that memories will not be blown away by the wind. Write to record history, and name each thing. Write what should not be forgotten. But then, why write novels? Probably because I come from Latin America, a land of crazy, illuminated people, of geological and political cataclysms—a land so large and profound, so beautiful and frightening, that only novels can describe its fascinating complexity.

A novel is like a window, open to an infinite landscape. In a novel we can ask all the questions, we can record the most extravagant, evil, obscene, incredible or magnificent facts—which, in Latin America, are not hyperbole, because that is the dimension of our reality. In a novel we can give an illusory order to chaos. We can find the key to the labyrinth of history. We can explore the past, attempt to understand the present and dream the future. In a novel we can use everything: testimony, chronicle, essay, fantasy, legend, poetry and other devices that might help us to decode the mysteries of our world and discover our true identity.

For a writer who nourishes himself or herself on images and passions, to be born in a fabulous continent is a privilege. In Latin America we don't have to stretch our imaginations. Critics in Europe and the United States often stare in disbelief at Latin American books, asking how the authors dare to invent those incredible lies of young women who fly to heaven wrapped in linen sheets; of black emperors who build fortresses with cement and the blood of emasculated bulls; of outlaws who die of hunger in the Amazon with bags full of emeralds on their backs; of ancient tyrants who order their mothers to be flogged naked in front of the troops and modern tyrants who order children to be tortured in front of their parents; of hurricanes and earthquakes that turn the world upside down; of revolutions made with machetes, bullets, poems and kisses; of hallucinating landscapes where reason is lost.

It is very hard to explain to critics that these things are not a product of our pathological imaginations. They are written in our history; we can find them every day in our newspapers. We hear them in the streets; we suffer them frequently in our own lives. It is impossible to speak of Latin America without mentioning violence. We inhabit a land of terrible contrasts and we have to survive in times of great violence.

Contrast and violence, two excellent ingredients for literature, although for us, citizens of that reality, life is always suspended from a very fragile thread.

The first, the most naked and visible form of violence is the extreme poverty of the majority, in contrast with the extreme wealth of the very few. In my continent two opposite realities

---

Vocabulary

cataclysms (kat′ə·kliz′əmz) *n. pl.:* violent upheavals that cause sudden changes.

labyrinth (lab′ə·rinth′) *n.:* maze; a complex, puzzling arrangement.

pathological (path′ə·läj′i·kəl) *adj.:* diseased.

Parade during carnival celebration. Oruro, Bolivia, 1995.

coexist. One is a legal face, more or less comprehensible and with a certain pretension to dignity and civilization. The other is a dark and tragic face, which we do not like to show but which is always threatening us. There is an apparent world and a real world—nice neighborhoods where blond children play on their bicycles and servants walk elegant dogs, and other neighborhoods, of slums and garbage, where dark children play naked with hungry mutts. There are offices of marble and steel where young executives discuss the stock market, and forgotten villages where people still live and die as they did in the Middle Ages. There is a world of fiction created by the official discourse, and another world of blood and pain and love, where we have struggled for centuries.

In Latin America we all survive on the borderline of those two realities. Our fragile democracies exist as long as they don't interfere with imperialist interests. Most of our republics are dependent on submissiveness. Our institutions and laws are inefficient. Our armed forces often act as mercenaries for a privileged social group that pays tribute to transnational enterprises. We are living in the worst economic, political and social crisis since the conquest of America by the Spaniards. There are hardly two or three leaders in the whole continent. Social inequality is greater every day, and to avoid an outburst of public rancor, repression also rises day by day. Crime, drugs, misery and ignorance are present in every Latin American country, and the military is an immediate threat to society and civil governments. We try to keep straight faces while our feet are stuck in a swamp of violence, exploitation, corruption, the terror of the state and the terrorism of those who take arms against the status quo.

But Latin America is also a land of hope and friendship and love. Writers navigate in these agitated waters. They don't live in ivory towers; they cannot remove themselves from this brutal

reality. In such circumstances there is no time and no wish for narcissistic literature. Very few of our writers contemplate their navel in self-centered monologue. The majority want desperately to communicate.

I feel that writing is an act of hope, a sort of communion with our fellow men. The writer of good will carries a lamp to illuminate the dark corners. Only that, nothing more—a tiny beam of light to show some hidden aspect of reality, to help decipher and understand it and thus to ini-

Vocabulary

discourse (dis′kôrs′) *n.*: conversation of ideas.
rancor (raŋ′kər) *n.*: anger; bitter hatred.

Our Waiting (1999) by Alfredo Castañeda.

Courtesy of Mary-Anne Martin Fine Art, New York.

tiate, if possible, a change in the conscience of some readers. This kind of writer is not seduced by the mermaid's voice of celebrity or tempted by exclusive literary circles. He has both feet planted firmly on the ground and walks hand in hand with the people in the streets. He knows that the lamp is very small and the shadows are immense. This makes him humble.

But just as we should not believe that literature gives us any sort of power, neither should we be paralyzed by false modesty. We should continue to write in spite of the bruises and the vast silence that frequently surrounds us. A book is not an end in itself; it is only a way to touch someone—a bridge extended across a space of loneliness and obscurity—and some-

times it is a way of winning other people to our causes.

I believe in certain principles and values: love, generosity, justice. I know that sounds old-fashioned. However, I believe in those values so firmly that I'm willing to provoke some scornful smiles. I'm sure we have the capacity to build a more gentle world—that doing so is our only alternative, because our present equilibrium is very fragile. In literature, we have been told, optimism is dangerous; it flirts with simplicity and is an insurrection against the sacred laws of reason and good taste. But I don't belong to that group of desperate intellectuals. Despair is a paralyzing feeling. It only benefits our enemies.

Response and Analysis

Reading Check

1. What does Allende think is the most important reason for writing?

2. Why does Allende write novels?

3. What answer does Allende give to critics who ask how Latin American writers can invent such incredible "lies"?

Thinking Critically

4. What do you think Allende means when she suggests a contrast between "a world of fiction created by the official discourse, and another world of blood and pain and love" (page 976)? What is ironic about her assertion that the world created by "official discourse" is actually the "fictional" world?

5. Describe how the structure of Allende's essay supports her points. How does she use a **comparison-contrast structure** to emphasize the "terrible contrasts" that define Latin America? Why does Allende nevertheless feel that Latin America is "a fabulous continent" and that it is "a privilege" to be born and to live there?

6. This is an **informal essay** in which Allende presents her own limited exploration of a very complex subject. What does the essay reveal about her convictions and values? Identify specific examples of her subjective point of view.

Extending and Evaluating

7. One purpose of writing is to bring about change. Where in this essay does Allende say that she agrees with this purpose? Explain your own ideas about the purposes of writing. Can you think of any books that have had a significant impact on the way people think or that have contributed to change in the world?

WRITING

Why Write?

In a brief informal essay, explore your own responses to the question *Why write?* What do you see as the primary purpose of writing novels, poems, plays, short stories? As a starting point, you might consider one book that has been important to you in your life and explain how that book fulfills one of the following purposes: to record aspects of human experience, to take us places we could not otherwise visit, to leave a record for future generations, to help us discover our unique identities, to change and expand our views of the world, to bring about social change, to feed the imagination and intellect, or to provide escapism and entertainment.

Vocabulary Development
Question and Answer

On a separate piece of paper, answer the following items about the underlined Vocabulary words. Be prepared to justify your answers.

1. Give examples of geological cataclysms.

2. Why is it easy to get lost in a labyrinth?

3. Why might you distrust someone who is a pathological liar?

4. Describe a discourse you might hear on the radio.

5. Why would a person who feels rancor toward you be unlikely to invite you to a party?

Connected Readings

Mightier Than the Sword: The Role of the Writer

International PEN . . . .**International PEN Charter**

Aleksandr Solzhenitsyn . . . .*from* **Nobel Prize Acceptance Speech, 1970**

Shu Ting . . . . **Perhaps . . .**

You have just read a portion of Isabel Allende's essay "Writing As an Act of Hope" and considered her views on the role of the writer in the world—in particular in Latin America. The next three selections you will read provide further viewpoints on the role of the writer. As you read, think about how these selections round out and extend Allende's points, bringing out such ideas as the power of imagination, the ways in which writers share common goals, the writer's need to write, and the reasons that literature is feared in repressive cultures. Note how the viewpoints and experiences expressed in these texts are similar to and different from one another and from Allende's essay. After you read, you'll find questions on page 984 that ask you to compare all four selections.

Cultural Points *of* View

Before You Read

PEN (the acronym originally stood for *Poets, Play-wrights, Essayists and Novelists*) is an international association of writers with a presence in nearly one hundred countries. Founded in England in 1921, PEN is nonpolitical and is not associated with any government or nation. The organization's goals are to create an international community of writers who know no national boundaries and who support and defend literature as a central contributor to world culture. PEN works on behalf of writers who are persecuted by governments for the peaceful exercise of their right to freedom of expression, and the organization has been responsible for speaking out on behalf of many writers whose work is censored or who have been imprisoned because of their writings. The public document that follows is the charter of International PEN; the charter is shared by PEN centers in nations all over the world.

PUBLIC DOCUMENT

INTERNATIONAL PEN CHARTER

The PEN Charter is based on resolutions passed at its International Congresses and may be summarized as follows:

PEN affirms that:

1. Literature knows no frontiers and must remain common currency[1] among people in spite of political or international upheavals.

2. In all circumstances, and particularly in time of war, works of art, the patrimony[2] of humanity at large, should be left untouched by national or political passion.

3. Members of PEN should at all times use what influence they have in favor of good

---

1. **currency** *n.:* here, the medium of exchange.

2. **patrimony** (pa'trə·mō'nē) *n.:* heritage.

understanding and mutual respect between nations; they pledge themselves to do their utmost to dispel race, class and national hatreds, and to champion the ideal of one humanity living in peace in one world.

4. PEN stands for the principle of unhampered transmission of thought within each nation and between all nations, and members pledge themselves to oppose any form of suppression of freedom of expression in the country and community to which they belong, as well as throughout the world wherever this is possible. PEN declares for a free press and opposes

arbitrary censorship in time of peace. It believes that the necessary advance of the world towards a more highly organized political and economic order renders a free criticism of governments, administrations and institutions imperative. And since freedom implies voluntary restraint, members pledge themselves to oppose such evils of a free press as mendacious[3] publication, deliberate falsehood and distortion of facts for political and personal ends.

---

3. **mendacious** (men·dā′shəs) *adj.:* false.

Cultural Points *of* View

Before You Read

Russian writer Aleksandr Solzhenitsyn (sōl′zhə·nēt′sin) (1918–   ) is among the most famous examples of an unfortunately all too common figure in the modern and contemporary world: the writer who has experienced years of imprisonment and exile for daring to expose the injustices of a repressive regime. Solzhenitsyn's imprisonment started after World War II, when he criticized premier Josef Stalin in a letter to a friend, an offense for which the writer spent eight years in prison (considered at the time to be a light sentence) and three more years in exile in central Asia. His masterpiece, *One Day in the Life of Ivan Denisovich* (1962), the tale of a typical day in a labor camp, was published in Russia during the brief political thaw that took place during premier Nikita Khrushchev's anti-Stalinist campaign. *The Gulag Archipelago* (1974), Solzhenitsyn's massive account of Stalin's labor camps (in which some sixty million Soviet citizens perished), was smuggled out of Russia and published in Paris; for

this offense, Solzhenitsyn, then aged fifty-five, was exiled from his homeland. He lived for about twenty years in the United States, returning to Russia in 1994 after having been granted Russian citizenship again.

When he was awarded the Nobel Prize in literature in 1970, Solzhenitsyn was not present. Sadly echoing the situation of another Russian writer, Boris Pasternak, who was awarded the prize in 1958 but was forced by Russian authorities to refuse it, Solzhenitsyn accepted the prize in absentia—fearful that if he left his country to go to Stockholm for the ceremony, he would not be allowed back in. His acceptance speech, part of which follows, was simply handed to the Swedish Academy; he never delivered it as a lecture. The prize was awarded to Solzhenitsyn "for the ethical force with which he has pursued the indispensable traditions of Russian literature."

from Nobel Prize Acceptance Speech, 1970

Aleksandr Solzhenitsyn

. . . I am cheered by a vital awareness of WORLD LITERATURE as of a single huge heart, beating out the cares and troubles of our world, albeit presented and perceived differently in each of its corners.

Apart from age-old national literatures there existed, even in past ages, the conception of world literature as an anthology skirting the heights of the national literatures, and as the sum total of mutual literary influences. But there occurred a lapse in time: readers and writers became acquainted with writers of other tongues only after a time lapse, sometimes lasting centuries, so that mutual influences were also delayed and the anthology of national literary heights was revealed only in the eyes of descendants, not of contemporaries.

But today, between the writers of one country and the writers and readers of another, there is a reciprocity[1] if not instantaneous then almost so. I experience this with myself. Those of my books which, alas, have not been printed in my own country have soon found a responsive, world-wide audience, despite hurried and often bad translations. . . .

Thus I have understood and felt that world literature is no longer an abstract anthology, nor a generalization invented by literary historians; it is rather a certain common body and a common spirit, a living heartfelt unity reflecting the growing unity of mankind. State frontiers still turn crimson, heated by electric wire and bursts of machine fire; and various ministries of internal affairs still think that literature too is an "internal affair" falling under their jurisdiction; newspaper headlines still display: "No right to interfere in our internal affairs!" Whereas there are no INTERNAL AFFAIRS left on our crowded Earth! And mankind's sole salvation lies in everyone making everything his business; in the people of the East being vitally concerned with what is thought in the West, the people of the West vitally concerned with what goes on in the East. And literature, as one of the most sensitive, responsive instruments possessed by the human creature, has been one of the first to adopt, to assimilate,[2] to catch hold of this feeling of a growing unity of mankind. And so I turn with confidence to the world literature of today—to hundreds of friends whom I have never met in the flesh and whom I may never see.

Friends! Let us try to help if we are worth anything at all! Who from time immemorial has constituted the uniting, not the dividing, strength in your countries, lacerated[3] by discordant[4] parties, movements, castes and groups? There in its essence is the position of writers: expressers of

---

1. **reciprocity** (res′·ə·präs′·ə·tē) *n.:* exchange, such as an exchange of views.

2. **assimilate** (ə·sim′·ə·lāt′) *v.:* absorb.
3. **lacerated** (las′·ər·āt·id) *v.* used as *adj.:* torn; wounded.
4. **discordant** (dis·kôrd′′nt) *adj.:* conflicting; not in harmony.

their native language—the chief binding force of the nation, of the very earth its people occupy, and at best of its national spirit.

I believe that world literature has it in its power to help mankind, in these its troubled hours, to see itself as it really is, notwithstanding the indoctrinations[5] of prejudiced people and parties. World literature has it in its power to convey condensed experience from one land to another so that we might cease to be split and dazzled, that the different scales of values might be made to agree, and one nation learn correctly and concisely the true history of another with such strength of recognition and painful awareness as it had itself experienced the same, and thus might it be spared from repeating the same cruel mistakes. And perhaps under such conditions we artists will be able to cultivate within ourselves a field of vision to embrace the WHOLE WORLD: in the center observing like any other human being that which lies nearby, at the edges we shall begin to draw in that which is happening in the rest of the world. And we shall correlate, and we shall observe world proportions.

And who, if not writers, are to pass judgment—not only on their unsuccessful governments (in some states this is the easiest way to earn one's bread, the occupation of any man who is not lazy), but also on the people themselves, in their cowardly humiliation or self-satisfied weakness? Who is to pass judgment on the lightweight sprints of youth, and on the young pirates brandishing their knives?

We shall be told: what can literature possibly do against the ruthless onslaught of open violence? But let us not forget that violence does not live alone and is not capable of living alone: it is necessarily interwoven with falsehood. Between them lies the most intimate, the deepest of natural bonds. Violence finds its only refuge in falsehood, falsehood its only support in violence. Any man who has once acclaimed violence as his METHOD must inexorably[6] choose falsehood as his PRINCIPLE. At its birth violence acts openly and even with pride. But no sooner does it become strong, firmly established, than it senses the rarefaction[7] of the air around it and it cannot continue to exist without descending into a fog of lies, clothing them in sweet talk. It does not always, not necessarily, openly throttle the throat, more often it demands from its subjects only an oath of allegiance to falsehood, only complicity[8] in falsehood.

And the simple step of a simple courageous man is not to partake in falsehood, not to support false actions! Let THAT enter the world, let it even reign in the world—but not with my help. But writers and artists can achieve more: they can CONQUER FALSEHOOD! In the struggle with falsehood art always did win and it always does win! Openly, irrefutably[9] for everyone! Falsehood can hold out against much in this world, but not against art.

And no sooner will falsehood be dispersed than the nakedness of violence will be revealed in all its ugliness—and violence, decrepit,[10] will fall.

That is why, my friends, I believe that we are able to help the world in its white-hot hour. Not by making the excuse of possessing no weapons, and not by giving ourselves over to a frivolous life—but by going to war!

Proverbs about truth are well-loved in Russian. They give steady and sometimes striking expression to the not inconsiderable harsh national experience:

ONE WORD OF TRUTH SHALL OUTWEIGH THE WHOLE WORLD.

And it is here, on an imaginary fantasy, a breach of the principle of the conservation of mass and energy, that I base both my own activity and my appeal to the writers of the whole world.

---

5. **indoctrinations** (in·däk′trə·nā′shənz) *n. pl.*: teachings.

6. **inexorably** (in·eks′ə·rə·blē) *adv.*: without fail; inevitably.

7. **rarefaction** (rer′ə·fak′shən) *n.*: thinness.

8. **complicity** (kəm·plis′ə·tē) *n.*: partnership in a wrongful act.

9. **irrefutably** (i·ref′yo͞o·tə·blē) *adv.*: without question.

10. **decrepit** (dē·krep′it) *adj.*: run-down; worn-out.

Cultural Points *of* View

Before You Read

The Chinese poet Shu Ting (1952–   ) is regarded as one of the finest contemporary Chinese poets. She was a core member of the group of Misty Poets—young Chinese poets who flourished in China from the late 1970s until the Tiananmen Square massacre in 1989. The Misty Poets were influenced by modernist Western literary movements, and they used obscure (or "misty") images and figures of speech in order to express social commentary and rebellion subtly. Although many of Shu Ting's fellow Misty Poets (including Bei Dao; see page 1078) fled China after 1989, Shu Ting remained in her country, though she keeps a low profile. Like other Misty Poets, Shu Ting writes poetry that is highly subjective, emphasizing the importance of individual feeling and perception. To understand how revolutionary this kind of individualistic poetry was, one should consider that under Mao Zedong and his Cultural Revolution, the only kind of acceptable poetry was simplistic, didactic poetry for the masses that expressed collective cultural ideals. Shu Ting's poem "Perhaps ..." might explain why, in spite of prevailing cultural views and government repression, writers will always feel compelled to write what they believe to be true and right.

POEM

Perhaps . . .

Shu Ting
translated by **Carolyn Kizer**

for the loneliness of an author

Crowd of people in China.

Perhaps these thoughts of ours
      will never find an audience
Perhaps the mistaken road
      will end in a mistake
5   Perhaps the lamps we light one at a time
      will be blown out, one at a time
Perhaps the candles of our lives will gutter out
      without lighting a fire to warm us.

Perhaps when all the tears have been shed
10   the earth will be more fertile
Perhaps when we sing praises to the sun
      the sun will praise us in return
Perhaps these heavy burdens
      will strengthen our philosophy
15   Perhaps when we weep for those in misery
      we must be silent about miseries of our own

Perhaps
Because of our irresistible sense of mission
We have no choice

Analyzing **Cultural Points** *of* **View**

Mightier Than the Sword: The Role of the Writer

The questions on this page ask you to analyze the views on the writer's role in society presented in the preceding four selections:

Isabel Allende . . . .*from* **Writing As an Act of Hope**
International PEN . . . .**International PEN Charter**
Aleksandr Solzhenitsyn . . .*from* **Nobel Prize Acceptance Speech, 1970**
Shu Ting . . . .**Perhaps . . .**

Comparing a Theme Across Cultures: The Role of the Writer

1. Review the notes you took on page 971 about the main idea(s) presented in each text. Write down what you think each selection is saying about the role a writer plays in the world and in the society he or she lives in. What common threads run through each selection?

2. How do you think each writer would answer this question: Why do people write novels, stories, plays, essays, and poems?

3. According to these texts, can writers change the world? If so, how? You might want to refer to your Quickwrite notes from page 971.

4. Imagine that Isabel Allende, Aleksandr Solzhenitsyn, and Shu Ting are at a PEN conference having a dialogue. Identify a passage from "Writing As an Act of Hope" that Solzhenitsyn might agree with. What passage from the International PEN Charter would Allende probably agree with most? What details in Allende's essay would Shu Ting find encouraging? How would Allende respond to Solzhenitsyn's speech?

North Carolina Competency Goal
2.01; 3.04; 4.03

SKILLS FOCUS

Pages 971–984 cover

Literary Skills
Analyze and compare cultural points of view on a topic.

Reading Skills
Compare main ideas across texts.

Writing Skills
Create a multimedia presentation.

WRITING

The Write Cause: A Multimedia Exploration

All over the world, writers have suffered from the restrictions imposed on them by repressive regimes that limit freedom of expression. Identify at least three writers whose works have been suppressed or censored in the past century. Research the stories behind these writers' experiences by using a variety of reliable print and media resources—books, Web sites, newspapers, magazines, television documentaries, radio transcripts, and so on. Prepare a multimedia presentation in which you share your findings about the injustices and censorship imposed on these writers. What exactly did the political regimes have to fear from these writers? Where are these writers today? End your presentation with suggestions for actions or policies that could protect writers now and in the future.

▶ **See "Creating a Multimedia Presentation," pages 1114–1119, for help with this assignment.**

Abioseh Nicol
(1924–1994)
Sierra Leone

Davidson Sylvester Hector Willoughby Nicol, who wrote under the pen name Abioseh Nicol (äb·ē·ō′se nē′kōl), was a man of many accomplishments. Born in Sierra Leone, a country in West Africa, Nicol, like many other African writers, studied abroad. The son of a pharmacist from Freetown, Sierra Leone, Nicol won a scholarship to study medicine at the University of London. He later became the first black African to receive a fellowship at Cambridge University. With doctorates in medicine and biochemistry, Nicol became a respected medical researcher, winning fame in medical circles for his research into the structure of insulin, the hormone used to treat diabetes.

Although primarily a scientist, Nicol was also a man of letters who valued the power of literature. After his years in England, Nicol returned to his homeland with a new perspective. Living in England in the 1950s, he had noticed that most literature about Africa was written by white Europeans. While Nicol recognized the skill of some of these authors, he also saw serious flaws in their portraits of Africans. Part of Nicol's motivation for writing was to address these flaws by writing stories that were truly told from an African perspective. He felt that African characters were often portrayed in disparaging ways, and he sought to correct this slanted view. When he first returned to Sierra Leone, he wrote "Upcountry," a poem that contrasted the rural villages of his youth to the new cities sprouting up along the Guinea coast. Nicol felt that the heart and spirit of the "real Africa" survived only in the countryside; not surprisingly, he set most of his works in small rural African villages.

Nicol excelled in a wide range of fields and made outstanding contributions in all of them. After teaching medicine in England and Nigeria, Nicol returned to Sierra Leone to serve as principal of Fourah Bay College and as vice-chancellor of the University of Sierra Leone. He was also his country's ambassador to the United Nations and was affiliated with the Red Cross, the World Health Organization, UNESCO, and just about every important West African conference and committee.

Despite his active careers in public service, health, science, and education, Nicol always found time to write. Best known for his 1965 collection, *The Truly Married Woman and Other Stories,* Nicol is regarded as one of Africa's best short story writers. He died in England in 1994.

Before You Read

Life Is Sweet at Kumansenu

Make the Connection

Quickwrite

Can you think of situations from real life or fiction (films, TV shows, books) in which an individual was caught between following the rules or advice of authority and following the dictates of his or her heart? Did the person end up following established rules, or did he or she challenge authority by following his or her heart instead? What was the outcome, and what do you think of the person's choice? Freewrite your thoughts.

Literary Focus

Foreshadowing

Sometimes a story's ending takes us completely by surprise. Other times, however, we are able to predict an ending (if we read carefully) because the writer has placed clues in the text. These clues **foreshadow,** or hint at, future events. Part of our delight after finishing such a story is seeing how many clues we noticed along the way—as well as how many details in the story make sense to us only at the end.

North Carolina Competency Goal
1.03; 4.05; 5.01; 5.03; 6.01

SKILLS FOCUS

Literary Skills
Understand foreshadowing.

Reading Skills
Compare cultures.

Foreshadowing is the use of clues to hint at what is going to happen later in the plot.

For more on Foreshadowing, see the Handbook of Literary and Historical Terms.

Reading Skills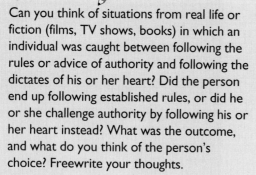

Comparing Cultures

Since this story is set in a culture very different from the one you live in, you may be puzzled by the way Bola and her West African family live and think. We quickly spot how people are different from us, but we may take for granted the characteristics that we all share. As you read "Life Is Sweet at Kumansenu," note any questions you have about Bola and her family. Also notice how many of the feelings expressed in this story—love, grief, and hope—are universal, shared by families everywhere.

Background

This story's characters are members of an extended Yoruba family. They live in a rural area in Nigeria, a West African country that was once a British colony. Many people in Bola's village have converted to Islam or Christianity, but they have not abandoned their traditional African beliefs. Almost all aspects of their everyday lives are affected by a strong belief in a spirit world.

Vocabulary Development

surreptitiously (sur′əp·tish′əs·lē) *adv.*: stealthily; sneakily.

cajoled (kə·jōld′) *v.*: coaxed with flattery, soothing words, or promises.

diffuse (di·fyoos′) *adj.*: not focused; scattered.

complacent (kəm·plā′sənt) *adj.*: self-satisfied; smug.

Traditional mud huts on the road to Kano, Nigeria.

LIFE IS SWEET AT KUMANSENU

Abioseh Nicol

The sea and the wet sand to one side of it; green tropical forest on the other; above it, the slow, tumbling clouds. The clean, round, blinding disk of sun and the blue sky covered and surrounded the small African village, Kumansenu.

A few square mud houses with roofs like helmets were here thatched, and there covered with corrugated zinc,[1] where the prosperity of cocoa and trading had touched the head of the family.

The widow Bola stirred her palm-oil stew and thought of nothing in particular. She chewed a kola nut rhythmically with her strong toothless jaws, and soon unconsciously she was chewing in rhythm with the skipping of Asi, her granddaughter. She looked idly at Asi, as the seven-year-old brought the twisted palm-leaf rope smartly over her head and jumped over it, counting in English each time the rope struck the ground and churned up a little red dust.

---

1. **corrugated zinc:** sheets made partially of zinc, a metal, that have been shaped into parallel ridges.

Bola herself did not understand English well, but she could easily count up to twenty in English, for market purposes. Asi shouted, "Six," and then said, "Nine, ten." Bola called out that after six came seven. "And I should know," she sighed. Although now she was old and her womb and breasts were withered, there was a time when she bore children regularly, every two years. Six times she had borne a boy child and six times they had died. Some had swollen up and with weak, plaintive cries had faded away. Others had shuddered in sudden convulsions, with burning skins, and had rolled up their eyes and died. They had all died; or rather he had died, Bola thought, because she knew it was one child all the time whose spirit had crept up restlessly into her womb to be born and mock her. The sixth time, Musa, the village magician whom time had now transformed into a respectable Muslim, had advised her and her husband to break the bones of the quiet little corpse and mangle it so that it could not come back to torment them alive again. But she had held on to the child and refused to let them mutilate it. Secretly, she had marked it with a sharp pointed stick at the left buttock before it was wrapped in a mat and taken away. When at the seventh time she had borne a son and the purification ceremonies had taken place, she had turned it <u>surreptitiously</u> to see whether the mark was there. It was. She showed it to the old woman who was the midwife[2] and asked her what it was, and she had forced herself to believe that it was an accidental scratch made while the child was being scrubbed with herbs to remove the placental[3] blood. But this child had stayed. Meji, he had been called. And he was now thirty years of age and a second-class clerk in government offices in a town ninety miles away. Asi, his daughter, had been left with her to do the things an old woman wanted a small child for: to run and take messages to the neighbors, to fetch a cup of water from the

earthenware pot in the kitchen, to sleep with her, and to be fondled.

She threw the washed and squeezed cassava leaves into the red, boiling stew, putting in a finger's pinch of salt, and then went indoors, carefully stepping over the threshold, to look for the dried red pepper. She found it and then dropped it, leaning against the wall with a little cry. He turned around from the window and looked at her with a twisted half smile of love and sadness. In his short-sleeved, open-necked white shirt and gray gabardine trousers, gold wristwatch, and brown suede shoes, he looked like the picture in African magazines of a handsome clerk who would get to the top because he

---

2. **midwife** *n.:* person who helps women in childbirth.
3. **placental** *adj.:* from the placenta, the organ through which a fetus in its mother's uterus is nourished and its wastes are removed.

Vocabulary

surreptitiously (sʉr'əp·tish'əs·lē) *adv.:* stealthily; sneakily.

ate the correct food or regularly took the correct laxative, which was being advertised. His skin was grayish brown and he had a large red handkerchief tied round his neck.

"Meji, God be praised," Bola cried. "You gave me quite a turn. My heart is weak and I can no longer take surprises. When did you come? How did you come? By truck, by fishing boat? And how did you come into the house? The front door was locked. There are so many thieves nowadays. I'm so glad to see you, so glad," she mumbled and wept, leaning against his breast.

Meji's voice was hoarse, and he said, "I'm glad to see you too, Mother," rubbing her back affectionately.

Asi ran in and cried, "Papa, Papa," and was rewarded with a lift and a hug.

"Never mind how I came, Mother," Meji said, laughing. "I'm here, and that's all that matters."

"We must make a feast, we must have a big feast. I must tell the neighbors at once. Asi, run

this very minute to Mr. Addai, the catechist,[4] and tell him your papa is home. Then to Mami Gbera to ask her for extra provisions, and to Pa Babole for drummers and musicians . . ."

"Stop," said Meji, raising his hand. "This is all quite unnecessary. I don't want to see *anyone*, no one at all. I wish to rest quietly and completely. No one is to know I'm here."

Bola looked very crestfallen. She was so proud of Meji and wanted to show him off. The village would never forgive her for concealing such an important visitor. Meji must have sensed this because he held her shoulder comfortingly and said, "They will know soon enough. Let us enjoy each other, all three of us, this time. Life is too short."

Bola turned to Asi, picked up the packet of pepper, and told her to go and drop a little into

---

4. **catechist** (kat′ə•kist′) *n.*: person who teaches the principles of a religion through questions and answers.

ing your throat. Are you ill?" She laid her hand on his brow. "And you're cold, too."

"It's the cold, wet wind," he said, a little harshly. "I'll go and rest now if you can open and dust my room for me. I'm feeling very tired. Very tired indeed. I've traveled very far today, and it has not been an easy journey."

"Of course, my son, of course," Bola replied, bustling away hurriedly but happily.

Meji slept all afternoon till evening, and his mother brought his food to his room and, later, took the empty basins away. Then he slept again till morning.

The next day, Saturday, was a busy one, and after further promising Meji that she would tell no one he was about, Bola went off to market. Meji took Asi for a long walk through a deserted path and up into the hills. She was delighted. They climbed high until they could see the village below in front of them, and the sea in the distance, and the boats with their wide white sails. Soon the sun had passed its zenith and was halfway toward the west. Asi had eaten all the food, the dried fish and the flat tapioca pancakes and the oranges. Her father said he wasn't hungry, and this had made the day perfect for Asi, who had chattered, eaten, and then played with her father's fountain pen and other things from his pocket. They soon left for home because he had promised that they would be back before dark; he had carried her down some steep boulders and she had held on to his shoulders because he had said his neck hurt so and she must not touch it. She had said, "Papa, I can see behind you and you haven't got a shadow. Why?"

He had then turned her around facing the sun. Since she was getting drowsy, she had started asking questions, and her father had joked with her and humored her. "Papa, why has your watch stopped at twelve o'clock?" "Because the world ends at noon." Asi had chuckled at that. "Papa, why do you wear a scarf always around your neck?" "Because my head would fall off if I didn't." She had laughed out loud at that. But soon she had fallen asleep as he bore her homeward.

the boiling pot outside, taking care not to go too near the fire or play with it. After the child had gone, Bola said to her son, "Are you in trouble? Is it the police?"

He shook his head. "No," he said, "it's just that I like returning to you. There will always be this bond of love and affection between us, and I don't wish to share it with others. It is our private affair and that is why I've left my daughter with you." He ended up irrelevantly, "Girls somehow seem to stay with relations longer."

"And don't I know it," said Bola. "But you look pale," she continued, "and you keep scrap-

Just before nightfall, with his mother dressed in her best, they had all three, at her urgent request, gone to his father's grave, taking a secret route and avoiding the main village. It was a small cemetery, not more than twenty years or so old, started when the Rural Health Department had insisted that no more burials were to take place in the back yard of households. Bola took a bottle of wine and a glass and four split halves of kola, each a half sphere, two red and two white. They reached the graveside and she poured some wine into the glass. Then she spoke to her dead husband softly and caressingly. She had brought his son to see him, she said. This son whom God had given success, to the confusion and discomfiture of their enemies. Here he was, a man with a pensionable clerk's job and not a poor farmer, a fisherman, or a simple mechanic. All the years of their married life, people had said she was a witch because her children had died young. But this boy of theirs had shown that she was a good woman. Let her husband answer her now, to show that he was listening. She threw the four kola nuts up into the air and they fell onto the grave. Three fell with the flat face upward and one with its flat face downward. She picked them up again and conversed with him once more and threw the kola nuts up again. But still there was an odd one or sometimes two.

They did not fall with all four faces up, or with all four faces down, to show that he was listening and was pleased. She spoke endearingly, she cajoled, she spoke severely. But all to no avail. She then asked Meji to perform. He crouched by the graveside and whispered. Then he threw the kola nuts and they rolled a little, Bola following them eagerly with her sharp old eyes. They all ended up face downward. Meji emptied the glass of wine on the grave and then said that he felt nearer his father at that moment than he had ever done before in his life.

It was sundown, and they all three went back silently home in the short twilight. That night, going outside the house toward her son's window, she had found, to her sick disappointment, that he had been throwing all the cooked food away out there. She did not mention this when she went to say good night, but she did sniff and say that there was a smell of decay in the room. Meji said that he thought there was a dead rat up in the rafters, and he would clear it away after she had gone to bed.

That night it rained heavily, and sheet lightning turned the darkness into brief silver daylight for one or two seconds at a time. Then the darkness again and the rain. Bola woke soon after midnight and thought she could hear knocking. She went to Meji's room to ask him to open the door, but he wasn't there. She thought he had gone out for a while and had been locked out by mistake. She

Vocabulary

cajoled (kə·jōld') v.: coaxed with flattery, soothing words, or promises.

opened the door quickly, holding an oil lamp upward. He stood on the veranda, curiously unwet, and refused to come in.

"I have to go away," he said hoarsely, coughing.

"Do come in," she said.

"No," he said, "I have to go, but I wanted to thank you for giving me a chance."

"What nonsense is this?" she said. "Come in out of the rain."

"I did not think I should leave without thanking you."

The rain fell hard, the door creaked, and the wind whistled.

"Life is sweet, Mother dear, goodbye, and thank you."

He turned around and started running.

There was a sudden <u>diffuse</u> flash of silent lightning, and she saw that the yard was empty. She went back heavily and fell into a restless sleep. Before she slept, she said to herself that she must see Mr. Addai next morning, Sunday, or better still, Monday, and tell him about all this, in case Meji was in trouble. She hoped Meji would not be annoyed. He was such a good son.

But it was Mr. Addai who came instead, on Sunday afternoon, quiet and grave, and met Bola sitting on an old stool in the veranda, dressing Asi's hair in tight, thin plaits.

Mr. Addai sat down and, looking away, he said, "The Lord giveth and the Lord taketh away." Soon half the village was sitting around the veranda and in the yard.

"But I tell you, he was here on Friday and left Sunday morning," Bola said. "He couldn't have died on Friday."

Bola had just recovered from a fainting fit after being told of her son's death in town. His wife, Asi's mother, had come with the news, bringing some of his property. She said Meji had died instantly at noon on Friday and had been buried on Saturday at sundown. They would have brought him to Kumansenu for burial. He had always wished that. But they could not do so in time, as bodies did not last more than a day in the hot season, and there were no trucks available for hire.

"He was here, he was here," Bola said, rubbing her forehead and weeping.

Asi sat by quietly. Mr. Addai said comfortingly, "Hush, hush, he couldn't have been, because no one in the village saw him."

"He said we were to tell no one," Bola said.

The crowd smiled above Bola's head and shook their heads. "Poor woman," someone said, "she is beside herself with grief."

"He died on Friday," Mrs. Meji repeated, crying. "He was in the office and he pulled up the window to look out and call the messenger. Then the sash broke. The window fell, broke his neck, and the sharp edge almost cut his head off; they say he died at once."

"My papa had a scarf around his neck," Asi shouted suddenly.

"Hush," said the crowd.

Mrs. Meji dipped her hand into her bosom and produced a small gold locket and put it around Asi's neck, to quiet her.

"Your papa had this made last week for your Christmas present. You may as well have it now."

Asi played with it and pulled it this way and that.

"Be careful, child," Mr. Addai said, "it is your father's last gift."

"I was trying to remember how he showed me yesterday to open it," Asi said.

"You have never seen it before," Mrs. Meji said sharply, trembling with fear mingled with anger.

She took the locket and tried to open it.

"Let me have it," said the village goldsmith, and he tried whispering magic words of incantation. Then he said, defeated, "It must be poor-quality gold; it has rusted. I need tools to open it."

"I remember now," Asi said in the flat, <u>complacent</u> voice of childhood.

The crowd gathered around quietly, and the setting sun glinted on the soft red African gold

---

Vocabulary

diffuse (di·fyoo͞s′) adj.: not focused; scattered.
complacent (kəm·plā′sənt) adj.: self-satisfied; smug.

of the dangling trinket. The goldsmith handed the locket over to Asi and asked in a loud whisper, "How did he open it?"

"Like so," Asi said and pressed a secret catch. It flew open and she spelled out gravely the word inside, "A-S-I."

The silence continued.

"His neck, poor boy," Bola said a little wildly. "That is why he could not eat the lovely meals I cooked for him."

Mr. Addai announced a service of intercession after vespers[5] that evening. The crowd began to leave quietly.

Musa, the magician, was one of the last to leave. He was now very old and bent. In times of grave calamity, it was known that even Mr. Addai did not raise objection to his being consulted.

He bent over further and whispered in Bola's ear, "You should have had his bones broken and mangled thirty-one years ago when he went for the sixth time, and then he would not have come back to mock you all these years by pretending to be alive. I told you so. But you women are naughty and stubborn."

Bola stood up, her black face held high, her eyes terrible with maternal rage and pride.

"I am glad I did not," she said, "and that is why he came back specially to thank me before he went for good."

She clutched Asi to her. "I am glad I gave him the opportunity to come back, for life is sweet. I do not expect you to understand why I did so. After all, you are only a man."

---

5. **service of intercession after vespers:** A service of intercession consists of prayers on behalf of someone. Vespers is an evening service.

Traditional Yoruba figurine from Nigeria.

Response and Analysis

Reading Check

1. How does Bola explain the death of her first six sons?

2. What reasons does Meji give for not wanting a feast or company during his visit home? What are his final words to his mother?

3. What shocking news does Bola hear at the end of the story? How does Asi prove that she *had* seen her father?

4. What does Musa, the village magician, tell Bola at the end? How does Bola respond?

Thinking Critically

5. What are the results of Bola's challenge to established tradition? Explain what the outcome of the story suggests about the author's views of institutional authority versus the laws of the human heart. Which do you think the author feels is more important and powerful? Refer to your Quickwrite notes. 🖉

6. Did the author prepare you for the surprise ending, or do you think the ending is artificial and tacked on? Go back to the very first descriptions of Meji, and note the various details the author uses to **foreshadow** the ending. Describe how foreshadowing is also used to provide suspense in the story.

7. Are the values presented in this story unique to a particular culture, or are they values that all people share? Despite its eerie details, would you say that this story is positive and life-affirming? Explain. 📖

8. Sometimes a story's **theme** is revealed in a single sentence or passage. Where is the theme stated in this story?

Extending and Evaluating

9. In his famous poem *In Memoriam,* British poet Alfred, Lord Tennyson (1809–1892) said, " 'Tis better to have loved and lost / Than never to have loved at all." Do you think Bola would agree with this sentiment? Do you agree with it? Explain.

WRITING

Analyzing the Impact of Cultural Beliefs

In a brief essay, analyze how cultural beliefs impact the subject and theme of this story. Could this story have taken place in a different time period or culture, or is an understanding of this story completely dependent on knowing the West African spiritual beliefs that underlie it? Be sure to point out the ways in which this story is specific to its culture of origin and ways in which it is universal. 📖

Vocabulary Development
Word Maps

surreptitiously   diffuse

cajoled   complacent

Make word maps for all the Vocabulary words listed above after you locate each word in the story to see how it is used. One has been done for you.

> complacent
>
> |
>
> **DEFINITION**
> "self-satisfied; smug"
>
> |
>
> **SYNONYMS**
> unworried; self-righteous
>
> |
>
> **EXAMPLE**
> someone who is too comfortable in his or her opinions

Chinua Achebe

(1930–   )
Nigeria

Chinua Achebe (chin'wä' ä·chä'bä) was born and grew up in the Ibo village of Ogidi when Nigeria was still a British colony. Although Achebe won a scholarship to study medicine, his love of literature and growing involvement with African nationalism led him to change careers. The nationalist movement after World War II brought about a new sense of self-awareness and confidence among Africans, and it occurred to Achebe that he and his fellow Africans had their own stories to tell. Achebe questioned the colonialist notion that African culture was inferior to the culture imposed by the European colonists. In keeping with his beliefs, Achebe dropped his first name, Albert, which his parents had given him in honor of Queen Victoria's husband.

In 1958, while working for the Nigerian Broadcasting Company, Achebe published his first novel, *Things Fall Apart*. The novel tells of an Ibo man whose life is destroyed by colonialism. This was the first of three novels that Achebe wrote to explore the Ibo past and the destructive effects of colonialism on African cultures and individual Africans.

In 1960, the new nation of Nigeria, with more than two hundred ethnic groups, was far from unified. The four largest ethnic groups—the Ibo, Hausa, Fulani, and Yoruba—constantly battled over land and power. Many of the frictions originated in the groups' very different religions, languages, and outlooks on life. Eventually, in 1967, things truly did fall apart. Achebe was one of many Ibo who supported an unsuccessful movement to secede from Nigeria and establish a new republic called Biafra. In the worst months of a bloody three-year civil war, about twelve thousand people, mostly children, starved to death each day. In all, between one and two million people died, many of them from disease and starvation. Several stories in Achebe's collection *Girls at War* (1973) describe the tragedies and horrors of those civil war years.

For Independent Reading

You may enjoy these stories by Achebe as well as his classic novel:

- "Marriage Is a Private Affair"
- "Civil Peace"
- *Things Fall Apart*

Dead Men's Path

Make the Connection

Quickwrite

People fight over things, but more often they fight over ideas or values. Nothing seems to anger people more than to have something that is important to them belittled by someone else. Can you recall a time when you became angry because someone disrespected something you value or believe in? Jot down notes on the details of this clash and its outcome.

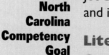

North Carolina Competency Goal
1.02; 1.03; 4.05; 5.01; 5.03; 6.01

Literary Focus

Conflict

At the heart of most fiction is a **conflict,** or struggle, between opposing characters, forces, or emotions. Conflict can be internal or external. An **internal conflict** is a struggle between competing needs, desires, and values within a character. An **external conflict** is a clash between two or more characters or between a character and some outside force, such as nature or society. A **cultural conflict** is a particular kind of external conflict in which the beliefs and values of one group or individual are pitted against those of another group or individual.

INTERNET

Vocabulary Practice
•
More About Chinua Achebe
Keyword: LE5 WL-7

Conflict is a clash or struggle between opposing characters, forces, or emotions.

For more on Conflict, see the Handbook of Literary and Historical Terms.

SKILLS FOCUS

Literary Skills
Understand conflict.

Reading Skills
Understand cultural differences.

Reading Skills

Understanding Cultural Differences

When you read a story that is set in a culture different from your own or a story that focuses on differences between the beliefs and values of the characters, it is helpful to identify and trace these cultural differences. As you read Achebe's story, identify the characters who have opposing ideas and note what these characters believe or value. You may want to use a chart like the following one to organize your ideas.

Character	What He or She Believes

If you make a few changes to the headings, you can also use a chart like this one to record cultural differences between yourself and the characters in a story.

Vocabulary Development

denigration (den′ə·grā′shən) *n.*: devaluation; belittlement.

superannuated (soo′pər·an′yoo·āt′id) *adj.*: no longer of use; out-of-date.

eradicate (ē·rad′i·kāt′) *v.*: remove all traces of; erase.

zeal (zēl) *n.*: passionate devotion to an ideal.

Ceremonies evoking the glory of the past. Benin.

Dead Men's Path

Chinua Achebe

Michael Obi's hopes were fulfilled much earlier than he had expected. He was appointed headmaster of Ndume Central School in January 1949. It had always been an unprogressive school, so the Mission authorities decided to send a young and energetic man to run it. Obi accepted this responsibility with enthusiasm. He had many wonderful ideas and this was an opportunity to put them into practice. He had had sound secondary school education which designated him a "pivotal teacher" in the official records and set him apart from the other headmasters in the mission field. He was outspoken in his condemnation of the narrow views of these older and often less-educated ones.

"We shall make a good job of it, shan't we?" he asked his young wife when they first heard the joyful news of his promotion.

"We shall do our best," she replied. "We shall have such beautiful gardens and everything will be just *modern* and delightful . . ." In their two years of married life she had become completely infected by his passion for "modern methods" and his denigration of "these old and superannuated people in the teaching field who

Vocabulary

denigration (den′ə·grā′shən) *n*.: devaluation; belittlement.

superannuated (soo′pər·an′yoo·āt′id) *adj*.: no longer of use; out-of-date.

would be better employed as traders in the Onitsha[1] market." She began to see herself already as the admired wife of the young headmaster, the queen of the school.

The wives of the other teachers would envy her position. She would set the fashion in everything . . . Then, suddenly, it occurred to her that there might not be other wives. Wavering between hope and fear, she asked her husband, looking anxiously at him.

"All our colleagues are young and unmarried," he said with enthusiasm which for once she did not share. "Which is a good thing," he continued.

"Why?"

"Why? They will give all their time and energy to the school."

Nancy was downcast. For a few minutes she became skeptical about the new school; but it was only for a few minutes. Her little personal misfortune could not blind her to her husband's happy prospects. She looked at him as he sat folded up in a chair. He was stoop-shouldered and looked frail. But he sometimes surprised people with sudden bursts of physical energy. In his present posture, however, all his bodily strength seemed to have retired behind his deep-set eyes, giving them an extraordinary power of penetration. He was only twenty-six, but looked thirty or more. On the whole, he was not unhandsome.

"A penny for your thoughts, Mike," said Nancy after a while, imitating the woman's magazine she read.

"I was thinking what a grand opportunity we've got at last to show these people how a school should be run."

Ndume School was backward in every sense of the word. Mr. Obi put his whole life into the work, and his wife hers too. He had two aims. A high standard of teaching was insisted upon, and the school compound was to be turned into a place of beauty. Nancy's dream-gardens came to life with the coming of the rains, and blossomed.

Beautiful hibiscus and allamanda hedges in brilliant red and yellow marked out the carefully tended school compound from the rank neighborhood bushes.

One evening as Obi was admiring his work he was scandalized to see an old woman from the village hobble right across the compound, through a marigold flower bed and the hedges. On going up there he found faint signs of an almost disused path from the village across the school compound to the bush on the other side.

"It amazes me," said Obi to one of his teachers who had been three years in the school, "that you people allowed the villagers to make use of this footpath. It is simply incredible." He shook his head.

"The path," said the teacher apologetically, "appears to be very important to them. Although it is hardly used, it connects the village shrine with their place of burial."

"And what has that got to do with the school?" asked the headmaster.

"Well, I don't know," replied the other with a shrug of the shoulders. "But I remember there was a big row some time ago when we attempted to close it."

"That was some time ago. But it will not be used now," said Obi as he walked away. "What will the Government Education Officer think of this when he comes to inspect the school next week? The villagers might, for all I know, decide to use the schoolroom for a pagan ritual during the inspection."

Heavy sticks were planted closely across the path at the two places where it entered and left the school premises. These were further strengthened with barbed wire.

Three days later the village priest of *Ani* called on the headmaster. He was an old man and walked with a slight stoop. He carried a stout walking stick which he usually tapped on the floor, by way of emphasis, each time he made a new point in his argument.

"I have heard," he said after the usual exchange of cordialities, "that our ancestral footpath has recently been closed . . ."

---

1. Onitsha (ō·nēʹchä).

"Yes," replied Mr. Obi. "We cannot allow people to make a highway of our school compound."

"Look here, my son," said the priest bringing down his walking stick, "this path was here before you were born and before your father was born. The whole life of this village depends on it. Our dead relatives depart by it and our ancestors visit us by it. But most important, it is the path of children coming in to be born . . ."

Mr. Obi listened with a satisfied smile on his face.

"The whole purpose of our school," he said finally, "is to eradicate just such beliefs as that. Dead men do not require footpaths. The whole idea is just fantastic. Our duty is to teach your children to laugh at such ideas."

"What you say may be true," replied the priest, "but we follow the practices of our fathers. If you reopen the path we shall have nothing to quarrel about. What I always say is: let the hawk perch and let the eagle perch." He rose to go.

"I am sorry," said the young headmaster. "But the school compound cannot be a thoroughfare. It is against our regulations. I would suggest your constructing another path, skirting our premises. We can even get our boys to help in building it. I don't suppose the ancestors will find the little detour too burdensome."

"I have no more words to say," said the old priest, already outside.

Two days later a young woman in the village died in childbed. A diviner was immediately consulted and he prescribed heavy sacrifices to propitiate[2] ancestors insulted by the fence.

Obi woke up the next morning among the ruins of his work. The beautiful hedges were torn up not just near the path but right round the school, the flowers trampled to death and one of the school buildings pulled down . . . That day, the white Supervisor came to inspect the school and wrote a nasty report on the state of the premises but more seriously about the "tribal-war situation developing between the school and the village, arising in part from the misguided zeal of the new headmaster."

---

2. **propitiate** (prō·pish′ē·āt) *v.:* please; pacify.

Vocabulary

eradicate (ē·rad′i·kāt′) *v.:* remove all traces of; erase.
zeal (zēl) *n.:* passionate devotion to an ideal.

Response and Analysis

Reading Check

1. How does the headmaster prevent the villagers from using the path?

2. What do the villagers do in response to the headmaster's action?

Thinking Critically

North Carolina Competency Goal
1.02; 1.03;
4.05; 5.03;
6.01

3. Why is the path so important to the priest and the villagers? What does its importance reveal about their values and beliefs?

4. Describe the headmaster's values and beliefs. In what ways are they representative of European, rather than African, cultural values? Why does the headmaster dismiss the beliefs of the priest and the villagers? You may want to consult your reading notes.

5. In the confrontation between Obi and the village priest, which man is more tolerant of the other's beliefs? Support your answer with evidence from the text. What point might the author be making here?

INTERNET
Projects and Activities
Keyword:
LE5 WL-7

6. In your opinion, does the villagers' action at the end of the story resolve or worsen the **conflict**?

7. Do you agree with the white inspector's report at the end of the story that there is a "tribal-war situation developing between the school and the village" and that this has resulted from "the misguided zeal of the new headmaster"? Why or why not? What other factors might have contributed to the conflict in this story?

Literary Skills
Analyze conflict.

Reading Skills
Understand cultural differences.

Writing Skills
State an opinion.

Vocabulary Skills
Answer questions about vocabulary words.

WRITING

Stating an Opinion

Conflicts over values and beliefs are not always resolved peacefully or to everyone's satisfaction. In fact, they often end in hatred, violence, and war. Write an opinion essay in which you suggest how to resolve cultural conflicts in ways that show respect for all parties. You may want to refer in your essay to "Dead Men's Path" or to the conflict and resolution you wrote about in your Quickwrite notes.

Vocabulary Development
In Your Own Words

Answer the following questions. In your responses, show that you understand the meaning of the underlined Vocabulary word.

1. How have vaccines helped to eradicate diseases like smallpox and polio?

2. How do you think employers should deal with superannuated computers?

3. When do you think zeal becomes misguided?

4. How can the law discourage the denigration of one cultural group by another?

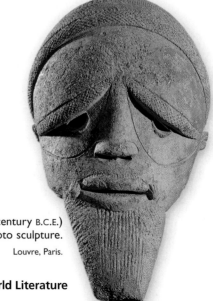

Male head (5th century B.C.E.) from Nigeria. Sokoto sculpture.

Louvre, Paris.

Grammar Link

Building Coherence: Using Direct References, Transitions, and Conjunctions

Transitional expressions are words and phrases writers use to help the reader follow their train of thought and see how ideas relate to one another. Writers connect ideas between sentences and paragraphs with **direct references, transitions,** and **conjunctions.**

Direct references are pronouns or key words and phrases that link sentences together. For example, the pronoun *his* and the adjective *progressive,* a synonym for the key word *modern,* directly refer to and link the ideas in this sentence.

> Michael Obi, the new headmaster, is determined to bring his rural Nigerian school into the modern age. His progressive ideas, however, conflict with the villagers' ancient traditions.

Use direct references by (1) referring to a noun or pronoun used earlier, (2) repeating a key word or phrase, or (3) substituting an appropriate synonym for a key word or phrase used earlier.

Transitions and **conjunctions** are words or phrases that indicate how ideas relate to each other. Such expressions may show how events relate in time or space; they can also indicate comparisons and contrasts, causes and effects, or examples and conclusions.

> Obi looks forward to making changes at the school. His wife, Nancy, is also highly ambitious.
> [*Also* links these ideas.]

Note the different purposes of the transitions and conjunctions included in the chart below.

PRACTICE

Improve the coherence of the following paragraph by adding direct references, transitions, and conjunctions to link ideas more smoothly.

> Nancy's beautiful gardens symbolize the couple's modern aspirations. Nancy's gardens stand in the way of a traditional path to the village's burial ground. Obi blocks the path in an effort to keep people from using the path. The gardens become the "heavy sacrifices" required to appease the villagers' unhappy ancestors.

Apply to Your Writing

Review a writing assignment you are working on now or have already completed. Connect ideas by adding direct references, transitions, and conjunctions between sentences and paragraphs.

▶ **For more help, see Sentence Combining, 10a–d, in the Language Handbook.**

North Carolina Competency Goal
1.03; 4.05; 5.03

Grammar Skills
Understand and use direct references, transitions, and conjunctions.

Time or Position	above, afterward, before, eventually, first, nearby, next, meanwhile, then, when
Comparison	again, also, and, besides, both, furthermore, in addition, likewise, moreover, similarly, too
Contrast	although, but, despite, however, in spite of, instead, neither . . . nor, nevertheless, still, yet
Purpose, Cause, or Effect	as, because, consequently, for, just as . . . so, since, so, so that, then, therefore
Summary, Conclusion, Example	as a result, for example, for instance, in fact, in other words, on the whole, overall, therefore, thus

Chinua Achebe   **1001**

Wole Soyinka

(1934–   )

Nigeria

In 1986, the Nigerian writer Wole Soyinka (wō′lā shô·yiŋ′kə) became the first black African to win the Nobel Prize in literature. He dedicated his acceptance speech to the political activist Nelson Mandela, then still in prison in South Africa. Like Mandela, Soyinka also had spent time in jail—under terrible conditions—for his political beliefs. Accused of supporting the state of Biafra in its war to secede from Nigeria, Soyinka was held as a political prisoner for more than two years, twenty-two months of which he spent in solitary confinement. Although he was denied writing materials, Soyinka managed to keep a diary by making his own ink and by writing on toilet paper, cigarette packages, and between the lines of the few books he secretly obtained. The results were eventually published as *The Man Died: Prison Notes of Wole Soyinka* (1972).

Akinwande Oluwole (*Wole* for short) Soyinka was born in western Nigeria. Raised as a Christian, Soyinka was also steeped in the ways of the Yoruba, a West African people with a long tradition of oral poetry and ritual dance, music, and drama. As a child, Soyinka was comfortable in both cultures, but as he grew older he became aware of a conflict between African traditions and Western ways. He addressed this clash of cultures in his autobiography *Ake: The Years of Childhood* (1981). Although Soyinka draws on his Yoruba heritage in his writing, he is more concerned with contemporary issues in Africa. He has criticized the African literary movement negritude for excessive nostalgia and emphasizing past glories. Soyinka has felt no need to trumpet the positive values of his African heritage: "A tiger does not shout its tigritude," he once declared.

After attending the University of Ibadan in Nigeria, Soyinka traveled to northern England to study drama at the University of Leeds. Soyinka's experiences in England were mixed. On the one hand, he received encouragement from his professors and wrote several well-regarded plays, some of which were produced. On the other hand, he suffered from racial prejudice.

Since his release from prison in 1969, Soyinka has often left Nigeria due to its political situation. In 1994, after being charged with treason and sentenced to death by the government, Soyinka once again left the country. He continued to write, finishing the second volume of his autobiography, *Ibadan, The Penkelemes Years* (1994). In 1996, he published *The Open Sore of a Continent,* a searing indictment of Nigeria's military dictatorship. Eventually, a new government emerged in Nigeria, and Soyinka returned to his homeland in 1998.

After the Deluge

Make the Connection

On the nightly news, in newspapers and magazines, in history textbooks, and online, you've probably come across accounts of leaders of various countries who have abused their power in sometimes unimaginable ways. Think of various dictators who ruled their countries brutally and profited personally while imposing untold hardships on their own people. What were some of their atrocities? What eventually happened to these dictators? Presuming they survived, what do you imagine their thoughts were as they looked back on their years in power?

Literary Focus

Irony

One of a writer's most powerful tools is irony. **Irony** is the difference between expectation and reality, between what is anticipated—or what would seem appropriate—and what actually happens. We see the irony, for example, when a chief executive who once made billions of dollars and moved in the most exclusive social circles ends up in an orange prison suit and chains. As you read this poem, be aware of how the writer uses irony to shape your feelings about the subject—an unnamed man the writer calls only "He."

Irony is the difference between expectations and reality.

For more on Irony, see the Handbook of Literary and Historical Terms.

Background

Throughout the 1960s, Soyinka experienced extensive persecution at the hands of the Nigerian government. He was arrested in 1967 because of his outspoken criticism of General Yakubu Gowon, who seized power in 1966. Nigeria—a country incredibly rich in natural resources and one of the world's leading oil exporters—has been systematically exploited by its rulers, resulting in the devastation of its economy. Nigeria was returned to civilian government in 1999.

The subject of this poem is a nameless dictator who, like many corrupt leaders, has diverted a fortune for his own uses while allowing his people to suffer poverty and deprivation. The word *deluge* in the poem's title means "destructive flood." In the Bible the Great Flood that destroyed the world's population—and which Noah survived in an ark—is called a deluge. A deluge can also refer to something that completely overwhelms.

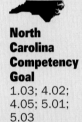

North Carolina Competency Goal
1.03; 4.02; 4.05; 5.01; 5.03

INTERNET

More About Wole Soyinka

Keyword: LE5 WL-7

Jean-Bedel Bokassa is crowned Emperor Bokassa I. Central African Republic, December 5, 1977.

Literary Skills Understand irony.

After the Deluge

Wole Soyinka

Once, for a dare,
He filled his heart-shaped swimming pool
With bank notes, high denomination
And fed a pound of caviar° to his dog.
5 The dog was sick; a chartered plane
Flew in replacement for the Persian rug.

He made a billion yen°
Leap from Tokyo to Buenos Aires,
Turn somersaults through Brussels,
10 New York, Sofia and Johannesburg.
It cracked the bullion° market open wide.
Governments fell, coalitions cracked
Insurrection° raised its bloody flag
From north to south.

15 He knew his native land through iron gates,
His sight was radar bowls, his hearing
Electronic beams. For flesh and blood,
Kept company with a brace° of Dobermans.
But—yes—the worthy causes never lacked
20 His widow's mite,° discreetly publicized.

4. caviar (kav′ē·är′) *n.:* fish eggs, an expensive gourmet food.

7. yen *n.:* Japan's basic unit of money.

11. bullion (bŏŏl′yən) *n.* used as *adj.:* gold and silver.

13. insurrection (in′sə·rek′shən) *n.:* rebellion.

18. brace *n.:* pair.

20. widow's mite: small amount of money or gift given voluntarily by someone who has limited resources.

He escaped the lynch days. He survives.
I dreamt I saw him on a village
Water line, a parched land where
Water is a god

25 That doles° its favors by the drop,
And waiting is a way of life.
Rebellion gleamed yet faintly in his eye
Traversing° chrome-and-platinum retreats. There,
Hubs of commerce smoothly turn without

30 His bidding, and cities where he lately roosted
Have forgotten him, the preying bird
Of passage.

They let him live, but not from pity
Or human sufferance.° He scratches life

35 From earth, no worse a mortal man than the rest.
Far, far away in dreamland splendor,
Creepers° twine his gates of bronze relief.
The jade-lined pool is home
To snakes and lizards; they hunt and mate

40 On crusted algae.

25. **doles** *v.:* gives frugally.

28. **traversing** (trə·vʉrsʹiŋ) *v.* used as *adj.:* traveling between.

34. **sufferance** *n.:* tolerance.

37. **creepers** *n. pl.:* vines.

Response and Analysis

Thinking Critically

1. What do stanzas 1–3 reveal about the character of the man who "knew his native land through iron gates" and kept a pair of Dobermans—large dogs that are often used as guard dogs?

2. Paraphrase the meaning of lines 19 and 20: "But—yes—the worthy causes never lacked/His widow's mite, discreetly publicized." How would you describe the speaker's **tone** in these lines?

3. What does the speaker mean by saying that the man escaped the "lynch days" (line 21)?

4. According to the fourth stanza, where does the speaker dream the man is now? How is the man now like the poor people he used to rule?

5. What line in the fourth stanza suggests that the man still hopes to regain his lost power?

6. Who do you think "They" are in the last stanza?

7. According to the final stanza, what has happened to the place where the man used to live?

8. What is the **ironic** contrast between the man's previous life—described in stanzas 1–3—and his present situation?

9. Strictly speaking, a deluge is a devastating flood or a catastrophic rainfall. What do you think *deluge* means in the context of this poem? Explain.

10. How do you think the speaker feels about the man he is describing? Who do you think the speaker might be? Use evidence from the poem to support your response.

Extending and Evaluating

11. Identify some historical or contemporary figures who are like the subject of this poem. What lines, in particular, remind you of those people?

WRITING
Comparing Poems

On page 480 is the poem "Jade Flower Palace," written by the Chinese poet Tu Fu in the eighth century. Like "After the Deluge," Tu Fu's poem presents a picture of a once-powerful man whose works are now in ruins. In an essay, compare "Jade Flower Palace" with "After the Deluge." In your essay, discuss differences between the two poems as well as similarities. Before you write, gather information in a chart like the following one:

	"After the Deluge"	"Jade Flower Palace"
Subject		
Images of power		
Images of destruction		
Use of irony		
Tone		

LISTENING AND SPEAKING
A Choral Reading

Present "After the Deluge" in a group reading. First, decide how many speakers you want to use. Then, assign parts of the poem to specific readers. Rehearse your choral reading before you present it to classmates; be sure you are satisfied that each speaker is expressing the right tone. Be sure also that the readers are attentive to run-on lines (as in lines 1–4) and end-stopped lines (as in line 11).

Introducing **Cultural Points** *of* **View**

Clashes of Cultures

You will be reading the three selections listed above in this Cultural Points of View feature on clashes of cultures. In the top corner of the pages in this feature, you'll find a globe. Smaller versions of the globe appear next to the questions on page 1015 that focus on the theme of cultural clashes. At the end of the feature (page 1021), you'll compare the various points of view expressed in the selections.

Examining the Issue: Clashes of Cultures

In contemporary world literature a powerful recurrent theme is the clash of cultures experienced by nations that have been under the control of a dominant industrialized culture from outside—usually Europe. In many colonized cultures indigenous, or native, customs and beliefs have been overshadowed—and sometimes nearly obliterated—by the dominant culture. Postcolonial writers pose questions about the future direction of their nations: Should they return to precolonial native traditions, synthesize the remnants of their culture with the best aspects of foreign colonial culture, or strike out in completely new directions? How can they reclaim or reforge a cultural identity when they have lost so much?

Queen Elizabeth II meeting local dignitaries. Tuvalu, October 1982.

Make the Connection

Quickwrite

Take some time to consider the idea of culture, which is often defined as the set of rules, traditions, beliefs, and behaviors that are shared by a specific group of people. What is American culture? To what other cultures—national, ethnic, religious—do you and your family belong? How do these various cultures define who you are as an individual, and how do they coexist in your life? Jot down your ideas.

Reading Skills

Comparing Points of View Across Texts

In order to compare the cultural points of view in the following selections, first determine which groups, people, or societies are in conflict. Then, identify each writer's point of view about the conflict.

SKILLS FOCUS

North Carolina Competency Goal
1.02; 1.03;
4.01; 4.05;
5.03; 6.01

Pages 1007–1021 cover

Literary Skills
Analyze cultural points of view on a topic.

Reading Skills
Compare points of view across texts.

Nadine Gordimer

(1923–   )

South Africa

In 1991, as Nelson Mandela was negotiating with the South African government to end minority rule, Nadine Gordimer became the first South African to receive the Nobel Prize in literature. Though she has always maintained that people are her subject and that politics interests her only in terms of its effects on human lives, Gordimer has unflinchingly explored the corrosive effects of apartheid in her works, providing insight into the damaging consequences the policy has had on the people of South Africa, both white and nonwhite. Her insight as a writer and social critic has been informed by her position as a white South African. "When you're born white in South Africa," she has observed, "you're peeling like an onion. You're sloughing off all the conditioning that you've had since you were a child."

Gordimer grew up in Springs, South Africa, a segregated gold-mining town located near Johannesburg. Both of her parents were Jewish immigrants, hailing from England and Lithuania, who provided Gordimer with a typical middle-class colonial upbringing. Gordimer recalled feeling lonely and isolated during her childhood "walled up among the mine dumps." She took refuge in the world of books and was inspired to start writing. By the time she was fifteen, her first story was published in a local weekly.

In 1949, after a year of study at the University of Witwatersrand, Gordimer moved to Johannesburg and began, in her writing, "to make sense of life." In that same year, *Face to Face,* her first short story collection, was published. Her next collection of short stories, *The Soft Voice of the Serpent and Other Stories* (which includes "The Train from Rhodesia"), was published in 1952. Her first novel, *The Lying Days,* appeared the following year.

Over the course of her long career, Gordimer has produced seventeen collections of short stories and fourteen novels, in addition to numerous articles and full-length works of nonfiction. Though three of her novels were initially banned in South Africa, her work has been widely admired abroad and has been translated into numerous languages.

Viewed as a whole, Gordimer's writings are a remarkable documentation of a country and a consciousness in constant change. Even though South Africa's policy of apartheid has ended, Gordimer still has a great deal to write about. As she points out, "Life didn't end with apartheid; new life began."

For Independent Reading

You may enjoy the following stories by Gordimer:
- "Once upon a Time"
- "Six Feet of the Country"
- "The Ultimate Safari"

Before You Read

The Train from Rhodesia

Cultural Points *of* View

In this story about a trainload of white tourists passing through a black African village in the 1950s, Gordimer's own cultural experiences from her life in South Africa inform her depiction of the huge social, economic, and political gulf between the races. In your opinion, what beliefs or situations contribute most to cultural clashes?

Literary Focus

Conflict and Setting

Conflict is the clash or struggle between opposing forces. **External conflicts** occur not only between individuals who disagree but also between groups whose interests cannot be reconciled. Cultural conflicts involving a clash of ideas, values, and traditions often involve an imbalance of power that results in unspoken but nevertheless obvious tensions.

Setting is the time and place of a literary work. A setting can be crucial to the central conflict of a work, as when a character has to struggle to survive against a force of nature, such as a storm. Setting also comes into play in conflicts that involve a character struggling against a culture, society, or political climate. As you read, note the ways in which the geographical, cultural, and political aspects of the setting give rise to the story's central conflict.

Conflict is a struggle or clash between opposing characters, forces, or emotions. **Setting** is the time and place in which a story occurs.

For more on Conflict and Setting, see the Handbook of Literary and Historical Terms.

Reading Skills

Understanding Cultural Impact on the Story

Although "The Train from Rhodesia" is a fictional work, Nadine Gordimer's experiences in South Africa clearly had an impact on the story. Gordimer lived in South Africa under apartheid (ə·pär'tāt')—the strict segregation of the nonwhite majority from the white minority. Thus, she witnessed racial prejudice in Africa firsthand. As you read, look for details that reveal the tensions between the two groups.

Background

Rhodesia was the name given by English colonizers to the country that borders South Africa to the north. After its independence in 1979, this country was renamed Zimbabwe, after the ancient African kingdom of Great Zimbabwe.

In this story, Gordimer does not use quotation marks to indicate dialogue. Pay attention to such speaker tags as "he laughed," "she said," and the like so that you will not be confused by who is speaking at different points in the story.

Vocabulary Development

interrogating (in·ter'ə·gāt'iŋ) v. used as *adj.*: inspecting; evaluating.

splaying (splā'iŋ) v. used as *adj.*: flattening; spreading out.

wryly (rī'lē) *adv.*: in a twisted manner.

atrophy (a'trə·fē) v.: shrink or waste away.

North Carolina Competency Goal
1.03; 4.03; 4.05; 5.01; 5.03

INTERNET

More About Nadine Gordimer

Keyword: LE5 WL-7

SKILLS FOCUS

Literary Skills
Understand conflict and setting.

Reading Skills
Understand cultural impact on the story.

The Train from

Nadine Gordimer

The train came out of the red horizon and bore down towards them over the single straight track.

The stationmaster came out of his little brick station with its pointed chalet roof, feeling the creases in his serge uniform in his legs as well. A stir of preparedness rippled through the squatting native venders waiting in the dust; the face of a carved wooden animal, eternally surprised, stuck out of a sack. The stationmaster's barefoot children wandered over. From the grey mud huts with the untidy heads that stood within a decorated mud wall, chickens, and dogs with their skin stretched like parchment over their bones, followed the piccanins[1] down to the track. The flushed and perspiring west cast a reflection, faint, without heat, upon the station, upon the tin shed marked "Goods," upon the walled kraal,[2] upon the grey tin house of the stationmaster and upon the sand, that lapped all around, from sky to sky, cast little rhythmical

---

1. **piccanins** (pik′ə·ninz) *n. pl.*: black children; a highly offensive term in the United States but in wide use among whites in South Africa at the time of this story.
2. **kraal** (kräl) *n.*: enclosure for domestic animals.

Rhodesia

Meeting the train in Bechuanaland, now Botswana. 1930s.

cups of shadow, so that the sand became the sea, and closed over the children's black feet softly and without imprint.

The stationmaster's wife sat behind the mesh of her veranda. Above her head the hunk of a sheep's carcass moved slightly, dangling in a current of air.

They waited.

The train called out, along the sky; but there was no answer; and the cry hung on: I'm coming … I'm coming….

The engine flared out now, big, whisking a dwindling body behind it; the track flared out to let it in.

Creaking, jerking, jostling, gasping, the train filled the station.

Here, let me see that one—the young woman curved her body farther out of the corridor window. Missus? smiled the old man, looking at the creatures he held in his hand. From a piece of string on his grey finger hung a tiny woven basket; he lifted it, questioning. No, no, she urged, leaning down towards him, across the height of the train towards the man in the piece of old rug; that one, that one, her hand commanded. It was a lion, carved out of soft, dry wood that looked

Nadine Gordimer 1011

like spongecake; heraldic, black and white, with impressionistic detail burnt in. The old man held it up to her still smiling, not from the heart, but at the customer. Between its vandyke[3] teeth, in the mouth opened in an endless roar too terrible to be heard, it had a black tongue. Look, said the young husband, if you don't mind! And round the neck of the thing, a piece of fur (rat? rabbit? meerkat?[4]); a real mane, majestic, telling you somehow that the artist had delight in the lion.

All up and down the length of the train in the dust the artists sprang, walking bent, like performing animals, the better to exhibit the fantasy held towards the faces on the train. Buck, startled and stiff, staring with round black and white eyes. More lions, standing erect, grappling with strange, thin, elongated warriors who clutched spears and showed no fear in their slits of eyes. How much, they asked from the train, how much?

Give me penny, said the little ones with nothing to sell. The dogs went and sat, quite still, under the dining car, where the train breathed out the smell of meat cooking with onion.

A man passed beneath the arch of reaching arms meeting grey-black and white in the exchange of money for the staring wooden eyes, the stiff wooden legs sticking up in the air; went along under the voices and the bargaining, interrogating the wheels. Past the dogs; glancing up at the dining car where he could stare at the faces, behind glass, drinking beer, two by two, on either side of a uniform railway vase with its pale dead flower. Right to the end, to the guard's van, where the stationmaster's children had just collected their mother's two loaves of bread; to the engine itself, where the stationmaster and the driver stood talking against the steaming complaint of the resting beast.

The man called out to them, something loud and joking. They turned to laugh, in a twirl of steam. The two children careered over the sand,

clutching the bread, and burst through the iron gate and up the path through the garden in which nothing grew.

Passengers drew themselves in at the corridor windows and turned into compartments to fetch money, to call someone to look. Those sitting inside looked up: suddenly different, caged faces, boxed in, cut off after the contact of outside. There was an orange a piccanin would like…. What about that chocolate? It wasn't very nice….

A girl had collected a handful of the hard kind, that no one liked, out of the chocolate box, and was throwing them to the dogs, over at the dining car. But the hens darted in and swallowed the chocolates, incredibly quick and accurate, before they had even dropped in the dust, and the dogs, a little bewildered, looked up with their brown eyes, not expecting anything.

—No, leave it, said the young woman, don't take it….

Too expensive, too much, she shook her head and raised her voice to the old man, giving up the lion. He held it high where she had handed it to him. No, she said, shaking her head. Three-and-six?[5] insisted her husband, loudly. Yes baas! laughed the old man. *Three-and-six?*—the young man was incredulous. Oh leave it—she said. The young man stopped. Don't you want it? he said, keeping his face closed to the old man. No, never mind, she said, leave it. The old native kept his head on one side, looking at them sideways, holding the lion. Three-and-six, he murmured, as old people repeat things to themselves.

The young woman drew her head in. She went into the coupé and sat down. Out of the window, on the other side, there was nothing; sand and bush; and thorn tree. Back through the open doorway, past the figure of her husband in the

---

5. **three-and-six:** three shillings and sixpence, a sum of money in the local currency.

Vocabulary

interrogating (in·ter′ə·gāt′iŋ) *v.* used as *adj.:* inspecting; evaluating.

---

3. **vandyke** *adj.:* pointed or irregular.
4. **meerkat** *n.:* type of mongoose.

corridor, there was the station, the voices, wooden animals waving, running feet. Her eye followed the funny little valance of scrolled wood that outlined the chalet roof of the station; she thought of the lion and smiled. That bit of fur round the neck. But the wooden buck, the hippos, the elephants, the baskets that already bulked out of their brown paper under the seat and on the luggage rack! How will they look at home? Where will you put them? What will they mean away from the places you found them? Away from the unreality of the last few weeks? The young man outside. But he is not part of the unreal-ity; he is for good now. Odd . . . somewhere there was an idea that he, that living with him, was part of the holiday, the strange places.

Outside, a bell rang. The stationmaster was leaning against the end of the train, green flag rolled in readiness. A few men who had got down to stretch their legs sprang on to the train, clinging to the observation platforms, or perhaps merely standing on the iron step, holding the rail; but on the train, safe from the one dusty platform, the one tin house, the empty sand.

There was a grunt. The train jerked. Through the glass the beer drinkers looked out, as if they could not see beyond it. Behind the flyscreen, the stationmaster's wife sat facing back at them beneath the darkening hunk of meat.

There was a shout. The flag drooped out. Joints not yet coordinated, the segmented body of the train heaved and bumped back against itself. It began to move; slowly the scrolled chalet

Mpisi and the Lion (20th century) by Allina Ndebele. Tapestry.

Johannesburg Art Gallery, South Africa.

moved past it, the yells of the natives, running alongside, jetted up into the air, fell back at different levels. Staring wooden faces waved drunkenly, there, then gone, questioning for the last time at the windows. Here, one-and-six baas!—As one automatically opens a hand to catch a thrown ball, a man fumbled wildly down his pocket, brought up the shilling and sixpence and threw them out; the old native, gasping, his skinny toes <u>splaying</u> the sand, flung the lion.

The piccanins were waving, the dogs stood, tails uncertain, watching the train go: past the mud huts, where a woman turned to look up from the smoke of the fire, her hand pausing on her hip.

The stationmaster went slowly in under the chalet.

The old native stood, breath blowing out the skin between his ribs, feet tense, balanced in the sand, smiling and shaking his head. In his opened palm, held in the attitude of receiving, was the retrieved shilling and sixpence.

The blind end of the train was being pulled helplessly out of the station.

The young man swung in from the corridor, breathless. He was shaking his head with laughter and triumph. Here! he said. And waggled the lion at her. One-and-six!

What? she said.

Vocabulary

splaying (splā′iŋ) *v.* used as *adj.*: flattening; spreading out.

He laughed. I was arguing with him for fun, bargaining—when the train had pulled out already, he came tearing after … One-and-six Baas! So there's your lion.

She was holding it away from her, the head with the open jaws, the pointed teeth, the black tongue, the wonderful ruff of fur facing her. She was looking at it with an expression of not seeing, of seeing something different. Her face was drawn up, <u>wryly</u>, like the face of a discomforted child. Her mouth lifted nervously at the corner. Very slowly, cautious, she lifted her finger and touched the mane, where it was joined to the wood.

But how could you, she said. He was shocked by the dismay of her face.

Good Lord, he said, what's the matter?

If you wanted the thing, she said, her voice rising and breaking with the shrill impotence of anger, why didn't you buy it in the first place? If you wanted it, why didn't you pay for it? Why didn't you take it decently, when he offered it? Why did you have to wait for him to run after the train with it, and give him one-and-six? One-and-six!

She was pushing it at him, trying to force him to take the lion. He stood astonished, his hands hanging at his sides.

But you wanted it! You liked it so much?

—It's a beautiful piece of work, she said fiercely, as if to protect it from him.

You liked it so much! You said yourself it was too expensive—

Oh *you*—she said, hopeless and furious. *You* … She threw the lion onto the seat.

He stood looking at her.

She sat down again in the corner and, her face slumped in her hands, stared out of the window. Everything was turning round inside her. One-and-six. One-and-six. One-and-six for the wood and the carving and the sinews of the legs and the switch of the tail. The mouth open like that and the teeth. The black tongue, rolling, like a wave. The mane round the neck. To give one-and-six for that. The heat of shame mounted through her legs and body and sounded in her ears like the sound of sand pouring. Pouring, pouring. She sat there, sick. A weariness, a tastelessness, the discovery of a void made her hands slacken their grip, <u>atrophy</u> emptily, as if the hour was not worth their grasp. She was feeling like this again. She had thought it was something to do with singleness, with being alone and belonging too much to oneself.

She sat there not wanting to move or speak, or to look at anything even; so that the mood should be associated with nothing, no object, word, or sight that might recur and so recall the feeling again…. Smuts blew in grittily, settled on her hands. Her back remained at exactly the same angle, turned against the young man sitting with his hands drooping between his sprawled legs, and the lion, fallen on its side in the corner.

The train had cast the station like a skin. It called out to the sky, I'm coming, I'm coming; and again, there was no answer.

Vocabulary

wryly (rī′lē) *adv.*: in a twisted manner.
atrophy (a′trə·fē) *v.*: shrink or waste away.

Response and Analysis

Reading Check

1. Who is waiting for the train approaching from the west? What does each of these people do when the train arrives?

2. Who are the people on the train?

3. What is the relationship between the young couple? What is the occasion for their trip?

4. What do the old carver and the young man on the train disagree about?

Thinking Critically

5. The story contrasts two **settings**—the interior world of the train and the exterior world of the station outpost. List details that highlight the differences between the two settings.

6. How is the train **personified**—that is, made to seem like a living thing? Find examples of words that describe the train as if it were alive. What do you think Gordimer is trying to suggest through her use of personification?

7. How does the young man view the old man and his carving? How does the woman view them? What does this **conflict** of values suggest about the couple's future?

8. What are the two main **conflicts** ultimately revealed in this story? Is either conflict resolved? Explain.

9. Why does the young woman on the train feel shame and regret? How do you think she views her own culture after this event?

Extending and Evaluating

10. What comment do you think Gordimer is making about race relations in this story? How do you think her experiences in South Africa influenced her to write this story?

WRITING

Analyzing Details

The critic Paul Gray describes Gordimer's portrayal of her homeland in this way: "An overriding injustice must be deduced from small, vividly realized details." Does his analysis apply to this story? In a brief essay, describe the picture of race relations you deduce from small details in the story.

Vocabulary Development
In Other Words

Read the following sentences from the story. Then, on a separate sheet of paper, write a synonym to replace each underlined Vocabulary word.

1. "A man passed beneath the arch . . . went along under the voices and the bargaining, <u>interrogating</u> the wheels."

2. ". . . The old native, gasping, his skinny toes <u>splaying</u> the sand, flung the lion."

3. "Her face was drawn up <u>wryly</u>, like the face of a discomforted child."

4. ". . . The discovery of a void made her hands slacken their grip, <u>atrophy</u> emptily. . . ."

North Carolina Competency Goal
6.01

INTERNET

Projects and Activities
Keyword:
LE5 WL-7

SKILLS FOCUS

Literary Skills
Analyze conflict and setting.

Reading Skills
Understand cultural impact on the story.

Writing Skills
Analyze details.

Vocabulary Skills
Replace vocabulary words with synonyms.

Connected Readings

Clashes of Cultures

Jamaica Kincaid . . . .*from* **On Seeing England for the First Time**

Derek Walcott . . . .**The Virgins**

You have just read Nadine Gordimer's short story "The Train from Rhodesia" and considered her views on culture clashes. The next two selections you will read provide further viewpoints on culture clashes. As you read, think about how these selections are similar to and different from one another. After you read, you'll find questions on page 1021 that ask you to compare all three selections.

Cultural Points *of* View

Before You Read

Jamaica Kincaid was raised on the lush Caribbean island of Antigua, which was a British colony for over three hundred years. The British forcibly enslaved people from Africa and brought them to Antigua to work on the island's sugar plantations. Today, the descendants of those Africans make up most of Antigua's population. Although Antigua won its independence in 1981, British influences are still strong on the island; the people speak English, and many of them belong to the Anglican (Episcopalian) Church. The school Kincaid attended was modeled on the British school system.

Born Elaine Potter Richardson to an Antiguan couple of African descent, Kincaid grew up in St. John's, Antigua's largest city. Antigua was still a British colony during Kincaid's childhood, and she came to hate the European colonialism that had exploited her people for so many centuries. An outspoken and strong-minded young person who often got into trouble at school, Kincaid left Antigua at the age of seventeen to become an au pair in New York, exchanging domestic services for her room and board. After attending college in New Hampshire, she began writing and publishing stories. Eventually, her writing skills landed her a job as a staff writer at *The New Yorker* magazine.

In this excerpt from her essay "On Seeing England for the First Time," Kincaid expresses her anger about her colonial upbringing. As she once remarked in an interview, "I never give up thinking about the way I came into the world, how my ancestors came from Africa to the West Indies as slaves. I just could never forget it."

from *On Seeing England for the First Time*

Jamaica Kincaid

When I saw England for the first time, I was a child in school sitting at a desk. The England I was looking at was laid out on a map gently, beautifully, delicately, a very special jewel; it lay on a bed of sky blue—the background of the map—its yellow form mysterious, because though it looked like a leg of mutton, it could not really look like anything so familiar as a leg of mutton because it was England—with shadings of pink and green, unlike any shadings of pink and green I had seen before, squiggly veins of red running in every direction. England was a special jewel all right, and only special people got to wear it. The people who got to wear England were English people. They wore it well and they wore it everywhere: in jungles, in deserts, on plains, on top of the highest mountains, on all the oceans, on all the seas, in places where they were not welcome, in places they should not have been. When my teacher had pinned this map up on the blackboard, she said, "This is England"—and she said it with authority, seriousness, and adoration, and we all sat up. It was as if she had said, "This is Jerusalem, the place you will go to when you die but only if you have been good." We understood then—we were meant to understand then—that England was to be our source of myth and the source from which we got our sense of reality, our sense of what was meaningful, our sense of what was meaningless—and much about our own lives and much about the very idea of us headed that last list.

At the time I was a child sitting at my desk seeing England for the first time, I was already very familiar with the greatness of it. Each morning before I left for school, I ate a breakfast of half a grapefruit, an egg, bread and butter and a slice of cheese, and a cup of cocoa; or half a grapefruit, a bowl of oat porridge, bread and butter and a slice of cheese, and a cup of cocoa. The can of cocoa was often left on the table in front of me. It had written on it the name of the company, the year the company was established, and the words "Made in England." Those words, "Made in England," were written on the box the oats came in too. They would also have been written on the box the shoes I

Single size egg coddler with "Made in England" stamp on the bottom.

was wearing came in; a bolt of gray linen cloth lying on the shelf of a store from which my mother had bought three yards to make the uniform that I was wearing had written along its edge those three words. The shoes I wore were made in England; so were my socks and cotton undergarments and the satin ribbons I wore tied at the end of two plaits of my hair. My father, who might have sat next to me at breakfast, was a carpenter and cabinet maker. The shoes he wore to work would have been made in England, as were his khaki shirt and trousers, his underpants and undershirt, his socks and brown felt hat. Felt was not the proper material from which a hat that was expected to provide shade from the hot sun should be made, but my father must have seen and admired a picture of an Englishman wearing such a hat in England, and this picture that he saw must have been so compelling that it caused him to wear the wrong hat for a hot climate most of his long life. And this hat—a brown felt hat—became so central to his character that it was the first thing he put on in the morning as he stepped out of bed and the last thing he took off before he stepped back into bed at night. As we sat at breakfast a car might go by. The car, a Hillman or a Zephyr, was made in England. The very idea of the meal itself, breakfast, and its substantial quality and quantity was an idea from England; we somehow knew that in England they began the day with this meal called breakfast and a proper breakfast was a big breakfast. No one I knew liked eating so much food so early in the day; it made us feel sleepy, tired. But this breakfast business was Made in England like almost everything else that surrounded us, the exceptions being the sea, the sky, and the air we breathed.

At the time I saw this map—seeing England for the first time—I did not say to myself, "Ah, so that's what it looks like," because there was no longing in me to put a shape to those three words that ran through every part of my life, no matter how small; for me to have had such a longing would have meant that I lived in a certain atmosphere, an atmosphere in which those three words were felt as a burden. But I did not live in such an atmosphere. My father's brown felt hat would develop a hole in its crown, the lining would separate from the hat itself, and six weeks before he thought that he could not be seen wearing it—he was a very vain man—he would order another hat from England. And my mother taught me to eat my food in the English way: the knife in the right hand, the fork in the left, my elbows held still close to my side, the food carefully balanced on my fork and then brought up to my mouth. When I had fi-

nally mastered it, I overheard her saying to a friend, "Did you see how nicely she can eat?" But I knew then that I enjoyed my food more when I ate it with my bare hands, and I continued to do so when she wasn't looking. And when my teacher showed us the map, she asked us to study it carefully, because no test we would ever take would be complete without this statement: "Draw a map of England."

I did not know then that the statement "Draw a map of England" was something far worse than a declaration of war, for in fact a flat-out declaration of war would have put me on alert, and again in fact, there was no need for war—I had long ago been conquered. I did not know then that this statement was part of a process that would result in my erasure, not my physical erasure, but my erasure all the same. I did not know then that this statement was meant to make me feel in awe and small whenever I heard the word "England": awe at its existence, small because I was not from it. I did not know very much of anything then—certainly not what a blessing it was that I was unable to draw a map of England correctly.

Cultural Points *of* View

Before You Read

The Nobel Prize–winning English-language poet Derek Walcott (1930–   ) was born and raised on St. Lucia, an island in the West Indies that was a colony of both France and England. The island's colonial history is marked by violence and tragedy, as the two European imperial powers periodically fought for control of it. Walcott studied the English classics in school and began writing poems of his own. His mother, an educator and seamstress, lent him the money to publish his first book of poetry when he was just eighteen. After graduating from the University College of West Indies in Jamaica, Walcott eventually moved to Trinidad, where he wrote poetry, plays, and reviews for the local paper. In 1964, Walcott's *Selected Poems* was published in the United States, starting his career

of international fame as a poet and playwright.

Many critics have suggested that Walcott is divided between cultures: black and white, Caribbean and British. But Walcott sees his own mixed racial and cultural heritage as symbolic of the new world and its inherent divisions. A major theme in Walcott's work is the clash of cultures in the Caribbean—the influences of U. S. and European colonialism and the island's own combination of African and Caribbean traditions.

The following poem is set in Frederiksted, one of the old port cities on the U.S. Virgin Island of St. Croix. Once the center of a booming sugar cane trade, Frederiksted's only industry today is tourism.

POEM

The Virgins

Derek Walcott

Down the dead streets of sun-stoned Frederiksted,
the first free port to die for tourism,
strolling at funeral pace, I am reminded
of life not lost to the American dream;
5   but my small-islander's simplicities
can't better our new empire's civilized
exchange of cameras, watches, perfumes, brandies
for the good life, so cheaply underpriced
that only the crime rate is on the rise
10 in streets blighted with sun, stone arches
and plazas blown dry by the hysteria
of rumor. A condominium drowns
in vacancy; its bargains are dusted,
but only a jeweled housefly drones
15 over the bargains. The roulettes spin
rustily to the wind—the vigorous trade
that every morning would begin afresh
by revving up green water round the pierhead
heading for where the banks of silver thresh.

Analyzing **Cultural Points** *of* **View**

Clashes of Cultures

The questions on this page ask you to analyze the views on cultural clashes expressed in the preceding three selections.

Nadine Gordimer . . . .**The Train from Rhodesia**

Jamaica Kincaid . . . .*from* **On Seeing England for the First Time**

Derek Walcott . . . .**The Virgins**

Comparing a Theme Across Cultures: Clashes of Cultures

1. What does each selection have to say about cultural clashes? What did you learn about the possible outcomes and misunderstandings that arise with coexisting cultures?

2. How are the views of the authors of these selections alike and different? With which point of view do you agree most? Refer to your reading notes (see page 1007).

3. Each of the authors in this feature uses **irony** to describe the injustice and misunderstandings created between different cultures. Explain the irony of each of the following details:

   • the young woman's reaction when the young man brings her the lion in "The Train from Rhodesia"

   • the title of "On Seeing England for the First Time," in light of where that event took place for the narrator

   • the representation of the "good life" and "the American Dream" in "The Virgins"

4. In your own life, have you ever experienced any cultural clashes? How does culture act as a lens that makes you see and interpret things in a particular way? Explain, referring to your Quickwrite notes from page 1007.

WRITING

Researching Cultural Clashes

Write a research report on the effects of colonialism on an emerging nation or culture. You can choose to further explore one of the cultures represented in this feature (South Africa, Antigua and other parts of the Caribbean) or another postcolonial culture. First, find information on that area's colonial and postcolonial history. Then, conduct research to uncover the effects that colonialism has had or is having on the culture. Prepare a research paper in which you report on your culture's post-colonial legacy and struggles. Support your points with quotations from postcolonial writers of that region. Present your report to the class.

▶ **See "Reporting Literary Research," pages 1098–1111, for help with this assignment.**

North Carolina Competency Goal
1.02; 1.03; 4.01; 4.05; 5.03; 6.01

SKILLS FOCUS

Pages 1007–1021 cover
Literary Skills
Analyze cultural points of view on a topic.

Reading Skills
Compare points of view across texts.

Writing Skills
Research cultural clashes.

Bessie Head

(1937–1986)
South Africa

Bessie Head was born in a South African mental hospital where her mother, a wealthy white woman, had been committed because of her relationship with Head's father, a black stableman. In the eyes of South Africa's apartheid (ə•pär′tāt′) society, which dictated complete separation between nonwhites and whites, Head's mother had committed a grievous offense, and she remained institutionalized for the rest of her life. Taken immediately from her mother at birth, Head was raised by foster parents, but at age thirteen she was sent to a missionary orphanage.

After a brief stint as a teacher, Head took a job as a journalist for *Drum* magazine. In 1960, she married a fellow journalist, Howard Head. As a nonwhite person living under South Africa's racist apartheid laws, Bessie Head faced severe discrimination in many areas of life, including education and housing. After her divorce in 1964, Head fled with her son, Howard, to live in exile in neighboring Botswana. There she wrote and worked as a gardener in a refugee community until her death from hepatitis at the age of forty-eight.

A hint of autobiography is present in much of Head's writing, which often deals with poor and emotionally abused black women, who are discriminated against on the basis of both race and sex. In her novels, historical chronicles, and short stories, Head examines African history and explores the effects of discrimination, exile, racism, and poverty. The theme of injustice, whether perpetrated by whites or nonwhites, is central in her writing.

Although Head's life was filled with tragedy, a sense of hope and optimism permeates her works. Her writing speaks of the importance of love and generosity in the face of corruption, oppression, and isolation. Her resilient characters convey a desire for peace and change in spite of seemingly hopeless circumstances. Ultimately, Head says, there are only two themes present in her writing: "that love is really good . . . and . . . that it is important to be an ordinary person."

The Prisoner Who Wore Glasses

Make the Connection

Quickwrite

Have you ever tried to assert yourself by asking to be treated a certain way? Write a few sentences about the pros and cons of acting assertively. Include some examples from your own life or from the experiences of people you know.

Literary Focus

Setting and Theme

The **setting** of a story is the time and place in which it occurs. Details of geography are often only a small part of setting in contemporary fiction. More important aspects of setting, such as political, social, and economic circumstances, can be useful when trying to determine a story's **theme,** or central idea about life.

This story is set in a South African prison farm in the era of apartheid, a system that lasted from the late 1940s until the early 1990s. What point about life in this time and place is the writer making in the story? As you read, note details of the setting that may help you determine the story's theme. Could this story have occurred in any other setting?

> **Setting** is the time and place of a story, play, or narrative poem.
> **Theme** is the central insight about life in a work of literature.
>
> *For more on Setting and Theme, see the Handbook of Literary and Historical Terms.*

Reading Skills

Identifying Political Influences

"The Prisoner Who Wore Glasses" takes place at a time when apartheid, or strict racial segregation, was the law of the land in South Africa. Members of the black majority were forced to live in "homelands," isolated areas far from decent jobs and schools. Protestors were often arrested and held for years as political prisoners. As you read the story, consider what Head is saying about the way apartheid affected all of South African society.

Background

Although Head did not live to see the end of apartheid, many of her writings anticipated that event. She wrote, "It is impossible to guess how the revolution will come one day in South Africa. But in a world where all ordinary people are insisting on their rights, it is inevitable. It is hoped that great leaders will arise there who remember the suffering of racial hatred and out of it formulate a common language of love for all people." In 1994, Nelson Mandela, a former political prisoner and winner of the Nobel Peace Prize, became the first black president of South Africa in that country's first democratic election.

North Carolina Competency Goal
1.02; 1.03; 4.01; 4.02; 4.05; 5.01; 5.03; 6.01

INTERNET
Vocabulary Practice
•
More About Bessie Head
Keyword: LE5 WL-7

SKILLS FOCUS

Literary Skills
Understand setting and theme.

Reading Skills
Identify political influences.

Vocabulary Development

perpetrated (pʉr′pə·trāt′id) *v.:* committed; done.

bedlam (bed′ləm) *n.:* chaos; complete disorder.

ruefully (rōō′fəl·ē) *adv.:* sorrowfully; with regret.

pivot (piv′ət) *n.:* central point on which something else depends.

The Prisoner Who Wore Glasses

Bessie Head

Prisoners in the fields. Rwanda, November 2003.

Scarcely a breath of wind disturbed the stillness of the day and the long rows of cabbages were bright green in the sunlight. Large white clouds drifted slowly across the deep blue sky. Now and then they obscured the sun and caused a chill on the backs of the prisoners who had to work all day long in the cabbage field. This trick the clouds were playing with the sun eventually caused one of the prisoners who wore glasses to stop work, straighten up and peer short-sightedly at them. He was a thin little fellow with a hollowed-out chest and comic knobbly knees. He also had a lot of fanciful ideas because he smiled at the clouds.

"Perhaps they want me to send a message to the children," he thought, tenderly, noting that the clouds were drifting in the direction of his home some hundred miles away. But before he could frame the message, the warder in charge of his work span[1] shouted: "Hey, what do you think you're doing, Brille?"

The prisoner swung round, blinking rapidly, yet at the same time sizing up the enemy. He was a new warder, named Jacobus Stephanus Hannetjie.[2]

His eyes were the color of the sky but they were frightening. A simple, primitive, brutal soul gazed out of them. The prisoner bent down quickly and a message was quietly passed down the line: "We're in for trouble this time, comrades."

"Why?" rippled back up the line.

"Because he's not human," the reply rippled down and yet only the crunching of the spades as they turned over the earth disturbed the stillness.

This particular work span was known as Span One. It was composed of ten men and they were all political prisoners. They were grouped together for convenience as it was one of the prison regulations that no black warder should be in charge of a political prisoner lest this prisoner convert him to his view. It never seemed to occur to the authorities that this very reasoning was the strength of Span One and a clue to the strange terror they aroused in the warders. As political prisoners they were unlike the other prisoners in the sense that they felt no guilt nor were they outcasts of society. All guilty men instinctively cower, which was why it was the kind of prison where men got knocked out cold with a blow at the back of the head from an iron bar. Up until the arrival of Warder Hannetjie, no warder had dared beat any member of Span One and no warder had lasted more than a week with them. The battle was entirely psychological. Span One was

assertive and it was beyond the scope of white warders to handle assertive black men. Thus, Span One had got out of control. They were the best thieves and liars in the camp. They lived all day on raw cabbages. They chatted and smoked tobacco. And since they moved, thought, and acted as one, they had perfected every technique of group concealment.

Trouble began that very day between Span One and Warder Hannetjie. It was because of the short-sightedness of Brille. That was the nickname he was given in prison and is the Afrikaans[3] word for someone who wears glasses. Brille could never judge the approach of the prison gates and on several occasions he had munched on cabbages and dropped them almost at the feet of the warder and all previous warders had overlooked this. Not so Warder Hannetjie.

"Who dropped that cabbage?" he thundered.

Brille stepped out of line.

"I did," he said meekly.

"All right," said Hannetjie. "The whole Span goes three meals off."

"But I told you I did it," Brille protested.

The blood rushed to Warder Hannetjie's face.

"Look 'ere," he said. "I don't take orders from a kaffir.[4] I don't know what kind of kaffir you think you are. Why don't you say Baas,[5] I'm your Baas, Why don't you say Baas, hey?"

Brille blinked his eyes rapidly but by contrast his voice was strangely calm.

"I'm twenty years older than you," he said. It was the first thing that came to mind but the comrades seemed to think it a huge joke. A titter swept up the line. The next thing Warder Hannetjie whipped out a knobkerrie[6] and gave Brille several blows about the head. What surprised his

---

1. **work span** *n.:* group or unit of workers.
2. **Jacobus Stephanus Hannetjie** (yä′kō·bōōs ste′fä·nōōs hä′net·ye).

3. **Afrikaans** (af′ri·käns′): an official South African language that developed from seventeenth-century Dutch.
4. **kaffir** (kaf′ər) *n.:* In South Africa, *kaffir* is a disparaging term for any black African.
5. **baas** (bäs): In South Africa, many white men once expected black Africans to address them as "baas" ("boss," "sir").
6. **knobkerrie** *n.:* short, heavy club with a knob at one end.

comrades was the speed with which Brille had removed his glasses or else they would have been smashed to pieces on the ground.

That evening in the cell Brille was very apologetic.

"I'm sorry, comrades," he said. "I've put you into a hell of a mess."

"Never mind, brother," they said. "What happens to one of us, happens to all."

"I'll try to make up for it, comrades," he said. "I'll steal something so that you don't go hungry."

Privately, Brille was very philosophical about his head wounds. It was the first time an act of violence had been <u>perpetrated</u> against him but he had long been a witness of extreme, almost unbelievable human brutality. He had twelve children and his mind traveled back that evening through the sixteen years of <u>bedlam</u> in which he had lived. It had all happened in a small, drab little three-bedroomed house in a small, drab little street in the Eastern Cape, and the children kept coming year after year because neither he nor Martha ever managed the contraceptives the right way, and a teacher's salary never allowed moving to a bigger house, and he was always taking exams to improve his salary only to have it all eaten up by hungry mouths. Everything was pretty horrible, especially the way the children fought. They'd get hold of each other's heads and give them a good bashing against the wall. Martha gave up somewhere along the line so they worked out a thing between them. The bashings, biting and blood were to operate in full swing until he came home. He was to be the bogeyman and when it worked he never failed to have a sense of godhead at the way in which his presence could change savages into fairly reasonable human beings.

Yet somehow it was this chaos and mismanagement at the center of his life that drove him into politics. It was really an ordered, beautiful world with just a few basic slogans to learn along with the rights of mankind. At one stage, before things became very bad, there were conferences to attend, all very far away from home.

"Let's face it," he thought <u>ruefully</u>. "I'm only learning right now what it means to be a politician. All this while I've been running away from Martha and the kids."

And the pain in his head brought a hard lump to his throat. That was what the children did to each other daily and Martha wasn't managing and if Warder Hannetjie had not interrupted him that morning he would have sent the following message: "Be good comrades, my children. Cooperate, then life will run smoothly."

The next day Warder Hannetjie caught this old man of twelve children stealing grapes from the farm shed. They were an enormous quantity of grapes in a ten-gallon tin and for this misdeed the old man spent a week in the isolation cell. In fact, Span One as a whole was in constant trouble. Warder Hannetjie seemed to have eyes at the back of his head. He uncovered the trick about the cabbages, how they were split in two with the spade and immediately covered with earth and then unearthed again and eaten with split-second timing. He found out how tobacco smoke was beaten into the ground and he found out how conversations were whispered down the wind.

For about two weeks Span One lived in acute misery. The cabbages, tobacco, and conversations had been the <u>pivot</u> of jail life to them. Then one evening they noticed that their good old comrade who wore the glasses was looking rather pleased with himself. He pulled out a four-ounce packet of tobacco by way of explanation and the comrades fell upon it with great greed. Brille merely smiled. After all, he was the father of many children. But when the last shred had disappeared, it occurred to the comrades that they ought to be puzzled. Someone said: "I say, brother. We're watched like hawks these days. Where did you get the tobacco?"

"Hannetjie gave it to me," said Brille.

There was a long silence. Into it dropped a quiet bombshell.

Vocabulary

perpetrated (pʉr′pə·trāt′id) v.: committed; done.
bedlam (bed′ləm) n.: chaos; complete disorder.
ruefully (roo′fəl·ē) adv.: sorrowfully; with regret.
pivot (piv′ət) n.: central point on which something else depends.

Yellow Houses: A Street in Sophiatown (c. 1940) by Gerard Sekoto.
Johannesburg Art Gallery, South Africa.

"I saw Hannetjie in the shed today," and the failing eyesight blinked rapidly. "I caught him in the act of stealing five bags of fertilizer and he bribed me to keep my mouth shut."

There was another long silence.

"Prison is an evil life," Brille continued, apparently discussing some irrelevant matter. "It makes a man contemplate all kinds of evil deeds."

He held out his hand and closed it.

"You know, comrades," he said. "I've got Hannetjie. I'll betray him tomorrow."

Everyone began talking at once.

"Forget it, brother. You'll get shot."

Brille laughed.

"I won't," he said. "That is what I mean about evil. I am a father of children and I saw today that Hannetjie is just a child and stupidly truthful. I'm going to punish him severely because we need a good warder."

The following day, with Brille as witness, Hannetjie confessed to the theft of the fertilizer and was fined a large sum of money. From then on Span One did very much as they pleased while Warder Hannetjie stood by and said nothing. But it was Brille who carried this to extremes. One day, at the close of work Warder Hannetjie said: "Brille, pick up my jacket and carry it back to the camp."

"But nothing in the regulations says I'm your servant, Hannetjie," Brille replied coolly.

"I've told you not to call me Hannetjie. You must say Baas," but Warder Hannetjie's voice lacked conviction. In turn, Brille squinted up at him.

"I'll tell you something about this Baas business, Hannetjie," he said. "One of these days we are going to run the country. You are going to clean my car. Now, I have a fifteen-year-old son and I'd die of shame if you had to tell him that I ever called you Baas."

Warder Hannetjie went red in the face and picked up his coat.

On another occasion Brille was seen to be walking about the prison yard, openly smoking tobacco. On being taken before the prison commander he claimed to have received the tobacco from Warder Hannetjie. Throughout the tirade from his chief, Warder Hannetjie failed to defend himself but his nerve broke completely. He called Brille to one side.

"Brille," he said. "This thing between you and me must end. You may not know it but I have a wife and children and you're driving me to suicide."

"Why don't you like your own medicine, Hannetjie?" Brille asked quietly.

"I can give you anything you want," Warder Hannetjie said in desperation.

"It's not only me but the whole of Span One," said Brille, cunningly. "The whole of Span One wants something from you."

Warder Hannetjie brightened with relief.

"I think I can manage if it's tobacco you want," he said.

Brille looked at him, for the first time struck with pity, and guilt.

He wondered if he had carried the whole business too far. The man was really a child.

"It's not tobacco we want, but you," he said. "We want you on our side. We want a good warder because without a good warder we won't be able to manage the long stretch ahead."

Warder Hannetjie interpreted this request in his own fashion and his interpretation of what was good and human often left the prisoners of Span One speechless with surprise. He had a way of slipping off his revolver and picking up a spade and digging alongside Span One. He had a way of producing unheard of luxuries like boiled eggs from his farm nearby and things like cigarettes, and Span One responded nobly and got the reputation of being the best work span in the camp. And it wasn't only take from their side. They were awfully good at stealing certain commodities like fertilizer which were needed on the farm of Warder Hannetjie.

Response and Analysis

Reading Check

1. Explain how Brille and the rest of Span One ended up in prison. Why do the warders keep prisoners of this type together? What is the effect of keeping these prisoners together?

2. What practices of the prisoners does the warder discover?

3. What happens when Hannetjie tells Brille to pick up his jacket? What prediction does Brille make?

Thinking Critically

4. Compare and contrast Brille's relationship with his children and his relationship with Hannetjie. What parallel might Head be drawing between Brille's home life, especially his children's behavior, and the nation of South Africa?

5. Compare and contrast Brille's and the warder's ways of asserting themselves. Which method is more effective? How do the two men's methods of self-assertion compare with your own? Refer to your Quickwrite notes.

6. Brille thinks to himself, "I'm only learning right now what it means to be a politician." What exactly is he learning, and why?

7. How is Brille able to break Hannetjie's nerve? How do the warder and the group of prisoners work together at the end of the story? Explain how this transformation occurs, and state whether you think it is realistic and believable.

8. Identify the **theme,** or central idea, of this story. How does the **setting**—especially the political backdrop of apartheid—contribute to this theme?

Extending and Evaluating

9. Nelson Mandela has said that "the oppressor must be liberated just as surely as the oppressed. A man who takes away another man's freedom is a prisoner of hatred." Does the behavior of the characters in "The Prisoner Who Wore Glasses" seem in keeping with the attitude expressed in this quotation? Explain.

WRITING

Writing a Dialogue

Suppose that Brille and Hannetjie live to see the end of apartheid in South Africa and that they meet on the street a few years later. Write a conversation they might have. In your dialogue, be sure to stay true to the characters as they are revealed in the story. With a partner, perform your dialogue for the class.

Vocabulary Development
Word-Information Charts

perpetrated   ruefully

bedlam   pivot

The chart below includes some basic information about the word *bedlam.* Using a dictionary, make similar charts for the rest of the Vocabulary words listed above.

bedlam
Meaning: *chaos; complete disorder*
Origin: *Middle English*
Synonym: *confusion*
Antonym: *order*
Example: *Teachers try to prevent classrooms from descending into bedlam.*

North Carolina Competency Goal
1.03; 4.02; 4.05; 5.03; 6.01

INTERNET
Projects and Activities
Keyword:
LE5 WL-7

Literary Skills
Analyze setting and theme.

Reading Skills
Identify political influences.

Writing Skills
Write a dialogue.

Vocabulary Skills
Create word-information charts.

Naguib Mahfouz
(1911–   )
Egypt

Naguib Mahfouz (nä·jēb' mä'fōōz), the best-known fiction writer in the Arabic language and the first Arab author to win the Nobel Prize in literature, grew up in a middle-class family similar to the one he depicts in his acclaimed thousand-plus-page *The Cairo Trilogy*— *Palace Walk* (1956), *Palace of Desire* (1957), and *Sugar Street* (1957). Mahfouz began sending stories to magazines while he was a philosophy student at the University of Cairo. When he received his first payment for a story, one anecdote goes, he exclaimed in disbelief, "One gets paid for them as well!"

For much of his life, Mahfouz was unable to depend on his writing for sufficient income. He worked as a civil servant for the Egyptian government in the Arts Administration, and later as head of the State Cinema Organization. Yet he has written more than forty novels and short story collections, several plays, and many film scripts. Almost all of his writing is set in Cairo, the city he knows and loves so well. "Like their author," writes the translator Denys Johnson-Davies, "his stories never travel abroad, not even to the Egyptian countryside."

Mahfouz's works are read widely throughout the Middle East, where he has popularized the novel and short story forms as workable alternatives to poetry, the traditional genre of the region. His writing addresses the social and political history of Egypt, the effects of time and change, the repression of women, the plight of the poor, moral decay among the upper classes, and the superficial values of modern society. Ironically, some of his books were banned in Arab countries—including Egypt—especially after he expressed support for the 1979 peace treaty between Egypt and Israel.

In 1988, the Nobel Prize in literature was awarded to Mahfouz "who, through works rich in nuance—now clear-sightedly realistic, now evocatively ambiguous—has formed an Arabian narrative art that applies to all mankind." Aware of how relatively unknown he was among non-Arab readers, Mahfouz commented, "I was told by a foreign correspondent in Cairo that the moment my name was mentioned in connection with the prize silence fell, and many wondered who I was." Since he was awarded the prize, his works have become more widely available in English.

When asked how he gets ideas for his stories, Mahfouz replied, "When you spend time with your friends, what do you talk about? Those things which made an impression on you that day, that week. . . . I write stories the same way. Events at home, in school, at work, in the street, these are the bases for a story."

Before You Read

The Norwegian Rat

Make the Connection

How do people react under the constant pressure of a threat that never seems to materialize? Imagine that a government tells its citizens to take precautions against an imminent natural disaster. The warnings go on for a long time, yet the disaster never happens. Still, the authorities stress that citizens should continue to take all precautions. How do you think most people would deal with such a situation?

Literary Focus

Ambiguity

Something that is ambiguous can have two or more possible meanings. Writers create **ambiguity** in literature by deliberately using words and sentences or presenting events in ways that are open to interpretation. An ambiguous story can prompt lively discussions among readers who disagree about its meaning, especially when each reader uses the same evidence from the story to express a different or contradictory interpretation. Ambiguity can deepen the complexity of a work, but it can also increase our enjoyment, allowing us to argue in favor of different understandings of what we've read. A literary work that is rich in ambiguity will lead readers into different streams of thought—multiple interpretations that all make sense in the context of the work.

> **Ambiguity** is a quality that allows something to be interpreted in several different—even contradictory—ways.
>
> *For more on Ambiguity, see the Handbook of Literary and Historical Terms.*

Reading Skills

Drawing Conclusions

When you read, you gather facts and details to make a judgment or draw a conclusion about the meaning of that evidence. Sometimes, when a story is ambiguous, you may find that all of your evidence allows you to draw two—or even more—equally valid conclusions. As you read this story, note details that seem significant and meaningful. Write down the conclusions you draw from these details.

Background

Rats have long been dreaded and despised by human beings. The Norwegian rat (*Rattus norvegicus*) is no exception: It can carry bubonic plague, typhus, salmonella, rabies, tularemia, and trichinosis. Rat-borne diseases have probably caused more deaths in the last millenium than all the wars humans have fought. No wonder that a sudden increase in an area's rat population would cause alarm.

Vocabulary Development

reiterating (rē·it′ə·rāt′iŋ) *v.*: repeating.

meticulously (mə·tik′yo͞o·ləs·lē) *adv.*: very carefully.

predominated (prē·däm′ə·nāt′id) *v.*: took control.

proliferation (prō·lif′ə·rā′shən) *n.*: rapid spread.

annihilated (ə·nī′ə·lāt′id) *v.*: destroyed completely.

voracity (vô·ras′ə·tē) *n.*: gluttony, especially in eating.

North Carolina Competency Goal
1.03; 4.03; 4.05; 5.01; 5.03

INTERNET

Vocabulary Practice
•
More About Naguib Mahfouz

Keyword: LE5 WL-7

SKILLS FOCUS

Literary Skills
Understand ambiguity.

Reading Skills
Draw conclusions.

The Norwegian Rat

Naguib Mahfouz

translated by **Denys Johnson-Davies**

Fortunately we were not alone in this affliction. Mr. A.M., being the senior householder
in the building, had invited us to a meeting in his
flat[1] for an exchange of opinions. There were not
more than ten people present, including Mr.
A.M., who, in addition to being the oldest among
us, held the most senior position and was also the
most well off. No one failed to show up—and
how could they, seeing that it had to do with the
rats and their likely invasion of our homes and
their threat to our safety? Mr. A.M. began in a
voice of great gravity[2] with "As you all know . . ."
and then set forth what the papers had been
reiterating about the advance of the rats, their vast
numbers, and the terrible destruction that would

---

1. **flat** *n.:* British for "apartment or suite of rooms on
   one floor."
2. **gravity** *n.:* seriousness; solemnity.

Vocabulary

reiterating (rē·it′ə·rāt′iŋ) *v.:* repeating.

be wrought[3] by them. Voices were raised around the room.

"What is being said is quite beyond belief."

"Have you seen the television coverage?"

"They're not ordinary rats; they're even attacking cats and people."

"Isn't it likely that things are a bit exaggerated?"

"No . . . no, the facts are beyond any exaggeration."

Then, calmly and with pride in being the chairman, Mr. A.M. said, "It has in any case been established that we are not alone. This has been confirmed to me by the Governor."

"It's good to hear that."

"So all we have to do is carry out instructions meticulously, both those that come directly through me and those that come by way of the authorities."

"And will this cost us a great deal?" it occurred to one of us to inquire.

He resorted to the Koran for a reply. " 'God does not charge a soul beyond its scope.' "

"The main thing is that the costs should not be excessive."

This time he resorted to a maxim. "An evil is not warded off by something worse."

At which more than one voice said, "We would hope that you will find us cooperative."

"We are with you," said Mr. A.M., "but do not rely upon us wholly. Rely too upon yourselves, starting at least with the obvious things."

"Absolutely so, but what are the obvious things?"

"Having traps and the traditional poisons."

"Fine."

"Having as many cats as possible in the stairwell and on the roofs. Also inside the flats if circumstances permit."

"But it's said that the Norwegian rat attacks cats."

"Cats are not without their use."

We returned to our homes in high spirits and with a sincere resolve. Soon, rats predominated over the rest of our worries. They made frequent appearances in our dreams, occupied the most time in our conversations, and came to engross us as life's main difficulty. We proceeded to take the precautions we had promised to, as we awaited the coming of the enemy. Some of us were saying that there was not long to go, while others said that one day we'd spot a rat darting past and that this would be the harbinger[4] of imminent danger.

Many different explanations were given for the proliferation of rats. One opinion was that it was due to the Canal towns being empty after the evacuation,[5] another attributed it to the negative aspects of the High Dam,[6] others blamed it on the system of government, while many saw in it God's wrath at His servants for their refusal to accept His guidance. We expended laudable[7] efforts in making rational preparations, about which no one was negligent. At a further meeting held at his home, the estimable[8] Mr. A.M., may God preserve him, said, "I am happy with the preventive measures you have taken, and I am pleased to see the entrance to our building swarming with cats. Certainly there are those who complain about the expense of feeding them, but this is of little importance when we think of our safety and security." He scrutinized our faces with satisfaction, then asked, "What news of the traps?"

One of us (an eminent[9] educator) answered. "I caught a skinny specimen—one of our local rats."

---

3. **wrought** (rôt) *v.:* made; formed.

4. **harbinger** (här′bin·jər) *n.:* something that foreshadows a future event.

5. **Canal towns . . . evacuation:** Suez Canal towns were evacuated during the Arab-Israeli wars of 1967 and 1973.

6. **High Dam:** rock-fill dam, finished in 1970, at Aswan, Egypt; erected to regulate Nile floodwaters.

7. **laudable** (lôd′ə·bəl) *adj.:* praiseworthy.

8. **estimable** (es′tə·mə·bəl) *adj.:* worthy of respect or esteem.

9. **eminent** (em′ə·nənt) *adj.:* distinguished; noteworthy.

Vocabulary

meticulously (mə·tik′yo͞o·ləs·lē) *adv.:* very carefully.
predominated (prē·däm′ə·nāt′id) *v.:* took control.
proliferation (prō·lif′ə·rā′shən) *n.:* rapid spread.

"Whatever a rat's identity, it's still harmful. Anyway, today I must inform you of the necessity, with the enemy at our gates, for being even more on your guard. Quantities of the new poison ground up in corn will be distributed to us. It is to be placed in vulnerable places such as the kitchen, though extreme care should be taken to protect children, poultry, and pets."

Everything happened just as the man said, and we told ourselves that we were truly not alone in the battle. Gratitude welled up in us for our solicitous[10] neighbor and our revered Governor. Certainly all this had required of us a lot of care on top of our daily worries. And unavoidable mistakes did occur. Thus a cat was killed in one home and a number of chickens in another, but there were no losses in terms of human life. As time went on we became more and more tense and alert, and the suspense weighed heavily on us. We told ourselves that the happening of a calamity was preferable to the waiting for it. Then, one day, I met a neighbor at the bus stop, and he said, "I heard from a reliable source the rats have <u>annihilated</u> an entire village."

"There was not a thing about this in the papers!"

He gave me a scornful look and said nothing. I imagined the earth heaving with hordes of rats as far as the eye could see and crowds of refugees wandering aimlessly in the desert. Good God, could such a thing come about? But what was so impossible about it? Had not God previously sent the Flood and the flocks of birds as mentioned in the Koran?[11] Would people tomorrow cease their daily struggle and throw all they possessed into the raging fires of battle? And would they be victorious, or would this spell the end?

At the third meeting, Mr. A.M. appeared in cheerful mood. "Congratulations, gentlemen," he said. "We are as active as can be. The losses are slight and will not, one hopes, recur. We shall become experts in matters of fighting rats, and

perhaps we shall be called upon in the future in other places. His Excellency the Governor is extremely happy."

One of our number began to complain. "The fact is that our nerves—."

But he was cut short by Mr. A.M. "Our nerves? Do you want to spoil our success with a thoughtless word?"

"When will the rats begin their attack?"

"No one can give a definite answer to that, and it is of no consequence so long as we are prepared for the battle." Then, after a pause, he continued. "Latest instructions are of special importance, relating as they do to windows, doors, and any apertures[12] in walls or elsewhere. Close all doors and windows and examine in particular the lower part of any door. If any space is found through which a mere straw could pass, seal it up completely with wooden planks. When doing the morning cleaning, the windows of one room should be opened, and while one person sweeps, another, armed with a stick, should stand at the ready. Then you should close the windows and move to the next room, where the same procedure should be followed. On finishing the cleaning, the flat should be left like a firmly closed box, whatever the weather."

We exchanged looks in glum[13] silence.

"It's impossible to go on like that," said a voice.

"No, you must maintain the utmost precision in carrying out . . ."

"Even in a prison cell there's . . ."

"We are at war, that is to say in a state of emergency. We are threatened not only with destruction but also with epidemics—God spare us. We must reckon with that."

We went on submissively carrying out what we had been ordered to do. We became more deeply submerged in a morass[14] of anticipation

_____

12. **apertures** (ap'ər·chərz) *n. pl.*: openings; gaps.
13. **glum** *adj.*: gloomy.
14. **morass** (mə·ras') *n.*: marsh or swamp; here, used figuratively for a difficult or perplexing situation.

_____

Vocabulary

annihilated (ə·nī'ə·lāt'id) *v.*: destroyed completely.

_____

10. **solicitous** (sə·lis'ə·təs) *adj.*: showing care or concern.
11. **Flood . . . Koran:** Suras 11:25–48 and 105:1–5; the flocks of birds dropped clay fragments on invading troops riding elephants.

and wariness, with the boredom and depression that accompany them. The nervous tension increased and was translated into sharp daily quarrels between the man of the house and his wife and children. We continued to follow the news, while the Norwegian rat, with its huge body, long whiskers, and alarming glassy look, became a star of evil that roamed in our imagi-nations and dreams and occupied the major part of our conversation.

At the last meeting, Mr. A.M. had said, "I've got some good news—a team of experts has been assigned to the task of checking the buildings, flats and locations exposed to risk, and all without any demand for additional rates."

It was indeed good news, and we received it

with universal delight, the hope being that we would be able to relieve ourselves of some of the distress we had been suffering. Then one day the concierge[15] informed us that a bureaucrat had inspected the entrance to the building, the stairwell, the roof, and the garage, and had pronounced favorably on the large bands of cats roaming about here and there. He had instructed the concierge to be extra vigilant and to inform him of any rat that might make its appearance, be it Norwegian or Egyptian.

One week after the meeting, the doorbell of our flat rang and the concierge gave us the good news that the bureaucrat was on his way and wished to have permission to make an inspection. The time was not convenient, because my wife had just finished preparing lunch, but I nevertheless hurried out to greet him. I found myself standing before a middle-aged, sturdily built man with a thick mustache, his square face with its short snub nose and glassy stare reminding me of a cat. I greeted him, concealing a smile that almost transformed itself into a laugh, and told myself that they really did have a flair for choosing their men. I walked ahead of him, and he proceeded to examine the traps and poisons, the windows and doors, nodding his head in approval. He did, however, find in the kitchen a small window covered over with a wire mesh of tiny holes, at which he said firmly, "Close the window."

My wife was on the point of protesting, but he snapped at her. "The Norwegian rat can gnaw through wire."

Satisfied that his order had been carried out, he sniffed at the smell of food, thus proclaiming his commendation.[16] I therefore invited him to eat. "Only a mean man refuses generosity," he answered simply.

Immediately we prepared a table for him alone, telling him that we had already eaten. He sat down as though in his own home and began gobbling up the food without any restraint or shyness—and with quite extraordinary voracity. Out of politeness, we left him to it. However, after a while I thought it best to check on him in case he might be in need of something. I gave him another helping, and while doing so I became aware of a dramatic change in his appearance. It seemed that his face reminded me no longer of a cat but of a rat, in fact of the Norwegian rat itself. I returned to my wife with my head spinning. I did not tell her what I had noticed but asked her to be pleasant to him and make him welcome. She was away for a minute or two, then returned, pallid,[17] and stared at me in stupefaction. "Did you see what he looks like when he eats?" she breathed.

I nodded, and she whispered, "It's quite amazing, unbelievable."

I indicated my agreement with a movement of my spinning head. It seems that our utter astonishment caused us to forget the passage of time, and we only came to when we heard his voice from the hallway calling joyfully, "May your house ever prosper!"

We rushed out, but he had reached the front door before us and had gone. All we glimpsed of him was his swaying back, then a swift about-face as he bade us farewell with a fleeting Norwegian smile. We stood behind the closed door looking at each other in bewilderment.

---

15. **concierge** (kän′sē·erzh′) *n.*: doorkeeper or custodian of an apartment building.
16. **commendation** (käm′ən·dā′shən) *n.*: approval; praise.

---

17. **pallid** (pal′id) *adj.*: pale.

Vocabulary

voracity (vô·ras′ə·tē) *n.*: gluttony, especially in eating.

Response and Analysis

Reading Check

1. How do the people prepare for the rat invasion?

2. Who inspects the narrator's home? Describe the way the narrator and his wife perceive this person at first. How does their perception change by the end of the story?

Thinking Critically

3. What sources of information about the rats do people in the story have access to? How reliable do you think these sources are? Explain.

4. What happens to people's emotions as preparations continue and the rat attack still has not occurred? Do you think there is psychological truth in the way Mahfouz presents his characters' reactions? Explain.

5. What conclusion(s) can you draw about the rat invasion? Do you think there really is an imminent invasion, or is something else happening? Explain, using specific details from the story.

6. **Ambiguity** abounds in the final scenes with the bureaucrat. Are the narrator and his wife under so much stress that they hallucinate? Or does the story suddenly move into the realm of **magic realism,** where realistic details are combined with incredible events? Are there any other possible explanations? Explain your opinion.

Extending and Evaluating

7. What does the government accomplish by having the people concentrate exclusively on an imminent rat invasion? What might the author be suggesting about the ways some countries' governments control and manipulate their citizens?

WRITING

Analyzing Allegory

An **allegory** is a story in which the characters, settings, and events stand for things beyond themselves, usually abstract or moral concepts. "The Norwegian Rat" can be read on a literal level, but it can also be interpreted symbolically. In a brief essay, explain what the story could represent on an allegorical level. What might the threatened invasion of the rats and the government's warnings to its citizens stand for? Use evidence from the story to back up your points.

North Carolina Competency Goal
1.03; 4.05; 5.03; 6.01

Vocabulary Development
What's the Difference?

Answer each question below on a separate sheet of paper. Underlined words are Vocabulary words.

1. What's the difference between *saying* and *reiterating*?

2. How is *meticulously* different from *carefully*?

3. What's the difference between *predominated* and *yielded*?

4. How does *proliferation* differ from *stagnation*?

5. What's the difference between *annihilated* and *survived*?

6. How do *voracity* and *restraint* differ?

---

go.hrw.com

INTERNET

Projects and Activities

Keyword: LE5 WL-7

SKILLS FOCUS

Literary Skills
Analyze ambiguity.

Reading Skills
Draw conclusions.

Writing Skills
Analyze allegory.

Vocabulary Skills
Answer questions about vocabulary words.

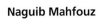

Yehuda Amichai
(1924–2000)
Israel

Like many Israelis of his generation, Yehuda Amichai (yə·hoo'də ä'mi·khī') spent much of his life as a soldier. During World War II he served in the Jewish brigade of the British army fighting against German forces in the Middle East. In 1948, after the state of Israel was formed and was attacked by neighboring Arab nations, Amichai fought with the special strike force of the Israeli army. Later, as an army reservist, he was often called upon to fight for his country.

Born to an orthodox Jewish family in southern Germany, Amichai escaped Nazi persecution when he was twelve years old. Like many other European Jews lucky enough to escape, Amichai and his family immigrated to British-controlled Palestine. They eventually settled in the city of Jerusalem, where the young Amichai continued his studies of Hebrew literature and the Bible. After serving as a soldier in the 1940s, Amichai completed his studies at Jerusalem's Hebrew University. By then he had already published several Hebrew-language poems in magazines, although his first poetry collection, *Now and in Other Days,* did not appear until 1955.

In addition to writing poems, novels, short stories, and plays, Amichai taught Hebrew literature both in Israel and abroad. Hebrew was not his first language; Amichai began learning it in Germany during his childhood religious studies, since ancient Hebrew is the language of Jewish scripture and ritual. Amichai won acclaim as one of the first Israeli writers to successfully combine Hebrew as it is spoken today with the rich cadences of ancient Hebrew. His characteristic style merges the informality of modern spoken Hebrew with the powerful poetic images found in the Hebrew Bible, or Old Testament.

At the heart of virtually all of Amichai's poetry is his concern with the effects that frequent warfare and a constant war-ready state have had on the Israeli consciousness.

from Laments on the War Dead

Make the Connection

Quickwrite ✏️

Conflicts in the Middle East, especially between the Israelis and the Palestinians, have gone on for decades. What effects do you think long-term conflicts between cultures or nations have on people? Can deeply entrenched conflicts ever be successfully resolved? Write your ideas.

Literary Focus

Repetition

Poets often use **repetition** to create rhythm, build suspense, or emphasize a particular word or idea. In **incremental repetition** a line or section of a poem or song is repeated with some variation in wording. Usually the variation adds important new information or expresses a significant change in meaning or attitude.

> **Repetition** is the repeating of a sound, word, phrase, line, or idea to create a musical or rhythmic effect, build suspense, or add emphasis.
>
> *For more on Repetition, see the Handbook of Literary and Historical Terms.*

Background

Driven by centuries of severe persecution and by a historical attachment to the land of Palestine, European Jews formed the Zionist movement in the late 1800s. The movement sought to establish a state where Jews could live free of oppression. Arabs had been Palestine's chief inhabitants for several centuries, but soon more and more Jews began settling in the area. In 1947, in the wake of world horror at the Holocaust, the United Nations voted to partition Palestine into a Jewish state and an Arab state. The plan proceeded, but on May 15, 1948, one day after the Jewish state of Israel came into being, neighboring Arab countries attacked it in the first of several Arab-Israeli wars.

Yehuda Amichai wrote his poetic sequence *Laments on the War Dead* soon after the Arab-Israeli war of 1973, when Egypt and Syria attacked Israel. Israel won the war, but at great cost, both economically and in terms of human lives.

The Damascus Gate in the Old City. Jerusalem. October 25, 2000.

North Carolina Competency Goal
1.02; 1.03; 4.05; 5.01; 5.03; 6.01

Literary Skills
Understand repetition.

Yehuda Amichai   **1039**

from Laments on the War Dead

Yehuda Amichai

translated by **Warren Bargad**
and **Stanley F. Chyet**

6

Is all this sorrow? I don't know.
I stood in the cemetery dressed
in the camouflage clothing of a live man, brown
pants and a shirt yellow as the sun.

5 Graveyards are cheap and unassuming.
Even the wastebaskets are too small to hold
the thin paper that wrapped the store-bought flowers.
Graveyards are disciplined, mannered things.
"I'll never forget you," reads
10 a small brick tablet in French.°
I don't know who it is who won't forget,
who's more unknown than the one who's dead.

Is all this sorrow? I think
so. "Be consoled in building the land." How
15 long can we build the land,
to gain in the terrible, three-sided
game of building, consolation, and death?
Yes, all this is sorrow. But
leave a little love always lit,
20 like the nightlight in a sleeping infant's room,
not that he knows what light is
and where it comes from, but it gives him
a bit of security and some silent love.

10. in French: Although Hebrew is Israel's chief language, an immigrant from Europe or elsewhere might also continue to use his or her first language, especially on a tombstone.

Response and Analysis

Thinking Critically

1. What two statements does the speaker make about graveyards in lines 5–8? What does the inscription on the small brick tablet prompt the speaker to wonder in lines 9–12?

2. What is the speaker's first answer to the opening question? How has his answer changed by lines 13–14? In what line of the poem does he arrive at his final answer?

3. Describe how the poet's use of **incremental repetition** helps to trace the development of the speaker's answer to the poem's opening question.

4. Identify another example of **incremental repetition** in the poem. What effect do the slight variations in wording, typical of incremental repetition, have on the meaning of the poem? Would the effect be the same if the words or phrases that recur were simply repeated word for word? Explain.

5. Whom might the speaker be quoting in line 14? What might the speaker's question in lines 14–17 reveal about modern Israeli experience?

6. Whom might the speaker be addressing in his request in lines 18–19? (Who should "leave a little love always lit"?)

7. Lines 18–23 present an **extended simile**—a comparison that is developed over several lines of a work. In your own words, state the comparison that is being made. How does this comparison help to bring an abstract concept down to earth? What advice might this comparison be giving to Israelis or war victims in general?

8. What would you say is the **theme** of this poem? In what part of the poem is the theme most directly expressed?

Extending and Evaluating

9. Would you say this poem ends on a positive or a negative note? Did your ideas about the resolution of long-standing conflicts change in any way after you read Amichai's poem? Take a look at what you wrote for your Quickwrite response.

WRITING

Writing an Elegy

Amichai's poem, which is part of a larger poetic sequence, can be viewed as an **elegy**—a poem of mourning or lament. Write an elegy in which you honor the memory of the victims of a war, natural disaster, crime, or other tragedy. In your poem, address the needs and feelings of survivors, as Amichai's poem does, and try to point to some possibility for renewal and healing.

Following (1998) by Michal Rovner.

Vénus Khoury-Ghata

(1937–   )
Lebanon

There's a story behind the unusual first name of Lebanese writer Vénus Khoury-Ghata. The name originally chosen for her was Dianne—"like Diana, the goddess from Greek mythology"—but when a neighbor announced that his new dog's name was also Dianne, Khoury-Ghata's mother decided to name her daughter after the Roman goddess of love and beauty, Venus. "I liked the name when I lived in Lebanon and was young and beautiful," Khoury-Ghata says. "But for some years now I hate my name. I see myself in old age, and with this name. . . . I'm a writer, and I lead a very austere life, and the name doesn't fit."

Khoury-Ghata began writing poetry in French when she was fifteen. Since then she has written many books of poetry and novels and has won several distinguished prizes for her work. She has also translated much contemporary Arabic poetry into French. "I lead a double life," she says. "One day I'll write a book revealing the life I lead in the light of day with the French language and my clandestine life with Arabic."

This double life began in her childhood. Khoury-Ghata was born in Lebanon near Beirut to middle-class Catholic parents who spoke mostly French. Her life in the city was one of harsh discipline, for her military father beat her and punished all of the children if they spoke Arabic. In the summers, however, there was a reprieve as the family—without her father—moved to her mother's village, Pshery, in the mountains north of Lebanon. The village had a claim to fame: It had been the hometown of the famous poet, artist, and mystic Khalil Gibran (1883–1931), whose most famous work, *The Prophet* (1923), has been a world-wide bestseller for decades, selling over nine million copies in the United States alone. In Gibran's village, Khoury-Ghata and her siblings were free of their father's tyranny and spoke the Arabic of the peasants. Khoury-Ghata was happy, something she could never be in Beirut. "In all my books I go back to the memory of this village, all the sources of my imagination come from there. . . . Pshery is the place that opened the doors of imagination before me, the peasants, life in nature, the earth. In all my stories I describe very pleasant peasants, simple people, not rich people but people of nature."

In 1975, civil war broke out in Lebanon. Supporters of the Palestine Liberation Organization and their Muslim allies were pitted against the Lebanese Maronite Christians, who were supported by Israel. By this time, Khoury-Ghata was divorced from her first husband and living in France. The war, which exploded shortly after she left Lebanon, reunited her with her children, who were sent to Paris for safety when violence tore Lebanon apart. The war left at least 100,000 people dead and Lebanon's beautiful, sophisticated cities lay in ruins. The war also left a residue of bitterness that is still palpable in the region.

Today, Khoury-Ghata lives in Paris, surrounded by a large garden. She has put memories of Beirut completely behind her. "I took shelter behind a white page," she says, "while shells rained down on Beirut."

Before You Read

Make the Connection

Quickwrite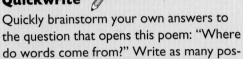

Quickly brainstorm your own answers to the question that opens this poem: "Where do words come from?" Write as many possibilities as you can think of, no matter how far-fetched or unusual they may seem.

Literary Focus

Figurative Language

Figurative language consists of words that are put together to make imaginative comparisons that express unexpected similarities between otherwise unrelated things. Although we expect to find figurative language in literature—especially poetry—it is used frequently in everyday speech, in such expressions as "Love is blind," "She's as grouchy as a bear," "We'll cross that bridge when we come to it." Such phrases demonstrate two key features of figurative language: It cannot be interpreted literally, and it helps us to grasp the meaning of one thing in terms of another thing that may be more familiar—or more emotionally and imaginatively suggestive—to us.

There are many kinds of figures of speech, but three are especially common. A **simile** compares two unlike things using a specific word such as *like* or *as:* "The road is *like* a ribbon of moonlight." A **metaphor** compares two unlike things without the use of a specific word of comparison—for example, "The road *is* a ribbon of moonlight." In **personification,** something nonhuman is spoken of as if it were human: "The moonlit road welcomed and reassured us."

Figurative language is language that is not literally true and that is always based on comparison. Three common figures of speech are simile, metaphor, and personification.

For more on Figurative Language, see the Handbook of Literary and Historical Terms.

Background

Khoury-Ghata constantly shifts back and forth between two languages in her mind: French and Arabic. French is Khoury-Ghata's language of choice in her daily life and work. But according to her translator Marilyn Hacker, the Arabic language, "like a distant lover or a lost country, becomes the subject of many of her poems."

The following verses come from a longer poem titled *Les Mots* (Words) in French. The poem creates a mythology that explains the origin of words—not just words from French or Arabic but words from all languages. In this poetic "creation myth," the poet imagines that words are made not only by people but also by the natural world itself—by pebbles, birds, water.

North Carolina Competency Goal
1.02; 1.03; 4.05; 5.01; 5.03; 6.01

INTERNET
More About Vénus Khoury-Ghata
Keyword: LE5 WL-7

Literary Skills
Understand figurative language.

Vénus Khoury-Ghata   **1043**

from Words

Vénus Khoury-Ghata

translated by **Marilyn Hacker**

Where do words come from?
from what rubbing of sounds are they born
on what flint do they light their wicks
what winds brought them into our mouths

5   Their past is the rustling of stifled silences
the trumpeting of molten elements
the grunting of stagnant waters

Sometimes
they grip each other with a cry
10   expand into lamentations
become mist on the windows of dead houses
crystallize into chips of grief on dead lips
attach themselves to a fallen star
dig their hole in nothingness
15   breathe out strayed souls

Words are rocky tears
the keys to the first doors
they grumble in caverns
lend their ruckus to storms
20   their silence to bread that's ovened alive

Response and Analysis

Thinking Critically

1. In lines 2–3, the speaker refers to "rubbing of sounds" and to "flint" and "wicks." What comparison does this **figurative language** suggest? (What are words being compared to?)

2. In line 6, sound and image are combined in a surprising way. This is an example of a descriptive technique called **synesthesia** (sin′əs·thē′zhə), in which an image that appeals to one sense, such as sight ("molten elements"), is conveyed in terms of an image that appeals to a different sense, such as sound ("trumpeting"). Where else do you see synesthesia in this stanza? What picture of the words' "past" do these images create in your mind?

3. According to the third stanza, what feelings and experiences can words express? Where do you see **personification** in this stanza, and what effect does it have on the stanza's meaning?

4. In the last stanza, the poet uses a series of **metaphors** to describe what words are and what they do. What does she compare words to? What is your interpretation of the final image: "bread that's ovened alive"?

Extending and Evaluating

5. Do you think Khoury-Ghata could have expressed the ideas in this poem without using so much figurative language, relying instead on other poetic elements, such as rhyme, repetition, or rhythm? How does the poet's use of figurative language support other literary elements in the poem, such as mood, tone, imagery, and theme? Explain why the use of figurative language might be especially appropriate and meaningful in a poem that is itself about words.

WRITING

Writing an Origin Myth

Write a brief imaginative narrative in verse or prose in which you explain the origin of words. For your narrative you will have to establish a time and place, characters, and a significant event that leads to the birth of words. Remember that myths often include transformations, or metamorphoses—marvelous changes of form. Be sure to refer to the ideas you brainstormed for your Quickwrite.

Comparing Poems

The poem that follows, by a Mexican poet, is also about words. In a brief essay, compare this poem to the excerpt from Khoury-Ghata's *Words*. Your essay should focus on two points of comparison: the figurative language used in each poem and how each poet seems to feel about the power of words.

> **The Word**
> comes out from the pen
> like a rabbit from a magician's hat
> astronaut who knows itself alone
> and weightless suspended on a line
> in space
> —Manuel Ulacia
> *translated by* Jennifer Clement

North Carolina Competency Goal
1.02; 1.03; 4.05; 6.01

SKILLS FOCUS

Literary Skills
Analyze figurative language.

Writing Skills
Write an origin myth. Compare poems.

Yasunari Kawabata

(1899–1972)

Japan

Yasunari Kawabata (yä´sōo·nä´rē kä´wä·bä´tä) was the first Japanese writer to win a Nobel Prize in literature. Primarily a novelist and short-story writer, Kawabata was deeply influenced by Japanese Buddhist scriptures and by the art and poetry of the Heian era (A.D. 794–1145). In his literary work he strove to achieve the same purity, delicacy, and suggestiveness that characterize the classic works of this period.

Kawabata's fiction also reflects his personal experience, which was marked by tragic loss and persistent loneliness. His father died when the boy was only two years old. A year later his mother died, followed by his sister shortly after. The young orphan was sent to live with his maternal grandmother, who took care of him for only a short time before she too died. For the next nine years, Kawabata lived with his ailing grandfather, whom he nursed through his final illness. When his grandfather died, Kawabata was sixteen and alone in the world. He had been keeping a diary since he was fourteen (published in 1925), which recorded the harrowing experience of caring for the dying old man. It is not hard to understand why themes of loneliness and death pervade Kawabata's work and why writing seemed to provide him with his most enduring solace.

Kawabata attended the Imperial University in Tokyo, where he studied English and Japanese literature. While at the university, he became involved with other young writers in a new literary movement called Neosensualism. Striving to capture pure feeling and the immediacy of a moment, these writers experimented with techniques derived from cubism, surrealism, and other European art movements; later, they adopted some of the techniques of Imagism, a Western poetic movement that was inspired by classical haiku. Kawabata developed a unique style that is hard to characterize in terms of either Eastern or Western models. The translator Edward Seidensticker says of Kawabata that "his best writing is episodic and wanting in grand climaxes, a stringing together of tiny lyrical episodes. . . . The linking, the relation of episode to preceding and following episode, is more important than the overall form."

In novels like *The Izu Dancer* (1926), *Snow Country* (1948), *Thousand Cranes* (1952), and *The House of the Sleeping Beauties* (1961), Kawabata depicts lonely men who seek comfort, even a kind of salvation, in the beauty of women. Sadly, however, these characters remain distanced from the objects of their idealization.

In 1972, alone in his studio, Kawabata took his own life, leaving no explanation for his action.

For Independent Reading

You may also enjoy the following stories by Kawabata:

- "The Silver Fifty-Sen Pieces"
- "The Grasshopper and the Bell Cricket"

The Jay

Make the Connection

Animal behavior often has a great deal to teach us. Think of some examples of how the behavior of animals can suggest the *best* aspects of human nature.

Literary Focus

Symbol and Theme

In literature, characters, animals, places, things, or events may function as **symbols**—that is, they stand not only for themselves but also for ideas that go beyond their literal meanings. For example, a horse in a story about a girl who is growing up may function both as a literal horse and as a symbol of the girl's growing independence and strength; a broken clock in a poem might symbolize the end of life. Because symbols suggest broader meanings, they are important clues to the **theme,** or central idea, of a work of fiction.

> A **symbol** is a person, a place, a thing, or an event that represents both itself and something beyond itself. The **theme** is the central idea of a literary work.
>
> *For more on Symbol and Theme, see the Handbook of Literary and Historical Terms.*

Reading Skills

Determining Meaning

To identify symbolic elements in a story, note prominent characters, settings, objects, and events, and look for words or images that are repeatedly associated with them. Do not expect symbols to be obvious or predictable, like a dove symbolizing peace or a snake symbolizing evil; writers often use unique, deeply personal symbols that can be interpreted only in the context of their work. Identifying and determining the meaning of symbols can help you uncover the theme of a story.

Background

Although best known for his novels, Kawabata also wrote as many as 146 of what he called *tanagokoro no shosetsu,* or "palm-of-the-hand stories." In their brevity and deceptive simplicity, these little stories recall the compactness of haiku poetry (see pages 446–454). "Many writers, in their youth, write poetry," Kawabata said. "I, instead of poetry, wrote the palm-of-the-hand stories. . . . [T]he poetic spirit of my young days lives on in them."

North Carolina Competency Goal
1.03; 4.05; 5.01; 5.03

INTERNET

Vocabulary Practice
•
More About Yasunari Kawabata
Keyword: LE5 WL-7

Literary Skills
Understand symbol and theme.

Reading Skills
Determine meaning.

Vocabulary Development

furtively (fʉr′tiv·lē) *adv.*: secretly; in a sneaky way.

winsome (win′səm) *adj.*: charming; pleasing.

intransigence (in·tran′sə·jəns) *n.*: stubbornness; refusal to compromise.

assiduously (ə·sij′ōō·əs·lē) *adv.*: diligently; industriously; painstakingly.

plaintively (plān′tiv·lē) *adv.*: sadly; sorrowfully.

The Jay

Yasunari Kawabata

translated by
Lane Dunlop
and **J. Martin Holman**

Since daybreak, the jay had been singing noisily.

When they'd slid open the rain shutters, it had flown up before their eyes from a lower branch of the pine, but it seemed to have come back. During breakfast, there was the sound of whirring wings.

"That bird's a nuisance." The younger brother started to get to his feet.

"It's all right. It's all right." The grandmother stopped him. "It's looking for its child. Apparently the chick fell out of the nest yesterday. It was flying around until late in the evening. Doesn't she know where it is? But what a good mother. This morning she came right back to look."

"Grandmother understands well," Yoshiko said.

Her grandmother's eyes were bad. Aside from a bout with nephritis[1] about ten years ago,

she had never been ill in her life. But, because of her cataracts, which she'd had since girlhood, she could only see dimly out of her left eye. One had to hand her the rice bowl and the chopsticks. Although she could grope her way around the familiar interior of the house, she could not go into the garden by herself.

Sometimes, standing or sitting in front of the sliding-glass door, she would spread out her hands, fanning out her fingers against the sunlight that came through the glass, and gaze out. She was concentrating all the life that was left to her into that many-angled gaze.

At such times, Yoshiko was frightened by her grandmother. Though she wanted to call out to her from behind, she would <u>furtively</u> steal away.

---

1. **nephritis** (nə·frīt′əs) *n.:* swelling of the kidneys.

Vocabulary

furtively (fʉr′tiv·lē) *adv.:* secretly; in a sneaky way.

This nearly blind grandmother, simply from having heard the jay's voice, spoke as if she had seen everything. Yoshiko was filled with wonder.

When, clearing away the breakfast things, Yoshiko went into the kitchen, the jay was singing from the roof of the neighbor's house.

In the back garden, there was a chestnut tree and two or three persimmon trees. When she looked at the trees, she saw that a light rain was falling. It was the sort of rain that you could not tell was falling unless you saw it against the dense foliage.

The jay, shifting its perch to the chestnut tree, then flying low and skimming the ground, returned again to its branch, singing all the while.

The mother bird could not fly away. Was it because her chick was somewhere around there?

Worrying about it, Yoshiko went to her room. She had to get herself ready before the morning was over.

In the afternoon, her father and mother were coming with the mother of Yoshiko's fiancé.

Sitting at her mirror, Yoshiko glanced at the white stars under her fingernails. It was said that, when stars came out under your nails, it was a sign that you would receive something, but Yoshiko remembered having read in the newspaper that it meant a deficiency of vitamin C or something. The job of putting on her makeup went fairly pleasantly. Her eyebrows and lips all became unbearably <u>winsome</u>. Her kimono,[2] too, went on easily.

She'd thought of waiting for her mother to come and help with her clothes, but it was better to dress by herself, she decided.

Her father lived away from them. This was her second mother.

When her father had divorced her first mother, Yoshiko had been four and her younger brother two. The reasons given for the divorce were that her mother went around dressed in flashy clothes and spent money wildly, but Yoshiko sensed dimly that it was more than that, that the real cause lay deeper down.

Her brother, as a child, had come across a photograph of their mother and shown it to their father. The father hadn't said anything but, with a face of terrible anger, had suddenly torn the photograph to bits.

When Yoshiko was thirteen, she had welcomed the new mother to the house. Later, Yoshiko had come to think that her father had endured his loneliness for ten years for her sake. The second mother was a good person. A peaceful home life continued.

When the younger brother, entering upper school, began living away from home in a dormitory, his attitude toward his stepmother changed noticeably.

"Elder sister, I've met our mother. She's married and lives in Azabu. She's really beautiful. She was happy to see me."

Hearing this suddenly, Yoshiko could not say a word. Her face paled, and she began to tremble.

From the next room, her stepmother came in and sat down.

"It's a good thing, a good thing. It's not bad to meet your own mother. It's only natural. I've known for some time that this day would come. I don't think anything particular of it."

But the strength seemed to have gone out of her stepmother's body. To Yoshiko, her emaciated stepmother seemed pathetically frail and small.

Her brother abruptly got up and left. Yoshiko felt like smacking him.

"Yoshiko, don't say anything to him. Speaking to him will only make that boy go bad." Her stepmother spoke in a low voice.

Tears came to Yoshiko's eyes.

Her father summoned her brother back home from the dormitory. Although Yoshiko had thought that would settle the matter, her father had then gone off to live elsewhere with her stepmother.

It had frightened Yoshiko. It was as if she had been crushed by the power of masculine indignation and resentment. Did their father

---

2. **kimono** (kə·mōʹnə) *n.:* long, loose-fitting traditional Japanese robe with wide sleeves.

Vocabulary

winsome (winʹsəm) *adj.:* charming; pleasing.

When her father said this kind of thing to her, Yoshiko wept.

If Yoshiko married, there would be no woman's hand to take care of her brother and grandmother. It had been decided that the two households would become one. With that, Yoshiko had made up her mind. She had dreaded marriage on her father's account, but, when it came down to the actual talks, it was not that dreadful after all.

When her preparations were completed, Yoshiko went to her grandmother's room.

"Grandmother, can you see the red in this kimono?"

"I can faintly make out some red over there. Which is it, now?" Pulling Yoshiko to her, the grandmother put her eyes close to the kimono and the sash.

"I've already forgotten your face, Yoshiko. I wish I could see what you look like now."

Yoshiko stifled a desire to giggle. She rested her hand lightly on her grandmother's head.

Wanting to go out and meet her father and the others, Yoshiko was unable just to sit there, vaguely waiting. She went out into the garden. She held out her hand, palm upward, but the rain was so fine that it didn't wet the palm. Gathering up the skirts of her kimono, Yoshiko assiduously searched among the little trees and in the bear-grass bamboo thicket. And there, in the tall grass under the bush clover, was the baby bird.

Her heart beating fast, Yoshiko crept nearer. The baby jay, drawing its head into its neck feathers, did not stir. It was easy to take it up into her hand. It seemed to have lost its energy. Yoshiko looked around her, but the mother bird was nowhere in sight.

Running into the house, Yoshiko called out, "Grandmother! I've found the baby bird. I have it in my hand. It's very weak."

dislike even them because of their tie to their first mother? It seemed to her that her brother, who'd gotten to his feet so abruptly, had inherited the frightening male intransigence of his father.

And yet it also seemed to Yoshiko that she could now understand her father's sadness and pain during those ten years between his divorce and remarriage.

And so, when her father, who had moved away from her, came back bringing a marriage proposal, Yoshiko had been surprised.

"I've caused you a great deal of trouble. I told the young man's mother that you're a girl with these circumstances and that, rather than treating you like a bride, she should try to bring back the happy days of your childhood."

Vocabulary

intransigence (in·tran′sə·jəns) *n.*: stubbornness; refusal to compromise.

assiduously (ə·sij′o͞o·əs·lē) *adv.*: diligently; industriously; painstakingly.

"Oh, is that so? Try giving it some water."

Her grandmother was calm.

When she ladled some water into a rice bowl and dipped the baby jay's beak in it, it drank, its little throat swelling out in an appealing way. Then—had it recovered?—it sang out, "Ki-ki-ki, Ki-ki-ki . . ."

The mother bird, evidently hearing its cry, came flying. Perching on the telephone wire, it sang. The baby bird, struggling in Yoshiko's hand, sang out again, "Ki-ki-ki . . ."

"Ah, how good that she came! Give it back to its mother, quick," her grandmother said.

Yoshiko went back out into the garden. The mother bird flew up from the telephone wire but kept her distance, looking fixedly toward Yoshiko from the top of a cherry tree.

As if to show her the baby jay in her palm, Yoshiko raised her hand, then quietly placed the chick on the ground.

As Yoshiko watched from behind the glass door, the mother bird, guided by the voice of its child singing <u>plaintively</u> and looking up at the sky, gradually came closer. When she'd come down to the low branch of a nearby pine, the chick flapped its wings, trying to fly up to her. Stumbling forward in its efforts, falling all over itself, it kept singing.

Still the mother bird cautiously held off from hopping down to the ground.

Soon, however, it flew in a straight line to the side of its child. The chick's joy was boundless. Turning and turning its head, its outspread wings trembling, it made up to its mother. Evidently the mother had brought it something to eat.

Yoshiko wished that her father and step-mother would come soon. She would like to show them this, she thought.

Vocabulary

plaintively (plān′tiv·lē) *adv.:* sadly; sorrowfully.

Bird on Branch (1916) by Watanabe Seitei.

Arthur M. Sackler Gallery, Smithsonian Institution, Washington, D.C.: Bequest of Robert O. Muller Collection (S2003.8.3270).

Response and Analysis

Reading Check

1. With whom does Yoshiko live?

2. What do you learn about the history of Yoshiko's family?

3. Why is the jay in the yard flying around and singing?

4. Why is Yoshiko sometimes "filled with wonder" around her grandmother?

5. What is Yoshiko preparing to do at the beginning of the story?

Thinking Critically

6. What can you infer about Yoshiko's father's feelings toward his first wife? How do these feelings extend to his relationship with his children?

7. How does Yoshiko react when her brother announces that he has met their mother? Why do you think she reacts this way?

8. How has Yoshiko's father proposed to make it up to her for the "trouble" he has caused her? How does she reconcile herself to her father's plan?

9. Yoshiko feels as though she has "been crushed by the power of masculine indignation and resentment." What does this statement mean? How is the way the women in this story—such as Yoshiko and her grandmother—relate to one another different from the way the men relate to each other?

10. Describe Yoshiko's emotions when she finds and tries to return the baby bird. What larger idea do you think the jay—and its reunion with its baby—**symbolizes**? How does this symbolism help you determine the **theme**, or overall meaning, of the story?

WRITING

Evaluating a Symbol

In a brief essay, evaluate the use of the jay as a **symbol** in Kawabata's story. Consider how the details and language used to describe the bird suggest broader ideas about human beings and human relationships. In your essay, be sure to address these questions: Why does Yoshiko wish she could show her father and stepmother the baby jay reuniting with its mother? How does Kawabata use the jay and its actions to make a comment about Yoshiko's family life?

Vocabulary Development
Complete the Meaning

furtively   assiduously

winsome   plaintively

intransigence

Fill in the blanks with the correct Vocabulary word from the list above.

1. The accused man showed his _____ by refusing to admit his guilt.

2. The stray cat _____ approached the treat we offered.

3. We worked _____ to complete the project on time.

4. The lost child wailed _____ in the last aisle of the supermarket.

5. My niece looked _____ in her old-fashioned velvet dress.

North Carolina Competency Goal
1.03; 4.05; 5.03; 6.01

INTERNET

Projects and Activities
Keyword:
LE5 WL-7

SKILLS FOCUS

Literary Skills
Analyze symbol and theme.

Reading Skills
Determine meaning.

Writing Skills
Evaluate a symbol.

Vocabulary Skills
Complete sentences with vocabulary words.

R. K. Narayan
(1906–2001)
India

In a life that spanned nearly the entire twentieth century, R. K. Narayan (nə·rī′ən) became India's best known and most internationally successful writer, introducing countless readers to Indian life while showing how similar human concerns are throughout the world.

Narayan was born in Madras and raised primarily by his grandmother, a strong woman steeped in the traditional lore of India—from healing remedies and horoscope readings to folk tales and domestic wisdom. In 1930, he graduated from Maharajah College in Mysore in southern India and worked briefly as a schoolteacher before embarking on a career as a full-time writer. Narayan used his experiences as a teacher as the basis for his first novel, *Swami and Friends* (1935), which was recommended to a publisher by his friend, the English writer Graham Greene.

Swami and Friends is also notable because it introduces readers to the imaginary town of Malgudi. Based on his hometown of Madras and also on Mysore, Narayan frequently sets his fiction in this town. Malgudi is a microcosm of India, containing all the various kinds of people, concerns, work, and conflicts found in any Indian city. Because Narayan returned repeatedly to his fictional village, many critics have compared him with the American writer William Faulkner, who returned again and again to his fictional Yoknapatawpha County. Both writers use the citizens of these fictional places to explore the complexities of the human condition.

Narayan had a long and productive career, publishing dozens of novels and hundreds of short stories. His curiosity about the lives of ordinary people, combined with his sense of the universality of human experience, resulted in fictional works that lovingly examine the intricacies of human relationships. In addition, he wrote travel books, collections of essays, and a memoir. He also published shortened prose versions of the classic Indian epics the *Ramayana* and the *Mahabharata*.

Narayan has proved to be as popular as he was prolific. His writing has been translated into every European language and into Hebrew as well. He was made an honorary member of the American Academy of Arts and Letters, and he received the Padma Bhushan, an award given in India for distinguished service to literature. Narayan died on May 13, 2001, in his home country of India.

For Independent Reading

You may also enjoy the following story by Narayan:
- "Like the Sun"

An Astrologer's Day

Make the Connection

A chance meeting, a careless choice, an unexpected delay—events like these can become golden opportunities, or they can lead to disaster. The outcomes of such occurrences often depend on how you react to them. Think about a time when you made the best of a coincidence and another time when you bungled an opportunity. How did each experience turn out? Why?

North Carolina Competency Goal

1.03; 4.02; 4.05; 5.01; 5.03

Literary Focus

Irony

Irony is a discrepancy between expectation and reality—between what appears to be true and what is actually true. **Situational irony** occurs when something happens that is the opposite of what is expected or appropriate. Often stories with surprise endings have an ironic twist. As you read this story, look for details in the astrologer's behavior that foreshadow the story's surprising—and ironic—ending.

INTERNET

Vocabulary Practice
•
More About R. K. Narayan

Keyword: LE5 WL-7

> **Irony** is the contrast between expectation and reality.
>
> *For more on Irony, see the Handbook of Literary and Historical Terms.*

Reading Skills

Making and Modifying Predictions

In a tense, suspenseful story such as this one, the writer works hard to make the events unpredictable. However, Narayan scatters clues throughout "An Astrologer's Day" that help explain the reasons behind the story's events. When you come across what appears to be a clue, jot down a prediction about what you think will happen. As you continue to read, modify your predictions based on what new clues tell you.

SKILLS FOCUS

Literary Skills
Understand irony.

Reading Skills
Make and modify predictions.

Background

The protagonist of this story practices Vedic astrology, also known as *Jyotish*, or the "Science of Light." Vedic astrology, an ancient art, is considered part of the Vedangas (scriptures) of the Hindu religion. A combination of ancient mathematics, astronomy, and spiritual beliefs, Vedic astrology is traditionally thought to have begun with Parashara Muni, a man who lived around 1500 B.C. Like its Western and Chinese counterparts, Vedic astrology is a form of divination—the practice of foretelling future events. This method of revealing truths about a person's character, health, and future by studying a horoscope—the positions of the stars and planets at the time of a person's birth—has flourished in India for several thousand years. Even today, Vedic astrologers are consulted to set dates for important events and to determine the compatibility of marriage partners.

Vocabulary Development

vociferousness (vō·sif′ər·əs·nəs) *n.*: loudness; noisiness.

municipal (myoo·nis′ə·pəl) *adj.*: of local government.

impetuous (im·pech′oo·əs) *adj.*: impulsive; forceful.

paraphernalia (par′ə·fər·nāl′yə) *n. pl.*: accessories; equipment.

piqued (pēkd) *v.* used as *adj.*: angry or irritated.

An Astrologer's Day

R. K. Narayan

Punctually at midday he opened his bag and spread out his professional equipment, which consisted of a dozen cowrie shells,[1] a square piece of cloth with obscure mystic charts on it, a notebook, and a bundle of palmyra[2] writing. His forehead was resplendent with sacred ash and vermilion,[3] and his eyes sparkled with a sharp, abnormal gleam which was really an outcome of a continual searching look for customers, but which his simple clients took to be a prophetic light and felt comforted. The power of his eyes was considerably enhanced by their position— placed as they were between the painted forehead and the dark whiskers which streamed down his

---

1. **cowrie** (kou′rē) **shells** *n. pl.*: smooth, brightly colored seashells; once known for their monetary value in regions of Africa and Asia.
2. **palmyra** (pal·mī′rə) *n.* used as *adj.*: A palmyra is a palm that grows in India. Strips from the leaves were used as writing materials by ancient Hindu scholars.

---

3. **sacred ash and vermilion** (vər·mil′yən): Ash and vermilion, a bright-red pigment, are religious markings that symbolize devotion to Hindu gods; also used in rituals.

cheeks: even a half-wit's eyes would sparkle in such a setting. To crown the effect he wound a saffron-colored[4] turban around his head. This color scheme never failed. People were attracted to him as bees are attracted to cosmos or dahlia stalks.[5] He sat under the boughs of a spreading tamarind tree[6] which flanked a path running through the town hall park. It was a remarkable place in many ways: a surging crowd was always moving up and down this narrow road morning till night. A variety of trades and occupations was represented all along its way: medicine sellers, sellers of stolen hardware and junk, magicians, and, above all, an auctioneer of cheap cloth, who created enough din all day to attract the whole town. Next to him in vociferousness came a vendor of fried groundnut,[7] who gave his ware a fancy name each day, calling it "Bombay Ice Cream" one day, and on the next "Delhi Almond," and on the third "Raja's Delicacy," and so on and so forth, and people flocked to him. A considerable portion of this crowd dallied before the astrologer too. The astrologer transacted his business by the light of a flare which crackled and smoked up above the groundnut heap nearby. Half the enchantment of the place was due to the fact that it did not have the benefit of municipal lighting. The place was lit up by shop lights. One or two had hissing gaslights, some had naked flares stuck on poles, some were lit up by old cycle lamps, and one or two, like the astrologer's, managed without lights of their own. It was a bewildering crisscross of light rays and moving shadows. This suited the astrologer very well, for the simple reason that he had not in the least intended to be an astrologer when he began life; and he knew no more of what was going to happen to others than he knew what was going to happen to himself next minute. He was as much a stranger to the stars as were his innocent customers. Yet he said things which pleased and astonished everyone: that was more a matter of study, practice, and shrewd guesswork. All the same, it was as much an honest man's labor as any other, and he deserved the wages he carried home at the end of a day.

He had left his village without any previous thought or plan. If he had continued there he would have carried on the work of his forefathers —namely, tilling the land, living, marrying, and ripening in his cornfield and ancestral home. But that was not to be. He had to leave home without telling anyone, and he could not rest till he left it behind a couple of hundred miles. To a villager it is a great deal, as if an ocean flowed between.

He had a working analysis of mankind's troubles: marriage, money, and the tangles of human ties. Long practice had sharpened his perception. Within five minutes he understood what was wrong. He charged three paise[8] per question, never opened his mouth till the other had spoken for at least ten minutes, which provided him enough stuff for a dozen answers and advices. When he told the person before him, gazing at his palm, "In many ways you are not getting the results for your efforts," nine out of ten were disposed to agree with him. Or he questioned: "Is there any woman in your family, maybe even a distant relative, who is not well disposed towards you?" Or he gave an analysis of character: "Most of your troubles are due to your nature. How can you be otherwise with Saturn[9] where he is? You have an impetuous nature and a rough exterior."

---

4. **saffron-colored** *adj.:* bright orange-yellow.
5. **cosmos or dahlia** (dal′yə) **stalks:** varieties of garden plants that produce bright flowers in autumn.
6. **tamarind tree:** tall, tropical tree having yellow flowers striped with red.
7. **groundnut** *n.:* type of plant with an edible root, such as the peanut.

8. **paise** (pī′se) *n. pl.:* plural form of *paisa,* a monetary unit equal to one hundredth of a rupee. The rupee is the basic monetary unit of India.
9. **Saturn:** In astrology the planet Saturn is believed to influence human behavior, causing a cold and melancholy disposition.

Vocabulary

vociferousness (vō·sif′ər·əs·nəs) *n.:* loudness; noisiness.
municipal (myo͞o·nis′ə·pəl) *adj.:* of local government.
impetuous (im·pech′o͞o·əs) *adj.:* impulsive; forceful.

Eastern Zodiac chart with illustrations and inscriptions
of signs in Sinhalese with English translations.

Victoria and Albert Museum, London.

R. K. Narayan   **1057**

Indian palm reader.

This endeared him to their hearts immediately, for even the mildest of us loves to think that he has a forbidding exterior.

The nuts vendor blew out his flare and rose to go home. This was a signal for the astrologer to bundle up too, since it left him in darkness except for a little shaft of green light which strayed in from somewhere and touched the ground before him. He picked up his cowrie shells and <u>paraphernalia</u> and was putting them back into his bag when the green shaft of light was blotted out; he looked up and saw a man standing before him. He sensed a possible client and said, "You look so careworn. It will do you good to sit down for a while and chat with me." The other grumbled some reply vaguely. The astrologer pressed his invitation; whereupon the other thrust his palm under his nose, saying, "You call yourself an astrologer?" The astrologer felt challenged and said, tilting the other's palm towards the green shaft of light, "Yours is a na-ture . . ." "Oh, stop that," the other said. "Tell me something worthwhile. . . ."

Our friend felt <u>piqued</u>. "I charge only three paise per question, and what you get ought to be good enough for your money. . . ." At this the other withdrew his arm, took out an anna,[10] and flung it out to him, saying, "I have some questions to ask. If I prove you are bluffing, you must return that anna to me with interest."

"If you find my answers satisfactory, will you give me five rupees?"

"No."

"Or will you give me eight annas?"

"All right, provided you give me twice as much if you are wrong," said the stranger. This pact was accepted after a little further argument. The astrologer sent up a prayer to heaven as the other lit a cheroot.[11] The astrologer caught a glimpse of his face by the match light. There was a pause as cars hooted on the road, jutka[12] drivers swore at

---

10. **anna** *n.:* Sixteen annas equal one rupee.
11. **cheroot** (shə·rōōt′) *n.:* type of cigar with both ends cut square.
12. **jutka** (jut′kä): Hindi (main language of India) for "two-wheeled carriage, hired out as a taxi."

Vocabulary

paraphernalia (par′ə·fər·nāl′yə) *n. pl.:* accessories; equipment.

piqued (pēkd) *v.* used as *adj.:* angry or irritated.

their horses, and the babble of the crowd agitated the semidarkness of the park. The other sat down, sucking his cheroot, puffing out, sat there ruthlessly. The astrologer felt very uncomfortable. "Here, take your anna back. I am not used to such challenges. It is late for me today. . . ." He made preparations to bundle up. The other held his wrist and said, "You can't get out of it now. You dragged me in while I was passing." The astrologer shivered in his grip; and his voice shook and became faint. "Leave me today. I will speak to you tomorrow." The other thrust his palm in his face and said, "Challenge is challenge. Go on." The astrologer proceeded with his throat drying up, "There is a woman . . ."

"Stop," said the other "I don't want all that. Shall I succeed in my present search or not? Answer this and go. Otherwise I will not let you go till you disgorge all your coins." The astrologer muttered a few incantations and replied, "All right. I will speak. But will you give me a rupee if what I say is convincing? Otherwise I will not open my mouth, and you may do what you like." After a good deal of haggling the other agreed. The astrologer said, "You were left for dead. Am I right?"

"Ah, tell me more."

"A knife has passed through you once?" said the astrologer.

"Good fellow!" He bared his chest to show the scar. "What else?"

"And then you were pushed into a well nearby in the field. You were left for dead."

"I should have been dead if some passerby had not chanced to peep into the well," exclaimed the other, overwhelmed by enthusiasm. "When shall I get at him?" he asked, clenching his fist.

"In the next world," answered the astrologer. "He died four months ago in a far-off town. You will never see any more of him." The other groaned on hearing it. The astrologer proceeded:

"Guru Nayak—"

"You know my name!" the other said, taken aback.

"As I know all other things. Guru Nayak, listen carefully to what I have to say. Your village is two days' journey due north of this town. Take the next train and be gone. I see once again great danger to your life if you go from home." He took out a pinch of sacred ash and held it to him. "Rub it on your forehead and go home. Never travel southward again, and you will live to be a hundred."

"Why should I leave home again?" the other said reflectively. "I was only going away now and then to look for him and to choke out his life if I met him." He shook his head regretfully. "He has escaped my hands. I hope at least he died as he deserved." "Yes," said the astrologer. "He was crushed under a lorry."[13] The other looked gratified to hear it.

The place was deserted by the time the astrologer picked up his articles and put them into his bag. The green shaft was also gone, leaving the place in darkness and silence. The stranger had gone off into the night, after giving the astrologer a handful of coins.

It was nearly midnight when the astrologer reached home. His wife was waiting for him at the door and demanded an explanation. He flung the coins at her and said, "Count them. One man gave all that."

"Twelve and a half annas," she said, counting. She was overjoyed. "I can buy some jaggery[14] and coconut tomorrow. The child has been asking for sweets for so many days now. I will prepare some nice stuff for her." "The swine has cheated me! He promised me a rupee," said the astrologer. She looked up at him. "You look worried. What is wrong?"

"Nothing."

After dinner, sitting on the *pyol*,[15] he told her, "Do you know a great load is gone from me today? I thought I had the blood of a man on my hands all these years. That was the reason why I ran away from home, settled here, and married you. He is alive."

She gasped. "You tried to kill!"

"Yes, in our village, when I was a silly youngster. We drank, gambled, and quarreled badly one day—why think of it now? Time to sleep," he said, yawning, and stretched himself on the *pyol*.

---

13. **lorry** (lôr′ē) n.: British for "truck."
14. **jaggery** (jag′ər·ē) n.: dark sugar made from the sap of certain palm trees.
15. *pyol* (pī′əl): Hindi for "mat used for sitting or sleeping."

Response and Analysis

Reading Check

1. Why has the astrologer chosen the spot under the tamarind tree to conduct business?

2. Summarize the types of advice the astrologer gives. Why is his advice taken by his customers?

3. What advice does the astrologer give to Guru Nayak?

Thinking Critically

4. Throughout the story, Narayan plants clues about secrets in the astrologer's past. What are these clues? What **predictions** did you make based on them? How did you modify your predictions as you came across later clues?

5. How does the astrologer use his knowledge of basic human psychology to tell people's fortunes? Base your response on specific examples of the astrologer's techniques described in the story.

6. When does the astrologer first glimpse the face of the stranger who appears at the end of the day? Why does the astrologer feel uncomfortable at this point? How does he reveal his discomfort?

7. Why does the astrologer first offer to give the man back his money and then press him for more money? Why is the astrologer's later statement that Guru Nayak cheated him **ironic**—that is, how is it different from what we expected?

8. Summarize the conflict that occurred between the astrologer and Guru Nayak when they were young men. What internal conflict do you think the astrologer is experiencing in this story?

Extending and Evaluating

9. Is the astrologer a clever hero or a devious trickster—or both? Explain.

Literary Criticism

10. Reviewer Shashi Tharoor concludes that even Narayan's best stories show little depth and "point to the banality of Mr. Narayan's concerns, the narrowness of his vision, the predictability of his prose, and the shallowness of the pool of experience and vocabulary from which he draws." Do you agree or disagree with this assessment, based on the story you've just read? Explain your position, using evidence from the story.

WRITING

Writing an Alternate Ending

Suppose that the astrologer had revealed his true identity as soon as he recognized Guru Nayak or that Nayak somehow recognized him during the course of their meeting. What do you think would have happened? Write an alternate ending to the story, staying true to the characters as Narayan has created them.

Vocabulary Development
Summarize the Story

vociferousness	paraphernalia
municipal	piqued
impetuous	

Write a brief summary of "An Astrologer's Day" using each of the Vocabulary words above. You may use any Vocabulary word more than once.

Zhang Jie

(1937–   )
China

Zhang Jie's childhood was marked by difficult circumstances. Raised in the Chinese capital, Beijing (bā·jiŋ′) (formerly Peking), Zhang grew up in dire poverty. Her father had abandoned the family a few months after her birth. She later observed that, in China at that time, her father had no binding, or legal, responsibility to his family.

Aware that women had more rights under China's new Communist government (established in 1949), Zhang joined the Communist Party as a young woman and supported government policy even when it meant compromising her own goals: She had hoped to study literature in college; instead she studied economics, which the government felt was more useful to society. Later, she was among many women who left their homes to work in factories or on farms in the hopes of improving China's shaky economy.

Zhang says of her early life that she was "like a darting dragonfly, with no goals in life and no substantial pursuits. Only through literature did I discover myself." She was not able to begin her writing career, however, until the Cultural Revolution ended and moderate leaders came into power. In 1978, Zhang won a national award for her story "The Music of the Forests." Three years later her novel *Leaden Wings* won China's Mao Dun Literary Prize.

Early in her career, Zhang wrote mainly about the problems of youth and love. Since that time, she has branched out to write about important contemporary social issues in China, including hypocrisy, corruption, bureaucracy, and discrimination against women. Zhang feels a responsibility to educate her readers about societal problems in order to effect change. She is considered a pioneer who highlighted women's problems long before Chinese authorities recognized them or took official action.

Among Chinese readers, Zhang Jie has enjoyed huge popularity, despite much controversy over her 1979 story "Love Must Not Be Forgotten," reprinted here. A huge success—especially among the young, who embraced its daring frankness—the story suggests that, for all the changes effected by the Communists, Chinese women still face centuries-old social pressures to marry and subordinate themselves to their husbands and families. Despite the easing of government censorship, Zhang's message—Chinese women were still being treated as second-class citizens—disturbed many Communist officials.

Even as Zhang's outspokenness and conviction were being praised abroad, her probing examinations of Chinese society were meeting with growing disapproval as China's government became more repressive in the late 1980s. After the brutal 1989 crackdown on the student pro-democracy movement in Beijing's Tiananmen Square, Zhang went into voluntary exile in the United States.

Before You Read

Love Must Not Be Forgotten

Make the Connection

Think back to a time when you were faced with a decision and someone convinced you to make a choice that you were unsure about. What was the result of that decision? Did you have any regrets?

Literary Focus

Flashback

A **flashback** is a scene in a movie, a play, or a story that interrupts the present action to show or tell what happened at an earlier time. Writers often use this device to develop a character or to give additional plot information. The flashbacks in "Love Must Not Be Forgotten" reveal the narrator's awareness of her mother's situation and feelings and serve to expand upon the story's theme.

North Carolina Competency Goal
1.03; 4.05; 5.01; 5.03

> **Flashback** is a scene in a narrative work that interrupts the present action to tell what happened at an earlier time.
>
> *For more on Flashback, see the Handbook of Literary and Historical Terms.*

Reading Skills

Analyzing Sequence of Events

Writers arrange events in ways that keep the reader's interest and best convey their ideas. As you read this story, keep track of when events shift from the present to the past and back again. Think about the following questions as you read:

- What parts of the narrative take place in the present?

SKILLS FOCUS

Literary Skills
Understand flashback.

Reading Skills
Analyze sequence of events.

- At what moments does the narrative shift to the past? How does the writer signal shifts between the past and the present?

- How are the diary entries written by the narrator's mother woven into this interplay of past and present?

Background

In 1949, Chinese Communists established the People's Republic of China under their military hero Mao Zedong (also spelled Mao Tse-tung). The new Communist regime instituted drastic social and economic changes and became increasingly oppressive. During Mao's Cultural Revolution, many moderate political figures were removed from power, imprisoned, and sometimes executed. China's writers were also silenced.

After Mao's death, in 1976, China came under more moderate leadership. Encouraged by the new spirit of openness, many writers emerged and began writing about past injustices and the need for reforms. But by the late 1980s, the government had become more repressive again. After the 1989 Tiananmen Square tragedy, few writers were allowed to publish within China, and those lucky enough to escape—like Zhang Jie—went abroad.

Vocabulary Development

prescience (presh'əns) *n.:* knowledge of something before it happens.

scrupulous (skroop'yə·ləs) *adj.:* acting in a strictly right or proper way.

strictures (strik'chərz) *n. pl.:* criticisms.

insuperable (in·soo'pər·ə·bəl) *adj.:* impossible to overcome.

Love Must Not Be Forgotten

Zhang Jie

translated by **Gladys Yang**

I am thirty, the same age as our People's Republic. For a republic thirty is still young. But a girl of thirty is virtually on the shelf.

Actually, I have a bona fide suitor. Have you seen the Greek sculptor Myron's *Discobolus*?[1] Qiao Lin[2] is the image of that discus thrower. Even the padded clothes he wears in winter fail to hide his fine physique. Bronzed, with clear-cut features, a broad forehead and large eyes, his appearance alone attracts most girls to him.

But I can't make up my mind to marry him. I'm not clear what attracts me to him, or him to me. I know people are gossiping behind my back, "Who does she think she is, to be so choosy?" To them, I'm a nobody playing hard to get. They take offense at such preposterous behavior.

Of course, I shouldn't be captious.[3] In a society where commercial production still exists, marriage, like most other transactions, is still a form of barter.

I have known Qiao Lin for nearly two years, yet still cannot fathom whether he keeps so quiet from aversion to talking or from having nothing

---

1. **Myron's *Discobolus*:** famous statue of a handsome athlete by this Greek sculptor of the fifth century B.C.
2. **Qiao Lin** (chyou′ lin′).

3. **captious** (kap′shəs) adj.: faultfinding; critical.

to say. When, by way of a small intelligence test, I demand his opinion of this or that, he says "good" or "bad" like a child in kindergarten.

Once I asked, "Qiao Lin, why do you love me?" He thought the question over seriously for what seemed an age. I could see from his normally smooth but now wrinkled forehead that the little gray cells in his handsome head were hard at work cogitating. I felt ashamed to have put him on the spot.

Finally he raised his clear childlike eyes to tell me, "Because you're good!"

Loneliness flooded my heart. "Thank you, Qiao Lin!" I couldn't help wondering, if we were to marry, whether we could discharge our duties to each other as husband and wife. Maybe, because law and morality would have bound us together. But how tragic simply to comply with law and morality! Was there no stronger bond to link us?

When such thoughts cross my mind I have the strange sensation that instead of being a girl contemplating marriage I am an elderly social scientist.

Perhaps I worry too much. We can live like most married couples, bringing up children together, strictly true to each other according to the law. . . . Although living in the seventies of the twentieth century, people still consider marriage the way they did millennia ago, as a means of continuing the race, a form of barter or a business transaction in which love and marriage can be separated. Since this is the common practice, why shouldn't we follow suit?

But I still can't make up my mind. As a child, I remember, I often cried all night for no rhyme or reason, unable to sleep and disturbing the whole household. My old nurse, a shrewd though uneducated woman, said an ill wind had blown through my ear. I think this judgment showed <u>prescience</u>, because I still have that old weakness. I upset myself over things which really present no problem, upsetting other people at the same time. One's nature is hard to change.

I think of my mother, too. If she were alive, what would she say about my attitude to Qiao Lin and my uncertainty about marrying him?

My thoughts constantly turn to her, not because she was such a strict mother that her ghost is still watching over me since her death. No, she was not just my mother but my closest friend. I loved her so much that the thought of her leaving me makes my heart ache.

She never lectured me, just told me quietly in her deep, unwomanly voice about her successes and failures, so that I could learn from her experience. She had evidently not had many successes—her life was full of failures.

During her last days she followed me with her fine, expressive eyes, as if wondering how I would manage on my own and as if she had some important advice for me but hesitated to give it. She must have been worried by my naiveté and sloppy ways. She suddenly blurted out, "Shanshan, if you aren't sure what you want, don't rush into marriage—better live on your own!"

Other people might think this strange advice from a mother to her daughter, but to me it embodied her bitter experience. I don't think she underestimated me or my knowledge of life. She loved me and didn't want me to be unhappy.

"I don't want to marry, mother!" I said, not out of bashfulness or a show of coyness. I can't think why a girl should pretend to be coy. She had long since taught me about things not generally mentioned to girls.

"If you meet the right man, then marry him. Only if he's right for you!"

"I'm afraid no such man exists!"

"That's not true. But it's hard. The world is so vast, I'm afraid you may never meet him." Whether married or not was not what concerned her, but the quality of the marriage.

"Haven't you managed fine without a husband?"

"Who says so?"

"I think you've done fine."

"I had no choice. . . ." She broke off, lost in thought, her face wistful. Her wistful lined face

Vocabulary

prescience (presh′əns) n.: knowledge of something before it happens.

reminded me of a withered flower I had pressed in a book.

"Why did you have no choice?"

"You ask too many questions," she parried, not ashamed to confide in me but afraid that I might reach the wrong conclusion. Besides, everyone treasures a secret to carry to the grave. Feeling a bit put out, I demanded bluntly, "Didn't you love my dad?"

"No, I never loved him."

"Did he love you?"

"No, he didn't."

"Then why get married?"

She paused, searching for the right words to explain this mystery, then answered bitterly, "When you're young you don't always know what you're looking for, what you need, and people may talk you into getting married. As you grow older and more experienced you find out your true needs. By then, though, you've done many foolish things for which you could kick yourself. You'd give anything to be able to make a fresh start and live more wisely. Those content with their lot will always be happy, they say, but I shall never enjoy that happiness." She added self-mockingly, "A wretched idealist, that's all I am."

Did I take after her? Did we both have genes which attracted ill winds?

"Why don't you marry again?"

"I'm afraid I'm still not sure what I really want." She was obviously unwilling to tell me the truth.

I cannot remember my father. He and Mother split up when I was very small. I just recall her telling me sheepishly that he was a fine handsome fellow. I could see she was ashamed of having judged by appearances and made a futile choice. She told me, "When I can't sleep at night, I force myself to sober up by recalling all those stupid blunders I made. Of course it's so distasteful that I often hide my face in the sheet for shame, as if there were eyes watching me in the dark. But distasteful as it is, I take some pleasure in this form of atonement."

I was really sorry that she hadn't remarried. She was such a fascinating character, if she'd

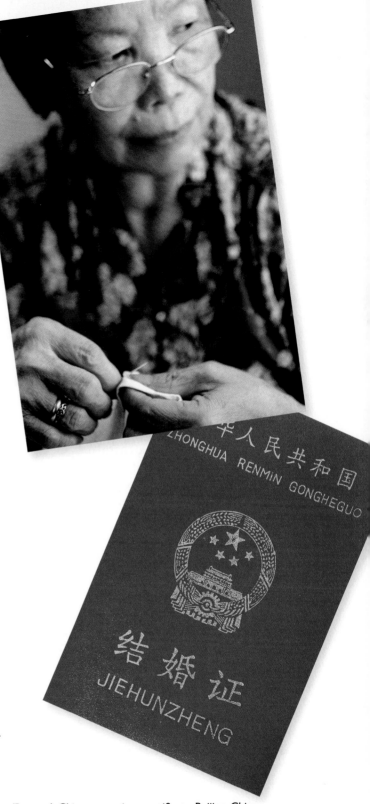

(Bottom) Chinese marriage certificate. Beijing, China.

married a man she loved, what a happy household ours would surely have been. Though not beautiful, she had the simple charm of an ink landscape. She was a fine writer, too. Another author who knew her well used to say teasingly, "Just reading your works is enough to make anyone love you!"

She would retort, "If he knew that the object of his affection was a white-haired old crone, that would frighten him away." At her age, she must have known what she really wanted, so this was obviously an evasion. I say this because she had quirks which puzzled me.

For instance, whenever she left Beijing on a trip, she always took with her one of the twenty-seven volumes of Chekhov's stories published between 1950 and 1955.[4] She also warned me, "Don't touch these books. If you want to read Chekhov, read that set I bought you." There was no need to caution me. Having a set of my own, why should I touch hers? Besides, she'd told me

---

4. **twenty-seven volumes of Chekhov's ... 1955:** complete stories of the Russian author Anton Chekhov (1860–1904), published in a Chinese edition in the 1950s.

this over and over again. Still she was on her guard. She seemed bewitched by those books.

So we had two sets of Chekhov's stories at home. Not just because we loved Chekhov, but to parry other people like me who loved Chekhov. Whenever anyone asked to borrow a volume, she would lend one of mine. Once, in her absence, a close friend took a volume from her set. When she found out, she was frantic, and at once took a volume of mine to exchange for it.

Ever since I can remember, those books were on her bookcase. Although I admire Chekhov as a great writer, I was puzzled by the way she never tired of reading him. Why, for over twenty years, had she had to read him every single day? Sometimes, when tired of writing, she poured herself a cup of strong tea and sat down in front of the bookcase, staring raptly at that set of books. If I went into her room then it flustered her, and she either spilt her tea or blushed like a girl discovered with her lover.

I wondered: Has she fallen in love with Chekhov? She might have if he'd still been alive.

When her mind was wandering just before her death, her last words to me were: "That set . . ." She hadn't the strength to give it its complete title. But I knew what she meant. "And my diary. . . 'Love Must Not Be Forgotten'. . . . Cremate them with me."

I carried out her last instruction regarding the works of Chekhov, but couldn't bring myself to destroy her diary. I thought, if it could be published, it would surely prove the most moving thing she had written. But naturally publication was out of the question.

At first I imagined the entries were raw material she had jotted down. They read neither like stories, essays, a diary, or letters. But after reading the whole I formed a hazy impression, helped out by my imperfect memory. Thinking it over, I finally realized that this was no lifeless manuscript I was holding, but an anguished, loving heart. For over twenty years one man had occupied her heart, but he was not for her. She used these diaries as a substitute for him, a means of pouring out her feelings to him, day after day, year after year.

No wonder she had never considered any eligible proposals, had turned a deaf ear to idle talk whether well meant or malicious. Her heart was already full, to the exclusion of anybody else. "No lake can compare with the ocean, no cloud with those on Mount Wu."[5] Remembering those lines I often reflected sadly that few people in real life could love like this. No one would love me like this.

I learned that toward the end of the thirties, when this man was doing underground work for the Party in Shanghai,[6] an old worker had given his life to cover him, leaving behind a helpless wife and daughter. Out of a sense of duty, of gratitude to the dead, and deep class feeling, he had unhesitatingly married the daughter. When he saw the endless troubles of couples who had married for "love," he may have thought, "Thank Heaven, though I didn't marry for love, we get on well, able to help each other." For years, as man and wife they lived through hard times.

He must have been my mother's colleague. Had I ever met him? He couldn't have visited our home. Who was he?

In the spring of 1962, Mother took me to a concert. We went on foot, the theater being quite near. On the way a black limousine pulled up silently by the pavement. Out stepped an elderly man with white hair in a black serge tunic suit. What a striking shock of white hair! Strict, scrupulous, distinguished, transparently honest—that was my impression of him. The cold glint of his flashing eyes reminded me of lightning or swordplay. Only ardent love for a woman really deserving his love could fill cold eyes like those with tenderness.

He walked up to Mother and said, "How are you, Comrade Zhong Yu?[7] It's been a long time."

"How are you!" Mother's hand holding mine suddenly turned icy cold and trembled a little.

They stood face to face without looking at each other, each appearing upset, even stern. Mother fixed her eyes on the trees by the roadside, not yet in leaf. He looked at me. "Such a big girl already. Good, fine—you take after your mother."

Instead of shaking hands with Mother, he shook hands with me. His hand was as icy as hers and trembling a little. As if transmitting an electric current, I felt a sudden shock. Snatching my hand away I cried, "There's nothing good about that!"

"Why not?" he asked with the surprised expression grown-ups always have when children speak out frankly.

I glanced at Mother's face. I did take after her, to my disappointment. "Because she's not beautiful!"

He laughed, then said teasingly, "Too bad that there should be a child who doesn't find her own mother beautiful. Do you remember in '53, when your mother was transferred to Beijing, she came to our ministry to report for duty? She left you outside on the veranda, but like a monkey you climbed all the stairs, peeped through the cracks in doors, and caught your finger in the door of my office. You sobbed so bitterly that I carried you off to find her."

"I don't remember that." I was annoyed at his harking back to a time when I was still in open-seat pants.

"Ah, we old people have better memories." He turned abruptly and remarked to Mother, "I've read that last story of yours. Frankly speaking, there's something not quite right about it. You shouldn't have condemned the heroine. . . . There's nothing wrong with falling in love, as long as you don't spoil someone else's life. . . . In fact, the hero might have loved her, too. Only for the sake of a third person's happiness, they had to renounce their love. . . ."

A policeman came over to where the car was parked and ordered the driver to move on. When

---

5. **Mount Wu:** one of a chain of picturesque mountains in eastern China.
6. **Party in Shanghai** (shaŋ'hī'): that is, the Communist Party in the large eastern Chinese city of Shanghai.
7. **Zhong Yu** (joŋ'yo͞o').

Vocabulary

scrupulous (skro͞op'yə·ləs) *adj.*: acting in a strictly right or proper way.

the driver made some excuse, the old man looked around. After a hasty "Goodbye" he strode back to the car and told the policeman, "Sorry. It's not his fault, it's mine. . . ."

I found it amusing watching this old cadre[8] listening respectfully to the policeman's strictures. When I turned to Mother with a mischievous smile, she looked as upset as a first-form[9] primary schoolchild standing forlornly in front of the stern headmistress.[10] Anyone would have thought she was the one being lectured by the policeman. The car drove off, leaving a puff of smoke. Very soon even this smoke vanished with the wind, as if nothing at all had happened. But the incident stuck in my mind.

Analyzing it now, I realize he must have been the man whose strength of character won Mother's heart. That strength came from his firm political convictions, his narrow escapes from death in the revolution, his active brain, his drive at work, his well-cultivated mind. Besides, strange to say, he and Mother both liked the oboe. Yes, she must have worshiped him. She once told me that unless she worshiped a man, she couldn't love him even for one day.

But I could not tell whether he loved her or not. If not, why was there this entry in her diary?

> "This is far too fine a present. But how did you know that Chekhov's my favorite writer?"
> "You said so."
> "I don't remember that."
> "I remember. I heard you mention it when you were chatting with someone."

So he was the one who had given her the *Selected Stories of Chekhov.* For her that was tantamount to a love letter. Maybe this man, who didn't believe in love, realized by the time his hair was white that in his heart was something which could be called love. By the time he no longer had the right to love, he made the tragic discovery of this love for which he would have given his life. Or did it go deeper even than that?

This is all I remember about him.

How wretched Mother must have been, deprived of the man to whom she was devoted! To catch a glimpse of his car or the back of his head through its rear window, she carefully figured out which roads he would take to work and back. Whenever he made a speech, she sat at the back of the hall watching his face rendered hazy by cigarette smoke and poor lighting. Her eyes would brim with tears, but she swallowed them back. If a fit of coughing made him break off, she wondered anxiously why no one persuaded him to give up smoking. She was afraid he would get bronchitis again. Why was he so near yet so far?

He, to catch a glimpse of her, looked out of the car window every day straining his eyes to watch the streams of cyclists, afraid that she might have an accident. On the rare evenings on which he had no meetings, he would walk by a roundabout way to our neighborhood, to pass our compound gate. However busy, he would always make time to look in papers and journals for her work. His duty had always been clear to him, even in the most difficult times. But now confronted by this love he became a weakling, quite helpless. At his age it was laughable. Why should life play this trick on him?

Yet when they happened to meet at work, each tried to avoid the other, hurrying off with a nod. Even so, this would make Mother blind and deaf to everything around her. If she met a colleague named Wang[11] she would call him Guo[12] and mutter something unintelligible.

It was a cruel ordeal for her. She wrote:

---

8. **old cadre** (ka′drē): here, former member of a cadre, or small unified group; in this case, a group of underground rebels.
9. **first-form** *adj.:* first-grade.
10. **headmistress** *n.:* female school principal.

11. **Wang:** common Chinese family name.
12. **Guo** (gwō): The names *Wang* and *Guo* are written in Chinese with similar characters. Because the narrator's mother is preoccupied, she confuses the two names.

Vocabulary

strictures (strik′chərz) *n. pl.:* criticisms.

We agreed to forget each other. But I deceived you, I have never forgotten. I don't think you've forgotten either. We're just deceiving each other, hiding our misery. I haven't deceived you deliberately, though; I did my best to carry out our agreement. I often stay far away from Beijing, hoping time and distance will help me to forget you. But when I return, as the train pulls into the station, my head reels. I stand on the platform looking round intently, as if someone were waiting for me. Of course there is no one. I realize then that I have forgotten nothing. Everything is unchanged. My love is like a tree the roots of which strike deeper year after year—I have no way to uproot it.

At the end of every day, I feel as if I've forgotten something important. I may wake with a start from my dreams wondering what has happened. But nothing has happened. Nothing. Then it comes home to me that you are missing! So everything seems lacking, incomplete, and there is nothing to fill up the blank. We are nearing the ends of our lives, why should we be carried away by emotion like children? Why should life submit people to such ordeals, then unfold before you your lifelong dream? Because I started off blindly, I took the wrong turning, and now there are <u>insuperable</u> obstacles between me and my dream.

Yes, Mother never let me go to the station to meet her when she came back from a trip, preferring to stand alone on the platform and imagine that he had met her. Poor mother with her graying hair was as infatuated as a girl.

Not much space in the diary was devoted to their romance. Most entries dealt with trivia: why one of her articles had not come off; her fear that she had no real talent; the excellent play she missed by mistaking the time on the ticket; the drenching she got by going out for a stroll without her umbrella. In spirit they were together day and night, like a devoted married couple. In fact,

Advertisement. China, 1930s.

they spent no more than twenty-four hours together in all. Yet in that time they experienced deeper happiness than some people in a whole lifetime. Shakespeare makes Juliet say, "I cannot sum up half my sum of wealth."[13] And probably that is how Mother felt.

He must have been killed in the Cultural Revolution. Perhaps because of the conditions then, that section of the diary is ambiguous and obscure. Mother had been so fiercely attacked for her writing, it amazed me that she went on keeping a diary. From some veiled allusions I gathered that he had questioned the theories advanced by that "theoretician" then at the height of favor and had told someone, "This

---

13. **Shakespeare . . . wealth":** In *Romeo and Juliet*, by William Shakespeare, Juliet makes this remark in describing her love for Romeo.

Vocabulary

insuperable (in·sooʹpər·ə·bəl) *adj.*: impossible to overcome.

is sheer Rightist[14] talk." It was clear from the tear-stained pages of Mother's diary that he had been harshly denounced; but the steadfast old man never knuckled under to the authorities. His last words were, "When I go to meet Marx,[15] I shall go on fighting my case!"

That must have been in the winter of 1969, because that was when Mother's hair turned white overnight, though she was not yet fifty. And she put on a black armband.[16] Her position then was extremely difficult. She was criticized for wearing this old-style mourning and ordered to say for whom she was in mourning.

"For whom are you wearing that, Mother?" I asked anxiously.

"For my lover." Not to frighten me she explained, "Someone you never knew."

"Shall I put one on too?" She patted my cheeks, as she had when I was a child. It was years since she had shown me such affection. I often felt that as she aged, especially during these last years of persecution, all tenderness had left her, or was concealed in her heart, so that she seemed like a man.

She smiled sadly and said, "No, you needn't wear one." Her eyes were as dry as if she had no more tears to shed. I longed to comfort her or do something to please her. But she said, "Off you go."

I felt an inexplicable dread, as if dear Mother had already half left me. I blurted out, "Mother!"

Quick to sense my desolation, she said gently, "Don't be afraid. Off you go. Leave me alone for a little."

I was right. She wrote:

> You have gone. Half my soul seems to have taken flight with you.
> I had no means of knowing what had become of you, much less of seeing you for

the last time. I had no right to ask either, not being your wife or friend. . . . So we are torn apart. If only I could have borne that inhuman treatment for you, so that you could have lived on! You should have lived to see your name cleared and take up your work again, for the sake of those who loved you. I knew you could not be a counterrevolutionary. You were one of the finest men killed. That's why I love you—I am not afraid now to avow it.

Snow is whirling down. Heavens, even God is such a hypocrite, he is using this whiteness to cover up your blood and the scandal of your murder.

I have never set store by my life. But now I keep wondering whether anything I say or do would make you contract your shaggy eyebrows in a frown. I must live a worthwhile life like you, and do some honest work for our country. Things can't go on like this—those criminals will get what's coming to them.

I used to walk alone along that small asphalt road, the only place where we once walked together, hearing my footsteps in the silent night. . . . I always paced to and fro and lingered there, but never as wretchedly as now. Then, though you were not beside me, I knew you were still in this world and felt that you were keeping me company. Now I can hardly believe that you have gone.

At the end of the road I would retrace my steps, then walk along it again. Rounding the fence I always looked back, as if you were still standing there waving goodbye. We smiled faintly, like casual acquaintances, to conceal our undying love. That ordinary evening in early spring a chilly wind was blowing as we walked silently away from each other. You were wheezing a little because of your chronic bronchitis. That upset me. I wanted to beg you to slow down, but somehow I couldn't. We both walked very fast, as if some important business were waiting for us.

---

14. **Rightist:** in politics, conservative or reactionary. Chinese politics during the Cultural Revolution was dominated by Rightist Party members.
15. **Marx:** Karl Marx (1818–1883), German-born economic philosopher and father of modern socialism; a revered figure by Chinese and other Communists.
16. **black armband:** traditional sign of mourning in China and elsewhere.

Relic 2 (2004) by Hung Liu.
Courtesy of Nancy Hoffman Gallery, New York.

How we prized that single stroll we had together, but we were afraid we might lose control of ourselves and burst out with "I love you"—those three words which had tormented us for years. Probably no one else could believe that we never once even clasped hands!

No, Mother, I believe it. I am the only one able to see into your locked heart.

Ah, that little asphalt road, so haunted by bitter memories. We shouldn't overlook the most insignificant spots on earth. For who knows how much secret grief and joy they may hide. No wonder that when tired of writing, she would pace slowly along that little road behind our window. Sometimes at dawn after a sleepless night, sometimes on a moonless, windy evening. Even in winter during howling gales which hurled sand and pebbles against the window pane. . . . I thought this was one of her eccentricities, not knowing that she had gone to meet him in spirit.

She liked to stand by the window, too, staring at the small asphalt road. Once I thought from her expression that one of our closest friends must be coming to call. I hurried to the window. It was a late autumn evening. The cold wind was stripping dead leaves from the trees and blowing them down the small empty road.

She went on pouring out her heart to him in her diary as she had when he was alive.

Right up to the day when the pen slipped from her fingers. Her last message was:

> I am a materialist, yet I wish there were a Heaven. For then, I know, I would find you there waiting for me. I am going there to join you, to be together for eternity. We need never be parted again or keep at a distance for fear of spoiling someone else's life. Wait for me, dearest, I am coming—

I do not know how, on her deathbed, Mother could still love so ardently with all her heart. To me it seemed not love but a form of madness, a passion stronger than death. If undying love really exists, she reached its extreme. She obviously died happy, because she had known true love. She had no regrets.

Now these old people's ashes have mingled with the elements. But I know that no matter what form they may take, they still love each other. Though not bound together by earthly laws or morality, though they never once clasped hands, each possessed the other completely. Nothing could part them. Centuries to come, if one white cloud trails another, two grasses grow side by side, one wave splashes another, a breeze follows another . . . believe me, that will be them.

Each time I read that diary, "Love Must Not Be Forgotten," I cannot hold back my tears. I often weep bitterly, as if I myself experienced their ill-fated love. If not a tragedy it was too laughable. No matter how beautiful or moving I find it, I have no wish to follow suit!

Thomas Hardy[17] wrote that "the call seldom produces the comer, the man to love rarely coincides with the hour for loving." I cannot judge them by conventional moral standards. What I deplore is that they did not wait for a "missing counterpart" to call them. If everyone could wait, instead of rushing into marriage, how many tragedies could be averted!

When we reach communism,[18] will there still be cases of marriage without love? Perhaps . . . since the world is so vast, two kindred spirits may never be able to answer each other's call. But how tragic! Could it be that by then we will have devised ways to escape such tragedies? But this is all conjecture.

Maybe after all we are accountable for these tragedies. Who knows? Should we take the responsibility for the old ideas handed down from the past? Because, if you choose not to marry, your behavior is considered a direct challenge to these ideas. You will be called neurotic, accused of having guilty secrets or having made political mistakes. You may be regarded as an eccentric who looks down on ordinary people, not respecting age-old customs—a heretic. In short, they will trump up endless vulgar and futile charges to ruin your reputation. Then you have to succumb to those ideas and marry regardless. But once you put the chains of an indifferent marriage around your neck, you will suffer for it for the rest of your life.

I long to shout: "Mind your own business! Let us wait patiently for our counterparts. Even waiting in vain is better than loveless marriage. To live single is not such a fearful disaster. I believe it may be a sign of a step forward in culture, education, and the quality of life."

---

17. **Thomas Hardy** (1840–1928): British author whose fiction often challenged conventional morality and ideas about romantic love. His characters are often destroyed by love.
18. **When we reach communism:** when we reach a communist ideal or perfect communist state, as the teachings of communism say will one day happen.

Response and Analysis

Reading Check

1. How does the narrator feel about her suitor, Qiao Lin? What are her feelings about marriage in general?

2. In the story, what is "Love Must Not Be Forgotten"? What private information does it reveal?

3. How does the narrator's mother feel about her own marriage? Why couldn't she marry the man she loved?

4. When did the mother's beloved die? What happened afterward?

Thinking Critically

5. Describe the relationship between the narrator and her mother. What does the narrator come to understand about her mother? How does this understanding affect the narrator's viewpoint?

6. What do the **flashbacks** involving the man the mother loved reveal about the kind of person he was and the reasons why the mother loved him?

7. This story starts in the present—as the narrator's story—and then shifts to the past to become her mother's story. Do you feel that the story does not hold together, or do you think it is a unified piece in spite of its shifts between present and past? Explain. What, if anything, unifies past and present in the story?

Extending and Evaluating

8. Do you think that the social pressures regarding marriage experienced by the narrator and her mother in Communist China exist to some degree for women in America today? Explain.

Literary Criticism

9. About "Love Must Not Be Forgotten," the American writer Annie Dillard wrote "Older [Chinese] critics criticized the story for its Western-style idealization of romantic love," while "young people in China said . . . such love is true and grand." Do you think this story treats love relationships realistically, or does it present an idealization of romantic love? Explain.

WRITING

Writing a Diary Entry

In the form of a diary entry, write your own views about love, marriage, independence, or one of the other related issues that Zhang Jie addresses. You may wish to respond directly to one or more of the declarations the narrator makes in the closing paragraphs of the story.

Vocabulary Development
Synonyms

prescience   strictures

scrupulous   insuperable

A **synonym** is a word that has the same or nearly the same meaning as another word. Choose the best synonym for each Vocabulary word below.

1. **prescience:** a. visibility b. symbol c. foreknowledge

2. **scrupulous:** a. immoral b. attentive c. whimsical

3. **strictures:** a. quotations b. conclusions c. criticisms

4. **insuperable:** a. insurmountable b. indefensible c. unbelievable

North Carolina Competency Goal
1.03; 4.05; 5.03; 6.01

INTERNET
Projects and Activities
Keyword:
LE5 WL-7

SKILLS FOCUS

Literary Skills
Analyze flashback.

Reading Skills
Analyze sequence of events.

Writing Skills
Write a diary entry.

Vocabulary Skills
Understand synonyms.

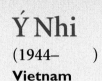

Ý Nhi
(1944–   )
Vietnam

Born in Quang Nam province, Ý Nhi (whose given name is Hoàng Thi Ý Nhi) was raised by her impoverished mother after her father left the family. Years later, Ý Nhi's father appeared again and out of concern for the family's well-being, he moved them all farther north in Vietnam where he had relocated.

Ý Nhi earned a degree in Vietnamese litera- ture and linguistics from the University of Hanoi. After graduation she worked in the Institute of Literature and then assumed editorial duties at the Liberation Literature and Arts Publishing House.

Ý Nhi's poems have appeared in a variety of anthologies. Her published collections of verse include *Coming Over to the River* (1978); *Street Trees, Waiting for the Moon* (1981); *Common Days* (1987); *Snow* and *The Face* (1991). She has received a number of prizes and honors, including the award of the Vietnam Writers' Association for her 1985 verse collection *Woman Knitting*.

Before You Read

Quang Binh

Make the Connection

Quickwrite

What might a person who returns to a favorite place after a long absence expect or hope to find? How would he or she feel? Jot down your ideas.

Literary Focus

Setting

The time and place of a literary work is its **setting.** In some works of literature, setting is an integral element of the **theme,** or overall meaning: The specific place and time of a work helps convey the writer's message.

> **Setting** is the time and place of a literary work.
>
> *For more on Setting, see the Handbook of Literary and Historical Terms.*

Background

After the defeat of Japan at the close of World War II, the Southeast Asian country of Vietnam suffered a thirty-year period of civil strife and foreign domination. In the 1950s, Vietnam was temporarily divided into Communist North Vietnam, with its capital at Hanoi, and noncommunist South Vietnam, with its capital at Saigon. In 1957, Communists in the South started a rebellion against the South Vietnamese government. This conflict escalated into the Vietnam War. The United States played a leading role in the conflict. At a 1973 peace conference, the combatants agreed to a cease-fire, and the United States withdrew its troops. Soon after, the North Vietnamese government invaded the South. Saigon fell to North Vietnamese forces, and the nation was reunified under a Communist government in 1975. Roughly a million Vietnamese refugees fled their homeland, migrating to other parts of the world.

North Carolina Competency Goal
1.02; 1.03;
4.02; 4.05;
5.01; 5.03;
6.01

SKILLS FOCUS

Literary Skills
Understand setting.

The Monk's Path (2004) by Hong Viet Dung.

Quang Binh

Ý Nhi

translated by **Marilyn Nelson**

The train has left;
its whistle blows carelessly.
Gray smoke fades along the lines of trees and reeds,
disappears over the uncountable sections of red earth,
5   pine trees, rice paddies.

Only I can recognize the face of *Quang Binh,*
suddenly realize this land so close to my heart.
After so much absence, so much silence, no promises to return;
my mind in tumult realizes this land is truly mine.

10 I understand my feelings now all those months and years
through all the rivers, forests, cities,
through the farewells, the meetings,
finally I am come back to that place that is my own.

I come back to the sand caves where winds still blow hard,
15 where at eighteen, younger brother, you died,
to where the bombs fell, and *Dong Hoi* citadel stood in silence,
to where you patched roads in tattered clothes as your hair
yellowed with illness.

I come back to the sandy hill that had no trees for cover,
20 where the harsh sunlight beat down on the old ramparts,
where, elder brother, you raised your voice softly above the grass
where your eyes turned slowly, vacantly toward the horizon.

I come back to the home of my youth,
to the cup of sim-leaf juice at *Quang Trach* in the afternoon,
25 to the night by the sea, waiting for the boat, sleepless, tense,
misjudging how the wind changed course by the bank of pine trees,
feet trampling over the thorns and pebbles
and white reed flowers leaning after dark shadows of men
and the deep purple *chac chiu,* red peonies,
30 the troops returning, the familiar yellow grass.
You said something, younger brother, in your black uniform.
I melted into the colors, the sights, the sounds,
part worried, part expectant, part anxious,
the colors flying passionately before the troops.
35 Through the long night we could hear the enemy guns firing
on the Southern banks,
our hearts flowed back to the head of the *Ben Hai* River.

To where the land opened up beneath our patient feet.
That purple blue sky, our eyes could never see enough of it.
40 That time when we had faith, when love was steadfast,
when our open palms met the open palms of our friends.

For a moment I see clearly
things not easy to see in the midst of life,
things of weight and gravity.
45 I've come back to my homeland, the land of my birth.
The train has gone, leaving me alone at the station.
I step onto the land, truly my land at last.

Response and Analysis

Thinking Critically

1. According to lines 1–5, what is the **setting** in which the speaker finds herself? How would you describe the atmosphere, or **mood,** suggested by this setting in the first stanza?

2. What realization suddenly grips the speaker in lines 6–9? Why do you think this realization comes as such a surprise to the speaker?

3. Whom does the speaker directly address in lines 14–18? According to the speaker, what happened to this person?

4. What elements or details in the fifth stanza (lines 19–22) contain parallels to elements or details in the fourth stanza (lines 14–18)? What do you think is the effect of this parallelism?

5. In the longest stanza (lines 23–37), the poet uses a number of sensory details that help convey a vivid description. Identify some of these details, and then explain how they contrast with other details that evoke a context of warfare.

6. In lines 38–41, how does the speaker contrast the present with the past? What is the effect of this contrast, in your view?

7. How does the poem's concluding stanza (lines 42–47) echo the opening stanza? What "moment" of illumination does the speaker experience at the end of the poem?

8. Ý Nhi uses a number of specific place names in this poem. Even though a reader might be unfamiliar with these places, what is the emotional effect of this technique?

Extending and Evaluating

9. Review your Quickwrite notes. How do the thoughts and feelings you listed compare or contrast with those of the speaker in "Quang Binh"?

WRITING

Writing a Reflective Essay

Jot down a few notes about the way this poem made you feel about war. Then, write a brief reflective essay on the topic. What did you learn about the nature of war from this poem? What are some of war's unintended consequences? You may want to share your essay with the class.

North Carolina Competency Goal
1.02; 1.03; 4.05; 5.03; 6.01

INTERNET

Projects and Activities
Keyword: LE5 WL-7

Literary Skills
Analyze setting.

Writing Skills
Write a reflective essay.

Bei Dao
(1949–   )
China

"**O**n the one hand poetry is useless," says the Chinese writer Bei Dao, the pen name of Zhao Zhenkai. "It can't change the world materially. On the other hand it is a basic part of human existence. It came into the world when humans did. It's what makes human beings human."

Bei Dao grew up in Beijing; his mother was a doctor and his father an administrator. At seventeen, he left school to join the Red Guard, a paramilitary group made up of students during China's Cultural Revolution (1966–1969). It was a time of chaos and terror in China when intellectuals were jailed, homes were searched, and books were banned. During the Cultural Revolution, Dao, like many other educated young men, was sent to the countryside to be "re-educated." For eleven years he worked as a construction worker. "Every day after exhausting work, I returned to a shack shared by a hundred workers. Reading and writing in the near-darkness in the shack brought me infinite pleasure. I found a secret world that belonged only to me." Disillusioned with China's government, he met secretly with friends who exchanged their writing and discussed Western books.

In 1978, Bei Dao co-founded an influential underground literary magazine called *Jintian* (Today). He took the pen name Bei Dao, suggested by a friend, to conceal his identity from the police. (Bei Dao means "northern island.") The poets associated with *Jintian*, including Bei Dao himself, came to be called the "Misty Poets," because their poetry seemed obscure and difficult to understand, or "misty." During Mao Zedong's Cultural Revolution, the only poetry that was allowed was didactic and simple political poetry for the masses, reflecting collective socialist ideals. The Misty Poets scandalized conservative critics by turning to Western models, such as Imagism, and creating an experimental poetry that was highly individualistic, ambiguous, and open to interpretation. "Our poetry was written in what amounted to a new language," Bei Dao explains, "which differed greatly from the official language to which people were accustomed. That was what got people excited." The government banned *Jintian* after two years, condemning Bei Dao's writing as subjective and obscure.

During the Tiananmen Square massacre in 1989 (see page 1079), Dao was a visiting writer in Berlin. The Chinese government refused to let him return, accusing him of helping to incite the pro-democracy protests. Separated from his wife and young daughter, who were not allowed to leave China, he says, ". . . the sense of solitude is very difficult, so I feel that I have to continue to write. Writing is the thing that sustains me and keeps me going. It is a form of self-preservation for me."

Bei Dao has taught in various universities in Europe and in America and currently lives with his daughter in northern California.

Requiem

Make the Connection

Quickwrite ✐

You sit staring at the TV screen as events unfold. The images play over and over; people comment; participants are interviewed. Think of significant national and world events that you have witnessed on TV. Choose one event, and write a journal entry telling what you remember about the event, what you saw, and how it made you feel.

Literary Focus

Mood

The **mood,** or atmosphere, of a literary work is the overall feeling that it evokes in a reader. You can usually describe a work's mood with one or two adjectives, such as *bitter, gloomy, joyful,* or *humorous.* Writers create mood by using descriptive details, images, sounds, figures of speech, and word connotations. The mood of a literary work may stay the same throughout the entire work, or it may shift.

> **Mood** is the overall emotion evoked by a work of literature.
>
> *For more on Mood, see the Handbook of Literary and Historical Terms.*

Background

During the evening of June 3 and the early morning hours of June 4, 1989, the Chinese government ordered tanks and troops into Tiananmen Square, in Beijing, to suppress a massive pro-democracy demonstration that had lasted for seven weeks. They fired on unarmed demonstrators and bystanders who tried to block their way. Students had begun the protest, sitting in the square and refusing to leave; workers and intellectuals had joined them until over one million people filled the square. The government had declared martial law on May 20, and when negotiations with the protestors failed, troops were ordered to clear the square. The Chinese Red Cross estimates that as many as 2,600 civilians were killed and 7,000–10,000 were wounded. The Goddess of Democracy, a student-made, thirty-foot-high statue, lay in ruins. The government quickly jailed and exiled dissidents, effectively putting an end to the pro-democracy movement.

A requiem (from the Latin word for "rest") is a Roman Catholic funeral mass or, by extension, any musical service, chant, or poem that honors the dead. Many of the great classical composers, including Giuseppe Verdi and Wolfgang Amadeus Mozart, composed requiems that set the words of the Latin mass to majestic, soaring music.

North Carolina Competency Goal
1.03; 4.05; 5.01; 5.03; 6.01

INTERNET

More About Bei Dao
Keyword: LE5 WL-7

SKILLS FOCUS

Literary Skills
Understand mood.

Golden stream bridges.
Forbidden City, Beijing, China.

Requiem

Bei Dao

translated by **Bonnie S. McDougall**
and **Chen Maiping**

for the victims of June Fourth

Not the living but the dead
under the doomsday-purple° sky
go in groups
suffering guides forward suffering
5   at the end of hatred is hatred
the spring has run dry, the conflagration° stretches unbroken
the road back is even further away

Not the gods but the children
amid the clashing of helmets
10   say their prayers
mothers breed light
darkness breeds mothers
the stone rolls, the clock runs backwards
the eclipse of the sun has already taken place

15   Not your bodies but your souls
shall share a common birthday every year
you are all the same age
love has founded for the dead
an everlasting alliance
20   you embrace each other closely
in the massive register of deaths

2. doomsday *n.* used as *adj.:*
Doomsday is Judgment Day,
the end of the world, or any
catastrophic day.

6. conflagration
(kän′flə·grā′shən) *n.:* big,
destructive fire.

Response and Analysis

Thinking Critically

1. Who are "the children / amid the clashing of helmets" in stanza 2? In stanza 3, whom is the poet addressing as "you"?

2. Why do you think each of the stanzas begins with the word *Not*? What other similarities can you find in the structure of each stanza?

3. How is stanza 3 different from stanzas 1 and 2? How would you paraphrase stanza 3?

4. Find images in the poem that seem surreal—irrational and dreamlike. (See, for example, lines 8–10.) What is their emotional effect?

5. How would you describe the poem's **mood**? How do the images contribute to that mood?

Extending and Evaluating

6. Here's how Bei Dao describes his poetic technique: "I try to introduce in my own poetry the technique of film montage, and by creating juxtaposed images and changes in speed, I want to arouse people's imaginations to fill in the substantial gaps between the words." Choose several lines from the poem that puzzle you. Then, discuss these lines with a small group of classmates. If you use your imaginations to fill in the gaps, how might you interpret those lines?

Literary Criticism

7. Bonnie S. McDougall, one of the translators of the poem, says that "In 'Requiem,' . . . there is a sense of faith and hope: It was hard for anyone in those days not to believe that this brutal use of terror must soon bring about the downfall of its perpetrators." Other critics, however, have described Bei Dao's "misty" poetry as gloomy and sad. Do you agree with either point of view? Do you find any sense of hope in "Requiem"? Explain.

WRITING

Writing a Poem

Look back at your Quickwrite notes, and write a free-verse poem about the event you recalled. Try to use vivid imagery, as Bei Dao does in "Requiem," to evoke a particular mood.

Writing a Letter

Write a letter to Bei Dao, responding to what he says about the importance of poetry (see the first paragraph of his biography on page 1078). Do you agree or disagree that poetry is central to human beings? Support your opinion by referring to your own experiences and to "Requiem" or poems by other authors. Do you think that a poem like "Requiem" can make a difference in society and change people's views?

North Carolina Competency Goal
1.02; 1.03; 4.05; 5.03; 6.01

INTERNET

Projects and Activities
Keyword:
LE5 WL-7

SKILLS FOCUS

Literary Skills
Analyze mood.

Writing Skills
Write a poem.
Write a letter.

Ha Jin

(1956–   )

China

Jin Xuefei, whose pen name is Ha Jin, grew up in a small, rural town in Liaoning Province on mainland China, where his father was a military officer. At fourteen, Jin volunteered for the People's Liberation Army (China's army) and worked as a telegraph operator near the Russian border, where the threat of a land invasion was considered serious. Jin was both patriotic and realistic about the situation: "I knew there might be a war, and so we were ready and knew if we had to die, we'd die."

At twenty-one, Jin began studying English; he wanted to read Friedrich Engels's (1820–1895) influential socialist work *The Condition of the Working Class in England* (1845) in its original English edition. In 1977, Jin entered Heilongjiang University, where he majored in English, and in 1985, he came to the United States to complete doctoral studies at Brandeis University, in Massachusetts. He had always intended to return to China, but news of the 1989 pro-democracy student protests and subsequent massacre by troops at Tiananmen Square, in Beijing, caused him to reconsider. Jin realized that he could never fulfill his ambition to be a writer in China because he would not be able to write openly and honestly; he chose to stay in the United States and write in English. "Unlike most exiled writers already established in their native language, I had no audience in Chinese, and so chose to write in English. To me, this meant much labor, some despair, and also, freedom."

Jin wrote most of his first book of poetry, *Between Silences* (1990), while he was still a graduate student working as a night watchman, a job that gave him a great deal of time to read and write. He began teaching at Emory College, in Atlanta, in 1993 after earning his Ph.D. from Brandeis. Memories of his tour of duty on the Russian border provided inspiration for *Ocean of Words* (1996), his first collection of short stories, with characters described by one critic as being "achingly human." It won the PEN/Hemingway Award. *In the Pond* (1998) is Jin's comic novella about the social injustice faced by a talented artist who must work in a fertilizer plant. His second novel, *Waiting* (1999), won the National Book Award. It depicts the conflict a Chinese army doctor endures as he attempts to divorce his loyal peasant wife in order to marry an educated woman.

Much of Jin's fiction dramatizes China's repressive government, depicting petty officials who impose their will on various characters in order to restrict their freedom. Jin says about his subject matter, "I guess we are compelled to write about what has hurt us most."

Ocean of Words

Make the Connection

If a person could not read at all, what problems might he or she encounter in life? Can you think of any situations in which being unable to read could be more than just embarrassing or problematic but actually dangerous—even life-threatening? Discuss these questions briefly with classmates.

Literary Focus

Character and Theme

A **character** in a story is an individual who may be static or dynamic. A **static character** does not change much during a story. A **dynamic character,** however, changes in some important way as a result of a story's events.

   Theme is the central insight about life in a work of literature. A theme can usually be stated as a generalization in just a sentence or two. Sometimes a character's words or actions—including the ways in which a character changes or evolves during the course of a story—can hint at the theme.

> A **character** is an individual in a story who may be **static** or **dynamic. Theme** is the central insight about life in a literary work.
>
> *For more on Character and Theme, see the Handbook of Literary and Historical Terms.*

Reading Skills

Comparing Historical and Contemporary Issues

During China's Cultural Revolution (1966–1976) the Communist government attempted to create radical social change through repression and violence. Books—especially those that contradicted the teachings of China's leader Mao Zedong—were banned, and intellectuals were regarded with extreme suspicion or purged from China's Communist Party. As you read this story, look for details that reveal the Cultural Revolution's attitude toward books and education. How is this attitude similar to or different from more recent attempts at censorship by repressive governments in other countries that you have read or heard about? Why might a government be against education and literacy? Describe the effects such a policy might have on a nation and its people.

Background

In this story the main character's frustrated attempts to become a member of the Communist Party of China are motivated not by ideology but by economic necessity. Zhou knows that citizens who apply for membership have to undergo extensive background and loyalty checks. But he also realizes that, since good jobs are available only to party members, joining is the only way he can assure his future financial stability.

North Carolina Competency Goal
1.03; 4.02; 4.03; 4.05; 5.01; 5.03

INTERNET

Vocabulary Practice
•
More About Ha Jin

Keyword: LE5 WL-7

SKILLS FOCUS

Literary Skills
Understand character and theme.

Reading Skills
Compare historical and contemporary issues.

Vocabulary Development

confiscate (kän′fis·kāt′) *v.*: seize by authority.

imminent (im′ə·nənt) *adj.*: about to happen.

enigma (i·nig′mə) *n.*: something baffling.

scathing (skā′thiŋ) *adj.*: extremely critical or severe.

resolution (rez′ə·lōō′shən) *n.*: firmness of purpose.

Ocean of Words

Ha Jin

Zhou Wen's last year in the People's Army[1] was not easy. All his comrades pestered him, because in their eyes he was a bookworm, a scholar of sorts. Whenever they played poker, or chatted, or cracked jokes, he would sneak out to a place where he could read alone. This habit annoyed not only his fellow soldiers but also the chief of the Radio-telegram Station, Huang Peng, whose rank was equal to a platoon commander's. Chief Huang would say to his men, "This is not college. If you want to be a college student, you'd better go home first." Everybody knew he referred to Zhou.

The only thing they liked about Zhou was that he would work the shift they hated most, from 1:00 A.M. to 8:00 A.M. During the small hours Zhou read novels and middle school textbooks instead of the writings by Chairman Mao, Marx, Lenin, and Stalin.[2] Often in the early morning he watched the eastern sky turn gray, pale, pink, and bright. The dawn was driving the night away from Longmen City bit by bit until, all of a sudden, a fresh daybreak descended, shining upon thousands of red roofs.

If not for the help of Director Liang Ming of the Divisional Logistics Department, Zhou's last year in the army would have been disastrous.

Liang and his family lived in a grand church built by nineteenth-century Russian missionaries, which was at the southern corner of the Divisional Headquarters compound. A large red star[3] stood atop the steeple. Within the church many walls had been knocked down to create a large auditorium, which served as the division's conference hall, movie house, and theater. All the fancy bourgeois[4] pews had been pulled out and replaced by long proletarian[5] benches, and Chairman Mao's majestic portrait had driven off the superstitious altarpiece.

The Liangs lived in the back of the church, as did the soldiers of the Radio-telegram Station. Because the antennas needed height, the radiomen occupied the attic, while the director's family had for themselves the three floors underneath. Whenever there was a movie on, the men at the station would steal into the auditorium through the rear door and sit against the wall, watching the screen from the back stage. They never bothered to get tickets. But except for those evenings when there were movies shown or plays performed, the back door would be locked. Very often Zhou dreamed of studying alone in the spacious front hall. Unable to enter it, he had to go outside to read in the open air.

One evening in October he was reading under a road lamp near the church. It was cloudy and

---

1. **People's Army:** China's army; also called the People's Liberation Army.
2. **Chairman Mao . . . Stalin:** Mao Tse-tung (1893–1976), Chinese Communist leader; Karl Marx (1818–1883), German-born economist and founder of modern socialism; Vladimir Ilyich Lenin (1870–1924), director of the 1917 Russian Revolution; Joseph Stalin (1879–1953), Soviet dictator.
3. **red star:** symbol of communism.
4. **bourgeois** (bōor-zhwä′) *adj.:* characteristic of the bourgeoisie, i.e., middle-class business owners or capitalists.
5. **proletarian** (prō′lə-ter′ē-ən) *adj.:* characteristic of the working class.

The Chairman Smiles. Poster.
Groninger Museum. Collection International Institute of Social History.
Stefan R. Landsberger, Amsterdam.

a snow was gathering, just as the loudspeaker had announced that morning. Zhou was so engrossed he didn't notice somebody approaching until a deep voice startled him. "What are you doing here, little comrade?" Director Liang stood in front of Zhou, smiling kindly. His left sleeve, without an arm inside, hung listlessly from his shoulder, the cuff lodged in his pocket. His baggy eyes were fixed on Zhou's face.

"Reading," Zhou managed to say, closing the book and reluctantly showing him the title. He tried to smile but only twitched his lips, his eyes dim with fear.

"*The Three Kingdoms!*"[6] Liang cried. He pointed at the other book under Zhou's arm. "How about this one?"

"*Ocean of Words,* a dictionary." Zhou regretted having taken the big book out with him.

"Can I have a look?"

Zhou handed it to the old man, who began flicking through the pages between the green covers. "It looks like a good book," Liang said and gave it back to Zhou. "Tell me, what's your name?"

"Zhou Wen."

"You're in the Radio Station upstairs, aren't you?"

"Yes."

"Do you often read old books?"

"Yes." Zhou was afraid the officer would confiscate the novel, which he had borrowed from a friend in the Telephone Company.

"Why don't you read inside?" Liang asked.

"It's noisy upstairs. They won't let me read in peace."

"Tickle their grandmothers!" Liang shook his gray head. "Follow me."

Unsure what was going on, Zhou didn't follow him. Instead he watched Liang's stout back moving away.

"I order you to come in," the director said loudly, opening the door to his home.

Zhou followed Liang to the second floor. The home was so spacious that the first floor alone had five or six rooms. Down the hall the red floor was shiny under the chandelier; the brown windowsill at the stairway was large enough to be a bed. Liang opened a door and said, "You use this room. Whenever you want to study, come here and study inside."

"This, this—"

"I order you to use it. We have lots of rooms. From now on, if I see you reading outside again, I will kick all of you out of this building."

"No, no, they may want me at any time. What should I say if they can't find me?"

"Tell them I want you. I want you to study and work for me here." Liang closed the door, and his leather boots thumped away downstairs.

Outside, snowflakes suddenly began fluttering to the ground. Through the window Zhou saw the backyard of the small grocery that was run by some officers' wives. A few naked branches were tossing, almost touching the panes. Inside, green curtains covered the corners of the large window. Though bright and clean, the room seemed to be used as a repository for old furniture. On the floor was a large desk, a stool, a chair, a wooden bed standing on its head against the wall, and a rickety sofa. But for Zhou this was heaven. Full of joy, he read three chapters that evening.

Soon the downstairs room became Zhou's haven. In the Radio Company he could hardly get along with anybody; there was a lot of ill feeling between him and his leaders and comrades. He tried forgetting all the unhappy things by making himself study hard downstairs, but that didn't always help. His biggest headache was his imminent discharge from the army: not the demobilization itself so much as his non-Party status. It was obvious that without Communist Party membership he wouldn't be assigned a good job once he returned home. Thinking him bookish, the Party members in the Radio Com-

6. **The Three Kingdoms:** popular novel that fictionalizes conflicts among warring Chinese states in the third century A.D.; first published in 1522 during the Ming dynasty. It is also known as *The Romance of the Three Kingdoms.*

Vocabulary

confiscate (kän′fis·kāt′) v.: seize by authority.
imminent (im′ə·nənt) adj.: about to happen.

Xinhua Dictionary.

pany were reluctant to consider his application seriously. Chief Huang would never help him; neither would Party Secretary Si Ma Lin. Zhou had once been on good terms with the secretary; he had from time to time helped Si Ma write articles on current political topics and chalked up slogans and short poems on the large blackboard in front of the Company Headquarters. That broad piece of wood was the company's face, because it was the first thing a visitor would see and what was on it displayed the men's sincere political attitudes and lofty aspirations. The secretary had praised Zhou three times for the poems and calligraphy on the blackboard, but things had gone bad between Zhou and Si Ma because of *Ocean of Words.*

The dictionary was a rare book, which Zhou's father had bought in the early 1950s. It was compiled in 1929, was seven by thirteen inches in size and over three thousand pages thick, and had Chinese, Latin, and English indexes. Its original price was eighty silver dollars, but Zhou's father had paid a mere one *yuan*[7] for it at a salvage station, where all things were sold by weight. The book weighed almost three *jin.* Having grown up with the small *New China Dictionary,* which had only a few thousand entries, Secretary Si Ma had never imagined there was such a big book in the world. When he saw it for the first time, he browsed through the pages for two hours, pacing up and down in his office with the book in his arms as if cradling a baby. He told Zhou, "I love this book. What a treasure. It's a gold mine, an armory!"

One day at the Company Headquarters the secretary asked Zhou, "Can I have that great book, Young Zhou?"

"It's my family's heirloom. I can't give it to anybody." Zhou regretted having shown him the dictionary and having even told him that his father had spent only one *yuan* for it.

---

7. **yuan** *n.:* basic monetary unit of China.

"I won't take it for free. Give me a price. I'll pay you a good sum."

"Secretary Si Ma, I can't sell it. It's my father's book."

"How about fifty *yuan*?"

"If it were mine I would give it to you free."

"A hundred?"

"No, I won't sell."

"Two hundred?"

"No."

"You are a stubborn, Young Zhou, you know." The secretary looked at Zhou with a meaningful smile.

From that moment on, Zhou knew that as long as Si Ma was the Party secretary in the company, there would be no hope of his joining the Party. Sometimes he did think of giving him the dictionary, but he could not bear to part with it. After he had refused Si Ma's request for the second time, his mind could no longer remain at ease; he was afraid somebody would steal the book the moment he didn't have it with him. There was no safe place to hide it at the station; his comrades might make off with it if they knew the secretary would pay a quarter of his yearly salary for it. Fortunately, Zhou had his own room now, so he kept the dictionary downstairs in a drawer of the desk.

One evening as Zhou was reading in the room, Director Liang came in, followed by his wife carrying two cups. "Have some tea, Little Zhou?" Liang said. He took a cup and sat down on the sofa, which began squeaking under him.

Zhou stood up, receiving the cup with both hands from Mrs. Liang. "Please don't do this for me."

"Have some tea, Little Zhou," she said with a smile. She looked very kind, her face covered with wrinkles. "We are neighbors, aren't we?"

"Yes, we are."

"Sit down, and you two talk. I have things to do downstairs." She turned and walked away.

"Don't be so polite. If you want tea, just take it," Liang said, blowing away the tea leaves in his cup. Zhou took a sip.

"Little Zhou," Liang said again, "you know I like young people who study hard."

"Yes, I know."

"Tell me, why do you want to study?"

"I don't know for sure. My grandfather was a scholar, but my father didn't finish middle school. He joined the Communist Army to fight the Japanese. He always wants me to study hard and says we are a family of scholars and must carry on the tradition. Besides, I like reading and writing."

"Your father is a good father," Liang announced, as if they were at a meeting. "I'm from a poor peasant's family. If a carrying pole stood up on the ground, my father couldn't tell it means 'one.' But I always say the same thing to my kids like your father says. You see, nowadays schools are closed.[8] Young people don't study but make revolution outside school. They don't know . . . about the revolution. For the revolutionary cause I lost my arm and these fingers." He raised his only hand, whose little and ring fingers were missing. The stumps quivered in the fluorescent light.

Zhou nerved himself for the question. "Can I ask how you lost your arm?"

"All right, I'm going to tell you the story, so that you will study harder." Liang lifted the cup and took a gulp. The tea gargled in his mouth for a few seconds and then went down. "In the fall of 1938, I was a commander of a machine-gun company in the Red Army,[9] and we fought against Chiang Kai-shek's[10] troops in a mountain area in Gansu. My company's task was to hold a hilltop. From there you could control two roads with machine guns. We took the hill and held it to protect our retreating army. The first day we fought a battle with two enemy battalions that attempted to take the hill from us. They left about three hundred bodies on the slopes, but our Party secretary and sixteen other

---

8. **schools are closed:** Schools and colleges were closed during China's Cultural Revolution.
9. **Red Army:** original name for the People's Liberation Army.
10. **Chiang Kai-shek's:** Chiang Kai-shek (1888–1975) was the leader of China's Nationalist Party who fled to Taiwan after being defeated by Mao Tse-tung's Communists.

Chinese forces enter Burma. January 1945.

men were killed. Another twenty were badly wounded. Night came, and we had no idea if all of our army had passed and how long we had to stay on the hill. At about ten o'clock, an orderly[11] came from the Regimental Staff and delivered a message. It had only two words penciled on a scrap of paper. I could tell it was Regimental Commander Hsiao Hsiong's bold handwriting.

"I turned the paper up and down, left and right, but couldn't figure out the meaning. I shouted to the whole company, 'Who can read?' Nobody answered. In fact, only the Party secretary could read, but we had lost him. You can imagine how outraged I was. We were all blind with good eyes! I beat my head with my fists

and couldn't stop cursing. Grabbing the messenger's throat, I yelled, 'If you don't tell me what the message is, I'll shoot you in the eye!'

"The platoon leaders saved the boy's life. They told me it wasn't his fault; he couldn't read either. And a messenger never knew the contents of a message, because if he was caught by the enemy they could make him tell them what he knew. Usually, he was ordered to swallow the message before it fell into the enemy's hands.

"What should we do now? We had no idea where our army was, although we had been told that if we retreated we should go to Maliang Village. That was twenty *li*[12] away in the north. Racking our brains together, we figured there

---

11. **orderly** *n.:* soldier who carries messages and performs personal services for a military officer.

12. ***li:*** Chinese measurement of distance; about one third of a mile.

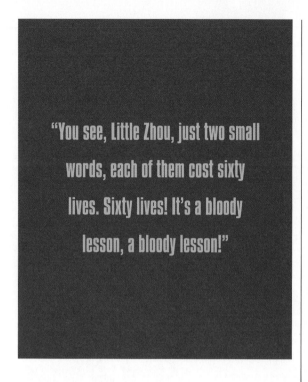

"You see, Little Zhou, just two small words, each of them cost sixty lives. Sixty lives! It's a bloody lesson, a bloody lesson!"

could be only two meanings in the message; one was to stay and the other to retreat, but we couldn't decide which was the one. If the message said to stay but we retreated, then the next day, when our troops passed the mountain without covering fire, there would be heavy casualties and I would be shot by the higher-ups. If the message said to retreat but we stayed, we merely took a risk. That meant to fight more battles or perhaps lose contact with our army for some time afterwards. After weighing the advantages and disadvantages, I decided to stay and told my men to sleep so we could fight the next day. Tired out, we all slept like dead pigs."

Zhou almost laughed, but he restrained himself. Liang went on, "At about five in the morning, the enemy began shelling us. We hadn't expected they would use heavy artillery. The day before they had only launched some mortar shells. Within a minute, rocks, machine guns, arms and legs, branches and trunks of trees were flying everywhere. I heard bugles buzzing on all sides below. I knew the enemy had surrounded us and was charging. At least two thirds of my men were already wiped out by the artillery—there was no way to fight such a bat-

tle. I shouted, 'Run for your lives, brothers!' and led my orderly and a dozen men running away from the hilltop. The enemy was climbing all around. Machine guns were cracking. We had only a few pistols with us—no way to fight back. We were just scrambling for our lives. A shell exploded at our rear and killed seven of the men following me. My left arm was smashed. These two fingers were cut off by a piece of shrapnel from that shell." Liang raised his crippled hand to the level of his collarbone. "Our regiment was at Maliang Village when we arrived. Regimental Commander Hsiao came and slapped my face while the medical staff were preparing to saw my arm off. I didn't feel anything; I almost blacked out. Later I was told that the words in the message were 'Retreat immediately.' If I hadn't lost this arm, Commander Hsiao would've finished me off on the spot. The whole company and twenty-two heavy machine guns, half the machine guns our regiment had, were all gone. Commander Hsiao punished me by making me a groom for the Regimental Staff. I took care of horses for six years. You see, Little Zhou, just two small words, each of them cost sixty lives. Sixty lives! It's a bloody lesson, a bloody lesson!" Liang shook his gray head and drank up the tea.

"Director Liang, I will always remember this lesson." Zhou was moved. "I understand now why you want us to study hard."

"Yes, you're a good young man, and you know the value of books and knowledge. To carry out the revolution we must have literacy and knowledge first."

"Yes, we must."

"All right, it's getting late. I must go. Stay as long as you want. Remember, come and study every day. Never give up. A young man must have a high aspiration and then pursue it."

From then on, Zhou spent more time studying in the room. In the morning, when he was supposed to sleep, he would doze for only an hour and then read for three hours downstairs. His comrades wondered why his bed was empty every morning. When they asked where he had been, he said that Director Liang had work for him to do and that if they needed him, just give the Liangs a ring. Of course, none of them dared go down to check or call the director's home.

Now the "study" was clean and more furnished. The floor was mopped every day. On the desk sat a cup and a thermos bottle always filled with boiled water. Liang's orderly took care of that. Occasionally, the director would come and join Zhou in the evenings. He wanted Zhou to tell him the stories in *The Three Kingdoms,* which in fact Liang knew quite well, for he had heard them time and again for decades. Among the five generals in the classic, he adored Guan Yu, because Guan had both bravery and strategy. After *The Three Kingdoms,* they talked of *All Men Are Brothers.*[13] Liang had Zhou tell him the stories of those outlaw heroes, which Liang actually knew by heart; he was just fond of listening to them. Whenever a battle took a sudden turn, he would give a hearty laugh. Somehow Zhou felt the old man looked younger during these evenings—pink patches would appear on his sallow cheeks after they had sat together for an hour.

Naturally Zhou became an <u>enigma</u> to his comrades, who were eager to figure out what he did downstairs. One afternoon Chief Huang had a talk with Zhou. He asked, "Why do you go to Director Liang's home so often, Young Zhou?"

"I work for him." Zhou would never reveal that he studied downstairs, because the chief could easily find a way to keep him busy at the station.

"What work exactly?"

"Sometimes little chores, and sometimes he wants me to read out Chairman Mao's works and newspaper to him."

"Really? He studies every day?"

"Yes, he studies hard."

"How can you make me believe you?"

"Chief Huang, if you don't believe me, go ask him yourself." Zhou knew the chief dared not make a peep before the director. Huang had better keep himself away from Liang, or the old man would curse his ancestors of eight generations.

"No, it's unnecessary. Zhou Wen, you know I'm not interested in what you do downstairs. It's Secretary Si Ma Lin who asked me about what's going on. I have no idea how he came to know you often stay in Director Liang's home."

"Thanks for telling me that, Chief Huang. Please tell Secretary Si Ma that Director Liang wants me to work for him."

After that, the chief never bothered Zhou again, but Zhou's fellow comrades didn't stop showing their curiosity. They even searched through his suitcase and turned up his mattress to see what he had hidden from them. Zhou realized how lucky it was that he had put his *Ocean of Words* downstairs beforehand. They kept asking him questions. One would ask, "How did you get so close to Director Liang?" Another, "Does he pay you as his secretary?" Another would sigh and say, "What a pity Old Liang doesn't have a daughter!"

It was true Director Liang had only three sons. The eldest son was an officer in Nanjing Military Region; the second worked as an engineer at an ordnance factory in Harbin; his youngest son, Liang Bin, was a middle school student at home. The boy, tall and burly, was a wonderful soccer player. One afternoon during their break from the telegraphic training, Zhou Wen, Zhang Jun, and Gu Wan were playing soccer in the yard behind the church when Liang Bin came by. Bin put down his satchel,[14] hooked up the ball with his instep, and began juggling it on his feet, then on his head, on his shoulders, on his knees—every part of his body seemed to have a spring. He went on doing this for a good three minutes without letting the ball touch the ground. The

---

13. ***All Men Are Brothers:*** popular novel from the Ming dynasty depicting the adventures of 108 heroic outlaws. It was one of the young Mao Tse-tung's favorite books. It is also known as *The Water Margin.*

14. **satchel** *n.:* bag for carrying books.

Vocabulary

enigma (i·nig′mə) *n.:* something baffling.

soldiers were all impressed and asked the boy why he didn't play for the Provincial Juvenile Team.

"They've asked me many times," Bin said, "but I never dare play for them."

"Why?" Gu asked.

"If I did, my dad would break my legs. He wants me to study." He picked up his satchel and hurried home.

Both Zhang and Gu said Director Liang was a fool and shouldn't ruin his son's future that way. Zhou understood why, but he didn't tell them, uncertain if Director Liang would like other soldiers to know his story, which was profound indeed but not very glorious.

Every day the boy had to return home immediately after school, to study. One evening Zhou overheard Director Liang criticizing his son. "Zhou Wen read *The Three Kingdoms* under the road lamp. You have everything here, your own

lamp, your own books, your own desk, and your own room. What you lack is your own strong will. Your mother has spoiled you. Come on, work on the geometry problems. I'll give you a big gift at the Spring Festival if you study hard."

"Will you allow me to join the soccer team?"

"No, you study."

A few days later, Director Liang asked Zhou to teach his son, saying that Zhou was the most knowledgeable man he had ever met and that he trusted him as a young scholar. Zhou agreed to try his best. Then Liang pulled a dog-eared book out of his pocket. "Teach him this," he said. It was a copy of *The Three-Character Scripture.*[15]

Zhou was surprised, not having expected the officer wanted him to teach his son classical Chinese, which Zhou had merely taught himself

---

15. *The Three-Character Scripture:* book for children containing Confucianist teachings on morality.

a little. Where did Liang get this small book? Zhou had heard of the scripture but never seen a copy. Why did a revolutionary officer like Liang want his son to study such a feudal book? Zhou dared not ask and kept the question to himself. Neither did he ever mention the scripture to his comrades. Instead he told them that Director Liang ordered him to teach his son Chairman Mao's *On Practice*,[16] a booklet Zhou knew well enough to talk about in their political studies. Since none of his comrades understood the Chairman's theory, they believed what Zhou told them, and they were impressed by his comments when they studied together.

As his demobilization drew near, Zhou worried desperately and kept asking himself, What will you do now? Without the Party membership you won't get a good job at home, but how can you join the Party before leaving the army? There are only five weeks left. If you can't make it by the New Year, you'll never be able to in the future. Even if you give the dictionary to Secretary Si Ma now, it's already too late. Too late to do anything. But you can't simply sit back waiting for the end; you must do something. There must be a way to bring him around. How?

After thinking of the matter for three days, he decided to talk to Director Liang. One evening, as soon as Zhou sat down in the room, the old man rushed in with snowflakes on his felt hat. "Little Zhou," he said in a thick voice, "I came to you for help."

"How can I help?" Zhou stood up.

"Here, here is Marx's book." Liang put his fur mitten on the desk and pulled a copy of *Manifesto of the Communist Party*[17] out of it. "This winter we divisional leaders are studying this little book. Vice Commissar Hou gave the first lecture this afternoon. I don't understand what he said at all. It wasn't a good lecture.

Maybe he doesn't understand Marx either."

"I hope I can help."

"For example," Liang said, putting the book on the desk and turning a few pages, "here, listen: 'An apparition—an apparition of Communism—has wandered throughout Europe.' Old Hou said an apparition is a 'spook.' Europe was full of spooks. I wonder if it's true. What's an 'apparition,' do you know?"

"Let's see what it means exactly." Zhou took his *Ocean of Words* out of the drawer and began to turn the pages.

"This must be a treasure book, having all the rare characters in it," Liang said, standing closer to watch Zhou searching for the word.

"Here it is." Zhou lifted the dictionary and read out the definition: "'Apparition—specter, ghost, spiritual appearance.'"

"See, no 'spook' at all."

"'Spook' may not be completely wrong for 'apparition,' but it's too low a word."

"You're right. Good. Tomorrow I'll tell Old Hou to drop his 'spook.' By the way, I still don't understand why Marx calls Communism 'an operation.' Isn't Communism a good ideal?"

Zhou almost laughed out loud at Liang's mispronunciation, but controlled himself and said, "Marx must be ironic here, because the bourgeoisie takes the Communists as poisonous snakes and wild beasts—something like an apparition."

"That's right." Liang slapped his paunch, smiling and shaking his head. "You see, Little Zhou, my mind always goes straight and never makes turns. You're a smart young man. I regret I didn't meet you earlier."

Here came Zhou's chance. He said, "But we can't be together for long, because I'll leave for home soon. I'm sure I will miss you and this room."

"What? You mean you'll be discharged?"

"Yes."

"Why do they want a good soldier like you to go?"

Zhou told the truth. "I want to leave the army myself, because my old father is in poor health."

---

16. ***On Practice:*** essay by Mao Tse-tung on political theory and its practice.
17. ***Manifesto of the Communist Party:*** document written by Karl Marx and Friedrich Engels (1820–1895) that contains most of the major communist doctrines.

"Oh, I'm sorry you can't stay longer."

"I will always be grateful to you."

"Anything I can do for you before you leave?"

"One thing, though I don't know if it's right to mention."

"Just say it. I hate men who mince words. Speak up. Let's see if this old man can be helpful." Liang sat down on the sofa.

Zhou pulled over the chair and sat on it. "I'm not a Party member yet. It's shameful."

"Why? Do you know why they haven't taken you into the Party?"

"Yes, because my comrades think I have read too much and I am different from them."

"What?" The thick eyebrows stood up on Liang's forehead. "Does Secretary Si Ma Lin have the same opinion?"

"Yes, he said I had some stinking airs of a petty intellectual. You know I didn't even finish middle school."

" . . . I'll talk to him right now. Come with me." Liang went out to the corridor, where a telephone hung on the wall. Zhou was scared but had to follow him. He regretted having blurted out what the secretary had said and was afraid Director Liang would ask Si Ma what he meant by "stinking airs of a petty intellectual."

"Give me Radio Company," Liang grunted into the phone.

"Hello, who's this? . . . I want to speak to Si Ma Lin." Liang turned to Zhou. "I must teach him a lesson."

"Hello," he said into the phone again. "Is that you, Little Si Ma? . . . Sure, you can tell my voice. Listen, I have a serious matter to discuss with you. . . . It's about Zhou Wen's Party membership. He is a young friend of mine. I have known him for a while and he is a good soldier, a brilliant young man. For what reason haven't you accepted him as a Party member? Isn't he going to leave soon?"

He listened to the receiver. Then he said out loud, "What? The devil take you! That's exactly why he can be a good Party member. What time are we in now?—the seventies of the twentieth century—and you are still so hostile to a knowl-edgeable man. You still have a peasant's mind.

Why does he have to stand the test longer than others? Only because he's learned more? You have a problem in your brain, you know. Tell me, how did we Communists defeat Chiang Kai-shek? With guns? Didn't he have American airplanes and tanks? How come our army, with only rifles plus millet, beat his eight million troops equipped with modern weapons?"

The smart secretary was babbling his answer at the other end. Zhou felt a little relieved, because the director hadn't mentioned what he had told him.

"That's rubbish!" Liang said. "We defeated him by having the Pen. Old Chiang only had the Gun, but we had both the Gun and the Pen. As Chairman Mao has taught us: The Gun and the Pen, we depend on both of them to make revolution and cannot afford to lose either. Are you not a Party secretary? Can't you understand this simple truth? You have a problem here, don't you?"

The clever secretary seemed to be admitting his fault, because the old man sounded less scathing now. "Listen, I don't mean to give you a hard time. I'm an older soldier, and my Party membership is longer than your age, so I know what kind of people our Party really needs. We can recruit men who carry guns by the millions, easily. What we want badly is those who carry pens. My friend Zhou Wen is one of them, don't you think? . . . Comrade Si Ma Lin, don't limit your field of vision to your own yard. Our revolutionary cause is a matter of the entire world. Zhou Wen may not be good in your eyes, but to our revolutionary cause, he is good and needed. Therefore, I suggest you consider his application seriously. . . . Good, I'm pleased you understood it so quickly. . . . Good-bye now." Liang hung up and said to Zhou, " . . . He's so dense." Zhou was sweating, his heart thumping.

Director Liang's call cleared away all obstacles. Within two weeks Zhou joined the Party. Neither Secretary Si Ma nor Chief Huang said a word

Vocabulary

scathing (skā′thiŋ) *adj.*: extremely critical or severe.

alluding to the call. It seemed the secretary had not divulged to anybody the lesson he had received on the telephone. Certainly Zhou's comrades were amazed by the sudden break-through, and he became more mysterious in their eyes. It was rumored that Zhou wouldn't be discharged and instead would be promoted to officer's rank and do propaganda work in the Divisional Political Department. But that never materialized.

The day before he left the army, Zhou went downstairs to fetch his things and say good-bye to Director Liang. No sooner had he entered the room than the old man came in holding some-thing in his hand. It was a small rectangular box covered with purple satin. Liang placed it on the desk and said, "Take this as a keepsake."

Zhou picked it up and opened the lid—a brown Hero pen[18] perched in the white cotton groove. On its chunky body was a vigorous in-scription carved in golden color: "For Comrade Zhou Wen—May You Forever Hold Tight the Revolutionary Pen, Liang Ming Present."

"I appreciate your helping my son," the old man said.

Too touched to say a word, Zhou put the pen into his pocket. Though he had taught the boy *The Three-Character Scripture*, Liang had helped him join the Party, which was an important event in anyone's life, like marriage or rebirth. Even without this gift, Zhou was the one who was indebted, so now he had to give something in return. But he didn't have any valuables with him. At this moment it dawned on him that his *Ocean of Words* was in the drawer. He took it out and presented it to Liang with both hands. "You may find this useful, Director Liang."

"Oh, I don't want to rob you of your inheri-tance. You told me it's your father's book." Liang was rubbing his hand on his leg.

"Please keep it. My father will be glad if he knows it's in your hands."

"All right, it's a priceless treasure." Liang's three fingers were caressing the solid spine of the tome. "I'll cherish it and make my son read ten pages of this good book every day."

Zhou was ready to leave. Liang held out his hand; for the first time Zhou shook that crippled hand, which was ice cold.

"Good-bye," Liang said, looking him in the eye. "May you have a bright future, Little Zhou. Study hard and never give up. You will be a great man, a tremendous scholar. I just know that in my heart."

"I will study hard. Take good care of yourself, Director Liang. I'll write to you. Good-bye."

The old man heaved a feeble sigh and waved his hand. Zhou walked out, overwhelmed by the confidence and resolution surging up in his chest. Outside, the air seemed to be gleaming, and the sky was blue and high. Up there, in the distance, two Chinese jet fighters were soaring noiselessly, ready to knock down any intruder. It was at this moment that Zhou made up his mind to become a socialist man of letters, fighting with the Revolutionary Pen for the rest of his life.

---

18. **Hero pen:** pen manufactured by the Hero Pen Factory of Shanghai, China (today the Hero Pen Company), a major supplier of pens in China.

Hero Pen.

Response and Analysis

Reading Check

1. What arrangement does Director Liang make with Zhou?

2. How much time does Zhou have left to serve in the People's Army? What worries him about his discharge?

3. What book does Zhou refuse to sell, and to whom? Why won't he sell the book?

4. How does Liang help Zhou? Why does he help him?

5. How does Zhou show his thanks to Liang at the end of the story?

Thinking Critically

6. Why is Zhou's being a "bookworm" so unacceptable to his fellow soldiers? What problems does it cause for him?

7. Explain what Zhou needs from Secretary Si Ma Lin. What does Zhou's refusal to sell his book to Si Ma Lin reveal about Zhou's **character**? Why is Zhou able to part with the book later?

8. State the **moral**, or lesson, that Liang's story about the loss of his arm teaches. What is his purpose in telling the story to Zhou? What does Liang value in Zhou?

9. In your opinion, is Zhou a **static** or a **dynamic** character? Explain your answer, citing evidence from the story.

10. Re-read Zhou's thoughts in the story's final paragraph. How do they point toward the **theme** of the story? How would you state this theme?

Literary Criticism

11. A review in *Publishers Weekly* of the book from which this story came states that "the author is at his best when telling the stories of soldiers forced to choose between ideology and love. Whether it is love of a woman or love of knowledge, Jin's characters make

hard choices that will move not just readers interested in China or the army life, but any reader vulnerable to good writing and simple human drama." Do you agree with this assessment, based on the story you have just read? Explain.

WRITING

Comparing Historical and Contemporary Issues

Research the events that took place during China's Cultural Revolution, paying particular attention to book banning and censorship. Then, in an essay, compare those events with more recent attempts at censorship by dictatorial governments of other countries.

Vocabulary Development
Analyzing Context Clues

Explain why the **context clues** in the following sentences are wrong. (The underlined words are Vocabulary words from the story.)

1. After federal agents confiscate your passport, you can legally travel across the border.

2. The skies will be clear for the next two weeks, so we should be prepared for imminent rain.

3. He is an enigma, always truthful and consistent in his behavior.

4. The writer was ecstatic after receiving the critic's scathing review of her novel.

5. Since I kept changing my mind, I knew I had achieved resolution.

FICTION
The Strength of a Mother's Love

Nectar in a Sieve is Kamala Markandaya's unsentimental tale of a family's struggle to survive continuous hardships, including poverty, drought, disease, and hunger in an Indian village. The story is told from the point of view of Rukmani, a young woman who has left her parents' home to marry a caring tenant farmer. Although Rukmani's faith is sorely tested through the years, she remains a steady source of strength for her family.

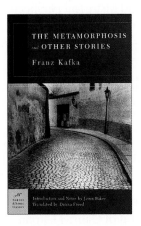

FICTION
A World of Nightmares

A traveling salesman wakes up one morning and discovers that he's been transformed into a repulsive insect. A visitor to a penal colony encounters an officer who is obsessed with a barbaric execution device. Where else would you expect to read of such nightmarish events but in a collection of Franz Kafka's compelling stories? *The Metamorphosis and Other Stories* is Donna Freed's translation of ten stories by the unrivaled modern master of surreal strangeness.

NONFICTION
Surviving to Bear Witness

Once you have read *Night*, Elie Wiesel's harrowing Holocaust testimony, you will never forget it. Wiesel was first exposed to the atrocities of the concentration camp when he was only fifteen. During his captivity in the camps, he struggled to survive and to hold on to his religious faith.

This title is available in the HRW Library.

ADDITIONAL READING

- *One Hundred Love Sonnets* is a mesmerizing introduction to the work of the Nobel laureate Pablo Neruda. These passionate poems, proclaiming Neruda's love for his wife, are presented in the original Spanish along with English translations by Stephen Tapscott.

- In *Kaffir Boy,* Mark Mathabane recounts the traumas he endured growing up under the tyranny of apartheid in a wretched South African ghetto. Despite the relentless cycle of violence and poverty in the ghetto, Mathabane went on to beat the odds, ultimately winning a scholarship to study in the United States.

- Alan Paton's novel *Cry, the Beloved Country* makes a powerful statement about the scourge of apartheid. The focus of the book is the tragic story of Stephen Kumalo, a Zulu pastor who leaves his rural village to find his son, Absalom, in the city of Johannesburg. Kumalo learns that his son has committed a grievous crime and must ultimately come to terms with this fact.

Reporting Literary Research

Writing Assignment
Write a formal research paper of at least 1,500 words on a topic that explores the impact of historical and cultural events on literature.

Literary research involves the study not only of literary works but also of sources that analyze and shed light on them. Such sources may be scholarly writings on the history and culture of a particular literary period, as well as critical studies focusing on the literary works themselves. Your research of such sources can expand your understanding of a literary work, its author, and the culture that produced it.

Prewriting

Choose and Narrow Down a Research Topic

Work from the General to the Specific Spend some time paging through this textbook and taking notes on possible topics. Which selections and which writers have you most enjoyed, and how might you examine them from a cultural and historical perspective? The best literary research papers are written in response to questions prompted by the literary texts themselves—questions that make you curious enough to search for the answers.

• How did Franz Kafka's life as a Jewish bureaucrat in early twentieth-century Prague affect the view of the world he presented in his stories and novels?

• How was the career of the poet Federico García Lorca affected by the political and social climate in Spain during the Spanish Civil War?

• What links exist between the cultural and political climate in South America and the magic realist fiction of Gabriel García Márquez?

Each of the questions above could lead to a topic that could become the focus of cultural and historical research. Be sure, however, that the topic you choose is narrow enough to be covered adequately. For example, examining how the works of contemporary South African writers reflect South African culture is too broad for a 1,500-word paper; the influence of South Africa's cultural and political climate on the writings of Nadine Gordimer is not.

SKILLS
FOCUS

Writing Skills
Write a literary research paper.

**North Carolina
Competency Goal**
6.01

Consider Purpose, Audience, and Tone

Why? Who? and What? Your **purpose** in this assignment is to inform your **audience**—probably your teacher and classmates—about the topic you've selected. Your research paper will be an original **synthesis,** or combination, of information compiled from your research, conclusions you've drawn, and your own insights. In formal research papers you should avoid slang, attempts to be humorous or mocking, flowery language, first- and second-person pronouns, and exclamation points. Try to strike an objective and relatively formal **tone** but avoid stuffiness and artificially elevated language that does not ring true.

Find and Record Sources

Make Your Research Plan After narrowing your topic, develop a list of research questions. You may want to use the *5W-How?* questions method. (This method answers the questions *Who? What? When? Where? Why?* and *How?*) Then, start searching for answers to these questions by consulting a general reference work, such as an encyclopedia or a Web site containing related key words. You can also use the card or online catalog of your school or local library; periodical indexes such as the *Readers' Guide to Periodical Literature;* and community resources such as museums, historical societies, and video stores (for documentary films). In your quest for cultural and historical information, try to use a variety of print and nonprint media sources.

Identify the Best Sources Once you have an overview of the big picture, look for specific sources of information.

- In your research, aim for a balance between primary and secondary sources. **Primary sources** consist of original, firsthand information—for example, letters, autobiographies, interviews, works of literature and art, and historical and cultural documents. **Secondary sources** consist of information about or derived from primary sources or other secondary sources, such as biographies, documentary films, and history books. The novels and stories by Gordimer that you read, as well as collections of Gordimer's letters, essays, and speeches, are primary sources, while a journal article written by a Gordimer scholar or a documentary about the author or about South Africa are secondary sources.

- In the process of identifying sources, you should be sure to check their **validity** and **reliability.** A source is reliable and valid when its facts are accurate and when its ideas are presented objectively. You will occasionally find, however, that sources—both primary and secondary—can be biased, or slanted, as well as inaccurate. In your search, give priority to information published by major universities or publishing companies. These sources provide a benchmark of credibility, which you can use to evaluate other sources.

TIP In formal academic writing, avoid trite expressions and clichés—unoriginal phrases that are so overused they have become lifeless and almost meaningless, such as "hailed by critics," "ample proof," "resting on his laurels," "by their very nature," "from time immemorial," "in the world today," "all walks of life," "the subject at hand," and so on.

TIP As you conduct research, think about how to prioritize and organize the information you are gathering so that you can effectively construct your thesis. In writing about Nadine Gordimer's works, for example, you may not need to start your research with a collection of ten articles on the culture of apartheid in South Africa; it might make more sense to begin by focusing on one or two of Gordimer's works, a collection of the author's essays, and a good general reference on South African history and culture.

- Another important research strategy is to look for information from all **relevant perspectives,** or points of view, on your topic. Look for sources revealing the perspectives of a variety of scholars—literary and historical—who have written about your topic or related matters. For a writer like Gordimer, try to find information from both African and American or British writers, as well as writers of other nationalities. Try not to become overly dependent on a single source or a single type of source.

Keep Track of Your Sources

For the convenience of your readers, you will need to provide exact details about every source you use in your research paper. You should include this information in a *Works Cited* list or a bibliography at the end of your report. Use these suggestions to help you keep track of your sources.

- **Make a source card, or bibliography card, for every source you use.** You may keep your list on three- by five-inch index cards, in a computer file, or on several pages of a notebook.

- **Number your sources.** Assign each source a number. Use the number on your note cards, rather than the author and title, when you take notes from a given source.

- **Record all publishing information.** Note everything you might need for your *Works Cited* list—for example, author and title, city of publication, name of publisher, and date. This book uses the Modern Language Association (MLA) format, often preferred by English teachers. Different formats include those of the *Chicago Manual of Style* or the American Psychological Association (APA).

- **Annotate your source card.** Write a short note about the contents of the source and your evaluation of the source.

- **Note the library call number or location of the source.** This information will save you time if you need to retrieve the source later.

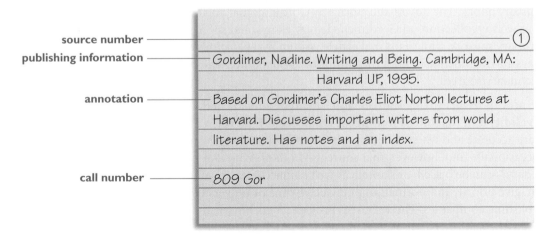

source number

publishing information

Gordimer, Nadine. Writing and Being. Cambridge, MA:
          Harvard UP, 1995.

annotation

Based on Gordimer's Charles Eliot Norton lectures at
Harvard. Discusses important writers from world
literature. Has notes and an index.

call number

809 Gor

Take Notes

As you take notes, use the guidelines below to decide how to record each piece of information—by direct quotation, paraphrase, or summary.

- **Direct quotation** Quote an author directly and exactly, including the original punctuation, capitalization, spelling, and emphasis. Enclose the passage in quotation marks. Since your paper should be a synthesis of information you derive from outside sources and of your own analysis, avoid using too many direct quotations. If you need only part of a quotation, you may use ellipsis points to show omissions from the quoted text. If you need to insert your own words into a quotation to clarify or explain it, place brackets around those insertions.

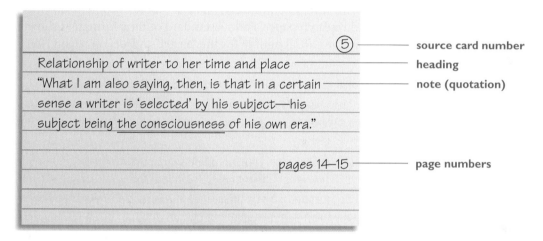

⑤	source card number
Relationship of writer to her time and place	heading
"What I am also saying, then, is that in a certain	note (quotation)
sense a writer is 'selected' by his subject—his	
subject being the consciousness of his own era."	
pages 14–15	page numbers

- **Paraphrase** When you want to use material from a source without directly quoting the source, paraphrase the information. When you paraphrase, you rewrite a passage completely, using your own words and style. An effective paraphrase is usually about the same length as the original.

- **Summary** When you want to use the main idea presented in a source, summarize the information. A typical summary is highly condensed—often one fourth to one third the length of the original.

> **TIP** Plagiarism is a serious academic offense in which you fail to give credit to an author whose words or ideas you either have used verbatim (word for word) or have simply replaced with synonyms. When you are paraphrasing, avoid plagiarizing by completely rewriting a passage in your own words and style. Always remember to cite the source.

Write Your Thesis Statement and Make an Outline

Identify Your Main Idea In a research paper your **thesis statement** is a sentence (occasionally two sentences) that clearly identifies your main idea. In essence, your thesis statement reflects the answers to your original research questions. The thesis statement serves as a signal or road map for your readers to let them know what to expect in your paper. Here is the thesis statement of the Writer's Model essay about Gordimer and South African culture:

In her fiction and nonfiction alike, Gordimer's work displays a complex, profound engagement with South African culture, as well as with the place of the writer in society.

TIP
• **Chronological order** can be used to discuss events in an author's or character's life in the order that they occurred.

• **Order of importance** can be used to discuss main ideas about an author's work. The main idea is often discussed last.

• **Logical order** groups ideas by the relationships among them—for example, cause-and-effect or comparison-contrast relationships.

Note that at this point your thesis statement is preliminary. You might change it later for reasons related to content or style.

Arrange Your Ideas After developing your thesis statement, create an outline by arranging your note cards according to their main-idea headings. Find an order that makes sense. You will probably end up using a combination of organizational patterns—for example, chronological order, order of importance, and logical order.

Organizing your ideas prepares you to write a **formal outline.** In its final form, such an outline can serve as a table of contents for the finished research paper. Follow standard outline format, as shown below in the partial outline for the Writer's Model on page 1105.

II. Gordimer's First Three Novels and Apartheid
  A. The Lying Days (1953)
    1. Search of Helen Shaw, white protagonist, for social identity
    2. Parallel with young Nadine Gordimer as member of a "minority-within-the-white-minority"
    3. Status of both figures as marginalized by society
  B. A World of Strangers (1958)
    1. Shift in narrator from insider to outsider point of view
    2. Toby Hood's dual life
      a. Relationship with Cecil Rowe, his white girlfriend
      b. Relationship with Steven Sitole, his black friend
    3. Voice of moral authority in novel: the social activist Anna Louw
  C. Occasion for Loving (1963)
    1. Prominence of interracial relationship between Ann and Gideon
    2. Background of violence in real life: the Sharpeville massacre
    3. Gordimer's pessimism: progress requires acceptance of racial separation

Document Sources

Reveal Your Sources To document a research report means to identify the sources from which the information in your paper came. In general, document all but the most widely known quotations (such as familiar Shakespearean or biblical phrases); all theories, ideas, and opinions other than your own; all survey data, research studies, and interviews conducted by someone other than yourself; and all obscure information represented as factual. You don't need to document common knowledge—information that can be found in standard reference works.

Place **parenthetical citations** (sources enclosed in parentheses) within the body of your paper as close as possible to the information they document. These references direct readers to the *Works Cited* list at the end of your report. For most citations, use the author's last name and the page number. If you name the author in the sentence, give only the page number in the citation.

GUIDELINES FOR GIVING CREDIT WITHIN A PAPER

Types of Sources	Content of Citation/Example
Sources with one author	Author's last name and a page reference, if any (Head 63)
Separate passages in a single source	Author's last name and page references, if any (Ettin 1, 5)
Sources with more than one author	All authors' last names; if over three, use first author's last name and the abbreviation *et al.* ("and others") (Bazin and Seymour 15)
Multivolume sources	Author's last name, plus volume and page reference (Roberts 2: 233)
Sources with a title only	Full title (if short) or shortened version with page reference (World Almanac 54)
Literary sources published in many editions	Author's last name, title, and division references (act, scene, canto, book, chapter, part, and line numbers) (Ham. 1.2.51–55)
Indirect sources	Abbreviation *qtd. in* before the source (qtd. in Ettin 45)
More than one source in the same citation	Citations separated with semicolons (Head 14; Temple-Thurston 67)
More than one source by a single author	Author's last name with title of works (if brief) or a shorter version of the title as necessary (Gordimer, Essential Gesture 105) **(refers in Works Cited to The Essential Gesture: Writing, Politics, and Places)**

In your *Works Cited* list, follow these guidelines.

- Center the words *Works Cited*.

- Begin each entry on a separate line. Double-space all entries.

- Alphabetize the sources by the authors' last names. If there is no author, alphabetize the item by its title, ignoring *A, An,* and *The* and using the first letter of the next word.

- If you use two or more sources by the same author, include the author's name only in the first entry. For all other entries, put three hyphens in place of the author's name, followed by a period (--- .).

Standard Reference Works

NOTE: When an author or editor is credited in a standard reference work, the source is listed under that person's name. Otherwise, the source is listed by the title of the book or article. Page number and volume numbers are not needed if the work alphabetizes entries. For common reference works, such as the *Encyclopædia Britannica*, the edition year is sufficient publication information.

Books

NOTE: Use shortened forms of publishers' names. For the words *University* and *Press*, use the letters *U* and *P*.

One Author

Clingman, Stephen. The Novels of Nadine Gordimer: History from the Inside. Amherst: U of Massachusetts P, 1992.

Two Authors

Bazin, Nancy Topping, and Marilyn Dallman Seymour, eds. Conversations with Nadine Gordimer. Jackson: UP of Mississippi, 1990.

Multiple Authors

Driver, Dorothy, et al. Nadine Gordimer: A Bibliography of Primary and Secondary Sources: 1937–1992. Bibliographical Research in African Literature Series. London: Hans Zell, 1993.

Selections Within a Book

From a Book of Works by One Author

Gordimer, Nadine. The Essential Gesture: Writing, Politics and Places. New York: Penguin, 1989.

Introduction, Preface, Foreword, or Afterword

Clingman, Stephen. Introduction. The Essential Gesture: Writing, Politics and Places. By Nadine Gordimer. New York: Penguin, 1989. 1-15.

Articles and Reviews from Magazines, Newspapers, and Journals

From a Periodical

Dinnage, Rosemary. "In a Far-Off Country." Rev. of None to Accompany Me, by Nadine Gordimer. Times Literary Supplement 9 Sept. 1994: 20.

From a Scholarly Journal

Bailey, Nancy. "Living Without the Future: Nadine Gordimer's July's People." World Literature Written in English 24 (1984): 215-24.

Other Sources

Interview

Interview with Stephen Clingman. Gordimer, Nadine. 27 Mar. 1987.

Material Accessed Through the Internet

Nobel e-Museum. 25 June 2003. Gordimer, Nadine. "Writing and Being." The Nobel Foundation, Stockholm. 18 July 2004. <http://www.nobel.se/literature/laureates/1991/gordimer-lecture.html>

PRACTICE & APPLY 1 Using the preceding instructions, select a topic for your literary research paper. Then, locate and record information from primary and secondary sources. Write a thesis statement, make a formal outline, and plan your paper's documentation. Be sure to follow the guidelines for making source cards (page 1100) and taking notes (page 1101).

Writing Skills
Analyze information. Write a thesis statement. Make an outline. Include a *Works Cited* list.

North Carolina Competency Goal
6.01; 6.02

Writing

Literary Research Paper

A Writer's Framework

Introduction

- Hook your readers with an interesting opening.

- Provide background information about the author, his or her works, and the period in which he or she wrote.

- Include a clear thesis statement.

Body

- Choose one or a combination of organizational patterns.

- Develop each main idea that supports your thesis.

- Add facts, details, and examples from your research.

- Use sources offering different perspectives.

Conclusion

- Restate your thesis.

- Bring your paper to an effective close by providing a final insight into your research or the significance of your topic.

A Writer's Model

Nadine Gordimer and the Consciousness of Place

Writing, Politics and Places. So reads the subtitle of The Essential Gesture, a collection of essays, speeches, and letters by the South African writer Nadine Gordimer, whose career has almost exactly overlapped with the history of apartheid in that country. Gordimer's choice of subtitle for The Essential Gesture is significant for the analysis of her distinguished body of work. In her fiction and nonfiction alike, Gordimer's work displays a complex, profound engagement with South African culture, as well as with the place of the writer in society. Taken together, Gordimer's works offer convincing evidence of her assertion that "a writer is 'selected' by his subject—his subject being *the consciousness* of his own era" (Selected Stories 14-15).

INTRODUCTION
Primary source

Thesis statement

(continued)

(continued)

As she said in a lecture given in 1995, "We are not only children of our time but of our place" (Gordimer, Living 225).

By the time Gordimer was awarded the Nobel Prize in literature in 1991, her steady output of fiction had made her the most celebrated writer from her native South Africa. As one critic has remarked, Gordimer's work has given us an "ongoing text" to set alongside the history of apartheid (Ettin 1).

Gordimer began publishing stories in 1937, when she was only fourteen, and her first full-length novel, The Lying Days, appeared in 1953. Gordimer's central theme in that novel is the struggle of a young white woman, Helen Shaw, to achieve social and political identity. As critics have pointed out (Head 35; Temple-Thurston 18), it is hard not to see parallels between Helen and the young Gordimer, who struggled to form her artistic identity as a member of what she later called "a minority-within-the-white-minority" (Essential Gesture 305). Both Helen Shaw and Gordimer, in fact, are triply marginalized: first, as whites on the margin of a black majority; then, as liberals in a conservative society; and finally, as women in a traditionally male-dominated culture.

In her second novel, A World of Strangers (1958), Gordimer shifts the point of view from inside South Africa to outside. In this work the narrator is a young and ultimately superficial visitor, Toby Hood, who travels from Britain to South Africa to represent his family's publishing firm. As the critic Dominic Head points out, Toby settles into a dual life, alternating between white high society and the black townships (48). He conceals his friendship with a black man, Steven Sitole, from his white girlfriend, Cecil Rowe. Toby, who has no political insight or interest, is gradually revealed to be an unreliable narrator. By contrast, the true voice of moral authority in the novel belongs to Anna Louw, a social activist who struggles to maintain an interracial marriage and must then undergo detention and imprisonment because of it (Temple-Thurston 26).

An interracial relationship is also an important element in Gordimer's third novel, Occasion for Loving (1963). Barbara Temple-Thurston considers this work "far more politically engaged than the first two novels" (30). In his analysis of Occasion for Loving, Dominic Head draws attention to an escalation of racially motivated state violence in this period, symbolized most powerfully by the Sharpeville massacre of 1960, in which police opened fire on a crowd of unarmed demonstrators, killing 67 and wounding 186. According to Head, "the failure of cross-racial personal contacts in Occasion for Loving"

(Margin labels:)

BODY
Direct quotation from secondary source

First main idea

Writer's conclusion

Specific examples

Author of quotation named in text

Connection of literature and history

suggests that at this moment in political and social history "progress requires an acceptance of separation" (63).

Two more representative novels, drawn from later periods of Gordimer's career, show her continuing engagement with cultural and political developments in South Africa. In July's People (1981), Gordimer dramatizes the primal nightmare of many South African whites: a violent revolution by the black majority that leaves Johannesburg in ruins. Bam and Maureen Smales escape from their comfortable suburban home with their family, becoming utterly dependent on their black servant July, who plays host to them at his country hut. The Smales are relieved to be rescued, but they cannot escape the consciousness of their comfortable social code (Folks). The resulting conflicts reveal Gordimer as a keen psychological observer of the corrosive effects of apartheid on both races.

In The House Gun (1998), Gordimer's plot unfolds in the post-apartheid era. Using the format of a courtroom drama, she tells the story of a young white architect, Duncan Lindgard, accused of murder and defended by a brilliant black advocate, Hamilton Motsamai. One of the novel's main themes is the anguish of Duncan's parents, Harald and Claudia, who struggle to comprehend the violence and grief and fear that have suddenly burst into their lives. Temple-Thurston considers The House Gun "a profound meditation on the philosophy and nature of violence" (150). In this connection it is worth noting that Gordimer, in a 1990 essay titled "How Shall We Look at Each Other Then?" declared that violence had "become the South African way of life. . . . The vocabulary of violence has become the common speech of both black and white" (Living 140, 142).

As Stephen Clingman has noted, Gordimer's fiction and nonfiction can be seen as "two different modes revolving around a single process" (13). Although she has resisted the label *crusader* (Gordimer, "Writing and Being" 130), Gordimer has been forceful and unwavering on the responsibility of writers to "reach out to grasp the hand of [our] society." It is this act that Gordimer, borrowing from a phrase from literary theoretician Roland Barthes, has named the "essential gesture" (Living 99).

In an eloquent address to university students titled "Speak Out: The Necessity for Protest," Gordimer reminds her audience that the tradition of protest in South Africa is both old and honorable, and she incisively quotes George Steiner: "Men are accomplices to that which leaves them indifferent" (Essential Gesture 91-92). In her Nobel lecture, Gordimer compares the writer to an explorer who plants a flag ("Writing and Being" par. 9). Elsewhere, she has

(continued)

Specific examples

Writer's conclusion

Specific examples

Link between primary source and literature

Second main idea

Specific examples

Additional examples from primary sources

Paraphrase

(continued)

described literature as "one of the most enduring means by which ideas cross frontiers and become universal" (Gordimer, Living 171). In her essay "A Writer's Freedom," Gordimer concisely sums up the writer's task: "All that the writer can do, as a writer, is to go on writing *the truth as he sees it*" (Essential Gesture 105). In portraying the truth about her society as she has perceived it, Gordimer has revealed a lifelong commitment and a many-faceted consciousness of her time and place. She has been, indeed, a "passionate interpreter of South African reality" ("Nadine Gordimer").

CONCLUSION

Final insight

Works Cited

Clingman, Stephen. Introduction. The Essential Gesture: Writing, Politics and Places. By Nadine Gordimer. New York: Penguin, 1989. 1-15.

Ettin, Andrew Vogel. Introduction. Betrayals of the Body Politic: The Literary Commitments of Nadine Gordimer. By Ettin. Charlottesville: UP of Virginia, 1993.

Folks, Jeffrey J. "Artist in the Interregnum: Nadine Gordimer's July's People." Critique: Studies in Contemporary Fiction 39.2 (1998): 115-126.

Gordimer, Nadine. The Essential Gesture: Writing, Politics and Places. New York: Penguin, 1989.

- - - . Living in Hope and History: Notes from Our Century. New York: Farrar, 1999.

- - - . Selected Stories. New York: Penguin, 1983.

- - - . "Writing and Being." Nobel e-Museum. 25 June 2003. The Nobel Foundation, Stockholm. 18 July 2004. <http://www.nobel.se/literature/laureates/1991/gordimer-lecture.html>

Head, Dominic. Nadine Gordimer. Cambridge: Cambridge UP, 1994.

"Nadine Gordimer." Twentieth-Century British Literature. Ed. Harold Bloom. 6 vols. New York: Chelsea, 1986.

Temple-Thurston, Barbara. Nadine Gordimer Revisited. New York: Twayne, 1999.

North Carolina Competency Goal
6.01; 6.02

INTERNET

More Writer's Models
Keyword:
LE5 WL-7

SKILLS FOCUS

Writing Skills
Draft and document a literary research paper.

PRACTICE & APPLY 2 Use the framework and the Writer's Model shown on pages 1105–1108 for help in drafting and documenting your literary research paper and creating a *Works Cited* list for it.

Revising

Evaluate and Revise Your Literary Research Paper

To make your paper the best it can be, read it over carefully at least twice. First, evaluate and revise the content and organization of your report. Then, evaluate and revise its style.

Use the guidelines in the following chart to evaluate and revise content and style. To answer the evaluation questions in the first column, use the tips in the second column. Then, if necessary, use the revision techniques suggested in the third column.

PEER REVIEW

Before you revise, trade papers with a peer and act as each other's editor. Another person can often spot problems that the writer cannot see. Your peer editor may be able to point out problems with organization or identify ideas in your paper that need more or better supporting details.

editor in charge

Rubric: Reporting Literary Research

Evaluation Questions	▶ Tips	▶ Revision Techniques
❶ Does the introduction hook the reader's attention, give background, and clearly state the thesis?	▶ **Circle** the hook, **underline** background information, and **bracket** the thesis statement.	▶ **Add** a quotation or interesting detail to hook readers. **Add** necessary background. **Add** a thesis statement.
❷ Does the body include only main ideas and supporting details that are relevant to the thesis?	▶ **Highlight** the main ideas. **Number** supporting details for each.	▶ **Delete** irrelevant ideas and details. **Add** details to support ideas with fewer than three supporting details.
❸ Are facts and ideas stated mainly in the writer's own words?	▶ **Star** sequences containing direct quotations. If more than one third of the sentences are starred, revise.	▶ **Replace** unnecessary direct quotations with paraphrases and summaries.
❹ Is the paper written in an objective and formal academic style that avoids slang, flowery or artificial language, and clichés and trite expressions?	▶ **Draw** a squiggly line underneath phrases or passages that are either too informal or too stilted. **Write Cl** above words or phrases that are clichés.	▶ **Rewrite** overly informal or flowery sentences to make them more formal yet natural sounding. **Replace** clichés and trite expressions with strong, direct, original language.
❺ Are sources credited when necessary? Are citations correctly placed and punctuated?	▶ **Place check marks** beside material that requires documentation from outside sources.	▶ **Add** parenthetical citations. **Correct** placement and punctuation of citations.
❻ Does the conclusion restate the thesis? Is the *Works Cited* list complete and correctly formatted?	▶ **Bracket** the restatement of the thesis. **Place an X** beside *Works Cited* entries of each source used in the body of the paper.	▶ **Add** a sentence or two restating the thesis. **Add** and **correct** *Works Cited* entries.

ANALYZING THE REVISION PROCESS

Study these revisions, and answer the questions that follow.

> Both Helen Shaw and Gordimer, in fact, are triply marginal-
> ized: first, as whites on the margin of a black majority; then, as
> liberals in a conservative society; and finally, as women in a
> traditionally male-dominated culture. Gordimer's central
> theme ~~or underlying message~~ in that novel is the struggle of
> a young white woman, Helen Shaw, to achieve social and
> *As critics have pointed out (Head 35; Temple-Thurston 18), it*
> political identity. It is hard not to see parallels between Helen
> and the young Gordimer, who struggled to form her artistic
> identity as a member of what she later called "a minority-
> within-the-minority" (Gordimer, Essential Gesture 305).

**North
Carolina
Competency
Goal**
6.01; 6.02

Responding to the Revision Process

1. Why did the writer move the first sentence?
2. Why did the writer delete information from the second sentence?
3. Why did the writer add information to the last sentence?

**SKILLS
FOCUS**

Writing Skills
Revise for content
and style.

PRACTICE & APPLY 3 Use the guidelines in this section to evaluate and revise the content and organization of your report. Then, evaluate and revise the style of your paper.

Publishing

Proofread and Publish Your Essay

Polish the Prose Don't allow careless errors in grammar, usage, and mechanics to destroy your credibility as an authority on your research topic. Instead, finish the job by proofreading your paper very carefully. Meticulously correct every error you find. While good content, organization, and style are the more impressive aspects of a paper, error-free writing is also impressive.

Publish Your Essay Your report synthesizes a good deal of information that supports the conclusions you have drawn, and it contains your hard-earned interpretations and insights. Don't let your work go to waste after sharing it with your teacher and classmates. Consider these publishing ideas in order to make your work available to others.

- Save your literary research project as a writing sample for a college application.
- If your school has a Web site or you know of a Web site focusing on a topic related to your paper, submit the report to the site creators for possible inclusion.

Reflect on Your Essay

Look Back Responding to the questions below will help you think about what this research project has meant to you and what you've learned about your strengths and challenges as a writer. Keep your answers along with a copy of your paper, and refer to both the next time you write a research report.

- What was the most interesting discovery your research produced? Why?
- What questions did your research answer that you had not asked or anticipated? Explain.

 PRACTICE & APPLY Following the guidelines in this section, proofread your research paper to correct any mechanical errors. Then, publish your essay in an appropriate forum and reflect on your literary research paper.

COMPUTER TIP

If you have access to advanced publishing software, consider using those tools to design and format graphics and visuals to enhance the content of your research paper. For more on graphics and visuals, see "Designing Your Writing," page 1157, in the Writer's Handbook.

SKILLS FOCUS

Writing Skills
Proofread and publish your essay. Answer reflection questions.

 **North Carolina Competency Goal** 6.01

Presenting Literary Research

Speaking Assignment
Adapt your literary research paper for an oral presentation to an audience.

Researchers in many fields—such as medicine, history, literature, and economics—publish their research in the form of articles and books. These same researchers also make oral presentations of their research results at various meetings and conferences. In this workshop you will do the same—adapt your written literary research report for an oral presentation.

Adapt Your Literary Research Paper

Tailor Your Content to Your Audience The purpose of your oral report will be to share the results of your research with an audience—in this case, your teacher and classmates. Adapting your literary research paper means putting it into a new form that will suit the requirements and restrictions of an oral presentation. Listeners, unlike readers, cannot control the pace at which they take in information; they will not be able to stop and think about information or re-read it. Therefore, you may need to simplify and clarify the material from your paper. Use the following suggestions for adapting your paper:

North Carolina Competency Goal
2.03; 3.03; 5.01; 5.03

- Reshape and focus your **introduction,** making it as lively as possible. Use an interesting fact, an intriguing quotation, or a challenging question to seize the attention of your audience right away.

- State your **thesis** clearly in the opening of your talk. Revisit your thesis in slightly different words throughout the presentation.

INTERNET
Speeches
Keyword:
LE5 WL-7

- Use your **conclusion** to repeat and emphasize your thesis; don't let your audience leave with any doubts about your main points. Try communicating a final insight into your topic with a relevant anecdote or a compelling quotation.

- Simplify your vocabulary, and break up long sentences into shorter ones. Try to make your report both informative and entertaining by using a combination of **exposition, narration,** and **description.**

- Include information from **primary** and **secondary** sources. Be sure to include information from all relevant perspectives on the topic.

SKILLS FOCUS

Listening and Speaking Skills
Present a literary research paper.

- At the beginning of your talk, tell your audience that you will be using information from a variety of sources. Do not cite sources except to identify the author of an important quotation or the source of a striking fact or conclusion. Practice smoothly integrating important quotations into your oral presentation. Transitional expressions, such as *according to, as the critic_____ has noted, in the author's words, in an interview with,* and so on, will help you signal to your audience that you are including a direct quotation.

Rehearse Your Presentation

Speak with Authority To make an impact as an authority on your subject, plan to deliver your presentation extemporaneously—that is, in a way that seems natural and not overly prepared, as one would expect from an expert on a topic. You should not memorize your presentation word-for-word; instead, you should create note cards with reminders of important points and the full text of important quotations. Rehearse your presentation until you are thoroughly familiar and comfortable with your material and able to deliver it in an assured manner using a formal, objective tone.

Practice Makes Perfect Once you are comfortable with the content of your presentation, begin to rehearse it using one or more of these rehearsal strategies: videotape your presentation, practice in front of a mirror, or present your report to your family or friends. Pay attention not only to the content of your presentation but also to performance details such as those listed in the chart below.

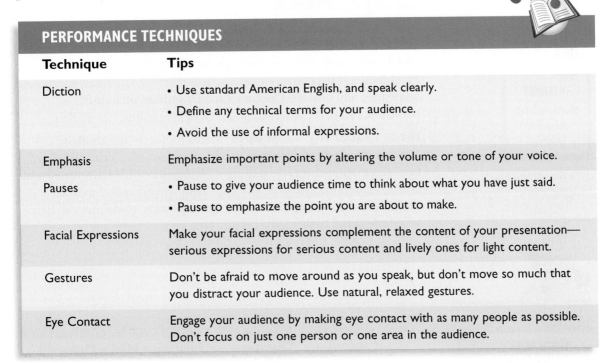

PERFORMANCE TECHNIQUES	
Technique	**Tips**
Diction	• Use standard American English, and speak clearly. • Define any technical terms for your audience. • Avoid the use of informal expressions.
Emphasis	Emphasize important points by altering the volume or tone of your voice.
Pauses	• Pause to give your audience time to think about what you have just said. • Pause to emphasize the point you are about to make.
Facial Expressions	Make your facial expressions complement the content of your presentation—serious expressions for serious content and lively ones for light content.
Gestures	Don't be afraid to move around as you speak, but don't move so much that you distract your audience. Use natural, relaxed gestures.
Eye Contact	Engage your audience by making eye contact with as many people as possible. Don't focus on just one person or one area in the audience.

Use Visuals Effectively Consider enhancing your presentation by using **visuals**—charts, graphs, photographs, or exhibits. If you decide to use visuals, think carefully about how to present them, and include them in your rehearsals. Visuals should be relevant to the part of the oral presentation you're delivering when you introduce them and large enough for the audience to see clearly.

North Carolina Competency Goal
6.01

SKILLS FOCUS

PRACTICE & APPLY 5 Follow the instructions in this workshop to adapt your literary research paper for an oral presentation.

Listening and Speaking Skills
Rehearse effective performance techniques.

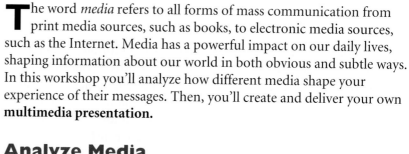

Creating a Multimedia Presentation

The word *media* refers to all forms of mass communication from print media sources, such as books, to electronic media sources, such as the Internet. Media has a powerful impact on our daily lives, shaping information about our world in both obvious and subtle ways. In this workshop you'll analyze how different media shape your experience of their messages. Then, you'll create and deliver your own **multimedia presentation.**

Analyze Media

Media Sources Each type of media has distinct characteristics that affect the way we experience its message. The messages that we receive and decode every day come through two categories of media sources. **Print media sources** include books, newspapers, magazines, pamphlets, billboards, and posters. **Electronic media sources** include films, television, radio, the Internet, audio CDs, DVDs, and CD-ROMs.

Media Literary Concepts Media literacy—the ability to analyze, interpret, and evaluate media messages—is a crucial skill in our information-saturated culture. It is important to be informed and critical readers and viewers who can "read" media messages and understand how they influence us. The following guidelines can help you understand basic media literacy concepts.

Quick guide

MEDIA LITERACY CONCEPTS	
Concept	**Questions for Analyzing Media Messages**
1. **All media messages are created by someone.** Individuals—alone or in groups—decide what elements to include in the message, what to leave out, and how to sequence them.	What is the point of view or experience of the message maker? Do I understand how the creator of the message has shaped it through choices in selecting, sequencing, and editing?
2. **Media messages are not reality; they are *representations* of reality that present a particular point of view.** For example, a television news account of a disaster will be edited to show a select few images and words.	What words, images, or sounds were used to create the message? What may have been omitted or selectively focused on?

(continued)

3. **Individuals interpret and respond to media messages differently.** Your interpretation of a media message is based on your own unique knowledge and experiences.

What does the message make me think or feel? Am I receptive to this message, or does something about it bother me?

4. **People create media messages for many purposes:** to inform, persuade, entertain, express ideas—and make money.

Who created the message? What is the main purpose of it? Might there be more than one purpose?

5. **Each type of mass media has unique characteristics.** Messages are shaped according to the media through which the message will be presented.

How does the form of a media affect the message that is being delivered?

Understand Media Strategies To be an effective media consumer, you should be able to **interpret** and **evaluate** some of the most common **media strategies.**

MEDIA STRATEGIES

Strategy	Examples
Language, which can be tailored to suit any purpose, audience, or message, is generally the main strategy for accomplishing a media purpose.	An informational television program aimed at teenage viewers might use fast-paced humor, current slang, and trendy references.
Visual representations, including film, art, photographs, charts, and maps, present information that a reader or viewer can respond to quickly.	A billboard showing a celebrity athlete wearing a particular brand of running shoes might influence a consumer to buy the same shoes.
Special effects, including computer-generated graphics, lighting, and audio effects, can highlight specific details and create illusions.	A television commercial might use CGI (computer-generated images) to show a dog performing miraculous feats of strength after eating a particular brand of dog food.
Symbols and stereotypes are used to convey information quickly in ways that an audience can easily recognize. A public **symbol** is a widely recognized person, place, thing, or event that stands both for itself and for something beyond itself. A **stereotype** is a generalized belief about an entire group of individuals, which is based on ideas that are overly simplistic or incorrect.	A political advertisement in a magazine might use the symbol of the American flag to show that a candidate stands for American values. A television commercial for a laptop computer might use the stereotype of a stressed and harried business traveler to promote the benefits of wireless technology.

PRACTICE & APPLY **1** Find a common topic that is treated in four different media sources, two print and two nonprint. Analyze the message in each source, and evaluate how successfully each message achieves its intended purpose.

Create and Deliver a Multimedia Presentation

Choose Your Topic A **multimedia presentation** integrates a speech or oral presentation with text, images, and audio. These media elements are balanced with the spoken part of the presentation. Author studies, surveys of literary movements, examinations of cultural and historical influences on literature—all of these and more lend themselves well to multimedia presentations. For this presentation you will examine a literary work to show how it reflects the country or culture from which it came, accessing cultural information from a variety of print and nonprint media sources.

To choose a topic, consider the contemporary literature in this anthology. You may already be interested in a particular country, author, literary movement, or cultural issue. When you select a topic, consider your **purpose** and **audience.** In this workshop your purpose will be to inform, and your audience will be your teacher and classmates.

Research Your Topic Use these research guidelines:

- Choose one or more pieces of literature that reflect the culture or country of your choice. For example, the short story "Dead Men's Path" by Chinua Achebe (page 996) reflects Nigerian culture.

- Analyze the literature, and determine what cultural ideas it reflects. "Dead Men's Path" is concerned with the tensions between modern and traditional beliefs in a postcolonial African country.

- Collect information about the culture from a wide variety of sources, both print and electronic. Take careful notes on any facts, examples, or quotations for possible use in your presentation.

- Document all your sources so that you give proper credit for others' words, images, or sounds.

Develop a Thesis Statement Write a clear **thesis statement** that encompasses your ideas and presents your focus. Here is one thesis statement for a presentation on "Dead Men's Path."

> In "Dead Men's Path," Chinua Achebe examines the tensions that result when traditional African beliefs clash with the modern ideas of westernized Africans who have turned away from ancient tribal culture.

TIP By documenting sources, you honor copyright laws and avoid the serious academic offense of plagiarism—using someone else's words, images, or sounds without giving proper credit. (See pages 1102–1104 for more on documenting sources.) Also, your audience members can then refer to your list of documented sources for further information.

SKILLS FOCUS

Media Skills
Analyze media. Create a multimedia presentation.

North Carolina Competency Goal
1.02

Select Media Choose text, images, and sounds that elaborate on the spoken content of your presentation. Use a wide range of media sources, including films, newspapers, magazines, CD-ROMs, online information, television, audio CDs, video, and electronic media–generated images. Consider what type of support is appropriate for each element of your presentation.

Use Media and Maximize Your Impact

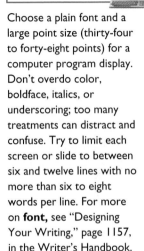

COMPUTER TIP

Choose a plain font and a large point size (thirty-four to forty-eight points) for a computer program display. Don't overdo color, boldface, italics, or underscoring; too many treatments can distract and confuse. Try to limit each screen or slide to between six and twelve lines with no more than six to eight words per line. For more on **font,** see "Designing Your Writing," page 1157, in the Writer's Handbook.

- **Text** refers to any words that appear on a poster, the screen of a video, a computer screen slide, and so on. For example, in a report on "Dead Men's Path," you might use text to provide a definition of postcolonialism or to present important quotations from the story. Limit the amount of text you expect your audience to read.

- **Images** are visual representations—everything from photos and charts to film clips and computer-generated animation. Images appeal to an audience's emotions and provide the necessary visual impressions of people, places, and things relevant to your topic. For "Dead Men's Path," you could show a map of Nigeria, a photograph of a Nigerian school and village, or video clips from a documentary about Nigeria. Be sure images are large and clear enough to be seen by everyone in the room, but don't overuse them; they should enhance and not compete with the spoken material. Cue video clips so that they show only the most important material.

- **Sounds** include sound files or other recordings of music, speeches, author readings, and sound effects. A recording of Chinua Achebe reading from his works or an example of traditional and modern Nigerian music could enhance an audience's understanding of "Dead Men's Path." Adjust sound levels: A recording of a speech should be loud enough for everyone in the audience to hear, but background music should not be intrusive.

Organize Your Presentation Follow the steps in the chart below to organize your multimedia presentation.

ORGANIZING A MULTIMEDIA PRESENTATION

1. Create **note cards** for key points and supporting details in the spoken part of your presentation.

2. Arrange cards by **order of importance.** Begin with the most important point, and end with the least important one or vice versa.

3. Use different color note cards to distinguish spoken content from media support. Insert each media card before the spoken content card that it will support.

4. Use your note cards to create an **outline** of your presentation. Check that your organization is sound and that the various media are properly integrated into your spoken presentation.

Here is part of an outline for a presentation on Nigerian culture and its impact on the story "Dead Men's Path."

Spoken Content

I. Introduce Nigeria as a postcolonial African country with many ethnic groups.
   A. Traditional tribal Nigerian culture
   B. Fusion of ancient and modern cultures

II. Discuss Achebe's use of oral traditions.
   A. African-derived English style
   B. Process of "re-storying" people

Media Support

- Use text definition for the word *postcolonial*.
- Show map of major ethnic regions: Yoruba, Hausa, and Igbo.
- Show photo collage of such items as masks, staffs, tribal clothing, and charms used in tribal rituals.
- Play recordings of call-and-response chanting along with jazz (Afrobeat).
- Show documentary video clip illustrating impact of modern world on Nigeria.
- Show text examples of Igbo proverbs and folklore from novel *Things Fall Apart* to illustrate flavor of Nigerian talk.
- Use audio clip from audiobook of *Things Fall Apart*.
- Use video clip from Chinua Achebe's interview on PBS.

PRACTICE & APPLY 2 Use the information that begins on page 1116 to choose your topic and plan an effective presentation.

TIP Use **transitions**—bridges between ideas—to help your presentation flow more naturally, especially when you are integrating media with your spoken content. For example, to introduce a recording of traditional Nigerian music, you might say, "Listening to this example of traditional Nigerian music can help you to understand the power and beauty of the tribal ways that the villagers in the story are trying to protect."

Practice Your Presentation In front of a group of friends or family members, rehearse your presentation exactly as you plan to give it. If you need to use the school's audiovisual equipment, arrange a rehearsal before or after school.

Your delivery is the key to your success; it will hold the whole presentation together. Express enthusiasm for your topic. Speak confidently and enunciate clearly. Use eye contact, facial expressions, and gestures to your advantage, and don't turn your back on the audience while using the audiovisual equipment.

Use the questions in the following chart to ask your rehearsal audience for feedback.

AUDIENCE FEEDBACK

- Which section of the spoken part of the presentation was most memorable? Why?

- Which of the multimedia elements were most effective? Why do you think so?

- How well did I combine the spoken content with text, images, and sound? Explain.

- What parts of the presentation, if any, were confusing? What made them confusing?

- How did my delivery affect the presentation? Explain.

Revise your presentation according to the responses of your rehearsal audience. Then, practice delivering your presentation a second time. Finally, deliver your presentation to your intended audience.

PRACTICE & APPLY 3 Practice your presentation for friends or family, and use the rehearsal feedback to revise and improve your multimedia presentation. Deliver your presentation to your intended audience.

TIP Check and double-check all of your audiovisual equipment in advance and be sure you are completely familiar and comfortable with it. Coordinating different parts of a presentation can be a challenge, so anticipate any potential problems and be prepared for emergencies that may force you to improvise.

North Carolina Competency Goal
6.01

SKILLS FOCUS

Media Skills
Rehearse and deliver a multimedia presentation.

Media Workshop: Creating a Multimedia Presentation **1119**

Test Practice   Like many other twentieth-century writers, Nazim Hikmet (1902–1963) and Aleksandr Solzhenitsyn (1918–   ) served time in prison and endured years of exile because of their political views. Hikmet, who was Turkish, was once sent to prison because Turkish military cadets were found reading his poetry. During one prison sentence he was forced to stand in latrines where excrement rose half a meter above the floor. He survived by singing all the songs he knew. Hikmet's political opponents continued to torment him even after Turkey formed a new democratic government. The writer spent his last years in exile, and his writings were banned for more than fifty years. The Russian writer Aleksandr Solzhenitsyn fought bravely for his country in World War II, but in a letter to a friend he referred to the Soviet premier Joseph Stalin as "the boss" in criminal's slang. For this "crime" he was held in prisons and labor camps for eight years. He described the brutalities of Stalin's penal system in his great work *The Gulag Archipelago* (1974). Because of this book, Solzhenitsyn was charged with treason, stripped of his Soviet citizenship, and exiled from his homeland until 1994, becoming the Soviet Union's best-known writer in exile.

DIRECTIONS: Read the following two selections. Then, read each multiple-choice question that follows, and write the letter of the best response.

Some Advice to Those Who Will Serve Time in Prison

Nazim Hikmet

translated by **Randy Blasing** *and* **Mutlu Konuk**

> If instead of being hanged by the neck
>   you're thrown inside
>   for not giving up hope
> in the world, your country, and people,
> 5   if you do ten or fifteen years
>   apart from the time you have left,
> you won't say,
>   "Better I had swung from the end of a
>   rope like a flag"—
> you'll put your foot down and live.
> 10 It may not be a pleasure exactly,

North Carolina Competency Goal
1.03; 4.05; 5.02; 5.03

SKILLS FOCUS

Pages 1120–1123 cover

Literary Skills
Compare and contrast literary works.

but it's your solemn duty
        to live one more day
            to spite the enemy.
Part of you may live alone inside,
15   like a stone at the bottom of a well.
But the other part
        must be so caught up
        in the flurry of the world
        that you shiver there inside
20   when outside, at forty days' distance, a leaf moves.
To wait for letters inside,
to sing sad songs,
or to lie awake all night staring at the ceiling
            is sweet but dangerous.
25 Look at your face from shave to shave,
forget your age,
watch out for lice
           and for spring nights,
       and always remember
30   to eat every last piece of bread—
also, don't forget to laugh heartily.
And who knows,
the woman you love may stop loving you.
Don't say it's no big thing:
35 it's like the snapping of a green branch
              to the man inside.
To think of roses and gardens inside is bad,
to think of seas and mountains is good.
Read and write without rest,
40 and I also advise weaving°
and making mirrors.
I mean, it's not that you can't pass
       ten or fifteen years inside
          and more—
45   you can,
        as long as the jewel
        on the left side of your chest doesn't lose
           its luster!

---

40. Hikmet learned to weave in prison.

from First Cell, First Love

from **The Gulag Archipelago**

Aleksandr Solzhenitsyn

translated by **Thomas P. Whitney**

You sit down and half-close your eyes and try to remember them all. How many different cells you were imprisoned in during your term! It is difficult even to count them. And in each one there were people, people. There might be two people in one, 150 in another. You were imprisoned for five minutes in one and all summer long in another.

But in every case, out of all the cells you've been in, your first cell is a very special one, the place where you first encountered others like yourself, doomed to the same fate. All your life you will remember it with an emotion that you otherwise experience only in remembering your first love. And those people, who shared with you the floor and air of that stone cubicle during those days when you rethought your entire life, will from time to time be recollected by you as members of your own family.

Yes, in those days they were your only family.

What you experience in your first interrogation cell parallels nothing in your entire *previous* life or your whole *subsequent* life. No doubt prisons have stood for thousands of years before you came along, and may continue to stand after you too—longer than one would like to think—but that first interrogation cell is unique and inimitable. . . . [1]

But it was not the dirty floor, nor the murky walls, nor the odor of the latrine bucket that you loved—but those fellow prisoners with whom you about-faced at command, and that something which beat between your heart and theirs, and their sometimes astonishing words, and then, too, the birth within you, on that very spot, of free-floating thoughts you had so recently been unable to leap up or rise to.

And how much it had cost you to last out until that first cell! You had been kept in a pit, or in a box, or in a cellar. No one had addressed a human word to you. No one had looked at you with a human gaze. All they did was to peck at your brain and heart with iron beaks, and when you cried out or groaned, they laughed.

For a week or a month you had been an abandoned waif,[2] alone among enemies, and you had already said good-bye to reason and to life. . . . Then all of a sudden you were alive again, and were brought in to your friends. And reason returned to you.

That's what your first cell is!

---

1. **inimitable** (i·nim'i·tə·bəl) *adj.:* incapable of being duplicated or copied.
2. **waif** (wāf) *n.:* person without a home or friends.

1. Hikmet's poem is addressed to —
   A his political opponents
   B his judges
   C a prisoner
   D a prison guard

2. Hikmet's advice could be described as —
   F bitter and despairing
   G upbeat and defiant
   H humorous and mocking
   J angry and cruel

3. Hikmet uses a metaphor in the last two lines to say what the prisoner must do to survive. Which statement below *best* states the meaning of these lines?
   A You can survive inside as long as your health holds out.
   B You can survive inside if you remain angry and defiant.
   C Those who survive hold on to their ideals and hope.
   D Those who survive hate their oppressors.

4. Why does Solzhenitsyn compare his first cell to his "first love"?
   F The cell is very private.
   G The cell was larger than expected.
   H He would no longer be interrogated in this cell.
   J It is the first place he encounters other prisoners like himself.

5. From the excerpt from "First Cell, First Love" we can infer that Solzhenitsyn experienced all of the following except —
   A being held in many cells as a prisoner
   B feeling tired of being among other prisoners like himself
   C longing for someone to talk to
   D feeling in danger of losing his mind

6. Which statement below *best* states one similarity between the writers?
   F Both writers regret writing works that offended the government.
   G Both writers saw prison as a minor part of their lives.
   H Prison changed the way both writers regarded the government.
   J Both writers describe things that helped them survive their prison experiences.

Essay Question

Both of these texts make use of the literary element of irony, which is the contrast or discrepancy between expectations and reality. In a brief essay, explore how each writer uses irony to present his views about political imprisonment. To find the irony, ask yourself what you would expect to find in a piece of writing about political imprisonment, and contrast it with what actually is stated in the texts.

Collection 7: Skills Review
Vocabulary Skills

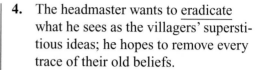

Context Clues

DIRECTIONS: Choose the answer that gives the best definition of the underlined word.

1. The hunger artist was so <u>emaciated</u> that his lean and bony body remained easily hidden in the hay.

    Emaciated means —

    A sheltered

    B completely exhausted

    C extremely thin

    D shy

2. The gods <u>chastise</u> Sisyphus and punish him by making him push a rock up a hill for eternity.

    Chastise means —

    F criticize harshly

    G reward lavishly

    H harm physically

    J imprison unjustly

3. Because the accident may have clouded his thinking, it's hard to tell whether the motorcycle driver is <u>lucid</u> or is hallucinating.

    Lucid means —

    A dizzy

    B clear-headed

    C unconscious

    D lying

4. The headmaster wants to <u>eradicate</u> what he sees as the villagers' superstitious ideas; he hopes to remove every trace of their old beliefs.

    Eradicate means —

    F ridicule

    G revise

    H disprove

    J eliminate

5. The baby bird sings <u>plaintively</u>, sadly calling out to its mother.

    Plaintively means —

    A in a simple style

    B sorrowfully

    C with urgency

    D unceasingly

6. During China's Cultural Revolution it was common for the repressive government to <u>confiscate</u> and remove books.

    Confiscate means —

    F seize

    G erase

    H rewrite

    J evaluate

North Carolina Competency Goal
6.01

Vocabulary Skills
Understand context clues.

Collection 7: Skills Review

Writing Skills

DIRECTIONS: Read the following paragraph from a draft of a student's literary research paper. Then, answer the questions below it.

(1) When Bessie Head wrote "The Prisoner Who Wore Glasses," apartheid was still in effect. (2) Apartheid—discrimination against nonwhites—was the social, economic, and political policy during the rule of South Africa's National party. (3) Following racial segregation, then territorial separation began. (4) Blacks were restricted to "homelands" and had to carry passports to enter South Africa; they were always threatened by a repressive police force, and arrest and imprisonment were commonplace. (5) At a press conference in November of 1966, Jean-Paul Sartre said that there were "twenty-five official prison farms" that relied on forced labor by black South Africans who had been arrested for minor infractions. (6) Sartre had won the Nobel Prize in literature two years earlier. (7) In her story about black prisoners and their white warder, Bessie Head underscores the power struggle that would eventually lead to the dismantling of apartheid in South Africa.

1. Which sentence would be a more effective opening for the passage?

   A Apartheid became official in South Africa in 1948, when the National party gained control of the government.

   B Bessie Head's short story "The Prisoner Who Wore Glasses" focuses on the racial oppression created by apartheid in post-colonial South Africa.

   C The institution of apartheid arose from the wish for a cheap labor system.

   D Jean-Paul Sartre was an influential existentialist writer.

2. How could Sentence 3 be rewritten to improve its structure?

   F At first there was segregation by races; soon, however, separation into territories was added.

   G There was racial segregation followed by a separation into territories.

   H At first there was racial segregation; this was followed by territorial separation.

   J After racial segregation there came separation into territories.

3. Which sentence should be deleted to improve the coherence of the paragraph?

   A Sentence 2

   B Sentence 4

   C Sentence 6

   D Sentence 7

4. Which sentence requires a Works Cited reference?

   F Sentence 3

   G Sentence 4

   H Sentence 5

   J Sentence 7

North Carolina Competency Goal
2.01; 4.03; 6.01

Writing Skills
Analyze a literary research paper.

Resource Center

The Parisian Novels (The Yellow Books), (1888) by Vincent van Gogh.

Reading Matters

When the Text Is Tough

Remember the reading you did back in first, second, and third grades? Big print. Short texts. Easy words. In high school, however, the texts you read are often filled with small print, long chapters, and complicated plots or topics. Also, you now find yourself reading a variety of material—from your driver's-ed handbook to college applications, from job applications to income-tax forms, from e-mail to e-zines, from classics to comics, from textbooks to checkbooks.

Doing something every day that you find difficult and tedious isn't much fun—and that includes reading. So this section of this book is designed for you, to show you what to do when the text gets tough. Let's begin to look at some reading matters—because, after all, reading *matters*.

READING UP CLOSE: HOW TO USE THIS SECTION

- **This section is for you.** Turn to it whenever you need to remind yourself about what to do when the text gets tough. Don't wait for your teacher to assign this section for you to read. It's your handbook. Use it.

- **Read the sections that you need.** You don't have to read every word. Skim the headings, and find the information you need.

- **Use this information to help you with reading for other classes,** not just for the reading you do in this book.

- **Don't be afraid to *re-read* the information** you find in Reading Matters. The best readers constantly re-read information.

- **If you need more help, then check the index.** The index will direct you to other pages in this book with information on reading skills and strategies.

Improving Your Comprehension

Comprehension, your ability to understand what you read, is a critical part of the reading process. Your comprehension can be affected by many factors. Think about each of the following types of texts, and rate your comprehension of each from 1 (*never understand*) to 5 (*always understand*):

A.   notes from friends
B.   e-mail messages from friends
C.   college applications
D.   job applications
E.   magazines
F.   computer manuals
G.   Internet sites
H.   school textbooks
I.   novels you choose
J.   novels your teachers choose for you

You probably didn't rate yourself the same for each type of text. Factors such as your interest level and the text's vocabulary level will cause your ratings to differ from text to text. Now, go back, and look specifically at items H, I, and J. How did you rate there? If you think your comprehension of those materials is low, then you'll want to study the next few pages carefully. They are filled with tips to help you improve your comprehension.

Visualizing the text.   The ability to visualize—or see in your mind—what you are reading is important for comprehension. To understand how visualizing makes a difference, try this quick test. At home, turn on a television to a program you enjoy. Then, turn your back to the television set. How long will you keep "watching" the program that way? Probably not long. Why not? Because it would be boring if you couldn't see what was happening. The same is true of reading: If you can't see in your mind what is happening on the page, then you probably will tune out quickly. You can improve your ability to visualize a text by practicing the following strategies:

READING UP CLOSE

▶ Monitoring Your Comprehension

Skilled readers often pay more attention to what they don't understand than to what they do. Here are some symbols you could put on self-sticking notes and place on texts as you are reading so that you can keep up with what's confusing you. Decide how you would use each symbol.

What reading problem could each sign indicate?

1.
2.   DEAD END
3.
4.
5.   YIELD
6.
7.
8.   STOP
9.
10. R X R

1. **Read a few sentences; then pause, and describe what is happening on the page.** Forcing yourself to describe the scene will take some time at first, but doing that will help in the long run.

2. **On a sheet of paper or a stick-on note, make a graphic representation of what is happening as you are reading.** For instance, if two characters are talking, draw two stick figures with arrows pointing between them to show yourself that they are talking.

3. **Discuss a scene or a part of a chapter with a partner.** Talk about what you "saw" as you were reading.

4. **Read aloud.** You might be having trouble visualizing the text because you aren't "hearing" it. Try reading a portion of your text aloud, using good expression and phrasing. As you hear the words, you may find it easier to see the scenes.

READING UP CLOSE

▶**Visualizing What You Read**

Read the following excerpt from "The Burning of Rome" (see page 324), and discuss what you "see":

And now came a calamitous fire . . . more violent and destructive than any that ever befell our city. . . . Breaking out in shops full of inflammable merchandise, it took hold and gathered strength at once; and being fanned by the wind soon embraced the entire length of the Circus, where there were no mansions with protective walls, no temple-enclosures, nor anything else to arrest its course. Furiously the destroying flames swept on, first over the level ground, then up the heights, then again plunging into the hollows. . . .

How's your metacognition? Your attention wanders for a moment as you are reading something, but your eyes don't quit moving from word to word. After a few minutes you realize you are several pages beyond the last point at which you can remember thinking about what you were reading. Then you know you need to back up and start over. This ability to think about your thinking—or, in this case, your lack of thinking—is called **metacognition.**

Metacognition refers to your ability to analyze what you are doing as you try to make sense of texts. A critical part of metacognition is paying attention to what you are reading. It's normal to find that your attention *sometimes* wanders while reading. If it always wanders, though, then try one of the following activities: (1) Keep paper and pen close, and jot down notes as you read; (2) read for a set amount of time (five minutes), and then stop and review what's happened since the last time you stopped. Lengthen this time as you find yourself able to focus longer. Take the following quiz to see what your metacognition level is:

READING UP CLOSE

▶**Measuring Your Attention Quotient**

The lower the score, the less you pay attention to what you are reading. The higher the score, the more you pay attention.

When I read, I

A. let my mind wander a lot

1	2	3
most of the time	sometimes	almost never

B. forget what I'm reading

1	2	3
most of the time	sometimes	almost never

C. get confused and stay confused or don't even realize I am confused

1	2	3
most of the time	sometimes	almost never

D. discover I've turned lots of pages and don't have a clue as to what I've read

1	2	3
most of the time	sometimes	almost never

E. rarely finish whatever I'm supposed to be reading

1	2	3
most of the time	sometimes	almost never

Try Think-Aloud. Comprehension problems don't appear only after you *finish* reading. Confusion occurs *as* you read. Therefore, don't wait until you complete your reading assignment to try to understand the text; instead, work on comprehending while reading by becoming an active reader.

Active readers **predict, connect, clarify, question,** and **visualize** as they read. If you don't do those things, you need to pause while you read to

- make **predictions**

- make **connections**

- **clarify** in your own thoughts what you are reading

- **question** what you don't understand

- **visualize** the text

Use the Think-Aloud strategy to practice your active-reading skills. Here is how Think-Aloud works: Read a selection of text aloud to a partner. As you read, pause to make comments and ask questions. Your partner's job is to tally your comments and classify each one according to the bulleted list above.

READING UP CLOSE

▶ **One Student's Think-Aloud**

Here's Steve's Think-Aloud for Petrarch's Sonnet 61 (page 682):

After reading entire sonnet once: I don't understand. He seems to be grateful for the pain he feels. Why would he say that? **(Question)**

After reading sonnet a second time: His description of love sounds kind of miserable. But he doesn't seem to mind. At the end he is focused only on this woman he loves. **(Comment/Clarification)**

After reading sonnet a third time: Even though he has had all these painful experiences as a result of his love for this woman—he mentions feeling like a prisoner and being wounded by love—maybe this sonnet is his way of saying that despite all the pain he feels, he thinks that love is worth it. **(Connection)**

Question the text.   This scenario may be familiar: You've just finished reading one of the selections in this book. Then you look at the questions that you'll be discussing tomorrow in class. You realize that you don't know the answers. In frustration you decide to give up on the questions.

While giving up is one way to approach the problem, it's not the best approach. In fact, what you need to do is focus *more* on questions—and focus on them while reading the text, not just at the end. This doesn't mean memorizing study questions before you read so that as you are reading you are thinking only about those questions. What it means is constantly asking yourself questions about characters, plot, point of view, setting, conflict, and even vocabulary while reading. You'll find that the more you question the text while reading, the more prepared you'll be to answer the questions at the end of the text.

READING UP CLOSE

▶ **Asking Questions While Reading**

Here is a list of questions you can use as you read literary selections. You should recopy this list on note cards and keep it close as you read.

Character Questions

1. Who is the central character? Is this character the narrator? What are the greatest strengths and greatest weaknesses of this character? What does this character discover by the story's end? Has he or she changed?

(continued)

2. Is the narrator telling the story while it is happening or while looking back? Can you trust this narrator? What if the narrator were a different character? How would the story change? What point of view does the narrator have— first person, limited third person, omniscient—and how does that point of view affect the narrator's authority?

3. Who are the other characters? What makes them important to the central character? What do their actions reveal about their personalities? How do your thoughts about the characters change as you read the story? Can you find specific points in the text where your feelings about characters shift? Could any character have been omitted from the story?

4. Which character do you like the best? What do you have in common with this character?

Plot, Setting, and Conflict Questions

1. What are the major events in the plot? Which events are mandatory in order for the story to reach the conclusion it does? What prior knowledge is necessary for understanding the plot?

2. How does the setting affect the story? Could you change the location or the historical context and have the same story? How does the author situate the reader in the setting? Is the setting believable?

3. What event creates the conflict? How does the central character react to the conflict? How do other characters react? How is the conflict resolved?

Re-reading and rewording. The best way to improve your comprehension is simply to **re-read.** The first time you read something, you get the basic idea of the text. The next time you read it, you revise your understanding. Try thinking of your first reading as a draft—like the first draft of an essay. As you revise your essay, you are improving your writing. As you revise your reading, you are improving your comprehension.

Sometimes, as you re-read, you find some specific sentences or even passages that you just don't understand. When that's the case, you need to spend some time closely studying those sentences. One effective way to tackle tough text is to **reword** the text:

1. On a piece of paper, write down the sentences that are confusing you.

2. Leave a few blank lines between each line that you write.

3. Then, choose the difficult words, and reword them in the space above.

While you wouldn't want to reword every line of a long text—or even a short one—this is a powerful way to help you understand key sentences.

READING UP CLOSE

▶ **One Student's Rewording**

Thomas tried rewording some of the *Iliad* (page 126, lines 1–6). Open your book to page 126, and read the original lines there. Then, see Thomas's changes below. Also, note that he has combined a Think-Aloud (see page 1132) with his rewording.

In this first part, Homer is calling on an "immortal one." The introduction on page 121 says that epics usually begin with a plea to a muse. What's a muse? OK, the introduction says the muses are these nine Greek goddesses of the arts and sciences. So I think Homer is asking this muse to help him by inspiring and guiding his writing—not a real song, but just an announcement. So it really could start by asking the Heavenly muse to speak of "Achilles' anger, doomed and ruinous, / that caused the Achaeans loss. . . ." The side note says the Achaeans are the Greeks. So Homer is basically saying, "Help me tell the story of Achilles' anger that led to the death of many brave Greek warriors."

Summarizing narrative text. Understanding a long piece of text is easier if you can summarize chunks of it. If you are reading a **narrative,** or a story (including a biography or an autobiography), then use a strategy called **Somebody Wanted But So (SWBS)** for help writing a summary of what you are reading.

SWBS is a powerful way to think about the characters in a narrative and to note what each does, what conflict each faces, and what the resolution is. As you write an SWBS statement for different characters or subjects within the same narrative, you are forcing yourself to rethink the narrative from different **points of view.**

Here are the steps for writing SWBS statements:

1. Write the words *Somebody, Wanted, But,* and *So* across the top of four columns.

2. Under the "Somebody" column, write a character's name.

3. Then, under the "Wanted" column, write what that character wanted to do.

4. Next, under the "But" column, explain what happened that kept the character from doing what he or she wanted.

5. Finally, under the "So" column, explain the eventual outcome.

If you're making an SWBS chart for a long story or novel, you might need to write several SWBS statements at different points in the story.

READING UP CLOSE

▶ One Student's SWBS Chart

Read this SWBS statement of the excerpt from the *Epic of Gilgamesh* (see page 23). Try writing an SWBS statement from the point of view of Enkidu.

Somebody	Wanted	But	So
Gilgamesh	wanted eternal life,	but the serpent seized the plant that restores lost youth,	so he had to face his mortality.

Summarizing expository text. If summarizing the information in a text is difficult, try a strategy called GIST.

1. Choose three or four sections of text you want to summarize.

2. Read the first section of text.

3. Draw twenty blank lines on a sheet of paper.

4. Write a summary of the first section of text using exactly twenty words—one word for each blank.

5. Read the next section of text.

6. Now, in your next set of twenty blanks, write a new summary statement that combines your first summary with whatever you want to add from this second section of text. You still have only twenty blanks to fill in, not forty.

Repeat this process one or two more times, depending on how many more sections of text you have to read. When you are finished, you'll have a twenty-word statement that gives you the gist, or overall idea, of the entire text.

READING UP CLOSE

▶ One Student's GIST

Study the GIST statements for the three paragraphs from the Aztec myth "Tata and Nena," found on page 65. Then, try your hand at creating the third GIST.

GIST 1 (for the first paragraph)

The god Tlaloc decides to destroy the world, but he gives two people instructions to follow in order to survive.

GIST 2 (adding the second paragraph)

The god Tlaloc destroys the world, but he spared the lives of two people who will later disobey his commands.

GIST 3 (adding the final paragraph)

____ ____ ____ ____ ____ ____ ____ ____ ____ ____ ____

Using question maps. Most readers at some point will struggle with a text. Some readers find reading poetry a struggle, but they can breeze through computer magazines. Others find the technical language in computer magazines difficult but read poetry easily. It's not whether you struggle with texts that matters; instead, what matters is what you *do* when you struggle.

If you are an independent reader, then you know how to find the answers on your own—independently—to whatever causes you to struggle. If you are a dependent reader, you expect others to do the explaining for you. Dependent readers often say, "I don't get it," and give up. Independent readers, by contrast, know what they don't get and then figure out how to get it.

If you think you are a dependent reader, try using a question map like the one below. As you complete the chart, you'll be mapping your way toward independent reading.

1. In the first column, **list your questions** as you are reading.

2. In the second column, **make notes about each question.** For instance, jot down what made you think about the question or what page you are on in the text.

3. In the third column, **list possibilities for finding answers.** Remember that re-reading the text is always a good idea. Other places to find answers include dictionaries (especially if you have questions about vocabulary), your own mind (sometimes the text gives you part of the information, and you must figure out the rest), or other parts of the book (especially if you are reading a science, math, or history book).

4. In the final column, **jot down answers to your questions** only after you've made notes about them and thought out where to find answers to them. If you can't answer your questions at this point, then it's time to see your teacher.

READING UP CLOSE

▶ One Student's Question Map

Here is a part of Denise's question map for the *Aeneid* (page 273):

Questions	Notes	Places to find answers	Answers
1. Who is Minerva?	p. 276, line 106	dictionary or encyclopedia	Roman goddess of war and the arts
2. Who is Cassandra?	p. 277, line 131	re-read text or ask teacher	A woman who makes prophecies that are never believed

Know some smart words. Sometimes you understand what you've read, but when it comes time to talk about or write about the selection, you can't find the words you want to use to discuss the plot, characters, theme, or author's writing style. Here's a list of words and phrases that can serve as a springboard to discussion. They are beginning points—you still must be able to explain why you chose those words or phrases.

Words and Phrases to Describe the Plot

Positive	Negative
realistic	unrealistic
good pace from scene to scene	plodding
suspenseful	predictable
well-developed ideas	sketchy ideas

Words and Phrases to Describe the Characters

Positive	Negative
original	stereotyped
well-rounded	flat
dynamic; able to change	static; unable to change

Words to Describe the Theme

Positive	Negative
subtle	obvious
unique	overworked
powerful	trivial

Words and Phrases to Describe the Author's Style of Writing

Positive	Negative
descriptive; filled with figurative language	boring; lacking imagery
original	filled with clichés
lively; full of action	plodding; slow-moving
poetic; lyrical	stilted

READING UP CLOSE

▶ Using Smart Words

Choose one of the stories you've read in *Elements of Literature* this semester and, using some of the words and phrases in the above list, describe the plot, characters, theme, and author's writing style. Remember to support your word choices with examples from the story.

Improving Your Reading Rate

If your reading concerns are more about getting through the words than figuring out the meaning, then this part of Reading Matters is for you.

If you think you are a slow reader, then reading can seem overwhelming. However, you can change your **reading rate**—the pace at which you read. All you have to do is practice. The point isn't to read so that you just rush over words—the I'mgoingtoreadsofastthatallthe-wordsruntogether approach. Instead, the goal is to find a pace that keeps you moving comfortably through the pages. Why is it important to establish a good reading rate? Let's do a little math to see why your silent-reading rate counts.

MATH PROBLEM!

If you read 40 words per minute (wpm) and there are 400 words on a page, how long will it take you to read 1 page? 5 pages? How long will it take if you read 80 wpm? 100 wpm? 200 wpm?

Words per Minute (wpm)	1 page @400 words/page	5 pages @400 words/page
40 wpm	10 minutes	50 minutes
80 wpm	5 minutes	25 minutes
100 wpm	4 minutes	20 minutes
200 wpm	2 minutes	10 minutes

Reading rate and homework. Now, assume that with literature homework, science homework, and social studies homework, you have forty pages to read in one night. If you are reading at 40 wpm, you are spending more than six *hours* just reading the information; but at 100 wpm, you spend only two hours and forty minutes. At 200 wpm, you'd finish in one hour and twenty minutes.

Figuring out your reading rate. To determine your silent-reading rate, you'll need three things: a watch or clock with a second hand, a book, and someone who will watch the time for you. Then, complete the following steps:

1. Have your friend time you as you begin reading to yourself.

2. Read at your normal rate. Don't speed just because you're being timed.

> **Example**
> 1st minute   180 words
> 2nd minute   215 words
> 3rd minute   190 words
>   585 words ÷ 3 = 195 wpm

3. Stop when your friend tells you that one minute is up.

4. Count the number of words you read in that minute. Write down that number.

5. Repeat this process several more times, using different passages.

6. Then, add the number of words together, and divide by the number of times you timed yourself. That's your average number of words per minute.

Reading Rate Reminders

1. **Make sure you aren't reading one word at a time with a pause between each word.** For instance, read the following rhyme. The first time you read it, pause between each word; the second time, pause only where you see the slash marks. Hear the difference the phrasing makes?

> Mary had a little lamb, / Its fleece was white as snow. / Everywhere that Mary went, / The lamb was sure to go.

Word-at-a-time reading is much slower than phrase reading.

2. **Make sure when you are reading silently that you really are reading silently.** As you read, avoid moving your lips or reading aloud softly. Also, don't use your finger to point to words as you read. Instead, use a bookmark to stay on the correct line while you practice your phrase reading.

3. **As you practice your fluency, remember that the single best way to improve your reading rate is simply to read more.** You won't get better at what you never do. Also, always remember that your rate will vary as your purpose for reading varies. Don't rush to read fast if that means understanding less.

Vocabulary Development

Fluency, reading rate, and comprehension are all connected to how quickly you recognize words and know what they mean. No matter how many words you study in school, you can't learn all the words you'll ever encounter. So you need to understand how words work— what *prefixes, suffixes,* and *roots* mean—so that when you encounter new words, you can see their components and figure out their meanings.

LATIN AND GREEK ROOTS, PREFIXES, AND SUFFIXES

Prefixes	Meaning	Examples
ad–	to	adapt, addict, adhere, admit
amphi–	both; around	amphibian, amphitheater
an–	without	anarchy, anesthesia, anonymous, anorexia
auto–	self	autobiography, autograph, automatic, automobile
co–	together	coauthor, cognate, coincide, cooperate
de–	opposite	deactivate, deform, degrade, deplete, descend
dis–	opposite	disagree, disarm, discontinue, disgust, dishonest
for–	not	forbid, forget, forgo
il–	not	illegal, illegible, illegitimate, illiterate, illogical
im–	not	imbalance, immaculate, immature
in–	not	inaccurate, inactive, inadvertent, incognito
ir–	not	irreconcilable, irregular, irresponsible
mal–	bad	maladjusted, malaise, malevolent, malice
pro–	before	progeny, prognosis, program, prologue
pro–	forward	proceed, produce, proficient, progress
re–	again	reappear, redistribute, redo, repaint, rewrite
sub–	under	subcontract, subject, submarine, subordinate
trans–	across	transatlantic, transcend, transcribe, transfer
un–	not	unable, uncertain, uncomfortable, unhappy

Roots	Meaning	Examples
–act–	do	action, actor, enact, react, transact
–aud–	hear	audible, audience, audition, auditorium
–cred–	believe	credit, credulous, discredit, incredible
–dic–	speak	contradict, dictate, diction, predict, verdict
–graph–	write	autograph, paragraph, phonograph, photograph
–loc–	place	allocate, dislocate, locate, location

(continued)

(continued)

–man–	hand	manipulate, manual, manufacture, manuscript
–mot–	move	demote, motion, motor, promote
–ped–	foot	pedal, pedestal, pedestrian
–pop–	people	populace, popular, population
–port–	carry	export, import, portable, porter, transport
–sign–	mark	insignia, signal, signature, significant
–spec–	see	inspect, respect, spectacle, spectator, suspect
–tract–	pull; drag	attract, contract, detract, subtract, traction, tractor
–vid–	see	evidence, provide, providence, video
–volve–	roll	evolve, involve, revolution, revolve, revolver

Suffixes	Meaning	Examples
–ade	action or process	blockade, escapade, parade
–age	action or process	marriage, pilgrimage, voyage
–ant	one who	assistant, defendant, immigrant, merchant, servant
–cle	small	corpuscle, cubicle, particle
–dom	state or quality of	boredom, freedom, martyrdom, wisdom
–ent	one who	parent, resident, regent, superintendent
–ful	full of	careful, fearful, joyful, thoughtful
–ic	relating to	comic, historic, poetic, public
–less	without	ageless, careless, thoughtless, tireless
–let	small	islet, leaflet, owlet, rivulet
–ly	resembling	fatherly, helpfully, motherly, scholarly
–ly	every	daily, monthly, weekly, yearly
–ment	action or process	development, embezzlement, government
–ment	state or quality of	amazement, amusement, predicament
–ment	product or thing	fragment, instrument, ornament
–or	one who	actor, auditor, doctor, donor

Word Family Tree

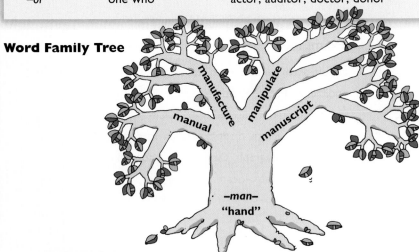

manufacture · manipulate · manual · manuscript

–man–
"hand"

The World of Work

The ability to read critically and write effectively is your driver's license to navigating today's world. Without strong reading and writing skills, you will feel as frustrated and powerless as you do in a traffic jam. A future college student must be able to write application essays and understand scholarship guidelines. A mechanic must be able to read instruction manuals to use new equipment. A renter must understand a lease before getting an apartment. A supervisor must be able to write an effective memo to present ideas. In your life and in the world of work, you will rely on reading and writing skills to learn new information, communicate effectively, and get the results you want.

Reading for Work and Life

To avoid getting stranded in life and in the world of work, you will need to learn to read **informative** and **persuasive documents.**

Informative Documents Informative documents are like road maps: They provide facts and information. They can also be good places to check when you want to verify or clarify information from other sources. If a friend writes down directions that you're uncertain about, you consult a map to verify the directions. Likewise, if you read on a Web site an angry customer's complaint about repairs on a computer you just bought, you could review the warranty to see if the information is valid. Two kinds of common informative documents are consumer documents and workplace documents.

Consumer Documents You've probably already made thousands of buying decisions in your life. As you get older, however, buying decisions often carry bigger consequences. Should you sign a six- or a twelve-month apartment lease? Should you buy or lease a car? Being informed about the details of major purchases can help you avoid costly mistakes. This information can be found in **consumer documents,** such as warranties, contracts, product information, and instruction manuals.

- **Warranties** describe what happens if the product doesn't work properly or breaks down. Warranties note how long the product is covered for repair or replacement, which repairs the warranty does and does not cover, and how to receive repair service.

> The SureFocus digital camera is guaranteed to be free of defects in material or workmanship under normal use for a period of one (1) year from the date of purchase. Equipment covered by the warranty will be repaired by SureFocus Repair Members WITHOUT CHARGE, except for insurance, transportation, and handling charges. A copy of this warranty card and proof of purchase must be enclosed when returning equipment for warranty service. The warranty does not apply in the following cases:
> - the camera has been damaged through abuse
> - leaking batteries or other liquids have caused damage to the camera
> - unauthorized repair technicians have attempted to service the camera

Contracts give details about an agreement that a buyer enters into with a company. A lease for an apartment or a car is a contract that defines the terms of the lease, including how long it lasts, what the responsibilities of the customer—also known as the lessee— and the landlord or car company are, how to end the lease, and what the penalties for breaking the lease are. A lease always includes a space for the customer's signature, which signifies agreement with the terms of the contract. Below is a portion of a typical apartment lease.

This apartment lease is entered into by <u>Althea Brown</u>, hereinafter "Lessee," and Sun Valley Apartments.

1. **Grant of Lease:** Sun Valley Apartments does hereby lease unto Lessee Apartment #<u>B-2</u>, located at <u>101 Saguaro Drive, El Cajon, CA</u>.

2. **Term of Lease:** This lease shall begin on the first day of August, 2006, and extend until the <u>first</u> day of <u>August, 2007</u>, after which the lessee can extend the lease month to month until terminated according to the terms described below.

3. **Rental Payments:** Lessee agrees to pay as rent the sum of <u>$800</u> per month each month during the term of this lease before the <u>fifth</u> day of each month.

Product information describes the basic features and materials of a product. Product information on the box of a cordless telephone, for example, would tell whether it has automatic redial, memory, caller ID, voice-mail, and other features.

Instruction manuals tell the owner how to set up, operate, and troubleshoot problems with a product. Instruction manuals also include safety precautions, diagrams, and descriptions of the product's features.

Workplace Documents Two common workplace documents—**procedure manuals** and **memoranda**—can tell you how to do your job and how to stay informed so you are both knowledgeable and effective.

Procedure manuals are the step-by-step directions that tell employees how to serve customers, operate machinery, report problems, request vacation, or do anything that the company wants performed in a certain way.

Memoranda—or memos—are the standard form of internal communication in many businesses. Memos are concise and usually address one topic, identified in the subject line. Headings or bullets may indicate the main ideas. Memos follow a standard format that includes the date, the recipient, the sender, and the subject at the top of the document, as shown in the example below.

Date: February 25, 2006
To: Sophia Cervenka
From: Cole Hurley
Subject: Computer Training

Training on the new software will begin Monday, March 13, 2006. Members of your department who are interested in receiving training should call me at extension 4390 by Friday, March 10, to sign up. Training will last from 8:00 A.M.–3:00 P.M. The next training session will be held on March 20.

Persuasive Documents While informative documents are like road maps, persuasive documents are like travel brochures, trying to influence a reader's destination. Persuasive documents try to persuade readers to believe or act in a certain way. It's important for you to be able to distinguish between informative and persuasive public documents. For example, a policy statement from a county commission about recycling might quote facts, but its primary purpose is to influence citizens to support the commission's position. By critically reading persuasive public documents, you can evaluate whether you agree or disagree. Persuasive public documents include **policy statements, political platforms, speeches,** and **debates**.

- A **policy statement** outlines a person's or group's position on an issue and sometimes provides the rationale for that position. For example, the mayor might issue a policy statement explaining why she supports or opposes a tax increase for school construction. The policy statement gives the main points for the mayor's position and may provide facts or use rhetorical devices to support the position. A policy statement may also include a **call to action,** or a request for readers to take a specific action. Some organizations issue policy statements to endorse specific legislation, hoping to win the support of the voting public or of the lawmakers who can create the legislation.

- A **political platform** outlines a political candidate's position on a variety of issues so voters know where the candidate stands. It may also set forth the candidate's goals and describe the beliefs that guide his or her positions. The positions and goals are known as the *planks* of the platform. The audience for a political platform is usually friendly to the candidate, and the platform is intended to rouse support and to persuade undecided voters. Sometimes a platform will also address and rebut opposing viewpoints. Below is an excerpt from the political platform of a city council candidate about the issue of noise pollution.

> Rocky Mount is a quiet and peaceful place that does not need more intrusion from the local government to reduce noise levels. We are not close to a major airport, so we do not hear the regular drone of airplanes. Concertgoers hear Beethoven and Mozart, not the loud rock groups that play in larger cities. Noise pollution is an occasional, not regular or excessive, problem that can be handled without more city ordinances. Therefore, I do not support the development of laws to address the nonexistent issue of noise pollution.

- A **persuasive speech** is designed to change an audience's attitudes or beliefs or to move an audience to action. A speaker may make persuasive arguments and address audience counterclaims by using reasoning and rhetorical devices such as repetition. (For more on **persuasive speaking,** see page 336.)

- A **debate** involves two teams who take turns discussing a controversial topic. The topic under discussion is called the *proposition.* One side argues for the proposition, and the other side argues against it. Each side also refutes, or argues against, its opponent's case.

Critiquing Persuasive Documents

Persuasive documents use logical, emotional, and ethical appeals to be convincing. Notice how these appeals are used to help you critique a document's validity and truthfulness.

- **Logical appeals** are based on reasons and supporting evidence. As you read, notice whether the evidence is based on reliable facts that can be confirmed through other, unbiased sources. If you are unsure, consult informative public documents, such as state laws, to verify the evidence. Notice whether the appeal makes sense and avoids fallacies, such as hasty generalizations or circular reasoning. A **hasty generalization** is a conclusion based on insufficient evidence. **Circular reasoning** occurs when the reason for an opinion is simply the opinion stated in different words.

- **Emotional appeals** rely on strong feelings to persuade readers. The writer may use examples that tug on heartstrings or arouse anger. Vivid language may make either positive or negative associations with the topic. Evaluate emotional appeals based on all of the evidence. If an argument is based primarily on emotion, the case may be weak. Watch out for signs of bias and stereotypes—including words such as *always* and *never*—that suggest the reasoning is unsound.

- **Ethical appeals** rely on the reader's sense of right and wrong. For example, a writer might persuade an audience to share a certain view by implying that the opposing position is unpatriotic or selfish.

Critique a persuasive document by seeing how fairly the writer treats the topic. Does the writer use credible evidence? Does he or she know enough about the topic to be believed?

PRACTICE & APPLY 1 Choose a persuasive public document, and critique its effectiveness and validity. Identify the appeals and the call to action, if any. Consult at least one informative public document to verify information presented in the persuasive document.

Writing for Work and Life

Writing is your passport to exciting places in life. A powerful résumé can win you the job of your dreams. A memo proposing cost-saving measures can earn you a promotion. A letter to your city council can lead to a new soccer field for a recreational league. Clear, effective writing is one of the best skills you can have as you enter the world of work.

Job Applications and Résumés One of the first places you will use writing beyond school will be in a job application or résumé. To fill out a **job application** completely and accurately, first read the instructions carefully. Type or write neatly in blue or black ink. Include all information requested. If a question does not apply to you, write *N/A* or *not applicable* in the blank. Proofread your completed form and neatly correct any errors. Finally, submit the form to the correct person.

A **résumé** summarizes your skills, education, achievements, and work experience. Prepare a résumé to use when you apply for a job or when you seek admission to a college or special program. Keep in mind that a résumé should be tailored to match the target audience. Select and highlight the skills and experiences that would most appeal to the employer or college reading the résumé. For a college or academic program, for example, you would highlight a strong GPA, successful class projects, and involvement in school clubs. The language would create a sophisticated, but not artificial, tone. For an employer, on the other hand, you would highlight work experience, both paid and volunteer, and the skills you learned on the job, using clear and direct language.

Here are some more tips to help you create a résumé:

- Give complete information about work experience, including job title, dates of employment, company, and location.

- Do not use *I;* instead, use short, parallel phrases that describe duties and activities.

- Proofread carefully. Mistakes on a résumé make the writer seem careless.

Business Letters Business letters are used to request, complain, inform, and thank. A proper business letter has a courteous, formal style and tone and is expected to follow a conventional format that includes six parts: a heading, inside address, salutation or greeting (*Dear Sir*), body, closing (*Sincerely*), and signature. Business letters often follow a block-style format (see the example below), in which all six parts of the letter align at the left margin. A modified block-style format is also used, in which the heading, closing, and signature are indented far to the right and every paragraph in the body is indented.

Your Street Address
Your City, State, and ZIP code — **Heading**
Date on which letter is written

Recipient's Title [Mr., Miss, Dr., Professor, Rev., etc.]
   and First and Last Name
Recipient's business title — **Inside Address**
Company Name
Street Address
City, State, and ZIP code

Dear [Title and Last Name of Recipient]: — **Salutation**

Body

In this paragraph, tell the recipient why you are writing, stating what you are requesting in clear and concise language.

In this paragraph, include information relevant to your goal, such as relevant facts about your background or questions you have for the recipient.

Here you thank the recipient in advance for whatever actions he or she may take in regard to your request in the first paragraph.

Sincerely,

Your Signature — **Closing**

Your Full Name

Word-Processing Features The appearance of workplace documents is important. Learn to use word-processing features to your advantage by making documents that are properly formatted.

- **Margins** Most word-processing programs automatically set side and top margins. You can adjust these default margins to suit your purpose.

- **Fonts** For most workplace documents, use a font that is businesslike and easy to read. For more on **fonts,** see page 1158.

- **Line spacing** Most letters and memos are single-spaced to conserve space, but longer reports are often double-spaced to allow room for handwritten edits and comments.

Integrating Databases, Graphics, and Spreadsheets Workplace documents often integrate databases, graphics, and spreadsheets into text. For example, a pie chart or a spreadsheet can show budget expenses, or a list of customers in a specific ZIP Code might be integrated from a database into a report. Add features such as these to communicate your ideas more effectively. Place a graphic close to the related text, and explain the graphic's context.

Résumé Format Word-processing features can help you create an attractive format for your résumé. Here are some guidelines to remember:

- Use wide margins for the top, bottom, and sides, and use double-spacing between sections to make the résumé easy to scan for information.

- Consider using a different font, boldface, and a larger point size for your name and for headings.

The following résumé was written by a student interested in a sales job. He highlighted skills and experiences that show his interpersonal skills and initiative and used an attractive, easy-to-read format.

MIGUEL GUERRERO
1902 Greig Street
Santa Rosa, CA 95403
(707) 555-0085
E-mail: mguerrero@fhs.k12.ca.us

EDUCATION
Senior, Forsythe High School
Grade-point average: 3.3 (B)

WORK EXPERIENCE
Summer 2005–present
Waiter, Starlite Restaurant
- Serve customers quickly and efficiently
- Train new employees in effective customer service
- Twice awarded Star Employee

Summer 2004
Campaign Volunteer, Antonio Suarez Campaign for Mayor
- Assisted in door-to-door campaigns
- Collected and input data for mailing list
- Organized teen volunteers to distribute flyers

SKILLS
Communication: Telephone sales, oral presentations
Computers: Word processing, Web design

ACTIVITIES
Debate team, soccer team, student government representative

REFERENCES
Janet Matteson, Owner   David Cho, Principal
Starlite Restaurant   Forsythe High School
(707) 555-0146   (707) 555-0013

PRACTICE & APPLY 2 Create a résumé for your dream job. Think about what experiences and skills you have that would appeal to a potential employer. Present this information in a clear, concise, and eye-catching way.

Writer's Handbook

The Writing Process

Effective writing involves a process. The steps in this process, called a **recursive** process because you may repeat them several times, are like those of a spiral staircase—you must travel around and around, yet with each revolution you ascend toward your goal. While each writer's process is slightly different, most effective writers follow the steps below.

STAGES OF THE WRITING PROCESS	
Prewriting	• Identify your purpose and audience.
	• Choose a topic and an appropriate form.
	• Formulate your thesis, or main idea, about the topic.
	• Gather information about the topic.
	• Organize information in a preliminary plan.
Writing	• Draft an introduction that seizes your readers' attention and provides necessary background information.
	• State your thesis clearly and assertively.
	• Develop body paragraphs that elaborate on key ideas.
	• Follow an organizational plan.
	• Draft a conclusion that restates your thesis and leaves readers with something to think about.
Revising	• Evaluate your draft.
	• Revise to improve its content, organization, and style.
Publishing	• Proofread your draft, and correct errors in spelling, punctuation, grammar, and usage.
	• Share your final draft with readers.
	• Reflect on your writing experience.

Throughout the writing process, make sure you do the following:

• **Keep your ideas coherent and focused.** Keep your specific purpose in mind to help you present a tightly reasoned argument. Evaluate every idea to make sure it will focus your readers on your main point, and make that point clear in your thesis statement.

- **Share your own perspective.** You bring your own ideas to every piece you write. Share not only information you've gathered but also your viewpoint on your topic. Let your natural voice shine through to readers.

- **Keep your audience in mind.** Consider your readers' backgrounds and interests. If your form is not assigned, choose a form that will grab your readers, such as a song, editorial, screenplay, or letter.

- **Plan to publish.** Labor over every piece as though it will be published or shared with an audience. Enlist the help of a classmate when you proofread a finished piece, and use the questions in the chart below. The numbers in parentheses indicate the sections in the Language Handbook that contain instruction on each concept.

QUESTIONS FOR PROOFREADING

1. Is every sentence complete, not a fragment or run-on? (8a, 9d–e)

2. Are punctuation marks used correctly? (12a–r, 13a–o)

3. Are the first letters of sentences, proper nouns, and proper adjectives capitalized? (11a, c)

4. Does each verb agree in number with its subject? (2a) Are verb forms and tenses used correctly? (3b–c)

5. Are subject and object forms of personal pronouns used correctly? (4a–e) Does every pronoun agree with a clear antecedent in number and gender? (2j)

When revising and proofreading, use the symbols below.

SYMBOLS FOR REVISING AND PROOFREADING

Symbol	Example	Meaning of Symbol
≡	805 Linden avenue	Capitalize a lowercase letter.
/	the First of May	Lowercase a capital letter.
∧	one ^of^ my friends	Insert a missing word, letter, or punctuation mark.
⌐	at the ^onset^ beginning	Replace a word.
℮	Give me a a number	Delete a word, letter, or punctuation mark.
∽	beleive	Change the order of letters.
¶	¶"Yes," she answered.	Begin a new paragraph.

Paragraphs

The Parts of a Paragraph

Paragraphs can be as different as oak trees are from pines. Some paragraphs are a single word; others run several pages. Their uses differ, too: A paragraph may present a main idea, connect one idea to another, emphasize an idea, or simply give the reader's eyes a rest in a long passage.

Many paragraphs in essays and other types of nonfiction, including workplace writing, develop one main idea. A main-idea paragraph is often built from a **topic sentence, supporting sentences,** and a **clincher sentence.**

PARTS OF A PARAGRAPH	
Topic Sentence	• an explicit statement of the paragraph's main idea or central focus
	• often the first or second sentence in a paragraph, but may appear at the end to emphasize or summarize
Supporting Sentences	• provide elaboration by supporting, building, or proving the main idea
	• often include details of the following types:
	sensory details: information about sight, sound, taste, smell, and texture
	facts: details that can be proved true
	examples: specific instances that illustrate a general idea
	anecdotes: brief stories about people or events that illustrate a main idea
	analogies: comparisons between ideas familiar to readers and unfamiliar concepts being explained
Clincher Sentence	• may restate the topic sentence, summarize supporting details, offer a final thought, or help readers refocus on the main idea of a long paragraph

TIP Not every paragraph has, or needs, a topic sentence. In fiction, paragraphs rarely have topic sentences. Paragraphs presenting time sequences (how-to instructions or histories, for example) may also lack topic sentences—the steps or events themselves focus the reader's mind. Finally, a paragraph may imply, or suggest, its main idea without directly stating it in a topic sentence. In your school writing, however, topic sentences are a help: They keep *you* focused on each paragraph's topic.

TIP Not every paragraph needs a clincher sentence. Use one for a strong or dramatic touch or for renewing a main idea in a lengthy or complicated paragraph.

Putting the Parts Together   You can clearly see the parts of a paragraph in the following example. Notice that its topic sentence expresses the paragraph's main idea and that the clincher sentence re-emphasizes it.

Topic Sentence
Supporting
Sentences

Clincher Sentence

> There are some differences between the heroes and quests of old and their contemporary versions, to be sure. These differences reflect the fact that popular entertainment today is more self-conscious than tales from the oral tradition, incorporating specifically contemporary concerns. For example, instead of relying on superhuman powers or the intervention of gods and goddesses, the heroes of the *Star Trek* universe rely on futuristic technology, scientific knowledge, and a sophisticated understanding of diverse alien cultures in order to succeed in their various quests. In this way, although the *Star Trek* adventures contain echoes of the heroic quest story, they are unmistakably a product of our time.

Qualities of Paragraphs

Think about trees again. Each type is so distinct: a pine with its needles and cones, a magnolia with its glossy leaves and huge blossoms. Yet, while different, each is a pleasing whole. Paragraphs achieve this wholeness, too, through two major qualities: **unity** and **coherence.**

Unity   Unity means that all of a paragraph's supporting sentences really fit the main idea—no pine cones should poke out among the magnolia blooms. In other words, all of the supporting sentences must work together and stay on the topic. Unity is achieved when

- all sentences relate to the paragraph's main idea—whether it is stated in a topic sentence or implied, or
- all sentences relate to a sequence of events

Coherence   When a paragraph has coherence, the ideas are arranged in an order that makes sense so that the reader moves easily from one idea to another. The paragraph flows; it doesn't bounce readers around or befuddle them. You can create coherence in a paragraph by paying attention to

- the order you use to arrange ideas
- the connections you make between ideas to show readers how the ideas are related

To create coherence through the arrangement of your ideas, choose the type of order that best fits your purpose. The chart below explains how to use the four main types of order.

TYPES OF ORDER

Order	When to Use	How It Works
Chronological	• to tell a story or relate an event • to explain a process • to show cause and effect	• presents events in the order they happen • shows how things change over time
Spatial	• to describe individual features • to create a complete visual picture	• arranges details by location in space—top to bottom, left to right, near to far, center to edge, and so on
Order of Importance	• to inform • to persuade	• arranges ideas and details from most important to least, or vice versa • places emphasis where the writer thinks it is most effective
Logical	• to inform or to persuade, often by classifying: defining, dividing a subject into parts, or comparing and contrasting	• groups ideas or details together in ways that illustrate the relationships between them; for example, as parts of a whole

TIP The types of order can overlap or can be used in combination. For example, to explain an effect, you might move **chronologically** through its causes, describing the first cause, which leads to the second cause, and so on. However, suppose that three simultaneous causes produce a single effect. You could discuss those causes in **order of importance.**

Guide readers through your clearly arranged ideas by pointing out the connections among them. Show connections by using **direct references** (repetition of ideas), **transitional expressions,** and **parallelism.** The chart on the next page details how you can use these three types of connections to add to the coherence of your writing.

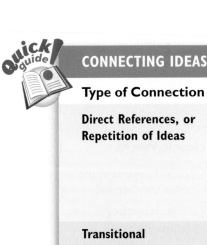

CONNECTING IDEAS

Type of Connection	How to Use It
Direct References, or Repetition of Ideas	• Refer to a noun or pronoun used earlier in the paragraph. • Repeat a word used earlier. • Substitute synonyms for words used earlier.
Transitional Expressions	• Compare ideas (*also, and, another, in the same way, just, like, likewise, moreover, similarly, too*). • Contrast ideas (*although, but, however, in spite of, instead, nevertheless, on the other hand, still, yet*). • Show cause and effect (*accordingly, as a result, because, consequently, for, since, so, so that, therefore*). • Indicate time (*after, at last, before, early, eventually, first, later, next, then, thereafter, until, when, while*). • Show place (*above, across, adjacent, behind, beside, beyond, down, here, in, near, over, there*). • Show importance (*first, last, less significant, mainly, more important, to begin with*).
Parallelism	• Use the same grammatical forms or structures to balance related ideas in a sentence. • Sparingly, use the same sentence structures to show connections between related ideas in a paragraph or composition.

PRACTICE & APPLY Develop two paragraphs on a single topic that interests you. First, choose two primary methods of organizing ideas on the topic (keeping in mind that you may use a combination of orders). Then, plan a topic sentence, a variety of supporting details, and a clincher sentence for each of your two paragraphs. Finally, draft your paragraphs, clearly organizing and connecting ideas and eliminating any ideas that detract from your focus.

The Writer's Language

Revising often focuses on a piece's content and organization. However, to communicate ideas effectively, you must work just as carefully to revise a piece's **style**—how you express those ideas. When revising your style, fine-tune your writing's **sound, word choice,** and **sentence variety,** and use **rhetorical devices** to grab readers' attention and make your ideas clear and interesting.

A Sound Style Keep your **audience** and **purpose** in mind to help you choose a suitable **voice, tone,** and **level of formality** for a piece of writing.

Voice In writing, voice is your unique personality on paper. Just as you recognize a friend's spoken voice, you can recognize the work of favorite writers by the unique way they express ideas. To evaluate your own writing voice, read your work out loud. If your writing doesn't sound natural, revise it to bring your personality to life.

Tone Tone reveals your attitude toward a topic and audience. Always use an appropriate tone for your audience and purpose. For example, if your purpose is to persuade readers to share your view on an important issue, your tone should be serious and respectful.

Level of Formality You wouldn't don formal wear for a beach party, and neither should you use a casual, informal style for a serious essay on a subject about which you care deeply. Match the level of formality to your subject, your audience, and your purpose. Look at these examples.

INFORMAL   Some people shouldn't own pets. Period.

FORMAL   Certain people should not own pets under any circumstances.

Word Choice Make sure your words express the ideas you want them to express. Every word should help create a clear, vivid picture of what you mean and communicate the connotation you want.

Precise Language Replace vague language in your writing with words that are distinct and strong. For example, you might describe a big boulder you saw on a hike as being as *huge as a car* or as *mammoth as a double-decker bus*. You could mention that the boulder *rumbled* down the hill or *squatted* by the path. Using **precise verbs, nouns,** and **adjectives** like these will make your writing clearer and more interesting.

Connotations As you choose words, notice their **connotations**—the emotional effects they create. For instance, the word *cheap* means "economical," but it also has the negative connotation of being poor in quality. The word *inexpensive* expresses the same idea as *cheap* but in a more positive way. Choose words carefully by considering their effects.

Reference Note

For more on **revising to add variety,** see **Revising for Variety,** 9g–i, in the Language Handbook.

Sentence Variety Readers can become bored with writing that uses the same types of sentences over and over. Create variety by varying the beginnings of your sentences and mixing simple, compound, and complex sentences.

Rhetorical Devices To give your ideas a greater impact, use the rhetorical devices of **parallelism, repetition,** and **analogy.**

Parallelism Just as a train stays on its tracks because they're parallel, readers will stay on track if your written ideas are grammatically parallel.

NOT PARALLEL	More lives are saved when **drivers wear seatbelts** and **motorcyclists are wearing helmets.**
PARALLEL	More lives are saved when **drivers wear seatbelts** and **motorcyclists wear helmets.**

You can also use parallelism for effect by using similar sentence structures to express related ideas.

Repetition Repeating important words or phrases can create an emotional response or underscore their significance. Use this technique sparingly to make your key ideas resonate with readers.

Analogy An analogy illustrates an idea by comparing it to something with similar characteristics. For example, you could say, "The politician worked the crowd as if he were selling the Fountain of Youth."

A Stylish Model Read the following passage, noting the writer's sound, word choice, sentence variety, and rhetorical devices.

A Writer's Model

Voice/tone

Repetition
Analogy
Connotation

Precise verbs

Credit cards are a ticket to an unpleasant lesson for college freshmen. One in five college students will rack up $10,000 in credit card debt by graduation. That's right—$10,000! Some people use credit as recklessly as play money. Unfortunately, the consequences for misusing credit cards are staggering. A $5,000 credit card debt can take up to 30 years and $15,000 to pay off—three times the value of the items purchased. Credit cards only look good until the bill comes due. I encourage students to stand firm and refuse the temptations dangled before them by credit card companies.

PRACTICE & APPLY Revise the paragraph below to improve its style. Add your own ideas as appropriate.

I think students should be allowed to bring cell phones to school. What if we need to call someone? Students have rights too. I think the school staff should quit treating us like babies. This rule just isn't fair and should be changed.

Designing Your Writing

A document must be designed to convey information in a way that is easy to understand and remember. In other words, the text arrangement and appearance and any visuals must support the content. You can create effective design and visuals by hand, or you can use advanced publishing software and graphics programs to design pages and to integrate other features into your word-processed documents.

Page Design

Lay It on the Line   If you want your documents to catch readers' attention, you must design them to be visually appealing and easy to read. Use the following design elements to improve readability.

- **Columns** arrange text in separate sections printed vertically side by side. Text in reference books and newspapers usually appears in columns. A **block** is a rectangle of text shorter than a page. The text in advertisements is usually set in blocks so that it may be read quickly. Blocks and columns are separated from each other by white space.

- A **bullet** (•) is a symbol used to highlight information in a text. Bullets separate information into lists like this one. Bullets attract attention and help readers remember information.

- A **heading** appears at the beginning of a section of text to tell readers what that section is about. A **subheading** indicates a smaller section within a heading. Headings and subheadings may be set off from other text in large, **boldface,** or *italic* type or in a different font.

- **White space** is any area on a page where there is little or no text or graphics. Usually, white space is limited to the margins and the spaces between words, lines, and columns. Advertisements usually have more white space than do books or articles.

- A **caption** appears under a photograph or illustration to explain its meaning and connect it to the text. Captions may appear in italics or in a smaller type size than the main text.

- **Contrast** refers to the balance of light and dark areas on a page. Dark areas contain blocks of text or graphics. Light areas have little type. A page with high contrast, or roughly balanced light and dark areas, is easier to read than a page with low contrast.

- **Emphasis** is how a page designer indicates to a reader which information on a page is most important. Because readers' eyes are drawn naturally to color, large and bold print, and graphics, these elements are commonly used to create emphasis.

Type

Letter Perfect The basic material of your document is the type. Your choice of different **cases** and **fonts** can pull the reader into the text, provide emphasis, and make your document easy to read.

Case The two cases of type are uppercase, or capital, letters and lowercase, or small, letters. You can vary case in these ways:

● **Uppercase letters** Text in all uppercase letters attracts readers' attention and may be used in headings or titles. Because text in all capital letters can be difficult to read, use all capitals only for emphasis, not for large bodies of text.

● **Small caps** Small caps are uppercase letters that are reduced in size. They are used in abbreviations of time, such as 9:00 A.M. and A.D. 1500. Small caps may be combined with capital letters for an artistic effect.

Font A font is one complete set of characters (such as letters, numbers, and punctuation marks) of a given size and design. The three types of fonts are explained in the chart below.

Quick guide

CATEGORIES OF FONTS		
Category	**Explanation**	**Uses**
decorative, or **script,** fonts	elaborately designed characters that convey a distinct mood or feeling	Decorative fonts are difficult to read and should be used in small amounts for an artistic effect.
serif fonts	characters with small strokes (serifs) at each end, such as the main type on this page	Because the strokes on serif characters help guide the reader's eyes from letter to letter, serif type is often used for large bodies of type.
sans serif fonts	characters such as these, formed of straight lines with no serifs	Sans serif fonts are easy to read and are used as headings, subheadings, and captions.

● **Font size** The size of the type in a document is called the font size or point size. In general, newspapers and textbooks use type measured at 12 points. Type for headings and headlines is larger, while captions are usually smaller.

● **Font style** Most text is set in roman (not slanted) style. *Italic*, or slanted, style is used for captions or book titles. Underscored or boldface type can be used for emphasis.

Visuals

Show, Don't Tell   If you wanted to tell about the weekly expenses and income from your summer lawn-care business, it would be more effective to show the information in a table than to list it in a paragraph. Visuals, or graphics, such as this must be accurate and appropriate. You can create visuals by hand or by using technology, such as advanced computer software and graphics programs. You can also add to a document's impact by integrating a database or spreadsheet into it. Here are some useful visuals.

TIP   Consider copying and pasting information from databases into your documents. For example, if you were writing a letter to your school administration proposing a senior class trip to a national park, you could paste information from a database comparing costs and available activities at several parks in your area. (Always give credit to your sources for such data.)

- **Graphs** present numeric information and can show trends or changes over time or how one thing changes in relation to another. A **bar graph** can also compare quantities at a glance, or note the parts of a whole. A **line graph** can compare trends or show how two or more variables interact, as in this example.

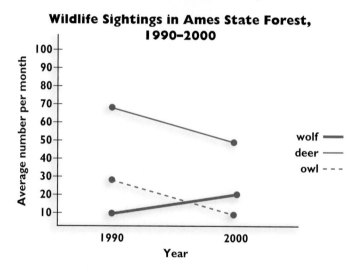

- **Tables** use rows and columns to provide detailed information arranged in an accessible way. A **spreadsheet** is a special kind of table created on a computer. The cells of a spreadsheet are associated with mathematical equations. Spreadsheets are especially useful for budgets or schedules in which the numbers are variables in an equation. In the spreadsheet below, the last column of each row calculates the average of the figures to the left of it.

First Quarter Grades					
Name	**Essay**	**Test**	**Speech**	**Project**	**Average**
Cooper, L.	84	78	81	92	84
Nguyen, H.	90	86	88	95	90
Torres, B.	88	94	91	90	91
Watt, K.	96	90	93	88	92

● **Pictures,** such as drawings and photographs, can show how something works, what something or someone looks like, or something new, unfamiliar, or indescribable. You can scan a copyright-free picture on the computer or paste it manually into your document. Place it near the reference in the text, and include a caption.

● **Charts** show relationships among ideas or data. A **flowchart** uses geometric shapes linked by arrows to show the sequence of events in a process. A **pie chart** is a circle divided into wedges. Each wedge represents a certain percentage of the total, as in this example.

How Energy Is Used Worldwide

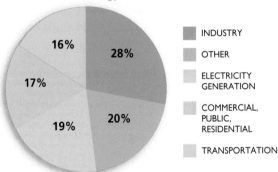

● **Time lines** identify the events that have taken place over a given period of time. (For an example of a time line, see page 2.)

PRACTICE & APPLY Choose and create the visual you think would most effectively communicate the following information using the guidelines in this section.

The estimated expenses for the Sanger High senior class trip are as follows: bus rental, $1,000; gas, $200; hotel, ten rooms at $45 per room for five days, or $2,250; food, $30 a day per person (ten people for five days), or $1,500. The total trip cost is $4,950.

Test Smarts

by Flo Ota De Lange *and* Sheri Henderson

Strategies for Taking Multiple-Choice Tests

Whatever you choose to do in the future, a high school diploma can open doors for you. It is a basic requirement for many, many jobs as well as for getting into college. But to get that diploma, you'll have to pass a lot of tests—pop quizzes in class, midterm exams, finals, your state's standardized tests required for graduation, and probably the SAT if you are thinking about college.

Taking tests doesn't have to be the scary nightmare many students make it out to be. With some preparation, you'll do just fine. The first thing you have to do, of course, is study, study, study! Read all your assignments at least once, and make sure you have mastered the skills being taught.

The following pages can help you prepare for all your standardized tests. They are designed to help you with three goals:

- to become familiar with the different types of questions you will be asked
- to learn some strategies for approaching the questions
- to discover the kinds of questions that give you trouble

Once you have met those goals, you will want to practice answering the kinds of questions that give you trouble until you feel comfortable with them. Here are some basic strategies that will help you approach your multiple-choice tests with confidence:

Stay Calm

You have studied the material, and you know your stuff, but you're still nervous. That's OK. A little nervousness will help you focus, but so will a calm body. **Take a few deep breaths** before you begin.

Track Your Time

First, take a few minutes to estimate how much time you have for each question. Then, set checkpoints for yourself—how many questions should be completed at a quarter of the time, half of the time, and so on. That way you can **pace yourself** as you work through the test.

Master the Directions

Read the directions carefully so you know exactly what to do and how to do it. If you are supposed to fill in a bubble, fill it in carefully. Be sure to match each question's number to the number on the answer sheet.

Study the Questions

Read each question once, twice, three times—until you are absolutely certain you know what the question is asking. Watch out for words like *not* and *except:* They tell you to look for choices that are false, different, or opposite.

Anticipate Answers

Once you are sure you understand the question, **anticipate the answer** before you read the choices. If the answer you guessed is there, it is probably correct. To be sure, though, check out each choice. If you understand the question but don't know the answer, eliminate any choices you think are wrong. Then, make an educated—not a wild—guess to choose one of the remaining choices. **Avoid distracters,** answer choices that are true but don't fit the question.

Don't Give Up

If you are having a hard time with a test, take a deep breath and **keep on going.** On most tests the questions do not get more difficult as you go, and an easier question is probably coming up soon. The last question on a test is worth just as many points as the first, so give it your all—all the way to the end.

Types of Test Questions

You will feel a lot more confident if you are familiar with the kinds of questions given on a test. The following pages describe and give examples of and tips for answering the different types of multiple-choice questions you'll find on many standardized tests.

Critical-Reading Questions

The critical-reading section of a test seeks to determine how well you can think analytically about what you read. This is not news to you. That is the purpose of every reading test you have ever taken. Although challenging tests may give you long, difficult readings and complicated questions, it helps to remember that you will find everything you need—including the answers—right there on the page.

Strategies for Critical-Reading Questions

Here are some tips for answering critical-reading questions.

- **Look for main ideas.** In this kind of test, pay special attention to the **introductory and concluding paragraphs,** in which writers often state their main idea. Read all footnotes or margin notes. As you read the passage, look for **key words, phrases,** and **ideas.** If you are allowed to write on the test, circle or underline them.
- **Look for structure.** Try to determine how the logic of a passage is developed by paying attention to **transition words** and the **pattern of organization.** Does the author build an argument brick by brick, using words and phrases such as *also, and, as well as, furthermore?* Does the author instead offer an argument with contrasts, using words and phrases such as *however, although, in spite of, nevertheless?* And finally, **what is the writer's point?**
- **Eliminate obviously wrong answer choices.** If the questions are long and complicated, it often helps to translate them into

plain English to be sure you understand what's being asked. Then, anticipate the possible answers. When you have eliminated the obviously wrong choices, put your finger on the choice you think is correct, and go back to the passage. **Check it.** Do not rely on memory. This is particularly important for vocabulary-in-context questions.

- **Watch out for traps.** Be wary of choices that use extreme words, like *always* and *never.* Look out for choices that are true but do not correctly answer the question—these are called *distracters.* Remember that questions using *except* or *least* or *not* are asking you to find the false answer. Trust your common sense.

We'll use the reading selection below to discuss a few of the most common kinds of critical-reading questions:

DIRECTIONS: Read the passage below. Then, read the questions that follow, and write the letter of the best answer.

from Acceptance and Nobel Lecture—1993
Nelson Mandela

We speak here of the challenge of the dichotomies of war and peace, violence and nonviolence, racism and human dignity, oppression and repres-
5 sion and liberty and human rights, poverty and freedom from want.

We stand here today as nothing more than a representative of the millions of our people who dared to
10 rise up against a social system whose very essence is war, violence, racism, oppression and repression, and the impoverishment of an entire people.

I am also here today as a represen-
15 tative of the millions of people across the globe, the antiapartheid movement, the governments and organizations that joined with us not to fight against South Africa as a country or

---

(continued)

20   any of its peoples but to oppose an
     inhuman system and sue for a speedy
     end to the apartheid crime against
     humanity.

         These countless human beings,
25   both inside and outside our country,
     had the nobility of spirit to stand in
     the path of tyranny and injustice with-
     out seeking selfish gain. They recog-
     nized that an injury to one is an injury
30   to all and therefore acted together in
     defense of justice and a common
     human decency. Because of their
     courage and persistence for many
     years, we can, today, even set the dates
35   when all humanity will join together
     to celebrate one of the outstanding
     human victories of our century.

         When that moment comes, we
     shall, together, rejoice in a common
40   victory over racism.

VOCABULARY-IN-CONTEXT QUESTIONS

ask you to define words within the context of the reading. If the word is fairly common, look out! A word's meaning in the reading may be an unusual or uncommon one. If it is a really tough word, read several lines above and several lines below the line in which the word is found. The meaning will be in there somewhere. Whatever you do, **always go back and check the reading** for vocabulary-in-context questions. Always.

I. The word *dichotomies* in line 2 is used to describe—

   A a separation of social classes

   B the establishment of groups

   C an ordering of topics

   D a division into opposites

   E a medieval hierarchy

Answer: All the choices refer to some kind of structure. Based on the context clue of the sets of opposites that follow the word *dichotomies,* you can figure out that **D** is the correct answer. If you've taken science courses, you have another clue in the Greek prefix *di–,* which means "twice; double" in words such as *dioxide.*

PARAPHRASING or RESTATING QUESTIONS

ask you to choose the best restatement of an idea, detail, or fact in the selection. You are not asked to make any judgments about the idea; instead, like an interpreter, you are simply asked to report accurately what the writer said. If the question is long and complex, put it into your own words **before** you read the choices. The answer is easier to find if you know what is being asked.

2. When Mandela speaks of "the apartheid crime against humanity" (lines 22–23), he is referring to how—

   A a social system that injures some injures all

   B like any social system, apartheid has its pros and cons

   C apartheid leads to crime

   D apartheid is a crime because it is illegal in South Africa

   E humanity has committed crimes against apartheid

Answer: Even if you didn't know that apartheid was the South African social and legal system of segregation, the sentence tells you that it is a "crime against humanity." Only **choice A** refers to this concept. **B, C,** and **D** do not paraphrase the speaker's meaning, and **E** says the opposite of his meaning.

INFERENCE QUESTIONS

ask you to read between the lines, to connect clues from the ideas in selections. You compile hints and key bits of information to arrive at the answer. Inference questions require careful reading in order to glean what is implied rather than stated outright.

3. The speaker would most likely agree that—

A South Africans alone are responsible for South Africa's problems

B apartheid could be overturned by a response from the world community

C there is a bright side to everything

D the law is the law and must be obeyed

E apartheid does not favor any one racial group over another

Answer: First, rule out any choices that are not true according to what is said in the speech. Choices **C, D,** and **E** can all be eliminated because they are contrary to what Mandela states directly. Choice **A** seems possible, and so does **B**. Re-read the speech. See that the third and fourth paragraphs make clear that the speaker believes apartheid is a world problem, not just South Africa's. Therefore, **choice B is the best answer.**

TONE or MOOD QUESTIONS ask you to infer the writer's attitude toward the subject. Pay attention to the descriptions of the subject. Are they positive, neutral, or negative? Is the writer hopeful, sad, admiring, wishy-washy, sarcastic? (A standardized test might use more difficult vocabulary words for those same words: *sanguine, melancholy, reverent, ambivalent, sardonic.*)

4. Which of the following words best describes Mandela's attitude toward his subject?

A amused   D bewildered

B resigned   E diplomatic

C impassioned

Answer: Mandela is clearly neither amused **(A)**, resigned **(B)**, nor bewildered **(D)**. His subject is serious, and he speaks with conviction about change. Although a Nobel Peace Prize acceptance speech is an occasion that may call for diplomacy **(E)**, Mandela is evidently passionate about his subject. Since *impassioned* is a synonym for *passionate,* **C is the best choice.**

MAIN-IDEA or BEST-TITLE QUESTIONS ask you to consider the big picture, much as you might do when you step back

from a still-life painting to focus on the entire effect rather than zoom in on the individual fruits and objects that create that effect. Ask yourself:

• What is the subject?
• What aspect of the subject does the writer address?
• What does the writer want me to understand about this aspect?

Main ideas are often found at the beginning or end of a selection. In choosing your answers, be wary of those that may be true but are either too specific or too general to reflect the message of *this* selection.

5. Which of the following titles is best for Nelson Mandela's speech?

A "Racism Defeated"

B "Apartheid in South Africa"

C "South Africa United"

D "Millions of People Unite"

E "A Stand Against Injustice"

Answer: **The best answer is E** since Mandela talks about the stand he and millions of others have taken against the injustice of apartheid. Racism has not yet been defeated, so **A** is not right. **B** and **D** are too general. **C** is irrelevant.

EVALUATING-THE-WRITER'S-CRAFT QUESTIONS ask you to look at the selection's organization, logic, and argumentative techniques. They often look like this:

6. In his speech the speaker makes his central point primarily by—

A attacking the specific persons responsible for apartheid

B praising the efforts of many people to combat apartheid

C warning the world against future apartheids

D counting the gains of apartheid

E describing in detail crimes against humanity

Answer: **The best answer is B;** the third through fifth paragraphs praise those who fight against apartheid. Choice **A** seems possible, but the word *specific* signals that it's not the right answer—Mandela never mentions any specific persons. You can eliminate **E** because although he mentions crimes against humanity, Mandela does not describe them in detail. Choices **C** and **D** do not relate to the speech.

Vocabulary Questions

You will encounter several types of vocabulary questions on standardized tests. They all test your knowledge of word meanings, both in and out of context.

SENTENCE-COMPLETION, or FILL-IN-THE-BLANK, QUESTIONS look easy, but they require your full attention. Here's a step-by-step way to approach each question:

- **Cover up the answer choices, and read the entire sentence carefully.** Most sentences contain clues to the intended meaning and thus to the word you want. Ask yourself, "What is this blank about?" and "What else does the sentence say about the subject of the blank?"
- **Look for clue words.** Pay special attention to words that change the direction of a sentence. Look for words that **reverse** the sentence's main idea, such as *no, not, although, however, but.* Look also for words that indicate that a **synonym** is wanted: *and, also, in addition, likewise, moreover.* Finally, look for words that suggest **cause and effect:** *thus, therefore, because, since, so.*
- **Anticipate answers.** Think of words that might best fill the blank.
- **Look at the choices.** If the word you guessed is there, it is probably the correct choice. You can double-check by eliminating any choices that are obviously wrong. Then, try *each* choice in the blank, and re-read the sentence *each* time to find the best fit. Take no shortcuts on this step.

Here are four fill-in-the-blank questions:

7. Meeting a Noah's ark-like emergency today would require an ocean freighter to hold the ten million species weighing a total of one thousand tons, says Clifford Pickover in "Keys to Infinity," but successfully preserving them from extinction would still be _____ because at least fifty members of a species are required to maintain genetic health.

   A feasible   **D** dubious

   B inappropriate   **E** effortless

   C abstruse

Answer: You are looking for a word that means "unlikely." How do you know that? Your clue lies in the part of the sentence that follows the word *because,* which tells you that it will take fifty times the two-by-two formula to keep the animals in good genetic shape. (Of course, a difficult test like the *SAT* will not give you a word as easy as *unlikely* as a choice.)

Let's imagine for a moment that those choices are all unfamiliar words, and maybe they are to you. You can still think them through. **Use what you know to eliminate incorrect answers.** You can eliminate **B** and **E**—the task described is neither inappropriate nor easy enough to be called effortless. Cross out **C** (*abstruse,* which means "difficult to understand"), because it doesn't fit the context either. **A** (*feasible,* which means "doable") and **D** (*dubious*) are the remaining choices. Choice **A** suggests the meaning that is opposite the context, so **D is the best answer.**

8. If it were possible to _____ a car body in a vat of human stomach acid, the acid would eat the car body, given enough time and assuming you could keep the vat from dissolving.

   A vacillate   **D** ostracize

   B vilify   **E** refurbish

   C immerse

Answer: **C is the correct answer,** the only choice that makes sense in the sentence. You have a great clue in the second half of this sentence, which tells you that the car would dissolve *in* the acid. This would, of course, require the car to be *in* the acid. Thus, you would look for a word like *soak* to fill the blank, so *immerse,* which means "plunge into a liquid," is your best choice.

Two Blanks to Fill In

Some sentence-completion questions have two blanks. The trick is to find the choice that fits both blanks correctly—in the order given. **As a shortcut, determine the choices that fit *one* blank, whichever blank seems easier to you.** Cross out all the choices that don't fit. **Then, consider *only* the remaining choices when filling in the other blank.**

9. Researchers have determined that the ability to wiggle one's ears and curl one's tongue is _____, much to the disappointment of kids who have spent hours trying to _____ these skills.

   A genetic, achieve

   B complicated, procure

   C unreliable, sustain

   D inherited, flaunt

   E acquired, relinquish

Answer: Before you look at the choices, make sense of the sentence. One clue lies in the word *disappointment,* which tells you that the kids are not successful in learning the skill. Another clue lies in the word *researchers,* which suggests that the blank word will be scientific. Since the kids couldn't learn the skills, the skills must be *inborn.*

Now, look at the choices. **You can immediately eliminate any first-blank choices that do not reflect the sentence's meaning**—in this case, eliminate any first-blank choices that do not mean "inborn." Strike out **E** (*acquired,* an antonym), **B** (*complicated*), and **C** (*unreliable*). Both **A** (*genetic*) and **D** (*inherited*) could fill the first blank.

Now, go on to the second blank, checking only the choices that fit the first blank—in this case, **A** and **D.** In this half of the sentence, you know you are looking for a verb that means "get; learn." **A** (*achieve*) is a possibil-

ity, but **D** (*flaunt*) doesn't work since it is not possible to flaunt what has not been acquired. Thus, **A is your best answer.**

10. Elephants, which are the largest animals walking the earth today, can _____ a number of human _____, including seasickness, colds, pneumonia, mumps, and diabetes.

    A recollect, infirmities

    B diagnose, junctures

    C acquire, tendencies

    D contract, maladies

    E atrophy, ailments

Answer: You know that the second blank will mean "illnesses" because the second half of the sentence lists quite a few human illnesses. The first blank will therefore mean something akin to the word *catch.*

For this question it might be easier to begin with the second blank. Remember that you are looking for a word that means "illnesses," so you can quickly eliminate **B** and **C.** Choices **A** (*infirmities*), **D** (*maladies*), and **E** (*ailments*) all fit the second blank.

Your next step is to check the first blank for choices **A, D,** and **E,** the only choices that fit the second blank. Which of them has a first-blank choice that means "catch"? Only **choice D** (*contract*) fits the meaning you need. (Yes, *acquire* also means "catch," but you've already eliminated **C** because the second blank doesn't fit.) **D is the best answer.**

Finally, try out the sentence to make sure that both words in choice D make sense.

ANALOGY QUESTIONS require that you figure out the relationship between one pair of words and then select another pair with the same relationship. Analogies use many kinds of relationships, including **cause and effect, part and whole, performer and related object, performer and related action, person or object, quality, synonym, antonym, characteristic, degree.** (For more about analogies, see pages 58 and 903.)

The more comprehensive your vocabulary, the better off you will be when you face an analogy question. If you are stumped, try breaking an unfamiliar word into its prefix, suffix, and root. In some tests the analogy questions get harder as you go, but don't give up. Everyone's vocabulary is different, and a word that seems difficult to others may be easy for you. Let's try one out:

11. TEACHER : STUDENTS : :

A actor : playwrights

B speaker : audience

C horse : corrals

D business owner : stocks

E luggage : airplanes

Begin by turning the first pair of words (the stem words) into a sentence that defines their relationship. Your sentence should begin with the first word in the pair and end with the second word; you fill in the middle. A sentence for item 11 might be *A teacher's job is to educate or inspire students.* Now, try each choice out within the same sentence: An actor's job is to educate or inspire playwrights? A speaker's job is to educate or inspire an audience? A horse's job is to educate or inspire corrals? (No way.) A business owner's job is to educate or inspire stocks? The job of luggage is to educate or inspire airplanes?

Answer: **B is the best answer** because it preserves the relationship and the kind of comparison being made. Both a teacher and a speaker are kinds of people. Students and audiences listen to them and—the teacher and the speaker hope—become educated or inspired as a result of what they hear. None of the other choices show the same relationship.

You may already have noticed that words in vocabulary questions are anything but commonplace. What's a student to do in the face of such *egregious, inordinate,* and *maliciously pedantic* word choices? Study them. Study them. Study them. The best way, though, to learn vocabulary words is to read. Read many different kinds of materials. Don't just skim over words you don't know: Look them up. Then, think about the meaning they add to the passage you are reading. If you follow those

suggestions, you'll increase your vocabulary *exponentially,* and questions on vocabulary tests will be much less *formidable.*

In the analogy questions that follow, the first uses easy words only; the second throws in some challenging words.

12. SHEEP : FLOCK : :

A milk : water

B street : road

C car : truck

D trees : orchard

E telephone : receiver

Answer: To define the relationship in the stem words, you might make up this sentence: *Sheep are part of a group called a flock.* Then, try out that same sentence with all of the choices. You can eliminate **A, B,** and **C** because none of them make sense in your sentence. **D** makes sense: Trees are part of a group called an orchard. **E** might have made sense if the words were in reverse order (a receiver is part of a telephone)—but they're not. **So D is the correct answer.** The analogy is based on the relationship of a part to a whole.

13. LUMINOUS : GLOWING : :

A burnished : beautiful

B murky : dark

C weathered : new

D distraught : erroneous

E inane : sagacious

Answer: **The answer is B.** The relationship in this analogy is that of synonyms: *Luminous* means the same as *glowing.* You can eliminate choices **C** and **E** (the word pairs are antonyms, not synonyms) as well as **D,** in which the words seem totally unrelated. The words in **A** aren't synonyms either (*burnished* means "bright," not "beautiful"), so that leaves only **B,** whose words (*murky, dark*) are indeed synonyms.

Multiple-Choice Writing Questions

Multiple-choice writing questions are designed to test your knowledge of standard written English. Some questions ask you to spot errors in a sentence's grammar or punctuation. Some ask you to spot the best written form of a sentence. Some ask when a paragraph is (or isn't) properly developed. You will need to know the rules of punctuation and grammar. Here are some question formats you might encounter:

IDENTIFYING-SENTENCE-ERROR QUESTIONS

ask you to look at underlined sections of a sentence and choose the section that includes an error. You are *not* expected to correct the error.

14. The average person <u>knows</u> about 50,000 of
A

the 150,000 words in a standard college dictionary, <u>have learned</u> most of <u>them</u> by
B   **C**

high <u>school, which means</u> 3,000 words per
D

year or eight every day. <u>No error</u>.
E

Answer: **The correct answer is B.** Replace the verb phrase *have learned* with the present participle *having learned.* The phrase *having learned most of them by high school* is a participial phrase that modifies *person.* Remember, however, that you are asked only to *find* the error, not to correct it or explain why it's wrong. By the way, have you picked up your eight words today?

IMPROVING-SENTENCES QUESTIONS

ask you to correct an underlined section by choosing the best version offered. It is helpful to find the error before you look at the answer choices. Then, anticipate how it could best be

corrected. The answers to questions like those are often confusing to read because they are long and very poorly written (remember that all but one of them are wrong). Take some time with such questions.

15. Over an average person's life span, his or her heart will pump about 50 million gallons, <u>which equals enough to fill a million bathtubs or filling fifty 10-ft-deep swimming pools being as big as football fields.</u>

   A which equals enough to fill a million bathtubs or to fill fifty 10-foot-deep swimming pools as big as football fields.

   B enough to fill a million bathtubs or fifty 10-foot-deep swimming pools as big as football fields.

   C which means a million bathtubs or fifty 10-foot-deep swimming pools as big as football fields will be filled by it.

   D enough to fill a million bathtubs with 10-foot-deep swimming pools being as big as football fields.

   E which is a million bathtubs, 10-foot-deep swimming pools, and football fields.

Answer: **The best answer is B.** Your next-best choice, **A,** says the same thing but with less economy. **C** is awkward and unnecessarily switches verb tenses; **D** and **E** totally garble the information.

IMPROVING-THE-PARAGRAPH QUESTIONS

present a paragraph followed by questions. You may be asked to pick a choice that combines or rewrites portions of sentences. You may be asked to decide which sentences could be added or removed from the paragraph. You may be asked which sentence could be used to strengthen the argument of the writer, or you may be asked to choose a thesis statement for the paragraph.

DIRECTIONS: Read the paragraph below. Then, find the best answer to the following questions.

(1) An initially beneficial chemical whose use had unintended consequences is DDT. (2) Beginning in 1939, this pesticide was used throughout the United States to exterminate disease-carrying and crop-eating insects. (3) This powerful chemical also helped India. (4) It helped India reduce cases of malaria from 75 million to fewer than five million. (5) In 1962, scientists began to realize that the chemical was passing through the food chain and harming some types of birds. (6) As a result of high concentrations of DDT in the birds' tissue, many species began laying thin-shelled eggs that cracked easily. (7) One result of widespread DDT spraying was the decline of some bird populations.

16. Which of the following choices represents the *best* way to combine sentences 3–4?

A This powerful chemical also helped India, it reduced cases of malaria from 75 million to fewer than five million.

B This powerful chemical also helped India by helping India to reduce cases of malaria from 75 million to fewer than five million.

C India also was helped by this powerful chemical, which had the effect of India's reducing cases of malaria from 75 million to fewer than five million.

D This powerful chemical also helped India to reduce cases of malaria from 75 million to fewer than five million.

E This powerful chemical also helped India: reduce cases of malaria from 75 million to fewer than five million.

Answer: You are looking for the sentence that contains all of the important information with the *least* amount of repetition. It takes careful reading to figure out that **the best answer is D,** which cuts the clutter and maintains the meaning. Answer **A** is a run-on sentence, so that's out. **B** is awkwardly repetitious; **C** makes the verb passive, increasing wordiness. The difference between choices **D** and **E** is slight—only a colon and the word *to.* That's enough to make **E** wrong (the rest of the sentence doesn't go with the colon) and **D** smooth, streamlined, and the only correct answer.

17. Which of the words below could *best* be inserted in sentence 5 immediately after "In 1962,"?

A also   **D** and

B however   **E** because

C but

Answer: **The best answer is B,** the only choice that makes sense in the context of the paragraph. Choice **B** (*however*) reflects the reversed direction of sentence 5, which clearly states that—unlike the information given in the preceding sentences—not everything about DDT was good.

Strategies for Taking Writing Tests

Writing a Response to Literature

When you are asked to respond to a literary passage on a writing test, the passage may be a short story, a novel excerpt, a poem, or a section of a play. No matter the type of passage, you'll need to understand not only its literal meaning, but also the deeper point the writer is making. Follow the steps below to write a response to a passage from a play. The sample responses provided are based on the prompt to the right. (The excerpt from *Oedipus Rex* appears on page 212.)

Prompt

In Part I of *Oedipus Rex*, Oedipus tells the Theban citizens: "You should have found the murderer . . . / I say I take the son's part, just as though / I were his son, to press the fight for him. . . ." In an essay, explain Oedipus's viewpoint and Sophocles' use of irony in this speech, given Oedipus's situation in the play.

THINKING IT THROUGH   Writing a Response to Literature

STEP 1 **Carefully read the prompt and the selection.** Be sure you can identify the task and the surface meaning of Oedipus's words.

I need to explain both what the passage means and the writer's deeper point. Oedipus is boasting that he will obtain justice for Laius and chastises the citizens of Thebes for failing to avenge the previous king's death. Since the reader knows that Oedipus is himself the murderer he seeks, these words are filled with irony. The words will come back to haunt Oedipus, serving as a punishment for his egotism.

STEP 2 **Draw a conclusion about the deeper meaning of the piece, and gather support for that conclusion.** Base your conclusion on your own knowledge and on details that seem important in the selection.

It seems like Oedipus is extremely arrogant. He is quick to accuse other people of wrongdoing and views himself as above reproach. His excessive pride is apparent when he tells the citizens that they "should have" acted in a certain way and says that he'll "press the fight for him / And see it won!" Such arrogance contributes to his downfall.

STEP 3 **Develop a thesis statement for your essay based on your conclusion and your evidence.**

The ironic "I take the son's part" speech from Oedipus Rex effectively demonstrates Oedipus's egotism, which ultimately leads to his undoing.

STEP 4 **Write your response.** Explain how examples you use from the text relate to each other and to your thesis. Write with an authoritative tone, and use precise language to explain the conclusion you have drawn. End your response by emphasizing your thesis in a memorable way. Proofread your finished response, and correct any errors in English-language conventions.

Writing a Response to Expository Text

Expository text provides information. A written **response to expository text** should demonstrate your understanding of the information provided and the organization of that information. To write a response to expository text for a test, use the steps below. The sample responses provided are based on the prompt to the right. ("When Timbuktu Was the Paris of Islamic Intellectuals in Africa" begins on page 532.)

Prompt

The article "When Timbuktu Was the Paris of Islamic Intellectuals in Africa" explains what life was like in medieval Timbuktu. Using examples from the article, write a brief essay explaining some ways in which the city has changed since medieval times.

THINKING IT THROUGH

Writing a Response to Expository Text

STEP 1 **Carefully read the prompt and the selection.** Make sure you understand what tasks the prompt calls for.

I need to pick out the main differences between life in medieval Timbuktu and life in the city today, giving examples of those differences.

STEP 2 **Decide on your general answer, and identify your main supporting points.** Skim the selection to identify the main points you will make to support your answer to the prompt.

The article describes the intellectual history and commercial activity of medieval Timbuktu.

STEP 3 **Develop a thesis statement for your essay.** Your thesis statement will sum up your main points and draw a conclusion about your topic.

Medieval Timbuktu was drastically different from the Timbuktu of today.

STEP 4 **Gather support for your thesis.** Choose details and examples from the selection that will provide strong support, and elaborate on them.

I can discuss the fact that Timbuktu was once a thriving cultural center and compare that image with the current description of the city as "a slumbering and decrepit citadel." I can also explain that the people of Timbuktu once "thrived on the commerce of gold, salt and slaves" and mention that now the city is located in "one of the poorest countries in the world." Finally, I can point out that in contrast to present-day Timbuktu, the city was once a major center of intellectualism where law, literature, and science manuscripts were being written.

STEP 5 Write your essay. Begin with an attention-getter, such as a question or a surprising statement. Organize ideas clearly and logically, using transitions to show readers the links between those ideas. Then, find and correct any errors in English-language conventions in your draft.

Writing a Biographical Narrative

Writing a **biographical narrative** requires you to do more than simply retell an event from someone's life. Through vivid descriptions and explanations, you must make readers feel that they, too, witnessed the event. To give a biographical narrative meaning, share a significant conclusion about the person involved in the event. To write a biographical narrative in response to a test prompt, follow the steps below. The sample responses provided are based on the prompt to the right.

Prompt

While everyone makes mistakes, some people handle them better than others. In a narrative, relate how someone you witnessed handled making a mistake, including the consequences of the way the mistake was handled. Note what this tells you about the person and how witnessing this event affected you.

THINKING IT THROUGH · Writing a Biographical Narrative

STEP 1 Carefully read the prompt, and choose a subject.

I need to explain what someone I saw make a mistake did—how they handled the mistake and what the consequences were. I'll tell about when my government teacher said something negative about a political candidate during class.

STEP 2 Identify the parts of the event you will relate. Outline in sequence the smaller events that make up your chosen event.

A student mentioned whom he supported in the upcoming election. Mrs. Jackson made a joke about the candidate that offended the student. Mrs. Jackson apologized and explained that she had strong opinions because she liked politics so much—that's why she became a government teacher—and she hoped we would also develop strong opinions, but express them more appropriately. Her apology started a great discussion.

STEP 3 Identify important details about the people, events, and setting. Details should be relevant and specific to bring the incident to life.

Mrs. Jackson's expressions and tone of voice are important, as are those of the student whose candidate she insulted.

STEP 4 Draw a conclusion based on the details. Decide why the incident is significant; this conclusion will be the basis for your narrative's thesis.

Mrs. Jackson showed what a good teacher she is by admitting her mistake and turning it into a thought-provoking lesson. I'll be careful now to back up my opinions rather than insult someone else's position.

STEP 5 Write your narrative. Provide context for readers in your introduction. Make your point of view clear and consistent, and make sure every detail you include helps support your thesis or bring the event to life. Finally, correct any errors in grammar, usage, and mechanics.

Writing an Expository Composition

Expository compositions explain. You might write an expository composition to tell how to do something, define a topic, compare and contrast two things, or explain causes and effects. No matter the task, expository writing should anticipate readers' questions and clear up any potential misunderstandings or biases about the topic. Use the steps below to write an effective expository composition for a test.

Prompt

Consider an important recent event in your community or in the larger world. In an essay, discuss what you think are the primary cause and the most important effect of the event. Support the cause and effect you identify with examples.

THINKING IT THROUGH · Writing an Expository Composition

STEP 1 Carefully read the prompt, and choose a topic you know well.

I need to explain the main cause and effect of an event. I'll pick the collapse that happened last month of the old two-lane bridge over Town Creek.

STEP 2 Identify the major parts of the topic.

The parts are one cause and one effect. There were lots of causes, including increased truck traffic and a recent flood, but the main cause is lack of funding for repairs. The main effect is increased traffic on the only other bridge over the creek.

STEP 3 Brainstorm background information and details about each part of the topic. Your essay will need to answer potential questions and clear up any misunderstandings or biases readers might have.

Voters opposed funding needed for repairs a few years ago because many thought that since the bridge had stood for so many years, the repairs were only cosmetic, not structural. Now those voters are paying the price with longer drives to cross the other bridge in heavy traffic while the old bridge is being rebuilt—at greater expense than the proposed repairs would have entailed.

STEP 4 Synthesize your ideas to plan a thesis. Draft a thesis sentence explaining the point made by all of your information about your topic.

The collapse of Old Town Creek Bridge was the result of an attempt to save money; now it is costing drivers both time and money as they are diverted to the only other bridge over the creek.

STEP 5 Write your essay. Don't just string together ideas in your draft. Instead, provide insight into your topic by thoroughly explaining your major points. Organize ideas in an easy-to-follow way, and connect them with transitional expressions to help guide readers. Finally, proofread and correct any errors in English-language conventions.

Writing a Persuasive Composition

In a **persuasive composition** written for a test, you must quickly identify a position and strong reasons and evidence that support that position. To make the most of your time, follow the steps below. The sample responses provided are based on the prompt to the right. Notice that in some cases it is faster and easier to develop a strong argument for a position that doesn't fit your views; your goal on a test is simply to write the best essay you can.

Prompt

Many states are considering enacting graduated driver's license laws, which limit such things as the time of day when teenagers may drive or the number of passengers they may carry. In an essay, explain whether you agree or disagree with such laws, and back up your position with evidence.

THINKING IT THROUGH • Writing a Persuasive Composition

STEP 1 **Carefully read the prompt, analyzing the situation and the task.**

The laws limit when teenagers can drive or how many people can ride with them. I have to decide based on evidence whether these laws are a good idea.

STEP 2 **Draft an opinion statement.** Choose the easiest position to defend.

Personally, I don't want my rights limited, but I think I can use stronger evidence if I pick the position in favor of graduated licenses. My opinion statement will be: Graduated license laws, while unpopular with teenagers, are a good idea.

STEP 3 **Identify reasons and evidence.** Use the acronym MATH (**M**oney, **A**ttitudes, **T**ime, **H**ealth/safety) to identify reasons and counterclaims.

Money: Graduated licenses will be more expensive to issue and enforce, but they might reduce expenses resulting from accidents caused by teen drivers.

Attitude: I have a friend who's a terrible driver but feels like he has the right to drive however he wants. These limits might change that attitude.

Time: Parents will waste time picking up teenagers from jobs if they have to work later than they're allowed to drive, but this is a minor problem.

Health/safety: Keeping teens from driving late at night or with a carload of friends might prevent a lot of accidents.

STEP 4 **Choose your two or three strongest reasons.** Use reasons and responses to readers' potential counterclaims that relate to the prompt.

I'll focus on the most important issues related to these laws—safety and money.

STEP 5 **Write your essay.** Write with a convincing, knowledgeable voice, and thoroughly explain your reasons and evidence. Organize your ideas in order of importance, finishing with your strongest reason to leave a lasting impression. Then, proofread your draft, and correct any errors in English-language conventions.

Writing an Analytical Composition

On a writing test, you may be asked to write an **analytical composition.** To do so, you must show insight in analyzing a statement, idea, or situation. Usually you will form a generalization and support it with evidence. Follow the steps below. The sample responses provided are based on the prompt to the right.

THINKING IT THROUGH   Writing an Analytical Composition

STEP 1 Read the prompt, and identify your general response to it. Make sure you understand any quotations or important ideas in the prompt.

The statement means that people often see that something is different and automatically think it's better even though it may not be.

STEP 2 Identify two or three pieces of strong supporting evidence.

The Edsel was supposed to be an innovative car in the 1950s, but it turned out to have a lot of problems and was a failure.

Another example is the designated hitter rule in baseball. People thought having a designated hitter batting in place of the pitcher would make the game more exciting, but it wound up making the games longer and making pitchers less well-rounded players.

STEP 3 Synthesize your ideas to plan a thesis statement. Draft a sentence or two explaining how your examples support your analysis.

When progress takes the form of a stylish new car that runs poorly or a new sports rule that winds up hurting the game, it isn't progress at all, but only novelty.

STEP 4 Organize your support. Depending on your topic, consider using order of importance, comparison and contrast, cause and effect, chronological order, or a combination of orders.

First, I'll discuss the Edsel because its problems were so obvious. Then, I'll explain the less obvious problems with the designated hitter rule. That order can lead into a final statement about how people should consider not only obvious problems but also more subtle ones when they're deciding whether something is truly progress or only novelty.

STEP 5 Draft your essay. Clearly explain what you think quotations or important ideas in the prompt mean, and state your thesis. Connect your ideas with transitional expressions, and elaborate on those ideas with details. Conclude by restating your thesis, and close with a memorable comment. Finally, correct any errors in grammar, usage, and mechanics.

Handbook of Literary and Historical Terms

ACMEISM **A literary movement from the early twentieth century that strove toward clear expression by using carefully chosen words and focusing on the real world.** Acmeism was a reaction to **symbolism,** which was a highly popular literary style in the early twentieth century. Acmeists rejected the vagueness and mysticism of symbolism and instead employed concrete images in their writing. Acmeism is typified by the works of the Russian poet Anna Akhmatova (Collection 7), who helped found the movement with her husband, Nikolay Gumilyov.

See page 891.

ALLEGORY **A story in which the characters, settings, and events stand for abstract or moral concepts.** An allegory can be read on one level for its literal meaning and on another level for its symbolic, or allegorical, meaning. Dante's *Divine Comedy* (Collection 5) is an example of an allegory. On a literal level, it tells of Dante's journey through Hell, Purgatory, and Paradise to reach God. On an allegorical level, his journey symbolizes every individual's quest for spiritual salvation.

See pages 648, 664, 1037.

ALLITERATION **The repetition of consonant sounds in words that are close to one another.** Alliteration occurs most often at the beginning of words, as in "broken bottle," but consonants within words may also alliterate, as in "always wide awake." Poets may use alliteration to achieve special rhythmic and musical effects, to emphasize particular images and moods, or to give their poems greater unity.

See page 514.
See also *Assonance.*

ALLUSION **A reference to a statement, person, place, event, or thing that is known from literature, history, religion, myth, politics, or some other field of knowledge.** For example, Czeslaw Milosz's poem "Song of a Citizen" (Collection 7) contains an allusion to the biblical book of Ecclesiastes. Allusions add depth of meaning to a work of literature by inviting comparisons.

See pages 110, 899.

CALVIN AND HOBBES © 1990 Watterson. Reprinted with permission of UNIVERSAL PRESS SYNDICATE. All rights reserved.

AMBIGUITY **The expression of an idea in language that suggests more than one meaning.** Writers who employ ambiguity do so to lead readers into several trains of thought, all of which make sense in the context of the work. In "Peonies" (Collection 3), Li Ch'ing-chao uses ambiguity to make readers wonder whether the poem is addressed to a flower or to a woman.

See pages 438, 1031.

ANALOGY **A comparison of two things to show that they are alike in certain respects.** Writers often make analogies to show how something unfamiliar is like something well known or widely experienced. For example, people often draw an analogy between creating a work of art and giving birth.

See pages 58, 191, 559.

ANECDOTE **A brief and sometimes witty story that focuses on a single interesting incident or event, often in order to make a point or teach a moral lesson.** Sometimes an anecdote reveals the character of a famous person. Taoists, Zen Buddhists, and Sufis (Collections 3 and 4), among others, use anecdotes to convey indirectly the teachings of their philosophies.

See page 564.

ANTAGONIST **The character or force that opposes or blocks the protagonist, or main character, in a narrative.** Usually the antagonist is human, like Hagen in "How Siegfried Was Slain" (Collection 5). Sometimes the antagonist can be supernatural, like Mephistopheles in *Faust* (Collection 6).

ANTICLIMAX See *Climax.*

ANTITHESIS **A contrast of ideas expressed in a grammatically balanced statement.** The following proverb from the Hebrew Bible balances opposite ideas:

> Faithful are the wounds of a friend; but the kisses of an enemy are deceitful.

See page 542.

APHORISM **A concise, sometimes witty saying that expresses a principle, truth, or observation about life.** "Don't cry over spilled milk" is a well-known aphorism that points to the uselessness of regretting things that cannot be changed.

APOSTROPHE **A figure of speech in which a speaker directly addresses an absent or dead person, a deity, an abstract quality, or something nonhuman as if it were present and capable of responding.** Apostrophe is commonly used in hymns to address a divine being.

See pages 45, 369.

ARCHETYPE **A pattern that appears in literature across cultures and is repeated through the ages. An archetype can be a character, a plot, an image, or a setting.** For example, the basic plot of the hero's quest is a recurring pattern in myths and other types of literature from different cultures around the world.

See pages 305, 307, 508.

ARTHURIAN ROMANCE **A verse narrative in an idealized world that deals with King Arthur and his knights of the Round Table.** The heroes of these romances are bound by the codes of chivalry and courtly love.

See pages 592, 624.
See also *Romance.*

ASIDE **Private words that a character in a play speaks to another character or to the audience that are not supposed to be overheard by others onstage.** Stage directions usually tell when a speech is an aside.

ASSONANCE **The repetition of similar vowel sounds followed by different consonant sounds in words that are close together.** For example, the long *a* sounds in "It's a great day for baseball" create assonance. Like **alliteration,** assonance may be used in poetry to create special rhythmic and musical effects, to emphasize particular images or moods, or to achieve unity.

See also *Alliteration.*

ATMOSPHERE The mood or feeling in a literary work. Atmosphere is usually created through descriptive details and evocative imagery. For example, a story set in a grimy factory town may create a gloomy atmosphere in which characters struggle against despair.

See also *Mood.*

AUTOBIOGRAPHY A written account of a person's own life. Autobiographies are unified narratives usually prepared for a public audience. Unlike **memoirs,** which often focus on particular events, autobiographies are usually quite comprehensive and introspective.

See also *Memoir.*

BALLAD A song or songlike poem, often from the oral tradition, that tells a story. Most ballads have a regular pattern of rhythm and rhyme and use simple language and refrains as well as other kinds of repetition. The ballads from China's *The Book of Songs* are among the most ancient recorded **folk ballads.** In the Middle Ages, folk ballads were composed by anonymous singers and were passed down orally from generation to generation before they were written down. Medieval ballads usually tell sensational stories of tragedy, adventure, betrayal, revenge, and jealousy. **Literary ballads** are composed and written down by known poets, usually in the style of the older folk ballads.

The typical ballad stanza in European literature is a quatrain with the rhyme scheme *abcb* (although this is by no means universal). The meter is often only loosely iambic, with four stresses in the first and third lines and three stresses in the second and fourth lines. The number of unstressed syllables in each line may vary.

See page 592.

BIOGRAPHY An account of a person's life written or told by another person. For example, Tacitus's historical account of imperial Rome, *The Annals* (Collection 2), includes a biography of the emperor Nero.

BLANK VERSE Poetry written in unrhymed iambic pentameter. "Blank" means that the poetry is unrhymed. "Iambic pentameter" means that each line contains five **iambs,** or metrical feet, each consisting of an unstressed syllable followed by a stressed syllable (ˇ ′). Blank verse was the most common metrical form used in English dramatic and epic poetry during the Renaissance. It is the verse form used, for example, in John Milton's epic poem *Paradise Lost.* Because blank verse lends itself easily to slight variations within the basic pattern and can mimic the natural rhythms of English speech, it has been used over the centuries by many poets writing in English. Here are the closing lines from *Paradise Lost,* describing Adam and Eve's departure from Paradise:

> The world was all before them, where to choose
> Their place of rest, and Providence their guide;
> They hand in hand, with wand'ring steps and slow,
> Through Eden took their solitary way.

BUDDHISM A religion whose followers seek an end to human suffering by renouncing desires and selfishness. Buddhism was founded in India in the sixth century B.C. by Siddhartha Gautama. After giving up a life of wealth and privilege, Siddhartha came to believe that suffering is caused by the desire for earthly things. He said that one can achieve inner peace only by renouncing this desire. Siddhartha's followers gave him the name Buddha, which means "enlightened one." Though it fell into decline and nearly disappeared from India in the first century A.D., Buddhism also spread to China, Japan, and many other countries. It continues to influence spiritual life throughout the world today.

See pages 349, 355, 363.

CADENCE The natural rise and fall of the voice. Poets who write in free verse try to imitate the natural cadences of spoken language.

See also *Rhythm.*

CANTO A subdivision in a long poem, similar to a chapter in a book. Dante's *Divine Comedy* (Collection 5), for example, is divided into one hundred cantos. The word *canto* comes from a Latin word for "song" and originally designated a section of a narrative poem that a minstrel could sing in one session.

See page 647.

CARPE DIEM *A Latin phrase that literally means "seize the day"—that is, "make the most of present opportunities."* The *carpe diem* theme appears in the ode "Carpe Diem" (Collection 2) by Horace and has commonly appeared in world literature through all times and cultures.

See pages 303, 681.

CATALOG *A lengthy list—often of gods, heroes, weapons, or geographical features—in an epic poem.*

CHAIN TALE *A type of folk tale that contains minimal plot, much repetition and rhythm, and a pattern that ties the tale together.* "Talk" (Collection 4) is an example of a chain tale. The paragraph that begins with the words "My yam said" ties the tale together.

See page 504.

CHANSON DE GESTE *A kind of epic poem composed in Old French from the twelfth to the fifteenth centuries, focusing on the heroic deeds of Charlemagne and other feudal lords.* Literally meaning "songs of deeds," *chansons de geste* such as the *Song of Roland* (Collection 5) share many characteristics with classical **epics.**

See page 592.

CHARACTER *An individual in a story, play, or narrative poem.* A character always has human traits, even if the character is an animal, such as the trickster Coyote in American Indian tales, or a god or monster, such as Odin and the Fenris Wolf in the Norse myth "The End of All Things" (Collection 2). Most characters, however, are ordinary human beings, like Qiao Lin in Zhang Jie's "Love Must Not Be Forgotten" (Collection 7).

The process by which the writer reveals the personality of a character is called **characterization.** A writer can reveal a character in the following ways:

1. By telling us directly what the character is like: humble, ambitious, impetuous, easily manipulated, and so on
2. By describing how the character looks and dresses
3. By letting us hear the character speak
4. By revealing the character's private thoughts and feelings
5. By revealing the character's effect on other people—showing how other characters feel about or behave toward the character
6. By showing the character's actions

The first method of revealing character is called **direct characterization.** When a writer uses this method, we do not have to figure out what a character's personality is like—the writer tells us directly. The other five methods of revealing a character are known as **indirect characterization.** When a writer uses these methods, we have to exercise our own judgment, putting clues together to figure out what a character is like—just as we do in real life when we are getting to know someone.

Characters can be classified as static or dynamic. A **static character** is one who does not change much in the course of a story. A **dynamic character,** on the other hand, changes in some important way as a result of the story's action. Characters can also be classified as flat or round. **Flat characters** have only one or two personality traits. They are one-dimensional—their personalities can be summed up by a single phrase. In contrast, **round characters** have more dimensions to their personalities—they are complex, solid, and multifaceted, like real people.

See pages 607, 757, 814, 882, 1083.

CHIVALRY *The system of ideals and social codes governing the behavior of knights and gentlewomen in feudal times.* The ideal knight was meant to be brave, honorable, and courteous; gentlewomen were meant to be chaste. The code of chivalry is reflected in medieval romance literature such as *Perceval* (Collection 5) by Chrétien de Troyes.

See pages 586, 592.

CHORUS *In classical Greek tragedies, a group of nameless onlookers who comment on and interpret the action of the play.* In most Greek tragedies, the Chorus consists of twelve or fifteen performers who dance as they sing their lines. In Sophocles' *Oedipus Rex* (Collection 2), the Chorus is used as a collective "actor" within the drama itself.

See page 201.

CLASSICISM *A European movement in art, literature, and music that advocates imitating the principles manifested in the art and literature of* ancient ("classical") Greece and Rome. Classicism emphasizes reason, clarity, balance, harmony, restraint, order, and universal themes. Classicism is often placed in direct opposition to Romanticism, with its emphasis on unrestrained emotions and personal themes. However, this opposition should be approached with caution, as it is sometimes exaggerated for effect. Classicism was particularly admired in art in the eighteenth century.

CLICHÉ **An expression that was fresh and apt when it was first coined but is now so overused that it has become hackneyed and stale.** "Busy as a bee" and "fresh as a daisy" are two examples. Clichés are often likened to **dead metaphors**—figures of speech ("leg of a chair," "mouth of a river") whose power to surprise has now been completely lost.

CLIMAX **The point of greatest emotional intensity or suspense in a plot when the outcome of the conflict becomes known.** The climax usually marks the moment toward the end of the plot when the conflict is decided one way or the other. After the climax, the story is usually resolved. Long works, such as novels, may have more than one climactic moment, though the greatest climax usually occurs last. At the **turning point** in a plot, something happens that seals the fate of the hero. The hero's fortunes begin to decline or improve. All the action leading up to this turning point is **rising action,** and all the action following it is **falling action.**

When something trivial or comical occurs at the point in a narrative when one expects something important or serious, the accompanying deflation is called an **anticlimax.**

See page 607.
See also *Plot, Dramatic Structure.*

COMEDY **In general, a story that ends happily.** The hero or heroine of a comedy is usually a character who overcomes a series of obstacles that block what he or she wants. Sometimes a comedy pits two young people who wish to marry against parental blocking figures who want to prevent the marriage. The wedding that concludes these comedies suggests the renewal of life or the formation of a harmonious society. Comedy is distinct from **tragedy,** in which a great person comes to an unhappy or disastrous end, often due to some tragic flaw in his or her personality.

See also *Tragedy.*

COMMUNISM **An economic and political theory that advocates the creation of a classless and stateless society in which economic goods are distributed equally.** The most famous Communist government is, of course, the now dissolved Soviet Union, a country that one could say perverted the ideals of Communism, since it had a ruling class that was better off than the working class. Human nature seems to prevent people from bringing into being a perfect Communist society.

CONCEIT **A fanciful and elaborate figure of speech that makes a surprising connection between two surprisingly dissimilar things.** A conceit may be a brief metaphor, or it may form the framework of an entire poem. One particularly important type of conceit is the **Petrarchan conceit.**

Petrarchan conceits get their name from the fourteenth-century Italian poet Petrarch, who developed them in his influential sonnet sequence. Poets influenced by Petrarch used these conceits to describe the beauty of the lady for whom they wrote. She invariably had hair of gold, lips of cherry red, and teeth of oriental pearl. Petrarchan conceits were also used to describe a paradoxical state.

CONFLICT **A struggle or clash between opposing characters, forces, or emotions.** In an **external conflict,** a character struggles against some outside force: another character, society as a whole, or some natural force. An **internal conflict,** on the other hand, is a struggle between opposing needs, desires, or emotions within a single character. Many longer works contain both internal and external conflicts that are often interrelated. In some works, such as Luigi Pirandello's "War" (Collection 7), the conflict between characters reflects larger cultural conflicts.

See pages 271, 389, 796, 996, 1009.

CONFUCIANISM **A philosophy founded in China by Confucius, which teaches that order, discipline, and social stability are the foundations of a good life.** Confucius's teachings were collected by his disciples in the *Analects* (Collection 3). The teachings later became the official state doctrine of China.

See pages 349, 358, 407, 408.

CONNOTATIONS All the meanings, associations, or emotions that a word suggests. For example, a clothing store might prefer to advertise its excellent "apparel" rather than its excellent "garments." Both words have the same literal meaning, or **denotation:** "articles worn to cover the body." *Apparel*, however, has connotations of elegance and sophistication, but *garments* does not. The same store would certainly not describe its clothing as "threads."

Notice the difference between the following pairs of words: *young/immature, ambitious/cutthroat, uninhibited/shameless, lenient/lax.* In each pair, the second word carries unfavorable connotations that the first word does not.

See page 776.
See also *Denotation*.

CONSONANCE The repetition of final consonant sounds after different vowel sounds. The words *boasts* and *jests* are examples of consonance. The term is also sometimes used to refer to repeated consonant sounds in the middle of words, as in *tilled field*. (Consonance, when loosely defined, can be a form of alliteration. **Alliteration,** however, usually refers to the repetition of initial consonant sounds.)

COUPLET Two consecutive lines of poetry that rhyme. The German epic poem *The Nibelungenlied* (Collection 5) was written in stanzas that consist of two rhymed couplets. When a couplet is written in iambic pentameter, it is called a **heroic couplet.** When a couplet forms a complete thought, it is called a **closed couplet.** Shakespeare's sonnets (Collection 5) end in closed couplets.

See pages 623, 679.

COURTLY LOVE A conventional medieval code of behavior that informed a knight of the proper way to treat his lady. The code was first developed by the troubadours of southern France and was extensively employed in European literature from the twelfth century throughout the medieval period.

See pages 586, 593.

CRISIS See *Dramatic Structure*.

DEISM The belief that God, after creating the universe, ceased to interfere with the laws of nature and society.

DENOTATION The literal, dictionary definition of a word. For example, a denotation, or dictionary definition, of the word *star* (as in "movie star") is an "eminent actor or actress," but the connotation is that of an actor or actress who is adored by fans and who leads a fascinating and glamorous life.

See page 776.
See also *Connotations*.

DENOUEMENT See *Plot*.

DESCRIPTION Writing that is intended to re-create a person, place, thing, event, or experience. Description uses **imagery**—language that appeals to the senses—to show how something looks, sounds, smells, tastes, or feels to the touch.

See also *Imagery*.

DEUS EX MACHINA Any artificial or contrived device used at the end of a plot to resolve or untangle the complications. The phrase is Latin and means "god from a machine." The phrase refers to a device used in ancient Greek and Roman drama: At the conclusion of the play, a god would be lowered onto the stage by a mechanical device so that he could save the hero and end the story happily. The term now refers to any device that resolves a plot in a forced or implausible way. Oscar Wilde's *The Importance of Being Earnest* and Charles Dickens's *Oliver Twist* both contain examples of *deus ex machina*.

DIALECT A way of speaking that is characteristic of a particular region or group of people. A dialect may have a distinct vocabulary, pronunciation system, and grammar. In the Middle Ages, when Latin was the literary language, writers such as Dante Alighieri (Collection 5) began writing for middle-class audiences in their own regional languages, or what are now interchangeably called dialects or **vernaculars.** Today one dialect usually becomes accepted as the standard for a country or culture. In the United States, the dialect used in formal writing and spoken by most TV and radio announcers is known as standard English.

Writers often use other dialects, however, to establish character or to create local color. The East London cockney dialect, and the lower-class background it betrays, are at the very heart of Bernard Shaw's famous play *Pygmalion*.

See page 594.

Handbook of Literary and Historical Terms

DIALOGUE Conversation between two or more people. Writers use dialogue to advance the action of a plot, to present an interplay of ideas and personalities, and to reveal the background, occupation, or social level of characters through **tone** and **dialect.**

DICTION A writer's or speaker's choice of words. Writers and speakers use different types of words depending on the audience they're addressing, the subject they're discussing, and the effect they're trying to produce. For example, the language a scientist would use in a scholarly article to describe a snowflake would be different from the language used by a poet.

Diction is an essential element of a writer's style. It may be, for instance, simple or ornate (big rooms/commodious chambers), general or specific (fish/fantailed goldfish), modern or old-fashioned (men's store/haberdashery). An important aspect of any writer's diction is the connotations that the words carry.

See page 794.

DIDACTIC LITERATURE A literary work that is meant to instruct, give advice, or convey a philosophy or a moral message. Much didactic literature, such as Zen parables (Collection 3), stems from religious or philosophical teachings. Secular works such as fables and maxims are also didactic in intent.

See page 542.
See also *Fable, Parable.*

DILEMMA TALE A type of moral tale, from the oral tradition, that does not have a resolution but instead ends with a question posed to the audience. Dilemma tales are particularly popular in Africa, where they are used to uphold community values by inspiring discussions of moral behavior.

See page 510.

DISSONANCE A harsh, discordant combination of sounds. The opposite of **euphony,** a pleasant combination of sounds, dissonance is usually created by the repetition of harsh consonant sounds. Dissonance is often used in poetry to communicate energy. Dissonance is also called **cacophony.**

DRAMA A story that is written to be acted out in front of an audience. Drama is one of the major genres, or forms, of literature. The earliest Western dramas originally had a **sacred** or **ritual** function and were used in religious ceremonies or services. In medieval Japan, a very formal and stylized mode of drama known as **Noh** also developed from religious sources.

In Europe during the Renaissance and Enlightenment, playwrights such as William Shakespeare, Molière, and William Congreve created dramas in several forms—satires, historical plays, comedies, tragedies, and tragicomedies (which combined elements of both comedy and tragedy). In the late nineteenth century, the Norwegian playwright Henrik Ibsen helped influence the direction of much modern drama by creating Realist plays about controversial subjects.

See pages 111, 199, 755.

DRAMATIC MONOLOGUE A poem in which a speaker addresses one or more listeners. The reactions of the listener, who remains silent, must be inferred by the reader. From the speaker's words, the reader learns the speaker's identity, as well as the situation, setting, and the identity of other characters.

See page 922.

DRAMATIC STRUCTURE The method of development of a play's plot. A typical dramatic structure in European literature, especially in the plays of Shakespeare, includes **exposition,** in which relevant background information is presented; **rising action,** which accelerates and adds complications to the plot; the **climax** (sometimes called the **turning point** or **crisis**), which is the moment of greatest emotional intensity or suspense; **falling action,** which unravels the complications; and the **resolution,** which settles the play's conflicts.

Greek tragedies such as *Oedipus Rex* have their own dramatic structure. It consists of the **prologue,** an opening scene that usually introduces you to the main character of the tragedy; the **parodos,** which is the first of the Chorus's lyric songs, or **choral odes,** in which they comment on the action of the drama; a regular alternation of dialogue between characters in the play and choral odes; and the **exodos,** which concludes the action of the play.

See page 199.

ELEGY A poem that mourns the death of a person or laments something lost. Elegies may lament the passing of life and beauty, or they may be meditations on the nature of death. A type of lyric poetry, elegies are usually formal in language and structure and solemn or even melancholy in tone. A modern example is Yehuda Amichai's "Laments on the War Dead" (Collection 7).

See page 539.

END-STOPPED LINE A line of poetry in which the meter and the meaning conclude with the end of the line. Often the end-of-line pause is marked with punctuation, though it need not be.

ENJAMBMENT (en·jam′mənt), also called run-on line. The use of run-on lines to complete a thought from one line of verse to the next. By cutting down on **end-stopped lines** (lines that conclude a thought with punctuation), enjambment enhances the flow of a poem's language and prevents a strict rhyme scheme or rhythm from sounding predictable and rigid.

See page 686.

ENLIGHTENMENT A name historians have applied to the eighteenth century. This period has been called the Age of Enlightenment and the Age of Reason because at that time, people began to rely on reason and experience, rather than superstition and Church authority, to gain an understanding of the world.

See page 601.

EPIC A long narrative poem that relates the great deeds of a larger-than-life hero who embodies the values of a particular society. Most epics include elements of myth, legend, folklore, and history. Their tone is serious and their language grand. Most **epic heroes** undertake quests to achieve something of tremendous value to themselves—like Gilgamesh (Collection 1)—or to their society—like the hero of Virgil's *Aeneid* (Collection 2).

Most ancient epics began as **oral epics,** also known as **primary epics,** which were performed by generations of anonymous storytellers and changed slightly with each retelling. The African epic *Sundiata* (Collection 4), for example, was passed down orally for hundreds of years by storytellers known as griots before it was written down in the 1950s. **Literary epics,** on the other hand, are created by individual writers, often from earlier models. Virgil's *Aeneid* is an example of a literary epic modeled after earlier Greek epics—Homer's *Iliad* (Collection 2) and *Odyssey*.

Many epics, particularly those in the western literary tradition, share standard characteristics and formulas known as **epic conventions,** including

- an **invocation,** or formal plea to a deity or some other spiritual power to inspire the poet
- action that begins **in medias res** (literally, "in the middle of things") and then flashes back to events that take place before the narrative's current time setting
- **epic similes,** or elaborately extended comparisons relating heroic events to simple, everyday events
- a consistently predictable **metrical structure** (originally intended as a memorization aid in oral performances of the epic)
- **stock epithets,** or descriptive adjectives or phrases used repeatedly with—or in place of—a noun or proper name, such as "the wine-dark sea" in Homer's *Odyssey*

See pages 21, 121, 269, 519, 607.

EPIC HERO An epic's larger-than-life main character whose mighty deeds reflect the values admired by the society that created the epic. Epic heroes usually undertake a dangerous journey or quest to supernatural realms to achieve a goal. They are often endowed with superior strength, knowledge, and courage. However, epic heroes can also possess human weaknesses. Gilgamesh (Collection 1) is an example of an epic hero, as is Sundiata (Collection 4).

See page 21.

EPIGRAM A brief, clever, and usually memorable statement that often contains a moral. Fables, such as those in the *Panchatantra* (Collection 3) and those by Jean de La Fontaine (Collection 5), often end with epigrams that summarize the message of the story.

See pages 383, 903.
See also *Maxim, Moral, Proverb*.

EPIPHANY In a literary work, a moment of sudden insight or revelation that a character experiences. The word *epiphany* comes from Greek and can be translated as "manifestation" or "showing forth." The term has religious origins that have been transferred to literature. James Joyce gave the word its literary meaning in an early draft of his novel *A Portrait of the Artist as a Young Man* (1914–1915).

See page 863.

EPITHET **An adjective or other descriptive phrase that is regularly used to characterize a person, place, or thing.** Phrases such as "Ivan the Terrible" and "Jack the Giant-Killer" are epithets. Homer created so many stock epithets in his *Iliad* (Collection 2) and *Odyssey* that his name has been permanently associated with a particular type of epithet. The **Homeric epithet** consists of a compound adjective that is regularly used to modify a particular noun. Famous examples are "the wine-dark sea," "the gray-eyed goddess Athena," and "rosy-fingered dawn."

See pages 38, 121.
See also *Epic.*

EPONYM **A real or mythical person from whose name the name of a nation, institution, idea, or term has been derived.** For example, Miguel de Cervantes' character Don Quixote (Collection 5) is the eponym for the word *quixotic,* which describes someone who is like Don Quixote—impractical, romantic, and visionary.

See page 110.

ESSAY **A short piece of nonfiction prose that examines a single subject from a limited point of view.** There are two major types of essays. **Formal essays** are usually serious and impersonal in tone. Because they are written to inform or persuade, they are expected to be factual, logical, and tightly organized. **Informal essays** (also called **personal essays**) generally reveal much about the personalities and feelings of their authors. They tend to be conversational in tone, and many are autobiographical in nature.

See page 973.

EXISTENTIALISM **A modern European movement in philosophy, religion, and art that asserts "existence precedes essence," that is, that the universe and everything in it exists but has no meaning and that people supply meaning through their actions.** Some existentialists, such as Albert Camus, emphasize that each person is free to make moral choices that define and give meaning to his

or her life. Through their choices and actions, human beings are responsible for what they make of themselves and their lives.

See pages 850, 898.

FABLE **A very brief story in prose or verse that teaches a moral or a practical lesson about life.** In **beast fables,** the characters are animals that behave and speak like human beings. Some of the most popular fables are those attributed to Aesop, a Greek slave who supposedly lived in the sixth century B.C. Other popular and widely influential fables include those collected in the *Panchatantra* (Collection 3).

See pages 383, 704.
See also *Parable.*

FALLING ACTION See *Dramatic Structure.*

FANTASY **A work that takes place in an unreal world and features incredible characters.** Works of fantasy often do not follow natural laws or normal logic; however, they usually have internal consistency.

FARCE **A type of comedy in which ridiculous and often stereotyped characters are involved in far-fetched, silly situations.** The humor in farce is based on crude physical action, slapstick, and clowning. Characters may slip on banana peels, get pies thrown in their faces, and knock one another on the head with ladders. The movies featuring Abbott and Costello, Laurel and Hardy, and the Marx Brothers are all examples of farces.

See also *Comedy.*

FASCISM **A nationalistic political philosophy that advocates centralized, one-party rule by a single charismatic dictator.** Fascism, strictly speaking, refers to the philosophy of Benito Mussolini's political party, which was founded in 1919 to oppose Communism in Italy. The word, however, was soon used to describe the philosophies of similar repressive, nationalistic political parties in other countries. The German Nazis were fascists, as were the regimes of Francisco Franco in Spain and Juan Peron in Argentina.

FEUDALISM **The economic, political, and social system of medieval Europe.** This system was basically composed of three classes: the feudal lords, who were powerful landowners; vassals, who did work or military service for the feudal lords in exchange for land; and serfs, who were servants to the lords and vassals and who were bound to their masters' land.

See page 591.

FIGURATIVE LANGUAGE See *Figure of Speech*.

FIGURE OF SPEECH A word or phrase that describes one thing in terms of another and is not meant to be understood on a literal level. Figures of speech (sometimes called **figurative language**) always involve some sort of imaginative comparison between seemingly unlike things. Some 250 types of figures of speech have been identified, but the most common are the **simile** (a heart like a comforting fire), the **metaphor** (the dark cloak of night), and **personification** (angry winds shouting through the canyon).

See pages 778, 857, 938, 1043.
See also Hyperbole, Metaphor, Onomatopoeia,
Personification, Simile, Symbol.

FLASHBACK A scene in a narrative work that interrupts the present action of the plot to "flash backward" and tell what happened at an earlier time. Flashback is one of the conventions of Homer's *Iliad* (Collection 2) and *Odyssey* that became a standard feature of many later epics. A less common narrative device is the **flashforward,** or scene that interrupts the present action to skip ahead to an event in the future.

See pages 122, 1062.

FOIL A character who is used as a contrast to another character. The use of a foil emphasizes the differences between two characters, bringing out the distinctive qualities in each. For example, in *The Nibelungenlied* (Collection 5), Hagen serves as a foil to Siegfried, thereby emphasizing Siegfried's heroic qualities.

See page 644.

FOLK TALE A story with no known author that originally was passed on from one generation to another by word of mouth. Folk tales belong to the oral tradition. Most folk tales are told for entertainment, although they may also teach moral values.

Legends, tall tales, fables, ghost stories, and fairy tales are all forms of folk tales.

FORESHADOWING Clues that hint at what is going to happen later in the plot. Foreshadowing arouses the reader's curiosity and builds suspense. In "An Astrologer's Day" (Collection 7), for example, R. K. Narayan includes details in his initial description of the astrologer to foreshadow the story's surprise ending.

See pages 122, 636, 986.

FRAME STORY A story that serves to bind together several different narratives. The *Panchatantra* (Collection 3), *The Thousand and One Nights* (Collection 4), and Boccaccio's *Decameron* (Collection 5) all use frame stories as a device for unifying various shorter stories.

See pages 383, 669.

FREE VERSE Poetry that has no regular meter or rhyme scheme. Free verse usually relies instead on the natural rhythms of ordinary speech. Poets writing in free verse may use alliteration, internal rhyme, onomatopoeia, repetition, or other devices to achieve their effects. They may also place great emphasis on imagery.

See page 895.

GENRE The category to which a literary work belongs. Examples of genres include drama, the epic, the novel, the short story, and lyric poetry.

GRIOT A traditional keeper of oral literature in West Africa. In the past, griots were responsible for memorizing and transmitting their nation's histories, laws, and literature. Today, griots can be storytellers or entertainers.

See page 496.

HAIKU A brief, unrhymed, three-line poem developed in Japan in the 1600s. In the original language, the first and third lines of a haiku have five syllables each, and the middle line has seven. Haiku generally juxtapose familiar images and present them in a compressed form, forcing the reader to make an imaginative leap to understand the connection between them.

See pages 363, 446, 448.

HINDUISM The central and most ancient religion in India, centered on the concepts of dharma, the caste system, karma, and reincarnation. Hinduism is characterized by a multitude of rituals, beliefs, and gods. It has no written doctrine and no religious leader.

According to Hindu belief, everyone is born with a unique **dharma,** which encompasses many concepts, including religion, duty, and ethics. Dharma requires that one fulfill one's station in life, whether it be lofty or humble. One's dharma unfolds through a person's lifetime based on the choices he or she makes. Sometimes one must act in unrighteous ways when following one's dharma.

A person's dharma is determined in part by his or her **caste,** or social class. In the Hindu tradition the caste system divides people into four different ranks of society. The four castes are the **Brahmans,** who were scholars, teachers, and priests; the **Kshatriyas,** who were rulers and warriors; the **Vaisyas,** who were merchants, artisans, and farmers; and the **Sudras,** who did menial work. There is also a caste called the untouchables, who were completely excluded from society.

Two other central concepts of Hinduism are karma and reincarnation. *Karma* is a word meaning one's actions in life, and **reincarnation** is the rebirth of a deceased person's soul in another body. If a person has good karma, he or she will be reincarnated into a higher caste. When one's soul is completely pure, it is united with Brahman, the ultimate spiritual reality.

See page 353.

HISTORY A genre of nonfiction that involves the recording of actual events as they happened or are likely to have happened. The earliest histories were objective writings that merely reported events. In ancient Greece, historical writing began to develop when Thucydides (Collection 2) posed difficult questions about the Peloponnesian War. Later, the ancient Roman writer Tacitus (Collection 2) incorporated his own beliefs and opinions into historical writing. A history is usually written in narrative form.

HUMANISM An intellectual movement of the European Renaissance that restored the study of the classics and focused on examining human life here and now. Humanists broke away from the focus on Christian theology that characterized medieval learning. Though humanists were still interested in theology and religious questions, the focus of their interest expanded to include earthly matters as well.

See page 596.

HYMN A lyric poem or song addressed to a divine being. Hymns praise the power and wisdom of a deity and often ask for divine help or mercy.

See page 367.

HYPERBOLE A figure of speech that uses exaggeration to express a strong sentiment or create a comic effect. Also called **overstatement,** hyperbole does not express the literal truth; however, it is often used to capture a sense of intensity or to emphasize the essential nature of something. For example, when we say we are "sweating to death" in a stuffy room, we are using a hyperbole to express extreme discomfort. Hyperbole is often used in **satire,** such as Voltaire's *Candide* (Collection 5), for ridiculing or exposing an opponent's vices or follies.

See page 298.

CALVIN AND HOBBES © 1993 Watterson. Reprinted with permission of UNIVERSAL PRESS SYNDICATE. All rights reserved.

IAMBIC PENTAMETER A line of poetry made up of five iambs. An **iamb** is a metrical foot, or unit of measure, consisting of an unstressed syllable followed by a stressed syllable (˘ ′). The word *preferred,* for example, is made up of one iamb. **Pentameter** is derived from the Greek words *penta* ("five") and *meter* ("measure"). Sonnets and blank verse use iambic pentameter. It is by far the most common verse line in English poetry because of its similarity to the natural rhythms of spoken English. Here, for example, are two lines of iambic pentameter from Shakespeare's *The Tempest:*

> His mother was a witch, and one so strong
> That could control the moon, make flows and ebbs

See page 679.
See also *Meter.*

IDIOM An expression peculiar to a particular language that means something different from the literal meaning of the words. *Fit to be tied* (very angry or upset) and *take a chance* (accept the risk of failure or loss) are idioms of American English.

See page 970.

IMAGERY Language that appeals to the senses. Most images are visual—that is, they appeal to the sense of sight. But imagery can also appeal to the reader's sense of hearing, touch, taste, or smell. Although imagery is an element in all types of writing that involve description, it is especially important in poetry.

See pages 175, 778, 891.

INCREMENTAL REPETITION A device widely used in ballads and other songs and lyrics whereby a line or lines are repeated with slight variations from stanza to stanza. Each repetition advances the plot of the narrative.

INDUSTRIAL REVOLUTION The period of social and economic change in nineteenth-century Europe following the replacement of hand tools by machines and power tools, which allowed manufacturers to increase production and save money. The perfection of the steam engine in the last half of the eighteenth century signaled the arrival of the age of the machine. The Industrial Revolution began on a small scale among textile manufacturers in the middle of the eighteenth century but soon spread rapidly. Most textile products were produced by steam-engine-powered machines by the early nineteenth century. As the nineteenth century progressed, other industries began to use steam engines to produce their goods. George Eliot uses the Industrial Revolution as the backdrop for *Silas Marner* (1861), and Charles Dickens satirizes its social effects in *Hard Times* (1854).

See pages 742, 750.

IN MEDIAS RES The technique of starting a story in the middle and then using a flashback to tell what happened earlier. *In medias res* is Latin for "in the middle of things." Epics, such as Homer's *Iliad* (Collection 2), traditionally begin *in medias res.*

See page 121.

IRONY A contrast or discrepancy between expectations and reality—between what is said and what is really meant, between what is expected and what really happens, or between what appears to be true and what is really true. Irony in literature falls into three major categories:

1. **Verbal irony** occurs when a writer or speaker says one thing but really means the opposite. If you tell a friend who shows up an hour late for an appointment, "I just love being kept waiting in the rain," you are using a form of verbal irony called sarcasm.
2. **Situational irony** occurs when what actually happens is the opposite of what is expected or appropriate. An example of situational irony takes place in Greek mythology when Zeus falls in love with a mortal woman named Semele. Zeus promises to give Semele anything she wants. To his dismay, she begs to see him in his true form as the Lord of Heaven. Zeus reluctantly agrees, and the brilliant splendor of the god burns her to death.
3. **Dramatic irony** occurs when the audience or the reader knows something important that a character in a play or story does not know. Dramatic irony can heighten a comic effect or generate suspense. In *Oedipus Rex* (Collection 2), for example, when the Corinthian messenger tells Oedipus that the King of Corinth has died of natural causes, Oedipus believes he has been released from the prophecy that says he

será

will murder his father. The audience, however, knows that the truth has yet to come to light.

See pages 202, 669, 814, 927, 965, 1003, 1054.

ISLAM Religion founded by Muhammad, who recorded revelations he received from Allah in the Koran. Followers of Islam believe in Allah, the all-powerful God; a hierarchy of angels; and a day of judgment. They also believe that Muhammad was the last in a long line of prophets through whom Allah spoke. The tenets of Islam are recorded in the Koran.

See pages 490–491, 497.

LAIS Medieval French stories written in verse and sung to the accompaniment of a lyre or lute. *Lais* were influenced by the ideals of courtly love and often include supernatural or fairy tale elements.

See page 593.

LEGEND A story about extraordinary deeds, based to some extent on fact. The African epic *Sundiata* (Collection 4), for example, is based on the life of a historical figure, Sundiata Keita, who reestablished the Mandingo Empire of Old Mali in 1235. Through many retellings over time, however, the facts of his life were greatly embellished, and Sundiata Keita became a legendary hero.

See page 518.

LYRIC POETRY Poetry that focuses on expressing private emotions or thoughts. Most lyric poems are short, and they usually imply rather than directly state a single strong emotion. The term *lyric* comes from ancient Greece, where lyric poems, such as those by Sappho (Collection 2), were recited to the accompaniment of a stringed instrument called a lyre. Today, lyric poets rely on the musical effects they can create with words (such as rhyme, rhythm, alliteration, and onomatopoeia).

See page 110.

MAGIC REALISM A literary style that combines incredible events with realistic details and relates them all in a matter-of-fact tone. Magic realism originated in Latin America, where authors such as Gabriel García Márquez and Julio Cortázar (Collection 7) drew on elements of surrealism and local folklore to create a style that is both timeless and innovative.

See pages 853, 956.

MAXIM A brief, direct statement that expresses a basic rule of human conduct or a general truth about human behavior. "It is better to give than to receive" is an example of a well-known maxim.

See page 408.
See also *Epigram, Moral, Proverb.*

MEMOIR A type of autobiography that usually focuses on a single time period or historical event. "A Good Day" by Primo Levi (Collection 7) is a memoir about the author's experiences at the death camp Auschwitz in 1944–1945.

See page 913.
See also *Autobiography.*

METAFICTION A type of postmodern fiction that self-consciously draws attention to its fictional qualities. Some examples of metafiction include stories in which the author is a character or in which a character knows he or she is in a work of fiction, as well as stories about a person writing or reading a story. The Italian writer Italo Calvino's novel *If on a winter's night a traveler,* in which the reader is a character, and Jorge Luis Borges's story "Borges and I" (Collection 7) are examples of metafiction.

See page 936.

METAPHOR A figure of speech that makes a comparison between two seemingly unlike things without using the connective words *like, as, than,* or *resembles.* A direct metaphor states that one thing is another, such as "the stars are icy diamonds." ("Stars like icy diamonds" is a simile.) Often metaphors are **implied:** "Against her black formal gown, she wore a constellation of diamonds" implies a comparison between diamonds and stars and between the black gown and a night sky.

An **extended metaphor** is a metaphor that is developed over several lines of writing or even through an entire poem or paragraph. Marie de France uses an extended metaphor that compares the love of Tristan and Iseult to the entwinement of a hazel tree and a honeysuckle in "Chevrefoil" (Collection 5).

A **dead metaphor** is a metaphor that has become so common that we no longer even notice that it is a figure of speech. Our everyday language is filled with dead metaphors, such as "the pinnacle of success," "a tower of strength," and "the root of the problem."

A **mixed metaphor** is the incongruous mixture of two or more metaphors. Mixed metaphors are usually unintentional and conjure up ludicrous images. "Those snakes in the grass pulled the rug out from under us."

See pages 618, 938, 1043.

"I thought it was only a metaphor when people said, 'My car died.'"

© The New Yorker Collection 1990 Ed Frascino from cartoonbank.com. All Rights Reserved.

METER A generally regular pattern of stressed and unstressed syllables in poetry. Meter is measured in units called feet. A **foot** consists of one stressed syllable and usually one or more unstressed syllables. The standard feet used in English poetry are the **iamb** (as in convínce), the **trochee** (as in bórrŏw), the **anapest** (as in cŏntrădíct), the **dactyl** (as in áccŭrăte), and the **spondee** (as in séawéed). In meters such as **iambic pentameter**—which consists of five iambs per line—other feet may be substituted occasionally. Such variations prevent the meter from sounding singsong and monotonous.

When we want to indicate the metrical pattern of a poem, we mark the stressed syllables with the symbol ´ and the unstressed syllables with the symbol ˘. Indicating the metrical pattern of a poem in this way is called **scanning** the poem, or **scansion**. Here, for example, is a passage from *The Tempest* with the scansion marked. Note how Shakespeare varies the basic iambic pentameter by substituting an anapest for one of the feet in the second line and by adding an extra unstressed syllable at the end of the third line.

> Thĭs blúe-eyed hág wăs híthĕr bróught wĭth chíld
> Ănd hére wăs léft bў thĕ sáilŏrs. Thóu, mў sláve,
> Ăs thóu rĕpórtst thȳsélf, wăst thén hĕr sérvănt

See pages 121, 679.

See also *Blank Verse, Epic, Iambic Pentameter.*

METONYMY A figure of speech in which something closely related to a thing or suggested by it is substituted for the thing itself. You are using metonymy if you call the judiciary "the bench," the monarch "the crown," or the president (or presidential staff) "the White House."

MIDDLE AGES The period in Europe between A.D. 500 and 1500. Also called the medieval period, the Middle Ages lie between the era of classical Greek and Roman culture and the rebirth of those values in the Renaissance. The Middle Ages is characterized by dominance of the Church; the ideals of chivalry and courtly love; and the economic, social, and military system known as feudalism.

See page 588.

MODERNISM A broad trend in literature and the other arts, from approximately 1890 to 1940, that reflected changes in the world, especially the impact of scientific works such as Sigmund Freud's writings on psychoanalysis. In general, modernist writers rejected the forms and values of the past and sought new forms to reflect the fragmentation and uncertainty they felt characterized modern life. Many modernist poets, for example, rejected traditional meter in favor of free verse. Novelists such as James Joyce employed a new technique called **stream of consciousness** to record the jagged monologue of their characters' thoughts.

See pages 842, 849.

MONOLOGUE A long, formal speech made by a character in a play. A monologue may be directed at another character or the audience.

See page 191.

MOOD **The overall emotion created by a work of literature.** Mood can usually be described with one or two adjectives, such as eerie, dreamy, jubilant, or angry. All of the elements of literature, from figures of speech to the language's rhythm, contribute to a work's mood.

See pages 422, 786, 1079.
See also *Atmosphere.*

MORAL **A lesson about life that a story teaches.** Fables often end with a moral that is clearly stated.

See pages 547, 704.
See also *Epigram, Maxim, Proverb.*

MOTIF **In literature, a word, character, object, image, metaphor, or idea that recurs in a work or in several works.** The rose is a motif that has recurred throughout centuries of love poetry. In *The Divine Comedy* (Collection 5), sin and punishment are recurring motifs. A literary motif always bears an important relationship to the theme of the work.

MOTIVATION **The reasons that compel a character to act as he or she does.** Motivation is revealed through a combination of the character's desires and moral nature and the circumstances in which he or she is placed. In "The Prisoner Who Wore Glasses" (Collection 7), Brille's desire for better treatment for himself and his fellow prisoners is the motivation for his behavior toward Hannetjie.

See pages 67, 271.
See also *Character.*

MYTH **An anonymous, traditional story that explains a belief, a custom, or a mysterious natural phenomenon.** Most myths grew out of religious rituals, and almost all of them involve the exploits of gods and heroes. Myths helped people understand and cope with things beyond human control. Every culture has its own mythology, but in the Western world, the most important myths have been those of ancient Greece and Rome. In twentieth-century literature, allusions to myths are often ironic, intended to reveal how diminished humanity has become in comparison with grand mythological figures.

See page 305.

NARRATIVE **Any work of literature, written or oral, that tells a story.** Narrative literature may be fictional (such as fairy tales and short stories) or nonfictional (such as autobiographies and histories); it may be prose, such as "Noah and the Flood" (Collection 1), or poetry, such as the *Iliad* (Collection 2). Narrative is distinguished from drama, which acts out, rather than tells, a story.

See page 67.

NARRATOR **The person or character who tells a story.** In fiction the narrator occupies any one of a variety of relations to the events described: from the center of the action to a distant, even objective, observer. A narrator may also be reliable or unreliable—if unreliable, the reader is made aware that the narrator's perceptions and interpretations of the action are different from those of the author. Such unreliable narrators can be deceitful or bumbling but are often just naive or highly impressionable characters.

NATURALISM **A radical offshoot of Realism that arose in France in the 1870s.** Naturalist writers, led by Émile Zola, considered free will an illusion and often showed their characters as helpless victims of heredity, fate, and their environment.

See page 752.
See also *Realism.*

NEOCLASSICISM **The revival of classical standards and forms during the late seventeenth and eighteenth centuries in Europe.** The neoclassicists valued the classical ideals of order, reason, balance, harmony, clarity, and restraint. In particular, they studied and tried to emulate the Roman poets Horace and Virgil (Collection 2).

NONFICTION **Prose writing that presents real events using either narrative or expository structures.** Nonfiction is distinguished from fiction—writing that is basically imaginative rather than factually true. Popular forms of nonfiction are autobiography, biography, and the essay. Other forms of nonfiction include newspaper articles, historical and scientific writing, and even personal diaries and letters.

NOVEL **A long fictional prose narrative, usually of more than fifty thousand words.** In general, a novel uses the same basic literary elements as a short story: plot, character, setting, theme, and point of view. A novel's length usually permits these elements to be more fully developed than they are in a short story. However, this is not always true of modern novels. Some are basically character studies, with only the barest plot structures. Others reveal little about their characters and concentrate instead on setting or tone or even on language itself.

Although some early prose narratives resemble novels in form, the novel as a distinct literary genre is widely considered to have emerged in Japan around A.D. 1000 with Lady Murasaki Shikibu's *Tale of Genji* and in Europe with the publication of Miguel de Cervantes' *Don Quixote* in 1605 (Collection 5).

OBJECTIVE WRITING **Writing that conveys facts and figures without introducing the writer's personal biases.** The purpose of objective writing is to inform. Newspaper reporters on current events usually write in an objective style.

See page 913.
See also *Subjective Writing*.

OCTAVE **An eight-line stanza or poem or the first eight lines of an Italian, or Petrarchan, sonnet.** The usual rhyme scheme of the octave in this type of sonnet is *abbaabba*. The octave, which is sometimes called the octet, is followed by a six-line sestet with the rhyme scheme *cdecde, cdcdcd, ccdeed,* or *cdcdee*.

ODE **A complex, generally lengthy lyric poem on a serious subject.** In English poetry, there are basically two types of odes. One is highly formal and dignified in style and is generally written for ceremonial or public occasions. This type of ode, called the **Pindaric ode,** derives from the choral odes of the ancient Greek poet Pindar, who wrote them in honor of the victors at the Olympics and other sacred games. The **Horatian ode,** like the lyrics of the Roman poet Horace for whom it is named, tends to be more personal and reflective in style.

ONOMATOPOEIA **The use of a word whose sound imitates or suggests its meaning.** Many familiar words, such as *clap, squish, snort,* and *whine,* are examples of onomatopoeia. In poetry, onomatopoeia can reinforce meaning while creating evocative and musical effects.

ORAL TRADITION **Literature not written down but instead passed from generation to generation by word of mouth.** Folk tales, proverbs, myths, and epics are among the types of literature that belong to the oral tradition. These works often reveal the wisdom and vitality found in a given culture.

See pages 495, 505.

OXYMORON **A figure of speech that combines apparently contradictory or opposing ideas.** "Living death," "cruel love," and "deafening silence" are oxymorons. The classic oxymoron "wise fool" is almost a literal translation of the term from the Greek: *Oxys* means "sharp" or "keen," and *moros* means "foolish."

See page 684.

PARABLE **A short, allegorical story that teaches a moral or religious lesson about life.** The most famous parables in Western literature are those told by Jesus in the Gospels of the New Testament, such as the parable "The Prodigal Son" (Collection 1).

See pages 83, 464.
See also *Allegory*.

PARADOX **An apparent contradiction that is actually true.** A paradox may be a statement or a situation; as a statement, it is a figure of speech. For example, to say that "she killed him with kindness" is a paradox. The statement challenges us to find an underlying truth that resolves the apparent contradiction.

See pages 371, 413, 929.

PARALLELISM **The repetition of words, phrases, or sentences that have the same grammatical structure or that compare and contrast ideas.** Parallelism is used frequently in literature that is meant to be read aloud, such as poetry and speeches, because it helps make the literature rhythmic and memorable. In much biblical writing, such as the Book of Psalms (Collection 1), the rhythm of parallelism helps to unify ideas, emphasize images, and heighten the emotional effect of the words. **Structural parallelism** (repetition of a word or an entire sentence pattern), **restatement** (repetition of an idea using different words), and **antithesis** (the balancing of contrasting ideas) are some of the ways writers achieve parallelism.

See page 76.

PARODY **The imitation of an artistic work for amusement or instruction.** Parodies use exaggeration or inappropriate subject matter to make a serious form or particular work of art seem laughable or to highlight its flaws. *Don Quixote* (Collection 5), for example, is a parody of medieval romances.

See page 688.

PASTORAL **A type of literature that depicts rustic life in idealized terms.** The term *pastoral* comes from the Latin word for "shepherd," and originally pastorals were about shepherds and nymphs. Today the term has a looser meaning and refers to any literary work, especially a poem, that portrays an idealized rural setting or that expresses nostalgia for an age or place of lost innocence.

PERSONIFICATION **A kind of metaphor in which a nonhuman thing or quality is talked about as if it were human.** For example, the familiar figure of a blindfolded woman holding a sword and a pair of scales is a personification of justice. The names of many everyday objects, such as the "hands of a clock," and many ordinary expressions, such as "an angry sky," involve personification. In poetry, personification invites the reader to view the world as if natural and inanimate objects possess the same feelings, qualities, and souls that people do. Li Ch'ing-chao's "Peonies" (Collection 3) contains examples of personification.

See pages 436, 932, 938, 942, 1043.

PERSUASION **Writing that tries to persuade the reader or listener to think or act in a certain way.** Examples of persuasion include political speeches, editorials, and advertisements, as well as many essays and longer works of literature. Persuasive writing may contain **logical appeals** (appeals to the intellect supported by factual evidence), **ethical appeals** (appeals that establish the writer's qualifications and sincerity), and **emotional appeals** (appeals that arouse feelings in the reader).

See page 181.

PLOT **The series of related events that make up a narrative, such as a story, a novel, or an epic.** The plot is the underlying structure of a narrative. Most plots are built on these "bare bones": A **basic situation,** or **exposition,** introduces the characters, setting,

and, usually, the narrative's major **conflict.** Out of this basic situation, complications develop, intensifying the conflict. **Suspense** mounts to a **climax**—the most exciting or tense part of the plot. At the climax, the outcome of the conflict is determined. Finally, all the problems or mysteries of the plot are unraveled in the **resolution,** or **dénouement.** Longer narrative works, such as novels, plays, or epics, often contain **subplots,** or minor plots interwoven with the main plot.

See also *Conflict, Dramatic Structure.*

POETRY **A kind of rhythmic, compressed language that uses figures of speech and imagery designed to appeal to our emotions and imaginations.** Most of the world's poetry falls into three major types: **lyric poetry,** the **ballad,** and the **epic.** Some specialized types of poetry, however, such as the **haiku** of Japan, defy these broad categorizations. Though poetry is one of the oldest forms of human expression, it is extremely difficult to define. The English Romantic poet William Wordsworth called it "the spontaneous overflow of powerful feelings," and the Japanese scholar Kamo Mabuchi claimed that it provides "without explanation the reasons governing order and disorder in the world."

See also *Ballad, Epic, Haiku, Lyric Poetry, Pastoral, Prose Poetry, Psalm, Rubá'i, Sonnet.*

POINT OF VIEW **The vantage point from which a writer tells a story.** There are three main points of view: **omniscient, first-person,** and **third-person-limited.**

In the **omniscient** (or "all-knowing") **point of view,** the person telling the story—the **narrator**—knows everything that's going on in the story. This omniscient narrator is outside the story, a godlike observer who can tell us what all the characters are thinking and feeling, as well as what is happening anywhere in the story. For example, in "The Ring" by Isak Dinesen (Collection 7), the narrator enters into the thoughts and secrets of every character.

In the **first-person point of view,** the narrator is a character in the story. Using the pronoun *I,* this narrator tells us his or her experiences but cannot reveal with certainty any other character's private thoughts. When we read a story in the first person, we hear and see only what the narrator hears and sees. We may have to be skeptical and interpret what this narrator says because a first-person narrator may or may not be objective, honest, or perceptive. Zhang Jie's short story

"Love Must Not Be Forgotten" (Collection 7) uses a first-person narrator.

In the **third-person-limited point of view,** the narrator is outside the story—like an omniscient narrator—but tells the story from the vantage point of only one character. The narrator goes where this chosen character goes and reveals this character's thoughts. The reader learns the events of the narrative through the perceptions of the chosen character. R. K. Narayan's "An Astrologer's Day" (Collection 7) is an example of a story told from the third-person-limited point of view.

See page 934.

POSTMODERNISM A trend in art and philosophy that reflects the late-twentieth-century distrust in the idea that there is a legitimate and true system of thought that can be used to understand the world and our place in it. Postmodernists, like the modernists, see contemporary life as fragmentary, but rather than regard the fragmentary condition of our world with horror, postmodernists look upon the fragments as materials that can be plundered and combined in new ways to create works of art. Postmodern writing typically experiments with nontraditional forms and allows for multiple meanings. The lines between real and imaginary worlds are often blurred, as is the boundary between fiction and nonfiction. Other characteristics of postmodern literature are cultural diversity and an often playful self-consciousness; that is, an acknowledgment that literature is not a mirror that accurately reflects the world, but a created world unto itself. Julio Cortázar's "The Night Face Up" (Collection 7), in which the experiences of a motorcycle accident victim intermingle with the events of an Aztec sacrifice, is an exemplary postmodern short story.

See pages 842, 851.

PROSE POETRY Poetry written in prose form but using poetic devices such as rhythm, imagery, and figurative language to express a single strong emotion or idea. This form of lyric poetry developed in the nineteenth century in France and was popularized by Charles Baudelaire and Arthur Rimbaud.

See page 433.

PROTAGONIST The main character in a work of fiction, drama, or narrative poetry. The protagonist is the character whose conflict sets the plot in motion. (The character or force that struggles against or blocks the protagonist is called the **antagonist.**) Most protagonists are rounded, dynamic characters who change in some important way by the end of the story. Whatever the protagonist's weaknesses, we usually identify with his or her conflict and care about how it is resolved.

See also *Antagonist, Character.*

PROVERB A short saying that expresses a common truth or experience, usually about human failings and the ways that people interact with one another. Proverbs often incorporate such literary elements as metaphor, alliteration, parallelism, and rhyme.

See page 514.
See also *Aphorism, Epigram, Maxim, Moral.*

PSALM A type of Hebrew lyric poem used as a sacred song or hymn. Psalms were originally sung to the accompaniment of a harp (the word *psalm* comes from a Greek verb meaning "to pluck"). Today the term is usually used to refer to any of the 150 poems that make up the Book of Psalms in the Old Testament. These lyric poems greatly influenced the development of **free verse** in the nineteenth and twentieth centuries.

See page 76.

PUN A play on the multiple meanings of a word or on two words that may sound alike but have different meanings. Many jokes and riddles are based on puns. ("When a clock is hungry, it goes back four seconds.") Shakespeare is regarded as one of the great punsters of all time.

QUATRAIN A four-line stanza or poem, or a group of four lines unified by a rhyme scheme. The quatrain is the most common verse unit in English poetry.

See page 679.
See also *Ballad, Rubá'i, Sonnet, Stanza.*

RATIONALISM A philosophy that advocates the idea that one should use reason rather than emotion when one is attempting to discover the truth. Rationalists believe that one must follow reason to determine what opinions are correct and what course of action one should take in a given situation. Rationalism stands in opposition to Romanticism, which emphasizes the value of intuition and emotion in arriving at truth.

See page 602.

REALISM **In literature and art, the attempt to depict people and things as they are, without idealization.** Realism as a movement developed during the mid–nineteenth century as a reaction against Romanticism. Realist writers believed fiction and drama should truthfully depict the harsh, gritty reality of everyday life without beautifying, sentimentalizing, or romanticizing it. Gustave Flaubert, Henrik Ibsen, and Anton Chekhov are considered Realist writers.

See pages 743, 752.
See also *Naturalism.*

REFORMATION **The break from Catholicism and the authority of the pope that resulted in the establishment of the Protestant churches in the sixteenth century in Europe.** Most scholars date the beginning of the Reformation to 1517, the year Martin Luther nailed his *Ninety-five Theses* to the door of a church in Wittenberg, Germany. The *Theses* criticized the Catholic Church's abuse of indulgences and called for reform. In response the Church leaders condemned Luther, and he was forced to break from the Catholic Church and begin his own religious movement.

See page 600.

REFRAIN **A repeated word, phrase, line, or group of lines.** Although refrains are most common in poetry and songs, they are sometimes used in prose, particularly speeches. Refrains are used to create rhythm, build suspense, or emphasize important words or ideas. An example of a refrain occurs in Baudelaire's poem "Invitation to the Voyage" (Collection 6).

RENAISSANCE **A French word meaning "rebirth," used to designate the period in European history beginning in Italy in the fourteenth century and ending in the seventeenth century when scientific truths began to challenge long-accepted religious beliefs.** The Renaissance was characterized by a renewal of interest in classical learning and a focus on the study of human life on earth, not only on God and eternity.

See page 595.

REPETITION **The intentional repeating of a sound, word, phrase, line, or idea in order to create a particular literary effect.** Many literary elements involve some kind of repetition. For example, **alliteration** repeats consonant sounds, **parallelism** repeats grammatical structures or ideas, **meter** repeats a regular pattern of stressed and unstressed syllables, and **refrains** repeat a line or group of lines. In **incremental repetition,** a line or section of a poem or song is repeated with some variation in wording. Usually, the variation adds significant new information or expresses a significant change in meaning or attitude. Yehuda Amichai's "Laments on the War Dead" (Collection 7) uses incremental repetition.

See pages 51, 403, 1039.
See also *Alliteration, Assonance, Consonance, Meter, Parallelism, Refrain, Rhyme.*

RESOLUTION See *Plot.*

RHETORIC **The use of language, particularly oratory, for persuasion.** In ancient Greece, rhetoric was considered the highest form of prose.

RHYME **The repetition of accented vowel sounds and all sounds following them in words that are close together in a poem.** "Lark" and "shark" rhyme, as do "follow" and "hollow." The most common type of rhyme, **end rhyme,** occurs at the ends of lines. **Internal rhymes** occur within lines.

When words sound similar but do not rhyme exactly, they are called **approximate rhymes** (or **half rhymes, slant rhymes,** or **imperfect rhymes**). "Lark" and "lurk" are approximate rhymes, as are "follow" and "halo."

The pattern of end rhymes in a poem is called its **rhyme scheme.** A rhyme scheme is indicated by assigning each new end rhyme a different letter of the alphabet. Many traditional forms of poems, such as the **Italian sonnet** and the Persian **rubá'i,** follow strict rhyme schemes. For example, most English translations of the rubá'i follow the rhyme scheme *aaba,* as the following example from Edward FitzGerald's translation of Omar Khayyám's *Rubáiyát* illustrates:

> A Book of Verses underneath the Bough, a
> A Jug of Wine, a Loaf of Bread—and Thou a
>   Beside me singing in the Wilderness— b
> Oh, Wilderness were Paradise enow! a

See page 514.

See also *Consonance, Couplet, Rubá'i, Sonnet.*

RHYTHM **The alternation of stressed and unstressed syllables in language.** Rhythm occurs naturally in all forms of spoken and written language. The most obvious kind of rhythm is produced by **meter,** the regular pattern of stressed and unstressed syllables found in some poetry. But writers can also create less structured rhythms by using different kinds of **repetition** (such as rhyme, alliteration, assonance, parallelism, and refrains) or by balancing long and short words, phrases, or lines. Such rhythms are common in **free verse.**

See also *Blank Verse, Free Verse, Meter.*

ROMANCE **Historically, a medieval European verse narrative chronicling the adventures of a brave knight or other hero who must overcome great danger for love of a noble lady or high ideal.** The stories of King Arthur and of his chivalrous knights of the Round Table, such as Perceval and Lancelot, are examples of **courtly romances.** Today the term has come to mean any story that presents a world that is happier, more exciting, or more heroic than the real world.

See pages 592, 624.

See also *Arthurian Romance.*

ROMANTICISM **A literary, artistic, and philosophical movement that developed in Europe during the late eighteenth and early nineteenth centuries as a reaction against neoclassicism.** Whereas neoclassicism (and classicism) emphasize reason, order, harmony, and restraint, Romanticism emphasizes emotion, imagination, intuition, freedom, personal experience, and the beauty of nature. However, many critics feel that the traditional opposition between Romanticism and classicism is all too often

forced and exaggerated. The works of the German poet and dramatist Johann Wolfgang von Goethe and the English poet William Wordsworth are closely identified with Romanticism.

See pages 742–743, 748.

RUBÁ'I (*plural:* **rubáiyát**) **A Persian word meaning "quatrain," or four-line verse.** The rubá'i is an ancient literary form that Persian poets used to express their thoughts on diverse subjects. In English translation, the most famous example is the *Rubáiyát of Omar Khayyám* (Collection 4), published by Edward FitzGerald in 1859. FitzGerald's translation is widely considered a masterpiece of English poetry in its own right.

See page 553.

RUN-ON LINE See *Enjambment.*

SARCASM **A kind of particularly cutting irony, in which praise is used tauntingly to indicate its opposite meaning.** The speaker's tone of voice can be an important clue in understanding this kind of irony. When someone gives you a gift that you think is tacky, you might say sarcastically, "What a thoughtful present!"

SATIRE **A kind of writing that ridicules human weakness, vices, or folly in order to bring about social reform.** Satires often try to persuade the reader to do or believe something by showing the opposite view as absurd or—even more forcefully—vicious and inhumane. To achieve their purpose, satirists may use exaggeration, irony, parody, and wit. Voltaire uses all these techniques in his scathing satire of European rationalism, *Candide* (Collection 5).

See page 709.

SCANSION See *Meter.*

SCIENCE FICTION **A form of imaginative fiction in which scientific facts, assumptions, or hypotheses form the basis of adventures in the future, on other planets, in other dimensions of space or time, or under new variants of scientific laws.** Although science fiction is usually set in the future, writers often use it to comment on the present, sometimes in the form of satire.

SESTET A six-line stanza or poem or the last six lines of an Italian, or Petrarchan, sonnet. The usual rhyme scheme of the sestet in an Italian sonnet is *cdecde, cdcdcd, ccdeed,* or *cdcdee.* It follows an eight-line octave with the rhyme scheme *abbaabba.*

See page 678.

SETTING The time and place of a story, play, or narrative poem. Usually, the setting is established early in a narrative through descriptive details and imagery. Longer works may have more than one setting. For example, Voltaire's *Candide* (Collection 5) begins in Europe but moves to South America and other parts of the globe.

Setting is often closely linked to the mood of a literary work. For example, the setting of "The Train from Rhodesia" (Collection 7) contributes to the story's mood of isolation. Setting may also reveal character by showing whether a character is in harmony with a particular place or in conflict with it. In "The Prisoner Who Wore Glasses" (Collection 7), for example, the prisoners' desire to be treated with dignity conflicts with the harsh conditions of a South African prison farm. Finally, setting may suggest a story's theme. In "I Have Visited Again" (Collection 6), for example, the neglected estate reinforces the poem's theme of the inevitability of change.

See pages 772, 957, 1009, 1023, 1074.
See also *Atmosphere, Mood.*

SHORT STORY A short fictional prose narrative. Although some ancient prose narratives (such as the Book of Ruth, Collection 1) resemble modern short stories, as a distinct genre the short story developed in the nineteenth century. Short stories are more limited than novels, usually having only one major character, plot, setting, and theme. A short story is usually built on a plot that consists of a basic situation or exposition, conflict, complications, climax, and resolution. However, many modern short stories concentrate less on what happens and more on revealing a character or evoking a vivid emotional effect.

SIMILE A figure of speech that makes a comparison between two seemingly unlike things by using a connective word such as *like, as, than,* or *resembles.* "A full moon like an accusing face," "hail hard as BB pellets," "an actor's hand opening more gracefully than a blossom," and "clouds resembling stuffed animals" are all examples of similes.

Like an extended metaphor, an **extended simile** is developed over several lines of writing or even through an entire poem or paragraph. An **epic** or **Homeric simile** is an elaborately extended simile that relates heroic events to simple, everyday events. Homer used many such similes in his epic poems, the *Iliad* (Collection 2) and the *Odyssey.*

See pages 121, 930, 1043.
See also *Epic, Figure of Speech, Metaphor.*

SOCIALISM A political movement that advocates the idea that the ownership and operation of the means of production and distribution should be owned by the community rather than by private individuals. This political movement is related to Communism in that it seeks to eliminate class distinctions within society.

SOLILOQUY A long speech in which a character who is usually alone onstage expresses his or her private thoughts or feelings. The soliloquy is an old dramatic convention that was particularly popular in Shakespeare's day.

See also *Monologue.*

SONNET A fourteen-line lyric poem, usually written in iambic pentameter, that has one of several traditional rhyme schemes. The oldest sonnet form is the **Petrarchan** (or **Italian**) **sonnet,** which was popularized by the fourteenth-century Italian poet Petrarch. This kind of sonnet is divided into two parts: an eight-line stanza called the **octave,** having the rhyme scheme *abbaabba,* and a six-line stanza called the **sestet,** having the rhyme scheme *cdecde, cdcdcd, ccdeed,* or *cdcdee.* The octave usually presents a problem, poses a question, or expresses an idea that leads up to the **turn** (called the *volta* in Italian), which marks a shift in the poem. The sestet then resolves, answers, or drives home the idea that was developed in the octave.

The other major sonnet form, which was widely used by Shakespeare, is known as the **Shakespearean** (or **English**) **sonnet.** It consists of three stanzas called **quatrains** followed by a concluding stanza called the **couplet.** The three quatrains often express related ideas or examples, and the couplet sums up the poet's conclusion or message. The most common rhyme scheme for the Shakespearean sonnet is *abab cdcd efef gg.* Subsequent generations of poets have developed many variations based on the Petrarchan and Shakespearean forms.

See pages 678, 681, 940.
See also *Couplet, Octave, Quatrain, Sestet, Stanza.*

SPEAKER The imaginary voice, or persona, assumed by the author of a poem. This voice is often not identified immediately or directly. Rather, the reader gradually comes to understand that a unique voice is speaking and that this speaker's characteristics must be interpreted as they are revealed.

See page 46.

SPEECH A more or less formal address delivered to an audience or assembly or the written or printed copy of this address. The use of the word *speech* to designate an address to an audience seems to have entered the English language in the sixteenth century. Speeches are most commonly delivered by politicians, political activists, and other public figures.

STANZA A group of lines in a poem that forms a single unit. A stanza in a poem is like a paragraph in prose: It often expresses a unit of thought. A stanza may consist of one line or any number of lines beyond that. Stanzas are usually named for the number of lines they contain or for the meter and rhyme scheme that they follow. A **couplet,** for example, consists of two lines, a **tercet** of three lines, and a **quatrain** of four lines.

See also *Rubá'i.*

STREAM OF CONSCIOUSNESS A writing style that tries to depict the random flow of thoughts, emotions, memories, and associations rushing through a character's mind. The term *interior monologue* is often used interchangeably with *stream of consciousness.* The Irish novelist James Joyce and the English novelist Virginia Woolf employ stream of consciousness in their writings.

See page 849.

STYLE The unique manner in which writers use language to express their ideas. Style is closely related to **diction,** or word choice, and, depending on what the author wants to communicate, can be formal or casual, plain or ornate, abstract or concrete, as well as comic, poetic, forceful, journalistic, and so on. Voltaire (Collection 5) is often studied for his style.

See pages 322, 456, 709.

SUBJECTIVE WRITING Writing that reveals and emphasizes a writer's personal feelings and opinions. Autobiographies and memoirs are examples of subjective writing.

See page 913.

SURREALISM A twentieth-century literary and artistic movement that sought to break down the barriers between rational and irrational thoughts and situations. Influenced by the psychoanalytic theories of Sigmund Freud, surrealist writers and artists sought to portray the inner workings of the unconscious mind by using dreamlike imagery.

See page 853.

SUSPENSE The uncertainty or anxiety a reader feels about what will happen next in a story. Writers often create suspense by including hints or clues that something—especially something unexpected or terrible—is going to happen.

See page 947.

SYMBOL A person, place, thing, or event that stands both for itself and for something beyond itself. Many symbols have become widely recognized: A lion is a symbol of majesty and power; a dove is a symbol of peace. These symbols are sometimes called **public symbols.** But writers often invent new, personal symbols, whose meaning is revealed in a work of poetry or prose. In "The Train from Rhodesia" (Collection 7), for example, the train becomes a symbol for social and economic barriers.

See pages 791, 1047.

SYMBOLISM A literary movement that began in France during the late nineteenth century and emphasized the use of highly personal symbols to suggest ideas, emotions, and moods. The French symbolists believed that emotions are fleeting, individual, and essentially inexpressible and that therefore the poet is forced to suggest meaning rather than directly express it. The leading Symbolists, such as Paul Verlaine and Arthur Rimbaud (Collection 6), were reacting against **realism** and **naturalism.**

> See pages 753, 791.
> See also *Naturalism, Realism.*

SYNECDOCHE **A figure of speech in which a part represents the whole.** The capital city of a nation, for example, is often spoken of as though it were the government: "Washington is claiming popular support for its position." Another example is "our daily bread" meaning food. Synecdoche is closely related to metonymy.

SYNESTHESIA **In literature, a term used for descriptions of one kind of sensation in terms of another.** For example, color may be described as sound (a "loud" yellow), sound as taste (how "sweet" a sound), odor as tangible (a "sharp" smell), and so on.

> See pages 454, 1045.

TANKA **A traditional, five-line form of Japanese poetry.** In the original language, tanka follows a strict form: The first and third lines contain five syllables each, and the second, fourth, and fifth lines contain seven syllables each.

> See pages 363, 440, 442.

TAOISM **A philosophy founded by Laotzu in China that teaches that wisdom can be gained by observing nature.** The principles of Taoism are expressed in the *Tao Te Ching,* a book of Laotzu's sayings and teachings. Taoists urge people to seek wisdom by ignoring society and contemplating Tao, the force that governs and unifies all of nature.

> See pages 349, 360, 413.

TERCET **A triplet, or stanza of three lines, in which each line ends with the same rhyme.** It is also either of the two three-line groups forming the sestet of a sonnet.

> See page 647.

TERZA RIMA **An interlocking, three-line stanza form with the rhyme scheme *aba bcb cdc ded,***

and so on. Terza rima is an Italian verse form originally used by Dante throughout *The Divine Comedy* (Collection 5).

> See page 647.

THEATER OF THE ABSURD **A type of modernist drama that reflects the belief that human existence is unreasonable and incoherent.** The theater of the absurd usually features characters that only speak in banalities and plots that go nowhere. The final scene of Samuel Beckett's *Waiting for Godot* typifies the beliefs of the theater of the absurd: One tramp says, "Well? Shall we go?" and the other responds, "Yes, let's go." The final stage direction, however, is *"They do not move."*

> See page 851.

THEME **The central idea or insight of a work of literature.** A theme is not the same as the subject of a work, which can usually be expressed in a word or two: old age, ambition, love. The theme is the idea the writer wishes to convey about the subject—the writer's view of the world or revelation about human nature. In "The Train from Rhodesia" (Collection 7), for example, Nadine Gordimer's subject is about the transitory contact between two cultures, but her theme is that alienation and emptiness are the results of treating others as less than human.

While some stories, poems, and plays have themes that are directly stated, most themes are **implied.** It is up to the reader to piece together all the clues the writer has provided about the work's total meaning. Two of the most important clues to consider are how the main character has changed and how the conflict has been resolved. In addition, long works such as novels and plays may have more than one theme.

> See pages 59, 83, 305, 804, 869,
> 965, 1023, 1047, 1083.

TONE **The attitude a writer takes toward the reader, a subject, or a character.** Tone is conveyed through the writer's choice of words and descriptions of characters and setting. Tone can usually be described with an adjective, such as amused, angry, indifferent, or sarcastic.

> See pages 303, 905.

TOTALITARIANISM **A system of government that advocates the rule of an absolute dictator or a single political party.** Totalitarian governments forbid any opposition to the government party or ruler to emerge within the state. Consequently, free speech and other liberties guaranteed in democracies are denied to those living under a totalitarian government. Bei Dao's poem "Requiem" laments a totalitarian regime's massacre of civilians.

TRAGEDY **A play, novel, or other narrative depicting serious and important events, in which the main character comes to an unhappy end.** In the traditional tragedy, the main character is usually dignified, courageous, and often high ranking. The character's downfall may be caused by a **tragic flaw**—an error in judgment or a character weakness—or the downfall may result from forces beyond his or her control. The tragic hero or heroine usually wins some self-knowledge and wisdom, even though he or she suffers defeat, possibly even death.

Tragedy is distinct from **comedy,** in which an ordinary character overcomes obstacles to get what he or she wants. Sophocles' *Oedipus Rex* (Collection 2) is an example of a tragedy. Dramas that contain elements of both tragedy and comedy are often called **tragicomedies.**

See page 199.

TRICKSTER **A universal figure in the myths and folk tales of many cultures who uses cunning to get the better of others who are usually bigger and stronger than he or she.** In the African oral tradition, the trickster is often an animal, such as a spider or a hare. The trickster's actions are usually entertaining but can also be destructive. "Why We Tell Stories About Spider" (Collection 4) is an example of a tale about a trickster.

See page 504.

TURN See *Sonnet.*

TURNING POINT See *Dramatic Structure.*

TZ'U **A poetic form originating in central Asia that requires the poet to supply words to accompany established musical patterns.** "Peonies" (Collection 3) by Li Ch'ing-chao is an example of this distinct, delicate poetic form.

See page 436.

UNDERSTATEMENT **A figure of speech that consists of saying less than what is really meant or saying something with less force than is appropriate.** Understatement is the opposite of **hyperbole,** or overstatement, and is a form of **irony.** To say, "It is a bit wet out there" after coming in from a torrential downpour is to use understatement. Understatement can be used to create a kind of deadpan humor, and it can contribute to an overall satiric tone, as in Cervantes' *Don Quixote* (Collection 5).

VEDAS **A collection of hymns and other writings that are considered sacred by followers of Hinduism.** The Vedas were brought to India by the Aryans, who migrated there around 1500 B.C. Hindus believe that gods directly revealed the Vedas to humans. Followers of Hinduism observe the rituals outlined in the Vedic texts even today.

See pages 352, 366.

VERNACULAR See *Dialect.*

WIT **A quality of speech or writing that combines verbal cleverness with keen perception, especially of the incongruous.** Wit may be a product of puns and wordplay, hyperbole, or verbal irony. Sei Shōnagon's *The Pillow Book* (Collection 3) offers many examples of wit in her **understated** descriptions of humorous situations, as the following example from her chapter titled "Hateful Things" illustrates:

> A man recites his own poems (not especially good ones) and tells one about the praise they have received—most embarrassing.

Language Handbook

▌ THE PARTS OF SPEECH

PART OF SPEECH	DEFINITION	EXAMPLES
NOUN	Names person, place, thing, or idea	poet, Jamaica Kincaid, Egyptians, tribe, nation, Japan, epic, *Sundiata,* realism
PRONOUN	Takes the place of one or more nouns or pronouns	
Personal	Refers to one(s) speaking (first person), spoken to (second person), spoken about (third person)	I, me, my, mine, we, us, our, ours you, your, yours he, him, his, she, her, hers, it, its, they, them, their, theirs
Reflexive	Refers to subject and directs action of verb back to subject	myself, ourselves, yourself, yourselves, himself, herself, itself, themselves
Intensive	Refers to and emphasizes noun or another pronoun	(See Reflexive.)
Demonstrative	Refers to specific one(s) of group	this, that, these, those
Interrogative	Introduces question	what, which, who, whom, whose
Relative	Introduces subordinate clause and refers to noun or pronoun outside that clause	that, which, who, whom, whose
Indefinite	Refers to one(s) not specifically named	all, any, anyone, both, each, either, everybody, many, none, nothing
ADJECTIVE	Modifies noun or pronoun by telling *what kind, which one, how many,* or *how much*	**a popular** ballad, **Indian** philosophy, **that** one, **the three young** brothers, **more** time
VERB	Shows action or state of being	
Action	Expresses physical or mental activity	describe, travel, fight, believe, consider, remember
Linking	Connects subject with word identifying or describing it	appear, be, seem, become, feel, look, smell, sound, taste
Helping (Auxiliary)	Assists another verb in expressing time, voice, or mood	be, have, may, can, shall, must, would
ADVERB	Modifies verb, adjective, or adverb by telling *how, when, where,* or *to what extent*	walks **slowly, quite** different, **somewhat** boldly, coming **here soon**
PREPOSITION	Relates noun or pronoun to another word	about, at, by, for, from, in, on, according to, along with, because of
CONJUNCTION **Coordinating**	Joins words or word groups Joins words or word groups used in the same way	and, but, for, nor, or, so, yet

Correlative	A pair of conjunctions that join parallel words or word groups	both . . . and, either . . . or, neither . . . nor, not only . . . but (also)
Subordinating	Begins a subordinate clause and connects it to an independent clause	although, as if, because, since, so that, unless, when, where, while
INTERJECTION	Expresses emotion	ah, wow, ugh, whew

2 AGREEMENT

AGREEMENT OF SUBJECT AND VERB

2a. **A verb should agree with its subject in number. Singular subjects take singular verbs. Plural subjects take plural verbs.**

SINGULAR   **She walks** to the market.
PLURAL   **They walk** to the market.

2b. **The number of the subject is not changed by a phrase or a clause following the subject.**

EXAMPLE
Arjuna, one of the Pandava brothers, **speaks** to Krishna.

2c. **Indefinite pronouns may be singular, plural, or either.**

(1) The following indefinite pronouns are singular: *anybody, anyone, anything, each, either, everybody, everyone, everything, neither, nobody, no one, nothing, one, somebody, someone,* and *something.*

EXAMPLE
Each of these stories **describes** the creation of the world.

(2) The following indefinite pronouns are plural: *both, few, many,* and *several.*

EXAMPLE
Both of the poems **were written** by Pablo Neruda.

(3) The indefinite pronouns *all, any, most, none,* and *some* are singular when they refer to singular words and are plural when they refer to plural words.

SINGULAR   **None** of the equipment **was damaged.** [*None* refers to *equipment.*]
PLURAL   **None** of the machines **were damaged.** [*None* refers to *machines.*]

2d. **A *compound subject* may be singular, plural, or either.**

(1) Subjects joined by *and* usually take a plural verb.

EXAMPLE
After rehearsal, **Juan, Anita,** and **Marcus are going** out to dinner.

A compound subject that names only one person or thing takes a singular verb.

EXAMPLE
His **friend** and **comrade** in arms **is** Patroclus.

(2) Singular subjects joined by *or* or *nor* take a singular verb.

EXAMPLE
Stephanie or **Mario wants** to write a sequel to Ovid's *Metamorphoses.*

(3) When a singular subject and a plural subject are joined by *or* or *nor,* the verb agrees with the subject nearer the verb.

EXAMPLE
Neither the **dancers** nor the **choreographer was** pleased with the routine.

2e. **The verb agrees with its subject even when the verb precedes the subject, as in sentences beginning with *here, there,* or *where.***

SINGULAR   Where **is** [*or* **where's**] **Malcolm**?
PLURAL   Here **are** [*not* here's] **Malcolm** and his **brother.**

2f. **A *collective noun* (such as *audience, flock,* or *team*) is singular in form but names a group of persons or things. A collective noun takes a singular verb when the noun refers to the group as a unit and takes a plural verb when the noun refers to the parts or members of the group.**

SINGULAR	The tour **group is** on the bus. [The group as a unit is on the bus.]
PLURAL	The tour **group are talking** about their plans. [The members of the group are talking to one another.]

2g. An expression of an amount (a length of time, a statistic, or a fraction, for example) is singular when the amount is thought of as a unit or when it refers to a singular word and plural when the amount is thought of as many parts or when it refers to a plural word.

SINGULAR	**Ten years is** how long the Trojan War lasts. [one unit]
PLURAL	**One fifth** of the juniors **are working** on a production of *Faust*. [The fraction refers to *juniors*.]

Expressions of measurement (length, weight, capacity, area) are usually singular.

EXAMPLE
Four and seven-tenths inches is the diameter of a compact disc.

2h. The title of a creative work (such as a book, song, film, or painting) or the name of an organization, a country, or a city (even if it is plural in form) takes a singular verb.

EXAMPLES
"**Unmarked Boxes**" **was written** by the Sufi poet Rumi.
The **United Nations was formed** in 1945.

2i. A verb agrees with its subject, not with its predicate nominative.

SINGULAR	The **subject** of the lecture **was** epic heroes.
PLURAL	**Epic heroes were** the subject of the lecture.

AGREEMENT OF PRONOUN AND ANTECEDENT

A pronoun usually refers to a noun or another pronoun. The word to which a pronoun refers is called its *antecedent*.

2j. A pronoun agrees with its antecedent in number and gender. Singular pronouns refer to singular antecedents. A few singular pronouns also indicate gender (feminine, masculine, or neuter). Plural pronouns refer to plural antecedents.

EXAMPLES
Voltaire wrote *Candide* after **he** moved to Geneva, Switzerland. [singular, masculine]
Ruth promises to stay with **her** mother-in-law. [singular, feminine]
Zen **masters** told **their** students parables. [plural]

2k. Indefinite pronouns may be singular, plural, or either.

(1) Singular pronouns are used to refer to the indefinite pronouns *anybody, anyone, anything, each, either, everybody, everyone, everything, neither, nobody, no one, nothing, one, somebody, someone,* and *something.* The gender of any of these pronouns is determined by the word or words that the pronoun refers to.

EXAMPLES
Each of the **boys** has brought **his** notebook.
One of the **girls** has injured **herself.**

If the antecedent may be either masculine or feminine, use both the masculine and feminine pronouns to refer to it.

EXAMPLE
Anyone who is going on the field trip needs to bring **his** or **her** lunch.

(2) Plural pronouns are used to refer to the indefinite pronouns *both, few, many,* and *several.*

EXAMPLE
Many of the spectators leapt from **their** seats and cheered.

(3) Singular or plural pronouns may be used to refer to the indefinite pronouns *all, any, most, none,* and *some.* These indefinite pronouns are singular when they refer to singular words and are plural when they refer to plural words.

SINGULAR	**None** of the renovated theater matches **its** original beauty. [*None* refers to the singular noun *theater.*]
PLURAL	**None** of the geese have left on **their** annual migration. [*None* refers to the plural noun *geese.*]

2l. A plural pronoun is used to refer to two or more singular antecedents joined by *and.*

EXAMPLE
Menelaus and Paris cannot settle **their** feud over Helen peacefully.

2m. A singular pronoun is used to refer to two or more singular antecedents joined by *or* or *nor*.

EXAMPLE
Either **Achilles or Hector** will lose **his** life.

2n. A collective noun (such as *club* or *family*) takes a singular pronoun when the noun refers to the group as a unit and takes a plural pronoun when the noun refers to the parts or members of the group.

SINGULAR   The **jury** reached **its** decision less than one hour later. [The jury decided as a unit.]

PLURAL   The **jury** disagree on how much importance **they** should give to one of the defendant's statements. [The members of the jury disagree.]

2o. The title of a creative work (such as a book, song, film, or painting) or the name of an organization, a country, or a city (even if it is plural in form) takes a singular pronoun.

EXAMPLES
I read ***Flowers of Evil*** and wrote a report on **it**.
The **United Arab Emirates** generates most of **its** revenue from the sale of oil.

3 USING VERBS

THE PRINCIPAL PARTS OF VERBS

Every verb has four basic forms called the *principal parts:* the *base form,* the *present participle,* the *past,* and the *past participle.* A verb is classified as *regular* or *irregular* depending on the way it forms its past and past participle.

3a. A *regular verb* forms the past and past participle by adding *–d* or *–ed* to the base form. An *irregular verb* forms the past and the past participle in some other way.

COMMON REGULAR AND IRREGULAR VERBS

The following examples include *is* and *have* in italics to show that helping verbs (forms of *be* and *have*) are used with the present participle and past participle forms.

BASE FORM	PRESENT PARTICIPLE	PAST	PAST PARTICIPLE
REGULAR			
attack	*is* attacking	attacked	*have* attacked
drown	*is* drowning	drowned	*have* drowned
occur	*is* occurring	occurred	*have* occurred
risk	*is* risking	risked	*have* risked
try	*is* trying	tried	*have* tried
use	*is* using	used	*have* used

IRREGULAR

be	*is* being	was, were	*have* been
bring	*is* bringing	brought	*have* brought
burst	*is* bursting	burst	*have* burst
come	*is* coming	came	*have* come
eat	*is* eating	ate	*have* eaten
go	*is* going	went	*have* gone
lead	*is* leading	led	*have* led
pay	*is* paying	paid	*have* paid
see	*is* seeing	saw	*have* seen
sing	*is* singing	sang	*have* sung
steal	*is* stealing	stole	*have* stolen
take	*is* taking	took	*have* taken
throw	*is* throwing	threw	*have* thrown

NOTE   If you are not sure about the principal parts of a verb, look in a dictionary. Entries for irregular verbs give the principal parts. If no principal parts are listed, the verb is a regular verb.

TENSES AND THEIR USES

3b. The *tense* of a verb indicates the time of the action or state of being that is expressed by the verb.

(1) The *present tense* is used mainly to express an action or a state of being that is occurring now.

EXAMPLE
The article **compares** Gilgamesh with other epic heroes.

The present tense is also used

- to show a customary or habitual action or state of being
- to convey a general truth—something that is always true
- to make a historical event seem current (such use is called the **historical present**)
- to summarize the plot or subject matter of a literary work or to refer to an author's relationship to his or her work (such use is called the **literary present**)
- to express future time

EXAMPLES

Every Friday, our teacher **gives** us a vocabulary quiz. [customary action]

Reptiles **are** coldblooded. [general truth]

The Greeks **establish** separate city-states, which **war** among themselves. [historical present]

The mighty Oedipus **becomes** blind and powerless. [literary present]

Tomorrow a surprise visitor **addresses** the entire school. [future time]

(2) The **past tense** is used to express an action or state of being that occurred in the past but did not continue into the present.

EXAMPLE

An expert on African sculpture **spoke** to our class.

(3) The **future tense** (*will* or *shall* + base form) is used to express an action or a state of being that will occur.

EXAMPLE

Rachel **will explain** the rules of the game.

NOTE *Shall* and *will* are both acceptable in forming the future tense.

(4) The **present perfect tense** (*have* or *has* + past participle) is used to express an action or a state of being that occurred at some indefinite time in the past.

EXAMPLE

Zhang Jie's writings **have caused** controversy in China.

The present perfect tense is also used to express an action or a state of being that began in the past and continues into the present.

EXAMPLE

The war **has raged** nonstop for nine years.

(5) The **past perfect tense** (*had* + past participle) is used to express an action or state of being completed in the past before some other past occurrence.

EXAMPLE

Enkidu **had died** before Gilgamesh left Uruk. [The dying occurred before the leaving.]

Be sure to use the past perfect tense in "if" clauses that express the earlier of two past actions.

EXAMPLE

If you **had seen** [*not* saw *or* would have seen] the film, you would have learned about Dante.

(6) The **future perfect tense** (*will have* or *shall have* + past participle) is used to express an action or state of being that will be completed in the future before some other future occurrence.

EXAMPLE

By this time next week, I **will** [*or* **shall**] **have finished** the *Inferno*.

3c. Avoid unnecessary shifts in tense.

INCONSISTENT	Sundiata pushed against the huge iron bar and manages to stand. [shift from past to present tense]
CONSISTENT	Sundiata **pushed** against the huge iron bar and **managed** to stand. [past tense]
CONSISTENT	Sundiata **pushes** against the huge iron bar and **manages** to stand. [present tense]

When describing events that occur at different times, use verbs in different tenses to show the order of events.

EXAMPLE

She **taught** school for several years, but now she **works** for a publishing company. [Because she taught at a specific time in the past, the past tense *taught* is correct. Because she works at the present time, the present tense *works* is correct.]

ACTIVE VOICE AND PASSIVE VOICE

3d. *Voice* is the form a transitive verb takes to indicate whether the subject of the verb performs or receives the action.

A verb is in the **active voice** when its subject performs the action (its object receives the action).

| ACTIVE VOICE | Francesco Petrarch **wrote** more than three hundred sonnets. |

A verb is in the **passive voice** whenever its subject receives the action (the verb has no object). A passive verb is always a verb phrase that includes a form of *be* and the past participle of an action verb.

| PASSIVE VOICE | More than three hundred sonnets **were written** by Petrarch. |

3e. Use the passive voice sparingly.

In general, the passive voice is less direct and less forceful than the active voice. In some cases, the passive voice also may sound awkward.

AWKWARD PASSIVE The people of Uruk are ordered to build a statue of Enkidu by Gilgamesh.

ACTIVE Gilgamesh **orders** the people of Uruk to build a statue of Enkidu.

Although you generally will want to use active voice rather than passive voice, the passive voice is not less correct than the active voice. In fact, the passive voice is useful in the following situations:

1. when you do not know the performer of the action

EXAMPLE
This epic **was written** four thousand years ago.

2. when you do not want to reveal the performer of the action

EXAMPLE
Her birthday **has been forgotten** for the second year in a row.

3. when you want to emphasize the receiver of the action

EXAMPLE
Noah **was rewarded** for his faithfulness.

4 USING PRONOUNS

CASE

Case is the form that a noun or a pronoun takes to indicate its use in a sentence. In English, there are three cases: *nominative, objective,* and *possessive.* Most personal pronouns have a different form for each case.

The Nominative Case

4a. A subject of a verb is in the nominative case.

EXAMPLES
They built the tower near the sea as **he** had requested. [*They* is the subject of the verb *built. He* is the subject of the verb *had requested.*]

4b. A predicate nominative is in the nominative case.

EXAMPLE
The only students who auditioned for the chorus were **she** and **Carlos.** [*She* and *Carlos* are predicate nominatives that follow the linking verb *were* and identify the subject *students.*]

PERSONAL PRONOUNS			
SINGULAR			
	NOMINATIVE	**OBJECTIVE**	**POSSESSIVE**
FIRST PERSON	I	me	my, mine
SECOND PERSON	you	you	your, yours
THIRD PERSON	he, she, it	him, her, it	his, her, hers, its
PLURAL			
	NOMINATIVE	**OBJECTIVE**	**POSSESSIVE**
FIRST PERSON	we	us	our, ours
SECOND PERSON	you	you	your, yours
THIRD PERSON	they	them	their, theirs

NOTE The form of a noun is the same for both the nominative case and the objective case. A noun changes its form for the possessive case, usually by adding an apostrophe and an s to most singular nouns and only an apostrophe to most plural nouns.

 For more information about forming possessives of nouns, see 13f.

The Objective Case

4c. An object of a verb is in the objective case.

EXAMPLES

Virgil's response comforts **him**. [*Him* is a direct object that tells *whom* Virgil comforts.]

The old boatman Charon gives **them** a stern warning. [*Them* is an indirect object that tells *to whom* Charon gives a warning.]

4d. An object of a preposition is in the objective case.

EXAMPLE

Who is that standing beside **her**? [*Her* is the object of the preposition *beside*.]

The Possessive Case

4e. A noun or a pronoun preceding a gerund is in the possessive case.

EXAMPLE

We were all thrilled by **Joetta's** [*or* **her**] scoring in the top 5 percent. [*Joetta's* or *her* modifies *scoring*, a gerund used as the object of the preposition *by*.]

Do not confuse a gerund with a present participle, which is a verb form that ends in *–ing* and may function as an adjective.

EXAMPLE

Dante saw **them** [*not* their] running after a banner. [*Them* is modified by the participial phrase *running after a banner*.]

SPECIAL PRONOUN PROBLEMS

4f. An appositive is in the same case as the noun or pronoun to which it refers.

EXAMPLES

Both poets, **Virgil and he**, tour Hell. [The compound appositive *Virgil and he* refers to the subject, *poets*.]

Souls swarm around them, **Virgil and him**. [The compound appositive *Virgil and him* refers to *them*, the object of the preposition *around*.]

4g. A pronoun following *than* or *as* in an elliptical construction is in the same case as it would be if the construction were completed.

An *elliptical construction* is a clause from which words have been omitted.

NOMINATIVE I see him more often **than she.** [I see him more often *than she sees him. She* is the subject in the elliptical construction.]

OBJECTIVE I see him more often **than her.** [I see him more often *than I see her. Her* is the direct object in the elliptical construction.]

4h. A pronoun ending in *–self* or *–selves* should not be used in place of a personal pronoun.

EXAMPLE

No one besides Alicia and **me** [*not* myself] wants to visit the museum.

4i. The pronoun *who* (*whoever*) is in the nominative case. The pronoun *whom* (*whomever*) is in the objective case.

EXAMPLES

Who wrote "Carpe Diem"? [*Who* is the subject of the verb *wrote*.]

To **whom** did Sappho write "Sleep, Darling"? [*Whom* is the object of the preposition *to*.]

CLEAR PRONOUN REFERENCE

The word that a pronoun stands for or refers to is called the *antecedent* of the pronoun.

4j. A pronoun should always refer clearly to its antecedent.

Avoid an ambiguous, a general, a weak, or an indefinite reference by

1. rephrasing the sentence, or

2. replacing the pronoun with an appropriate noun, or

3. giving the pronoun a clear antecedent.

AMBIGUOUS After Paul Verlaine and Arthur Rimbaud parted company, he gave up poetry. [The antecedent of *he* is unclear. Did Verlaine or Rimbaud give up poetry?]

CLEAR Arthur Rimbaud gave up poetry after he and Paul Verlaine parted company.

GENERAL Candide is optimistic despite his suffering. That is clear. [*That* has no specific antecedent.]

CLEAR That Candide is optimistic despite his suffering is clear.

WEAK	Our dog Hank is jealous of my new baby sister. To help him get over it, I try to give him extra attention. [The antecedent of *it* is not expressed.]
CLEAR	To help our dog Hank get over his jealousy of my new baby sister, I try to give him extra attention.

INDEFINITE	In this article it explains why the Viking settlers finally left Greenland. [*It* is not necessary to the meaning of the sentence.]
CLEAR	This article explains why the Viking settlers finally left Greenland.

5 USING MODIFIERS

A *modifier* is a word or group of words that limits the meaning of another word or group of words. The two kinds of modifiers are *adjectives* and *adverbs*.

5a. Use an *adjective* to limit the meaning of a noun or a pronoun. Use an *adverb* to limit the meaning of a verb, an adjective, or another adverb.

COMPARISON OF MODIFIERS

5b. *Comparison* refers to the change in the form of an adjective or an adverb to show increasing or decreasing degrees in the quality the modifier expresses.

The three degrees of comparison are *positive, comparative,* and *superlative.*

1. Most one-syllable modifiers form the comparative and superlative degrees by adding *–er* and *–est.*

2. Some two-syllable modifiers form the comparative and superlative degrees by adding *–er* and *–est.* Other two-syllable modifiers form the comparative and superlative degrees by using *more* and *most.*

3. Modifiers of more than two syllables form the comparative and superlative degrees by using *more* and *most.*

4. To show a decrease in the qualities they express, all modifiers form the comparative by using *less* and the superlative by using *least.*

POSITIVE	COMPARATIVE	SUPERLATIVE
soft	softer	softest
thirsty	thirstier	thirstiest
slowly	more slowly	most slowly
skillfully	less skillfully	least skillfully

☞ For information about adding suffixes such as *–er* and *–est* to words, see 14e–j.

5. Some modifiers form the comparative and superlative degrees in other ways.

POSITIVE	COMPARATIVE	SUPERLATIVE
bad (ill)	worse	worst
far	farther (further)	farthest (furthest)
good (well)	better	best
little	less	least
many (much)	more	most

5c. Use the comparative degree when comparing two things. Use the superlative degree when comparing more than two.

COMPARATIVE	Although both the *Iliad* and the *Aeneid* describe the same events, the *Iliad* is the **older** epic. [comparison of two epics]
SUPERLATIVE	Of the three epics I read, the *Mahabharata* is the **longest.** [comparison of three epics]

5d. Avoid a double comparison or a double negative. A *double comparison* is the use of two comparative forms (usually *–er* and *more* or *less*) or two superlative forms (usually *–est* and *most* or *least*) to modify the same word. A *double negative* is the use of two negative words where one is enough.

EXAMPLES
Who is the **noblest** [*not* most noblest] of King Arthur's knights?
I know **nothing** [*not* don't know nothing] about the Enlightenment.

5e. Include the word *other* or *else* when comparing one member of a group with the rest of the group.

ILLOGICAL	Achilles is stronger than any of the Greek warriors. [Achilles is one of the Greek warriors. Logically, Achilles cannot be stronger than himself.]
LOGICAL	Achilles is stronger than any of the **other** Greek warriors.

5f. Avoid comparing items that cannot logically be compared.

ILLOGICAL	Egypt's ancient monuments are more famous than any other country. [The sentence makes an illogical comparison between monuments and a country.]
LOGICAL	Egypt's ancient monuments are more famous than those of any other country. [The sentence makes a logical comparison between monuments.]

PLACEMENT OF MODIFIERS

5g. Avoid using a *misplaced modifier*—a modifying word, phrase, or clause that sounds awkward because it modifies the wrong word or group of words.

To correct a misplaced modifier, place the word, phrase, or clause as close as possible to the word or words you intend it to modify.

MISPLACED	The servant revealed the bag of gold to his angry master hidden in the ground. [What was hidden in the ground: the gold or the servant's master?]
CLEAR	The servant revealed **to his angry master** the bag of gold hidden in the ground.
MISPLACED	I researched more about John Harrison, who invented a clock to measure longitude after I saw the program.
CLEAR	**After I saw the program,** I researched more about John Harrison, who invented a clock to measure longitude.

5h. Avoid using a *dangling modifier*—a modifying word, phrase, or clause that does not sensibly modify any word or words in a sentence.

You may correct a dangling modifier by

- adding a word or words that the dangling word, phrase, or clause can sensibly refer to
- adding a word or words to the dangling word, phrase, or clause
- rewording the sentence

DANGLING	Paying no attention to the noblemen, the fishing continued. [Who paid no attention to the noblemen?]
CLEAR	Paying no attention to the noblemen, the hermit continued fishing.
CLEAR	The hermit paid no attention to the noblemen and continued fishing.

6 PHRASES

WHAT IS A PHRASE?

6a. A *phrase* is a group of related words that is used as a single part of speech and that does not contain a verb and its subject.

EXAMPLE

The *Epic of Gilgamesh,* **a poem of ancient Mesopotamia, was rediscovered in 1839.**
[*A poem of ancient Mesopotamia* functions as a noun, *was rediscovered* is a verb, and *in 1839* functions as an adverb.]

THE PREPOSITIONAL PHRASE

6b. A *prepositional phrase* begins with a preposition and ends with the *object of the preposition,* a word or word group that functions as a noun.

EXAMPLE

Along the way to the finish line cheered crowds **of spectators.** [The noun *way* is the object of the preposition *along.* The noun *finish line* is the object of the preposition *to.* The noun *spectators* is the object of the preposition *of.*]

An object of a preposition may be compound.

EXAMPLE

The old woman ignored the advice **of her friends and neighbors.** [Both *friends* and *neighbors* are objects of the preposition *of.*]

(1) An *adjective phrase* is a prepositional phrase that modifies a noun or a pronoun. An adjective phrase tells *what kind* or *which one.*

EXAMPLE

The happy village experienced seven years **of prosperity.** [*Of prosperity* modifies the noun *years.*]

An adjective phrase usually follows the word it modifies. That word may be the object of another preposition.

EXAMPLE

He rode alone on his journey **from Camelot.** [*From Camelot* modifies *journey,* the object of the preposition *on.*]

More than one adjective phrase may modify the same word.

EXAMPLE

Alexander Pushkin's exile **to his mother's estate for his beliefs** influenced his poetry. [The phrases *to his mother's estate* and *for his beliefs* modify the noun *exile.*]

(2) An *adverb phrase* is a prepositional phrase that modifies a verb, an adjective, or an adverb. An adverb phrase tells *how, when, where, why,* or *to what extent* (*how long* or *how far*).

As you can see in the example below, more than one adverb phrase can modify the same word. The example also shows that an adverb phrase, unlike an adjective phrase, can precede the word it modifies.

EXAMPLE

In 1835, Pushkin returned **to the estate for a visit.** [Each phrase modifies the verb *returned. In 1835* tells *when, to the estate* tells *where,* and *for a visit* tells *why.*]

VERBALS AND VERBAL PHRASES

A *verbal* is a form of a verb used as a noun, an adjective, or an adverb. A *verbal phrase* consists of a verbal and its modifiers and complements.

Participles and Participial Phrases

6c. A *participle* is a verb form that is used as an adjective. A *participial phrase*

consists of a participle and all the words related to the participle.

The two kinds of participles are the *present participle* and the *past participle.*

(1) *Present participles* end in *–ing.*

EXAMPLE

The giant left Thor **scratching his head.** [The participial phrase modifies the noun *Thor.* The noun *head* is the direct object of the present participle *scratching.*]

(2) Most *past participles* end in *–d* or *–ed.* Others are irregularly formed.

EXAMPLE

Filled with jealousy, Hagen plots Siegfried's death. [The participial phrase modifies the noun *Hagen.* The adverb phrase *with jealousy* modifies the past participle *filled.*]

Gerunds and Gerund Phrases

6d. A *gerund* is a verb form ending in *–ing* that is used as a noun. A *gerund phrase* consists of a gerund and all the words related to the gerund.

EXAMPLES

For the rats in the fable, **hanging a bell on the cat** seems the best solution. [*Hanging a bell on the cat* is the subject of the verb *seems.* The adverb phrase *on the cat* modifies the gerund *hanging.*]

The frightened rodents avoid **putting their plan into action.** [*Putting their plan into action* is the direct object of the verb *avoid. Plan* is the direct object of the gerund *putting.* The adverb phrase *into action* modifies the gerund *putting.*]

Infinitives and Infinitive Phrases

6e. An *infinitive* is a verb form that can be used as a noun, an adjective, or an adverb. An infinitive usually begins with *to.* An *infinitive phrase* consists of an infinitive and all the words related to the infinitive.

EXAMPLES

The three friends promised **to meet later.** [The infinitive phrase acts as a noun and is the direct object of the verb *promised.* The adverb *later* modifies the infinitive *to meet.*]

She had a great desire **to visit Moscow.** [The infinitive phrase acts as an adjective and modifies the noun *desire. Moscow* is the direct object of the infinitive *to visit.*]

The Greeks leave a giant horse **to trick the Trojans.** [The infinitive phrase acts as an adverb and modifies the verb *leave.* The noun *Trojans* is the object of the infinitive *to trick.*]

Athena helps **the Greeks build the horse.** [The sign of the infinitive, *to,* is omitted. The infinitive has a subject, *Greeks,* making the entire construction an **infinitive clause.** The infinitive clause acts as a noun and is the direct object of the verb *helps.*]

APPOSITIVES AND APPOSITIVE PHRASES

6f. An *appositive* **is a noun or a pronoun placed beside another noun or pronoun to identify or explain it. An** *appositive phrase* **consists of an appositive and its modifiers.**

An appositive or appositive phrase usually follows the word it identifies or explains.

EXAMPLES
Have you read Rilke's poem **"Black Cat"?** [The appositive *"Black Cat"* identifies the noun *poem.*]

Rilke was born to German-speaking parents in Prague, **the modern capital of the Czech Republic.** [The entire phrase *the modern capital of the Czech Republic* identifies the noun *Prague.*]

For emphasis, however, an appositive or an appositive phrase may precede the word that it explains or identifies.

EXAMPLE
A riot of colorful sights, intriguing aromas, and surprising noises, a Cairo bazaar is great fun to visit. [The appositive phrase explains why a Cairo bazaar is fun to visit.]

7 CLAUSES

7a. A *clause* **is a group of words that contains a verb and its subject and that is used as part of a sentence. There are two kinds of clauses: the** *independent clause* **and the** *subordinate clause.*

THE INDEPENDENT CLAUSE

7b. An *independent* (or *main*) *clause* **expresses a complete thought and can stand by itself as a sentence.**

EXAMPLE
    SUBJECT   VERB
Pablo Neruda wrote numerous love sonnets. [one independent clause]

THE SUBORDINATE CLAUSE

7c. A *subordinate* (or *dependent*) *clause* **does not express a complete thought and cannot stand alone as a sentence.**

EXAMPLE
    SUBJECT   VERB
that **Julio Cortázar lived** in exile in France

The thought expressed by a subordinate clause becomes complete when the clause is combined with an independent clause to create a complete sentence.

EXAMPLE
I read **that Julio Cortázar lived in exile in France.**

The Adjective Clause

7d. An *adjective clause* **is a subordinate clause that modifies a noun or a pronoun.**

An adjective clause always follows the word or words that it modifies. Usually, an adjective clause begins with a **relative pronoun** (such as *that, which, who, whom, whose*). A relative pronoun both relates an adjective clause to the word or words the clause modifies and performs a function within its own clause by serving as a subject, an object of a verb, an object of a preposition, or a modifier.

EXAMPLES
Jamaica Kincaid, **who wrote *Annie John,*** started writing for a teenage girls' magazine. [The relative pronoun *who* relates the adjective clause to the noun *Jamaica Kincaid* and serves as the subject of the verb *wrote.*]

The relic **for which Perceval is searching** is the Holy Grail. [The relative pronoun *which* relates the adjective clause to the noun *relic* and serves as the object of the preposition *for.*]

An adjective clause may begin with a ***relative adverb,*** such as *when* or *where.*

EXAMPLES
My uncle Robert told us about the time **when he backpacked across the island of Luzon.** [The adjective clause modifies the noun *time.*]
He first flew to Manila, **where he stocked up on supplies.** [The adjective clause modifies the noun *Manila.*]

The Noun Clause

7e. A *noun clause* is a subordinate clause that may be used as a subject, a predicate nominative, a direct object, an indirect object, or an object of a preposition.

Words that are commonly used to introduce noun clauses include *how, that, what, whether, who, whoever,* and *why.*

EXAMPLES
That Dr. Faust cannot know more troubles him. [subject]
Knowledge is **what Faust desires.** [predicate nominative]
Mephistopheles believes **that Faust thinks too much.** [direct object]
The teacher will give **whoever can recite the speech** ten points. [indirect object]
The teacher will give ten points to **whoever can recite the speech.** [object of a preposition]

The word that introduces a noun clause may or may not have another function in the clause.

EXAMPLES
Do you know **who wrote *Faust*?** [The word *who* introduces the noun clause and serves as the subject of the verb *wrote.*]

The Chorus at first denies **that Oedipus killed his father.** [The word *that* introduces the noun clause but does not have any function within the noun clause.]

The Adverb Clause

7f. An *adverb clause* is a subordinate clause that modifies a verb, an adjective, or an adverb.

An adverb clause, which may come before or after the word or words it modifies, tells *how, when, where, why, to what extent,* or *under what condition.* An adverb clause is introduced by a ***subordinating conjunction***—a word or word group that relates the adverb clause to the word or words the clause modifies.

EXAMPLES
He acted **as though he had seen a ghost.** [The adverb clause modifies the verb *acted,* telling *how* he acted.]
Jane is taller **than her grandmother is.** [The adverb clause modifies the adjective *taller,* telling *to what extent* Jane is tall.]
They stayed longer **than I thought they would.** [The adverb clause modifies the adverb *longer,* telling *to what extent* their stay was longer.]

The Elliptical Clause

7g. Part of a clause may be left out when the meaning can be understood from the context of the sentence. Such a clause is called an *elliptical clause.*

EXAMPLES
While [he was] **painting,** Rembrandt concentrated completely on his work.
Ken may ride with us **if he wants to** [ride with us].
This job took longer **than the last one** [took].

 For more about using pronouns in elliptical constructions, see 4g.

8 SENTENCE STRUCTURE

SENTENCE OR FRAGMENT?

8a. A *sentence* is a group of words that has a subject and a verb and expresses a complete thought.

EXAMPLES
The *Mahabharata* is most likely the longest poem ever written.
How would you compare the conflicts in the *Iliad* and the *Aeneid*?
What a welcome sign the rainbow was!

Only a sentence should begin with a capital letter and end with a period, a question mark, or an exclamation point. Do not be misled by a group of words that looks like a sentence but that either does not have a subject and a verb or does not express a complete thought. Such a word group is called a *sentence fragment.*

| FRAGMENT | Although he wastes his father's money. |
| SENTENCE | Although he wastes his father's money, the son is forgiven. |

SUBJECT AND PREDICATE

8b. A sentence consists of two parts: a subject and a predicate. A *subject* tells *whom* or *what* the sentence is about. A *predicate* tells something about the subject.

In the following examples, all the words labeled *subject* make up the **complete subject,** and all the words labeled *predicate* make up the **complete predicate.**

EXAMPLES

| SUBJECT | PREDICATE |
| My mother and I | laughed throughout the show. |

| PREDICATE | SUBJECT | PREDICATE |
| For twenty-five years | Sundiata | ruled Mali. |

The Simple Subject

8c. A *simple subject* is the main word or group of words that tells *whom* or *what* the sentence is about.

EXAMPLE

The last **challenge** for the hero is Soumaoro. [The complete subject is *the last challenge for the hero.*]

The Simple Predicate

8d. A *simple predicate* is a verb or verb phrase that tells something about the subject.

EXAMPLE

Have you **read** "A Problem"? [The complete predicate is *have read "A Problem."*]

The Compound Subject and the Compound Verb

8e. A *compound subject* consists of two or more subjects that are joined by

a conjunction—usually *and* or *or*—and that have the same verb.

EXAMPLE

Gilgamesh and **Enkidu** go on a quest together.

8f. A *compound verb* consists of two or more verbs that are joined by a conjunction—usually *and, but,* or *or*—and that have the same subject.

EXAMPLE

Truth **enlightens** the mind, **frees** the spirit, and **strengthens** the soul.

How to Find the Subject of a Sentence

8g. To find the subject of a sentence, ask *Who?* or *What?* before the verb.

(1) The subject of a sentence is never within a prepositional phrase.

EXAMPLES

A long **line** of moviegoers snaked around the block. [What snaked? Line snaked. *Moviegoers* is the object of the preposition *of.*]

In the clearing hung the soft **scent** of jasmine. [What hung? Scent hung. *Clearing* is the object of the preposition *in. Jasmine* is the object of the preposition *of.*]

(2) The subject of a sentence expressing a command or a request is always understood to be *you,* although *you* may not appear in the sentence.

| COMMAND | Identify the sword that Roland carries. [Who is being told to identify? *You* is understood.] |

The subject of a command or a request is *you* even when the sentence also contains a **noun of direct address**—a word that names or identifies the one or ones spoken to.

| REQUEST | Maria, [you] please read the first verse of *The Song of Roland.* |

(3) The subject of a sentence expressing a question usually follows the verb or a part of the verb phrase. Turning the question into a statement will often help you find the subject.

| QUESTION | Have you seen the intricate carving on this horn? |
| STATEMENT | **You** have seen the intricate carving on this horn. [Who has seen? You have seen.] |

| QUESTION | Did the epic differ from the historical account? |
| STATEMENT | The **epic** did differ from the historical account. [What differed? Epic differed.] |

(4) The word *there* or *here* is never the subject of a sentence.

EXAMPLES
There is the Mona Lisa. [What is there? The Mona Lisa is there.]
Here are my **books** on other great painters. [What are here? Books are here.]

COMPLEMENTS

8h. A *complement* is a word or a group of words that completes the meaning of a verb or a verbal. The four main kinds of complements are *direct objects, indirect objects, objective complements,* and *subject complements.*

The Direct Object and the Indirect Object

8i. A *direct object* is a noun, a pronoun, or a word group that functions as a noun and tells *who* or *what* receives the action of a transitive verb.

EXAMPLES
Siegfried never suspected **him.** [Suspected whom? him]
Borges wrote **poems** and **stories.** [Wrote what? poems and stories—compound direct object]

8j. An *indirect object* is a word or word group that comes between a transitive verb and a direct object. An indirect object, which may be a noun, a pronoun, or a word group that functions as a noun, tells *to whom, to what, for whom,* or *for what* the action of the verb is done.

EXAMPLES
For her birthday she bought **herself** a flashy necklace. [Bought for whom? herself]
We should give **practicing for the concert** our full attention. [Should give our full attention to what? practicing for the concert]

The Objective Complement

8k. An *objective complement* is a word or word group that helps complete the meaning of a transitive verb by identifying or modifying the direct object. An objective complement, which may be a noun, a pronoun, an adjective, or a word group that functions as a noun or an adjective, usually follows the direct object.

EXAMPLES
The fox calls the rooster **brother.** [The noun *brother* identifies the direct object *rooster.*]
The Greeks hope to make the city **theirs.** [The pronoun *theirs* modifies the direct object *city.*]
Please don't think me **foolish.** [The adjective *foolish* modifies the direct object *me.*]

 NOTE A *transitive verb* is an action verb that takes an object, which tells who or what receives the action.

The Subject Complement

8l. A *subject complement* is a word or a word group that completes the meaning of a linking verb or a verbal and that identifies or modifies the subject. The two kinds of subject complements are *predicate nominatives* and *predicate adjectives.*

(1) A *predicate nominative* is a word or group of words that follows a linking verb and refers to the same person, place, thing, or idea as the subject of the verb. A predicate nominative may be a noun, a pronoun, or a word group that functions as a noun.

EXAMPLES
In this African tale, the eldest brother is the wisest **one.** [The pronoun *one* identifies the subject *brother.*]
Chekhov's main characters are **Sasha Uskov and his uncle.** [The two nouns *Sasha Uskov* and *uncle* are a compound predicate nominative that refers to the subject *characters.*]

(2) A *predicate adjective* is an adjective that follows a linking verb and that modifies the subject of the verb.

EXAMPLES
At first glance, this poem seems **simple.** [The adjective *simple* modifies the subject *poem.*]
The room is **cold** and **damp.** [The two adjectives *cold* and *damp* are a compound predicate adjective that modifies the subject *room.*]

 For a list of linking verbs, see Part 1: The Parts of Speech.

Language Handbook

SENTENCES CLASSIFIED ACCORDING TO STRUCTURE

8m. According to their structure, sentences are classified as *simple, compound, complex,* and *compound-complex.*

(1) A *simple sentence* has one independent clause and no subordinate clauses.

EXAMPLE
Most of the villagers had not traveled more than forty miles from home.

(2) A *compound sentence* has two or more independent clauses but no subordinate clauses.

EXAMPLES
Dante is afraid, but Virgil beckons him to follow.
The final circle is reserved for traitors; each one is frozen beneath the ice.

(3) A *complex sentence* has one independent clause and at least one subordinate clause.

EXAMPLE
The narrator feels that her mother died happy. [The independent clause is *the narrator feels.* The subordinate clause is *that her mother died happy.*]

(4) A *compound-complex* sentence has two or more independent clauses and at least one subordinate clause.

EXAMPLE
The chief cannot believe the men, but once they leave, his own stool speaks to him! [The two independent clauses are *the chief cannot believe the men* and *his own stool speaks to him.* The subordinate clause is *once they leave.*]

SENTENCES CLASSIFIED ACCORDING TO PURPOSE

8n. According to their purpose, sentences are classified as *declarative, interrogative, imperative,* and *exclamatory.*

(1) A *declarative sentence* makes a statement. It is followed by a period.

EXAMPLE
The lock on the front door is broken.

(2) An *interrogative sentence* asks a question. It is followed by a question mark.

EXAMPLE
Would you mind singing something else?

(3) An *imperative sentence* makes a request or gives a command. It is usually followed by a period. A very strong command, however, is followed by an exclamation point.

EXAMPLES
Forward me the message when you get the chance.
Please turn off the light.
Be careful out there!

(4) An *exclamatory sentence* expresses strong feeling or shows excitement. It is followed by an exclamation point.

EXAMPLES
What a talented writer she was!
We won!

 For more information about using end marks, see 12a–e.

---

9 SENTENCE STYLE

WAYS TO ACHIEVE CLARITY

Coordinating Ideas

9a. To *coordinate* two or more ideas, or to give them equal emphasis, link them with a connecting word, an appropriate mark of punctuation, or both.

EXAMPLE
The train finally arrived, **and** dozens of passengers rushed to board it.

Subordinating Ideas

9b. To *subordinate* an idea, or to show that one idea is related to but less important than another, use an adverb clause or an adjective clause.

EXAMPLES
The young woman is furious **because the young man did not pay a fair price for the wooden lion.** [adverb clause]
She thinks of the artist **who worked so hard to carve it.** [adjective clause]

Using Parallel Structure

9c. Use the same grammatical form (*parallel structure*) to express ideas of equal importance.

(1) Use parallel structure when you link coordinate ideas.

EXAMPLE
In the winter I usually like **to ski** and **to skate.** [infinitive paired with infinitive]

(2) Use parallel structure when you compare or contrast ideas.

EXAMPLE
Einstein liked mathematical **research** more than laboratory **supervision.** [noun contrasted with noun]

(3) Use parallel structure when you link ideas with correlative conjunctions (*both . . . and, either . . . or, neither . . . nor,* or *not only . . . but also*).

EXAMPLE
Capoeira is both a **dance form** and a **martial art.** [Note that the correlative conjunctions come directly before the parallel terms.]

When you revise for parallel structure, you may need to add an article, a preposition, or a pronoun before each of the parallel terms.

UNCLEAR	I admire the poems of Verlaine more than Rimbaud.
CLEAR	I admire the poems of Verlaine more than **those of** Rimbaud.

OBSTACLES TO CLARITY

Sentence Fragments

9d. Avoid using a *sentence fragment*—a word or word group that either does not contain a subject and a verb or does not express a complete thought.

 For more information about sentence fragments, see 8a.

Here are two common ways to correct a sentence fragment.

I. Add words to make the thought complete.

FRAGMENT	The Trojans around Hector's pyre. [The verb is missing.]
SENTENCE	The Trojans **gathered** around Hector's pyre.

2. Attach the fragment to the sentence that comes before or after it.

FRAGMENT	From the boat the girl sees her family. Waving goodbye to her. [participial phrase]
SENTENCE	From the boat the girl sees her family **waving goodbye to her.**

 NOTE Sentence fragments can be effective when used in expressive and creative writing and in informal writing.

Run-on Sentences

9e. Avoid using a *run-on sentence*—two or more complete thoughts that are run together as if they were one complete thought.

The two kinds of run-on sentences are *fused sentences* and *comma splices.* A **fused sentence** has no punctuation or connecting word at all between the complete thoughts. A **comma splice** has just a comma between the complete thoughts.

FUSED SENTENCE	Roland tries to break his sword it shatters the rock.
COMMA SPLICE	Roland tries to break his sword, it shatters the rock.

You can correct run-on sentences in several ways.

I. Make two sentences.

EXAMPLE
Roland tries to break his sword**. It** shatters the rock.

2. Use a comma and a coordinating conjunction.

EXAMPLE
Roland tries to break his sword**, but** it shatters the rock.

3. Change one of the independent clauses to a subordinate clause.

EXAMPLE
When Roland tries to break his sword, it shatters the rock.

4. Use a semicolon.

EXAMPLE
Roland tries to break his sword**;** it shatters the rock.

5. Use a semicolon and a conjunctive adverb.

EXAMPLE
Roland tries to break his sword**; however,** it shatters the rock.

Unnecessary Shifts in Sentences

9f. Avoid making unnecessary shifts in subject, in tense, and in voice.

AWKWARD	Grandma goes to the farmers' market, where the freshest produce is. [shift in subject]
BETTER	**Grandma** goes to the farmers' market, where **she** finds the freshest produce.
AWKWARD	Faust follows the Devil at first but eventually found salvation. [shift in tense]
BETTER	Faust **follows** the Devil at first but eventually **finds** salvation.
AWKWARD	Lyle spent four hours at the library, but no books on his research topic were found. [shift in voice]
BETTER	Lyle **spent** four hours at the library, but he **found** no books on his research topic.

REVISING FOR VARIETY

9g. Use a variety of sentence beginnings.

Putting the subject first in a declarative sentence is not wrong, but starting every sentence with the subject can make your writing boring. To add variety to your sentences, rearrange sentence parts to vary the beginnings. The following examples show how a writer can revise sentences to avoid beginning with the subject every time.

SUBJECT FIRST	**Arjuna** is dejected and afraid and does not want to fight against his own relatives.
SINGLE-WORD MODIFIERS FIRST	**Dejected** and **afraid,** Arjuna does not want to fight against his own relatives.
SUBJECT FIRST	The **Bhagavad-Gita,** completed by 300 A.D., is a dialogue between Arjuna and Krishna.
PARTICIPIAL PHRASE FIRST	**Completed by 300 A.D.,** the Bhagavad-Gita is a dialogue between Arjuna and Krishna.
APPOSITIVE PHRASE FIRST	**A dialogue between Krishna and Arjuna,** the Bhagavad-Gita was completed by 300 A.D.

Varying Sentence Structure

9h. Use a mix of simple, compound, complex, and compound-complex sentences in your writing.

EXAMPLE
Aeneas first learns of the Greek attack in a dream. [simple] Hector appears to tell him that Troy is being destroyed. [complex] He wakes up and intends to arm himself, but the priest Panthus dashes his hopes of retaking the city. [compound] Aeneas runs through the burning town, gathering a group to him. [simple] After they overpower an enemy band, the Trojans disguise themselves as Greeks, but then their own side attacks them. [compound-complex]

 For information about the four kinds of sentence structure, see 8m.

Revising to Reduce Wordiness

9i. Avoid using unnecessary words in your writing.

The following guidelines suggest some ways to revise wordy sentences.

1. Take out a whole group of unnecessary words.

WORDY	King Mark sends Tristan back home to Wales, where he lives.
IMPROVED	King Mark sends Tristan back home to Wales.

2. Replace pretentious words and expressions with straightforward ones.

WORDY	In *Candide,* a young man of great simplicity and considerable honesty goes on a series of adventures that can scarcely be believed.
IMPROVED	In *Candide,* a **simple** and **honest** young man goes on a series of **incredible** adventures.

3. Reduce a clause to a phrase.

WORDY	The Fisher King possesses the Holy Grail, which is the cup that was used at the Last Supper.
IMPROVED	The Fisher King possesses the Holy Grail, **the cup used at the Last Supper.**

4. Reduce a phrase or a clause to one word.

WORDY	At that point in time, the hostess returns.
IMPROVED	**Then,** the hostess returns.

10 SENTENCE COMBINING

COMBINING BY INSERTING WORDS AND PHRASES

10a. Combine related sentences by taking a key word (or using another form of the key word) from one sentence and inserting it into another sentence.

ORIGINAL	The famous magician Harry Houdini performed impossible escapes. The escapes only seemed impossible.
COMBINED	The famous magician Harry Houdini performed **seemingly** impossible escapes. [The verb *seemed* becomes the adverb *seemingly*.]

10b. Combine related sentences by taking (or creating) a phrase from one sentence and inserting it into another.

ORIGINAL	Have you read the poem "To Hélène"? It was written by Pierre de Ronsard.
COMBINED	Have you read the poem "To Hélène" **by Pierre de Ronsard**? [prepositional phrase]

COMBINING BY COORDINATING IDEAS

10c. Combine related sentences whose ideas are equally important by using coordinating conjunctions (*and, but, or, nor, for, so, yet*) or correlative conjunctions (*both . . . and, either . . . or, neither . . . nor, not only . . . but also*).

The relationship of the ideas determines which connective will work best. When joined, the coordinate ideas form compound elements.

ORIGINAL	"Song of a Citizen" was written by Czeslaw Milosz. "The Poor Poet" was also written by him.
COMBINED	"Song of a Citizen" **and** "The Poor Poet" were written by Czeslaw Milosz. [compound subject]
ORIGINAL	The farmer had closed his market stall for the afternoon. We decided to buy fresh produce somewhere else.
COMBINED	The farmer had closed his market stall for the afternoon, **so** we decided to buy fresh produce somewhere else. [compound sentence]

Another way to form a compound sentence is to link independent clauses with a semicolon or with a semicolon and a conjunctive adverb (such as *however, likewise,* or *therefore*) followed by a comma.

EXAMPLES
She was willing to compromise; he was not.
They moved to Dorsetshire; **however,** they stayed there only a few months.

COMBINING BY SUBORDINATING IDEAS

10d. Combine related sentences whose ideas are not equally important by placing the less important idea in a subordinate clause (adjective clause, adverb clause, or noun clause).

ORIGINAL	I read about the life of Queen Nefertiti. She ruled Egypt from 1353 to around 1341 B.C.
COMBINED	I read about the life of Queen Nefertiti, **who ruled Egypt from 1353 to around 1341 B.C.** [adjective clause]
	or
COMBINED	Queen Nefertiti, **whose life I read about,** ruled Egypt from 1353 to around 1341 B.C. [adjective clause]
ORIGINAL	The injured thief points his knife at Lise. She thinks that he wants her ring.
COMBINED	**When the injured thief points his knife at Lise,** she thinks that he wants her ring. [adverb clause]
ORIGINAL	Sigismund asks Lise about her wedding ring. He asks her where she lost it.
COMBINED	Sigismund asks Lise **where she lost her wedding ring.** [noun clause]

 For more information about subordinate clauses and subordinating ideas, see 7c–g and 9b.

Language Handbook

11a. Capitalize the first word in every sentence.

EXAMPLE
The man who succeeds Oedipus as king is Creon.

(1) Capitalize the first word of a sentence following a colon.

EXAMPLE
The Sphinx posed a riddle: What walks on four legs by morning, two at noon, and three at night?

(2) Capitalize the first word of a direct quotation.

EXAMPLE
After winning, Brian said, "**W**e couldn't have done it without the support of the good people of Raleigh."

When quoting from another writer's work, capitalize the first word of the quotation only if the writer has capitalized it in the original work.

EXAMPLE
After winning, Brian acknowledged "**t**he support of the good people of Raleigh."

(3) Traditionally, the first word of a line of poetry is capitalized.

EXAMPLES
Blest be the day, and blest the month and year,
Season and hour and very moment blest,
The lovely land and place where first possessed
By two pure eyes I found me prisoner.
   —Francesco Petrarch, *Sonnet 61,*
     translated by Joseph Auslander

NOTE Some writers do not follow this rule. Whenever you quote from a writer's work, always use capital letters exactly as the writer uses them.

11b. Capitalize the first word in the salutation and the closing of a letter.

EXAMPLES
Dear John,   **D**ear Sir or Madam: **S**incerely,

11c. Capitalize proper nouns and proper adjectives.

A **common noun** is a general name for a person, a place, a thing, or an idea. A **proper noun** names a particular person, place, thing, or idea. A **proper adjective** is formed from a proper noun. Common nouns are capitalized only if they begin a sentence (also, in most cases, a line of poetry), begin a direct quotation, or are part of a title.

COMMON NOUNS	PROPER NOUNS	PROPER ADJECTIVES
dramatist	**S**hakespeare	**S**hakespearean performer
country	**R**ussia	**R**ussian diplomat
mountains	the **A**lps	**A**lpine flora

In most proper nouns made up of two or more words, do not capitalize articles (*a, an, the*), short prepositions (those with fewer than five letters, such as *at, of, for, to, with*), the mark of the infinitive (*to*), and coordinating conjunctions (*and, but, for, nor, or, so, yet*).

EXAMPLES
Speaker **o**f **t**he **H**ouse **o**f **R**epresentatives
American **S**ociety **f**or **t**he **P**revention **o**f **C**ruelty
   to **A**nimals

NOTE When you're not sure whether to capitalize a word, check a dictionary.

(1) Capitalize the names of most persons and animals.

GIVEN NAMES	**I**sak	**P**ablo
SURNAMES	**D**inesen	**N**eruda
ANIMALS	**B**abe	**S**eabiscuit

NOTE Some names contain more than one capital letter. Usage varies in the capitalization of *van, von, du, de la,* and other parts of many multiword names. Always verify the spelling of a name with the person, or check the name in a reference source.

EXAMPLES
La **F**ontaine   **O**'**K**eefe   **a**l-**K**hansa   **M**ac**A**dam
Van **A**llen   **I**bn **S**ina   **v**an **E**yck   **d**a **G**ama

(2) Capitalize the names of nationalities, races, and peoples.

EXAMPLES
Japanese   **C**aucasian   **H**ispanic   **C**elt

(3) Capitalize brand names. Notice that the noun that follows a brand name is not capitalized.

EXAMPLES
Sealtest milk   **W**onder bread   **C**rest toothpaste

(4) Capitalize geographical names.

TYPE OF NAME	EXAMPLES	
Towns, Cities	**S**tratford-on-**A**von **R**io de **J**aneiro	**D**ublin **S**outh **B**end
Counties, Townships	**M**arion **C**ounty **B**rooklyn **B**orough	**A**lexandria **T**ownship **L**afayette **P**arish
States, Territories	**O**klahoma **Y**ucatán	**N**orth **C**arolina **Y**ukon **T**erritory
Regions	the **M**iddle **E**ast **W**estern **H**emisphere	the **L**ake **D**istrict the **S**outhwest
Countries	**E**ngland	**C**osta **R**ica
Continents	**S**outh **A**merica	**E**urope
Islands	**L**ong **I**sland	**B**ritish **I**sles
Mountains	**H**imalayas **P**ikes **P**eak	**M**ount **R**ainier **S**ierra **N**evada
Other Landforms and Features	**C**ape of **G**ood **H**ope **D**eath **V**alley	**I**sthmus of **C**orinth **B**lack **F**orest
Bodies of Water	**I**ndian **O**cean **B**ering **S**trait	**R**ed **S**ea **S**an **F**rancisco **B**ay
Parks	**H**awaii **V**olcanoes **N**ational **P**ark **P**oint **R**eyes **N**ational **S**eashore	
Roads, Highways, Streets	**R**oute 42 **I**nterstate 75	**K**ing **A**venue **T**hirty-fourth **S**treet

NOTE Words such as *city, state,* and *county* are often capitalized in official documents such as proclamations. In general usage, however, these words are not capitalized.

OFFICIAL USAGE
the State of Iowa

GENERAL USAGE
the state of Iowa

NOTE Words such as *north, western,* and *southeast* are not capitalized when they indicate direction.

EXAMPLES
north of London
heading **s**outhwest

NOTE The second word in a hyphenated number begins with a small letter.

EXAMPLE
Forty-**s**econd Street

(5) Capitalize the names of organizations, teams, business firms, institutions, buildings and other structures, and government bodies.

TYPE OF NAME	EXAMPLES
Organizations	**D**isabled **A**merican **V**eterans **P**rofessional **P**hotographers of **A**merica
Teams	**R**iver **C**ity **E**astside **B**ombers **H**arlem **G**lobetrotters
Business Firms	**A**aron's **C**arpets **N**ational **B**roadcasting **C**orporation
Institutions	**O**xford **U**niversity **S**outhern **C**hristian **L**eadership **C**onference
Buildings and Other Structures	**L**incoln **C**enter for the **P**erforming **A**rts the **G**reat **W**all of **C**hina
Government Bodies	**U**nited **S**tates **C**ongress **H**ouse of **C**ommons

NOTE Do not capitalize words such as *democratic, republican,* and *socialist* when they refer to principles or forms of government. Capitalize such words only when they refer to specific political parties.

EXAMPLES
The citizens demanded **d**emocratic reforms.
Who will be the **R**epublican nominee for governor?

NOTE Do not capitalize words such as *building, hospital, theater, high school,* and *post office* unless they are part of a proper noun.

(6) Capitalize the names of historical events and periods, special events, holidays and other calendar items, and time zones.

TYPE OF NAME	EXAMPLES	
Historical Events and Periods	Middle Ages	Reign of Terror
Special Events	Super Bowl	Pan-American Games
Holidays and Other Calendar Items	Monday November	Memorial Day National Book Week
Time Zones	Eastern Daylight Time (EDT) Central Mountain Time (CMT)	

NOTE Do not capitalize the name of a season unless it is being personified or used as part of a proper noun.

EXAMPLES
We moved here last fall.
This month Fall begins painting the leaves in brilliant hues.
The Fall Festival is next week.

(7) Capitalize the names of ships, trains, aircraft, spacecraft, monuments, awards, planets and other heavenly bodies, and any other particular places and things.

TYPE OF NAME	EXAMPLES	
Ships	*Merrimac*	**U.S.S.** *Nautilus*
Trains	*Zephyr*	*Hill Country Flyer*
Aircraft	*Enola Gay*	*Spruce Goose*
Spacecraft	*Atlantis*	*Magellan*
Monuments	Mount Rushmore National Memorial Effigy Mounds National Monument	
Awards	Nobel Prize	Medal of Freedom
Planets and Other Heavenly Bodies	Neptune Big Dipper	Polaris Cassiopeia
Other Particular Places and Things	Hurricane Alma Marshall Plan	Silk Route Union Jack

NOTE Do not capitalize the words *sun* and *moon*. Do not capitalize the word *earth* unless it is used along with the proper names of other particular places, things, or events.

EXAMPLES
The equator is an imaginary circle around the earth.
Is Mercury closer to the sun than Earth is?

☞ For more information about the names of particular places and things, see the discussion of proper nouns in 11c.

11d. Do not capitalize the names of school subjects, except names of languages and course names followed by a number.

EXAMPLES
French   art   Algebra I

11e. Capitalize titles.

(1) Capitalize a title belonging to a particular person when it comes before the person's name.

EXAMPLES
General Patton   Dr. Sanchez   President Clinton

In general, do not capitalize a title used alone or following a name. Some titles, however, are by tradition capitalized. If you are unsure about capitalizing a title, check in a dictionary.

EXAMPLES
Who is the prime minister of Britain?
When was Ann Richards governor of Texas?
The Prince of Wales met earlier today with European leaders.

A title is usually capitalized when it is used alone in direct address.

EXAMPLE
Good afternoon, Sir [*or* sir], may I help you?

(2) Capitalize a word showing a family relationship when the word is used before or in place of a person's name, unless a possessive comes before the word.

EXAMPLES
I asked Mom if Uncle Bob is named after her uncle Roberto.

(3) Capitalize the first and last words and all important words in titles of books, periodicals, poems, stories, essays, speeches, plays, historical documents, movies, radio and television programs, works of art, musical compositions, and cartoons.

TYPE OF NAME	EXAMPLES	
Books	*The Hunchback of Notre Dame*	*Annie John*
Periodicals	*National Geographic*	*Time*
Poems	"I Have Visited Again"	"The Guitar"
Stories	"The Train from Rhodesia "	"An Astrologer's Day"
Essays and Speeches	"Of Experience"	Funeral Speech of Pericles
Plays	*Oedipus Rex*	*Faust*
Historical Documents	Magna Carta	Treaty of Versailles
Movies	*Robin Hood: Prince of Thieves*	*Clueless*
Radio and TV Programs	*A Prairie Home Companion*	*Frontline*
Works of Art	*The Kiss*	*March of Humanity*
Musical Compositions	*War Requiem*	"Tears in Heaven"
Cartoons	*For Better or For Worse*	*Jump Start*

NOTE Unimportant words in a title include articles (*a, an, the*), short prepositions (those with fewer than five letters, such as *of, to, in, for, from, with*), and coordinating conjunctions (*and, but, for, nor, or, so, yet*).

☞ For information about which titles should be italicized and which should be enclosed in quotation marks, see 13b and 13d.

11f. Capitalize the names of religions and their followers, holy days and celebrations, holy writings, and specific deities and venerated beings.

TYPE OF NAME	EXAMPLES	
Religions and Followers	Christianity Muslim	Buddhist Judaism
Holy Days and Celebrations	Easter Passover	Ramadan Holy Week
Holy Writings	Bible Talmud	Koran I Ching
Specific Deities and Venerated Beings	Allah Dalai Lama	God Jehovah

NOTE The words *god* and *goddess* are not capitalized when they refer to mythological deities. The names of specific mythological deities are capitalized, however.

EXAMPLES
The Greek god of the sea was Poseidon.

12 PUNCTUATION

END MARKS

12a. A statement (or declarative sentence) is followed by a period.

EXAMPLE
The old man described the land of Eldorado.

12b. A question (or interrogative sentence) is followed by a question mark.

EXAMPLE
Has anyone tried to produce a miniseries based on the *Iliad*?

12c. A request or command (or imperative sentence) is followed by either a period or an exclamation point.

EXAMPLES
Turn the music down, please. [request]
Hang on to the rail as you go down the stairway.
[mild command]
Watch out! [strong command]

12d. An exclamation (or exclamatory sentence) is followed by an exclamation point.

EXAMPLE
How the sight filled us with fear!

TYPE OF ABBREVIATION	EXAMPLES
Personal Names	Peter H. Lee R. K. Narayan
Organizations, Companies	Co. Inc. Ltd.
Titles Used with Names	Ms. Sr. Dr.
Times of Day	A.M. (or a.m.) P.M. (or p.m.)
Years	B.C. (written after the date) A.D. (written before the date)
Addresses	St. Blvd. P. O. Box
States	S.C. Calif.

12e. An abbreviation is usually followed by a period.

If an abbreviation with a period ends a sentence, do not add another period. However, do add a question mark or an exclamation point if one is needed.

EXAMPLES
The store opens at 10 A.M.
Does the store open at 10 A.M.?

Some abbreviations, including those for most units of measurement, are written without periods.

EXAMPLES
AM/FM, CIA, CNN, PC, NASA, SOS,
cc, ft, lb, kw, ml, psi, rpm [but in. for inch]

NOTE Use a two-letter state code when the ZIP Code is included. Two-letter state codes are not followed by periods, and no comma is placed between the state code and the ZIP Code.

EXAMPLE
Lexington, **KY** 40505

COMMAS

12f. Use commas to separate items in a series.

EXAMPLE
Nadine Gordimer, Elie Wiesel, and Anton Chekhov are among the writers we are studying.

If all the items in a series are linked by *and, or,* or *nor,* do not use commas to separate them.

EXAMPLE
Dante drew on Homer **and** Plato **and** Virgil.

12g. Use a comma to separate two or more adjectives preceding a noun.

EXAMPLE
Perceval is a humble, innocent knight.

When the last adjective before a noun is thought of as part of the noun, the comma before the adjective is omitted.

EXAMPLE
I've finally found a decent, affordable used car.
[*Used car* is thought of as one unit.]

12h. Use a comma before *and, but, or, nor, for, so,* and *yet* when they join independent clauses.

EXAMPLE
We could read the book first, or we could wait until after we have seen the movie.

You may omit the comma before *and, but, or,* or *nor* if the clauses are very short and there is no chance of misunderstanding.

12i. Use commas to set off nonessential clauses and nonessential participial phrases.

A *nonessential* clause or phrase is one that can be left out without changing the meaning of the sentence.

NONESSENTIAL CLAUSE	The poet Saadi, **who was born around 1213,** lived as a wandering holy man.
NONESSENTIAL PHRASE	His sayings, **stated simply and directly,** express Sufi wisdom.

 For more information about phrases, see 6a–f. For more on clauses, see 7a–g.

An *essential* clause or phrase is one that cannot be left out without changing the meaning of the sentence. Essential clauses and phrases are *not* set off by commas.

ESSENTIAL CLAUSE The writer **who received the Nobel Prize in literature in 1990** was Octavio Paz.

ESSENTIAL PHRASE The servant **traveling alongside Candide in South America** is the prudent Cacambo.

12j. Use commas after certain introductory elements.

(1) Use a comma after a one-word adverb such as *first, next, yes,* or *no* or after any mild exclamation such as *well* or *why* at the beginning of a sentence.

EXAMPLE
No, I have not yet read *The Pillow Book.*

(2) Use a comma after an introductory participial phrase.

EXAMPLE
Looking calm, Jill walked to the podium.

(3) Use a comma after two or more introductory prepositional phrases or after a single long one.

EXAMPLE
After the fall of Sosso, nothing remained.

(4) Use a comma after an introductory adverb clause.

EXAMPLE
After I had locked the car door, I remembered that the keys were still in the ignition.

12k. Use commas to set off elements that interrupt a sentence.

(1) Appositives and appositive phrases are usually set off by commas.

EXAMPLES
Julio Cortázar's first story collection, *Bestiary,* was published in 1951.
South Americans drink yerba maté, **a kind of tea.**

Sometimes an appositive is so closely related to the word or words near it that it should not be set off by commas. Such an appositive is called a *restrictive appositive.*

EXAMPLE
The writer **Alexander Pushkin** died after a duel.

(2) Words used in direct address are set off by commas.

EXAMPLE
Your research paper, **Dylan,** is quite interesting.

(3) Parenthetical expressions are set off by commas.

Parenthetical expressions are remarks that add incidental information or that relate ideas to each other. Some common parenthetical expressions are *for example, I think, moreover,* and *on the other hand.*

EXAMPLE
Some dogs make good helpers; Labradors, **for example,** can be patient and obedient.

 NOTE A contrasting expression introduced by *not, rather than,* or a similar term is parenthetical. Set it off by commas.

EXAMPLE
Paul Verlaine, **not Arthur Rimbaud,** wrote "The Sky Is Just Beyond the Roof."

12l. Use a comma in certain conventional situations.

(1) Use a comma to separate items in dates and addresses.

EXAMPLES
On April 8, 1300, Dante begins his journey.
Send complete entries to 315 Wayne Court, Dinuba, CA 93618.

(2) Use a comma after the salutation of a personal letter and after the closing of any letter.

EXAMPLES
Dear Alicia,   Yours truly,

(3) Use commas to set off abbreviations such as *Jr., Sr., RN, M.D., Ltd.,* or *Inc.*

EXAMPLES
Is Jorge Rivera, Jr., in your class?
She is the owner of Flowers by Arthurine, Inc.

SEMICOLONS

12m. Use a semicolon between independent clauses that are closely related in thought and are not joined by *and, but, for, nor, or, so,* or *yet.*

EXAMPLE
The rain had finally stopped; a few rays of sunshine were pushing through breaks in the clouds.

12n. Use a semicolon between independent clauses joined by a conjunctive adverb or a transitional expression.

A *conjunctive adverb*—such as *furthermore, however,* or *nevertheless*—or a *transitional expression*—such as *for instance, in fact,* or *that is*—indicates the relationship of the independent clauses that it joins.

EXAMPLE

The snow made traveling difficult**;** **nevertheless,** we arrived home safely.

12o. Use a semicolon (rather than a comma) before a coordinating conjunction to join independent clauses that contain commas.

EXAMPLE

To trace the ancient pilgrimage route to Santiago de Compostela, the hikers could start in Tours, France, cross the Pyrenees to Roncesvalles, Spain, and then head west**;** or they could start in Arles, France, cross the mountains at Col de Somport, Spain, and then join the main route at Puente la Reina. [commas within the clauses]

12p. Use a semicolon between items in a series if the items contain commas.

EXAMPLE

The summer reading list includes the *Odyssey,* by Homer**;** *Orlando furioso,* by Ludovico Ariosto**;** and *Don Quixote,* by Miguel de Cervantes.

COLONS

12q. Use a colon to mean "note what follows."

(1) Use a colon before a list of items, especially after expressions such as *as follows* and *the following.*

EXAMPLE

Collection 7 includes poems by the following authors**:** Rainer Maria Rilke, Federico García Lorca, Czeslaw Milosz, and Pablo Neruda.

 NOTE Do not use a colon before a list that directly follows a verb or a preposition.

EXAMPLES

The textbook includes poems by Rainer Maria Rilke, Federíco Garcia Lorca, Czeslaw Milosz, and Pablo Neruda. [The list directly follows the preposition *by.*]

The main characters in Anton Chekhov's "A Problem" are Sasha Uskov, Ivan Markovitch, and the otherwise unnamed Colonel. [The list directly follows the verb *are.*]

(2) Use a colon before a quotation that lacks a speaker tag such as *he said* or *she remarked.*

EXAMPLE

His father's response surprised him**:** "I'm proud of you, son."

 For information about punctuating quotations that do have speaker tags, see 13c.

(3) Use a colon before a long, formal statement or quotation.

EXAMPLE

The patient awakens in what he thinks is a dream**:** "It was unusual as a dream because it was full of smells, and he never dreamt smells. First a marshy smell, there to the left of the trail the swamps began already, the quaking bogs from which no one ever returned."

12r. Use a colon in certain conventional situations.

EXAMPLES

12**:**01 A.M. [between the hour and the minute]

Mark 3**:**10 [between chapter and verse in referring to passages from the Bible]

To Whom It May Concern**:** [after the salutation of a business letter]

*Sundiata***:** *An Epic of Old Mali* [between a title and a subtitle]

13 PUNCTUATION

ITALICS

Italics are printed characters that *slant to the right like this.* To indicate italics in handwritten or typewritten work, use underlining.

13a. Use italics (underlining) for words, letters, and symbols referred to as

such and for foreign words that have not been adopted into English.

EXAMPLES

The words *hiss* and *clang* are examples of onomatopoeia.

You typed *ie* instead of *ei.*

The motto *e pluribus unum* appears on all United States coins.

13b. Use italics (underlining) for titles of books, plays, long poems, periodicals, newspapers, works of art, films, television series, long musical compositions, recordings, comic strips, computer software, court cases, trains, ships, aircraft, and spacecraft.

TYPE OF NAME	EXAMPLE	
Books	*Webster's New World Thesaurus*	
Plays	*Oedipus Rex*	
Long Poems	*Epic of Gilgamesh*	
Periodicals	*Sports Illustrated*	
Newspapers	*The Boston Globe*	
Works of Art	*The Persistence of Memory*	
Films	*It's a Wonderful Life*	
TV Series	*Austin City Limits*	
Long Musical Compositions	*The Planets*	
Recordings	*Unforgettable*	
Comic Strips	*Doonesbury*	
Computer Software	*Netscape Communicator*	
Court Cases	*Marbury v. Madison*	
Trains, Ships, Aircraft, and Spacecraft	*Orient Express* *Enola Gay*	*Queen Elizabeth 2* *Apollo 13*

NOTE The article *the* before the title of a book, periodical, or newspaper is neither italicized nor capitalized unless it is part of the official title. The official title of a book appears on the book's title page. The official title of a periodical or newspaper is the name on its masthead, usually found on the editorial page.

EXAMPLES
What role do the gods play in the *Iliad*?
I found this information in *The New York Times*.
My mom looks through the *Sun-Times* every morning.

☞ For a list of titles that are enclosed in quotation marks, see 13d. For information about capitalizing titles, see 11e(3).

QUOTATION MARKS

13c. Use quotation marks to enclose a *direct quotation*—a person's exact words.

(1) A direct quotation usually begins with a capital letter.

EXAMPLE
Anthony J. D'Angelo wrote, "**G**ive more than take."

However, when the quotation is only a part of a sentence, do not begin it with a capital letter.

EXAMPLE
Chuang Tzu explains that the difference between himself and the butterfly is "**o**nly due to their changing material forms."

Do not use quotation marks to enclose an *indirect quotation* (a rewording of a direct quotation).

DIRECT QUOTATION	Al said, "I'm going fishing today."
INDIRECT QUOTATION	Al said that he is going fishing today.

(2) When the expression identifying the speaker divides a quoted sentence, the second part begins with a lowercase letter.

EXAMPLE
"Common sense," explained Albert Einstein, "**i**s the collection of prejudices acquired by age eighteen." [Notice that each part of a divided quotation is enclosed in quotation marks.]

When the second part of a divided quotation is a new sentence, the first word begins with a capital letter.

EXAMPLE
"Petrarch described his beloved in ideal terms," Mr. Owusu noted. "**L**ater writers used the same language in their own love poetry."

(3) When used with quotation marks, other marks of punctuation are placed according to the following rules.

● Commas and periods are always placed inside the closing quotation marks.

EXAMPLES
"Read these lines," he said, "and tell me what you think they mean."

- Semicolons and colons are always placed outside the closing quotation marks.

EXAMPLES

Miriam's first response was "Why me?"; nevertheless, she planned the project well.

Discuss one of the following themes in R. K. Narayan's "An Astrologer's Day": fate, honesty, or redemption.

- Question marks and exclamation points are placed inside the closing quotation marks if the quotation itself is a question or an exclamation. Otherwise, they are placed outside.

EXAMPLES

"Where were you?" Pedro asked

How I enjoyed "The Guitar"!

(4) When quoting a passage that consists of more than one paragraph, put quotation marks at the beginning of each paragraph and at the end of only the last paragraph in the passage.

EXAMPLE

"We all got up. We held our damp blankets more tightly around us. And we forced ourselves to move a few steps, to turn around where we were.

"Suddenly a cry rose up from the wagon, the cry of a wounded animal. Someone had just died."

—Elie Wiesel, *Night,*
translated by Stella Rodway

(5) Use single quotation marks to enclose a quotation within a quotation.

EXAMPLE

According to Ssu-ma Ch'ien, the people "all said, 'Cheng was not the only able one—his sister too has proved herself a woman of valor!'"

(6) When writing *dialogue* (a conversation), begin a new paragraph every time the speaker changes, and enclose each speaker's words in quotation marks.

EXAMPLE

"I don't want to marry, mother!" I said, not out of bashfulness or a show of coyness. I can't think why a girl should pretend to be coy. She had long since taught me about things not generally mentioned to girls.

"If you meet the right man, then marry him. Only if he's right for you!"

"I'm afraid no such man exists!"

—Zhang Jie, "Love Must Not Be Forgotten,"
translated by Gladys Yang

13d. Use quotation marks to enclose titles of short works, such as short stories, poems, essays, articles, songs, episodes of television series, and chapters and other parts of books.

TYPE OF NAME	EXAMPLE
Short Stories	"The Night Face Up" "A Problem"
Poems	"You May Forget But" "On Her Brother"
Essays	"A History of Eternity" "Essay on the Origin of Language"
Articles	"Mystery Mountain of the Inca"
Songs	"Crazy in Love" "Happy Birthday to You"
TV Episodes	"The Long Goodbye" "Here Comes the Sun"
Chapters of a Book	"Effective Visual Design" "Muslim Spain"

NOTE Neither italics nor quotation marks are used for the titles of major religious texts or for the titles of historical or legal documents.

EXAMPLES

the Bible

Code of Hammurabi

Bill of Rights

Monroe Doctrine

 For a list of titles that are italicized, see 13b.

ELLIPSIS POINTS

13e. Use three spaced periods called *ellipsis points* (. . .) to mark omissions from quoted material and pauses in a written passage.

ORIGINAL For a second the eyes of both followed it. It rolled a few inches toward him and stopped before his bare foot. In a hardly perceivable movement he kicked it away and again looked into her face.

—Isak Dinesen, "The Ring"

(1) If the quoted material that comes before the ellipsis points is not a complete sentence, use three ellipsis points with a space before the first point.

EXAMPLE
Describing the moment when Lise drops the ring, the narrator says, "It rolled a few inches . . . and stopped before his bare foot."

(2) If the quoted material that comes before the ellipsis points is a complete sentence, use an end mark before the ellipsis points.

EXAMPLE
The narrator says of the thief, "In a hardly perceivable movement he kicked it away. . . ."

(3) If one sentence or more is omitted, ellipsis points follow any end mark that precedes the omitted material.

EXAMPLE
The moment was tense: "For a second the eyes of both followed it. . . . In a hardly perceivable movement he kicked it away and again looked into her face."

(4) To show that a full line or more of poetry has been omitted, use a line of spaced periods that is as long as the line of poetry above it.

ORIGINAL   And many a council I have seen,
           Or reverend chapter with its dean,
               That, thus resolving wisely,
               Fell through like this precisely.
                   —Jean de La Fontaine, *Fables,*
                       translated by Elizur Wright, Jr.

ONE LINE   And many a council I have seen,
OMITTED   . . . .
               That, thus resolving wisely,
               Fell through like this precisely.

APOSTROPHES

Possessive Case

13f. The *possessive case* of a noun or a pronoun indicates ownership or relationship. Use an apostrophe in forming the possessive case of nouns and indefinite pronouns.

(1) To form the possessive of a singular noun, add an apostrophe and an *s*.

EXAMPLES
Roland's sword   the flower's petals

NOTE   When forming the possessive of a singular noun that ends in an *s* sound, add only an

apostrophe if the addition of *'s* will make the noun awkward to pronounce. Otherwise, add *'s*.

EXAMPLES
Ms. Rodgers' class   the witness's testimony

(2) To form the possessive of a plural noun ending in *s*, add only the apostrophe.

EXAMPLES
the players' uniforms   the volunteers' efforts

(3) Form the possessive of only the last word in a compound word, in the name of an organization or business, or in a word group showing joint possession.

EXAMPLES
brother-in-law's car
Ralph Merrill and Company's products
Macbeth and Lady Macbeth's plan

NOTE   When a possessive pronoun is part of a word group showing joint possession, each noun in the word group is also possessive.

EXAMPLE
Chen's, Ramona's, and **my** project

(4) Form the possessive of each noun in a word group showing individual possession of similar items.

EXAMPLE
Pushkin's, Tolstoy's, and Chekhov's plays

(5) Possessive forms of words indicating time, such as *minute, day, month,* and *year,* and words indicating amounts in cents or dollars require apostrophes.

EXAMPLES
four weeks' vacation   a dollar's worth

(6) To form the possessive of an indefinite pronoun, add an apostrophe and an *s*.

EXAMPLES
no one's fault   somebody else's jacket

Contractions

13g. Use an apostrophe to show where letters, words, or numbers have been omitted in a contraction.

EXAMPLES
let us . . . . **let's**   she would . . . . . **she'd**
you will . . . . . **you'll**   1998 . . . . **'98**

The word *not* can be shortened to *–n't* and added to a verb, usually without changing the spelling of the verb.

EXAMPLES
do not . . . . **don't**   should not . . . **shouldn't**
EXCEPTION
will not . . . **won't**

Plurals

13h. Use an apostrophe and an *s* to form the plurals of all lowercase letters, some uppercase letters, numerals, and some words referred to as words.

EXAMPLES

There are two *c*'s and two *m*'s in *accommodate*.
Try not to use so many *I*'s in your cover letter.
[Without the apostrophe, the plural of the pronoun *I* would spell *Is*.]

NOTE You may add only an *s* to form the plurals of words, numerals, and capital letters if the plural forms will not cause misreading. However, it is never wrong to use an apostrophe in such cases and is usually a good idea to do so.

EXAMPLE

The Black Death struck Europe in the mid **1300s** [*or* **1300's**].

HYPHENS

13i. Use a hyphen to divide a word at the end of a line.

- Do not divide a one-syllable word.

EXAMPLE

I **cringed** [*not* cring-ed] when I heard that tasteless joke.

- Divide a word only between syllables.

EXAMPLE

They read the contract and signed the **docu-ment** [*not* docum-ent].

- Divide an already hyphenated word at the hyphen.

EXAMPLE

Naomi expected to return without her **daughters-in-law** [*not* daugh-ters-in-law].

- Do not divide a word so that one letter stands alone.

EXAMPLE

Paradise Lost by John Milton is a famous English **epic** [*not* e-pic] that is based on the book of Genesis.

13j. Use a hyphen with compound numbers from twenty-one to ninety-nine and with fractions used as modifiers.

EXAMPLES

thirty-seven
a **three-fourths** majority [*but* **three fourths** of the voters]

13k. Use dashes to set off abrupt breaks in thought.

EXAMPLE

The playwright handles her material—I should say lack of material—quite well.

13l. Use dashes to set off appositives or parenthetical expressions that contain commas.

EXAMPLE

Several of the Russian writers—Pushkin, Tolstoy, and Chekhov, for example—led fascinating lives.

13m. Use a dash to set off an introductory list or group of examples.

EXAMPLE

The Song of Roland and *The Nibelungenlied* share many elements—oral origins, historical references, and fatal betrayals.

PARENTHESES

13n. Use parentheses to enclose informative or explanatory material of minor importance.

EXAMPLES

A *roman à clef* (literally, "novel with a key") is a novel about real people to whom the novelist has assigned fictitious names.
The Taj Mahal (see the photo on page 317) was completed in 1648. [The *s* in *see* is lowercase because the parenthetical sentence is within a complete sentence.]
The Taj Mahal was completed in 1648. (See the photo on page 317.) [The *S* in *See* is capitalized and a period follows *page 317* because the parenthetical sentence is not within another sentence but instead stands on its own.]

BRACKETS

13o. Use brackets to enclose an explanation within quoted or parenthetical material.

EXAMPLE

The newspaper article stated that "at the time of that Democratic National Convention [in Chicago in 1968] there were many protest groups operating in the United States."

14 SPELLING

UNDERSTANDING WORD STRUCTURE

Many English words are made up of roots and affixes (prefixes and suffixes).

Roots

The **root** of a word is the part that carries the word's core meaning.

ROOT	MEANING	EXAMPLES
–fin–	end, limit	final, infinite
–gram–	write, writing	grammar, epigram
–tract–	pull, draw	tractor, extract
–vit–	life	vitamin, vital

Prefixes

A **prefix** is one or more letters or syllables added to the beginning of a word or word part to create a new word.

PREFIX	MEANING	EXAMPLES
contra–	against	contradict, contrast
inter–	between, among	interstate, interact
mis–	not, wrongly	misfire, misspell
re–	back, again	reflect, refinance

Suffixes

A **suffix** is one or more letters or syllables added to the end of a word or word part to create a new word.

SUFFIX	MEANING	EXAMPLES
–fy	make, cause	verify, pacify
–ish	suggesting, like	smallish, childish
–ist	doer, believer	artist, humanist
–ty	quality, state	cruelty, certainty

SPELLING RULES

 NOTE Always keep in mind that the best way to be sure you have spelled a word correctly is to look the word up in a dictionary.

ie and *ei*

14a. Write *ie* when the sound is long e, except after *c*.

EXAMPLES
relieve   chief   field   conceit   deceive
EXCEPTIONS
either   leisure   neither   seize   protein

14b. Write *ei* when the sound is not long e.

EXAMPLES
reign   foreign   their   sovereign   weight
EXCEPTIONS
ancient   view   friend   mischief   conscience

 NOTE Rules 14a and 14b apply only when the *i* and the *e* are in the same syllable.

–cede, –ceed, and –sede

14c. The only English word ending in *–sede* is *supersede*. The only words ending in *–ceed* are *exceed*, *proceed*, and *succeed*. Most other words with this sound end in *–cede*.

EXAMPLES
concede   precede   recede   secede

Adding Prefixes

14d. When adding a prefix, do not change the spelling of the original word.

EXAMPLES
over + run = **over**run   mis + spell = **mis**spell

Adding Suffixes

14e. When adding the suffix *–ness* or *–ly*, do not change the spelling of the original word.

EXAMPLES
gentle + ness = gentle**ness**   final + ly = final**ly**

EXCEPTIONS

For most words ending in *y*, change the *y* to *i* before adding *–ness* or *–ly*.

heavy + ness = heav**iness**   ready + ly = read**ily**

NOTE One-syllable adjectives ending in *y* generally follow rule 14e.

EXAMPLES

shy + ness = shy**ness**   sly + ly = sly**ly**

14f. Drop the final silent *e* before a suffix beginning with a vowel.

EXAMPLES

awake + en = awak**en**   race + ing = rac**ing**

EXCEPTIONS

Keep the final silent *e*

- in a word ending in *ce* or *ge* before a suffix beginning with *a* or *o*
  peac**eable**   courag**eous**
- in *dye* and in *singe* before *–ing*
  dy**eing**   sing**eing**
- in *mile* before *–age*
  mil**eage**

NOTE When adding *–ing* to words that end in *ie*, drop the *e* and change the *i* to *y*.

EXAMPLES

die + ing = d**ying**   lie + ing = l**ying**

14g. Keep the final silent *e* before a suffix beginning with a consonant.

EXAMPLES

care + less = care**less**   sure + ty = sure**ty**

EXCEPTIONS

nine + th = nin**th**   judge + ment = judg**ment**
true + ly = tru**ly**   wise + dom = wis**dom**

14h. For words ending in *y* preceded by a consonant, change the *y* to *i* before any suffix that does not begin with *i*.

EXAMPLES

heavy + est = heav**iest**
accompany + ment = accompan**iment**
verify + ing = verif**ying**

14i. For words ending in *y* preceded by a vowel, keep the *y* when adding a suffix.

EXAMPLES

enjoy + ing = enjo**ying**   play + ed = pla**yed**

EXCEPTIONS

day + ly = da**ily**   lay + ed = la**id**
pay + ed = pa**id**   say + ed = sa**id**

14j. Double the final consonant before a suffix that begins with a vowel if the word *both* (1) has only one syllable or has the accent on the last syllable *and* (2) ends in a single consonant preceded by a single vowel.

EXAMPLES

rap + ing = ra**pping**   refer + ed = refe**rred**

EXCEPTIONS

- For words ending in *w* or *x*, do not double the final consonant.
  bow + ed = bow**ed**   tax + able = tax**able**
- For words ending in *c*, add *k* before the suffix instead of doubling the *c*.
  picnic + k + ing = picnic**king**

FORMING THE PLURALS OF NOUNS

14k. Remembering the following rules will help you spell the plural forms of nouns.

(1) For most nouns, add *–s*.

EXAMPLES

beagle**s**   senator**s**   taxi**s**   Saxon**s**

(2) For nouns ending in *s, x, z, ch,* or *sh,* add *–es.*

EXAMPLES

glass**es**   waltz**es**   brush**es**   Perez**es**

(3) For nouns ending in *y* preceded by a vowel, add *–s.*

EXAMPLES

journey**s**   decoy**s**   Saturday**s**   Kelley**s**

(4) For nouns ending in *y* preceded by a consonant, change the *y* to *i* and add *–es.*

EXAMPLES

comed**ies**   cavit**ies**   theor**ies**   sk**ies**

EXCEPTIONS

For proper nouns, add *–s.*
Gregory**s**   Kimberly**s**

(5) For some nouns ending in *f* or *fe,* add *–s.* For others, change the *f* or *fe* to *v* and add *–es.*

EXAMPLES

belief**s**   loa**ves**   giraffe**s**   wi**ves**

EXCEPTIONS

For proper nouns, add *–s.*
DeGroff**s**   Rolfe**s**

(6) For nouns ending in *o* preceded by a vowel, add *–s.*

EXAMPLES

radio**s**   cameo**s**   shampoo**s**   Matsuo**s**

(7) For nouns ending in *o* preceded by a consonant, add *–es*.

EXAMPLES
torped**oes**   ech**oes**   her**oes**   potat**oes**

For some common nouns ending in *o* preceded by a consonant, especially those referring to music, and for proper nouns, add only an *–s*.

EXAMPLES
phot**os**   haird**os**   sol**os**   sopran**os**   Spir**os**

(8) The plurals of a few nouns are formed in irregular ways.

EXAMPLES
g**ee**se   m**e**n   child**ren**   m**i**ce   t**ee**th

(9) For a few nouns, the singular and the plural forms are the same.

EXAMPLES
deer   series   Chinese   Sioux

(10) For most compound nouns, form the plural of only the last word of the compound.

EXAMPLES
courthous**es**   seat belt**s**   four-year-old**s**

(11) For compound nouns in which one of the words is modified by the other word or words, form the plural of the noun modified.

EXAMPLES
son**s**-in-law   passer**s**by   mountain goat**s**

(12) For some nouns borrowed from other languages, the plural is formed as in the original languages. In a few cases, two plural forms are acceptable.

EXAMPLES
analysis—analys**es**   phenomenon—phenomen**a** *or* phenomenon**s**

(13) To form the plurals of figures, most uppercase letters, signs, and words referred to as words, add an *–s* or both an apostrophe and an *–s*.

EXAMPLES
1500**s** *or* 1500**'s**   B**s** *or* B**'s**
$**s** *or* $**'s**   *and***s** *or* *and***'s**

> **NOTE** To avoid confusion, add both an apostrophe and an *–s* to form the plural of all lowercase letters, certain uppercase letters, and some words used as words.

EXAMPLES
The word *fictitious* contains three *i***'s**. [Without an apostrophe, the plural of *i* could be confused with the word *is*.]
Sebastian usually makes straight A**'s**. [Without an apostrophe, the plural of *A* could be confused with the word *As*.]
Because I mistakenly thought Isak Dinesen was a man, I used *his***'s** instead of *her***'s** in my paper. [Without an apostrophe, the plural of *his* would look like the word *hiss* and the plural of *her* would look like the pronoun *hers*.]

> **NOTE** In names, ***diacritical marks*** (marks that show pronunciation) and capitalization are as essential to correct spelling as the letters themselves. If you're not sure about the spelling of a name, check with the person whose name it is, or consult a reference source.

EXAMPLES
François   Lagerlöf
Van Doren   van Gogh
Márquez   Marín
de Vega   al-Khansa

---

15 GLOSSARY OF USAGE

The Glossary of Usage is an alphabetical listing of expressions with definitions, explanations, and examples. Some of the examples are labeled *standard, nonstandard, formal,* or *informal.* The label **standard** or **formal** identifies usage that is appropriate in serious writing and speaking (such as in compositions and speeches). The label **informal** indicates standard English that is generally used in conversation and in everyday writing such as personal letters. The label **nonstandard** identifies usage that does not follow the guidelines of standard English usage.

accept, except   *Accept* is a verb meaning "to receive." *Except* may be a verb meaning "to leave out" or a preposition meaning "excluding."

EXAMPLES
Why doesn't Achilles **accept** Hector's request for a proper burial? [verb]
The contest rules **except** employees of the sponsoring firm and their families. [verb]
Our group will donate all of the food **except** the cans on the top shelf. [preposition]

affect, effect   *Affect* is a verb meaning "to influence." *Effect* may be either a verb meaning "to bring about or to accomplish" or a noun meaning "the result [of an action]."

EXAMPLES
How does the conversation on the train **affect** the woman's view of her husband? [verb]
The student council hopes to **effect** changes in the recycling program. [verb]
Winning the Nobel Peace Prize had a positive **effect** on the organization's image. [noun]

all ready, already   *All ready* means "all prepared." *Already* means "previously."

EXAMPLES
Are you **all ready** for the audition?
We have **already** read "The Guitar."

all right   *All right* means "satisfactory," "unhurt; safe," "correct," or, in reply to a question or to preface a remark, "yes." *Alright* is a misspelling.

EXAMPLES
Does this look **all right** [*not* alright]?
Oh, **all right** [*not* alright], you can go.

all the farther, all the faster   Avoid using these expressions in formal situations. Use *as far as* or *as fast as.*

EXAMPLE
Is that **as fast as** [*not* all the faster] Chris can run?

all together, altogether   *All together* means "everyone in the same place." *Altogether* means "entirely."

EXAMPLES
The runners were **all together** at the starting line.
To say that the king wants Tristan to leave is not **altogether** true.

allusion, illusion   An *allusion* is an indirect reference to something. An *illusion* is a mistaken idea or a misleading appearance.

EXAMPLES
The Great Denial that Dante mentions is likely an **allusion** to the abdication of Pope Celestine V.
Thor is flabbergasted to discover that the king's stronghold is just an **illusion.**
People invested in the company under the **illusion** that it would be successful.

a lot   Avoid this expression in formal situations by using *many* or *much.*

EXAMPLE
Many [*not* a lot] of my friends work part time after school and on weekends.

already   See **all ready, already.**

altogether   See **all together, altogether.**

among   See **between, among.**

and etc.   *Etc.* stands for the Latin words *et cetera,* meaning "and others" or "and so forth." Always avoid using *and* before *etc.* In general, avoid using *etc.* in formal situations. Use one of its meanings instead.

EXAMPLE
We are comparing the main female characters in Greek and Roman epics: Helen, Penelope, Dido **and others** [*or* **etc.** *but not* and etc.].

any one, anyone   The expression *any one* specifies one member of a group. *Anyone* means "one person, no matter which."

EXAMPLES
Any one of these plans might work.
Anyone who finishes the writing may read quietly.

as   See **like, as.**

as if   See **like, as if.**

at   Avoid using *at* after a construction beginning with *where.*

NONSTANDARD	Where does the last servant hide his gold at?
STANDARD	Where does the last servant hide his gold?

a while, awhile   *A while* means "a period of time." *Awhile* means "for a short time."

EXAMPLES
We waited for quite **a while** before being seated.
The hikers rested **awhile** and then continued their trek.

bad, badly   *Bad* is an adjective. *Badly* is an adverb. In standard English, *bad* should follow a sense verb, such as *feel, look, sound, taste,* or *smell,* or other linking verb.

EXAMPLE
The prospects for fair weather look **bad** [*not* badly].

because   In formal situations, do not use the construction *reason . . . because.* Instead, use *reason . . . that.*

EXAMPLE
The **reason** Perceval stays quiet about the Grail is **that** [*not* because] he thinks it would be rude to speak up.

being as, being that   Avoid using either of these expressions for *since* or *because.*

EXAMPLE
Because [*not* being as *or* being that] Perceval is a knight, we expect him to behave chivalrously.

beside, besides *Beside* means "by the side of" or "next to." *Besides* means "in addition to" or "other than" or "moreover."

EXAMPLES
Returning to her place, Mia found a note **beside** her cafeteria tray.
No one **besides** Sarah knows the correct answer.
Let me pay for lunch; **besides,** you paid last time.

between, among Use *between* to refer to only two items or to more than two when comparing each item individually to each of the others.

EXAMPLES
The reward money will be divided **between** Chang and Marta.
Sasha explained the difference **between** assonance, consonance, and alliteration. [Each item is compared individually to each of the others.]

Use *among* to refer to more than two items when you are not considering each item in relation to each other item individually.

EXAMPLE
The reward money will be divided **among** the four girls.

bring, take *Bring* means "to come carrying something." *Take* means "to go carrying something."

EXAMPLES
I'll **bring** my copy of *The Sorrows of Young Werther* when I come over.
Please **take** the model of the Trojan horse to the library.

bust, busted Avoid using these words as verbs. Instead, use a form of *break* or *burst,* depending on the meaning.

EXAMPLES
The window is **broken** [*not* busted].
The water main has **burst** [*not* busted] open.

can, may Use *can* to express ability. Use *may* to express possibility.

EXAMPLES
Can you play the guitar?
It **may** rain later.

cannot (can't) help but Avoid using *but* and the infinitive form of a verb after the expression *cannot (can't) help*. Instead, use a gerund alone.

NONSTANDARD	I can't help but laugh when I look at that photograph.
STANDARD	I can't help **laughing** when I look at that photograph.

compare, contrast Used with *to, compare* means "to look for similarities between." Used with *with, compare* means "to look for both similarities and differences between." *Contrast* is always used to point out differences.

EXAMPLES
The poet **compares** the person seeing the cat **to** a madman and an insect in amber.
We **compared** Jamaica Kincaid's style **with** that of Zhang Jie.
My paper will **contrast** Omar Khayyám's and Saadi's different attitudes toward worldly things.

could of See **of.**

double subject Avoid using an unnecessary pronoun after the subject of a sentence.

EXAMPLE
Sappho [*not* Sappho she] wrote "Don't Ask Me What to Wear."

due to Avoid using *due to* for "because of" or "owing to."

EXAMPLE
All schools were closed **because of** [*not* due to] inclement weather.

effect See **affect, effect.**

either, neither *Either* usually means "one or the other of two." In referring to more than two, use *any one* or *any* instead. *Neither* usually means "not one or the other of two." In referring to more than two, use *none* instead.

EXAMPLES
Either of the two quotations would be appropriate to use at the beginning of your speech.
You should be able to find ample information about **any one** of those four poets.
Neither of the Perez twins is in school today.
None of the seniors have voted yet.

etc. See **and etc.**

every day, everyday *Every day* means "each day." *Everyday* means "daily," "ordinary," or "usual."

EXAMPLES
Every day presents its own challenges.
The party will be casual; wear **everyday** clothes.

every one, everyone *Every one* specifies every single person or thing of those named. *Everyone* means "everybody, all of the people named."

EXAMPLES
Sei Shōnagon wrote **every one** of these entries.
Did **everyone** read "Embarassing Things"?

except See **accept, except.**

farther, further Use *farther* to express physical distance. Use *further* to express abstract relationships of degree or quantity.

EXAMPLES

Your house is **farther** from school than mine is.

The United Nations members decided that **further** debate was unnecessary.

fewer, less Use *fewer* to modify a plural noun and *less* to modify a singular noun.

EXAMPLES

Fewer students are going out for football this year.

Now I spend **less** time watching TV.

good, well Avoid using the adjective *good* to modify an action verb. Instead, use the adverb *well,* meaning "capably" or "satisfactorily."

EXAMPLE

We did **well** [*not* good] on the exam.

Used as an adjective, *well* means "in good health" or "satisfactory in appearance or condition."

EXAMPLES

I feel **well.**

It's eight o'clock, and all is **well.**

had of See **of.**

had ought, hadn't ought Do not use *had* or *hadn't* with *ought.*

EXAMPLES

Your application **ought** [*not* had ought] to have been sent in earlier.

She **ought not** [*not* hadn't ought] to swim so soon after eating lunch.

illusion See **allusion, illusion.**

imply, infer *Imply* means "to suggest indirectly." *Infer* means "to interpret" or "to draw a conclusion."

EXAMPLES

Although he sounds brave, Catullus **implies** that he feels uncertain about rejecting his love.

Based on his questions, we can **infer** that the poet would welcome her back.

in, in to, into *In* generally shows location. In the construction *in to, in* is an adverb followed by the preposition *to. Into* generally shows direction.

EXAMPLES

He had left his class ring **in** the locker room.

A kind person turned it **in to** the main office.

After finding his brothers dead, Yudhistra waded **into** the lake to perform their funeral rites.

infer See **imply, infer.**

irregardless, regardless *Irregardless* is nonstandard. Use *regardless* instead.

EXAMPLE

Regardless [*not* irregardless] of the danger, he continued his journey.

its, it's *Its* is the possessive form of *it. It's* is the contraction of *it is* or *it has.*

EXAMPLES

The community is proud of **its** school system.

It's [it is] a symbol of peace.

It's [it has] been cooler today.

kind of, sort of In formal situations, avoid using these terms for the adverb *somewhat* or *rather.*

| INFORMAL | The end of the story is kind of ambiguous. |
| FORMAL | The end of the story is **rather** [*or* **somewhat**] ambiguous. |

kind of a(n), sort of a(n) In formal situations, omit the *a(n).*

| INFORMAL | What kind of a poem is "Invitation to the Voyage"? |
| FORMAL | What **kind of** poem is "Invitation to the Voyage"? |

kind(s), sort(s), type(s) With the singular form of each of these nouns, use *this* or *that.* With the plural form, use *these* or *those.*

EXAMPLES

This type of engine performs more economically than any of **those types.**

less See **fewer, less.**

lie, lay The verb *lie* means "to rest" or "to stay, to recline, or to remain in a certain state or position." Its principal parts are *lie, lying, lay,* and *lain. Lie* never takes an object. The verb *lay* means "to put [something] in a place." Its principal parts are *lay, laying, laid,* and *laid. Lay* usually takes an object.

EXAMPLES

The statue shows the Buddha **lying** on a couch as he achieves enlightenment. [no object]

Visitors to the shrine **lay** flowers at the base of the statue. [*Flowers* is the object of *lay.*]

like, as In formal situations, do not use *like* for *as* to introduce a subordinate clause.

| INFORMAL | Everything turned out just like the seer predicted. |
| FORMAL | Everything turned out just **as** the seer predicted. |

like, as if In formal situations, avoid using the preposition *like* for the compound conjunction *as if* or *as though* to introduce a subordinate clause.

INFORMAL	The heavy footsteps sounded like they were coming nearer.
FORMAL	The heavy footsteps sounded **as if** [*or* **as though**] they were coming nearer.

might of, must of See **of.**

neither See **either, neither.**

nor See **or, nor.**

of *Of* is a preposition. Do not use *of* in place of *have* after verbs such as *could, should, would, might, must,* and *ought* [*to*]. Also, do not use *had of* for *had.*

EXAMPLES
If I **had** [*not* had of] known about the shortcut, I **would have** [*not* would of] been here sooner.

Avoid using *of* after other prepositions such as *inside, off,* and *outside.*

EXAMPLE
This hymn was found **inside** [*not* inside of] a tomb.

off, off of Do not use *off* or *off of* for *from.*

EXAMPLE
You can get a program **from** [*not* off of] the usher.

on to, onto In the expression *on to, on* is an adverb and *to* is a preposition. *Onto* is a preposition.

EXAMPLES
The lecturer moved **on to** her next main idea.
She walked **onto** the stage.

or, nor Use *or* with *either;* use *nor* with *neither.*

EXAMPLES
The list of authors does not include **either** Octavio Paz **or** [*not* nor] Gabriel García Márquez.
Neither Octavio Paz **nor** Gabriel García Márquez is on the list of authors.

ought See **had ought, hadn't ought.**

ought to of See **of.**

raise See **rise, raise.**

reason . . . because See **because.**

refer back Since the prefix *re–* in *refer* means "back," adding *back* is generally unnecessary.

EXAMPLE
Aeneas's speech **refers** [*not* refers back] to his escape from Troy.

rise, raise The verb *rise* means "to go up" or "to get up." Its principal parts are *rise, rising, rose,* and *risen. Rise* never takes an object. The verb *raise* means "to cause [something] to rise" or "to lift up." Its principal parts are *raise, raising, raised,* and *raised. Raise* usually takes an object.

EXAMPLES
Her blood pressure **rose** as she waited. [no object]
Roland **raised** the horn for one final blast. [*Horn* is the object of *raised.*]

should of See **of.**

sit, set The verb *sit* means "to rest in an upright, seated position." Its principal parts are *sit, sitting, sat,* and *sat. Sit* seldom takes an object. The verb *set* means "to put [something] in a place." Its principal parts are *set, setting, set,* and *set. Set* usually takes an object.

EXAMPLES
The women **sit** in the parlor. [no object]
Please **set** the groceries on the table. [*Groceries* is the object of *set.*]

some, somewhat In formal situations, avoid using *some* to mean "to some extent." Use *somewhat.*

EXAMPLE
Ivan Markovitch was somewhat surprised [*not* surprised some] by Sasha's request for one hundred rubles.

sort(s) See **kind(s), sort(s), type(s)** and **kind of a(n), sort of a(n).**

sort of See **kind of, sort of.**

take See **bring, take.**

than, then *Than* is a conjunction used in comparisons. *Then* is an adverb meaning "at that time" or "next."

EXAMPLES
Oedipus ends the play wiser but unhappier **than** he once was.
He had, after all, unknowingly murdered his father and **then** married his mother.

that See **who, which, that.**

their, there, they're *Their* is a possessive form of *they.* As an adverb, *there* means "at that place." *There* is also used to begin a sentence. *They're* is the contraction of *they are.*

EXAMPLES
The Trojans mourned **their** dead hero.
The whole club was **there** for the banquet.
There are three reasons why we should wait.
They're my closest friends.

Language Handbook

theirs, there's *Theirs* is a possessive form of the pronoun *they*. *There's* is the contraction of *there is*.

EXAMPLES
The treasure is **theirs** now.
There's an allusion to the Bible in the poem.

them Do not use *them* as an adjective. Use *those*.

EXAMPLE
Have you seen **those** [*not* them] murals by Judith Baca at the art museum?

then See **than, then.**

there See **their, there, they're.**

there's See **theirs, there's.**

they're See **their, there, they're.**

this here, that there Avoid using *here* or *there* after *this* or *that*.

EXAMPLE
This [*not* this here] poem was written by the Indian playwright Kalidasa.

try and, try to Use *try to*, not *try and*.

EXAMPLE
Let's **try to** [*not* try and] reproduce one of these beautiful Moorish tile patterns.

type, type of Avoid using the noun *type* as an adjective. Add *of* after *type*.

EXAMPLE
What **type of** [*not* type] characters appear in both Zen and Christian parables?

type(s) See **kind(s), sort(s), type(s).**

ways Use *way*, not *ways*, when referring to distance.

EXAMPLE
The Phoenicians sailed a long **way** [*not* ways] to reach what is now northwestern France.

well See **good, well.**

when, where Do not use *when* or *where* to begin a definition.

NONSTANDARD	A caesura is where you break or pause in a line of poetry.
STANDARD	A caesura is **a break or pause in a line of poetry.**

where Do not use *where* in place of *that*.

EXAMPLE
I read **that** [*not* where] you won a scholarship.

where . . . at See **at.**

who, which, that *Who* refers to persons only. *Which* refers to things only. *That* may refer to either persons or things.

EXAMPLES
In the *Epic of Gilgamesh,* Utnapishtim is the character **who** [*or* that] resembles Noah.
The Wei dynasty, **which** lasted from A.D. 386 to around 535, was started by foreign nomads.
Where is the set of cups **that** you made in pottery class?

who's, whose *Who's* is the contraction of *who is* or *who has*. *Whose* is the possessive form of *who*.

EXAMPLES
Well, look **who's** [who is] here!
Who's [who has] read all of the play?
Whose treasure is it?

would of See **of.**

your, you're *Your* is a possessive form of *you*. *You're* is the contraction of *you are*.

EXAMPLES
Is that **your** car?
I can see that **you're** tired.

1236 Resource Center Language Handbook

Glossary

The glossary that follows is an alphabetical list of words found in the selections in this book. Use this glossary just as you would use a dictionary—to find out the meanings of unfamiliar words. (Some technical, foreign, and most obscure words in this book are not listed here but instead are defined for you in the footnotes that accompany many of the selections.)

Many words in the English language have more than one meaning. This glossary gives the meanings that apply to the words as they are used in the selections in this book. Words closely related in form and meaning are usually listed together in one entry (for instance, compassion and compassionate), and the definition is given for the first form.

The following abbreviations are used:

adj.	adjective
adv.	adverb
n.	noun
pl.	plural
v.	verb

Each word's pronunciation is given in parentheses. A guide to the pronunciation symbols appears at the bottom of every other page. For more information about the words in this glossary or for information about words not listed here, consult a dictionary.

A

absurd (ab·surd′) *adj.:* so unreasonable as to be ridiculous; meaningless.
acquittal (ə·kwit′′l) *n.:* act of clearing a person of charges of wrongdoing.
adjured (ə·joord′) *v.:* commanded as under oath.
afflicted (ə·flikt′id) *v.:* brought suffering upon.
affront (ə·frunt′) *n.:* intentional insult.
allay (a·lā′) *v.:* to relieve; calm.
ameliorate (ə·mēl′yə·rāt′) *v.:* make better.

amorous (am′ə·rəs) *adj.:* showing love or desire.
ample (am′pəl) *adj.:* roomy; large.
annihilated (ə·nī′ə·lāt′id) *v.:* destroyed completely.
apathy (ap′ə·thē) *n.:* lack of interest or feeling; indifference.
apparition (ap′ə·rish′ən) *n.:* ghost or ghostlike figure that appears unexpectedly.
appeasing (ə·pēz′iŋ) *v.* used as *n.:* relieving; quieting.
arduous (är′joo·əs) *adj.:* difficult.
assiduously (ə·sij′oo·əs·lē) *adv.:* diligently; industriously; painstakingly.
atrophy (a′trə·fē) *v.* shrink or waste away.
avowal (ə·vou′əl) *n.:* acknowledgment.

B

bedlam (bed′ləm) *n.:* chaos; complete disorder.
beguiled (bē·gīld′) *v.:* deceived.
benediction (ben′ə·dik′shən) *n.:* blessing; gift.
beneficent (bə·nef′ə·sənt) *adj.:* kind; helpful.
bounty (boun′tē) *n.:* reward; generosity.

C

cache (kash) *n.:* hiding place for goods or valuables.
cajoled (kə·jōld′) *v.:* coaxed with flattery, soothing words, or promises.
calamitous (kə·lam′ə·təs) *adj.:* disastrous.
candor (kan′dər) *n.:* honesty and frankness; fair, unbiased attitude.
cataclysms (kat′ə·kliz′əmz) *n. pl.:* violent upheavals that cause sudden changes.
censuring (sen′shər·iŋ) *v.* used as *n.:* expressing strong disapproval of.
chastise (chas·tīz′) *v.:* punish; criticize harshly.
clambered (klam′bərd) *v.:* climbed with difficulty.

---

at, āte, cär; ten, ēve; is, īce; gō, hôrn, look, tool; oil, out; up, fur; ə *for unstressed vowels, as* a *in* ago, u *in* focus; ′ *as in* Latin (lat′′n); chin; she; thin; *the*; ŋ *as in* ring (riŋ); zh *as in* azure (azh′ər)

commiserate (kə·miz′ər·āt′) v.: feel pity for or sympathize with.

complacent (kəm·plā′sənt) adj.: self-satisfied; smug.

compunction (kəm·puŋk′shən) n.: feeling of remorse or guilt.

condemned (kən·demd′) v.: judged guilty.

confiscate (kän′fis·kāt) v.: seize by authority.

convulsed (kən·vulst′) v. used as adj.: shaken uncontrollably, as with laughter or weeping.

covenant (kuv′ə·nənt) n.: solemn agreement or contract.

D

debilitating (dē·bil′ə·tāt′iŋ) v. used as adj.: weakening.

decrepit (dē·krep′it) adj.: worn-out by old age.

deluge (del′yōōj′) n.: great flood.

denigration (den′ə·grā·shən) n.: devaluation; belittlement.

deployed (dē·ploid′) v.: stationed military troops.

derision (di·rizh′ən) n.: ridicule; scorn.

despicable (di·spik′ə·bəl) adj.: hateful; abominable.

destitute (des′tə·tōōt′) adj.: abandoned.

dexterously (deks′tər·əs·lē) adv.: nimbly.

diffuse (di·fyōōs′) adj.: not focused; scattered.

disconcert (dis′kən·surt′) v.: unsettle; confuse.

discourse (dis′kôrs′) n.: conversation of ideas.

discretion (di·skresh′ən) n.: prudence; quality of being cautious about one's behavior.

disdain (dis·dān′) n.: scorn.

disillusion (dis′i·lōō′zhən) n.: disenchantment; disappointment.

dispel (di·spel′) v.: remove; drive away.

dissipated (dis′ə·pāt′id) adj.: wasted by excessive drinking and gambling.

dominion (də·min′yən) n.: rule; absolute authority.

duress (dōō·res′) n.: pressure; force.

E

edifying (ed′i·fī′iŋ) v. used as adj.: morally instructive.

efface (ə·fās′) v.: erase.

elated (ē·lāt′id) v. used as adj.: very happy.

eloquence (el′ə·kwəns) n.: graceful and persuasive speech.

emaciated (ē·mā′shē·āt′id) v. used as adj.: extremely thin; wasted away.

emulate (em′yōō·lāt′) v.: imitate.

endure (en·door′) v.: withstand; undergo.

enigma (i·nig′mə) n.: something baffling.

enmity (en′mə·tē) n.: hostility.

enterprise (ent′ər·prīz′) n.: undertaking.

entreat (en·trēt′) v.: beg; plead with.

eradicate (ē·rad′i·kāt′) v.: remove all traces of; erase.

errant (er′ənt) adj.: rambling; wandering off course or beyond set limits (often used in the phrase *knight-errant*).

eschew (es·chōō′) v.: shun; avoid.

expedient (ek·spē′dē·ənt) n.: something that is useful or helpful.

exulting (eg·zult′iŋ) v. used as adv.: rejoicing greatly.

F

feigned (fānd) v.: pretended.

fervent (fur′vənt) adj.: very intense in feeling.

fidelity (fə·del′ə·tē) n.: loyalty.

forged (fôrjd) v.: made a metal object by heating and hammering.

formidable (fôr′mə·də·bəl) adj.: causing fear.

fostered (fôs′tərd) v.: brought up in a nurturing way.

furtively (fur′tiv·lē) adv.: secretly; in a sneaky way.

futile (fyōōt′'l) adj.: useless.

G

grandiloquent (gran·dil′ə·kwənt) adj.: pompous or overblown in speech or writing.

H

habitual (hə·bich′ōō·əl) adj.: done repeatedly by habit.

I

imminent (im′ə·nənt) adj.: about to happen.

immutable (i·myōōt′ə·bəl) adj.: unable to be changed.

impartial (im·pär′shəl) adj.: not favoring one thing over another.

imperceptible (im′pər·sep′tə·bəl) *adj.*: not plain or distinct.

impervious (im·pʉr′vē·əs) *adj.*: unaffected by.

impetuous (im·pech′o͞o·əs) *adj.*: impulsive; forceful.

implacable (im·plak′ə·bəl) *adj.*: incapable of being pacified.

implored (im·plôrd′) *v.*: begged earnestly for.

impregnable (im·preg′nə·bəl) *adj.*: incapable of being captured.

incantations (in′kan·tā′shənz) *n. pl.*: chants or songs with magical qualities.

incongruous (in·käŋ′gro͞o·əs) *adj.*: not fitting; out of place.

incredulity (in′krə·do͞o′lə·tē) *n.*: disbelief; doubt.

indignation (in′dig·nā′shən) *n.*: anger resulting from injustice.

inert (in·ʉrt′) *adj.*: lacking the power to move or act.

inextricable (in·eks′tri·kə·bəl) *adj.*: unable to be disentangled.

ingenious (in·jēn′yəs) *adj.*: original; clever.

inscrutable (in·skro͞ot′ə·bəl) *adj.*: hard to understand; unknowable.

insignificant (in′sig·nif′i·kənt) *adj.*: unimportant.

instigation (in′stə·gā′shən) *n.*: urging on to an evil act.

insuperable (in·so͞o′pər·ə·bəl) *adj.*: impossible to overcome.

interminable (in·tʉr′mi·nə·bəl) *adj.*: endless.

interrogating (in·ter′ə·gāt′iŋ) *v.*: used as *adj.*: inspecting; evaluating.

intimation (in′tə·mā′shən) *n.*: hint.

intransigence (in·tran′sə·jəns) *n.*: stubbornness; refusal to compromise.

intrepid (in·trep′id) *adj.*: fearless; extremely brave.

inverted (in·vʉrt′ed) *v.* used as *adj.*: turned upside down.

invoking (in·vōk′iŋ) *v.* used as *adj.*: calling upon.

irreproachable (ir′i·prō′chə·bəl) *adj.*: innocent.

itinerant (ī·tin′ər·ənt) *adj.*: traveling; moving from place to place.

J

juxtaposed (juks′tə·pōzd′) *v.* used as *adj.*: placed side by side.

K

kindred (kin′drid) *n.*: family; relatives.

L

labyrinth (lab′ə·rinth′) *n.*: maze; a complex puzzling arrangement.

levity (lev′i·tē) *n.*: lack of seriousness; disrespectful lightness or improper gaiety.

livid (liv′id) *adj.*: grayish blue, as if bruised.

loath (lōth) *adj.*: reluctant.

lucid (lo͞o′sid) *adj.*: rational.

M

manifest (man′ə·fest′) *adj.*: revealed.

melancholy (mel′ən·käl′ē) *n.*: sadness.

meticulously (mə·tik′yo͞o·ləs·lē) *adv.*: very carefully.

mundane (mun·dān′) *adj.*: pertaining to the world.

municipal (myo͞o·nis′ə·pəl) *adj.*: of local government.

N

nascent (nas′ənt) *adj.*: starting to grow.

nocturnal (näk·tʉr′nəl) *adj.*: of or pertaining to the night.

O

obscurity (əb·skyoor′ə·tē) *n.*: lack of fame.

ominous (äm′ə·nəs) *adj.*: seeming to threaten evil or misfortune; sinister.

omnipotent (äm·nip′ə·tənt) *adj.*: all-powerful.

opaque (ō·pāk′) *adj.*: not allowing light to penetrate.

---

at, āte, cär; ten, ēve; is, īce; gō, hôrn, look, to͞ol; oil, out; up, fʉr; ə *for unstressed vowels, as* a *in* ago, u *in* focus; ′ *as in* Latin (lat′′n); chin; she; thin; *the*; ŋ *as in* ring (riŋ); zh *as in* azure (azh′ər)

P

paraphernalia (par'ə·fər·nāl'yə) *n. pl.*: accessories; equipment.

pathological (path'ə·läj'i·kəl) *adj.*: diseased.

pedant (ped''nt) *n.*: teacher who emphasizes details or rules instead of genuine learning.

penchant (pen'chənt) *n.*: fondness for.

pensive (pen'siv) *adj.*: thinking seriously.

perfidious (pər·fid'ē·əs) *adj.*: wicked; unfaithful.

permeated (pʉr'mē·āt'id) *v.*: spread throughout.

perpetrated (pʉr'pə·trāt'id) *v.*: committed; done.

perpetually (pər·pech'oo·əl·ē) *adv.*: constantly.

pestilence (pes'tə·ləns) *n.*: deadly disease.

petrified (pe'trə·fīd') *adj.*: paralyzed with shock or fear.

pettiness (pet'ē·nis) *n.*: insignificance.

piety (pī'ə·tē) *n.*: religious devotion.

piqued (pēkd) *v.* used as *adj.*: angry or irritated.

pivot (piv'ət) *n.*: central point on which something else depends.

plaintively (plān'tiv·lē) *adv.*: sadly; sorrowfully.

plight (plīt) *n.*: unfortunate condition.

pompous (päm'pəs) *adj.*: self-important.

predatory (pred'ə·tôr'ē) *adj.*: relating to hunting and feeding on other animals.

predominated (prē·däm'ə·nāt'id) *v.*: took control.

prescience (presh'əns) *n.*: knowledge of something before it happens.

prevaricate (pri·var'i·kāt') *v.*: avoid the truth; lie.

primal (prī'məl) *adj.*: original.

pristine (pris·tēn') *adj.*: pure; unspoiled.

procured (prō·kyoord') *v.*: secured; brought about by effort.

prodigious (prō·dij'əs) *adj.*: very large; huge.

proliferation (prō·lif'ə·rā'shən) *n.*: rapid spread.

propitiate (prō·pish'ē·āt') *v.*: pacify; satisfy.

prudent (proo'dənt) *adj.*: careful in behavior; cautious.

R

rancid (ran'sid) *adj.*: spoiled.

rancor (raŋ'kər) *n.*: anger; bitter hatred.

razing (rāz'iŋ) *v.* used as *n.*: tearing down completely.

reckoning (rek'ən·iŋ) *n.*: assignment of rewards or punishments for actions.

recompense (rek'əm·pens') *v.*: repay; reward.

reiterating (rē·it'ə·rāt'iŋ) *v.*: repeating.

replenish (ri·plen'ish) *v.*: refill or make complete again; resupply.

reprehensible (rep'ri·hen'sə·bəl) *adj.*: deserving of criticism or blame.

reprimand (rep'rə·mand') *n.*: rebuke; scolding.

reproach (ri·prōch') *v.*: scold; express disapproval.

reprobation (rep'rə·bā'shən) *n.*: disapproval.

reproved (ri·proovd') *v.*: expressed disapproval of.

resolutely (rez'ə·loot'lē) *adv.*: firmly; determinedly.

resolution (rez'ə·loo'shən) *n.*: firmness of purpose.

revere (ri·vir') *v.*: respect deeply.

ruefully (roo'fəl·ē) *adv.*: sorrowfully; with regret.

S

sabotage (sab'ə·täzh') *v.*: damage.

scathing (skā'thiŋ) *adj.*: extremely critical or severe.

scorned (skôrnd) *v.*: rejected.

scrupulous (skroop'yə·ləs) *adj.*: acting in a strictly right or proper way.

scrutinized (skroot''n·īzd') *v.*: looked at closely and carefully.

siege (sēj) *n.*: sustained attempt to obtain control.

sinister (sin'is·tər) *adj.*: threatening harm or evil.

slanderous (slan'dər·əs) *adj.*: insulting to others.

solace (säl'is) *n.*: comfort in times of trouble.

solicitously (sə·lis'ə·təs·lē) *adv.*: in a caring or concerned way.

somber (säm'bər) *adj.*: dark; dismal.

sonorous (sə·nôr'əs) *adj.*: having a rich, full sound; grand-sounding.

splaying (splā'iŋ) *v.* used as *adj.*: flattening; spreading out.

staidness (stād'nəs) *n.*: soberness.

stealthily (stelth'ə·lē) *adv.*: in a sly way.

stoically (stō'i·kəl·lē) *adv.*: calmly; without emotion.

strictures (strik'chərz) *n. pl.*: criticisms.

suavely (swäv'lē) *adv.*: smoothly.

subdue (səb·doo') *v.*: conquer; cultivate.

submissiveness (səb·mis'iv·nis) *n.*: obedience; lack of resistance.

subsided (səb·sīd'id) *v.*: sank; moved to a lower level.

subversive (səb·vʉr'siv) *adj.*: seeking to overthrow a government or other established system.

sufficed (sə·fīst') *v.*: satisfied; had a need met.

sumptuous (sump′ch͞oo·əs) *adj.:* lavish.

superannuated (s͞oo′pər·an′y͞oo·āt′id) *adj.:* no longer of use; out-of-date.

supplication (sup′lə·kā′shən) *n.:* humble request.

surreptitiously (sʉr′əp·tish′əs·lē) *adv.:* stealthily; sneakily.

symmetrical (si·me′tri·kəl) *adj.:* evenly matched; corresponding in form.

T

tempered (tem′pərd) *v.:* strengthened by heating and sudden cooling.

tenacious (tə·nā′shəs) *adj.:* persistent; tough.

tenuous (ten′y͞oo·əs) *adj.:* insubstantial; flimsy.

terminate (tʉr′mə·nāt′) *v.:* end.

thwarted (thwôrt·ed) *v.* used as *adj.:* hindered; blocked.

transgression (trans·gresh′ən) *n.:* act that goes beyond limits set by laws.

translucent (trans·l͞oo′sənt) *adj.:* allowing some light to pass through.

turbulent (tʉr′byə·lənt) *adj.:* disorderly; unruly.

U

undeterred (un·dē·tʉrd′) *adj.* used as *adv.:* un-obstructed; without restriction.

undulating (un′jə·lāt′iŋ) *v.* used as *adj.:* moving in a wavelike manner.

V

vanquishing (vaŋ′kwish·iŋ) *v.* used as *n.:* conquering.

venerate (ven′ə·rāt′) *v.:* revere.

versatile (vʉr′sə·təl) *adj.:* able to do many things.

vivacity (vī·vas′ə·tē) *n.:* liveliness.

vociferousness (vō·sif′ər·əs·nəs) *n.:* loudness; noisiness.

void (vɔid) *n.:* empty space.

voracity (vô·ras′ə·tē) *n.:* gluttony, especially in eating.

W

winsome (win′səm) *adj.:* charming; pleasing.

wisps *n.:* thin strands.

writhes (rī*th*z) *v.:* squirms in agony; contorts the body.

wryly (rī′lē) *adv.:* in a twisted manner.

Z

zeal (zēl) *n.:* passionate devotion to an ideal.

---

at, āte, cär; ten, ēve; is, īce; gō, hôrn, look, t͞ool; ɔil, ɔut; up, fʉr; ə *for unstressed vowels, as* a *in* ago, u *in* focus; ′ *as in* Latin (lat′′n); chin; she; thin; *the*; ŋ *as in* ring (riŋ); zh *as in* azure (azh′ər)

Spanish Glossary

Glosario

El siguiente glosario es un listado en orden alfabético de palabras que aparecen en las selecciones de este libro. Puede usarse como si fuera un diccionario: para buscar el significado de las palabras desconocidas.

Muchas palabras de la lengua española tienen más de un significado. Las definiciones de este glosario se ajustan al contexto en el que se usan las palabras en las selecciones del libro. Las palabras que están muy relacionadas en cuanto a su forma y su significado generalmente se mencionan juntas en una entrada (por ejemplo, compasión y compasivo), y se da la definición de la primera forma.

Se usan las siguientes abreviaturas:

adj.	adjetivo
adv.	adverbio
s.	sustantivo
pl.	plural
v.	verbo

Consulta un diccionario para obtener más información acerca de las palabras del glosario o de palabras que no aparecen aquí.

A

absurd/absurdo *adj.*: tan irracional que llega a ser ridículo; sin sentido.

acquittal/absolución *s.*: acción de librar a una persona de los cargos que le corresponden por haber actuado mal.

adjured/exhortar *v.*: ordenar como bajo juramento.

afflicted/afligir *v.*: causar sufrimiento.

affront/insulto *s.*: ofensa.

allay/aplacar *v.*: aliviar; calmar.

ameliorate/mejorar *v.*: perfeccionar.

amorous/amoroso *adj.*: que muestra amor o deseo.

ample/amplio *adj.*: espacioso; grande.

annihilated/aniquilar *v.*: destruir por completo.

apathy/apatía *s.*: falta de interés o sentimientos; indiferencia.

apparition/aparición *s.*: fantasma o figura fantasmal que aparece cuando nadie lo espera.

appeasing/aliviar *v.*: mitigar, tranquilizar.

arduous/arduo *adj.*: difícil.

assiduously/aplicadamente *adv.*: diligentemente; laboriosamente; concienzudamente.

atrophy/atrofiar *v.*: encoger o consumir.

avowal/reconocimiento *s.*: confesión.

B

bedlam/locura *s.*: caos; desorden total.

beguiled/embaucar *v.*: engañar.

benediction/bendición *s.*: don; regalo.

beneficent/caritativo *adj.*: amable; servicial.

bounty/dádiva *s.*: recompensa; generosidad; tesoro.

C

cache/escondite *s.*: lugar donde se ocultan bienes u objetos valiosos.

cajoled/engatusar *v.*: convencer con halagos, palabras tranquilizadoras o promesas.

calamitous/catastrófico *adj.*: desastroso, calamitoso.

candor/franqueza *s.*: honestidad; actitud justa, abierta e imparcial.

cataclysms/cataclismos *s. pl.*: agitaciones violentas que producen cambios repentinos.

censuring/censura *s.*: acción de desaprobar algo con severidad.

chastise/reprender *v.*: castigar; criticar severamente.

clambered down/descender *v.*: bajar.

commiserate/compadecer *v.*: sentir pena por otra persona o comprender su sufrimiento.

complacent/petulante *adj.*: satisfecho de sí mismo; presumido.

compunction/cuidado *s.*: interés; atención.

condemned/condenar *v.*: juzgar culpable.

confiscate/confiscar *v.*: apoderarse de los bienes de alguien (en especial, si lo hace una autoridad).

convulsed/agitarse *v.*: sacudirse de forma descontrolada, como, por ejemplo, al reír o llorar.

covenant/pacto *s.*: acuerdo o contrato.

D

debilitating/extenuante *adj.*: que cansa o debilita.

decrepit/decrépito *adj.*: muy desgastado por la edad.

deluge/diluvio *s.*: gran inundación.

denigration/denigración *s.*: desvalorización; menosprecio.

deployed/estacionar *adj.*: desplegar tropas militares.

derision/escarnio *s.*: desprecio; burla.

despicable/despreciable *adj.*: aborrecible; abominable.

destitute/desamparado *adj.*: abandonado.

dexterously/hábilmente *adv.*: con destreza.

diffuse/disperso *adj.*: que no está concentrado; esparcido.

disconcert/desconcertar *v.*: alterar; confundir.

discourse/discurso *s.*: exposición de ideas.

discretion/discreción *s.*: prudencia; acción de comportarse con cautela.

disdain/desdén *s.*: desprecio.

disillusion/desilusión *s.*: desencanto; decepción.

dispel/disipar *v.*: eliminar; hacer desaparecer.

dissipated/disipado *adj.*: entregado con exceso a la bebida y al juego.

dominion/señorear *v.*: dominar con autoridad absoluta.

duress/coacción *s.*: presión; fuerza.

E

edifying/edificante *adj.*: moralmente instructivo.

efface/eliminar *v.*: borrar.

elated/eufórico *adj.*: muy feliz.

eloquence/elocuencia *s.*: modo de hablar lleno de gracia y persuasión.

emaciated/escuálido *adj.*: extremadamente delgado; consumido.

emulate/imitar *v.*: emular.

endure/tolerar *v.*: aguantar; sufrir.

enigma/enigma *s.*: algo desconcertante.

enmity/enemistad *s.*: hostilidad.

enterprise/empresa *s.*: tarea.

entreat/rogar *v.*: suplicar.

erradicate/erradicar *v.*: borrar todas las huellas; eliminar.

errant/andante *adj.*: que deambula; que se aparta del recorrido o va más allá de los límites establecidos (se utiliza a menudo en la frase *"caballero andante"*).

eschew/abstenerse *v.*: rechazar; evitar.

expedient/recurso *s.*: algo que es útil o práctico.

exulting/exultante *adj.*: extremadamente alegre.

F

feigned/fingir *v.*: aparentar.

fervent/ferviente *adj.*: muy intenso en sentimiento.

fidelity/fidelidad *s.*: lealtad.

forged/forjar *v.*: dar forma a un objeto de metal por medio del calor y de martillazos.

formidable/temible *adj.*: que causa temor.

fostered/adoptado *v.*: criado con muchos cuidados.

furtively/furtivamente *adv.*: secretamente; con disimulo.

futile/fútil *adj.*: inútil.

G

grandiloquent/grandilocuente *adj.*: pomposo o rimbombante al hablar o al escribir.

H

habitual/habitual *adj.*: que se realiza repetidamente por hábito.

I

imminent/inminente *adj.*: que está por suceder.

immutable/inmutable *adj.*: que no se puede modificar o cambiar.

impartial/imparcial *adj.*: que no prefiere una cosa sobre otra; que no tiene en cuenta o abandona todo apego por las cosas.

imperceptible/imperceptible *adj.*: que no es claro ni nítido.

impervious/inmune *adj.*: que no es afectado por algo.

impetuous/impulsivo *adj.*: impetuoso; precipitado.

implacable/implacable *adj.*: que no se puede suavizar; aguerrido.

implored/implorar *v.*: rogar.

impregnable/inexpugnable *adj.*: imposible de capturar.

incantations/conjuros *s. pl.*: cánticos o canciones con características mágicas.

incongruous/inapropiado *adj.*: que no corresponde; que está fuera de lugar.

incredulity/incredulidad *s.*: duda; descreimiento.

indignation/indignación *s.*: enojo por una injusticia.

inert/inerte *adj.*: que no tiene la capacidad de moverse o actuar.

inextricable/inextricable *adj.*: imposible de desenredar o descifrar.

ingenious/ingenioso *adj.*: original; inteligente.

inscrutable/inescrutable *adj.*: difícil de comprender; indescifrable.

insignificant/insignificante *adj.*: sin importancia.

instigation/instigación *s.*: incitación a cometer una maldad.

insuperable/insuperable *adj.*: imposible de vencer.

interminable/interminable *adj.*: eterno.

intimation/indicio *s.*: pista.

intransigence/intransigencia *s.*: obstinación; negativa a llegar a un acuerdo.

intrepid/intrépido *adj.*: que no siente temor; muy valiente.

inverted/invertido *adj.*: que está al revés.

invoking/invocando *v.*: convocando; llamando.

irreprochable/intachable *adj.*: inocente.

itinerant/itinerante *adj.*: ambulante; que se mueve de un lado a otro.

J

juxtaposed/yuxtapuesto *adj.*: colocado uno junto al otro.

K

kindred/familia *s.*: parientes.

L

labyrinth/laberinto *s.*: lugar con muchos caminos que se entrecruzan; disposición compleja y confusa.

levity/frivolidad *s.*: falta de seriedad; ligereza irrespetuosa o alegría que no resulta apropiada.

livid/lívido *adj.*: azul grisáceo, como por un golpe o por el frío.

loath/reacio *adj.*: poco dispuesto a hacer algo.

lucid/lúcido *adj.*: racional.

M

manifest/manifiesto *adj.*: revelado.

melancholy/melancolía *s.*: tristeza.

meticulously/meticulosamente *adv.*: con mucho cuidado.

mundane/mundano *adj.*: que se refiere al mundo; que muestra predilección por la seguridad y la ganancia.

municipal/municipal *adj.*: del gobierno local.

N

nascent/naciente *adj.*: que empieza a crecer; nuevo.

nocturnal/nocturno *adj.*: relacionado con la noche.

O

obscurity/oscuridad *s.*: anonimato.

ominous/(mal) agüero *s.*: que sugiere maldad o desgracia; siniestro.

omnipotent/omnipotente *adj.*: todopoderoso.

opaque/opaco *adj.*: que no deja pasar la luz.

P

paraphernalia/bártulos *s. pl.*: útiles, equipamiento.

pathological/patológico *adj.*: que causa enfermedad.

pedant/pedante *s.*: maestro que enfatiza los detalles o las reglas en lugar de lo que se debe aprender.

penchant/afición *s.*: gusto por algo.

pensive/imaginativo *adj.*: que tiene muchas ideas o que piensa seriamente en algo.

perfidious/pérfido *adj.:* malvado, desleal.

permeated/impregnar *v.:* esparcirse por todos lados.

perpetrated/cometer *v.:* realizar.

perpetually/permanentemente *adv.:* constantemente.

pestilence/pestilencia *s.:* enfermedad mortal.

petrified/petrificado *adj.:* paralizado por el impacto o el miedo.

pettiness/pequeñez *s.:* insignificancia.

piety/piedad *s.:* devoción religiosa.

piqued/ofenderse *v.:* enojarse o irritarse.

pivot/eje (central) *s.:* punto central del que depende otra cosa.

plaintively/lastimeramente *adv.:* tristemente.

plight/aprieto *s.:* situación difícil.

pompous/pomposo *adj.:* pedante.

predatory/depredador *adj.:* que caza y se alimenta de otros animales.

predominated/predominar *v.:* tomar control.

prescience/clarividencia *s.:* conocimiento de algo antes de que suceda.

prevaricate/mentir *v.:* evitar la verdad; andar con rodeos.

primal/primitivo *adj.:* original.

pristine/prístino *adj.:* puro; inmaculado.

procured/procurar *v.:* conseguir; lograr con esfuerzo.

prodigious/inmenso *adj.:* muy grande; enorme.

proliferation/proliferación *s.:* rápida multiplicación.

propitiate/propiciar *v.:* calmar; satisfacer.

prudent/prudente *adj.:* cuidadoso en su conducta; cauto.

R

rancor/aborrecimiento *s.:* enojo; odio implacable.

rancid/rancio *adj.:* echado a perder.

razing/arrasar *v.:* destrozar por completo.

reckoning/pagar (por una acción) *v.:* sufrir un castigo por las acciones realizadas.

recompense/recompensa *s.:* compensación; retribución.

reiterating/reiterar *v.:* repetir.

replenish/reponer *v.:* llenar o completar nuevamente; reabastecer.

reprehensible/reprensible *adj.:* que merece ser criticado o cargar con la culpa.

reprimand/reprimenda *s.:* reto; regaño.

reproach/reprochar *v.:* regañar; mostrar desaprobación.

reprobation/reprobación *s.:* desaprobación.

reproved/recriminar *v.:* expresar desaprobación.

resolutely/resueltamente *adv.:* firmemente, con determinación.

resolution/determinación *s.:* propósito firme.

revere/venerar *v.:* respetar profundamente.

ruefully/arrepentido *adj.:* apenado.

S

sabotage/sabotear *v.:* dañar.

scathing/mordaz *adj.:* extremadamente crítico o severo.

scorned/desdeñar *v.:* rechazar.

scrupulous/escrupuloso *adj.:* que actúa de forma estrictamente correcta o apropiada.

scrutinized/inspeccionar *v.:* observar detenidamente.

siege/asedio *s.:* sitio; intento continuo de tomar control.

sinister/siniestro *adj.:* que amenaza con un daño o una maldad.

slanderous/difamatorio *adj.:* ofensivo para otros.

solace/solaz *s.:* consuelo en momentos difíciles.

solicitously/solícito *adj.:* bondadoso o preocupado.

somber/lúgubre *adj.:* oscuro; sombrío.

sonorous/sonoro *adj.:* de sonido intenso y vibrante.

splaying/extender *v.:* aplanar.

staidness/sobriedad *s.:* seriedad.

stealthily/clandestinamente *adv.:* a escondidas.

stoically/estoicamente *adv.:* con calma; sin emoción.

strictures/críticas *s. pl.:* comentarios negativos.

suavely/elegantemente *adv.:* con suavidad y sofisticación.

subdue/sojuzgar *v.:* conquistar; someter.

submissiveness/sumisión *s.:* obediencia; falta de resistencia.

subsided/descender *v.:* pasar a un nivel más bajo.

subversive/subversivo *adj.:* que trata de derrocar al gobierno o a cualquier otro sistema establecido.

sufficed/saciarse *v.:* satisfacer; cubrir una necesidad.

sumptuous/suntuoso *adj.:* lujoso.

superannuated/anticuado *adj.:* que ya no se usa; obsoleto.

supplication/postración *s.:* pedido humilde; súplica.

surreptitiously/subrepticiamente *adv.:* furtivamente; a escondidas.

symmetrical/simétrico *adj.:* parejo; que tiene la misma forma.

T

tempered/templado *adj.:* que se reforzó por el calor y el enfriamiento repentinos.

tenacious/tenaz *adj.:* persistente; resistente.

tenuous/endeble *adj.:* frágil; poco sólido o insustancial.

terminate/finalizar *v.:* terminar.

thwarted/frustrar *v.:* dificultar; bloquear.

transgression/transgresión *s.:* acto que excede los límites impuestos por las leyes.

translucent/traslúcido *adj.:* que deja pasar algo de luz.

turbulent/turbulento *adj.:* desordenado; revoltoso.

U

undeterred/libremente *adv.:* sin restricciones ni obstáculos.

undulating/ondulante *adj.:* que se mueve como una ola.

V

vanquishing/derrotar *v.:* conquistar.

venerate/venerar *v.:* reverenciar.

versatile/versátil *adj.:* que puede hacer muchas cosas.

vivacity/viveza *s.:* animación.

vociferousness/barullo *s.:* ruido; alboroto.

void/vacío *s.:* lugar donde no hay nada.

voracity/voracidad *s.:* glotonería, especialmente al comer.

W

winsome/encantador *adj.:* agradable; grato.

wisps/jirones *s.:* trozos de tela desgarrados o arrancados; hebras delgadas.

writhes/retorcerse *v.:* se estremece de dolor; contrae el cuerpo.

wryly/irónicamente *adv.:* de manera retorcida.

Z

zeal/fervor *s.:* devoción apasionada por un ideal.

Acknowledgments

For permission to reprint copyrighted material, grateful acknowledgment is made to the following sources:

Isabel Allende: "Writing As an Act of Hope" by Isabel Allende from *Paths of Resistance: The Art and Craft of the Political Novel,* edited by William Zinsser. Copyright © 1989 by Isabel Allende. Published by Houghton Mifflin, 1989.

American Poetry Review: "Such a moon" by Yosa Buson, translated by Lucien Stryk and Takashi Ikemoto from *American Poetry Review 3* (May–June 1976). Copyright © 1976 by American Poetry Review.

Ballantine Books, a division of Random House, Inc.: "Tata and Nena" and "Deucalion" from *Parallel Myths* by J. F. Bierlein. Copyright © 1994 by J. F. Bierlein.

The Baltimore Sun Company: From "Holocaust Survivors Bring Memories" by Lisa Pollak from *The Baltimore Sun,* November 4, 2003. Copyright © 2003 by The Baltimore Sun Company.

Bantam Books, a division of Random House, Inc., www.randomhouse.com: "The Second Teaching: Philosophy and Spiritual Discipline" from *Bhagavad-Gita,* translated by Barbara Stoler Miller. Translation copyright © 1986 by Barbara Stoler Miller.

Tony Barnstone: "Avoiding fishnet" by Yosa Buson, translated by Tony Barnstone and from "The Cannibal Hymn," translated by Tony Barnstone and Willis Barnstone from *World Poetry: An Anthology of Verse from Antiquity to Our Time* by Katharine Washburn, John S. Major, and Clifton Fadiman. Copyright © 1998 by Tony Barnstone.

Beacon Press, Boston: "Daisies" from *Why I Wake Early* by Mary Oliver. Copyright © 2004 by Mary Oliver.

Bilingual Press/Editorial Bilingüe, Arizona State University, Tempe, AZ: "Better Death Than Suffer the Affronts of Growing Old" from *Sor Juana Ines de la Cruz: Poems,* translated by Margaret Sayers Peden. Copyright © 1985 by Bilingual Press/Editorial Bilingüe.

Robert Bly: "The Guitar" by Federico García Lorca from *Lorca and Jimenez: Selected Poems,* chosen and translated by Robert Bly. Copyright © 1973 by Robert Bly. Published by Beacon Press, Boston, 1973.

Estate of J.C.E. Bowen: "The tyranny of silence" by Qulzum from *Poems from the Persian,* translated by John Charles Edward Bowen. Copyright © 1964 by J.C.E. Bowen. Published by Blackwell Publishing, London, 1948.

George Braziller, Inc.: From *Maupassant* by Michael G. Lerner. Copyright © 1975 by Michael G. Lerner.

Cambridge University Press, UK: "The Prodigal Son" and "The Talents" from *The New English Bible,* edited by William Safire. Copyright © 1961, 1970 by the Delegates of the Oxford University Press and Cambridge University Press.

Jennifer Sibley Clement: "The Word" by Manuel Ulacia, translated by Jennifer Clement. Copyright © 1995 by Jennifer Clement.

Rosica Colin Limited: From *Candide* by Voltaire, translated by Richard Aldington. Copyright © by The Estate of Richard Aldington.

Columbia University Press, 562 W. 113th St., New York, NY 10025: From "What the Effect of Love Is" from *The Art of Courtly Love* by Andreas Capellanus, translated by John Jay Parry. Copyright © 1960 by Columbia University Press. "Poem 93: Here is a Tree Older Than the Forest Itself" and "Poem 40: I Climb the Road to Cold Mountain" from *Cold Mountain: 100 Poems by the T'ang poet Han-shan,* translated by Burton Watson. Copyright © 1970 by Columbia University Press. From *The Pillow Book of Sei Shōnagon,* translated by Ivan Morris. Copyright © 1991 by Ivan Morris. Excerpt from "Kamo Mabuchi: Kokuiko," translated by Heinric Domulin from *Sources of Japanese Tradition,* compiled by Ryusaku Tsunoda, William Theodore de Bary, and Donald Keene. Copyright © 1958 by Columbia University Press.

Da Capo Press, a member of Perseus Books, L.L.C.: From Introduction from *Hannibal Crosses the Alps* by John Prevas. Copyright © 1998 by John Prevas.

Darhansoff, Verrill, Feldman Literary Agents: "Everything Is Plundered" by Anna Akhmatova from *Poems of Akhmatova,* translated by Stanley Kunitz with Max Hayward. Copyright © 1967, 1968, 1972, 1973 by Stanley Kunitz and Max Hayward.

Discovery Communications, Inc.: "Explorer: Legendary El Dorado Pinpointed" by Rossella Lorenzi from *Discovery News,* August 9, 2002. Copyright © 2002 by Discovery Communications, Inc.

Doubleday, a division of Random House, Inc.: "Psalm 23" from *Psalms I: 1–50* (The Anchor Bible) by Mitchell Dahood. Translation, Introduction, and Notes copyright © 1966 by Doubleday, a division of Random House, Inc. "Old Pond" by Matsuo Bashō from *An Introduction to Haiku* by Harold G. Henderson. Copyright © 1958 by Harold G. Henderson.

Doubleday, a division of Random House, Inc. and electronic format by permission of **American University in Cairo Press:** "The Norwegian Rat" from *The Time and the Place and Other Stories* by Naguib Mahfouz, translated by Denys Johnson-Davies. Copyright © 1991 by American University in Cairo Press.

Doubleday, a division of Random House, Inc. and electronic format by permission of **Harold Ober Associates Inc.:** "Dead Men's Path" from *Girls at War and Other Stories* by Chinua Achebe. Copyright © 1972, 1973 by Chinua Achebe.

Doubleday, a division of Random House, Inc. and electronic format by permission of **Hiroaki Sato:** "One lone pine tree" and "Drops of dew" by Saigyo from *From the Country of Eight Islands,* translated by Hiroaki Sato and Burton Watson. Copyright © 1981 by Hiroaki Sato and Burton Watson.

Dutton Signet, a division of Penguin Group (USA) Inc. and electronic format by permission of **The Octagon Press Ltd.:** "Saadi of Shiraz," edited by Idries Shah, from *The Way of the Sufi* by Idries Shah. Copyright © 1968 by Idries Shah.

Elling O. Eide: "Spring Thoughts" from *Poems of Li Po,* translated by Elling O. Eide. Copyright © 1983 by Elling O. Eide.

Encyclopaedia Britannica: From "Luigi Pirandello" from *Encyclopaedia Britannica, 1994–2001.* Copyright © 2001 by Encyclopaedia Britannica.

Farrar, Straus and Giroux, LLC: From Book 1, "Quarrel, Oath and Promise," Book 22, "Desolation Before Troy," and Book 24, "A Grace Given in Sorrow," from *The Iliad,* translated by Robert Fitzgerald. Translation copyright © 1974 by Robert Fitzgerald. All rights reserved. "Russia 1812" by Victor Hugo, translated by Robert Lowell from *Imitations* by Robert Lowell. Copyright © 1959 by Robert Lowell; copyright renewed © 1987 by Harriet, Sheridan, and Caroline Lowell. "Freedom to Breathe" from *Stories and Prose Poems* by Alexander Solzhenitsyn, translated by Michael Glenny. Translation copyright © 1971 by Michael Glenny. "The Virgins" from *Sea Grapes* by Derek Walcott. Copyright © 1976 by Derek Walcott.

Foreign Languages Press, Beijing: "Love Must Not Be Forgotten" and from "Biographical Note—My Boat" by Zhang Jie, translated by Gladys Yang from *Love Must Not Be Forgotten,* edited by

Gladys Yang. Copyright © 1986 by Foreign Languages Press.

Leslie Garis: Quote by Jamaica Kincaid from "Through West Indian Eyes" by Leslie Garis from *The New York Times,* October 7, 1990. Copyright © 1990 by Leslie Garis.

Graywolf Press, Saint Paul, Minnesota: "Words" and excerpt from "Why I Write in French" by Vénus Khoury-Ghata, and from Introduction by Marilyn Hacker from *She Says* by Vénus Khoury-Ghata, translated by Marilyn Hacker. English translation from the French copyright © 2003 by Marilyn Hacker.

Grove/Atlantic, Inc.: "Song 103: O Oriole, Yellow Bird" and "Song 130: What Plant Is Not Faded?" from *The Book of Songs,* translated by Arthur Waley. Copyright 1937 by Arthur Waley.

Harcourt, Inc.: "Charles Baudelaire: L'Invitation au Voyage" from *Things of This World* by Richard Wilbur. Copyright © 1956 and renewed © 1984 by Richard Wilbur. This material may not be reproduced in any form or by any means without the prior written permission of the publisher. From *Conversations with Czeslaw Milosz* by Ewa Czarnecka and Aleksander Fiut, translated by Richard Lourie. Translation copyright © 1987 by Ewa Czarnecka, Aleksander Fiut, and Czeslaw Milosz.

Harcourt, Inc. and electronic format by permission of **Stanislaw Baranczak:** "In Praise of Feeling Bad About Yourself" from *View with a Grain of Sand* by Wislawa Szymborska, translated by Stanislaw Baranczak and Clare Cavanagh. Copyright © 1993 by Wislawa Szymborska; English translation copyright © 1993 by Stanislaw Baranczak and Clare Cavanagh; copyright © 1995 by Harcourt, Inc.

Harcourt Inc. and electronic format by permission of **Benedict Fitzgerald on behalf of the Fitzgerald Children:** From "Antigone" from *The Antigone of Sophocles, An English Version* by Dudley Fitts and Robert Fitzgerald. Copyright 1939 by Harcourt Inc.; copyright renewed © 1967 by Dudley Fitts and Robert Fitzgerald. CAUTION: All rights, including professional, amateur, motion picture, recitation, lecturing, performance, public reading, radio broadcasting, and television are strictly reserved. Inquiries on all rights should be addressed to Harcourt, Inc., Permissions Department, Orlando, FL 32887-6777. Part I and Part II ("Prologue" and "Parados") from *The Oedipus Rex of Sophocles: An English Version* by Dudley Fitts and Robert Fitzgerald. Copyright 1949 by Harcourt, Inc.; copyright renewed © 1977 by Cornelia Fitts and Robert Fitzgerald. CAUTION: All rights, including professional, amateur, motion picture, recitation, lecturing, performance, public reading, radio broadcasting, and television are strictly reserved. Inquiries on all rights should be addressed to Harcourt, Inc., Permissions Dept., Orlando, FL 32887-6777.

Harmony Books, a division of Random House, Inc.: From *Bhagavad Gita: A New Translation* by Stephen Mitchell. Copyright © 2000 by Stephen Mitchell.

HarperCollins Publishers, Inc.: From Chapters I, II, and VII from *Don Quixote* by Miguel de Cervantes, A New Translation by Edith Grossman; Introduction by Harold Bloom. Translation copyright © 2003 by Edith Grossman. "Tuesday Siesta" from *No One Writes to the Colonel and Other Stories* by Gabriel García Márquez, translated by J. S. Bernstein. English translation copyright © 1968 by Harper & Row Publishers, Inc. "Song of a Citizen" from *The Collected Poems: 1931–1987* by Czeslaw Milosz. Copyright © 1988 by Czeslaw Milosz Royalties, Inc. "When people see some things as beautiful" and "Do you want to improve the world?" by Lao-tzu, "The supreme good is like water" by Po Chü-i, and quote by Po Chü-i from *Tao Te Ching: A New English Version* translated by Stephen Mitchell. Translation copyright © 1988 by Stephen Mitchell. From "First Cell, First Love" from *The Gulag Archipelago 1918–1956: An Experiment in Literary Investigation* by Aleksandr Solzhenitsyn, translated by Thomas P. Whitney. Copyright © 1973 by Aleksandr I. Solzhenitsyn; English translation copyright © 1973, 1974 by HarperCollins Publishers, Inc. From *The First Circle* by Aleksandr Solzhenitsyn, translated by Thomas P. Whitney. English translation copyright © 1968 by HarperCollins Publishers, Inc.

HarperCollins Publishers, Inc. and electronic format by permission of **George Fischer and Victor Fischer:** From *The Life of Mahatma Gandhi* by Louis Fischer. Copyright 1950 by Louis Fischer.

Harvard University Press, Cambridge MA: From Introduction from *Greek Religion* by Walter Burkert, translated by John Raffan. Copyright © 1985 by Basil Blackwell Publishers and the President and Fellows of Harvard College.

Corinna Hasofferett and Vénus Khoury-Ghata: Quotes by Vénus Khoury-Ghata from "Destiny's Choice" by Corinna Hasofferett from *Corinna Hasofferett and Jacket Magazine.* Copyright © 1995 by Corinna Hasofferett and Vénus Khoury-Ghata. "Destiny's Choice" also appears in *Noffey Haneffesh (Once She Was a Child)* by Corinna Hasofferett, Hudna Press, Israel, 2003.

David Higham Associates Limited: From *Goethe's Faust, Part I and Part II,* translated by Louis MacNeice. Copyright 1951, 1954 by Frederick Louis MacNeice; copyright renewed © 1979 by Heidi MacNeice. "Life Is Sweet at Kumansenu" from *The Truly Married Woman and Other Stories* by Abioseh Nicol. Published by Oxford University Press.

Hill and Wang, a division of Farrar, Straus & Giroux, LLC and electronic format by permission of **Georges Borchardt, Inc. for Les Editions de Minuit:** From *Night* by Elie Wiesel, translated by Stella Rodway. Copyright © 1960 by MacGibbon & Kee; copyright © renewed 1988 by The Collins Publishing Group. Originally published as *La Nuit.*

Bertha Hilton: From *A History of the Romans* by Frank C. Bourne. Copyright © 1966 by D. C. Heath and Company; copyright renewed © 1994 by Frank C. Bourne.

Henry Holt and Company, LLC: "Talk" from *The Cow-Tail Switch and Other West African Stories* by Harold Courlander and George Herzog. Copyright © 1947, 1974 by Harold Courlander.

IBEX Publishers, Inc.: "Donkeys Inside Panniers" and "The Soup of the Soup of the Duck Soup" from *Mulla's Donkey and Other Friends,* adapted by Mehdi Nakosteen. Copyright © 1974 by Mehdi Nakosteen.

Indiana University Press, Bloomington, Indiana: From "Laments on the War Dead" by Yehuda Amichai from *Israeli Poetry,* selected and translated by Warren Bargad and Stanley F. Chyet. Copyright © 1986 by Indiana University Press. "The Creation," from "The Four Ages," and "The Story of Daedalus and Icarus" from *Ovid: Metamorphoses,* translated by Rolfe Humphries. Copyright © 1995 by Indiana University Press.

International African Institute, London: "The Five Helpers" from *Tales Told in Togoland* by A. W. Cardinall. Copyright © 1936 by International African Institute.

International PEN: Charter of International PEN. Copyright © 2003 by International PEN, the authors, the photographers, and Javelin Complete Ltd.

The Jewish Publication Society: "Noah and the Flood" from Genesis 6:5–9:29 from *The Torah: The Five Books of Moses.* Copyright © 1962 by The Jewish Publication Society.

Johnson & Alcock Ltd.: "The Prisoner Who Wore Glasses" from *Tales of Tenderness and Power* by Bessie Head. Copyright ©1989 by The Estate of Bessie Head. "I Have Visited Again" from *The Bronze Horseman: Selected Poems of Alexander Pushkin,* translated by D. M. Thomas. Translation copyright © 1982 by D. M. Thomas. Published by Secker & Warburg, 1982.

Alfred A. Knopf, a division of Random House, Inc.: "The Myth of Sisyphus" from *The Myth of Sisyphus and Other Essays* by Albert Camus, translated by Justin O'Brien. Copyright © 1955, 1983 by Alfred A. Knopf, a division of Random House, Inc.

Labyrinth Press, a division of Baker Book House Company: From "Chevrefoil" from *The Lais of Marie de France,* translated by Robert Hanning and Joan Ferrante. Copyright © 1978 by Robert W. Hanning and Joan Ferrante.

Lifestyle Media, Inc.: From "Perfect Circles" by Kimberly Gdula from *Dance Spirit,* September 1, 2001. Copyright © 2001 by Lifestyle Media, Inc.

Los Angeles Times and **Aaron Naparstek:** From "Versed in Traffic Control" by Maggie Farley from *Los Angeles Times*, May 18, 2002. Copyright © 2002 by Los Angeles Times. Naparstek's honku also appear in *Honku: The Zen Antidote to Road Rage*, Villard 2003.

MacNeil/Lehrer Productions: From *The NewsHour with Jim Lehrer*, December 23, 2003. Copyright © 2003 by MacNeil/Lehrer Productions.

Julian Mates, c/o George Brazillier, Inc.: From "The Here and Now" from *Renaissance Culture: A New Sense of Order*, edited by Julian Mates and Eugene Cantelupe. Copyright © 1966 by Julian Mates and Eugene Cantelupe.

Estate of Edward Powys Mathers: "Dates" from "The Tale of Young Nur and the Warrior Girl" from *The Book of the Thousand Nights and One Night* by E. Powys Mathers. Published by The Casanova Society, London, 1923.

Helen Schary Motro: From "An ignoble fast" by Helen Schary Motro from *The Christian Science Monitor*, September 26, 2003. Copyright © 2003 by Helen Schary Motro.

Regeen Najar for The Philosophical Library, New York: From *Out of My Later Years* by Albert Einstein. Copyright 1950 by the Philosophical Library, Inc.

National Geographic Society: "Pharaohs of the Sun" by Rick Gore from *National Geographic*, April 2001. Copyright © 2001 by National Geographic Society. "Zen Garden's Calming Effect Due to Subliminal Image?" by Hillary Mayell from *National Geographic*, September 25, 2002. Copyright © 2002 by National Geographic Society.

National Public Radio, Inc.: From "Sumerian Tablets" by Daniel Zwerdling from *National Public Radio: All Things Considered*, May 2, 1998. Copyright © 1998 by National Public Radio, Inc.

Navajivan Trust: From "Speech, March 23, 1922" by Mohandas Gandhi.

New Directions Publishing Corporation: "Requiem" from *Old Snow* by Bei Dao, translated by Bonnie S. McDougall and Chen Maiping. Copyright © 1991 by Bei Dao. From Preface by Bonnie S. McDougall from *Old Snow* by Bei Dao, translated by Bonnie S. McDougall. Preface copyright © 1991 by Bonnie S. McDougall. "Moonrise" by Hilda Doolittle from *Collected Poems, 1912–1944*, edited by Louis L. Martz. Copyright © 1982 by the Estate of Hilda Doolittle. "Dreaming of Li Po" by Tu Fu from *The Selected Poems of Tu Fu*, translated by David Hinton. Copyright © 1988, 1989 by David Hinton. "The Parable of the Old Man and the Young" from *The Collected Poems of Wilfred Owen*. Copyright © 1963 by Chatto & Windus, Ltd. "Viento, Agua, Piedra," "Wind, Water, Stone," and "A Tree Within" from *Collected Poems 1957–1987* by Octavio Paz. Copyright © 1979, 1985, 1987, 1988 by Octavio Paz; copyright © 1984 by Octavio Paz and Eliot Weinberger. "Peonies" from *Complete Poems of Li Ch'ing-Chao*, translated by Kenneth Rexroth and Ling Chung. Copyright © 1971 by Kenneth Rexroth and Ling Chung. "Jade Flower Palace," "Night in the House by the River," and "Loneliness" by Tu Fu from *One Hundred Poems From the Chinese*, translated by Kenneth Rexroth. Copyright © 1971 by Kenneth Rexroth. "Doesn't he realize..." by Ono no Komachi from *Women Poets of Japan*, translated by Kenneth Rexroth and Ikuko Atsumi. Copyright © 1977 by Kenneth Rexroth and Ikuko Atsumi. "Pine Tree Tops" from *Turtle Island* by Gary Snyder. Copyright © 1974 by Gary Snyder.

The New York Times Agency: From "Baltic Soil Yields Evidence of a Bitter End to Napoleon's Army" by Michael Wines from *The New York Times*, September 14, 2002. Copyright © 2002 by The New York Times Company. From "When Timbuktu Was the Paris of Islamic Intellectuals in Africa" by Lila Azam Zanganeh from *The New York Times*, April 24, 2004. Copyright © 2004 by The New York Times Company.

Nguyen Ba Chung: "Quang Binh" by Y Nhi from *Six Vietnamese Poets*, translated by Nguyen Ba Chung and Kevin Bowen. Copyright © 2002 by Y Nhi; translation copyright © 2002 by Nguyen Ba Chung and Kevin Bowen.

The Nobel Foundation: From Nobel Lecture by Alexander Solzhenitsyn from *Nobel Lectures, Literature 1970*. Copyright © 1970 by The Nobel Foundation. From "Towards the Splendid City" from Nobel speech by Pablo Neruda, December 13, 1971. Copyright © 1971 by The Nobel Foundation. From Nobel Lecture by Naguib Mahfouz from *Nobel Lectures, Literature 1981–1990*. Copyright © 1988 by The Nobel Foundation. From Nobel Peace Prize acceptance speech by Nelson Mandela. Copyright © 1993 by The Nobel Foundation.

North Point Press, a division of Farrar, Straus and Giroux, LLC: "The Jay" from *Palm-of-the-Hand Stories* by Yasunari Kawabata, translated by Lane Dunlop and J. Martin Holman. Translation copyright © 1988 by Lane Dunlop and J. Martin Holman. All rights reserved.

Northwestern University Press, Evanston, IL: "Why We Tell Stories About Spider" from *West African Folktales*, collected and translated by Jack Berry; edited and with an Introduction by Richard Spears. Copyright © 1991 by Northwestern University Press.

W. W. Norton & Company, Inc.: From *The Divine Comedy* by Dante Alighieri, translated by John Ciardi. Translation copyright © 1954, 1957, 1959, 1960, 1961, 1965, 1967, 1970 by The Ciardi Family Publishing Trust. "Sixth Day, Tenth Story" (retitled "Brother Onion") from *The Decameron* by Giovanni Boccaccio, translated by Mark Musa and Peter Bondanella. Copyright © 1982 by Mark Musa and Peter Bondanella. From *The Song of Roland*, translated by Frederick Goldin. Copyright © 1978 by W. W. Norton & Company, Inc. From Chapter XVI from *The Greek Way* by Edith Hamilton. Copyright 1930, 1943 by W. W. Norton & Company, Inc; copyright renewed © 1958, 1971 by Dorian Reid.

Harold Ober Associates Inc.: "Icarus's Flight" by Stephen Dobyns. Copyright © 1996 by Stephen Dobyns. First appeared in *Ploughshares*, Winter 1996/97.

Oberlin College Press: "Conversation Among Mountains" and "Taking Leave of a Friend" by Li Po from *Five T'ang Poets*, translated by David Young, FIELD Translation Series 15. Copyright ©1990 by Oberlin College.

Robert J. Ormsby: Poem # 8 "Wretched Catullus, Leave off Playing the Fool" from *Catullus: The Complete Poems for Modern Readers*, translated by Reney Myers and Robert J. Ormsby. Copyright © 1972 by Reney Myers and Robert J. Ormsby.

Oxford University Press, UK: "The End of All Things" from *Tales of the Norse Gods*, retold by Barbara Leonie Picard (OUP, 2001). Copyright © 1953 by Barbara Leonie Picard.

Pantheon Books, a division of Random House, Inc.: "The Night Face Up" from *End of the Game and Other Stories* by Julio Cortázar, translated by Paul Blackburn. Copyright © 1963, 1967 by Random House, Inc. "Coyote and the Origin of Death" from *American Indian Myths and Legends*, edited by Richard Erdoes and Alfonso Ortiz. Copyright © 1984 by Richard Erdoes and Alfonso Ortiz. "The Butterfly," "The Missing Axe," "The Lost Horse," and "Wagging My Tail in the Mud" from *Chinese Fairy Tales and Fantasies*, edited and translated by Moss Roberts. Copyright © 1979 by Moss Roberts.

Peter Pauper Press, Inc.: Haiku by Bashō, Buson, Issa, and Onitsura from *Haiku Harvest: Japanese Haiku Series IV*, translated by Peter Beilenson and Harry Behn. Copyright © 1962 by Peter Pauper Press. From *African Proverbs*, compiled by Charlotte and Wolf Leslau. Copyright © 1962, 1985 by Peter Pauper Press.

Pearson Education Limited: From "The Lion's Awakening" and from "The Words of the Griot Mamadou Kouyaté" from *Sundiata: An Epic of Old Mali* by D. T. Niane, translated by G. D. Pickett. Copyright © 1965 by Addison Wesley Longman Ltd.

Penguin Books Ltd.: Poems 70, 85, and 107 from *The Poems of Catullus*, translated by Peter Whigham (Penguin Classics, 1966). Copyright © 1966 by Peter Whigham. "The Exordium," "The Cessation," "Daylight," and "Comfort" from *The Koran*, translated by N. J. Dawood (Penguin Classics 1956, Fifth revised edition 1990). Copyright © 1956, 1959, 1966, 1968, 1974, 1990, 1993,

1997, 1999, 2003 by N. J. Dawood. "The Fisherman and the Jinnee" from *Tales From the Thousand and One Nights,* translated by N. J. Dawood (Penguin Classics 1954, Revised edition 1973). Translation copyright © 1954, 1973 by N. J. Dawood. "How Siegfried Was Slain" from *The Nibelungenlied,* translated by A. T. Hatto (Penguin Classics 1965, revised edition 1969). Copyright © 1965, 1969 by A. T. Hatto. "The Piece of String" from *Selected Short Stories* by Guy de Maupassant, translated by Roger Colet (Penguin Classics, 1971). Copyright © 1971 by Roger Colet. "Expression of Feelings, VII" by Yuan Mei from *The Penguin Book of Chinese Verse,* edited by A. R. Davies, translated by Robert Kotwall and Norman L. Smith (Penguin Books, 1962). Translation copyright © 1962 by Robert Kotwall and Norman L. Smith. "Night" from *The Rig Veda,* translated by Wendy Doniger O'Flaherty (Penguin Classics, 1981). Copyright © 1981 by Wendy Doniger O'Flaherty. From *The Epic of Gilgamesh,* translated by N. K. Sandars (Penguin Classics 1960, Third Edition 1972). Copyright © 1960, 1964, 1972 by N. K. Sandars.

The Permissions Company on behalf of Copper Canyon Press: "Perhaps" from *Carrying Over* by Shu Ting, translated by Carolyn Kizer. Copyright © 1988 by Carolyn Kizer.

The Permissions Company on behalf of the Estate of Angel Flores: "The Guitar" by Federico García Lorca, translated by Rachel Benson and Robert O'Brien from *An Anthology of Spanish Poetry from Garcilaso to García Lorca in English Translation with Spanish Originals,* edited by Angel Flores. Copyright © 1961 by Angel Flores.

Permissions Company on behalf of Writer's House LLC: "Time" from *Selected Poems of Gabriela Mistral,* translated by Doris Dana. Copyright © 1961, 1964, 1970, 1971 by Doris Dana.

Persea Books, Inc., New York: "Some Advice To Those Who Will Serve Time in Prison" from *Poems of Nazim Hikmet,* translated by Randy Blasing and Mutlu Konuk. Translation copyright © 1994, 2002 by Randy Blasing and Mutlu Konuk.

Estate of Luigi Pirandello, c/o Avv. Giovanna Cau: "War" from *The Medals and Other Stories* by Luigi Pirandello. Copyright 1939 by Luigi Pirandello.

Princeton University Press: "In Praise of Self-Deprecation" from *Sounds, Feelings, Thoughts: Seventy Poems* by Wislawa Szymborska, translated and introduced by Magnus J. Krynski and Robert A. Maguire. Copyright © 1981 by Princeton University Press.

Publishers Weekly: From review of *Ocean of Words* by Ha Jin from *Publishers Weekly,* 1996. Copyright © 1996 by Cahners Business Information, Inc.

Random House, Inc.: "Sonnet 15" and "Sonnet 61: Blest be the day, and blest the month and year" from *The Sonnets of Petrarch* by Francis Petrarch, translated by Joseph Auslander. Copyright 1931 by Longmans, Green and Co., a division of Random House, Inc. From *The Aeneid* by Virgil, translated by Robert Fitzgerald. Copyright © 1980, 1982, 1983 by Robert Fitzgerald. "After the Deluge" from *Mandela's Earth and Other Poems* by Wole Soyinka. Copyright © 1988 by Wole Soyinka.

Random House, Inc. and electronic format by permission of **Stephen Mitchell:** From *Letters to a Young Poet* by Rainer Maria Rilke, translated by Stephen Mitchell. Copyright © 1984 by Stephen Mitchell. "Black Cat" and "I, 5" from "Sonnets to Orpheus" from *The Selected Poetry of Rainer Maria Rilke,* translated by Stephen Mitchell. Copyright © 1982 by Stephen Mitchell.

Random House, Inc. and **Rungstedlund Foundation:** "The Ring" from *Anecdotes of Destiny* by Isak Dinesen. Copyright © 1958 by Isak Dinesen.

Schocken Books, a division of Random House, Inc.: "On Her Brother" by Al-Khansa, translated by Willis Barnstone and "Sonnet XXIII" by Louise Labé from *A Book of Women Poets: From Antiquity to Now,* translated and edited by Aliki and Willis Barnstone. Copyright © 1980 by Schocken Books, a division of Random House, Inc.

Scribner, an imprint of Simon & Schuster Adult Publishing Group: "The Hunger Artist" from *The Metamorphosis, In The Penal Colony and Other Stories* by Franz Kafka, translated by Joachim Neugroschel. Translation copyright © 1993, 1995, 2000 by Joachim Neugroschel.

Scribner, an imprint of Simon & Schuster Adult Publishing Group and electronic format by permission of **The Arthur Waley Estate, c/o John Robinson:** From *The Analects of Confucius,* translated by Arthur Waley. Copyright © 1938 by George Allen and Unwin, Ltd.

Simon & Schuster Adult Publishing Group, electronic format by permission of **The Balkin Agency, Inc.:** "The Wooden People: A Quiché Mayan Myth" from *Popol Vuh,* translated by Dennis Tedlock. Copyright © 1985, 1996 by Dennis Tedlock.

Stanford University Press, www.sup.org: "Unseen by men's eyes" by Tsurayuki, "Though I Go to You" by Ono no Komachi, and "The sight of the flowers" by Mitsune, translated by Helen Craig McCullough from *The First Imperial Anthology of Japanese Poetry* by Kokin Wakashu. Copyright © 1985 by the Board of Trustees of the Leland Stanford Jr. University. "Now that the blossoms…" by Ki no Tsurayuki from *Traditional Japanese Poetry, An Anthology,* translated by Steven Carter. Copyright © 1991 by the Board of Trustees of the Leland Stanford Jr. University.

Etsuko Terasaki: "A flower of waves" by Lady Ise, translated by Etsuko Terasaki with Irma Brandeis from *A Book of Women Poets From Antiquity to Now,* edited by Willis and Aliki Barnstone. Translation copyright ©1980 by Etsuko Terasaki.

Thomson Learning Global Rights Group: "Sonnet: To Hélène" by Pierre de Ronsard from *Western Literature II: The Middle Ages, Renaissance, Enlightenment* by Robert Hollander and A. Bartlett Giamatti. Copyright © 1971 by Heinle, a division of Thomson Learning Global Rights Group, www.thomsonrights.com.

Threshold Books: "Unmarked Boxes" from *Open Secret: Versions of Rumi,* translated by John Moyne and Coleman Barks. Copyright © 1984 by Threshold Books.

Anthony Thwaite: From Introduction by Ki Tsurayuki from *The Penguin Book of Japanese Verse,* edited and translated by Geoffrey Bownas and Anthony Thwaite (Penguin Books, 1964). Translation copyright © 1964 by Geoffrey Bownas and Anthony Thwaite.

Time, Inc.: From "Person of the Century: Mohandas Gandhi (1869–1948)" by Johanna McGeary from *Time,* December 31, 1999. Copyright © 1999 by Time, Inc. From "All the Right Questions" by Anita Hamilton from *Time,* April 5, 2004. Copyright © 2004 by Time, Inc.

Charles E. Tuttle Co., Inc., Boston, MA, and Tokyo, Japan: "Muddy Road," "A Parable," "The Thief Who Became a Disciple," and "The Taste of Banzo's Sword" from *Zen Flesh, Zen Bones,* compiled by Paul Reps. Copyright © 1957 by Charles E. Tuttle Co., Inc.

David Unger: "The Censors," translated by David Unger from *The Censors* by Luisa Valenzuela. Copyright © 1976, 1978, 1988 by Luisa Valenzuela. Translation copyright © 1988 by David Unger. First published in *Short Shorts,* edited by Irving Howe, published by David Godine, Boston, 1982.

The University of California Press: From pp. 96–99 from *Ancient Egyptian Literature,* Three Volumes, translated by Miriam Lichtheim. Copyright © 1973, 1980 by The Regents of the University of California. "You are the herdsman of evening," "Sleep, darling," "We drink your health," "You may forget but," "Tonight I've watched," "Don't ask me what to wear," and "He is More Than a Hero" from *Sappho: A New Translation* by Mary Barnard. Copyright © 1958 by The Regents of the University of California; copyright renewed © 1984 by Mary Barnard.

The University of Chicago Press: From Introduction and from *The Panchatantra,* translated from the Sanskrit by Arthur W. Ryder. Copyright 1925 by The University of Chicago; copyright renewed 1953 by Mary E. Ryder and Winifred Ryder. From *The Sumerians: Their History, Culture, and Character* by Samuel Noah Kramer. Copyright © 1963 by The University of Chicago. All rights reserved.

The University of Georgia Press, Athens, GA: "The Grail" from *Perceval or The Story of the Grail* by Chrétien de Troyes, translated by Ruth Harwood Cline. Copyright © 1983 by Ruth Harwood Cline.

The University of Michigan: Excerpts from "An Interview with Visiting Bei Dao: Poet in Exile" from *Journal of the International Institute*, vol. 2, no. 1, 2000. Copyright © 2000 by The Regents of the University of Michigan.

University of Texas Press: "Sonnet XLIX" and "Sonnet LXXI" and from Dedication from Pablo Neruda from *100 Love Sonnets/Cien Sonetos de Amor* by Pablo Neruda, translated by Stephen Tapscott. Copyright © 1959 by Pablo Neruda and Fundación Pablo Neruda; copyright © 1986 by the University of Texas Press.

University of Virginia Press: From "Invitation to Travel" from *The Flowers of Evil and Other Poems* by Charles Baudelaire, translated by Francis Duke. Copyright © 1965 by University of Virginia Press.

Viking Penguin, a division of Penguin Group (USA) Inc.: From Book 22, "The Death of Hector" from *The Iliad* by Homer, translated by Robert Fagles. Translation copyright © 1990 by Robert Fagles. "An Astrologer's Day" from *Malgudi Days* by R. K. Narayan. Copyright © 1972, 1975, 1978, 1980, 1981, 1982 by R. K. Narayan. "Rama and Ravana in Battle" from *The Ramayana* by R. K. Narayan. Copyright © 1972 by R. K. Narayan. "The Train from Rhodesia" from *Selected Stories* by Nadine Gordimer. Copyright © 1952 by Nadine Gordimer.

Viking Penguin, a division of Penguin Group (USA) Inc. and electronic format by permission of **Giulio Einaudi Editore S.p.A.:** "A Good Day" from *If This Is a Man (Survival in Auschwitz)* by Primo Levi, translated by Stuart Woolf. Copyright © 1958 by Giulio Einaudi Editore S.p.A.; copyright © 1959 by Orion Press, Inc.

Viking Penguin, a division of Penguin Group (USA) Inc. and electronic format by permission of **The Wylie Agency, Inc.:** "Borges and I" from *Collected Fictions* by Jorge Luis Borges, translated by Andrew Hurley. Copyright © 1998 by Maria Kodama, translation copyright © 1998 by Penguin Putnam Inc.

Wadham College, Oxford: "Primitive Song" (retitled "Elephant-Hunter, Take Your Bow!") from *Primitive Song* by C. M. Bowra. Copyright © 1962 by C. M. Bowra.

The Arthur Waley Estate, c/o John Robinson: "Madly Singing in the Mountains" by Po Chü-i from *Chinese Poems*, translated by Arthur Waley (Second Edition, Unicorn Books, 1961). Copyright © 1961 by Arthur Waley. From "Twelve Poems" by T'ao Ch'ien from *Translations from the Chinese* by Arthur Waley. Copyright 1919 and renewed 1947 by Arthur Waley.

Weatherhill, an imprint of Shambhala Publications, Inc.: "An old silent pond" by Matsuo Bashō, translated by Harry Behn from *One Hundred Frogs: From Renga to Haiku to English* by Hiroaki Sato. Copyright © 1983 by John Weatherhill, Inc.

Wiley Publishing, Inc., a subsidiary of John Wiley & Sons, Inc.: Symbols from Pronunciation Key from *Webster's New World™ College Dictionary*, Fourth Edition. Copyright © 2000, 1999 by Wiley Publishing, Inc. All rights reserved.

The H. W. Wilson Company: Quotes from "Luisa Valenzuela" from *World Authors 1980–1985*. Copyright © 1991 by The H. W. Wilson Company.

Diane Wolkstein: From "Inanna Spoke," translated by Diane Wolkstein and Samuel Noah Kramer from *Inanna: Queen of Heaven and Earth* (HarperCollins, 1983). Copyright © 1983 by Diane Wolkstein and Samuel Noah Kramer.

The Wylie Agency, Inc.: "On Seeing England for the First Time" by Jamaica Kincaid from *The Best American Essays*, 1992. Copyright © 1992 by Jamaica Kincaid.

Yale University Press: "Most Beautiful Youth Who Ever Happened" and "The Voice of the Wild Goose" from *Literature of Ancient Egypt*, edited by William Kelly Simpson, translations by R. O. Faulkner, Edward F. Wente, Jr., and William Kelly Simpson. Copyright © 1972 by Yale University.

Zephyr Press: "Before spring there are days like these..." from *The Complete Poems of Anna Akhmatova*, translated by Judith Hemschemeyer, edited and introduced by Roberta Reeder. Translation copyright © 1989, 1992, 1997 by Judith Hemschemeyer.

Zoland Books, an imprint of Steerforth Press: From *Ocean of Words* by Ha Jin. Copyright © 1996 by Ha Jin.

Sources Cited

From "Ha Jin: In His Own Words" from *BookBrowse.com 1977–2001.*

Quote by Margot Arce de Vazquez from *Gabriela Mistral: The Poet and her Work* as quoted in *Contemporary Authors*. Published by Gale Group Literary Database, 2003.

Quote on Akhmatova's poetry by Nicholas G. Gumilyov from *Contemporary Authors*. Published by Gale Group Literary Database, 2003.

Quote about magical realism by Luisa Valenzuela from *Time* magazine as quoted in *Contemporary Authors*. Published by Gale Group Literary Database, 2003.

Quote on Russian fiction by Anatole France.

Quote by Stephen Mitchell from *Tao Te Ching: A New English Version*, translated by Stephen Mitchell. Published by HarperCollins, New York, 1988.

From "Torture by Happiness" from *Nightingale Fever: Russian Poets in Revolution* by Ronald Hingley. Published by Knopf, New York, 1981.

Quote by Derek Walcott from *The New Yorker*, February 9, 2004, pg. 46.

Quote by Alfred Nobel from *The Nobel Foundation* Web site, 2002.

Quote from *Arthur Rimbaud* by Enid Starkie. Published by Norton, New York, 1947.

Quote by Roger Colet from *Guy de Maupassant: Selected Short Stories*, translated by Roger Colet. Published by Penguin, UK, 1971.

Quote by Guy de Maupassant from *Maupassant: A Lion In the Path* by Francis Steegmuller. Published by Random House, New York, 1949

Quote by Rainer Maria Rilke from *The Selected Poetry of Rainer Maria Rilke*, translated by Stephen Mitchell. Published by Random House, New York, 1989.

From "The Problem" from *Rediscovering the Parables* by Joachim Jeremias. Published by Scribner's, New York, 1966.

"Writing is the mother..." (Sumerian Proverb) from *Cradle of Civilization* by Samuel Noah Kramer. Published by Time-Life Books, NY, 1967.

From "Conclusion" from *Alexander Pushkin* by Walter N. Vickery. Published by Twayne, 1970, Boston.

From letter by Arthur Rimbaud to his daughter, June 23, 1891, from *Rimbaud: Complete Works, Selected Letters, Translation, Introduction, and Notes* by Wallace Fowlie. Published by University of Chicago Press, Chicago and London, 1966.

Quote from "Yasunari Kawabata" by Edward Seidensticker from *World Authors 1950–1970*. Published by H. W. Wilson, New York, 1975.

Picture Credits

The illustrations and/or photographs on the Contents pages are picked up from pages in the textbook. Credits for those works can be found either on the textbook page on which they appear or in the list below.

iii: The Detroit Institute of Art, USA/Founders Society Purchase/Bridgeman Art Library; viii: © Musée des arts Asiatiques-Guimet, Paris/Art Resource, New York; A01: Photograph © 1987 The Metropolitan Museum of Art; A03: © Erich Lessing/Art Resource, New York; A05: © Bildarchiv Preussischer Kulturbesitz/Art Resource, New York; A06: © Scala/Art Resource, New York; A09: © Private Collection/Art Resource, New York; A10: Superstock Inc.; A11: Marc & Evelyn Bernheim/Woodfin Camp; A12 (top) The Art Archive/National Museum, Damascus, Syria/Dagli Orti; A13: Dean Conger/CORBIS; A14: © Bildarchiv Preussischer Kulturbesitz/Art Resource, New York; A16: © Scala/Art Resource, New York; A18: © 2004 Estate of Pablo Picasso/Artists Rights Society (ARS), New York © John Bigelow Taylor/Art Resource, New York; A20: Victoria & Albert Museum, London/The Bridgeman Art Library International; A42: Courtesy of the Oriental Institute of the University of Chicago; 2: (top) Photodisc/Getty Images; 2: (bottom) © Bildarchiv Preussischer Kulturbesitz/Art Resource, New York; 3: (bottom) The Bridgeman Art Library International; 4: The Art Archive/Musée du Louvre, Paris/Dagli Orti; 5: (left) © Réunion des Musées Nationaux/Art Resource, New York; 5: (right) akg-images; 7: The Art Archive/British Museum/Eileen Tweedy; 8: Roger Wood/CORBIS; 9: The Art Archive/San Zeno Maggiore Verona, Italy/Dagli Orti (A); 12: © Erich Lessing/Art Resource, New York; 13: © Werner Forman/Art Resource, New York; 14: The Bridgeman Art Library International; 15: The Art Archive/British Library; 17: (left) © Erich Lessing/Art Resource, New York; 17: (right) West Semitic Research/Dead Sea Scrolls Foundation/CORBIS; 18: (bottom) The Art Archive/British Museum/Eileen Tweedy; 18: (top) The Bridgeman Art Library International; 19: © Erich Lessing/Art Resource, New York; 20: The Art Archive/Musée du Louvre, Paris/Dagli Orti (A); 22: The Art Archive/Musée du Louvre, Paris/Dagli Orti (A); 29: The Art Archive/Archaeological Museum, Aleppo, Syria/Dagli Orti; 30: © Werner Forman/Art Resource, New York; 32: © Bildarchiv Preussischer Kulturbesitz/Art Resource, New York; 37: Araldo De Luca; 39: The Art Archive/Egyptian Museum, Cairo/Dagli Orti (A); 41: The Image Bank/Getty Images; 43: © Bildarchiv Preussischer Kulturbesitz/Art Resource, New York; 45: The Art Archive/Egyptian Museum, Cairo/Dagli Orti; 47: (background) Kenneth Garrett/National Geographic Image Collection; 48: Photograph © 2004 Museum of Fine Arts, Boston; 49: © Bildarchiv Preussischer Kulturbesitz/Art Resource, New York; 50: © The Jewish Museum, New York/Art Resource, New York; 55: © Bildarchiv Preussischer Kulturbesitz/Art Resource, New York; 57: © Bill Aron/PhotoEdit; 59: The Art Archive/The Bodleian Library, Oxford; 60: Philadelphia Museum of Art/CORBIS; 63: © Jewish Museum, New York/Superstock Inc.; 64: © Erich Lessing/Art Resource, New York; 68: © Victoria & Albert Museum, London/Art Resource, New York; 71: © 2004 Artist Rights Society (ARS), New York/ADAGP, Paris © Réunion des Musées Nationaux/Art Resource, New York; 76: The Art Archive/Biblioteca del Studio Teologico Accademico Bressanone/Dagli Orti; 77: © The Pierpont Morgan Library/Art Resource, New York; 78: © Scala/Art Resource, New York; 79: Richard T. Nowitz/CORBIS; 80: Courtesy of Vivian Linder, Seattle; 82: The Bridgeman Art Library International; 84: © Scala/Art Resource, New York; 87: (top left) Cover from GILGAMESH; A Verse Narrative by Herbert Mason (Boston: Mariner Books, 2003). Reprinted by permission of Houghton Mifflin Company. All Rights Reserved; 87: (top right) Cover from THE OXFORD HISTORY OF ANCIENT EGYPT edited by Ian Shaw (2002). By permission of Oxford University Press. Cover illustration from a watercolor of a painted relief, early 19th Dynasty tomb of Setyl, by Henry Salt. © Copyright The Trustees of The British Museum; 87: (bottom left) Cover: THE ILLUSTRATED HEBREW BIBLE, 75 SELECTED STORIES. Adapted by Ellen Frankel. Abradale Press/Harry N. Abrams, Inc. Courtesy of Fair Street Productions; 88: © Phil McCarten/PhotoEdit; 100: (bottom left) © Erich Lessing/Art Resource, New York; 100: (background) Kevin R. Morris/CORBIS; 102: (top) © Nimatallah/Art Resource, New York; 102: (bottom) © Erich Lessing/Art Resource, New York; 103: (top) akg-images; 103: (center) © Scala/Art Resource, New York; 104: (top) © Erich Lessing/Art Resource, New York; 104–105: (bottom) akg-images; 105: (top) © Scala/Art Resource, New York; 107: © Réunion des Musées Nationaux/Art Resource, New York; 108: (top left) © Réunion des Musées Nationaux/Art Resource, New York; 108–109: (bottom) © Bildarchiv Preussischer Kulturbesitz/Art Resource, New York; 109: (top) © SEF/Art Resource, New York; 110: The Art Archive/Archaeological Museum, Sparta/Dagli Orti; 111: Bettmann/CORBIS; 112: (top) © Bildarchiv Preussischer Kulturbesitz/Art Resource, New York; 112: (center) The Art Archive/Jan Vinchon Numismatist, Paris/Dagli Orti; 115: © Scala/Art Resource, New York; 116: © Scala/Art Resource, New York; 117: Digital Vision/Getty Images; 118: © Scala/Art Resource, New York; 119: © Giraudon/Art Resource, New York; 120–121: © Scala/Art Resource, New York; 123: © Erich Lessing/Art Resource, New York; 124: (bottom left) The Bridgeman Art Library International; 124: (bottom right) © Scala/Art Resource, New York; 124–125: (background) Wolfgang Kaehler/CORBIS; 125: (bottom left) © Scala/Art Resource, New York; 126: © Erich Lessing/Art Resource, New York; 129: © Gilles Mermet/Art Resource, New York; 131: © Scala/Art Resource, New York; 133: The Bridgeman Art Library International; 137: The Art Archive/Musée du Louvre, Paris/Dagli Orti; 140: © Gilles Mermet/Art Resource, New York; 141: The Art Archive/Archaeological Museum, Istanbul/Dagli Orti; 147: Chris Hellier/CORBIS; 149: The Minneapolis Institute of Arts, Gift of funds from Ruth and Bruce Dayton; 150: © Scala/Art Resource, New York; 155: Photograph © 2004 Museum of Fine Arts, Boston; 158: © Alinari/Art Resource, New York; 165: © Erich Lessing/Art Resource, New York; 169: The Bridgeman Art Library International; 170: © Giraudon/Art Resource, New York; 172: © Alinari/Art Resource, New York; 174: The Art Archive/Archaeological Museum, Sparta/Dagli Orti; 175: The Bridgeman Art Library International; 177: © Victoria & Albert

Index of Skills

The boldface page numbers indicate an extensive treatment of the topic.

Quatrain, 553, 679, 707, 732, **1193,** 1196, 1197
Quixotic hero, **688**
Realism, **1194**
    magic, **956, 1188**
Refrain, **403,** 505, **786, 1194**
Renaissance sonnet, **681**
Repetition, **51, 57, 403,** 616, 893, **1039, 1194,** 1195
Resolution, 1182, 1192
Restatement, 1191
Rhetoric, **181, 1194**
Rhetorical question, 301
Rhyme, 514, **1194–1195**
Rhyme scheme, 1194
Rhyming sounds, 895
Rhythm, **1195**
Rising action, 1180, 1182
Romance, **624,** 633, **1195**
    Arthurian, 623, **624, 1177**
    courtly, 1195
Romanticism, **1195**
Round character, 882, **1179**
Rubá'i, 552, **553,** 557, 1194, **1195**
Sarcasm, **1195**
Satire, 677, **709,** 723, **1195**
Scansion, 1189
Science fiction, **1195**
Sestet, 678, 732, **1196**
Setting, **772, 957, 1009, 1023, 1074, 1196**
Shakespearean sonnet, 679, 732, **1196–1197**
Short story, **1196**
Simile, 369, 778, **857, 930,** 955, **1043, 1196**
    epic, **121,** 171, 296, **1183, 1196**
    extended, 955, 1041, **1196**
Situational irony, **669, 814, 965, 1054, 1187**
Slant rhyme, 893, 1194
Soliloquy, **1196**
Sonnet, **678–679, 681, 1196–1197**
    Petrarchan, **678–679,** 732, **1196**
    Shakespearean, **679,** 732, **1196–1197**
Sound effects, 893
Speaker, **46,** 922, **1197**
Speech, **1197**
Spondee, 1189
Stanza, **1197**
Static character, **882, 1083, 1179**
Stock epithet, **121, 1183–1184**
Story, frame, **383, 669, 1185**
Stream of consciousness, **1189, 1197**
Structural parallelism, 1191
Style, **322, 456, 1197**
    diction, **456, 1182,** 1197
    syntax, **456**
    tone, **456**
Subjective writing, **1197**
Subplot, 1192
Surrealism, **1197**
Suspense, 399, **947,** 1192, **1197**
Symbol, 454, **622, 791,** 880, **1197**
Symbolism, **1197–1198**
Symbolist poetry, **791**

Synecdoche, **1198**
Synesthesia, **454, 1045, 1198**
Syntax, **456**
Tanka, **440, 442, 1198**
Tercet, 647, 1197, **1198**
Terza rima, 647, **1198**
Theater of the absurd, **1198**
Theme, **59,** 66, 86, 201, 445, 775, **804, 869,** 893, 957, 963, **965, 1023,** 1029, 1074, **1083, 1198**
Third-person-limited point of view, **1192–1193**
Time and sequence
    flashback, 121, 122, **1062, 1185**
    foreshadowing, **122, 633, 636, 644,** 812, 969, **986, 1185**
Tone, 48, 301, **303,** 454, **456, 905, 1198**
Traditional essay. *See Formal essay.*
Tragedy, **199, 263,** 1180, **1199**
Tragic flaw, **199,** 263, **1199**
Tragic hero, **199, 263**
Tragi-comedy, 1199
Translation, interpreting literature
    through, *170*
Trickster, **504, 576, 1199**
Trochee, 1189
Turn, 678, 1196. *See also* Sonnet.
Turning point, 607, 1180, 1182.
    See also Climax.
Tz'u, **436, 1199**
Understatement, **1199**
Utopian literature, **720**
Vedas, 366, **1199**
Verbal irony, 197, **814, 969, 1187**
Vernacular. *See Dialect.*
Verse
    blank, **1178**
    dactylic hexameter, 307
    free, **895, 1185**
    iambic pentameter, 679, **1187,** 1189
Volta, 678, 1196. *See also* Sonnet.
Wit, **1199**

VOCABULARY SKILLS

Affixes, 173, 1141–1142
Analogy, 736, **903**
    analyzing, **58**
Analyzing
    context clues, 920, 1096
    word analogies, **58**
Antonyms, 58, 98, 172, **535**
Choosing words, 644, 889
Completing sentences with vocabulary
    words, 1052
Connotation, **776**
Context clues, **535,** 580, 920, 1096, 1124
Definition, **535**
Denotation, **776**
Difference in vocabulary word
    meanings, 802, 1037
Etymology, 296, 677, **724**
Etymology chart, 296, 677
Etymology map, 724
Graphic organizers
    etymology chart, 296, 677

    etymology map, 724
    Indo-European roots chart, 387
    question and answer chart, 963
    semantic maps, 189, 399, 867
    word information charts, 265, 1029
Greek prefixes, 173, 1141
Greek roots, 173, 1141–1142
Greek suffixes, 173, 1142
Idioms, **970**
Indo-European word families and roots, 387
In your own words, 462, 1000
Jargon, **970**
Latin prefixes, 173, 1141
Latin roots, 173, 1141–1142
Latin suffixes, 173, 1142
Multiple-choice tests
    analogy questions, 1166–1167
    sentence-completion or fill-in-the-
        blank questions, 1165–1166
Narrative, summarizing a, 633
Prefixes
    Greek, **173,** 1141
    Latin, **173,** 1141
Question and answer, 770, 963, 978
Question and answer chart, 963
Replacing vocabulary words with
    synonyms, 1015
Restatements, **535**
Roots
    Greek, 173, 1141–1142
    Latin, 173, 1141–1142
Semantic mapping, 189, 399, 867
Sentence sense, 381, 812, 955
Story, summarizing the, 969
Substituting words, 666
Suffixes
    Greek, 173, 1142
    Latin, 173, 1142
Summarizing a narrative, 633
Summarizing with vocabulary words,
    534, 633, 969, 1060
Synonyms, 58, 98, 172, **197,** 342, **535,** 821, 911, 1015, **1073**
Test Practice, 98, 342, 484, 580, 736, 836, 1124
Test Smarts. *See* Multiple-choice tests.
True or false statements, 880
Vocabulary Development, 36, 57, 58, 66, 74, 172, 173, 189, 197, 265, 296, 328, 381, 387, 399, 462, 534, 535, 616, 633, 644, 666, 677, 702, 723, 724, 770, 776, 802, 812, 821, 867, 880, 889, 903, 911, 920, 955, 963, 969, 970, 978, 994, 1000, 1015, 1029, 1037, 1052, 1060, 1073, 1096, 1141–1142
Vocabulary words, summarizing with, 534, 633, 969, 1060
Word differences, 802, 1037
Word information charts, 265, 1029
Word maps, 994
Words with multiple meanings, 484

LISTENING AND SPEAKING / MEDIA SKILLS

INDEPENDENT READING

Index of Art

Index of Authors and Titles